THE NEW INTERPRETER'S® BIBLE

IN TWELVE VOLUMES

VOLUME I	General Articles on the Bible; General Articles on the Old Testament; Genesis; Exodus; Leviticus
VOLUME II	Numbers; Deuteronomy; Introduction to Narrative Literature; Joshua; Judges; Ruth; 1 & 2 Samuel
VOLUME III	1 & 2 Kings; 1 & 2 Chronicles; Ezra; Nehemiah; Esther; Additions to Esther; Tobit; Judith
VOLUME IV	1 & 2 Maccabees; Introduction to Hebrew Poetry; Job; Psalms
VOLUME V	Introduction to Wisdom Literature; Proverbs; Ecclesiastes; Song of Songs; Book of Wisdom; Sirach
VOLUME VI	Introduction to Prophetic Literature; Isaiah; Jeremiah; Baruch; Letter of Jeremiah; Lamentations; Ezekiel
VOLUME VII	Introduction to Apocalyptic Literature; Daniel; Additions to Daniel; Hosea; Joel; Amos; Obadiah; Jonah; Micah; Nahum; Habakkuk; Zephaniah; Haggai; Zechariah; Malachi
VOLUME VIII	General Articles on the New Testament; Matthew; Mark
VOLUME IX	Luke; John
VOLUME X	Acts; Introduction to Epistolary Literature; Romans; 1 Corinthians
VOLUME XI	2 Corinthians; Galatians; Ephesians; Philippians; Colossians; 1 & 2 Thessalonians; 1 & 2 Timothy; Titus; Philemon
VOLUME XII	Hebrews; James; 1 & 2 Peter; 1, 2, & 3 John; Jude; Revelation
INDEX	Subjects and Themes; Ancient Literature; Persons in the Bible; Persons outside the Bible; Places in the Bible; Places outside the Bible; Biblical Languages: Hebrew and Greek; Maps, Charts, and Illustrations; Excursuses; Reference Lists; Abbreviations

INDEX

Editorial Board

THE NEW INTERPRETER'S® BIBLE

GENERAL ARTICLES
&
INTRODUCTION, COMMENTARY, & REFLECTIONS
FOR EACH BOOK OF THE BIBLE
INCLUDING
THE APOCRYPHAL/DEUTEROCANONICAL BOOKS
IN
TWELVE VOLUMES

INDEX

[redacted]

ABINGDON PRESS
Nashville

THE NEW INTERPRETER'S BIBLE
INDEX

This book is printed on recycled, acid-free paper.

Library of Congress Cataloging-in-Publication Data
The New Interpreter's Bible: general articles & introduction, commentary, & reflections for each book of the Bible, including the Apocryphal/Deuterocanonical books.
p. cm.
Full texts and critical notes of the New International Version and the New Revised Standard Version of the Bible in parallel columns.
Includes bibliographical references.
ISBN 0-687-03916-9 (index: alk. paper)
1. Bible—Commentaries. 2. Abingdon Press. I. Bible. English. New International. 1994. II. Bible. English. New Revised Standard. 1994.
BS491.2.N484 1994
220.7'7—dc20   94-21092   CIP

10/04

PUBLICATION STAFF
President and Publisher: Neil M. Alexander
Editorial Director: Harriett Jane Olson
Reference Unit Director: Paul Franklyn
Reference Project Director: Charles B. Puskas.
Production Editor: Elizabeth R. Lindsey
Hebrew and Greek Editor: Jennifer L Koosed
Software Production Composer: B. Gayl Hinton
Production and Design Manager: Walter E. Wynne
Copy Processing Manager: Sylvia S. Street
Prepress Manager: Glenn R. Hinton
Publishing Systems Analyst: Michael V. Barker
Prepress Systems Technician: Phillip D. Elliott
Print Procurement Coordinator: Martha K. Taylor

04 05 06 07 08 09 10 11 12 13 — 10 9 8 7 6 5 4 3 2 1

MANUFACTURED IN THE UNITED STATES OF AMERICA

FOCUS AND FEATURES OF THE NEW INTERPRETER'S® BIBLE INDEX

The New Interpreter's Bible Index and *The New Interpreter's Bible: A Commentary in Twelve Volumes* share the same goal — to bring the best in contemporary biblical scholarship into the service of the church to enhance preaching, teaching, and study of the Scriptures. Two controlling principles shaped *The New Interpreter's Bible:* (1) form serves function and (2) maximize ease of use. The same goal and controlling principles guided the creation of this index to the twelve-volume commentary series, which has set a high standard in the interpretation and exposition of the Scriptures. As a result, function and purpose for the benefit of the user take precedence over dependence on any format or structure that might become too perplexing or cumbersome. In this intentional manner, *The New Interpreter's Bible Index* seeks to point out and facilitate reference to the various topics in *The New Interpreter's Bible.*

While the CD-ROM version of *The New Interpreter's Bible* can formulate complete searches and serve as a concordance by displaying every occurrence of a word in its immediate context, *The New Interpreter's Bible Index* addresses a dilemma sometimes created by the CD-ROM. When preparing a sermon or planning a Bible study, the attempts by the CD-ROM user to find substantial discussion that significantly addresses the queries that prompted the search are often impeded. The search for noteworthy discussion of, for example, "God as Creator/Sustainer" can overwhelm the CD-ROM user with thousands of locators for "God." The indexers of this volume used the CD-ROM database to locate and manually sift through the hundreds of topics, thousands of entries, and millions of page number references contained in all twelve volumes of the commentary. This enormous endeavor was undertaken to determine, capture, and secure for *The New Interpreter's Bible* reader only the best and most useful references.

The focus and features of *The New Interpreter's Bible Index* are in agreement with the working premise of the American Society of Indexers as stated on its website: an index is not an outline, nor is it a concordance. It is an intelligently compiled list of topics covered in the work, prepared with the reader's needs in mind. Concentrating only on those entries that substantially address the topics and advance discussion for the reader's needs, we of Abingdon Press formulated the following indexes and helpful features:

- SUBJECTS AND THEMES — covers subjects like chariots and themes like God's will
- ANCIENT LITERATURE — includes hundreds of sources and non-canonical writings
- PERSONS IN THE BIBLE — names all whom the Bible regards as persons or personal beings
- PERSONS OUTSIDE THE BIBLE — names many of the persons or personal beings discussed in the commentary who are not named in the Bible

- ♦ PLACES IN THE BIBLE — features all that the Bible regards as places and dwellings
- ♦ PLACES OUTSIDE THE BIBLE — features those places and dwellings mentioned in the commentary but not mentioned in the Bible
- ♦ BIBLICAL LANGUAGES: HEBREW AND GREEK — includes not only the original language, transliteration, and translation, but also a handy transliteration key that can be used with any of the twelve volumes
- ♦ LISTS OF MAPS, CHARTS, AND ILLUSTRATIONS — references all of the charts and graphical features found in the commentary
- ♦ EXCURSUSES — provides further expositions of biblical topics
- ♦ REFERENCE LISTS — covers everything from the plagues on Egypt to the miracles of Jesus to the women mentioned in the Bible
- ♦ ABBREVIATIONS — gathers together in one place all of the abbreviations from the twelve volumes

The format of *The New Interpreter's Bible Index* has been carefully designed to meet the needs of its intended audience of students, teachers, and preachers of the Scriptures. Special features include:

Main Headings. These take into consideration the reader's search strategy and include carefully selected subheadings that are useful. In order to avoid becoming another commentary on a commentary, the indexers did not attempt to provide every small grouping of entries with its own specific subheading.

Cross-References. These were included wherever it was helpful to do so. They will guide the reader to other relevant headings.

Format. The easy-to-read format, with large, clear type, make the index readily accessible to all readers.

Accuracy. The indexers sought for accuracy in page references, also paying close attention to any discrepancies that might exist between the printed version and *The New Interpreter's Bible* CD-ROM database.

Scope. The coverage of the index is wide-ranging, providing access to such diverse discussion in the commentary as the Qumran scrolls, the teachings of Jesus, animals in the Bible, the temple curtains, the Jordan River, and both the transliterations and translations of thousands of Hebrew, Aramaic, and Greek words.

Many scholars and editors worked together for one year to conceive, compile, and present *The New Interpreter's Bible Index,* including: Rebecca Burgoyne, Steve Cook, Paul Franklyn, Douglas Hagler, Gayl Hinton, Heath Jones, Lynn Kauppi, Jennifer Koosed, Elizabeth Lindsey, Bobbie Morris, Charles Puskas, Nanette Ryan, Susannah Southard, Linda Spicer, Deborah Wiseman, and Ed Wynne.

CONTENTS

INDEX

Subjects and Themes ____ 1

Ancient Literature ____ 209

Persons in the Bible ____ 227

Persons outside the Bible ____ 279

Places in the Bible ____ 287

Places outside the Bible ____ 317

Biblical Languages: Hebrew ____ 321

Biblical Languages: Greek ____ 412

Maps, Charts, Illustrations ____ 495

Excursuses ____ 499

Reference Lists ____ 501

Abbreviations ____ 509

SUBJECTS AND THEMES

A

ABBA

See under GOD, NAMES FOR/TITLES OF *in PERSONS IN THE BIBLE*

ABIB

(month in Jewish calendar) **1:**275; **2:**412

ABLUTION, ABLUTIONS

1:281, 1060–61; **12:**71

ABOMINATION

OF DESOLATION **4:**440, 442; **5:**611; **7:**114, 128, 143, 147; **8:**690; **9:**404; **12:**693; IN THE OT AND APOCRYPHA **1:**1127; **2:**351, 379, 421, 475, 834; **3:**115, 996; **4:**85, 701; **5:**556, 570, 651, 724; **6:**640, 1153, 1168, 1176–77, 1261, 1307, 1386, 1458, 1574; **7:**288, 864; IN PROVERBS **5:**2, 55, 77, 117, 119, 127, 149, 151, 158–60, 211, 213, 245; IN THE NT **8:**684, 690; **9:**302, 312–15; **10:**492; **12:**403, 589, 636, 681, 685

ABRAHAM'S BOSOM

9:25, 315–17, 357

ABSTINENCE

IN THE OT AND APOCRYPHA **1:**998; **2:**234, 615, 264, 1140; **3:**838, 1134; **7:**93, 232, 792, 799; IN THE NT **10:**151, 869, 872, 877; **11:**103, 574, 631–32, 664, 783, 812

ABYSS

4:920; **5:**590, 833–34; **6:**935; **7:**528; **9:**187, 252; **10:**663; **11:**415; **12:**492, 613, 630–31, 638, 642, 651, 656, 702, 707, 716

ACACIA

1:890; **2:**1248

ACCENT, ACCENTS

GALILEAN **9:**67; LINGUISTIC/MUSICAL/POETIC **1:**801; **2:**376; **4:**308; **5:**67; **7:**266

ACCEPTANCE

BY GOD OF HUMANS **8:**223–24, 291, 473; **9:**128, 293; **10:**463, 548; **11:**78, 195, 261, 284; BY HUMANS OF GOD/JESUS **8:**223, 291; **9:**560, 587, 724; **10:**363, 382; **11:**702–3, 765; BY HUMANS OF OTHERS **8:**223, 472, 673; **9:**104, 108; **10:**919; **11:**54, 224, 629, 799

ACCESS

TO GOD IN THE OT **1:**51, 278, 541–42, 552, 854, 906–7; **2:**26, 40, 283, 428, 1093; **3:**574, 647; **4:**1131; **5:**643, 730; **6:**752–54, 1549, 1577, 1591; **7:**418, 421, 425, 750, 861; TO GOD/JESUS/THE KINGDOM IN THE NT **3:**115; **8:**724; **9:**344–45, 496, 524, 549, 551, 587, 604, 611, 613, 643, 669, 672, 679, 742, 745, 777, 853; **10:**546, 974, 988; **11:**69, 312, 370, 400–401, 402, 408, 411, 413, 416, 442; **12:**40, 57, 91–92, 95, 106, 114, 117, 120, 149, 152, 155, 158–60, 166, 168, 407, 435, 531, 650, 705; TO GIFTS/ATTRIBUTES OF GOD IN THE NT **9:**144, 345, 461, 650, 664, 742, 764, 781; **10:**315, 320, 515–16, 525, 736, 820, 822; **11:**211, 219, 270, 400, 566–67, 572, 615, 632, 634, 637–38, 640; **12:**617, 646

ACCURSED

IN THE OT AND APOCRYPHA **4:**30, 249, 295, 471, 736; **5:**280, 471, 473, 552–53; **7:**248; IN THE NT **8:**455; **10:**572, 697, 1002; **11:**206, 390; **12:**351, 405, 724, 734. *See also* ANATHEMA

ACCUSER

2:629; **4:**223; **5:**218–19; **6:**1138, 1147, 1307; **7:**865; **9:**268–70, 309, 446, 588; **10:**398; **12:**306, 583, 624

ACROSTIC

4:310, 330, 716–17, 776–79, 809, 813–14, 1132, 1135–36, 1166–67, 1259; **5:**257, 260, 262, 619, 641, 863, 867; **6:**66, 1018, 1020–21, 1024, 1036, 1057, 1059, 1071

ADAR

(month in Jewish calendar) **3:**379, 712; **4:**101, 270, 297; IN THE BOOK OF ESTHER **3:**857, 859, 875, 896, 899, 922, 925, 929–30, 933–35, 937–38, 953, 967

ADJURATION

2:356; **4:**368; **5:**368, 374, 388, 389–90, 412, 429

ADONAI/ADONAY

See under GOD, NAMES FOR/TITLES OF *in PERSONS IN THE BIBLE*

ADOPTION

OF BELIEVERS IN THE NT **10:**591, 593, 597–98, 601, 606; **11:**92, 281, 284–86, 292, 337, 372–74, 378, 435, 678; **12:**649; OF ISRAEL/THE KING **1:**717; **4:**689; **5:**463; **6:**123, 1226; **8:**359; OF JESUS AS THE CHRIST **8:**359, 528; **10:**591;

ADORATION

1:210, 799, 843, 920, 1067; **3:**400, 539; **4:**813, 928, 934; **5:**409, 425, 571, 693; **6:**814; **7:**268; **9:**172; **11:**266, 564; **12:**27, 438, 604

ADULTERY

1:610, 850; **2:**62–63, 128, 327, 333, 1284–85, 1288, 1305; **3:**18; **4:**496, 556; **5:**558, 689; **6:**211; **7:**216; **11:**435; **12:**163, 195, 443; EXAMPLES IN NARRATIVES **1:**609–10, 850; **2:**62, 547, 865, 875–76, 963, 1223, 1271, 1279, 1283, 1293, 1305; **3:**332, 416, 423, 1141; **6:**258, 685, 692, 794; **7:**169, 180, 182, 206, 224; **8:**134; JESUS' VIEW OF **1:**1143;

ADULTERY *(continued)*
2:457; **5:**80; **8:**190–92, 608, 645; **9:**628, 630; LAWS REGARDING **1:**428, 848, 851, 1126–27, 1141, 1143; **2:**9, 62–63, 66–67, 336, 380, 455, 457, 474, 629, 1284–85; **3:**741; **4:**553, 557, 882; **5:**752, 765; **6:**1241, 1321, 1331; **7:**182, 208, 236; **8:**134, 190–92, 608, 645; **9:**313–14, 628; **10:**559, 725; AS A METAPHOR **5:**44, 46, 65–66, 71, 101, 474–75, 751–52; **6:**490–91, 603, 620, 653, 750, 1223–24, 1241, 1316, 1320–21, 1329–30; **7:**184, 198, 224, 245, 256; **11:**147; **12:**351, 581; TEACHINGS AGAINST **5:**64–66, 78–81, 83–85, 254, 406; **6:**750, 1310, 1319–21; **7:**241, 256; **10:**445–47, 559, 725; **11:**642, 791; **12:**78

ADVENT
OF GOD/KINGDOM OF GOD **2:**613, 1141, 1217; **6:**1121, 1130–31; **7:**664; **8:**114–15, 156–57, 164, 189, 232, 268, 314, 329, 364, 477, 718; **9:**244; OF JESUS/THE MESSIAH **1:**277; **3:**432, 563; **6:**815; **7:**108; **8:**90, 119, 125, 134, 138, 142, 144, 149, 153, 156–58, 167, 175, 186–87, 189, 195–96, 258, 266, 268, 286, 292–94, 319, 321, 360, 364, 406, 440, 450; **9:**497, 738, 747–48, 764, 770–71, 776, 826; **11:**279; **12:**22, 253, 323, 439, 516, 532; SEASON OF THE CHURCH YEAR **1:**96, 206, 212; **2:**55, 236, 1217, 1259; **4:**780, 965, 1001, 1018, 1038, 1186, 1196; **7:**538, 570, 572, 873; **8:**150, 533, 537, 659–60; **9:**53, 66; **12:**4, 64

ADVERSARY
1:800, 822, 931; **2:**631, 975, 1266; **3:**47, 93, 96, 865, 919, 1099, 1161; **4:**332, 624; **5:**293, 323; **6:**1444; **7:**8, 124, 375, 609; **9:**165, 337, 766; **11:**269, 316; **12:**467–68; GOD AS **1:**751; **4:**411, 457–58, 555; **10:**400; GOD'S **6:**1523; **7:**604, 654. *See also under* SATAN *in PERSONS IN THE BIBLE*

ADVOCATE
AGAINST GOD **4:**457, 460–61, 508, 569; **5:**311; **12:**392, 649; GOD AS **1:**726, 773; **4:**861; **7:**355, 357–58, 366, 424, 587; JESUS AS **8:**279, 321, 390, 425; **9:**428, 588, 747, 771; **12:**43, 367, 376, 388, 492, 649; SPIRIT AS **9:**747, 771; **11:**490; **12:**367, 376, 388, 492, 649, 705

AEON
1:191; **10:**811, 819, 821–23, 825; **11:**69, 74, 85, 138, 150, 422, 438, 450

AESTHETICS
1:78, 139, 313; **5:**384, 547, 570; **6:**1066; **10:**383, 605; **12:**556

AFRICAN/AFRICAN AMERICAN
1:148, 154, 156–60, 182, 195, 490, 874; **2:**595, 656, 711, 1051; **4:**548; **5:**170, 247, 364, 367–68, 371, 374, 379, 382–85, 390, 394, 397, 401, 404–6, 408–9, 412–13, 415–16, 418–24, 426, 428–29; **6:**119; **7:**246, 701, 717; **10:**171, 189, 484; **11:**278, 457; CHURCHES (*see under* CHURCH)

AGAPE
LOVE FEASTS **12:**492–93

AGATE
6:1392; **12:**723

AGE
BRONZE AGE **1:**215, 221, 244, 246–49, 251–54, 257–59, 266, 276, 1126; **2:**163, 557, 572, 581, 612, 615–16, 626, 635, 637, 639, 641, 662, 685, 688, 694, 779; TO COME **1:**191; **3:**390; **5:**226; **6:**271; **8:**189, 422; **9:**143, 177, 226–28, 230, 349, 370; **10:**419, 427, 439, 464, 524–25, 528, 530, 546, 631, 690, 701, 703, 705–6, 718; **11:**203, 360, 614, 632, 637, 813; **12:**75, 106, 521, 606, 677; END OF THE **1:**166, 1158, 1160; **4:**771, 1089; **6:**223; **8:**138, 256, 259; **9:**488, 704, 762; **10:**384, 786, 822, 886, 938, 980; **12:**12, 113, 259, 567, 636; IRON AGE **1:**215–20, 224, 226, 244, 247–48, 251–52, 258–59; **2:**557, 572, 615, 626, 688, 779, 832; **6:**1347–48; NEW **1:**35, 41, 46, 199, 1106, 1161; **2:**32, 60, 311; **3:**402, 407, 409, 462, 464, 469, 496, 514, 835; **5:**343; **6:**39–40, 68–69, 147, 201, 217, 225; **7:**219, 327–28, 538, 565, 655, 699–700; **8:**167, 189, 555, 601; **9:**31, 334, 538, 585, 693, 738, 741, 748, 778, 781, 784, 796, 842, 844; **10:**37, 402, 419, 427, 451, 516, 597, 701, 705–7, 727–28, 735, 737, 811–12; **11:**249, 296, 591, 614, 636, 638, 640, 643, 648, 650, 678–79, 695, 701, 715, 721, 723–24, 726–27, 729, 732, 734, 748, 852; **12:**394, 398, 412, 519, 524, 527, 531, 535, 593–94, 603, 615, 635, 686, 704–5, 710, 720; NEW AGE (MODERN) **10:**343, 463, 596, 615; **11:**291, 636, 640; PRESENT **1:**191; **8:**163, 349, 690; **10:**378, 701, 705, 707, 820; **11:**202, 208, 218, 384, 390, 458, 461, 463, 621, 811, 830, 857, 871, 873, 901; **12:**36, 530, 626, 657, 669, 704, 711, 717

AGE, OLD
OF LIFE **1:**486, 515, 598; **2:**332, 546, 629, 661, 810, 941, 988, 1223; **3:**13, 18, 28, 536, 1015, 1043, 1069–70; **4:**331, 381, 441, 636, 958–59, 961, 1052; **5:**263, 277, 328, 353–55, 357, 462, 478–79, 685, 687, 760, 801, 867; **6:**196, 405–6; **7:**529; **9:**45, 346, 861; **11:**818; AS OPPOSED TO NEW AGE **8:**189; **10:**728–29, 822, 983; **11:**202, 224, 243, 272, 278, 625, 633, 650, 678, 680, 708, 715, 723–25; **12:**264, 730

AGNOSTIC, AGNOSTICISM
5:250, 276, 466, 547; **9:**349; **10:**532; **12:**49

AGONY
1:390, 772; **2:**501; **3:**1005; **4:**208, 359, 397, 419, 728, 1029; **6:**185, 212, 467, 469, 528, 580,

629, 1057, 1156, 1438; **7:**395, 584, 692; **9:**317; **10:**606–7, 697; **12:**512, 524, 646, 648, 667; OF JESUS **8:**630; **9:**190, 433, 456, 463, 712, 752, 789, 803

AGORA
1:223; **4:**254; **10:**233, 239, 242, 244–45, 253, 255, 864, 867

AGRARIAN
1:214, 227, 651, 865–66, 869, 870–72, 952; **2:**64, 587, 659, 667, 670, 684, 697, 755, 919, 957; **5:**3, 108, 147, 173, 192, 213, 239, 687, 828; **6:**1216, 1399, 1471; **7:**738; **8:**51; **9:**271; **10:**376, 827, 987

AGRICULTURE
1:215, 217–19, 221, 225, 255, 329, 623, 1133; **2:**356, 405, 410, 414, 445, 502, 668, 711–12; **3:**457; **4:**510; **5:**74, 213, 314, 319, 350, 690; **6:**255, 281; **7:**424, 565, 813, 817; **9:**296; **10:**827; **12:**15, 74, 76

AIR, POWER OF
11:393

AKKADIAN
1:232–33, 237, 242, 1018, 1105, 1134, 1172; **2:**87, 614, 678; **3:**201, 205, 710; **5:**3, 6–9, 94, 174, 400; **6:**1126, 1138, 1165, 1174, 1179, 1221, 1234, 1326, 1382, 1388, 1394, 1429, 1516, 1538, 1566; **7:**62–63, 84, 90, 257, 406, 715

ALABASTER
5:346; **6:**988; **9:**169–70, 172

ALEPH
(Hebrew letter) **1:**1187; **4:**390, 718, 1166, 1168; **5:**607; **6:**1018; **7:**601, 686

ALIEN, ALIENS
1:171, 186, 291, 458, 483, 492, 527, 704–5, 722, 825, 836, 1052, 1070, 1113, 1131, 1165; **2:**406, 468, 491, 503, 510, 563, 567, 629, 635–36; **3:**468, 551, 619–20, 850, 1018; **4:**451, 545, 548, 597, 615, 632, 1105, 1169–70, 1178, 1264; **5:**44, 68, 71–72, 207; **6:**174, 237–38, 377, 874, 1189, 1408, 1601–2; **7:**88, 161, 258, 268, 293, 334, 778, 780, 793, 868, 874; **8:**314; **9:**229; **10:**378, 935; **12:**135, 137, 170, 239, 246 (*see also* FOREIGNER); RESIDENT **1:**317, 419, 490, 527, 705, 868, 870–71, 874, 924, 998, 1080, 1117, 1119–20, 1135, 1149, 1165, 1171, 1173; **2:**22, 33, 86–87, 127, 129, 150–51, 265, 369, 379, 411–13, 459, 462, 470, 477, 481, 634–35, 876, 915–16, 1202; **3:**429, 618, 747, 820, 1114; **4:**16, 202, 476, 513, 725, 733, 854; **6:**169, 1601–2; **7:**357–58, **9:**336; **10:**32, 111, 125, 219–20; **11:**358; **12:**137, 146, 235, 239, 241, 243, 246, 248, 305, 319

ALIENATION
1:172, 368, 892, 962; **2:**415, 514, 1306, 1310, 1316–17, 1341; **3:**518; **4:**395–97, 457–58, 474, 476, 488, 492, 511, 544, 583, 631, 687, 952, 1029, 1043, 1055, 1087, 1128; **5:**64, 477, 551, 860; **6:**959, 970; **7:**34, 225, 585; **8:**50, 97, 100, 132, 174, 190, 500; **9:**303–4; **10:**225, 377; **11:**56, 98, 133, 572, 609, 625, 636, 673, 680, 682, 688–89, 711, 720–21, 727, 733; **12:**222–24, 236, 238, 294, 670, 685; FROM GOD **1:**367, 376; **2:**1119, 1127, 1129, 1149; **3:**636; **4:**450, 502, 581, 660, 970, 997, 1001, 1029, 1042; **5:**487; **6:**381, 1170, 1188; **7:**261; **8:**500; **10:**49–50; **11:**29, 276, 321, 391, 400, 606, 625, 646; **12:**672, 685

ALLEGORY
AS A LITERARY FORM **2:**186, 442, 1293; **3:**523; **4:**452, 876, 999–1000; **5:**354, 370–71, 381, 550, 689; **6:**16, 1225, 1242, 1252, 1295, 1320, 1335; **7:**192, 215, 466, 468; **8:**181, 212, 230, 298–99, 305, 308, 326, 450, 453, 672; **9:**383; **10:**663; **11:**283, 299–303, 305–6, 308; **12:**55, 156, 711; AS A METHOD OF BIBLICAL INTERPRETATION **1:**46, 48–49, 69, 79, 82, 86, 89–96, 98, 102, 163, 193; **6:**142, 1225, 1409; **7:**215, 493; **8:**218, 381, 390, 413–14, 417, 449–50, 671; **9:**178, 271, 363, 570; **11:**301–3, 305, 308–9; **12:**156

ALLELUIA
3:1062, 1065; **4:**1100; **5:**263; **12:**695. *See also* HALLELUJAH

ALLIANCE
1:264, 700, 964; **2:**624, 634, 651, 770, 773, 818, 1212, 1249, 1279, 1347; **3:**36–37, 40, 49, 58, 61, 81, 87, 90, 93, 118, 207, 251, 253, 265, 529, 536, 542, 544, 597, 629, 1102, 1109; **4:**20, 132–33, 143, 160, 169, 189; **5:**459; **6:**37, 168, 182, 230–31, 239, 253–54, 259, 291, 293, 354, 599, 858, 1250, 1324, 1349, 1360, 1402; **7:**140–42, 246, 445, 449, 595, 631, 661, 675, 691, 729; **8:**414; **9:**437; **10:**318, 360; **11:**702; **12:**661; TRIBAL (EARLY ISRAEL) **2:**558, 1224–25, 1230, 1252, 1345; **3:**160, 168, 181, 544, 551, 553, 564, 568, 586, 602, 1112

ALLOTMENT
OF LAND **2:**221, 254, 580, 657–58, 667–68, 671, 673, 684, 686, 701, 706, 735–37, 863; **3:**52, 746; **4:**1170, 1172; **5:**324; **6:**626, 820, 894, 1579, 1581, 1600, 1604–6

ALLOY
6:61, 477, 1312

ALMIGHTY
See under GOD, NAMES FOR/TITLES OF *in PERSONS IN THE BIBLE*

ALMOND, ALMONDS
1:218; **2:**140; **5:**355; **6:**579, 583–84, 874; **7:**406

ALMS
3:1001, 1015–16, 1018, 1055–56, 1064; **4:**925;

ALMS *(continued)*
5:107, 119, 664, 675, 693, 718, 732; **8:**76, 200–201; **9:**247, 260–61, 306, 326, 347, 472; **10:**77, 85, 162, 170, 321–22, 756; **12:**194
ALMUGWOOD
3:82
ALOES
2:190; **5:**405; **6:**1230
ALPHA AND OMEGA
See under GOD, NAMES FOR/TITLES OF *in PERSONS IN THE BIBLE*
ALPHABET
1:10, 230–31, 294, 304; **2:**35, 96; **4:**555, 684, 716, 718, 776–77, 809, 813, 1090, 1132, 1166, 1168; **5:**257, 261, 438, 650, 756; **6:**1017–18, 1029, 1046, 1059, 1067, 1179; **7:**601, 686; **8:**187
ALTAR
ASYLUM AT (*see under* ASYLUM); BUILDING AN **1:**299, 393, 424, 567, 577, 584, 652, 880, 931; **2:**484, 487, 561, 587, 635–36, 706–7, 797, 1016–17, 1019, 1080, 1380–81; **3:**124, 126, 251, 421, 423–26, 426, 485, 505, 690–92, 694, 696, 794, 802; **4:**11, 189; **6:**940, 1177; **7:**143; **9:**675; HORNS ON THE **1:**900, 1033–35, 1040, 1049, 1061, 1066; **2:**264; **3:**22, 33, 787, 1144; **6:**707–8, 1534, 1555–56, 1566, 1568–69; **7:**376, 811; **12:**632, 676; INCENSE **1:**278, 900, 915–16, 960, 972, 1013, 1033–35, 1045, 1061, 1067, 1070; **2:**78, 137, 140, 988; **3:**486, 536, 591; **4:**34, 198; **5:**517; **6:**174, 1549; **9:**45–46; **12:**104; SACRIFICE ON THE **1:**93, 281, 393, 495–96, 861, 881, 900, 989–90, 1005, 1009–10, 1012–13, 1024–25, 1033–35, 1044, 1049, 1118; **2:**81, 151, 220, 771, 792, 796–97, 1012, 1381; **3:**425, 473, 499, 599, 712, 1151; **4:**197–98; **5:**797, 859; **6:**56, 940, 942, 1534, 1558, 1564, 1577; **7:**114, 143; **8:**33, 212, 435, 690; **9:**45–46; **10:**516, 918; **11:**214; **12:**5, 41; OF WISDOM **2:**561, 706–7
AMAZEMENT
See ASTONISHMENT
AMBASSADOR
4:35, 102, 160, 217–18, 270, 286, 888; **5:**208, 626; **11:**95, 369, 462–63, 898–99, 901
AMBER
6:1114, 1129, 1560
AMBUSH
2:627, 631, 772, 817, 885, 1147–48; **4:**56–57, 115, 141, 150, 176, 211, 930; **5:**12, 37–38, 715, 787; **6:**717; **7:**252, 290–91; **10:**312, 325
AMEN
1:22, 29, 176, 954, 963; **2:**63, 491–92, 494, 855; **3:**24, 408, 457, 532, 592, 781, 800–801, 1041, 1166, 1173; **4:**948, 1146; **6:**109, 396, 552, 785, 827; **7:**695; **8:**187, 205, 226, 255, 257–58, 369, 374, 379, 391, 408, 411, 439, 450, 467, 470, 475; **9:**107, 264, 345, 348, 409, 458, 532, 549, 645–46, 726, 861; **10:**433, 629–30, 696, 768–69, 965, 967, 1002; **11:**40, 202, 347, 416, 545–46; **12:**4, 54, 269, 531, 586, 695, 734
AMETHYST
6:1392; **12:**723
AMULET, AMULETS
2:65, 344, 352; **4:**277, 1048; **5:**48; **6:**1203, 1206; **9:**188; **11:**563
ANAGOGICAL
1:50
ANALOGY
1:163, 196, 963; **2:**53, 140, 249, 343, 404, 408, 608, 760, 774, 1091; **3:**447, 715, 1079; **4:**52, 303, 305, 361, 380, 402, 453, 551, 553, 556–57, 626, 674, 1072–73, 1111, 1171; **5:**7, 102, 141, 486, 547, 598, 644, 679, 715–16, 730, 732, 740, 746–47, 768, 830, 834; **6:**53–54, 317, 361, 376, 393, 443, 447, 601, 603, 645–46, 675, 715, 774, 835, 1376, 1428, 1439, 1487–88, 1494, 1596; **7:**210, 407, 487, 509–10, 522–23; **8:**59, 212, 269, 298, 309, 311, 336, 371, 445, 556, 576; **9:**293, 321, 330, 552, 718, 755–56, 780, 809; **10:**567, 677, 683, 709, 804, 827, 851, 864, 947, 957; **11:**77, 195, 228, 256, 263–65, 269, 281, 283–84, 295, 305, 345, 439, 627, 704–5, 809; **12:**28, 46, 74, 76, 81, 112, 116, 152–53, 167, 246, 259, 285, 295, 305, 614, 672
ANATHEMA
1:16; **3:**746; **10:**337, 479, 624, 628, 1002; **11:**18, 206–7, 315, 347. *See also* ACCURSED
ANCHOR
AS A METAPHOR **1:**216, 325, 337, 422, 439; **2:**127, 158, 229; **3:**610, 1132; **4:**787, 823, 1167; **6:**1064, 1342; **10:**348; **11:**191, 389, 423, 796; **12:**81, 83, 121, 165
ANCIENT OF DAYS
See under GOD, NAMES FOR/TITLES OF *in PERSONS IN THE BIBLE*
ANGEL
1:73, 89, 241, 291, 452, 464, 510, 557, 661, 711, 794, 849–50, 876–77, 934, 937–39, 1018, 1157; **2:**91, 161, 585, 612–13, 727, 736, 744–45, 747–48, 750, 755, 796–97, 834, 841, 845–47, 850, 861, 887, 1259, 1381–82; **3:**108, 140, 171, 423, 975, 980, 983, 985, 989, 1003, 1008, 1010, 1022–26, 1028, 1031, 1040, 1043–44, 1051–53, 1055–57, 1170; **4:**72, 204, 296, 348, 460, 478, 570, 587, 819; **5:**167, 524, 623, 730, 853; **6:**13, 332, 526, 531, 994; **7:**2–3, 8–9, 11–12, 65, 67, 74, 105, 107, 137, 149, 179, 182, 193, 283–84,

515, 527, 736–37, 748, 750–53, 756–58, 764–66, 769–74, 778–79, 782–84, 827; **8:**25, 36, 64–65, 134–36, 146–48, 163, 175, 206, 246, 375, 499–500, 520, 530, 533, 631, 729–31; **9:**23–24, 28, 45–48, 50–52, 55, 58, 65–66, 95, 159, 190, 245, 316, 378, 381, 426, 433, 440, 456, 462, 468–69, 528, 578, 712, 838; **10:**105, 123, 144, 163–64, 168–69, 175, 180, 182, 230, 311, 349; **11:**151, 164–66, 206, 271, 389–90, 436, 564, 708, 724; **12:**27, 29, 33, 41, 47, 350–51, 524, 527, 533, 535, 557, 565, 567, 571, 575–87, 589, 591, 594, 598, 601–4, 609, 611, 613, 619, 630–32, 637–39, 641–42, 646, 648, 656–57, 666–68, 676–77, 681–82, 692, 694–96, 699, 705–8, 716, 722–24, 732–34; OF CHURCH(ES) **12:**566–67, 569, 574–78, 581, 583, 585, 589, 614, 646, 667, 734; OF DARKNESS/DEATH **10:**181; **11:**389–90, 436; **12:**602; OF DESTRUCTION **2:**1381; **3:**423, 656; **10:**913; OF EVIL **1:**89; **7:**67; **9:**51; **11:**390; **12:**350, 488; FALL OF **5:**621; **7:**150; **8:**163, 291; **12:**488, 645; OF GOD **1:**454, 794; **2:**791, 845–46, 1188, 1313, 1315; **3:**962, 1011, 1023, 1032; **4:**51; **5:**160; **7:**182, 194; **11:**760; GUARDIAN **1:**876; **2:**79, 528; **4:**1048; **5:**730; **10:**180; OF INTERPRETATION **7:**736, 748, 750, 752–53, 756, 758, 764, 769, 773, 777–78, 782–84; OF THE LORD **1:**452, 489, 562; **2:**412, 544, 733, 747–48, 756–57, 796, 842, 846, 1381; **3:**140, 173, 269, 423, 424–25, 483, 996; **4:**100, 266; **5:**96; **6:**295, 579; **7:**150, 164; **8:**268, 499; **9:**19, 46, 69, 468, 475–76, 485; **10:**104, 106, 108, 143, 178–79, 181; MULTITUDES OF **9:**66; **12:**620–26, 695. *See also by name in PERSONS IN THE BIBLE*

ANGELIC HOST

1:272, 288, 289; **3:**1057; **4:**1271; **6:**206, 213, 227; **7:**65, 113, 150, 168, 751–52, 783; **9:**29, 65, 95; **12:**33, 621, 624, 634, 642, 666, 695, 722–23

ANGELS OF THE SEVEN CHURCHES

12:571, 667, 675, 720, 733

ANGER

1:373, 555, 565, 665, 715; **2:**124, 136, 167, 246, 363, 633, 803, 1055–57, 1102, 1119, 1123, 1126, 1128–29, 1135, 1192, 1203; **3:**386, 777, 1003; **4:**21, 289–90, 359, 371–72, 380, 382, 384, 397, 535, 562–63, 586, 837, 900, 1041–42, 1127, 1228–30; **5:**334, 422, 523; **6:**108, 279, 498, 530, 609, 658, 729, 1034, 1043–44, 1072, 1170, 1257, 1274, 1438; **7:**42, 95–96, 143, 189, 473, 481, 484, 493, 518, 522, 525, 569, 587, 613; **8:**148, 190, 196, 634, 668; **9:**22, 222, 545; **11:**181, 319, 327, 347, 431, 453, 460, 645–46; **12:**48, 181, 187, 651, 666, 675; DIVINE **1:**282, 389, 395, 477, 715, 932–33, 937, 1165; **2:**40, 100, 140, 160, 179, 183, 197–200, 300, 319, 356, 363, 528, 732, 750, 756–58, 767, 802, 824–25, 996–97, 1011, 1055–57, 1102, 1249, 1380–81; **3:**112, 124, 126, 282; **4:**229, 240, 242, 247, 377, 381, 410, 415, 442, 458, 463, 476, 486, 493, 503, 513, 556, 569, 592, 704, 726, 833, 916, 973, 990, 995, 1017, 1036, 1040, 1042, 1087, 1092; **5:**211, 593, 619, 656, 678, 808; **6:**127, 129, 133, 161, 204–5, 256, 353, 371, 386, 394, 477, 493, 582, 608, 648, 665, 679–80, 711, 717, 723, 733–34, 757, 766, 775, 812, 874, 891, 900, 926, 955, 958, 982, 1038, 1043–44, 1052, 1054–55, 1140, 1165, 1171, 1177, 1185, 1235, 1242, 1257, 1282, 1288, 1299, 1304, 1312, 1370, 1471, 1537, 1574; **7:**115, 219, 278, 288, 296–97, 366, 377, 478, 514, 537, 541, 569, 575–76, 589, 597, 613, 746–47, 753–54, 760, 789, 792, 816; **9:**258; **11:**642; **12:**388, 672, 675, 712; HUMAN ANGER AT GOD **2:**1249, 1263; **4:**319, 368, 371–72, 557; **6:**698, 1043–44, 1054–55, 1072, 1170; **7:**402, 473, 481; **8:**616; **12:**522; PROPHETIC **1:**68; **2:**1088; **3:**238; **6:**547, 627, 698, 1299, 1311, 1383; **7:**613; RIGHTEOUS **2:**756, 1055, 1057, 1203; **5:**543; **6:**493; **7:**126, 553; **11:**645; “SLOW TO ANGER” **1:**477, 946, 988; **2:**125, 741; **3:**811; **4:**234, 671, 780; **5:**141, 143, 150, 162, 179, 219, 561, 619, 655; **6:**57, 697, 702, 711, 717, 1140, 1166, 1318; **7:**319, 408, 472–73, 518, 525, 553, 602; **12:**204, 358

ANGUISH

2:748, 1271, 1339; **3:**347, 777, 903; **4:**208, 313, 391, 395, 637, 801, 899, 1173; **5:**258, 384, 485, 499, 536; **6:**122, 431, 436, 448, 451, 454, 461, 508, 517, 545, 631, 693, 805, 821, 957–58, 1167, 1268, 1298, 1367, 1418; **7:**148, 666, 682; **9:**780; **10:**586, 627; **11:**296; CORPORATE **1:**719; **4:**582, 954, 984; **5:**534, 586; **6:**119, 346, 449–51, 477, 521, 625, 628, 1030, 1057, 1370, 1415; **7:**316, 587, 677–78; **11:**707; GOD’S **3:**777; **6:**346, 563, 629–30, 632, 648, 655; **11:**646; INDIVIDUAL **1:**488, 973; **2:**633, 1129, 1271, 1340–41; **3:**1004; **4:**385–87, 391, 395, 535, 564, 631; **5:**4, 258, 584; **6:**185–86, 436, 440, 457, 460, 503, 521, 563, 614–15, 619, 629–32, 648, 665, 697, 704, 1139, 1455; **7:**232, 644; **8:**707; **10:**628–29, 636, 680; **11:**120, 296, 404; **12:**444; OF JESUS (*see under* JESUS THE CHRIST *in PERSONS IN THE BIBLE*

ANIMAL, ANIMALS

1:218–20, 349, 352, 359, 362–63, 364–65, 375, 390, 395, 449, 747, 1075–76, 1119–21; **2:**183–84, 194, 316, 387, 399, 454, 1120, 1206; **3:**759, 1026, 1154, 1159; **4:**41, 206, 256, 458, 484, 488, 510, 608–9, 611–12, 615, 618, 622, 624, 708, 763; **5:**72, 126, 255, 311–12, 526, 591, 746; **6:**143, 1176, 1201, 1269, 1377, 1464, 1528, 1584; **7:**55, 192, 262, 467, 478, 482–83, 487,

ANIMAL, ANIMALS *(continued)*
514, 523, 808; **8:**277, 403, 658; **9:**230, 273–74, 367; **12:**167; CLEAN/UNCLEAN **1:**316, 391, 393, 399, 986, 1000, 1052, 1076, 1080–82, 1097, 1120, 1187–89; **2:**147–48, 397–98, 849–50, 853; **4:**64; **8:**32, 582–83; **12:**692; HIDE(S) **1:**1049, 1066, 1082; **6:**820; IMAGERY **2:**316; **4:**510, 609, 618, 708, 763; **5:**69, 85, 585; **6:**142–43, 163, 260, 276–77, 380, 601, 685, 896, 1269, 1314, 1516, 1532, 1564; **7:**53, 55, 74–75, 101–3, 185, 192, 234, 289, 293, 375, 482, 808; **8:**403, 582–83, 585; **9:**282, 409; **10:**847; **11:**847; **12:**112, 167, 603–4, 692; LAWS RELATED TO **1:**281, 399, 567, 785, 865–67, 870, 988, 1013, 1025, 1027, 1039, 1049, 1051–54, 1097, 1119–21, 1151–52, 1165; **2:**126, 151, 387, 420, 452, 493, 767, 849–50, 853; **4:**510; **5:**797; **6:**282, 1149, 1546, 1558, 1580, 1589; **7:**375; **8:**277; **9:**284, 358; SACRIFICE OF **1:**280–81, 393, 494, 498, 785, 861, 988–89, 991, 998, 1009, 1011–13, 1015–17, 1020, 1025, 1027, 1034–35, 1039–40, 1046, 1049, 1051–54, 1061–62, 1111–12, 1119, 1151–52, 1188–89; **2:**126, 151, 229–33, 420, 832; **3:**346, 610, 647, 708; **4:**41, 206, 421, 877; **5:**591, 797; **6:**276, 282, 1284, 1463, 1466, 1527–28, 1546, 1558, 1564, 1589, 1592–93, 1605; **7:**467, 846, 862; **8:**196; **10:**704, 893; **12:**107, 110, 112, 114–15, 158, 269; WORSHIP OF **5:**417, 445, 526, 536, 540–41, 543–45, 570. *See also* BEAST; CREATURE; CREEPING THING; *by individual species name*

ANKLETS
3:1147

ANNUNCIATION
OF JOHN'S BIRTH **8:**64, 67, 69; **9:**11, 15, 21, 33, 43–44, 47–48, 52, 58–59, 69, 80, 434; OF JESUS' BIRTH **2:**1259; **8:**64–65, 67, 69, 134; **9:**11, 13–14, 21, 33, 49–53, 55, 58, 62, 69, 71, 73, 77, 91, 381, 426, 442, 456, 487; **12:**4

ANOINT (*OR* ANOINTS, *ETC.*)
1:91, 225, 542, 585, 888, 907, 919–20, 976, 1017, 1047, 1060–61, 1071, 1099, 1101, 1148; **2:**163, 1040; **3:**143, 215, 217, 469, 1147; **4:**110; **5:**114, 326–27, 461; **6:**513, 1228, 1266, 1337, 1393; **7:**128, 771; **8:**22, 206, 466, 594, 622, 699; **9:**17, 104–6, 160, 316; **10:**79; **11:**451; **12:**222, 376, 400, 404, 406–8, 410, 414, 423, 426, 439, 449, 453–54, 587; THE DEAD **8:**465–66, 498, 695, 698, 701, 730; **9:**450, 465, 468–69, 472, 685–86, 701–3; JESUS **1:**897; **2:**603; **6:**1497; **8:**26, 58, 169, 464–66, 498, 528, 695, 697–701, 726, 730; **9:**105, 169–70, 172, 415, 450, 465, 468, 472, 481, 685–86, 690, 699, 701–3, 707, 710, 722, 804, 836; A KING **2:**606, 816, 926, 953, 961, 982, 1023, 1032, 1036, 1037–44, 1046, 1053, 1060–61, 1086, 1092, 1094–95, 1097–99, 1101, 1107–8, 1119, 1121, 1145, 1211, 1213, 1223, 1233–34, 1293, 1345, 1347; **3:**20, 143–44, 209, 212, 215–17, 366, 468–69; **4:**1036, 1131; **5:**164, 708, 846, 851; **6:**122

ANOINTED ONE, THE
See under JESUS THE CHRIST, NAMES FOR/TITLES OF *in PERSONS IN THE BIBLE*

ANT
5:74–75, 107, 255

ANTELOPE
See GAZELLE

ANTHROPOLOGY, ANTHROPOLOGICAL
1:141, 150, 179, 184, 214, 323–24, 1076; **2:**22, 558; **3:**874; **4:**712; **5:**61, 125, 138, 152, 160, 283, 447; **6:**8, 23, 531, 1101; **8:**206, 264, 315, 476, 513; **9:**525, 553, 555, 672; **10:**526, 867, 900; **11:**23, 326, 330, 347; **12:**37, 54, 273, 436, 446–47

ANTHROPOMORPHIC
MORPHISM **1:**49, 70, 72, 90, 322, 351, 803, 1010–11; **4:**312; **6:**649, 653, 665, 680, 874, 960, 1118–21, 1130, 1155, 1291; **7:**518, 836; **8:**532; **11:**290

ANTICHRIST
See ANTICHRIST *in PERSONS IN THE BIBLE*

ANTINOMIAN, ANTINOMIANISM
3:501; **7:**108; **10:**325, 360, 475, 485, 489–90, 540, 823; **12:**475, 489, 492, 497–98

ANTITHESIS
1:178, 814, 955; **2:**646, 815, 1192, 1371; **3:**396, 587; **4:**382, 689, 753, 908, 1240, 1263; **5:**109–11, 116–17, 120–21, 128, 143, 230, 238, 301, 305, 311, 326, 341, 345, 477, 519, 573, 579, 585–86, 590; **6:**92, 489, 1188, 1198, 1207, 1261, 1271, 1283–84, 1311, 1316, 1337, 1364, 1461, 1465, 1467, 1469, 1484, 1485; **7:**181, 489, 615; **8:**188, 190, 191, 193, 195, 408, 541, 708; **9:**135, 257, 339, 667, 711, 808; **10:**419, 454, 481, 486, 543, 549, 555, 609, 662; **11:**63, 66, 78, 94, 105, 252, 305–6, 414, 441–42, 507, 622, 768, 798, 808–9, 820, 830–31, 843, 845; **12:**65, 102, 204, 209, 348, 361, 428, 514

APHORISM
2:1007; **5:**296, 675, 689, 692; **8:**298; **9:**249, 255, 260, 330, 347–48, 386, 557, 697; **10:**337, 916; **11:**815, 846; **12:**178, 197, 199, 202, 209, 436, 453, 657

APOCALYPSE
1:288; **6:**206–7, 227; **7:**1–5, 22, 654; **8:**345; **10:**64; **11:**409; **12:**328, 505, 507, 509, 512, 514, 517, 519, 527, 534, 542, 546, 553, 556, 560, 568, 574, 577, 595, 616, 670, 688, 695, 701, 709, 722; THE APOCALYPSE (BOOK OF REVELATION) **1:**8, 16; **6:**218; **10:**388, 390–91; **11:**673; **12:**503,

505–17, 530, 541, 545, 547–48, 550–52, 554–55, 559–63, 570, 584–85, 589, 596, 601, 607–8, 612, 614, 712, 730, 733–34; EXTRABIBLICAL **1:**15, 289, 314, 1194; **5:**558; **7:**2, 6–7, 11–14, 122; **8:**103; LITTLE **7:**11; **8:**310; IN THE OT **1:**288; **6:**43, 206–7, 210, 218, 225, 227, 273–74, 1513; **7:**5, 9–10, 144; IN THE NT **1:**8, 16; **6:**206, 218; **7:**1–2, 15; **8:**51, 310, 429, 439–43, 445, 457, 528, 687; **10:**376, 388, 391, 424; **12:**97, 328, 506, 509, 515, 519, 530; MATTHEW 24/MARK 12-13 **8:**123, 429, 440–42, 457; **12:**519

APOCALYPTIC

BEAST (*see under* BEAST); DISCOURSE **7:**7, 15, 874; **8:**258, 428, 446, 474, 518, 630, 654, 659, 663, 671, 683, 700; **9:**331, 407; **12:**510, 516, 548, 550; ESCHATOLOGY **6:**207, 223, 277, 1513–14; **10:**10, 63; GROUPS/MOVEMENT(S) **1:**289; **6:**228; **7:**1, 14, 118; **8:**259; IMAGERY/MOTIFS/THEMES **1:**394; **3:**1098; **6:**207, 221, 227; **8:**309, 442; **9:**90, 224, 263, 265, 452; **11:**304, 391, 411, 724, 726, 728, 748; **12:**431, 505–6, 530, 541, 550, 616, 670, 687; LITERATURE **1:**46, 289, 364; **3:**948; **4:**577, 618, 675; **6:**84, 113, 156, 206, 228–29, 274, 934, 981, 1513; **7:**1–4, 22–23, 63, 106, 114–15, 118, 128, 149, 164, 382, 429, 654; **8:**446, 631, 687; **9:**91, 167, 458, 787; **10:**822; **11:**206, 566, 590; **12:**85, 97, 347, 403, 412, 506, 510, 519–21, 531, 550, 567, 596; THEOLOGY (*see under* THEOLOGY); UNDERSTANDING/WORLD VIEW **1:**288; **4:**488; **6:**67, 73, 83, 223, 255, 961; **7:**1, 7, 15, 429; **8:**157, 262, 309; **10:**438, 822; **11:**88, 704, 708, 714, 724, 734, 748, 900; **12:**375, 530, 543, 596, 720; VISION(S) (*see under* VISION)

APOCALYPTICISM

1:288–89; **6:**37, 448, 982; **7:**1–2, 4–5, 7, 10–11, 13–16, 103, 106, 149; **8:**37–38, 40, 455; **9:**499; **11:**683–84, 715, 728, 741, 753; **12:**85, 410, 412, 435, 519–20, 554, 713, 716

APODICTIC, APODEICTIC

1:311, 869–70, 1138; **2:**328, 1056; **3:**718; **6:**1206, 1259; **8:**189; **11:**172

APOLOGETICS

1:71, 73, 80; **8:**153, 393; **9:**473; **10:**240, 314; **12:**447

APOSTASY

1:78, 306, 404, 1118; **2:**198, 344, 389, 391, 393–95, 420–21, 436, 452, 520, 526–28, 714, 731–32, 750, 754, 756–57, 760, 766, 787, 899, 988, 1017, 1026–27; **3:**5, 125, 169–70, 251, 497, 511, 514–15, 524–25, 551, 566, 577, 587, 591, 597–98, 602, 611, 632, 635, 643–44, 650, 733, 735, 746; **4:**19, 32, 44, 46, 240, 1000; **5:**562; **6:**72, 285, 477, 489–90, 492, 516, 573, 584, 589, 599–601, 610, 618, 620–21, 646, 656, 670, 685, 692–93, 702, 707, 716, 721–22, 750, 761, 873, 920, 1160, 1167, 1274–75, 1279, 1286, 1509, 1575–76; **7:**291, 305, 318, 323, 325, 594; **8:**29, 36; **9:**242, 253, 857; **10:**101, 205, 225, 254, 282, 283, 293; **11:**713, 756, 758, 796, 838; **12:**49, 75, 78, 122, 124, 127, 137, 159–60, 352, 443–44, 522, 543, 581

APOSTLE

4:503; **8:**73, 95, 102, 103, 410, 528, 539, 600, 731; **9:**6, 137, 159, 224, 310, 323; **10:**38, 49, 98, 115, 140, 161, 167, 169, 415, 602, 653, 745, 753, 758, 762, 780, 797, 902, 904, 909–11, 937, 949; **12:**45–46, 230, 233–34, 246, 323, 333, 360, 366, 530, 537, 562, 704–5, 722; GREAT (*see under* GREAT); TO THE GENTILES (PAUL) **8:**46; **9:**118, 487; **10:**401, 407, 682, 701, 798; **11:**91, 112, 173, 218, 236, 293, 355, 614, 785. *See also* PAUL THE APOSTLE *in PERSONS IN THE BIBLE*; PETER *in PERSONS IN THE BIBLE*

APOSTLES' CREED

See under CREED

POSTOLIC FATHERS/CHURCH FATHERS

See CHURCH: FATHERS

APPAREL

1:906, 908; **3:**692, 1086, 1142; **6:**453, 1228; **7:**765; **9:**468; **11:**801; **12:**592, 693. *See also* CLOTHES, CLOTHING

APPEAL TO CAESAR

BY PAUL **9:**363; **10:**322, 324–26, 330–31, 359

APPLE

1:26, 914; **5:**218, 317, 346, 389, 395; **7:**296, 309; **11:**880; OF THE EYE **4:**740; **5:**419, 730; **6:**681, 1343; **7:**760–61; **8:**283

APRON

2:909; **5:**843

AQUEDUCT

8:718

ARAMAIC, ARAMAISM

1:22, 26, 28, 31, 39, 70–71, 101, 129, 179, 233–34, 237, 239, 241, 249, 292, 294, 297, 302, 303, 314; **2:**613, 627, 739, 772, 833; **3:**93, 265, 379, 666, 675–76, 699, 707–8, 711–12, 718, 720, 722, 748, 761, 801, 833, 848, 860–62, 899, 929, 947, 951, 955, 969, 976–77, 979, 1017; **4:**47, 184, 188–89, 325, 355, 467, 501, 690; **5:**6, 94, 198, 207, 251, 258, 270–71, 332, 604, 642, 674, 777, 780, 808; **6:**293, 642, 660, 831, 986, 1016, 1240, 1250, 1330, 1378, 1393, 1429, 1507; **7:**3, 13, 19, 32, 51, 64–65, 72, 74–75, 81, 83, 88–89, 91, 100, 102, 111–12, 117, 122, 124, 156, 158, 163, 174, 185, 187–88, 192–93, 465, 653, 715, 738, 804, 846; **8:**6, 29, 46, 75, 80, 90, 107, 108, 148, 158, 202, 204, 210, 286, 308, 345, 360, 436, 471, 492, 528, 550, 556, 562, 568, 571,

ARAMAIC, ARAMAISM *(continued)*
590, 612, 666, 722; **9:**18, 105, 124, 151, 190, 234, 418, 433, 454, 531, 549, 822, 830, 842; **10:**112, 161, 217, 307, 337, 593, 778, 857, 1002; **11:**226, 285, 290, 374, 501; **12:**183, 230, 245, 323, 474. *See also* SYRIAC VERSION(S) *in ANCIENT LITERATURE*

ARCH
3:1167; **7:**53; **10:**894; **11:**402

ARCHAEOLOGY, ARCHAEOLOGICAL
1:6, 182, 184, 214–15, 216–17, 219, 221, 225, 246–55, 256, 258–59, 262, 264–65, 268, 327, 388, 695, 805, 996, 1054, 1081; **2:**315, 556, 557, 558, 615–16, 669, 694, 700, 724, 934, 1237; **3:**6, 52, 82, 280, 591, 765, 769, 1174; **5:**28, 80; **6:**10, 577, 1160, 1349; **7:**192, 203, 333, 534–35, 855; **8:**35, 674; **10:**271, 314, 774; **11:**361, 471, 675–76, 682; **12:**571

ARCHAEOLOGIST(S)
1:19, 214, 219, 246–47, 250–51, 253–54, 258, 990; **2:**557, 615–16, 755; **3:**28, 300; **4:**156, 241; **5:**102; **6:**10, 1119, 1143, 1301, 1540, 1555, 1566; **7:**620, 751, 848; **8:**228, 539, 606, 673, 719; **10:**380, 773

ARCHANGEL
1:287–89; **3:**1038; **7:**13; **12:**488–90, 571, 649. *See also* ANGEL

ARCHER
3:220; **6:**1049; **7:**810

ARCHETYPE, ARCHETYPES
1:210, 278, 394; **3:**377; **4:**1128; **8:**79, 699; **12:**532

ARCHISYNAGOGOS
LEADER OF THE SYNAGOGUE **10:**775

ARCHITECTURE
1:221, 226, 247, 251, 278–79; **2:**14, 54; **4:**787, 1184; **5:**64, 147; **6:**1532; **7:**53, 111, 118; **8:**439, 686; **10:**429; **11:**365, 405, 430; **12:**15, 551

ARK OF NOAH
1:56, 257, 316, 370, 389, 391–94, 1005; **4:**328–29; **5:**523, 526, 552–53; **6:**212, 278; **12:**134, 633

ARK OF THE COVENANT/TESTIMONY/CONGREGATION
1:277–78, 364, 889–91, 893, 897, 924, 931, 960, 972, 979, 998–99, 1007, 1012, 1033, 1066, 1111, 1113; **2:**21, 32, 36, 52–55, 79–80, 83, 89, 94–98, 126, 140, 151, 198, 246, 254–55, 328, 363–65, 367, 384, 487, 520, 546, 589, 599–600, 607, 871, 949, 952–53, 955, 959–60, 962, 969, 974–75, 987, 992–93, 995–1015, 1017–19, 1022, 1148, 1051, 1063, 1073, 1079, 1139, 1188, 1197–98, 1201, 1236–37, 1240, 1243, 1246–52, 1256, 1270, 1286, 1324–25, 1327, 1345, 1354; **3:**33, 39–40, 69–70, 75, 78, 104, 150, 345, 365, 368, 370, 382–87, 388, 390, 393–96, 399–402, 405–7, 432–33, 438, 445, 461, 473, 484, 494, 496–99, 501–2, 505, 606, 618, 644, 647–48, 692, 839, 842, 993; **4:**34, 77–78, 198, 741, 772–73, 865, 868, 905, 919, 927, 944–45, 992, 999, 1013, 1064, 1075, 1104, 1130, 1181, 1211–12, 1279; **5:**282, 517, 523, 526, 552, 556, 757; **6:**13, 102, 212, 261, 278, 294, 453, 575, 708, 772, 891, 925, 1118–20, 1179, 1183, 1319, 1349, 1393–94, 1533–34, 1560, 1575; **7:**231, 252, 272, 667, 722, 774, 836; **8:**364, 446; **10:**474; **11:**364; **12:**58, 104, 134, 569, 630, 644, 672

ARM
1:606, 1033, 1054; **2:**651, 1108, 1154; **3:**106, 629, 752; **4:**297, 517, 554, 572, 857, 984; **5:**134; **6:**388, 892, 1147, 1161, 1209, 1247, 1420–21, 1430; **8:**431; OF GOD **1:**796, 801; **4:**296, 616–17, 623, 857, 996, 1035, 1072; **5:**13, 183, 486; **6:**256, 338, 388, 441, 443, 448, 455, 460–61, 465–66, 502, 733, 911, 1147, 1161, 1288, 1420; **9:**56, 716; **11:**294

ARMAGEDDON
10:606; **11:**88; **12:**543–44, 677

ARMLET
2:1201–3

ARMOR
2:1108, 1110–15, 1120, 1198, 1206; **3:**166, 368, 553, 775, 996, 1008, 1084, 1143, 1147, 1161; **4:**89, 130, 153, 210, 624; **5:**229, 326, 486; **6:**134, 394, 1516; **7:**145; **9:**242, 245, 341, 430; **10:**728–29; **11:**361, 458–64; **12:**299–300, 632; **3:**1008; OF GOD **4:**749; **5:**46; **11:**463, 909. *See also* ARMS: AS WEAPONRY; BREASTPIECE/BREASTPLATE; COAT: OF MAIL

ARMORY
2:484, 513; **3:**67, 769; **6:**194, 915

ARMS
1:57, 232, 400, 445, 499, 572, 1054, 1126, 1148; **2:**861; **3:**532, 1049; **4:**572, 602, 1209; **5:**72, 354, 373, 393, 398, 719, 721, 824; **6:**1228, 1247, 1269, 1419–21, 1466; **7:**136, 258, 336; **8:**637; **9:**29, 170, 296, 302, 454, 861; **10:**530, 957; **11:**297; **12:**561, 598; AS WEAPONRY **1:**740; **2:**300, 648, 651, 878, 884, 1103, 1111–14, 1134, 1167; **3:**102, 1090; **4:**106, 122, 152, 212, 223, 250, 1276; **5:**194, 442, 525; **6:**186, 853, 858, 1356, 1421; **7:**7, 64, 67, 137, 144, 151, 194, 248, 258, 757; **8:**690; **9:**430; **11:**459, 462, 645, 724; **12:**605, 646, 700 (*see also* ARMOR; WEAPONS)

ARMY
1:118, 226, 249, 269, 820; **2:**34, 39, 162, 439, 461, 547, 646, 775–76, 779–81, 788–89, 795, 816–17, 821, 825, 830, 838, 885, 1070, 1109,

1111–13, 1183, 1205, 1230, 1280, 1336, 1346, 1352, 1376; **3:**27, 50, 150, 192, 201–2, 205, 212, 221, 269, 289, 294, 379, 384, 414, 416, 445, 530–31, 533, 538, 542, 581, 871, 995, 1023, 1095, 1101, 1105–6, 1113, 1118, 1123, 1127, 1132, 1140, 1144, 1158, 1167, 1178; **4:**16, 30, 35–36, 47, 57–60, 62–64, 66–67, 85, 88–89, 91, 93, 95, 100, 110–11, 114, 121, 125, 127, 129, 133–35, 138, 140, 143, 145, 154, 157, 174, 177, 193, 228–30, 248, 254–55, 262, 264, 290, 295–96, 436, 442, 485; **5:**143, 418, 724, 806, 834; **7:**65–67, 107, 140, 308, 354, 366, 371, 386, 547, 582, 594, 609–10, 613, 616, 635, 679, 709, 770, 805, 810, 817, 836; **8:**228, 443; **9:**88, 366, 404; **10:**93, 170; **11:**138, 233, 617, 842; **12:**82, 144, 539, 544, 713; BABYLONIAN **1:**267; **2:**406, 826; **3:**871–72, 1097, 1123; **6:**559, 628, 648, 655, 722, 733, 797, 805, 819–20, 830, 834, 848, 851, 865, 882–83, 1081, 1085, 1143, 1245, 1366, 1410–11, 1420, 1455, 1534; **7:**454; OF DAVID/SAUL **1:**261; **2:**219, 547, 1070, 1079–81, 1110–13, 1120–21, 1139, 1152, 1174–75, 1197, 1201, 1212, 1216, 1237, 1278, 1280, 1283, 1286, 1324, 1346–47, 1350–52, 1376; **3:**27, 376–77; **5:**174, 724; EGYPTIAN/OF PHARAOH **1:**266, 795; **2:**109, 253, 370, 809; **3:**286; **4:**592; **5:**525, 529, 531, 591, 612, 818; **6:**831, 848, 882, 1077, 1326, 1364, 1402–3, 1405–6, 1413, 1415, 1420, 1436, 1438; **7:**25; **8:**537; **11:**64; **12:**672; OF GOD/YAHWEH **2:**585, 612, 733, 747; **3:**379, 552, 563; **4:**517, 612, 773; **6:**156, 213, 1130, 1317, 1504; **7:**10, 67, 316–17, 324, 333, 783, 836; **9:**65; **10:**999; **12:**494, 583, 664, 700, 714; OF GOG **6:**1516–17, 1522, 1527, 1529, 1532; OF ISRAEL **1:**261; **2:**96, 246–47, 252, 439, 584, 736–37, 747, 752, 756, 779, 787–88, 796, 802–4, 807, 1001–2, 1081, 1113, 1191, 1201–2, 1268, 1332, 1375, 1380; **3:**49–50, 217, 236, 245, 338, 370, 380, 382, 413, 422, 460, 547, 560, 562, 586, 590–91, 600, 628, 772, 775; **4:**71, 78, 85, 89, 111, 138, 148, 151–52, 156, 175, 250, 276, 297; **6:**108, 809, 857–58, 1194–95; **7:**122, 344, 403, 814, 828; **12:**351

AROMA
1:916, 1010, 1013, 1015–16, 1018, 1024, 1036; **2:**126; **5:**380; **6:**1558; **11:**58

ARROW
1:538; **2:**1289; **3:**166, 220, 237–38, 553, 649; **4:**459, 486, 624, 930, 1047; **5:**485, 630, 736, 765; **6:**183, 295, 657, 1049, 1499; **7:**810

ARSENAL
1:76, 757; **4:**335, 419; **5:**390, 671; **6:**1296, 1414, 1522; **7:**136, 167, 464, 683; **8:**50; **9:**436; **11:**137, 560; **12:**43

ART, ARTS
1:1, 6–7, 63, 87, 109, 113, 121, 139–40, 142, 145, 359, 376–77, 898, 922, 941; **2:**192, 307, 332, 510, 514, 546, 616–17, 1284; **3:**55, 889, 1080, 1083; **4:**224, 315, 322, 351, 488, 1221; **5:**57, 72, 94, 102, 118, 155, 205, 218, 281, 294, 351, 417, 503, 513, 543, 584, 591, 690, 773, 807–8, 813; **6:**412, 654, 1066, 1093, 1095, 1203, 1275; **7:**147, 209; **8:**2, 218; **9:**145, 260, 362, 369, 413; **10:**247, 267, 371, 379–80, 382–83, 783; **11:**189, 566, 737, 796; **12:**25, 56, 324, 513, 542, 550–52; PERFORMING/VISUAL **1:**6–7, 139–40, 145, 897, 922; **2:**88, 192, 861, 1288; **3:**55, 129, 448, 1080, 1162; **4:**608–9; **5:**80, 155, 205, 294, 322, 439, 513, 543, 546–47, 557–58, 813; **6:**1022, 1066, 1563; **7:**53, 111, 118, 147, 377, 529, 611–12, 862; **8:**321, 497; **9:**91, 196, 296, 465; **10:**244, 247, 813, 957; **11:**548, 709; **12:**550–52, 694, 696

ARTIFICER
5:546; **6:**1131

ARTILLERY
4:87; **6:**1480

ARTISAN, ARTISANS
1:223, 921, 961–62, 964, 976; **3:**68, 477–79; **4:**533, 1098; **5:**11, 546–47, 552, 557, 625, 702, 812–13; **6:**176, 944, 1004, 1075; **7:**29, 260, 756; **8:**12, 13, 514; **9:**9–10; **10:**270, 377, 773; **11:**675

ASCENSION
3:865; **4:**870; **6:**139; **10:**40, 46; DEATH, RESURRECTION, AND ASCENSION OF JESUS (*see under* JESUS THE CHRIST *in PERSONS IN THE BIBLE*); OF ELIJAH **3:**173, 179; **5:**851

ASCENT, ASCENTS
2:78, 1248; **3:**381, 839; **4:**57, 63, 74, 100, 150, 281, 726, 1014–15, 1176, 1183; **5:**252; **7:**504, 511; **8:**174; **10:**290; **12:**596, 630, 677; OF GOD/PERSON/SOUL TO HEAVEN **1:**49, 94, 96; **4:**1014–15; **5:**151; **7:**5, 11, 13; **8:**723; **9:**489, 551, 610, 732, 782, 788, 843–44; **11:**361, 372, 382, 384, 411, 421, 567, 639; **12:**82, 294, 515, 518, 520–21, 565, 592, 596, 603–4, 619, 630, 643

ASCENTS, SONG OR SONGS OF
4:309, 653, 658, 664, 1176–78, 1180, 1183–85, 1187, 1189, 1192, 1194–95, 1197–98, 1200, 1202–3, 1205, 1208, 1210–11, 1214, 1216, 1219, 1223–24, 1227, 1231

ASCETICISM
1:96, 288; **3:**1019, 1113–14, 1180; **5:**72; **7:**122, 126, 400; **8:**4, 352; **9:**767; **10:**869; **11:**386, 562, 631–32, 635, 642, 653, 813; **12:**523, 543

ASHAMED
1:362, 799; **2:**438, 1340; **3:**755; **4:**43, 69, 389, 502, 705, 800, 1126; **5:**455, 616, 673–74,

ASHAMED *(continued)*
827–28; **6:**63, 202, 248, 402, 477, 647, 670, 912, 1238, 1240, 1492, 1530, 1562; **7:**124, 176, 180, 243, 588, 832; **8:**32, 627; **9:**307, 354, 408; **10:**423–24, 426, 443, 505, 517, 532, 546, 590, 595, 714; **11:**154, 490, 537–38, 595, 835, 837–39, 844; **12:**40, 137

ASHERAH
1:233, 239; **2:**277, 286, 420, 569–70, 687, 766, 797; **3:**116, 118, 124, 135, 139, 162, 276, 1108; **6:**1175–76; **7:**224, 226, 240, 272, 779

ASHES
1:1014, 1019, 1044; **2:**81, 99, 137, 151–52, 247, 320, 719, 1192, 1305; **3:**380, 501, 797, 805, 901–2, 959–60, 1002, 1087, 1113–14, 1142, 1145; **4:**281, 355, 434, 463, 539, 1087; **5:**460, 567, 834; **6:**432, 808, 813, 1049, 1217, 1342, 1395, 1491, 1579; **7:**189–90, 528, 684, 872; **9:**46, 410; **12:**107; DUST AND **4:**546, 628–29, 713; **5:**705, 731, 823; **6:**919; **7:**312; AND SACKCLOTH **3:**902, 959–60, 1113, 1142; **4:**63; **8:**205–6; **9:**84, 221

ASP
5:715. *See also* SERPENT; SNAKE

ASS, ASSES
1:219, 242, 365, 453; **2:**767, 841; **4:**38, 351, 387, 421, 510, 545, 547, 597, 608, 610–11, 624; **5:**715, 791; **6:**53, 265–66, 601–2, 1224, 1232; **7:**234, 261, 292, 405, 781, 807; **8:**25; **9:**321; **11:**103; **12:**351; BALAAM'S **1:**242; **12:**351; DUMB **4:**421; ISRAEL AS "A WILD ASS IN HEAT" **6:**601–2, 1224, 1232; **7:**234, 261, 292, 781; JAWBONE OF AN **2:**767, 841; JOB AND THE WILD **4:**387, 597, 610–11, 624; JOB'S BRAYING FRIENDS **4:**545; MESSIAH RIDING AN **7:**807; UNBELIEVERS YOKED AS **11:**103; WILD **1:**453; **4:**387, 421, 510, 545, 547, 597, 608, 610–11, 624; **5:**715; **6:**265, 266, 601–2, 1224, 1232; **7:**234, 261, 292. *See also* MULE

ASSASSIN, ASSASSINS
2:770, 782, 827, 1209, 1229–30; **3:**139, 205, 294, 786–87; **6:**1080, 1258, 1345; **10:**298, 312, 325; **11:**751; **12:**405

ASSEMBLY
DIVINE/HEAVENLY **1:**42, 241–42, 273, 278, 345; **4:**450, 518, 773; **5:**757; **6:**336, 338, 341, 369, 579, 588, 717, 751–52, 962, 968, 1114, 1393; **11:**615; GENERAL/REPRESENTATIVE **1:**39; **2:**599, 1007, 1016, 1018, 1046–47, 1128; **3:**20, 78, 384–85, 467–68, 473, 494, 496, 499, 574, 608, 616, 667, 669, 687, 693, 725, 740, 742–43, 768, 780, 783, 800, 802, 804, 882; **4:**51, 66, 82, 87, 101, 164–65, 1221; **5:**160, 269, 652, 693; **6:**56, 872, 943, 1330, 1435; **7:**51, 258, 550, 674, 685, 696, 827; **8:**346, 379; **9:**125, 155, 442, 447, 464, 489; **10:**56, 59, 88, 105, 114, 124, 168, 197, 203–4, 206, 208–9, 214, 239, 245, 273, 847; **11:**194, 430, 651, 688; **12:**156, 619; GREAT **1:**306; **2:**752; **3:**732, 804; **4:**26, 77, 161; **5:**14; **7:**877; OF A RELIGIOUS CONGREGATION **1:**40, 591, 960, 1035, 1156, 1159–60; **2:**89, 124, 135–36, 152, 636, 641, 893, 901, 919, 946, 1112; **3:**98, 156, 460–61, 470, 494, 616, 669, 686, 687, 733, 746, 757, 781, 794, 804–6, 842, 1117; **4:**72, 165, 685–86, 782–83; **5:**268–69, 473, 652, 781; **6:**159, 654, 1348, 1408, 1534, 1570; **7:**266, 312, 320–21, 550, 666, 696, 702; **8:**379; **9:**155, 287, 393, 442; **10:**96, 145, 211, 231, 295, 807, 847; **11:**223, 359, 410, 430, 436, 561, 575, 615, 649, 651, 677–78, 688–89, 808–9, 814, 819, 892; **12:**48, 55, 60, 121, 154, 158, 163, 192–95, 200–201, 221–22, 463–64; SOLEMN **3:**802, 805; **6:**56; **7:**320, 666; **12:**287

ASTARTE
1:1135; **2:**569–70, 755, 757, 1017, 1198; **4:**80, 276, 945; **6:**345, 638, 1360, 1392; **7:**779

ASTONISHMENT
OVER A DIVINE ACT **1:**795, 818, 826, 881, 948; **2:**1115, 1043–44; **3:**129, 735, 1154; **4:**990; **5:**506; **6:**400, 466, 468–69, 613, 758, 1086, 1497, 1499, 1503, 1596; **7:**67, 635, 784; **8:**62–63, 219, 240, 328, 511, 541, 549, 589–90, 603, 650–51, 665, 732; **9:**59, 66, 103, 110–11, 242, 284, 386, 472, 485, 550, 565, 585, 843; **10:**57, 78, 85, 88, 139–40, 167, 180, 198, 405; **12:**292

ASTROLOGER, ASTROLOGERS
6:412; **7:**44, 50, 63, 72, 618; **8:**140, 143–44

ASTROLOGY, ASTROLOGICAL
1:344, 599; **3:**882; **5:**626, 663, 672; **6:**412, 660; **7:**4–5, 111, 558; **8:**24, 29, 142–44; **11:**362, 391, 460, 627, 636; **12:**521

ASTRONOMY, ASTRONOMICAL
1:117; **2:**36; **3:**630; **4:**34; **5:**502, 506; **6:**660; **7:**4, 11, 167–68; **8:**691; **9:**329; **11:**378, 411, 415

ASYLUM
2:265, 268, 501, 697, 919; **3:**22, 33, 787; **4:**125; **6:**169, 1179; AT ALTARS **2:**264, 268; **3:**22, 33, 787; **4:**125, 222, 645, 721, 736, 786, 905, 912, 919, 922, 958; **6:**1179, 1566; CITIES OF **1:**4; **2:**169, 263–65, 268, 696–97; **12:**81 (*see also* CITY: OF REFUGE)

ATHEISM
1:285; **4:**729, 731; **5:**35, 118; **6:**550; **7:**58, 65–67, 104, 422; **8:**15, 17–18, 22, 164, 291, 459; **9:**257; **10:**246; **12:**49, 514, 684

ATONEMENT
1:204, 913, 915–17, 933, 988, 998–99, 1001, 1007, 1011–12, 1024, 1027, 1032–33, 1035–37, 1039, 1041, 1044, 1047, 1051–52, 1061, 1065–67, 1085, 1099, 1101, 1112–14, 1119–20,

1144, 1159; **2:**33, 78–79, 81–82, 129, 140, 151–52, 197, 247, 264; **3:**22, 346, 603, 608–10, 612, 618; **4:**122, 277, 933; **5:**592, 797, 808, 842; **6:**457, 463–64, 1584; **7:**376; **8:**32, 34–35, 399, 493, 495–96, 654; **9:**69, 457, 495, 499, 713–15, 837; **10:**466–67, 476–77, 480, 531, 551, 575; **11:**98, 202, 214, 276, 312, 798; **12:**38, 43, 60, 83, 107, 122, 283, 369, 387, 388, 391, 406, 428, 439, 444; AND THE TEMPLE **1:**282, 999; **2:**81–82; **3:**311, 346, 606–13, 691, 802–3, 1151; **4:**122, 933; **5:**797, 859; **6:**1585; **8:**34–35, 405, 431, 438–39, 493; **9:**69, 376; **10:**82, 474; **12:**58

ATONEMENT, DAY OF
1:275, 282, 890, 916, 999, 1003, 1010–11, 1033, 1070, 1074, 1098, 1104, 1107, 1110–11, 1113–14, 1156, 1159, 1171, 1174; **2:**81, 127, 194, 230–33, 236; **3:**609, 612, 691, 802–3, 805, 1113, 1151, 1158; **4:**1003; **5:**611, 678, 859; **6:**1176, 1491, 1585; **7:**528; **8:**33, 205, 405, 555; **9:**130, 376; **10:**82, 346, 467, 474, 476–77, 610; **11:**257, 288; **12:**41, 58–60, 82, 85, 104, 106–7, 110, 112–13, 116, 166–67. *See also under* FEASTS/FESTIVALS

AUGURY
8:24

AUGUSTAN COHORT
10:345

AUTHOR OF LIFE
See under JESUS THE CHRIST, NAMES FOR/TITLES OF *in PERSONS IN THE BIBLE*

AUTHORITY
OF THE BIBLE **1:**6, 34–37, 43, 49, 50–51, 53–55, 57, 59–60, 62–63, 103–4, 108, 119, 186, 189–90, 197; **2:**681; **5:**246; **6:**170; **7:**76; **8:**85; OF GOD **1:**20, 36, 57, 62, 108, 119, 802, 1017; **2:**88, 416–17, 426, 490, 526, 961, 963, 988, 1031, 1063, 1098, 1128; **3:**72, 75, 304, 395, 552, 704, 706; **4:**52, 306, 862; **5:**187, 466, 726; **6:**48, 161, 257, 294, 587; **7:**3, 103, 105, 263, 372, 510, 513, 570, 707, 790–91; **8:**295, 411, 520, 541, 551, 624, 714; **9:**99, 164, 378; **10:**21, 81, 92, 247, 342, 356, 664; **11:**758; **12:**345, 348, 489–90, 494, 496, 500, 593, 603; OF JESUS/CHRIST **1:**190; **8:**168, 229, 232, 255–56, 282, 448, 468, 503, 528, 541, 597, 621, 696; **9:**110, 367, 378, 436, 508, 535, 630; **10:**40, 73, 84, 232; **11:**342, 746; **12:**90, 569; OF THE KING **1:**259, 697, 745, 1017; **2:**298, 419, 425, 592, 811, 819, 855, 958–59, 961, 963, 970, 1023, 1027, 1053, 1061, 1063, 1072–73, 1086–87, 1109, 1128, 1157–58, 1178, 1192–94, 1212–13, 1250, 1314, 1319, 1355, 1380; **3:**13–14, 100, 152–53, 238, 677, 703, 720, 897, 905; **4:**222, 819, 862–63, 1130; **5:**214, 334; **6:**109, 134, 743, 1391; **7:**52, 64, 82, 103, 570, 573, 731; **8:**168, 282, 323, 597; **11:**216, 342, 644, 682; OF THE LAW **1:**37, 685; **2:**468; **3:**669; **4:**413; **9:**306, 409, 825; **10:**139, 911; **11:**276, 802, 870; **12:**475; OF THE LORD **1:**758, 817; **2:**613; **3:**718; **6:**175, 698; **7:**13, 570; **11:**154, 172; OF PAUL **10:**199, 204, 288, 317; **11:**12, 14, 49, 111, 116, 133, 141, 175–76, 201, 218, 351, 607, 861; OF THE PRIESTS **1:**736; **2:**135, 139, 431, 538, 970, 988, 1027, 1072, 1140; **4:**7; OF THE PROPHET **1:**41; **2:**108, 1061, 1063, 1027, 1072–73, 1086–87; **3:**137, 144, 152, 171, 209, 215, 217, 238, 469, 538, 592, 702, 711, 976; **6:**67, 574, 577, 579, 582, 586, 667, 709; **7:**788, 790, 798, 800, 824; **10:**73, 175, 232, 345; **11:**724; OF RELIGIOUS OFFICIALS **1:**1034, 1036; **2:**193, 1072; **3:**303, 306, 513; **5:**801; **6:**257; **9:**164, 378, 553, 630; **10:**5, 8, 22, 24, 97, 101, 105, 107, 109, 112–13, 115, 140, 160, 165, 175, 178–79, 188–89, 193–94, 197–200, 204, 238, 252–53, 266, 268–71, 333–34, 350, 377; **11:**164; **12:**61; SPIRITUAL **7:**188; **10:**14, 24, 29, 45, 49, 63, 69, 71, 73, 78–79, 88, 91–92, 95–96, 100, 104, 109, 112–13, 115, 121, 139, 160, 165, 171, 175, 179–81, 206, 231–32, 238, 242, 244, 246, 249, 253, 263, 267, 270, 274, 285, 288–89, 293–94, 317, 319, 322, 341, 345–46, 353

AUTHORSHIP
APOSTOLIC **1:**15, 48; **8:**106, 235; **9:**498–99; **12:**318, 366; DIVINE **1:**33, 37, 45, 55, 120, 126, 130; MOSAIC **1:**38, 56, 308–9, 677, 839, 995; **2:**273; **4:**1040; OTHER **1:**73, 79, 120, 129, 213, 997; **2:**22, 105, 108, 179, 952, 1113; **3:**937, 1176; **4:**655–56, 1188; **5:**20, 32, 270, 390, 438, 442, 608, 624, 818; **6:**28–30, 33–34, 66, 140, 246, 256, 313, 356, 575, 660, 797, 842, 916, 1016, 1093, 1097, 1110, 1376, 1408, 1505, 1513; **7:**50, 199, 342, 352–53, 363, 390, 535, 554, 563, 650, 652–53; **8:**4, 106, 517–18; **9:**5, 207, 498, 500, 862–63; **10:**5, 384; **11:**19, 471, 473, 577–78, 624, 720, 777, 859; **12:**6, 183, 230, 233–34, 319, 323–24, 365–66, 473, 514, 560; PAULINE **8:**47; **10:**372, 789–90; **11:**471, 473, 579–80, 583, 682–83, 776, 780–81, 785, 859; **12:**6; PSEUDONYMOUS **1:**70; **6:**933; **7:**2–3; **11:**351, 366, 577, 582, 587, 664, 683, 776, 779–81; **12:**183, 186, 232–34, 323–24, 328, 473–75, 521

AUTONOMY
AS HUMAN FREEDOM **1:**81, 113, 362, 366, 368–69, 726, 739, 786, 926, 963; **2:**566, 997, 1267, 1271, 1281, 1355, 1377; **3:**883; **4:**254, 290, 299, 397, 411–12, 502, 541, 661, 667, 669, 686–87, 689, 693, 695, 712, 724, 729, 731, 753, 822, 890–91, 913, 931, 978, 1042, 1225, 1261; **5:**337, 423; **6:**248, 665, 712, 767, 852, 956; **7:**162, 822; **9:**760; **11:**196, 310, 321; **12:**401, 583, 613, 652; OF THE TEXT **1:**114–16, 122, 138–39, 141, 144

AVENGER OF BLOOD
2:265, 435, 563, 696, 1314–15; **3:**1144
AWE
AS RESPONSE TO ANOTHER HUMAN OR GROUP **2:**1110–11, 1119, 1121; **3:**45, 858, 1098; **5:**400, 859; **6:**202; **7:**44, 861; **8:**686; **9:**449; **10:**478, 757; **11:**58, 229, 444, 626; **12:**504, 634, 657; AS RESPONSE TO GOD/JESUS *or* ACTS OF GOD/JESUS **1:**362, 475, 541–43, 736, 801, 836, 838, 881, 883, 897, 938, 942, 964, 1160; **2:**338, 1252; **3:**191, 998, 1062, 1065; **4:**314, 519, 560, 616, 701, 837, 990, 1269; **5:**254, 283, 306, 384, 506, 648, 696, 852, 861; **6:**18, 102, 248, 482, 957, 994, 1131, 1363, 1370, 1388; **7:**3, 106, 603, 720–21, 861; **8:**65, 264, 511, 590, 633, 729; **9:**29, 125, 284, 369, 417, 476, 596; **10:**71, 486, 644, 696; **11:**58, 64, 67, 373, 378–80, 444, 512, 626, 657, 874; **12:**62, 156, 159–61, 168, 172, 204, 297–98, 504, 522, 634, 657
AWL
1:1172
AWNING
6:1374
AXE
5:348
AXLE
5:787; **6:**1116
AYIN
(Hebrew letter) **3:**704; **4:**718, 1168; **7:**601, 686

B

BAAL, BAALS
1:233, 236–37, 239, 274–76, 840, 1067, 1147, 1181; **2:**185, 189, 277, 286, 306, 364, 374, 399, 480, 534, 569–70, 600, 729, 755, 757, 766, 772, 791, 792–93, 797, 802, 810, 841, 1005, 1017–18, 1029, 1062, 1230, 1274; **3:**21, 124–28, 130–31, 133, 135–36, 138–39, 142–43, 145–46, 150, 156, 158, 162, 178, 180, 183–84, 214–15, 224–26, 228, 230, 234, 276, 285, 357, 382, 575, 582, 598, 635, 678; **4:**51, 197, 290, 395, 469, 485–86, 518, 592, 621–22, 792–93, 945–46, 1097, 1220, 1268; **5:**36, 71, 227, 397, 430, 622, 667, 673, 800; **6:**9, 21, 159, 180, 217, 597, 599–601, 607, 640, 655, 670, 679, 707, 721, 750, 913, 1002, 1114, 1213, 1224, 1360–61, 1387, 1393, 1434; **7:**25, 101, 105, 113–14, 143, 167–68, 188–89, 200, 202–3, 206, 224–26, 234–35, 239, 244, 258, 264, 277, 288, 602, 717, 779, 828; **8:**343, 580; **10:**676; **11:**214; **12:**581, 725
BAAL-BERITH
2:635, 792
BAALISM (*OR* BAALIST, BAALIZATION *ETC.*)
1:949; **2:**1213; **3:**138, 225–26; **4:**793, 934, 947; **7:**203
BAAL-ZEBUB
See BAAL-ZEBUB/BAAL-ZEBUL/BEELZEBUL *in PERSONS IN THE BIBLE*
BABOONS
3:82; **5:**313
BACKSLIDE (*OR* BACKSLIDING, BACKSLIDERS, *ETC.*)
2:824; **3:**338, 390, 425, 522, 533, 536, 539, 542, 581, 590, 631, 637, 643–44, 649; **4:**262; **5:**141; **6:**493, 1135, 1261, 1446
BADGER, BADGERS
(animal) **1:**1080; **4:**597; **5:**255
BAG
2:1112; **5:**683; **6:**1583; **8:**595; **9:**171, 177, 194, 220, 422, 429–30
BAGPIPE
7:63
BAKE (*OR* BAKES, *ETC.*)
1:217, 224, 294, 411, 615, 814, 1017, 1019, 1159, 1181; **2:**127, 1139, 1185; 1303; **3:**140, 768; 1003; **5:**302, 395; **6:**638, 1149, 1154, 1558, 1591; **7:**234, 257, 261, 293; 779; **8:**311; **9:**123, 236, 277, 542
BAKER
1:614–15; **2:**1029; **3:**437; **7:**256–57
BALANCE, BALANCES
FOR MEASUREMENT **4:**925; **5:**748; **6:**627, 1583; **7:**84, 416. *See also* SCALE; WEIGHTS AND MEASURES
BALDNESS
1:1095, 1097; **6:**81, 168, 886, 1578; **7:**547; **10:**928, 931; **12:**482
BALLAD
2:156, 166–67, 184, 191, 774, 787
BALM
5:219, 347; **6:**643, 648, 650, 826, 883, 1379; **11:**859; IN GILEAD **6:**648, 650, 826, 883
BALSAM
2:1243
BAN (*OR* BANS, *ETC.*)
1:700, 1026; **2:**168, 276, 614, 901, 919; **3:**245, 430, 574, 742, 757, 842, 848; **4:**47–48, 74, 82, 232, 250, 261; **5:**339; **6:**212, 1310, 1344, 1494, 1577–78; **7:**25, 620; **10:**90, 105, 107, 628, 972, 1002; (HEB: *HEREM*) GIVEN TO/DEVOTED TO GOD **1:**32, 700, 1189; **2:**163, 168, 255–56, 276, 393, 589, 613–14, 739, 1047, 1087, 1089, 1148; **3:**87, 135, 152–53, 430, 574, 742, 926, 932, 1171–72, 1180; **4:**21, 46, 74, 82, 156; **6:**212; **10:**628
BAND
1:742, 780, 978, 1179; **2:**162, 339, 589, 618,

625, 803, 827, 959, 1036, 1041–42, 1167, 1174, 1193; **3:**93, 238, 775; **4:**58, 60, 97, 114–15, 1100; **5:**12, 80, 196, 742, 834; **6:**14, 653–54, 808, 872, 1178, 1345; **7:**124; **8:**45, 405, 653; **9:**292; **11:**722; **12:**259, 272, 599

BANDAGE (*OR* BANDAGES, *ETC.*)
6:627, 1420; **7:**249; **9:**230

BANISHMENT
1:365, 374, 841; **2:**963, 1302, 1315; **3:**722, 742, 753, 895, 1062; **4:**1042; **6:**211, 1207, 1432; **7:**278, 506; **8:**543; **10:**698

BANK, BANKS
OF RIVER OR SEA **1:**246, 287; **2:**338, 371, 486, 561, 584, 587, 607, 649, 674, 696, 706–8, 714; **3:**176–77; **4:**114; **5:**758; **6:**1404; **7:**111, 136, 148, 593, 616, 837; **8:**111, 327, 339, 643, 664; **9:**271; **12:**598

BANNER (*OR* BANNERS, *ETC.*)
1:104, 255, 820; **2:**37, 98, 164; **3:**531; **4:**1079; **5:**418; **6:**548, 912, 1374; **9:**579, 657; **12:**713

BANQUET (*OR* BANQUETS, BANQUETING, *ETC.*)
1:224, 279, 1024, 1026–27; **2:**78, 153, 1037–38, 1042, 1132–33, 1248, 1249; **3:**755–56, 856–58, 875, 878–80, 883, 889, 899, 907–11, 917, 918, 993–94, 1033, 1042, 1124, 1158; **4:**22, 177, 218, 345–46; **5:**15, 95, 101, 103–4, 366, 624, 668, 692, 696–97, 784; **6:**186, 206, 216–18, 228, 236, 471, 473, 478, 498, 543, 702, 810, 1527; **7:**40–41, 81, 84, 400; **8:**204, 226, 235, 309, 323–25, 417, 473, 553, 555, 598, 601, 603, 614–15, 699, 704, 707; **9:**22, 25–26, 35, 126–27, 130–31, 133, 144, 169–70, 196, 234, 263–64, 272, 278–79, 283, 286–90, 306, 317, 343, 393, 419, 425–26, 458; **10:**715; **11:**443, 838; **12:**40, 603; AS DIVINE SACRIFICAL MEAL **1:**278, 1024–27; **2:**1038; **3:**993–94; **6:**216; ESCHATOLOGICAL **6:**206, 217–18, 227–28, 471–73, 478, 498, 543, 810; **8:**204, 226, 235, 309, 324–25, 417, 473, 603, 614; **9:**22, 25, 35, 131, 133, 144, 169–70, 196, 234, 263, 278–79, 283, 286, 288–91, 306, 317, 343, 393, 419, 425–26, 458; **10:**715; **12:**603; EUCHARISTIC **2:**78, 153; **8:**323, 553, 601, 704, 707; FUNERARY **5:**696–97; **6:**702; GREAT **1:**1026; **6:**1527; **9:**26, 35, 283, 288, 306, 458; TO HONOR A GUEST **2:**1042; **3:**1142, 1158; **4:**117, 345; **5:**624, 784; **9:**26, 126–27; **11:**838; ROYAL **1:**244; **2:**1248; **3:**756, 857–58, 878–80, 883, 889, 899, 908–11, 917; **4:**218; **5:**95; **7:**81; **8:**417, 598; WEDDING (*see under* WEDDING); WISDOM'S **5:**100–101, 104, 668, 692; **11:**443

BAPTISM
1:16, 55, 103, 201, 204, 208–11, 398, 460, 838, 843, 853, 909, 919; **2:**15, 38, 40, 54, 67, 97, 141, 152, 167, 237, 609; **3:**198, 355, 395, 619, 688, 1145, 1158; **4:**854, 1025; **5:**327; **6:**710, 1497; **7:**873; **8:**26, 44, 46, 82, 110, 147, 150, 157–60, 165, 270, 352, 364, 366, 392, 398, 471, 527, 531–33, 535–56, 550, 565, 631, 647, 653; **9:**8, 81, 83–85, 87–88, 90, 99, 266, 378, 381, 385, 432, 442, 487, 529, 534, 550, 558, 560, 624, 665, 724, 774, 834, 847; **10:**30, 50, 54–55, 59, 62, 67–68, 70–71, 139, 144, 149, 152, 161, 167, 169, 211, 236, 253, 260–63, 307, 410, 420, 495, 512, 533–41, 543, 545–49, 559, 572, 584–85, 589, 603, 664, 698, 729–30, 788, 798, 807, 847, 856, 883, 894, 914, 916, 945, 948; **11:**73, 105, 243, 249, 251, 255, 263, 271–74, 328, 381, 389, 391, 400, 404, 422–23, 430, 438, 451, 497, 538, 574, 596, 623–25, 628–29, 637, 643, 678, 792, 829, 877; **12:**46, 68, 71, 75–76, 113, 121, 127, 180, 229, 241–42, 250, 260, 262–64, 268, 273, 276, 282, 292–93, 295–96, 298, 303, 337, 407, 439, 498, 569, 625; AND APOSTLE'S CREED **1:**208; OF BELIEVERS **1:**103; **2:**656; **3:**354; CHRISTIAN (*see under* CHRISTIAN); AND CIRCUMCISION **1:**460; **2:**609; AND COVENANT **1:**853; AND DIPPING/IMMERSING/WASHING **1:**919; **2:**67; **3:**198, 1145, 1158; **8:**157; AND DISCIPLES **8:**504; **9:**212, 401, 487; **10:**788; AND THE EXODUS **1:**209–11, 398; **2:**602, 604; **10:**534; OF FIRE **7:**873; **8:**158, 532–33; **9:**85–86, 160; **10:**54, 262, 266; OF JESUS (*see* JESUS THE CHRIST: BAPTISM AND TEMPTATION OF *in PERSONS IN THE BIBLE*); AND REPENTANCE **1:**16, 843, 903; **2:**97; AS SACRAMENT **2:**15, 38, 40, 54, 141, 152, 168, 237; **3:**395, 688; **5:**327; **6:**710; AS IN THIRST FOR GOD **4:**854

BAPTIST
See JOHN THE BAPTIST *in PERSONS IN THE BIBLE*

BAPTIZE (*OR* BAPTIZES, BAPTIZER, *ETC.*)
1:179, 191, 199, 201–2, 210, 212, 460; **2:**603, 656, 1045; **3:**706, 1143; **4:**514, 854; **6:**641, 1497, 1564; **7:**77, 327; **8:**111, 115, 157–63, 274–75, 385, 410, 504, 521, 525, 530–32, 534, 536, 543, 653; **9:**27, 83, 85–87, 90, 92, 160, 212, 266, 378, 401, 487–88, 529, 560; **10:**22, 41, 53, 67–68, 70, 96, 106, 138–39, 144, 167, 169, 256, 262–63, 307, 382, 520–21, 534–35, 537–39, 541–42, 548, 551, 558–59, 581, 706, 762, 788, 801, 804, 807–8, 810, 882, 913–14, 945, 982, 1000; **11:**184, 243, 271–74, 281, 291, 320, 420, 431, 456, 480, 538, 643; **12:**9, 35, 64, 121, 180, 206, 229, 262, 296, 298, 407, 588

BAR
OF WOOD OR METAL **1:**896; **2:**53, 536; **3:**505, 764, 768, 770; **4:**602–3; **5:**112; **6:**377, 386, 1418, 1452, 1518; **7:**506, 618, 758; **8:**627

BARBARIAN, BARBARIANS
4:182, 202, 229, 266; **5:**349; **6:**1304, 1512; **7:**118; **10:**355, 422, 644

BARBER, BARBERS
5:309; **6:**1150
BARLEY
1:217–18, 275, 759, 1020, 1157–58, 1161; **2:**127, 232, 356, 593, 899, 910, 921–22, 930–31, 1359; **3:**1001; **6:**1149, 1203, 1379, 1584; **7:**231, 309, 430; **8:**601; **9:**118; **12:**612; HARVEST (*see* HARVEST: BARLEY/GRAIN/WHEAT)
BARN, BARNS
5:49–50, 323; **6:**389; **8:**211, 405; **9:**256, 259
BARREN
1:219, 239, 329, 420, 422, 429, 463, 475, 486, 517, 520, 522, 877, 1142; **2:**546, 600, 846, 900, 910, 959, 973, 975, 977, 980, 983; **3:**1049, 1051; **4:**191, 368, 448, 452, 610, 819, 1201; **5:**132, 473, 475, 724; **6:**386, 432, 441, 447, 449, 1503–4, 1222, 1599, 1607; **7:**198, 202, 234, 236, 239, 250, 253, 264–65, 267, 270, 274, 276, 307–8, 314, 664, 686; **9:**45, 181, 271; **10:**659; **11:**304, 802; **12:**95, 136, 264, 635. *See also* CHILDLESS
BASIN, BASINS
1:224, 279, 918, 972, 1034, 1066, 1160; **2:**55, 77, 678, 738; **3:**485–86, 608–9, 679; **5:**327; **6:**1546. *See also* BOWL
BASKET, BASKETS
1:102, 391, 615, 622, 699, 701, 782, 892, 1047, 1163; **2:**480; **3:**223, 775–76; **5:**261, 348, 499; **6:**1165; **7:**31, 377, 407, 414, 777, 779; **8:**182, 601, 618; **9:**148, 363, 408, 594, 918–19; **11:**138, 160. *See also under* BREAD
BASTARD, BASTARDS
6:1233; **7:**220, 293; **12:**151
BAT, BATS
(animal) **6:**73; **11:**425
BATH, BATHS
1:1098; **2:**152, 1284, 1289; **3:**198, 1158; **6:**1583–84; **7:**179, 220; **9:**308, 316, 723–24; **11:**877
BATHING
2:151, 1283–85, 1289; **3:**167, 1143, 1147, 1158; **4:**156, 216, 538; **5:**326, 397; **7:**176, 179; **9:**724; **11:**451
BATTALION, BATTALIONS
1:783, 1182; **2:**1087, 1331; **8:**584; **9:**399
BATTERING RAM, RAMS
6:195, 242, 1143, 1302, 1366
BATTLE
AGAINST CHAOS/PRIMEVAL **1:**274–75, 800; **2:**600; **4:**487, 518, 602, 617, 619, 622, 773, 1054, 1096; **7:**101–2, 601; ARRAY **4:**296; **7:**683; COSMIC **2:**790, 859; **3:**1177; **4:**518, 1054; **6:**935; **8:**752; COSMOGONIC **4:**368, 410, 519; CRY (CRIES) **2:**96; **4:**78, 518, 868; **5:**764; **6:**625, 1302; **7:**666, 682–83; DEFEAT IN **7:**355, 805; ESCHATOLOGICAL **1:**287; **7:**5; **11:**726–28; **12:**699–700; FIELD OF **2:**440, 547, 999, 1002, 1007, 1013, 1112, 1197–98, 1202, 1207, 1336, 1361; **3:**368, 551, 736; **4:**297, 691; **6:**37, 156, 159, 1341, 1497, 1532; **7:**49, 334, 355; **9:**202; **11:**225, 326; FINAL **1:**289; **2:**1183, 1188, 1207, 1324, 1335–36; **4:**127; **6:**1086, 1106, 1512–13, 1523; **7:**5, 129, 304, 333–34; **10:**984; **12:**649; GOD/THE LORD/YAHWEH AND **2:**600, 637, 1007, 1112, 1243; **6:**55, 751, 1515, 1523; **7:**836; MESSENGER(S) **2:**1002, 1201–2, 1287, 1323; **3:**21; **6:**293; MESSIANIC **1:**74; PLAN(S) **1:**10; **2:**613, 1183; **11:**165; PREPARATION FOR **1:**789; **2:**781, 837, 1185, 1207, 1330; **3:**148, 416, 1127; **4:**25, 61, 87, 758, 917, 1054; **5:**229, 486; **10:**959; **12:**713; REPORT(S) **2:**1201, 1240; **3:**337–38, 414–15, 532, 552, 560, 628, 929; VICTORY IN **2:**365; **4:**1129; **6:**337, 354; **9:**707. *See also* SIEGE; WAR
BATTLEMENTS
3:591
BEAM, BEAMS
1:224, 285, 1017; **2:**1108, 1361; **3:**378; **4:**624, 1097; **6:**11, 753, 1551; **7:**618; **8:**722; **9:**249, 321, 348; **11:**896
BEANS
1:218; **3:**204; **10:**606
BEAR, BEARS
(animal) **1:**771, 1179; **2:**1111, 1332; **3:**178; **4:**605; **5:**167, 239, 715, 764, 849; **6:**141, 866, 1049, 1464, 1593; **7:**101–2, 105; **12:**656
BEARD (*OR* BEARDS, BEARDED, *ETC.*)
1:1061, 1096, 1135, 1147; **2:**859, 1142, 1279, 1352; **3:**733; **4:**538, 1214; **5:**415, 809; **6:**168, 1000, 1150, 1342, 1578
BEAST, BEASTS
1:27, 88, 219–20, 288, 359, 366, 748, 1000, 1052, 1127, 1180, 1187–88; **2:**452–53, 530, 981, 1087, 11112; **3:**728, 761, 948; **4:**212, 337, 608, 632, 905, 946, 969; **5:**10, 49, 85, 95, 124, 139, 237, 243, 252, 254–55, 285, 310, 585, 715; **6:**143, 225–26, 260, 282, 405–6, 1049, 1210, 1214, 1269, 1404, 1434, 1437, 1464, 1471–73, 1497, 1499, 1527–28, 1580, 1593; **7:**3, 7–10, 55, 63, 71, 74–75, 100–105, 108, 112, 143, 308, 468, 489, 528; **8:**18, 692; **9:**284; **10:**401, 705, 987; **11:**458; APOCALYPTIC **1:**88, 288; **6:**226, 282, 1434–35; **7:**3, 8–10, 63, 102–3, 105–7, 112, 143; **8:**691; **11:**51, 205; **12:**205, 504–5, 509, 513, 516–17, 519, 525–27, 529, 532, 535, 537–38, 541, 543–44, 548–49, 566, 576–77, 579–81, 583, 585, 589, 591–95, 603–4, 606, 609, 611–13, 616, 619, 624, 626, 631–33, 638–39, 642, 644, 649–53, 655–60, 663–69, 672–73, 676–78,

680–87, 692–93, 699–703, 707, 712–17, 720–22, 724–25, 730, 733–35; OF BURDEN **3:**728, 761; OF THE FIELD **1:**359, 365–66; **3:**1154; **4:**608, 624; **6:**213, 1249, 1521; **7:**74; HORNED/STRONG **2:**981; MARK OF THE **11:**51; **12:**601, 614, 618, 654, 676, 686, 700; PUNISHING **6:**1049; THE SERPENT **1:**359, 366. *See also* ANIMAL

BESTIAL BEHAVIOR
4:228, 969; **5:**85, 124, 252

BEATEN, BEATING
THE BREAST **7:**610; **9:**342, 462; **10:**697; GRAIN **1:**1163; **2:**229; **5:**174; **6:**227, 579; OIL **2:**229; PHYSICAL **1:**155, 702, 728, 730, 863–64, 1037; **2:**184, 861, 878; **3:**710; **4:**210; **5:**181, 199, 207, 369, 412–13, 425; **6:**722, 848–49, 1241; **7:**210, 233, 262; **8:**100, 487, 670, 688, 719; **9:**229–30, 264, 351–54, 443, 449, 451, 819; **10:**233, 297, 308, 319, 682, 757, 775; **11:**22, 157, 164, 294, 453; **12:**140–41; SILVER **6:**1378

BEATITUDE, BEATITUDES
3:571, 1064–65; **4:**683, 805, 847–48, 864, 1013–14, 1058, 1201, 1256, 1263–64; **5:**552; **8:**719; **9:**55, 161, 179, 223, 225, 243, 250, 263–64, 317–18, 476; **10:**937; **12:**677, 696; IN MARK AND LUKE **1:**129; **4:**673, 774, 1134; **5:**550; **8:**76, 80, 84, 89, 104, 171, 175–81, 183, 210, 217, 436, 538; **9:**25, 105, 143–45, 147, 196, 317–18; **10:**891; **11:**99; **12:**192, 291

BEAUTY
1:59, 344, 666, 889, 897, 906–8, 960, 964; **2:**373, 1206; **3:**68, 429, 464, 479, 484; **4:**32, 43, 314, 449, 534, 786, 959, 1066, 1229; **5:**93, 119, 172, 343, 357, 366, 395, 415–17, 419, 440, 442–43, 486, 498, 509, 512, 522, 599, 671, 679, 801, 824–25; **6:**389, 925, 972, 980–81, 1022, 1041, 1066, 1228, 1230, 1232, 1240, 1324, 1369, 1373, 1375, 1382–83, 1388, 1391, 1394–95, 1426, 1432; **7:**177–78; **9:**74, 398, 405; **10:**126, 516, 596, 606, 695, 916; **11:**378, 609, 696, 709; **12:**146, 284–85, 402, 566, 696, 723; AESTHETIC **1:**889, 960, 964; **2:**1206; **3:**429, 479, 484; **4:**43, 1279; **5:**443, 509, 512, 671, 825, 834; **6:**1041, 1066, 1373, 1391, 1394, 1426, 1595; **9:**75, 259, 398; **10:**695; **11:**284–85; OF APPEARANCE **1:**383, 393, 428, 666, 906; **2:**1165–66, 1206; **3:**68, 868, 871, 882, 885, 905, 962, 1080, 1086–87, 1130, 1132, 1147–50, 1153–55, 1159, 1165, 1177, 1182; **4:**32, 635; **5:**80, 93, 119, 122, 263, 370, 372, 375, 382–83, 388, 402–4, 416–19, 630, 764–65; **6:**81, 1230, 1232, 1321, 1324; **7:**176–80; **12:**566; OF CREATION **1:**344, 361; **2:**373; **4:**604, 623; **5:**546–47, 550, 731, 815, 818; **10:**516, 606; **11:**378–79; OF GLORY/HOLINESS OF/OF TORAH **1:**897, 907–8; **3:**464; **4:**534, 1066; **6:**980–81; **10:**126

BED, BEDS
1:308, 610, 659, 698, 745, 1104, 1125; **2:**123, 167, 309, 340, 781, 877, 1127, 1185, 1230, 1232, 1303; **3:**189, 777, 871, 885, 962, 1132, 1151, 1160–61; **4:**31, 306, 388, 395, 443, 462, 530, 684, 807, 1195, 1275–76; **5:**49, 75, 85, 205, 225, 274, 316, 323, 341, 351, 388, 400, 607, 753; **6:**237, 490–91, 1230, 1246, 1442–43, 1488; **7:**95, 100, 258, 375, 585, 620; **9:**123–25, 180, 330, 332, 578–80, 751, 787; **10:**161, 657; **11:**805; **12:**139, 163, 527, 581

BEDCHAMBER
1:745; **2:**1303; **3:**1151, 1161–62

BEE, BEES
1:1143; **2:**718, 850; **5:**74, 306, 625, 708; **6:**113

BEELZEBUL
See BAAL-ZEBUB/BAAL-ZEBUL/BEELZEBUL *in PERSONS IN THE BIBLE*

BEGGAR, BEGGARS
1:178; **4:**548; **8:**195, 212, 655; **9:**12, 29, 194, 237–38, 314, 316–17, 320, 322, 335, 338, 348, 353–55, 357, 482, 652; **10:**76–78, 84–85, 88, 161; **11:**287, 291, 459, 696

BEGINNING AND END
See GOD, NAMES FOR/TITLES OF: ALPHA AND OMEGA *in PERSONS IN THE BIBLE*

BEGOTTEN
See under JESUS THE CHRIST, NAMES FOR/TITLES OF: ONLY BEGOTTEN *in PERSONS IN THE BIBLE*

BEHEAD (*OR* BEHEADS, BEHEADING, *ETC.*)
2:1198, 1230; **3:**1076, 1088, 1160–62; **7:**33; **8:**598; **9:**13, 194–95, 219, 281; **10:**178; **12:**707, 713

BEHEMOTH
4:337, 596–97, 614–19, 621, 624–25, 627; **5:**11, 98, 536, 678; **12:**710. *See also* MONSTER

BEKA, BEKAS
See COIN; WEIGHTS AND MEASURES

BELIEF, BELIEFS
BASIC/FUNDAMENTAL **4:**372, 454, 508, 552; **5:**139; **7:**663; **10:**621; BEDROCK/CENTRAL/CORE **2:**68; **3:**1168; **6:**1155, 1275, 1395, 1409; **9:**693; **10:**9, 104, 222, 274, 335, 336, 338, 340, 749; CHRISTIAN **2:**681; **3:**523; **8:**85, 520; **10:**18, 151, 240, 252, 485, 519, 575, 718, 727, 740; **11:**608, 696; **12:**246, 447; COMMON/SHARED **1:**50, 195, 442; **3:**1065; **8:**73; **10:**71, 100, 700, 784; **11:**236, 404; FAITH AND **1:**42, 48, 50–51, 61, 63, 195, 442, 448; **2:**167, 275, 300, 350, 375, 377, 440, 467, 529–30, 681, 760, 1001, 1022, 1236; **3:**344, 532, 680, 868, 873, 906, 1009, 1168; **4:**200, 372, 436, 492–94, 504, 513, 583, 737, 872–73; **5:**121, 153, 186, 506, 547, 609, 717; **6:**40, 95, 164, 223, 240, 262, 752, 1083, 1143–44, 1169, 1338–39, 1370,

BELIEF, BELIEFS *(continued)*
1409, 1480, 1497, 1511; **7:**64, 161, 624, 635, 642–44; **8:**64, 86, 250–51, 573, 641, 679, 716; **9:**546, 602, 611, 621, 650, 678, 688, 693, 746, 841, 850; **10:**18, 70, 85, 151, 260, 263, 276, 320, 336, 382–83, 453, 468, 478, 481–82, 492, 499, 663–64, 672–73, 700, 709, 711, 732, 813, 974, 983; **11:**240, 314, 404–5, 525, 530–31, 713, 747, 795, 831, 851; **12:**3, 71, 95, 131, 133, 146, 198, 285, 423, 435, 437, 442, 462, 716; IN GOD(S)/THAT GOD . . . **1:**236; **2:**79, 280, 365, 512, 521, 941; **3:**867, 1009; **4:**191, 512–13, 572, 595, 1001; **5:**244, 505, 627, 660, 678, 717, 759, 780, 860; **6:**982, 1291, 1395, 1409; **7:**313, 513, 545, 550, 624, 636, 643, 663, 666; **8:**31, 64; **9:**584; **10:**92, 374, 498, 528, 661, 664, 672, 732, 758; **11:**607, 831; **12:**329, 435, 712; IN JESUS/THAT JESUS . . . **7:**644; **8:**30, 42, 73; **9:**521, 555, 575, 626, 653, 746; **10:**664, 673, 700, 709; **11:**607; **12:**391, 435; IN THE RESURRECTION **1:**230, 288; **4:**241; **6:**222–23; **8:**676; **9:**346, 388; **10:**151, 335, 664; **11:**502, 528; **12:**703; SYSTEM OF **3:**1103; **4:**372, 614; **11:**636

BELL, BELLS
1:907, 1001, 1060, 1172; **2:**89; **3:**576; **4:**370, 531; **5:**356, 395, 843, 859; **6:**244, 549, 920, 1352; **7:**839, 861; **10:**408, 464, 900

BELLOWS
1:350; **5:**434; **6:**1313; **10:**812

BELOVED DISCIPLE
See BELOVED DISCIPLE *in PERSONS IN THE BIBLE*

BELT, BELTS
1:222; **2:**718, 1120; **3:**171, 217; **4:**58, 601; **6:**1325, 1375, 1377, 1380; **7:**136; **8:**532; **9:**81, 152, 171, 861; **10:**289, 605; **11:**459–60; **12:**561, 598

BENEDICTION, BENEDICTIONS
1:210–11, 558, 584, 634, 636, 660, 1066, 1068; **2:**66, 69, 194, 1174, 1235; **3:**20, 198, 333, 437, 442, 619; **4:**352, 939–40, 1000, 1176–77, 1201, 1203, 1216–17, 1229; **5:**332, 615–16, 731, 801, 866; **8:**202, 391; **9:**105, 234–35, 242, 504–5, 510, 657–58, 765, 871; **10:**58, 88, 284, 379–80, 382, 798; **11:**188, 345–47, 546, 556, 666, 668–69, 689, 735, 770, 827, 829–30, 854, 858–59, 879, 889, 903; **12:**4, 11, 20, 70, 161, 171–72, 309, 450, 500, 734; AGAINST HERETICS **9:**504, 510, 657–58, 765, 871; EIGHTEEN **5:**801, 866; **8:**202, 391; **9:**105, 235; **10:**498; **12:**138

BENEDICTUS
1:209; **9:**21, 58–59, 61

BENEFACTOR, BENEFACTORS
1:291, 716, 727; **2:**481, 527, 1230; **3:**35, 594, 892, 894, 913, 919, 1182; **4:**85, 291; **5:**179, 596, 781; **6:**608, 1277; **8:**545, 650–51, 682; **9:**171, 363, 424; **10:**246, 249, 519, 762, 782; **11:**31, 352, 364, 372, 376–77, 380, 401, 405, 410, 412, 416, 424, 432, 675, 677; **12:**461–63

BERYL
6:1116, 1392; **7:**136; **12:**561, 598, 723

BESTIALITY
1:1126–27, 1141

BETROTH (*OR* BETROTHS, BETROTHED, *ETC.*)
1:474, 553, 1134; **7:**225, 309; **8:**130; **9:**51–52; **10:**793, 884, 889; **11:**82, 147–48, 173

BETROTHAL
2:457; **3:**981–82, 1033, 1037–38, 1062; **6:**515; **9:**51, 565; **11:**36, 146, 149

BEWITCH
11:250, 253

BIER
2:1208, 1225; **4:**462; **9:**157, 209

BIGAMY
8:645

BINDING AND LOOSING
4:605; **8:**346; **9:**847; **12:**584

BIOGRAPHY
1:137; **3:**1103; **6:**14–15, 23, 576, 1324; **8:**68, 72, 109, 519–20; **9:**10–12; **10:**30, 138, 372–74, 377

BIRD, BIRDS
1:240, 341, 345, 349, 352, 364, 389, 391–93, 395, 401, 615, 716, 1013–14, 1025, 1036–37, 1076, 1098, 1100–1101, 1106; **2:**13, 108, 178, 235, 397–98, 453, 918, 1112, 1289, 1359; **3:**135, 996, 1002, 1058, 1154; **4:**254, 256, 442, 451, 524, 532, 539, 581, 605, 608–12, 721, 741, 898, 945, 1013, 1097, 1271; **5:**26, 28, 38, 85, 120, 180, 206–7, 230, 254, 312, 349, 355, 357, 393, 485, 502, 585, 593, 618, 630, 714, 719–20, 747, 768–69, 793, 834; **6:**7, 74, 117, 195, 243, 261, 277, 646–47, 702, 704, 708, 965, 996, 1009, 1077, 1167, 1243, 1245, 1252–53, 1336, 1405, 1425, 1428, 1435, 1497, 1499, 1521, 1523, 1526–28, 1563, 1580; **7:**55, 73, 75, 239, 258, 260, 262–63, 266, 269, 278, 280, 314, 371, 594, 674; **8:**24, 211, 229, 311, 570–71, 577–79; **9:**98, 119, 177–80, 217, 259–60, 275–76, 282; **10:**433, 596, 987; **12:**205, 636, 692, 699–700, 702; AS A METAPHOR FOR GOD (*see* GOD, METAPHORS FOR *in PERSONS IN THE BIBLE*); PHOENIX **4:**539; OF PREY **1:**446, 1081; **2:**339; **3:**112, 127, 129; **4:**530, 608; **6:**175, 679, 1525, 1527; **7:**447; **9:**333; SACRIFICE **1:**1013, 1098, 1100–1101

BIRTH
1:241, 326, 329, 353, 372, 375, 382, 418, 420, 468, 481, 485–86, 488, 491, 500, 515, 517, 520–21, 523, 544, 552, 554–55, 558–59, 585–87, 606, 686, 696, 698–99, 701, 838, 1067, 1084,

1085; **2:**12, 16, 123, 168, 211, 214–15, 300, 324, 370, 406–7, 411, 413–14, 432, 447–48, 459, 474, 660, 760, 762, 767, 798, 840–41, 843, 845, 895–96, 933, 942–43, 945, 953, 958, 960, 969, 970–71, 973, 977, 979–80, 983, 994, 996, 1004, 1135, 1144, 1170, 1207, 1239, 1242, 1283, 1297–98; **3:**23–24, 43, 342, 353, 388, 390, 442, 576, 759, 833, 1014, 1023; **4:**356, 364, 366–69, 371–72, 380, 415, 440, 448, 452, 545, 547, 597, 602, 604, 609, 634, 689, 838, 862, 908, 959, 961, 965, 1025, 1070, 1186; **5:**9, 92, 159, 306–7, 325–26, 400, 411, 471, 497, 511, 513, 534, 580, 630, 651, 721, 736, 745, 846; **6:**5, 11, 99, 112–13, 116, 121–24, 139, 202, 293, 321, 375, 396, 418, 421, 471, 509, 547, 562, 575, 580, 697, 728–29, 805, 828, 1015, 1226, 1230, 1236, 1316, 1319, 1425, 1458; **7:**31, 73, 108, 164, 169, 187, 206, 218, 224, 239, 270, 273, 283, 290–91, 550, 572, 606, 707, 852; **8:**17, 19, 35, 38, 46, 49, 64–67, 69, 102, 110, 126, 137–38, 142–43, 149, 152, 175, 289, 310, 355, 442, 519, 592; **9:**6, 10, 13, 17, 33, 42–48, 54–55, 57–60, 62–63, 65–69, 71–73, 75, 77–78, 80–81, 84–85, 90, 92, 94, 98, 112, 284, 345, 378, 399, 434, 442, 445, 462, 464, 476, 478, 518, 549–52, 554–55, 646, 653, 691, 780; **10:**77, 241, 374, 398, 427, 432, 500, 550, 597, 605–6, 686, 888, 938; **11:**69, 180, 236–37, 239–41, 284, 293, 296–98, 304, 318, 391, 393, 397, 403, 470, 475, 515, 525–26, 530, 613, 656, 702, 711, 802, 900; **12:**29, 42, 136, 138, 142, 181, 189, 204, 213, 223, 410, 413–16, 436, 447, 549, 569, 616, 635, 645, 648–49, 651–53, 729; OF A CHILD **1:**372, 825; **2:** 933, 970; **3:**93, 145; **4:**1143; **6:**116; **7:**218; **8:**32, 65; **9:**43, 48–50, 56, 63, 66, 70–71, 521, 780; **12:**255; OF THE CHURCH **1:**46, 91; **2:**1045; **9:**139; AND/TO DEATH **1:**225, 363; **2:**399, 448, 456; **4:**352, 593, 1182; **5:**327, 823; **9:**384; **12:**62, 155, 187–88; OF/TO ISRAEL **1:**354, 519, 560; **2:**106, 504; **8:**169; OF JESUS/CHRIST (*see* JESUS THE CHRIST: BIRTH AND GENEOLOGY OF *in PERSONS IN THE BIBLE*); OF JOHN (*see under* JOHN THE BAPTIST *in PERSONS IN THE BIBLE*); NARRATIVE **1:**519; **3:**576; **8:**66–67, 140, 143, 152, 227; **9:**14, 68, 72–73, 77–78, 90, 101; NEW **1:**210; **2:**168, 413, 447–48, 896; **9:**521, 549–52, 555, 714, 780; **10:**938; **11:**900; **12:**231, 250, 260, 262, 276; PANGS **3:**1014; **8:**442; **9:**55; **10:**597, 888; **11:**296, 298, 302, 613; **12:**569, 729; OF/TO A SON **1:**462, 1084; **2:**810, 845–46, 976, 1002; **3:**43, 187; **7:**218–19; **9:**76; STORY **1:**692; **2:**861, 952, 976–77, 1182; **7:**218; **8:**126–27, 135, 137–40, 150, 160, 226, 234, 297, 319, 359, 460, 464, 486, 529; **9:**66, 603; VIRGIN (*see under* VIRGIN)

BIRTHRIGHT
1:488, 515–18, 522–24, 535–37, 539, 541, 555, 564, 659, 812; **2:**429, 474, 550, 810, 846, 1341; **3:**337, 358, 1089; **6:**1273; **8:**484, 670; **9:**255, 301–3, 638; **10:**393; **12:**5, 154, 158, 399

BISHOP
8:103, 105; **9:**310; **10:**810; **11:**480, 482, 775, 778, 805, 859, 864, 867; **12:**283, 454

BIT
FOR A HORSE **6:**294

BITTER
1:57, 190, 534, 537, 806, 808, 897; **2:**63, 394, 421, 461, 474, 476, 506, 513, 530, 546, 833, 892, 897, 899, 904–5, 909, 911, 942, 1089, 1118, 1217, 1225, 1250, 1252, 1297, 1313; **3:**33, 208, 399, 541, 667, 780; **4:**36, 85, 188, 310, 362, 369–70, 395, 402, 409, 419, 439–41, 459, 485, 507–8, 525, 669, 762, 857–58, 954, 1011, 1111, 1171; **5:**67, 207, 230, 258, 301, 409, 440, 476, 616, 757, 824, 862; **6:**94, 412, 601, 810, 1030, 1052, 1054, 1103, 1153, 1160, 1267, 1273, 1290, 1292, 1295–96, 1359, 1369, 1438; **7:**54, 147, 220, 380, 388, 390, 417, 454, 547; **8:**70; **9:**439–40, 457–58; **10:**225, 252, 437, 718; **11:**308, 318, 525, 529; **12:**125, 209, 216, 630, 639, 676; FRUIT **1:**524; **9:**149, 302, 642; HERBS **2:**87; **8:**472; **9:**418; WATER **1:**806–7; **2:**99, 253; **3:**178; **5:**621, 807

BITTERNESS
2:63, 68, 422, 461, 892, 909–12, 941–42, 973, 975, 1192; **3:**801; **4:**356, 372, 395, 397, 434, 440, 459, 479, 508, 535, 614, 634, 764, 953, 1028; **5:**140, 410, 617; **6:**305, 655, 1049; **7:**112, 388, 548; **8:**148, 667; **9:**298, 691; **10:**458; **11:**430–32, 645, 655, 663, 860; **12:**154, 419, 434, 630; WATER OF **2:**63, 68

BITUMEN
1:473, 699

BLACK, BLACKS
1:70, 116–17, 219, 411, 556, 1097; **3:**370, 554, 921; **4:**258, 331, 371, 488; **5:**364, 367–68, 371, 374, 379, 382–85, 390, 394, 397, 401, 404–6, 408–9, 412–13, 415–16, 418–24, 426, 428–29; **6:**49, 176; **7:**784, 872; **9:**101, 152; **10:**606; **11:**709; **12:**610, 612. *See also* AFRICAN/AFRICAN AMERICAN

BLASPHEMY (*OR* BLASPHEMIES, BLASPHEMOUS, *ETC.*)
1:57, 297, 1011, 1039, 1109, 1114, 1138, 1163, 1164–65; **2:**128, 195, 321, 420, 804; **3:**156, 269, 271, 629, 733, 811–12; **4:**100–101, 275, 319, 321, 330, 449, 465, 517, 520, 525; **5:**170, 317, 642, 660; **6:**133, 294, 318, 394, 742, 773, 1044, 1048, 1218, 1388–89; **7:**189, 192, 560, 860; **8:**234, 241, 258, 420, 480, 550–51, 557–58, 561, 565, 713–14; **9:**13, 122–24, 126, 172, 194, 253,

BLASPHEMY *(continued)*
280, 441, 580, 647, 675, 677–79, 820–21; **10:**105, 121–23, 126, 131, 199, 434, 722, 724; **11:**219, 267, 277, 461; **12:**123, 301, 443, 577, 585, 609, 656–57, 660, 676, 681, 684, 721

BLAST
OF DIVINE BREATH OR TRUMPET **1:**804, 836; **2:**88–89, 198, 588, 1367; **3:**561; **4:**869, 1003–4; **5:**347, 859; **6:**226, 1116, 1448, 1537; **7:**15, 371, 666, 682–83; **8:**537; **12:**629–30, 632, 643, 676–77. *See also under* TRUMPET

BLEACH
1:883

BLEMISH (*OR* BLEMISHES, *ETC.*)
1:1051, 1150–52; **2:**151, 229, 232, 421; **3:**117, 612, 680; **4:**421; **5:**550, 797; **6:**718, 1223, 1585, 1586, 1588–89, 1593; **7:**39, 227, 859, 862; **9:**287; **11:**440, 512, 606; **12:**12, 108, 256, 336, 351, 353, 357, 359, 492, 500

BLESS (*OR* BLESSES, *ETC.*)
1:156, 159, 242, 328, 398, 423–24, 439–40, 517, 527, 536–37, 559, 595, 612, 653, 659, 666, 780, 869, 973, 1066–67, 1141; **2:**65–66, 69, 182, 188–91, 193, 195, 212, 482, 534, 549, 758, 775, 780, 787, 945, 973, 987, 1138, 1250, 1256–57, 1324; **3:**22, 56, 88, 179, 592, 625, 806, 985, 1008, 1039, 1041–42, 1051, 1055, 1057, 1062, 1064–65, 1119, 1167, 1173; **4:**64, 310, 346, 349, 353, 356, 360, 452, 681, 702, 737, 790, 814, 927, 937, 946, 999, 1061, 1065, 1078, 1089, 1091, 1096, 1100, 1106, 1126, 1139, 1145, 1190, 1216–17, 1219–21, 1259; **5:**75, 106, 530, 532, 843, 859; **6:**396, 585, 661, 828, 1008, 1510, 1537, 1570; **7:**330, 358, 393, 429, 528, 660, 811, 821; **8:**29, 32, 82, 347, 601; **9:**30, 84, 107, 139, 147, 152, 226–27, 250, 287, 327, 344, 420, 462, 480, 488–90; **10:**41, 74, 83, 125, 152, 169, 213, 838, 841, 962; **11:**40, 83, 160, 190, 258, 275, 279, 375, 442, 537; **12:**42, 80, 88, 203–5, 290, 296, 315, 597, 710, 732; BLESS GOD/THE LORD **1:**440, 869; **2:**775, 787; **3:**22, 1008, 1040, 1042, 1051, 1055, 1057, 1064–65; **4:**310, 346, 353, 356, 360, 452, 681, 702, 783, 1065, 1089, 1091, 1096, 1100, 1145, 1216–17, 1219–21; **5:**843; **6:**795; **7:**237; **9:**29, 243; **11:**40, 42–43, 83, 160, 791; **12:**203–5, 710; AND CURSE(S) **1:**332, 402–3, 435, 845, 1115, 1178, 1180, 1186; **2:**184, 272–73, 289–90, 339, 367, 375, 485, 491–92, 495, 499–503, 505, 636, 788, 816, 870, 1062–64; **3:**178, 752, 995, 1062; **4:**229, 366; **5:**55, 120, 270, 436, 575, 615, 668; **6:**74, 78, 204, 733, 1075–76, 1472, 1496; **7:**252, 526, 663, 680, 703, 853, 860; **8:**31, 82; **10:**460, 659–60; **11:**258–59, 276; **12:**76; GOD/THE LORD BLESSES **1:**211, 398, 660; **2:**65–66, 194, 846, 1261; **3:**332, 984, 1025, 1042; **4:**682, 1216; **5:**162, 667; **7:**861; **9:**145; **11:**372; GOD'S/THE LORD'S BLESSING **1:**424–25, 442, 512, 567, 580, 696, 1041, 1134; **2:**14, 65, 69, 388, 776, 797; **3:**77, 81, 355, 382, 388, 403, 422, 437–38, 451, 457, 461, 522–23, 525, 580, 594, 611, 619, 624, 800, 1001, 1042, 1052, 1120; **4:**1216–17, 1273; **5:**239, 651; **6:**766, 793, 795, 826, 860; **7:**52, 102, 691; **9:**255, 458, 489; **11:**34, 39–40, 43, 48, 255, 262, 275, 346, 378, 460; **12:**71, 178, 200, 290

BLESSEDNESS
4:375, 381, 485, 635, 694, 1201; **5:**53, 408, 467, 469–71, 473–74, 480, 484, 486, 498, 513, 536, 552–53; **6:**1472; **7:**8; **8:**177–78, 204; **9:**54–55, 242, 245, 349; **10:**612, 817, 891, 997; **11:**40, 294, 829; **12:**222, 253, 291–92, 310

BLIGHT
1:1037, 1099; **4:**592; **5:**75; **6:**336; **7:**380; **10:**659

BLINDNESS
AND DEAFNESS (*see under* DEAF); DIVINE **6:**1070–71; MORAL OR METAPHORICAL **1:**818, 1100; **2:**129, 167, 179, 511, 858, 860, 1232; **3:**984; **4:**388, 564, 582, 637; **5:**140, 167, 464, 560, 586; **6:**361, 364, 369–72, 374, 377, 381, 389–90, 393, 490, 544, 763, 860, 1229; **7:**268, 683; **8:**22, 63, 239, 383–84, 398–400, 565, 614, 656, 677; **9:**178, 341, 343, 356, 579, 587, 656, 661, 663–64, 716, 821; **10:**194; **11:**66, 291, 442, 486; **12:**337–38, 716; PHYSICAL **1:**475, 535; **2:**179, 840, 858; **3:**201, 975, 984, 989, 1002–3, 1010, 1023, 1028, 1039, 1050; **5:**291, 330, 471, 596; **6:**1195; **7:**826; **8:**123, 223, 399, 619; **9:**355, 579, 653, 656, 660–61, 663–64; **10:**151, 190, 194, 337. *See also under* EYE; HEALING

BLOOD
OF AN/THE ANIMAL **1:**399, 988, 1111, 1119; **8:**32; **12:**110; AVENGER OF BLOOD *OR* BLOOD AND VENGEANCE/ REVENGE **1:**375, 848; **2:**265, 268, 333, 422, 435, 563, 629, 696, 1230, 1314–16, 1326; **3:**430, 1144; **6:**1336–37; **7:**810; **12:**158, 617; BODY AND **1:**193; **8:**473; **9:**422–23; **10:**938; OF THE BULL **1:**912, 1111 (*see also* BULL); OF THE COVENANT **1:**881, 1027, 1062; **7:**809, 811; **8:**472, 704, 720; **9:**420; **12:**9, 110, 123, 127, 353; FEUD **1:**375, 579; **2:**696, 967, 1174, 1230; **3:**930; FLESH AND **1:**167–68, 464, 557, 600, 748, 1081; **2:**827; **3:**395, 656, 1163; **5:**101, 426, 716; **6:**338, 499, 912, 1325, 1432, 1527; **9:**576, 608, 610, 614; **10:**560, 988, 993; **11:**63, 216, 460; **12:**10, 40, 64, 155, 571, 703, 728; FLOW OF **1:**1085, 1105; **2:**151; **8:**587; **9:**345, 833–34; HUMAN **1:**377, 1135; **2:**266; INNOCENT **2:**493, 1169, 1229; **3:**655,

737; **4:**189–90; **5:**77; **6:**626, 723, 740, 742, 1063, 1270; **7:**181, 631; OF JESUS/CHRIST/THE LORD **2:**83; **3:**612; **6:**815; **8:**473, 704; **9:**723; **10:**476, 519, 938; **11:**78, 284, 372, 398; **12:**108, 158, 247–48, 258; OF THE LAMB **1:**777, 1053; **2:**51; **6:**1564; **12:**548, 583, 602, 613, 618, 624, 626, 650–51, 659, 721, 733; AND OFFERING **1:**777, 912, 916, 986, 999, 1005, 1010, 1012–13, 1024–27, 1033–37, 1040, 1043, 1048–49, 1061–62, 1066, 1072, 1085, 1099, 1101, 1111–12, 1135; **2:**151, 1376; **3:**346, 608–9, 612, 617–18, 647, 959; **6:**1546, 1564, 1568–69; **8:**720; **9:**833; **10:**474; **11:**435; **12:**74, 104, 106–8, 118, 120, 142, 155, 158, 387; RITE **2:**81; **3:**346, 608, 612, 618, 647; SACRIFICIAL **1:**881, 1012, 1026, 1033, 1053, 1099; **3:**22, 485; **8:**472; **9:**723; **10:**476; **12:**113; SPILL(ED/ING/S) **1:**374, 1027, 1120; **2:**1169; **6:**1063, 1307; **12:**158

BLOODGUILT
2:200, 265, 445, 447, 453, 461, 696, 966, 1126, 1138, 1157, 1161, 1164–65, 1168–71, 1179, 1199, 1202, 1222, 1225, 1227, 1229–31, 1315, 1357–59; **3:**27, 35; **4:**254; **6:**84, 211, 1168, 1261, 1306–7, 1310–11, 1333, 1336; **7:**336; **8:**437

BLOODSHED
1:264, 1118; **2:**267, 421, 763, 1049; **3:**1008; **4:**886–88; **5:**558; **6:**39, 88, 218, 276, 1058, 1084, 1103, 1168, 1180, 1306–7, 1309–11, 1315, 1329–30, 1333–34, 1336–37, 1397, 1476, 1488–89, 1522; **7:**236, 482, 559–60, 598, 613, 646; **8:**670; **9:**270, 370, 437

BLUE
1:896; **2:**53, 128; **4:**67; **5:**341, 593; **6:**1321, 1374

BOAR
8:584

BOARD
ON A BOAT OR SHIP **1:**391–92; **6:**1374; **7:**500, 527; **10:**352–53, 356. *See also* PLANKS

BOAT, BOATS
1:232, 391; **3:**409, 714; **5:**485, 787; **6:**722, 724, 743, 775, 1484; **7:**467, 527; **8:**69, 84, 170, 230, 237, 300, 304, 314–15, 323, 327–30, 341, 525, 561, 568–69, 580–81, 600, 603, 614–15, 617, 671; **9:**116–17, 142, 176, 184, 187, 195, 596, 865; **10:**345–46, 348–49, 352, 598, 898, 932; **11:**469, 498. *See also* GALLEYS; SAILOR; SHIP

BODY, BODIES
OF/IN CHRIST **1:**211–12, 1150; **2:**587, 745, 790, 818, 912; **3:**1065; **4:**965, 1038; **5:**189, 227; **7:**67, 96; **8:**471; **9:**761; **10:**525, 559, 710, 726, 787, 804, 806, 823, 833, 850, 865, 918, 922, 935–36, 938, 941, 947–49, 956; **11:**123, 226, 229, 243, 296, 335, 338, 357–58, 360, 367, 378, 386, 394, 403–4, 408, 413, 418, 420, 422–24, 429–31, 443, 449–52, 456, 458, 461, 493, 504, 565, 606, 626, 643–44, 648, 650, 669, 779, 873; **12:**403, 484; DEAD **1:**1071, 1074, 1147–49; **2:**445, 767, 1135; **3:**14, 1002, 1179–80; **4:**254, 277; **6:**539, 549, 813, 825, 1009; **7:**613, 727, 829; **8:**443, 505, 535, 723; **9:**834, 836; **11:**260; **12:**108, 110; AND FLESH **1:**383, 1104, 1119–20; **3:**370; **4:**354, 833; **5:**49, 68, 425, 518; **9:**485, 834; **10:**542, 551–52, 574–75, 592, 682, 710, 729–30, 863, 865–66, 922, 987; **11:**88, 137, 321, 398, 423, 451–52, 490–91, 565, 572, 578, 606, 613, 623–26, 633–34, 642; **12:**105, 120, 295, 703; HUMAN **1:**92, 685, 706; **2:**54, 60; **4:**390, 852; **5:**354, 370, 398, 405, 407–8; **6:**1500; **7:**400; **10:**500, 823, 949; **12:**108; OF JESUS **2:**67; **8:**500–501, 726; **9:**465, 468, 544, 686, 702, 800, 835–36, 840–42; **10:**343, 540; **12:**74, 107, 115, 117, 727; OF LAW(S) **1:**65, 68, 861; **2:**927; ONE **1:**32; **2:**818, 884; **3:**382; **5:**140; **10:**525, 708–10, 726–27, 749, 759, 863, 865–66, 882, 918, 920, 935–36, 938, 945, 947; **11:**226, 242, 338, 344, 398, 400, 413, 420, 422, 425, 432, 648, 650; OF SIN **10:**539–40; **11:**243; AND SOUL **1:**18, 89, 288, 568, 1075, 1119; **3:**998, 1004, 1058; **4:**241, 286, 737, 852; **5:**152, 162, 440, 460, 475, 498, 511–12, 518, 567, 579; **6:**1500; **8:**264, 531; **9:**88, 346, 402, 687; **10:**707, 823, 866, 989; **11:**84, 399, 438, 450–52, 504, 536, 566–67, 623; **12:**53, 253, 292, 599; SPIRITUAL **1:**288; **10:**987; **11:**536

BODYGUARD
2:1148, 1180, 1376; **3:**718; **4:**154; **6:**994

BOIL (*OR* BOILS, *ETC.*)
AS IN BOILING LIQUID **1:**872, 1024, 1026; **2:**398, 987; **3:**647; **4:**625; **5:**135, 664; **6:**451, 469, 579, 584, 1062, 1066, 1334–35, 1337, 1591–92; **7:**839; **11:**317; **12:**401, 426; AS IN SKIN ERUPTION **1:**753–54, 1096; **2:**1006; **3:**271; **4:**358; **5:**335, 529, 584; **6:**301

BOLDNESS
AS IN CONFIDENCE/FAITH **2:**130, 359, 808, 872, 1183, 1263, 1297; **3:**1181; **4:**948; **6:**358, 517; **8:**19; **9:**782, 808, 810, 835; **10:**9, 15, 54, 92–93, 104, 108, 367–68, 753; **11:**407, 411, 413, 488, 662, 798, 807; **12:**46, 55, 119–20, 125, 140, 164, 168, 379, 422, 431, 442

BOLSTER
2:776, 810, 824; **3:**386, 532; **4:**17; **5:**442, 543; **6:**342, 347, 378, 389, 517; **7:**720; **8:**193; **9:**765; **10:**928; **11:**124, 191, 451; **12:**398, 442, 445, 476

BOLT
ON A DOOR **5:**748, 772; **9:**236; OF LIGHTNING (*see* LIGHTNING)

BOND, BONDS
1:68, 74, 224, 277, 284, 352–53, 500, 591, 781, 872–73, 1076; **2:**82, 292, 343, 393, 410, 466, 482–83, 752, 817, 896, 1208; **3:**224, 382, 518, 522, 986, 1022, 1033, 1041–42, 1045, 1173; **4:**47, 191, 308, 358, 368, 414, 429, 442–43, 463, 496, 510–11, 554–55, 611, 689, 953, 1013; **5:**69, 77, 119, 121–22, 144, 185, 363, 391, 401, 428, 499, 561–63, 654, 689, 747, 790; **6:**454, 531, 627, 806, 1222, 1233, 1289, 1309, 1331, 1471–72, 1502; **7:**169, 206, 229, 234, 237, 312, 319, 438, 605–6, 663, 674, 866; **8:**54, 471–72, 645; **9:**183, 318, 525, 771; **10:**550, 566, 613, 615, 647, 814, 862–63; **11:**292, 297, 338, 386, 404, 420, 424, 462, 464, 466, 485, 544, 613, 616, 625, 648, 745–46, 896; **12:**124, 485, 612–13, 634

BONDAGE, BONDAGES
1:83, 157, 160, 190, 210, 616, 683, 685, 706, 713, 721, 725, 735, 737, 751, 755, 770, 773, 785, 788–89, 799, 804, 806, 808, 812, 830, 834, 837, 862, 873, 949, 957, 1166, 1172, 1174, 1180; **2:**510, 901, 930, 977, 988, 1002–3, 1011, 1029, 1047; **3:**76, 104, 277, 294, 669, 736; **4:**370, 610, 754, 1207, 1220; **5:**823; **6:**282, 335, 376, 378, 413, 432, 454–55, 477, 499, 703, 832, 1263, 1291; **7:**296, 662, 690, 722, 732, 780, 801; **9:**106, 114, 125, 185, 336, 414, 478; **10:**596, 604, 924; **11:**29, 213, 247, 260–61, 269, 276, 288–91, 302–4, 310, 313, 355, 509, 627, 638, 887; **12:**40–41, 325, 673, 707, 710

BONE, BONES
1:217, 219, 229–30, 290, 353, 601, 674, 789–90, 1081–82; **2:**90, 151, 190, 571, 635, 718, 816, 860, 1198, 1252, 1357, 1359; **3:**106; **4:**228, 359, 395, 463, 477, 484, 526, 564, 618, 704, 763, 801, 805, 819, 833, 1087, 1244; **5:**49, 75, 144, 152, 159, 160, 322, 460, 599, 772, 846, 852, 855; **6:**8, 222, 301, 338, 640, 657, 750, 813, 822, 956, 1009, 1081, 1089, 1106, 1128, 1159, 1169, 1186, 1334–35, 1337, 1345, 1497–1504, 1506, 1523, 1525–26; **7:**5, 272, 362, 402; **8:**488; **9:**834; **10:**93, 575, 617; **11:**139; **12:**54; DRY **1:**229; **2:**860; **5:**599, 846; **6:**222, 1106, 1128, 1497–1504; **7:**5; AND FLESH **1:**353; **2:**816, 1233, 1346; **4:**354; **6:**1499–1500; **9:**485; **10:**710; **11:**451

BOOK OF LIFE
5:343; **6:**84; **9:**224, 658; **10:**969; **11:**540; **12:**571, 583, 601, 654, 657, 682, 715, 724, 730, 734

BOOTH, BOOTHS
1:1160; **2:**412, 1286; **3:**691, 801–4, 1075, 1133; **4:**63, 786; **6:**54, 1038; **7:**348, 426–27, 471, 481, 519, 521–22, 527; **8:**630–31; **9:**27, 204, 207, 616. *See also* TABERNACLE; TENT

BOOTHS, FEAST/FESTIVAL OF
See under FEASTS/FESTIVALS

BOOTY
1:440–42; **2:**11, 120–21, 123, 148, 163, 202, 245–48, 256, 562, 615, 651, 657, 808–9, 1089, 1266; **3:**152, 156, 561, 925, 932; **4:**55, 163, 277; **5:**261, 484; **6:**195, 212, 337, 467–68, 899, 1078, 1228, 1380, 1410, 1518; **7:**454, 685; **12:**87, 352

BORN
AGAIN **3:**637; **9:**552, 554–55, 566; **10:**155, 481; **12:**250, 254, 263, 276; ANEW **2:**168; **11:**296, 900; **12:**250, 254, 258, 260, 262–63, 265, 276; OF A/THE VIRGIN **9:**8, 50, 95; **12:**43, 62, 155; OF WATER **9:**345, 550, 555; OF WOMAN **4:**440, 450, 517; **5:**459; **10:**930

BORROW (*OR* BORROWS, *ETC.*)
CROSS-CULTURAL OR LITERARY **1:**13, 87, 105, 115, 156, 395, 1023, 1075; **2:**568, 655, 709, 732–33, 736, 740, 840, 1316; **3:**317, 364, 377, 388, 390, 399, 406, 418, 421–23, 429, 461–62, 473, 477–78, 484, 498, 529–30, 539, 591, 616, 629, 643–44, 665, 896, 980, 1091, 1098; **4:**352, 497, 914, 955, 990, 1223; **5:**21–22, 80, 142, 201, 206, 214, 275, 327, 331, 422, 441, 455, 459, 469, 473–74, 485, 503, 592, 631, 647, 729, 736, 823; **6:**16, 123, 510, 598, 987, 1090, 1130–31, 1140, 1230, 1296, 1391, 1394, 1444; **7:**32, 50–51, 62, 83, 145, 151, 302, 335, 344, 352, 407, 468, 519, 571, 576, 578, 663–64, 696, 703, 760, 818; **8:**65; **9:**169; **11:**690; **12:**28, 31, 37, 41, 49, 54, 64, 137, 158, 167, 179, 271, 327, 336, 352, 484; OR LEND **3:**186, 199, 779; **4:**829; **5:**567, 570, 736; **6:**697; **7:**83; **8:**570, 659, 671; **9:**370; **12:**128

BORROWER
1:867; **2:**467; **3:**780; **5:**775; **6:**211; **8:**195

BOTTLE, BOTTLES
1:90; **4:**810; **6:**891, 1595–96; **10:**469, 617; **11:**52

BOTTOMLESS PIT
9:282; **12:**631, 682, 684

BOUNDARIES, TRIBAL
2:437, 636; **3:**364

BOUNDARY STONE, STONES
See under STONE

BOW
OF A SHIP **10:**352; AS A VERB **1:**601, 628, 634–35, 659, 772, 838, 841; **2:**747, 871, 1297, 1319, 1358; **3:**177, 479, 866, 869, 872, 894, 919, 923, 951, 956, 1148–49; **4:**306, 701, 792, 964, 1020, 1061, 1069, 1091, 1232; **5:**562, 674, 765, 859; **6:**72, 397, 403, 407, 461, 509, 549, 1206, 1303, 1537, 1588; **7:**65, 67, 76, 160, 183, 188, 699, 838; **8:**186; **10:**719, 738, 749; **11:**509–10, 516; **12:**29, 306, 650, 730; AS A WEAPON **1:**242, 400,

660; **2:**1205–7; **4:**111, 486, 539, 546, 930, 981; **5:**578; **6:**68, 156, 183, 189, 900, 1038, 1523; **7:**218, 256, 258, 653, 809–10, 814; **8:**367; **12:**612

BOWELS
5:411, 664; **10:**50; **11:**484, 499; **12:**419, 467

BOWL, BOWLS
1:745, 890, 1026; **2:**678, 788; **3:**485, 487, 679, 728; **4:**34, 303, 349, 353; **5:**355–57; **7:**54, 400, 769–70; **8:**182, 470; **10:**950; **11:**855; **12:**535, 538, 562, 592, 604–5, 609, 620, 630, 632, 659, 672, 675–77, 680, 722, 732. *See also* BASIN

BOX, BOXES
2:365, 1001, 1248; **3:**70, 1182; **4:**594, 635; **5:**330; **6:**1116; **7:**293; **8:**431, 676; **10:**227; **11:**847; **12:**250

BRACELETS
3:1147; **6:**1228, 1329–30

BRAID (*OR* BRAIDS, BRAIDED, *ETC.*)
2:841, 858; **11:**801; **12:**432, 467

BRAMBLE, BRAMBLES
2:635, 816–17; **9:**151

BRANCH (*OR* BRANCHES, *ETC.*)
OF A FAMILY **1:**52, 183, 325, 405, 408, 415; **2:**701, 892, 1259; **3:**22, 318, 344–45, 357–58, 451; **6:**84, 140, 143, 1272, 1274, 1506; **7:**737, 739, 744, 763, 766–68, 785–87, 788, 807, 811, 814; **8:**147; **9:**505, 658, 696, 757–58; **11:**183; AS A KINGLY OR MESSIANIC FIGURE **6:**84, 140; **7:**737, 739, 766, 768, 788, 807, 811, 814; **8:**147; **10:**511; OF A LAMPSTAND/RIVER **1:**1017, 1163; **2:**80; **3:**386, 431; **4:**166; **5:**765; **6:**1404, 1595; **7:**769; **12:**596; NATURAL **6:**516; **10:**680, 684–85; OF A TREE OR AS A METAPHOR **1:**393, 615, 666, 1100, 1159–60; **2:**412, 1336; **3:**135, 801–2; **4:**154, 257, 286, 470–71, 540, 608, 1155; **5:**475, 605, 651, 719, 721, 807; **6:**175, 516, 874, 1177, 1211, 1216–17, 1219, 1244, 1246–48, 1252–53, 1271–74, 1422, 1425–27, 1430, 1435, 1484, 1506, 1514; **7:**75–77, 240, 411, 771; **8:**403, 577–78, 658, 674; **9:**179, 275–76, 357, 367, 542, 706–8, 739, 755, 756–61, 833; **10:**564, 568, 601, 680, 683–86, 709, 999–1000; **11:**284, 404; **12:**621; AND VINE IMAGERY **1:**615; **6:**1211, 1216–17, 1219, 1244, 1246–48, 1271–74, 1506; **9:**739, 755–60; **12:**468, 710

BRASS
9:171, 399; **12:**597

BREACH (*OR* BREACHES, *ETC.*)
AS A NOUN **1:**53, 404, 628, 956; **2:**452, 468, 614, 853, 878, 1171, 1304; **3:**542, 581, 587, 722, 737; **4:**459, 881; **5:**81, 557; **6:**194, 499, 598, 600–601, 614, 620–21, 646, 650, 655, 809, 853, 859, 948, 1171, 1194, 1201, 1315; **7:**224, 252, 261, 829; **8:**34; **9:**26, 446, 563, 566, 588, 660; **10:**931; **11:**645, 857; **12:**34, 60, 75, 105, 123, 163; AS A VERB **1:**383, 1181; **3:**293; **4:**40, 223, 256, 349, 459, 546; **5:**173; **6:**1079, 1088, 1151, 1161, 1201, 1358, 1366, 1418; **7:**610; **9:**822; **10:**782, 855

BREAD
1:654–55, 779, 805, 812–16, 877, 892, 913, 1019, 1021, 1047, 1051, 1062, 1181; **2:**355, 412, 608–9, 804, 807, 901, 903, 988, 1036–37, 1042, 1110, 1249, 1276; **3:**127, 612, 782, 909, 1017; **4:**311, 328, 500, 698, 991, 1098, 1175; **5:**4, 63–64, 102, 104, 166, 181, 186–87, 255–56, 303, 351, 395, 578–79, 708, 720, 752, 765, 776, 818–19; **6:**238, 255, 456, 481–82, 638, 849, 1061, 1148–49, 1153, 1176, 1203, 1212, 1228, 1230, 1342, 1438, 1517; **7:**193, 265, 411, 448–49, 779, 834; **8:**163, 165–66, 204, 207, 213, 247, 309, 324–26, 342, 468, 471, 556, 609, 617, 703–4; **9:**14–15, 97–100, 118, 171, 193–97, 220, 231, 234–36, 238, 276, 287, 302, 316, 318, 320, 418–21, 422–23, 466, 479–83, 486, 490, 538, 576, 593–94, 596, 599–600, 603, 607, 612–14, 625, 668–69, 858, 864; **10:**352, 918, 934–36, 938; **11:**130, 768; **12:**104; BASKET **1:**622, 782; **5:**261; BREAK(S) BREAD/BROKE(N) BREAD **1:**190–91; **3:**612; **9:**26, 421, 726; **10:**71–72, 277–78, 901; AND COMMUNION/EUCHARIST **1:**91, 816, 892; **2:**1276; **8:**601; **9:**196–97, 480, 538–39, 606–8, 612–14; **10:**352, 934–35; **11:**234; **12:**75; AND CUP **2:**1276; **3:**612; **8:**471, 703–4; **9:**418–23; **10:**918, 934–35, 938; DAILY **1:**1020, 1159, 1164; **3:**813; **4:**509, 770, 790, 1226; **5:**126, 253; **8:**209; **9:**597; **11:**752; EAT(EN/S) **1:**704; **2:**127; **5:**262, 343; **6:**1149, 1154, 1343; **7:**122, 410, 772; **8:**703; **9:**166, 284; GIFT OF **1:**812, 814–15, 892; **9:**599–600, 612; OF HEAVEN (*see under* HEAVEN); HOLY **2:**247, 1138–40; **9:**136; LEAVENED **1:**777; **7:**380; **9:**415; **10:**848; LIVING BREAD/BREAD OF LIFE **1:**209, 813, 1022; **4:**824; **5:**15; **9:**4, 513, 592, 598, 600–608, 611–14, 694; OF THE PRESENCE **1:**890, 892–93, 1011, 1067, 1072, 1163, 1166; **2:**1139–41, 1143; **3:**477, 485–86, 608; **4:**852, 999; **9:**133, 136; **12:**103; UNLEAVENED, FEAST OF (*see* FEASTS/FESTIVALS: OF PASSOVER/UNLEAVENED BREAD; PASSOVER AND FEAST OF UNLEAVENED BREAD); AND WATER **1:**490; **2:**68, 163; **3:**844; **4:**311; **5:**720; **6:**190, 1148, 1196, 1343, 1361; AND WINE **1:**208, 440; **2:**68; **5:**340, 720; **7:**862; **8:**471, 601, 703–4; **9:**165–66, 591, 608; **11:**234; **12:**86. *See also* LOAF

BREAKFAST
9:860, 864–65; **10:**351

BREAST, BREASTS
1:458, 666, 913, 990, 1026, 1053–54, 1062; **2:**106, 910; **3:**625, 894; **4:**233, 763, 1208; **5:**69,

BREAST, BREASTS *(continued)*
368, 379–80, 388, 390, 402, 415–16, 419, 425–26, 428, 432–33, 526, 663, 731, 765, 809; **6:**421, 1041, 1227, 1319, 1327; **7:**224, 270, 376, 610; **9:**23, 245, 342, 404, 450–52, 462–63, 498; **10:**606, 697; **12:**141

BREASTPIECE/BREASTPLATE
1:888, 905–7, 973, 1061; **2:**162, 220; **5:**486, 593, 618, 834, 843; **6:**1392; **7:**136, 146; **10:**692; **11:**459; **12:**632, 645, 723. *See also* ARMOR

BREATH, BREATHS
1:230, 289, 739, 767, 1157; **2:**104, 613, 926, 1089; **3:**129, 510, 1004, 1057, 1178; **4:**51, 396, 443, 452, 476, 514, 517, 519, 523, 563, 576, 800, 838, 923–24, 1099, 1220, 1236, 1278–79; **5:**188, 279, 298, 311, 354, 355, 397, 426, 460, 772; **6:**141, 293, 331, 403, 1065, 1115–16, 1154, 1179, 1499–1500, 1502–3; **7:**50, 83, 194, 506, 824; **8:**420; **9:**290, 301, 410; **10:**247, 419, 508, 607, 696, 700, 763, 835; **11:**347, 381, 417, 459, 737, 760; **12:**431, 700, 703; OF GOD **4:**377, 517, 526, 568, 591, 810, 1099; **5:**479, 504, 507; **6:**331, 1292; **11:**759; OF LIFE **1:**350, 383, 391; **4:**242, 1099; **5:**567; **6:**221, 364, 990, 1500; **9:**846; **12:**642; AND WIND **4:**377, 519, 591, 838, 1220, 1236; **5:**279, 311; **6:**1115, 1116, 1500, 1502; **10:**419

BREATHE (*OR* BREATHES, *ETC.*)
1:337, 350, 746, 946; **2:**633; **4:**439, 463, 1271, 1278; **5:**97, 311, 497, 567–68, 525, 624, 724; **6:**1500, 1502; **8:**105; **9:**461, 484, 846, 848; **10:**575, 724; **11:**400, 704, 760, 851; **12:**433, 542, 595, 686

BREECHES
1:1060; **6:**243

BRETHREN
3:381; **4:**188–89; **7:**67, 77; **8:**18; **9:**428; **10:**806, 901; **11:**707; **12:**259, 543, 612, 624, 650, 669, 704, 717

BRIBE (*OR* BRIBES, *ETC.*)
1:260, 828–29, 870; **2:**369, 420, 832–33, 858, 860, 1026, 1061; **3:**118, 251, 695, 700, 785, 897, 904, 918–19; **4:**107, 177, 222, 224, 242, 276, 783, 1000; **5:**151–52, 167, 170, 172, 193–94, 242, 318, 611, 740; **6:**60, 92, 95, 598, 1260, 1310; **7:**417, 561, 585, 683; **8:**124, 500; **9:**279, 337

BRIBERY
1:828, 870, 920; **2:**493; **3:**556; **4:**105, 223, 733; **5:**167, 170, 239, 693; **6:**63, 627, 742, 1310; **7:**390

BRICK, BRICKS
1:221, 411, 724, 727, 735, 925, 1180–81; **2:**656; **5:**34; **6:**127, 1143–44, 1150–51, 1194, 1301; **7:**31, 40, 66, 618; **10:**41; **11:**46; **12:**374

BRICKMAKER
1:727; **5:**812

BRICKYARD
1:892

BRIDAL
1:553; **2:**1118, 1122, 1305; **5:**400; **6:**597–98, 1228; **9:**558, 565; **11:**82, 148; CHAMBER **3:**979–80, 982, 1008, 1029, 1031, 1033; **8:**359; **11:**450–51. *See also* WEDDING

BRIDE, BRIDES
1:553, 837; **2:**234, 455, 629, 741, 903–4, 926, 939, 941, 1331; **3:**90, 979–80, 982, 1008, 1026, 1029, 1033, 1038–39, 1043; **4:**313, 862; **5:**13, 44, 84, 96, 400, 403, 405, 407, 419, 421, 425, 445, 491, 498, 509, 512, 720, 829; **6:**88, 337, 431, 477–78, 547, 573, 596, 602–3, 670–71, 685, 826, 995, 1228, 1492; **7:**281, 286, 320; **8:**449–50; **9:**51, 263, 289, 558, 565; **10:**447; **11:**450–51; **12:**29, 579, 664, 681, 686, 694–95, 721–22, 734; CHRIST/JESUS AS BRIDE/BRIDEGROOM **1:**184; **7:**227–28; **8:**235–36, 449–50; **9:**557–58, 565; **10:**559; **11:**82, 147–48, 152, 173, 359, 450–52; **12:**664, 694, 734; OF GOD/YAHWEH **6:**1319, 1321, 1329; **7:**236; **9:**558; **11:**359; **12:**686; OF THE LAMB **12:**579, 664, 681, 694, 722; PRICE **1:**867; **2:**629, 930, 1122; **7:**231

BRIDEGROOM, BRIDEGROOMS
1:241, 718; **4:**312; **5:**400, 407, 419–20, 512; **6:**87–88, 826, 1342, 1492; **7:**227–28, 320; **8:**79, 450–51, 555; **9:**51, 130–31, 262, 538–39, 557–58, 570, 752; **11:**147; **12:**29, 686, 694, 721; FRIEND(S) OF THE **6:**87; **9:**558, 752

BRIDESMAID, BRIDESMAIDS
8:123, 449–51

BRIDLE, BRIDLES
4:210, 299; **11:**74; **12:**203

BRIER, BRIERS
6:89, 226, 265, 378, 482, 485, 544, 1123, 1396–97, 1451

BRIMSTONE
1:329, 473, 475; **2:**877; **4:**470; **5:**723

BROAD PLACE
1:530; **4:**748, 801, 1154, 1170

BRONZE
1:218, 223, 900–901, 915, 972–73, 1138, 1180; **2:**137, 536, 738, 1266; **3:**67, 116, 251, 429, 473, 485–86, 526, 768, 800; **4:**107, 160, 163, 165, 388, 390, 471, 486, 546, 591, 618, 624; **6:**586, 696, 1178, 1306, 1312–13, 1360, 1364, 1377–78, 1538, 1540, 1546, 1549; **7:**21, 54–55, 81, 83, 136, 189, 567, 782–83; **9:**171; **11:**460; **12:**561, 567, 598, 694; AGE (*see under* AGE)

BRONZE SEA
3:485, 679; **6:**925

BROOD
OF OFFSPRING **3:**967; **4:**612; **5:**475, 524; **8:**157; **9:**83, 372; AS A THOUGHTFUL ATTITUDE **1:**942, 1133; **5:**319
BROOK
OF WATER **1:**447; **3:**802; **5:**133; **6:**698–99, 1348, 1474; **7:**547; **9:**801
BROOM, BROOMSTICK
3:140, 348; **6:**159
BROTH
5:8; **6:**1337
BROTHER, BROTHERS
OF JESUS **8:**103; **9:**100; **10:**178–79; **11:**217; **12:**473–75, 481; KEEPER **1:**374, 1139; LOVE **2:**432; **9:**304; **12:**290, 423; AND SISTERS IN THE FAITH/LORD **1:**25, 377, 476, 574, 1015; **2:**467, 493, 522; **3:**592, 616, 821; **8:**298, 363; **10:**805, 840, 975; **11:**338, 587. *See also* SIBLINGS; SISTER
BROTHERHOOD
2:460, 475; **3:**520; **7:**362; **11:**736; **12:**275
BUCKET, BUCKETS
2:190; **5:**355, 541; **9:**566–67
BUCKLE, BUCKLES
AS A FASTENER **4:**58, 130, 148, 165; **6:**1129; AS A VERB **2:**859
BUCKLER, BUCKLERS
4:819; **5:**403; **6:**1516, 1524
BUGLE
10:959
BUL
(month in Canaanite calendar) **3:**62, 69
BULL, BULLS
1:273, 912–13, 916, 931, 963, 1035, 1039, 1051, 1061–62, 1110–11, 1119, 1158; **2:**78, 81, 84, 126–27, 185, 187, 189, 230, 232–33, 771, 797; **3:**104, 135–36, 142, 485, 647, 691, 709, 712, 730, 962, 993; **4:**71, 459, 618, 635, 763; **5:**681, 798, 850; **6:**915, 925, 1115, 1528, 1546, 1568–69, 1585–86, 1589; **7:**53, 62, 235, 809; **10:**423; **12:**60, 74, 104, 247; CALF **1:**1034–35, 1065, 363–64 (*see also* CALF). *See also* COW
BULLOCK
10:474
BULRUSHES
1:391; **3:**575
BULWARK
4:487; **5:**526; **6:**379, 493; **7:**40; **11:**775
BUNDLE
5:683, 742, 787; **6:**1194; **11:**317, 424, 457; OF THE LIVING **2:**1168
BURDEN, BURDENS
1:17, 63, 148, 199, 219, 225, 364, 366, 553, 827, 862, 946, 1044, 1128, 1180; **2:**297, 331, 404, 407, 574, 596, 716, 860, 908, 974, 1027, 1048, 1145, 1171, 1175, 1309; **3:**53–54, 58, 61, 102, 140, 300, 438, 470, 498, 518, 622, 624, 645, 723, 728, 741, 761, 773, 777, 782–83, 819, 848, 1071; **4:**241, 303, 501, 513, 579, 631–32, 684, 713, 754, 896, 899–900, 1004, 1088, 1128; **5:**15, 108, 173–74, 230, 295, 454, 463, 584, 597, 627–28, 676, 688, 690, 745; **6:**55, 79, 119, 150, 159, 170, 191, 254, 296, 370, 405–7, 436, 454, 545, 563, 581, 583, 585, 589, 698, 710, 729, 753, 831, 921, 1051, 1069, 1132, 1139, 1194, 1232, 1255, 1340, 1450, 1455; **7:**42, 138, 275, 310, 500, 507, 585, 779, 801, 804, 826, 853, 862; **8:**32, 54, 80, 275, 277, 395, 431, 470, 540, 590; **9:**248–50, 359, 496, 542, 599, 773; **10:**327, 462–63, 767, 787, 834, 904, 938, 939, 987, 997; **11:**9, 12, 32, 71, 115–16, 145, 150, 169, 170, 243, 332–35, 339, 621, 662, 664, 700, 767, 821, 824–25, 867; **12:**23, 74, 86, 90, 96, 421, 581, 612, 721; OF GUILT **3:**423, 610; **5:**584; **11:**243; OF LEADERSHIP **2:**104–6, 112; PROPHETIC **6:**586, 596, 676, 702, 727; OF SIN(S) **4:**1076, 1112; **6:**371, 1446
BURIAL
1:240, 281, 306, 308, 334, 418, 434, 489, 503–4, 514–15, 571, 577, 598, 656, 658–59, 664, 667–70, 674; **2:**12, 50, 65, 149, 198, 445, 448, 546, 564, 569, 647, 707, 709, 718–19, 1055, 1212, 1217, 1225, 1230, 1336, 1357, 1359; **3:**36, 108, 113, 177, 221, 242, 286, 368, 424, 543, 570, 580–81, 587, 590, 600, 631, 649, 981–82, 984, 996, 998, 1001–2, 1014–15, 1069, 1181–82; **4:**111, 149, 241, 254, 281, 352, 494, 524, 1195; **5:**174, 322, 337, 697, 742, 809, 837; **6:**457, 466, 723, 741, 830, 963, 1009, 1106, 1176, 1442–44, 1497, 1516, 1524–26; **7:**266, 567, 666, 683; **8:**32, 124, 230, 248, 465–67, 470, 488, 491, 493–95, 498, 523, 531, 639, 695, 697–99, 724–26, 728, 730; **9:**13, 37, 169, 174, 316, 367, 450, 464–68, 470, 472, 514, 634, 686, 690–92, 701–2, 704–5, 799–800, 808, 815, 833, 835–36, 841, 843–44; **10:**106, 126, 161, 342, 538; **11:**274, 623–24, 628; **12:**139, 155, 489
BURNING
1:411, 866, 1010, 1013, 1024–25, 1035, 1044, 1067, 1138; **2:**36, 80, 104, 316, 648, 842, 853, 1087, 1359; **3:**106, 389, 543, 648, 723, 819, 1026; **4:**12, 40, 55, 58, 66, 82, 175, 198, 305, 395, 465, 624, 1087, 1206; **5:**126, 226, 247, 446, 578, 585, 700; **6:**133, 242, 256, 271, 277, 335, 365, 540, 640, 727, 821, 850, 1002, 1038, 1151, 1153, 1177, 1317, 1330, 1337, 1546; **7:**65, 168, 256, 328, 371, 676, 685, 765; **9:**84, 86, 252, 452, 480; **10:**271, 274, 893; **11:**461; **12:**76, 310, 597, 630, 682, 694, 712; ANGER/NOSTRILS/WRATH **1:**931, 934; **2:**36; **4:**55, 305, 624; **5:**328; **6:**128, 670,

BURNING *(continued)*
711, 727, 1038, 1063, 1279, 1338, 1523; **7:**317, 357, 402, 478, 514, 517–18, 524–25, 685; BUSH **1:**692, 704, 711, 794, 824, 1000, 1008; **2:**585, 612; **6:**874; **7:**138, 164; **8:**423; **9:**389, 443, 475, 632; **10:**127; CITY/TOWN(S) **2:**246, 648; **4:**175, 851; **6:**850, 1038, 1150–51, 1330; **9:**252; COAL(S)/LAMP(S)/LAMPSTAND(S)/LIGHT(S)/TORCH(ES) **1:**893, 900–901, 1163, 1166; **2:**80, 992; **3:**485, 487, 568; **4:**190; **5:**220, 261; **6:**414, 515, 1115, 1182–83, 1560; **7:**371; **9:**263, 632; **10:**715; **12:**104, 599, 630; HUMANS **1:**495, 1138; **2:**25, 831, 833–34, 842; **4:**46, 243, 281, 471, 813, 1285–86, 1327, 1526; **6:**640; **9:**252; **12:**682; INCENSE **1:**1017, 1045, 1067, 1111, 1164; **2:**137–38, 141, 220; **3:**37, 40, 346, 442, 591, 607; **4:**40; **6:**1159, 1576; **9:**46, 48; **11:**58; **12:**104; OF A/THE SCROLL **4:**40; **6:**769, 839–40, 956

BURNT OFFERING, OFFERINGS
See under OFFERING

BURY (*OR* BURIES, *ETC.*)
1:242, 455, 503–4, 584–86, 660, 667, 669, 674; **2:**159, 252, 448, 520, 555, 561, 582, 717, 752, 816, 859, 907, 1198, 1336, 1359; **3:**109, 157, 168–69, 220, 238, 282, 286, 756, 864, 975, 979–80, 989, 993, 995–96, 998, 1001–2, 1016, 1028, 1041; 1056, 1069, 1071, 1182; **4:**111, 152, 198, 263, 277, 370, 524, 756; **5:**134, 232, 322, 397, 591; **6:**223, 276, 640, 721, 850, 1009, 1059, 1438, 1442–43, 1445, 1501–3, 1525–26, 1561; **7:**82, 548; **8:**14, 58, 105, 124, 230, 313–14, 322, 423, 493–94, 726, 730; **9:**217, 229, 317, 361, 465–66, 468, 475, 691, 730, 835–36; **10:**50, 98–99, 132, 138, 538, 559, 684, 976; **11:**243, 389, 574; **12:**43, 62, 139, 246, 250, 295

BUSH, BURNING
See under BURNING

BUSHEL, BUSHELS
1:1098, 1188; **2:**108, 921; **3:**58, 722; **5:**346, 499; **6:**1583; **7:**774, 777; **8:**182, 575; **9:**308

BUTTER
1:219, 1026; **6:**1292

BUZZARD, BUZZARDS
3:967; **4:**611

BYWORD
4:223, 546, 858; **5:**829; **6:**1062, 1207, 1237, 1322, 1330; **9:**152; **10:**638

C

CABINET
KING'S ADVISORY GROUP **3:**8, 49–50, 52, 58; **9:**311

CAGE (*OR* CAGES, *ETC.*)
3:480, 996; **5:**714; **6:**195, 243, 1077; **7:**594

CAKE, CAKES
1:912–13, 1019, 1157; **2:**1185, 1303; **3:**112, 140, 363; **4:**469; **5:**139, 193, 312; **6:**638–39, 873, 1379; **7:**193, 234, 256–57, 261–62, 779; **8:**213; **10:**683; BARLEY **6:**1149; RAISIN **7:**231

CALAMUS
See CANE: FRAGRANT

CALDRON
6:1186, 1334, 1336–37; **7:**691

CALENDAR
1:73, 210, 218, 275, 286, 316, 1109, 1156; **2:**32, 36, 230, 233, 236, 331–32, 411, 414–15, 593; **3:**61–62, 305, 399, 406, 431, 441, 480, 506, 606, 622, 649, 751, 803, 938; **4:**18–19, 110, 157, 168, 189, 253, 268–69, 280, 367; **5:**185, 308, 502, 731, 787, 834; **6:**168, 176, 265, 934, 1537; **7:**4, 718; **8:**3, 33, 39, 166, 702; **9:**80; **10:**271, 320; **11:**205, 283, 288, 291, 415, 437, 631; CHRISTIAN/CHURCH **1:**189, 199; **2:**232, 235, 1217; CULTIC **2:**9, 11, 23, 89, 169, 202, 223, 230, 232–33, 235; **3:**646; **4:**8; **7:**674; **8:**692; FESTAL/FESTIVAL **1:**871, 874, 950–51; **2:**289, 409, 412–14; **3:**104; JEWISH **1:**69; **3:**805, 899; **4:**40, 297; **6:**1454; LITURGICAL **2:**32; **3:**803; **5:**731, 787; **11:**288, 415; RELIGIOUS CONVICTION(S) **1:**316; **3:**506, 649; **5:**834; **8:**33

CALF, CALVES
1:93, 225, 463, 927, 931–32, 937–38, 941, 945, 947, 949–50, 1034–35, 1066, 1164; **2:**151, 363–64, 1012, 1185; **3:**104, 522, 598, 993; **5:**715; **6:**141, 831, 1131, 1168; **7:**202, 203, 205, 213, 235, 259–61, 263, 265, 272, 275, 288, 419, 579, 779, 872–73; **8:**309, 537; **12:**107, 110, 117; FATTED **1:**1026; **2:**771; **9:**301, 303; GOLDEN **1:**396, 689, 930, 956, 1023, 1056, 1063, 1065; **2:**47, 63, 106, 125, 188, 197, 198, 220, 362–63, 365, 687, 792, 804, 809, 826, 871, 887; **3:**104, 106, 226, 252, 617, 811, 1137, 1139; **4:**730, 778, 844, 885, 991, 1000, 1087–88, 1092, 1111, 1133, 1150, 1205; **5:**159, 562; **6:**74, 456, 649, 657, 1167–68, 1201, 1279, 1509; **7:**205, 260; **10:**433, 563, 638–39, 662; **11:**266; **12:**588. *See also* COW

CALL (*OR* CALLS, CALLING, *ETC.*)
TO DISCIPLE(S)/DISCIPLESHIP **4:**815, 1252, 1277; **8:**169–70, 183, 188, 195, 215, 220, 228, 230, 234, 256, 277, 300, 351–52, 383, 394, 500, 552–53, 562, 594, 694, 709; **9:**111, 114–15, 118, 126, 129, 137, 139, 142, 152, 193, 216–18, 293–94, 309, 402, 469, 533–34, 711, 751, 779, 864; **12:**170; DIVINE/GOD'S/THE LORD'S **1:**199, 238, 426, 1063; **2:**293–94, 994, 1044; **3:**145, 332; **4:**819; **5:**394; **6:**354, 400, 540, 587–88; **8:**539; **9:**118; **10:**145, 282, 345, 349, 798–9, 906; **11:**75, 204, 215, 395, 419, 482, 533, 649, 702, 719, 829; **12:**481; BY GOD/THE LORD/YAHWEH

1:190, 306, 719–20, 1049; **2:**503, 797–98, 994, 1044; **4:**248; **6:**104, 347, 358, 375, 429, 563, 580, 582, 586, 588, 868, 956, 1370, 1464; **7:**204, 219, 328, 437, 670; **8:**126, 416; **9:**352; **10:**52, 124, 127, 285, 374, 425, 603, 676, 797–98, 811, 888, 937; **11:**149, 533, 648, 702, 746, 836; **12:**60–61, 246, 269, 481, 483; ON GOD/THE LORD/YAHWEH/THE NAME OF THE LORD **1:**435, 528; **2:**767, 853, 859, 945, 1016; **3:**194, 332, 904; **4:**212, 249, 275, 277, 290, 426, 569, 747, 883, 1000, 1027, 1075, 1243; **5:**531, 533, 856; **6:**147, 184, 202, 294, 329, 503, 542, 545, 692, 827, 917, 957–58, 1056; **7:**122, 124–26, 160, 326, 328, 483, 506, 517, 675, 699, 797, 815; **9:**100, 350, 798; **10:**59, 65, 68–96, 72, 99, 206, 210, 307, 630, 653, 665–67, 670, 690, 1002; TO MINISTRY **3:**145, 1043; **7:**216; NARRATIVE(S)/STORY (STORIES) **1:**692; **2:**991, 1036, 1040–42; **5:**377; **6:**12, 19, 319, 330–31, 348, 420, 429, 514, 573, 579, 583–87, 596, 878, 1121, 1124, 1132; **7:**138, 204, 219; **8:**253, 539; **9:**117, 140, 531, 534, 546, 710, 857, 860; **11:**190, 215. *See also* VOCATION

CAMEL, CAMELS
1:219–20, 511, 557, 754, 1075, 1080; **2:**808, 1193; **3:**565, 1044, 1106, 1142; **4:**345, 351; **6:**195, 254, 337, 601, 899, 1224, 1351, 1380; **7:**801; **8:**395, 436, 650–51; **9:**151, 202, 296, 348, 350, 359–60; HAIR **3:**1142; **9:**81, 163

CAMP
1:58, 174, 813, 836, 932, 986, 995, 1035, 1098, 1112; **2:**4–5, 10–13, 15–16, 21, 25–27, 31, 34, 36–41, 47, 50–51, 53–56, 59–60, 64–66, 68–69, 77, 80–83, 86–87, 89, 91–92, 94–95, 97, 99–100, 104–9, 111–12, 126, 136, 140–41, 149, 151–52, 164, 169, 170, 199, 201–2, 229, 235, 247, 255, 262–64, 461, 606, 625, 627, 639, 736, 1001, 1030, 1079, 1110–11, 1113, 1174–75, 1195, 1201, 1286, 1330–32; **3:**207–9, 217, 363, 379, 551, 622, 894, 932, 960, 996, 1028, 1088, 1093, 1124, 1148, 1150, 1156, 1158–59, 1161–62, 1170–71; **4:**54, 63–64, 66, 78, 110, 141, 204, 247, 276, 282; **5:**525, 628, 765, 853; **6:**647, 1147, 1156, 1167, 1510, 1531; **7:**122; **10:**822; **11:**310, 461; **12:**702; ARRANGEMENT/LAYOUT **2:**12, 15, 23, 25–27, 36–38, 51, 59, 170; ENEMY **1:**286; **2:**803; **3:**871, 1075, 1093, 1149, 1173; **4:**66; INSIDE/WITHIN **1:**1098; **2:**4, 26, 60–61, 66–67, 104, 107, 170; ISRAELITE **2:**4, 10, 13, 22, 25, 38, 80, 82, 189, 190, 193, 199, 245, 618; **4:**82; **6:**1319; OUTSIDE **1:**995, 1035, 1044, 1061, 1066, 1070, 1097–98, 1100–1101, 1165; **2:**26, 39, 60, 80, 104, 106–8, 110, 151, 247; **3:**1158; **9:**325; **12:**107, 167, 170, 531, 668, 728

CANAL, CANALS
2:668; **3:**726; **4:**229, 604, 1227; **5:**607, 758, 818; **6:**180, 943, 1081, 1109–10, 1120, 1129, 1136, 1175, 1182, 1184, 1246, 1360, 1401, 1403–4, 1407, 1413, 1425, 1434, 1516, 1529; **7:**111; **8:**247; **10:**761

CANDLE (*OR* CANDLES, CANDLESTICKS, *ETC.*)
1:1044; **6:**244; **9:**46, 181, 245, 632; **10:**676; **11:**377, 760, 896

CANE
5:296; FRAGRANT **1:**1061; **5:**757; **6:**379, 1379

CANNIBALISM
1:1181; **2:**503, 505; **3:**204; **5:**311; **6:**128, 952, 1043, 1062, 1153; **7:**557, 674; **9:**373

CANON
1:5, 7–21, 31, 35, 37, 40, 43–44, 46–49, 61, 65–67, 70, 83, 85–86, 94, 100–102, 126, 129–30, 132, 134–35, 139, 147, 161, 168–70, 188, 190, 283, 285, 292, 296, 305, 321, 354, 924, 927, 952; **2:**273, 893, 946, 958, 1024, 1065; **3:**370, 513, 663, 716, 747, 803, 859, 867, 896, 972, 977, 1079; **4:**503, 642, 666, 1174; **5:**27, 278, 281–82, 330, 337, 349, 359, 364, 368, 390–91, 448, 620, 633–34, 651; **6:**18, 22–23, 48, 85, 148, 169–70, 214, 313, 315, 339, 875, 1099, 1210, 1240, 1438; **7:**2, 22–23, 175, 302, 339, 352, 408, 467, 493, 623; **8:**6, 28, 72, 106; **9:**486, 589; **10:**26–27, 31–32, 37, 147, 370–71, 383–90, 548, 716, 971; **11:**194–95, 319, 353–54, 582, 853, 867; **12:**4, 70, 161, 287, 324, 329, 366, 370, 420, 455, 468, 494; OF THE OT (*see under* OLD TESTAMENT); OF THE NT (*see under* NEW TESTAMENT)

CANONIZE, CANONIZATION
1:47, 71, 135, 152, 314, 823; **2:**719, 893; **3:**976, 1081; **6:**1071; **8:**72; **10:**27, 31, 379, 384, 388, 390; **11:**218, 582, 886; **12:**177, 368, 493, 701

CANOPY
2:199; **3:**1088, 1151, 1161–62, 1165, 1180; **4:**312; **5:**400; **6:**84, 866, 1431, 1555; **7:**758

CANTICLES
(not the book Canticles) **1:**205; **9:**25, 55, 71, 116

CAPITAL
CHARGE/CRIME/OFFENSE **1:**240, 867, 1174; **2:**128, 289, 334, 379, 443, 448; **3:**156, 787; **4:**1127; **6:**773, 1208, 1230, 1251, 1261, 1310, 1331, 1448, 1452; **7:**208; **8:**234, 240, 480, 485, 712; **9:**677, 816, 824; **10:**131; **11:**469, 473–74, 521, 547–48; CITY **1:**10, 221–22, 224, 233, 262, 266, 269–70, 1126; **2:**279, 365, 560–61, 602, 634, 663, 673, 683, 736, 740, 816, 962, 1127, 1147, 1209, 1211–13, 1216, 1224, 1235–36, 1240, 1244, 1247, 1249, 1266, 1273, 1279–80, 1284, 1300, 1319–20, 1323, 1326, 1358; **3:**18, 52, 55, 58, 87, 93–94, 103, 113, 124, 128, 132, 147, 158, 164, 197, 212, 223, 242, 245, 253, 364, 377, 381, 416, 457, 522, 525–26, 556, 562, 587, 630, 636, 706–7, 751, 828, 871, 878, 992–93, 995, 1008,

CAPITAL *(continued)*
1097, 1112; **4:**30, 129, 253, 270, 313, 872–73; **5:**365, 419, 426, 439, 853; **6:**7, 36, 74, 81, 107–9, 174, 183, 186, 235, 262, 556, 715, 774–75, 792, 814, 834, 897, 1013, 1030, 1065, 1076, 1079, 1081, 1151–52, 1157, 1191, 1215, 1217, 1221, 1224–26, 1236, 1245, 1293, 1302, 1306–7, 1309, 1312, 1316, 1319–20, 1322, 1324, 1329, 1336, 1338, 1347, 1351, 1378–80, 1389, 1403, 1422, 1429, 1440, 1443, 1595; **7:**111, 179, 267, 275, 293, 342, 362, 375–76, 442, 447, 456, 458, 493, 533–34, 543, 567, 572, 594–96, 606, 623, 661, 691–92; **8:**142, 622; **9:**451; **10:**181, 189, 317, 325, 404, 415, 422, 623, 732, 755, 757; **11:**675, 838, 884; EXECUTION/PUNISHMENT **1:**352, 377, 399, 404, 850, 863, 870, 873, 1051, 1118, 1134, 1142, 1164–65; **2:**139, 332–33, 394, 421, 434, 436, 455, 666, 1114, 1160, 1310; **3:**722, 742; **5:**305; **6:**95; **7:**144; **8:**134, 482; **10:**813; **11:**214, 485; FINANCIAL **1:**162, 218, 226, 1165; **2:**404, 406, 408, 454, 456–57, 462, 467, 476, 493; **3:**144, 176, 779; **5:**192, 205, 238, 272; **6:**650; **8:**453; LETTER **1:**27, 302, 1164; **10:**961

CAPTAIN
1:609; **3:**18, 172–73, 177; **4:**10, 36, 56, 97, 206, 227, 275; **6:**293, 859, 994; **7:**84, 470, 474, 476–77, 485–86, 492, 495, 497–99, 500, 502, 505–6, 513–14, 523, 527, 580; **9:**277; **10:**105, 346; **12:**401; OF THE GUARD (*see under* GUARD); OF THE TEMPLE (*see under* JERUSALEM TEMPLE *in PLACES IN THE BIBLE*)

CAPTIVITY
1:883, 1051, 1181; **2:**859–61, 864, 871, 926, 997; **3:**76, 79, 151, 192, 198, 242, 302, 677, 713, 735, 773, 802, 810, 992–93; **4:**856, 1037, 1092, 1105, 1230; **5:**446, 532, 556, 692, 797; **6:**18, 81, 282–83, 407, 411–12, 454, 576, 697, 703, 722, 793, 796, 866, 975, 977–78, 1016, 1047, 1075, 1214–15, 1402, 1418, 1514, 1529; **7:**27, 30, 38, 74, 94, 136, 144–45, 181, 279, 312, 330, 451, 550, 554, 610, 703, 715, 811, 821; **8:**323, 720; **9:**638, 861; **10:**288, 457, 571, 659; **11:**276, 294, 304, 373, 421, 625, 858; **12:**55, 83, 636, 657; BABYLONIAN **1:**95, 992, 1060; **3:**295; **4:**1065; **5:**862; **7:**702, 781; **10:**447, 660

CARAVAN (*OR* CARAVANS, CARAVANEERS, *ETC.*)
1:565; **2:**459, 787; **3:**510, 687; **4:**388; **5:**400; **6:**254, 1379, 1467, 1525; **7:**449; **9:**63; **10:**163

CARBUNCLE
1:1096

CARCASS
1:281, 1075, 1080, 1082; **2:**445, 767, 850, 853; **3:**608; **5:**67, 859; **6:**159, 1405, 1427, 1432, 1435, 1437, 1523; **12:**167

CARE
DIVINE/GOD'S/THE LORD'S/PROVIDENTIAL/YAHWEH'S **1:**355, 370, 392, 565, 699, 707; **2:**21, 82, 355–57, 389, 484, 512, 519, 527, 641, 1240; **3:**395, 500, 728, 730, 809–10, 1057; **4:**80, 183, 193, 257, 414, 442, 585, 597, 602, 610, 669, 741, 899, 959, 1181; **5:**446, 479, 526, 536, 547, 552–54, 561–62, 567, 788; **6:**190, 248, 259–61, 270, 281, 283, 285, 602, 607, 614, 646, 669, 680, 892, 1265, 1279, 1461; **7:**194, 264, 527, 814; **8:**63, 211, 214; **9:**254, 260, 338, 347, 695, 797; **10:**878; **11:**728

CARNAL, CARNALIT
3:624; **5:**407, 736, 748, 752–53; **6:**532, 546; **7:**245; **12:**69

CARNELIAN
6:1392; **12:**592, 723

CARPENTER, CARPENTERS
2:1100, 1242; **3:**692; **4:**513–14; **5:**446, 417, 536, 548, 550, 557, 566–68, 570, 812; **6:**388, 1374; **7:**412; **8:**317–18, 592; **9:**52

CARPET, CARPETS
1:1049; **11:**847

CARRIAGE
5:400

CART (*OR* CARTS, CARTED, *ETC.*)
2:960, 1012, 1248–49; **3:**393, 395, 1173; **5:**282, 787; **6:**94, 1312, 1533; **7:**366, 605; **8:**13

CARVING, CARVINGS
1:225, 890; **5:**829; **6:**1554–55; **7:**29, 61; **8:**583

CASLEU
See CHISLEV

CASSIA
1:1061; **5:**757; **6:**1379

CASTLE
3:1085; **5:**513; **9:**242, 245; **11:**207, 386

CASUISTIC LAW
1:237, 1137; **2:**328, 380; **3:**718; **6:**1134, 1206, 1208, 1210, 1212, 1258, 1260, 1262, 1446, 1448; **8:**33, 189–90, 193, 197–98, 378, 435

CAT, CATS
2:1153; **3:**1089; **4:**270, 611; **5:**397; **6:**989, 997, 1418; **9:**311

CATARACT, CATARACTS
1:234; **3:**1049; **6:**1071, 1407; **7:**424, 670

CATERPILLAR, CATERPILLARS
4:312; **5:**241

CATHOLIC
CANON/BIBLE **1:**5, 8, 10, 17–18; EPISTLE(S)/LETTER(S) **1:**8, 15; **5:**14; **10:**32, 371, 389; **12:**177, 229, 329, 365, 411, 466, 475; UNIVERSAL **1:**152; **3:**731; **8:**89;

10:17, 26, 28–31, 51, 147, 281, 371, 380, 384, 390; **11:**228, 646; **12:**326, 390, 474, 476, 669

CATTLE
1:219–20, 433, 754, 767, 780–81, 821, 1009, 1013–15, 1019, 1024, 1081, 1134, 1143, 1152, 1179; **2:**52, 83, 107, 127, 160, 188, 246, 248, 364, 606, 1029, 1080, 1088–89; **3:**337, 347, 353, 355, 647, 782, 814, 1091, 1114, 1139, 1154; **4:**347, 453, 467, 590, 618, 992, 1271; **5:**220, 243, 297, 695, 791, 812; **6:**113, 195, 406, 1257, 1425, 1436, 1518, 1592; **7:**311, 314, 335, 411, 527, 758; **9:**285, 298, 543; **10:**337. *See also* COW

CAULDRON
See CALDRON

CAVALRY
3:525, 1177; **4:**63, 67, 69, 89, 110–11, 130, 152, 174–75, 265; **5:**182; **6:**194; **7:**124, 140, 147, 613, 635, 814; **8:**584; **12:**544

CAVE, CAVES
1:270, 293–94, 475, 504, 515, 659; **2:**549, 647–48, 795, 1144, 1157–58, 1376; **3:**142, 144, 980, 1182; **4:**39, 46, 545; **5:**271, 394, 407, 550, 634, 636, 867; **6:**73, 1079, 1458; **7:**14, 421, 448, 481; **9:**63, 113, 363, 374; **12:**144, 146, 614; BURIAL **1:**503, 515; **2:**65; **3:**1181; QUMRAN (*see* QUMRAN, KHIRBET *in PLACES IN THE BIBLE and PLACES OUTSIDE THE BIBLE*)

CEDAR, CEDARS
FROM/IN/OF LEBANON **3:**692; **5:**415, 757; **6:**137, 740, 742, 1295, 1373, 1422, 1424–25; **7:**817–18; **8:**577; TREE(S) **1:**1098, 1100; **2:**151, 190, 1242, 1244, 1256; **3:**58, 82, 242, 429, 474, 477, 693, 1058; **4:**618; **5:**400, 405, 433, 502; **6:**73, 127, 386–87, 584, 740, 742–43, 1105, 1217, 1244–46, 1252–53, 1272–73, 1360, 1422–23, 1425–29, 1435, 1439, 1444, 1469, 1554, 1595; **7:**817; **9:**275–76

CEILING
4:193; **5:**355; **6:**1541, 1554; **12:**597

CELESTIAL
2:35; **3:**164, 422, 551, 658; **4:**518; **5:**699; **6:**1393; **7:**113, 117, 683, 770, 772; **10:**989; **11:**206, 291; **12:**711; ARMY/FORCES/HOST(S) **3:**176–77, 180, 201–2, 207, 237, 552, 563; BEING(S) **6:**1394; **7:**137–38; **12:**350; BODY (BODIES) **5:**545–46; **10:**989; **11:**282; POWER(S) **3:**179, 426; **11:**282

CELIBATE, CELIBACY
1:287; **2:**153, 833–35; **3:**1133, 1162; **5:**629; **6:**571; **8:**123, 387, 834; **10:**869, 872, 874; **11:**645; **12:**163, 686

CENSER, CENSERS
1:1069, 1111; **2:**137–40; **3:**591; **5:**592; **6:**1176, 1534; **12:**630, 694

CENSUS
1:226, 754, 918, 972, 1187; **2:**3–4, 8, 10, 23, 31–35, 40, 51–53, 59, 80, 95, 126, 169, 202–3, 207, 211–15, 247–48, 267, 679, 953, 957, 964, 968, 1355, 1380, 1382–83; **3:**232, 320, 332, 336, 338, 352–53, 358, 379, 414, 421–24, 426, 436, 456–57, 530, 538, 547, 586, 685; **4:**348; **5:**656, 724; **6:**6, 84; **8:**420, 673; **9:**62–63, 73, 386; **12:**620, 723; FIRST **2:**23, 27, 37, 48, 50, 122, 207, 212–13, 213, 263; SECOND **2:**10–11, 33–34, 37, 48, 52, 136, 159, 169, 180, 200, 207–8, 213, 215, 262–63, 753. *See also* TAX: CENSUS/POLL

CENTURION
1:483; **7:**502; **8:**60, 63, 226, 228, 337, 493, 526–28, 628, 696, 722, 724; **9:**13–14, 24, 28–29, 34, 45, 99, 154–57, 174, 208, 322, 341–42, 447, 450–51, 458, 461–62, 464, 472, 574; **10:**129, 162, 308, 313, 345–46, 351–52; **11:**233; CENTURION'S CONFESSION **8:**724; **9:**14, 29, 156; ROMAN (*see under* ROMAN)

CEREAL, CEREALS
1:218; **2:**411, 1114; **3:**847; **6:**1148, 1558, 1580; **7:**309; OFFERING(S) (*see under* OFFERING)

CEREMONY
1:241, 268, 307, 316, 318, 659, 1011–12, 1014, 1023, 1025, 1028, 1034–35, 1048, 1054, 1060–62, 1067, 1070, 1084, 1098–99, 1110–13, 1158, 1160; **2:**83–84, 475, 480, 519, 635, 706, 714, 771, 1016, 1047, 1056, 1062–63, 1237, 1249, 1251; **3:**8, 20, 68, 70–71, 75, 77, 217, 386, 390, 394, 433, 469, 518, 591, 609, 645–47, 666, 692–93, 699, 705, 721, 796, 803, 805–6, 840, 841–42, 1039–41, 1043, 1082, 1158, 1182; **4:**106, 689, 755, 772, 862, 916, 1090; **5:**399–401, 425; **6:**82, 122–23, 499, 1259, 1491, 1537–38, 1568; **7:**31, 312, 381, 580, 583, 666, 683, 729, 789; **8:**278; **9:**46, 75, 81, 366, 369–70, 418, 420–21, 542; **10:**274; **11:**533; **12:**107, 110, 167, 260, 729; CEREMONIAL LAW (*see under* LAW); COVENANT(ING) CEREMONY/COVENANT RENEWAL CEREMONY **1:**689, 879; **2:**96, 561, 563, 635, 816, 1224; **3:**100, 103, 284; **4:**880–81; **6:**949; **10:**490–91

CHAFF
4:439, 484, 493, 685; **5:**63, 188, 485; **6:**175, 227, 238, 271, 649, 1002; **7:**288, 416; **8:**158; **9:**86, 133, 160, 315, 321

CHAIN, CHAINS
1:190, 210, 622; **2:**1287, 1289, 1305–7, 1309–10, 1314; **3:**293, 332, 345, 353, 355, 364, 560, 575, 615, 636, 650, 654, 835, 858, 1125, 1170; **4:**62, 401, 471, 557; **5:**58, 122, 141, 167, 255, 318, 465, 491, 583, 585, 698, 772, 792, 798; **6:**403, 831–32, 851, 1023, 1049, 1168,

CHAIN, CHAINS *(continued)*
1228, 1265, 1329; **7:**82, 138, 261, 495, 505, 731; **8:**64, 129, 149, 525, 583; **9:**88, 95, 164, 187–88, 211, 221, 312, 349; **10:**66, 179, 289, 297–98, 327, 341, 360, 603, 652, 668, 782, 975; **11:**42, 51, 63, 211, 289, 338, 424, 442, 444, 458, 462–63, 488, 556, 569, 661, 665, 668, 843, 846–47; **12:**28, 40, 275, 288, 315, 347, 434, 452, 488, 669, 707

CHAIR, CHAIRS
1:1104; **2:**788, 1135; **4:**287; **6:**919, 1119, 1209, 1488; **10:**813; **11:**43, 88

CHAMBER, CHAMBERS
1:221, 279, 838; **2:**199, 687, 771–72, 1225, 1303; **3:**729, 741, 820, 846–47, 850, 914, 1151; **4:**71, 590, 626, 1097; **5:**85–86, 101–2, 269, 380, 397, 399–400, 428–29; **6:**19, 839, 1106, 1176, 1542, 1545–48, 1551–52, 1557–58, 1578, 1582, 1591; **7:**11, 91, 189, 320; **8:**589; **10:**617, 750, 813, 894; **11:**88, 756; **12:**116, 126, 636; BRIDAL/WEDDING (*see under* BRIDAL); INNER **2:**79; **3:**1090, 1161; **5:**669; **12:**58, 167; ROOF **2:**771–72. *See also* BEDCHAMBER; ROOM

CHAMBERLAIN
10:181

CHAMPION, CHAMPIONS
AS ADVOCATE/HERO **1:**59, 193, 255, 696, 716; **2:**620, 673, 1099, 1108–12, 1144; **3:**128, 355, 378, 438, 533, 1144; **4:**410, 513, 519, 539; **5:**407, 798, 849; **7:**8; **8:**30; **10:**155, 271, 864; **12:**40–41, 43

CHANCELLOR
4:137, 206–7, 265, 276, 280; **10:**270

CHANNEL (*OR* CHANNELS, CHANNELING, *ETC.*)
1:70, 170, 223, 390, 417, 483, 580, 623, 654, 742; **2:**49, 167, 193, 431, 771, 991, 993–94, 1100, 1333, 1224; **3:**426, 429, 467–68, 503, 718; **4:**377, 517, 530, 604, 626; **5:**192, 642, 652; **6:**227, 1387; **7:**771; **9:**145, 235, 364; **10:**562, 828, 963, 975, 994; **11:**41, 122, 497, 636; **12:**701, 729

CHANT (*OR* CHANTS, *ETC.*)
1:205, 297; **4:**67, 309, 711, 1079; **5:**316, 366, 377, 716, 849; **6:**190, 636, 1016, 1437; **7:**528; **9:**282, 372, 456, 479; **10:**728; **11:**310, 649

CHAOS
1:95, 275, 341–42, 356, 394, 696, 699, 739–40, 742–43, 764–68, 771, 779, 800, 802, 901; **2:**13, 39, 235, 726–27, 755, 811, 818, 820, 827, 840, 862–63, 865–66, 869, 872, 875, 884, 886, 888, 957, 982, 1064, 1366, 1368; **3:**948, 1032; **4:**63, 154, 319, 336, 368, 380, 410, 415, 423, 465, 487, 511, 518, 520, 540, 571, 597, 602, 607, 619, 631, 711, 772–23, 865, 899, 931, 977, 1001, 1007, 1054, 1117, 1190; **5:**25, 72, 121, 138, 180, 254, 294, 333, 408, 536, 611, 833–34; **6:**39, 77–79, 157, 161, 185, 207, 210–12, 214, 216, 225–27, 254, 277, 335, 401, 455, 477, 614, 619, 765, 864, 959, 970, 1018, 1034–35, 1043–44, 1066, 1069, 1185, 1210, 1338, 1512, 1521, 1538, 1564; **7:**92, 100, 102, 107, 325, 342, 654, 679, 797, 815, 836; **8:**232, 444, 582–83, 585, 593; **9:**56, 91, 184, 545, 829; **10:**272, 455, 505, 526, 588, 718, 720, 804, 965, 967; **11:**325, 329, 384, 536, 598; **12:**357–58, 508, 528, 555, 615, 619, 632–34, 636, 644, 656, 678, 685, 716; DRAGON/MONSTER (*see* MONSTER: CHAOS/DRAGON/SEA); FORCE(S) OF **1:**274, 774, 892; **2:**600; **3:**840; **4:**395, 1035, 1050, 1054, 1062, 1236; **6:**528, 1537; **7:**101, 601, 654; **8:**232, 327, 580; POWER(S) OF **1:**279, 720, 766, 780, 795, 799–801, 902; **2:**976; **5:**76; **7:**8, 101; **8:**328, 580; THREAT OF **1:**701, 767, 774, 804; **2:**1365, 1368; **4:**1190; WATERY/WATERS OF **1:**274, 336, 394, 795, 799; **3:**1029; **4:**487, 518, 747, 865, 1096; **6:**380, 477, 1425; **8:**584, 730; **9:**596. *See also under* COSMOS; CREATION)

CHARCOAL
9:809

CHARGER, CHARGERS
7:609

CHARIOT (*OR* CHARIOTS, CHARIOTEERS, *ETC.*)
1:282–83, 622, 669, 795, 804, 877; **2:**603, 637, 651, 662, 685, 733, 739–40, 746, 779, 781, 788, 1202, 1206, 1266, 1319; **3:**17, 137–38, 151, 166–67, 176, 180, 201, 219–20, 224, 416, 462, 511, 519, 551–52, 649, 870, 914; **4:**51, 280, 287, 306, 347–48; **5:**382, 386–87, 420, 555; **6:**72, 74, 194, 196, 260, 375, 834, 886, 1111, 1116–20, 1129, 1172, 1175–76, 1182–84, 1232, 1366–67, 1442, 1528, 1538, 1555; **7:**147, 609–10, 612–13, 635, 653, 730, 737, 751, 757, 760, 782–84; **9:**367, 399, 480; **12:**520, 591–92, 596–98; DIVINE/THRONE **6:**1116–17, 1118–20, 1172; **12:**520, 591–92, 596–97

CHARISMA
2:103, 111–13, 139, 220, 1332; **3:**39, 176; **10:**160, 380, 383, 524, 872, 949, 951; **11:**27, 43, 330, 904; **12:**573

CHARISMATA
10:693, 710, 787, 799, 821, 830, 872, 941, 943–45, 949, 965, 993; **11:**143, 424

CHARITY
1:847, 874; **2:**379, 404, 467, 481; **3:**975, 982, 984, 986, 987, 989, 993, 995–96, 1001–3, 1016; **4:**534, 541, 593; **5:**351, 609, 780; **6:**1034; **7:**692;

8:200, 557, 698; **9:**320; **10:**161, 759, 957; **11:**332, 422, 429, 432, 889, 894–95; **12:**287, 313, 443

CHARM (*OR* CHARMING, *ETC.*)
2:738, 974, 1164, 1207, 1319; **3:**768, 905, 1147; **4:**381; **5:**348–51, 367, 372, 404, 407, 415–16, 557, 806; **6:**74, 266; **10:**775; **11:**537; **12:**725; SNAKE CHARMER (*see under* SNAKE)

CHASM
1:2; **3:**599; **4:**443; **5:**117, 364, 367, 408, 644; **9:**318; **12:**403

CHASTENING, CHASTENED
1:197; **2:**963, 1169, 1358; **3:**632; **4:**234, 569, 1154; **5:**316; **6:**34, 631, 1356; **7:**661, 663, 826; **8:**35; **10:**639, 939; **11:**22

CHASTITY
1:90, 1124; **3:**1162; **5:**397, 405, 407, 433, 765; **7:**176, 209; **8:**391; **10:**271; **11:**814

CHEESE
1:219

CHEESEMAKER
See under GOD, METAPHORS FOR *in PERSONS IN THE BIBLE*

CHEMOSH
1:274, 1189; **2:**166, 198, 830–31, 907; **3:**96, 184; **6:**890–92, 894, 920, 1489

CHERUB, CHERUBS
1:359, 890, 1111; **2:**1367; **6:**1118–19, 1179, 1182–84, 1392–95, 1554, 1560. *See also* ANGEL

CHERUBIM
1:278, 364–65, 890, 893, 1111; **2:**79–80, 83, 330, 364, 1001, 1248; **3:**70, 75, 104, 269, 386, 462, 484, 1178; **4:**441, 999, 1003, 1075; **6:**102, 751, 1118–20, 1131, 1172, 1179, 1182–84, 1186, 1189, 1393–94, 1554–55; **7:**167, 774; **12:**104, 597, 729. *See also* ANGEL

CHEST
BOX **1:**112; **2:**98, 168, 1001; **3:**72, 232, 580; **6:**1118; **12:**104; AS PART OF THE BODY **4:**624; **5:**60, 415; **7:**312; **9:**148, 834; **12:**218, 561

CHIASM
1:344, 392, 399, 404, 420; **3:**327, 329–30, 332, 376, 1084, 1104, 1124, 1148; **4:**310, 653, 740, 1023; **5:**133, 350, 866; **7:**478, 495, 504–6, 513; **8:**113, 139, 317; **9:**432–33, 601–2; **10:**702, 724; **11:**501, 603; **12:**60, 106, 125–26, 149, 275

CHIASTIC
1:388, 399–400, 420, 427, 518, 802, 923; **2:**355, 445, 584, 1000; **3:**320, 330, 345, 376, 415, 431, 525, 594, 618, 635, 842, 1104, 1130; **4:**52, 192, 449, 552–53, 686, 694, 705, 721, 724, 740–41, 748, 777, 783, 806, 902, 912, 939–40, 963, 983, 1009, 1020, 1024, 1041–42, 1050, 1057, 1068, 1082–83, 1190, 1227, 1239, 1247, 1263; **5:**10, 162, 207, 262, 452; **6:**974, 1198, 1243, 1322; **7:**100, 168, 239, 284, 344, 384–85, 439, 686, 736, 773, 778, 789; **8:**113, 115, 154, 255, 261, 269, 271, 317, 422; **9:**11, 76, 214, 303, 316–17, 432–33, 667; **10:**142, 165; **11:**488; **12:**103, 276. *See also* CONCENTRIC

CHIEF
COMMANDER IN **2:**577, 1237; **3:**34; **4:**51, 67; **5:**145; **6:**149, 182, 1190, 1232, 1402, 1406; **12:**669; GOD **1:**273, 1018; **2:**527, 830, 1017; **6:**101, 217, 894, 912, 920; AS LEADER **1:**614–15, 1147; **2:**199–200, 527, 658, 1174, 1226, 1268, 1375, 1380; **3:**33–34, 49–50, 58, 132, 192, 265, 379, 442, 478, 782, 826, 882, 1042; **4:**36, 95–97, 260, 487, 886–87; **6:**133, 330, 839, 858, 866, 941, 1168, 1386, 1443, 1512, 1516; **7:**15, 82, 88, 477, 804; **8:**346, 564; **9:**85, 310, 353, 356–59, 362, 400, 458; **10:**104, 191, 198, 273, 540; **11:**790, 798, 813–14; **12:**172, 315, 540, 599; PRIEST(S) (*see under* PRIEST)

CHILD, CHILDREN
OF ABRAHAM (*see* CHILDREN OF ABRAHAM *in PERSONS IN THE BIBLE*); FEMALE **9:**69; **11:**361; FIRSTBORN **2:**391, 834; **6:**1283–84, 1530; **9:**66, 69; OF GOD **1:**159, 210, 1184; **2:**300, 327, 488, 1170; **3:**688, 723; **4:**632, 769, 981, 1025; **5:**12, 170, 463, 485, 534, 591, 788, 801; **6:**47, 82, 531; **8:**28, 166, 195, 358, 371; **9:**4, 147, 153, 370, 390, 496, 513, 521, 524–25, 552, 636, 639–41, 698, 703, 732, 775, 832, 843, 845–46; **10:**299, 511, 591, 593–94, 596–97, 607, 643, 868; **11:**69, 92, 199, 249, 272, 278, 280, 284, 286, 305, 310, 358, 363, 374, 435, 440, 512, 678, 721; **12:**40, 250, 372, 375–76, 379, 402, 410–11, 413, 416, 421, 424, 427, 430, 435–37, 440, 518, 539; OF ISRAEL **1:**75, 165–66, 560; **2:**197, 546, 706, 900; **3:**358; **5:**590; **6:**432, 1122; **7:**231–32; **8:**359; **9:**235, 278; **10:**166, 534, 550, 563; **11:**67, 69; **12:**247, 258, 264, 267, 602, 620–21, 629; LITTLE **4:**770; **5:**94–95; **6:**77, 141, 414; **8:**374, 647; **9:**211, 345, 350; MALE **1:**786; **2:**233, 933, 975; **4:**877; **8:**358; **9:**42, 69, 77, 649, 651; **11:**361; PRODIGAL (*see under* PRODIGAL); SACRIFICE **1:**494, 1138–39; **2:**50, 391, 570, 619; **3:**250, 255, 276, 598, 635; **4:**82, 1111; **5:**542; **6:**635, 640, 721, 1230, 1284, 1290

CHILDLESS
1:451, 520, 712; **2:**845–86, 958–59, 970, 977, 979–81, 983; **3:**1051; **4:**485; **5:**253, 377, 467, 473–75; 479–81, 485, 489, 563, 829; **6:**431–33, 447, 449; **7:**686; **9:**45, 52, 60, 452; **11:**304; **12:**136. *See also* BARREN

CHISLEV
(month of the Hebrew calendar) **2:**544; **3:**742, 751; **4:**40, 190–91, 197; **9:**675

CHOIR
1:1020; **2:**1217; **3:**300, 305, 345, 446–47, 495, 561, 610, 826, 837–40; **4:**900, 1072; **6:**169, 301; **7:**665; **9:**311; **10:**820; **11:**121, 417, 445; HEAVENLY **12:**643, 676; LEVITE/LEVITICAL CHOIR *or* TEMPLE CHOIR **2:**214; **3:**501, 847; **4:**657; **7:**665, 671

CHOSEN
CITY/COMMUNITY **1:**283, 418, 424, 475, 484; **3:**115, 168, 761; **6:**38, 62, 67, 974; FAMILY/LINE **1:**325, 416, 419, 429, 442, 454–55, 461, 515, 580–81, 595, 655; **3:**317; GOD'S/THE LORD'S/YAHWEH'S **1:**74, 196, 435, 452, 461, 467, 484, 497, 510, 537, 593, 612, 978, 1061; **2:**140, 350, 386, 388, 397, 631, 670, 735, 790, 802, 825, 840, 946, 1036, 1045–46, 1048–51, 1099, 1111, 1236, 1250, 1252, 1280, 1331, 1366–68; **3:**87, 93, 268, 362, 421, 753, 1065; **4:**19, 178, 234, 465, 668–69, 733, 748, 940, 1129, 1142, 1210, 1213, 1220, 1271; **5:**304, 624; **6:**3, 62, 68, 109, 133, 223, 240, 363, 432, 478, 662, 677, 743, 762, 974, 1065, 1082; **7:**56, 75, 181, 370, 456, 541, 573–74, 576, 718, 856; **8:**28, 357; **9:**49, 137, 456–57, 463, 560, 568; **10:**49, 79, 166, 171, 268, 338, 413, 445–46, 783, 815, 827, 914, 987, 989; **11:**62, 76, 245–46, 259, 275, 358–59, 410; **12:**60, 192, 200, 265–66, 272, 449; ONE **1:**414, 428, 467, 484, 489, 510, 541, 568; **2:**773, 1046, 1048, 1050–51, 1098, 1212, 1252, 1331; **3:**94; **6:**363; **7:**75, 502; **8:**36; **9:**18–19, 207, 232, 454, 456–57, 463, 560; **10:**152; ONES **1:**429, 484–85, 492, 518, 539, 591, 623; **2:**34; **3:**317, 402; **4:**1105, 1110; **7:**169; **9:**21, 338, 355, 793; **10:**636, 914; **11:**844; PEOPLE **1:**163, 419, 441, 452, 455, 591, 623, 752; **2:**363, 385, 670, 773; **3:**40, 197, 243, 244, 285, 402, 867, 956–57, 960, 967, 1017; **4:**19, 234, 465, 704, 1220, 1225; **5:**232, 802; **6:**88, 155, 551, 767, 900, 918, 1082, 1455; **7:**330, 354, 415, 456, 560, 574, 576, 816, 829; **8:**28–29, 291, 501; **9:**49, 568, 571; **10:**405, 413, 445, 446, 586, 614, 634, 669; **11:**594, 844, 872, 876; **12:**266–67, 524, 585

CHRIST
See JESUS THE CHRIST *in PERSONS IN THE BIBLE*

CHRISTIAN
BAPTISM(S) **8:**26, 161; **9:**550; **10:**67–68, 263, 307; **11:**271–72, 643; **12:**71, 241, 292, 295, 439; BELIEF(S) (*see under* BELIEF); BIBLE **1:**16–18, 33, 37, 41, 45–47, 49, 83, 85, 228; **3:**1075, 1079, 1081; **5:**1; **10:**3, 383–85, 391; **12:**24, 735; CANON (*see under* NEW TESTAMENT); CHURCH(ES) **1:**16, 85, 95, 105, 108, 120, 163, 190, 200, 204, 291; **2:**98; **3:**319, 364, 447, 855, 868; **4:**642, 845, 888, 1128, 1151; **5:**63, 705; **6:**49, 139, 550, 929, 946; **7:**10, 156, 328, 583; **8:**2, 15, 29, 73; **9:**387, 421; **10:**486, 547; **11:**190, 218, 245, 308, 353, 397, 492, 545, 610, 824, 872; **12:**195, 312, 378, 654, 661, 708, 730; COMMUNITY (*see under* COMMUNITY); CONGREGATION (*see under* CONGREGATION); CONSCIENCE (*see under* CONSCIENCE); DISCIPLE(S)/DISCIPLESHIP **2:**681; **5:**690; **8:**186, 259–60, 390–92, 395, 399, 457, 466, 513; **9:**129–30, 429, 865; **10:**30, 130, 155, 261, 290; DOCTRINE(S) (*see under* DOCTRINE); DOCUMENTS (*see under* DOCUMENT); EDUCATION **1:**201–2, 212; **8:**377; **9:**197; **10:**671; **11:**456, 621; **12:**340; ETHICS **8:**197, 215, 637; **9:**101, 146, 278, 409; **10:**435, 548, 726; **11:**621, 873–74; **12:**195, 490, 499; EXISTENCE (*see under* EXISTENCE); FAITH (*see under* FAITH); FELLOWSHIP (*see under* FELLOWSHIP); GOSPEL (*see under* GOSPEL); HOPE **5:**825; **6:**551, 822; **7:**429; **9:**473, 784–85; **10:**509, 513, 631; **11:**382, 386, 538, 640, 790, 862, 871; **12:**50, 200, 250, 262, 273, 292; LITERATURE (*see* LITERATURE: BIBLICAL/CHRISTIAN/RELIGIOUS); MESSAGE(S) **1:**47, 84, 110, 196; **4:**803; **5:**15; **7:**457; **8:**158, 167–68, 264, 467, 486, 503; **9:**40; **11:**206, 208, 218, 348, 462, 660, 857, 870; **12:**83; MINISTRY **6:**1464; **8:**398; **10:**55, 144, 201, 286, 382, 618, 631; **11:**617, 867; **12:**575 (*see also* MINISTRY, CHRISTIAN); ORIGIN(S) **1:**20–21, 44; **8:**38, 52, 55; **10:**5; **12:**573; PREACHER(S) **1:**21; **3:**348; **9:**662; **10:**14; **11:**184, 194–95, 219, 340, 618, 696, 772; **12:**237–38, 255, 260, 304; PREACHING **1:**45, 84, 191, 196; **2:**112; **8:**33, 374, 536, 675; **10:**14, 240, 406; **11:**195, 208, 217, 278, 309, 339, 606, 721; **12:**28, 76, 78, 383, 437; SACRAMENT(S) **1:**539; **2:**15, 141, 152, 168, 194; **10:**72; **11:**452; SCRIPTURE(S) **1:**17, 33–34, 45–47, 83, 85–86, 110, 152, 155, 188–89, 192, 194, 779; **6:**339, 382, 403–4; **7:**771; **10:**385; **11:**195; SERVICE **3:**432, 523; **8:**171; **11:**493, 838; SUFFERING **9:**292; **10:**109; **11:**42; **12:**296–97, 281–82, 310, 313; THEOLOGIAN(S) (*see under* THEOLOGIAN); THEOLOGY (*see under* THEOLOGY); TRADITION(S) **1:**50, 83, 89, 100, 107, 127–28, 140, 157–58, 192, 199, 272, 304, 499, 586, 737, 776, 843, 854, 916; **2:**54–55, 68, 90, 98, 112, 152, 194, 235–36, 284–85, 325, 550, 912, 1326; **3:**299, 619, 928, 998, 1019, 1114; **4:**23, 243, 477, 503, 519, 556–57, 742, 756; **5:**99, 264, 366, 377, 389, 548, 634; **6:**1, 1140, 1504, 1564; **7:**93, 232, 431, 729, 857, 873; **8:**29, 85, 96, 119, 156, 175, 195, 262, 295, 314, 332, 345, 433, 708; **9:**147, 162, 339, 391, 419, 490, 518, 650, 685, 702, 706, 733; **10:**376, 383, 418, 578, 589, 610, 644, 713, 730, 823, 973; **11:**191, 239, 323, 335, 414, 627, 794, 812, 833; **12:**5, 13, 28, 133, 231, 234, 315, 324, 340, 345, 347, 353, 369, 420, 440, 468, 513–14, 524, 536, 553–54, 652; UNITY (*see under* UNITY); WORSHIP (*see under* WORSHIP); WRITING(S) **1:**14, 20, 43, 45–46, 85, 188–92, 194; **2:**587; **4:**586; **5:**23, 430; **7:**339;

8:1–2, 515; **9:**278, 331; **10:**438, 604, 724, 727; **12:**11, 74, 180, 193, 258, 275, 278, 285, 352, 403, 488

CHRISTIANITY

EARLY/EARLIEST **1:**13, 21, 127, 131, 136, 315; **2:**564; **3:**1133, 1145, 1151; **4:**243; **5:**96; **7:**2, 14–15, 89, 150; **8:**12, 20, 27, 39–40, 43–45, 47, 54–55, 72, 80, 82, 93, 98, 106–7, 109, 153, 156, 177, 187, 193, 214, 221, 253, 266, 268, 286–87, 289, 325, 345, 375, 416, 418, 427, 431, 447, 457, 470, 491, 529, 595, 633, 654, 702; **9:**191, 510, 579, 799; **10:**27, 31, 260, 267, 366, 384, 388–89, 415, 472, 524, 537, 650, 701, 726, 763, 788; **11:**652–53, 674, 680, 730, 784, 869; **12:**34, 82, 177, 194, 326, 357, 369, 395, 475–76, 482, 488, 546, 573, 599, 635, 705, 729; GENTILE **8:**95, 332, 357; **9:**840; HISTORY OF **2:**719; **3:**898; **7:**67; **8:**5, 44, 54; **10:**143; **11:**792, 834, 853; **12:**709; JEWISH **1:**193; **8:**54, 95–97, 128, 192, 200, 202, 371; **9:**840; **11:**240; **12:**182, 476; JOHANNINE **8:**103; **12:**368, 376, 403, 449, 467–68; JUDAISM AND **1:**43–44, 308, 315, 317; **2:**284, 329, 353, 399, 407; **3:**972; **4:**383, 557, 963, 1156; **5:**98, 164, 244, 341, 350; **6:**662, 815, 1013, 1016; **7:**2, 26; **8:**40, 118, 377; **9:**523, 636, 745; **10:**632; **11:**239, 302; **12:**21, 24, 64–65, 84, 95, 106–7, 128, 492, 588, 709; PAULINE **1:**129; **8:**46–47, 49, 95; **10:**266, 375; **11:**674, 784, 839; PRIMITIVE **1:**13, 191; **12:**369

CHRISTOLOGY

1:815, 854; **3:**390; **4:**794; **5:**301; **7:**857; **8:**29, 42, 74, 109, 110, 118, 135, 158–59, 165, 178, 180, 188, 202, 217–18, 220, 249, 262, 266, 344, 350–51, 353–58, 361, 367, 396, 398, 403, 455, 491, 511, 534, 543, 555, 572, 578, 627; **9:**3, 13, 27, 95, 101, 112, 118, 140, 196, 203, 225–26, 326, 392, 496, 498, 502, 522, 553, 555, 569, 589–90, 626, 633, 650, 672, 679, 863; **10:**20, 376, 387, 417–18, 472, 572, 575, 586, 662–63, 665, 682, 712, 717, 738, 823, 864; **11:**186, 283, 382, 386, 569–71, 576, 579, 696, 784, 798, 831, 872, 877; **12:**5–7, 10, 12, 22–24, 27–32, 40, 42–43, 47, 60, 62, 65, 74, 84, 86, 92, 98–99, 114, 116, 132, 138, 155, 161, 165, 180, 183, 213, 240, 278, 280, 288, 375, 426, 441; CLAIM(S) **1:**902, 914; **2:**1141; **8:**177, 186, 263, 287, 356; **9:**134, 456, 528, 680, 689, 743; **10:**66, 84, 914; **11:**795; **12:**299, 387; FORMULA(TION) **1:**787, 946; **5:**507; **10:**386, 488, 509, 768; **11:**26, 383, 609; **12:**61; INTERPRETATION **4:**477; **8:**221; **9:**479, 623; **10:**20, 262; **11:**638; **12:**37

CHRONICLES

1:156, 501; **2:**4, 763, 1240; **3:**750, 941; **5:**371; **6:**12, 1078, 1226; **9:**9, 72, 241, 413, 488; 1 CHRONICLES **1:**652, 960, 963; **2:**199, 673, 696, 894, 1212; **3:**712, 727, 745, 756, 824–26, 832, 842, 1014; **4:**47, 348, 838; **5:**849; **7:**42; **8:**129; **9:**737; 2 CHRONICLES **1:**262, 266, 281; **2:**87, 214, 579; **3:**802; **4:**72, 85, 212, 222, 503; **5:**441, 515; **6:**117, 284, 1110; **7:**361, 534; **9:**249; 1 AND 2 CHRONICLES **1:**8, 11, 43, 65, 76, 129, 250, 252–53, 256, 260, 264, 268, 309, 314, 325, 996; **2:**89, 256, 543, 580, 1357; **3:**663–64, 677, 690, 692, 713–14, 753, 806, 825–26, 976; **4:**8, 212, 555; **5:**273, 696; **6:**2, 50, 944, 1526; **7:**52, 305, 473, 736, 794, 804; **8:**29, 97

CHRONOLOGY

1:54, 56, 102, 250, 253, 257, 262, 265, 284, 306, 314, 321, 336, 382, 389, 391–92, 1057; **2:**32, 77, 87, 278, 300, 378, 546, 1071, 1265, 1358; **3:**101, 538, 690, 698, 702, 751, 796, 833, 834; **4:**18–19, 114, 160, 191, 216, 227–28, 230; **5:**502; **6:**99, 201, 560, 932, 939–40, 942, 1326; **7:**121, 404, 436; **8:**81, 110–11, 130, 159, 319, 323, 336, 400–401, 403, 430, 439, 463, 478, 494, 496; **9:**62, 72, 80, 415, 451, 493, 543, 674, 704–5, 707, 719, 823; **10:**10, 14, 25, 40, 42, 275, 330, 372–73; **11:**163, 193, 221; **12:**90, 94, 96, 105, 367, 410, 505, 570; OLD TESTAMENT (*see under* OLD TESTAMENT); NEW TESTAMENT (*see under* NEW TESTAMENT)

CHRYSOLITE

6:1116, 1392; **12:**599, 723

CHRYSOPRASE

12:723

CHURCH, CHURCHES

AFRICAN AMERICAN/BLACK **1:**157–58; **2:**1307; **5:**247; **6:**119; **11:**329, 457; ANGEL(S) OF (*see under* ANGEL); ANGLICAN **2:**1383; **7:**253, 280; AUTHORITY OF **1:**36, 49–52, 55, 193; **8:**44; **10:**270, 289, 322; **11:**574, 599, 900; **12:**467, 493, 712; BEGINNING/BIRTH OF **1:**46, 85, 91; **2:**670, 1045; **9:**139, 847–48; **10:**134; **12:**535; CATHOLIC/ROMAN CATHOLIC **1:**1, 23, 26, 28, 34, 50, 52, 58, 101, 205; **2:**719; **3:**861; **5:**635, 788; **6:**244; **7:**253; **8:**6, 318; **10:**31, 390; **11:**238, 775; **12:**166, 390; CHRISTIAN **1:**16, 85, 95, 105, 108, 120, 163, 190, 200, 204, 291; **2:**98; **3:**319, 364, 447, 855, 868; **4:**642, 845, 888, 1128, 1151; **5:**63, 705; **6:**49, 139, 550, 929, 946; **7:**10, 156, 328, 583; **8:**2, 15, 29, 73; **9:**387, 421; **10:**486, 547; **11:**190, 218, 245, 308, 353, 397, 492, 545, 610, 824, 872; **12:**195, 312, 378, 654, 661, 708, 730; COLOSSIAN **11:**580, 590, 668, 884, 892; CORINTHIAN **1:**133, 1073; **3:**395; **10:**252, 255–56, 732, 775, 777–78, 788, 798, 801, 803–4, 807–8, 811, 814, 817, 840, 854, 863, 880, 892, 927, 944, 951, 959, 969, 972, 1000; **11:**48, 135, 253, 274, 329, 358, 644, 674, 725, 812; **12:**7, 118, 232, 444, 578; DISCIPLINE **3:**629; **8:**123, 311, 372, 377, 379; **11:**875; **12:**454; DOCTRINE **1:**58,

CHURCH, CHURCHES *(continued)*
90; **8:**379; **9:**680; **10:**750; **12:**269; EARLY **1:**5, 19–20, 48–49, 58, 61, 84–86, 91–92, 133, 170, 182, 200, 205, 208, 211–12, 782, 823, 837, 898, 980, 1001, 1011, 1072, 1121, 1136; **2:**602–3, 609, 642, 702, 1030, 1051, 1161; **3:**348, 612; **4:**672–73, 700, 863, 888, 954, 1011, 1025, 1067, 1112, 1182, 1209; **5:**92, 199, 552, 635; **6:**105, 112, 124, 868; **7:**95, 425, 700; **8:**2, 21, 27, 29, 37, 59, 78–80, 89, 93, 109, 204, 256, 296, 334, 427, 449, 569, 618, 638, 647; **9:**9, 30, 72–73, 82, 118, 127, 130, 137–38, 144, 165, 194, 196–97, 202, 205, 207, 219, 224, 233–34, 238, 253, 264, 288, 293, 310, 313, 336, 339, 381–82, 395, 421, 429–30, 479, 499, 504, 520, 528, 544, 550–51, 558, 570, 587, 593, 612, 623, 679, 702, 723, 737, 799, 834, 838, 858, 861; **10:**17, 214, 266, 370, 371, 385, 507, 537, 608, 664, 711; **11:**40, 79, 148, 228, 232, 274, 297, 638, 649, 673, 802, 815, 822; **12:**24, 28, 37, 61, 66, 75, 77, 94, 116, 121, 126, 163, 255, 290, 324, 353, 365–66, 390, 456, 466, 485–86, 498, 546, 625, 683; EARLY CHRISTIAN **2:**1255, 1259; **3:**501; **4:**1154; **8:**82; **11:**364, 423, 819; ELDERS **10:**203, 214, 283; **11:**194; **12:**314; EPHESIAN **10:**266, 269, 282, 1002; **11:**791; **12:**574, 575; EXISTENCE OF **11:**384, 410, 466, 574, 689; **12:**230, 523; FAITH OF **1:**19, 47–48, 58–59, 61, 132; **6:**143; **8:**64, 149, 238, 342, 358, 500; **9:**339; **10:**11, 27; **11:**307; FATHER(S) **1:**14, 75, 168, 290, 1001, 1112; **2:**833; **3:**868, 932; **5:**635; **6:**337; **8:**89, 100, 201, 211; **9:**5, 7, 504, 623, 679; **11:**476, 507; **12:**486; FIRST-CENTURY **1:**13; **8:**27; **12:**493; GALATIAN **10:**383, 756, 880; **11:**113–14, 183–85, 188, 191, 193, 206, 221, 225, 271, 302, 307, 309, 311–12, 315–17, 323–24, 327, 331, 334–35, 337, 339, 341, 345–47, 674; GENTILE **8:**202, 503; **9:**382; **10:**505, 513, 685–86, 701, 995; **11:**115, 228, 262, 300, 412; **12:**235; HISTORY OF **1:**19, 33, 200, 228; **2:**609, 617, 702, 1143; **3:**576; **4:**1112; **6:**728; **7:**8, 565, 776; **8:**167, 202, 212, 275, 288, 351, 448, 509; **9:**3, 665, 734, 767, 847, 865; **10:**53, 671, 766, 813, 823, 875; **11:**248, 618, 650, 892; **12:**119, 125, 456, 543, 713; JEWISH **10:**9, 146, 168, 180, 189, 200, 205–6, 211–12, 218–19, 221, 253, 291–92, 312, 319, 376; JOHANNINE **12:**398–99, 404, 407, 412, 418, 426, 456, 468; LEADER(S) IN **1:**23, 94, 1150; **2:**906, 983, 1044, 1227; **3:**418, 738; **4:**243; **7:**576; **8:**48, 104, 287, 375, 448; **9:**263, 310, 382, 425, 847; **10:**24, 132, 139, 168, 188–89, 206, 231, 259, 263, 282, 285, 292, 295, 767, 968; **11:**193, 229, 425, 493, 516, 656, 659, 701, 703, 704, 707–8, 727, 731, 792, 806, 809, 869, 875, 891, 893; **12:**68, 182, 314–17, 340, 398, 473, 481; LIFE OF **1:**46, 83, 90, 92, 95, 109, 189, 201–2, 205, 208–9, 211–12, 816, 838; **2:**38, 237, 945, 995, 1030, 1045, 1050, 1064; **4:**1101, 1175; **5:**127; **8:**3, 93, 112, 118, 128, 202–3, 205, 300, 332, 381, 387, 473; **9:**128, 181, 249, 490, 494, 614, 624, 649, 672, 679, 695, 703, 708, 754, 776–78, 798, 847, 848; **10:**44, 92, 132, 465, 702, 712, 714, 927, 950, 960, 968; **11:**277–78, 310, 317, 330, 492, 688, 690, 701, 720, 744; **12:**64, 155, 164, 237, 273, 371, 377, 386, 408, 441, 451, 468; MEMBER(S/SHIP) **1:**202–4, 1073; **2:**84, 130, 142, 1013, 1031; **3:**738; **5:**676; **8:**40, 48, 56, 287, 363, 378, 436, 553, 602; **9:**339; **10:**19, 506, 765; **11:**202, 254, 272, 332, 346, 422, 424, 456, 475, 496, 521, 657, 688, 691, 695–96, 700–701, 711–12, 720, 736, 746, 809, 812, 818, 884, 891; **12:**69, 78, 80, 162, 307, 315, 357, 396, 419, 447, 449, 476, 482–83, 490, 497, 500, 518, 568, 577–78, 581, 717, 728; ORTHODOX **1:**8; **2:**604; **4:**503; **5:**448; **8:**318; **11:**417, 805; PAULINE **8:**47–49; **9:**73; **10:**32, 225, 227, 266, 277, 367, 857, 969; **11:**38, 218, 354, 419, 580, 602, 644, 653–54, 656, 659, 662–63, 667–68, 781, 812; **12:**239; PHILIPPIAN **11:**472, 474–75, 481, 485, 495, 513, 519, 539, 681; PROTESTANT **1:**202–7; **2:**83, 230, 702; **9:**87, 613; **10:**210, 485, 644; ROMAN **1:**14; **5:**448; **10:**357, 366, 370, 404, 406–7, 420, 422–23, 427, 438, 488, 501, 504–5, 514–15, 537, 558, 597, 623, 626, 681, 697, 701, 713–14, 731, 739, 746, 753, 755, 761–63, 775; **11:**194, 417, 675; **12:**10, 233, 318, 324, 705; SECOND-CENTURY **9:**498, 504; **11:**811; SEVEN **1:**1166; **5:**102; **12:**235, 370, 532, 535, 562, 566–67, 569, 571, 579, 587, 611, 626, 642, 654, 667, 675, 717, 720, 733; THEOLOGIANS **1:**58; **9:**498, 737, 861; THESSALONIAN **11:**673, 675, 680–81, 693–94, 696, 699, 701, 704, 707, 710, 714–15, 721, 725, 745–46; TRADITIONS OF **1:**52, 55, 100, 168, 193, 199; **4:**805, 1176; **6:**105, 285; **7:**873; **8:**95, 325; **9:**379, 504, 778; **10:**182; **11:**348, 883; **12:**468, 486, 683; WALL(S) (*see under* WALL)

CINNAMON
1:1061; **4:**635; **5:**757; **6:**1230

CIRCUMCISION
1:68, 89, 291, 316, 332, 401, 455, 459–61, 504, 576, 579, 581, 584, 718, 720, 845, 1084, 1086, 1182; **2:**127, 580, 603, 606–9, 634, 642; **3:**850; **4:**11–12, 16, 32, 39, 48, 258, 675, 1154; **5:**611, 673, 798, 842; **6:**606, 656, 1389, 1442–44, 1574; **8:**35, 42, 44, 46–47, 80, 98, 196; **9:**58, 68–69, 542, 579, 619–20; **10:**11, 125, 169, 204–7, 209, 214, 219, 226, 294, 413, 446, 448–49, 451, 459, 461, 481, 487, 493–96, 498, 504, 580, 585, 658, 661, 690, 693, 704, 731, 736, 747, 788, 880–81, 950; **11:**17, 76, 93, 113, 185–86, 196–97, 199, 202, 206–7, 213, 217, 221–28, 231–39, 244, 249,

251–53, 255–56, 259, 262–64, 271–74, 277, 284, 290–91, 295, 297–98, 301, 305, 307, 311–14, 316–18, 320–24, 327–28, 337–40, 342–45, 347–48, 362, 364, 389, 404, 488, 524–26, 529, 531, 534, 568, 572, 623–25, 633, 644, 783, 865, 867, 872; **12:**193, 197, 295, 298, 726; OF THE HEART **1:**89, 1086, 1182; **2:**377; **6:**656; **10:**561; **11:**397, 524; PARTY **11:**227–28, 274, 317, 322, 347; SPIRITUAL **1:**460; **11:**397, 624; UNCIRCUMCISED **1:**460, 578, 735, 783, 1134; **2:**603, 609, 1079, 1197, 1206; **3:**574, 872, 962; **4:**33; **5:**842; **6:**454–55, 626–28, 643, 656, 1389, 1430, 1442–44, 1574; **10:**8, 59–60, 129, 131, 134, 160, 164, 167–71, 182, 203–9, 211–14, 218–20, 226, 258, 284, 293–95, 442, 446, 448–49, 453, 480, 482–83, 493–95, 561, 731, 778, 882; **11:**186, 194, 222–29, 258, 273, 278, 300–301, 305, 328, 342–43, 348, 397, 625; UNCIRCUMCISION **6:**1389, 1442; **10:**442, 448, 561, 657–58, 736, 880–81; **11:**93, 226, 284, 298, 314, 318, 344, 348, 362, 396, 625, 644; **12:**197

CISTERN, CISTERNS
1:226, 600, 1082; **3:**1158; **4:**156, 264, 842; **5:**68, 355–57; **6:**293, 600, 608, 849, 859; **8:**157; **9:**284, 566

CITADEL, CITADELS
1:222, 224, 248, 279; **2:**1237; **3:**751, 756, 793–94, 840, 878, 886, 899, 904, 932–33, 1167; **4:**36, 66, 71, 87–88, 90, 96, 98, 109, 115, 118–19, 121, 125, 134–35, 138, 141, 146, 152, 156, 159, 164–65, 171–72, 193, 217, 222, 228, 257, 261, 297, 873; **5:**612; **6:**67, 740, 1083, 1430; **7:**143, 147, 567; **8:**20; **10:**670

CITIZENSHIP
1:868; **2:**470, 1031; **3:**761, 926; **4:**10–11, 217–18, 935; **5:**597, 624; **7:**34, 129; **8:**49, 674; **10:**298, 305, 366, 378, 576, 755, 822, 988; **11:**397, 402, 471, 496, 498, 535, 785, 879; **12:**138, 235–36, 277, 287, 711; GREEK/ROMAN **1:**291; **5:**439–40, 442, 597; **10:**9, 130, 234, 236, 309, 326–27, 329, 374; **11:**157, 535, 887

CITY, CITIES
AUTHORITIES **10:**239–40; OF BLOODSHED **6:**1103, 1306–7, 1310–11, 1315, 1333–34, 1336–37; **7:**482, 598, 613; CANAANITE **1:**273, 278; **2:**212, 739, 743, 747, 766, 788; CAPITAL **1:**10, 221–22; **2:**740, 962, 1236, 1284, 1300, 1319, 1323, 1326; **3:**18, 58, 164, 223, 993, 995; **5:**365, 419, 853; **6:**81, 108–9, 183, 262, 556, 715, 774–75, 814, 834, 1013, 1030, 1065, 1076, 1081, 1191, 1215, 1224, 1338, 1351; **7:**293, 342, 362, 376, 533–34, 543, 567, 595; **8:**142 (*see also under* CAPITAL); CITY-STATE(S) **1:**230, 246–48, 255–56, 259, 261, 269, 481, 577, 878; **2:**212, 637, 1206, 1266, 1280; **3:**353; **4:**5, 8, 206; **5:**205; **6:**36, 182, 1213, 1349, 1358–61, 1367, 1369–71, 1384, 1398, 1410, 1596; **7:**333, 360–61, 425; **8:**17, 21, 24; OF DAVID (*see* DAVID, CITY OF *in PLACES IN THE BIBLE*); ELDERS (*see under* ELDERS); OF GOD/THE LORD/YAHWEH **2:**1238; **3:**115, 384; **4:**204, 864–65, 872, 874, 1023, 1037, 1183; **5:**112, 621; **6:**214, 613, 773, 813, 982, 1595; **7:**804; **12:**136, 138, 709, 712; GREAT (*see under* GREAT); HEAVENLY **6:**214; **11:**304; **12:**11, 141, 153, 158, 585, 694, 711, 720; HOLY **1:**189; **2:**547, 1236, 1238; **3:**452, 669, 824–25, 840, 850, 1064; **4:**7, 193, 214, 289; **5:**555; **6:**46–47, 54, 84, 175, 217–18, 262, 284, 417–18, 454–56, 509, 733, 773, 813, 1061; **7:**127, 161, 560, 565; **8:**129, 164, 179, 402; **9:**353, 370, 459; **10:**8, 13, 19, 40, 57, 59, 95, 110, 114, 123, 130, 134, 145–47, 167, 178, 204, 214, 258, 270, 275–76, 287–91, 296, 306, 320, 359; **12:**136, 266, 579, 594, 642, 649, 702, 711, 720, 722, 726, 734; OF MOAB **2:**184; OF PALMS **2:**738, 770; OF REFUGE **1:**863; **2:**127, 203, 218, 262–66, 268, 320, 434–36, 563, 630, 634, 661, 695–98, 700, 1332; **3:**347, 1144; **12:**81; OF RIGHTEOUSNESS **6:**47, 60–61, 448, 477–79, 547; SACRED **6:**94, 161, 236, 261–62, 1107, 1537, 1606; **7:**556; OF THE SUN **6:**1418; WALL(S) OF (*see under* WALL)

CIVIL
DISOBEDIENCE **1:**714, 737; **2:**666; **6:**183; **7:**56, 64–65, 91–92; **10:**109; LAW **1:**68, 870, 872, 1001, 1019, 1037, 1040, 1128, 1131; **2:**8, 62, 127, 265, 376, 379, 384; **4:**7, 165, 413; **5:**246; **6:**56, 1206; **7:**64; **8:**142; **9:**128, 227, 304; **10:**233, 309, 398–99, 855, 911–12; **11:**403; RELIGION **9:**86, 386; **10:**271; RIGHTS **1:**157, 162; **2:**978, 1209; **6:**183, 658; **7:**694, 717; **9:**304; **11:**329, 493

CIVILIZATION, CIVILIZATIONS
1:59, 71, 214, 246–47, 375, 377, 996; **2:**18, 64, 192, 327, 337, 426; **4:**190, 488, 604, 1221; **5:**2, 94, 327, 842; **6:**157, 159, 161; **7:**112, 139, 606; **8:**583–84; **10:**644; **12:**612–13, 639, 678, 697; WESTERN **1:**166; **2:**336, 422; **7:**118, 396

CLAN, CLANS
1:216, 245, 258–60, 273, 423, 590–91, 593, 652, 714, 845, 848, 1139; **2:**33, 35, 47, 51, 54, 80, 122, 139, 200, 207–8, 211–13, 217–18, 221, 265–66, 297, 305, 328, 333, 404, 417, 419, 422, 437, 460, 466–67, 488, 580, 628, 629–31, 673, 683, 696, 706, 724, 735, 740, 765, 772, 781, 783, 788, 796, 822, 900–901, 913–14, 916, 918, 935, 939, 973, 1047, 1166, 1170, 1211, 1222, 1236, 1352; **3:**156, 217, 248, 318, 327, 328–30, 332–33, 336, 338, 344–46, 352–53, 357, 363, 393–94, 436, 442, 450–51, 556, 561, 645, 648, 678, 994, 1039, 1143–44; **4:**44, 106, 206, 222–23, 554, 562; **5:**22, 77, 140, 230; **6:**93, 96,

CLAN, CLANS *(continued)*
828, 834, 1168, 1259, 1593; **7:**206, 675, 805, 807, 826–27, 829, 835, 839; **11:**414, 690, 702

CLASPS
1:896; **4:**34

CLAY
1:215, 217, 224, 349, 411, 606, 1019; **2:**363, 656, 803; **3:**421; **4:**378–79, 434, 568, 603; **5:**308, 536, 550, 567–68, 570, 715, 793, 860; **6:**247, 249, 254, 402, 406, 528, 571, 629, 712, 714–15, 717–18, 721–22, 1312, 1438, 1502; **7:**21, 49, 54–55, 105, 189; **9:**653–54; **10:**429, 622, 640–41, 670, 677; **11:**718; IDOL(S) **5:**446, 450, 536, 565–68; POT(S)/POTTERY **1:**1048, 1082, 1098; **6:**866, 1061; **7:**55; **8:**334 (*see also* POT; POTTERY); TABLET(S) **2:**614; **3:**707; **6:**10, 12; **10:**380

CLEAN
1:394, 615, 816, 918, 1012–13, 1044, 1074, 1081–82, 1096, 1098, 1101, 1117, 1120; **2:**83, 151, 310, 398, 915, 1295; **3:**194, 276, 348, 437, 500, 518, 788; **4:**71, 412, 419, 773, 781, 783, 886–87, 969; **5:**282, 827; **6:**55, 117, 381, 414, 626, 718, 1191, 1334, 1337–38, 1451, 1491, 1496, 1563, 1579, 1607; **7:**381, 663, 673, 728–29, 765, 767; **8:**40, 334, 515, 544–45; **9:**46, 119–21, 152, 245, 247–48, 325–26, 342, 724, 739, 755; **10:**171, 479, 640, 728, 740, 742, 851; **11:**55, 440, 791, 807, 833, 845–46; **12:**65, 296, 523, 585, 654, 660, 672, 681; ANIMAL(S) (*see* ANIMAL: CLEAN/UNCLEAN); CEREMONIALLY/RITUALLY **1:**1019, 1026, 1051, 1085, 1148; **2:**147, 151; **4:**277; **5:**793; **6:**103, 549; **8:**156, 495; CONSCIENCE (*see under* CONSCIENCE); DECLARED/PRONOUNCED **1:**1096–98, 1100; **8:**225, 545; FOOD (*see* FOOD: CLEAN/UNCLEAN); HAND(S) (*see under* HAND); AND UNCLEAN **1:**316, 344, 391, 399, 836, 923, 985, 987–88, 997, 999–1000, 1003, 1071–72, 1074–77, 1080–83, 1096–98, 1104, 1106; **2:**13, 397, 399; **3:**994; **4:**39, 440–41; **6:**211, 213, 1314, 1578, 1579; **7:**728; **8:**331, 582–83, 607; **9:**120, 131; **10:**163, 168, 189, 740; **11:**866

CLOAK, CLOAKS
1:610, 622; **2:**388, 454, 469–70, 472, 809, 918, 928–29, 1090, 1184; **4:**130, 500, 602; **5:**187, 412; **6:**77, 1138, 1144, 1228; **8:**19, 195, 403, 603, 628, 656, 658; **9:**194, 247, 367, 370–71, 430, 548, 713; **10:**308, 450, 905; **11:**49, 815, 846, 857; **12:**30, 234, 660

CLOSET, CLOSETS
1:170; **3:**359, 600, 1018; **5:**324; **8:**201

CLOTH, CLOTHS
1:224, 234, 1060–61, 1082; **2:**53, 1140; **3:**226, 901, 927, 1003, 1142; **4:**394; **5:**261–62, 499, 679, 830; **6:**301, 529, 1193, 1228, 1342, 1374, 1377, 1379; **7:**609; **8:**236, 249, 555, 649; **9:**62–63, 65, 199, 260, 362, 455, 465, 471–73, 501, 814, 837, 841, 844; **10:**176, 231–32, 342, 858; **12:**681

CLOTHES, CLOTHING
1:217, 219, 223, 230, 281–82, 350, 362, 364, 535, 541, 586, 598, 600, 604, 621–22, 639, 645, 665, 770, 777, 883, 908–9, 912, 986, 1014, 1082, 1095–98, 1100, 1105, 1111, 1114, 1134, 1148; **2:**81, 124, 151–52, 246, 247, 349, 355, 357, 369, 454, 469, 484, 631, 789, 804, 850–51, 926, 987, 1002, 1127–28, 1157, 1201–2, 1225, 1297, 1359; **3:**208, 426, 562, 601, 728, 776, 783, 813, 821, 838, 901–4, 908, 914, 995, 998, 1003, 1016, 1058, 1130, 1142–43, 1147; **4:**43, 63, 77, 99, 105, 141, 352, 412–13, 431, 500, 510, 524, 538, 553, 914, 928, 1097; **5:**142, 261–62, 357, 497, 505, 547, 625, 688–89, 737, 776, 787 818–19; **6:**81–82, 182, 203, 293, 451, 515, 684, 795, 972, 977, 980, 981, 988, 995, 1000, 1009, 1135, 1228, 1245, 1259, 1326, 1330, 1383, 1450, 1464, 1491, 1586, 1578–79, 1593; **7:**31, 41, 44, 64, 93, 129, 220, 225, 231, 233, 312, 371, 528, 765, 767; **8:**156, 210, 217, 224, 418, 456, 491, 532, 544, 555, 584–85, 587–88, 595, 630, 634, 648–49, 681, 683, 722; **9:**21, 81, 84, 119, 163–64, 186, 205, 259–60, 402, 468, 485, 692, 705, 722, 799, 819, 829–31, 836, 843; **10:**162, 199, 232, 254, 458, 728–29, 947; **11:**84, 157, 429, 440, 451, 457, 463, 643, 648, 657, 699, 763, 801, 828; **12:**30, 50, 87, 148, 163, 197, 257, 263, 401, 457, 498, 573, 599, 624, 664, 694, 723, 725, 733. *See also* APPAREL; GARMENT; RAIMENT; *types of clothing by name*

CLOUD, CLOUDS
1:90, 274, 288, 391, 399–400, 882–83, 887, 938–39, 954, 980, 1008, 1135; **2:**69–70, 86–91, 94, 96–97, 107, 122, 338, 385, 534, 789, 826, 1005, 1367; **3:**70, 78, 494, 496, 502; **4:**197, 314, 367, 394, 484, 501, 518–19, 540, 581, 590, 592, 598, 602, 604–5, 691, 747, 823, 1004–5, 1069, 1076, 1220; **5:**118, 161, 219, 340, 350, 356, 525, 585, 798, 834; **6:**84, 88, 159, 214, 343, 509, 548, 988, 1005, 1013, 1038, 1055, 1071, 1114–15, 1117, 1119, 1160, 1183, 1271–72, 1366, 1414, 1418, 1422, 1425, 1427–28, 1435, 1466, 1512, 1517; **7:**15, 103, 316, 602, 666, 682–83; **8:**364, 366–67, 537, 630; **9:**51, 205–7, 268, 399, 407, 410; **10:**43, 131, 474, 534, 661, 914, 957; **11:**64, 724, 728; **12:**403, 492, 505, 591–92, 597, 638, 643, 668, 710, 734; DENSE/THICK **1:**835–36; **2:**88; **10:**615; AND FIRE **1:**688, 788–89, 794, 979; **4:**1105; **5:**517; **7:**758; **10:**513, 581, 593; OF GLORY **1:**831, 978–79, 1007; **3:**137, 496, 502; **4:**198; **6:**1117; PILLAR OF **1:**688, 788, 938, 1179;

2:108, 110, 126; **3:**811; **4:**1075; **5:**517, 585, 621, 757, 758; **6:**1510; **10:**513, 556, 581, 593; RIDING THE CLOUDS/CLOUD RIDER **1:**289; **2:**755, 1367; **3:**127; **4:**945, 1097; **6:**159, 180, 1119; **7:**8–9, 105, 113, 168, 762; **8:**444, 691, 714; **9:**18, 206, 407; **10:**131, 661; **11:**728; **12:**582–83, 734; STORM **1:**265; **2:**340; **3:**600; **6:**1089, 1108, 1113; **7:**653; OF WITNESSES **5:**860; **9:**590; **10:**384; **11:**117; **12:**148, 155, 511

CLUB, CLUBS
AS A WEAPON **4:**486, 624; **6:**915, 1178, 1420, 1524; **7:**192, 194; **9:**436

COAL, COALS
1:31, 1070, 1111; **3:**140; **4:**197, 305, 624, 721; **5:**220, 714, 772; **6:**103–4, 1115, 1172, 1182–83, 1334, 1337, 1394, 1560; **7:**371, 699; **10:**715; **11:**329

COAST, COASTS
1:245, 666, 1018, 1081; **2:**646, 662, 719; **3:**242, 251, 878, 1108; **4:**4, 30, 130, 150, 168, 170, 173, 202, 219, 275, 792, 1010; **5:**261; **6:**202, 305, 1221, 1356, 1358–59, 1370, 1384, 1396, 1596; **7:**202; **9:**451; **10:**189, 191, 240, 345, 348, 754, 469, 878

COASTLAND, COASTLANDS
1:408; **2:**88, 662; **3:**1117, 1127; **4:**96; **6:**12, 145, 182, 212, 347, 349, 352, 354, 357, 362–63, 365, 420, 429, 431, 460, 501, 1358, 1367–68, 1373, 1378, 1382, 1429, 1523; **7:**103, 141; **10:**755; **11:**215

COAT, COATS
1:598–600, 645, 868–69; **3:**217; **9:**359, 374; **10:**131, 423, 741; OF MAIL **2:**1112; **4:**624

COCK
4:605; **8:**475, 715; **9:**428, 438, 733

CODE
1:949, 993–94, 1040, 1076, 1137, 1143; **2:**276, 292, 378–79, 416, 460, 783, 825, 878, 904, 1102; **3:**594, 1181; **4:**292, 500, 551, 556, 684; **5:**200, 547, 675; **6:**95, 828, 832, 1304; **7:**176, 573, 675; **8:**48, 217, 321, 332, 386, 448, 517, 545, 623; **9:**236, 254; **10:**254, 378, 440, 707, 910; **11:**186, 328, 386, 460, 625, 654–60, 823, 839; **12:**237, 314, 505–6, 552, 555, 561, 726; COVENANT **1:**689, 831, 855, 861, 1165, 1170; **2:**876; **6:**1258; **7:**355, 674, 774; HOLINESS **1:**986–87, 993–95, 1003, 1074, 1115, 1117, 1123, 1126–27, 1156, 1172, 1178; **2:**474; **3:**616, 721; **4:**1006; **6:**597, 1152, 1154, 1206, 1258, 1309; **7:**776; **11:**225; **12:**260–61, 489; HOUSEHOLD **11:**353, 367, 434, 441–42, 444, 446, 449, 452–55, 553, 555, 559, 576, 579, 641, 644, 649, 652–54, 658–59, 661–62, 909; **12:**278, 280, 284; LAW/LEGAL *or* CODE OF HAMMURABI **1:**9–10, 284–85, 291, 379, 489, 1165; **2:**63, 272–73, 278–79, 289, 293, 319, 322, 323, 327, 349, 366, 369, 373, 378–81, 384, 387, 393–94, 419, 427, 440–41, 453, 456, 461, 468, 470, 481, 484, 486, 491, 500, 503–4, 876, 965; **3:**547, 722; **5:**7, 144; **6:**10, 20–21, 1226, 1463; **7:**660, 774; **8:**31–32, 645; **9:**148; **11:**186, 338; **12:**523; MORAL **2:**455; **10:**86, 403, 479, 483, 587, 849; **12:**334; WORD **6:**919; **10:**786, 813, 815, 835, 906, 915, 923–24, 977, 983; **11:**39, 92; **12:**318

CODEX (*OR* CODICES, *ETC.*)
1:11, 18, 65, 296; **3:**800; **5:**636; **8:**3, 8–9; **9:**623, 874; **11:**390, 857. *See also by title in ANCIENT LITERATURE*

COFFER, COFFERS
2:771, 1187; **3:**54, 104, 700; **4:**60; **5:**717; **7:**41, 272; **8:**322

COHORT, COHORTS
AS COMPANION **1:**882; **2:**311; **3:**932; **6:**852, 1317, 1527, 1533; **7:**801; **8:**477, 719; **9:**801; **10:**153, 167; **11:**49, 82; AS MILITARY UNIT **10:**162, 297, 345

COIN, COINS
1:6, 250, 268, 1132; **4:**38, 137, 154, 168, 178, 393; **7:**54, 84, 113; **8:**165, 267, 420, 488, 663, 673–74, 683; **9:**12, 23, 35, 88, 171, 174, 193–94, 252, 272, 294–96, 298, 300, 303, 318, 320, 336, 386, 395–96, 543; **10:**269; **11:**52, 401, 417, 580; **12:**433; BEKA **3:**510; COPPER **8:**104, 682; **9:**21, 24, 171, 193, 252, 269, 336, 363, 395; DENARIUS (DENARII) **8:**76, 393, 673; **9:**21, 170–71, 230, 252, 269, 296, 361–62, 386, 396; DIDRACHMA **9:**171; DRACHMA(S) **3:**1055; **4:**218; **8:**105, 371, 383; **9:**171, 296; GOLD TALENTS **1:**262; **3:**84, 431, 728; **6:**1361; HALF-SHEKEL **1:**918; **2:**35; **3:**510, 721; **8:**33, 41; **9:**171; SHEKEL **1:**314, 504, 600, 865, 918, 1039, 1042, 1136, 1173, 1187–89; **2:**35, 52, 77–78, 148, 245, 247, 454, 456, 629, 1037; **3:**424, 510–11, 580, 721, 782, 798, 819, 995; **6:**1149, 1583; **7:**231, 735, 822; **8:**33, 41, 371; **9:**69, 171; SILVER **3:**692; **6:**171, 193–94, 296; TALENT **1:**251, 262; **2:**35; **3:**84, 264, 416, 431, 467, 468, 722, 728, 780, 897, 904, 911, 995; **4:**104, 108, 248; **5:**565, 611; **6:**389, 1361; **8:**61, 123, 382, 383, 450, 451, 453; **9:**265, 310, 353, 361–64; **10:**829; TWO SIDES OF THE SAME COIN *or* TWO SIDES OF ONE COIN **1:**574; **5:**139, 145; **6:**433, 529, 1138; **8:**41; **10:**85, 547, 677; **11:**338; **12:**273, 393. *See also* MONEY; WEIGHTS AND MEASURES

COLA
(poetic form) **2:**66; **5:**650, 673

COLLAR
5:688–89; **7:**605

COLLECTION
ASCENTS (OF PSALMS) **4:**1180, 1219; OF BOOKS **1:**8,

COLLECTION *(continued)*
13, 19–21, 37, 135, 188, 193–94, 296, 535; **3:**4; **5:**2; **6:**12, 17–18; **7:**139; **8:**29; DAVIDIC (OF PSALMS) **4:**658, 664, 852, 881, 964, 1231, 1243, 1246–47, 1250, 1254–55, 1258; OF DOCUMENTS/TEXTS/WRITINGS **1:**37, 43, 126, 130, 189, 296; **2:**521; **6:**839; **11:**194; **12:**28; HALLEL (OF PSALMS) **4:**1138, 1148–49, 1153, 1155; KORAH(ITE) (OF PSALMS) **3:**561; **4:**658, 852, 1019; OF MONEY/OFFERING/TITHES (*see under* TITHES); OF POEMS **2:**637, 1205; OF PROPHECIES **6:**66, 147, 230, 878, 882; **12:**733; OF PROVERBS/MAXIMS **1:**43, 240; **3:**1016; **5:**609; OF PSALMS **3:**561; **4:**309, 643, 653, 655–58, 662, 664–65, 688, 755, 852, 857, 881, 963–64, 1019, 1053, 1057, 1060–61, 1064, 1069, 1072, 1074, 1077, 1138, 1148–49, 1153, 1155, 1176, 1180, 1183, 1187, 1192, 1194, 1197, 1199–1200, 1202, 1204, 1208, 1210, 1214, 1216, 1231, 1243, 1246, 1250, 1254–55, 1258, 1264, 1267–68, 1270, 1272, 1278; **8:**33, 35; **11:**780; OF SAYINGS **1:**2, 19; **5:**14, 30, 105, 215, 225, 349; **6:**17, 19, 126; **7:**234, 625, 648; **8:**91, 95–96, 176, 509, 641, 651; **9:**12, 244, 258, 268, 306, 330, 713; OF TAXES **1:**222; **2:**33, 149; **3:**452; **7:**738; **9:**62

COLONY, COLONIES
1:234, 248, 250, 267, 285, 851, 990; **2:**595, 668–69, 1073; **3:**457, 1108, 1118; **4:**12–13, 63, 82, 189, 725; **6:**202, 1378; **7:**28, 76, 866; **9:**121; **10:**175, 231, 233, 355, 739, 774, 875; **11:**58, 470, 535, 675, 871; **12:**248

COLOPHON
1:995, 1024, 1043, 1055, 1147–48, 1151, 1155, 1163, 1170, 1190; **3:**946, 970–71; **6:**1266, 1273, 1432, 1437, 1605; **9:**560; **12:**442

COLORS
1:598, 896, 906, 1060; **2:**53, 55; **3:**357, 1151; **4:**67; **5:**408, 557; **6:**1245; **7:**751, 782–83; **12:**592, 632

COLOSSIANS, LETTER TO THE
1:8, 13, 160; **2:**321; **3:**417; **4:**672; **5:**16; **8:**48; **9:**4; **10:**370, 373, 534, 538, 687, 709, 720–21, 761, 767–68, 789–90, 949, 969–70; **11:**353–55, 357–58, 362, 364, 369–70, 374–75, 380, 382–85, 389, 396–98, 400, 407–9, 414, 416, 423, 427, 429, 434–35, 441, 446, 453, 465–66, 473, 479, 504, 684, 884, 899, 903; **12:**27, 41, 69, 230, 232, 246, 278, 280, 284, 388, 398, 562, 573, 625

COLT
4:421; **7:**807–8; **8:**153, 358, 403, 658; **9:**17, 353, 367, 455, 707

COMEDY
1:141; **3:**1155–56; **5:**7; **6:**1291; **10:**198; **12:**276

COMFORT
1:69, 92, 158, 184, 201, 380, 400, 600, 673, 796, 1036; **2:**376, 1094, 1177; **3:**55, 562, 564, 753, 887, 957, 1024; **4:**320, 357, 362, 383, 388, 395, 457, 462, 537, 540, 631, 635, 722, 765, 768, 839, 901, 960–61, 983, 1021, 1170–71, 1208–9; **5:**113, 182, 198, 296, 298, 311, 335, 384, 398, 628, 645–46, 651, 676, 720, 818, 853; **7:**7, 12, 114, 138, 148–49, 340, 398, 400, 412, 538, 545, 561, 599, 603, 753–54, 869; **8:**50, 52, 178, 195, 395, 574; **9:**52, 144, 194, 440, 663, 747, 753; **10:**93, 154, 221, 225, 349, 381, 385, 446, 521, 614, 616, 645, 699, 703, 746; **11:**3, 33, 41–44, 53–54, 101, 109, 111, 157, 163, 289, 483, 492, 497–99, 517, 521, 547, 666, 690, 712, 715, 727–28, 762–63, 844, 847, 855–56; **12:**81, 123, 229, 234, 254, 263, 267, 280, 292, 313, 316, 319, 358, 402, 424, 482, 588, 625, 646, 730; MY/THE PEOPLE **1:**1182; **4:**240, 309, 1043; **6:**339, 810; **7:**754; **9:**70; WORD OF **1:**400, 636, 671, 673; **4:**431; **6:**424, 457, 476, 551, 572, 797, 810, 1305; **7:**562, 606; **9:**596, 763; **11:**733; **12:**567, 577; FOR ZION **6:**319, 335, 424, 443, 447, 456, 547, 1033, 1044; **7:**754; **9:**70

COMFORTER
See under GOD, NAMES FOR/TITLES OF *in PERSONS IN THE BIBLE*

COMMANDMENT, COMMANDMENTS
FIRST **1:**42, 74–75, 351, 586, 840–41, 846, 852, 867, 869, 871, 877; **2:**288, 329, 343, 380, 421, 441, 470, 543; **3:**173, 257; **4:**736, 1004; **5:**658; **6:**222, 597, 712; GOD'S/THE LORD'S/YAHWEH'S **1:**38, 70, 72, 75, 277, 1127; **2:**218, 252, 263, 267, 288, 312, 329, 339, 346, 348, 356, 369–70, 375–76, 403, 454, 503–4, 518–19, 759, 1071–72, 1089; **3:**62–63, 109, 255, 433, 526, 539, 620, 622, 645, 720, 753–54, 995, 1014, 1055, 1068; **5:**33, 180, 652, 655, 658, 758; **6:**244, 961–62, 968, 1517; **8:**277, 332, 607, 608, 643; **9:**349, 671; **10:**880; **11:**243, 258, 443, 591; **12:**398, 422, 427, 431–32, 435–37, 452, 495, 498, 565, 585, 651, 666–67, 734; GREAT **1:**207; **3:**1015; **5:**307; **6:**641; **8:**123, 189, 213, 215, 401, 409, 419, 423, 442, 450, 466, 679; **9:**233, 704–5; KEEP/OBSERVE **1:**277, 281, 283, 1127; **2:**289, 322, 354, 371, 373, 482, 511–12, 1071; **3:**255, 433, 539, 752–54, 821, 1014, 1068; **4:**50, 232, 241; **5:**33, 45–46, 63, 180, 282, 333, 359, 650–51; **6:**968; **7:**747; **8:**42, 390; **9:**349, 733–34, 746–47, 749, 758, 861; **10:**659, 880; **11:**243, 251, 258, 322, 433, 829; **12:**376, 390, 398–99, 422–24, 427, 435, 437, 565, 651, 666–67, 734; SECOND **1:**843, 846; **2:**288, 314, 316–17, 321, 329, 362–63, 397; **6:**72, 74, 176

COMMANDMENTS, TEN
See DECALOGUE; TEN COMMANDMENTS

COMMENTARY, COMMENTARIES
BIBLE/BIBLICAL/SCRIPTURE **1:**1, 10, 73, 75, 77–79, 81, 127, 140, 183; **6:**1099; **9:**834; **10:**16, 62; **12:**560; CRITICAL **11:**188; EXEGETICAL **1:**110; **12:**101, 550; INTERPRETIVE **1:**778, 868; **7:**242; **9:**662, 841, 861

COMMERCE
1:7, 245, 262, 266, 515, 906, 998; **2:**192, 404, 414, 570, 639, 787; **3:**693, 848; **4:**448; **5:**74, 117, 119, 121, 155, 186, 261, 313, 351, 543, 754, 767, 768, 773; **6:**414, 892, 1363–64, 1368, 1388, 1394, 1570, 1596; **7:**140, 416, 581, 679, 700, 839; **9:**332, 830; **10:**261, 775, 906–7; **11:**170; **12:**271, 694, 696

COMMISSION
AUTHORIZATION/CHARGE **2:**1041, 1121, 1128, 1274; **3:**140, 144, 332, 394, 409, 424, 429, 436, 547, 715, 720, 761, 1051, 1069; **4:**350, 771; **5:**687, 842; **6:**13, 42, 99, 100–105, 107, 110, 118, 133, 243, 361, 371, 394–95, 401, 580–83, 585, 587–89, 680, 758, 792, 811, 825, 865, 878, 882, 1101, 1108, 1121, 1128–30, 1208, 1335; **7:**138, 376, 404, 510–11, 753, 765, 820–22, 824; **8:**56, 64–66, 69, 326, 366, 410, 500, 503, 731; **9:**105, 117–18, 128, 137, 187–88, 219, 222, 225, 308, 426, 439, 487–90, 569, 759, 857, 861, 864; **10:**24, 62, 115, 130, 134–35, 145–47, 150, 195, 224, 226, 281, 305, 307–8, 333, 337–39, 383, 405, 415, 420, 422–23, 427, 452–53, 455, 529, 603, 667, 754, 906; **11:**40, 62, 202, 211, 216, 219, 233, 242, 270, 408, 413, 488, 520, 540, 559, 661, 777, 787, 793–95, 799, 814, 829, 837, 841, 855, 858, 861–63, 871; **12:**92, 246, 601, 630, 639, 646; GREAT **7:**429; **8:**124, 256, 401, 418, 498, 500–501, 503; **9:**486, 704; OFFICIAL GROUP **2:**1383; **3:**666, 669, 726–28, 731, 742–43, 745, 796, 847; **4:**169; **6:**1526; SINS OF **5:**55, 350; **6:**380, 1461, 1463; **12:**443

COMMON
(BEFORE THE) COMMON ERA **1:**65, 230, 1170, 1194; **5:**7; **7:**148, 156; **8:**40; **10:**477; **11:**480; **12:**232; BELIEF(S) **1:**50; **3:**1065; **8:**73; **10:**71; **11:**236; FORM(S/ULA) **1:**237, 594; **2:**631, 1078; **3:**1026; **5:**752; **6:**585; **7:**631; **8:**78, 555; **9:**628, 732; **11:**454; GOOD(S) **1:**871; **2:**53, 684, 1195; **3:**714, 761; **4:**541; **5:**176, 182, 300; **6:**69; **7:**263, 279; **8:**45, 48; **10:**73, 98, 786, 788, 825, 830, 910, 941, 943–50, 959, 962; **11:**142–43, 179, 800; LANGUAGE/VOCABULARY **1:**161, 411; **2:**534; **3:**4; **4:**983; **5:**1, 270; **7:**22; **8:**202; **9:**224; **10:**7; **12:**129, 206; LECTIONARY **2:**12, 714, 1259; **5:**266; **6:**1497; **7:**219, 280, 596, 623, 641, 643, 873; **8:**362; **9:**612; **11:**329, 658; **12:**262, 276, 286, 297, 377, 438, 455, 510; LIFE **1:**190–91; **4:**823; **6:**926; **7:**755; **8:**18, 181, 299; **9:**779; **10:**23, 42, 71–74, 95, 98, 101, 115, 697, 727, 825; **11:**248, 272, 332, 338, 499; **12:**43, 686, 728–29; MEAL(S) **1:**287; **8:**44; **9:**235; **10:**238, 277; **11:**232; **12:**587; MOTIF(S) **1:**475; **2:**138; **3:**1155, 1178–79; **4:**314, 402, 410, 469; **7:**43, 74; **8:**216; **9:**538; PATTERN(S) **2:**1370; **3:**1085; **5:**102; **6:**81, 724; **7:**736; **8:**62, 66; **9:**286, 363, 372; **10:**23; PEOPLE **1:**1035; **2:**817, 894; **4:**12; **5:**241, 272; **7:**467; **8:**414, 531, 545, 552, 650; PRACTICE(S) **1:**88, 452; **2:**474–75, 635, 1005, 1297; **3:**1108; **4:**169, 624; **6:**94, 866; **7:**635; **8:**16, 279; **9:**63, 829–30, 833; **10:**73, 98; **11:**341; **12:**495; THEME(S) **3:**1023, 1144; **4:**193; **5:**142, 765; **6:**76, 92, 99, 180, 229, 253, 255, 933, 1306; **7:**522, 748, 813, 868; **8:**383; **9:**20, 144, 219, 294, 319; **10:**230; **11:**426, 453, 698; **12:**355, 563; THEOLOGY **1:**274, 315; **3:**804; **7:**377; **9:**494; **10:**15, 224; TRADITION(S) **1:**129, 209; **3:**1179; **7:**381; **9:**8, 117, 401, 699, 814; **10:**608; **11:**424; **12:**11, 232; WORSHIP **1:**1156; **10:**73, 406–7, 746

COMMONWEALTH
1:307–8, 314–15, 317; **3:**358; **4:**281; **6:**516; **9:**53; **11:**284, 304, 396–98, 402, 496, 535; **12:**540, 712

COMMUNICATION, COMMUNICATIONS
1:21, 36, 47, 49, 63, 76, 115, 118, 124, 143, 361, 389, 412, 414, 534, 598, 1135; **2:**83, 218, 234, 460, 932, 1153, 1205; **4:**240, 371, 392; **5:**76, 97, 110, 155, 208, 268, 398, 720; **6:**190, 294, 564, 566, 686, 722, 1081, 1088, 1099, 1125–26, 1299; **7:**629, 751, 877; **8:**3, 12, 47, 56, 71, 107, 109–10, 144, 193, 294, 299, 304, 341–42, 518; **9:**14, 51, 222, 663; **10:**8, 379–80, 761, 790, 913, 959; **11:**31, 33, 102, 370, 385, 409, 455, 474, 520, 542, 559, 595, 611, 643, 669, 728, 785, 831, 834, 846, 856, 860; **12:**15–16, 67, 72, 142, 160, 370, 383–84, 459, 506, 571, 697; DIVINE AND OTHER COMMUNICATION BETWEEN GOD AND HUMANS **1:**35, 39, 41–42, 44, 49–50, 56, 58, 61, 63, 229, 345, 364, 412, 541–42, 953; **2:**14–15, 21, 110, 160, 218, 429, 932, 1073, 1192, 1261; **3:**22, 724; **4:**334, 569, 899, 1054, 1169; **5:**644, 852; **6:**5, 10, 68, 92, 294, 545–46, 564, 722, 750, 1044, 1088, 1139, 1209–10, 1454, 1487; **7:**106, 327, 419, 493, 544, 751, 852–53; **8:**24; **9:**51, 777, 797–98; **10:**367, 799; **11:**860; **12:**97, 571, 603 (*see also* MESSENGER)

COMMUNION
1:53, 535, 682, 837, 880, 883, 888–89, 891–93, 900, 919, 938, 943, 972, 974, 990, 999, 1021, 1024, 1026, 1052, 1062, 1067; **2:**82–83, 429, 633, 1057, 1088, 1383; **3:**108; **4:**445, 742, 764, 786, 852, 1014, 1044, 1216; **5:**398, 423, 481, 560; **6:**216–17, 456; **7:**169, 304, 309, 311–12, 318–19, 322–23, 325, 334; **8:**25, 275, 327;

COMMUNION *(continued)*
9:692, 694, 741, 748–50, 784; **10:**162, 825, 918, 939; **11:**179, 233, 310, 593; **12:**241, 269, 287, 310, 337, 383–86, 566, 569, 695; SACRAMENT OF **1:**208, 210, 212; **2:**55, 67, 83, 168; **3:**395, 464, 612, 619; **4:**742; **6:**815; **10:**813, 918, 939; **11:**310; **12:**310, 569; OF (THE) SAINTS **2:**912; **4:**765, 1030; **10:**916; **11:**39; **12:**390

COMMUNITY
OF BELIEVERS **3:**693; **5:**644; **7:**458; **8:**97; **9:**27, 421, 480, 490, 840; **10:**22, 57, 93, 96, 176, 212, 278, 288, 785, 788–89, 809, 812, 847, 850, 855–57, 931, 941, 956, 959, 962, 965, 972; **11:**10–11, 104, 175, 179, 430, 512, 521, 611, 690–91; **12:**49, 154, 292; CHRISTIAN **1:**5–6, 14, 104, 161, 163, 192, 460, 779, 815; **2:**38–39, 141–42, 768, 818; **3:**1043; **4:**23; **5:**208; **6:**700, 759, 777, 816; **7:**862; **8:**68, 71, 73, 85, 92, 97–99, 102–3, 118, 153, 156, 158, 165, 175, 178, 180, 196, 211, 230, 238, 258, 262, 274, 278–79, 292, 297–98, 334, 337, 373–74, 378–79, 383–84, 386–87, 390, 392, 420, 431–32, 437, 450, 503–4, 602, 604, 608, 678; **9:**30, 59, 146, 211, 276, 406, 499, 510, 525, 550, 575, 610, 647, 650, 664, 734, 759–60, 762, 767–68, 774, 776–77, 798, 844, 853; **10:**30, 73, 209, 253, 278, 378, 422, 478, 711–13, 717, 724, 726, 743, 800, 809, 825, 865, 901, 1003; **11:**39, 195, 207–8, 217, 225, 228, 232, 277, 363, 370, 405, 421, 424, 430–31, 469, 475, 481, 484, 489, 495–96, 499, 501, 513, 516–17, 525, 529–30, 537, 540, 546–47, 627, 645, 650–51, 683, 701, 866, 880; **12:**34, 46, 74–75, 78, 129, 148, 155, 160, 162–63, 205, 212, 239, 245, 269–70, 275, 277–78, 280, 290, 310–11, 328, 396, 403, 413, 449, 456, 460; EARLY CHRISTIAN **1:**83; **4:**1156; **7:**847, 867; **8:**93, 257, 519, 573; **9:**163, 540; **11:**227; OF FAITH **1:**20–21, 34, 90, 112, 135, 148, 163, 168, 171, 183, 189–91, 314, 323, 326–27, 341, 377, 395, 401, 418, 426, 430, 435, 455, 460, 468, 476, 479, 482–84, 490, 492, 517, 529, 539, 558–60, 569, 580, 586, 594, 607, 611–12, 623, 655, 661, 776, 778, 786–87, 816, 825, 837, 853, 951, 963, 979, 1114; **2:**193, 237, 367, 616, 681, 753, 789, 896, 902, 920, 946, 978, 1021, 1030–31, 1044–45, 1064–65, 1267, 1294, 1299, 1317; **3:**36, 47, 78, 95, 137–38, 214, 257, 344–45, 347–48, 370, 380, 396, 461, 467, 576, 624, 1121, 1125; **4:**495, 690, 787; **6:**49, 64, 85, 119, 138, 148, 568, 577, 586, 641, 667, 680, 686, 704, 724, 734, 753–54, 756, 776–77, 813–14, 821, 827, 835, 853, 860, 868, 875, 917, 1035, 1207, 1305; **7:**490, 780, 800, 823–24, 830, 832–34, 840, 866; **8:**180–81, 207, 293, 298, 330, 377, 574; **9:**139, 402, 490, 496–97, 499, 507, 533–34, 540, 559, 572, 589–90, 650, 672, 711, 714, 728, 733, 738, 744–45, 747, 757, 760, 764–67, 771, 773, 777–78, 780, 785, 788–89, 791–98, 846–49, 853, 855, 863–64; **10:**46, 49, 51, 73, 85, 96, 98, 112, 128, 155, 167–68, 180, 209–10, 221–22, 255, 257, 294, 329, 357, 369, 371, 375, 377, 380, 384–88, 390, 846, 855, 868, 938, 972; **11:**195, 279, 314, 321, 329, 346, 413, 701, 712, 842, 877, 896; **12:**9, 15, 19, 23, 49, 78, 81, 95, 145, 152, 159, 161, 192, 194–95, 200, 203, 216, 221–22, 224, 236, 238–39, 271, 273, 304, 307, 319, 409, 486, 490; OF GOODS **1:**287; **10:**10, 15, 22–23, 28, 35, 49, 65, 67, 72–73, 97–98, 100, 110–11, 113, 115, 137, 139, 162, 169, 176–77, 182, 203, 235, 274, 283, 285, 294, 357; INCLUSIVE (*see* INCLUSIVE/EXCLUSIVE); JEWISH **1:**65, 67–68, 77–80, 289–91, 296, 301, 313; **2:**398, 413, 935; **3:**95, 358, 672, 680, 688, 694, 704, 716, 722, 773, 780, 860, 890, 971; **4:**23, 196, 514, 746, 912; **5:**439–40, 442, 490, 542–43, 565, 597, 610, 627, 643, 652, 664, 688, 750; **6:**228, 759, 989, 1016; **7:**24–25, 32, 116, 126, 141–42, 146, 155–56, 175, 178, 182, 192, 442, 771, 866; **8:**40, 94, 97, 99–100, 372, 494, 515, 548, 682, 684, 688; **9:**156, 506, 543, 587–88, 648; **10:**72, 194, 239, 253, 330, 360, 406, 850; **11:**214, 232, 364–65, 404, 525; **12:**85; JEWISH CHRISTIAN **8:**95, 139; **9:**506; **10:**292; **11:**239; **12:**588; OF JEWS AND GENTILES **8:**99, 292, 496; **11:**277

COMPASS
DIRECTION/POINTS **1:**214; **4:**508; **6:**316, 376, 430–31, 433, 456, 548, 1114, 1130, 1294, 1500, 1601; **7:**690–91; **10:**359; **11:**47; **12:**391, 434, 722

COMPASSION
ACT(S) OF **1:**1184; **2:**825, 1158–60, 1279; **3:**1042; **6:**877; **8:**223, 266; **9:**86, 187, 466; DIVINE (OF GOD/THE LORD) **2:**528, 757; **3:**76, 503, 525, 656, 998, 1042; **4:**387; **5:**366, 564, 628, 656, 678; **6:**528, 604, 665, 694, 808, 810, 813, 853, 1530; **7:**223, 473, 490, 528, 685, 753, 815–16; **8:**121, 251–52, 337; **11:**41, 515; JUSTICE AND **2:**289, 405, 463, 1030, 1057; **5:**159; **6:**600, 832; **7:**352, 607; **9:**86, 88, 339; LOVE AND **2:**286, 393, 513; **4:**947, 954, 983, 1091–92, 1260; **5:**391; **8:**667; **11:**484, 151; MERCY AND/OR **1:**1149; **2:**727, 825; **3:**1042; **4:**995; **5:**536, 541, 543, 562, 564; **6:**521, 692, 767, 1530; **8:**551; **11:**41; **12:**180–81

CONCENTRIC, CENTRICALLY
1:696, 836, 1076, 1081; **3:**327, 368, 597, 1151; **4:**1219; **5:**101, 106, 108, 411, 446, 494, 528, 536; **6:**1116, 1375, 1377; **7:**344; **8:**151–56, 174, 503, 731; **10:**587; **12:**16–17, 84, 172; STRUCTURE **4:**1097; **5:**444–45, 452, 503, 509–11, 515, 517, 550, 557, 561, 566, 569, 571 (*see also* CHIASTIC)

CONCUBINE, CONCUBINES
1:501, 515, 585; **2:**456, 492, 729, 742, 782, 791, 810, 816, 825, 835, 872, 875–79, 884–88, 899, 970, 1055, 1213, 1222–23, 1242, 1293, 1324, 1330–31, 1359; **3:**14, 32, 90, 318, 329, 353, 388, 522, 868, 888–91; **4:**21, 32, 63, 222; **5:**255, 297, 332, 377, 412–13, 419–20, 426; **6:**1309, 1325; **7:**81, 93, 232, 267, 275
CONCUPISCENCE
5:298, 749
CONDEMNATION
1:62, 78, 283, 991, 1085, 1127, 1190; **2:**315, 406, 492, 514, 631, 684, 748, 887; **3:**40, 96, 153, 156, 196, 226, 511, 737, 1016; **4:**501, 554, 835, 1004; **5:**117, 173, 200, 316, 340, 354, 384, 475, 484, 536, 766, 849, 851; **6:**53, 63, 74, 82, 89, 92, 94, 155, 159, 176, 189, 197, 204, 259, 371, 380, 438, 499, 545–46, 548, 563, 599, 679, 703, 724, 794, 853, 872, 975, 982, 1503; **7:**41–42, 50, 142, 145–46, 178, 182, 200, 205, 224, 244–45, 264, 267, 278, 283, 362, 396, 534–35, 539, 553, 556, 558, 576, 582, 597, 606, 614, 694, 831, 865; **8:**21, 63, 144, 212, 214, 226, 287, 408, 412, 414, 418, 494, 516, 595, 598, 669, 682–83, 714; **9:**88, 126, 166, 170, 242–43, 248–49, 278, 336, 375, 384, 392–96, 440, 448, 462, 478, 560, 630, 645, 732, 824; **10:**79, 129, 140, 196, 234, 247, 310, 400, 413, 435, 440, 443, 450, 454, 524, 528–29, 550–51, 566, 574–76, 579–80, 589, 613, 619, 628, 648, 676, 678, 721, 736, 738, 742; **11:**65–66, 102, 233, 373, 437, 483, 530, 563, 572, 632, 644, 656, 794, 806, 879; **12:**158, 179–80, 215, 221–22, 224, 301, 347, 424, 432, 477, 485, 491, 494, 498, 681, 693, 695, 725
CONDUIT
3:31, 146; **4:**402, 469; **5:**59, 298; **6:**107, 1164, 1209; **10:**363, 828; **11:**256
CONEY
(animal) **1:**1080
CONFESSION, CONFESSIONS
OF FAITH **1:**16, 337; **2:**15, 480, 484, 837; **3:**198; **4:**722, 736; **6:**163, 606, 859–60; **7:**72, 93, 382; **8:**68, 174, 261, 344, 410, 455, 619; **9:**100, 254, 609, 611, 660, 689, 691, 782, 840, 850, 852; **10:**18, 106, 144, 150, 246, 318, 320–22, 482; **11:**538; **12:**12, 23, 25, 28, 165, 405; OF GOD **1:**338, 499, 543, 635; **2:**194; **4:**627, 722; **6:**531; **8:**149; **9:**191; **11:**267, 831, 835; **12:**181, 724; OF GUILT **1:**629, 639, 641, 758; **5:**459, 484, 579; **6:**602; OF JESUS, THE LORD **8:**80, 261, 270, 341, 351, 362, 366, 459, 519, 527, 529, 580–81, 621–22; **9:**17, 56, 111–12, 137, 144, 156, 198–201, 205, 211, 255, 442, 454, 457, 461, 477, 594, 611, 661, 850; **10:**132, 166, 375, 664, 672, 732, 941–42; **11:**502, 628; **12:**199, 245, 424, 425, 428, 435, 437, 439–40, 457, 716; PRAYER(S) OF **1:**207; **6:**930–31, 937, 939, 945–46, 948–49, 957, 960, 971; **7:**122, 126, 129, 160–61; **9:**324, 370; PUBLIC **1:**498, 607, 629, 639; **3:**666; **4:**554; **6:**949; **9:**250; **10:**144, 209, 320, 375; OF SIN(S) **1:**644, 673, 1051; **2:**78, 83, 126, 946, 1060, 1295, 1381; **3:**427, 502, 525, 553, 666, 669, 735, 750, 797–98, 809–13; **4:**110, 669, 704, 805, 975, 1000, 1088, 1110, 1174, 1250, 1252; **5:**808; **6:**58, 85, 103, 257, 371, 466, 529, 606, 649, 690, 692, 704, 810, 920, 946, 948–49, 957, 959, 1053–54, 1058, 1067; **9:**126; **12:**222, 225, 386, 416, 666
CONFIRMATION
1:40, 62, 541, 600; **2:**193, 220, 510, 615, 636–37, 842, 846–47, 1043, 1056, 1088, 1097, 1284; **3:**271, 939, 1068, 1161; **4:**286, 628, 891, 1241; **5:**480, 528, 598, 655; **6:**10, 117, 278, 359, 419, 584, 647, 786, 794, 815, 849, 874–75, 1276, 1278, 1335, 1338, 1393, 1460; **7:**641; **8:**394, 693; **9:**21, 65–66, 91–92, 105–6, 125, 156, 163, 186, 485–86, 525, 624, 687, 741, 791, 835, 845; **10:**20, 24, 43, 57, 151–52, 154, 161, 164, 171, 174–75, 208, 234, 247, 261, 292, 321, 494, 636, 660, 739, 799, 815; **11:**28, 36, 58–59, 65, 115, 117, 124, 130, 157, 168, 227, 285–86, 304, 484, 545, 558, 613; **12:**71, 75, 80–81, 125, 131, 265, 338, 340, 357, 375, 408, 423, 442
CONFISCATE (*OR* CONFISCATES, CONFISCATION, *ETC.*)
1:579, 900; **2:**657, 1029, 1273–74; **3:**159, 722, 742, 920; **4:**34, 105, 125, 207–8; **5:**612; **6:**1400, 1582, 1590; **11:**305; **12:**9, 42, 77
CONGREGATION
1:3, 46, 200–204, 206–8, 211, 696–98, 813, 1032, 1035, 1037, 1060, 1066–67, 1072, 1097–98, 1163; **2:**15, 33–35, 39–40, 48, 50–51, 60, 64–66, 68–69, 77, 79–81, 86–87, 89, 95–96, 123–24, 127, 130, 135–36, 138–41, 151, 153, 160, 197, 199, 214, 248, 265, 268, 366, 587, 601, 641–42, 697, 708, 1003, 1267; **3:**447, 501, 538, 608–11, 687, 693, 747, 783, 800–801, 828, 938; **4:**64, 72, 107, 165, 243, 519, 697, 764–65, 769, 783, 785, 792, 796, 869, 881, 900, 917, 937, 975, 1066, 1078, 1133, 1145–46, 1150, 1216, 1223, 1280; **5:**268–69, 828, 837, 859; **6:**60, 68, 148, 221, 628, 637, 920, 1134, 1206, 1451, 1574; **7:**245, 508, 515, 561, 565, 675; **8:**38, 95, 311, 346, 375, 378–80, 431; **9:**86, 92, 112, 287, 360, 554, 671, 778, 811; **10:**9, 19, 28, 42, 52, 68, 78, 99, 114–15, 132–33, 139, 155, 161, 171, 175–77, 181–82, 189, 191, 194, 201–2, 204–7, 210–11, 215, 218, 220, 223, 225, 227, 230–31, 238, 252–54, 256, 258, 261, 263, 267,

CONGREGATION *(continued)*
277, 285–86, 293, 295, 299, 347, 377–80, 391, 697, 777, 788, 804, 814, 818, 823, 836, 846, 857–58, 869, 873, 875, 879, 882, 885, 893, 916, 923, 934, 943, 950, 960, 967, 970, 993; **11:**5, 25, 83, 133, 209, 230, 243, 245, 253, 297, 309, 317, 332, 345, 372, 386, 459–61, 480, 567, 594, 682–83, 824, 853, 878, 892–93; **12:**12, 24, 48, 52, 59, 68, 71, 77–78, 80, 125–28, 137, 149, 151, 153, 155, 158, 161–69, 171, 173, 195, 200, 219, 288, 310, 328, 406, 408, 431, 433, 455–56, 464, 482, 485; CHRISTIAN **4:**883; **5:**327; **6:**113; **8:**180, 379; **10:**172, 235, 257, 261, 281, 371, 422; **12:**396; ENTIRE/WHOLE **1:**210, 1006, 1035, 1039, 1071, 1165–66; **2:**33, 49, 81, 89, 127, 138, 141, 159, 217, 249, 707; **3:**713, 804; **4:**7, 1217; **5:**664; **6:**1534; **9:**489; **10:**55, 115, 212, 363, 380, 778; **11:**731, 879; **12:**55, 449; OF ISRAEL/THE ISRAELITES **1:**960, 999, 1005–6, 1071; **2:**26, 36, 47, 81, 89, 94, 124, 135, 138, 153, 220, 229, 249; **4:**1231; **6:**1534; **10:**363, 848; LOCAL **1:**59, 202; **3:**539; **4:**758; **8:**378; **10:**113, 177, 224, 263; **11:**21, 599, 603; **12:**449

CONQUEST
1:164, 175, 197, 250, 308, 441, 804, 820, 877, 1189; **2:**8–9, 19–20, 120–23, 126, 158–59, 161–63, 165–67, 181–82, 192, 207, 220, 248–50, 252, 255–56, 291, 299, 307, 310, 343, 487, 511, 520, 541, 543, 552, 559–60, 563–64, 575, 585, 600, 607, 611, 626–27, 636–37, 639–40, 646, 648–49, 654–55, 661–62, 665, 668, 673, 681, 696, 706, 711, 715, 717, 735–37, 747–48, 752, 865, 871, 885, 886, 969, 1023, 1055, 1205, 1238–40, 1266, 1289, 1355; **3:**101, 151, 332, 346, 353, 355, 377, 384, 569, 678, 730, 782, 810–11, 827, 829, 1106, 1144, 1165; **4:**18, 30, 81, 869, 945, 999–1000, 1035, 1228; **5:**21, 45, 159, 162, 194, 261, 536, 542, 695, 862; **6:**174, 186, 584, 628, 655, 741, 758, 762, 783, 842, 858, 866, 876, 932, 943–46, 1347, 1437; **7:**23, 26, 30, 34, 44, 58, 62, 66, 72, 81, 90, 102, 112–13, 122, 145–46, 151, 178, 187, 357, 361, 399, 454, 456, 550, 594, 638, 699, 738, 797, 823; **8:**62, 130, 142, 328, 426, 670; **9:**437, 844; **10:**975; **11:**343, 471; **12:**398–99, 435, 457, 576, 583, 587, 609, 611, 642, 657, 667, 696, 714; ALEXANDER'S **1:**247; **3:**878; **7:**26; OF CANAAN **1:**248, 253–55, 307, 689, 875; **2:**248, 555–56, 571, 620, 634, 646–47, 670, 724, 726, 728, 731–33, 735–36, 745, 747–48, 752, 816; **3:**4, 1115, 1119, 1172; **7:**455, 550; ISRAELITE **1:**175, 253–54; **2:**285, 393, 746, 749; OF JERICHO **2:**300, 308, 562, 590, 620, 803; **12:**140, 142; OF THE LAND **1:**438, 949; **2:**161, 165, 266, 352, 376, 481, 565, 584, 723; **4:**84, 944; **5:**631; **12:**53, 142; NARRATIVE/STORY (STORIES) **1:**314; **2:**10, 255, 257, 556, 562, 577, 588, 593, 606, 625, 630, 655, 684, 691, 706, 715, 870

CONSCIENCE
1:568, 629, 893, 990, 1025, 1040, 1067, 1128, 1134; **2:**405, 408, 442, 925; **3:**503, 1145; **4:**290, 523; **5:**237, 331, 584, 768, 801; **6:**763, 777, 852, 1053; **7:**94, 96, 616; **8:**136, 371, 695; **10:**320, 355, 400, 411, 442, 618, 673, 721, 732, 739–42, 744, 888, 920–23; **11:**45, 47, 49, 74, 91, 165, 243, 310, 438, 795, 811, 831, 866; **12:**74, 105–6, 108, 110, 113–15, 117, 121, 166, 281, 292, 295–96, 298, 423–24, 625, 646; CHRISTIAN **6:**787; **10:**627, 721; **11:**457; CLEAN/CLEAR **5:**13; **10:**309, 835, 921; **11:**791, 807, 833; **12:**169, 291; GUILTY **1:**1060; **5:**584; **7:**718; **10:**322; INDIVIDUAL **1:**53, 55; **2:**492; **11:**218; WEAK **1:**1121; **10:**733, 899; **11:**105

CONSECRATE (*OR* CONSECRATES, *ETC.*)
1:277, 542, 907, 912, 976, 989, 1045, 1048, 1062, 1066, 1070, 1099, 1135, 1158, 1166, 1171–72, 1188; **2:**47, 51, 65, 80–81, 106, 247, 307, 332, 845, 870; **3:**80, 437, 467, 542, 580, 602, 609–10, 656, 768, 1112, 1154; **4:**55, 197, 1214; **6:**156, 562, 580, 588, 740, 1284, 1568–69, 1605; **7:**272, 680, 727; **9:**69, 794; **10:**45, 189, 215, 258, 281, 293, 311, 683; **11:**58, 215, 532, 606, 649, 812, 815, 845; **12:**64

CONSECRATION
1:209, 785, 905, 912, 998, 1003, 1015, 1017, 1020, 1039, 1044, 1046, 1052, 1056–57, 1059–62, 1066–67, 1099, 1139, 1158–59, 1166, 1188–89, 1191; **2:**47, 64, 80–81, 92, 307, 403, 528, 845, 847, 870, 1012; **3:**610–11; **4:**1214; **6:**548, 640, 1107, 1110, 1491, 1565, 1567–69, 1578, 1585; **7:**455, 678, 727; **9:**88, 354, 461, 793–94; **10:**14, 36, 213, 215, 294; **11:**802; **12:**39, 404, 407

CONSOLATION
1:69, 99; **2:**833; **3:**33; **4:**331, 382, 450, 457–58, 491, 494, 520, 629, 867, 1059; **5:**474, 487, 764; **6:**339, 485–86, 804, 932, 958, 971, 979, 1045, 1438; **7:**94, 262, 599, 813; **8:**178, 577; **9:**25, 70–71, 73, 179, 445, 478, 738–39, 770; **10:**170, 517, 823, 960; **11:**3, 33, 40–42, 54, 101, 109, 111, 499, 520, 686, 688, 700, 706, 709, 712, 723–27, 753; **12:**402, 416, 423, 631, 646; BOOK OF CONSOLATION **6:**563, 568, 572, 744, 797, 811, 819, 1530; OF ISRAEL **6:**339; **8:**178; **9:**70–71, 73, 445, 478; POEM OF CONSOLATION **6:**930–32, 934, 937, 939, 971, 973, 978

CONSTELLATION, CONSTELLATIONS
1:213, 219, 226; **6:**377, 396, 1285; **9:**610, 787,

794, 863; **10:**215, 808; **12:**418, 511; STELLAR **2:**569; **4:**410, 598, 605; **5:**547; **6:**156, 412; **7:**389

CONSUL
4:102, 104–5, 169

CONSUMPTION
AS A DISEASE **1:**1149, 1180; **6:**1153; AS AN ACT OF USING **1:**67, 219, 224–25, 539, 852, 923, 1049; **2:**13, 398, 1030; **3:**820; **4:**199; **5:**166, 312, 849; **6:**628, 712, 1153, 1196, 1501, 1580, 1582; **7:**40, 44, 187; **8:**649; **9:**256, 316; **10:**7, 250; **12:**401, 477, 634, 639, 686, 693

CONTENTMENT
2:1350; **4:**471, 1261; **5:**86, 150, 211; **11:**544, 548, 588, 827–28; **12:**163

CONTRIBUTION, CONTRIBUTIONS
AS OFFERING, OFTEN MONETARY **1:**218, 260, 1054; **2:**570, 1377; **3:**52, 232, 300, 379–80, 438, 447, 467, 469, 478, 487, 613, 618, 624, 645, 648, 687, 721–22, 728–31, 794, 820, 841–42, 844, 846–47, 850–51, 993, 1018; **5:**242, 625, 631, 717; **6:**1290, 1584, 1593, 1600, 1604–6; **7:**206; **8:**371; **10:**996; **11:**112, 116, 118, 124, 175, 483, 520, 543, 633, 720

CONTRITE
1:1174; **2:**825; **4:**887, 1042; **5:**121; **6:**380, 492, 502, 514; **7:**162, 295

CONVERSION
OF CORNELIUS **7:**700; **9:**155; **10:**15, 146, 149, 160, 162–63, 164, 168–71, 203, 206–8, 363; **11:**251; OF THE ETHIOPIAN EUNUCH **3:**1168; **10:**134–35, 140, 142, 144–45; FORCED **1:**270; **3:**1078, 1125, 1127; OF PAUL/SAUL **10:**35, 130, 132, 146–47, 149–55, 176, 293, 306–9, 314, 333–34, 337, 342–43, 373, 375, 415, 460, 480, 530, 585, 653, 718; **11:**193, 243, 394, 412, 531, 785, 790, 796; **12:**518, 522, 735; RELIGIOUS **1:**93, 155, 175, 568, 624, 776, 1164; **2:**193, 753; **3:**192, 195, 966, 1062, 1078, 1119, 1127, 1168–69; **4:**1151; **5:**49, 61, 135, 246, 484, 536, 541–42, 544, 557, 562, 575, 595, 721; **6:**181, 607, 1408; **7:**56, 72, 77, 145, 193–94, 263, 281, 286–87, 328, 428–29, 469, 488, 500, 513, 669, 698–700; **8:**17, 23, 29, 46, 177, 217, 239, 261, 392, 399, 418, 444, 533; **9:**46, 118, 554, 765; **10:**14, 35–36, 59, 67, 70, 73, 79, 81, 83, 130, 132, 134, 140, 155, 162, 175, 188, 190, 205–8, 226, 230, 235–36, 243, 245–46, 249, 254, 256, 269, 271, 338, 341, 481, 533, 550, 564, 604, 688, 825, 917, 975; **11:**69, 104, 163, 204, 215, 220, 253, 272, 285, 287, 362, 364, 367, 375, 381, 387, 389, 392, 394, 400, 403, 405, 419–20, 428, 430–31, 435, 437, 446, 625, 680, 695, 719, 796, 859, 876–77, 885; **12:**182, 184, 204, 208–10, 212–15, 221, 283, 294, 334, 336–38, 353, 476, 534, 549, 712

CONVICTION, CONVICTIONS
BASIC/CORE/FUNDAMENTAL **1:**148; **2:**505, 642; **4:**468, 675, 848; **6:**164, 407, 946; **8:**353; **10:**5, 10, 38, 101, 133, 143, 167, 249, 277, 381, 384, 735, 842, 930, 935; **11:**22, 166, 608, 856; RELIGIOUS **1:**86, 539; **2:**445, 1066; **3:**58; **4:**250; **5:**759; **6:**110, 161; **7:**830; **8:**689; **9:**379; **10:**234; **11:**219, 619; **12:**179, 467; THEOLOGICAL **1:**190, 328, 537, 872; **2:**467; **3:**532; **5:**790; **9:**611, 625, 743; **10:**26, 31, 167, 226, 235, 342, 371, 377, 380–81, 388, 631, 930; **12:**277

CONVOCATION
1:1156, 1179; **2:**232–33, 236, 492; **3:**801

COOK (*OR* COOKS, *ETC.*)
1:521, 1017, 1019–20, 1048–49; **2:**1029; **3:**647, 1057; **4:**240; **5:**8, 230; **6:**386, 388, 1299, 1333–37; **7:**257; **8:**436; **10:**712

COOKING
UTENSILS/VESSELS **1:**1082, 1104; **6:**549, 1186, 1333–34, 1336; **7:**839; **12:**108. *See also* UTENSILS

COPPER
1:215, 1019; **2:**12; **4:**529; **5:**328, 567, 570, 715; **6:**1312, 1334, 1336, 1338, 1371; **7:**161, 362; **8:**104, 682; **9:**21, 24, 171, 193, 252, 269, 336, 363, 395

COPPERSMITH
11:857

COR
See WEIGHTS AND MEASURES

CORBAN
8:606, 645

CORD, CORDS
1:605; **2:**40, 128, 588, 594, 685, 1266, 1366; **4:**622, 682, 689, 1202–3; **5:**316, 355–56, 579, 689; **6:**1002, 1137, 1141, 1145, 1538, 1596; **7:**857; **9:**285

CORINTHIANS
1:14, 160; **4:**888; **8:**553, 677, 702, 705; **9:**153, 220, 310; **10:**254, 256, 321, 377; **11:**211, 253, 310, 315, 369, 404, 423, 452, 480, 504, 534, 543, 614, 814, 891; **12:**4, 10, 578, 615; 1 CORINTHIANS **1:**133, 156, 182, 804; **2:**609; **4:**888; **5:**814; **8:**703, 732; **9:**421, 468, 485; **10:**252–53, 292, 373, 513, 521, 535, 709–10; **11:**201, 234, 423–24, 603, 775, 783; **12:**4, 192, 287, 304, 409, 530, 560, 708; 2 CORINTHIANS **3:**469; **5:**176; **7:**785; **8:**20; **10:**252–53, 259, 373, 380, 550, 555, 560–61, 598, 602, 607, 617, 626, 718, 732, 752, 756, 759; **11:**222, 227, 334, 459, 479, 487, 577, 587; **12:**232; 1 AND 2 CORINTHIANS **1:**8, 13; **10:**215, 761; **11:**354, 489, 883

CORN
1:1071; **2:**838; **7:**314; **8:**138

CORNERSTONE
1:1124; **2:**477; **4:**811; **5:**263; **7:**729, 814; **8:**670–71; **9:**72, 382, 384; **10:**89, 342; **11:**150, 396, 402; **12:**24, 237, 256, 265–66, 268, 312, 701, 722

CORRECTION, CORRECTIONS
DIVINE/BY WISDOM **4:**375–76, 381, 383, 463, 569; **5:**41, 103, 124, 139, 149, 152, 167; **6:**127, 547, 602, 619, 629, 631, 638–39, 653, 655, 664, 670, 692, 722, 769; **7:**249, 664–65, 671, 693, 695–97; **8:**58–60; **9:**783, 803; **10:**80, 289; **11:**311; **12:**151; MUTUAL/SELF **10:**936–37, 939; **11:**287, 311, 331–32, 334, 338, 443; **12:**223–24; SCRIBAL/TEXTUAL **1:**1, 25, 132, 295; **2:**678, 718; **3:**424, 688; **4:**562; **5:**182; **6:**567–68, 792, 1337; **7:**424, 442; **8:**515; **9:**560, 783; **11:**286, 601, 684; TIME OF **12:**105–6

CORRELATION
1:67, 86, 143, 147; **2:**743; **3:**523, 571; **4:**304, 493, 801, 964; **5:**93, 99, 237, 341, 530, 534, 542, 565, 659, 702, 768; **6:**6, 312, 449, 467, 527, 608, 641, 647, 715, 788, 1253, 1339; **7:**486; **8:**22, 83, 433, 671, 684; **9:**80, 144, 351; **10:**372, 941; **11:**143, 846–47, 862, 871; **12:**146, 290

CORRUPTION
1:390, 394, 750, 828, 1018, 1021, 1085, 1143; **2:**298, 420, 423, 494, 866, 949, 957, 960, 966, 969–70, 977, 986–87, 994, 997, 1017, 1023, 1026, 1030; **3:**370, 832, 860, 894, 951, 966; **4:**312, 412, 481, 488, 517, 724, 731; **5:**140, 160, 174, 243, 351, 381, 549, 552, 559, 672; **6:**47, 57–58, 60, 72, 82, 94, 134, 142–43, 161, 610, 627, 629–30, 684, 750, 755, 958, 982, 1210, 1236, 1314–15, 1432, 1444, 1566; **7:**147, 175, 181–82, 184, 189, 200, 213, 236, 254, 256, 267, 275, 417, 534, 624, 631, 693–94, 729, 774, 776, 781, 792, 848, 862; **8:**309, 537, 608, 720; **9:**53, 85, 127, 241, 247–48, 251, 309, 312, 364, 373; **10:**193, 399, 431–32, 500–501, 504, 511, 525–26, 538, 588, 596, 604, 606, 851, 924, 987; **11:**203, 337–40, 678, 847; **12:**215, 219, 330–31, 336–38, 340, 347–48, 351–53, 358, 361, 516, 533, 535, 538, 644, 712; TEXTUAL **1:**297, 301; **2:**135; **6:**670, 762, 782, 859; **7:**667; **9:**557

COSMETIC, COSMETICS
1:600; **2:**324; **3:**885, 888–89, 1086, 1143, 1147; **4:**635; **5:**80, 194, 388; **7:**224; **9:**151; **12:**284

COSMOGONY, COSMOGONIC
4:367–68, 410, 487, 519, 591, 604; **5:**9–11, 663; **6:**343, 345; **12:**596

COSMOLOGY, COSMOLOGICAL
1:49, 56, 84; **2:**36, 39, 49, 60, 415; **4:**441, 595–96, 598, 794, 823, 1096, 1220; **5:**10, 26, 138, 293, 430, 647; **7:**4, 839; **8:**250, 580, 584–85, 723–24; **9:**411, 519, 525; **10:**699; **11:**377–78, 382, 385, 390–91, 393, 396, 414–15, 421, 438, 565, 567–68, 579, 618, 622, 627, 632, 638; **12:**94, 436, 531, 596, 634

COSMOS
1:76, 321, 356, 647, 760; **2:**886, 982; **3:**810, 956; **4:**314, 336, 371, 420–21, 427–28, 496, 508, 516–20, 528–29, 533, 535, 557, 597, 601–2, 614, 626, 752–53, 867, 906, 964, 974, 1007, 1052, 1061, 1069, 1097, 1142, 1181, 1271–72; **5:**10, 12, 15, 25–26, 64, 85, 89, 91, 93, 101–4, 149, 159, 186, 217, 294, 331, 442, 448, 451, 455–56, 465, 486–87, 503–6, 516, 522–23, 526, 530, 532, 557, 562, 577–78, 593–94, 596, 729, 759, 817, 834; **6:**142, 159, 276, 588, 717, 751, 812, 826, 962, 1007, 1395; **7:**2–3, 9, 11, 198, 317, 334, 421, 478, 504, 654, 785, 837; **8:**37, 732; **10:**244, 426, 598, 618–19, 936, 994; CHAOS AND **1:**342; **2:**886, 982; **4:**410, 487, 518, 520, 597, 747, 772, 974, 1096–97; **5:**25, 294, 834; **7:**654; **12:**634; ENTIRE/WHOLE **1:**368, 477, 504; **4:**410, 531, 669, 1066, 1069, 1079, 1224–25; **6:**213, 229, 375, 454; **7:**317, 422; **8:**23, 692; **10:**478, 495, 511, 589, 596, 607; **11:**23, 378, 386, 416, 420; FORCES OF THE **5:**442, 456, 486–87, 526, 532, 577–78, 594; **8:**561; **11:**410, 420; ORDER AND **1:**179, 281, 319, 337, 342–43, 356, 396, 504; **4:**336–37, 421, 487, 496, 597, 747, 752–53, 772, 1066, 1069, 1096–97, 1142; **5:**10, 31, 89, 93–95, 97, 101, 103–4, 107, 159, 210, 442, 504, 562, 729, 834; **6:**812, 826–27; **7:**654, 785, 837; **11:**378, 415, 636; **12:**634, 687; ORIGIN AND **1:**179, 337; **4:**518, 1224–26; **5:**88, 94–95, 210, 455, 460, 503, 506, 577; **12:**596; WISDOM AND **4:**528, 531, 533, 601–2; **5:**10, 31, 85, 88–89, 91, 93–94, 101–4, 107, 210, 331, 442, 448, 456, 486–87, 503–6, 516, 522–23, 526, 530, 532, 562, 578, 594; **11:**374, 415, 605, 636; **12:**521

COTTON
2:595

COUCH, COUCHES
AS FURNITURE **1:**1230; **3:**919; **5:**387–88, 613; **6:**1230, 1329–30, 1443; **7:**375; **9:**730

COUNSEL
1:41, 90, 240, 420, 763–64; **2:**190, 549, 749, 878, 1011, 1259, 1325–26, 1330–32; **3:**282, 294, 458, 518, 570–71, 577, 587, 916, 1063, 1120; **4:**51, 236, 287, 347, 424, 428–29, 450, 483, 502, 517, 538, 601, 686, 811, 938, 1010, 1116; **5:**44, 55, 91, 127, 147, 158, 181, 190, 195, 206, 211, 230, 328, 334, 491, 510, 605, 682, 693, 740, 749, 758, 775, 784, 787–88, 805–6, 812, 825; **6:**109, 141, 180–81, 238, 244, 262, 342, 366, 396, 404, 412, 529, 560, 716, 793, 841, 851–52,

916, 1168, 1186; **7:**605, 655, 662, 664, 751, 787; **8:**189, 222, 351, 382, 420, 646; **9:**148, 212, 232, 286, 386, 771; **10:**379, 441, 793, 852, 871–72, 878; **11:**107, 285, 335, 337, 339, 437, 546, 801–2, 806–7, 815, 818, 823–24, 828, 847, 864, 869–70, 875; **12:**288, 388, 393, 395, 408, 410, 430, 444, 454, 583, 587; OF GOD **2:**178; **4:**424, 596, 601, 737; **5:**122, 227, 518; **6:**253, 407, 792; **8:**532; **10:**281; OF PAUL **10:**846, 848–49, 869–75, 877–78, 880–81, 883–85, 887, 891–93, 917–18, 921, 923, 941, 949, 972; **11:**10, 16, 107, 124, 130, 134, 199, 216, 311, 322, 329–31, 338–39, 546, 777, 866; WISE **2:**1304; **3:**577, 916, 1118; **4:**51, 540; **5:**30, 118, 129, 190, 242, 510

COUNSELOR, COUNSELORS
1:644, 915; **2:**1320; **3:**150, 452, 518, 530, 570, 577, 580, 721, 723, 953, 1077, 1158–59; **4:**458, 539, 589, 1169; **5:**92–95, 122, 172, 275, 586, 604, 626, 805, 833, 837; **6:**60–61, 180–81, 357; **7:**52, 62–63, 72, 82, 92, 245, 567, 693–94, 754; **9:**747, 775; **10:**43; **11:**880; **12:**55

COUNCIL, COUNCILS
1:7, 12, 14, 16, 19, 52, 100–101, 222, 273, 579, 748; **2:**629, 658, 1331; **3:**217, 456, 458, 1114, 1123, 1137; **4:**6, 51, 71, 161, 182, 191, 243, 281, 450, 779, 1006, 1066; **5:**55, 62, 311, 448; **6:**328, 334, 752, 754, 1367; **7:**444, 751; **8:**259, 480–81; **9:**14, 18, 147, 161, 201, 370, 401, 442–43, 448, 465, 696; **10:**89–91, 101, 104–8, 122, 131, 168–69, 176, 178, 204–5, 207–9, 212, 217–19, 221, 225, 239, 245–46, 259, 309–10, 312, 315, 318, 894; **11:**194, 221, 225, 228, 397, 825; **12:**277, 486, 597; COUNCIL OF CHURCHES **1:**24, 60; COUNCIL OF JAMNIA **1:**8–9, 11, 306; **5:**634; **8:**98; COUNCIL OF JERUSALEM **1:**1121; **3:**1078, 1154; **4:**223; **5:**448; **8:**46, 717; **10:**8, 32, 35–36, 59, 65, 88, 147, 169, 175–76, 193, 202–3, 205–12, 214–15, 217, 222, 224–26, 252, 254, 258, 291–94, 373; **11:**193; COUNCIL OF NICAEA **1:**7, 305; COUNCIL OF TRENT **1:**5, 12–13, 16–17, 52, 60, 100; **5:**448, 635; **8:**6; **9:**847; DIVINE/HEAVENLY **1:**240, 277–78, 345, 352, 384, 412–13; **3:**164, 422, 552, 810; **4:**347, 351, 461, 792–93, 1035, 1093; **6:**5, 10, 19, 93, 103–4, 319, 327, 329, 330–31, 332, 334, 336–37, 341, 343, 345, 349, 352, 355, 359, 361, 363–64, 375, 387, 390, 393, 423, 429, 441, 448, 453, 455, 476, 515, 547, 575, 582, 588, 751–52, 755, 852, 1129, 1208, 1513; **7:**103, 137, 444; OF ELDERS **9:**111, 442; **10:**282, 306; **11:**814; SECOND VATICAN COUNCIL **1:**1, 20, 61, 100, 198, 202, 205; **3:**1019; **4:**72; **12:**444

COURAGE
1:152, 186, 624, 666, 680, 682, 691, 719, 740, 763, 765, 817, 933, 940, 949; **3:**381, 418, 431, 520, 538, 543, 561, 629, 723, 783, 869, 901, 906, 918, 920, 959, 983, 1005, 1009, 1023–24, 1040, 1042, 1049, 1090, 1129–30, 1139; **4:**16, 58, 241–42, 248, 258, 266, 290, 436, 445, 504, 579, 612, 723, 749, 785, 787, 802–3, 839, 903, 1070, 1170, 1193, 1253; **5:**211, 291, 294, 327, 419, 510, 674–75, 687, 693, 860; **6:**119, 183, 238, 281, 283, 358, 503, 613, 974, 977–82, 1067, 1253, 1264, 1305, 1311; **7:**21, 31, 42, 53, 96, 102, 125, 129, 138, 144, 175, 183, 207–8, 555, 632, 713, 722–23, 725, 796; **8:**263, 328, 495; **9:**334, 401, 738, 783–85; **10:**101, 109, 311, 349–50, 357, 519, 661; **11:**84, 207, 355, 412, 488, 493, 516–17, 635, 698–99, 761, 901; **12:**46, 55, 140, 254, 295, 297, 318, 401, 599, 722

COURIER, COURIERS
3:602, 925; **5:**812; **7:**164; **12:**384, 465

COURT, COURTS
1:189, 223, 233, 241, 247, 270, 459, 593, 609, 615, 622, 689, 725, 739, 767, 772, 828, 851, 866, 869, 874, 898, 900–901, 916, 960, 972, 1035, 1037, 1041; **2:**52–53, 379, 435, 560–61, 567, 576, 585, 602, 637, 649, 657–58, 660, 682, 687–89, 749, 953, 956, 962–63, 1095, 1118, 1121, 1126, 1145, 1217, 1225, 1262, 1303, 1315, 1319, 1326; **3:**3, 18, 45, 51–52, 54, 162, 164, 381, 423, 456, 460, 502, 552, 554, 556, 720, 753, 861–64, 866–67, 870, 874, 877–79, 882–83, 887–90, 892, 894, 899, 905, 908, 911, 916, 918, 931, 941, 949–50, 960, 994, 996, 1098, 1118, 1147; **4:**109, 116, 163, 212, 240, 260, 269, 327, 363, 410, 421, 697, 820, 861, 1125; **5:**1, 5–6, 10–11, 20, 30, 143, 145, 193, 199, 205–6, 213, 215, 218–19, 222, 245, 271, 322, 334–35, 339, 359, 698, 783, 859; **6:**52, 63, 78, 88, 95, 109, 180, 183, 247, 284, 433, 485, 598, 600, 602, 606, 619, 621, 657, 716, 739–42, 745, 751, 773, 775, 807, 811, 839, 848, 850–51, 898, 943, 956, 1041, 1072, 1134, 1176, 1198, 1208, 1307, 1402, 1563; **7:**19–21, 28, 36–37, 39, 42, 44, 49–53, 62–63, 81, 88, 94, 103, 139, 144, 150–51, 175, 180, 184, 200, 213, 224, 234, 252, 254, 256–57, 260, 329–30, 388, 416, 612, 694; **8:**15, 18, 100, 190–91, 195, 259, 267, 279, 321, 405, 482, 559–60, 597–99, 646, 674, 688–89, 696, 700, 712, 714, 720; **9:**249, 259, 268–71, 309, 345, 395, 442, 588, 634, 820; **10:**95, 109, 124, 129, 194, 214, 233–34, 239, 256, 273, 289, 297, 313, 326, 330, 333, 366, 399–400, 458–59, 614, 623, 738, 777, 785, 834, 856, 858, 943, 947; **11:**7, 11, 265, 382, 625, 858; **12:**192, 422, 424, 432, 522, 684; CASE(S) **1:**870; **2:**832–33; **4:**435; **5:**173, 218; **7:**330, 334; **8:**195; **10:**122, 255, 853, 868; OF DAVID **1:**242; **2:**281, 558–60, 602, 628, 967, 1256, 1347–48; **3:**13, 22, 50; DIVINE **1:**241–42; **2:**602, 831; **4:**347–48; **5:**757;

COURT, COURTS *(continued)*
7:73, 677–78, 767; **12:**158, 592; DOCUMENTS **1:**233; **3:**13, 358; **7:**50; FOREIGN **3:**870, 888; **5:**231; **7:**53, 139, 144; HEAVENLY **1:**345, 382, 890; **3:**552; **4:**347, 773; **5:**95, 122, 133, 208; **6:**101–3, 336, 362–63, 455; **7:**5, 9–10, 65, 105, 632, 663, 765, 771, 861; **8:**163, 691–92; **9:**252; **10:**854; **11:**490, 493, 823; **12:**521; HIGH(ER) **1:**828; **3:**50, 556; HISTORY/HISTORIAN **2:**953, 956, 963; **3:**13; **5:**1; **9:**259; INNER **2:**1113; **3:**485, 496, 704; **4:**99; **6:**1175, 1177–79, 1183, 1533–34, 1544–45, 1548, 1557, 1560, 1566, 1570, 1577–79, 1588–89, 1591; **7:**320; **9:**399; OF LAW **2:**336, 526, 696, 934, 938; **3:**46, 422, 555; **5:**24, 77, 127, 149, 172, 176, 213, 242; **6:**16, 90, 296, 585, 598; **7:**417, 663, 675, 677, 703; **8:**211; **9:**304; **10:**88, 345; **11:**98, 237; **12:**15, 131, 217, 568, 729; OFFICIAL(S)/OFFICER(S) **1:**614; **2:**1038, 1268, 1354; **3:**18, 50, 556, 870, 886; **4:**881; **6:**128, 560, 944; **7:**44, 63, 618, 670; **10:**143; OPEN/OUTER **1:**1034–35, 1147; **2:**50, 54, 633; **3:**496–97, 580; **4:**71; **6:**1106, 1175, 1533, 1542, 1544, 1557–58, 1569–70, 1578–79, 1588–89, 1591, 1597; PERSIAN (*see under* PERSIAN); ROMAN (*see under* ROMAN); ROYAL **1:**224, 248; **2:**292, 419, 639, 1274, 1319; **3:**32, 54, 560, 676, 695, 892, 1159; **4:**44, 135, 214; **5:**4–5, 7, 22, 121–22, 215, 217, 222; **6:**8, 108, 175, 194, 839, 850; **7:**44, 256–57, 263, 301, 670, 753; **8:**643; **9:**737; **12:**521; OF SAUL **2:**966, 1094, 1097, 1101, 1103, 1108, 1132, 1135, 1138, 1140, 1224; TEMPLE **3:**345, 442, 485, 495, 561, 575, 580–81, 599, 607–9, 647–48, 768; **4:**99; **6:**634, 722; **8:**408, 439; **9:**542–43, 632; **11:**703

COURTYARD, COURTYARDS
1:216, 218, 224, 634, 1010, 1033, 1040, 1044–45, 1048, 1061, 1066, 1070, 1072, 1112, 1118; **2:**52–53, 77, 934; **3:**913, 1049; **4:**11, 291; **6:**925, 996, 1534; **8:**479, 481, 539, 552, 712; **9:**12, 37, 117, 169, 236, 253, 437–38, 441–42, 632, 808–9, 841; **10:**77, 106, 894

COUSIN, COUSINS
1:176, 511, 537, 1181; **2:**737, 921, 930, 935, 1081, 1108, 1212; **3:**522, 868–69, 884, 889, 903, 916, 940; **5:**428; **7:**544; **8:**318; **9:**51; **10:**191, 225, 611, 685, 697; **11:**667; **12:**455

COVENANT
WITH ABRAHAM **1:**458, 527, 584, 988, 1082, 1181–82; **2:**20, 608; **3:**337; **4:**66, 188, 582, 1104–5; **5:**473; **6:**355, 362, 366, 1154, 1238; **7:**864; **9:**21, 84; **10:**402, 413, 464, 466, 482, 484, 490, 494, 555, 655, 699; **11:**76, 263–66, 302; **12:**110; ARK OF THE **1:**277, 999, 1007, 1012, 1033, 1066, 1113; **2:**21, 79, 94, 96, 98, 140, 328, 365, 599, 960, 969, 995, 999, 1001, 1005–6, 1013, 1015, 1148, 1236–37, 1324; **3:**69–70, 150, 393, 395, 400, 406, 461, 496, 606, 993; **4:**34, 78; **6:**453, 575, 891, 925, 1118, 1179, 1183, 1349, 1560, 1575; **7:**272, 722; **8:**364; **10:**474; **12:**58, 104, 644, 672; BOOK OF THE COVENANT **1:**37, 286, 861, 880–81, 1115, 1156; **2:**128, 273, 277, 379–80, 386, 420, 493; **3:**285, 646, 747; **4:**881; **5:**12, 14, 962, 968; CODE (*see under* CODE); COMMUNITY **1:**39–40, 813, 851, 870–71, 875; **2:**328, 460, 463, 863, 942, 1022, 1029–31, 1064, 1280, 1294, 1354; **3:**137, 987; **5:**207, 339; **6:**389, 783, 918, 1574; **7:**320, 662–64, 699; **8:**269, 292, 311, 380, 671; **9:**69, 75, 336, 619, 645, 656; **10:**25, 77, 83, 142, 167, 205, 209, 212, 307; **11:**239, 246, 345, 442; **12:**162; CONDITIONAL (SUZERAINTY) **2:**1262; **11:**76; WITH DAVID **1:**447; **2:**147, 962, 1090, 1120, 1223, 1233, 1371; **3:**95, 239, 304, 395, 406–8, 461, 464, 496, 498–500, 529–30, 565, 575; **4:**660, 1040, 1074, 1081, 1104, 1255, 1271; **5:**553, 843; **6:**22, 464, 482–83, 527, 739, 1268, 1461, 1470; **9:**391; **11:**76, 404; ETERNAL/PERPETUAL **1:**924; **2:**962; **3:**530; **5:**842–43, 849; **6:**502, 504, 821, 915, 1082, 1238, 1274, 1471–72; **7:**811; **10:**42; **11:**76; **12:**4, 172; EVERLASTING **1:**316, 401, 457; **2:**1370–72; **3:**408; **4:**888, 1105; **5:**843; **6:**210–11, 214, 336, 362, 477, 483, 502, 513, 915, 1461, 1469, 1530, 1569, 1577; **7:**319, 325, 334, 732, 809; **10:**831; **11:**76; FAMILY **1:**1042; **3:**609; **10:**410, 429, 467, 482, 484, 487, 493, 495, 503–4, 604; FORM(S)/FORM(S) OF/FORMULA **1:**276, 312, 723, 735, 830, 913, 950, 1023; **2:**20, 99, 612, 1061, 1120, 1262; **3:**568, 1040; **4:**880; **6:**669, 671, 715, 809, 812, 948, 1188, 1470, 1473, 1511; **7:**319, 761, 795, 810, 815, 833; **10:**550; **12:**673; WITH GOD/THE LORD/YAHWEH **1:**74, 76, 932, 947, 949, 1098; **2:**20, 79, 147, 278, 293, 319, 320, 350, 357–58, 363, 377, 482, 487, 681, 726–27, 729, 731, 744, 750, 752, 849, 863, 866, 1090, 1133, 1184, 1249, 1262, 1372; **3:**70, 72, 95, 393, 395, 406–7, 424, 461, 497, 512, 575, 1102; **4:**136, 188, 1134; **5:**33, 44; **6:**53, 361, 453, 485, 641, 758, 762, 815, 1076, 1118, 1215, 1250, 1315, 1415, 1471, 1517, 1519, 1574; **7:**39, 162, 198, 220, 223, 226, 252, 261, 270, 296, 548, 664, 683, 700, 809; **8:**30, 704; **9:**179, 383, 423; **10:**42, 54, 111, 209, 399, 426, 458–59, 461, 490, 494, 617; **11:**76, 132, 187, 246, 264, 276, 302, 316, 396, 403, 436, 451, 456, 529, 703, 790, 876; **12:**110, 158; WITH ISRAEL **1:**66, 316, 861, 927, 947, 1179; **2:**314–15, 327, 365, 482, 512, 612, 635, 749, 796, 1221; **3:**69–70, 72, 94, 304, 461, 497, 512, 575, 956, 1040; **5:**33; **6:**19–21, 815, 827, 1010, 1242, 1250, 1560; **7:**209–10, 215, 220, 227, 262, 675; **9:**45, 96, 345, 347, 349, 469, 542; **10:**398–99, 404, 428, 452, 458–59, 564, 568, 622; **11:**227, 258, 402, 844, 865; **12:**591; LAWSUIT (*see under* LAWSUIT); NEW

1:38, 285, 306, 317, 679, 681, 686, 893, 927, 951, 1086; **2:**511, 616, 642, 1030; **3:**617; **5:**46, 242; **6:**8, 19, 21, 257, 448, 451, 545, 671, 710, 812, 815–16, 950, 1085; **7:**226, 565, 798, 811; **8:**346, 399, 468, 653, 671, 704, 707; **9:**60, 420–21, 423, 427; **10:**54, 209, 406, 429, 442, 448–50, 453, 460, 483–84, 512, 545, 557, 560–61, 604, 614, 623, 625, 640, 649, 655, 660, 666–67, 671, 699; **11:**3, 14, 28, 34, 57, 61, 63–67, 72–73, 75, 81, 302, 307–8, 428, 459, 618; **12:**19, 100–101, 105, 107–10, 113–18, 120–23, 129, 156, 158, 166, 533, 713; WITH NOAH **1:**328–29, 332, 391–92, 398–402, 417, 446, 458, 941, 1076; **4:**608, 1272; **5:**621, 842; **6:**211, 214, 477; **7:**663, 665, 675, 696; **11:**76; **12:**592; OBLIGATION(S) **2:**747, 755, 843, 886, 1268, 1273–74; **6:**1084, 1122, 1152, 1189, 1248, 1254, 1296, 1331, 1458, 1484, 1491; **7:**859; **10:**400, 420, 429; **11:**227, 230, 258; OLD **1:**686, 706, 734, 955, 1062; **6:**671, 815; **8:**472; **11:**28, 64, 69, 302, 308; **12:**30, 100–102, 123, 158, 166, 568, 593; PEOPLE OF THE **1:**679, 933, 937; **2:**460, 1030–31, 1240; **3:**173, 413, 427, 497, 522, 576, 600, 615, 656–58; **4:**23, 71, 136, 184, 582; **5:**384, 390; **6:**257, 364, 451, 814, 872, 1218, 1338, 1415, 1487; **7:**319, 322–23, 366, 541, 544, 683–84, 762, 865; **8:**30, 33, 42, 291, 346, 356, 379, 471–72; **9:**59, 87, 227, 346; **10:**205, 405, 447, 449, 458–61, 471, 473, 481–82, 487, 495, 555, 611, 614, 623, 634, 638, 644, 655, 660; **11:**187, 236–37, 239, 313, 357, 403, 456, 460; **12:**493; RELATIONSHIP(S) **1:**38, 458, 1014, 1019; **2:**286, 320, 322, 328, 349–50, 365, 481, 749, 752, 768, 962, 1027, 1063, 1065, 1258, 1276, 1281; **3:**69, 80, 395, 496–98, 506; **6:**19, 361, 600, 618, 671, 808, 815, 1082, 1209, 1331, 1505, 1509, 1531, 1569, 1585, 1593; **7:**224, 313, 354, 662, 674, 860, 865; **10:**126, 220–21, 420, 646; **11:**75, 185, 255, 259, 261; **12:**92, 101, 154; SALT **1:**1018–19, 1021; **2:**78, 147; **3:**530, 699; **6:**1569; **8:**181, 640–41; SIGN OF THE **1:**400; **2:**603; **6:**214, 548, 1309; **10:**461, 494; **11:**396, 524; **12:**592; SINAI **1:**830, 839, 860; **2:**1255; **3:**1040; **6:**211, 1470, 1472–73; **7:**660, 663, 674–75, 683, 690, 864; **11:**303; **12:**110, 530; TERMS OF THE **1:**446; **2:**271, 276–77, 500; **3:**158; **12:**84; THEOLOGY **2:**350, 1254; **3:**77, 94, 1040; **6:**671; **7:**395; **10:**399, 449, 472, 494, 560–61, 671; **11:**844; **12:**127

COVERING, COVERINGS

AS A NOUN **1:**185, 483, 794, 889–91; **2:**53, 77, 79; **3:**1142; **4:**218, 518, 1236; **5:**262, 356; **6:**237, 1003, 1203, 1230, 1392; **7:**101, 779; **10:**263, 927–32, 934, 969; **12:**681, 723; AS A VERB OR GERUND *(esp. as hiding)* **1:**391, 405, 552, 746, 771, 794, 889–90, 1097; **2:**594; **3:**394, 484, 1142; **4:**518, 819, 1047; **5:**111, 127, 167, 179, 238, 355–56, 619, 775; **6:**196, 276, 389, 642, 1195, 1228, 1429, 1512, 1517; **7:**559; **10:**443, 758, 761; **11:**69; **12:**42, 223, 304

COVERLET, COVERLETS

6:1380

COVET (*OR* COVETS, COVETOUS, *ETC.*)

1:849, 852, 926, 950, 1133; **2:**321, 328, 335–36, 380, 423, 452, 669, 807, 865, 871, 1100; **3:**88, 155, 159, 430, 468, 479, 1017; **4:**170, 495, 534, 593; **5:**55–56, 64, 80, 232, 612; **6:**9, 1260, 1341, 1582; **7:**66, 178, 548, 550, 557; **9:**393; **10:**140, 263, 285–86, 562–63, 725; **11:**143, 435, 642, 645–46, 819, 827; **12:**77, 530, 669, 713

COW, COWS

1:225, 620–21, 771, 801, 949, 1025, 1066, 1081, 1118, 1149; **2:**148, 1012; **5:**715; **6:**82, 141, 883, 1149; **7:**242, 275, 374, 376; **9:**399; RED **2:**81, 151. *See also* BULL; CALF; CATTLE; HEIFER

CRAFT, CRAFTS

1:217; **2:**80, 620, 772, 808; **3:**28, 478, 1133; **4:**203, 414; **5:**92, 118, 205, 234, 502, 570, 702, 813; **6:**32, 73, 410, 661, 1275, 1304; **7:**226, 465, 596, 696; **8:**327; **10:**63; **11:**298, 741; **12:**694, 713

CRAFTSMAN, CRAFTSMEN

1:236, 921; **3:**329, 478, 480, 487; **5:**58, 281, 570; **6:**387, 990, 1004, 1078, 1081, 1293, 1360; **7:**31; **8:**14, 592, 640; **9:**502; **10:**271

CRAFTSMANSHIP

1:861; **5:**94; **6:**388, 393, 405; **9:**461

CREATION

ACCOUNT(S)/MYTH(S)/NARRATIVE(S)/STORY **1:**56, 74, 85, 182, 246, 316, 323, 336, 340–42, 344, 346, 349, 353–54, 409, 425, 430, 458, 720, 743, 845, 884, 1076; **2:**11, 39, 48, 229, 325, 398, 403, 529, 532, 542, 551, 600; **3:**1041; **4:**532, 602, 614, 626, 754, 810, 974, 1072, 1096, 1140, 1224, 1269; **5:**99, 102, 314, 454, 456, 504, 516, 519, 523, 621, 663, 757, 823; **6:**142, 212, 214, 225–26, 255, 343, 380, 395, 528–30, 758, 965, 1007, 1425, 1500, 1521; **7:**748, 865; **8:**386; **9:**519, 524–25, 643; **10:**596, 699; **11:**79, 288, 800; **12:**205; ACT(IVITY/S) OF **1:**102, 342, 344–45, 699, 977, 1132; **2:**18, 448; **4:**528, 533, 603, 670, 711, 1051, 1062; **5:**10–11, 251, 606, 619; **6:**335, 355, 380, 448–49, 477, 546, 821; **7:**754; **8:**29; **10:**696; **11:**358, 382, 403, 608; **12:**53; AND CHAOS **1:**279, 311, 336, 341–42, 344, 356, 394, 699, 743, 765, 767, 794–95, 799–802, 902; **2:**13, 39, 234–35, 600, 886, 1368; **3:**1029; **4:**319, 395, 411, 415, 423, 465, 487, 511, 518, 520, 597, 602, 607, 617, 711, 773, 974, 1007, 1050, 1054, 1096; **5:**408, 536, 834; **6:**210–12, 225–26, 277, 335, 380, 401, 448, 477, 614, 1425, 1434–35, 1521, 1564; **7:**101, 601, 815; **8:**328; **9:**91;

CREATION *(continued)*
10:526; **11:**598; **12:**357, 358, 656; OF THE COSMOS/EARTH/UNIVERSE/WORLD **1:**38, 67, 74, 232, 278, 289, 321, 355, 357, 365, 845, 884; **2:**546; **4:**288, 411, 518, 533, 601–2, 608, 631, 1078, 1099, 1224, 1226, 1279; **5:**26, 88, 94, 98, 442, 455, 506, 523, 577–78, 580; **6:**190, 621, 782, 1425, 1537; **7:**528; **9:**519; **10:**822; **11:**377; **12:**358; CREATIO EX NIHILO/CREATION OUT OF NOTHING **1:**342, 356, 426, 805; **10:**498, 616; DOCTRINE OF **1:**85, 196, 356, 922; **7:**840; **12:**132; TO ESCHATON **1:**199; **8:**292–93; **12:**65, 98; GOD/LORD OF **1:**84, 89, 176, 353–54, 356, 375, 399, 403, 409, 413–14, 567, 699, 721, 843, 851, 874, 893, 925–26; **2:**20, 194, 221, 534, 542, 555, 601, 983; **3:**402, 479; **4:**288, 423, 486, 496, 504, 557, 589, 593, 598, 602–3, 614, 630–32, 1035, 1078, 1100, 1226, 1236, 1261; **5:**46, 97, 101, 139, 188, 205, 254, 396, 408, 492–93, 503, 505, 516, 541, 547, 550, 553, 570–71, 599, 730; **6:**140, 198, 247, 349, 375, 515, 551, 786, 828, 965, 1130, 1469, 1563; **7:**55, 310, 544, 785; **8:**196, 229, 291, 386; **9:**524, 749, 790; **10:**375, 432, 465, 472, 504–5, 511, 615, 645, 822, 901; **11:**375, 608; **12:**313; IMAGERY **1:**179, 278–79, 341, 344, 902; **2:**80, 1317; **4:**366, 414, 595, 598, 604, 626, 631, 974, 1053, 1190, 1236; **5:**53, 93, 107, 112, 254, 599, 212, 254, 405, 417, 541, 546, 578, 598, 817–18; **7:**664, 674, 724, 772, 857; **8:**292; **9:**925; **11:**190, 377, 385, 400; **12:**190, 377, 385, 400; NEW **1:**316, 337, 343, 346, 393, 458, 699, 795, 902, 922, 962, 976, 1086; **2:**18, 21, 38–39, 235, 267, 1044; **3:**810; **4:**874, 888–89; **5:**33, 232, 520, 530, 598–99; **6:**143, 381, 387, 467, 472, 544–48, 551, 810–11, 1171; **7:**355, 766, 824; **8:**36, 126, 160, 181, 392, 472; **9:**52; **10:**68, 343, 528, 540, 556, 581, 605–6, 608, 625, 680, 695, 699, 728, 765, 786, 811–12, 822, 866, 924, 930, 977, 980, 986, 989; **11:**23, 26–27, 66, 69, 92–95, 105, 138, 187, 190, 196, 199, 208, 219, 234, 247, 249, 272–73, 278–79, 288, 298, 310, 314, 320, 324, 341, 344–45, 348, 362–63, 370, 393, 397, 400, 403, 405, 412, 427, 435, 442, 466, 570, 574, 599, 601, 610, 644; **12:**357, 532, 594, 656, 729; ORDER OF **1:**323, 329, 342, 356, 369, 607; **2:**13, 39, 235, 398, 1371; **4:**71, 410, 495–96, 594, 604, 608; **5:**35, 54, 62, 98, 134, 208; **6:**139, 646, 812, 1564, 1607; **7:**601, 673, 757, 772, 818, 839; **10:**596, 717, 930; **12:**160, 205, 479, 489–90; THEOLOGY (*see under* THEOLOGY)

CREATIONIST
1:257

CREATOR
1:14, 63, 65, 84, 121, 124, 179–80, 323, 335, 344, 347, 355, 439–40, 492, 510, 512, 522, 574, 743, 746, 758–59, 800, 809, 835, 844–46, 867, 871, 875, 925–26, 955, 1000, 1085, 1103–4, 1157; **2:**321, 488, 527–30, 602, 981; **3:**402, 810, 813, 956; **4:**197, 439, 465, 497, 500, 556, 681, 752, 810–11, 934, 976, 1053, 1061, 1094, 1099, 1236, 1263, 1271; **5:**10, 27, 35, 49, 71, 78, 101–2, 121, 145, 167, 173, 186, 251–52, 254, 264, 354, 356, 497, 503, 506, 516, 546–47, 557, 567–68, 607, 617–19, 627–28, 639, 641, 648, 671, 726, 729, 757, 759, 788, 800, 802, 807, 815, 817–19, 825, 833–35; **6:**248, 294, 344, 377, 393, 418, 597, 661, 786–87, 953, 1096, 1114, 1140, 1171, 1291, 1309, 1514, 1524; **7:**279, 368, 382–83, 389, 672, 675, 680, 683, 865–66; **8:**204, 214, 259, 357, 394, 471, 608, 678; **10:**22, 92–93, 199, 338, 349, 374, 399, 405, 416, 424, 431–34, 444–46, 482–83, 499, 515, 523, 526, 561, 596, 605, 616, 634, 640–41, 728, 748, 754, 769; **11:**291, 380, 415, 420, 428, 442, 460, 504, 571, 597–98, 629, 636, 642, 645, 847, 879, 901; **12:**29–30, 136, 240, 269, 274, 281, 284, 308, 312, 391, 569, 594, 666, 713; OF THE COSMOS/UNIVERSE **1:**362; **4:**519; **5:**102, 146, 186, 547, 759; **6:**621, 822; **12:**591; GOD **1:**85, 179, 375, 490, 577, 716, 750, 759–60, 844; **2:**191, 219; **4:**450, 597, 602, 619, 1072; **5:**6, 92, 94, 546; **6:**225, 782, 1004; **7:**93, 382, 468; **8:**206, 291; **10:**246–47, 340, 399, 404, 428, 449–50, 477–78, 488, 500, 503–4, 507, 520–21, 524, 529–30, 586, 591, 600, 618, 644, 647, 716, 815, 901; **11:**400, 608, 663; GOD/THE LORD/YAHWEH AS **1:**124, 174, 338, 341, 349, 355, 381, 395, 409, 416, 425, 429, 438, 440–42, 455, 475, 512–13, 536, 539, 556, 591, 722, 844, 997; **2:**139, 221, 407, 982; **3:**468, 478, 523, 1041; **4:**241, 360, 414, 487, 516, 519, 581, 589, 596, 608, 1264; **5:**10, 146, 175, 196–97, 456, 519–20, 546, 593, 599; **6:**960, 967–68, 1425, 1473, 1486; **7:**168–69, 373, 380, 484–85, 487, 660, 680, 772, 803, 813, 815–16, 824, 839–40; **8:**132, 264, 291, 315; **10:**249, 400–401, 426, 431, 433, 477, 498, 500, 642, 670, 698, 704, 738, 823, 901, 963; **11:**377, 414–15, 570, 663, 829; **12:**24, 181, 330, 529, 593, 634, 638; SOVEREIGN **3:**269, 273; **8:**291–92; **10:**19, 96, 391, 405, 431. *See also* GOD, NAMES FOR/TITLES OF *in PERSONS IN THE BIBLE*

CREATURE, CREATURES
1:67, 326, 335, 337, 341, 343–46, 349, 351, 353, 355–56, 362, 368, 368–70, 381, 390, 395–96, 716, 739, 743, 747, 809, 845, 977, 988, 997, 1000, 1009, 1042, 1070, 1075–76, 1081, 1082, 1103, 1118–19, 1120, 1149; **2:**129, 235, 316, 332, 364, 397–99, 448, 493, 1141, 1297; **3:**70, 82, 127, 129, 363, 1032; **4:**359, 368, 379, 394, 427, 428, 439, 442, 495, 520, 530, 532, 557, 576, 593, 597, 611, 614, 616–19, 621, 624, 632, 669–70, 702, 753, 811, 823, 824, 927, 1090,

1092, 1097–99, 1098, 1150, 1224–25, 1232, 1260, 1272, 1277–80; **5:**13, 35, 40, 46, 75, 90–92, 98, 126, 133, 141, 155, 158–59, 164, 172, 189, 226, 232–33, 251, 254, 311, 553, 570, 578, 599, 648, 678, 730, 764, 801, 823, 834; **6:**40, 140–41, 143, 157, 211, 213, 225, 278, 470, 532, 544, 708, 965, 1061, 1066, 1086, 1115–16, 1119, 1129–31, 1176, 1179, 1182–83, 1201, 1252, 1284, 1306, 1346, 1392–94, 1404, 1472, 1499, 1523, 1538, 1596; **7:**8, 236–37, 279, 482–83, 497, 521, 523, 675–76, 683; **8:**148, 206, 229, 264, 288, 292, 432, 679; **9:**259; **10:**246, 356, 433, 508, 526, 639, 641, 668, 704–5, 873, 956, 977; **11:**159, 287, 373, 394, 400, 462, 554, 569, 579, 597–98, 607, 879; **12:**29–30, 42, 181, 187, 189, 204–5, 225, 275, 402, 591–92, 601–2, 604–5, 610, 612–13, 624, 631–32, 634, 664, 666, 672, 676, 695, 700, 734; FLYING/WINGED **1:**890, 1080; **2:**164; **4:**905, 919, 1181; **7:**167, 774; OF GOD **1:**176, 365, 377, 394, 419, 846, 849, 1171; **2:**129; **4:**517, 593, 615, 618, 1272; **5:**75, 101, 135, 139, 175, 179, 516, 545, 599, 731; **6:**630, 919; **7:**724; **9:**693; **10:**698, 913, 956, 994; **12:**189; HUMAN **1:**846; **5:**306; **6:**124, 528, 717, 860; **7:**483, 521, 721; **10:**430; **11:**321, 377; **12:**264–65, 277; LIVING **1:**92, 352, 390–92, 400, 430, 1009; **4:**608, 1272; **5:**311, 523; **6:**142, 214, 217, 548, 1113, 1115–17, 1120, 1128, 1131, 1175, 1182–84, 1212, 1214, 1245, 1394, 1406, 1422, 1437, 1521, 1528; **7:**192, 382; **11:**510; **12:**205, 593, 598, 613, 696; SEA/WATER **1:**398, 1081; **2:**13; **4:**597, 618; **5:**598; **6:**226, 1432; **8:**324; **12:**205; SWARMING **1:**398, 1080; **6:**1596; WILD **2:**357; **4:**609–10; **6:**142, 226, 277–78. *See also* ANIMAL; BEAST; CREEPING THING

CREDIT
1:120, 557, 758, 794; **2:**673, 681, 782–83, 803–5, 808, 945, 1055, 1081, 1111, 1169, 1176, 1192, 1203, 1243, 1267, 1309, 1315, 1340, 1361, 1375; **3:**415, 418, 468, 513, 611, 617, 619, 747–48, 777, 909, 918, 927, 938, 962, 966, 969, 1055, 1162, 1165; **4:**57, 382, 589, 611, 1199; **5:**351, 365, 389, 819, 825, 849; **6:**37, 1015, 1066, 1360, 1427; **7:**482, 511, 611; **8:**79, 315, 570, 574, 590; **9:**147, 560, 737; **10:**180, 314, 812, 815, 817, 825, 941; **11:**17, 19, 42, 45, 59, 95, 141, 164, 166, 234, 544, 838; **12:**200; FINANCIAL **1:**445, 528, 851, 950; **3:**533; **4:**815, 878; **5:**175, 198, 200, 205, 351, 659, 660, 789; **6:**357; **8:**455; **10:**490, 759, 776; **11:**627; **12:**281

CREDITOR, CREDITORS
1:770, 772, 868, 872, 1042; **2:**469, 566–67, 593, 596, 659; **3:**186, 779–81, 783, 789, 979; **4:**511; **5:**199–200, 205, 775–76; **6:**14, 211, 1259; **7:**647–48; **8:**435; **9:**269

CREED, CREEDS
1:47, 57, 61, 212, 804, 947–48; **2:**480; **3:**562, 1065; **4:**695, 736, 753; **5:**317, 377, 622; **6:**223, 403; **7:**529, 579; **8:**39–40, 153, 227, 424; **9:**78, 125, 162, 392; **10:**382, 384, 866, 916, 977; **11:**829, 846; **12:**23, 31, 75, 457, 468, 716; APOSTLES' CREED **1:**208; **4:**736, 1131, 1146, 1181; **12:**26, 43, 62, 155; NICENE CREED **5:**99; **9:**764; **12:**435

CREEDAL
1:181, 209, 312, 563, 636, 789; **2:**480–81; **3:**1119; **4:**802, 1020–21; **5:**628; **6:**403, 1292; **7:**319, 588; **8:**526, 528, 695–96, 730; **9:**92; **10:**898, 977; **11:**39, 149, 382, 501, 724, 784, 798, 835, 839, 847, 873; **12:**24, 26, 327, 375, 390

CREEPING THING, THINGS
1:345, 716; **4:**1100, 1271; **6:**1086, 1176, 1521

CREMATION
3:996; **6:**1395; **7:**402

CRESCENT, CRESCENTS
2:808

CRIB, CRIBS
5:139; **9:**63, 67; **11:**159

CRIME, CRIMES
1:374, 629, 639, 671, 851, 1037, 1041–42; **2:**61, 265, 333, 432, 435, 437, 445, 453, 468, 627, 630, 707, 740, 886–88, 1031, 1087, 1089, 1114, 1160, 1223, 1293, 1295, 1297, 1300, 1305, 1309–10, 1346; **3:**43–44, 220, 568, 882, 897, 920; **4:**48, 182, 210, 435–36, 460, 483, 485, 504, 510–11, 513, 553, 577, 626, 1059, 1126–27, 1199; **5:**37, 54, 146, 151, 187, 254, 314, 337, 752, 775, 790, 800, 860; **6:**47, 63, 65, 84, 157, 213, 243, 270, 296, 439, 500–01, 585, 600, 626, 637, 653, 723, 786, 807, 872–73, 882, 918, 1130, 1138–39, 1168, 1185–86, 1212, 1214, 1219, 1241, 1253, 1264, 1307–10, 1315, 1317, 1330, 1363, 1400, 1489, 1538; **7:**176–77, 180, 205, 227, 236, 252–53, 256, 261–63, 267, 269, 333, 353–55, 357, 361–64, 370, 441, 443, 450, 454, 561, 597, 616, 631–32, 648, 663–64, 677, 692; **8:**15, 193, 197, 714, 723; **9:**28, 272, 374, 446, 448, 458, 818; **10:**107, 255, 309, 321, 326, 330, 356, 367, 427, 433, 451, 476; **11:**342, 898; **12:**311, 343, 415, 549, 660; CAPITAL (*see* CAPITAL: CHARGE/CRIME/OFFENSE); CAPITAL EXECUTION/PUNISHMENT (*see under* CAPITAL); AND PUNISHMENT(S) **1:**240, 412, 629, 665, 868, 1051, 1142, 1165; **2:**328, 448, 613, 628, 630, 1087, 1114, 1160, 1310; **3:**424, 551, 773, 814; **4:**182, 210, 218, 248, 254, 297, 367, 460, 1126–27, 1228; **5:**69, 112, 122, 136, 175, 187, 254, 752; **6:**47, 82, 93, 243–44, 270, 439, 585, 723, 786, 831, 865, 874, 894,

CRIME, CRIMES *(continued)*
1085, 1123, 1130, 1139, 1155, 1171, 1214, 1238, 1241, 1253, 1264, 1330–31; **7:**333, 355, 441, 541, 548, 550–51, 558, 560, 561, 597, 663–64, 677; **9:**446; **10:**356, 433, 434, 476; **12:**311

CRIMINAL, CRIMINALS
1:1143; **2:**272, 379, 422, 434–35, 441, 447–48, 453, 1100, 1143, 1148, 1226, 1341; **4:**165, 281, 331, 337, 340, 421, 436, 455, 480, 508, 511, 512, 632, 636, 874; **5:**127, 132, 143, 155, 176, 189, 217, 246; **6:**56, 88, 247, 1206, 1452, 1489; **7:**176, 676; **8:**60, 486, 627, 710; **9:**52, 441, 452, 456–59, 461, 463, 818, 829–30; **10:**255, 318–19, 399, 436; **11:**260, 843, 846, 885; ACT(S)/BEHAVIOR **2:**276, 335, 432, 434–35, 437, 448; **4:**626; **10:**234, 273, 314, 360; **11:**432

CRIMSON
1:896; **2:**55, 151, 1207; **3:**332, 583; **5:**403; **6:**56; **7:**3

CRIPPLE (*OR* CRIPPLES, CRIPPLING, *ETC.*)
1:566, 574, 748, 872, 1009, 1015, 1148; **2:**407, 1230, 1273; **3:**418; **5:**186; **6:**218, 1077, 1099, 1395, 1421; **7:**42, 502; **9:**22, 24–26, 29, 98, 106, 123, 128, 134, 272, 274, 287, 290, 316, 354, 370, 458, 462, 478, 734; **10:**84–85, 88, 188; **11:**547, 705, 721; **12:**71

CRITICISM
AUDIENCE **1:**125, 134; BIBLICAL **1:**55, 57, 59, 107, 113, 115, 120, 125–26, 167, 197; **2:**539; **6:**1118; CANONICAL **1:**21, 125, 134–35, 147–48, 314, 682; COMPOSITION **1:**125, 134; **8:**84, 93; DECONSTRUCTION/DECONSTRUCTIONISM **1:**105, 112, 115, 125, 145; FORM **1:**125–26, 131, 133, 136, 139, 311–12; **2:**539; **4:**303, 642–44, 646, 648–52, 665–66, 669, 890, 1033, 1254; **5:**2, 6; **6:**15–16, 34, 285, 311–12, 314, 319, 322, 327, 331, 347–48, 352–54, 362, 385, 393, 401, 405, 410, 418, 428, 440, 481, 489, 491, 498, 500, 519, 525–26, 538, 541, 1388; **7:**342–43, 355, 535, 595; **8:**50, 68, 72, 77–81, 83, 86, 92–93, 108, 336, 366, 509–11, 519; **9:**501; HIGHER/LOWER **1:**113, 125, 131, 194; **3:**1076; **8:**1; HISTORICAL/HISTORICAL CRITICAL *(incl. traditio-historical)* **1:**1–4, 6, 34, 54–58, 78–80, 103–5, 107–8, 112–13, 125, 128, 131–35, 148–49, 159, 162–63, 167–68, 182, 194–95, 197–98, 252, 254–55, 257, 313, 315, 335, 341, 683, 828, 1028; **2:**278, 378, 441, 539–40, 546, 724, 953–55; **3:**153; **4:**454, 558, 642; **5:**2, 671; **6:**310, 312, 366, 576, 1090, 1092, 1094–95; **7:**67; **8:**90; **9:**507; **10:**371; **11:**309; **12:**255, 503, 544; INTERCULTURAL **1:**168, 171–73; LITERARY/LITERARY CRITICAL **1:**104–5, 109, 111, 115–16, 125, 134, 136, 140–41, 147, 182, 198, 236, 256, 313, 323, 328, 576, 681; **2:**539, 540, 954; **3:**891, 1082; **6:**314, 1090, 1094; **8:**84, 91, 93, 107–9, 175, 355, 512; **9:**510; **10:**13; METHOD OF STUDY OF TEXT **1:**20, 34, 57, 108, 113; **2:**286, 327, 541, 725, 1123; **3:**866; **5:**467, 547; **9:**737; **10:**178, 195, 218, 324; NARRATIVE **1:**105, 125, 142–44; **8:**68, 84, 86, 108, 516; **9:**33; NEW **1:**54–56, 111, 114, 116, 118, 136, 313; **2:**539; **4:**302; **6:**1095; READER-RESPONSE **1:**105, 118–20, 125, 134, 137, 143–44, 167–68, 197; **7:**471; **8:**108; REDACTION/REDACTION CRITICAL **1:**125, 131, 133–34, 139; **6:**28, 32, 314, 1092; **7:**341–42, 535, 539; **8:**83–86, 93, 96, 108, 119, 230, 511–13, 521; **9:**32; **12:**328; RHETORICAL/RHETORICAL CRITICAL **1:**105, 125, 140, 143, 182; **2:**539–40, 548; **4:**642–43, 651–52, 655, 665–66; **6:**323, 569; **7:**343, 491, 535, 668; **8:**108; **11:**684, 744, 770; **12:**331, 480; SOCIAL/SOCIAL CRITICAL *or* SOCIAL SCIENTIFIC/SOCIAL SCIENCE **1:**681, 697, 722, 774, 809, 844, 872; **2:**725; **8:**15, 513; SOURCE/SOURCE CRITICAL **1:**125–26, 132, 134, 322–23, 391, 417, 444, 604, 794, 994; **6:**32–33, 285; **8:**75, 77, 108; **9:**106, 509, 517, 619; **12:**545, 708; STRUCTURALISM/POST-STRUCTURALISM **1:**107, 109, 112, 115, 122, 125, 140, 141, 143, 145; **2:**539–40, 548; TEXTUAL/TEXT CRITICAL **1:**17, 28, 49, 76, 125, 131–32, 139, 301–2; **2:**748; **3:**48, 796, 800; **6:**331, 336, 546, 1422; **8:**1–7, 9; **9:**470; **11:**762; **12:**545; TRADITION/TRADITIO-CRITICAL/TRADITIO-HISTORICAL **1:**131, 255; **8:**78, 93; **9:**685, 693, 806

CROCODILE, CROCODILES
4:615, 622; **6:**1104, 1401, 1403–5, 1434, 1516

CROSS
1:92, 170, 178, 449, 955, 977, 1101; **2:**505, 798, 810, 1141, 1209, 1299; **3:**145, 417, 619; **4:**673–74, 692, 731, 762, 802–3, 849, 909, 931, 974, 992, 997, 1001, 1048, 1055, 1070, 1076, 1083, 1093, 1137, 1143, 1179, 1182, 1188, 1203, 1229, 1230, 1241; **5:**51, 291, 330, 377, 553; **6:**396, 680, 704, 718, 723, 815, 1072, 1504; **7:**396, 687; **8:**153, 161, 164, 166, 198, 280, 349, 356, 365–66, 396, 404, 428, 437, 486, 491–92, 500, 512, 520, 526, 561, 580, 591, 624–27, 632, 654, 696, 705, 708, 713, 720, 722–25, 731; **9:**18, 28, 43, 72, 108, 175, 206–7, 217, 233, 334, 341, 360, 413, 415, 433, 440–41, 447, 451, 453–56, 459, 461–63, 465, 478, 552, 571, 635, 819, 827, 830–31, 834, 836–37, 842, 844, 861; **10:**261, 342, 376, 387, 467, 471, 474, 477, 482, 485, 502–3, 520, 523, 529, 531, 551, 566, 573–76, 578–79, 590, 614, 617, 635, 644, 671, 745, 754, 811–13, 817–18, 868, 916; **12:**10, 42, 43, 92, 113, 117, 147, 149, 151, 261, 270, 283, 288, 353, 516, 530–31, 568, 607, 611, 638, 649–50, 694; BEAR/CARRY **4:**702, 728, 924, 928, 1179, 1191,

1277; **8:**124, 195, 488–89, 627, 654, 722; **9:**292–93, 450–51, 800, 829; **12:**167, 170; BLOOD OF **3:**427; **11:**398, 435, 572, 578, 601, 603–4, 609; OF CHRIST/JESUS **1:**204, 1120; **2:**98; **3:**582; **4:**672, 800, 812, 835, 906, 914, 947, 954, 981, 1030, 1073, 1093, 1206; **5:**114, 547, 552; **7:**232, 317, 335; **8:**262, 271, 491, 512, 628, 694, 722, 732–33; **9:**373, 450, 544, 552, 555, 829–30, 832–33, 835, 837; **10:**478, 720, 807–9, 817; **11:**208, 314, 342, 475, 535; **12:**167, 261; DEATH ON/DIE(D/S) ON **1:**1015, 1027, 1114; **2:**835, 861; **3:**783; **8:**73, 511, 516, 527, 529, 550, 590; **9:**19, 331, 714–15, 732, 737, 827, 833, 837; **10:**470; **11:**187, 240, 244, 251, 260, 276, 284–85, 378, 396, 440, 450, 509, 535, 626; **12:**82, 107, 113–14, 166; INSCRIPTION ON THE **9:**450, 829–30; OVER **1:**69, 1127; **2:**161–62, 607, 771; **3:**176; **4:**1205; **6:**457; **7:**101, 252; **10:**227, 851; **11:**104; OVER JORDAN/THE RIVER **2:**181, 249, 276, 312, 320, 486, 510, 584, 772, 788, 838; **4:**36; PARADOX OF **3:**227; **8:**632, 696, 706; AND RESURRECTION **1:**209–10; **4:**669, 674, 728, 766, 895, 924, 1248; **6:**734; **7:**328, 785; **8:**295, 529, 618; **9:**208, 214; **10:**521, 537, 606, 615, 617; **11:**228, 322; **12:**709; SCANDAL OF **4:**673; **5:**14; **8:**520, 632, 732; **11:**316; **12:**681; SIGN OF **5:**328; **11:**405, 538; TAKE UP **4:**673, 975, 1029, 1055; **6:**440, 607; **8:**351, 513, 522, 626–27, 651, 683, 707, 722; **9:**4, 27, 98, 201–3, 352, 711, 714; **10:**707, 730; **12:**605; THEOLOGY OF (*see under* THEOLOGY); WAY OF/TO **4:**1119; **6:**550, 795; **8:**281, 350; **9:**13, 203, 217, 352; **10:**809; **11:**207, 628

CROW, CROWS
(bird) **5:**349; **6:**988, 1005; "THE COCK CROWS" **8:**475, 715; **9:**428, 438

CROWN
1:264, 448, 654, 1135, 1148; **2:**163, 1169, 1201–3, 1239, 1300; **3:**155–56, 211, 230, 377, 416, 421, 457, 569, 592, 914, 927, 959; **4:**125, 133, 137, 159, 178, 475, 679, 692, 932, 934, 1092, 1211, 1274; **5:**125, 142–43, 162, 167, 233, 254, 318, 400, 454, 461, 475–76, 486, 650–51, 823; **6:**236, 981, 1228, 1245, 1252, 1303, 1329, 1425, 1496, 1590; **7:**766, 786–88, 811; **8:**674; **10:**645, 654, 754, 909; **11:**6, 78, 112, 173, 469, 486, 536, 708, 842, 856; **12:**181, 187–88, 190, 201, 216, 305, 315, 533, 536, 571, 585, 599, 611, 693; GOLD(EN) **4:**122, 154, 286; **5:**843; **12:**631, 648, 668; PRINCE **1:**720; **2:**521, 1136, 1205, 1309; **3:**39, 93, 184, 551; **6:**99, 112, 121, 123–24; **7:**828–29; ROYAL **3:**882, 889, 908; OF THORNS **8:**488; **9:**822. *See also* DIADEM

CRUCIBLE
1:186; **4:**509; **5:**58; **6:**1312; **9:**403

CRUCIFIXION
1:898, 955; **2:**90, 447, 1231–32, 1358; **3:**426, 612, 1143; **4:**278, 673–74, 728, 874, 1073, 1156; **6:**440, 468–69; **7:**569–70; **8:**66, 71, 73, 81, 124, 150, 163, 268, 296, 350, 354–55, 396, 398, 401–2, 405, 438, 463–64, 470–71, 486, 488, 490–91, 494–96, 498–501, 503, 528, 543, 590, 696–97, 703, 705, 722–24, 726; **9:**13, 18–19, 28, 37, 174, 202, 352, 369, 376, 381–82, 429, 448, 450–57, 460–65, 468, 470, 477, 485, 488, 493, 514, 528, 544, 552, 595, 704–5, 713, 719, 799–800, 811, 816, 818, 820, 823, 827, 829–33, 836–37, 845, 861; **10:**20, 66, 106, 418, 465, 467, 474, 502, 540, 650, 745, 811, 813, 817, 957; **11:**26, 81, 167, 176, 217, 242, 244, 250–51, 255, 260–61, 276, 293, 328, 343–44, 357, 492, 509, 515, 537, 604, 609, 628, 650, 839; **12:**40, 42, 76, 240, 302, 384, 404, 439, 441, 516, 532, 560, 611, 677; AND RESURRECTION **1:**838; **2:**1232; **4:**954; **8:**39, 110, 119, 149, 245, 400, 480, 492–93, 501; **9:**278, 351, 466, 552, 610, 635; **11:**492; **12:**42, 240, 302, 404. *See also* JESUS THE CHRIST: CRUCIFIXION, RESURRECTION, AND ASCENSION OF *in PERSONS IN THE BIBLE*

CRUSE
3:186

CRYSTAL, ROCK
12:591, 597, 672, 724

CUB, CUBS
(animal) **1:**665, 771; **2:**1332; **5:**167; **6:**1266, 1269–70, 1272–73; **7:**101, 612

CUBIT, CUBITS
1:391; **2:**36, 79, 108, 167, 264, 268, 309, 599, 701, 1110; **3:**61, 63, 67, 484–85, 708, 759, 768, 911; **6:**1119, 1393, 1540–43, 1547–53, 1555, 1557, 1559, 1566–67, 1581–82, 1592, 1596, 1604–7; **7:**774; **8:**214, 247; **9:**259, 398; **12:**723

CUCUMBER
6:54, 986–87, 1009

CULT
1:127, 282–83, 306, 311–12, 316, 373, 459, 680, 890–91, 907, 925, 978, 991–92, 1126, 1135, 1138; **2:**8, 23, 41, 47, 77–78, 88, 100, 106, 137, 148–49, 152, 228, 246, 250, 257, 283, 562, 564, 567, 570, 572, 574–75, 615, 626, 628, 655, 689, 702, 726, 755, 1376; **3:**250, 677, 710, 761, 1061–62, 1078, 1124–25, 1182; **4:**9, 11, 39, 82, 218, 232–33, 257, 504; **5:**2, 34, 408, 511, 542, 544, 549, 557, 562, 620, 633, 669, 696, 855–56; **6:**10, 119, 122, 148, 238, 244, 262, 318, 473, 484, 540, 639, 826, 892, 940, 1175, 1177, 1404, 1573–74, 1578, 1588; **7:**6, 54, 62, 72, 117, 137, 143, 146, 198, 205, 213, 226, 231, 235, 239–40, 244–45, 256, 259–61, 263, 265, 267, 270, 272, 288, 352, 380, 606, 627, 661, 717, 751, 826,

CULT *(continued)*
859, 861; **8:**13, 25, 33, 35, 78, 526, 539, 683, 730; **9:**164, 386–87, 543; **10:**42, 125, 200, 270, 320, 404, 477, 516, 604, 615, 718, 732; **11:**361, 383, 411, 470–71, 510, 564, 678, 696, 792, 807; **12:**46, 571, 625, 684; OF ARTEMIS **10:**270–73; **11:**361, 792; OF BAAL **2:**755; **3:**156, 214–15; **4:**793; **6:**707; **7:**239; CENTRAL/CENTRALIZATION **1:**255; **2:**87, 148–49, 232–33, 265, 279, 384, 386–87, 487, 568, 570, 627–28, 706; **3:**677; **6:**1285; OF THE DEAD **3:**1061, 1182; **4:**241; **5:**697; **6:**491, 1561; OF THE EMPEROR/CAESAR CULT/STATE CULT **10:**404, 604, 615; **11:**383, 470–71, 510; **12:**571, 684; FERTILITY **2:**755; **5:**101; **6:**57, 62–63, 601, 604, 1002; **7:**202, 241, 249, 258, 265; FUNCTIONAL **4:**504, 650–51; IMPERIAL **7:**4, 10; **8:**16; **10:**230, 515, 719, 739, 754, 774, 894; **11:**205, 535; **12:**658, 685; ISRAELITE **2:**87, 246, 420–21, 574; **3:**835; **5:**619–20; **6:**542; **7:**200, 203, 234, 261, 322; JERUSALEM **1:**252, 256, 309; **3:**722, 1062; **6:**464; **7:**352, 839; **10:**704; MYSTERY **5:**496; **6:**176; **8:**25–26; **9:**177–78; **10:**374, 533; **11:**532, 561, 567, 653, 807; **12:**204; OBJECT(S) **1:**889, 891; **2:**96, 139, 255, 276, 351–52, 384, 808; **3:**115, 260, 276; **6:**62, 1175, 1569; **7:**61, 205, 233; **8:**663; PAGAN **1:**1018, 1127; **4:**185, 230; **5:**544; **8:**663; **10:**273; **11:**364, 561; PROSTITUTE/PROSTITUTION **1:**1135; **2:**462; **3:**118, 168; **4:**232; **5:**84; **6:**1160; **7:**202–3, 215, 224, 241, 365; SACRIFICIAL **1:**285, 316, 992; **2:**11, 25; **3:**691, 800; **4:**205–6, 211; **5:**629, 797, 849; **6:**62, 639, 1564; **7:**12, 394, 579, 861; **8:**33–34, 665, 678; **10:**461; TABERNACLE/TEMPLE (*see under* JERUSALEM TEMPLE *in PLACES IN THE BIBLE*); OF YAHWEH **2:**563, 565, 600, 635, 641, 666, 687, 706; **6:**1176, 1287; **7:**205, 419

CULTURE
AMERICAN **1:**202, 330, 464; **2:**656; **3:**998; **4:**480, 667, 669, 687, 720, 1119, 1146; **5:**145, 182; **6:**776, 1325; **8:**615; **9:**149, 554; **12:**213; CONTEMPORARY/MODERN/PRESENT **1:**66, 464; **2:**38, 111, 236, 268; **3:**612; **4:**471, 541, 637, 891, 1119; **5:**20, 247; **6:**120, 143, 213, 413, 711, 1592; **9:**649; **10:**435–36, 858; **12:**206, 588, 728; DOMINANT **1:**169, 186; **2:**920; **6:**1017, 1034, 1072; **7:**34, 85, 95; **11:**228, 405; **12:**595, 616, 685, 687; GREEK/HELLENISTIC **1:**268; **3:**1109, 1144; **5:**275, 759, 828; **7:**4, 10, 105, 118; **8:**13, 40–41, 45; **9:**519; **10:**231, 298, 374, 377, 397; **12:**123, 151; HUMAN **4:**453, 607, 610; **5:**95, 97, 160, 360; **12:**606–7; ISRAELITE/ISRAEL'S **1:**273; **2:**65, 108; **3:**347, 430; **4:**82; **5:**58, 81, 125, 172, 185, 220, 793; **6:**1224; **7:**211; JEWISH **1:**66, 77; **3:**1133, 1144; **8:**336; **11:**229; MEDITERRANEAN **1:**162; **5:**673; **8:**56; **9:**362; **11:**173, 347; **12:**485; NEAR EASTERN **1:**80, 323, 335; **5:**134; **9:**584; ORAL **1:**200–201, 592; **5:**60, 152, 174, 179; **8:**669; **10:**305; PATRIARCHAL **1:**25, 559; **2:**1171; **3:**803; **4:**241; **5:**20, 35, 400; **7:**615; **8:**138, 386; **12:**686; POPULAR **2:**1289; **3:**1024, 1183; **7:**313; **10:**64, 273, 532; **11:**893; **12:**340, 416; ROMAN/GRECO-ROMAN **3:**1144, 1150; **5:**776; **7:**7, 10; **8:**46, 553; **10:**8, 554, 755; **11:**470, 653, 701; **12:**137; SECULAR **3:**868; **4:**753, 779, 1137; **6:**946; **9:**82; **10:**85, 249; SURROUNDING **2:**39, 757; **6:**73; **8:**56; **10:**45, 244, 714; **12:**212, 523, 588; WESTERN **1:**6, 115, 151, 1026; **2:**214, 234; **3:**890; **5:**291; **6:**946, 969; **7:**155, 561; **8:**314, 345, 377; **10:**484, 547, 722, 928; **11:**207, 229; **12:**415

CUNEIFORM
1:230–32, 238, 267, 1018; **2:**755; **4:**18, 31, 157; **5:**3; **7:**80

CUP, CUPS
1:615, 638–39; **3:**612; **4:**722, 736, 738, 768, 916, 977, 1149; **5:**147; **6:**655, 815, 897, 913, 1065, 1154, 1338; **7:**250, 454, 825–26; **8:**398, 471, 476, 640, 703–5, 707–8; **9:**132, 247, 251, 311, 329, 418–22, 432–33, 803, 832–33; **10:**918; **12:**639, 678, 680–81; AND BREAD **2:**1276; **8:**703; **9:**418–23; **10:**918, 934–35, 938; OF SALVATION **4:**681, 1146, 1148–49; OF WINE **6:**684, 765–66; **8:**653, 658; **10:**934; **12:**681, 692; OF WRATH **6:**413, 449, 451, 453, 571, 764–66, 892, 896, 1065; **7:**826; **8:**398; **12:**678, 681, 692–93

CUPBEARER
1:614–15, 620; **3:**265, 751, 755–56; **9:**458

CURDS
2:788; **4:**303, 485; **5:**255; **6:**112–13

CURSE (*OR* CURSES, *ETC.*)
1:236, 242, 306, 363, 403–5, 423–24, 428, 452, 483, 490, 535, 537–38, 577, 713, 821, 842, 847, 1004, 1164, 1175, 1180–81; **2:**62–63, 68, 177–78, 182, 185–87, 195, 250, 352, 375, 485, 487–94, 500–503, 505, 537, 559–60, 588, 601, 607–8, 612, 619–20, 626, 665, 681, 711, 816–17, 869, 910, 986, 1080, 1206, 1225, 1229, 1270; **3:**179, 184, 497, 569, 582, 657, 668, 781, 797, 817, 842, 894, 1002, 1065; **4:**156, 234, 349, 366–69, 371–72, 376, 471, 508, 512, 522–23, 525–26, 553–55, 602, 621, 631, 702, 1128; **5:**57, 160, 213, 219, 224, 231, 237, 245, 253, 322, 436, 473–74, 476, 479, 617, 655, 659, 664, 746, 823–24; **6:**64, 119, 211, 390, 527, 544, 661, 670, 717, 728–29, 750, 831, 891, 952, 1008, 1062, 1159, 1263, 1348, 1351, 1472, 1499; **7:**74–75, 248, 270, 272, 330, 381, 431, 574, 576, 611, 660, 665, 679–80, 688, 690–93, 752–54, 757, 774–75, 778, 792, 797, 826, 859, 862, 865, 870, 876; **8:**28, 31–32, 82, 100, 163, 407, 481, 595, 661, 703; **9:**147; **10:**85, 190, 310, 628, 663, 714, 741, 941; **11:**61, 76, 199, 202,

206–8, 243, 256–62, 266, 268, 276–77, 284, 286, 303–4, 308, 322, 345, 439, 457, 563; **12:**203–5, 563, 645, 720, 734; AND BLESSING(S) **1:**332, 402–3, 435, 845, 1115, 1178, 1180, 1186; **2:**184, 272–73, 289–90, 339, 367, 375, 485, 491–92, 495, 499–503, 505, 636, 788, 816, 870, 1062–64; **3:**178, 752, 995, 1062; **4:**229, 366; **5:**55, 120, 270, 436, 575, 615, 668; **6:**74, 78, 204, 733, 1075–76, 1472, 1496; **7:**252, 526, 663, 680, 703, 853, 860; **8:**31, 82; **10:**460, 659–60; **11:**258–59, 276; **12:**76; COVENANT/OATH **3:**76, 282, 497, 503, 657; **4:**471, 510; **6:**621, 865, 1084, 1154, 1215, 1254, 1351, 1472, 1499; **7:**304, 306–7, 322–23, 381, 411, 775; **11:**456; **12:**616; DIVINE **1:**452; **2:**189, 198, 447, 501, 505; **3:**332, 388, 1071; **4:**452; **5:**53, 55, 427; **7:**330; **8:**545; **10:**107, 418; **11:**260, 305, 444; **12:**315; GOD **1:**869, 1164; **4:**321, 329, 346, 350, 353–54, 356, 358, 366, 523, 525, 601, 627; THE GROUND **1:**312, 363, 374, 380, 393; **6:**544; **7:**382; THE HEBREWS/ISRAEL/THE PEOPLE **1:**242; **2:**179–86, 189–90, 195, 197, 245–46, 665; **3:**844; **7:**579; **11:**257; **12:**351, 491, 579; LIST(S) OF **2:**491, 493, 500; **3:**645, 1064; **6:**1491; **10:**659; THE SERPENT **1:**363, 405; **4:**368, 621; **6:**544; THREAT OF **2:**177, 375, 489; **7:**876; **11:**206

CURTAIN, CURTAINS
5:383, 583; **12:**120–21; TABERNACLE/TEMPLE (*see under* JERUSALEM TEMPLE *in PLACES IN THE BIBLE*). *See also* PARTITION

CUSHION, CUSHIONS
7:502; **8:**580; **9:**184, 730

CUSTODIAN, CUSTODIANS
1:237, 866–67, 978; **2:**364, 366, 430, 515, 521, 1013, 1249; **3:**48; **7:**862, 876; **8:**657; **10:**20, 109, 206, 281; **11:**199, 265, 281, 320

CYMBAL, CYMBALS
3:386, 394, 447, 692, 840, 1177; **4:**1279

CYNIC, CYNICS
5:824; **6:**1198; **7:**675, 679; **8:**18–20, 264, 595, 681; **10:**698, 722, 820, 833, 870, 881; **11:**111, 121, 458–59, 544, 561, 567, 582, 698–99, 828, 831

CYNICISM
1:486; **2:**1231–32, 1263; **3:**46; **4:**454, 481; **5:**365, 422, 773; **6:**380, 827; **7:**74, 103, 516, 612, 675–76, 723; **8:**18–19, 720; **9:**49, 458; **10:**109, 588; **11:**418; **12:**434

CYPRESS
TREE/WOOD **3:**82; **5:**757; **6:**482, 1422, 1554; **7:**296, 609, 817

D

DAGGER, DAGGERS
2:171, 1216; **5:**127, 771; **12:**645

DALET
(Hebrew letter) **1:**293; **7:**497–98, 601–2

DAMN (*OR* DAMNED, DAMNATION, *ETC.*)
3:370; **4:**349, 928; **5:**322, 345; **6:**580, 602, 724, 750, 1189, 1310; **8:**183, 216, 305, 332, 641; **9:**101, 482, 641; **10:**107, 245, 308, 435, 716, 852, 857; **11:**747; **12:**77, 444

DANCE (*OR* DANCES, *ETC.*)
1:180, 802–3, 932; **2:**547, 727, 741, 749, 757, 833, 853, 886, 987, 1121, 1188, 1193, 1248–49, 1250–51; **3:**135, 394, 401, 576, 903, 1108–9, 1139, 1173–74; **4:**644, 797, 1274–75, 1280; **5:**72, 121, 275, 304, 355, 421, 425, 652, 690, 700, 861; **6:**809–10, 815, 825, 1070, 1298, 1415; **7:**63, 107, 137, 667; **8:**321–22; **9:**166, 303, 349, 482, 542; **10:**746; **11:**444, 548, 640; **12:**32

DANIEL, BOOK OF
1:5, 8, 11, 18–19, 43, 46, 65, 230, 241, 268, 285, 288–90, 292, 294, 303, 620, 1182; **2:**541, 855; **3:**301, 417, 856, 867, 869–70, 873, 929, 966, 1015, 1080, 1083, 1086, 1091, 1099, 1101, 1108–9, 1142, 1154, 1176; **4:**6, 8, 23, 38, 40, 51, 104, 193, 212, 227, 256, 328, 343, 363, 487, 503, 516, 568, 577, 608, 616, 805, 1244; **5:**1, 258, 271, 273, 285, 291, 332, 654, 672, 699, 793; **6:**13, 206–7, 223, 226, 228, 260, 449, 547, 930–32, 934–35, 945, 948–50, 989, 1130, 1213, 1388, 1502; **7:**18–36, 155–57, **8:**29, 30, 32, 36, 38–40, 50–51, 151, 356, 361, 442, 448, 516, 627, 631, 675, 690, 692; **9:**48, 346, 382, 404, 407, 486; **10:**400–401, 447, 475, 634, 650, 661, 723; **11:**382–83, 812; **12:**143, 504–5, 518–26, 532, 541, 543, 546, 560–61, 566–67, 603–4, 639, 681, 685–86, 711, 724, 733

DAPPLED
3:402; **5:**382; **7:**784; **12:**610

DARK, DARKNESS
1:342–44, 446, 766–68, 771, 780, 784, 789, 890, 892, 902; **2:**178, 321, 338, 376, 982, 1367–68; **3:**40, 43, 47, 81, 97, 114, 145, 167, 201, 295, 759, 980, 1002, 1061, 1069, 1087; **4:**307, 368, 409, 422, 459, 462, 465, 468, 486, 501, 518, 520, 547, 591, 602–3, 680, 787, 824, 837, 873, 1021, 1026–30, 1047, 1070, 1105, 1117–18, 1177, 1180, 1185, 1236, 1251; **5:**44, 84, 319, 321, 354, 356, 383, 446, 529, 583–86, 591, 596, 835; **6:**10, 98, 122, 156, 158, 160, 344, 359, 364, 367, 369–70, 394, 401, 411, 422, 438, 478–79, 483, 505, 508, 521, 685, 750, 1009, 1049, 1176, 1194, 1425, 1438, 1503, 1512; **7:**52, 91, 118, 169, 317, 321, 325, 334, 349, 392–93, 558, 586, 603, 679, 682, 750, 782; **8:**167, 210, 226, 264, 425, 492–93, 543, 723–24; **9:**60, 65, 244–45, 252, 371, 443, 450, 460–61, 506, 520, 525, 548,

DARK, DARKNESS *(continued)*
634, 643, 686, 713, 718, 730, 802, 804, 824, 826; **10:**21, 339, 445, 598, 629, 701, 729–30; **11:**65–66, 75, 282, 361, 377, 384, 390, 394, 422, 428, 434, 436, 438, 440, 451, 460, 566, 596, 661, 690, 726; **12:**189, 212, 267, 269, 276, 347, 351–52, 369, 374, 377, 391, 394–96, 400, 419, 426, 436, 478, 482, 488–89, 492, 497, 500, 516–17, 611, 615, 631, 633, 649, 676, 684, 723; ANGEL OF **11:**389, 390, 436; CHILDREN/SONS OF **1:**289; **3:**757; **5:**12; **6:**73, 228; **7:**15; **8:**195; **11:**389, 420, 437, 443; **12:**665; DAY(S) OF **4:**210, 451; **5:**353; **6:**72, 156; **7:**666, 682, 872; DEEP/THICK **2:**88; **3:**70–71, 78; **4:**367, 423, 430, 510–11, 577, 601, 603, 768; **6:**119, 510, 602; **7:**103, 316, 666, 682–83; **12:**158; FORCES OF/POWER(S) OF **3:**417; **4:**368, 1236; **9:**430, 435–38, 460, 463; **10:**365, 427, 534, 589; **11:**360, 570–71, 596; **12:**515, 529; AND LIGHT **1:**287, 289, 767–68, 892; **3:**554, 982, 984; **4:**250, 310, 367, 415, 470, 511, 529–30, 598, 603; **5:**59, 76, 302, 585, 598, 670; **6:**94, 123, 188; **9:**520, 524, 553, 663, 665, 713, 857; **10:**334, 434, 728; **11:**289, 381, 437, 441, 513, 593, 726; **12:**75, 381, 385–86, 393–94, 516, 701; PLAGUE OF **1:**688, 765; **5:**417, 580, 583, 585, 592; **6:**1435; **12:**158; WALK(ED/ING/S) IN **1:**892; **3:**992; **4:**537, 903; **5:**300, 485; **6:**369, 438, 509; **9:**602, 632; **12:**372, 379, 385

DARK VALLEY
See SHADOW, VALLEY OF THE

DART, DARTS
4:624; **11:**462

DATE, DATES
FRUIT/TREE **1:**275, 1071; **6:**1176; **7:**309; **9:**367

DAUGHTER
1:238–40, 242, 264, 375, 476, 511, 537, 554, 578, 580, 622, 659, 703, 718, 862, 867, 1084, 1124, 1126, 1139, 1142, 1147, 1149; **2:**212, 214, 234, 393, 428, 559, 592, 628, 737, 741, 749, 757, 853, 876–77, 905, 917, 927, 931, 1284, 1315; **3:**37, 160, 214, 227–28, 280, 330, 353, 368, 414, 522, 551, 565, 573, 741, 757, 768, 788, 832, 833–34, 849, 886, 889, 914, 983, 989, 994, 1007, 1039–43, 1050–51; **4:**127, 132, 176, 218, 243, 328, 861; **5:**5, 24, 38, 76, 90, 363, 397, 425, 428, 553, 629–30, 695, 745, 765, 790, 829; **6:**657, 691, 811, 1038, 1041, 1055, 1059, 1061–62, 1065, 1214, 1220, 1222–24, 1235–36, 1240, 1269–70, 1318, 1321, 1347, 1358, 1360, 1364, 1402, 1438, 1579; **7:**73, 140–41, 184, 187, 208, 216–18, 226, 253, 295, 770, 828, 864, 865; **8:**59, 237, 321, 337, 358, 613; **9:**87–88, 91, 98, 158, 189, 273–74, 359, 574; **10:**321; **11:**147–48, 456; BABYLON **3:**1171; **6:**160, 406, 410–13, 423, 913; **7:**760–61; DAUGHTER-IN-LAW **1:**600, 606, 652, 1125, 1141; **2:**683, 903, 904–6, 908, 910, 921–22, 925, 930, 933, 942, 999, 1002; **3:**328, 914, 987; **4:**556; **6:**1310, 1380; **9:**267; DAUGHTER ZION/DAUGHTER OF ZION **1:**30; **6:**54, 81, 83, 294, 410, 413, 423, 431, 454, 547, 615, 913, 1020–21, 1023, 1027, 1029–30, 1032–36, 1038–46, 1052, 1059, 1061, 1065–66, 1069; **7:**702, 761, 808; **8:**704; **9:**367; OF GOD **8:**137; **11:**639; OF JAIRUS **1:**1106; **4:**787; **8:**63, 587–88, 612, 619, 630, 634, 707, 729; **9:**24, 155, 175, 190–91, 205, 415, 432, 486, 684; **10:**540; OF JEPHTHAH **2:**551, 724, 729, 741, 748, 762–63, 766–67, 782, 821, 827, 830–31, 833–35, 837–38, 842, 860, 872, 884, 886, 1080; **3:**1174; **5:**127, 412, 629; **7:**385–86; **8:**598; OF PHARAOH **1:**298, 699–701; **3:**67, 81, 87, 90, 93; **6:**432, 1343; **12:**140; OF SAUL **2:**546, 1120–21, 1127, 1139, 1170, 1224, 1233, 1248, 1250–52, 1359; **3:**368, 395; WOMAN'S **2:**804; **8:**62, 337, 590; **9:**155

DAVID, CITY OF
See DAVID, CITY OF *in PLACES IN THE BIBLE*

DAWN
OF DAY **1:**566–67; **2:**182, 185, 235, 614, 854, 992; **3:**201, 776, 1028; **4:**368, 597–98, 602–3, 624, 626, 631, 906, 926, 929; **5:**400, 419, 645, 676, 731; **6:**515; **7:**250, 252, 317, 521, 525, 667, 694, 697, 783; **8:**543, 722; **9:**60, 488; **10:**277, 676, 727–29; **11:**410, 438; **12:**343, 619; "DEER OF THE DAWN" **4:**609, 656; AS EXPRESSION OF NEWNESS *(e.g., dawn of faith)* **1:**27, 77, 166, 247, 768; **2:**282, 511; **3:**381, 396, 654; **5:**2, 308, 313, 447, 503; **7:**568, 654, 766, 770; **8:**50, 167, 266, 270; **10:**398, 464, 526, 701, 727–28; **11:**701; **12:**635; AS NAME OF FOREIGN GODS **4:**906; **6:**159, 344

DAY, DAYS
OF ATONEMENT (*see* ATONEMENT, DAY OF); OF CHRIST **11:**46, 288, 483, 485–86, 513, 516, 536; FORTY **1:**391–92, 882, 887, 930, 1085; **2:**126, 1110; **3:**142, 996; **6:**1145, 1147, 1412; **7:**122, 511–12, 528; **8:**163, 535, 600; **9:**97–99, 485, 488, 705; **10:**40–41, 43, 45, 47; GREAT (*see under* GREAT); OF JUDGMENT (*see* JUDGMENT DAY); LAST (*see* LAST DAY/LATTER DAY); OF THE LORD/YAHWEH **2:**602, 613; **3:**179; **4:**46, 210, 532, 612; **5:**117, 303; **6:**22, 39, 42, 65, 70–73, 84, 98, 113, 156, 188, 194, 210, 216, 227, 277, 300, 500, 709, 767, 805–6, 883, 885–86, 1102, 1157, 1162, 1165–67, 1169, 1201, 1277, 1303, 1314, 1342, 1344, 1412–14, 1435, 1461, 1466, 1524, 1529, 1578; **7:**267, 302, 304–5, 311–13, 316–18, 320, 323–24, 326–29, 331, 333–36, 344, 366, 393, 435–36, 438–43, 449, 451, 453–54, 493, 660–61, 663–66, 669, 675–86, 688, 691, 696, 699–700, 702, 723, 827, 836, 847,

852, 875–76; **8:**531; **9:**47, 83, 158, 195, 220, 234, 264, 330, 332, 460; **10:**64, 82, 375, 799–800, 847, 852; **11:**46, 54, 229, 438, 483, 723, 725–28, 741, 747, 750, 755, 758, 760; **12:**121, 343, 345, 495, 543, 566, 614, 616, 631, 677, 703; THE LORD'S **4:**1156; **6:**335, 709, 919; **7:**313; **8:**279; **12:**248, 566, 569; MEMORIAL (*see under* MEMORIAL); OF PREPARATION **8:**697, 702; **9:**493, 452, 704–5, 719, 814, 823, 833; SEVEN **1:**278, 316, 321, 375, 391–92, 460, 553, 557, 742–43, 913, 924, 1057, 1060, 1062, 1065, 1084, 1096, 1098, 1100, 1104–6, 1156–60, 1171; **2:**90, 110–11, 151, 162, 232–33, 412–13, 415, 588, 606–7, 1010, 1043, 1055, 1068, 1071, 1297; **3:**123, 221, 802, 1002, 1142; **4:**358, 366, 370–71, 561; **5:**809; **6:**1111, 1128, 1132, 1447, 1453, 1488, 1499, 1526, 1569, 1586; **7:**122; **8:**468; **9:**69, 119, 414, 616; **10:**357; **12:**104, 525, 629; SEVENTH **1:**346, 815, 845, 871, 924, 926, 1065, 1086, 1098, 1132, 1156, 1160–61, 1180; **2:**212, 233, 332, 850; **3:**712, 882, 1002; **6:**942, 1420, 1454, 1585; **7:**722; **9:**542, 622; **12:**53, 271; THIRD **1:**88, 836, 1026–28, 1051, 1057, 1133; **2:**1201; **3:**712, 962, 1142; **6:**10, 223, 1149; **7:**250, 380; **8:**322, 348–49, 729–30; **9:**18, 201, 206, 280–81, 351–52, 419, 468–69, 478, 481, 486, 536, 687; **10:**348, 976; **12:**62 (*see also* THIRD DAY); THREE **1:**217, 392, 496, 556, 615, 628, 715, 768, 1121; **2:**19, 94, 96–97, 253, 586, 594, 600, 850, 1193, 1232, 1351, 1381; **3:**43, 46, 177, 726, 730, 742, 759, 1041, 1093, 1156; **4:**46, 125, 626; **5:**204, 809; **6:**367, 1129; **7:**380, 504–5, 509, 511–12, 526; **8:**296, 348–49, 363, 614–15, 652, 660, 685, 695, 713, 723, 728; **9:**77, 201, 243, 281, 352, 458, 536, 687; **10:**151, 161, 325; **12:**43, 59

DAY STAR
2:191; **6:**159, 344

DEACON, DEACONS
2:54; **8:**103, 398, 432; **9:**425; **10:**761–62, 766, 828, 969; **11:**38, 135, 151, 471, 480, 482, 775, 779, 802, 804, 806–7, 810, 813, 822, 864, 869

DEACONESS
10:762. *See also* DEACON

DEAD, ABODE OF THE
5:341; **7:**506; **12:**302

DEAD SEA SCROLLS
See DEAD SEA SCROLLS *in ANCIENT LITERATURE*; QUMRAN/SCROLLS *in ANCIENT LITERATURE*

DEAF, DEAFNESS
1:1180; **2:**511; **3:**592; **5:**91, 355; **6:**247, 249, 281, 283, 361, 364, 369–72, 376–78, 381, 388–89, 393, 442, 544; **7:**267; **8:**63, 69, 522, 572, 590, 612, 618–19; **9:**58, 161, 178, 241–42, 244–45, 287, 340, 374; **10:**616, 626, 700; **11:**254; **12:**510; AND BLIND **1:**1133; **2:**492; **4:**569; **6:**281, 317, 334, 364, 368, 370–71, 376–77, 388, 391, 410, 544; **8:**619; **9:**178, 287

DEATH
OF CHRIST **1:**191, 1015, 1042, 1120; **2:**82; **3:**502, 612; **6:**723, 816; **7:**10, 409; **9:**714; **10:**372, 382, 387, 529, 559, 786, 808–9, 811–12, 818, 822, 849, 869, 918, 935–38, 973, 977–78, 981, 983–84, 989, 993–94; **11:**26, 69, 75, 81, 85, 88, 91–92, 95, 98–99, 138, 176, 187, 195, 199, 203–4, 219, 228, 235, 240, 243–47, 249, 251, 256, 260–62, 270, 274, 276, 284, 289, 326, 344, 347, 355, 373, 376, 396, 400, 435, 450, 529, 536–37, 556, 570, 572–73, 600, 606, 609–10, 623, 626–28, 630, 633, 636, 643, 678, 734, 799, 843; **12:**40, 94, 108–9, 118, 300, 441, 569–70, 642 (*see also* JESUS THE CHRIST: CRUCIFIXION, RESURRECTION, AND ASCENSION OF *in PERSONS IN THE BIBLE*); OVERCOME **8:**589; **9:**844; **11:**63; PENALTY **1:**374, 606, 863, 923, 1126, 1134, 1141–43, 1164–65; **2:**128, 286, 329, 422, 434, 446–48, 470, 493, 587, 628, 669, 756, 1080, 1358; **3:**34, 156, 1031; **4:**165, 829, 1127; **5:**752; **6:**109, 258, 278, 775, 1135, 1234, 1448; **7:**189, 209, 229, 278, 831; **8:**279, 551, 712–13; **9:**628, 815–16, 819–20; **10:**326, 336, 360, 434, 586; **12:**123, 271; POWER(S) OF **1:**479, 690, 746, 755, 804, 892; **2:**60, 66, 97–98, 152, 1008, 1297–99; **3:**1029; **4:**223, 457, 471, 878–79, 898; **5:**430; **6:**218, 367; **8:**346; **9:**690–91, 694–95, 699, 708, 740; **11:**208; **12:**40; POWER OVER **5:**563; **8:**590; **11:**42, 208; PUT TO **1:**238, 281, 852, 873, 1101, 1142, 1182; **2:**393, 421, 441, 446, 455, 457, 614, 641, 648, 886, 1053, 1055–56, 1126, 1292, 1346–47; **3:**32, 34, 215, 370, 1141; **4:**87, 212; **6:**469, 1214, 1219, 1258, 1309; **7:**190, 229; **8:**30, 463; **9:**88, 401, 428, 449; **10:**181, 467, 539, 542, 579, 598, 704; **11:**214, 328, 435, 585, 641–42, 645; **12:**151, 292–93, 303, 710; AND RESURRECTION **1:**13, 84, 91, 189, 192, 199, 210; **2:**90; **3:**78, 185, 188, 738, 997; **4:**442, 738, 754, 765, 766, 830, 870, 874, 879, 903, 938, 954, 1001, 1022, 1048, 1119, 1131, 1143, 1156, 1226, 1252, 1280; **5:**15, 343; **6:**223, 469, 1171; **7:**2, 4, 10, 15, 317; **8:**52, 71–72, 112, 138, 188, 198, 245, 249, 325, 341, 360, 476, 511, 632, 657, 671, 698, 732; **9:**30–31, 117, 200–201, 206–7, 210, 215, 351, 460, 486–87, 490, 533, 537, 545, 671, 681, 695, 710, 715, 722, 726, 780, 785, 842, 848; **11:**26, 69, 82, 85, 92, 99, 139, 205, 218–19, 228, 246–49, 274–75, 283, 285, 308, 313, 317, 326, 344, 384, 480, 491, 502, 573, 600, 608–10, 614, 628, 636, 639, 643, 678–79, 689, 715, 724–25, 734; **12:**42, 64, 93, 180, 213, 255, 292–93, 297; SECOND **12:**492, 517, 577, 613, 708, 722; SIN AND **1:**209–10, 820; **2:**789, 861, 1326,

DEATH *(continued)*
1372; **3:**114, 370, 587; **4:**906, 1042, 1044, 1055; **5:**77, 111, 557, 630, 764, 823; **9:**690, 714; **10:**62, 66, 250, 399, 427, 511–13, 523–25, 528, 531–33, 535, 537, 540–41, 543, 546, 550–51, 553, 555–56, 560–61, 565–68, 571, 574, 576, 578, 585, 588–90, 598, 618, 625, 634, 643–44, 664, 681; **11:**66, 72, 87, 246, 321, 389, 395, 505–6; **12:**31, 43, 313, 345, 443–44, 500

DEBT, DEBTS
1:226–27, 239, 262, 377, 704, 770, 862, 950, 1039–42, 1170, 1172–74; **2:**265–68, 379, 404, 406–7, 471, 566–68, 573, 578, 590, 592–96, 628, 656, 659, 670, 687, 696, 711, 1198; **3:**186, 199, 540, 569, 583, 779, 783, 797, 819, 851; **4:**125, 401, 500, 511; **5:**187, 198, 200, 205, 746, 775; **6:**282, 305, 436, 831–32; **7:**141, 200, 365, 800–801; **8:**202–5, 382, 453, 726; **9:**147, 170, 230, 235, 269, 289, 307–8, 393; **10:**67, 253, 423, 435, 479, 491, 540, 549, 558, 591, 600, 604, 696, 724–25, 727, 756; **11:**31, 124, 351, 365, 404, 545, 617, 834, 899; **12:**386, 554, 646; SLAVE(RY/S) **1:**227, 862, 864–65, 872; **2:**406, 408, 470, 566, 570, 589–90, 593–95, 609, 626, 630; **3:**780; **6:**14, 21; **7:**416, 550, 822; **8:**720

DEBTOR, DEBTORS
1:770, 772, 868, 872, 1041–42, 1173; **2:**404, 469, 592, 594, 659; **3:**186, 540, 625, 779–80; **4:**125; **5:**199–200, 205; **6:**211, 1259, 1261, 1450; **7:**647–48, 801; **8:**202; **9:**169–70, 269–71, 307–9; **10:**591–92, 601

DECALOGUE
1:38–39, 42, 129, 311, 315, 831, 839, 840, 844, 847, 849, 852, 854, 880, 949–50, 1131, 1178; **2:**128, 235, 291, 322, 328, 449, 470, 492, 544; **3:**1015; **4:**773, 881–82, 1003–4; **5:**80, 558, 622, 730, 842; **6:**176, 620, 628, 637, 641, 702, 710, 1258–59, 1261, 1309; **7:**236, 548, 859, 868; **8:**32, 189–91, 222, 277, 333–34, 390, 645, 648; **9:**105, 314; **10:**725; **11:**456; **12:**193, 195. *See also* TEN COMMANDMENTS

DECK
OF A BOAT/SHIP **6:**1374

DEDICATION, FEAST OF
See under FEASTS/FESTIVALS

DEEP
DARKNESS **1:**501; **3:**78; **4:**367, 423, 430, 511, 577, 601, 603, 768; **6:**510; THE DEEP **1:**203, 274, 342, 356, 392, 495, 718; **4:**420, 531–32, 603, 624–25, 823, 853, 886, 952, 984, 1028, 1054, 1098, 1118, 1205; **5:**92–93, 663, 833; **6:**13, 212, 965, 1369, 1422, 1425, 1428–29; **7:**101, 505–6, 750; **10:**659, 663; **12:**581; SHADOW(S) **4:**430; SLEEP **1:**353, 446; **2:**1175–76; **4:**378; **5:**180; **6:**243; **7:**115, 497, 518; **11:**438; WATER(S) **1:**203; **4:**951, 1205; **5:**172, 185; **9:**115–16; **11:**169

DEER
1:667, 1081; **3:**782; **4:**311, 598, 608–10, 656, 854; **5:**69, 406, 433; **6:**18; FALLOW **1:**1081. *See also* DOE; FAWN; ROE; STAG

DEFILE
1:1011, 1071, 1075, 1077, 1106, 1147–48; **2:**60, 64, 66, 170, 198, 445, 447; **3:**871, 1144; **4:**40, 101, 286, 1111; **5:**634; **6:**150, 189, 201–4, 255, 603, 1167, 1209, 1258, 1282, 1286, 1310, 1388, 1458, 1489, 1509, 1561, 1579; **7:**44, 161, 334; **8:**32, 607–8; **9:**248; **10:**168, 219–20, 317; **11:**260; **12:**489, 726

DEFILEMENT
1:581, 584, 586, 997, 999, 1060–62, 1074, 1085, 1147, 1148; **2:**15, 23, 26, 47, 56, 60, 62–69, 123, 149, 151, 170, 233, 248, 445; **3:**582, 1009; **4:**230, 257, 285–86, 995; **5:**533–34; **6:**454–55, 603–4, 1063, 1159, 1161, 1314, 1316, 1394, 1488–89, 1492, 1534, 1574; **7:**53, 553, 567, 728, 829; **8:**122, 330, 333, 335, 608, 663, 684; **9:**242, 815; **10:**831, 851, 899; **11:**103, 105, 430, 442, 451, 866; **12:**108, 336, 351–52, 664, 681

DELIVERER
2:647, 725, 767, 770, 773, 779, 795, 797, 802, 819, 825, 841, 845, 847, 849, 853–54, 863, 953, 1016, 1040–41, 1053–55, 1062, 1110–11; **3:**236, 949, 1113, 1115, 1130, 1165, 1177; **4:**40; **6:**516, 1386; **7:**281; **8:**135, 361; GOD AS (*see under* GOD, METAPHORS FOR *in PERSONS IN THE BIBLE*); JESUS AS (*see under* JESUS THE CHRIST, NAMES FOR/TITLES OF *in PERSONS IN THE BIBLE*)

DELUGE
1:56, 306, 308; **4:**603, 608; **6:**1117, 1128, 1213, 1314; **7:**674, 696; **12:**646. *See also* FLOOD

DEMON, DEMONS
1:1112; **2:**614; **3:**975, 977, 980, 989, 1008–10, 1026, 1029, 1031, 1033, 1037, 1040–41, 1048; **4:**611; **5:**384; **6:**655; **7:**501; **8:**62, 64, 223, 232, 285, 296, 368, 536, 541, 543, 580, 584–85, 609, 633–36, 665, 708; **9:**110, 113, 186–87, 192, 209–10, 241–45, 273, 355, 619, 644–45, 671; **10:**232, 268–69, 451, 649; POSSESSED BY **8:**62, 64, 232, 285, 368, 521, 535, 543, 546, 551, 562, 583, 591, 609, 665; **9:**113, 187–88, 242, 355, 730; TABLE OF **10:**912

DEMONIAC, DEMONIACS
8:62, 232, 481, 581–85, 589, 609–10, 634; **9:**20, 111, 113, 166, 175, 184, 186–91, 326, 370; **10:**232, 269; **12:**631

DEMONOLOGY
5:502; **11:**627

DEMYTHOLOGIZE (*OR* DEMYTHOLOGIZED, DEMYTHOLOGIZATION, *ETC.*)
1:110, 195, 197, 375; **2:**387–88; **3:**70; **6:**213, 1425; **10:**268–69; **11:**309; **12:**313, 404, 507–8, 546

DENARIUS, DENARII
See under COIN

DENIAL (*OR* DENIES, *ETC.*)
CHRIST/JESUS **1:**1063; **2:**753, 810; **8:**285, 351, 523, 624, 626, 707, 715–16, 730; **9:**12, 202, 207, 253, 391, 423, 425, 428, 438–39, 449, 589, 644, 733; **11:**56; **12:**43, 345, 435, 485–86; OF CHRIST/JESUS **7:**834; **8:**287, 705; **9:**252–53, 711, 733; **10:**981; **11:**844; **12:**403, 412, 443, 485–86; SELF-DENIAL (*see* SELF-DENIAL)

DEPOSE (*OR* DEPOSES, *ETC.*)
1:665, 821; **2:**562, 589, 606, 988, 1065, 1345; **3:**17, 31, 118, 242, 245, 251, 285, 287–88, 290, 872; **4:**792, 1088; **6:**133, 559, 743, 1272, 1326, 1387; **7:**52, 128, 631, 678; **8:**8; **9:**55, 88, 363, 697

DEPOSIT (*OR* DEPOSITED, DEPOSITION, *ETC.*)
OF FUNDS/THINGS LEFT AT A HOLY PLACE **1:**124, 219, 242, 1040; **3:**847, 877, 975, 989, 995–96, 1011, 1014, 1017, 1044; **4:**34, 207–8, 211, 223; **5:**188, 827; **6:**509, 1591; **7:**61, 822; **10:**96, 907; **11:**376, 830, 837–39, 841–42; **12:**250; GEOLOGI CAL **1:**388, 473; **3:**692–93, 736; **6:**1336, 1361, 1378; **12:**489; OF WRITING(S) **1:**38, 112, 231, 311, 315, 860, 880; **6:**797; **10:**182; **11:**659; **12:**367–68

DEPTHS
OF CHAOS/SHEOL/WATERS, ETC. **1:**616, 799–800; **4:**313, 332, 463, 519, 529–32, 590, 624, 764, 797, 951–52, 1028, 1118, 1204–7, 1220, 1236; **5:**69, 101, 149, 254, 590, 593, 757; **6:**343, 388, 411, 728–30, 850, 1057, 1445; **7:**101, 479–80, 506, 510, 589, 750; **8:**221; **10:**668

DEPUTIES, DEPUTY
2:435; **3:**698; **4:**60, 62, 68, 140, 222, 289; **6:**1361; **7:**787; **12:**283

DESCENT
1:311, 334, 427, 447, 643, 647, 651, 954; **2:**110, 742, 763, 821, 1126, 1129, 1205, 1340; **3:**169, 502, 1159; **4:**100, 488; **5:**120, 354, 618, 834, 866; **6:**365, 962; **7:**6, 480, 495, 497, 504, 507, 509–11; **8:**34, 366, 631; **9:**301, 529, 600; **10:**123; **11:**501; **12:**42, 630; ANCESTRY **1:**325; **2:**558, 656, 711, 933, 1030, 1268; **3:**217, 329, 344, 441, 450, 667, 678, 684, 691, 805–6, 842, 846, 849; **6:**1568; **7:**58, 206, 210, 224, 291; **8:**137, 157, 359, 526; **9:**84, 391, 638, 678; **10:**417–18, 777; **11:**526; **12:**90, 734; INTO DEATH/HADES/SHEOL **1:**447; **4:**603; **6:**1104, 1176–77, 1358–59, 1368, 1423, 1427, 1429, 1438, 1440; **7:**93, 504, 506–7, 509–10; **10:**663; **11:**421; **12:**294; OF GOD/JESUS/THE SPIRIT **1:**412, 946; **2:**25, 32, 90; **4:**603; **6:**365, 492; **8:**366, 528, 534–35; **9:**91, 529, 532, 551–52, 559, 600, 603, 610, 732, 782, 844; **10:**416, 630; **11:**421, 501, 600; **12:**42, 82, 116, 294, 592

DESERT
1:92, 215, 219–20, 255, 258, 620, 666, 991, 995, 999, 1081, 1112, 1144; **2:**8, 14, 18, 94–95, 97, 160, 169, 185, 189, 308, 355–56, 374, 555, 589, 602, 605, 607, 609, 627, 660, 677, 752, 795, 802, 865, 1088, 1193; **3:**9, 93, 139–40, 337, 726, 730, 1004, 1019, 1040, 1155; **4:**44, 48, 58, 133, 137, 141, 198, 247, 380, 530, 598, 604, 607, 621, 1041, 1117; **5:**51, 192, 194, 302–3, 375, 390, 399–400, 402, 437, 441, 446, 469, 494, 516, 525, 528, 531–32, 534, 540, 560, 573–75, 577–78, 583, 585, 590–93, 598, 757; **6:**8, 43, 146, 149, 185–86, 188–89, 280–81, 335–36, 365, 367, 375, 378, 407, 432–33, 436, 447, 455, 614, 708, 711, 914, 981, 1103, 1118, 1146, 1161, 1217, 1247, 1266, 1271, 1279–82, 1284, 1288–90, 1294, 1319, 1330, 1338, 1351, 1397, 1401, 1434, 1472, 1491, 1504, 1511, 1601, 1607 **7:**71–72, 224, 269–70, 273, 362, 455, 691, 701; **8:**66, 156, 270, 325, 376, 478, 520, 525, 535, 543, 600, 614, 705, 707; **9:**97, 184, 242, 268, 300, 479; **10:**143, 850; **11:**463, 721, 876; **12:**55, 82, 95, 97–98, 101–4, 117, 266, 268, 428, 565, 591, 649, 651, 680, 725–26. *See also by name in PLACES IN THE BIBLE*

DESIGN (*OR* DESIGNED, DESIGNATION, *ETC.*)
ARCHITECTURAL/CRAFT **1:**222, 251, 353, 394, 896–98, 900–901, 906, 927, 972, 1056, 1061; **2:**399; **4:**336, 614, 616, 630–31; **5:**9, 618, 627, 679; **6:**342, 388, 1374, 1549, 1562, 1607; **7:**738, 839; **9:**171; **10:**434, 462, 469, 994; **11:**23, 298; **12:**265, 728; DIVINE/GOD'S **1:**349; **2:**399; **4:**319, 598, 601–2, 611–13, 623, 629, 1052, 1098, 1100; **6:**133, 204, 247, 344, 364–65, 390, 407, 439, 460, 465; **9:**42, 50, 59, 67, 77, 81; **10:**343, 578, 857, 943; **11:**269, 242, 256, 263, 269, 298, 376, 410; **12:**98; BY GOD **1:**884; **2:**1029, 1036, 1039; **3:**1031; **4:**611, 613, 634; **6:**401, 1141; **7:**638, 731; **9:**463; **10:**494; **11:**277; **12:**711;

DESIRE, DESIRES
FOR DEATH/LIFE **3:**1017; **4:**363, 395, 416, 479, 705, 796, 815, 1021; **12:**358; DIVINE/GOD'S/LORD'S/YAHWEH'S **2:**121, 997, 1057, 1295; **3:**1178; **4:**734, 854, 887, 1004; **6:**564, 605, 649, 1171, 1349; **9:**742, 798; **11:**728, 874; EVIL/WICKED **5:**44, 126; **11:**427, 642; **12:**178, 187, 258, 273, 336, 355, 494; FLESHLY/PHYSICAL/SEXUAL **1:**383; **2:**457, 1302–4, 1310; **3:**871, 1159–60; **5:**71, 75, 364,

DESIRE, DESIRES *(continued)*
753; **6:**492; **7:**178, 210; **8:**191; **9:**521; **10:**563, 729–30, 874; **11:**186, 311, 325–26, 634, 642, 718; **12:**239, 272, 337, 352; FOR A KING **2:**1027, 1032, 1049; **9:**595; FOR REVENGE/VENGEANCE **2:**763, 766, 790, 1055, 1160, 1263, 1310; **3:**934, 1099; **4:**669, 1125–27, 1227–29; **6:**160, 278–79, 718, 1349, 1357, 1438; **7:**333, 484, 563, 576, 588; FOR WISDOM **1:**361; **5:**509; **7:**178; **11:**443

DESOLATING SACRILEGE
4:11, 39, 71, 232; **8:**429, 442, 445, 657, 689, 693, 730; **9:**704

DESTINY
1:116, 159, 317, 363, 521, 538, 601, 697, 788–89, 825, 837, 878, 882, 924–25, 938, 1026; **2:**187, 192, 350, 495, 521, 534–35, 603, 745, 931, 981–82, 1038–39, 1165, 1185, 1226, 1234, 1288; **3:**5, 113, 273, 303, 402–3, 426, 518, 969, 1086, 1160; **4:**402, 675, 689, 695, 712, 717–18, 721, 725, 811, 819, 822, 849, 857, 876, 891, 913, 924, 928, 931, 1007, 1041, 1066, 1099, 1221, 1225, 1237, 1252, 1279; **5:**2, 9, 282, 299, 301, 313, 327, 329, 337, 339, 341, 350, 359, 464–65, 486–87, 556, 677, 790; **6:**189, 328, 347, 375, 401, 406, 428, 430–31, 465, 471, 491, 515, 540, 548, 551, 580, 608, 640, 642, 699, 702, 717, 766, 787, 852, 1263, 1598; **7:**45, 55, 107, 129, 354, 638; **8:**310, 314, 316, 319, 386, 414, 455, 463, 657; **9:**42, 77, 245; **10:**29, 49, 96, 122–23, 126, 147, 150, 152, 214, 237, 256, 266, 270, 273, 275, 283, 288, 291, 305, 311, 323, 327, 338, 341, 344, 348–49, 352, 357, 359, 366, 602, 816, 852, 975; **11:**6, 112, 344, 376, 386, 412, 494, 535, 547, 718, 792, 847; **12:**188, 247, 251, 268, 401, 412, 575, 653, 713, 730; ETERNAL/ULTIMATE **5:**114, 311, 339; **6:**462; **8:**217, 484; **10:**820, 857; **12:**402, 577, 632, 658, 720; OF ISRAEL/THE NATION/THE PEOPLE **1:**697, 834, 841, 877, 924, 979; **2:**187, 293, 364, 513, 962, 1366; **3:**278; **5:**692; **6:**378, 381, 462, 664; **10:**19, 192, 419, 747; **11:**375, 874; **12:**266, 521; THEOLOGICAL **3:**304; **6:**540

DESTROY, UTTERLY
2:349, 1087–88; **6:**1257; **7:**424; **12:**682

DESTROYER, DESTROYERS
1:697, 777; **2:**140, 615, 797, 910; **4:**21, 414, 866; **5:**185, 446, 459, 464, 471, 536, 591–92; **6:**185–86, 270, 431, 693, 740, 813, 891–92, 912, 1043, 1388; **7:**54, 75, 293, 345, 373, 382, 485, 493, 505–6, 509, 680, 691; **8:**343; **10:**181, 913, 920; **12:**631–32

DESTRUCTION, DEVOTED TO
See under DEVOTED

DETERMINSIM
1:287, 601; **5:**285, 303, 456, 626, 788; **6:**134, 717; **9:**279, 388, 416, 423; **10:**109

DEUTERONOMIST
See under DEUTERONOMY, BOOK OF

DEUTERONOMY, BOOK OF
1:38, 129, 294, 315, 828; **2:**5, 10–11, 47, 170, 219, 250, 747, 753, 1061; **3:**4, 26, 278, 993, 1014; **4:**44, 50, 814, 857, 881–82, 1110, 1167; **5:**492, 532, 560, 564, 627, 655; **6:**50, 443, 671, 1118, 1491; **7:**204, 662; **9:**312; **11:**258; D DEUTERONOMIST *(also known as D)* **2:**297–98, 307, 309–10, 563, 567, 572, 575–76, 579, 589–90, 593, 606, 620, 626, 629, 634, 639, 641, 657–60, 665, 678, 684, 687–89, 697, 714, 952, 954, 956, 1020, 1257, 1270; **3:**26, 28, 35, 37, 88, 124, 406, 408, 432, 503, 506, 518, 522, 525, 590, 600, 651; **5:**555; **6:**693; **7:**260, 272; **8:**30; DEUTERONOMIC HISTORY **1:**129, 307; **2:**420, 895; **4:**57; **6:**949; **8:**41; DEUTERONOMISTIC HISTORY **1:**166, 317; **2:**6, 96–97, 166, 254, 264, 274, 291, 556–62, 564–65, 568–69, 572–75, 579–80, 588–90, 600–601, 607–9, 612, 626–27, 634–36, 639, 649, 658–60, 673, 687–88, 701, 711, 714, 718, 724, 727, 861, 865, 945, 952, 956, 969–70, 996–97, 1101, 1019, 1032, 1060, 1199, 1203, 1229, 1233, 1254–55, 1270, 1276; **3:**4, 695, 705, 1119; **4:**1167; **5:**329, 850, 853; **6:**2, 6, 158, 176, 284–86, 297, 303, 443, 455, 599, 621, 693, 751, 1521, 1561; **7:**204–6, 594, 764

DEVIL, DEVILS
1:97, 360, 363, 586, 1112, 1118; **2:**759, 872; **3:**426, 1108; **4:**347, 1048, 1055; **5:**227, 496, 742, 791; **6:**98, 226, 1130, 1155, 1445, 1534; **7:**562, 676; **8:**151, 163–65, 223, 232, 290, 310, 315, 333, 335, 341, 354, 424, 455, 459, 491; **9:**14, 27, 79, 97–101, 110–11, 178–79, 186–87, 235, 241, 282, 413, 416, 436, 442, 456, 611, 641–46, 713, 722, 730, 752–53, 772; **10:**166, 274; **11:**355, 423, 429–31, 460, 548, 806–7, 846, 849; **12:**40–41, 43, 209–10, 252, 303, 317, 376, 379, 382, 398, 400, 403, 411–13, 416, 418, 489–90, 516, 532–34, 577, 649–51, 661, 667, 703, 707–8, 712, 714–15

DEVOTED
1:2, 10, 90, 96, 216, 283, 287, 300, 306, 323, 526, 604, 786, 924, 949, 1019, 1021, 1072; **2:**540, 557, 568–69, 647, 670, 739, 787, 841, 871–72, 894, 954, 1018, 1044, 1066, 1110, 1149, 1197, 1251, 1270; **3:**138, 304, 343, 344, 358, 388, 407, 445–46, 461–62, 464, 470, 474, 496, 544, 552, 555, 612, 622, 624, 628, 631, 646, 981, 1082, 1086, 1178; **4:**47, 361, 431, 467, 641, 657, 1020–21, 1050; **5:**25, 84, 255, 319, 322, 673;

6:19–20, 310, 750, 933, 1205, 1319; **7:**215, 254, 353, 415, 567; **8:**32, 45, 75, 78, 93, 224, 279, 359, 384, 393, 429, 547, 555, 700, 708; **9:**11, 62, 136, 165, 168, 176, 191, 195, 260–61, 265, 269, 309, 375, 402, 414, 433–34, 486, 858, 863; **10:**44, 135, 256, 1000–1001; **11:**12, 19, 52, 55, 101, 121, 131, 179, 332, 419, 453, 645, 843; **12:**26, 86, 180, 197, 217, 221, 261, 705; TO DESTRUCTION/GOD **1:**867, 1048, 1128, 1187, 1189; **2:**255, 393, 743; **4:**67, 665, 991, 1174; **5:**33; **6:**877; **8:**179; **11:**152, 533; TO THE LORD/YAHWEH **1:**845; **2:**519, 590; **3:**96, 576; **4:**82; **6:**203, 212, 1580; **7:**567; **9:**69; THING **2:**147; **6:**1580

DEVOUT
1:57, 88–89, 1109; **2:**109; **3:**132, 643, 736, 1001, 1114; **4:**156, 243; **5:**463, 671, 808, 833, 837; **6:**50, 60, 491; **8:**46, 626; **9:**45, 49, 69–72, 179, 201, 217, 233, 250, 255, 341, 461, 464–65, 487; **10:**19, 55–57, 59, 63, 70, 72, 76–78, 81, 84, 88, 105, 132, 146, 150–51, 162–64, 188, 192, 194–96, 237–38, 244, 291, 305, 307, 312, 343, 362–63, 426, 461, 464, 505–6, 529, 590, 600, 759; **11:**141, 277, 289, 331, 392, 529; **12:**62, 387, 423

DEW
1:536, 813; **2:**802–3, 826, 1206; **3:**127; **4:**539, 598, 604, 1214; **5:**54, 180, 411, 541, 578, 708, 732, 757, 834; **7:**164, 252–53, 263, 288, 296, 574, 576, 796; **10:**975; **12:**710

DIADEM, DIADEMS
1:912, 1061; **4:**13, 31, 105; **5:**454, 486, 592; **6:**982; **7:**766, 839; **12:**593, 649, 656, 699. *See also* CROWN

DIAMOND, DIAMONDS
6:707, 1126; **8:**314

DIASPORA
1:288, 290–91, 336, 1181; **2:**866; **3:**402, 723, 855, 858, 870, 872, 890, 898, 935, 940–41, 949, 969, 977, 987, 1154; **4:**183–84, 199, 1024; **5:**490, 542–43, 565; **6:**313, 315, 377, 378, 430, 441, 448, 456, 935, 940, 1080, 1098, 1408, 1505, 1512, 1517, 1527, 1531; **7:**20, 28, 43, 50, 72, 89, 91–93, 95, 100, 111, 122, 124, 136, 155, 169, 194, 667, 699–700, 811, 860; **8:**27, 29, 33, 40, 42, 660; **9:**451; **10:**10, 28, 68, 97, 120, 133, 135, 143, 146–47, 151, 161, 169, 191–93, 198–200, 205, 213, 218, 220, 222, 226, 230, 238, 243, 252, 254–55, 267, 284, 292, 294, 296, 305, 318, 326, 363, 461, 626, 661, 698, 754; **11:**535, 561, 631, 696, 799, 820; **12:**183, 246, 272; EASTERN **3:**856, 859, 860, 959, 977; **7:**5–6, 20, 112; JEWS **3:**858, 912, 1098, 1113; **4:**562; **7:**103, 105, 121, 810; **8:**40–41, 371; **10:**36, 53, 112, 121, 150, 175, 236, 261; JUDAISM **1:**290; **7:**95; **8:**54; **10:**121, 130, 319, 374

DIDRACHMA
See under COIN

DILL
6:238

DINNER, DINNERS
1:634; **2:**1039; **3:**908, 1002, 1005, 1160; **4:**359; **5:**206, 461, 624; **6:**1330; **7:**400; **8:**14, 105, 234–35, 407, 416–18, 546, 593, 698–99; **9:**22, 26, 169–70, 286–87, 306, 393, 701; **10:**850, 858, 893, 900, 921, 923, 934, 964; **11:**104

DIRGE, DIRGES
2:1205; **4:**111; **5:**273; **6:**20, 59–60, 82, 158, 163, 167–68, 186, 190, 655, 805, 890, 1019–21, 1266, 1268, 1273–74, 1367–68, 1371, 1373, 1382, 1384–85, 1391, 1429, 1432, 1434; **7:**385–86, 468, 595, 601. *See also under* FUNERAL

DISABILITY, DISABILITIES
1:707, 809, 1133; **6:**281; **8:**62, 223; **9:**134; **10:**545; **11:**342

DISCERN
GOD/GOD'S GRACE/WILL, ETC. **1:**131, 558; **2:**111, 737, 994–95, 1014, 1100, 1258; **3:**167, 868, 906; **4:**845, 889, 1175; **6:**827, 1130, 1412; **8:**189; **10:**38, 52, 209, 212; **11:**437; THE SPIRIT(UAL) **1:**49; **2:**193, 195; **10:**211, 825; **12:**72

DISCHARGE, DISCHARGES
1:316, 1003, 1060, 1074–75, 1085–86, 1096, 1101, 1104–6, 1149; **2:**54, 60–63, 67, 147, 988; **3:**386, 536; **4:**51; **5:**407; **6:**443, 451, 1030, 1234, 1306; **8:**238, 332, 588; **9:**217, 488; **10:**725, 988; **11:**839

DISCIPLE, DISCIPLES
2:200, 753, 804, 810, 847; **3:**1182; **5:**15; **8:**102–3; 116, 158, 169–71, 191, 205–6, 260–61, 270, 346, 350–51, 392, 397, 494, 503, 539, 548, 578, 618, 626, 637, 648–49, 654; **9:**4, 13–17, 21–30, 114, 117–18, 127–28, 130, 138–40, 150, 177, 184, 187, 190, 193–94, 198, 201–3, 211–13, 216–26, 231–32, 291–94, 424–26, 475, 486–87, 530–34, 592, 596–97, 702–3, 710–11, 725–27, 746–50, 759, 783, 809–11, 835–37, 845–48, 856–65; **10:**24, 48–49, 100, 112, 153, 176, 209, 227, 270, 290, 305; **11:**531, 601, 617, 813; **12:**14, 233, 393, 456, 705; BELOVED (*see* BELOVED DISCIPLE *in PERSONS IN THE BIBLE*); "DISCIPLE WHOM JESUS LOVED" **9:**498, 500, 729, 808, 834, 840, 860; **12:**366; OF JOHN **8:**159, 234–36, 270, 536, 548, 556, 725; **9:**15, 25, 426, 530, 533, 557, 560; **12:**571; OF MOSES **9:**588, 659, 809; OUTSIDE THE NT **1:**294; **3:**176, 179, 199, 201, 214, 217, 1019; **5:**13; **6:**313; **7:**204, 528, 711; **8:**19; OF PAUL **10:**262, 267, 969; **11:**369, 582, 634. *See also under* MULTITUDE

DISCIPLESHIP
1:103, 178, 853; **2:**200, 1031, 1093; **3:**145; **4:**673, 928, 1191, 1252; **5:**170, 642; **6:**607–8; **7:**129; **8:**52, 54, 109, 112, 116, 118, 159, 169–70, 178, 180, 182, 201, 210, 217, 219, 220, 222, 229–30, 235, 239, 262, 285, 288, 298, 304, 313–14, 316, 349–50, 353, 359, 367, 370, 390–91, 395, 400, 443, 450–51, 467, 483, 501, 503–4, 515, 537, 540, 548, 566, 574, 578, 625–28, 636, 638, 641, 648–50, 653–54, 674, 678, 707; **9:**27, 78, 98, 117, 126–29, 133, 136–37, 139–40, 150–54, 179, 192, 198, 201–7, 210–11, 216, 226, 250, 261, 291–93, 321–25, 346, 348–49, 402, 427, 439, 481, 499, 515, 530–31, 534, 548, 572, 632, 640–41, 659, 702–3, 710, 714, 720, 726, 729, 733–34, 758, 808–10, 812, 835, 840, 842–43, 861–62, 864–65; **10:**10, 20, 44, 109, 222, 617; **11:**298, 809, 813, 820, 860, 877; **12:**72, 127, 164, 167, 239–40, 423, 437, 575, 657; ASPECT/ESSENCE/MEANING/NATURE OF **8:**223, 239, 263, 270, 275, 298, 328–29, 349–50, 352, 384, 396, 502; **9:**34, 149, 193, 205, 533, 733; CALL TO **4:**928, 1277; **8:**170, 183, 228, 230, 234, 256, 352, 394, 500, 552–53; **9:**111, 114–15, 118, 126, 129, 139, 142, 152, 216–18, 293–94, 469, 533–34, 864; **12:**170; CHRISTIAN **2:**681; **5:**690; **8:**186, 260, 390, 395, 399, 457, 466, 513; **9:**129–30, 429; **10:**30, 130, 155, 261, 290; COST OF **4:**821, 1055; **5:**190; **8:**255, 261, 352, 366; **9:**272, 283, 293–94, 306; **10:**290; LIFE OF **8:**157, 181, 195, 373, 375, 392, 425; **9:**153, 703

DISCIPLINE
1:55, 57, 81, 109, 116, 122, 167, 543, 681, 727, 783, 836, 839, 841, 848, 861, 874, 891, 897, 916, 972, 1073; **2:**112, 256, 613, 629, 633, 1271; **3:**518, 1017, 1019, 1138, 1181; **4:**185, 233, 242, 334, 376, 381, 563, 564, 572, 630, 704, 787, 833, 837, 882, 1058, 1245; **5:**30, 33–34, 50, 59, 68, 70, 80, 123–24, 131, 133–34, 139, 149, 152, 163, 180–82, 188–89, 199, 206, 244–45, 469, 536, 553, 606, 610, 613, 620, 627, 638, 643, 650, 652, 654, 669–70, 685, 687–88, 690, 695, 745, 768, 772, 777, 786, 860; **6:**7, 98, 337, 346, 451, 602, 626, 631, 653, 821, 835, 1087, 1299, 1533, 1563–64, 1592; **7:**152, 231, 258, 583; **8:**78, 83, 93, 97, 99, 112, 123, 212, 214, 258, 304, 308, 377, 458, 607, 666; **9:**448; **10:**320, 606, 617, 782, 804, 825, 841, 851, 909–10, 915, 937, 939; **11:**22, 112, 175, 206, 253, 306, 325, 331, 431, 453, 456, 470, 531, 567, 645, 656, 741, 768, 782, 792, 795, 809, 811, 813, 816, 822, 824–25, 829, 841–42, 847, 852, 864–65, 878; **12:**19, 129, 150, 286, 338, 423, 437, 444, 461, 464, 467–68, 511, 587, 705; DIVINE/GOD'S **4:**381, 383, 499, 630; **5:**627; **12:**147, 150–52, 155, 595; FAMILY/HOUSEHOLD/ PARENTAL **2:**355, 416, 446, 494; **5:**141, 207; **12:**151; MANUAL OF DISCIPLINE **1:**10; **3:**1158; **4:**1285; **5:**690; SELF-DISCIPLINE (*see* SELF-DISCIPLINE); SPIRITUAL **2:**977; **9:**248, 482; **10:**729–30

DISCRETION
2:633; **3:**597, 721, 727, 903–4; **4:**89, 330; **5:**43, 302, 331; **6:**304; **9:**555, 697; **11:**123, 281. *See also* PRUDENCE

DISCUS
4:216, 218

DISEASE, DISEASES
1:216, 428, 431, 629, 744, 753, 808–9, 986, 1003, 1046, 1052, 1074–75, 1080, 1086, 1095, 1097–98, 1100, 1005, 1110, 1180; **2:**15, 59–60, 66–67, 199, 351, 447, 461, 469, 514, 901, 1006–7, 1225, 1381; **3:**178, 192, 197–98, 245, 544, 998, 1024, 1051; **4:**193, 292, 340, 355, 360, 436, 445, 453, 469, 471–72, 524, 547, 704–6, 833, 1047, 1083, 1087; **5:**56, 68, 407, 542, 624, 736, 807–8, 860; **6:**450, 460, 693, 704, 956, 1169, 1223, 1466; **7:**107, 248, 381, 431, 728; **8:**33, 329, 545–46, 619; **9:**99, 111, 120–21, 126, 175, 208, 222, 272, 316, 319, 325, 344, 580; **10:**22, 358, 445, 463; **11:**294, 455, 517, 625, 769; **12:**58, 205, 213, 219, 390, 525, 616, 646, 678, 730; HANSEN'S/SCALY/SKIN **1:**1094–96, 1098, 1100, 1104–5, 1149; **2:**59–60, 67, 104, 147, 469; **3:**251, 592; **4:**355, 401; **8:**224, 544–45, 587; **9:**119 (*see also* LEPROSY). *See also* SICKNESS

DISH, DISHES
1:890, 1026; **2:**78; **3:**276, 487, 679; **4:**34; **5:**181, 327; **6:**718, 988, 1338; **8:**703–4; **9:**46, 247, 286, 418

DISHONOR
2:775–76, 865, 1250, 1359; **3:**1137; **4:**208, 236, 349; **5:**172, 187, 616, 705, 862; **6:**692, 956, 990, 1002, 1004, 1009, 1030, 1214, 1223–24, 1321, 1442, 1483; **7:**224; **8:**654, 670; **9:**401, 584, 645; **10:**108–9, 447, 500, 929, 987; **11:**509, 536, 824, 845; **12:**10, 485, 487

DISOBEDIENCE
1:363, 366, 496, 679, 695, 750, 753, 814, 960–61, 986, 1118–19, 1133, 1137, 1178, 1180–81; **2:**127, 159, 162, 179, 215, 298–99, 306, 319–20, 339, 490, 501–2, 504, 511, 513, 518, 526, 551, 587, 606, 627, 630, 731, 739, 741, 746, 749, 757, 779, 843, 853, 863, 865, 875, 885–86, 888, 960, 1063, 1065, 1086–87, 1089, 1091–93, 1255; **3:**9, 80–81, 94, 105, 107–10, 114, 257, 278, 294, 305, 338, 359, 370, 500–501, 526, 542, 580, 592, 617, 649, 657, 722, 810–12, 882, 897; **4:**355, 463, 592, 670, 684, 752, 754, 805, 882, 895, 992, 1076, 1106,

1118, 1203, 1252; **5:**55, 523, 567, 584, 764; **6:**211, 228, 370–71, 402, 442, 526, 542, 545, 606, 618–19, 629, 639, 648, 653, 669–71, 692, 704, 708, 711, 734, 751, 759, 761–62, 769, 772, 777, 811–12, 821, 828, 831, 834–35, 838, 853, 864–65, 868, 872–73, 920, 925, 948, 952, 956, 958, 962–63, 970, 975, 1152, 1188, 1208, 1391, 1495, 1509, 1522; **7:**63, 94, 310, 475, 480, 482, 486, 495, 501, 511, 522, 524, 541, 553, 576, 578, 589, 662, 680, 683, 718, 789, 797, 800; **8:**31, 33, 35, 163, 545, 585, 612; **9:**264, 375; **10:**130, 349, 492, 496, 523–24, 526, 529, 579, 611, 637, 677, 682, 687, 694–95; **11:**138, 259, 262, 268, 343, 389, 391, 504–6, 509, 642; **12:**45, 49, 52, 64, 128, 266, 293, 351, 376, 485, 488; ACT(S) OF **1:**684, 927; **3:**278; **6:**521, 544, 1279; **8:**544; **11:**625; **12:**34; CIVIL **1:**714, 737; **2:**666; **6:**183; **7:**56, 64–65, 91–92; **10:**109; CONSEQUENCE(S)/PUNISHMENT/RESULT(S)/RETRIBUTION FOR/OF **2:**306, 319, 355, 501, 505; **3:**153, 501, 995; **4:**1062–63; **6:**949, 959; **8:**31; **11:**258; OF ISRAEL/THE PEOPLE **2:**320, 363, 511, 743; **3:**811; **4:**1110–11, 1205; **6:**948–50, 1245; **7:**661; **10:**398, 454, 529, 639

DISPERSION
1:77, 326, 336, 412, 541, 665, 667, 1182; **2:**324, 413–14, 537; **3:**278, 940; **4:**852, 1154, 1167, 1177–78, 1180, 1183, 1187, 1192; **5:**14, 642–43, 852; **6:**316, 335, 548, 767, 1282, 1306, 1489; **7:**301, 759, 760, 783, 794, 797, 814, 816; **8:**29, 35, 40, 42; **9:**621; **10:**306; **12:**182, 186, 189, 246–47, 266

DISTAFF
5:262

DISTRIBUTION OF GOODS
1:851; **10:**73, 101, 115

DISTRICT, DISTRICTS
1:222; **2:**659, 678, 683, 694, 822; **3:**48, 51–53, 337, 456, 732, 765, 767–70, 953, 1111; **4:**56, 60, 108, 125, 136, 140, 171; **6:**1159, 1294, 1581–82; **7:**438, 709, 731; **8:**342; **10:**197–98, 231; **11:**48, 470

DIVERSITY
1:3, 19, 43, 46, 59, 147, 161, 180, 185, 215, 218, 234, 245–46, 284, 292, 295, 375, 413–14, 668, 940; **2:**39, 54, 324, 378, 540–44, 546, 587, 642; **3:**700, 747; **4:**86, 108, 288, 1025, 1034, 1144, 1148; **5:**25–26, 34, 49, 60, 72, 75, 81, 226–27, 244; **6:**4, 6, 18–19, 110, 130, 155, 208, 345, 677, 946, 970, 1018; **7:**251, 464, 477, 849; **8:**14, 16, 27, 43, 48, 50, 53, 703; **9:**87, 503, 505–6, 642, 761, 808, 831; **10:**93, 112–13, 171, 226, 252, 370, 385, 388, 709–10, 773, 789, 794, 804, 825, 868, 943, 949; **11:**208, 310, 403, 420, 425, 444, 867; **12:**91, 177; THEOLOGICAL **1:**19, 21, 43; **10:**32, 369, 389–90

DIVINATION
1:237, 317, 556, 639, 1131, 1135; **2:**68, 178, 182, 184–85, 187–88, 193–95, 246, 428, 665, 809, 1082, 1089; **3:**28, 255, 276; **4:**1066; **5:**4, 160, 542, 793; **6:**74, 120, 393, 577, 1002, 1198–99, 1201, 1203, 1302, 1315; **7:**833; **8:**16, 23–25; **9:**130; **10:**230, 232

DIVINE COUNSEL
See under COUNSEL

DIVINE PRESENCE
See under GOD, NAMES FOR/TITLES OF *in PERSONS IN THE BIBLE*

DIVINER, DIVINERS
1:237; **2:**177–78, 180, 182–84, 187, 189, 192–94, 246, 665, 1010–11; **3:**285, 896; **6:**4, 15, 72, 794, 1159, 1200, 1203, 1208, 1304; **7:**5, 53, 82, 558, 813–14; **8:**24

DIVINITY OF CHRIST/JESUS
See under JESUS THE CHRIST *in PERSONS IN THE BIBLE*

DIVORCE, (*OR* DIVORCES, *ETC.*)
BILL OF **6:**436; FROM MARRIAGE **1:**67, 286, 490, 577, 1125–26, 1148–49; **2:**234, 454–57, 467–68, 629, 876, 907; **3:**95, 673, 686, 716, 725, 735, 739, 741–43, 745–46, 768, 796, 842, 849, 994, 1016; **4:**555, 1137; **5:**11, 170, 255, 280, 765; **6:**436, 603–4, 1223, 1579; **7:**140, 224, 457, 686, 864–67; **8:**73, 82, 123, 134, 136, 187, 191–93, 196, 319, 321–22, 384–86, 394, 519, 598, 642–46, 664, 673; **9:**267, 306, 312–14; **10:**171, 195, 235, 793, 849, 869, 875–79, 882–83, 885, 891; **11:**43, 84, 451, 455, 615, 809, 820; **12:**270, 277, 280, 415, 581

DOCETIC (*OR* DOCETICS, *ETC.*)
1:431, 454, 523; **8:**137, 495; **9:**101, 550, 608, 610, 834; **10:**823; **12:**373

DOCTOR, DOCTORS
1:101, 808; **2:**66, 666; **3:**544; **4:**256; **5:**733, 807–8; **8:**587, 590; **9:**6, 107, 128, 865; **10:**445; **11:**667; **12:**536, 538. *See also* PHYSICIAN

DOCTRINE, DOCTRINES
1:12, 35, 43, 50–52, 54, 57–58, 60, 90, 96, 99, 101, 103–4, 119, 201, 977, 1164; **2:**319, 350, 356, 377, 386, 441–42, 505–6, 596, 670–71, 1365; **3:**582, 658, 700, 1145; **4:**419, 695, 981, 1237; **5:**12, 25, 276, 283, 285, 314, 324, 328, 340, 371, 454–55, 752; **6:**40, 105, 109, 134, 177, 248, 1292, 1497; **7:**28, 129, 150, 189, 249, 636, 640, 642, 718; **8:**24, 90, 186, 195, 213, 264, 275, 288, 294, 298, 352–53, 356, 379, 399, 405, 420, 448, 457, 495, 503–4; **9:**30, 490, 677, 679–80, 751; **10:**261, 285, 375, 407, 424, 442, 465–67, 489, 531–32, 556, 589, 618, 661, 676, 706, 716,

DOCTRINE, DOCTRINES *(continued)*
750; **11:**235, 238, 240, 248, 362, 391, 489, 825, 844, 853; **12:**95, 200, 230, 234, 248, 264, 269, 283, 294, 304, 325–27, 336, 341–42, 344–46, 350–51, 353, 356, 360–61, 366, 376–77, 454, 458, 468, 475–76, 479, 486, 490, 497, 529, 538, 661, 687, 713; CHRISTIAN **1:**14, 40, 59, 93, 100, 140; **2:**1341; **4:**765; **5:**327; **12:**342, 357, 543, 554; OF CREATION **1:**85, 196, 356, 922; **7:**840; **12:**132; DEUTERONOMIC **2:**280, 300, 307–8, 441–42, 502, 504, 519; OF JUSTIFICATION BY FAITH **3:**540; **10:**403, 420, 426, 468, 514, 749; **11:**275; OF RESURRECTION **1:**229; **4:**737–38, 742, 877, 970, 1045; **5:**313; **7:**249; **8:**422; **9:**389; **12:**531; OF RETRIBUTION/RETRIBUTIVE JUSTICE **2:**504–5, 1365; **3:**926, 985; **4:**446, 705, 835, 848, 952; **5:**2; **6:**1139, 1153, 1210, 1252; **7:**537

DOCUMENT, DOCUMENTS
ARAMAIC **3:**675; **5:**604; CATHOLIC **7:**227; **12:**326, 476; CHRISTIAN **7:**14, 129; **8:**43; **9:**498; **11:**814; **12:**24, 58, 117, 413; COURT/ROYAL **1:**233; **3:**13, 358; **7:**50; DOCUMENTARY HYPOTHESIS **1:**80, 307, 310–13, 678; **2:**6–7; **6:**33; EXILIC/POST-EXILIC **1:**680; **3:**300; GNOSTIC **9:**519, 742; HISTORICAL **1:**18, 121, 163; **3:**6, 22, 260; **8:**10, 90–91; PRIESTLY/P **1:**80, 993, 1115; **3:**624 (*see also* PRIESTLY WRITER); SOURCE **2:**274, 952; **3:**675, 685, 811; **4:**183; **6:**1376; **11:**183

DOE
1:666; **4:**609, 656; **5:**69, 406. *See also* DEER

DOG, DOGS
1:223, 771; **2:**462, 673, 803, 1112, 1158, 1223, 1274, 1326; **3:**112, 167, 1028, 1050; **4:**439, 544, 572, 605, 763, 913–14; **5:**312, 340, 342–43, 357, 675, 715, 746; **6:**98, 198, 359, 1321, 1389; **7:**117, 125; **8:**212, 336, 610–11; **9:**316; **10:**230; **11:**247, 488, 524–26, 529; **12:**352, 668, 733

DOGMA, DOGMAS
1:55–57, 105, 149, 309, 367; **2:**370, 648, 1233; **5:**98, 759; **6:**105, 110, 1035; **7:**639; **8:**18, 318; **11:**476; **12:**24, 75

DOGMATIC, DOGMATICS
1:54–56, 108; **4:**362, 578–79, 625; **5:**63, 247, 655; **6:**473; **7:**874; **8:**318; **10:**450, 466, 635, 664; **11:**207, 378, 775

DOGMATISM
4:578; **8:**91; **9:**767

DOMINATION
1:247–49, 264, 363, 398, 804, 840, 921; **2:**635, 649, 958, 1240; **3:**168, 1082, 1095, 1099, 1125; **4:**105, 610, 661, 712, 717, 973, 1146, 1192, 1209; **5:**387, 397, 408, 423; **6:**556, 609, 786, 788, 795, 852, 1355, 1560; **7:**26, 28, 31, 33, 44, 105, 145, 227, 595, 638, 676, 692, 779–80; **8:**125, 128, 541; **9:**59–60, 405; **11:**307, 383, 451, 573, 628; **12:**203, 548; ASSYRIAN **1:**244, 250, 263–65; **2:**566, 572; **3:**612; **6:**36, 102, 556, 1076–77, 1380; BABYLONIAN **1:**244, 263–64, 266; **6:**559, 762, 768–69, 778, 782, 784, 786, 791–92, 794, 806, 850, 858, 925; FOREIGN/BY THE NATIONS **3:**302, 714, 814; **4:**661, 717, 1146, 1192; **6:**741, 758, 795, 804; **7:**42, 588; **8:**657; **9:**59; MALE **2:**455, 457, 476; **7:**175; **11:**660; PERSIAN **1:**267; **3:**723; **7:**757, 840; PHILISTINE **2:**1068, 1205, 1222, 1243

DOMINION
1:289, 335, 343, 345–46, 350–51, 355, 363, 365, 372, 398, 536, 845, 1018; **2:**166, 399; **4:**30, 395, 516, 519, 623, 711–13, 764, 840, 872, 877, 964, 1006, 1091, 1130, 1142, 1259, 1272; **5:**314, 454, 490, 516, 563; **6:**439, 965, 1305, 1349, 1473, 1561; **7:**10, 100, 102–6, 108, 309, 567, 730–32, 739, 804, 807, 810, 835, 837; **8:**564, 627, 628, 654, 691; **9:**234, 367, 596; **10:**495, 528, 536, 543, 558, 852, 963; **11:**287, 303, 382–83, 389, 436, 442, 452, 508, 510, 571, 596, 598, 602–3, 627–28, 636, 661; **12:**37, 42, 305, 430, 461, 519, 526–27, 544, 550, 562, 591, 612, 643–44, 673, 686–87, 699

"DO NOT DESTROY"
4:656

DOOR
1:52, 55, 159, 221, 373, 392, 475, 714, 760; **2:**37, 66, 430, 629, 671, 711, 830, 833, 877, 1305; **3:**205, 355, 386, 486, 532, 630, 643, 785, 883; **4:**193, 504, 553, 572; **5:**67, 95, 159, 174, 219, 225, 242, 307, 409, 411–13, 433, 596, 714, 748, 772, 798, 825; **6:**35, 74, 212, 214, 242, 619, 744–45, 773, 792, 805, 853, 925, 1006–7, 1189, 1225, 1231, 1546, 1554; **7:**13, 189–90, 336; **8:**15, 271, 543, 592; **9:**221, 236, 239, 263, 265, 278–79, 282, 298, 314, 324, 480, 667; **10:**164, 180, 205, 221, 227, 262, 471, 480, 504, 568, 577, 618, 776–77, 817, 993, 997; **11:**41, 43–44, 55, 56, 61, 207, 378, 387, 462, 564, 569, 662, 691, 796, 849; **12:**49, 66, 132, 136, 221, 303, 418, 456, 468, 512, 584, 587–88, 591, 594–95, 646, 687, 699, 729, 732; NARROW **8:**60; **9:**12, 35, 277–79; OF THE TENT OF MEETING/TABERNACLE **1:**1060; **2:**60, 65–66, 89, 199, 217, 228

DOORKEEPER, DOORKEEPERS
4:1014; **8:**346; **9:**279. *See also* LEVITE; PORTER; PRIEST; WATCHMAN

DOORPOST, DOORPOSTS
1:42, 776, 778–79, 1157; **2:**51, 344; **3:**264, 273, 599; **6:**102, 1260, 1555, 1561, 1585–86; **9:**833, 837

DOT, DOTS
1:294, 297; **2:**626; **6:**1319; **9:**162; **12:**408

DOUAY VERSION
7:91
DOUBLE-MINDED
1:947; **12:**182, 188, 192–93, 195, 198, 209, 211–12, 222, 224
DOUBLE-TONGUED
5:680; **11:**806; **12:**204
DOUGH
1:781; **2:**127; **3:**713, 820; **6:**456; **7:**231, 256–57; **8:**617; **9:**276, 654–56; **10:**683, 847–48, 851; **11:**315
DOVE, DOVES
1:392–93, 1013, 1025, 1036, 1086, 1099, 1105; **2:**65; **3:**757; **4:**96, 635, 656, 945, 974; **5:**393, 411; **6:**365, 367, 509, 1167; **7:**234, 256, 258, 261, 269, 278, 470, 493; **8:**160, 534, 663; **9:**90–91, 373, 529, 543; **10:**315, 390, 764, 857, 999–1000; "DOVE ON FAR-OFF TEREBINTHS" **4:**656; DUNG **3:**204
DOWRY
1:511, 553, 557; **2:**222; **3:**37, 81; **4:**193; **9:**298
DOXOLOGIES, DOXOLOGY
1:510, 745, 760, 800, 802, 825–26, 948, 981; **2:**981, 994, 1169, 1261, 1366–67; **3:**319, 403, 468, 722–23, 809, 812; **4:**335, 380–81, 410–11, 424, 428–30, 475, 575, 658–59, 794, 848, 963–64, 1034, 1079, 1112, 1265, 1278; **5:**164, 598–99; **6:**23, 212, 621, 708, 812, 1128; **7:**382, 422, 855, 858; **8:**205; **9:**30, 692; **10:**382, 412, 630, 674, 695–96, 757–58, 765, 767–69, 982; **11:**188, 202, 352, 359, 360, 413, 416–17, 441, 486, 545–46; **12:**20, 35, 171, 231, 256, 267, 305, 307, 329, 360, 478, 480, 500, 518, 563
DRACHMA, DRACHMAS
See under COIN
DRAGNET
8:314
DRAGON, DRAGONS
1:233, 274; **2:**600; **3:**948–49, 969, 1026, 1098, 1165; **4:**368, 395, 410, 615, 621, 624, 974; **5:**764, 833; **6:**207, 225–28, 254, 1105, 1401, 1404, 1427, 1432–37; **7:**10, 101, 157, 187, 190, 192–94; **9:**282; **10:**232; **12:**529, 533, 535, 541, 558, 591, 594, 603, 612, 614, 647–53, 656–58, 672, 677, 685, 700, 707, 717. *See also* MONSTER; RAHAB
DRAWERS OF WATER
3:820; **6:**1574
DREAD
1:428, 720, 766, 801, 908, 956; **2:**181, 195, 552, 593, 1001; **3:**1084–85; **4:**234, 360, 370, 412, 415, 507, 509, 519, 572, 631; **5:**112, 394, 673; **6:**388–89, 509, 1444; **7:**402, 664, 720; **8:**660; **9:**449; **11:**175, 442; **12:**158, 410; FEAR AND **1:**398; **2:**339; **3:**1106; **4:**96, 608; **5:**670; **7:**588; **12:**634; OF GOD/THE LORD **1:**766; **2:**1055
DREADFUL
1:191, 713, 854, 881, 905, 907, 935, 1027, 1139; **4:**572; **5:**536, 583, 585, 592, 823, 834; **6:**1069, 1154, 1327, 1369–70, 1383; **7:**227, 272, 416, 481, 555, 684; **8:**714; **9:**400; **10:**132; **11:**42; **12:**156, 525, 603
DREAM, DREAMS
1:42, 142, 165–66, 173, 196, 273, 277, 481, 483, 488, 519, 540–41, 543, 556–57, 599, 601, 614–16, 620–21, 623, 627–28, 643, 653, 659, 671, 740, 874, 877–78, 962; **2:**110, 549, 586, 669, 688, 757, 767, 920, 1161, 1183, 1207, 1209, 1372; **3:**39–40, 945–49, 951, 968–70, 1078, 1098, 1120; **4:**35, 296, 378, 444, 484, 487, 559, 568–70, 878, 1042, 1083, 1195, 1199, 1245; **5:**71, 131, 244, 317, 366–67, 390, 397, 409, 411–12, 422, 426, 429, 498, 502, 510, 515, 517, 592, 610, 639, 792–93, 860; **6:**9–10, 48, 183, 242, 339, 396, 414, 605, 752–53, 811, 1174, 1208, 1371, 1511; **7:**29, 43, 49–53, 55–58, 61, 72, 74–75, 95, 100–101, 106, 111, 139, 187, 284, 750, 813; **8:**38–39, 130, 134, 143, 146, 175, 365, 486, 537; **9:**63, 73, 78, 208, 256, 319, 359, 362, 370, 450, 532; **10:**69, 179, 256, 590, 759, 809, 943, 975; **11:**348, 469, 635, 760, 768; **12:**22, 46, 447, 489, 507–8, 514, 544, 603, 634; OF DANIEL/NEBUCHADNEZZAR **7:**36, 44, 54, 73–74, 100, 114, 136–37; **9:**275, 382; **12:**521; INTERPRETATION/INTERPRETING **1:**333, 598, 613–16, 620, 623, 639; **2:**392; **3:**28, 871, 1138; **4:**50, 193, 296; **5:**1, 281, 525; **6:**9–10, 752–53; **7:**8, 49, 50, 54, 57, 73, 82, 116; **8:**23, 25, 140; **9:**458; **12:**521; OF JACOB **1:**333, 540–42; **7:**284, 750; **9:**532; OF JOSEPH/PHARAOH **1:**598–99, 601, 620–22, 634, 1149; **3:**949; **7:**111; **9:**42; AND/OR VISION(S) **1:**42; **4:**377, 395, 569; **7:**5, 106–7, 326, 558; **12:**329, 343, 504–5
DRESS (*OR* DRESSES, *ETC.*)
1:117, 276, 605, 888, 905–6, 912, 1111; **2:**275, 454, 636, 656, 872, 1103, 1359; **3:**148, 903, 908, 927, 938, 962, 1080, 1087, 1134, 1147; **4:**165, 216; **5:**386, 779; **6:**82, 127, 244, 318, 602, 989, 1321, 1560, 1586; **7:**3, 66, 137, 483, 514, 609, 660, 678, 767; **8:**267, 431, 451, 532, 544, 719; **9:**74, 152, 163–64, 316, 320, 337, 438, 446, 692, 819–20, 822, 827, 858, 861; **10:**179, 432, 487, 568; **11:**378, 800–801; **12:**192, 613, 672, 728
DRINK
1:399, 742, 812, 817, 1071; **2:**63, 166, 781, 802, 845, 1170, 1376; **3:**106, 127, 265, 378, 879, 909, 998, 1017, 1019; **4:**298, 303, 450, 576, 612, 698, 768–69, 823, 878, 977, 1131, 1245; **5:**68, 208,

DRINK *(continued)*
220, 258, 343, 462, 613, 720, 784; **6:**93–94, 96, 197, 293, 413, 481, 601, 626, 647, 655, 684, 766, 834, 1149, 1167, 1196, 1327, 1461, 1528; **7:**122, 231, 250, 400, 454, 483, 514, 666, 792; **8:**398, 456, 471, 476, 491–92, 653, 704–5, 707, 723; **9:**46, 48, 131, 231, 418–21, 456, 565–66, 607, 610, 623, 626, 832, 857; **10:**714, 882, 911, 914–15, 918, 962; **11:**233, 805, 873; **12:**264, 266, 612, 639, 666, 676, 678, 681; EAT AND **1:**118, 881, 931–32, 1020, 1083; **2:**876; **3:**136, 983, 1039, 1065; **4:**228, 770, 1015; **5:**303, 307–8, 312, 333, 336–37, 340, 343, 406, 461, 683; **6:**195, 197–98, 490; **7:**93, 400; **8:**294; **9:**26, 137, 166, 256–57, 260, 280, 421, 426, 486; **10:**463, 823, 934, 937, 939, 982, 991, 993; **12:**287, 712; FOOD AND **1:**439, 614; **2:**149, 461, 878, 918, 1166–67; **3:**601; **4:**770, 768–70; **5:**15, 64, 103–4, 298, 303, 319, 337, 364, 758, 779; **6:**1208; **7:**231, 233, 267, 312; **8:**63, 456, 472; **9:**220, 247, 601, 608; **10:**150, 312, 731, 741, 841, 913–16, 934; **11:**562, 631, 633–34; **12:**105, 166; OFFERING(S) (*see under* OFFERING); STRONG **1:**1070–71; **2:**229, 850, 975–76; **4:**177; **5:**30, 183, 185, 741; **6:**93, 237, 243, 1579; **8:**722

DROMEDARY
1:1080. *See also* CAMEL

DROPSY
8:63; **9:**24, 35, 272–73, 283–84, 285, 465

DROSS
3:311, 632; **4:**533; **5:**62, 166, 218, 226, 654; **6:**60–61, 478, 1062, 1104, 1306, 1311–13, 1337

DROUGHT, DROUGHTS
1:217, 220, 427; **2:**178, 356, 374, 1063; **3:**81, 126–28, 130, 132, 135, 137, 144, 500, 779; **4:**51, 381, 592, 605, 609, 685; **5:**68, 194, 219, 531; **6:**211–12, 604, 690, 692, 750, 1314, 1469, 1473, 1485–86, 1563; **7:**236, 250, 289, 304, 306, 309–14, 318, 323–25, 352, 380, 582, 601, 717–18, 725; **9:**91

DRUNK, DRUNKEN
1:343, 473; **2:**975–76; **3:**150; **4:**176; **5:**765, 784; **6:**94–95, 236–38, 472, 1329–30; **7:**42, 454, 616, 811; **8:**598–99; **10:**64; **11:**328, 438, 441–42; **12:**681; FROM STRONG DRINK **1:**404, 476, 1071; **2:**559, 978, 1045, 1169, 1287, 1309; **3:**427, 871, 881–82, 959, 1076, 1160–61; **4:**22, 176–77, 630; **5:**69, 76, 185, 349, 389, 784; **6:**702, 891–92, 913, 1065, 1327, 1347, 1528; **7:**257, 454; **8:**703–4; **9:**245, 264, 409; **10:**728, 777, 934, 939; **11:**424, 442, 727; **12:**257, 624, 631, 650, 680–81, 684, 686, 692, 694, 717

DRUNKENNESS
1:403–4, 476, 1071; **2:**64, 973, 1045; **3:**1017, 1019; **4:**177; **5:**558, 784; **6:**236, 239, 243, 684, 765; **7:**81, 256, 454, 647; **9:**179, 301, 409; **10:**730; **11:**442, 451; **12:**303

DRY BONES, VALLEY OF THE
1:229; **2:**860; **5:**599; **6:**222, 1089, 1128, 1136, 1175, 1497–99, 1504

DUALISM, DUALISMS
1:287, 384, 684; **5:**456, 570, 788; **6:**98; **7:**4; **8:**37, 216, 218, 330, 335, 385, 420, 455, 459, 501, 573; **9:**634; **10:**375, 419, 485, 588, 592, 705, 722, 730; **11:**330, 362, 384–85, 390, 394, 431, 436, 438, 568, 593, 608, 623, 636, 638; **12:**181–82, 187, 203–4, 212, 325, 395, 426–27, 476, 539, 555, 586, 733

DUALISTIC
1:287; **4:**348, 487, 504; **5:**330, 423; **6:**1500; **7:**5, 10; **8:**125, 157, 181, 210, 264, 285, 287, 291–92, 310, 315, 330, 333–34, 385, 420, 460, 476, 487; **9:**506, 521, 763, 793; **10:**463, 535, 730; **11:**374, 390, 393, 434, 440, 565, 568, 610, 622, 632, 635–36, 690; **12:**98, 198, 368, 414, 457, 467, 508, 534, 547, 579, 676

DUMB
3:442; **6:**281, 283, 1222; **9:**287; **12:**306, 508

DUNG
2:151; **3:**204, 959; **4:**484; **6:**1149; ASCETICISM/MOURNING **3:**959, 1087, 1142; **6:**293, 1154, 1159; IDOLS **6:**1205–6, 1258, 1277, 1282, 1307, 1321–22, 1417, 1457, 1489, 1491, 1575; AS MANURE **1:**218–19; **2:**659

DUNGEON, DUNGEONS
5:525; **6:**370, 378, 391, 449; **7:**670

DUST
1:288, 349, 353, 363–64, 434, 445, 748; **2:**62–63, 151, 687; **3:**136, 147, 236, 473, 637, 776, 1004, 1102, 1105; **4:**4, 141, 349, 358, 380, 394, 443, 459, 464, 471, 478, 524, 530, 532, 617, 709, 763–65, 1041, 1099, 1169; **5:**232, 294, 311, 313, 355, 541, 525, 651, 787, 823–24, 827; **6:**95, 175, 242, 247, 449, 509, 996, 1005, 1366, 1382, 1438, 1502; **7:**5, 139, 148, 164, 272, 309, 321, 361–62, 365, 408, 547, 565, 602; **8:**257, 595–96; **9:**194, 220, 222, 231, 346, 460; **10:**196, 206, 254, 272, 308, 498, 592, 884, 988; **11:**504; **12:**468, 694; AND ASHES **4:**546, 628–29, 713; **5:**705, 731, 823; **6:**919; **7:**312; **12:**700

DWELLING PLACE
1:25, 541, 893, 1008, 1187; **2:**386; **3:**71, 75; **4:**603, 733, 773, 958, 979, 981, 1013, 1025, 1041, 1044, 1047, 1097, 1142; **5:**517, 679; **6:**256, 262, 527, 546, 555, 626, 635–37, 642, 733, 766, 772–73, 968, 1034, 1038, 1387, 1394; **7:**14, 250, 739, 754; **9:**242, 740, 748, 815; **10:**128, 568, 831, 833, 848, 966; **11:**893; **12:**82, 160, 692, 724

DYE (*OR* DYES, *ETC.*)
3:368, 1003; **4:**67; **5:**262; **6:**661, 1374, 1379, 1442; **7:**44, 609; **9:**296; **12:**571
DYSENTERY
1:1180

E

EAGLE, EAGLES
1:29, 343, 834, 837; **2:**1004, 1207; **4:**256, 310, 312–13, 612; **5:**254, 422; **6:**260–61, 892, 896, 1065, 1115, 1131, 1244–49, 1252, 1455, 1469, 1499, 1523; **7:**12, 260, 447, 527, 547; **8:**719; **9:**91, 171, 333; **11:**303; **12:**267, 526–27, 533, 592, 598, 631, 651–52, 666
EAR, EARS
1:543, 684, 882, 897, 946, 1172; **2:**54, 511, 570, 706, 901, 933, 935, 992, 1040, 1325; **3:**355, 390, 520, 542, 580, 651, 1066, 1080, 1105; **4:**164, 335, 348, 377, 430, 440, 449, 524, 538, 628, 843; **5:**61, 64, 91, 152, 174, 186, 193, 196, 218, 241, 272, 316, 328, 346, 349, 385, 388, 390, 393, 455, 550, 652, 664; **6:**8, 98, 175, 243, 245, 265, 271, 344–46, 358, 369–71, 376–77, 380, 436–38, 440, 448, 451, 482–83, 516, 521, 529, 544, 546, 621, 627–28, 724, 754, 786, 838, 1127, 1190, 1193, 1196, 1228, 1242, 1292, 1296, 1326–27, 1330, 1338, 1386, 1488, 1497, 1537, 1599; **7:**30, 161, 170, 375, 477; **8:**3, 477, 619, 696, 709; **9:**136, 188, 245, 252, 326, 590, 716, 718, 761, 803, 810–11; **10:**63, 65, 129, 131, 182, 362, 376, 379, 480, 537, 570, 668, 677, 705, 734, 906; **11:**43, 194, 243, 277, 321, 782, 842, 846, 855; **12:**33, 70, 72, 88, 115, 155, 384, 482; OF CORN/GRAIN **1:**620–21, 1020; **2:**838; **6:**174; **9:**133; **12:**710; DEAF (*see* DEAF); "GIVE EAR" **1:**206; **4:**700, 894, 898, 999, 1243, 1250; **5:**490; **6:**963, 1466; **11:**241; **12:**276; GOD'S/THE LORD'S/YAHWEH'S **1:**835; **3:**752, 1178; **4:**1086; **6:**440, 477, 646, 649, 1190; **12:**222–23, 290; RIGHT **1:**1062, 1099, 1101; **9:**435–36; UNCIRCUMCISED **6:**626–28; **10:**129, 131; "WHOEVER HAS EARS TO HEAR" **3:**525; **5:**64, 89, 174, 316; **6:**408; **8:**268, 568; **9:**293; **10:**63, 463, 478, 744; **12:**511, 556, 716
EARLY RAIN, RAINS
1:1113; **7:**324; **10:**665
EARNEST
AS A PROMISE/MONEY **1:**1159; **3:**364, 505, 562, 657; **5:**164; **6:**477; **11:**49, 84, 86; **12:**75
EARRING, EARRINGS
1:584; **2:**809; **3:**1147; **5:**387; **6:**1167, 1228, 1329
EARTH, THE
CREATION OF **1:**67; **4:**601; **6:**782; **12:**357; EXPLOITATION AND **1:**335, 346; **2:**399; **6:**1465; **7:**676; **12:**217, 219, 720; FACE OF THE **1:**409, 414, 939; **2:**109, 182, 345, 885; **3:**112, 177; **4:**256; **5:**293; **6:**17, 786, 1279, 1464; **7:**666, 675; **12:**283; FILL(ED/ING/S/) **1:**346, 398, 409, 412–13, 750; **4:**806, 809, 811; **5:**454; **6:**144, 548; **11:**444; **12:**593; FOUR CORNERS OF THE **6:**335, 376, 431, 1165, 1531; **7:**101, 169; **12:**619, 704; HEAVEN AND **1:**206, 277–78, 325, 342, 349, 383, 412, 442, 510, 512, 713, 716, 767, 924, 954, 981; **2:**14, 32, 319, 593, 1336; **3:**269, 407, 704, 706, 1165; **4:**46, 71–72, 295, 486, 934, 1145–46, 1180, 1190, 1216–17, 1273, 1279; **5:**93, 377; **6:**52, 294, 344, 388, 391, 401–2, 414, 448, 544–45, 575, 661, 752, 766, 787, 883–84, 913, 988, 1005; **7:**382, 578, 680, 718, 730, 748, 750, 754, 774, 782, 839; **8:**41, 187, 503; **9:**55, 65, 224, 409, 462, 532, 551; **10:**246, 482, 618; **11:**40, 396, 565, 568, 599, 640; **12:**96, 159, 357, 531, 541, 551, 588, 594, 605, 630–31, 686, 715, 720, 727–28; NEW **1:**166, 980, 1175; **4:**1269; **6:**528, 542, 544, 551; **7:**3; **8:**36, 392; **10:**596; **11:**345; **12:**330–31, 336, 338, 361, 527, 532, 558, 591, 703, 713, 718, 720, 730; SUBDUE THE **1:**346, 351, 364, 372; WHOLE **1:**411–13, 748, 768, 978, 1160; **3:**401, 1101, 1110; **4:**31, 1142; **6:**20, 102, 104–5, 144, 156, 158–59, 206, 210–12, 407, 477, 541, 606, 877–78, 913, 915, 1435; **7:**62, 543, 683, 739, 751–52, 754, 756–57, 770–71, 773–74, 780, 782–83; **8:**492; **9:**405; **10:**247; **12:**267, 526, 592, 603, 646, 692
EARTHENWARE
6:820; **10:**773; **11:**81, 83–84, 86, 137, 164, 166, 845
EARTHQUAKE, EARTHQUAKES
1:473; **2:**789, 1078–79, 1367; **3:**142, 704, 1098, 1178; **4:**51, 382, 410, 441, 592–93, 865, 916; **6:**97, 211–12, 242, 1196, 1469, 1499, 1521; **7:**317, 352, 366, 381, 417, 481, 602, 723, 836; **8:**15, 223, 230, 327, 441–42, 493, 499; **9:**400, 402, 407, 468, 829; **10:**230, 233–34; **11:**580; **12:**573, 614, 630, 636, 643, 677
EASTER
1:7, 15, 110, 201, 209–10, 212, 720, 768, 804, 836; **2:**55, 97, 194, 846, 1008; **4:**797, 938, 948, 1070, 1138, 1216, 1273, 1280; **5:**323; **7:**724; **8:**3, 92, 256, 259, 337, 348, 434, 493, 495, 503–5; **9:**17, 24, 74, 468, 470, 472–73, 478, 481, 490, 494, 610, 695, 748, 780, 785, 838, 840–41, 844–45, 847–48, 857; **10:**3, 40, 44–46, 58, 67, 100, 342–43, 419, 534, 540, 547, 590, 614, 671, 683; **12:**4, 64, 90, 254, 262, 276, 286, 377, 384, 415, 419, 438, 441; DAY/SUNDAY **1:**189, 1161; **2:**90, 236; **4:**854, 1156; **5:**303, 731; **8:**628, 660; **9:**437, 483, 488, 778, 844, 848; **10:**44; **11:**639;

EASTER *(continued)*
12:441; MORNING **2:**846; **8:**143, 497, 505, 726; **10:**728; POST-EASTER **8:**73, 77–79, 85, 93, 102–3, 134, 158, 163, 167–69, 175, 177, 186–87, 189, 211, 214, 217, 220, 225, 230, 238, 254, 256, 258–59, 261–63, 265, 273, 275, 287, 289, 296, 300, 329, 356–57, 363–64, 366, 371, 391, 397–98, 406, 409, 414, 417, 480, 486, 500, 503; **9:**17, 117, 144, 193, 253, 472–73, 847; **10:**30; **11:**724, 808; PRE-EASTER **8:**73–74, 79, 81–82, 85, 93, 95, 102, 110, 168–69, 230, 254, 258, 265, 295, 300, 308, 329, 356–57, 365–66, 499–500, 623; **9:**199; **11:**808; VIGIL **4:**1073, 1226, 1252; **6:**1497

EAST WIND
1:794; **4:**330, 525, 604, 872; **6:**1245, 1271–72, 1382–83; **7:**213–14, 281–82, 292–93

EBONY
6:1371, 1377–78

ECCLESIASTES
1:8–9, 11, 19, 29, 31, 45, 65, 79, 135, 301, 1190; **2:**371, 399, 544; **3:**88, 474, 911; **4:**178, 326–27, 352, 377, 423, 443, 493–95, 593, 838–39, 877, 1030; **5:**1, 11–12, 20, 25, 50, 86, 107, 122, 141, 164, 194, 197, 211, 229, 239, 253, 256, 364–65, 430, 446, 455, 459, 461, 466, 498, 518, 567, 603–5, 608, 613, 618, 620, 625, 629, 644, 646, 651, 654, 659, 678, 692, 742, 758, 800, 813, 849, 862; **6:**190, 197–98, 962; **8:**29; **11:**780; **12:**521

ECCLESIASTICAL
1:35, 50, 51–56, 103, 167, 203, 309–10, 705, 1121; **2:**142, 616, 1031, 1214, 1227, 1244, 1258, 1382; **3:**364, 844; **4:**1206; **5:**55; **8:**3, 5, 43–44, 97, 103, 308, 314; **9:**425, 503; **10:**24, 182, 204, 206; **11:**218, 253, 775–76, 805, 900; **12:**168, 269, 298, 399, 467, 510, 536–37, 543, 551, 565

ECCLESIOLOGY (*OR* ECCLESIOLOGICAL, *ETC.*)
1:59, 198, 815, 853, 882, 960; **4:**975; **8:**2, 109, 110, 135, 161, 223, 266, 342, 344, 353, 396, 398, 474; **9:**669, 672–73, 766–67, 863; **10:**213, 244, 665, 700–701; **11:**186, 330, 361, 449, 455, 570, 613, 776, 781; **12:**269, 390, 428, 452, 461, 464, 533, 555, 712, 717

ECLIPSE
LUNAR/SOLAR **2:**87, 647; **4:**367; **5:**730; **7:**328, 417; **9:**460; **12:**529

ECSTASY
2:1042; **4:**383, 728, 1029; **5:**397, 411; **6:**750; **7:**106, 497; **10:**163, 514; **11:**285

ECSTATIC
2:107, 110, 134, 190, 982, 1128; **3:**911, 1051; **4:**383; **6:**752, 1090; **7:**111, 351, 407; **8:**24, 730; **10:**57, 62, 78; **11:**91, 567, 660; **12:**520

EDEN, GARDEN OF
See GARDEN: THE GARDEN *in SUBJECTS AND THEMES*; EDEN, GARDEN OF *in PLACES IN THE BIBLE*

EDICT, EDICTS
1:527, 1172; **2:**315; **3:**677, 705, 715, 720–21, 875, 897, 899–901, 914, 918, 922–25, 930, 966–67, 1109; **4:**166, 269; **6:**399, 1513; **7:**89, 514–15, 790; **10:**253, 406, 762; **12:**125, 140, 146

EDIFICATION
1:72, 98–99, 101–2; **2:**928; **3:**396; **8:**104; **10:**309, 381, 794, 896, 920, 923–24, 945–46, 950, 956, 958–63, 965, 967; **11:**70, 91, 141, 161, 172–73, 177, 430, 678, 726–27, 731; **12:**221, 223

EDUCATION
1:3, 55, 200, 202, 211–12, 231, 291, 765; **2:**218, 281, 315, 336, 376, 494, 519, 749, 759, 987, 1289, 1341; **3:**453, 998; **4:**138, 200, 216, 218–19, 234, 327, 381, 993, 1175; **5:**5, 38, 134, 149, 155, 367, 389, 547, 667, 670–71, 674, 676, 688–89, 745, 788, 813, 867; **6:**90, 310, 1216, 1240, 1331, 1451; **7:**118, 144, 151; **8:**16, 18, 540, 574, 620; **9:**42, 56, 204, 276, 377; **10:**24, 88, 92, 96, 130, 253, 260–62, 298, 306, 336, 342, 374, 783, 808, 813, 860; **11:**134, 363, 412, 452–53, 457, 611, 850, 871; **12:**15, 68, 70, 151–52, 155, 324, 392, 447, 474, 482

EGG, EGGS
2:453; **3:**1163; **4:**611–12; **6:**568, 708; **8:**24; **9:**238

EL
See under GOD, NAMES FOR/TITLES OF *in PERSONS IN THE BIBLE*

ELDER
1:524; **2:**49, 335, 435, 659; **3:**288, 556, 1019, 1087; **4:**291; **5:**5, 93, 77; **6:**1238, 1316–17, 1319, 1347, 1508; **7:**179, 182, 184, 525, 701; **8:**223; **9:**301, 303; **10:**52, 208, 306, 637; **11:**779, 818, 822, 864, 867, 895; **12:**314–15, 365–66, 370–76, 378, 383–84, 386, 388–91, 393–96, 398–401, 403–10, 412–16, 418–20, 422–40, 443–47, 449–54, 456–58, 460–68, 624

ELDERS
1:75, 182, 221–22, 503, 669, 714–15, 718, 817, 825, 834–35, 945, 1023, 1035, 1060, 1066, 1119–20; **2:**54, 81, 179, 297, 312, 417, 431, 435, 455–56, 467, 470, 633, 715, 738, 750, 752–53, 756, 821, 824–25, 827, 830–31, 836, 885, 934–35, 938–39, 1001–2, 1023, 1027–31, 1038–39, 1042–44, 1049–50, 1055, 1061, 1098, 1233, 1331; **3:**147, 151, 156, 223, 678, 704–6, 712, 742, 954, 1130, 1137, 1141–42, 1148, 1173; **4:**145, 159, 163, 281, 419, 449, 450, 477,

538, 562–63, 1172; **5:**6–7, 14, 77, 126, 170, 262–63, 479–80, 510–11, 556, 687, 790, 827; **6:**9, 21, 76, 78, 127, 774–75, 785, 860, 943, 1064, 1070, 1086, 1168, 1176, 1179–80, 1205–6, 1285–87, 1374, 1459; **7:**155, 175–84, 306, 320, 534, 541, 560, 877; **8:**153, 162, 332, 420, 491, 518, 605–7, 657, 669, 673, 710, 712; **9:**76, 137, 154, 260, 376–77, 381–82, 388, 393, 442, 477, 629, 696; **10:**52, 88, 105, 120, 146, 169, 177, 181, 200, 203, 207–8, 210–11, 214, 221, 226, 266, 278, 280–86, 292, 295, 318, 325, 329, 341, 860; **11:**211, 399, 422, 480, 634, 712, 775, 787, 816, 818, 822–25, 863–64, 878; **12:**131, 169, 222, 224, 283, 308, 314–16, 399, 577, 592–93, 602, 604–5, 611, 624, 631, 650, 664, 668, 693, 696, 699; ASSEMBLY/COUNCIL OF **5:**693; **9:**111; **10:**59, 282, 306; **11:**814; CHURCH **10:**203, 214, 283; **11:**194; **12:**314; CITY/COMMUNITY/TOWN/VILLAGE **1:**259; **2:**379, 417, 436, 445–46, 448, 454, 628–29, 659, 667; **3:**205, 704, 1087; **5:**93, 213; **6:**1137; **7:**278, 301, 390; OF ISRAEL **1:**714, 1065; **2:**138, 482, 999, 1000–1001, 1003, 1023, 1026–28, 1045, 1213, 1224, 1226, 1230, 1233–34, 1283; **3:**137, 377, 393; **6:**15, 1118, 1155, 1176, 1205, 1276, 1352, 1463, 1494; OF JERUSALEM **3:**932; **10:**59, 206; OF THE JEWS **1:**299; **3:**704, 706, 711, 932; **7:**770, 788; **9:**155, 464; OF JUDAH **1:**821; **2:**570, 1194, 1211, 1346; **6:**1174, 1176, 1205; AND PRIESTS **1:**881, 883; **4:**99; **5:**213; **6:**721; **7:**301; **8:**349, 409–11, 413–14, 463–64, 477, 480, 483, 501; **9:**111, 201, 281, 331, 376, 382, 414, 436, 442, 445, 469; **10:**312, 329–30; SEVENTY **1:**880–81; **2:**5, 9, 12, 21, 99, 105–8, 112, 134, 189, 193, 219–20, 254, 298, 324; **3:**137; **4:**219; TWENTY-FOUR **10:**705; **12:**695, 707

ELECT

THE/OF GOD **1:**287, 518, 523–24, 537, 612, 665; **2:**91, 520; **3:**80, 309, 313, 317, 319, 464, 733, 753; **4:**205, 859; **5:**446, 470, 492, 620–21, 647; **6:**69, 83, 148, 206–7, 222, 227–28, 278, 328, 344, 356, 516, 588, 860, 917, 1266, 1363, 1513; **7:**4, 9, 12–15, 328, 370, 425, 688, 690, 703; **8:**157, 211, 416, 418–19, 442–44, 447, 526, 532–34, 538, 572, 577, 627, 690–93; **9:**144, 278, 338–39, 408, 611; **10:**86, 171, 241, 374–75, 387, 613, 636, 676, 689; **11:**269, 271, 319, 346, 373, 375, 377, 381–82, 384, 389–90, 408, 410–11, 415–17, 419–20, 423, 428–29, 436, 529, 587, 647, 747, 798, 823, 843, 861, 867; **12:**247, 265, 455, 509, 538–40, 544, 583, 585, 619, 646, 654, 664–65, 682, 697, 703–5, 708–9, 713

ELECTION

1:165, 337, 417, 424, 447, 459, 517, 524, 591, 1082; **2:**350, 359, 469, 635, 669–70, 953, 1097, 1109, 1114, 1236; **3:**24, 71–72, 77, 90, 93, 95, 114, 119, 317, 319, 462, 664, 809–10; **4:**21, 859, 1078; **5:**324, 441; **6:**52, 93, 108, 262, 355, 358, 369, 375, 377, 386, 389, 402, 516, 527, 547, 580, 918, 1170, 1278, 1353; **7:**264, 328, 346, 369–70, 423, 767, 854–56, 870, 872; **9:**137, 226, 279, 338, 426, 676, 724, 759, 763; **10:**372, 446, 635, 643, 675–76, 797–98, 807, 814, 847, 879; **11:**223, 239, 372–74, 376–78, 381, 385, 392–93, 411, 414, 419–20, 423, 435, 649, 687–88, 727, 748; **12:**188, 247, 298, 330–31, 337–40, 359, 453, 538–39; DIVINE/GOD'S/THE LORD'S/YAHWEH'S **1:**518, 523, 667; **2:**49, 140, 286, 308, 349–50, 359, 426, 431, 463, 466, 481, 556, 1050, 1063; **3:**23, 39, 56, 76, 87, 96, 115, 319, 332, 461, 464; **4:**197, 868; **5:**320, 836; **6:**163, 196, 239, 295, 300, 516, 580, 597, 1166, 1305; **7:**204, 269, 277, 861; **8:**30, 129, 574; **9:**91, 611; **10:**192, 210, 375, 378, 814; **11:**373, 376–77, 393, 419, 746, 762; **12:**217, 263; OF ISRAEL **1:**166, 317, 355, 835; **2:**359, 481, 1063; **3:**94, 307, 309, 313, 995; **4:**197, 213, 868, 1141; **5:**281; **6:**140, 157, 516, 1349; **7:**204, 289, 369; **8:**30; **9:**139, 145; **10:**375

ELECT LADY

12:379, 448–50, 452–53, 456, 460

EL ELOHE ISRAEL

See under GOD, NAMES FOR/TITLES OF *in PERSONS IN THE BIBLE*

EL ELYON/ELYON

See under GOD, NAMES FOR/TITLES OF *in PERSONS IN THE BIBLE*

ELEMENT, ELEMENTS

OF THE COSMOS/CREATION/NATURE/UNIVERSE **4:**1061, 1097; **5:**9, 532, 536, 545, 549, 569, 577–78, 596–97, 818; **7:**683; **9:**189; **11:**283, 287, 292; ELEMENTAL SPIRITS **1:**160; **11:**282, 565–66, 622, 627, 631–33, 637, 639, 696; FOUR **1:**691; **2:**1366–67; **3:**982; **4:**366, 604; **5:**252–53, 293, 532, 546, 577–78, 597; **6:**1095; **7:**683; **10:**74; **11:**282, 390, 565–66; **12:**33, 357

ELEPHANT, ELEPHANTS

4:16, 60, 89, 98, 133, 266, 270, 282, 286, 296; **5:**612; **6:**1374; **7:**102, 140

ELEVEN, THE

DISCIPLES MINUS JUDAS ISCARIOT **8:**477, 502, 732; **9:**8, 13, 37, 193, 359, 462, 466, 469, 476, 480–81, 483–84, 486, 488–90, 704–5, 730, 846; **10:**40, 44, 49, 51

ELOAH

See under GOD, NAMES FOR/TITLES OF *in PERSONS IN THE BIBLE*

ELOHIM

See under GOD, NAMES FOR/TITLES OF *in PERSONS IN THE BIBLE*

ELOHIST, ELOHISTIC
(also known as E) **1:**129, 310, 322, 417; **2:**5, 180; **4:**658, 893, 1013
ELOI, ELOI, LAMA SABACHTHANI
8:492
EL SHADDAI/SHADDAI
See under GOD, NAMES FOR/TITLES OF *in PERSONS IN THE BIBLE*
EMBALM, EMBALMING
1:600, 669; **5:**812; **8:**143; **9:**691
EMBASSY
4:143, 160–61, 164, 169, 171, 198, 270, 298; **7:**792, 798–99; **11:**463
EMBROIDERY
5:843
EMENDATION, EMENDATIONS
SCRIBAL/TEXTUAL **1:**25–26, 29–30, 32, 671, 1138; **2:**599, 613, 916, 936, 1212; **3:**52, 205, 332, 484, 522, 562, 644, 647, 712, 740, 743, 766, 776, 779, 797, 825–26, 828, 832, 1149; **4:**380, 411, 415, 452, 462, 478–79, 511, 530, 546, 577, 587, 590, 619, 622, 624, 690, 853, 908, 1198, 1275; **5:**132, 144, 182, 192, 225, 226, 237, 243–44, 251, 316, 339, 345, 354, 420; **6:**72, 356, 405, 466–67, 1177, 1379, 1389, 1391, 1415, 1428, 1582; **7:**237, 255–58, 279, 292, 303, 375, 419, 547, 602, 604, 609–10, 846; **8:**4, 84–85; **9:**6, 418, 557; **10:**27; **11:**102
EMERALD
6:1360, 1392; **12:**592, 723
EMIM, THE
2:306, 654
EMISSION
1:281, 1104–5, 1149; **2:**1135; **6:**1578, 1592
EMMANUEL
See under JESUS THE CHRIST, NAMES FOR/TITLES OF *in PERSONS IN THE BIBLE*
EMOTION, EMOTIONS
1:57, 179, 373, 496, 598, 600, 643, 803, 1025, 1127; **2:**437, 551, 750, 775, 908, 922, 1129, 1269, 1284; **3:**44, 90, 386, 448, 668, 693, 842, 869, 884, 910, 914, 916, 923, 933, 962, 1024, 1031, 1080, 1105, 1129; **4:**59, 236, 359–60, 382, 398, 441, 463, 465, 520, 526, 535, 592, 597, 632, 828, 1195; **5:**127, 141, 143, 150, 155, 230, 243, 301, 364, 366, 377, 379, 384, 390, 391, 396–97, 410, 413, 426, 434, 628, 664, 760; **6:**160–61, 402, 609, 976, 1045, 1059, 1155, 1171, 1196, 1223, 1274, 1322, 1368, 1371, 1421, 1438; **7:**8, 95, 231, 318, 414, 447, 499, 523–24, 866; **8:**22, 207, 210, 486, 544, 671; **9:**303, 370–71, 433, 545, 690–91, 837; **10:**296, 726; **11:**20, 40, 102, 297, 414, 462, 543, 558–59, 611, 650, 661, 735, 770–71, 894, 899; **12:**60, 77, 359–60, 478, 496, 500, 506, 508, 560, 594, 615; DIVINE **4:**556; **5:**328; **6:**1140, 1152, 1235, 1343; **7:**233, 296; HUMAN **2:**1341; **3:**714; **4:**311, 441; **5:**140, 153, 395; **6:**1345; **7:**576, 690; **8:**529; **11:**484
EMPEROR, EMPERORS
1:201, 291, 428; **3:**381, 636, 680, 714, 855, 878, 913, 951, 966, 970, 1124; **4:**7, 9–10, 17, 211, 240, 286, 292, 431, 1131; **5:**439–40, 490, 544, 557, 597, 622; **6:**20; **7:**7, 10, 20–21, 25, 32, 42–44, 49–50, 53, 57–58, 62, 64–67, 73–77, 89, 92–93, 112, 141, 146–47, 150–51, 738, 757, 776; **8:**15–16, 123, 164, 180, 343, 401, 409, 419–20, 488, 659, 663, 673–74, 684, 689, 712, 718, 730; **9:**80, 88, 171, 199, 252, 363, 385–86, 405, 460, 543, 822–23; **10:**214, 304, 313, 324–27, 333, 342, 349, 357, 359–60, 366–67, 404, 406, 415, 423, 624, 665, 717, 748, 774, 782, 866; **11:**205, 377, 383, 401, 405, 417, 470–71, 510, 535, 546, 677, 760, 784, 909; **12:**76, 163, 234–35, 239, 275–76, 278, 280, 284, 287, 485, 493, 514, 533, 571, 578, 658, 683–84, 729; WORSHIP **7:**146; **12:**234–35, 578, 658
EMPOWER (*OR* EMPOWERS, EMPOWERING, *ETC.*)
1:62, 381; **2:**90–91, 141, 187, 214, 350, 659, 684, 1042, 1045, 1053, 1055, 1057, 1365–66; **3:**177, 179, 239, 462, 681; **4:**416, 470, 670, 803, 1067, 1191; **5:**321, 331, 408; **6:**134, 258, 396, 440, 1111; **7:**126, 151; **8:**115, 195, 263, 585; **9:**52, 103, 153, 197, 203, 740, 746, 846; **10:**22, 28, 37, 40–42, 44, 46, 55, 57, 62, 92, 95, 144, 167, 210, 221, 226, 278, 307, 343, 367, 384, 387, 584, 830; **11:**220, 325, 334, 344, 595; **12:**200, 222, 301, 449
EMPOWERMENT
1:622, 772; **2:**684, 1045, 1055, 1070, 1306; **3:**681; **4:**789–90, 1264; **5:**340; **6:**457, 1201; **7:**648, 720–21; **9:**27, 92, 403, 486, 848; **10:**43, 58, 139; **11:**326, 850, 858
EMPTIED
1:190, 685, 885, 914, 979, 1099; **3:**128, 656, 914; **6:**914; **7:**267, 810; **9:**46; **10:**808, 952, 983; HIMSELF **3:**783; **4:**759; **11:**503, 508, 527, 546, 887
ENCAMPMENT, ENCAMPMENTS
1:219, 562, 1019; **2:**32–33, 36–37, 51, 53, 92, 121, 190, 272, 312, 1286; **6:**1351; **7:**43, 803, 806; **9:**373; **12:**714
ENCHANTER, ENCHANTERS
6:77; **7:**44, 50, 53, 72, 82
ENCHANTMENT, ENCHANTMENTS
2:187–88; **3:**979; **6:**412–13, 491; **7:**468
END, THE
OF THE AGE **1:**166, 246, 254, 259, 1158, 1160;

4:771, 1089; **6:**223; **8:**138, 256, 259; **9:**488, 704, 762; **10:**384, 786, 822, 886, 938, 980; **12:**12, 113, 259, 567, 636; IN/OF DEATH **1:**818; **2:**862; **4:**424; **6:**217; **7:**414; **9:**645; **10:**546, 942; **12:**721; OF HISTORY **1:**74; **2:**91; **6:**1511; **7:**303; **8:**45, 50–52, 211, 346, 455; **10:**38, 85–86; **11:**615; **12:**252, 709, 711; OF LIFE/OF HIS LIFE **2:**709, 809, 816, 841, 1123, 1179; **3:**1068; **4:**111; **5:**86, 326–28, 356, 476, 651, 709, 790; **6:**301, 1276; **7:**414; **9:**282, 410–11, 721, 734, 753; **12:**85, 138, 509; OF TIME **4:**648; **6:**67, 84; **7:**10, 15, 327, 724, 873; **8:**144, 187, 361; **9:**200, 202–3, 402, 404, 411; **10:**363, 660–61, 689; **11:**719; **12:**259, 312, 526 (*see also under* TIME); TIME(S) **2:**191; **3:**409; **4:**96; **5:**486; **6:**175, 614, 1511; **7:**10, 15, 115, 117, 149, 568, 585, 874; **8:**30, 38–39, 44–45, 50, 163, 441, 523, 526, 529, 532–33, 572, 627, 631, 640, 657, 663, 676, 680, 683–90, 692–93, 695, 707, 728–29, 731; **9:**15, 224, 282, 333, 402, 409; **10:**10, 336, 799–800, 811, 829, 854, 936, 957, 980–81, 983–84; **11:**23, 28, 50, 69, 76, 82–84, 90, 120, 173, 357, 360, 373, 442, 461, 492, 573, 576, 579, 701, 704, 712, 716, 723, 728, 747, 748, 756; **12:**324, 348, 357, 412, 478–79; OF THE WORLD **1:**394; **3:**1098; **4:**113, 675, 752; **6:**587; **7:**14–15, 108, 115, 564–65, 684; **8:**39, 46, 49, 53, 203, 222, 439–44, 687, 691, 694; **9:**161, 167, 202, 398–411; **10:**885; **11:**386, 463; **12:**505, 535–36, 635, 711–12, 727

END(S) OF THE EARTH
1:288; **2:**200, 982; **3:**390, 479, 512, 1062; **4:**30, 55, 159, 532, 690, 764, 771, 872, 934–35, 937, 939–40, 964, 1229; **5:**64, 160, 454, 505, 562; **6:**68, 202, 212, 331, 353–55, 365, 376, 391, 402, 433, 460–61, 471, 1083–84, 1245; **7:**73, 326, 571, 807; **8:**445, 577; **9:**21, 41, 104, 367, 374, 460, 469, 479, 487; **10:**15, 19, 24, 32, 35, 41–42, 44, 46, 59, 82, 84, 146–47, 160, 182, 189, 195, 204, 213, 227, 256, 275, 278, 283, 291, 327, 334, 338, 342, 357, 359, 361, 389–90, 498, 668; **11:**215, 303; **12:**22

ENEMIES, ENEMY
OF THE CHURCH **2:**1003; **10:**132, 155, 693; OF THE CROSS **11:**475, 535, 537; OF GOD/THE LORD/YAHWEH **1:**822, 933; **2:**255, 442, 502, 530, 749, 776, 787, 789–90, 885, 1001, 1007–8, 1022, 1087, 1092, 1134, 1148, 1158, 1165, 1188, 1194, 1248–49, 1368; **3:**551, 773, 777, 1163; **4:**410, 414, 617, 723, 726, 862, 895, 947, 952, 1009–11, 1028, 1073, 1256, 1276; **5:**211, 247, 569; **6:**60, 98, 137, 156, 194, 228, 249, 402, 501, 547, 681, 710, 785, 911, 919, 1042, 1413; **7:**163, 316, 323, 334–35, 395, 429, 441, 455, 603, 606, 610, 616, 639, 664, 683, 688, 693, 696, 754; **8:**680; **9:**224, 804; **10:**519; **11:**220, 319, 462; **12:**212, 703; OF ISRAEL **1:**819–21; **2:**190, 439, 731, 733, 763, 766, 782, 820, 841, 858, 1085, 1179, 1238, 1279; **3:**150, 894, 1084, 1130, 1168; **6:**948, 1065; **7:**9, 360, 402, 422, 493; OF JESUS/CHRIST **4:**924; **8:**547, 555, 562, 565, 606, 617, 625, 649, 673, 680, 697–98, 700, 706, 713–14, 716, 718, 725–26; **9:**423, 581; **12:**31, 41

ENGINES
OF COMMERCE, WAR, ETC. **4:**88, 156, 216; **5:**311, 313

ENGLISH BIBLE
1:22, 25–27, 297–98, 1054, 1112; **2:**548, 952; **3:**772; **5:**720, 603; **11:**703, 895; GENEVA BIBLE **12:**537–39, 549, 713; GOOD NEWS BIBLE **1:**22, 30–31; **5:**270; **11:**895; JERUSALEM BIBLE/NEW JERUSALEM BIBLE **1:**31–32, 1194; KING JAMES VERSION/AUTHORIZED VERSION **1:**5, 23–24; **4:**72; **8:**7; **11:**895; **12:**6; NEW AMERICAN BIBLE **1:**28–29; NEW ENGLISH BIBLE **1:**22, 25–27; **11:**895; NEW INTERNATIONAL VERSION **1:**5, 27–28; NEW KING JAMES VERSION **7:**539; **11:**85; NEW REVISED STANDARD VERSION **1:**5, 24–25; NUMBERING OF CHAPTERS/VERSES **1:**297–98; REVISED ENGLISH BIBLE **1:**22, 25–27; **11:**895; TANAKH **1:**29–30; TYNDALE'S VERSION **1:**24–25, 1042, 1112; **8:**202

ENGRAVED (*OR* ENGRAVING, *ETC.*)
3:484; **4:**478; **5:**592; **6:**707–8, 710, 1325, 1391–92; **7:**766; **9:**642; **12:**723

ENTHRONEMENT
1:802; **2:**1319; **3:**36, 575, 857, 867; **4:**257; **6:**122–23, 1119–20; **10:**92, 416; COLLECTION OF PSALM(S) **3:**1176; **4:**1061; **7:**683; **8:**503; FESTIVAL OF (*see under* FEASTS/FESTIVALS); OF GOD/JESUS/THE LORD/YAHWEH **1:**774, 802; **2:**79, 88, 1248; **3:**69; **4:**717, 772, 792, 868–69, 871, 939, 1035, 1053, 1064, 1075, 1131, 1139, 1273; **6:**213; **7:**103; **9:**827, 830; **10:**617, 723; **11:**389; **12:**10, 25–26 (*see under* FEASTS/FESTIVALS)

ENVOY, ENVOYS
1:241; **2:**184, 771, 1278–79; **3:**630, 698; **4:**5, 102, 160, 169, 172, 204, 218, 269, 283, 461; **6:**303–4, 559, 879, 1078, 1233, 1326, 1329, 1347–48, 1361, 1398; **7:**136; **9:**88; **11:**95, 706, 708, 899; **12:**45, 465, 467, 567, 569, 642

ENVY
AS A NOUN **1:**528, 555, 852; **2:**510, 1123, 1352; **4:**105, 212; **5:**6, 55–56, 144, 170, 207, 210, 285, 311–13, 316, 465, 496, 549, 557; **6:**205; **7:**95; **8:**608, 719; **9:**244, 643; **11:**11, 324, 327, 329–30, 332, 338, 488, 493, 576, 663, 827, 876, 879; **12:**179–81, 203, 205–6, 210–13, 215–19, 221, 223–25, 263, 269, 276, 405, 491, 493, 530

EPHAH
See under WEIGHTS AND MEASURES
EPHESIANS, LETTER TO THE
1:8, 13, 16, 160, 963; **3:**417; **4:**1025; **5:**36, 401; **6:**759; **7:**334, 866; **8:**48; **9:**461; **10:**266, 272, 370, 373, 379, 381, 390, 538, 687, 702, 709, 767–68, 789–90, 932, 949, 969–70; **11:**284, 535, 577–78, 649, 662, 668, 684, 808; **12:**146, 230–32, 246, 278, 280–81, 284, 294, 304, 398, 509, 523, 531, 653, 723
EPHOD
1:23, 888, 905–7, 973, 1061; **2:**162, 220, 764, 791–92, 808–11, 870, 987–88, 1079, 1081–82, 1139–40, 1148, 1152–53, 1183, 1192–93, 1243, 1249; **5:**592, 843; **7:**232
EPIGRAPHY (*OR* EPIGRAPHIC, *ETC.*)
1:244, 248–50, 252, 255–58, 261–62, 264–65, 996; **4:**193
EPILEPSY, EPILEPTIC
4:1181; **8:**368, 546; **9:**34, 158, 192, 204, 208; **11:**165
EPIPHANY
1:908, 1184; **3:**140; **4:**208–10, 253, 263, 276, 287; **6:**501, 508, 513; **7:**393, 602; **8:**64–65, 145, 510, 580, 584, 603–4, 630–31; **9:**184, 540, 712, 856–57, 859; **10:**150, 179, 227, 306, 966; **11:**58, 759, 829, 831, 836, 855; CHURCH-YEAR SEASON **2:**55; **4:**794, 960–61, 965, 1052, 1067, 1233; **8:**145
EPISTLE, EPISTLES
CATHOLIC **1:**8, 15; **5:**14; **10:**32, 371, 389; **12:**177, 229, 329, 411; GENERAL **1:**135; **8:**3; **10:**377; **12:**229, 365; JOHANNINE **1:**14; **9:**426, 499, 559; **10:**377; **12:**239, 365–66, 368–69, 370, 372, 374–75, 377, 393, 405, 413, 461, 468; PASTORAL **8:**22, 48–49, 54; **9:**336, 338, 359; **10:**285, 370, 789, 969–70, 972; **11:**218, 330, 353, 480, 577, 580, 659, 664, 667, 775–77, 797, 832, 835, 862, 877; **12:**232, 234, 271, 278, 285, 454, 573; PAULINE/PAUL'S **1:**13, 15–16, 85, 97, 110, 135, 155, 190–91, 209, 211; **5:**276; **8:**6, 29, 528, 654, 708; **9:**410; **11:**354, 362, 398, 408–9, 471–72, 883; **12:**34, 255, 325, 449, 466, 650, 728; SERMON-EPISTLE **12:**55, 84, 95, 118, 127
EQUALITY
1:62, 170, 183–84, 353, 555, 864, 1036; **2:**457, 669, 808; **3:**358, 442–43, 447, 451, 1004, 1120; **4:**413, 1011; **5:**37, 199, 332, 447, 497; **6:**486, 609; **7:**108, 358, 396, 580, 676, 681; **9:**25, 389, 677; **10:**424, 499, 866, 886, 930, 932; **11:**24, 115, 124, 232, 272, 278, 899; **12:**261, 285, 287; WITH GOD **3:**783; **4:**759; **6:**358; **9:**584, 677; **11:**502–3, 507–9, 527
EROS
1:843; **5:**66; **10:**435; **11:**646
ESCAPE, ROCK OF
2:1154
ESCHATOLOGY
1:179, 287; **3:**512; **4:**184; **5:**113, 800; **6:**66; **7:**4–5, 7, 10, 13–14, 439, 699, 874; **8:**29, 35–37, 39, 118, 144, 205, 222, 234, 259, 264, 351, 428–29, 445, 520; **9:**333, 497, 553, 585, 663–65, 741, 784, 790, 796, 862; **10:**25, 82, 462, 477, 623, 655, 688, 700–701, 705; **11:**96, 186, 224, 313, 360, 375, 573, 579; **12:**98, 269, 276, 312–13, 327–28, 410, 513, 519, 525, 527, 531–32, 545–46, 553, 555, 615, 684, 703, 705, 709, 711–12, 716, 721; APOCALYPTIC **6:**207, 223, 277, 1513–14; **10:**10, 63; CHRISTIAN **1:**290; **12:**357; INAUGURATED **3:**417; **8:**195, 365; **10:**514, 598–99, 606, 612, 661, 706, 720, 729; OT/JEWISH **7:**428, 430; **8:**40, 226; **11:**572; OVERREALIZED **10:**719, 722; **11:**683, 725; REALIZED **1:**177; **3:**407; **8:**299; **9:**553, 570, 584–85, 602, 784; **10:**538, 616; **11:**458, 576, 578, 639, 684; **12:**475, 555, 713
ESTHER, BOOK OF
1:5, 8–12, 18, 28–29, 43, 51, 65, 186, 241, 284–85, 286, 294, 592, 697, 896, 1061; **2:**552, 1044; **3:**756, 978, 1081, 1086–87, 1091, 1095, 1098, 1102–3, 1113, 1118, 1124, 1132, 1142–43, 1147, 1167, 1171–72, 1187; **4:**297; **5:**119, 189, 273, 285, 291, 334, 363–64, 606; **6:**449, 945, 1524; **7:**21, 30, 32, 41, 43, 50, 56, 63–64, 81, 93, 124, 156; **8:**29, 41, 66, 598; **10:**718; ADDITIONS TO (*see* ADDITIONS TO ESTHER *in ANCIENT LITERATURE*)
ETERNAL
LIFE **1:**350, 364, 853, 1125; **2:**167–68; **3:**370, 1004, 1018, 1071; **4:**737, 824, 854, 1044, 1101; **5:**4, 53, 120, 451, 605, 627; **6:**223, 414, 608, 711, 1383, 1423; **7:**336; **8:**36–37, 40, 74, 201, 275, 390–92, 648, 651, 676, 705; **9:**25, 177, 226–28, 230, 344–47, 349–50, 497, 552–53, 555, 558–59, 561, 566, 584, 587, 589, 599, 602, 604–5, 608, 610–11, 664, 676, 689, 694, 711, 714–15, 723, 751, 774, 789, 824, 827; **10:**59, 70, 85, 165, 193–96, 218–19, 222, 254, 262, 322, 335, 338, 378, 438, 509, 520, 525, 530, 546, 549, 574, 584, 604, 657; **11:**27, 336–37, 829, 877, 879; **12:**260, 338, 372, 379, 381–84, 399, 401, 404, 409, 419–20, 423, 424, 431, 440–43, 446–47, 450, 461, 479, 497–98, 704; PUNISHMENT **6:**549, 1409, 1445, 1480; **7:**15; **11:**749–50; **12:**74, 488, 497
ETERNITY
1:436, 458, 573; **4:**484, 1036, 1042, 1086–87, 1093, 1099; **5:**306, 313, 464, 644, 645; **6:**342,

369, 401, 407, 452, 469; **8:**455; **9:**473, 643; **11:**416, 771; **12:**61, 86, 360, 385, 411, 535, 552, 570, 657, 715

ETHICAL
BEHAVIOR(S)/OUTCOME(S)/PERFORMANCE(S)/RESPONSE(S) **1:**517, 1131–32; **2:**221; **3:**736; **6:**57; **7:**632; **11:**507, 733; **12:**686; CHOICE(S)/CONCERN(S)/DECISION(S)/DILEMMA(S)/ISSUE(S)/QUESTION(S)/TEST(S) **1:**81–82, 853, 889; **2:**336, 445; **3:**109, 821, 1109, 1156; **4:**82, 290, 292, 775, 1237; **5:**313, 330, 451, 609, 781; **6:**1, 19, 832; **7:**77; **8:**189, 219, 251; **9:**378; **10:**89; **11:**516–17, 873; CONDUCT/DEMAND(S)/IMPERATIVE(S)/NEED(S)/OBLIGATION(S)/RESPONSIBILITIES **1:**135; **2:**221, 327, 374–75; **3:**723; **4:**552, 555; **5:**452–54, 460, 462, 465, 477, 544, 807; **6:**1122; **8:**177, 219; **9:**145, 147, 254, 733–34; **10:**339, 534, 605, 706, 726; **11:**514, 593, 692, 701; **12:**5, 394, 424, 475; EXHORTATION(S)/NORM(S)/REQUIREMENT(S)/STANDARD(S)/SYSTEM(S)/TRADITION(S) **1:**81; **3:**570, 811; **4:**164–65, 168; **5:**827; **6:**1, 20–21; **7:**89, 345, 395–96; **8:**177; **9:**147, 286, 331, 409; **10:**203, 462; **11:**358, 367, 393, 413, 418, 423, 429, 431, 438, 507, 515, 555, 573, 621, 641, 662, 873–74; **12:**335–36; INJUNCTION(S)/PRINCIPLE(S) **1:**68, 1124, 1131; **2:**369; **3:**737; **11:**454; **12:**290, 667; INSTRUCTION(S)/LESSON(S)/TEACHING(S) **1:**76–77, 1158, 1164; **5:**10, 307, 787, 790; **7:**340; **8:**21, 41; **9:**83, 101, 147, 278, 493; **11:**128, 362, 428, 516, 619, 652, 660; **12:**156, 327–28, 355, 479; PERSPECTIVE(S)/REFLECTION(S)/UNDERSTANDING(S) **1:**872; **2:**285; **3:**487; **5:**440, 447, 451, 453, 596; **6:**19; **8:**386; **10:**726; REFORM(S) **9:**83–85

ETHICS
1:2, 49–50, 121, 178, 227, 868, 872, 897, 1124, 1132, 1143, 1175, 1190; **2:**26, 129, 255, 567; **3:**34–35, 179, 556, 592, 620, 1144; **4:**16, 48, 184, 292, 453, 552–53, 555, 626, 775; **5:**155, 312–13; **6:**7, 641, 1259; **7:**129, 145, 582; **8:**18–19, 118, 148, 178, 193, 197, 220, 222, 251, 294, 313, 372, 379, 404, 455; **9:**187; **10:**382, 384, 404, 533, 542, 700, 702, 705–6, 726, 728, 732; **11:**187, 420, 476, 514–16, 579, 718, 784, 873; **12:**4, 181, 260, 327–28, 341, 360, 513; CHRISTIAN (*see under* CHRISTIAN); SOCIAL **1:**1004, 1115, 1123, 1128, 1133; **2:**195, 220; **3:**555, 664; **7:**340; **12:**184, 213, 225

ETHNARCH
3:1113, 1118; **4:**164–65, 168; **5:**843

ETHNOGRAPHY, ETHNOGRAPHIC
1:214, 220, 226, 255–56, 258; **7:**122

ETHNOLOGICAL
1:403, 432, 476, 577

ENTHNOPOLITICAL
7:168

EUCHARIST
1:91, 193, 205, 209–11, 776, 784, 816, 836, 845, 892, 1114, 1184; **2:**15, 38, 40, 54, 141–42, 152, 230; **3:**1065; **4:**816, 1149; **7:**228; **8:**74, 82, 124, 212, 326, 467, 469–70, 472–73, 601, 695, 704; **9:**117, 195–97, 480, 495, 528, 539, 606–8, 610, 612–14, 719, 759, 834, 858; **10:**234, 352, 450, 535, 730, 759, 934; **11:**234; **12:**75, 123, 264, 269, 439, 493, 569

EUNUCH
3:751, 885, 889, 903, 919, 951, 1077, 1106, 1158–59; **5:**441, 467, 473–76, 480, 485, 489, 552, 563, 630, 681, 740, 779; **6:**485, 850; **9:**345; **10:**142–45; ETHIOPIAN EUNUCH (*see* ETHIOPIAN EUNUCH *in PERSONS IN THE BIBLE*)

EVANGELISM
1:196, 199, 202, 823; **2:**1030; **3:**487; **4:**993; **8:**219, 264, 314, 376; **9:**197, 358; **10:**70–71, 155, 254, 623, 755, 759, 911; **11:**484, 664, 778, 796, 807; **12:**288, 358

EVANGELIST
2:325; **3:**501; **4:**578; **6:**365, 434, 451, 1209; **7:**254; **8:**74, 81, 83–85, 93, 95, 108, 151, 172, 245, 466, 509–11, 514, 518, 520, 525, 541, 548, 550, 559, 562–63, 565, 603, 607, 614–15, 640, 684, 693, 731–32; **10:**70, 145, 198, 289, 422, 753, 817, 959; **11:**422, 591, 855, 859; **12:**561

EVENING
1:88, 103, 341, 343, 346, 1009, 1044, 1070, 1082, 1105, 1120, 1163; **2:**80, 90, 151–52, 236, 543, 876, 992, 1202, 1287, 1289; **3:**616, 1002; **4:**367, 393, 912, 1041–42, 1206; **5:**394, 396, 485, 733; **6:**175, 1194–95, 1339, 1342, 1453, 1588; **7:**58, 89, 309, 365, 667, 694; **8:**323–24, 451, 463, 468, 470, 481, 494, 498, 663, 697, 702, 725; **9:**100, 195, 233, 287, 290, 320, 323, 373, 390, 414–15, 428, 479, 719, 722, 759, 805, 838, 845, 848, 856; **10:**100, 277, 361, 526; OFFERING(S)/SACRIFICE(S) **1:**1044, 1157; **2:**229; **3:**399, 691, 733, 735, 819, 821, 1143; **4:**1243, 1245; **6:**1589; **8:**33; PRAYER(S) **1:**67, 205, 207; **2:**229; **4:**1245; **8:**204; **10:**76–77; **12:**510, 660

EVERLASTING
1:448, 458, 460–61, 492, 504; **2:**1255, 1257, 1259, 1262–63; **3:**117, 242, 401, 498, 502, 810, 1062, 1099; **4:**234, 240, 310, 689, 934, 973, 1041, 1173, 1238; **5:**401, 525, 720; **6:**282, 483, 509, 661, 711, 717, 768, 934, 960, 971–72, 974, 975, 977, 980, 982, 1430–31; **7:**55, 65, 105, 125, 312, 771; **8:**654, 691–92; **9:**460, 823; **11:**436, 459; **12:**241, 356, 405; COVENANT (*see under* COVENANT); LIFE **3:**568; **4:**242; **5:**53; **6:**218, 1502; **7:**148; **9:**346

EVERY VALLEY
9:22, 81

EVIL
ACTS/ACTIONS/DEED(S) **1:**478, 672; **2:**15, 59, 359, 887, 1119; **5:**12, 50, 75, 337, 678; **6:**607, 673, 1066, 1452; **7:**93, 220, 239, 333, 544, 553; **9:**151; **10:**567; **11:**389, 391, 437, 606, 625; **12:**633, 667; AGE **1:**160; **8:**541, 671–72, 675, 688, 696, 709; **10:**377, 718, 822; **11:**184, 196, 202, 206–8, 215, 219, 225, 229, 240, 244, 247, 269, 340, 344, 374, 442, 638, 643; ANGEL(S) **1:**89; **7:**67; **9:**51; **11:**390; **12:**350, 488; DESIRE(S) **11:**427, 642; **12:**187, 258, 273, 336, 355, 494; DO(ES/ING/NE) **1:**640; **2:**725, 760, 763, 766, 774, 779, 792, 795, 845, 854, 863–64, 1134, 1160, 1165, 1168; **3:**123, 247, 277, 287, 289–90, 292, 452, 526, 658, 705, 849, 1056; **4:**32, 36, 97, 471, 576, 626, 890, 1245; **5:**112, 127, 160, 247, 316, 678, 724; **6:**53, 56, 379, 448, 746, 986, 1250; **7:**142, 515, 551, 585, 868; **8:**165, 559; **9:**135–36, 589, 816; **10:**454, 533, 721; **11:**27, 524; **12:**204, 242, 372; "THE EVIL ONE" (*see under* SATAN *in PERSONS IN THE BIBLE*); EYE(S) **2:**185; **4:**913; **5:**784; **6:**1144; **9:**641; **11:**250, 294; FORCE(S)/POWER(S) OF **1:**85, 204, 210, 274, 435, 601, 739; **2:**136, 790, 1114; **3:**426, 563, 576, 731, 758; **4:**190, 487, 763, 909, 914, 974, 1243; **5:**801; **6:**74, 98, 208, 226, 228; **7:**3, 10, 12, 15, 49–50, 100, 128, 335, 429, 636; **8:**62, 64, 163, 205, 232, 292–93, 346, 357, 580, 594; **9:**186, 224, 244, 417, 713, 793, 804, 810; **10:**178, 428, 729; **11:**268, 282, 318, 352, 355, 390–91, 393, 410, 460, 463, 498, 509, 564–65, 570, 573, 627–28, 678, 708, 759; **12:**252, 297, 317, 399, 436, 536, 631, 653, 660, 704; GOOD AND (*see* GOOD: AND/OR EVIL); GOOD FOR/FROM/OVER EVIL *or* EVIL FOR/FROM/OVER GOOD **2:**819, 1159–60, 1164, 1167, 1171; **4:**176, 503; **5:**168, 220, 717; **6:**926; **7:**8; **10:**124, 192, 533, 701, 715; **12:**68, 72, 152, 286; HEART **1:**393, 398; **2:**1111; **7:**382; **8:**234; **12:**49; INTENT(S)/INTENTION(S) **1:**991–92; **4:**52, 63, 1058; **5:**194; **6:**741, 1279; KING(S) **1:**264; **2:**551, 1063, 1159; **4:**503; **6:**117, 159; **8:**146; PURGING **1:**1144; **2:**392, 455; **6:**1495; **8:**269; IN THE SIGHT OF GOD/THE LORD **2:**760, 770, 776, 779, 795, 798, 824, 1089; **3:**121, 123, 169, 243, 247, 277, 287–90, 292; SIN AND/OR **1:**176, 365, 384, 425, 435, 479, 594, 671, 673; **7:**334; **10:**399, 823, 847; SPIRIT(S) **2:**454, 817–18, 831, 1101–4, 1109, 1119, 1121, 1126–29, 1149; **3:**1029; **5:**809; **7:**501; **8:**23–24, 62, 296, 525, 541; **9:**51; **10:**234, 269; **11:**563, 627, 653; **12:**41, 294, 297, 677, 700; AND SUFFERING (*see under* SUFFERING); SYMBOL(S) OF **2:**901; **3:**948; **5:**11; **6:**918; **12:**653; WAY(S) **1:**72, 74, 470; **2:**782, 885; **3:**110; **5:**46, 464; **6:**752, 761, 793, 860, 1215, 1290, 1446, 1448–50, 1492; **7:**314

EWE, EWES
1:491–42, 1098; **2:**1292; **3:**14, 18, 152; **4:**609; **5:**403, 418; **6:**1274; **7:**468–69

EXALTATION
3:24, 295, 671, 1026; **4:**50, 396, 585, 738, 1136, 1139, 1145, 1275; **6:**326, 462–63, 471, 489, 492, 504, 508–9, 515, 665, 1252–53; **7:**509, 745, 754, 830, 834; **8:**30, 37, 623, 632, 653, 678, 680, 713; **9:**18, 55, 315, 790, 799; **10:**144; **11:**355, 382, 389, 391–92, 415, 438, 458, 490, 501–2, 516; **12:**188, 192, 210, 216, 316, 686; OF CHRIST/JESUS **8:**40, 631, 695, 732–33; **9:**205, 463, 478, 488, 552, 635, 713, 816, 819, 827, 830, 842; **10:**178; **11:**360–61, 372, 374, 378, 381–83, 385–86, 392, 402–3, 409, 419, 450, 458, 460, 463, 501–2, 509–10, 514–15, 536, 538, 545, 571–72, 638, 808; **12:**7, 10–12, 21–25, 29–30, 34, 38, 40, 42, 46, 61–62, 68–69, 90, 94–95, 108, 172, 519, 531, 569, 589, 593, 644, 702–3; OF GOD/YAHWEH **1:**796; **4:**585, 1139; **6:**71, 73, 469, 658, 708; **8:**733

EXCAVATE (*OR* EXCAVATING, EXCAVATION, *ETC.*)
1:104, 214–15, 219, 221, 224, 229, 233, 247, 251, 265, 1054, 1081; **2:**615, 636, 688; **3:**70, 82, 178, 768, 773, 838, 878, 889, 1174; **4:**328; **6:**7, 577, 1176, 1596; **7:**352, 376, 810; **8:**228

EXCELLENCE
2:1165; **3:**63, 337, 594, 618; **4:**236, 296; **5:**64, 117, 132, 205, 331; **7:**88; **9:**76; **11:**213, 613, 690, 721; **12:**188, 274, 337

EXCELLENT
4:202; **5:**64, 327, 694, 813; **6:**238; **7:**82, 88; **11:**541, 559, 807, 877; **12:**78, 597; MORE **1:**849; **4:**1193; **7:**502, 526; **11:**340; **12:**24, 100; MOST **4:**935; **5:**366, 377; **9:**9, 40; **10:**7

EXCLUSION
1:169, 182, 259, 292, 314, 369, 455, 598, 601, 656, 1135, 1151, 1165, 1189; **2:**201, 328, 460–61, 469, 529, 589, 625, 642, 707, 711, 810, 1238; **3:**19, 225, 422, 531, 575, 842, 1134; **4:**368, 461, 510, 545, 547–48, 611, 654, 952; **5:**199; **6:**389, 516–17, 970, 1190, 1296, 1331; **7:**200, 511, 547; **8:**10, 79; **9:**129, 345, 400, 648, 663; **10:**41, 205, 311, 434, 448, 480, 685, 690; **11:**273, 305, 327, 401–2, 436, 530, 609, 750, 763; **12:**158, 224, 456, 467, 617, 649, 652, 686; OF WOMEN **1:**182, 186; **8:**196

EXCLUSIVE
See INCLUSIVE/EXCLUSIVE

EXCOMMUNICATE (*OR* EXCOMMUNICATION, *ETC.*)
1:459, 777, 920, 923, 1051, 1118, 1142; **2:**87,

128, 151; **3:**741; **6:**1209, 1212; **8:**33, 101, 378–79; **9:**504, 765–66; **10:**82, 111, 852; **11:**211, 795; **12:**444, 456, 464, 467

EXECRATE (*OR* EXECRATES, EXECRATION, *ETC.*)
2:191, 1236; **4:**107; **7:**611, 613

EXECUTE (*OR* EXECUTES, *ETC.*)
PUT TO DEATH **1:**186, 265–66, 290, 306, 537, 705, 863, 865, 923, 933, 1165; **2:**199, 265–66, 447–48, 455, 585, 627, 629–31, 646, 648, 719, 1100, 1159, 1229, 1266, 1314–15, 1358–59; **3:**690, 717, 892, 950, 996, 1001; **4:**40, 48, 93, 223, 233, 262, 281, 285, 290; **5:**484, 772, 818; **6:**443, 560, 716, 742, 773–74, 795, 851, 925, 943, 995, 1079, 1261, 1403, 1442; **7:**95, 671, 765, 787; **8:**156, 269, 385, 464, 528, 531, 536, 563, 593, 598, 643, 656, 668, 688, 712, 718–19, 723; **9:**52, 370, 465, 830, 835–36; **10:**74, 132, 150, 178, 312, 374; **11:**403, 417, 607; **12:**167, 657

EXECUTION
OF A PERSON **1:**459, 697, 865, 870, 905, 1138, 1142; **2:**125, 151, 198, 199, 392, 447–48, 455, 470, 562, 613, 627, 629, 808, 810, 964, 1201, 1266, 1273, 1355, 1357–58; **3:**27, 33–34, 581, 923, 932, 1090, 1118, 1171; **4:**17, 19, 40, 47, 92, 95, 182, 233, 286, 874; **5:**797; **6:**412, 772, 774, 794, 851, 857, 925, 1172, 1179–80, 1191, 1235, 1299, 1310, 1345, 1489; **7:**64, 90, 833; **8:**194, 319, 370, 396, 414, 479, 482, 488, 490–91, 493, 526, 531, 598, 627–28, 636, 643, 714, 718–19, 722–23, 726; **9:**195, 448, 451, 454–55, 465, 646, 816, 820, 829–30, 861; **10:**43, 79–80, 85, 105, 122, 125, 129–31, 146, 179, 234, 309, 342; **11:**474, 493, 601; **12:**311, 540, 605

EXECUTIONER
2:792; **3:**980; **4:**242, 974; **6:**276, 1307; **7:**66, 346; **10:**235, 454; **12:**445

EXHORTATION, EXHORTATIONS
ETHICAL **1:**81; **8:**177; **9:**286, 331, 409; **11:**358, 367, 393, 413, 418, 423, 429, 431, 438, 507, 515, 555, 573, 621, 641, 662; **12:**335; TO FAITHFULNESS **11:**560, 585, 619; TO HOLINESS/TO BE HOLY **1:**1115, 1137, 1142; **11:**419, 560, 585, 641; TO JUSTICE **5:**437, 442, 444, 449, 451, 456; MORAL **1:**99, 185, 192; **8:**42; **10:**371, 378, 382; **11:**188, 320–21, 424, 440, 443, 716; **12:**177–79, 181, 200, 210, 272, 299, 329, 371; PROPHETIC **4:**651, 729, 880, 890, 1003, 1060–61; **6:**637, 641, 740; **8:**31; **12:**735; TO REPENT **7:**281; **10:**140, 247; TO WISDOM **5:**411, 449, 488

EXILE
ASSYRIAN **2:**864; **3:**995; **6:**196, 596; **7:**265, 267, 278–79, 330; BABYLONIAN **1:**9, 65, 209, 268, 284, 307, 312, 365, 422, 996, 1060, 1181–82; **2:**5, 504, 520, 557, 565, 579–80, 687, 723, 725, 731, 736, 864, 895, 996, 1024, 1063, 1209, 1258, 1317; **3:**313, 332, 598, 607, 636, 654, 656, 665, 667, 674, 677, 679, 708, 737, 931, 959, 1016, 1112; **4:**196–97, 404, 442, 661, 852, 1043, 1065, 1072, 1190, 1195, 1207; **5:**21, 244, 274, 720, 801; **6:**14, 31, 37, 49, 142, 145, 155, 159–60, 188, 197, 201, 203–4, 207, 226, 232, 236, 247–48, 252, 255, 258, 273, 276, 280–82, 284, 297, 304, 312, 315, 322, 328–29, 335, 439, 443, 449, 454, 463, 484, 560, 582, 731, 743, 757–58, 793–94, 797, 806, 815, 819, 851, 858, 867, 874, 912, 934, 940–43, 945, 947, 952, 958, 980, 1075, 1121, 1147, 1157, 1185, 1215, 1286, 1313, 1344, 1410, 1446, 1458, 1466, 1526; **7:**2, 3, 23, 31, 139, 147, 176, 199, 206, 217, 249, 301, 396, 437, 438, 489, 553, 563, 567–68, 571–72, 626, 671, 708, 738, 765, 772, 847; **8:**34–35; **10:**398, 661, 675; **12:**236, 246, 533, 535, 569, 596; EXODUS AND **1:**518; **2:**547; **10:**643, 657; RETURN FROM **1:**83, 209, 268, 307; **3:**301, 313, 364, 436, 538, 636, 668, 672, 675–76, 680, 708, 714, 751, 770, 831, 1062, 1112; **4:**8, 122, 663, 673, 730, 790, 795, 843, 1016, 1073, 1087, 1091, 1105, 1117–19, 1121, 1133, 1141, 1143, 1153–56, 1177, 1187, 1195, 1225, 1272; **5:**720; **6:**145, 484, 604, 783, 796, 801–1, 911, 914, 961, 969, 1276, 1538; **7:**206, 223, 232, 568, 572, 708–10, 752; **10:**644–45, 655, 659–60, 696; **11:**259; **12:**596; SPIRITUAL **3:**302, 365, 501, 602, 611; **10:**129–30, 362; THEOLOGY AND (*see under* THEOLOGY); WILDERNESS AND **1:**805, 898, 906–8; **2:**865; **3:**313; **4:**1043–44, 1105, 1117, 1143, 1224; **6:**283, 371, 432, 449, 455, 491, 601; **7:**235, 265–66, 278–79, 346, 396; **10:**129; **12:**258, 569

EXILIC PERIOD
1:237, 252, 367; **2:**7, 37, 229; **3:**4, 738, 994; **6:**157, 356, 499, 525, 812, 1045, 1079–81, 1092, 1537; **7:**43, 90, 162, 436, 555, 586; **12:**101; DOCUMENTS **1:**680; **3:**300; PRE-EXILIC PERIOD **1:**312, 316, 997, 1170–71; **3:**301–2, 327, 329; **6:**785, 1083, 1117, 1196, 1464; **7:**372; POST-EXILIC PERIOD **1:**285, 309, 591, 961, 1113, 1190; **2:**9, 11, 47, 109, 137, 214, 274, 283, 579, 613, 760, 865, 902, 942; **3:**95, 295, 300, 305, 319–20, 345, 394, 417, 441, 450, 499, 570, 580, 623, 667, 768, 795, 842, 847, 886, 993–94, 1016, 1063, 1086, 1099, 1117; **4:**325, 347, 887; **5:**370, 555; **6:**148, 226–27, 273, 276, 280, 491, 525, 1087–88; **7:**124–25, 181, 362, 466, 626, 846; **8:**29, 31, 35–36

EXISTENCE
CHRISTIAN **5:**208; **7:**643; **8:**189, 328; **10:**516, 588, 590; **11:**271, 500, 555, 574, 620, 639–40, 645;

EXISTENCE *(continued)*
12:146, 376, 390, 413, 416, 460, 575; OF THE CHURCH **11:**384, 410, 466, 574, 689; **12:**230, 523; BY/OF/WITH GOD/YAHWEH **1:**279, 342, 947; **4:**402, 661, 1104; **5:**834; **6:**759, 1057; **7:**52–53, 64; **8:**529; **9:**550, 646; **12:**42; HUMAN **1:**318, 326, 354, 624, 803, 808, 830, 848, 850; **2:**488, 1057, 1299, 1341; **4:**241, 378, 380, 393–94, 396, 402, 451, 497, 517, 520, 523, 556, 629–30, 731, 1041–42, 1075, 1087, 1199; **5:**56, 78, 93, 129, 159, 237, 252, 303, 328, 430, 434, 456, 525, 652, 679, 721, 753, 793, 815; **6:**658, 677, 734, 813; **7:**636; **8:**264, 351; **9:**550, 552, 589, 790; **10:**247, 253, 323, 336, 378, 544, 588, 595, 901; **11:**120, 272, 321, 509, 561, 608, 634, 705; **12:**188, 204, 216, 504, 521, 530, 553, 589; OF ISRAEL **1:**789, 803, 830–31, 835, 923, 937; **2:**300, 350, 355, 416, 485, 957, 1240; **3:**26, 248; **4:**1041, 1088; **5:**531; **6:**5–6; **7:**12, 593, 848; PRE-EXISTENCE **2:**577; **5:**511–12; **7:**571; **8:**150, 275, 529; **9:**516, 518, 520, 523, 528, 646; **11:**283, 502, 504; **12:**7, 12, 21–24, 29, 42, 61–62, 99, 446, 586, 657

EXODUS
BOOK OF **1:**8, 12, 67–69, 165, 175, 238, 294, 298–99, 307, 309, 427–29, 434, 452, 486, 488, 593–95, 601, 611, 630, 645, 647, 652, 654–55, 670–72, 674, 996, 1007, 1056, 1132; **2:**5–6, 10–11, 33, 181, 250–51, 253, 406, 543, 546, 547, 560, 600, 602, 629, 723, 752–53, 760, 876, 1021, 1030; **3:**467, 1119, 1176; **4:**19, 72, 159, 754, 801, 933, 937, 991, 1062, 1112, 1150; **5:**10, 14, 78, 149, 186, 262, 441, 443, 525, 529, 531–32, 540, 542, 561, 578, 583, 585, 591, 596, 818, 842; **6:**282, 355, 628, 745, 809, 1072, 1164; **7:**50, 52, 150, 355, 357, 381, 421; **8:**30–31, 323, 492, 530; **9:**347; **11:**64, 69, 266; **12:**103, 142, 267, 269, 387, 560, 562, 604, 609, 672; EVENT **1:**18, 37, 79, 83, 93, 164, 209–10, 248, 254–55, 257, 274–75, 277, 308, 311–12, 317, 327, 341, 433, 445, 447, 452, 473, 518, 560, 593, 600, 627, 652, 660, 669, 995, 1008, 1018, 1057, 1136, 1159, 1164, 1171; **2:**3, 16, 19–20, 32–33, 39, 50, 68, 70, 77, 81, 86–87, 89, 91, 94–96, 99, 109–10, 120, 125, 128–29, 136, 138, 159, 161–62, 166, 181–82, 188, 190, 218–19, 222, 250, 252–54, 294, 297, 342, 411, 504, 544, 547, 589–90, 600, 602, 604, 607, 613, 619, 626, 641, 660, 673, 724, 781, 792, 804, 901, 1001–1004, 1006, 1010, 1014, 1022, 1027, 1029, 1038, 1047, 1062, 1087, 1366; **3:**61, 72, 77, 93–94, 96, 104, 150, 179, 184, 255, 273, 277, 294–95, 304, 408, 464, 483, 497, 501, 664, 668, 671, 676–80, 687, 713–14, 721, 726, 730, 735, 753–54, 809–11, 827, 829, 866, 896, 899, 948, 956–57, 1001, 1106, 1129, 1137; **4:**80, 190, 212, 313, 513, 663, 673, 717, 741–42, 748, 768, 790, 795, 800–801, 810, 843, 857, 872–73, 916, 934, 937–38, 944–46, 959, 963, 973–74, 977, 980, 984, 990–91, 996, 1000, 1021, 1028, 1035, 1062, 1065–66, 1072–73, 1076, 1078, 1087–88, 1091–92, 1104–6, 1112, 1117, 1133–34, 1138, 1141–42, 1149, 1153–56, 1177, 1181, 1219–20, 1224–25, 1247, 1251–52, 1269, 1275; **5:**21, 96, 113, 441–43, 450, 469, 487, 494, 518, 520, 522, 525, 528–36, 543, 546, 553, 569, 579, 580, 591, 593, 596–99, 606, 621; **6:**19, 38, 112, 137, 145–46, 157, 181, 282, 284, 297, 344, 365, 372, 375–76, 378, 400–401, 420–21, 432, 443, 447–48, 456, 473, 526–27, 529, 575, 597, 599, 693, 697, 703, 733–34, 745, 815, 882, 950, 958, 974, 994, 1099, 1118, 1172, 1238, 1274–75, 1279, 1319, 1402, 1420, 1435, 1437, 1473, 1510; **7:**65, 101, 265, 277, 281, 346, 355, 357, 365–66, 369, 424–25, 583, 586, 588–89, 683, 699, 722, 815, 823, 839, 855, 857; **8:**28, 33, 533; **9:**15, 195, 198–99, 346–47, 421, 460, 478, 594, 596, 600–601, 603, 612–13, 616, 632, 637–38, 668; **10:**43, 54, 180, 181–82, 191–92, 338, 416, 429, 510, 533–37, 541, 545–48, 550–53, 555, 563, 576, 590, 596, 598, 605, 619, 624, 635, 638–40, 657, 670, 677, 680, 778, 793, 838, 902, 910, 913–16, 920, 935, 937, 939; **11:**40, 43, 64, 99, 160, 608; **12:**53, 59, 81, 95, 128, 139, 142, 156, 339, 532, 554, 591, 673, 725–26; NARRATIVE/STORY **1:**170, 274, 290, 427, 429, 670; **2:**252–53, 461, 480, 600, 834, 1011, 1062, 1112; **3:**1139; **4:**82, 198, 582, 984, 1054, 1105, 1264; **5:**442, 525, 528, 573, 584, 586, 594, 596, 598; **6:**282; **7:**355; **8:**94; **9:**542, 605; **10:**267, 433, 457, 511–13, 525, 547–48, 563, 581, 585, 593, 608, 611, 622, 638–39, 913–14, 918; **11:**124, 166, 266–67; **12:**267, 725; NEW **1:**209; **2:**600, 1011; **3:**432, 718; **4:**916, 917, 938, 1065, 1072, 1088, 1105, 1143, 1205, 1275; **6:**315, 430, 432, 1147, 1289, 1461, 1466, 1491, 1502; **7:**223, 235, 258, 287, 297, 396; **8:**535; **9:**59, 837; **10:**471, 510–13, 525, 533–35, 537, 541, 546–47, 550–52, 556, 564, 591, 608, 643; **11:**106, 166; SECOND **3:**678; **4:**1195; **5:**45; **6:**335, 482, 1103, 1288, 1509; **7:**815

EXORCISM
2:150; **3:**980; **8:**23–24, 59, 62, 64, 117, 223, 228, 232, 244, 285, 337, 348, 365, 367, 368, 511, 521, 529, 539–41, 543, 545, 561, 580, 583–85, 591, 623, 633–34, 637; **9:**118, 160, 174–75, 186–88, 208–9, 241–44, 247; **10:**138, 140, 232–33, 267–69

EXPIATION
1:986, 1005, 1010, 1024–25, 1036, 1039–40, 1061, 1066–67, 1109, 1111–12; **2:**65, 77, 140,

266, 963, 1354–55, 1358–59; **6:**227, 430, 440, 442, 464, 529, 1489; **8:**34; **9:**664–65, 837; **10:**476; **11:**373; **12:**41, 376, 388, 391, 395, 414, 435, 441, 446

EXTORT (*OR* EXTORTS, EXTORTION, *ETC.*)
1:1033, 1041; **2:**82, 609; **4:**925; **5:**340; **6:**530, 637, 742, 1261, 1310, 1315; **7:**77, 285, 293; **8:**720; **9:**85, 359, 393, 543; **10:**323, 463

EYE, EYES
APPLE OF THE (*see under* APPLE); BLIND **1:**178, 1149; **2:**992; **3:**1029; **5:**64, 241, 300, 328; **6:**364, 369, 376, 378, 544, 621, 767; **7:**89, 279; **8:**619; **9:**113, 150, 160, 269, 287, 298, 354, 356, 358, 652, 656–57; **10:**338, 463; **12:**337, 587; EVIL (*see under* EVIL) **11:**250, 294; "(AN) EYE FOR (AN) EYE" **1:**46, 377, 1165; **2:**436, 888; **5:**541; **6:**90, 278, 1483; **9:**148; GOD'S/THE LORD'S/YAHWEH'S **1:**70, 390, 573, 1142, 1172; **2:**80, 139, 374, 864, 871, 982, 986–87, 1101, 1041, 1262, 1283–84, 1287, 1291, 1293–94, 1324, 1326, 1345, 1367; **3:**7, 117, 227, 241, 244–45, 248, 250, 704, 706, 1154, 1178–79; **4:**21, 348, 448, 517, 577, 741; **5:**66, 127, 141, 151, 163, 225, 454, 615, 708, 724, 800; **6:**440, 477, 637, 718, 920, 1064, 1071, 1167, 1180, 1190, 1281, 1503–4, 1510–11; **7:**291–92, 506, 760, 767, 769–70, 780, 806, 823, 826; **9:**439; **11:**629; **12:**54, 267, 303, 673; GOUGING OF AN **2:**858, 1054; **6:**1176, 1251; **8:**191, 405, 640; LIDS *(in reference to dawn)* **4:**624; OF A NEEDLE **7:**801; **8:**395, 650; **9:**151, 202, 348, 350, 359–60; OF THE **4:**740; **5:**419, 730; **6:**681, 1343; **7:**760–61; **9:**283; OPEN **1:**178, 361, 402, 489; **2:**184, 190; **3:**189, 403, 752, 1049, 1064; **5:**246, 775, 860; **6:**265, 364, 369–70, 378, 433, 451, 482; **7:**89, 91, 548, 750, 826; **8:**136; **9:**238, 352, 354, 360, 477, 480, 484, 486, 489, 533, 560, 569, 572, 657; **10:**170, 338, 424, 541; **12:**9, 337, 552, 569

EYEWITNESS, EYEWITNESSES
2:752–53; **3:**22, 43; **4:**22, 288; **6:**195, 296, 842, 872; **7:**306; **8:**89, 106, 491; **9:**7, 30–31, 40–41, 225, 227, 486, 488, 490, 500, 522, 693, 833–34, 858, 863; **10:**13, 15, 43, 63, 65, 81, 105, 192, 214, 243, 376; **12:**253, 342–43

EZEKIEL, BOOK OF
1:8–9, 11, 65, 76, 96, 229–30, 239, 278, 282–83, 290, 733–34, 838, 881, 993, 1010, 1028, 1034, 1104, 1138; **2:**38, 230, 355, 427, 504, 1002; **3:**70, 362, 462, 514, 587, 656, 679, 735, 1069; **4:**256, 314, 329, 346, 404, 591, 898, 975; **5:**46, 381, 401, 419, 455, 544, 555, 557, 631, 634, 647, 663, 800, 818, 836; **6:**2, 5, 7, 8, 12–13, 15, 18–19, 21–22, 66, 82, 101, 103, 149, 183, 186, 222, 257, 310, 320, 331, 449, 464, 467, 490, 492, 568, 576, 579, 581, 608, 629, 638, 702, 794, 812, 940, 942–43, 945, 1020; **7:**5, 111, 138, 150, 162, 177, 179, 189, 192, 268, 302, 312, 323, 339, 348, 375, 382, 386, 428, 430–31, 435, 440, 472, 489, 544, 548, 693, 756, 775, 779–80, 804, 807, 817, 820, 822, 822–23, 831, 833, 837, 846; **8:**28, 41, 360, 601; **9:**93; **10:**145, 447–49, 451, 831; **11:**261; **12:**505, 512, 515, 520–21, 561, 566, 591–92, 595–96, 598–99, 603, 615, 619, 638–39, 681, 685–86, 711, 722–23, 726–27

EZRA, BOOK OF
1:11, 292; **3:**1077; **4:**77, 163; **5:**270, 607, 632–34, 759, 855; **6:**400, 527, 551; **7:**3, 52–53, 126, 178, 723, 738–39, 763, 788, 866; **12:**519

EZRA AND NEHEMIAH, BOOKS OF
1:8, 43, 65, 250, 252, 268–69, 303, 314, 996; **2:**543, 760, 894, 902, 923, 942; **3:**299–300, 305, 328, 461, 511, 518, 554, 615, 657, 987, 1016, 1069; **4:**119, 199, 1195; **5:**37, 44, 273, 862; **6:**315, 318, 399, 444, 474, 546, 946; **7:**21, 27–30, 32, 43–44, 52, 121, 138, 175, 488, 847, 864, 866; **8:**28, 36, 41

F

FABLE, FABLES
2:815–18; **3:**241, 587, 1108, 1163; **5:**8; **6:**1103, 1243–47, 1251–52, 1268–70, 1272, 1274; **7:**466, 468; **9:**476

FACE
OF GOD/THE LORD/YAHWEH **1:**564, 566–70, 573, 942, 1179; **2:**91, 277; **3:**500, 617, 1015, 1064, 1066; **4:**350, 357, 439, 458–59, 601, 624, 627, 678, 698, 720, 722, 727, 740–42, 764, 774, 785–86, 801, 852–53, 857–58, 872, 903, 927, 940, 952–53, 999, 1035, 1061, 1088, 1099, 1104, 1251; **5:**237, 395, 506; **6:**477, 733, 917, 1207, 1217, 1530–31, 1555; **7:**249, 557; **8:**31, 375; **11:**64, 69; **12:**571, 594, 625, 724; MY **1:**633, 841, 939, 940; **3:**1088, 1124, 1165, 1167; **4:**310, 510, 853; **6:**711, 1167, 1203, 1207, 1237, 1484, 1529; **7:**263; **11:**64, 237, 438; **12:**597, 681

FAITH
OF ABRAM/ABRAHAM **1:**431, 445, 447–49, 460, 468, 486, 495, 497, 591; **4:**50; **10:**414, 465, 487–88, 491–92, 497–502, 506, 690; **11:**256, 275, 528; **12:**79–80, 135, 138, 141, 184; ACT(S) OF **1:**495, 679, 875; **2:**19; **4:**366, 436, 695, 1001, 1028, 1030, 1044; **6:**345; **8:**250; **9:**500, 708; **10:**22; **12:**133, 138, 140, 197–98, 436, 462; AFFIRMATION OF **2:**904; **3:**631; **4:**690, 727, 766, 770, 809, 824, 864, 899, 916, 930, 968, 1021, 1048; **6:**49, 85, 222; **7:**442; **11:**378; **12:**406; ARTICLES OF **1:**16; **2:**350, 514; **3:**1168; **5:**330; BIBLICAL **1:**57, 183, 196, 721, 730, 747, 760, 765, 790, 803, 808, 821, 823, 830, 837, 839, 843, 848, 852, 877,

FAITH *(continued)* 941–42, 947, 952; **2:**1123; **3:**137, 980; **4:**938, 983, 996, 1269; **5:**45, 135, 176, 188, 267, 330, 456, 547; **6:**73, 177, 228, 1043; **7:**34, 319, 639, 655; **10:**247, 342, 387; **12:**287; IN CHRIST **1:**61; **4:**243; **7:**328, 643; **8:**352, 455, 591; **10:**204, 213, 231, 250, 321–23, 382, 502; **11:**273, 318, 357, 375, 527–28, 554, 617, 619, 792, 794, 807, 851; **12:**32, 71, 78, 523; CHRISTIAN **1:**7–8, 14, 16–17, 34, 48, 63, 104, 110, 155, 183, 192, 195–96, 681, 773, 804, 883, 951, 954–55; **2:**152, 652, 1209, 1231, 1368; **3:**347, 380, 480, 659, 997, 1071; **4:**1230; **5:**398; **6:**176, 245, 608, 759, 875; **7:**34, 44, 67, 128, 644; **8:**26, 86, 92, 137, 181, 186, 196, 222, 245, 249–50, 261, 263–64, 282, 319, 325, 334, 337, 345, 356, 366, 368, 418, 448, 472–73, 505, 528, 628, 632, 679; **9:**293, 305, 472, 495, 545, 559, 649, 679, 743, 757, 766, 784; **10:**27, 121, 171, 182, 214, 226, 255, 260, 262, 375, 385, 387, 391, 410, 424, 451, 453, 465, 467–68, 470, 473, 480, 495, 501–2, 507, 548, 603, 660–61, 664, 672–73, 688–89, 692, 711, 735, 742, 745, 765, 786, 813; **11:**161, 184, 205, 207, 218, 291, 307, 312, 319, 352, 369, 379, 381, 450, 492, 590, 628, 795, 820, 831, 833, 844, 861; **12:**4, 7, 11, 24, 31, 64, 72, 95, 127, 252, 254–55, 262, 269, 287, 291, 338, 394, 395–96, 427, 456, 716; CHURCH'S **1:**19, 48, 58, 59, 61, 132; **6:**143; **8:**149, 238, 342, 358, 500; **9:**339; **10:**11, 27; **11:**307, 319, 695, 714, 745–46; COMMUNITY OF (*see under* COMMUNITY); CONFESSION/CONFESSING **1:**16, 337; **2:**15, 480, 484, 837; **3:**198; **4:**722, 736; **6:**163, 606, 859–60; **7:**72, 93, 382, 527; **8:**68, 174, 225, 261, 344, 354, 410, 455, 459, 619; **9:**100, 254, 609, 611, 660, 689, 691, 782, 840, 850, 852; **10:**18, 106, 144, 150, 246, 318, 320–22, 482; **11:**538, 829; **12:**12, 23, 25, 28, 165, 405; COVENANT(AL/ED) **1:**843, 951; **2:**1021–23, 1031, 1280, 1327; **5:**50; **6:**621; **7:**289, 502; DEEDS/WORKS OF **12:**184, 187, 191, 196–98; FOREBEAR(S) IN (THE) **1:**594; **2:**651; **9:**566; **12:**19, 129, 163, 286, 390; GENUINE/TRUE **2:**346; **3:**532, 577; **4:**1149; **5:**50; **7:**644; **9:**153, 322; **10:**506; **12:**200, 251, 713; IN GOD **1:**63, 161, 163, 431, 447, 476, 496–97, 500, 528, 696; **2:**18, 20, 39, 99, 300, 320, 440, 511, 528, 530, 753–54, 759, 762, 837, 960; **3:**650, 758, 1109, 1120; **4:**50, 514, 579, 648, 651, 694, 722, 747, 749, 755, 785, 800, 809, 876, 886, 920, 929–30, 974, 1083, 1110, 1146, 1149, 1171, 1178, 1180; **5:**337, 532; **6:**257, 262, 550, 868, 1044, 1058, 1099, 1400, 1480; **7:**156, 163, 624, 635, 662, 675, 697, 788; **8:**32, 149, 275, 443, 608, 616, 635; **9:**78, 153, 257, 260, 322, 381, 717; **10:**70, 187, 349–50, 384, 463, 488, 501, 507, 602, 611, 650, 663, 665, 747, 935; **11:**23, 404, 695, 813, 829, 862; **12:**24, 70–71, 127, 138–41, 195, 254, 273; AND HOPE **1:**426; **2:**480, 514; **3:**386, 403, 873; **4:**690, 777, 779, 787, 828, 958, 993, 1001, 1028, 1030, 1206–7; **6:**164, 1051; **7:**442; **9:**417; **10:**615, 745, 757, 953–54, 956–57; **12:**135, 259; OF ISRAEL **1:**78, 132, 191, 678, 690, 713–14, 723, 768, 793, 795, 796, 799, 803, 820, 825–26, 830, 834–35, 848, 877–78, 923–94, 927, 933, 937, 978, 980, 1135; **2:**275, 293, 327–29, 352–53, 366, 388, 394, 480, 519, 529, 757, 1018, 1022, 1236, 1258; **3:**467, 629, 1168; **4:**513, 671, 747, 819, 1008, 1021, 1097, 1232; **5:**490, 506, 548; **6:**670, 751–52; **9:**823; **10:**124, 305, 897; **11:**214, 267; **12:**13, 96, 142; IN/OF JESUS **1:**48; **7:**328; **8:**70, 76, 102, 118, 137, 286, 288, 337, 344, 352, 354, 384, 427, 618, 632, 634, 651; **9:**154, 156, 191, 261, 507, 532, 552, 559, 570, 576, 587, 589, 601–3, 621, 637, 647–48, 663–65, 678, 688–89, 694, 713, 716–17, 746, 748, 765–66, 835, 853; **10:**150, 334, 339, 371, 386–87, 470, 473, 644, 646, 653, 662, 673, 680, 686, 695, 698, 749; **11:**237–39, 269–70, 318, 385, 404, 792; **12:**177, 180–81, 192–94, 200–201, 224, 424, 431, 435, 437, 440, 451, 653, 667, 715; JEWISH **1:**199, 270, 290, 822, 1164; **2:**283; **4:**247; **7:**53, 94, 118; **8:**132, 202, 264, 291, 624; **9:**541; **10:**125, 133, 258, 268, 314, 321, 333, 336, 374, 688; JUSTIFICATION/JUSTIFIED BY **3:**486, 540; **4:**674; **6:**272, 641; **8:**42; **9:**772; **10:**403, 420, 426, 428, 439, 465, 468, 470, 481, 486–89, 497, 499, 503, 505, 509, 514, 549, 580, 590, 603–4, 615, 658, 686, 725, 733, 736, 744, 747, 749–50, 767; **11:**27, 183, 275, 393; LACK OF **1:**794, 818; **2:**21, 99, 160, 169–70, 249, 255–56, 300, 513, 1082, 1114; **3:**205, 208, 426, 522, 543, 628; **6:**118; **8:**226, 251, 324, 329, 341, 369, 510, 549, 579–80, 592, 603, 635, 696, 699, 730; **9:**260, 279, 616, 690, 716, 764; **10:**343; LIFE/ LIVES OF **1:**7–8, 14, 16, 34, 147, 152, 201, 325, 327, 701, 719, 882, 934, 1132, 1190; **2:**16, 39, 66, 90, 97, 141, 169, 236, 255–56, 601, 732, 790, 798, 820, 826, 911, 1014; **3:**540; **4:**646, 727, 802, 821, 975, 1156, 1233; **5:**50; **6:**198, 227–28, 575, 585, 661, 1291; **8:**451; **9:**495, 535, 553, 561, 569, 572, 581, 589, 597, 626, 665, 695, 754, 757, 797, 853, 865; **10:**27, 122, 125, 380, 384–85, 388, 548, 785–86, 794, 798, 821, 825, 827, 829–30, 833, 837, 842, 848, 850, 852, 856, 862, 865, 869–70, 877–78, 887, 898, 907, 910, 912–13, 918, 922, 927, 934, 938, 950, 955–56, 959, 963, 968, 973, 975, 980, 990–92, 1003; **11:**18, 23, 27, 38–39, 61, 69–70, 78, 83–84, 88, 93, 105, 110, 116, 122, 137–38, 145, 148, 152, 160, 167, 171, 173, 176, 178–79, 417,

594, 867; **12:**13, 55, 64, 131, 135, 140, 146, 154–55, 238, 258, 340, 440, 596; LIVING **1:**86; **2:**55, 821; **3:**533, 547, 594, 650, 998; **4:**787, 828, 1221, 1248; **5:**75, 717; **7:**623, 640–44, 655; **8:**458; **9:**84, 291; **10:**425, 693, 935; **11:**43, 244, 259, 641, 816, 829; **12:**126, 133, 241, 259, 458; IN/OF THE LORD **2:**327, 353, 393, 395, 440, 1195; **3:**5, 104, 198, 205, 346, 542, 560, 649; **4:**1220; **6:**163, 255, 814; **7:**328, 527; **10:**282, 386–87; **11:**384, 386, 894; NEW **1:**46, 825; **3:**310, 583, 1168; **8:**136, 261; **10:**138, 407; **11:**791–92; PEOPLE OF (THE) **2:**827, 1031, 1154, 1180, 1185–86, 1231, 1277; **4:**557, 727, 1181; **6:**109, 164, 261, 1209, 1219; **7:**34, 612, 732; **9:**139, 804, 863; **10:**222; **12:**712; PROFESSING/PROFESSION OF **4:**648, 651, 671, 693–94, 696, 722, 737–38, 749, 772, 785, 789, 806, 822, 824, 840, 857, 876, 890, 922–23, 968, 976, 1004, 1013, 1044, 1046, 1057, 1083, 1110, 1146, 1171, 1176, 1178, 1180, 1204, 1206, 1220, 1225, 1241, 1277; **6:**550; **9:**253, 637, 648; **12:**240; RELIGIOUS **2:**286, 321, 366, 827, 1231, 1269; **3:**506, 522, 978, 1120; **5:**652; **6:**120, 161, 278; **7:**192, 633; **9:**305; **10:**69; **11:**829; RULE OF **1:**8, 42, 47–48, 50, 90; **2:**275; **10:**29, 51, 111, 284, 384–85; **11:**867; SHARED **2:**366; **10:**114, 769; **11:**862, 895; **12:**250; STATEMENT(S) OF **1:**496, 636; **6:**1051; **7:**64–65, 697; **8:**238; **9:**691, 694; **10:**263; **11:**417, 792, 813, 816, 829; **12:**18, 21, 23–24, 46, 189; AND/OR/WITH WORKS **1:**19; **2:**596; **5:**186, 232; **6:**272; **8:**42; **10:**222, 413; **11:**238, 258, 314, 362, 389; IN YAHWEH **1:**511, 824, 949; **6:**93, 95, 163, 181, 253, 1082, 1156, 1412; YAHWISTIC **1:**513, 624; **2:**182, 282; **6:**38, 181, 1082, 1169, 1437

FAITHFULNESS

OF CHRIST **10:**378, 387; **11:**240, 244, 263, 323, 528; TO THE COVENANT **1:**39, 459, 460; **2:**726, 757; **4:**51, 71, 299; **6:**1489; **7:**580; **8:**459; **10:**400, 402–4, 407, 410–11, 413–14, 426–27, 452, 464–66, 469–74, 477–78, 481–82, 484, 488, 495, 497, 500, 502–5, 513–14, 523, 525, 530, 535, 546–47, 584, 590, 594, 596, 601, 611, 617, 621–22, 644–45, 654–55, 678, 769; **11:**76, 246; **12:**616; DIVINE/GOD'S/THE LORD'S/YAHWEH'S **1:**327, 426, 447, 449, 501, 557, 666; **2:**215, 306, 716, 740, 752, 768, 795–96, 820, 893, 912, 945–46, 1060, 1062, 1064, 1091–92, 1212, 1324, 1352; **3:**5, 96–97, 497, 500; **4:**747, 778, 797, 803, 806, 854, 858, 861, 863, 894, 927, 960, 961, 991, 995, 998, 1022, 1034–36, 1038, 1043, 1047, 1054, 1073, 1082, 1173–74; **5:**134, 441, 446, 451, 469–70, 481, 534, 596, 656; **6:**53, 120, 358, 432, 463, 472, 599, 697, 809, 811, 1239; **7:**560, 693, 800; **8:**423, 674; **9:**260, 389, 403, 453, 487, 612; **10:**11, 15, 25, 28, 45, 49, 56–57, 59–60, 68, 73, 80–82, 135, 146, 165, 182, 194, 210, 247, 311, 327, 410–11, 413, 420, 425–26, 452–53, 455, 464, 466, 470, 474, 478, 482, 488, 504, 513, 525, 560, 584, 591, 594, 620–23, 626, 640, 644, 647, 655, 699, 747, 759, 800, 916, 981; **11:**3, 40, 42–43, 48–49, 51–52, 76, 94, 160, 240, 270, 291, 346, 765, 847; **12:**40, 77–78, 82–83, 266, 524; TO GOD/THE LORD/YAHWEH **1:**499; **2:**256, 716, 738, 872, 932; **3:**5, 96, 169, 473, 603, 813, 1017; **4:**258, 662, 814, 821, 861, 1048, 1137, 1174–75, 1201, 1227, 1229; **5:**477, 509; **6:**213, 261, 772, 811, 876; **7:**580, 582, 717; **8:**674; **9:**213, 281, 339, 349, 766; **10:**20, 32, 40, 44, 235, 298, 386–87, 655; **11:**708, 829; **12:**13, 58; TO THE GOSPEL **8:**651; **10:**601; **11:**555, 558, 560, 585, 619; OF JESUS **10:**222, 387, 405, 410, 413, 467, 468–70, 474, 476, 502, 525, 531; **11:**187, 195, 240, 246, 269, 278, 313; TO JESUS **9:**129, 211, 424, 426, 670, 747; **10:**45, 222; UNFAITHFULNESS **1:**459; **2:**62, 217, 355, 526, 726, 731, 738, 742, 745, 749–50, 755, 760–62, 832, 864, 958; **3:**8, 81, 89–90, 95–96, 119, 137, 170, 226, 253, 278, 302–3, 307, 329, 338, 358, 370, 377, 524, 544, 591, 598, 607, 617, 654, 656, 657, 741, 746; **4:**991, 996, 1035, 1043; **5:**67, 69, 79, 442, 512, 560, 567; **6:**82, 204, 211, 477, 658, 698, 1143, 1241–42; **7:**216, 224, 231, 798, 848, 851, 863–65; **8:**134, 295, 429; **10:**453, 685, 747; **11:**76, 240, 261, 308, 844; **12:**154

FAITHLESSNESS

2:256, 298, 319, 513, 520, 732, 767, 969, 1060; **3:**277, 598–99, 733, 742, 850; **4:**494, 882, 899, 991–92, 1003, 1104, 1106, 1110, 1112, 1203; **5:**474, 476, 532, 560; **6:**577, 585, 596, 598, 605–8, 620, 694, 750, 772, 1140, 1223, 1241; **7:**142, 206, 244, 507, 575, 589; **9:**209; **10:**68, 378, 410, 413, 428, 452–53, 462, 635; **11:**703, 844; **12:**45, 49, 78, 211

FALCON

4:611

FALL (*OR* FALLEN, *ETC.*)

OF ADAM **8:**535; **10:**470, 512, 624; **11:**503–4; OF ANGEL(S) **5:**621; **7:**150; **8:**163, 291; **12:**488, 645; ASLEEP **2:**858, 1157; **7:**527; **8:**450–51, 707–8, 722; **9:**6, 263, 432; **11:**727; **12:**355; OF ASSYRIA/NINEVEH **1:**95, 266; **3:**1069–70; **6:**1427; **7:**593, 596–97, 599, 603, 605, 610, 616, 661; AWAY **1:**1094; **2:**350, 488; **3:**417, 500, 636, 658, 1144; **6:**77, 540, 574; **7:**242; **8:**267, 270, 288, 442, 515; **9:**29, 179, 428, 765; **10:**676, 984; **11:**177, 204, 240, 274, 319, 347, 689, 812, 815; **12:**5, 9, 73, 74–76, 78, 137, 266, 277, 575; OF BABYLON **3:**690; **6:**185–86, 406–7, 520, 911; **7:**81; **9:**404; **12:**522, 558, 630, 666, 677, 689, 692, 695, 697; CREATION AND **1:**367; **5:**441;

FALL *(continued)*
10:407; THE FALL **1:**367–68, 381, 401; **5:**558, 725, 764; **8:**356; **10:**511–12, 563, 596; **11:**384, 504, 508, 510; **12:**43, 521, 532, 575, 645; FESTIVAL OF HARVEST (*see under* FEASTS/FESTIVALS); OF ISRAEL **3:**255, 1119; **7:**200, 205, 219; **10:**406; **12:**55; OF JERUSALEM **1:**230, 260, 264, 282–83, 306, 314, 399, 467, 477–78, 1181; **2:**612; **3:**3, 293, 768; **4:**95, 205, 972; **6:**197, 277, 519, 574–75, 576, 769, 866, 1015, 1075, 1081–82, 1088, 1149, 1254, 1339, 1350, 1354, 1358–59, 1370, 1373, 1401, 1447, 1453, 1456, 1466, 1474; **7:**141, 330, 362, 441, 550, 582, 626, 671; **8:**77, 343; **9:**405; **10:**9, 402, 461; **12:**544, 596; OF JUDAH **2:**546; **3:**286, 656, 1119; **6:**842; **7:**336, 438; FROM PARADISE **6:**1394–95; RISE AND **1:**194, 220, 256; **2:**413, 415, 818; **4:**178; **6:**36, 787, 1273; **7:**367, 635–36; **8:**29; **11:**385; **12:**526; OF SAMARIA/NORTHERN KINGDOM **1:**263–64, 282, 467; **2:**319, 556, 560, 568, 573, 586, 635–36, 660; **3:**3, 11, 101, 251–52, 255, 261, 274, 602; **6:**127–28, 231, 235–36, 599, 1322; **7:**342, 363, 372, 534, 542, 582, 660, 664; OF SATAN **2:**790; **9:**98–99, 225; **11:**806; **12:**529; SHORT **1:**28, 95; **2:**298, 300, 437, 748, 811, 819, 887, 1372; **3:**1082; **4:**389; **5:**97–98, 140, 153, 303, 331; **6:**21, 366, 597, 1139; **7:**768; **8:**189; **10:**552, 696; **11:**69, 71, 155, 257; **12:**52, 69, 154, 161, 589, 659, 660; BY THE SWORD **4:**43; **6:**156, 261, 294, 1186, 1339, 1343, 1354, 1418, 1458; **7:**258; **9:**405; **12:**527

FALLOW
1:871, 1170–72; **2:**404, 407, 659, 668; **3:**657, 819; **4:**555; **8:**577; **11:**145; DEER **1:**1081; GROUND **7:**276

FALSE
ACCUSATION(S) **2:**436, 454; **4:**289, 468, 504, 645, 708, 740, 742, 930; **5:**56, 480, 597, 765; **6:**1309; **7:**179; **8:**685, 718; **9:**359; **10:**122; **11:**320, 825; **12:**283, 291, 301; APOSTLE(S) **10:**732; **11:**87, 133, 151; **12:**573, 722; CHRIST(S)/MESSIAH(S) **8:**246, 459, 526, 528, 687, 690–91, 693; **10:**417; **12:**403; GOD(S)/IDOL(S) **1:**896, 1010; **2:**255, 528, 602, 757; **3:**255, 1110, 1123; **4:**697, 736; **5:**557, 559, 562; **6:**180, 599, 661, 1006, 1008–10; **7:**67, 363, 575; **10:**463, 640, 898; **11:**214, 289, 428, 696; **12:**447, 652, 661; GOSPEL(S) **9:**203; **11:**186, 206–7, 229, 488, 492; PROPHECY/PROPHECIES **2:**381, 430; **3:**164; **6:**9, 48, 585, 694, 743, 752, 755, 773, 777, 782, 785, 792, 805, 1102, 1191, 1210, 1411; **7:**833–34; **8:**217, 690; **11:**812, 815; **12:**343, 427, 531, 588, 650, 658; PROPHET(S) (*see under* PROPHET); RELIGION **2:**528; **6:**176, 318, 407, 421, 542, 549; **7:**553; **10:**243; TEACHERS **8:**39, 157; **10:**284; **11:**353, 409, 423, 436, 782, 787, 789–90, 865–66; **12:**324–32, 334, 336–37, 339, 341–45, 347–60, 473–80, 482–98, 500, 522; TEACHING **8:**606; **9:**40; **10:**284; **11:**208, 315, 362, 399, 423, 557, 775, 777, 781–82, 791, 794, 812, 863, 865; **12:**457, 479; TESTIMONY **2:**380; **4:**820; **5:**77, 126, 179, 213, 339; **7:**774–76; **10:**124, 297; WITNESS(ES) **1:**852, 866, 870; **2:**334, 423, 436, 865; **4:**433–34, 477, 496, 702, 773, 882; **5:**76–77, 139, 143, 179, 182, 219, 558; **6:**742; **7:**93, 182; **8:**334, 480–81, 484, 501, 712, 723; **9:**373, 443, 544; **10:**120, 122–23, 725, 979; WORD(S) **1:**727–28, 1041; **5:**131; **6:**613, 620, 622, 752; WORSHIP **1:**844, 1118, 1139; **2:**198, 255; **3:**994; **5:**441, 445–46, 506, 529, 536, 543, 556, 569–71; **6:**211, 378, 389, 394, 478, 491, 527, 541–46, 548, 550, 635; **7:**62; **8:**333; **10:**125; **11:**292; **12:**585

FAMILY
CHOSEN **1:**419, 429, 435, 442, 454–55, 515, 580–81, 595, 655; COVENANT (*see under* COVENANT); DISCIPLINE (*see under* DISCIPLINE); EXTENDED **1:**216, 258, 326, 517; **2:**33, 330, 447, 459, 466, 467–69, 472, 476, 573, 592, 618, 629, 683, 918, 935, 1136; **3:**725, 1071, 1080, 1144; **4:**476, 1214; **5:**189, 230, 660, 860; **7:**696–97; **8:**593; **9:**318; **11:**331, 338, 414, 737; OF GOD **2:**1170; **3:**514, 520, 531; **4:**969, 1215–16; **5:**170, 199, 773, 801; **8:**262, 298, 315, 374, 378, 383, 392, 432, 611; **9:**832, 843; **10:**486, 496, 519, 742, 744, 797, 799, 807, 809, 827, 840, 850, 901, 916, 996; **11:**202, 208, 211, 251, 271, 276, 280, 284–85, 290–91, 337, 678, 680, 695, 808; **12:**270, 392, 398–99, 427, 490; HEAD OF THE **1:**578–79, 1124; **2:**446, 452, 473–74, 901; **3:**210, 725; **9:**420; **11:**455, 801; HOLY **8:**147; **9:**70, 72; **12:**474, 482; LIFE **1:**186, 201, 216, 329, 372, 405, 504, 635, 673, 998; **2:**234, 276, 324, 343, 447, 477, 502; **3:**731, 986, 989; **4:**174, 287; **6:**1045, 1240; **8:**387; **10:**241; **11:**663, 736; LINE/LINEAGE/TREE **1:**332, 378, 416, 476, 534; **2:**47, 128, 136, 213, 416, 819, 886, 892, 894, 897, 932, 941–44, 1099; **3:**318, 363, 451; **6:**140, 389; **8:**130, 319, 422; **9:**95, 567; NEW **1:**230, 426, 584; **2:**468; **4:**634–35; **8:**298, 324, 378, 567, 571, 592, 637, 651, 688, 700, 708; **9:**182, 832, 843; **10:**414, 483, 494, 807, 842; RELATION(S/SHIPS) **1:**405, 520, 523, 534, 591, 595, 1004, 1115, 1123, 1139; **2:**109, 975, 1208; **3:**522, 1037; **4:**191, 313, 347, 753; **5:**180; **6:**810–11; **7:**865, 876; **8:**322; **9:**293, 303–4, 536, 748; **10:**593; **11:**280, 455, 873; **12:**721

FAMINE, FAMINES
1:240, 329, 399, 427–30, 527, 530, 599, 621–23, 627, 633, 635, 644–45, 651, 653–55, 674, 695, 759, 1181; **2:**356–57, 374, 480, 503, 666, 899–901, 905, 935, 945, 1357–59, 1381; **3:**81,

132, 137, 190, 199, 204–5, 207, 208–10, 293, 423, 779, 941, 1179; **4:**50, 113, 328, 381, 391, 423, 445, 452, 524, 592; **5:**54, 120, 230, 620, 656, 692, 818, 851; **6:**168, 174, 412, 450, 620, 675, 690–91, 693, 704, 792, 831, 865, 867, 873, 925, 956, 1009, 1015, 1150–51, 1153, 1161, 1167, 1194, 1199, 1210, 1212, 1214–15, 1296, 1462, 1469, 1473, 1485–87, 1492–93, 1563; **7:**312, 345, 380–81, 383, 582, 690, 833–34; **8:**15, 441–42, 690; **9:**255, 301–2, 344, 372, 400, 402, 404, 407; **10:**175, 177–78, 181, 289, 756, 759; **11:**221, 617–18, 697; **12:**609, 612, 636, 693

FARE

PAID **1:**224; **6:**1149; **7:**495, 527

FARMER, FARMERS

1:217, 220, 226, 255, 311, 350, 372–73, 654, 785, 865–66; **2:**233, 411, 434, 659, 668, 810; **3:**779; **4:**202, 511, 934; **5:**107, 192, 239, 314, 334, 584, 625, 746, 768, 812–13; **6:**8, 205, 235, 237–38, 244, 266, 277, 690, 811, 915, 1592; **7:**250, 309, 333–34, 551, 708; **8:**279, 303, 311, 553, 570, 577, 592, 610–11; **9:**35, 86, 177, 254, 269, 298, 323, 357; **10:**716; **11:**696, 842, 846–47

FARTHING

5:732

FAST, FASTS

FROM FOOD **1:**1155, 1159; **3:**156, 355, 728, 803, 805, 866, 902, 905, 908, 911, 938, 940, 962, 1058, 1087, 1113, 1132, 1147; **6:**15, 498, 690, 839, 942, 1177; **7:**52, 122–26, 136, 308, 311–12, 318, 321, 513, 790, 792, 798; **8:**205–6, 555, 557; **9:**130, 318, 342; **10:**151–52, 163, 312, 346, 461

FASTING

1:314, 1074, 1110, 1113, 1159; **2:**233, 1185, 1202, 1297; **3:**560, 669, 728, 733, 805, 905, 946, 959, 1058, 1079, 1113–14, 1130, 1132–33, 1162; **4:**63, 270, 281; **5:**797; **6:**498–99, 503, 1150, 1343; **7:**42, 52, 93, 122–26, 136, 178, 194, 529, 744, 746, 786, 789–90, 792–93, 797–99; **8:**34, 39, 59, 79, 163, 196, 201, 205–6, 235–36, 548, 554–55, 557, 606; **9:**34, 127, 129–31, 133, 342, 421; **11:**157, 562–65, 567, 575, 594, 631–32, 634–35, 647; AND CONFESSION **2:**1018, 1021; **3:**805; AND PRAYER **1:**1110; **3:**871, 1056, 1058, 1075, 1130, 1133–34, 1139, 1151; **5:**323, 363; **6:**503, 943; **7:**92, 123, 125, 137; **8:**200; **9:**130, 336; **10:**189, 200–201; **11:**223; **12:**687

FAT

1:219, 620, 645, 1062; **2:**726, 771–73, 830, 841, 1207; **3:**782, 801, 811; **4:**224, 451; **5:**241, 355; **6:**174, 277, 379, 1461, 1463, 1467–68, 1473, 1528; **7:**192; **11:**88, 431; **12:**148; DIETARY REGULATIONS REGARDING **1:**1003, 1006, 1027, 1043, 1052–53, 1082; AS PART OF OFFERINGS (*see under* OFFERING)

FATE

IDEA OF *(esp. in Wisdom writings)* **3:**985; **4:**60, 363, 376, 400, 404, 440, 462, 483–84, 486, 493, 495, 503, 586; **5:**4, 9, 16, 45, 57, 98, 133, 193, 282–83, 285, 300–301, 310–11, 313, 319, 323, 339–40, 342–43, 460, 583, 692, 705, 720; **6:**407, 686, 717, 1219, 1264–65; **8:**17, 24–25, 273, 349, 625; **9:**77; **11:**58, 563; **12:**401, 733; OF THE RIGHTEOUS/OF THE WICKED **1:**236; **3:**551; **4:**340, 363–64, 377, 401, 422, 427, 446, 448, 452, 466–68, 470, 481–83, 489, 491–92, 497, 499–501, 503, 523–24; **5:**522; **6:**348, 491, 1135, 1263; **8:**314

FATHER, FATHERS

APOSTOLIC/CHURCH **1:**14, 75, 168, 290, 1001, 1112; **3:**868, 932; **6:**337; **8:**89, 100, 201, 211; **9:**5, 7, 504, 623, 679; **11:**476, 507; **12:**486; GOD AS OF OUR/THEIR/YOUR FATHER(S) **1:**528, 636, 652, 666, 671, 1173; **3:**338, 501, 522, 531, 533, 573, 581–82, 646, 1063; **5:**463; **6:**530; **8:**202, 290, 666; **9:**641; **11:**688, 736, 745 (*see also* GOD, NAMES FOR/TITLES OF *in PERSONS IN THE BIBLE*); HEAVENLY (*see* GOD, NAMES FOR/TITLES OF: FATHER IN HEAVEN *in PERSONS IN THE BIBLE*); AND MOTHER **1:**847, 1141, 1147–48; **2:**200, 332, 629, 913, 1145; **3:**180, 981, 1045; **4:**306, 416; **5:**207, 400; **6:**363, 1309, 1458; **7:**831; **8:**322, 333, 606, 645; **9:**71, 77, 167, 217, 347, 349; **10:**863; **11:**451; HOUSE **1:**216, 577, 605; **2:**33, 455, 592–93, 629, 804, 850, 876–77, 904, 907, 1110, 1148; **3:**328, 725, 752; **4:**1013; **5:**231, 364, 397, 428; **6:**1257; **9:**20, 27, 77, 91, 201, 281, 302, 318, 373–74, 543, 740–41; **10:**58; **12:**246; AND SON **1:**211, 404, 489, 499, 651, 653, 955, 1124, 1147; **2:**1080–81, 1133, 1207, 1254, 1257, 1313, 1315–16, 1333, 1342; **3:**345, 473, 1069; **5:**3, 15, 58, 180, 558, 610, 654, 659–60, 668; **6:**381, 551, 1083, 1579; **7:**206, 208, 859; **8:**161, 274–75, 417, 436, 504; **9:**158, 178, 224–26, 302–3, 305, 487, 496, 523–24, 531, 583–86, 588, 598, 678, 751, 757, 764, 788, 790, 795–96, 798; **10:**57, 416, 580, 615, 696; **11:**590; **12:**390, 407, 431, 435, 517, 535, 562, 664

FATHERHOOD

(esp. of God) **3:**1038; **5:**463; **7:**865; **8:**212; **9:**161, 238; **10:**497; **11:**290–91

FATHERLESS

6:1069; **12:**86, 94

FATHOM, FATHOMS

1:410; **3:**1137; **4:**332, 450; **6:**1451; **9:**327; **10:**352, 695, 821–22, 982; **11:**594, 685; **12:**525

FATLING, FATLINGS
2:1088, 1249; **6:**141, 1528
FATTED
1:1026; **2:**771; **3:**782; **5:**150; **9:**301, 303; **10:**698
FAUNA
1:316, 365; **5:**402, 405, 408; **6:**277, 1274, 1595; **7:**525
FAWN, FAWNS
1:666; **5:**69, 390, 402, 426; **6:**690; **7:**376. *See also* DEER
FEAR
AND DREAD **1:**398; **2:**339; **3:**1106; **4:**96, 608; **5:**670; **6:**389; **7:**588; **12:**634; GOD/YAHWEH **1:**498, 629, 795, 1174; **2:**14, 340, 345, 369, 594; **3:**945, 1017, 1179; **4:**534–35, 547, 764, 810, 938, 1017, 1092, 1133, 1135–37, 1181, 1201; **5:**33, 46, 50, 63, 282, 317, 359, 652, 705, 725; **6:**438, 957; **7:**272–73; **9:**252, 337, 339, 459; **10:**191, 194; **12:**140, 258, 275, 278, 498, 529, 631, 644, 666, 695; OF GOD/YAHWEH **1:**483, 494, 496, 795, 1133, 1135, 1172; **2:**10, 879, 1370–71; **3:**501, 562, 775, 780, 782–83, 982, 1179; **4:**376, 413, 449, 508, 814–15; **5:**33–34, 161, 260, 647–48, 650, 656, 668, 720; **6:**528, 957, 961, 1345, 1349, 1467; **7:**498, 500, 557; **8:**264; **9:**252, 337; **10:**101, 457–58, 685; **11:**442, 657; **12:**62, 284, 666; OF ISAAC **1:**557–58; **5:**239, 696; OF THE LORD **1:**361; **2:**876, 1259; **3:**556, 1017, 1065, 1068; **4:**529, 533–34, 679, 752, 812–15, 1133–34; **5:**10, 12, 19, 24, 29, 33, 35, 43, 45, 47–48, 52–53, 63, 91, 100, 103, 105, 112, 117, 132, 141, 143, 150–53, 158–59, 161, 163, 176, 181–82, 198, 207, 229, 263–64, 281, 320, 332, 608, 626–27, 638, 646, 648–51, 655, 663, 733, 737, 761, 823–25; **6:**118, 141, 248, 271, 294, 619, 774, 822; **7:**177; **9:**336, 337; **11:**90, 453, 654; THE LORD **2:**344, 369; **4:**681, 1133–35, 1145, 1201; **5:**33, 49, 139, 145, 163, 207, 616–17, 650, 654; **6:**447, 621, 1501; **9:**385; **11:**90, 657; **12:**275; AND TREMBLING **1:**494; **2:**995; **3:**681, 1170; **4:**296; **5:**676; **6:**1266, 1496; **7:**319; **8:**63, 588; **10:**817, 830; **11:**340, 511–12
FEASTS/FESTIVALS
1:68–69, 204, 209, 225, 275, 286, 344, 448, 553, 683, 726–27, 783–87, 871, 875, 898, 912, 931, 986, 1009, 1021, 1024–27, 1052, 1086, 1132, 1156, 1158–60; **2:**38, 69, 86–87, 89–91, 108, 148, 152, 189, 229–30, 233, 410–12, 414–15, 548, 569, 824, 850, 859, 876, 886, 893, 912, 1042, 1134–35, 1166, 1169, 1224, 1309; **3:**17–20, 68, 75, 77, 104, 106, 347, 499, 506, 538, 602, 616–17, 646–47, 649, 691–92, 801, 806, 844, 857, 859–61, 899, 905, 927, 929, 934–35, 937–40, 1001–2, 1005, 1039, 1050–51, 1069, 1167, 1176; **4:**3, 11, 23, 37, 39–41, 67, 93, 101, 184, 190, 191, 202, 228, 243, 297, 345, 357, 795, 868, 937, 944, 1003, 1005, 1061, 1070, 1111, 1156, 1269; **5:**63, 85, 89, 95, 102, 104, 153, 266, 274, 349, 363, 389, 425, 509, 525, 651, 720, 758, 784; **6:**93–94, 123, 270, 490, 635, 638, 702, 808, 810, 883, 939, 994, 1043, 1106, 1115, 1159, 1277, 1329, 1395, 1499, 1527–28, 1537–38, 1589; **7:**36, 40–41, 78, 80–81, 85, 180, 205, 256, 260, 264–67, 269–70, 273, 285–86, 365, 380, 400, 414, 418, 663, 674, 703, 707, 715, 724, 726, 839, 873; **8:**3, 33, 235, 407, 418, 436, 486, 615, 659–60, 663, 700; **9:**22, 127, 170, 255–56, 278, 285, 289, 291, 304, 316, 382, 415, 418, 448, 458, 476, 482, 513, 538, 543, 545, 616, 619, 622, 632, 648, 673, 675; **10:**220, 278, 461, 736, 776, 848–49; **11:**147, 185, 283, 288, 291, 343, 377, 631; **12:**24, 193, 287, 350, 359, 475, 482, 492, 511, 551, 576, 624, 699, 712, 726; AGAPE/LOVE **12:**492–93; ATONEMENT/YOM KIPPUR **1:**275, 890, 916, 986, 999, 1033, 1109, 1131; **3:**803; **4:**93, 116, 122; **5:**859; **7:**528; 833; **12:**94, 104 (*see also* ATONEMENT, DAY OF); OF BOOTHS/SUKKOT/TABERNACLES **1:**67, 275, 311, 403, 1065, 1113, 1156–57, 1159–61, 1171; **2:**230–31, 233, 412, 519, 1286; **3:**69, 75, 78, 104, 106, 305, 494, 499, 666, 668–69, 670, 684, 691, 796, 797, 801–5, 813, 839, 993, 1001, 1133; **4:**18, 64, 72, 122, 178, 182, 184, 190, 196, 199, 257, 868, 1003, 1014, 1061, 1155; **5:**266; **6:**549, 859, 939, 946; **7:**264–65, 267, 269–70, 273, 285, 663, 665, 673, 674, 703, 722, 839; **8:**33, 364, 630–31, 658; **9:**206, 542, 614, 616, 619, 622, 632, 634, 654, 674–75; **12:**621; CALENDAR **1:**871, 874, 950–51; **2:**289, 409, 411–14; **3:**104; OF DAPHNAE **4:**67, 228; OF DEDICATION/HANUKKAH **3:**840, 936, 1145, 1162; **4:**3, 23, 72, 122, 182, 184, 190, 795; **8:**33, 658, 663; **9:** 513, 542, 673–75, 675, 726; **11:**493; **12:**726; OF ENTHRONEMENT **4:**868, 944, 1053, 1061; OF FIRSTFRUITS/PENTECOST/WEEKS **1:**311, 1065, 1156–59, 1161; **2:**50, 230, 232, 236, 412, 893; **3:**305, 538, 937, 1001; **4:**64, 276; **10:**53, 305, 683 (*see also* PENTECOST); OF HARVEST (SPRING/AUTUMN) **1:**871, 1156; **2:**232, 233, 235–36; **3:**691, 713, 802; **4:**933, 939; **6:**1537; **7:**265, 273, 414; **9:**616; **10:**53; OF INGATHERING **1:**871, 1156, 1159, 1161; **2:**230, 233, 480; **7:**264, 674–75, 703; LOVE **5:**389; **6:**1329; **12:**350, 359, 475, 482, 492; MESSIANIC **2:**152; **8:**339; **12:**580; NEW YEAR'S **1:**311; **3:**860, 948; **4:**649, 868, 1053, 1064; **6:**946, 1570; **7:**76, 80, 202, 393, 683; OF PASSOVER/UNLEAVENED BREAD **1:**275, 773, 777, 781, 785–87, 871, 912, 949, 1050, 1156–59, 1161; **2:**50, 51, 87, 90, 127, 230, 232–33, 236, 411–12, 573,

590, 594, 605, 796; **3:**285, 305, 615–18, 646, 648, 713, 1001; **5:**591; **6:**1575, 1586; **7:**674; **8:**453, 468, 470, 472, 497, 659, 697, 702; **9:**414–15, 418, 420, 446, 493, 507, 542, 710, 721, 823; **10:**179, 276, 848, 849, 852 (*see also* PASSOVER AND FEAST OF UNLEAVENED BREAD); PURIM **3:**856–57, 859–60, 870, 872, 875, 896–97, 899, 928–29, 935–36, 938–40, 953, 967, 969–71; **4:**101, 514; **5:**363; OF ROSH HASHANAH/ TRUMPETS **1:**275, 1115, 1155–56, 1159; **3:**937; **4:**1003, 1004, 1279; **8:**205; WEDDING (*see* WEDDING: BANQUET/FEAST)

FEET

See FOOT

FELLOWSHIP

1:287, 1098; **2:**919; **3:**332, 364, 380, 487, 522, 554, 619; **4:**366, 368, 445, 461–62, 790; **5:**645; **6:**390, 451, 470, 526, 946–47; **7:**184, 325; **8:**275, 326, 347, 472, 551; **9:**298, 334, 472, 722; **10:**70–71, 73, 78, 98, 114, 236, 252, 422, 486, 700, 744, 749, 767, 776, 786–87, 794, 807, 844, 847–52, 874, 877, 918, 964, 967; **11:**24, 39, 53–54, 105, 114, 179, 196, 201, 226, 229, 235, 243, 295, 305, 313, 338, 399, 481, 497, 499, 517, 529, 544, 563, 690, 809, 860, 878, 892–93, 895; **12:**12, 66, 68, 76, 116, 168, 173, 195, 304, 310, 383–84, 386–87, 403, 466, 475; IN/WITH CHRIST/JESUS **6:**339; **7:**254; **9:**23, 128, 197, 288, 305, 421, 473, 613, 723, 728, 858; **10:**817, 923; **11:**497; **12:**389; CHRISTIAN **6:**586; **10:**28, 74, 182, 214, 220, 260, 262, 278, 375, 506, 733, 763; **11:**484, 489, 893; **12:**383, 454; IN/WITH GOD/THE LORD/YAHWEH **1:**169, 987, 997, 1007, 1024, 1039, 1052–53, 1066–67, 1085, 1100, 1159; **2:**78, 488; **3:**484, 514, 582, 586, 612, 619, 658; **6:**414, 516, 1597; **7:**309, 319, 768; **8:**504; **9:**53, 224, 228, 279, 349; **11:**529; **12:**369, 383, 389; MEAL **1:**1133; **8:**25, 472; **9:**127, 421, 481; **12:**492, 493; OFFERING(S) (*see under* OFFERING); TABLE **1:**890, 892; **2:**608, 609; **9:**25–27, 128, 278, 480; **10:**168, 278, 677; **11:**231, 232, 234, 235, 245

FENCE, FENCED

1:1184; **3:**135, 736; **4:**923; **5:**56, 121; **6:**996, 1201; **7:**618; **8:**413; **9:**380; **10:**480, 850–51; **11:**173, 399; **12:**586

FERRET

AS A VERB **4:**349; **5:**310; **6:**1276; **7:**679; **8:**100, 299

FERTILITY CULT, CULTS

2:755; **5:**101; **6:**57, 62–63, 601, 604, 1002; **7:**202, 241, 249, 258, 265

FESTAL

APPAREL, LETTER, ETC. **1:**7, 15, 777, 871, 908, 951; **2:**387; **3:**104, 993; **4:**649, 968, 1003, 1035, 1090, 1176, 1190; **5:**102, 340; **7:**273, 765, 804; **9:**707; **10:**917; **11:**438, 883; **12:**158, 624, 650

FESTIVAL

See FEASTS/FESTIVALS

FETTER, FETTERS

3:655; **4:**586; **5:**610, 688–89; **6:**1161, 1194; **7:**30, 125, 169, 258, 616; **11:**424

FEVER, FEVERS

1:1180; **4:**177, 331; **5:**382; **7:**262; **8:**228, 546; **9:**111, 200; **10:**305, 356; **12:**636

FIELD, FIELDS

1:118, 215–18, 223, 225–26, 329, 350, 359, 363–66, 425, 504, 517, 536, 758, 866–67, 869, 871, 1100, 1118–19, 1120, 1133, 1134, 1136, 1158–59, 1172, 1180, 1188–90; **2:**151, 161, 164, 166, 181, 187–88, 367, 374, 403, 453, 467, 471, 540, 541, 547, 614, 651, 668, 817, 846, 853, 897, 901, 910, 913–17, 922–23, 930, 933–36, 945, 995, 1012, 1048, 1051, 1053, 1055, 1126, 1134–35, 1167, 1206, 1216, 1283, 1286, 1315, 1332; **3:**144, 590, 779–80, 802, 820–21, 842, 1102, 1132–33, 1154; **4:**46, 381, 510–11, 532, 545, 608, 624, 626, 1066; **5:**93, 134, 139, 232–33, 261, 282, 305, 314, 318, 351, 383, 386, 389–90, 420, 427, 687–88, 765; **6:**8, 9, 54, 93, 169, 238, 247, 249, 266, 295, 332, 338, 343, 387, 465, 579, 615, 646, 647, 679, 797, 809, 816, 819–21, 822, 834, 850, 851, 853, 896, 914, 950, 986, 1072, 1148, 1190, 1201, 1220, 1226, 1246, 1252–53, 1294, 1319, 1351, 1425, 1429, 1432, 1435, 1473, 1499, 1523, 1524, 1526, 1582, 1590; **7:**41, 244, 286, 308, 314, 330, 386, 390, 448, 548, 560, 618; **8:**15, 229, 278, 303, 311–13, 315, 446, 484, 539, 577, 579, 658; **9:**21, 66, 133, 255, 259, 275, 301, 303, 323, 330, 332, 349, 367, 374, 404, 451, 569; **10:**49, 97, 423, 579, 614, 716, 827, 828, 841, 947; **11:**143, 329; **12:**219; OF BLOOD **8:**484; GOD'S **1:**963; **10:**806, 827; LILIES OF THE **3:**88; **5:**327, 547; MISSION **1:**155; **10:**217, 224–25, 276, 283, 288, 333, 759; **11:**417

FIG, FIGS

1:218; **2:**356; **3:**271; **5:**393; **6:**236, 301, 571, 756–58, 793; **7:**411, 414; **9:**85, 151, 357, 367; TREE(S) **3:**82, 637, 658; **4:**159, 166; **6:**293, 807; **7:**226, 244, 273, 308, 431, 550, 618, 767; **8:**123, 163, 400, 401, 407–8, 445, 523, 660–61, 663, 665, 672, 693; **9:**239, 270–72, 373, 408, 532, 704–5; **12:**205, 614, 727

FIGURED SPEECH

10:784, 803, 861; **11:**13, 29

FIGUREHEAD

1:274; **2:**617, 1212; **3:**1097; **10:**357

FILIGREE
6:1392; **12:**723
FINE
CLOTH(ES/ING)/GARB/GARMENTS **2:**789, 1140; **6:**203, 1380; **9:**163, 393, 454; FLOUR (*see under* FLOUR); GOLD **6:**965, 1061; **11:**277; LINEN **5:**461; **6:**1378; **9:**316, 337, 465; **12:**694–95; PAID AS A PENALTY **1:**864–65, 1033; **3:**654; **5:**160; SILENCE **3:**142–44, 146
FINERY
1:896; **2:**1103; **6:**1438; **8:**267
FINGER OF GOD
See under GOD, NAMES FOR/TITLES OF *in PERSONS IN THE BIBLE*
FIR TREE
6:1373, 1425–26
FIRE
ALTAR/OFFERING AND **1:**912–13, 1011–13, 1017, 1019–20, 1024, 1026, 1035, 1044, 1067, 1070, 1164; **2:**25, 49, 65, 126, 137, 140, 147, 151, 214, 229, 316, 791, 796–97, 842; **3:**135–36, 425, 498–99, 819; **4:**197–98, 281; **5:**469, 471, 843; **6:**103, 261, 1286, 1394; **9:**46; **12:**133, 630, 668; AND BRIMSTONE **1:**329, 475; **2:**877; **4:**470; **6:**723; CLOUD AND/PILLAR OF **1:**688, 788–89, 794, 979, 1066, 1179; **2:**126; **3:**811; **4:**197, 1105; **5:**446, 417, 517, 580, 585; **7:**758; **9:**632; **10:**513, 556, 581, 593; **12:**638; CONSUMING/DEVOURING **1:**800, 882; **2:**15, 88, 319; **3:**173; **4:**305, 624; **6:**63, 256, 271, 620, 1395; **7:**662; **9:**266; **11:**64; **12:**123, 156, 161; DESTRUCTION BY **1:**1019; **2:**99, 138–39; **5:**446, 524, 579; **6:**850, 894, 1182, 1384, 1394; **7:**381, 695; **12:**330, 356–57, 702; FROM GOD/THE LORD/YAHWEH **1:**1067; **2:**88, 100, 104, 319, 589, 842, 1367; **3:**425; **5:**430, 851; **6:**271, 627, 1038, 1315, 1576; **7:**355, 406, 699; FROM HEAVEN **1:**1044; **2:**603; **3:**137–38, 144, 169, 173, 179, 184, 587; **4:**197; **6:**1531; **7:**381; **12:**714; OF JUDGMENT **6:**1151; **7:**10; **9:**86, 266; **12:**357, 476, 479, 672, 694; LAKE OF **7:**10; **12:**612, 700, 702–3, 708, 714–15, 722; PASS THROUGH **1:**1138; **2:**247, 428; **6:**61, 381, 1283, 1286; PURIFYING/REFINER'S/REFINING **6:**60, 103, 629, 718; **7:**65, 116, 833, 873; **9:**86, 160, 266; **12:**694; AND SMOKE **1:**446; **2:**321, 1367; **4:**623; **6:**84, 543; **7:**328, 875; **12:**632; STRANGE **1:**1070; **2:**49; **3:**725; **5:**72, 843; TEST(ED/ING) BY/IN **5:**469, 534, 580; **8:**640; **10:**829; TONGUES OF **10:**54; **12:**522, 597; WALL OF **7:**758, 774–75
FIREBRANDS
7:375
FIREPAN, FIREPANS
1:1069; **9:**46
FIRMAMENT
1:279, 341, 344, 391, 394; **2:**194; **4:**752, 823, 1279; **6:**1116; **12:**591, 597–98, 635
FIRST
BORN **1:**291, 306, 375, 422, 494, 498–99, 524, 553, 555, 585, 604–6, 660, 665, 717–18, 720, 771–73, 779–80, 782, 785–87, 869, 949–50, 1011, 1158–59, 1187, 1189; **2:**26, 35, 37, 47–48, 50–52, 54, 79–81, 83, 86, 90, 140, 147–49, 211–12, 252, 263–64, 391, 406, 412, 446–48, 474, 476, 535, 588, 609, 619, 629, 683–84, 834–35, 904, 1305; **3:**17, 112, 120, 176, 184, 337, 345, 353, 451, 522, 820, 825, 994, 1063; **4:**64, 243, 313, 449–50, 469, 524, 877, 992, 1105; **5:**15–16, 49, 93–94, 446, 529, 590–92, 621, 668; **6:**62, 376, 400, 640, 809, 1283–84, 1398, 1442, 1530, 1579, 1586; **7:**392, 580, 691, 700, 828, 830; **8:**359; **9:**63, 66, 69, 834–35; **10:**416, 421, 591, 601, 637, 769, 980, 981; **11:**63, 323, 358, 373, 570, 572–73, 597, 599, 602–5, 607–9; **12:**29, 154, 158, 562, 586, 620; FRUIT(S) **1:**28, 311, 458, 785, 869, 871, 883, 950, 1017–20, 1022, 1065, 1086, 1131, 1156, 1158–61; **2:**50, 147, 149, 230, 232, 236, 378, 406, 428, 480–81; **3:**624, 666, 798, 820, 850, 993, 1001, 1154; **4:**64; **5:**49; **6:**598; **7:**15, 325, 643, 674; **8:**33; **9:**159, 197, 542; **10:**517, 585, 597, 682–84, 762, 980–82, 992; **11:**63, 599, 605, 725, 762; **12:**181, 187, 189, 204–5, 252, 310, 649, 664–65, 669, 703; RIPE **2:**121; **6:**236
FIRSTLING, FIRSTLINGS
1:373, 1019; **2:**148, 403; **9:**69
FISH, FISHING
1:233, 341, 345, 716, 742, 989, 1076, 1081; **2:**13, 107, 398; **3:**848, 975, 985, 988, 1025–27, 1029, 1031–33, 1048–50, 1056; **4:**622; **5:**38, 72, 193, 312, 502, 593, 725; **6:**214, 703, 1364, 1401, 1404–5, 1434, 1435, 1521, 1595–96, 1607; **7:**55, 463–64, 467, 469–71, 474, 478–83, 485, 487, 490–92, 502–7, 509, 511–12, 518–21, 526–28, 638, 674, 837; **8:**63, 165, 169–70, 213, 247, 296, 314, 324–26, 372, 539, 571, 601, 614; **9:**26, 110, 115–18, 139, 175–76, 190, 196, 221, 238, 439, 469, 481, 484, 486, 490, 503, 594, 597, 612, 614, 856–58, 859, 864–65; **10:**161, 987; **11:**332; **12:**351, 636
FISHERMAN, FISHERMEN
6:703, 1364; **8:**169–71, 539–40, 552, 580; **9:**34, 114–18, 128, 133, 136, 139, 370, 530, 808; **12:**230, 233, 323
FLAG, FLAGS
1:869; **2:**652, 849; **3:**546; **4:**973; **5:**229, 245; **6:**920, 1374; **9:**227, 387; **11:**118; **12:**297

FLAGON, FLAGONS
1:890; **9:**286
FLAGSTAFF
6:255
FLASK, FLASKS
6:721; **9:**169–70, 172
FLAX
1:759, 1044; **2:**593
FLEA, FLEAS
2:1006, 1158, 1175; **4:**439; **5:**26
FLEET
1:240; **2:**1154, 1217; OF SHIPS **1:**247; **3:**511; **4:**243, 260, 270; **6:**1360, 1367, 1371
FLEETING
1:980; **3:**529, 657, 1148; **4:**395, 440, 483–84, 492, 509, 838–39, 1044, 1087, 1199; **5:**341, 353–54, 433, 459, 597, 613; **6:**400; **7:**252–53, 263; **8:**694; **9:**482, 806; **10:**73; **11:**475; **12:**140, 145, 509
FLESH
BECOME/MADE **1:**63, 1184; **3:**502; **4:**643, 673, 787, 866, 1070; **5:**97; **6:**124; **9:**496, 516, 522, 524–25, 545, 576, 605, 610, 625, 659, 742–43, 746, 775, 790, 834; **12:**382, 400, 457, 515, 517, 587, 705; AND BLOOD **6:**1432, 1527; **9:**576, 608, 610, 614; **10:**560, 988, 993; **11:**63, 216, 460; **12:**10, 40, 63, 155, 571, 703, 728; AND BONE(S) **5:**144; **9:**485; COME IN THE **1:**85; **10:**631; **12:**373, 375–76, 403, 428, 435, 439, 452, 457; HEART AND/OF **3:**574; **6:**1188, 1487, 1492, 1495, 1574; ONE **1:**353–54, 361, 1125, 1128, 1147; **5:**121, 129, 140, 232, 765; **7:**865; **8:**386, 643; **10:**863, 865, 922; **11:**451–52; REALM OF THE **10:**553; **12:**300, 302–3; THORN IN THE **2:**798; **3:**527; **10:**939; **11:**27, 85, 294; WORD BECOME/MADE **1:**63; **3:**502; **4:**643, 866, 1070; **5:**97; **9:**496, 516, 522, 524, 525, 545, 576, 605, 610, 625, 775, 790, 834; **12:**515, 517, 587, 705
FLESHPOT, FLESHPOTS
1:434, 809, 812; **10:**546; **12:**725
FLIES/FLY
(insect) **1:**393, 688, 749–51, 1081; **2:**127; **3:**170, 1117; **4:**992, 1105; **5:**67, 72, 162, 346, 529, 540, 573; **6:**113, 883; **9:**241, 863; AS A VERB **1:**1081; **4:**380, 484; **5:**72, 75, 206–7, 254, 830; **6:**1244; **7:**239, 269, 447, 618, 653, 748, 760, 774; **9:**51; **10:**571; **11:**118; **12:**597–98, 636, 699
FLINT, FLINTY
2:608, 718; **5:**531; **6:**1126; **11:**237
FLOAT, FLOATS
1:424, 606, 661, 699, 1148; **3:**199; **5:**356; **6:**4, 1404; **9:**116; **12:**646
FLOCK, FLOCKS
1:206, 217–20, 275, 425, 433, 552, 556, 599, 605, 653, 703, 754, 767, 821, 1009, 1013–14, 1039, 1150–51, 1190; **2:**78, 148, 246, 249, 351, 367, 374, 399, 403, 406–7, 414, 668, 788, 923, 1029, 1110, 1166–67, 1233–34, 1292; **3:**336, 380, 424, 518, 608, 647, 745, 820, 1050; **4:**36, 224, 349, 381, 422, 510, 539, 544, 609–10, 626, 768, 790, 998–99; **5:**28, 30, 112, 233–34, 385–86, 403, 418; **6:**141–42, 144, 265, 337, 339, 356, 378, 527, 625, 664, 685, 744, 766, 896, 913, 915, 978, 1289, 1335, 1351, 1461–70, 1472–73, 1487, 1492, 1494, 1509, 1593; **7:**41, 242, 245–46, 263, 351, 376, 408, 411, 478, 483, 514, 554, 567, 571, 574, 619, 741, 811, 813–15, 818, 820–24, 833–34; **8:**252, 376, 378, 474, 512, 521, 532, 560; **9:**65–66, 260, 296, 310, 667–72, 698, 702–3, 793, 804, 861; **10:**263, 283–86, 290, 381, 624, 764; **12:**172, 315, 317
FLOG (*OR* FLOGS, *ETC.*)
1:84; **2:**471; **3:**710, 722; **4:**210, 254; **5:**160; **8:**258, 487–88, 491, 495; **9:**351–52, 401, 447–49, 469, 818–19; **10:**107–8, 122, 234, 308; **11:**22, 157, 161, 214, 294, 346; **12:**144, 151
FLOOD, FLOODS
1:230, 232, 316, 323, 329, 332, 336, 341, 346, 377, 379–81, 383–84, 389–96, 398–403, 405, 407, 410, 415, 417–18, 435, 750, 800, 901, 924, 941; **2:**20, 39, 123, 127, 182, 398, 549, 552, 600, 647, 872, 1088, 1243; **3:**317, 333, 388, 1009; **4:**202, 368, 382, 401, 450, 486, 501, 590, 592–93, 619, 793, 829, 951, 1054, 1058, 1072, 1272; **5:**38, 55, 94, 381, 430, 445, 523, 593, 605, 621, 674, 823; **6:**117, 180, 212, 236, 305, 335, 381, 477, 481, 548, 885, 1117, 1128, 1177, 1214, 1352, 1443, 1463, 1469, 1522; **7:**58, 128, 147, 310, 345, 389, 414, 417, 422, 505–6, 527, 602, 610, 813; **8:**29, 132, 218; **9:**91, 152, 330–32; **10:**521; **12:**134, 160, 241, 293–95, 298, 305, 330, 347–48, 350, 356, 358, 488, 533, 633, 651 (*see also* DELUGE); ACCOUNT/NARRATIVE/STORY **1:**316, 336–37, 335, 343, 356, 374–75, 381, 388, 394–95, 403, 411, 473, 477, 699; **2:**120, 123, 267, 1050, 1091; **4:**328, 730, 1279; **5:**4, 518; **6:**214, 548, 1168, 1314, 1394, 1471; **7:**382; POST-FLOOD **1:**379, 398–99, 403, 405, 417; **6:**1463; WATERS **1:**356, 398; **4:**525, 833, 951; **6:**117, 375, 477–78, 481; **7:**674
FLOOR, FLOORS
1:216–17; **2:**62, 78, 772, 1185; **3:**486; **4:**783; **5:**278; **6:**528, 584, 1551, 1554; **7:**189, 324; **9:**298, 479, 730; **10:**206, 549; **11:**230; **12:**597; THRESHING (*see under* THRESHING)
FLORA
5:405, 408; **6:**277, 1274, 1595; **7:**525

FLOUR
1:91, 219, 224, 913, 1017, 1036, 1045–46, 1098–99, 1158; **2:**77, 229, 233, 468, 1139; **3:**190, 424, 452; **6:**1228, 1338, 1558, 1589; **7:**261, 777, 779; **8:**24, 298, 309, 311; **9:**24, 276, 427; **12:**710; FINE **1:**91, 1017, 1036, 1045–46, 1098–99, 1158; **3:**452; **6:**1228, 1589; **9:**427

FLOWER, FLOWERS
3:680; **4:**304, 440, 443; **5:**364, 389, 393–95, 405, 427, 459, 461, 607, 784, 818; **6:**236, 332, 336, 338, 387, 499, 1166, 1554; **7:**769; **9:**259, 409, 458; **10:**592, 768; **12:**28, 273, 415, 552

FLUTE, FLUTES
4:331; **5:**348–49, 809, 859; **7:**63; **8:**238; **9:**166, 366, 542; **10:**959; **11:**709

FLUX, BLOODY
8:588

FODDER
3:132; **4:**510; **7:**411; **9:**302

FOLD
OF PEOPLE/SHEEP, ETC. **2:**738; **3:**320, 380, 781, 1168; **4:**381, 771; **6:**744, 915, 1144, 1269, 1351, 1466; **7:**554; **9:**148, 669; **10:**260; **12:**283

FOLLY
1:763–64; **2:**321, 327, 370, 455, 1029, 1078–79, 1168, 1304; **3:**426, 501, 515, 518–19, 530, 542, 551, 586–87, 649; **4:**286, 379, 496, 572, 593, 833; **5:**11, 25, 29, 31, 34, 35, 38, 44, 49, 54–55, 59, 63–71, 75, 78, 85–86, 89–90, 97, 101–3, 105, 107, 109, 112, 114, 133–35, 138–42, 150–51, 154, 161, 178, 188, 199, 206–7, 211, 225, 230–31, 243, 245, 281, 285, 293, 295–97, 300, 346, 348, 476, 506, 524, 543, 586, 605, 614, 627, 629, 658, 674, 692, 719, 720, 760, 850; **6:**128, 253–54, 265, 454, 493, 1274, 1349, 1361, 1383, 1406, 1420; **7:**403, 481; **9:**205, 255, 257, 292, 312; **10:**167, 426, 431, 433, 444, 665, 675, 809–11, 822, 841, 920, 974, 982–83; **11:**134, 158, 160, 442–43, 515, 850; **12:**198, 405, 568, 614, 635, 677; DAME/LADY/WOMAN **5:**4, 12, 31, 37, 40, 68, 100, 102–4, 153, 185; WISDOM AND **5:**24, 33, 35–36, 37, 40, 44–46, 53, 71, 78–79, 83–86, 89, 101, 103–5, 107–8, 127–28, 134, 160, 174, 186, 189, 212, 242, 287, 344–45; **10:**833; **11:**166, 441

FOOD, FOODS
CLEAN/UNCLEAN **1:**1074–75, 1083, 1127; **2:**13, 399, 842, 845; **3:**994; **4:**40; **7:**265, 267; **8:**156; **10:**163; **11:**232, 866; AND DRINK **1:**439, 614; **2:**149, 461, 878, 918, 1166–67; **3:**601; **4:**768–70; **5:**15, 64, 103–4, 298, 303, 319, 337, 364, 758, 779; **6:**1208; **7:**231, 233, 267, 312; **8:**63, 456, 472; **9:**220, 247, 601, 608; **10:**150, 312, 731, 741, 841, 913–16, 934; **11:**562, 631, 633–34; **12:**105, 166; LAW(S)/REGULATIONS **1:**1082, 1104, 1106; **2:**13; **3:**1147; **8:**196, 333–34; **9:**579; **10:**219–20, 461, 481, 580, 661; **11:**231–32, 251, 274, 323, 362, 364, 534; OFFERED/SACRIFICED TO IDOLS **1:**1121; **3:**994; **10:**778, 897, 915, 921, 972; **12:**545, 578–79, 581, 687, 722; OFFERING(S) (*see* OFFERING); PROVIDE(D/ING/R/S) **1:**362, 521, 654, 666, 814, 989, 1025; **2:**355, 406, 911; **3:**205, 458, 619, 624; **4:**608, 619, 768, 770, 1098; **6:**68, 203, 271; **7:**267; **8:**13, 63, 163–64, 324, 456, 601, 614, 660; **12:**125; RICH/SUMPTUOUS **1:**279, 666; **5:**614, 779; **6:**236; **8:**681; **9:**278; **12:**598; SOLID **6:**112; **10:**825, 856; **11:**69; **12:**68–69, 152, 264; AND WATER **2:**18, 21, 1193; **3:**132; **4:**311; **5:**573; **6:**76, 189, 191, 271, 293, 388, 1281, 1348, 1410, 1464; **8:**615; **9:**130. *See also by type of food*

FOOL, FOOLS
1:240, 763–64, 925; **2:**184, 673, 762, 773, 1142, 1164–69, 1171, 1175, 1225, 1304; **3:**88, 543, 912, 915, 1017, 1124; **4:**379, 398, 454, 545, 561, 605, 729, 877–78, 886; **5:**5, 11–12, 30, 64, 85, 91, 102, 104, 106, 111–12, 126, 135, 139–41, 148, 150, 162, 167, 170, 172–73, 178, 186, 194, 211, 215, 223–25, 230, 232, 243, 255, 301–3, 311–12, 314, 317, 322–23, 345–46, 349, 567, 614, 674, 709, 716, 721, 740, 862; **6:**265, 389, 708; **7:**181, 188–89, 213, 266–67; **8:**60, 190; **9:**25, 35, 144, 250, 254–60, 302, 306–7, 316, 319, 332, 337, 347, 357, 370, 381, 402, 459; **10:**507; **11:**15, 30, 154, 157, 163, 168; **12:**173; KING'S **6:**759, 769

FOOT, FEET
1:29, 90, 207, 391, 393, 473, 530, 622, 645, 665, 718, 802, 864, 1019, 1025, 1060, 1062, 1096, 1099, 1106, 1111, 1148, 1184; **2:**79, 167, 309, 355, 374, 475, 589, 673, 781, 788–89, 859, 916, 924, 926, 938, 1028, 1110, 1154, 1157, 1216–17, 1230, 1273–74, 1325; **3:**61, 67, 70, 137, 158, 348, 421, 484, 658, 911, 919, 923–24, 938, 956, 985, 1026, 1029, 1049; **4:**85, 240, 355, 376, 440, 538, 552–53, 712, 733, 741, 763, 781–82, 946, 1180–81; **5:**54, 61, 67, 70, 76–77, 80, 85, 178, 207, 219, 242, 254, 328, 370, 414, 425, 550, 553, 630, 764–65, 807, 853, 860; **6:**18, 102, 113, 236, 243, 336, 438, 457, 509, 810, 1109, 1115, 1121, 1136, 1161, 1175, 1228, 1299, 1343, 1346, 1351–52, 1434, 1436, 1457, 1461, 1497, 1500, 1503, 1540–41, 1548–49, 1551–53, 1555, 1557, 1560, 1576, 1595; **7:**53, 55, 102, 115, 125, 137, 366, 371, 501, 526, 606–7, 632, 676, 679, 774, 836; **8:**13, 213, 247, 309, 314, 332, 500, 588, 595, 640; **9:**24, 26, 60–61, 100, 116, 152, 169–70, 186–87, 190, 194, 220, 222, 229, 231–32, 287, 302–3, 316, 321–22,

326, 367, 371, 374, 377, 388, 458, 475, 478, 484–85, 490, 692, 701–3, 761, 842; **10:**45, 95–96, 98, 100–101, 131, 164, 196, 233, 289, 306, 352, 484, 541, 570, 605, 612, 614, 623, 667, 671, 710, 765, 884, 981–82; **11:**139, 205, 383, 459, 536–37, 820; **12:**9, 115, 153, 264, 468, 561, 565, 567, 581, 598–99, 617, 635, 638, 648, 656–57, 694, 696, 703, 732–33; AS A MEASUREMENT (*see under* WEIGHTS AND MEASUREMENTS); AS A PLACE (*e.g., foot of the mountain*) **1:**222, 834, 932; **2:**277, 362, 887; **3:**1124; **5:**859; **6:**528; **8:**634; **9:**834; **10:**482, 644; SET **1:**367, 538; **3:**332; WASHING **2:**1286; **5:**411; **6:**1265; **7:**526; **8:**136, 196; **9:**172, 425–26, 509, 514, 690, 701–3, 705, 711, 719–29, 731–33, 735, 741, 758–59, 763, 797, 803, 810; **11:**820

FOOTSTOOL, FOOTSTOOLS
1:1111; **2:**79, 96, 1001; **3:**70, 402, 460–61, 511, 1144; **4:**1075, 1130; **6:**1038, 1119, 1560; **7:**836; **10:**129; **12:**5, 37, 115, 728

FORBEAR (*OR* FOREBEARS, FOREBEARING, *ETC.*)
1:70, 161, 166, 459, 518, 593–94; **2:**294, 300, 310, 320, 339, 483, 560, 596, 651, 688; **3:**140, 680, 688, 737, 806; **5:**70; **6:**8, 381, 421, 968, 1254, 1265, 1291; **7:**273, 448, 456, 735–36; **8:**29; **9:**566, 603; **10:**30, 510, 586, 851, 914–15, 920; **11:**833, 834; **12:**19, 129, 137, 146–47, 149, 163, 286, 390, 552

FORDS
1:313; **2:**601, 772, 838, 1332

FOREHEAD, FOREHEADS
1:92, 907, 1147; **2:**1112; **3:**805; **4:**555; **5:**328, 693; **6:**1002, 1126, 1140, 1175, 1179, 1214–15, 1296; **8:**431; **12:**538, 585, 604, 618–19, 625, 631, 656, 658, 663–64, 681, 705, 707, 724

FOREIGN
ALLIANCE(S) **1:**40; **3:**95, 511; **4:**143; **5:**474; **6:**173, 175, 180, 182, 253–54, 257, 304, 1329, 1402; COURT(S) **3:**870, 888; **5:**231; **7:**53, 139, 144; GOD(S) **1:**85, 580, 584, 586, 1075; **2:**197, 714–15, 763, 770, 824, 827, 841, 843, 854, 1016–18, 1029, 1047; **3:**90, 115, 129, 257, 713, 1109; **5:**44; **6:**356–57, 600, 722, 989, 1233; **7:**115, 665, 864–65; **8:**35; LAND(S) **1:**560, 1171; **2:**389, 459, 502, 550, 825, 858, 886; **3:**129, 198, 733, 782, 1109, 1171; **4:**479, 1227; **5:**784; **6:**145, 187, 198, 967, 1420; **7:**21, 146, 242, 268, 286–87, 297, 469, 481, 495, 588; **10:**353, 471; WIVES/WOMAN/WOMEN **2:**109, 245–46, 738, 740, 782, 841, 843, 894, 901–2, 918–19, 923, 926, 941–42; **3:**37, 40, 88, 90, 95–96, 115, 129, 133, 158, 214, 260, 511, 666, 669, 673, 730, 733, 735, 738–43, 747, 797, 805, 818, 835, 842, 849, 1016; **5:**44, 230–31, 384, 605, 629, 669, 765; **6:**1023, 1223; **7:**269, 864–66

FOREIGNER, FOREIGNERS
1:461, 473, 527, 610, 704–5, 783, 1136, 1152, 1163; **2:**12, 109, 426, 459, 463, 467, 512–13, 547, 549, 569, 736, 738, 740–41, 761–62, 841–42, 849, 863, 870, 876, 878–79, 894, 900, 913, 916, 918–19, 920, 925, 928, 931, 932, 942, 946, 1324, 1339; **3:**37, 58, 61, 76, 79, 87, 93–96, 156–57, 257, 328, 332, 390, 497, 502, 547, 574, 618, 649, 654, 666, 670, 678, 691, 732–33, 741–42, 745, 747–48, 797, 805, 810, 813, 818–19, 838, 842, 849–50, 956, 1016; **4:**21–22, 69, 87, 228, 233, 476, 1256; **5:**84, 187, 321, 384, 474, 632, 705, 746, 798, 800–801; **6:**40, 54, 60, 180, 191, 284, 471, 484–86, 505, 516, 549, 859–60, 986, 1169, 1186, 1330, 1416, 1427–28, 1467, 1574, 1578; **7:**42, 53, 63, 76, 82, 92, 95, 118, 146, 161–62, 168, 180, 184, 193, 257–58, 261, 330, 333, 354, 425, 451, 472, 476, 489, 620, 672, 805; **8:**23, 140, 150; **9:**326–27, 336; **10:**135, 143–44, 623; **12:**40, 107, 136–37, 146; MARRIAGE TO **1:**40; **2:**841; **3:**158, 818, 849–50; **5:**44, 632; **7:**864–65, 866. *See also* ALIEN

FOREKNOWLEDGE
1:420, 460; **5:**510, 591; **6:**1249, 1283; **9:**367, 416, 422–23, 610, 646, 773; **10:**66, 600–603, 675; **11:**393; **12:**247–48, 251, 259, 485, 586

FORERUNNER, FORERUNNERS
1:97, 293, 876; **3:**22, 130, 432, 1134; **4:**51, 973; **5:**120, 542; **6:**338, 470; **7:**205; **8:**156–57, 362, 365, 532; **9:**15, 46, 50, 82, 85, 90, 164, 219, 267, 520, 529; **10:**160; **11:**611; **12:**82, 120, 246, 282, 288, 293, 315

FORESAIL
10:353. *See also* SAIL

FORESKIN, FORESKINS
1:1134; **2:**550, 1118, 1122–24, 1250; **4:**33; **6:**812, 1574; **11:**252, 271, 315, 343, 624; **12:**295

FOREST, FORESTS
1:215–16, 425; **2:**685, 816, 1336; **3:**758; **4:**416, 534, 626, 632; **5:**93, 298, 314; **6:**99, 133, 136, 194, 247, 249, 266, 342, 657, 972, 1217, 1292, 1294–95, 1304, 1345, 1472, 1524; **7:**310, 574, 648, 817; **8:**157; **10:**244, 472, 509–10; **12:**101, 433, 526; OF LEBANON (*see* LEBANON, FOREST OF *in PLACES IN THE BIBLE*); TREES OF THE **6:**52, 388, 1217

FORGETFULNESS, LAND OF
6:1503

FORGIVENESS
1:207, 282, 484, 572, 671–73, 822, 870, 890–91, 934, 945, 961–62, 1028, 1033, 1039, 1041, 1061, 1067, 1111–13, 1120, 1180, 1182, 1184; **2:**125, 127, 130, 139, 741, 749, 753, 759, 826,

FORGIVENESS *(continued)*
1089, 1160–61, 1168, 1316, 1341, 1381; **3:**76, 196, 425–26, 497, 500–503, 617, 619, 632, 658, 753, 777, 813, 847, 931; **4:**211, 234, 556, 702, 753, 777–78, 805–6, 838, 843, 884–87, 933, 935, 992, 995, 998, 1000, 1044, 1076, 1091–93, 1117–18, 1171, 1175, 1187; **5:**159, 401, 669, 693, 730, 797, 800; **6:**317, 320, 339, 365, 370–71, 380, 386, 393, 402, 414, 417, 467, 478, 527, 530, 544, 547, 597, 619, 639, 691, 827, 840, 920, 934, 949, 958, 1057, 1140, 1170, 1221, 1239, 1278, 1497; **7:**116, 122, 124, 126, 160, 219, 279, 287, 406, 408–9, 414, 577, 589, 766; **8:**64, 112, 123, 201, 214, 223, 234–35, 269, 287, 372, 377, 379–82, 448, 484, 531, 547, 549–51, 555, 557, 564–65, 566, 572, 624, 667; **9:**12, 36, 56, 78, 121, 126, 169, 172–73, 177–78, 234–35, 253–54, 272, 291, 302, 304, 320, 322, 324, 329, 352, 360, 428, 455, 461, 463, 701; **10:**15, 59, 66–68, 77, 90, 132–33, 146, 176, 199, 206, 262, 322, 338–39, 427, 485, 493, 504, 506, 638, 647, 693, 953; **11:**34, 52–55, 88, 110, 112, 154, 247, 257, 377, 398, 405, 420, 431–32, 439–40, 607, 625, 627, 630, 648–50, 660; **12:**57, 60, 74, 92, 110, 117, 124, 127, 374, 386, 391, 398, 443–44, 543; DIVINE/OF GOD/THE LORD/YAHWEH **1:**934, 1035, 1057, 1065, 1114; **2:**125, 129, 152, 234, 825, 1294, 1317; **3:**332, 423, 497, 502, 540, 543, 560, 612, 620; **4:**396, 667, 674, 806, 811, 839, 885, 992, 1093, 1111, 1205–6, 1229; **5:**484, 678, 734, 772, 797; **6:**272, 379, 408, 605, 619, 812, 825, 839, 1169; **7:**198, 227, 528; **8:**33, 202, 204–5, 212, 234, 286, 382, 565, 666; **9:**172–73, 305; **10:**65, 68, 85, 130, 133, 140, 146, 171, 307, 338–39, 342, 461; **11:**430, 629–30, 664; **12:**390, 646; GRACE AND **1:**1057; **2:**1317; **3:**738; **5:**190; **7:**537; **8:**217, 379; **9:**343; **10:**47; MERCY AND **1:**318; **5:**563, 733; **7:**227, 569, 589; **8:**666; **9:**343; **12:**114–15; OF SIN(S) **1:**207, 1001, 1110, 1114, 1159; **3:**295, 421, 497, 1145; **4:**396, 674, 806, 811, 1043; **5:**45, 772; **6:**339, 379, 469, 948; **7:**583; **8:**157, 159, 207, 232, 284, 399, 455, 471–72, 532–33, 536, 551, 553, 654, 704; **9:**22, 83, 90, 105–6, 122–23, 125, 487, 579, 847; **10:**65, 68, 73, 107, 167, 169, 188, 193, 219, 247, 334, 472, 477, 487, 494, 504, 534, 647, 680; **11:**54, 187, 202, 247, 276, 312, 373, 375, 378, 392, 571, 596, 629; **12:**101, 116–17, 223, 224, 390, 392

FORK
AS A UTENSIL **1:**987; **9:**86; IN THE ROAD **1:**488; **6:**1293, 1301, 1347

FORM
CRITICISM (*see under* CRITICISM); FINAL FORM OF THE TEXT **1:**129, 135, 139, 142, 314, 678, 835, 927, 934; **2:**540, 725, 953–56, 1032; **3:**4; **7:**868; **8:**93–94, 108 (*see also* REDACTOR); HUMAN **1:**92, 362, 425, 446, 452, 458, 462–64, 562, 565, 568–69, 585, 661; **2:**316, 809; **4:**1213; **6:**386, 1115–16; **8:**550, 689; **11:**505, 509, 527; **12:**592

FORNICATION
2:198; **3:**1016; **5:**557–59, 614, 639, 751; **6:**1224, 1321, 1329–30; **7:**216, 239, 241–42, 245; **8:**190, 192; **9:**640; **10:**220–21; **11:**194, 225, 435, 642, 718; **12:**74, 78, 154, 163, 530, 578–79, 581, 614, 631, 633, 636, 644, 646, 651, 653–54, 664, 666, 675, 680–81, 683, 686–87, 692–93, 695–96, 717, 721–22, 724

FORNICATOR, FORNICATORS
3:159; **5:**752; **12:**76, 154, 163, 733

FORT, FORTS
4:66, 100, 276; **6:**195, 242, 1407

FORTIFICATION, FORTIFICATIONS
1:216, 221, 222–23, 225, 247, 251, 259, 261, 265; **2:**20, 121, 123; **3:**58, 81–82, 84, 416, 522, 628, 1098; **4:**85, 116, 145, 150, 156, 164, 229, 865; **6:**508; **7:**82, 534, 560; **8:**20; **9:**373

FORTRESS, FORTRESSES
1:293; **2:**613, 652, 1366; **3:**268, 286, 467, 520–21, 525, 547, 756, 768, 793, 967; **4:**38, 119, 159, 168, 175–76, 228, 717, 747, 800, 864–65, 872, 912–14, 923, 958, 1047, 1059; **5:**113, 245; **6:**6, 202–3, 586, 808, 1080, 1359, 1361, 1364, 1374, 1382, 1418; **7:**147, 250–51, 263, 275, 334, 447–48, 618, 635, 647, 681, 809; **8:**267, 270, 319, 598, 643, 720; **9:**245, 446, 802; **10:**311–12; **11:**138, 304, 459

FORTUNE
1:261, 828, 1026; **3:**28, 336, 338, 538, 921; **4:**164, 171; **5:**9, 68, 526, 677, 715, 781, 824; **6:**120, 372, 531, 805, 1072, 1383; **8:**17, 21, 686; **9:**296; **10:**232, 250; **11:**488, 828; BAD/ILL **3:**1141; **4:**412; **9:**479; CHANGE/REVERSAL(S)/TURN OF **3:**145, 937; **4:**462, 1017; **5:**254, 293, 475–76, 527; **6:**382, 528, 531, 1044, 1061; **7:**13, 41, 52, 56, 64, 74–75, 84, 93, 95, 105–6, 118, 188–89, 194, 376, 403, 647, 680, 699–700, 703; **9:**314; **10:**349; GOOD **1:**555, 645; **2:**513, 620, 752, 1183, 1188; **3:**271, 994–95, 1042; **4:**358, 364, 443, 451–52, 468, 492, 524, 554, 635, 801, 847; **5:**668, 708; **7:**40; **9:**255, 298, 326–27, 479; **10:**51, 334; **11:**44, 403, 494

FORTY
1:1085; **2:**471; **3:**782, 1023, 1095, 1109; **4:**210, 266; **5:**167, 327; **6:**691, 948, 1490, 1549, 1592; **7:**31; **8:**151, 719; **9:**16, 398; **10:**311–12, 325, 773; **11:**157; **12:**390, 457; DAYS **1:**391–92, 669, 1085; **2:**126, 1110; **3:**996; **6:**1145, 1147, 1412; **7:**511–12, 528; **8:**535, 600; **9:**97–99, 485, 488,

705; **10:**40–41, 43, 45, 47; DAYS AND (FORTY) NIGHTS **1:**391, 882, 887, 930; **3:**142; **7:**122; **8:**163; YEAR(S) **1:**18, 216, 253, 262–63, 991–92, 995; **2:**3, 126, 158, 219, 249, 305, 355, 546, 607, 739, 764, 768, 777, 789, 809–10, 817, 820–22, 838, 841, 845, 859, 1002, 1018, 1213, 1234; **3:**28, 61, 83, 102, 233, 802, 1068, 1182; **4:**190; **6:**48, 1126, 1147, 1401, 1407, 1598; **8:**535; **9:**99; **10:**127; **12:**48, 50

FORUM
1:59; **2:**540, 935; **4:**101; **5:**527–28; **6:**1004; **7:**29; **8:**14, 629; **10:**357, 774, 864, 894

FOUNDATION
FOR A BUILDING **2:**89, 872; **3:**487, 668, 691–93, 705, 736, 838; **4:**198, 314, 596; **6:**237, 318, 342, 413, 516, 585, 640, 1595; **7:**728–29, 770, 780, 789, 796; **8:**345; **9:**151–53, 292; **10:**549, 828; **11:**409, 502, 810, 846; **12:**53, 113, 259, 264, 657, 704; GOD/JESUS AS **2:**327, 431; **4:**465, 737, 1051, 1136; **6:**57; **7:**444, 577; **10:**755, 829–30, 832, 941; **11:**402, 845; **12:**264, 585; PETER AS **8:**342, 345, 347; **9:**861

FOUNTAIN, FOUNTAINS
1:356; **4:**441, 854, 946; **5:**60, 69, 355, 327, 405–6; **6:**212, 963, 1564; **7:**293, 335, 829; **10:**894; **12:**635; OF LIFE **5:**111, 132, 143, 161, 220; OF LIVING WATER **5:**68; **6:**608, 698, 709, 963; OF WISDOM **5:**172; **7:**12; **12:**524

FOWL
1:1009; **2:**78; **3:**782

FOWLER, FOWLERS
5:812; **7:**258, 262–63, 266–67

FOX, FOXES
1:365; **2:**842, 852; **3:**772–73; **5:**394, 746; **9:**217, 281–83

FRACTURE (*OR* FRACTURES, *ETC.*)
1:51, 430; **6:**10, 477; **7:**24, 741, 820, 833, 865; **10:**49, 434–35, 602, 890; **11:**14, 248, 337, 457; **12:**404, 517, 616

FRAGRANCE, FRAGRANCES
1:916; **5:**387, 388, 405–6, 415, 426, 461, 469, 504–5, 818; **9:**458, 701; **11:**57–58, 61, 106, 138, 710. *See also* PERFUME

FRAME
FOR CARRYING TABERNACLE/TEMPLE UTENSILS **1:**689, 894

FRANKINCENSE
1:920, 1018, 1036; **2:**78; **3:**512, 846–47; **5:**403, 757; **6:**379, 1558; **8:**143; **12:**694

FREE CHOICE/FREE WILL
1:287, 720; **2:**462, 595, 1136, 1310, 1341; **3:**1137; **4:**248; **5:**308, 398, 456, 610, 626–28, 638, 651, 718, 721, 726, 752, 788; **6:**134, 657; **7:**328, 369, 372; **9:**279, 348, 388, 417, 423, 712; **10:**906; **11:**121, 123, 126, 129, 815; **12:**326, 525; FREEWILL OFFERING(S) (*see under* OFFERING)

FREEDMAN, FREEDMEN
10:120–24, 763, 881; **11:**401

FREEDOM
OF CHRIST **8:**372, 375; **10:**508, 781, 861, 895, 901, 906–7, 910, 928, 944; **11:**72, 184, 207, 273, 276, 300, 310, 438, 644, 657; **12:**275, 278, 281, 283, 286–87, 325, 350, 475; OF GOD **1:**236, 282, 465, 838, 846, 888, 907, 932, 938, 979; **2:**462, 671, 1010, 1014, 1078, 1082; **3:**78, 185, 714, 985, 997; **5:**23, 33, 163; **6:**366, 382, 396, 400, 402, 432–33, 642, 717, 1264; **7:**391, 411, 476, 485, 800; **9:**113; **12:**56; FROM THE LAW **8:**46, 277, 332; **9:**314; **10:**513, 552, 555, 559, 586; **11:**186, 194, 210, 213, 222, 227, 242, 295, 297, 300, 305–7, 316, 334, 340, 347, 357, 617; OF RELIGION **1:**165; **3:**1108; **6:**109, 602; **7:**26, 108; **10:**182, 299; FROM SIN **1:**160; **5:**251; **9:**714; **10:**508, 540, 545; **11:**328; **12:**305, 500; AND SLAVERY **1:**151, 156, 490, 615, 872, 1134; **2:**324, 408; **3:**414, 1108; **4:**106; **7:**279, 606; **8:**20; **9:**637–38; **10:**410, 464, 511–12, 534, 536, 542–44, 546–48, 551, 560, 880–81, 883–84, 902, 906–7, 909–10; **11:**76, 199, 225, 249, 273, 284, 292, 299, 302–3, 321–22, 887, 900; **12:**107, 156, 286, 333

FREE WILL
See FREE CHOICE/FREE WILL

FRIEND, FRIENDS
1:604–6, 942, 1027, 1114; **2:**13–15, 40, 110, 671, 673, 733, 756, 758, 760, 804, 908, 914, 934, 1030, 1080, 1132–35, 1137, 1149, 1153, 1194, 1208, 1303, 1309, 1319, 1325, 1330–31, 1353; **3:**293–94, 379, 919, 966, 1001, 1117; **4:**106, 127, 130, 140, 143, 147, 154, 232, 242, 255, 268, 287, 330–33, 362, 389, 433, 449, 460–61, 477, 492, 503, 548, 564, 680, 848, 897, 1026, 1029, 1045, 1079, 1172; **5:**4, 8–9, 11, 159–60, 175, 230–32, 330, 342, 363, 393, 395, 416–17, 455, 459, 479–80, 505, 509, 519, 524, 557, 613, 617, 680, 682–84, 715, 736, 747, 768, 771, 775, 781, 790, 805, 808; **6:**158, 358, 362–63, 403, 604, 658, 681, 728, 807, 832, 1361, 1510; **8:**195, 394, 477, 484, 492, 703; **9:**4, 23, 46, 127, 170, 236, 287, 301, 342, 356, 394, 401, 423, 434, 453, 570, 775, 822; **10:**189, 342, 360, 631, 809, 918, 921, 994; **11:**20, 29–30, 44, 46, 48, 50, 55, 98, 112, 173, 294, 298, 335, 417, 699, 885, 891–92, 894, 898; **12:**123, 459; OF THE BRIDEGROOM **6:**87; **9:**558, 752; OF GOD/YAHWEH **1:**938, 1027; **2:**13, 15, 40, 110, 671, 756, 758, 760; **3:**560, 1038; **5:**11, 330, 502, 563, 565; **6:**88, 358, 363, 403, 604, 1510; **9:**40; **12:**182, 189, 198, 200, 211, 213; OF JESUS **2:**14; **8:**703;

FRIEND, FRIENDS *(continued)*
9:4, 23, 170, 758, 775; **10:**208, 342; OF THE KING **3:**50, 457; **4:**122, 171, 223, 242; **7:**143, 187; OF THE WORLD **12:**178, 182, 189, 198, 200, 211–12, 221–22

FRIENDSHIP
1:133, 579, 1024, 1026; **2:**15, 420, 546, 966, 1115, 1129, 1132, 1134, 1136–37, 1153, 1208, 1212, 1276, 1277, 1279, 1315; **3:**700; **4:**102, 107, 143–44, 147, 161, 171, 275, 288, 340, 357, 385, 388–89, 538, 547, 559; **5:**30, 77, 167–68, 175, 228–29, 231–32, 391, 505, 511, 513, 558, 610, 614, 638–39, 681–84, 701, 709, 715, 746–47, 771, 805, 823; **6:**1360; **7:**42, 96, 229, 438, 585; **8:**18, 350, 425, 641, 709; **9:**75, 236, 286, 327, 730, 758–59, 763; **10:**71, 100–101, 114, 253, 261, 296, 354, 446, 956, 994, 1002; **11:**20, 28–30, 46, 48–49, 52, 95, 101, 107, 109, 112, 140, 169–70, 173, 177, 294–95, 297–98, 409, 419, 690, 744, 756, 904; **12:**181–82, 433; WITH GOD/THE LORD/YAHWEH **1:**1021; **2:**14, 715; **5:**280, 437, 447, 502, 504; **12:**178, 198–99, 209, 212, 216, 221–22, 224–25

FRINGE, FRINGES
1:21, 255, 258, 537, 767, 839; **2:**105; **3:**1040; **4:**548, 632; **5:**227; **6:**10, 183, 541, 1203; **8:**431–32; **9:**190–91, 417; **10:**763; **12:**550, 553, 670

FROG, FROGS
1:688, 743–46, 750; **4:**992, 1105; **5:**186, 229, 231, 244, 529, 540, 573, 584, 593, 598, 716; **10:**716; **12:**677

FRONTLETS
5:843

FROST
3:1070; **4:**598, 604, 1268; **5:**485, 525, 578–79, 618, 660, 834; **6:**840; **12:**636

FRUIT, FRUITS
1:88, 124, 218, 236, 350, 361–62, 374, 405, 555, 1071, 1160, 1163, 1180; **2:**120–21, 123, 319, 340, 471, 480, 483, 536, 901; **3:**637; **4:**256, 441, 452, 470, 510, 608, 1000; **5:**53, 71, 103, 120, 126, 131, 218, 234, 365, 389, 405, 475, 523, 524, 598, 619, 681; **6:**84, 89, 226–27, 238, 265, 277, 602, 675, 708, 757, 1079, 1165, 1176, 1216–17, 1245, 1253, 1271, 1351, 1473, 1597; **7:**42, 74, 234, 273, 296, 308–9, 407, 411, 414, 527, 585, 618; **8:**314, 413, 570–71, 577, 660, 664, 693; **9:**84, 150–52, 239, 289, 408, 418, 458, 570, 642, 756–57; **10:**531, 601; **12:**152, 492, 614, 694, 710, 724; BEAR(ING/S) **2:**1212; **3:**205, 1051; **4:**685, 909; **5:**113, 176, 473; **6:**521, 1252, 1484; **7:**270, 837; **8:**305, 570–71, 578; **9:**83, 141, 176–80, 271–72, 310, 359, 402, 755, 757–61; **10:**512, 514, 559–60; **11:**37, 485, 569, 591, 595; BITTER **1:**524; **9:**149, 302, 642; FIRST (*see under* FIRST); OF LABOR(S) **1:**1161, 1166; **5:**119, 298, 302, 319, 511; **6:**78, 710; **10:**757; **11:**491; OF THE SPIRIT **10:**450, 585, 848; **11:**51, 196, 199, 324, 328–30, 339, 415, 420, 593, 678, 718, 846; **12:**649; TREE(S) **1:**1134; **2:**816; **3:**1058; **4:**1271; **5:**768; **6:**174; **7:**324, 837; **8:**435; **10:**462; OF THE TREE(S) **1:**351, 361, 383, 1133; **3:**820, 1041; **8:**217, 408; **9:**742; OF THE VINE OR VINEYARD **6:**1216; **8:**471, 674; **9:**383, 418–19

FRYING PAN, PANS
1:1017, 1020; **5:**126; **7:**393. *See also* GRIDDLE; POT

FUEL, FUELS
FOR BURNING **1:**215; **3:**144; **4:**484; **6:**305, 386, 388, 1149, 1211, 1217, 1335, 1524; **7:**770; **11:**493

FULFILLMENT
OF THE (DIVINE) BLESSING **1:**381, 409; **2:**35, 40; **3:**506; OF GOD'S WILL **1:**127; **3:**98, 145, 179, 226; **4:**862; **6:**140; **9:**203; **11:**242; **12:**401; OF GOD'S WORD/THE WORD **1:**449, 486; **3:**217, 377; **6:**456, 851, 874, 1305; **11:**323; OF THE LAW **1:**605, 607; **2:**211, 266, 513; **5:**798; **8:**189, 547; **9:**68, 70, 120, 207; **10:**725; **11:**322–24, 340, 343, 346, 357, 485, 502; **12:**193; OF THE PROMISE(S) OF GOD/JESUS/YAHWEH **1:**165–66, 307–8, 317, 404, 418, 430, 442, 446, 449, 453–55, 467, 486, 488, 497–98, 500, 515, 530, 567, 574, 581, 659; **2:**124, 126, 180–81, 215, 234, 262, 510, 1261; **3:**24, 33, 35–36, 234, 289, 409, 474, 505, 617, 671, 754; **4:**711; **5:**733; **6:**363, 443, 457, 463, 471, 509, 515, 544, 547, 1282, 1447, 1454, 1502; **7:**330, 355, 767; **8:**36, 67, 132, 144, 271, 529; **9:**55, 59, 69–71, 106–7, 110, 167, 202, 352, 420, 426, 445, 508, 608, 648, 671–72, 699, 841, 843, 846, 857–58; **10:**46, 126–27, 132, 284, 405, 464, 505, 511, 525, 654–55, 671, 756; **11:**268, 276, 304; **12:**138, 336–37, 343, 356, 488, 534; OF (THE) PROPHECY **1:**87; **3:**113, 160, 162, 173, 203, 209, 221, 223, 676, 728; **6:**786, 1413; **7:**84, 489; **8:**38, 690; **9:**440; **10:**57, 72, 81, 150, 208, 353, 415–16, 450; **12:**261, 561; OF (THE) SCRIPTURE(S) **1:**84; **8:**97, 147, 150, 152–53, 186, 356, 403; **9:**20–22, 41–44, 80, 98, 106, 108, 351, 373, 404, 423, 430, 456, 475, 478–79, 486–87, 531–33, 793, 831, 833–34, 836; **10:**41, 196, 691; **11:**262; TIME OF **7:**667; **8:**38, 63, 186, 305; **9:**372, 422, 537, 567, 572, 617, 748, 766, 780, 783; **10:**126; **11:**96, 409, 615; OF A VOW **1:**239, 281, 584–85, 1051; **2:**64, 236, 265, 391, 1319; **4:**503, 933, 1149; **6:**1002, 1569; **7:**828; **8:**598; **10:**258

FUNERAL, FUNERALS
1:573, 593, 670, 1124, 1147–48; **2:**64, 149, 168, 399, 1195, 1209; **3:**238, 543, 631, 649, 1002; **4:**430, 491, 494, 631, 767, 1045, 1111, 1182; **5:**322, 355, 471; **6:**16, 92, 168, 198, 702, 1016, 1252, 1564; **7:**647; **8:**238, 269, 589, 612, 676, 726, 730; **9:**74, 159, 166, 465, 695; **10:**714; **11:**387, 859; **12:**730; BANQUET(S) **5:**696–97; **6:**702, 1342; DIRGE(S)/SONG(S) **4:**352; **6:**158, 170, 805, 1019, 1021; **7:**344, 349, 385, 414, 595, 601; ROYAL/STATE **1:**669; **2:**1222, 1225; **6:**741; **9:**466

FURNACE, FURNACES
4:379; **5:**460, 470, 654, 851; **6:**261, 277, 1312–13, 1337, 1501; **7:**64–65, 93, 146, 150, 160, 164, 168, 169, 822; **8:**314; **9:**318; **12:**525, 561, 631; FIERY **1:**285; **2:**541; **3:**871; **4:**50–51; **6:**164, 1306; **7:**53, 65, 81, 160, 168; **12:**144, 521

FURNISHING, FURNISHINGS
1:689, 885, 896, 972, 976; **2:**83, 385, 520, 1003; **3:**62, 68, 251, 433, 462, 478, 484–85, 644; **4:**67, 72, 222; **5:**85, 275; **6:**1107, 1553; **7:**717; **12:**103–4, 391

FURNITURE
1:223, 225, 889–90, 901, 916, 920, 999, 1045, 1113; **2:**246; **4:**203; **6:**260; **7:**44, 709; **8:**246, 249; **12:**5, 82, 87, 103, 108, 116

FURROW, FURROWS
4:555; **5:**688, 692; **7:**286, 366; **9:**217

G

GALL
OF LIVER **3:**1026, 1033, 1049–51; **4:**459, 485; **7:**526; **8:**490

GALLEYS
6:271. *See also* BOAT; SHIP

GALLOWS
3:857, 875, 892, 910–11, 919–20, 934; **5:**118; **6:**1156; **9:**310

GAME
CONTEST **1:**359, 366, 469, 497, 569, 640, 646, 765, 769, 925, 1136, 1139; **2:**684, 885, 1153, 1216; **3:**552–53, 908–9, 918, 923; **4:**5, 32, 130, 217–18, 305–6, 428; **5:**89, 188, 323–24, 395, 397, 525; **6:**74, 257, 376, 608, 788, 1143–45, 1244, 1265, 1292, 1315, 1329, 1370; **8:**269, 275; **9:**166–67, 178, 286–87, 440, 767; **10:**52, 326, 617, 751, 759, 775, 846, 894, 909; **11:**298, 300, 379, 424, 632, 813, 842, 844, 856; **12:**116, 298, 571, 659; WILD **1:**535–36, 989, 1009, 1117, 1120; **2:**549, 1175

GANGRENE
11:841, 845–46

GARDEN
2:18, 182, 190, 701; **3:**155, 768, 919; **5:**69, 71, 95, 140, 368–69, 375, 388, 404–7, 417, 420, 433, 461, 512, 607, 627, 746, 758, 823–24; **6:**174, 280, 543, 742, 745, 1009, 1194, 1561; **7:**176–79, 263, 430–31; **8:**309, 311, 436; **9:**275, 705, 712, 799, 801–3, 810, 836–37, 843–44, 846; **10:**592, 768; **11:**163; **12:**576, 630; OF EDEN (*see* EDEN, GARDEN OF *in PLACES IN THE BIBLE*); THE GARDEN *(i.e., the Eden/Paradise garden)* **1:**77, 350–52, 360, 362, 364, 367–68, 372, 374, 376, 428; **2:**551; **4:**440–41, 1042; **5:**405, 584; **6:**528, 545, 1252, 1393, 1599; **7:**167; **8:**535, 537; **10:**526, 563; **11:**163; **12:**576, 694, 724; OF GOD/THE LORD **1:**359, 434–35, 473; **4:**1051; **6:**335, 1392–93, 1423, 1426, 1595; **7:**750; **12:**723. *See also by name in PLACES IN THE BIBLE*

GARLAND, GARLANDS
3:1078, 1108, 1139; **5:**143, 626, 650–51; **6:**236, 336, 1342; **10:**198

GARMENT, GARMENTS
1:74, 362, 586, 605, 610, 1048, 1056, 1060–61, 1097, 1111, 1114, 1120, 1134, 1148; **2:**128, 163, 220, 453, 809, 850, 918, 926, 928, 987, 1079, 1090, 1179, 1207, 1279, 1305; **3:**95, 914, 1084, 1086, 1142–43, 1147; **4:**67, 77, 286, 310, 312, 429, 459, 862; **5:**262, 275, 341, 400, 486, 553, 613, 648, 679, 830, 843; **6:**11, 122, 437, 449, 453, 503–4, 515, 784, 979–80, 1178, 1230, 1253, 1368, 1380, 1392, 1429, 1558, 1597; **7:**44, 64, 148, 232, 365, 767, 799, 832, 866; **8:**33, 79, 195, 236, 238, 480, 491, 555, 588–89, 595, 633, 658, 710, 723; **9:**84, 131, 147–48, 163, 190–91, 263, 367, 369–70, 450, 454–55, 831; **10:**670; **11:**274, 412, 438, 440, 648; **12:**257, 599, 613, 695; HEM OF A **5:**648; **6:**11, 102, 105; **9:**455; KING'S/ROYAL **1:**622; **4:**862, 1053; **5:**688; LINEN **1:**1044, 1110, 1114; **3:**914, 1158; **5:**262; **6:**1578; RENDING OF **3:**94; **5:**305; **6:**1150; TORN **2:**1090, 1305, 1309, 1325; **3:**94, 177, 237, 733; **5:**305, 798; **6:**840, 1143, 1150; **7:**318; **8:**480, 714; TRAIN OF A **8:**33; WHITE **1:**1110; **5:**341; **8:**630, 731; **11:**272; **12:**699. *See also* CLOTHES, CLOTHING

GARRISON, GARRISONS
2:1000, 1070, 1078–79, 1376; **4:**9, 57, 60, 87, 115, 117–19, 121, 132–33, 138, 145, 150, 152, 156, 174, 222–23, 228–29, 261, 276; **5:**612; **7:**25, 29–30, 138, 143, 147, 609; **9:**373

GATE, GATES
1:221–22, 224, 239, 413; **2:**38, 340, 371, 570, 629, 787, 855, 934, 939, 941, 1002, 1225, 1286, 1319, 1340; **3:**164, 205, 208, 299, 363, 505, 575, 751, 753, 756, 761, 764–66, 770–71, 784, 838, 967, 1049, 1065, 1085, 1087, 1098, 1148, 1155, 1159; **4:**147, 379, 413, 547, 603, 626, 644, 1077, 1118, 1183; **5:**88, 142, 159, 211, 218, 263, 491,

GATE, GATES *(continued)*
687; **6:**194, 211, 221, 236, 510, 635, 647, 690, 721, 740, 746, 773, 797, 822, 899, 996, 1107, 1137, 1176, 1194, 1218, 1300, 1302, 1364, 1367, 1429, 1518, 1540–41, 1546–47, 1570, 1578, 1587, 1607; **7:**82, 111, 349, 380, 389–90, 394, 416, 451, 610, 618, 758, 783, 801; **8:**62, 293, 346, 395, 693, 719; **9:**25, 144, 157, 279, 316–19, 399, 458, 482, 602, 667, 669, 672–73, 742; **10:**164, 180, 198, 230; **11:**846; **12:**41, 401, 534, 585, 597, 697, 716, 722, 724, 735; OF THE CITY **1:**223, 261, 503; **2:**854–55, 935, 1280, 1339; **3:**130, 133, 162, 223, 766, 768, 793, 848, 851; **4:**101, 537–38, 1024, 1198; **5:**40, 89, 204, 262–63, 400; **6:**1030, 1039, 1195, 1606; **7:**390, 452, 527, 694; **8:**216; **9:**290, 348; **10:**231; **12:**167, 720, 722, 733; OF HEAVEN **1:**277, 542; **3:**658; **7:**750, 770, 782–83; **12:**531, 729; INNER **6:**1106, 1543–46, 1549, 1557, 1588; **9:**399; NORTH **6:**1175–76, 1178, 1543, 1548, 1573, 1591, 1595; OUTER **6:**1106, 1542, 1544–45, 1549, 1589; **10:**179; PRISON **8:**230; SOUTH **6:**1543; TEMPLE (*see under* JERUSALEM TEMPLE *in PLACES IN THE BIBLE*); TWELVE **3:**364; **6:**1593, 1606–7; **12:**694, 722–23; WEST **3:**451. *See also by name in PLACES IN THE BIBLE*

GATEKEEPER, GATEKEEPERS
2:199; **3:**300, 363, 394, 400, 436, 450–53, 575–76, 648, 686, 718, 745, 770, 788, 793, 817, 824, 826, 835, 838, 842, 848, 851; **8:**293; **9:**667, 668; **10:**137; **12:**457, 722

GAZELLE, GAZELLES
5:395, 389–90, 433

GEM, GEMS
3:82; **4:**531; **5:**415, 498; **6:**1061, 1371, 1392; **7:**474; **9:**156, 304; **11:**144. *See also* JEWELS AND PRECIOUS STONES; STONES: PRECIOUS; *by individual type*

GEMARA/GEMARAH
1:68, 315

GENDER
1:24, 27, 31, 105, 148, 168, 181, 184–85, 187, 214, 242, 783; **2:**222, 452, 454, 530, 551, 727, 776, 1114, 1168, 1252; **3:**96, 506, 507, 688, 747, 872, 924, 1086, 1132, 1142, 1148, 1167; **4:**565; **5:**35, 44, 46, 82, 84, 108, 207, 242, 365–66, 426; **6:**11, 82, 337, 345, 608, 670, 693, 961, 1046, 1224, 1241–42, 1392; **7:**206, 208–9, 220, 227–29, 232, 245, 250, 297, 475–76, 493, 495, 502, 505, 535; **8:**54, 338, 546, 611; **9:**108, 333, 571, 843; **10:**114, 431, 509, 571, 699, 766, 870, 912; **11:**85, 255, 273, 274, 279, 310, 337, 404, 455, 457, 611, 869; **12:**188, 194–95, 287, 374, 449, 486, 550, 620

GENEALOGY
1:283, 308, 325–27, 336–37, 349, 372, 375, 379–81, 390, 403, 405, 408, 411–12, 415–16, 422, 501, 514, 554, 559, 590–91, 593, 595, 598, 606, 652, 693, 700, 723, 733, 735–36, 905, 908, 1164; **2:**26, 33, 47–49, 135–36, 199, 212–15, 576, 673, 687, 701, 933, 941, 943, 945, 962, 988, 1037, 1100, 1284; **3:**301, 305, 317–20, 327–30, 332–33, 336–38, 344–46, 352–53, 355, 357–58, 363, 367–68, 436, 445, 447, 526, 590, 655, 669, 688, 693, 701, 717–18, 747, 769–70, 786, 794, 825–26, 836, 838–39, 886, 889, 894, 948, 992, 1042, 1131–32, 1143, 1181; **5:**523, 631; **6:**5, 941; **7:**659, 670, 787; **8:**97, 160; **9:**93; **11:**790; **12:**86–87, 90, 97; OF JESUS (*see* JESUS THE CHRIST: BIRTH AND GENEALOGY OF *in PERSONS IN THE BIBLE*)

GENERAL
MILITARY COMMANDER **1:**269, 290; **2:**264, 738, 774–76, 779, 781, 783, 788, 795, 803–4, 818, 830, 841, 878, 1044, 1062, 1202, 1273, 1280, 1351; **3:**6, 33, 192, 194, 199, 212, 214, 871, 894, 1075–77, 1089–90, 1095, 1101, 1106, 1113, 1118–19, 1140, 1145, 1148, 1159, 1167, 1182; **4:**91, 104–5, 125, 135, 137, 140, 178, 188–89, 193, 248, 255, 641, 691, 981; **5:**143, 237, 261, 643; **6:**119, 932, 1403, 1411; **7:**24, 65, 111–12, 117, 139–41, 151; **8:**343, 490; **9:**49, 290, 366, 370, 373, 405; **11:**458, 548, 675, 842; **12:**168, 614

GENERAL EPISTLES
1:8, 135; **8:**3; **10:**370, 377; **12:**177, 229, 365

GENERATION
NEW **1:**38, 57, 78, 166, 325, 418, 513, 695, 776, 850; **2:**3, 215, 300, 316, 324, 521, 555, 589, 606–7, 727, 729, 732, 747, 751–53, 755, 766, 826, 843, 847, 865, 886, 1024; **3:**338, 402, 443, 532, 537, 555, 569, 598, 602, 607, 693; **4:**1119; **5:**70; **6:**18, 49, 50, 321, 338, 344, 358–59, 379, 390, 418, 442, 448, 456–57, 459–60, 467, 476, 526, 940, 1282; **9:**548, 853; **10:**266, 294, 766; NEXT **1:**42, 279, 468, 500, 529, 630, 763–64; **2:**120, 124, 199, 389, 627, 750, 752, 754, 810; **3:**353, 396, 437, 443, 546, 582, 840; **5:**8, 19, 58–59, 70, 132, 134, 625, 777; **6:**337, 515, 675, 707; **7:**362; **8:**48; **9:**749; **10:**11, 112, 282, 284, 636; **11:**869; **12:**324; PRESENT **1:**36, 56; **2:**316, 501, 512; **3:**560, 615, 671, 735; **4:**405, 1110; **6:**305, 370, 379, 380, 527, 543–44, 1198, 1262; **7:**284, 285; **8:**436–37, 693, 694; **11:**892

GENESIS
1:677, 691, 693–94, 696, 699, 712, 714–15, 723, 733–34, 764, 799, 849, 924, 927, 932–33, 937, 979, 985; **2:**7, 10–11, 48, 221, 291–92, 297, 322,

342, 385, 479–80, 529, 540–41, 543–44, 546–48, 551, 555, 560, 613, 680, 761, 877, 943, 950; **3:**317–19, 332, 810, 996, 1038, 1062, 1143; **4:**232, 288, 296, 328–29, 343, 345, 440, 449, 470, 488, 495, 532, 614, 622, 626, 712, 793, 810, 1042, 1078, 1092, 1096, 1099, 1224, 1271–72; **5:**1, 10, 16, 50, 71, 99, 182, 280, 311, 314, 369, 405, 428, 454, 464–65, 479, 487, 504, 506, 523–26, 541, 567, 598, 634, 729–30, 753, 818; **6:**13, 45, 84, 183, 213–14, 277, 354–55, 361, 366, 441, 527–30, 542, 544, 548, 614, 618–19, 815, 1138, 1213, 1391, 1393–95, 1425, 1444, 1471, 1473, 1500, 1516, 1521, 1530; **7:**3, 12, 21, 39, 41, 50, 73, 90, 142, 150, 164, 283, 284, 287, 345, 357, 362, 369, 381, 389, 548, 573, 597, 674, 692, 750, 855–56, 860, 865; **8:**31, 36, 126, 160, 291, 643; **9:**94, 219, 475, 519, 524, 567, 619, 643; **10:**413, 432–33, 463–64, 471, 487–88, 490–92, 494–96, 498, 500, 505–6, 513, 525–26, 535, 550, 563, 596, 610, 636, 765; **11:**194, 252, 255–56, 261, 264–65, 269, 300–6, 309, 390, 451, 502–3, 505, 508, 604, 802; **12:**22, 43, 83, 86, 89, 129, 135–36, 138, 154, 198, 205–6, 294, 330, 356, 358, 418, 520–21, 532, 596, 634, 725

GENESIS, BOOK OF
1:690, 694, 706, 712, 786, 789–90, 847; **2:**35, 148, 319, 466, 546, 752; **3:**317, 319, 483, 1056; **4:**754, 1150; **5:**529, 621; **8:**125

GENTILE, GENTILES
JEWS AND **1:**169; **2:**603; **3:**869, 954; **4:**182, 211, 222, 276; **6:**516; **7:**643; **8:**40–41, 99, 102, 182, 292, 408, 414, 416, 443, 496, 516, 610, 687, 693; **9:**71, 698; **10:**25, 32, 133, 188, 197, 226, 334, 339, 341, 365, 368, 390, 406–7, 410, 413, 428, 437–38, 441, 451, 468, 472, 484, 489, 503, 525, 643, 645, 647, 667, 684, 687, 689, 731, 733, 756, 833, 869; **11:**186, 195, 199, 223, 225, 227–29, 231–35, 241–43, 245, 248, 257, 262, 268, 272, 276–77, 284, 290–91, 295, 298, 308, 313, 344, 346, 397, 399, 422, 431, 456, 529, 682, 707; **12:**405; MISSION **8:**44, 46, 49–50, 52, 54, 95, 98, 105, 149, 229, 256, 296, 406, 435, 486, 492, 503, 610; **9:**374, 570; **10:**9, 11, 32, 46, 85, 161, 164–65, 168, 171, 174, 190, 195, 203, 364, 372, 375, 389–90, 402, 478, 623, 667–68, 684, 688; **11:**222–24, 227–28, 232, 304, 607, 613, 615–16; MISSION TO THE **6:**1357; **8:**100, 337, 435, 489, 687; **9:**9, 187, 710; **10:**65, 160, 169, 170, 195, 208, 214, 292, 294, 312, 317, 333, 338, 624, 667; **11:**113, 186, 215, 221, 222, 230, 232, 242, 300

GEOGRAPHY
1:213–14, 245, 695, 705, 788; **2:**36, 38, 54, 158, 164–65, 606, 680, 1018, 1218, 1235; **3:**336, 344, 859, 1023, 1028; **4:**22, 110, 603; **5:**232; **6:**188, 218, 1027, 1533–34, 1563; **7:**519; **8:**111, 231, 323, 327, 363, 396, 500, 520, 543; **9:**110, 325, 565, 659; **10:**140, 154, 189, 339

GEOLOGY (*OR* GEOLOGICAL, *ETC.*)
1:215, 278, 388, 439, 473; **2:**316, 357, 373; **3:**178; **4:**1099, 1192; **7:**167–68, 437, 836

GHOST
2:91, 606, 953, 967, 1086, 1090, 1095, 1182, 1184–87, 1191, 1218; **3:**1055; **5:**314, 651; **6:**242, 1342, 1474; **7:**107, 137; **8:**328, 500; **9:**190, 485, 489, 596, 846; HOLY GHOST (*see* HOLY GHOST *in PERSONS IN THE BIBLE*)

GIANT, GIANTS
1:438; **2:**19–21, 120, 122–23, 255, 300, 359, 363–64, 514, 646, 654–55, 662, 689, 906, 1108, 1110, 1114, 1361; **3:**24, 378, 413, 415–17, 1127; **4:**386, 594; **5:**95, 312, 725, 749; **6:**960, 965–66, 1464, 1549; **7:**6, 13, 644; **9:**542; **10:**155, 523; **12:**78, 347, 420, 645

GIFT, GIFTS
OF BREAD **1:**812, 814–15, 892; **9:**599–600, 612;
DIVINE **1:**528, 590; **2:**120, 129, 147, 165, 218, 221, 262, 266, 448, 1014, 1370; **3:**386, 420, 513; **4:**902; **5:**11, 125, 175, 193, 340, 647, 651, 659, 765; **6:**671, 759, 935; **11:**306, 385; **12:**352;
OF/TO GOD **1:**38, 40, 190, 321, 425, 430, 490, 624, 659, 735, 787, 818, 847, 878, 922, 954, 964, 990, 1010, 1017–18, 1062, 1158, 1173; **2:**82–83, 91, 129–30, 193–94, 277, 300, 307–8, 343–44, 352, 357, 359, 402–4, 406–7, 423, 448, 467, 480, 534, 790, 940, 973, 975, 977–78, 980, 982, 995, 997, 1019, 1156–157, 1266, 1382; **3:**35, 40–41, 55, 80, 278, 370, 437, 448, 510, 523, 560, 630, 948, 986, 995, 997, 1005, 1010, 1024, 1043, 1051, 1063, 1071, 1154; **4:**197, 400, 523, 667, 674, 793, 797, 810, 815, 830, 857, 902, 954, 1042, 1098, 1100, 1175, 1198, 1201, 1225; **5:**46, 49, 96, 180, 188, 282, 294, 298, 303, 307–8, 311, 319–21, 364, 408, 461, 494, 498, 511–12, 629, 645, 647, 663, 683, 806; **6:**56, 141, 255, 759, 809, 813, 965, 968, 1188, 1229, 1347, 1505; **7:**309, 324, 328, 428, 574, 643; **8:**33, 160, 192, 197, 304, 316, 387, 535, 651; **9:**254, 272, 285, 390, 397, 490, 553, 555, 557, 559, 561, 571–72, 600, 612, 688, 721, 743, 747, 775, 789, 791–92, 804, 864–65; **10:**23, 57, 71, 169, 421, 465, 471, 501, 514, 531, 539, 546, 574, 575, 621, 648, 654, 662, 710–11, 799, 820, 823, 830, 837, 840, 865, 872, 897; **11:**43, 69, 78, 87, 119, 261, 275, 292, 356, 370, 392, 394, 411, 423, 481, 497, 513, 679, 719, 732, 876; **12:**78, 117, 153, 178, 182, 184, 189, 198–99, 212, 225, 307, 408, 423, 431; GOOD/GOOD AND PERFECT **1:**190,

GIFT, GIFTS *(continued)*
368, 940, 1086; **2:**129, 130; **3:**997; **4:**704, 797; **6:**754; **7:**42, 400; **8:**192, 196–97, 203; **10:**72; **11:**381, 635, 765; **12:**181, 187, 190, 199, 210, 222, 256; OF GRACE **1:**318; **2:**488, 494, 970, 975, 977–78, 1019, 1157, 1194; **4:**445; **5:**70; **6:**759; **9:**523, 538, 597, 796; **10:**449, 471, 528, 547, 996; **11:**29, 131, 420, 836; **12:**264; OF THE HOLY SPIRIT **2:**236; **5:**102; **6:**550; **9:**833, 847, 849; **10:**23, 57–58, 67–68, 97, 107, 139, 140, 167–69, 453, 548; **11:**265, 335, 719; **12:**34–35, 71, 497; OF THE LAND **1:**445, 734; **2:**91, 99, 125, 127, 129–30, 150, 159, 219, 249, 298, 300, 308, 414, 755; **3:**35, 304, 497, 562, 671, 612, 813; **4:**857; **5:**21; **6:**1338; **7:**309; OF LIFE **1:**780, 808; **2:**877; **3:**1005, 1042, 1051; **4:**414, 674, 704, 758, 824, 954; **5:**307–8, 532, 568, 570, 834, 859; **7:**388; **9:**525, 575, 606, 608–9, 614, 626, 686, 694, 699, 743, 795, 834; **10:**575; **11:**391; **12:**287; OF/TO THE LORD/YAHWEH **1:**805, 927, 962, 1042, 1133; **2:**1229; **3:**418, 536, 562; **5:**174; **6:**1233, 1309, 1348, 1593; **9:**255; **11:**842; PERFECT **12:**181, 187–88, 190, 199, 201, 218, 222; SPIRITUAL (*see under* SPIRITUAL)

GIRDLE
5:843

GLASS
1:4; **2:**1276; **5:**330, 355; **6:**965, 1023; **7:**620; **10:**502, 624, 954; **12:**194, 441, 551, 558, 591, 592, 663, 671–72, 723; WATER/WINE **5:**264, 303; **8:**651

GLAZE, GLAZING
5:226; **6:**714, 1245; **11:**250

GLEANING, GLEANINGS
2:471, 916–19, 923, 925, 931, 935, 945; **3:**522; **6:**174, 626; **7:**448

GLORIFICATION
1:84, 794–96; **2:**39, 811, 1262; **3:**54, 192, 941; **4:**58, 882; **6:**510, 516, 541, 545, 547, 1290, 1397, 1494, 1495; **7:**65, 321, 564; **9:**539–40, 645, 711–12, 732, 746, 749, 758, 774, 783, 788, 790–91, 799, 827, 833, 836, 843, 855, 858, 863–64; **10:**509, 519, 539, 550, 585, 597, 601, 603–4, 609, 612–13, 615, 830, 865–66; **11:**67, 71, 83, 515, 677–78, 682, 744, 746, 750–51, 762, 765; **12:**305, 553; OF JESUS **3:**928; **9:**527, 616, 623, 686, 708–10, 712, 714–15, 717–18, 732, 771, 789, 792, 795, 830, 833, 841–43, 846, 851, 860; **11:**755; **12:**404

GLORY
CLOUD OF (*see under* CLOUD); DIVINE (*see under* GOD, METAPHORS FOR *in PERSONS IN THE BIBLE*); OF GOD **1:**569, 682, 813, 882, 884, 902, 913, 940, 953–58, 981, 1020, 1066–67, 1083, 1139; **2:**49, 91, 194, 321, 631, 887, 997, 1002, 1011; **3:**70, 78, 418, 624, 688, 1065; **4:**198, 299, 713, 792, 794, 863, 928, 959, 996, 1016–17, 1065, 1069, 1076, 1139, 1144, 1146, 1260, 1273, 1275; **5:**46, 121, 222, 291, 494, 504, 507, 731; **6:**335, 359, 369, 388, 403, 406, 408, 418, 455, 508, 545, 547–49, 552, 658, 685–86, 956, 969, 972, 980–82, 1084, 1089, 1118, 1121, 1131, 1139, 1175, 1179, 1183, 1189–91, 1494, 1560, 1570; **7:**167, 713, 714; **8:**182, 549, 633, 733; **9:**72, 124, 126, 326, 331, 369, 488, 497, 522, 539, 588, 597, 619, 658–59, 661, 686, 690, 692, 699, 717, 732, 749, 789–90, 795–96, 798, 850; **10:**131, 150, 428, 433, 454–55, 470, 500, 510, 513, 516, 519, 526, 538–39, 575, 590, 602, 604, 668, 686, 696, 698, 746, 921, 996; **11:**28, 64, 67–69, 71, 75, 77, 81–83, 118, 144, 167, 220, 275, 313, 372, 376–77, 416, 486, 494, 504–6, 510, 513, 515, 545, 690; **12:**12, 238, 260, 269, 274, 318, 584, 592–93, 666, 672, 686, 705, 722–23, 729–30, 733; OF THE LORD/YAHWEH **1:**689, 759, 792, 882, 907, 978, 1056, 1065–67; **2:**11, 25, 88, 124–26, 135, 138–40, 160, 193, 780; **3:**70, 477, 498, 1056; **4:**214, 792; **5:**143, 507, 730; **6:**84, 210, 212, 280–81, 330, 336, 685, 1086, 1089, 1101–2, 1107, 1109–11, 1113, 1117–21, 1128–30, 1136, 1143, 1152, 1172, 1175, 1180, 1182–85, 1188–90, 1254, 1529, 1532, 1534, 1438, 1540, 1555, 1559–60, 1562–65, 1570, 1573, 1588, 1591; **7:**321; **8:**439; **9:**65, 71, 81, 479; **11:**65, 67–71, 126, 216, 438, 504, 746, 751, 762; **12:**541

GLOSSOLALIA
8:201; **10:**55, 599, 794, 943–45, 950, 959–61, 967, 980; **11:**91, 142

GLUTTON, GLUTTONY
2:1166; **5:**783; **6:**1237; **7:**85; **8:**269, 324; **9:**23, 127, 165, 167; **11:**535

GNASH, GNASHING
4:458, 820, 829; **5:**777; **7:**178; **8:**226, 311, 314, 418; **9:**278; **10:**436

GNAT, GNATS
1:688, 747–48, 925; **4:**1105; **5:**529, 540, 573, 584, 593; **8:**436; **9:**202, 348

GNOSTICISM
1:14; **5:**232; **8:**54, 83, 291; **9:**498, 506, 517, 521, 756; **10:**30, 705, 897; **11:**503, 527, 561, 568, 604, 722, 775, 783, 830; **12:**69, 82, 85, 368, 474, 476, 520, 531

GNOSTICS
1:14, 46, 85; **8:**53; **9:**498, 506; **10:**823; **11:**88, 184, 400, 422, 438, 450–51, 489; **12:**325, 475

GOAD, GOADS
1:67; **5:**327, 413; **9:**442; **10:**337; **12:**669

GOAT, GOATS
FEMALE **1:**1025, 1035–36; **2:**127; **1:**217, 219–20,

245, 600, 605, 916, 986, 999, 1011, 1013–14, 1024, 1033, 1051, 1066, 1072, 1080, 1098, 1111–12, 1118, 1125, 1152; **2:**230, 232–33, 589, 685, 832, 846, 879, 1127, 1166; **3:**522, 608–9, 691, 714, 721, 901, 967, 1003, 1007, 1142; **4:**597–98, 608–11, 1100; **5:**345, 386, 395, 403, 418, 715; **6:**157, 277, 467, 1377, 1528, 1546, 1569; **7:**36, 108, 111–13, 116–18, 139, 376; **8:**33; **9:**303, 361; **10:**474, 642; **11:**87; **12:**74, 104, 107, 110, 117, 247, 704, 717; HAIR **1:**219–20; **2:**1127; **3:**901, 1003; MALE/HE-GOAT(S) **1:**1035, 1110, 1118, 1158; **2:**78, 127; **3:**712, 730; **5:**255; **6:**277, 1461, 1568, 1586; SHEEP AND **1:**218–20, 1000, 1009, 1076, 1081; **2:**148; **3:**647; **4:**609; **7:**148, 411; **8:**455; WILD **4:**598, 608–9, 611; **6:**277, 1528. *See also* KID

GOD, METAPHORS FOR

See GOD, METAPHORS FOR *in PERSONS IN THE BIBLE*

GOD, NAMES FOR

See GOD, NAMES FOR/TITLES OF *in PERSONS IN THE BIBLE*

GOD, SON OF

See under JESUS THE CHRIST, NAMES FOR/TITLES OF *in PERSONS IN THE BIBLE*

GODDESS, GODDESSES

1:233, 239, 242, 622, 1026, 1125; **2:**164, 178, 276, 344, 374, 385, 392, 410, 612, 755, 772, 797, 1017, 1198; **3:**421, 886, 1108; **4:**11, 39–40, 85, 193, 211, 243, 276, 329, 331–32, 395, 492, 603, 618, 621; **5:**4–5, 13, 27, 53, 63, 84, 90, 94, 101, 397, 503, 511, 569, 651, 757; **6:**21, 638, 707, 1003, 1019, 1160, 1175, 1176, 1221, 1395, 1399, 1418, 1435, 1471, 1495; **7:**10, 200, 202, 224, 240, 419, 610, 612, 614; **8:**13–14, 21, 25, 368, 712; **9:**171; **10:**271, 274, 404; **11:**361, 440, 567, 682

GODLESS

2:1371; **4:**17, 57, 87, 91, 113, 116, 119, 250, 332, 400, 402, 577, 586; **5:**117–18, 141, 170, 462, 530; **6:**60, 128, 132, 353, 394, 396, 454; **7:**638; **9:**220, 460; **11:**398, 417, 791, 811, 847; **12:**356, 509, 579, 703, 712

GODLY

1:188, 382, 624, 1073, 1113, 1128; **2:**13, 872; **4:**724, 948; **5:**19, 25, 38, 49–50, 62, 70, 78, 108, 110, 113–14, 161, 198, 208, 210, 237, 261, 377, 532, 772; **6:**371, 389, 972, 981, 1063; **7:**181, 865; **8:**172; **9:**147; **10:**439, 485, 815, 849; **11:**53, 109–10, 815, 851–52, 871; **12:**276, 287, 291, 330, 336–38, 348, 352, 357–58, 413, 509

GODS

FALSE **1:**1010; **2:**255, 528, 602, 757; **3:**1110; **4:**697, 736; **5:**557, 559, 562; **6:**180, 599, 661, 1008–10; **7:**67, 363, 575; **10:**640; **11:**214, 289, 428, 696; **12:**447, 652; FOREIGN **1:**85, 580, 584, 586, 1075; **2:**197, 714–15, 763, 770, 824, 827, 841, 843, 854, 1016–18, 1029, 1047; **3:**90, 115, 129, 257, 713, 1109; **5:**44; **6:**356–57, 600, 722, 989, 1233; **7:**115, 665, 864–65; **8:**35; OTHER **1:**236, 259, 272, 276, 285, 528, 585–86, 688, 757, 759, 800, 825, 838, 840–42, 861, 869, 871, 949, 1118; **2:**21, 148, 197–98, 276, 280, 329, 344, 356, 374, 380, 392–93, 503, 511, 529–30, 714, 731, 748, 750, 755–60, 767–68, 792, 796, 798, 819, 821, 824, 854–55, 864, 871, 1020, 1027, 1175; **3:**96, 129, 138, 173, 195, 219, 255, 477, 599–600, 636, 645, 733, 849, 956, 959; **4:**30, 32, 38, 44, 50, 204, 736, 843, 995, 1006–7, 1145, 1170, 1221; **6:**7, 9, 21, 49, 82, 159, 176, 222, 281, 329, 341, 358, 379, 492, 559, 585, 596–602, 606, 620, 636–39, 655, 661–62, 670, 680, 684–85, 692–93, 741, 750, 761, 796, 872–73, 875, 892, 896, 913, 987, 989, 994, 1019, 1189–190, 1208, 1224, 1278, 1280, 1286, 1302; **7:**147, 226, 230–31, 235, 289–90, 419, 614, 674, 675, 779; **8:**22, 163; **9:**153, 374; **10:**413, 433, 922, 930; **11:**148, 361, 784, 808; **12:**735; STRANGE **2:**529, 535; **10:**245

GOLD

CROWN(S) **4:**122, 154, 286; **5:**843; **12:**631, 648, 668; (EAR)RING(S) **1:**937; **2:**809; **4:**635; **5:**218; **6:**1167–68; **12:**194; **1:**164, 622, 861, 900–901, 906, 932, 972, 1110, 1138; **2:**78, 220, 245, 247, 363, 669, 760, 808, 1011–12, 1207, 1266, 1300; **3:**82, 87, 116, 168, 273, 290, 311, 432, 475, 484–85, 487, 510, 512, 526, 632, 864, 927, 1065, 1080; **4:**34, 148, 163, 165, 169, 218, 331, 434, 440, 509, 529, 531, 533, 554, 591; **5:**62, 91, 112, 119, 226, 355, 400, 446, 469–71, 534, 536, 551, 566–67, 570, 580, 695, 759, 824, 859; **6:**8, 74, 783, 1061–62, 1119, 1168, 1179, 1182, 1377, 1392–93; **7:**55, 61–62, 81–83, 136, 424, 724, 766, 771; **8:**104, 143, 435; **9:**171, 399; **10:**578, 829; **11:**277, 469, 801; **12:**87, 251–52, 265, 561, 598, 605, 681, 693–94, 723; OVERLAID WITH **1:**889, 915; **3:**511; **6:**990, 998; PLATED **1:**890, 1061; **3:**462, 484; **6:**1010; **7:**194; PURE **1:**890, 1163; **3:**531; **6:**1360; **10:**661; **12:**723; AND SILVER **1:**239, 715, 770, 782, 849, 888, 961; **2:**393, 809, 1011; **3:**424, 462, 474, 679, 687, 708, 721, 728, 1132; **4:**67, 104, 222, 369, 502, 524; **5:**271, 297, 536, 550, 585, 687, 825, 849; **6:**71–72, 407, 509, 662, 944, 965, 969, 988, 990, 1010, 1167, 1220, 1224, 1230, 1325, 1371, 1518; **7:**21–22, 54, 57, 81, 140, 147, 189, 194, 235, 260, 787–88, 805; **9:**363, 396; **11:**845; **12:**261, 633; TALENTS **1:**262; **3:**84, 431, 728; **6:**1361

GOLDEN CALF, CALVES

See under CALF

GOLDEN RULE, THE
1:998, 1133; **3:**1017–19; **8:**171, 210, 213–15; **9:**146–47
GOLDSMITHS
3:768, 770
GOOD
CREATION **1:**359–60, 365, 401, 513, 517; **5:**126, 232; **6:**387, 1473; **8:**291; **10:**428, 526, 823; **11:**291; AND/OR EVIL **1:**88, 141, 350, 361, 405, 574, 640, 672; **2:**256, 442, 1109, 1314; **3:**654, 1041, 1086, 1172; **4:**470–71, 483–84, 486–88, 504, 547, 557, 581; **5:**12, 29–30, 46, 70–71, 73, 109, 112, 114, 116–17, 119, 121, 125–28, 134, 140, 142, 148–49, 151, 160, 167, 170, 180, 247, 285, 306, 330, 456, 498, 544, 552, 559, 570, 574, 616, 708, 724, 787, 801; **6:**92, 94, 210, 228, 545, 733, 777, 787, 935, 990, 1001, 1058, 1487, 1495; **7:**2–5, 9, 101, 373, 868; **8:**70, 444; **9:**151, 244, 347, 416–17, 553, 663, 722; **10:**93, 108, 527, 570, 641; **11:**87, 393, 435, 625, 627; **12:**72, 160, 427, 579, 652, 654; FOR/FROM/OVER EVIL **2:**819, 1159–60, 1164, 1167, 1171; **4:**176, 503; **5:**168, 220, 717; **6:**926; **7:**8; **10:**124, 192, 533, 701, 715; **12:**68, 72, 152, 286; GOD/THE LORD/YAHWEH IS **1:**209, 1051; **2:**1013; **4:**464, 814, 970, 1119; **5:**329; **6:**1051, 1492; **7:**373, 541, 633; **11:**812; **12:**264; NEWS **1:**15, 84, 122, 190–93, 199, 511, 645, 707, 735, 804, 814, 841; **2:**267, 893, 902, 912, 1051, 1057, 1201–3, 1230, 1295, 1316, 1327, 1339; **3:**21, 24, 56, 88, 96, 197, 208–9, 295, 402, 509, 525, 612, 643, 738, 996, 1041, 1168; **4:**270, 403, 669, 672, 674, 692, 694–95, 698, 706, 724, 731, 769, 778, 787, 794, 797, 803, 811, 814–16, 824, 830, 835, 840, 843, 845, 849, 854, 867, 878, 882, 888, 903, 917–18, 920–21, 945, 948, 969–70, 993, 995, 998, 1015, 1017, 1025, 1042, 1044, 1052, 1055, 1065–67, 1070, 1073, 1089, 1091, 1106, 1112, 1118–19, 1128, 1131, 1151, 1170, 1182, 1185–86, 1188, 1190, 1196, 1204, 1206–7, 1209, 1225–26, 1229, 1235–36, 1238, 1252, 1260–61, 1267, 1269, 1277; **5:**152–53, 170, 220, 298, 306, 349, 645, 708; **6:**39–40, 49, 55, 58, 68–69, 112, 113, 117, 124, 136–38, 142, 146, 148, 157–58, 160, 180–81, 213, 226, 229, 237, 240, 247, 266–67, 270–71, 278, 281–83, 305, 366, 408, 457, 513, 691, 694, 728, 754, 806, 810, 813–14, 865, 867–68, 918, 920, 926, 972, 1085, 1188, 1191, 1292, 1356, 1364, 1413, 1450, 1452, 1477, 1492, 1501, 1503, 1563; **7:**91, 307, 425–26, 561, 569, 575, 588–89, 606; **8:**89, 106, 132, 174, 289–90, 329, 352, 501, 528–31, 533, 536–37, 539–40, 585, 596, 608; **9:**25, 29, 41, 47, 65–66, 86, 105, 108, 112, 116, 121, 131–32, 143, 167, 174, 194, 196–97, 199, 274, 281, 313, 349, 360, 374, 377, 389, 398, 401, 442, 457, 459, 463, 473, 479, 487, 490, 496, 507, 554–55, 573, 581, 662–63, 743, 754, 776, 840, 843–44; **10:**45–46, 63, 66, 140, 144–45, 180, 198–99, 202, 208, 227, 246, 267, 278, 283, 308, 364, 415, 423, 428, 438, 448, 463, 469, 599, 667, 672, 675, 936; **11:**152, 166, 186, 195, 205, 275, 289, 292, 298, 385, 483, 628, 629, 651, 691, 711, 797, 843, 895; **12:**10, 52, 55, 70, 162, 197, 238, 240, 248, 253, 257, 260, 263, 266, 302, 615, 666; SHEPHERD (*see* GOD, METAPHORS FOR *in PERSONS IN THE BIBLE*; JESUS THE CHRIST, METAPHORS FOR *in PERSONS IN THE BIBLE*); WAY **1:**178; **3:**497, 501; **4:**313, 501; **6:**628–29, 631; **10:**658; WORK(S) **2:**931; **3:**501, 538, 580, 625, 761, 1003; **5:**138, 320, 678, 730, 867; **8:**183, 201, 408, 413, 698; **9:**73, 83, 279, 726; **10:**161, 166, 199, 339, 420, 446, 448, 574, 686, 725, 993; **11:**30, 119, 130, 239, 314, 337, 356, 389, 393–95, 419, 431, 441, 483–84, 486, 531, 555, 593, 595, 805, 841, 845, 852, 866, 870, 872–80; **12:**9, 121, 128, 274, 337, 444
GOOD FRIDAY
1:96, 189, 697; **2:**90, 97, 236, 1003; **5:**731; **6:**440, 1017; **8:**493, 660; **9:**130, 826; **10:**342; **12:**4, 441
GOSPEL, GOSPELS
APOCRYPHAL **1:**14; **8:**137, 147, 558, 710; **9:**76; CHRISTIAN **1:**84, 891; **2:**1050, 1232; **3:**612; **6:**381; **7:**301; **8:**250; **9:**437, 473; **10:**31, 106, 143, 249, 311, 335, 343, 362, 548, 717, 733, 750; **11:**219, 340, 493–94, 567, 610, 635, 696, 749; **12:**545, 606, 701; CONCERNING/OF JESUS CHRIST **1:**84, 174, 190; **2:**855; **8:**518, 530, 536, 539; **9:**300; **10:**427, 554, 591, 604, 618, 627, 750; **11:**131, 207, 796, 842; **12:**661; FORM(S/ULA/ULATION) OF **8:**83, 108, 509, 529; **9:**6, 13, 503–4, 509, 850, 863; **11:**152, 208, 218, 291, 620, 780, 794; **12:**515; OF JESUS **6:**551; **9:**479, 718; **10:**127, 188, 192, 239, 312, 413–14, 420, 423, 426, 502, 505, 528, 604, 619, 621, 631, 636, 655, 666, 672, 676, 681, 687, 695–96, 718, 733; **12:**155; MESSAGE **1:**60–61, 169, 190–91, 193, 199; **2:**357; **4:**728; **6:**516; **7:**44; **8:**108, 163, 271, 296, 533, 690; **9:**708; **10:**67, 79, 241, 274, 341, 404, 415, 424, 427, 432, 445, 451, 504, 629, 645, 754; **11:**206, 211, 232, 239, 252, 255, 319, 351, 492, 541, 569, 579, 594, 607, 615, 635, 648, 870; **12:**515, 529, 533, 666; NARRATIVE(S) **1:**209, 836, 880; **2:**1008; **8:**66–67, 70, 134, 245, 298, 460; **9:**45, 91, 98, 113, 158, 160, 248, 503, 508–9, 516, 523–24, 530–31, 533, 544–46, 551, 554, 558, 575, 580, 588, 591, 594, 608, 635, 651, 661, 679, 681, 709, 713, 721, 729, 777, 784, 806, 810, 824, 832, 838, 850, 853–54, 856, 863; **10:**40, 72, 80, 423, 730; **11:**247; **12:**64; OF PAUL

10:192, 201, 234, 261, 267, 283–84, 305, 322, 329, 333–34, 362, 376, 380–82, 418, 427, 450, 484, 505, 549, 717, 811, 813, 830, 835–36, 868, 877, 927, 973, 980; **11:**24, 74, 82, 148, 167, 199, 202, 205, 210, 217, 226, 242, 246–47, 260, 287, 291, 308, 318, 340, 348, 553, 567, 569–70, 570, 575–77, 579, 588, 591, 611, 613, 620, 623, 636, 640, 662, 678, 680–81, 705, 778, 794, 797, 836; **12:**62, 239; PREACH(ES/ED/ING) THE **1:**190–91, 195, 199; **3:**624; **5:**814; **8:**267, 535, 557, 565, 593, 602, 627–28, 687–88, 690; **9:**196, 487; **10:**105–6, 140, 150, 155, 188, 239, 339, 374, 666, 773, 793, 815, 905–7, 910, 913, 973, 977; **11:**7, 18, 45, 55, 63, 90, 134, 144, 149, 190, 213, 216, 218, 225, 245, 256, 279, 298, 363, 372, 422, 461–62, 475, 488, 674, 699; **12:**164, 237, 253, 255, 260, 294, 482, 632, 713; PROCLAIM/PROCLAMATION OF THE **1:**86, 414; **2:**768, 855; **6:**1563; **7:**801; **8:**602, 729; **9:**41, 65, 220, 225, 292, 313, 479, 679; **10:**21, 31, 70, 74, 91, 95, 103, 113, 126–27, 138, 140, 153, 162, 165, 197–98, 227, 232, 241, 283, 311, 335, 341, 356, 359, 367, 419, 426–27, 617, 768–69, 811, 935, 982; **11:**55, 75, 183, 201–2, 215, 219, 225, 229, 277, 280, 293, 309, 320, 348, 355, 461, 462, 481, 488, 490, 492, 537, 541, 547, 558, 560, 569, 585, 591, 607, 612, 614, 617–18, 651, 662–63, 678, 694, 698, 700, 836, 858; **12:**245, 260, 293, 302, 345, 479, 537, 696, 713; SOCIAL **1:**109; **7:**396; **9:**324; **10:**596; **11:**877; SPREAD(ING/S) THE **1:**1166; **8:**627, 706; **10:**32, 130, 390, 638; **11:**57, 61, 82, 216, 232, 288, 425, 462, 483; SYNOPTIC **1:**132, 168; **4:**673; **5:**15; **6:**1564; **7:**15, 869, 876; **8:**4, 29, 35, 40, 57–59, 61–62, 68, 73–77, 81–83, 92, 222, 298–99, 348, 359, 460, 513, 702; **9:**124, 138, 166, 176, 202, 212, 346, 410, 415, 418, 451, 493–94, 497, 501–2, 504, 509, 523, 528, 530–32, 534, 539, 543–44, 549, 552, 593, 611–12, 619–20, 675, 684–85, 691, 698, 701, 707, 711, 717, 719, 757, 762, 799, 802–3, 808, 810, 814–15, 818, 820, 829, 831–33, 840, 846, 849; **10:**115, 137; **11:**673, 756, 780; **12:**42, 84, 105, 369, 395, 403, 704, 727; TRADITION(S) **8:**62, 70, 77–78, 80, 193, 323, 356, 517; **9:**40, 207, 210, 216, 644, 684; **10:**43, 45, 115, 129–30, 198, 389, 718, 740; **11:**608, 620, 794; **12:**193, 223, 283, 328, 357, 561; WRITER(S) **1:**179; **2:**983; **4:**673, 765–66, 802, 849, 874, 1156, 1186; **5:**307; **7:**873; **8:**45, 50–51, 72–73, 77, 84, 86, 568; **9:**179, 454, 585, 612, 693; **10:**521; **11:**149, 756; **12:**74

GOSSIP
2:1123; **4:**260, 495; **5:**118, 167, 173, 182, 226, 331, 349, 735–36, 772; **6:**629, 654, 657, 1483; **7:**20; **10:**297; **11:**645, 806, 821–22, 825, 876, 879; **12:**218, 276

GOURD, GOURDS
1:218; **3:**485; **6:**1247; **7:**520

GOVERNMENT, GOVERNMENTS
1:180, 213–14, 262, 265, 267, 581, 594, 623, 694–95, 702, 770, 828, 934, 1143; **2:**16, 96, 148, 376, 384, 431, 487, 564, 577, 608–9, 617, 629, 649, 669, 679, 681, 719, 811, 855, 977, 1051, 1213; **3:**28, 35, 48, 50, 52–53, 55, 132, 667, 680, 700, 708, 715, 735, 878, 883, 887, 924, 941, 953, 966, 1114, 1118; **4:**12–13, 96, 113, 166, 232, 260, 265, 282, 287, 454, 867, 935, 965, 1011, 1084; **5:**91–92, 136, 143, 153, 214, 217, 227, 233, 242–43, 245–46, 258, 377, 498, 525, 801; **6:**38, 61, 64, 90, 124, 143, 265, 413, 580, 582, 745–46, 826, 851, 958, 1069, 1376, 1413, 1415, 1417; **7:**57, 62, 77, 81, 83, 102, 112, 342, 367, 428–29, 557, 559, 569, 594, 619, 624, 635, 638–40, 694, 700, 728; **8:**103, 148, 194, 420, 477, 494, 496, 628, 660; **9:**304, 379, 658; **10:**589, 716–17, 719, 723, 912; **11:**454, 677, 726, 761, 768, 797; **12:**9, 76, 234, 274, 277; CENTRAL **1:**314; **2:**417, 558, 615, 681; **3:**55; **4:**271; DIVINE **6:**582–83, 586–88, 596, 751, 754, 1595; FORM(S)/SYSTEM(S) OF **2:**426, 504, 716, 818, 961; **3:**48; **4:**102, 105, 254; **6:**5; **7:**558; **12:**219; OFFICIAL(S) **3:**137, 525; **4:**125; **5:**237; **7:**560; **8:**195; ROMAN (*see under* ROMAN)

GOVERNOR, GOVERNORS
1:224, 248, 265, 267–69, 1017; **2:**570, 718; **3:**12, 52, 293, 622, 666–67, 673, 679, 681, 685–87, 693, 702–6, 709–10, 730, 741, 748, 751, 757, 768, 775, 781–83, 787, 789, 793–94, 796, 815, 846–49, 899, 953, 1112; **4:**55–56, 62, 95, 105, 129, 135, 140–41, 165, 197, 206, 214, 223, 233, 247–49, 260–61, 275, 282, 286, 289, 516, 1084; **5:**517, 801, 859; **6:**582, 826, 842, 857–59, 943, 994, 1415, 1593; **7:**141, 162, 708–9, 715–16, 719, 738, 770, 847, 860; **8:**485, 717, 719; **9:**62, 212, 310, 385; **10:**313–14, 341, 737; **11:**138, 401, 760; GOD AS **1:**722, 814, 861; OF JUDAH **1:**268; **2:**306, 688; **3:**293, 691, 708, 782, 793; **6:**560, 857, 942, 1348; **7:**715, 730–31, 737, 765, 770; ROMAN (*see under* ROMAN)

GRACE
IN/OF/THROUGH CHRIST/JESUS **3:**433, 619; **9:**534, 540, 591, 597, 599, 630, 852; **10:**807, 936, 984; **11:**29, 73, 179, 191, 204, 208, 313, 317, 328, 347–48, 373, 663, 834, 877; **12:**69, 127, 316; DIVINE **1:**337, 951; **2:**21, 111, 300, 345, 412, 480, 488, 970, 1050, 1082, 1154, 1255, 1298; **3:**145, 295, 332, 364–65, 376, 381, 408, 421, 427, 429, 497, 501–2, 542, 568, 570, 632, 636, 657, 736;

GRACE *(continued)*
4:806; **5:**59, 108, 150, 170, 189–91; **6:**57, 1239; **8:**533; **10:**22, 60, 97–98, 144, 334, 356, 382, 387, 579, 603, 672; **11:**481, 871, 876, 900; **12:**353; AND FORGIVENESS **1:**1057; **2:**1317, 1366; **3:**426–27, 738; **5:**190; **7:**537; **8:**217, 379; **9:**343; **10:**47; OF GOD **1:**1036, 1073; **2:**130, 301, 356, 407, 494, 633, 670, 911, 940, 946, 970, 973, 975–78, 983, 989, 1007–8, 1014, 1019, 1050–51, 1082, 1099–1100, 1115, 1124, 1157, 1241, 1255, 1258–59, 1267, 1317, 1326–27, 1365–67, 1381; **3:**5, 40, 81, 88, 129, 167, 208, 234, 236, 244, 271, 274, 277, 287, 303, 407, 426, 433, 452, 630–31, 658, 681, 724, 738, 771; **4:**191, 312, 488, 632, 671, 701, 704, 706, 731, 753, 781, 783, 806–7, 815, 885–86, 888–89, 991–92, 1004, 1076, 1088–89, 1093, 1104, 1106, 1112, 1134, 1175, 1187, 1191, 1198, 1206, 1225, 1251, 1252, 1260; **5:**55, 122, 298, 323, 446, 479, 529; **6:**55, 346, 370, 379, 418, 468, 470, 485, 493, 601, 734, 758–59, 814, 1140, 1172, 1292, 1458; **7:**164, 370, 537, 800; **8:**62, 145, 157, 205, 218, 221, 288, 394, 533, 647; **9:**31, 60, 66, 73, 78, 86, 92, 107–8, 113, 128, 131, 173, 195, 197, 254, 279, 285, 288, 298, 305, 311, 324, 327–28, 333, 342–43, 346, 348, 383–84, 473, 479, 534, 561, 571, 591, 597, 665, 759, 796–97, 852; **10:**21–22, 47, 72, 85, 93, 96–98, 101, 128, 163, 176, 188, 194, 201, 208, 218–19, 223, 233, 256, 281–86, 322, 339, 343, 348, 350, 358, 376, 387, 466, 468, 471, 478–79, 482, 528, 531, 533, 537, 549, 579, 591, 605, 676, 680–81, 707, 753, 787, 798–800, 807–9, 814, 826–27, 830, 837, 840–41, 845, 847, 849, 852, 880, 884, 888, 914, 916, 918, 936, 938–39, 943, 948, 954–55, 957, 963, 974, 977, 982–84, 990, 994, 996, 1001–3; **11:**3, 23, 28, 38, 45–47, 57, 59, 69, 73, 75, 82–83, 87, 96, 99, 118–22, 130–32, 139, 144–45, 149, 165–67, 186, 202, 204, 207–8, 215, 226, 231–32, 234, 244–46, 248, 253, 260, 263–64, 268, 277–78, 284, 291, 308, 313, 317, 319, 337–38, 344, 347–48, 373, 377, 392–94, 407–8, 410, 413, 466, 484–86, 504, 517, 530, 569, 576, 590–91, 610, 621, 663, 669, 715, 746, 860, 871, 873–74, 877, 880, 900; **12:**38–39, 42, 75–76, 78, 123, 134, 154, 166, 232, 248, 261, 269, 318, 411, 485–86, 540, 729; GOD'S/THE LORD'S GREAT **10:**96–98, 101, 110, 177; JUSTIFICATION BY **1:**190, 193; **2:**1255, 1259; **3:**503; **4:**674, 807; **10:**517, 533; AND (THE) LAW **1:**196; **2:**199, 484, 488, 513; **11:**191; OF THE LORD **1:**409, 1191; **2:**408, 511; **10:**60, 169, 209, 225, 765, 1003; **11:**347, 546, 770–71, 794, 903; **12:**734; AND LOVE **1:**84, 1142; **2:**346; **4:**704, 706; **10:**484, 602, 840; **11:**179, 394; MEANS OF **1:**40, 1036; **2:**489; **3:**310, 386, 464–65, 487, 497; **4:**1015; **5:**63; **10:**234, 525, 744; AND MERCY **1:**1036; **2:**125, 904, 1326; **3:**137, 421, 738; **4:**1088–89, 1134, 1174; **5:**446, 470; **6:**421, 605, 1155; **9:**630; **10:**678, 694, 924; **12:**160, 482; AND PEACE **4:**1188; **10:**380, 421; **11:**38, 202, 208, 369–70, 481, 588, 770, 862; **12:**178, 247–48, 250, 334; SAVING **2:**1050, 1082; **6:**759; **7:**164; **9:**253; **10:**8, 21, 85, 98, 126, 176, 235, 345, 349, 352; **11:**836, 876–77; **12:**534; SIN AND **1:**190; **2:**1049; **3:**737, 738; **10:**523, 530, 539, 543, 548–49, 551, 877; **11:**41, 166, 389; THEOLOGY OF (*see under* THEOLOGY); AND TRUTH **1:**946, 955; **3:**502; **5:**308; **6:**470; **9:**523–24, 598, 600, 659; **12:**593

GRACIOUS
1:84, 207, 274, 329, 337, 423, 554–55, 568–69, 573–74, 635–36, 686, 770, 925, 940, 942, 946, 957, 1008, 1018, 1184; **2:**65–66, 300, 428, 480–81, 670, 741, 747, 757, 780, 803, 866, 1013, 1030, 1207, 1212, 1324; **3:**198, 278, 332, 379, 382, 407, 470, 499, 525, 529, 542, 552, 582, 602, 612, 617, 630–31, 636, 718, 723, 727, 730–31, 756, 758, 761, 793–94, 1153; **4:**67, 411, 502, 554, 671–72, 733–34, 768, 770, 778–79, 783, 805, 811, 829, 833, 838, 848, 934, 983, 999, 1004, 1020–21, 1042, 1088, 1134, 1136, 1138, 1142, 1149, 1173–74, 1187, 1205, 1247, 1250, 1252, 1259, 1261, 1267; **5:**118, 151, 161, 193, 234, 238, 562, 663, 665, 683, 732, 861; **6:**421, 472, 478, 650, 758–59, 793, 1278; **7:**319, 347, 391, 484, 753, 800, 859, 861; **8:**214, 274, 292, 383–84; **9:**58, 73, 106, 172, 727, 850, 864; **10:**246, 286, 444, 847; **11:**119, 129, 202, 216, 239, 273, 285, 304, 306–7, 327–28, 337, 352, 373, 382, 409, 411, 637, 646, 648, 662, 896, 904; **12:**5, 42, 50, 173, 258, 276, 595; ACT(S)/ACTION(S)/ACTIVITY **1:**364, 413, 449, 517, 1152; **2:**969, 1274; **4:**191, 806, 990–92, 1004, 1236; **5:**825; **6:**217, 478, 482; **7:**523; **8:**33, 62, 172; **11:**187, 204, 246, 255, 271, 512, 514, 516, 576, 591, 871; **12:**43, 107, 127, 260; GIFT(S) **1:**1051; **4:**824, 1125; **5:**320, 859; **8:**400; **9:**865; **11:**245, 277, 337; **12:**145, 287; GOD/LORD/YAHWEH AS **1:**277, 390, 449, 988, 1098; **2:**359, 479, 484, 796, 1257; **3:**484, 611, 617, 637, 731; **4:**191, 200, 502, 674, 697, 733, 781, 797, 806, 815–16, 824, 839, 885, 933–34, 940, 984, 990–92, 1001, 1004, 1025, 1087, 1236, 1260; **5:**173, 186, 320, 562, 825; **6:**57, 217, 332, 420, 478, 482, 809, 812, 1281, 1497; **7:**124, 264, 319, 369, 472–74, 553, 725, 736, 750, 801; **8:**172, 394; **9:**46, 51, 56, 91, 118, 296; **10:**133, 170, 387, 403, 516; **11:**208; **12:**145, 265, 308; "GRACIOUS, SLOW TO ANGER" **2:**741; **4:**671, 780; **5:**561, 655; **6:**697,

717, 1140, 1166; AND MERCIFUL **1:**940; **3:**239, 617, 811–12; **4:**913, 1133, 1148; **7:**472–73, 477, 486, 518, 525
GRACIOUSNESS
1:196, 208, 411, 442, 475, 567, 569, 572–73, 628–29, 636, 679, 746, 892, 927, 937, 945–46, 948, 951–52, 961, 1021; **2:**674, 804, 807, 1207–8, 1248, 1257, 1262, 1292–93, 1297; **3:**197, 332, 587, 692, 714, 736; **4:**202, 348, 570, 990; **6:**421, 821; **7:**345, 518, 800; **8:**611; **9:**540, 616, 865; **10:**318, 355; **11:**64, 136, 360, 373, 376, 389, 391, 410, 434–35, 441; **12:**248, 585, 625
GRAFT (*OR* GRAFTS, *ETC.*)
1:994; **2:**481; **6:**815, 1272; **10:**11, 627, 680, 684–86, 693, 709; **11:**114, 284, 404
GRAIN, GRAINS
1:217–19, 224–25, 536, 539, 620–22, 627, 629, 634, 695, 986, 1017, 1020, 1043, 1133, 1149, 1159, 1163, 1189; **2:**127, 147–48, 228, 230, 403, 412, 467–68, 471, 589, 607, 609, 668, 670, 796, 835, 853, 893, 909, 913, 915, 919, 921, 923, 930–31, 935, 945, 1005, 1029, 1110, 1141, 1152; **3:**128, 205, 624, 779, 820, 846–47; **4:**224, 381, 387, 511, 513, 555, 593, 636, 685; **5:**139, 188, 237–38, 261, 731, 768, 824, 827; **6:**93, 174, 227, 235, 238, 943, 1148, 1176, 1492, 1580, 1583–84, 1589, 1593, 1605; **7:**258, 261, 275, 296, 309, 314, 319, 323, 329, 333–34, 360, 366, 390, 406, 416, 424–25, 771, 777–78, 811; **8:**59, 61, 278, 435, 554, 556–57, 576; **9:**86, 114, 133, 148, 256, 307–8, 321, 711; **10:**353, 989; **11:**470, 822; **12:**136, 552, 710; HARVEST (*see* HARVEST: BARLEY/GRAIN/WHEAT) OFFERING(S) (*see under* OFFERING); PARCHES **1:**1017; **2:**921
GRANARY, GRANARIES
1:621; **2:**374; **7:**314; **9:**86
GRAPE, GRAPES
1:218, 223, 275, 403, 536, 615, 665, 1179; **2:**64, 121–22, 467, 471, 668, 849; **3:**624, 847; **4:**452, 511; **5:**427, 607, 699, 757; **6:**88–89, 544, 892, 1033, 1216–17, 1246, 1580; **7:**213, 265, 268–69, 272–73, 309, 329, 333, 430, 448, 679; **8:**670; **9:**151, 757; **10:**574; **11:**710; HARVEST (*see under* HARVEST); SOUR **1:**25, 239; **2:**125; **3:**650; **4:**404; **6:**1219, 1254, 1257, 1264–65; **8:**652; WILD **6:**88–89; **9:**757
GRASS
1:196, 290; **2:**181, 188; **3:**680; **4:**356, 513, 604, 618, 770, 1051, 1087; **5:**56, 150, 337, 547; **6:**95, 141, 168, 331–32, 336, 338–39, 343, 387, 451, 529, 690, 1499; **7:**74, 576; **8:**324, 601; **9:**21, 259–60, 409, 597; **10:**616; **11:**452; **12:**266, 273, 612, 710
GRASSHOPPER, GRASSHOPPERS
1:1081; **5:**355; **6:**343
GRATITUDE
1:81, 239, 277, 280, 373, 393, 555, 572, 786, 871, 883, 901, 913, 926, 939, 963, 1009, 1051–52, 1099, 1184; **2:**277, 285, 359, 388, 403, 406, 412, 413, 482, 817, 819, 908, 911, 995, 1212, 1347; **3:**19, 28, 108, 189, 407, 610, 1052, 1055, 1061; **4:**537–38, 540, 572, 632, 647, 727, 769, 782, 786, 790–91, 815–16, 857, 879, 887, 895, 903, 933–35, 940, 990, 992–93, 995, 1058, 1061, 1070, 1077, 1079, 1110, 1126, 1134, 1147–49, 1155, 1202, 1223–25, 1279; **5:**327, 499, 501, 550, 579, 612, 676, 689, 716, 776, 860–61; **6:**305, 439, 808, 1452; **7:**236, 357, 509, 721; **8:**591, 726; **9:**29, 75, 111, 169–70, 173, 308, 325–29, 362, 369–70; **10:**170, 318, 461, 478, 592, 603, 605, 637, 644, 816, 830, 923; **11:**31, 119, 297, 475, 482–83, 543, 617, 620, 648–49; **12:**124, 159–60, 345, 467; TO GOD/YAHWEH **1:**372, 424, 427, 492, 572, 1051; **4:**647, 783, 882–83, 891, 961, 1120, 1122, 1237, 1241; **10:**815; **11:**485, 548, 732
GRAVE, GRAVES
AS A BURIAL PLACE **1:**306, 585, 600, 1027, 1075, 1159; **2:**65, 104, 108, 449, 603, 687, 826, 1092, 1182, 1336; **3:**109, 238, 282, 581, 756–57, 769, 785, 839, 975, 984, 998, 1004, 1017, 1028, 1033, 1041–42, 1132, 1182; **4:**243, 296, 332, 352, 370, 442, 461, 636, 1028; **5:**38, 45, 125, 231–32, 253, 291, 300, 302, 337, 341, 354–55, 430, 460, 628, 651, 779; **6:**94, 158, 196, 223, 343, 433, 466–68, 640, 691, 702, 998, 1388, 1439, 1442–43, 1498, 1502–4, 1516, 1526; **7:**421, 505–6, 606, 724; **8:**319, 423, 436, 676; **9:**248, 251, 315, 471–73, 485, 585, 687, 692, 841; **10:**342, 541, 592; **11:**32, 85, 282, 419; MARKER **3:**998; **4:**443; **5:**779; **6:**1170, 1345; **8:**387; **12:**433
GRAVEL
4:463; **5:**187; **6:**1049
GRAVEN IMAGE, IMAGES
1:276; **2:**809–10; **5:**549; **8:**663
GRAY
1:1098; **2:**1061; **3:**370, 1153; **4:**343, 450, 488, 603; **5:**93, 162, 188, 317, 479, 687; **7:**257, 775, 783; **9:**101, 810; **10:**851–52; **12:**610
GREAT
APOSTLE **9:**118; **11:**355, 460, 795, 856; ASSEMBLY **1:**306; **2:**752; **3:**732, 804; **4:**26, 77, 161; **5:**14; **7:**877; BANQUET **1:**1026; **6:**1527; **9:**26, 35, 283, 288, 306, 458; CITY **3:**1097, 1100; **6:**157, 618, 741, 1384; **7:**111, 482–83, 493, 501, 522–23, 597, 694; **10:**258, 266; **12:**632, 642, 677, 683,

GREAT *(continued)*
693–94, 720; COMMANDMENT(S) **1:**207; **3:**1015; **5:**307; **6:**641; **8:**123, 189, 213, 215, 401, 409, 419, 423, 442, 450, 679; **9:**233, 704; CROWD(S) **6:**1589; **8:**560; **9:**137, 142, 176, 208, 707; **12:**148, 621; DAY **1:**845, 999, 1003, 1107, 1156, 1160; **3:**673, 804–5; **6:**221–22; **7:**223, 276, 666, 669, 681–82, 875; **9:**542; **10:**398, 691; **12:**566, 614, 667, 677, 699; KING **1:**267, 780, 801, 1151–52; **3:**704, 706, 859, 909, 1065, 1095, 1101; **4:**5, 865, 872–73, 979, 1060–61; **5:**92, 128; **6:**329, 556, 1083, 1159, 1393, 1430; **7:**21, 62, 248–49, 263, 272, 275, 869; **8:**402; **10:**66; MULTITUDE **3:**560; **4:**212; **6:**156; **7:**124, 354; **12:**557, 618, 621, 624–26, 629, 649, 666, 672, 695; NATION(S) **1:**308, 422–23, 488, 623, 652, 654, 931; **2:**35, 177, 180, 194, 215, 221, 477, 481; **3:**1095, 1098, 1103, 1106; **5:**564; **6:**432, 913, 968, 1364, 1425; **7:**367, 425; SEA/SEA MONSTER **1:**739, 800; **2:**262; **3:**865; **6:**1364, 1429, 1601; **7:**101; VOICE **12:**557, 564, 621, 643, 721

GREED
1:434, 477, 730, 755, 757, 760, 814, 850, 852, 878, 941, 1132; **2:**67, 195, 356, 723, 790, 872; **3:**159, 192, 332; **4:**485, 488, 534, 593, 749, 769, 787, 815, 848–49, 878–79, 891, 1079, 1112, 1199; **5:**55, 117, 132, 135, 152, 192, 206, 241, 264, 566, 612, 675, 772–73, 801; **6:**96, 239, 628, 630, 777, 1167, 1332, 1338, 1364, 1369, 1400, 1460, 1485, 1518; **7:**236, 268, 287, 416, 541, 549, 565, 585, 638, 694, 781, 804; **8:**204, 467, 649; **9:**84, 247, 251, 255, 257, 306, 312, 314, 362–64, 384, 702, 804; **10:**100–101, 232, 234, 322–23, 835, 998; **11:**129, 428, 430–31, 434–36, 629, 635, 642, 645–46, 702; **12:**163–64, 317, 344, 350–51, 491, 495

GREEK
BIBLE/CANON/OLD TESTAMENT/SEPTUAGINT/SCRIPTURE(S) **1:**8, 11–13, 43, 292, 300–301, 304; **2:**271; **4:**730; **6:**223, 966, 1092; **7:**156, 175; **11:**590, 850; **12:**9–10; CULTURE **1:**268, 290–91; **3:**1144; **5:**271, 759, 828; **7:**105, 118; **8:**13, 41, 45; **10:**231, 298; FORM/GRAMMAR/STYLE/SYNTAX **3:**1109; **4:**181, 184, 217–18, 305; **5:**642; **6:**731, 944; **8:**376, 436; **9:**531; **10:**769; **11:**237, 255, 355, 567, 588, 624, 649, 667; **12:**183, 230, 562–63, 578, 659; AND HEBREW TEXT(S) **1:**5, 17, 100; **5:**669, 692; HISTORIAN(S) **1:**267; **3:**1106, 1119; **4:**6, 34, 144, 169, 202, 218, 228; **6:**1398; **7:**61; JEW AND/OR **2:**1051; **8:**45; **10:**196, 209, 440, 484–85, 630, 665–66, 766, 882; **11:**115, 268, 272, 278, 644; **12:**239; LANGUAGE *or* KOINE/NT/SEPTUAGINT **1:**26, 114, 191; **3:**1108; **5:**652; **8:**13, 40–41, 106; **9:**9, 329; **10:**855; **11:**206, 256; **12:**4, 178; LETTER/PHRASE/TERM/WORD, ETC. **1:**2, 9, 17, 38, 178, 300, 304, 985, 1160; **3:**751, 768, 959, 962, 971, 1001, 1078, 1084, 1109, 1114, 1123, 1138; **4:**39, 56, 89, 106, 184, 188, 190, 217, 236, 250, 269, 290, 305, 653, 770, 843, 1024; **5:**15, 96, 262, 437, 439, 461, 463, 497, 498, 504, 507, 542, 552, 557, 562, 584, 642–43, 647, 652, 659, 670, 672, 787; **6:**4, 731, 934, 943, 952, 956–57, 960–61, 963, 974, 976–77, 994–95; **7:**63, 161, 177, 179–82, 188, 192, 616; **8:**37, 142, 164, 166–67, 176, 187, 201, 278, 298, 324, 358, 360, 395, 425, 436, 536, 545, 600, 688, 697; **9:**85, 128, 155, 171, 190, 196, 200, 227, 234, 236, 259, 295, 318, 329, 348, 367, 419, 497, 523, 531–32, 539, 546, 549–52, 599, 633–34, 641, 646, 657, 667, 677, 687, 690, 721, 748, 751, 758–59, 772, 779–81, 820; **10:**7, 113, 138, 161, 282, 374, 415, 440, 453, 459, 490, 642, 703, 768, 777, 790, 798, 800, 821, 828, 837, 938–39, 950, 952–53, 991; **11:**33, 46, 50, 63, 70, 75, 79, 92, 105, 109, 131, 167, 226, 234, 251, 253, 371, 375, 388–89, 392–93, 399, 402–3, 409, 422, 428, 435, 480–81, 484, 487–88, 491, 496–97, 500, 514, 522, 524, 526, 530, 533, 540–41, 544, 567, 588–89, 622, 624, 667, 688, 699, 703, 707, 711, 714, 717–18, 745, 755–58, 766, 827, 871, 895; **12:**6, 37, 81, 210, 230, 245, 246–47, 252–53, 259, 264, 282–83, 300–301, 333, 383, 388–89, 412, 454, 464, 478, 528, 533, 594, 611, 632, 659; LITERATURE/POETRY **1:**291, 462; **4:**168, 182, 211, 236, 243, 305; **5:**439, 510; **7:**50; **8:**204; **9:**117; **10:**247; **11:**204, 496, 501, 720; **12:**62, 82, 98, 148, 296; MANUSCRIPT(S)/MSS **1:**25, 101, 299, 302–4; **3:**743, 969, 1049; **4:**43, 63, 119, 143; **5:**553, 606–7, 611, 662, 719, 750, 756; **6:**985; **8:**3–5, 130, 211, 368, 742; **9:**316, 615, 874; **10:**17, 961, 1010; **11:**121, 230, 259, 500; **12:**14, 38, 53, 70, 136, 141, 333, 413, 747; NOVEL(S) **3:**1079–81, 1105, 1115, 1129, 1132, 1144, 1147–48, 1159; **10:**345; **11:**682; NT **1:**17, 25, 101, 131; **8:**1, 5–8, 91, 151, 231; **9:**471; **12:**150; PHILOSOPHER(S)/PHILOSOPHY **1:**18, 88, 192, 197, 290, 1014; **5:**14, 275, 301, 303, 460, 436, 498, 503, 505, 510, 518, 546–47, 579, 584, 597–98, 625; **7:**686; **8:**17, 677; **9:**506, 519, 758; **10:**71, 246; **11:**653, 864, 871; **12:**98; RECENSION(S)/VERSION(S) **1:**5, 28, 46; **2:**391, 737, 1199; **3:**3–4, 61, 862, 866, 886, 923, 945, 949, 969, 970–71, 976, 1069; **4:**22; **5:**448, 479, 765; **6:**180, 654, 696, 826, 839, 930–31; **7:**27, 62, 74, 83, 88, 149, 155–56, 174; **10:**64; **11:**72, 512; **12:**230, 233, 518; RELIGION **4:**39; **6:**223; **8:**21–22; **10:**271; RHETORIC **1:**192; **5:**606, 642; **11:**363; **12:**7, 22; TEXT(S) **1:**10–11, 30, 728, 730, 751; **2:**1079–80, 1109, 1119, 1122, 1266, 1287, 1381; **3:**87, 861–62,

1055; **4:**60, 125, 622; **5:**479, 559, 561, 608, 621, 634, 636, 642, 664, 666–67, 670, 683, 692, 697, 702, 705, 720, 729, 767, 779, 805, 818, 842, 859, 866; **6:**105, 567, 660, 761–62, 782, 859; **7:**72, 91, 189; **8:**1, 5–7, 29, 75, 91, 205, 308, 439, 544; **9:**108, 358, 418, 518, 543, 546, 549, 558–60, 566, 623, 667, 676, 689–90, 702, 722, 730, 741, 752, 758, 773, 794, 802–3, 808, 820, 831; **10:**258, 306, 336, 546, 656; **11:**205, 215, 225, 241, 259, 263, 269, 271, 285, 293, 295, 313–14, 320, 324–25, 355, 410, 483, 486, 589, 591, 599, 707, 883; **12:**31, 36–37, 50, 77, 86, 89, 110, 119, 122, 158, 187, 230, 246–47, 264, 440, 443, 446, 448–49, 459; TRANSLATION(S)/TRANSLATOR(S) **1:**42, 94, 284, 290, 293, 294–95, 300–301, 985, 1094; **2:**950; **3:**45, 95, 860, 956, 977, 1144; **4:**20, 36, 39, 111, 183, 218, 241, 657; **5:**118, 120, 268, 382, 558, 610, 642, 688–89, 692, 709, 765, 779, 828, 842; **6:**112, 635, 647, 722, 766, 784, 793, 809, 878, 930, 931, 941, 957, 1024; **7:**155–56, 242, 667; **8:**29, 152, 663; **10:**374; **11:**69, 790, 876; **12:**7, 9, 13, 28, 247, 518

GREEN
1:399, 430, 1098, 1143; **2:**55, 595, 1209; **3:**356; **4:**380, 402–3, 441, 445, 767; **5:**291, 317, 388, 824; **6:**142, 1336, 1466; **7:**236; **8:**661, 663; **9:**418, 452–53; **12:**610, 631; GRASS **4:**770; **8:**324, 601; TREE(S) **6:**601, 1159–60, 1224, 1296, 1430

GREETING
1:208, 635, 653, 1023; **2:**12, 65, 916, 1071, 1166, 1352; **3:**379, 699, 704, 721, 1025, 1050–51; **4:**127, 135, 154, 168, 188, 192, 255, 354, 547, 1061, 1156; **5:**400, 419, 682–83; **7:**51, 273; **8:**65, 438, 477, 500, 673; **9:**61, 134, 172, 220, 346, 435, 485, 536, 688, 690, 707, 846, 849; **10:**152, 379–80, 397, 421, 761, 763, 765; **11:**38, 178–79, 201–2, 341–42, 352–53, 367, 369–71, 377, 432, 465–66, 479, 481, 522, 554, 556, 588, 664, 668, 744, 770, 789–90, 832–33, 861–62, 878, 892, 899, 903–4; **12:**14, 178, 182, 184–86, 195, 232–33, 246–47, 333, 395, 429, 450, 454, 460, 481, 562, 568, 582

GRIDDLE, GRIDDLES
1:1019, 1049; **6:**1143. *See also* FRYING PAN

GRIEF
1:285, 389, 600, 707, 803, 1071, 1148; **2:**505, 748, 911–12, 945, 963, 967, 1002, 1021, 1086, 1090, 1092, 1094, 1097–98, 1136, 1192–93, 1195, 1198–99, 1201–3, 1205–9, 1232, 1240, 1247, 1297–99, 1303, 1305, 1309, 1318, 1337, 1339–42, 1355, 1371; **3:**353, 355, 458, 671, 733, 740–41, 806, 849, 901–2, 923, 981, 984, 1004, 1007–8, 1023, 1033, 1142; **4:**230, 304, 331, 351–52, 357–60, 371–72, 381–82, 459, 464, 571–72, 631–32, 669, 703–6, 719, 801, 852, 899, 1087, 1169, 1227–30; **5:**141, 230, 245, 295–96, 328, 557, 622, 696, 764, 777, 779, 809, 849; **6:**158, 170, 174, 202, 217, 658, 805, 956, 974, 980, 1015, 1017, 1019, 1021–22, 1030, 1034, 1036, 1044–45, 1051, 1058, 1070, 1072, 1081, 1104, 1177, 1194, 1196, 1201, 1274, 1299, 1340, 1343, 1345, 1383, 1450, 1452; **7:**142, 169, 272, 312, 318, 385, 385–86, 392, 417, 613; **8:**197, 714; **9:**27, 144, 159, 188, 207, 321, 432–33, 463, 485, 695, 779, 842, 844; **10:**199, 411, 445, 621, 624, 626–28, 631–32, 653, 666, 696, 766, 815, 984, 994; **11:**24, 50, 53, 99, 109, 121, 442, 707, 725; **12:**169, 211, 282, 441, 606, 693; DIVINE **1:**380, 395; **6:**78, 1343; **7:**386, 583; PROPHET'S **6:**15, 170, 1015, 1059, 1198, 1268, 1292, 1296, 1340, 1343, 1345, 1371, 1455; **7:**220, 232, 386

GRIND (*OR* GRINDS, *ETC.*)
1:932, 1017; **2:**859–60; **3:**554; **4:**463, 553; **5:**354–55; **6:**411, 762; **8:**446; **9:**330, 332–33; **12:**437

GROVE, GROVES
2:190, 853; **3:**1108; **6:**63; **7:**41, 241, 756; **9:**380, 801

GRUMBLING, GRUMBLINGS
4:1111; **5:**455, 532, 573; **9:**294, 358, 603–5, 609, 612; **10:**735, 916; **11:**37; **12:**55, 169, 195, 203, 221, 224, 317, 495

GUARD, GUARDS
CAPTAIN OF THE **1:**609, 614; **6:**860, 1079; **10:**180; DUTY **2:**36, 82, 89, 148; **3:**776; **6:**968, 1574–76, 1605; AS A NOUN **1:**221, 783; **2:**95, 199; **3:**18, 20, 33, 49, 230, 345, 451, 457, 574–75, 773, 775, 777, 793–94; **4:**78, 148, 283, 309, 395, 524; **5:**66, 133, 354, 394, 409, 731, 748; **6:**532, 606, 1541, 1558, 1574, 1577; **7:**11, 30, 32, 163, 618, 806; **8:**124, 369, 401, 459, 477, 497–501, 712, 716; **9:**387, 468, 473, 704; **10:**179, 314, 616, 758; **11:**128, 138, 160, 458, 463, 473; **12:**160, 273; PALACE **1:**223; **3:**574, 576; **11:**488; PRAETORIAN **11:**473; AS A VERB/TO BE ON **1:**22, 214, 240, 353, 399, 543, 712, 861, 866, 873, 897, 908, 950, 1148, 1174; **2:**4, 37, 50, 81, 254, 336, 981, 1006, 1027, 1031, 1136, 1167, 1192–93, 1195, 1304; **3:**152, 156, 574, 793–94, 911, 1085; **4:**306, 583, 610, 736, 1047, 1069, 1181, 1198, 1243; **5:**5, 60–61, 66, 161, 179, 198, 396, 672–73, 829; **6:**102, 345, 356, 394, 456, 479, 754, 1009, 1374, 1393–94, 1410, 1578; **7:**115, 352, 516, 769, 827, 839, 861; **8:**12, 20, 61, 102, 250, 375, 380, 453; **9:**25, 126, 163, 243, 392, 394, 409; **10:**86, 155, 179, 212, 291, 293, 299, 417, 670, 709, 823; **11:**104, 150, 160, 423, 438,

GUARD, GUARDS *(continued)*
458, 541, 548, 622, 635, 646, 756, 837; **12:**453, 476, 489, 646
GUARDIAN, GUARDIANS
1:44, 359, 876; **2:**79, 365–66, 456, 482, 520, 527, 529; **3:**223, 358, 848, 1039; **4:**34, 38, 85, 219, 228, 254–55, 265, 280, 282, 309, 1083; **5:**66, 244, 397, 433, 644, 663, 837, 867; **6:**577, 739, 775, 994, 1360, 1393–94; **7:**694; **8:**681; **9:**133, 310, 377; **10:**840; **11:**279, 281, 283, 310, 400, 640, 819–20; **12:**283, 315, 446, 490, 492; ANGEL(S) (*see under* ANGEL)
GUEST, GUESTS
1:462, 474, 634–35, 977, 1149; **2:**221, 850, 918, 1042, 1292, 1320, 1347; **3:**21–22, 129, 133, 918; **4:**176, 202, 476, 768, 770, 840; **5:**101, 103, 206, 400, 425, 485, 596–97, 624, 651, 668, 776, 784; **6:**481, 858, 1176, 1327, 1329, 1527–28; **7:**680; **8:**235, 322, 466, 543, 546, 552, 555, 599; **9:**22–23, 25–26, 128, 169–70, 172, 222, 236, 284, 286–91, 303, 317, 343, 393, 479–80, 594, 722; **10:**231, 239, 356, 363, 367, 827; **12:**235, 469, 489, 511; INVITED **1:**1024; **2:**1038; **4:**934; **5:**95; **7:**664–66, 678; **8:**416; **9:**289–90; ROOM(S) **3:**187, 210; **9:**63, 416; **11:**902
GUILE, GUILELESS
4:356; **5:**103, 502; **9:**659; **12:**263–64, 269, 276
GUILT
1:274, 428, 482–84, 527–28, 530, 563, 600, 604, 606, 610, 629–30, 639–41, 671–73, 866, 870, 890, 908, 933, 986, 1034–37, 1039, 1049, 1052, 1061, 1072, 1109, 1112, 1114, 1133, 1144, 1165, 1182; **2:**61–63, 78, 82, 125, 127, 130, 215, 217–18, 220, 234, 255, 265, 309, 392, 422, 436, 445, 447–48, 470–71, 492, 505, 628, 630, 758, 877, 884, 886–87, 963, 1030, 1168–69, 1226, 1231, 1284, 1289, 1294–95, 1298, 1314, 1326–27, 1354–55, 1359, 1366–68; **3:**34, 205, 208–9, 223, 302, 422–23, 497, 500, 503, 598, 610, 713, 735, 737–38, 742, 801, 804, 897, 903, 1003, 1099, 1145; **4:**110, 372, 412, 420–21, 431, 460, 554, 575, 579, 645, 678, 777, 804–5, 807, 833, 885–87, 910, 912, 935, 1055; **5:**77, 140, 190, 193, 198, 254, 452, 455, 470–71, 485, 568, 525, 584–86, 596, 674, 690, 736, 819; **6:**63, 69, 103, 204, 225, 227, 302, 371–72, 379, 381, 431, 450–51, 526, 528, 530, 597–98, 602, 637, 692, 699, 807, 915, 952, 958, 1010, 1023, 1030, 1072, 1139–41, 1145–47, 1156, 1170, 1180, 1189, 1228, 1236–37, 1282, 1291, 1302, 1369, 1452, 1476–77, 1488, 1547, 1576–77; **7:**34, 76, 92, 180, 183, 198, 244–45, 249, 272–73, 288, 295, 369, 411, 419, 499, 536, 551, 553, 583, 597, 663, 729, 739, 747, 765–67, 774, 778; **8:**15, 193, 213, 228, 249, 288, 369, 415, 478, 483–84, 486–87, 551, 709; **9:**145, 197, 358, 394, 438–39, 446, 458, 465, 714, 772, 775, 810, 815; **10:**66–67, 79–80, 109, 130, 192, 233, 297, 320, 322, 324, 330, 334, 343, 345, 456, 464, 472, 588–89, 924; **11:**237, 243, 332, 389, 571, 596, 629, 794; **12:**83, 147, 306, 423–24; BLOODGUILT (*see* BLOODGUILT); CONFESSION(S) OF **1:**629, 639, 641, 758; **5:**459, 484, 579; **6:**602; AND INNOCENCE (*see under* INNOCENCE); OFFERING(S) (*see under* OFFERING)
GULF
OF WATER **1:**214, 246, 822; **2:**254, 1209; **3:**242, 251; **6:**1325, 1348, 1418, 1474; **7:**67, 118, 151, 362, 437, 603; **10:**348; AS A GAP **1:**988, 997, 1048, 1072; **2:**14–15, 40, 594; **3:**636; **4:**383, 450; **5:**250, 312–13, 665, 819; **6:**109, 1088, 1389; **10:**820; **11:**404
GUM
1:1018; **5:**757; **6:**1379; **8:**143
GUTTER
6:1566–67
GYMNASIUM
1:286; **4:**6, 9–10, 12, 32, 42, 182–83, 216–18, 258; **5:**439–40, 611; **7:**25

H

HABAKKUK
WRITINGS OF **1:**267; **4:**30, 530, 977; **5:**198, 332; **6:**3, 18, 395, 762; **7:**194, 346, 382, 678; **9:**642; **10:**193–94, 425–26, 428; **11:**190, 259; **12:**126
HABIRU/HAPIRU
1:695
HADES
See HADES *in PLACES IN THE BIBLE*
HAGGADAH
8:29, 278; **9:**418
HAGGAI
WRITINGS OF **1:**268; **3:**675, 690–91, 695, 705; **4:**1121, 1195, 1267; **6:**20–21; **7:**736–38, 750, 760, 764–65, 770, 789, 796, 803, 848, 852, 855; **12:**159
HAIL, HAILSTONES
1:688, 755, 758–60, 763, 771; **2:**646–47, 877; **3:**1057; **4:**197, 598, 604, 747, 992, 1105, 1268; **5:**446, 486, 529, 577, 598, 818, 846; **6:**236, 256, 1202, 1383, 1522; **7:**810; **12:**630, 636, 644, 649, 672, 678
HAIR, HAIRS
1:218, 1071, 1094, 1096–98, 1100, 1135, 1148, 1171; **2:**62–65, 528, 726, 841–42, 845, 850, 858–59, 861, 888, 975, 1080, 1314–15, 1336; **3:**171, 688, 733, 848, 850, 895, 1087, 1142, 1147, 1161, 1163; **4:**64, 256, 378, 411; **5:**93,

162, 188, 206, 355, 370, 382, 401–2, 404, 414–15, 418, 422, 479, 687, 768, 809; **6:**10–11, 81, 1000, 1150–51, 1154, 1157, 1174, 1222, 1227, 1266, 1342, 1382, 1435, 1466, 1497, 1511, 1538, 1578–79; **7:**13, 31, 103, 192, 226, 257, 376, 528, 547; **8:**206, 435, 480; **9:**119, 169–70, 252, 254, 398, 402–3, 701; **10:**293–94, 785, 928–29, 931; **11:**801; **12:**561, 567, 599, 631

HALAKAH
8:183, 278; **10:**538; **11:**701

HALF-SHEKEL
See under COIN

HALF-TRIBE
2:309, 788; **3:**338

HALLELUJAH
3:447, 539, 1062, 1065; **4:**664, 1100, 1138–39, 1149, 1219, 1221, 1262–63, 1267, 1270, 1274, 1278; **5:**263; **12:**695

HALLOW (*OR* HALLOWS, HALLOWED, *ETC.*)
1:504, 696, 923, 1084, 1172; **4:**1076; **5:**651; **6:**1219, 1537; **8:**202–3; **9:**235; **11:**537; **12:**298, 566

HAMMER, HAMMERS
2:781; **3:**920; **4:**513–14; **6:**755, 913, 915, 1022, 1200; **8:**218; **10:**431, 484, 604, 693

HAMSTRING
2:651

HAND, HANDS
CLEAN **1:**482, 919, 1060, 1075; **4:**773, 782; **6:**221; DIVINE **1:**374; **2:**773, 783; **5:**350; **6:**664, 1483, 1506, 1508; **7:**694; OF GOD/THE LORD/YAHWEH **1:**84, 189, 368, 729, 739, 765, 787, 800, 889, 1076; **2:**339, 501, 756, 773, 804, 905, 909, 921, 945, 996–97, 1005–7, 1010–14, 1016, 1019, 1020–22, 1049, 1063, 1073, 1149, 1164, 1180, 1266, 1325; **3:**183, 462, 469, 573, 680, 704, 718, 723, 727, 731, 735, 737, 756, 758, 867–68, 915, 928, 1005, 1063, 1176; **4:**78, 241, 387, 428, 474, 547, 576, 581, 741, 802, 833, 857, 1000, 1130–31; **5:**303, 335, 340, 345, 411, 449, 461, 467–69, 486, 489, 502, 531, 574, 577, 656, 702; **6:**7, 97, 113, 127, 133, 221, 261, 327, 359, 369, 387, 407–8, 431, 443, 456, 531, 619, 699, 733–34, 766, 848, 860, 867, 891, 912–13, 1089, 1111, 1118, 1128, 1136, 1174, 1186, 1201, 1209, 1355, 1437, 1453, 1497, 1499, 1538; **7:**10, 56–57, 314, 395, 407, 550, 635–36, 731, 760–61, 833; **8:**707, 731–32; **9:**59–60, 71, 326, 331, 391; **10:**131, 175, 178, 190, 718, 816; **11:**69, 571, 574, 638; **12:**42, 91, 94, 292, 297, 712; GOD'S RIGHT **1:**84, 189, 800; **4:**470–71, 857, 984, 1130–31; **5:**345; **7:**417; **8:**73, 427, 713, 731–32; **9:**331, 391, 442–43, 488; **10:**131, 611; **11:**382, 384, 421, 571, 574, 638; **12:**12, 22–23, 26, 30–31, 41–42, 90–92, 94, 97, 149, 172, 330, 479, 601; WITH A HIGH **1:**1033, 1039, 1109; **2:**250; **9:**264; **10:**579; LAYING ON OF **1:**667, 1011, 1017, 1024–25, 1049; **2:**81, 162, 220; **3:**609; **8:**23; **9:**111, 273; **10:**113, 139, 152, 356; **11:**223, 779, 814, 833, 864; **12:**70–71; LEFT **1:**1160; **2:**771, 773, 782; **5:**345, 429; **6:**1523; **8:**398; **9:**134, 542; LEPROUS/WITHERED **1:**716; **2:**804; **3:**108; **8:**59, 63, 247, 558; **9:**114, 134, 209, 211, 284, 355 (*see also under* WITHER); MIGHTY/POWERFUL **1:**715, 729, 820, 1157; **2:**481; **3:**752, 756; **6:**1288, 1420, 1499; **12:**316–17; RIGHT **1:**84, 189, 237, 511, 585, 659, 800, 1062, 1099, 1160; **2:**762, 771, 1050, 1227, 1238, 1313; **3:**24, 195, 205, 208, 364, 402, 612, 776, 1171; **4:**44, 289, 297, 348, 617, 681, 737, 740–41, 857, 916, 972–73, 984, 1000, 1035, 1072, 1125, 1128, 1130–31, 1154, 1181, 1227–28, 1247–48; **5:**345, 429, 715; **6:**334, 354, 388–89, 402, 437, 527, 1038, 1084, 1294, 1391, 1523; **7:**417, 511, 522–23, 597, 731, 765; **8:**73, 398, 427, 713, 731–32; **9:**134, 331, 391, 442, 443, 488, 730; **10:**131, 611; **11:**113–14, 226, 229, 382, 384, 421, 571, 574, 638; **12:**5, 12, 22–23, 26, 30–31, 33, 41–42, 90–92, 94, 97, 149, 172, 330, 479, 567, 599, 601, 658; STRETCH OUT THE **3:**106; **4:**289, 296, 328, 349, 350, 546; **5:**675; **6:**56, 432, 454, 693, 1183, 1212, 1232, 1352, 1354, 1475, 1538; **7:**257, 691, 699; **8:**298, 328, 558; **9:**135, 861; **10:**175; WASHING THE **1:**1104, 1120; **2:**445, 808; **4:**412, 773, 781; **6:**244; **8:**331–33, 335, 486; **10:**361; **12:**298

HANDBREADTH, HANDBREADTHS
See under WEIGHTS AND MEASURES

HANDKERCHIEF, HANDKERCHIEFS
10:268

HANDMAID, HANDMAIDEN
1:91; **6:**822, 1605; **10:**956

HANDPIKE, HANDPIKES
6:1524

HANGING (*OR* HANGINGS, HANGED, *ETC.*)
AS EXECUTION **1:**615; **2:**198, 447, 627, 1332, 1358; **3:**857, 868, 892, 911, 923, 934, 938, 967, 1008, 1167; **4:**472; **5:**118, 384; **6:**396, 1156, 1489; **7:**51; **8:**484, 723; **9:**166, 310, 352, 458, 833; **10:**106; **11:**260; AS A WALL DECORATION **2:**53; **6:**1374, 1393

HANUKKAH
See FEASTS/FESTIVALS: OF DEDICATION/HANUKKAH

HAPPINESS
1:115, 1160; **2:**337, 502, 504; **3:**1050, 1057; **4:**312, 345, 394, 571, 665–68, 670, 686–87, 691–92, 694, 734, 759, 779, 786, 790, 805–6, 815, 829, 843, 847–48, 873, 931, 968, 970, 1012, 1014–15, 1035, 1058–59, 1110, 1133–34,

HAPPINESS *(continued)*
1136–37, 1154, 1168, 1172, 1197, 1200–1201, 1245, 1247, 1256, 1260, 1264–65; **5:**10–11, 49, 95, 180, 280, 282–83, 285, 290, 298, 300–301, 303, 307–8, 311, 320, 337, 340–41, 343, 354, 365, 367, 395, 498, 650–51, 681, 731, 765, 784; **6:**266, 278, 588, 892; **7:**270; **8:**177, 565; **9:**202, 397, 646; **10:**244, 521, 614, 617, 891; **11:**79, 345

HARBOR, HARBORS
FOR SHIPS **4:**159, 275; **6:**1360; **10:**346, 348, 355; **11:**405

HARLOT (*OR* HARLOTS, HARLOTRY, *ETC.*)
1:68, 73, 579, 605–6, 1118; **2:**743, 775; **3:**205, 1090; **5:**13, 84, 384; **6:**547, 596, 603–4, 702, 807, 1220, 1224, 1233, 1241–42, 1317, 1319, 1321, 1325, 1330, 1362; **7:**3, 215, 216, 224, 286, 296, 330; **9:**23, 34, 167, 169–70, 172, 178, 359, 370; **10:**863; **11:**147; **12:**351, 579, 686

HARNESS (*OR* HARNESSES, *ETC.*)
3:269, 645; **5:**386, 534, 541, 593, 652; **7:**275, 609; **8:**23; **9:**321, 597; **10:**968; **11:**394; **12:**29

HARP, HARPS
2:1103–4, 1232; **3:**386, 394, 447; **4:**331, 853, 876, 960, 1228; **5:**597; **6:**159, 1330, 1362, 1366; **9:**366; **10:**959; **12:**604, 664, 672, 694

HARPIST
1:236; **12:**664

HARPOON
4:622

HARROW
7:275

HART
4:854

HARVEST
1:218, 226, 875, 950, 1019–20, 1158, 1160–61, 1171–72, 1188; **2:**233, 403, 406, 411–13, 467, 471, 480, 483, 888, 915, 1206; **3:**368, 370, 552, 624; **4:**90, 233, 276, 368, 381, 603, 941, 1003, 1196; **5:**49, 75, 107, 114, 140, 161, 180, 223, 308, 687, 824–25; **6:**93, 123, 169, 173–76, 227, 238, 265, 1400, 1580; **7:**253, 265, 448, 722; **8:**67, 217, 252, 286, 303–4, 306, 311, 314, 570, 573–78, 670–71; **9:**86, 133, 151, 176–77, 179–81, 222, 256, 261, 408, 542, 569–70, 572; **10:**199, 413, 422, 531, 757, 920, 980, 992; **11:**16, 44, 130–31, 328, 337, 339, 485–86, 846, 900; **12:**82, 118, 223, 288, 558, 663, 665, 667–68, 699; BARLEY/GRAIN/WHEAT **1:**275, 536, 1157–58, 1163; **2:**412, 593, 893, 899, 910, 922, 935, 1063, 1359; **3:**624, 1001; FALL/SPRING **1:**1156; **3:**691; **7:**273; **9:**616; FESTIVAL (*see under* FEASTS/FESTIVALS); GRAPE **1:**403, 536, 665, 1179; **3:**847; **7:**309, 333, 448; SEASON/TIME **1:**217, 275, 871, 1133, 1159; **2:**893, 926; **5:**3, 185, 219; **9:**219; **3:**32–33

HATE
1:141, 598, 695, 821, 822, 842, 866, 1127, 1133; **2:**200, 551, 651, 818, 1056, 1340; **3:**138, 1017, 1062, 1064; **4:**291, 701, 782, 800, 882, 948, 951, 1069, 1070, 1124–25, 1178, 1203, 1215, 1229; **5:**33, 96, 103, 111–12, 131, 135, 149–50, 152, 161, 167, 179, 218, 247, 276, 291, 301, 306–7, 339, 341, 564, 724, 771; **6:**56, 679, 874, 1186; **7:**270, 334, 391, 515, 548, 683, 856, 865–66; **8:**195, 210, 213, 352, 375, 667; **9:**147, 292, 309, 348, 402, 649–50, 711, 759, 762–64, 766, 768; **10:**567–68, 637, 711; **11:**332, 403, 432; **12:**395–96, 412–13, 418–20, 432–34

HATRED
1:270, 377, 537, 541, 598–99, 821, 892; **2:**265, 549, 649, 1123, 1225, 1237, 1304–7; **3:**804, 850, 855, 960, 1163; **4:**38, 97, 205, 269, 278, 471, 749, 824, 906, 1105, 1125, 1185, 1237; **5:**91, 111, 149, 226, 285, 312, 422, 597, 745, 801, 862; **6:**160, 502, 550–51, 796, 1086, 1325, 1327, 1358, 1474, 1478–79, 1486; **7:**333, 362, 482, 493, 548, 576, 701; **8:**551, 598, 667, 688, 692; **9:**617, 734, 762–65, 765–66, 768, 793, 846, 863; **10:**312, 588–89, 720, 898; **11:**79, 177, 340, 374, 645, 879; **12:**211, 234, 377, 393–95, 413, 418–20, 422, 424, 433, 443, 491, 575, 616

HAUGHTY, HAUGHTINESS
1:726, 763; **3:**1108, 1113, 1144, 1178; **4:**625, 1082, 1208; **5:**77, 161, 192, 454, 536, 675; **6:**73, 81–82, 914, 1237, 1362, 1386, 1395, 1427; **7:**699; **9:**641; **10:**528, 816, 822, 847, 856, 937; **11:**103, 830, 849; **12:**123, 127, 231, 315

HAWK
4:598, 612; **6:**544; **11:**62

HAY
3:487; **5:**75, 131; **7:**406

HEAD
CHRIST AS **5:**16; **7:**228; **10:**709, 928, 949; **11:**357–58, 370, 372, 375, 381, 383–84, 386, 400, 403, 449, 450, 455, 571, 602–3, 605, 623, 632, 636–37; COVERING(S) **1:**185; **6:**1203; **10:**263, 926–33, 969; OF FAMILY/HOUSEHOLD **1:**238, 578–79, 1124; **2:**333, 446–47, 452, 473–74, 476, 628, 715, 901; **3:**209–10, 725; **5:**397; **9:**420; **10:**803; **11:**455, 652–53, 656, 801, 825, 838, 891; **12:**345

HEADDRESS, HEADRESSES
1:1061; **2:**164; **3:**914

HEADSHIP
2:702; **3:**328; **10:**949; **11:**455, 601, 603, 623, 628, 632

HEALING (*OR* HEALINGS, *ETC.*)
1:178, 192, 430, 484, 628, 731, 747, 784, 808–9, 829, 838, 840, 846, 977, 1010, 1027, 1095; **2:**21,

67, 152, 163–64, 549, 753, 892, 1011, 1102, 1109, 1208; **3:**6, 108, 190, 192, 194, 197–98, 201–2, 214, 500, 526, 618, 656, 659, 975, 984, 988–89, 1023, 1025–26, 1029, 1032–34, 1039–40, 1042, 1045, 1048–52, 1056, 1061, 1065; **4:**211, 381, 391, 421, 675, 703–4, 736–37, 847, 1091, 1118–19, 1127, 1265, 1269; **5:**53, 60, 90, 126, 141, 242, 401, 574–75, 624, 807–8; **6:**43, 103, 249, 255, 299, 301–2, 432, 478, 493, 498–99, 627, 647–48, 650, 653, 692, 694, 698, 709, 768, 807–8, 814, 825–27, 883, 958, 1034, 1035, 1044, 1209, 1241, 1345, 1597; **7:**55, 106, 115, 206, 229, 234, 250, 253–54, 263, 277, 279, 295, 297, 418, 873–74; **8:**62–64, 111, 121–22, 174, 207, 217, 222–24, 228, 232, 234, 237, 240–41, 245, 251, 256, 280, 285–86, 322, 324, 329, 331, 337–39, 368, 385, 400, 511, 520–22, 525, 539, 541–51, 553, 555–56, 558–59, 561, 565–66, 585, 588–92, 595–96, 602, 609, 611–14, 618–20, 628, 632, 634, 646, 654–55, 678, 696, 706; **9:**10, 12, 24, 29, 34, 36, 56, 103, 109–11, 113–14, 116, 118–26, 142, 154–57, 160–61, 172, 174–75, 178, 189–92, 194, 208, 211, 241, 272–74, 283–85, 324–27, 329, 353–55, 436, 446, 462, 473, 513, 535, 573, 575–76, 578–80, 584, 594, 597, 599, 619–20, 629, 636, 651, 653–54, 656–60, 680, 849; **10:**65, 76–78, 80, 83, 89, 97, 99, 133, 151 52, 160 62, 166, 170, 199, 230, 232, 235, 273, 307, 356, 451, 505, 597, 602, 605, 693, 699, 710, 754, 943; **11:**15, 253, 611, 650, 860; **12:**64, 71, 153, 213, 222–23, 617, 630, 634, 720, 724; OF THE BLIND **1:**178; **8:**63, 148, 239, 287, 594, 614, 621, 634, 656; **9:**335, 353–57, 369, 503, 513, 651, 665, 671, 691, 727, 764; DIVINE/GOD'S **1:**981; **2:**110, 112, 344; **3:**544, 985, 1023, 1050; **4:**703; **5:**574; **6:**302; **7:**164, 718; **8:**549, 585, 593, 635, 733; **10:**161–62, 198, 268, 358, 606; GIFT OF **3:**1003; **8:**336; MIRACLE(S) **3:**14, 631; **6:**302; **8:**285, 545, 549, 594, 600, 603, 611–13, 623, 625, 655–56; **9:**135, 284, 325, 508, 513, 576, 578, 581, 591, 616, 651–53, 661, 663; **10:**78, 80–81, 85, 198, 277, 949; NARRATIVE(S)/STORY(STORIES) **3:**1055; **8:**59, 62–64, 239, 368, 522, 543, 546, 551, 586, 589, 609, 619; **9:**125, 133, 135, 326, 353, 574, 576, 578, 581, 584, 591, 652–54, 663, 687; **10:**161, 170, 198, 267; POWER OF **1:**465; **2:**12, 67, 142, 167–68, 344, 804, 1102; **7:**856; **8:**244, 546, 548–49, 585, 587, 589, 592–93, 603, 621, 623, 635; **9:**653; **10:**84, 162, 198, 268, 356, 358; ON THE SABBATH **8:**277, 547; **9:**122, 134, 274, 284–85; OF THE SICK **3:**271; **4:**395; **5:**503; **8:**122, 326; **9:**56, 111–13, 160, 194–95, 576; **10:**21, 445; **12:**224

HEALTH
1:239, 365, 568, 685, 809, 866, 1023, 1036, 1075; **2:**15, 55, 59–60, 62, 67–68, 99, 190, 195, 200, 236, 332, 336, 374, 378, 398, 428, 431, 446–47, 460, 463, 468, 472, 719, 727, 741, 763, 782–83, 835, 872, 1232; **3:**198, 777, 981, 984, 1005, 1024, 1051, 1055; **4:**51, 138, 255, 359–60, 369, 444, 472, 495, 627, 833, 1127; **5:**10–11, 49–50, 55, 60, 68, 90, 108, 118, 141, 162, 163, 237, 354, 382, 404, 498, 510, 547, 550, 553, 568, 574, 579, 639, 650, 778, 808; **6:**96, 143, 189, 301, 304, 379, 825–26, 1061, 1219, 1501; **7:**263, 378, 388, 403, 419; **8:**23, 228, 543, 546, 565; **9:**136, 186, 203, 241, 269, 327, 339, 370; **10:**7, 78, 81–82, 850–51, 898; **11:**228, 287, 371, 494, 635, 824; **12:**211, 222, 247, 380, 459–60, 482, 710, 730; CARE **1:**223, 765, 850; **2:**66–67, 167; **3:**783, 1018; **4:**166; **6:**1465; **7:**700; **8:**553; **9:**865; OF THE COMMUNITY **1:**870, 1100; **2:**141–42, 237; **3:**850; **7:**725; **10:**115, 787–88, 823–24, 857, 971; **12:**31; GOOD **1:**643; **2:**69; **3:**983, 1023; **4:**192, 452; **5:**765; **8:**37; **9:**52; **10:**726; **12:**461; PHYSICAL **1:**1100; **2:**69; **3:**1024; **4:**797; **5:**809; **10:**115; **11:**791; SPIRITUAL **1:**1027; **3:**1024; **4:**1113; **8:**620, 686; **9:**244, 324, 328; **10:**263; **11:**338, 431; **12:**486. *See also* DISEASE; SICKNESS

HEART, HEARTS
OF BELIEVERS **1:**51; **3:**620; **10:**419, 516, 523; **11:**69; **12:**101, 276; CHANGING/TURNING THE **1:**793, 849, 931; **2:**824, 825; **3:**76, 396, 421, 497, 592, 635, 713–14, 1181; **4:**27, 170, 253; **5:**182, 484–85, 545; **6:**612, 650, 759, 774, 794, 865, 1492; **7:**671, 877; **8:**34, 646; **9:**47–48, 60, 81; **10:**448, 715; **11:**9, 110; **12:**733; CLEAN **2:**1295; **4:**886–87; **6:**1191; **9:**342; **11:**791, 846; DIVINE/GOD'S/THE LORD'S/YAHWEH'S **1:**260, 389, 396, 715, 823; **2:**756, 758, 958–59, 988, 1024, 1044–45, 1065, 1099, 1111, 1128, 1156, 1195, 1262, 1333, 1366; **3:**497, 582, 658; **6:**444, 620, 629, 655, 658, 670, 680, 684, 686, 691–92, 809–10, 812, 814, 1052, 1058, 1140, 1161, 1190, 1274; **7:**801; **10:**521; **12:**605; EVIL **1:**393, 398; **2:**1111; **7:**382; **8:**234; **12:**49; HARDEN THE **1:**717, 729–30, 751, 754, 762, 793, 816; **2:**637; **3:**167; **4:**1062; **5:**182, 239, 664; **6:**529, 531, 822, 1087, 1397; **8:**69, 328, 333; **10:**267, 638, 669; **11:**904; **12:**49; HUMAN **1:**389, 393, 398, 405, 1186; **2:**267, 276, 355, 359, 377, 549, 1100, 1342; **3:**409, 539; **4:**191, 348, 471, 488; **5:**46, 61, 63, 77, 129, 141, 149, 158, 166, 172, 183, 285, 384, 390, 410, 448, 487, 520, 526, 678, 833; **6:**156, 708, 812, 1460; **7:**263, 382; **8:**69, 551; **9:**312, 314; **10:**42, 208, 432, 434, 442–43, 599; **11:**63, 72, 463; **12:**213, 219, 222, 424, 533, 611; INCLINATIONS OF THE **1:**393, 398, 405; **2:**549; **5:**285, 353, 356; **7:**382; AND MIND(S) **1:**51–52, 417, 1106; **2:**377, 759, 988; **3:**396, 447, 462,

HEART, HEARTS *(continued)*
501, 532; **4:**191, 605, 782, 828, 1166, 1208, 1227; **5:**491, 519; **6:**27, 296, 620–21, 629, 646, 656, 673–74, 684, 691, 754, 810, 812, 840, 1049, 1460; **7:**74, 313, 584, 636; **10:**241, 343, 381, 422, 432, 541, 705, 769, 811, 835, 900; **11:**69, 413, 517, 541, 548; **12:**117, 218; NEW **1:**962; **2:**1043; **4:**188; **5:**46, 61; **6:**21, 758–59, 812, 816, 823, 825, 1264, 1266, 1492, 1496, 1522; **7:**382; **10:**442, 448, 453; PURE IN/OF **1:**482, 1060, 1075; **3:**1145; **4:**742, 773, 774, 969, 970; **5:**199; **8:**179–81, 196, 313; **9:**74, 151, 395–96; **12:**182, 213, 260, 724; UNCIRCUMCISED **1:**89, 460, 1086, 1182; **2:**377, 513; **3:**574; **5:**798; **6:**643, 656, 812, 1574; **10:**129, 561, 659; **11:**397, 524

HEARTH, HEARTHS
6:242, 1566–67, 1569, 1592

HEAT
1:217, 946, 1164, 1180, 1188; **2:**40, 547, 1055, 1188, 1207, 1216, 1323; **3:**220, 878, 1051, 1125; **4:**368, 388, 463, 511–12, 592, 603, 752, 1177, 1180, 1269; **5:**219–20, 340, 485, 577, 616, 732; **6:**217, 305, 371, 469, 601, 631, 698, 708, 840, 1033, 1063, 1071, 1224, 1306, 1312; **7:**164, 256–57, 261, 314, 528, 774–75, 837; **8:**393; **9:**268, 411, 565; **10:**330, 356, 986; **11:**318, 696, 778; **12:**625

HEATHEN
1:1126; **3:**869, 931, 959–60; **4:**525, 691; **7:**85; **8:**213; **9:**277

HEAVEN
ASCEND TO **1:**278, 1068; **3:**179; **4:**420; **5:**252, 256, 341, 852; **6:**20, 935, 1114, 1463; **7:**12; **9:**221, 551, 782; **10:**43, 47; **11:**362, 421; **12:**99, 533, 611; BREAD FROM/OF **1:**209–10, 805, 812–16, 892; **5:**598; **8:**204; **9:**600, 603, 605–6, 608, 612, 660, 757; **12:**75; COME DOWN FROM/DESCEND FROM **1:**43, 815, 1022; **2:**38, 91; **3:**138, 498; **5:**252, 609; **6:**935, 961, 1055, 1531; **7:**3; **9:**91, 215, 468, 551–52, 600–603, 608, 612–13, 782; **10:**663, 668; **11:**421; **12:**99, 302, 522, 558, 638, 646, 678, 692, 706–7, 711, 714, 720, 722; CREATOR/MAKER OF **1:**442, 512, 716; **3:**269, 1165; **4:**1145–46, 1180, 1216–17; **6:**294, 344, 388, 391, 401, 414, 787; **7:**382, 839; AND EARTH **1:**206, 277, 278, 325, 342, 349, 383, 412, 442, 510, 512, 541, 713, 716, 767, 924, 954, 981; **2:**14, 32, 319, 593, 1336; **3:**269, 407, 438, 704, 706, 1165; **4:**46, 71–72, 295, 344, 357, 486, 934, 1145–46, 1180, 1190, 1216–17, 1271, 1273, 1279; **5:**93, 377; **6:**52, 294, 344, 388, 391, 401–2, 414, 448, 544–45, 575, 661, 752, 766, 787, 883–84, 913, 988, 1005; **7:**382, 578, 680, 718, 730, 748, 750, 754, 774, 782, 839; **8:**41, 187, 503; **9:**55, 224, 409, 462, 532, 551; **10:**125, 246, 482, 618; **11:**40, 396, 565, 568, 640; **12:**82, 96, 159, 357, 531, 541, 551, 588, 594, 605, 630–31, 638, 686, 720, 727–29; FIRE FROM/OF **1:**1044; **2:**603; **3:**137, 144, 169, 173, 179, 184, 587; **4:**197; **7:**381; GATE(S) OF **1:**277, 542; **3:**658; **7:**750, 770, 782–83; **12:**531, 729; GOD/LORD OF/IN **1:**510, 512; **2:**90, 593; **3:**666, 678, 704–6, 708, 710, 715, 752–53, 756, 758, 761, 1039, 1101; **4:**11, 1225; **5:**574; **6:**399; **7:**13, 52, 72, 114, 125, 181, 468, 470, 485, 498, 501, 718, 730; **8:**503, 631; **9:**55, 224; **10:**246, 349, 482; **11:**640, 657; **12:**588, 593, 643–44, 666; HIGHEST **1:**277; **3:**75, 78; **5:**648; **9:**29, 60, 65, 369, 445, 488; **12:**82; HOST(S) OF **1:**287; **2:**569, 603; **3:**164, 632, 810, 813, 1057, 1179; **6:**10, 40, 101, 206, 210, 212–13, 227, 277, 334, 344, 884, 913, 1130, 1177; **7:**5, 10, 65, 113–14, 126, 168, 376, 421, 751, 755; **9:**65, 369; **10:**128–29; **12:**509, 593, 604, 606, 624, 705; KINGDOM OF **2:**872; **4:**774, 882, 1070; **5:**291, 323, 343; **7:**9, 178; **8:**107, 154, 156, 159, 167, 178, 188, 194, 196, 203, 211, 226, 279, 285, 288–94, 301, 305, 308, 311, 314, 321, 341, 346, 353, 357, 360, 365, 374, 387, 394, 416–17, 442, 450, 455, 460, 471; **9:**313, 345; **10:**130; **12:**626, 712; NEW **1:**166, 980, 1175; **4:**1269; **6:**544, 551; **7:**3; **8:**36, 392; **12:**330, 357, 527, 532, 541, 558, 605, 703, 713, 718, 720, 730; SATAN FROM/IN **1:**289; **9:**98; **12:**112, 650, 695, 707; TAKEN UP TO **1:**288; **3:**175; **4:**51; **9:**9, 215; TREASURE(S) OF **3:**592, 880, 1018; **5:**565; **6:**1383; **8:**210; **9:**144, 260, 309, 347; **11:**545, 590; VOICE FROM **6:**365–66; **8:**366; **9:**13–14, 18, 91–92, 95, 98, 111, 153, 192, 204–6, 209, 442, 461, 476, 712; **11:**215; **12:**159, 638–39, 643, 664, 667, 721, 735

HEBREW
BIBLE **1:**8, 10–11, 18, 22, 29, 38, 71, 78, 83, 140, 163, 175, 189, 192, 244–45, 252, 292, 294, 296–97, 307; **2:**96, 104, 271, 273, 275, 284, 291–92, 376–77, 398, 548, 893–94, 916, 943, 950, 1108, 1171; **3:**39, 126, 150, 155, 299, 348, 663, 772, 860, 879–80, 890, 945, 953, 956–57, 982, 1103, 1171; **4:**31, 63, 301–2, 309–10, 313–14, 378, 434, 704, 1167; **5:**22, 268–69, 273, 276, 278–79, 281, 285, 293, 303, 306, 311, 320, 322–23, 325, 328, 332, 339–41, 355–56, 359, 439–40, 479, 632–34, 642, 644, 813; **6:**1, 4, 11, 15, 20, 22, 95, 140, 161, 211, 223, 226, 929, 934–35, 949, 960, 966, 968–69, 985, 987, 998, 1007, 1018, 1023, 1092, 1110–11, 1171, 1210, 1222, 1238–39, 1257, 1259, 1296, 1301, 1308, 1354, 1389, 1420, 1450, 1466, 1474, 1484, 1531, 1566, 1590, 1595, 1602; **7:**2–6, 19, 22, 27, 112, 121, 148, 151, 155–56, 188, 200, 208, 220,

251, 469, 477, 497, 548, 597, 602–3, 605, 671, 852; **8:**28, 65, 89, 130, 151, 163, 171, 186, 272, 291; **10:**240, 469, 673; **11:**887; **12:**255, 677, 735; BIBLICAL **1:**24, 30, 78, 104, 197; **4:**308; **5:**198, 270, 279, 306, 332, 340; **8:**359; CANON **1:**10–12, 29, 43–44; **2:**274–75, 291; **5:**125, 244, 271, 438; **6:**49, 190; **7:**435; **8:**94; **9:**249; LANGUAGE **1:**66, 73, 99, 292, 294, 298, 1181; **2:**776; **3:**713, 858; **4:**199, 308, 753; **5:**269, 289; **7:**110, 848; **11:**526; LITERATURE **1:**77; **2:**981; **4:**427; **5:**345, 356, 359; **7:**343; SCRIPTURE(S) **1:**5, 8–11, 16, 40, 44, 47, 71, 73, 81, 83–86, 88, 93, 126, 163, 189–92, 194; **2:**336, 1122; **3:**977; **4:**16, 19–20, 22, 30, 67, 82, 96, 159, 177, 193, 199; **5:**273, 448; **6:**48, 50, 67, 84, 96, 98, 109, 112, 142, 227–28, 1057, 1080, 1140, 1152, 1153, 1159, 1194, 1196, 1212, 1222, 1230, 1258, 1314–15, 1341, 1366, 1379, 1386, 1393–94, 1397–98, 1425, 1434, 1437, 1457, 1467, 1496, 1521, 1529, 1540; **7:**112; **9:**41, 45, 70, 196, 249, 336, 342, 385, 389, 393, 486; **10:**374, 398, 446, 458, 487; **12:**283; TEXT(S) **1:**5, 9, 17, 28–29, 31, 70, 73, 82, 94, 100, 290, 292–95, 298, 300–303, 373, 380, 715, 728, 738, 757, 863, 869, 976, 1012, 1080, 1097, 1125, 1180; **2:**96, 569, 593, 608, 697, 737, 739, 748, 832, 893, 901, 904, 909, 916, 926, 950, 1042, 1048, 1069, 1109, 1119–20, 1168, 1249, 1287, 1304, 1381; **3:**27, 43, 45, 48–49, 51, 58, 61, 63, 80, 101, 158, 205, 212, 272, 416, 487, 655, 713, 737, 743, 766, 773, 775–76, 779, 784, 811, 831, 834–35, 860–61, 881–82, 884, 888, 892, 903, 913, 923, 955–56; **4:**20, 183, 346, 352, 379, 426, 462, 502, 511, 529, 544, 546, 578, 582, 586, 591, 690, 763, 845, 890, 895, 968, 1014, 1024, 1058, 1111, 1118, 1259; **5:**110, 118, 126, 157, 162, 219, 270, 279, 300, 316, 345, 382, 438, 610, 612, 618, 636, 642–43, 645, 664, 667, 670, 687–89, 693, 695, 720, 725, 779, 808, 812, 818, 828, 837, 842, 850, 852; **6:**108, 112, 116, 159, 567, 635–36, 654, 660, 696, 731, 761–62, 766, 791, 1016, 1114, 1187, 1311, 1314, 1329–30, 1429, 1473, 1516, 1552, 1582; **7:**148, 156, 163, 167–68, 211, 218, 230–31, 303, 366, 399, 419, 427–28, 442, 447–49, 456, 495, 499, 506, 536–37, 542, 547, 568, 582, 641–42, 653, 665, 667, 731, 848, 871, 875; **8:**28–29, 152, 156, 228; **9:**219; **10:**144, 362, 425, 748; **11:**7, 9, 48, 115, 126, 139

HEBREWS, THE

GOD OF **1:**715, 725–26, 742, 750, 753, 757, 759, 763, 773; **4:**298; LETTER TO **1:**8, 14–16, 19, 419–20, 430, 439, 442, 686, 854, 893, 898, 908, 914, 916, 920, 1001, 1027, 1051, 1114, 1136; **2:**97, 596, 827, 879; **3:**339, 465, 543, 576, 592, 611–12, 1024; **4:**738, 845, 1063; **5:**35, 50, 507, 527, 860; **6:**816; **7:**643, 811; **8:**17, 21, 29, 34, 41–42, 495, 666; **9:**94, 101, 376, 408, 420, 425; **10:**370–71, 377–79, 388, 470, 474, 586, 613; **11:**259; **12:**229, 253, 255, 353, 370–71, 376, 388, 444, 523, 531, 575. *See also* HEBREWS *in PERSONS IN THE BIBLE*

HEDGE

4:349–50, 354, 360, 370, 586, 600; **5:**151, 294; **6:**89, 1009, 1392, 1394; **9:**127; **10:**348, 352, 354; **11:**399

HEDONISM (*OR* HEDONIST, *ETC.*)

5:297–98, 337, 462; **6:**197; **7:**263; **8:**18; **9:**256–57; **10:**730; **11:**289, 760; **12:**190, 678

HEIFER, HEIFERS

1:93, 1119–20; **2:**445, 850, 1098; **5:**687; **6:**914; **7:**213, 234, 241–43, 274–75, 314; RED **2:**9, 99, 150, 152, 247; **3:**1002; **4:**106; **6:**1491, 1579; **12:**107, 110. *See also* CALF; COW

HEIR, HEIRS

1:37, 73, 236, 241, 243, 247, 260, 291, 330, 433, 436, 445, 454, 504, 605, 718, 720, 771, 773, 780, 1124; **2:**211, 221, 234, 245, 273, 446–47, 457, 474, 476, 580, 630, 634, 641, 680, 702, 928, 930, 932–33, 935, 937, 940, 943, 974, 1120, 1133, 1213, 1248, 1269, 1274, 1309, 1319, 1357–58; **3:**4, 8, 13–14, 17–21, 23, 31, 33, 112, 168–69, 176, 214, 223, 228–30, 233, 290, 328, 353, 380, 389, 409, 438, 464, 486, 512, 522, 560, 573, 603, 607, 699, 713, 730, 747, 803, 869, 889, 911, 994, 1009; **4:**4, 182, 255, 451, 1088, 1128; **5:**24, 170, 255–56, 300, 319, 343, 801; **6:**8, 311, 894, 1189, 1223, 1457; **7:**731–32, 770, 807; **8:**42, 101–2, 119, 126, 130, 132, 140, 226, 290, 294, 346, 359, 637, 653, 670; **9:**230, 381–82, 636; **10:**71, 192, 374, 387, 496, 511, 591–94, 600–601, 604, 607, 622–23, 644, 690, 698, 855, 857; **11:**199, 255, 263–65, 273–74, 278, 280–83, 286, 289, 292, 301, 305, 308, 346, 357, 411, 867, 877; **12:**12, 22, 29, 35, 52, 81, 117, 134–35, 140, 181–82, 192, 195, 200, 217, 236, 250, 285, 287, 302

HELL

See HELL *in PLACES IN THE BIBLE*

HELLENISM

1:270; **4:**182, 202; **5:**439–40, 570, 584, 597, 606, 622, 624–26, 656, 673, 692; **7:**27, 118, 122; **8:**40, 178; **9:**388, 506, 519; **12:**179, 223

HELMET, HELMETS

2:1112; **5:**486; **6:**1374; **10:**692; **11:**459, 462

HELPER, HELPERS

1:352; **2:**344, 374, 646; **3:**197, 379, 395, 678, 727, 959, 1144; **4:**148, 182, 518, 540, 679, 719, 865, 893–95, 1247; **5:**305, 805; **6:**260, 1232, 1415, 1442; **7:**125; **8:**375, 730; **9:**229; **10:**190, 270, 834; **11:**480; **12:**232

HEM
OF A GARMENT **5:**648; **6:**11, 102, 105; **9:**455
HEMORRHAGE, HEMORRHAGES
1:1033, 1106; **3:**1002; **7:**253; **8:**223, 238; **9:**24, 60, 175, 189–91, 322
HEN, HENS
1:184; **2:**918; **5:**255; **7:**251; **9:**282–83, 372
HERALD, HERALDS
1:622; **3:**50, 265; **4:**307; **6:**10, 19–20, 336–37, 357, 413, 441, 443, 455, 490, 513, 575, 596, 752, 1159, 1528; **7:**62, 332, 374, 376, 416, 632, 641; **8:**19; **9:**558; **10:**82, 176, 245, 448, 672; **11:**106, 799, 836; **12:**82, 238, 260
HERB, HERBS
1:349–50; **2:**87; **3:**1040; **5:**90, 574, 807–8; **8:**309, 311, 472; **9:**247–48, 418; BITTER **2:**87; **8:**472; **9:**418
HERD, HERDS
1:217–21, 425, 433, 653, 754, 767, 781, 821, 1190; **2:**78, 351, 374, 399, 403, 406–7, 414, 1193, 1292; **3:**608, 647, 868, 890, 1050; **4:**349, 351, 467, 492, 510, 605; **5:**3, 7; **6:**665, 1568; **7:**213, 245–46, 282, 376, 478, 483, 514; **8:**231, 583–84; **9:**186–87, 191, 783; **10:**415
HERDER, HERDERS
1:219–20; **6:**834
HERDSMAN, HERDSMEN
1:433; **3:**538; **6:**205, 420, 1465, 1592; **7:**340–42, 411
HERESY, HERESIES
1:15, 47, 57–58, 77, 100–101, 195, 208; **3:**104; **4:**582; **6:**473, 1015; **7:**560–61; **8:**13; **9:**679; **10:**320, 330; **11:**207, 277; **12:**27, 43, 78, 121, 165, 326, 344, 360, 366, 428, 475, 476, 710
HERITAGE
1:49, 71, 78, 152, 159, 195, 201, 246, 254, 272, 275, 327, 467, 591, 652, 671; **2:**415, 601, 652, 673, 753, 1175, 1314, 1352; **3:**278, 307, 319, 332, 358, 364, 395, 536–37, 565, 622, 630, 691, 693, 795, 813, 842, 994, 1039; **4:**18, 48, 166, 287, 380, 484, 510, 552, 737, 869, 919, 945, 947, 1058, 1110, 1172, 1198; **5:**11, 32, 148, 200, 294, 365, 400, 493, 544, 606, 658, 843; **6:**74, 403, 411, 479, 500, 571, 575, 577, 654, 678–81, 913, 918, 920, 1083, 1155, 1240, 1346, 1389, 1457; **7:**200, 202, 321, 330, 358, 401, 465, 659, 672, 699; **8:**27, 145; **9:**58, 69, 84, 86–87, 98, 302, 421, 464, 528, 606, 638, 640, 644, 649; **10:**46, 155, 212, 215, 375, 670; **11:**236, 375, 382, 404, 659, 665, 768, 781, 785; **12:**22, 59, 212, 285, 328, 339–40, 357–58, 383, 409, 420, 427; CULTURAL **1:**35, 161, 166, 261, 270; **8:**57; ISRAELITE **3:**400; **5:**452–53; **7:**761; **9:**100, 300; **11:**302, 308, 867, 874; JEWISH **1:**46; **9:**421, 638, 644; **10:**8, 16, 155, 211, 214, 222, 226, 253, 255, 259, 267, 277, 294, 310, 362, 848, 898, 935; **11:**38, 40, 132, 239, 352, 403, 411–12, 430–31, 783–84, 861; **12:**345; RELIGIOUS **1:**154, 451, 624; **3:**635; **7:**560; **9:**195, 648; **10:**135, 294; **11:**867
HESED
1:475, 483, 492, 510–11, 563, 611, 615, 659, 801, 842, 946, 1142; **2:**904, 908, 925, 930–32, 945–46, 1120, 1133–36, 1159, 1208, 1212, 1218, 1223, 1230, 1258, 1273–74, 1276–77, 1279, 1281, 1324, 1331; **3:**95, 304, 496, 498–99, 736; **4:**51, 388, 663, 670–71, 701, 748, 768, 844, 872–83, 885, 913, 983, 1020, 1034, 1078, 1082, 1091, 1116–17, 1121, 1126, 1150, 1171, 1232, 1255; **5:**181, 185, 609, 833, 837; **6:**336, 597, 809, 1051–52; **7:**42–43, 163, 236, 252, 319, 507, 518, 580; **8:**425; **9:**84, 523; **11:**345, 790, 876
HEWERS
OF STONE/WOOD **3:**58, 820; **6:**1574
HEXATEUCH
1:307–8, 311–12
HIDE, HIDDEN
APOCRYPHA(L) **1:**8, 11, 45; THE FACE *(sometimes of God)* **1:**282, 712; **2:**804, 942; **4:**1086; **5:**196; **6:**118, 711, 1484, 1529; GOD **1:**938, 978; **6:**477; **12:**515; FROM GOD/THE LORD/YAHWEH **1:**361–62, 373–74; **4:**512, 596, 930; **5:**11, 185, 619; **6:**207, 248; **7:**291, 679; **9:**256; **12:**617; HIDDEN/REVEALED **1:**286, 289; **2:**338; **3:**1025; **4:**428; **5:**14, 217, 252, 626, 670; **6:**382, 827; **7:**13, 181, 189–90, 194; **8:**274, 309–10, 447; **9:**34, 55, 173, 180, 224; **10:**595, 821–23; **11:**324, 374, 407, 409, 572, 613, 615–16, 636, 639, 807; **12:**56, 518, 525, 530, 560, 588, 615; KNOWLEDGE **4:**420, 422, 426; **5:**626, 647, 663; **8:**534; **11:**357, 374, 415, 572, 575, 613, 615–16, 619, 639; **12:**571; MYSTERY **2:**431; **4:**426; **5:**626; **11:**374, 559, 807; THING(S) **1:**286; **4:**422, 428, 529, 530, 876, 990; **5:**252, 670; **6:**421, 825; **9:**55; **10:**841, 960; **11:**65; **12:**518, 581; TREASURE (*see under* TREASURE); WISDOM **4:**424; **5:**14; **6:**937, 964, 965–66, 969; **9:**226; **10:**820, 822, 833; **11:**409, 415
HIDE, HIDES
See under ANIMAL
HIERARCHY
1:44, 176, 355, 598, 861; **2:**21, 37, 39, 52–53, 108, 113, 136, 141, 149, 430, 631, 808, 1192; **3:**358, 803, 882, 894, 1123; **4:**122, 255, 517, 544, 613; **5:**158, 208, 217, 658, 806; **7:**7, 206–7, 660; **8:**178, 355; **9:**80, 439, 760; **10:**24, 132, 137, 928; **11:**142, 208, 272, 276, 291, 454–55, 480, 653; **12:**464, 509, 565

HIEROGLYPH (*OR* HEIROGLYPHIC, *ETC.*)
1:230–32, 249; **5:**134, 160
HIGH PLACE, PLACES
CHRIST/JESUS AS **1:**1150; **8:**666; **9:**391; **12:**12, 18–19, 26, 34, 39, 41–46, 57–64, 71, 81–82, 84, 86, 92–94, 96–97, 100, 106, 112–14, 116, 155, 159, 172, 388; AS A SHRINE **1:**259; **2:**391, 570–71, 1206, 1208; **3:**37, 39–40, 80, 90, 104, 106, 115, 118, 168, 232, 248, 251, 260, 265, 276, 279, 473, 536, 539, 564, 569, 580–81, 597, 635–36, 644; **5:**846; **6:**67, 168, 556, 920, 1157, 1159–61, 1168–69, 1230, 1285–86, 1290, 1309, 1325, 1464, 1477, 1526, 1575–76; **7:**202–3, 241, 261, 272, 543, 602, 693; **9:**252
HIGH PRIEST
See under PRIEST
HIGHWAY, HIGHWAYS
1:178, 1160; **2:**161, 166; **5:**40, 51, 75, 151, 161; **6:**107, 145, 181, 280–82, 325, 330, 332, 335–36, 376, 500, 515, 1339, 1345, 1378, 1408; **8:**13, 156, 533; **12:**392. *See also by name in* PLACES IN THE BIBLE
HILL, HILLS
1:180, 217, 251, 278, 439, 475, 557, 1015, 1143; **2:**121, 123, 126, 385, 592, 648, 681, 685, 717, 719, 853–55, 1006, 1038, 1175, 1217, 1237; **3:**39, 90, 150, 155, 173, 597, 628, 686, 759, 765, 1109, 1124; **4:**45, 47, 66, 71, 119, 129, 156, 217, 312, 450, 747, 773, 1024, 1100, 1180–81; **5:**93, 403, 764; **6:**221, 606, 685, 972, 1023, 1160, 1128, 1472; **7:**275, 321, 335, 354, 376, 559, 560, 564, 610, 679; **8:**121, 175, 182, 490; **9:**22, 81, 454, 462, 463; **10:**395, 758; **12:**527, 713; COUNTRY **1:**245–48, 251, 257–59, 261–62, 264, 268, 828; **2:**122, 297, 308, 534, 557, 582, 594, 606, 641, 662, 685, 715, 739, 744, 779, 837, 863, 900, 1079, 1153, 1215–16, 1385; **3:**52, 82, 100, 150, 353; **4:**146, 152; **5:**262; **7:**218, 542; **9:**54, 59, 110, 300; HIGH **1:**1119; **4:**307; **6:**255, 601, 604, 1159–60, 1224, 1285, 1466; **7:**543; HOLY **1:**281; **4:**689, 694, 733, 853, 1014; **7:**454; MOUNTAINS AND **3:**1058; **4:**313, 1142, 1180; **6:**73, 355, 477, 1159, 1427, 1474, 1483; **7:**273, 577–78, 583, 602 (*see also* MOUNT, MOUNTAIN)
HINGE, HINGES
OF A GATE *or* FIGURATIVELY **1:**349, 432, 995; **4:**654, 686, 704, 1211, 1275; **5:**225; **6:**211, 547, 1427, 1507, 1555, 1581; **8:**316; **9:**688, 694; **10:**860, 909, 980; **12:**216, 372
HIPPOPOTAMUS, HIPPOPOTAMUSES
1:1081; **4:**615, 618
HISS (*OR* HISSES, *ETC.*)
4:1140, 1240; **6:**914, 1041, 1382; **7:**605, 691
HISTORICAL JESUS
See JESUS, HISTORICAL
HISTORICAL ACCURACY
1:253, 263; **2:**1070; **3:**82, 904, 1102; **4:**656, 690, 694, 1105; **6:**282, 939; **9:**95, 815; **10:**27, 31, 389; **11:**221
HISTORICITY
1:56, 91, 104, 116, 163, 254, 257, 327, 516; **2:**541, 724, 1201, 1203; **3:**43, 569, 699, 859, 879, 978, 1077; **5:**217; **6:**576, 1270, 1354; **7:**22, 44, 341; **8:**78, 80; **9:**160, 693; **10:**235
HISTORY
OF (ANCIENT) ISRAEL **1:**18, 47, 78, 95, 129, 131–33, 136, 213, 234, 244–45, 248, 250, 252–53, 257, 260, 276, 306, 308, 310, 317, 327, 420, 422, 426, 430, 432, 438, 441, 447, 467, 515, 593, 665, 861, 1056; **2:**6–8, 36, 69, 96, 98, 178, 183, 187–88, 252, 264, 291–92, 300, 326, 345, 355–56, 363, 367, 430, 479, 488, 500–501, 503–4, 511, 513, 529, 541, 543, 560–61, 612, 626, 635, 673, 680, 715, 724, 727, 732, 752, 755, 760, 776, 809–10, 816, 819, 837, 845, 864, 953–54, 960, 969, 1019, 1254, 1262, 1332; **3:**4, 6, 236, 252–53, 364, 407, 424, 494, 602, 735, 802, 811, 813, 820, 956, 1014, 1093, 1115, 1118, 1168, 1172; **4:**6, 765, 868, 1000, 1017, 1050, 1112, 1134, 1203, 1224; **5:**2, 14, 21, 149, 160, 364–65, 371, 377, 530, 534, 543, 591, 606, 620, 836; **6:**5, 35, 50, 284, 285, 364, 377, 413, 429, 442–43, 464, 519, 555–56, 575–77, 598, 614, 950, 958, 1015, 1099, 1103, 1141, 1147, 1160, 1168, 1198, 1225, 1242, 1274–75, 1278, 1280, 1320, 1333, 1338, 1386, 1491; **7:**3, 6, 16, 272–73, 319, 358, 408, 424, 458, 574, 579, 726, 741, 775, 823, 830; **8:**29–30, 41, 149, 271, 410; **9:**4, 21, 41, 91, 95, 207, 249, 383, 456, 542, 638; **10:**66, 99, 121–22, 124–26, 364, 505, 513, 534, 563, 624–25, 660, 662, 671, 747; **11:**779, 828, 861; **12:**9, 52–53, 55, 99, 140, 143–44, 534, 727; BIBLICAL **1:**54, 70, 131, 171, 201, 203, 268; **2:**467, 569; **3:**1076, 1102; **6:**297; **7:**40; **12:**504; OF CHRISTIANITY **2:**719; **3:**898; **7:**67; **8:**5, 44, 54; **11:**792, 853; **12:**709; OF THE CHURCH **1:**19, 200; **2:**617, 702, 1143; **3:**576; **4:**1112; **6:**728; **7:**8, 565, 776; **8:**167, 202, 212, 275, 288, 351, 448, 509; **9:**3, 665, 734, 767, 847, 865; **10:**671, 766, 813, 823, 875; **11:**248, 618, 650, 892; **12:**125, 456, 543, 713; DEUTERONOMIC (*see under* DEUTERONOMY, BOOK OF); DEUTERONOMISTIC (*see under* DEUTERONOMY, BOOK OF); END OF **1:**74; **2:**91; **6:**1511; **7:**303; **8:**45, 50–52, 211, 346, 455; **10:**38, 85–86; **11:**615; **12:**252, 709, 711; GOD IN/OF **1:**170; **2:**98, 483–84; **3:**36, 1168; **5:**2, 519; **6:**98, 129, 138, 161, 194, 359, 786–88, 1185; **7:**442; **8:**158, 304; **10:**462, 625; HUMAN **1:**85, 91, 431, 680, 712–13; **2:**370, 505, 530, 601, 981–82, 994, 1091, 1104,

HISTORY *(continued)*
1217, 1238, 1259, 1298, 1333, 1383; **3:**24, 96, 159, 226, 381, 563, 656, 867, 868, 985; **4:**299, 577, 687, 811, 887; **5:**40, 93, 307, 311, 333, 506–7, 523, 598; **6:**98, 140, 755, 982, 1291, 1305, 1531; **7:**8–9, 11–13, 327, 422, 596, 612, 615, 672, 718, 847; **8:**504; **9:**4, 20, 52, 67, 95–96, 161, 347, 417, 519, 524, 571; **10:**42, 45; **11:**211, 547, 640, 829; **12:**56, 255, 516, 520, 567, 569–70, 609, 682, 701–2, 705, 735; OF INTERPRETATION **1:**21, 36, 83, 330, 359, 1125; **2:**195, 213, 394, 724, 830, 833; **3:**872; **4:**899, 1027; **6:**50, 92, 122, 285, 311, 366, 403, 434, 451, 461, 468; **7:**8; **8:**279; **9:**495, 623, 649, 699, 840; **10:**68, 124, 369–70, 384, 481, 602; **11:**192, 308; **12:**197, 222, 503–4, 506–7, 528, 555, 602, 659; ISRAELITE **1:**127, 136, 164, 244, 251–53, 257, 275, 286, 408; **3:**3, 407, 1118–20, 1123–24, 1132, 1139; **5:**13, 621, 696; **6:**2, 6, 8, 14, 1213; **7:**126, 466; **8:**41; **10:**628; PRIESTLY (*see under* PRIESTLY WRITER); SALVATION (*see under* SALVATION); TEXTUAL **1:**10, 69, 78, 128–29, 135, 295, 682; **2:**996, 1109, 1261, 1270; **3:**417, 862; **4:**362; **6:**867, 1092; **9:**504, 615, 627; **10:**17, 378; TRADITION **1:**2, 131–35, 244, 308, 403, 451; **2:**6–7, 177, 579; **5:**26, 62; **6:**129; **7:**339, 342; **8:**76–80, 85, 94, 129, 202, 549; **9:**169, 615, 627, 737; **11:**852–53; WORLD **1:**41, 166, 308, 407; **2:**559; **3:**1099; **4:**8, 488, 1005, 1052, 1224; **6:**164, 203, 262, 274, 1130; **7:**3, 378, 415, 636, 847; **8:**51, 129; **9:**4, 62; **10:**416, 427, 432, 624–25, 664, 701, 763; **11:**203; **12:**535, 548

HOLIDAY, HOLIDAYS
1:1113; **2:**911; **3:**189, 355, 869, 927, 935, 937–39, 967, 971, 1025, 1132, 1162; **4:**934; **7:**273; **8:**574, 660; **9:**327; **10:**757

HOLINESS
1:45, 67, 103, 272, 280–81, 283, 567, 707, 718, 720, 784, 833, 836–37, 839, 843, 861, 873, 881, 883, 887–88, 892, 897, 905, 907–9, 914–15, 918, 920, 922, 925, 935, 941–42, 964, 974, 980, 987, 995, 997–99, 1003–5, 1019, 1021, 1040, 1045–46, 1062, 1070, 1074, 1076–77, 1082–84, 1098, 1100, 1115–16, 1121–24, 1127–28, 1131–33, 1135–37, 1139, 1141–44, 1146–50, 1152, 1155, 1157, 1160, 1161, 1163–64, 1166, 1191; **2:**15, 20–23, 25–26, 32–34, 47, 52–55, 60–62, 64, 67–69, 82–83, 91, 135–36, 139–40, 142, 147, 152–53, 160, 170, 229, 235, 247, 281, 331–32, 349, 388, 394, 397, 399, 403, 445, 614, 981, 1012, 1140–41, 1143, 1249; **3:**386, 393, 484, 506, 561, 576, 624, 848, 997, 1008; **4:**71, 185, 191, 194, 197, 205, 211, 281, 377, 773, 1054, 1075–76, 1134; **5:**67, 464, 486, 558, 668, 726; **6:**13, 414, 467, 493, 531–32, 543, 549, 636, 662, 933, 1161, 1290, 1397, 1399, 1512, 1514, 1522, 1533–34, 1558, 1562–64, 1576, 1578–79, 1591–92, 1597; **7:**106, 136, 148, 376, 455, 727, 728, 748, 779, 836, 839–40; **8:**212, 331, 335, 376, 379, 532, 551–52, 555, 675, 678; **9:**59, 349, 374, 391; **10:**11, 155, 214, 411, 419, 421, 539, 546, 548, 552, 588, 593, 599, 601, 605, 630, 700, 704, 711, 792, 815, 823, 832, 845, 847, 849–52, 855, 865–66, 868–69, 882–83, 886–87, 893; **11:**5, 10, 45, 103–5, 219, 359–60, 377–78, 393, 399, 414, 419, 428–31, 435–36, 443, 450–51, 455, 461, 463, 515, 558, 560, 585, 593, 596, 607, 641, 661, 690, 692, 701, 714, 716–19, 721, 732–33, 736, 798; **12:**153, 247–48, 258, 265, 267, 277, 358, 446, 492, 498, 579, 597, 604, 668, 723, 726, 729–30; CODE **1:**986–87, 993–95, 1003, 1074, 1115, 1117, 1123, 1126–27, 1156, 1172, 1178; **2:**474; **3:**616, 721; **4:**1006; **6:**597, 1152, 1154, 1206, 1258, 1309; **7:**776; **11:**225; **12:**260–61, 489; DIVINE **1:**280; **2:**20–21, 25–26, 49, 59–60, 134, 147, 150–51, 160, 164, 528; **4:**384; **6:**493, 1168, 1206, 1510, 1574; OF GOD **1:**281, 707, 712, 718, 721, 836–38, 849, 876, 883, 888, 898, 908, 913, 921–24, 942, 963, 974, 988, 994–95, 997–98, 1001, 1009, 1024, 1057, 1072, 1105–6, 1124, 1131, 1151–52; **2:**4–5, 11, 13, 15, 21, 25, 39, 59–60, 62, 82, 92, 98, 104, 141, 152, 169, 262, 289, 395, 491, 796, 1014, 1140, 1252; **3:**1009; **4:**520, 1070, 1076, 1112; **6:**7, 358, 522, 526, 580, 972, 1106, 1491, 1495, 1519, 1530; **7:**417, 639; **8:**203, 333, 335, 545, 551; **9:**239; **11:**242, 440, 719; **12:**123, 152, 258, 261, 285, 672, 728; OF THE LORD/YAHWEH **1:**836; **6:**597, 1316, 1399, 1519, 1523

HOLM TREE
6:387

HOLOCAUST, HOLOCAUSTS
1:32, 80, 697, 1011, 1013; **2:**147, 505, 649, 1007, 1092, 1103, 1149, 1368; **3:**710, 873, 887, 890, 926; **4:**277, 404, 465, 513–14, 675, 1229; **5:**129, 327, 580; **6:**138, 694, 815, 981, 1010, 1038, 1058, 1071–72, 1129, 1156, 1170, 1211, 1237, 1253, 1345, 1395, 1504; **7:**262, 279, 700; **10:**170, 621, 697; **11:**195, 404, 810; **12:**507

HOLY
CITY (*see* JERUSALEM *in PLACES IN THE BIBLE*); DAY(S) **1:**986, 1156, 1160–61; **2:**331; **3:**819, 848, 940, 1025; **4:**41, 125, 233, 569, 1003; **5:**611; **6:**500; **7:**394, 416; **9:**719; **10:**275, 750; **11:**362; FAMILY **8:**147; **9:**70, 72; **12:**474, 482; GROUND/SOIL **1:**273, 278, 499, 1000; **6:**579; **10:**127; HILL/MOUNTAIN(S) **1:**273, 278, 281, 359; **2:**316; **4:**71, 689, 694, 733, 853, 872, 1014, 1023, 1075; **5:**516, 586; **6:**39, 67, 142, 144, 207, 227, 242, 325, 454, 483, 485, 489–91, 500, 513, 542, 546,

549, 552, 1083, 1103, 1115, 1289–90, 1393–94, 1430, 1530, 1595; **7:**454, 795; **10:**143; **12:**664; HOLY GHOST (*see* HOLY GHOST *in PERSONS IN THE BIBLE*); HOLY GOD (*see under* GOD, NAMES FOR/TITLES OF *in PERSONS IN THE BIBLE*); "HOLY, HOLY, HOLY" **1:**209, 1131; **6:**105; **12:**507, 592; HOLY OF HOLIES (*see under* JERUSALEM TEMPLE *in PLACES IN THE BIBLE*); HOLY ONE (*see under* GOD, NAMES FOR/TITLES OF *in PERSONS IN THE BIBLE*); HOLY SPIRIT (*see* HOLY SPIRIT *in PERSONS IN THE BIBLE*); LAND (*see* HOLY LAND *in PLACES IN THE BIBLE*); TO THE LORD/YAHWEH **1:**869, 907; **2:**349, 397; **3:**729; **4:**198; **6:**1605; **7:**749, 766, 839; **11:**271; MOST (*see under* GOD, NAMES FOR/TITLES OF *in PERSONS IN THE BIBLE*); NAME (*see under* GOD, NAMES FOR/TITLES OF *in PERSONS IN THE BIBLE*); NATION **1:**688, 830, 891, 997, 1009, 1082, 1098, 1124; **2:**136, 349–50; **3:**319, 926; **5:**67, 583–86; **6:**588; **8:**32; **10:**567; **12:**241, 267, 269, 285, 312, 603, 721; ONES **1:**90, 288; **4:**39, 460, 736; **5:**341, 436, 505, 585, 591; **7:**9, 72, 100, 105–7, 117, 783, 836; **8:**147, 691–92; **9:**18, 367; **11:**370, 372, 382–83, 386, 389, 403, 407, 410, 419, 435–36, 481, 593–94, 714, 750; **12:**33, 494, 597; PEOPLE **1:**997, 1077, 1082, 1084; **2:**15, 38, 323, 397; **3:**733; **4:**184; **5:**463; **6:**326, 510, 514, 516, 527, 529, 532, 1206; **7:**149; **8:**157, 332, 431; **11:**301, 529, 593–94, 615, 649, 719; **12:**243, 256–58, 261, 267, 657; PLACE(S) *or* MOST HOLY PLACE **1:**897–98, 907, 916, 976–77, 1033–34, 1040, 1045, 1048, 1061, 1072, 1110–11, 1113–14, 1147, 1155, 1163; **2:**349, 407, 410, 1198, 1238–39; **3:**80, 484, 494, 576, 736; **4:**39, 198, 205, 732, 973, 1279; **5:**337; **6:**38, 67, 102, 108, 239, 281–82, 509, 640, 1260, 1389, 1555, 1558, 1576, 1582; **7:**128, 162, 205, 252, 376, 561, 727, 787; **8:**201, 405, 442–43, 493, 516; **9:**118, 133, 697; **10:**122, 127, 137, 297, 474, 832; **12:**82, 103–6, 113, 116, 120, 569, 672, 725–27; PRESENCE (*see under* GOD, NAMES FOR/TITLES OF *in PERSONS IN THE BIBLE*); SCRIPTURE(S) **1:**29, 37, 161, 188; **3:**63, 364, 381, 1077, 1172; **7:**537; **10:**768; **12:**457; SEPULCHRE **8:**490; THING(S) **1:**67, 908, 935, 1019, 1021, 1039, 1040, 1148–49, 1155; **2:**1140–41; **3:**346, 393, 437, 624, 745; **4:**39; **5:**72, 491; **6:**1309, 1314, 1577–78; **8:**212; WAR(S) (*see* WAR: HOLY/JUST); WEEK **1:**189; **2:**90, 236; **4:**956, 960; **6:**1017; **9:**685, 704–5, 719, 799, 811, 869; **11:**417; **12:**4

HOMICIDE
2:263, 265–67, 333, 432, 436, 453; **3:**556, 574; **5:**797; **6:**1190

HOMOSEXUALITY (*OR* HOMOSEXUAL, *ETC.*)
1:285, 474, 477, 844, 1126–27, 1141; **2:**877, 1208; **5:**391; **9:**126; **10:**28, 171, 433–35, 858; **11:**791–92; **12:**489–90

HONEY
1:1018, 1071; **2:**356, 767, 842–43, 850, 1080; **3:**112, 126, 624, 736; **4:**485, 1004; **5:**66–68, 162, 211, 219, 230, 379, 405–6, 415, 758, 818, 555; **6:**112, 1125, 1228, 1377–78; **8:**532; **9:**81; **11:**50; **12:**639; MILK AND (*see under* MILK)

HONOR (*OR* HONORS, *ETC.*)
1:280, 428–30, 554, 577–79, 581, 604–5, 634–35, 720, 734, 745, 863, 867, 896, 916, 1037, 1139, 1147, 1150; **2:**54, 406, 413, 423, 474, 480, 482, 547, 549, 659, 762, 780, 817, 1014, 1111, 1127, 1140, 1180, 1188, 1198, 1201, 1206, 1213, 1217, 1222, 1226, 1230, 1250, 1274, 1279, 1283, 1285, 1287, 1304–5, 1351, 1360; **3:**28, 39–40, 83, 87, 156, 345, 363, 388, 409, 443, 469, 474, 570, 581, 618, 631, 911–12, 914–15, 918–19, 951, 980, 1041, 1050, 1069, 1071, 1087, 1181; **4:**23, 69, 160, 169, 172, 236, 291–92, 340, 349, 361, 489, 537–38, 541, 544–46, 551, 555–56, 595, 613, 693, 696, 711–12, 862, 960, 1014, 1024, 1044, 1066, 1097–98, 1133, 1260; **5:**13, 37, 49, 55, 68, 103, 119, 133, 187, 214, 223–25, 345–46, 426, 475, 498, 525, 616, 624, 627, 638, 641, 658–60, 667, 670, 673, 680, 693, 703, 705, 720, 814, 824, 828; **6:**199, 217, 806, 852, 914, 952, 958, 1009–10, 1061, 1117, 1167, 1176, 1223, 1234, 1309, 1316, 1439, 1442, 1483, 1526; **7:**21, 51, 63, 75, 77, 83, 105, 140, 176, 187, 206, 208–10, 225, 239, 245, 321, 635, 647, 779, 849, 858–59; **8:**16, 321–22, 359, 513, 519, 522, 533, 546, 550, 567, 592, 599, 637, 652–54, 681–82, 699; **9:**26, 46, 107, 124, 127–28, 170, 211, 227, 236, 248, 250, 252, 285, 287, 290, 308–9, 347, 358, 378–79, 393–94, 472, 574; **10:**234, 290, 438, 442, 447, 551, 578, 580, 711, 721, 762, 774, 782, 802, 828, 832, 867, 947, 992; **11:**16, 21, 27, 57, 81, 141, 153, 158, 169, 173, 176, 348, 377, 446, 480, 489, 503, 507, 510, 513, 516, 520, 680, 734, 751, 819, 822, 824, 838–39, 845; **12:**11, 124, 138, 170, 180, 192, 195, 234, 266, 273, 275, 285, 345, 481–82, 485, 593, 597; DIVINE/GOD'S **2:**364; **3:**611, 956, 967; **4:**348, 361, 556, 613, 629; **6:**952, 981, 1287; **7:**587; **8:**277–78; **10:**653; **12:**251; FATHER/MOTHER/PARENTS **1:**405, 847, 1131, 1141; **2:**332; **3:**1014–15; **5:**48, 616, 658, 660; **6:**1309; **8:**606, 645; **9:**77, 347, 349; **11:**656; AND GLORY **2:**791, 1207; **4:**697, 712, 923, 1198; **5:**226, 231; **7:**272, 647; **10:**440, 930; **12:**37–39, 42, 61, 251, 269, 282, 594, 605; GOD/THE LORD/YAHWEH **1:**759, 844, 940, 1132; **2:**411, 988, 1007, 1013–14, 1093, 1252; **3:**432, 468, 594, 654, 967; **4:**38, 51, 361, 733, 822, 835, 871, 882, 885, 1127, 1272; **5:**49–50, 144, 628, 658, 861; **6:**78, 244, 378,

HONOR *(continued)*
382, 953; **7:**716–18; **8:**203, 277; **9:**136, 466, 584; **10:**432, 448, 468, 567, 694, 827, 883, 921, 922; **11:**510, 527, 733; **12:**192, 251, 273, 274, 337; PLACE(S) OF **1:**601, 659, 1141; **2:**789; **3:**402; **4:**256; **5:**222, 705, 715, 828; **6:**808; **7:**827, 862; **8:**431, 707; **9:**286–87, 336, 343, 353, 393; **10:**494; AND RICHES/WEALTH **3:**469, 474, 546, 551, 1068; **4:**925, 1198; **5:**53, 227, 320, 498, 663; **6:**1061; **7:**54, 724; AND SHAME (*see under* SHAME)

HOOK, HOOKS
1:1171; **2:**35, 759, 1237; **3:**468, 484; **4:**119, 622; **5:**207; **6:**23, 68–69, 180, 294, 1269, 1401, 1404, 1434–35, 1516, 1547; **7:**332, 377, 612; **8:**539; **9:**313

HOPE
APOCALYPTIC **8:**392; **11:**686, 704, 722–23, 731, 736; IN CHRIST/GOD/JESUS/THE LORD/YAHWEH **1:**280, 479, 735, 1017; **2:**66, 80, 283, 514, 864, 976–77, 1011, 1021, 1039, 1137, 1258–59, 1297, 1370, 1381; **3:**208, 273, 382, 403, 497, 970; **4:**200, 524, 650, 660, 679, 695, 709, 722, 777, 809, 834, 837, 839, 850, 854, 902, 1030, 1059, 1086, 1088, 1196, 1206; **5:**182, 469, 524, 656, 825; **6:**118, 320, 733, 1056, 1169, 1486; **7:**183, 295, 478, 514, 540, 570, 588, 700, 816; **8:**365, 725; **9:**336, 340, 381, 406, 417, 707, 754; **10:**25, 140, 335, 342, 376, 510, 924; **11:**42, 269, 375, 499, 691, 811, 819, 846; **12:**259, 302, 500; CHRISTIAN **4:**1217; **5:**825; **6:**551, 822; **7:**429; **9:**473, 784–85; **10:**509, 513, 604, 631; **11:**382, 386, 538, 640, 790, 862, 871; **12:**50, 200, 250, 262, 273, 281, 292, 316; ESCHATOLOGICAL **2:**1039, 1092; **3:**474, 562, 830; **5:**134; **7:**439, 797; **8:**144, 180, 348; **10:**524, 749; **11:**224, 313, 640; **12:**274, 281, 284, 497, 509; FAITH AND **1:**153, 426; **2:**480, 514; **3:**386, 403, 560, 873; **4:**690, 749, 777, 779, 787, 828, 958, 993, 1001, 1028, 1030, 1206–7; **6:**164, 1051; **7:**442; **9:**49, 334, 417; **10:**512, 615, 745, 757, 953–55, 957; **11:**385; **12:**135, 139, 259; FOR THE FUTURE **1:**635; **2:**128, 480–81, 503, 506, 520, 534, 1102, 1205, 1234, 1372, 1382; **3:**390, 475, 505, 562, 1008; **4:**1086, 1129, 1211; **6:**138, 768, 791, 797, 812, 877, 1408, 1478; **7:**321, 551, 561, 589, 685, 691; **8:**37; **9:**753, 785, 797; **10:**444, 510, 516, 591, 604, 614, 953; **11:**318, 337, 615, 862; **12:**188, 254, 340, 431, 500, 518, 520; OF ISRAEL **2:**393, 504, 983, 1029, 1099; **4:**1208; **5:**469, 543; **6:**531; **9:**70; **10:**318, 336, 340; MESSAGE OF **2:**319, 489, 512–13, 520, 526; **3:**873, 972; **6:**148, 797; **7:**219, 458, 538, 553, 607, 660, 708, 800; **8:**692; **12:**40, 662; MESSIANIC **2:**866, 1259, 1260; **8:**142, 353; **10:**702; **12:**602; FOR/OF RESURRECTION **2:**1232; **5:**717; **6:**223; **9:**159, 346; **10:**24, 310, 315, 318, 335–36, 340, 342, 607; **11:**337; **12:**231, 716; FOR/OF SALVATION **3:**947; **7:**234, 281; **8:**144, 535, 659; **10:**692, 829; **11:**411, 459, 591; **12:**653; SIGN(S) OF **1:**630; **2:**92, 128, 727; **3:**122, 738, 1065; **6:**123–24; **7:**665; **10:**606; **12:**297; SOURCE OF **1:**464; **2:**1092; **4:**854, 991; **7:**91, 648, 748; **12:**587

HORN, HORNS
1:28, 219, 288, 953, 1082, 1118; **2:**91, 188, 230–32, 588, 613, 980–83, 1098, 1366; **3:**22, 446; **4:**48, 71, 80, 109, 276, 459, 635, 763, 976–77, 1035, 1212–13, 1271–72, 1279; **5:**229, 867; **6:**13, 892, 1411, 1431, 1534, 1555, 1568–69; **7:**8–9, 76, 100, 102–3, 105, 112–13, 116, 321, 403, 567, 737, 744, 751, 755–57, 760, 778, 780; **9:**19, 59, 282, 313, 359, 378; **11:**460; **12:**538, 543–44, 603, 649, 656, 657, 658, 681–82, 684–85; OF THE ALTAR (*see under* ALTAR); RAM'S (*see under* RAM)

HORNET, HORNETS
1:562, 877; **5:**542

HORSE, HORSES
1:90, 116, 219, 666, 754, 795, 799, 802, 804, 1001; **2:**651, 788, 1101, 1208, 1266, 1319; **3:**17, 54, 87–88, 132, 176, 180, 201, 207–8, 221, 237, 265, 474, 511, 759, 914, 925; **4:**210, 299, 306, 598, 610–12, 624, 801, 980; **5:**182, 196, 346, 382, 387, 593, 777; **6:**72, 74, 98, 195, 255, 260, 293, 375, 549, 647, 886, 1177, 1196, 1232, 1248, 1312, 1321, 1325, 1366, 1377–78, 1442, 1516–17, 1528; **7:**295, 403, 547, 635, 653, 737, 748, 750–52, 756–57, 760, 770, 782–84, 807, 814, 826, 839; **8:**309, 403; **9:**367, 480; **11:**526; **12:**87, 203, 551, 610, 612, 631–32, 699–700; DEDICATED TO THE SUN **6:**1177; **7:**783; WAR **4:**598, 610, 612, 624; **6:**646; **7:**807, 814; **8:**309, 403; **9:**367; WHITE **5:**382; **7:**784; **9:**431; **12:**517, 525, 533, 538, 558, 566, 580, 583, 603, 610–12, 682–83, 698–700, 702, 704, 706, 720

HORSEMAN, HORSEMEN
2:1202, 1206; **3:**17, 176, 180; **4:**210, 348; **5:**709; **6:**1232, 1324; **7:**366, 635; **9:**431; **12:**530, 611, 632, 699

HOSANNA, HOSANNAS
1:1160; **4:**1155; **8:**403–4; **9:**369, 707–8; **12:**531, 621, 624

HOSEA
THE WRITINGS OF **1:**262, 265, 660, 679; **2:**142, 187, 198, 606, 1050; **4:**313, 400; **5:**36, 45, 113, 369, 419, 430, 558; **6:**2, 6, 11–12, 17–19, 45, 53, 57, 62, 82, 176, 227, 331, 543, 608, 657, 1241, 1326, 1355, 1471; **7:**339, 343, 386, 436, 559, 583, 685–86, 843, 853, 864; **8:**151, 235, 256, 333; **9:**452, 558; **10:**642–43, 863, 866; **11:**75, 646; **12:**579

HOSPITALITY
1:462–64, 467, 473–74, 511, 522, 580, 599, 704–5, 825, 1136; **2:**191, 459, 467, 774, 783, 804, 807, 846, 876–79, 918, 923, 967, 1166–67, 1193, 1211, 1270, 1273, 1292, 1309; **3:**28, 187, 202, 783, 844, 908, 986–87, 1024, 1038, 1124, 1159; **4:**143, 176, 421, 538, 554, 1098, 1214; **5:**596–97, 715; **6:**1327; **7:**449, 704; **8:**13, 257, 472, 546, 553, 595, 637, 640–41, 649, 651, 681; **9:**27, 35, 131, 172, 194, 197, 220, 236, 283, 285, 358, 362, 393, 426, 429, 479–80, 483, 538, 540, 565, 640, 722–24, 727, 730; **10:**22, 164, 231, 234–35, 239, 278, 292, 355–56, 358, 367, 801; **11:**22, 405, 668, 804–5, 820, 825, 858, 902; **12:**12, 66, 140, 142, 162, 170, 194–95, 199, 304, 373, 454, 462–66, 468, 475, 489

HOSTAGE, HOSTAGES
1:764–65, 767, 882; **2:**1089; **3:**242, 353, 587, 654; **4:**11, 31, 93, 104, 115, 119, 121, 140–41, 151, 216, 264, 283; **7:**141; **12:**83, 155

HOSTS
CELESTIAL AND/OR TERRESTRIAL **3:**176, 179–80, 237; **5:**757, 833; **6:**40, 378, 421, 527, 635, 892; **7:**113–14, 126, 129, 329, 332, 456; **11:**372, 415, 436; **12:**604, 648; GOD OF **2:**959, 962, 1095, 1199, 1235, 1237; **4:**913, 1000, 1035; **5:**251; **6:**196, 812, 883; **7:**347, 376, 382, 783; **11:**214; **12:**291; OF HEAVEN **1:**287; **2:**569, 603; **3:**164, 632, 810, 813, 1057, 1179; **6:**10, 40, 101, 206, 210, 212–13, 227, 277, 334, 344, 884, 913, 1130, 1177; **7:**5, 10, 65, 113–14, 126, 168, 376, 421, 751, 755; **9:**65, 369; **10:**128–29; **12:**509, 593, 604, 606, 624, 705; LORD OF (*see under* GOD, NAMES FOR/TITLES OF *in PERSONS IN THE BIBLE*); YAHWEH OF **7:**753–54, 760, 783, 790, 826, 839

HOUR, HOURS
1:178, 201–2; **3:**403, 612, 863; **5:**308, 340, 357, 385, 627, 709, 784; **6:**414, 797, 1057, 1349, 1384, 1455, 1563; **7:**447, 609, 694; **8:**61, 206, 247, 372, 393, 448, 469, 476, 492, 577, 601, 636, 708, 722; **9:**46, 48, 90, 97, 179, 202, 245, 259, 263–64, 301, 361, 383, 399, 408, 410, 418, 434–39, 454, 460, 465, 480, 497, 514, 531, 565, 567–68, 570–72, 584–85, 616, 647, 671, 678, 686, 698, 703, 710, 712–13, 715, 717, 721, 723, 726, 730, 732–33, 735, 738, 741, 750, 752–53, 765–66, 770, 778–81, 783, 785, 789, 792–95, 797, 799–800, 802–3, 821, 823, 827, 829–30, 832, 842, 852, 855, 863–64; **10:**64, 92, 313, 982–83; **11:**225, 348, 425, 728, 760; **12:**64, 144, 375, 379, 399–400, 403–4, 406, 420, 517, 585, 589, 631, 666, 668, 682, 693, 728; OF JESUS **9:**507–9, 513, 536–37, 539, 621, 653, 681, 701–3, 710, 712–13, 718–21, 727, 729–30, 732–33, 738, 740, 746, 748–49, 759, 768, 772–73, 781, 783–84, 787–88, 790–91, 795–800, 809, 813, 821, 825, 831–32, 840, 852, 857, 860, 862, 864

HOUSE
ANCESTRAL/FATHER'S **1:**216, 577, 605; **2:**33, 35, 37, 48, 51, 140, 455, 592–94, 629, 715, 804, 850, 876–77, 904, 907, 1039, 1110, 1148; **3:**328, 725, 752, 785, 994; **4:**1013; **5:**231, 364, 397, 428; **6:**1257, 1564, 1576; **9:**20, 27, 77, 91, 201, 281, 302, 318, 373–74, 543, 740–41; **10:**58; **12:**246; CHURCH(ES) **8:**514–15; **9:**244; **10:**254, 312, 762–64, 799, 814, 1002; **11:**417, 648, 659, 668, 674–75, 884, 891–93, 902–3; **12:**10, 162, 460; OF DAVID **1:**1182; **2:**283, 426, 556–72, 574–77, 579, 585–86, 589, 601–3, 606, 609, 612, 614, 619–20, 630, 634–35, 637, 639, 641, 646, 666, 671, 673, 678, 680, 687–88, 696, 701–2, 715, 717, 1002, 1045, 1134, 1215, 1218, 1247, 1262, 1276, 1365; **3:**35, 95, 102, 114, 117, 227, 287, 295, 319, 407, 565, 568–70, 573, 576, 839; **4:**310, 1183, 1211; **6:**107, 413, 481, 734, 739–40, 742, 1015, 1252–53, 1266, 1272, 1299; **7:**427, 741, 825–26, 828–31; **8:**135; **9:**15, 134, 354, 445, 834; **10:**598; **11:**526; **12:**61; OF GOD/THE LORD/YAHWEH **1:**251, 278–79, 542–43, 585, 1014, 1024, 1027, 1054, 1071, 1139, 1148, 1151; **2:**110, 389, 726, 871, 896, 993, 1239, 1256–57, 1297; **3:**37, 40, 58, 68, 75, 104, 228, 233, 273, 347, 405, 425, 437, 477, 679, 714, 722–24, 730, 786, 798, 819–20, 826, 828, 839, 1062, 1065; **4:**116, 198, 310, 644, 701, 741, 769, 823, 927, 933, 954, 1013–14, 1024, 1054, 1097, 1183, 1195, 1211, 1216; **5:**95, 138, 316; **6:**67, 272, 301, 399, 471, 500, 509, 542, 546, 550–51, 722, 724, 809, 860, 925, 940, 942, 946, 949, 966–67, 1115, 1189, 1492, 1538, 1540, 1557, 1564; **7:**242, 260, 717, 720, 754, 765, 770, 787, 796, 804, 839; **8:**278, 664–65; **9:**77, 133, 249, 310, 343, 543, 740; **10:**128; **11:**808, 810; **12:**46, 120, 256, 265, 311, 316, 599, 725, 727; OF ISRAEL **1:**555, 560, 991, 1117; **2:**939, 941–42, 1249; **3:**393, 1165; **4:**1072; **5:**561; **6:**78, 88, 467, 584, 598, 629, 656, 661, 669, 714, 718, 1075, 1084, 1102–3, 1123, 1125–27, 1132, 1134–35, 1138, 1140–41, 1143, 1145–47, 1151, 1176, 1180, 1186, 1194, 1205–7, 1209, 1216–17, 1242, 1244, 1248, 1250, 1254, 1258, 1262, 1264, 1284–86, 1290, 1312, 1329, 1331, 1343, 1396–97, 1401, 1406, 1408, 1411, 1420–21, 1431, 1445–46, 1448, 1450–51, 1453, 1455, 1464, 1474, 1479, 1484, 1487, 1490, 1492, 1494, 1496–97, 1499, 1501, 1505–6, 1514, 1526, 1529–31, 1539, 1561–62, 1573–74, 1577–78, 1582, 1584; **7:**218, 244, 253, 375, 386, 528, 797, 826; **8:**226, 286, 336, 474; **9:**420, 757; **10:**78, 96, 125, 140, 210, 214, 219, 237, 267, 304, 339, 511; **11:**337;

HOUSE *(continued)*
12:639, 681, 723; OF JACOB **1:**654; **2:**1259; **4:**34; **6:**65, 68, 72, 246–48, 417–18, 596, 598, 1277–78, 1399; **7:**417, 424, 455; **9:**51, 354, 381, 413, 426; **10:**128; OF JOSEPH **1:**22, 259, 638, 656; **2:**729, 732–33, 742–45, 747–48, 1346; **3:**479; **7:**455, 814–15; OF JUDAH **2:**1211; **3:**109, 317, 328, 775; **6:**15, 17, 295, 584, 1145, 1147, 1177, 1349, 1351–53; **7:**218, 248, 775, 797, 799–800, 814, 826; **9:**420; OF PRAYER **2:**389, 896; **3:**502, 618; **6:**471; **8:**201, 406, 408, 661, 663–65, 673; **9:**373, 432; **10:**143; ROYAL **1:**223, 225–26, 283; **2:**384, 988, 1194; **3:**70, 368, 370, 408, 522, 608; **4:**144; **5:**138; **6:**11, 17, 61, 64, 196, 231, 328, 482, 1272, 1299; **7:**834; OF SAUL **2:**547, 562–63, 575, 641, 1126, 1132, 1134–35, 1157, 1199, 1202, 1215–16, 1218, 1222–24, 1226, 1229–30, 1238, 1246, 1250–51, 1270, 1273, 1276–77, 1319, 1325–26, 1346–47, 1357–58; **3:**14, 27, 368, 381, 886; **5:**186

HOUSEHOLDER, HOUSEHOLDERS
2:595, 1195; **4:**476; **6:**9; **9:**250, 262; **11:**657, 659, 902; **12:**281, 284

HOUSEHOLD OF GOD
1:468; **4:**767; **10:**817; **11:**284, 396, 401, 784, 795, 804, 808, 813; **12:**243, 265, 311, 313, 669, 722

HOWLING
6:157, 1000; **7:**546; **8:**583; **11:**697

HUMANITY OF CHRIST/JESUS
1:46, 51, 96, 208; **8:**137, 355, 491; **9:**522; **10:**417, 419, 823; **11:**476, 515, 607; **12:**10, 43

HUMANKIND
1:85, 126, 157–58, 160, 246, 273, 321, 329, 335–36, 349, 353–54, 381, 384, 388–89, 393, 395, 411, 413, 435, 748, 1076; **2:**191, 329, 336–37, 448, 487, 495, 512, 515, 830, 826, 912, 945, 1141; **4:**368, 395, 528, 533, 605, 666, 670, 725, 730, 753, 772, 777, 793, 840, 1052, 1066, 1069, 1075, 1080, 1099, 1112, 1252–53; **5:**36, 77, 125, 142, 160, 163, 275, 306, 310, 312–14, 321, 323, 332, 340–41, 381, 395, 639, 660, 716, 725, 726, 731, 825; **6:**73, 144, 400, 406, 544–45, 548, 787, 822, 965, 1171, 1471; **7:**280, 325, 382, 521, 603, 671, 674–75, 683, 686, 699, 721, 732, 804, 806, 824; **9:**53, 134, 515, 603; **10:**90, 247, 250, 424, 457, 459, 466, 478, 532, 546, 554, 576–77, 581, 596, 661, 696, 698; **11:**167, 184, 191, 373, 398, 400, 421, 460, 798; **12:**13, 39, 43, 68, 247, 300, 443, 585, 632, 646, 649, 676, 703, 709, 713; CREATION OF **1:**345, 349; **2:**1088; **4:**754, 1043, 1150; **6:**375, 391; **8:**583; HISTORY OF (*see also* HISTORY: HUMAN) **1:**372; **2:**286; **4:**1221; **5:**93; **10:**563

HUMILITY
1:1111; **2:**110, 112, 762, 827, 871, 995, 1031, 1122, 1262–63, 1345, 1371; **3:**40–41, 274, 359, 402, 409, 514, 520, 571, 706, 737, 914, 966, 1024, 1043, 1055, 1068, 1095, 1113–14, 1137, 1144–45, 1162; **4:**46, 334, 503, 632, 679, 738, 778–79, 783, 811, 859, 863, 887, 992, 1011, 1038, 1100, 1204, 1208–9; **5:**77, 117, 151–52, 161, 163, 198, 222, 225, 316, 320, 519, 563, 586, 610, 638, 645–46, 649, 652, 656, 661–63, 665, 680, 693; **6:**550–51, 1361; **7:**138, 319, 685, 807; **8:**374, 433; **9:**25, 35, 67, 150, 154, 173, 272, 283, 285, 287–88, 323–24, 327–28, 340, 342, 349–50, 367, 426, 863; **10:**230, 282, 451, 483, 589, 607, 644–45, 671, 696, 698, 708–9, 726–27, 743–44, 758, 817; **11:**123, 136, 219, 329, 331–32, 335–36, 339, 420, 424–25, 443, 499, 515, 517, 562, 647, 660, 820, 846, 876, 879–80; **12:**60, 130, 190, 212, 290–91, 315–18, 467, 512, 670, 705

HUMOR
1:85, 559, 723; **2:**770, 773, 1157, 1188; **3:**22, 201, 858, 1082–83, 1087, 1103, 1168; **5:**225, 255, 629, 768; **7:**185, 469–70, 497, 524; **9:**131, 276; **11:**317, 664

HUNCHBACK
1:1149

HUNTER (*OR* HUNTERS, HUNTING, *ETC.*)
1:90, 180, 489, 1120; **2:**550, 1157–58; **4:**370, 415, 467, 469, 608–9, 618, 621–22; **5:**85, 133, 509, 616, 668, 680, 687, 714, 719–20, 771; **6:**359, 703, 913, 1194, 1250, 1269, 1401, 1404, 1408, 1434, 1516; **7:**55, 347, 371, 482, 612; **8:**249

HURRICANE
4:72, 865; **5:**70; **6:**302, 766

HUSBAND, HUSBANDS
1:868, 1105; **2:**234, 266, 875–76, 903–4; **3:**986; **5:**695, 765; **6:**608–9, 629, 693, 702, 1236, 1241, 1331, 1321; **7:**209–10, 225, 232; **8:**645; **9:**313; **10:**872, 885, 928, 932; **11:**455, 652–55, 801, 820, 869–70; **12:**284–85, 287, 420; AND WIFE **1:**185, 372, 454, 513; **3:**882, 986, 1039, 1040; **5:**36, 46, 129, 144, 505, 629, 765; **6:**104, 596, 609, 702, 1265; **7:**57, 198, 209, 233, 236, 297, 585; **8:**386, 645; **9:**267, 332; **10:**762–63, 793, 869, 871–73, 875–79, 885, 888, 929; **11:**435, 446, 452, 455, 644, 654–55, 801–2, 809; **12:**284–85, 287, 289, 314 (*see also* WIFE)

HUSBANDRY
1:218, 375; **4:**488; **5:**314; **6:**9, 255

HYMN, HYMNS
1:9–10, 156–57, 163, 183, 200–201, 203–5, 206, 210, 232–34, 274, 279, 289, 644, 799–800, 802, 1067; **2:**94, 161, 214, 651–52, 774, 979–81, 1029; **3:**142, 400–401, 407, 427, 432,

447, 469, 496, 540, 562, 681, 771, 809, 1056–57, 1061, 1063, 1065, 1113, 1177–78; **4:**20, 34, 51, 67, 71, 73, 81, 165–66, 198, 200, 254, 256, 264, 296, 326, 397, 398, 429, 519, 585, 596–97, 648–49, 671, 672, 710, 722, 742, 748, 751, 792, 865, 924, 928, 944, 981, 984, 1025, 1051, 1057, 1073, 1079, 1090–91, 1096, 1099, 1103, 1106, 1196, 1206, 1219, 1223, 1256, 1262, 1267, 1270, 1273–74; **5:**4, 6, 11, 13, 15–16, 30, 91, 93, 125, 164, 219, 257, 259, 262–63, 273, 308, 367, 377, 397, 479, 618, 638, 646–48, 719, 756–57, 815, 817–18, 833–34, 835, 836, 859, 860; **6:**16, 18, 23, 67, 104–5, 121, 123, 129, 212, 216, 221, 339, 349, 361, 365, 367–68, 385, 388, 390, 393, 395, 399, 417–18, 428–30, 438, 543, 730, 795, 948–49, 971, 1305, 1404, 1465, 1607; **7:**10, 52, 89, 160–61, 168, 344–45, 347, 352, 380–81, 384, 422, 508, 535, 588–89, 595, 600, 625–26, 653–55, 660, 666, 683, 697, 699, 724; **8:**30, 35, 36, 37, 39, 67, 314, 474, 659, 705, 732; **9:**60, 224, 324, 366–67, 516, 517–18, 521–23, 665, 790, 823, 853; **10:**223, 382, 442, 940; **11:**70, 123, 375, 382, 383, 396, 405, 436–37, 438, 440, 441–42, 444, 461, 476, 493, 500–501, 503, 507, 509–10, 548, 570, 576, 597–99, 601–5, 607–11, 649, 651, 662, 728, 763, 843; **12:**23–24, 62, 86, 93, 95, 130, 149, 213, 254, 294, 297, 563, 593, 595, 602, 615, 643, 644, 650, 672, 676; OF CHRIST **11:**96, 502–3, 554–55, 558–59, 574, 607–8, 909; OF PRAISE **2:**787, 980; **3:**840, 1179; **4:**26, 97, 148, 158, 166, 303, 375; **5:**257, 260, 263, 598, 641, 817, 863; **6:**102, 147, 207, 228, 270, 728, 868, 918, 1352, 1425; **7:**162, 394, 803, 824; **9:**59, 787; **10:**696; **11:**606, 611; **12:**561, 615, 644; OF THANKSGIVING **1:**10, 280; **3:**431, 637, 1176; **4:**795; **6:**122–23, 147–48, 428, 430; **9:**642, 834 (*see also* THANKSGIVING HYMNS *in ANCIENT LITERATURE*)

HYPOCRISY
1:1021; **2:**1359; **4:**236, 336, 427, 472, 724, 882–83; **5:**163, 194, 226, 652, 654, 824; **6:**244, 499, 550, 848; **7:**245–46, 253–54, 268, 287, 419; **8:**143, 188, 196, 431, 435–36, 470, 480, 501; **9:**74, 152, 172, 251–53, 263, 268, 281, 312, 393–94, 818; **10:**108, 223, 310, 330, 443; **11:**234, 343, 791, 811, 833

HYPOCRITE, HYPOCRITES
3:1114; **4:**782–83, 882, 925; **5:**163, 771, 786; **6:**244; **8:**143, 188, 200–201, 420, 429, 431, 448, 673; **9:**151, 251, 268, 285, 342; **11:**79

HYSSOP
1:1012, 1098, 1100; **2:**151; **4:**886; **5:**502; **9:**833; **12:**110

I

I AM
"I AM WHO I AM" (*see under* GOD, NAMES FOR/TITLES OF *in PERSONS IN THE BIBLE*); SAYINGS **8:**74; **9:**204, 494, 534, 596, 601–2, 632, 634, 646, 693, 742, 755–57, 802, 869; TETRAGRAMMATON **5:**748; **7:**290, 498; **10:**630 (*see also* TETRAGRAMMATON)

ICE
1:344; **4:**598, 605; **5:**219, 577–78, 618, 834; **6:**305; **12:**597

IDLE, IDLENESS
1:1157; **5:**64, 262, 568, 791; **8:**393; **10:**382; **11:**156, 730–31, 747, 765, 767, 770, 821, 865

IDOLATRY
1:165, 285, 314, 1118, 1132, 1178; **2:**106, 195, 197–98, 313–21, 352, 355, 442, 714, 756, 762, 774, 790–91, 806–9, 886, 869–70, 1017, 1020, 1027, 1064, 1089, 1213; **3:**104, 158, 226, 581, 894, 1142, 1221; **4:**82, 198, 582, 822, 886, 1017, 1111, 1221, 1235; **5:**417, 446, 474, 536, 548–49, 551, 554, 556–73, 622, 696, 702, 849; **6:**73–74, 176, 342–43, 354, 389, 399, 403, 407, 414, 418, 527, 640, 662, 714, 874, 987, 1192, 1205–6, 1224, 1276, 1286, 1306, 1458, 1463, 1489, 1509; **7:**30, 81, 185, 190, 204, 210, 288–89, 295, 394, 544, 553, 576, 660, 665, 676, 780–81, 805, 864; **8:**33, 41, 673; **9:**300, 374, 640; **10:**8, 22, 129, 195, 220, 222, 243–47, 249, 271, 410, 428–35, 445, 492, 499, 506, 640, 724, 741, 748, 809, 887, 898, 913–14, 916–18; **11:**79, 97, 223–24, 232, 287, 327, 347, 434–35, 628, 642, 645, 828, 866; **12:**154, 297, 301, 305, 325, 443, 446, 491, 521, 529, 578–80, 587–88, 595, 632–33, 664, 684, 726

IDOLS
See IMAGE

IGNORANCE
1:366, 467, 1033, 1113; **2:**546; **3:**658; **4:**475, 591, 604; **5:**13, 41, 85, 252, 256, 296, 306, 311, 584, 648, 675, 740, 749, 834; **6:**243, 281, 619, 647, 970; **7:**728; **8:**22, 34; **9:**135, 178, 264, 477, 479, 663, 730, 763, 821; **10:**21, 23, 57, 62–63, 67, 77, 79–81, 85, 89, 91, 108, 197, 199, 246, 329, 338, 339, 567, 579; **11:**276, 282, 287, 428, 636, 721

IMAGE, IMAGES
DIVINE/OF GOD **1:**123, 343, 345–46, 350, 352–53, 364, 380–81, 396, 399, 445, 565, 661, 995, 1042, 1165; **2:**408, 488, 495, 790, 808; **3:**998; **4:**197, 349, 358, 397, 414, 423, 439, 459, 464, 510, 519, 530, 537, 546, 553, 572, 593, 609, 712, 840, 947, 1072, 1236; **5:**93, 121, 390, 464, 465–66, 486, 504, 507, 549, 730; **6:**19, 55, 530, 716, 1306; **7:**242, 252, 280, 603, 653, 655, 679, 732, 784; **8:**582–83,

IMAGE, IMAGES *(continued)*
666, 673; **9:**92, 296, 669; **10:**428, 433, 463, 595, 600, 602, 604, 607, 769; **11:**74, 130, 216, 290, 400, 504, 506–9, 597, 605, 628, 644, 678, 901; **12:**206, 374, 416; GRAVEN **4:**463; **5:**187; **6:**1049 (*see also* IDOLATRY); OF JEALOUSLY **6:**1175; OF LIGHT (*see* LIGHT: IMAGES/SYMBOLS OF); MOLTEN **2:**810, 869–70; **7:**262, 293, 606

IMAGINATION
AND BIBLICAL INTERPRETATION **1:**157, 185–86, 195, 730, 768; **2:**956–58, 1377; **4:**412, 464, 519, 556, 654, 765; **5:**823, 860; **6:**191, 359, 811; **9:**744; **11:**627; **12:**506–7, 514, 523, 552, 555, 560, 562, 595, 615, 670; IN EARLY JUDAISM **1:**68–69; **8:**96, 183; AND EXODUS OR PASSOVER **1:**324, 355, 683–85, 697–98, 712, 722, 803, 873, 884–85

IMMANENCE
2:90; **3:**72, 497; **4:**1075, 1092; **5:**506–7, 519; **11:**71, 608; **12:**389, 543, 603

IMMANUEL
See under JESUS THE CHRIST, NAMES FOR/TITLES OF *in PERSONS IN THE BIBLE*

IMMORALITY
IN EARLY JUDAISM **1:**237, 287–88; IN THE OT AND APOCRYPHA **1:**232, 350, 364, 383–84, 412, 447, 997, 1179; **2:**718; **3:**1004; **4:**241, 443, 470, 685; **5:**4, 13, 15, 128, 274, 276, 286, 293–94, 306, 313, 340, 355, 437, 441, 447–56, 464–70, 475–76, 480, 487, 491, 510–11, 556, 563–65, 571, 598, 809; **6:**223, 1009, 1395, 1500; **7:**582; IN THE NT **1:**18; **8:**17, 36–37, 138, 264, 351, 423, 675–77; **9:**346, 388, 390, 643–45; **10:**438–42, 580, 954, 989; **11:**27, 536, 831, 836; **12:**330, 336–38, 552, 703, 716; SEXUAL **1:**1121; **2:**842, 860; **3:**732; **5:**245; **6:**794, 1309; **7:**245; **8:**18–19, 42, 321; **9:**567; **10:**219–20, 253, 532, 707, 729–30, 776, 779, 844, 847, 860, 861–63, 913–15; **11:**173, 358, 426–27, 430, 434–36, 452, 535, 642, 645–46, 653, 718; **12:**163, 325, 345, 485, 579, 680; AND WORSHIP **1:**1135, 1179; **3:**452, 569; **5:**577; **10:**431, 438, 602; **11:**428, 431; **12:**350, 353, 479

IMPALEMENT
2:198–99; **3:**934

IMPEDIMENT, SPEECH
1:1073; **2:**31, 126, 214, 821, 838; **11:**153

IMPRISONMENT
OF DANIEL **7:**89–91, 95; OF JEHOIACHIN **2:**502; OF JEREMIAH **6:**848–49, 52; **7:**810; OF JOHN THE BAPTIST **8:**266, 270–71, 319, 531; **9:**11, 87, 102, 160; OF JOSEPH **1:**615; **5:**524; OF JUDAH *or* ISRAEL AS A NATION **6:**206, 213, 228, 368, 370–72, 377, 381, 396, 401, 449, 586, 721, 1081; OF MICAIAH **2:**164; OF PAUL **8:**688; **9:**9, 230; **10:**282, 297–98, 314, 326, 368, 379; **11:**278, 355, 365, 369, 406–7, 411–13, 438, 459, 462–66, 473–74, 478, 484–85, 487–89, 492–95, 525, 546, 558–59, 569, 661–67, 780–81, 843, 856, 884–85, 902–3; PRACTICED IN ISRAEL **5:**136; **7:**663; OF SAMSON **2:**840

IMPURITY, RITUAL
1:281–82, 986, 1085, 1104, 1148; **2:**13–15, 59–61, 110, 151, 1011; **3:**506, 616, 687, 712, 793, 1160; **4:**82, 995; **5:**85, 793; **6:**1166–69, 1307, 1337, 1488, 1494, 1533–34, 1558, 1563–68, 1574, 1582, 1585, 1592; **8:**212, 332, 436, 531, 544, 583, 587–88, 607; **9:**191, 537; **10:**214, 255; **11:**428, 866; **12:**112, 692. *See also* PURIFICATION; RITUAL

INCANTATIONS
1:1134; **2:**68; **5:**688; **6:**1124, 1203, 1398, 1537; **7:**89, 611; **8:**541; **10:**84, 273

INCARNATION
1:200; **2:**1368; **4:**874, 1070, 1073, 1076, 1213, 1217; **5:**14; **6:**700, 875; **8:**41, 150, 245; **9:**496–97, 518, 521–26, 532–33, 545, 552, 572, 581, 601, 608–10, 661–64, 679, 691, 695, 715, 732, 743–45, 747–49, 768, 775–76, 782–84, 789–90, 795–96, 798, 836–37, 844; **10:**663; **12:**39–40, 61, 293, 375, 439, 452

INCENSE
1:919–20, 1013, 1017–20, 1069, 1148, 1163–64; **6:**56, 102, 945, 1159, 1176, 1230, 1285, 1330; **7:**860; **9:**45–47, 436; ALTAR (*see under* ALTAR); DISH FOR **1:**1111; **6:**1534

INCEST
1:404, 476, 1124–25, 1141; **2:**222, 1303; **3:**332; **4:**435; **5:**408; **7:**253; **8:**192; **9:**313; **12:**681

INCLUSIVE/EXCLUSIVE
COMMUNITY **1:**185, 417, 424, 860; **5:**690; **6:**1357, 1599; **8:**647; **9:**602, 673; **10:**196; **11:**529–30; MIXED MARRIAGE **3:**156, 846, 850; **5:**632; **10:**226–27, 683

INCULTURATION
See SYNCRETISM

INDICTMENT
See LAWSUIT

INDIVIDUAL, INDIVIDUALISM
1:852, 866, 1184; **2:**54, 715, 1194, 1203; **3:**348, 821; **4:**138, 449, 541; **5:**119, 160–61; **6:**96, 119; **8:**18, 299, 557, 646; **9:**761; **10:**249, 825, 944, 963; **11:**215, 310, 737, 766; **12:**127, 153, 262, 386

INGATHERING, FEAST OF
See under FEASTS/FESTIVALS

INHERITANCE
BIRTHRIGHT (*see* BIRTHRIGHT); AS CHILDREN/PEOPLE OF GOD **3:**364; **7:**761; **8:**180; **9:**639–41; **10:**685, 692, 840, 856–57; **11:**106, 263–70, 279, 284–91;

12:416; COMPARED TO WISDOM **5:**327, 669, 757; AND ESCHATOLOGY *(i.e., in a heavenly realm, as heirs of God's promises)* **3:**417, 956; **6:**547, 661, 679, 968; **9:**227–28, 346, 381; **10:**284, 405, 411, 464, 495–96, 500, 511–12, 550–51, 556, 585, 590–94, 604; **11:**273, 276–77, 301, 305, 327, 372, 375–76, 382–86, 389, 404, 436, 442, 590, 593, 658, 877; **12:**109, 135–36, 141, 241, 250, 276, 283–84, 296, 553, 716; IN FAMILY/MARRIAGE *(incl. Levirate marriage)* **1:**273, 605–6; **2:**23, 211–18, 235, 245–46, 265, 289, 379, 245–47, 456–57, 467, 473, 582, 668–71, 683–84, 928, 936–37, 943; **3:**994, 1042, 1050; **5:**77–78, 120, 187, 239; **6:**9, 442, 491, 500, 820, 1070, 1223, 1479; **8:**132, 647; **11:**281–82; OF LAND **1:**847, 948, 1143, 1172, 1188–89; **2:**8–12, 34, 169–70, 202, 220–23, 248–50, 263, 654, 658, 853, 870; **3:**87, 156–57, 307, 470, 956, 1115, 1172; **4:**995, 1172, 1198; **6:**442, 500, 626, 661, 679, 1188, 1457, 1600; **7:**455, 539–41, 548–50, 553; **10:**192; AND THE PRIESTHOOD *or* AMONG PROPHETS **1:**1142; **2:**254, 263, 365, 687, 739; **3:**176, 346, 436; **4:**734; **6:**1579, 1581; WITHIN ROYAL CIRCLES **1:**913; **2:**1153; **3:**155–56; **6:**9, 1590

INIQUITY
AND THE CONSEQUENCES OR PUNISHMENT OF **1:**85, 481, 947–48, 1072; **2:**63–64, 125, 741; **3:**577; **4:**450, 778, 806, 886, 1059, 1092; **5:**159, 655, 678; **6:**54, 57, 195–96, 222, 254, 451, 466, 470, 529, 543, 685, 693, 812, 957, 1038, 1102, 1135, 1145–49, 1154–55, 1167, 1219, 1254, 1262, 1282, 1302, 1343, 1448–52, 1514, 1575–76; **7:**236, 263, 269, 273, 369, 484; **9:**61, 105

INN
9:63, 230

INNER BEING/INNER PERSON
1:1074; **2:**1098; **5:**60, 144, 150–53, 166, 225; **10:**554, 571–72; **11:**92, 414, 417

INNOCENCE
AND GUILT **1:**482, 639–40, 886; **2:**62–63, 265, 445, 449, 471, 1168, 1222–31; **4:**460, 912; **5:**77, 736; **6:**69, 450, 602; **7:**183, 598, 663, 774; **8:**483, 486; **9:**197, 446, 458, 810, 815; **10:**192, 330; FROM SIN **2:**706, 739, 1126; **3:**736–37; **4:**46, 412, 439, 450, 669, 912, 1250; **6:**1138

INNOCENTS, SLAUGHTER OF THE
1:87, 587, 697, 771; **6:**1345; **8:**147–49; **9:**71–72

INQUIRE OF GOD
2:1048, 1152, 1184–85, 1358; **3:**425; **6:**145

INSCRIPTIONS
1:6, 231–33, 239, 246–51, 267, 291, 990, 1001; **3:**48–54, 320, 678, 748, 761, 878, 1017; **4:**202, 277; **5:**4, 461; **6:**12, 1260–61, 1516, 1537; **7:**50, 61–62, 76, 360, 362, 729, 804; **8:**25, 247, 673; **11:**364, 397, 460, 470, 540, 564, 863, 872; **12:**409, 571

INSECTS
1:747, 1076, 1080–81; **2:**12–13; **5:**345, 540, 570, 830; **6:**113, 996; **7:**431, 528; **12:**634

INSPIRATION AND REVELATION
1:33–64; **11:**409, 462, 505, 1167; **12:**343, 360, 581

INSTRUCTION
IN THE CHURCH **1:**47, 154, 191; **4:**779; **7:**863; **8:**171, 206, 211, 350, 369, 398, 456, 514, 626; **9:**233; **10:**176–77, 263, 367; **11:**335, 340, 362, 422, 456, 717, 852; **12:**68, 71, 315, 449, 454, 476, 485, 497; PUPILS AND SCHOOL **1:**98; **5:**269, 604; **8:**16; **11:**851; AS WISDOM *(often in the home)* **1:**233, 343; **2:**272, 312, 993, 1017; **3:**26, 1014–19; **4:**562; **5:**3, 24, 37, 43, 54, 58, 66, 68–69, 181, 258, 262, 604–8, 616, 654, 689, 700, 790; **9:**12; **11:**456

INSTRUMENTS
See MUSICAL INSTRUMENTS

INTEGRITY
2:628; **4:**412, 525, 709; **5:**256, 484; **6:**606, 657; **9:**151; **10:**223; **11:**207, 249, 346; **12:**386, 421, 461, 467, 669, 686

INTERCESSION
JUDICIAL **4:**467; **12:**106, 383; PRAYER **2:**100, 112, 139, 141–42, 163, 188, 363–66; **4:**669; **6:**73, 103, 637–38, 649, 676, 691, 716, 734, 865; **7:**270, 408, 691–92; **9:**794–96; **10:**598–600, 607; **11:**43, 380, 416, 479, 485, 661, 735; **12:**91, 163, 443–45

INTEREST
MONETARY **1:**868; **3:**780; **5:**238, 775; **11:**31

INTERMEDIARY
1:127; **3:**130, 140, 145; **4:**460, 569; **5:**97; **6:**8–9, 15, 1209, 1447, 1460; **7:**150, 478, 750–52, 757, 847, 852; **11:**265–67, 566; **12:**23, 81, 602

IRONY AND SATIRE
1:535, 595, 606, 715, 816; **2:**136, 728, 922; **3:**22, 857–58, 984, 1023–24, 1088–89, 1103, 1114, 1118; **4:**313, 324, 362, 369, 377, 401, 421, 434, 636; **5:**430; **6:**56, 72, 159, 168, 202, 247, 385–89, 406, 692, 743, 882, 1226, 1290–91, 1295, 1420, 1523, 1528, 1596; **7:**469; **8:**67, 229, 481, 488, 491, 501, 566, 685, 710, 719; **9:**476, 494, 587, 625, 698, 813, 816; **10:**64, 106, 131, 176, 245, 267, 289, 306, 310, 319, 602, 629, 781, 804, 818, 838, 855; **11:**7, 11, 26, 31, 58, 62, 101, 146, 154, 176, 236; **12:**173, 189, 198, 216, 464, 485

IRRIGATION
1:215, 245; **2:**374; **3:**155; **5:**192, 194, 298, 758; **6:**180, 1264, 1425

ITALIAN COHORT
10:162
IVORY
1:225; **2**:1232; **3**:70, 82, 511; **4**:862; **5**:426, 564, 829; **6**:1360, 1374, 1378; **7**:63, 376

J

JACKAL, JACKALS
3:948; **4**:611, 632; **6**:157, 335, 378, 914, 1061, 1201, 1523; **7**:546, 855
JAIL
See PRISON
JAMES, LETTER OF
CHRISTOLOGY OF **10**:387; INTRODUCTION TO **12**:177–84; AND LUTHER **1**:16, 19, 102; **10**:386; PLACE IN THE CANON **1**:14–20, 51, 102; **10**:370–71, 386
JAR, JARS
1:814, 816; **3**:140; **4**:23; **6**:684; **7**:777; **8**:702; **9**:170, 180, 416, 538, 569; **11**:718
JEALOUSY
OF GOD **1**:842; **2**:199–201; **6**:1235, 1322, 1481, 1483; **7**:753; **8**:654; **10**:917–18, 920; HUMAN **1**:376; **2**:62, 64, 68, 455, 1103, 1119, 1121–23, 1127–29, 1144, 1192, 1205, 1252; **3**:525; **4**:379, 461, 995, 997; **5**:81, 230, 430, 543; **6**:205, 345–46, 532, 597, 919, 1144, 1153, 1155, 1189–90; **10**:729, 804, 807, 825, 961; **11**:44, 172, 327, 420, 423, 492, 876; **12**:209, 211, 493; HUMAN ON BEHALF OF GOD **3**:142; IMAGE OF **6**:1175; OF JEWS AND FOLLOWERS OF JESUS **10**:104, 126, 194, 196–97, 201, 624, 653, 669, 672, 680, 682, 691, 756, 825; OF MARCION'S OT GOD **1**:84; OFFERING OF **1**:1018; **2**:62–63
JEHOVAH
MARCION'S OT GOD **1**:84–86
JEREMIAH, BOOK OF
BIOGRAPHY **6**:15; COMMISSIONING REPORT/CALL NARRATIVE **6**:13; COMPARED TO JONAH **7**:487; COMPOSITION OF **6**:3–4, 17–18, 563–66; DEPICTION OF DIVINE EMOTIONS **6**:1140; DIVINATION **6**:15; ETHICS **6**:21–22; HISTORICAL CONTEXT **6**:555–60, 573–74; HISTORIOGRAPHY **6**:14; MARITAL AND SEXUAL IMAGERY IN **5**:381, 401, 419; **7**:544; NATURE OF TEXT **1**:294, 301–2; **6**:567–68; PLACE IN THE CANON **1**:8, 11, 65; **5**:634; **6**:2; REINTERPRETED BY DANIEL **7**:121–22, 192; REINTERPRETED BY OBADIAH **7**:440–41; RELATIONSHIP TO DEUTERONOMY AND THE DEUTERONOMISTIC SCHOOL **2**:275, 514, 687–88; **3**:1119; RELATIONSHIP TO THE CHRONICLER **3**:655–56; UNDERSTANDING OF FALSE AND TRUE PROPHECY **6**:49; USE BY HEBREWS **12**:100–101, 108–9, 112–18; USE BY LUKE **9**:374; USE BY MATTHEW **8**:148, 344, 406, 480, 486; USE BY ZECHARIAH **7**:747, 752, 820–22; USE OF LAMENT FORM **6**:16; VIEW OF BABYLON **6**:413; AND WISDOM TRADITION **5**:687
JEREMIAH, LAMENTATIONS OF
1:1013–26; JOB AND **4**:458–60, 464, 475; PLACE IN THE CANON **1**:8, 11, 65; RELATIONSHIP TO DEUTERONOMY AND THE DEUTERONOMISTIC SCHOOL **2**:501, 504–5, 514; THIRD ISAIAH AND **6**:431, 437. *See also* LAMENTATIONS, BOOK OF
JEREMIAH, LETTER OF
INTRODUCTION TO **6**:985–91; PLACE IN THE CANON **5**:634–35; **7**:441. *See also* JEREMIAH, LETTER OF *in ANCIENT LITERATURE*
JESUS, HISTORICAL
1:55, 104, 110, 148, 168–69; **4**:947; **8**:77, 79–81, 83, 85–86, 90, 94, 110, 170, 172, 176, 187, 191, 200, 235, 239, 256, 259, 274, 296, 299, 310, 325, 347–48, 434, 511, 622; **9**:113, 196, 497, 518, 522–23; **10**:167, 189, 198, 375, 389; **11**:140, 607; **12**:70, 120, 149–50, 155, 167, 565
JESUS, METAPHORS FOR
See JESUS THE CHRIST, METAPHORS FOR *in PERSONS IN THE BIBLE*
JESUS, TITLES FOR
See JESUS THE CHRIST, NAMES FOR/TITLES OF *in PERSONS IN THE BIBLE*
JEWELS AND PRECIOUS STONES
COMPARED TO WISDOM **4**:529–31; ON THE HIGH PRIEST'S ROBES **1**:106; ON THE KING OF TYRE'S ROBES **6**:1392; IN REVELATION **12**:723; IN ZECHARIAH'S FOURTH VISION **6**:766. *See also* GEM; STONE: PRECIOUS; *by individual type*
JOB, BOOK OF
1:819; **2**:505, 671; **4**:713, 835; **6**:640; **10**:454; INFLUENCE ON BARUCH **6**:962, 1291; INFLUENCE ON TOBIT **3**:918; INTRODUCTION TO **4**:319–41; JEWISH INTERPRETATION OF **1**:72; PLACE IN THE CANON **1**:8, 11, 65; POETIC REPETITION IN **4**:314; AS WISDOM LITERATURE **5**:1–2, 10, 12–13
JOEL, BOOK OF
AS USED BY ACTS **10**:59, 64–66, 68–69, 71, 81, 83, 89–90, 93, 99, 107, 121, 152, 167, 169, 175, 192–93, 195, 197, 203, 206, 209–10, 213, 218, 288, 368; INTRODUCTION TO **7**:301–4; MESSAGE OF **4**:1196; PLACE IN THE CANON **7**:436; PRIESTLY IMAGERY IN **6**:123; AS USED BY ROMANS **10**:625, 665–66; AS USED IN REVELATION **12**:614, 631, 678
JOHN, GOSPEL OF
COMPARED WITH 1 JOHN **12**:385, 442; AS EVIDENCE FOR THE HISTORICAL JESUS **1**:81–82; INTRODUCTION TO **9**:493–514; PLACE IN THE CANON **1**:8, 13, 15–18; PROLOGUE **5**:15; RELATIONSHIP TO JOHANNINE LETTERS **12**:367–68; SOURCES OF **1**:76–77; UNIQUENESS OF **1**:73–74

JOHN, LETTERS OF
INTRODUCTION TO **12:**365–80; RELATIONSHIP TO THE GOSPEL **9:**499

JOHN, REVELATION TO
See REVELATION, BOOK OF

JONAH, BOOK OF
INTRODUCTION TO **7:**463–91; PLACE IN THE CANON **7:**436

JOSHUA, BOOK OF
ANOMALIES OF HISTORICAL NARRATIVE **1:**306–7; ASIAN AMERICAN INTERPRETATION OF **1:**164–65; HISTORY OF ANCIENT ISRAEL AND **1:**253, 257, 260; INTRODUCTION TO **2:**555–82; LITERARY PECULIARITIES **2:**545–47; PLACE IN THE CANON **1:**8, 11–12, 65

JOT
8:187

JOY, JOYS
1:1161; **3:**396, 693–94, 714, 801, 804, 839–40, 844, 1052; **4:**738, 1196; **5:**731; **6:**123–24, 339; **11:**709; IN ACTS **10:**575, 616–17, 741, 744; AMIDST SUFFERING **5:**95; IN BARUCH **7:**703; IN 2 CORINTHIANS **11:**483, 491, 493–94, 499, 514, 520–22, 536, 543, 546; IN CREATION AND WISDOM **5:**285, 303, 319; IN HEBREWS **12:**113, 190; IN JAMES **12:**254–55; IN JEREMIAH **6:**977–78; IN JOHN **10:**138; IN 1-3 JOHN **12:**695; IN THE LITURGY OF THE CHRONICLER **3:**984–85, 1063, 1065; IN LUKE **9:**558, 560, 758, 779–80, 784–85, 844, 846; IN 1 PETER **12:**384–85; IN PHILIPPIANS **11:**708, 732; IN ROMANS **11:**120–21; IN SECOND ISAIAH **6:**729, 810–11, 825–26; IN THE THEOLOGY OF ECCLESIASTES **6:**545; IN 1 THESSALONIANS **11:**149, 153; IN TOBIT **4:**483–84; TRANSITORY **4:**797; IN WORSHIP **3:**467–68; IN ZEPHANIAH **9:**29, 43, 46, 56, 294, 298, 305, 369

JUDAISM
AND AUTHENTIC JESUS SAYINGS AS BACKGROUND TO JOHN 1 **10:**17; BIBLICAL INTERPRETATION AS COMPARED TO CHRISTIANITY **1:**284–91; BIBLICAL INTERPRETATION WITHIN **1:**84–85, 87; CANON OF **1:**9, 39–40, 43–45, 305–9; **2:**893; **3:**663; **8:**97–102; AND CHRISTIANITY **1:**845–46; **8:**97–102, 277; AND CONTEMPORARY IDOLATRY **7:**4–7, 15–16; AS CONTEXT FOR THE NT **8:**80; DEVELOPMENT OF AS A DISTINCT RELIGION **1:**308–10, 315; AS DISTINCT FROM YAHWISM AND EARLY ISRAELITE RELIGION **6:**662; AND DIVORCE **5:**813; FIRST APPEARANCE OF THE WORD **4:**292; AND FORGIVENESS **5:**745; AND GALATIANS **11:**652–56; AND THE GOSPEL OF JOHN **9:**519; AND THE GOSPEL OF MATTHEW **8:**193; AND THE IDEA OF IMMORTALITY **5:**734; AND MESSIANISM AND MESSIANIC EXPECTATION **4:**8–16, 231–32, 258; AND MIRACLE STORIES **8:**331–32; NEGATIVE ATTITUDE TOWARD WOMEN IN LATER **5:**765; AND OATHS **8:**197; AND THE ORIGINS OF APOCALYPTICISM **8:**27–42; AND PAUL **10:**398–400; AND THE PENTATEUCH **1:**779; **11:**308–9; **12:**24, 64–65, 588; PERSECUTION UNDER ANTIOCHUS IV **4:**182, 202; PORTRAYAL IN THE WESTERN TEXT OF ACTS **10:**374–75; POST-EXILIC AND THE TORAH **1:**65–82, 126–27; AND RIGHTEOUSNESS **11:**195, 213, 228; AND RITUAL HAND WASHING **9:**504–7, 646–50; AND THE SABBATH **1:**1109–10; AND THE SERMON ON THE MOUNT **8:**246–47; AND SUICIDE **5:**14; **11:**605; TEMPLE CODES AND **12:**725–27; VIEWS ON MANUAL LABOR AND TORAH STUDY **6:**8; AND WISDOM LITERATURE AND TRADITIONS **5:**313, 454; AND YOM KIPPUR **1:**289–90; **2:**191; **4:**863, 1001, 1131, 1156; **7:**789; **12:**709

JUDAIZE (*OR* JUDAIZERS, JUDAIZING, *ETC.*)
10:11, 489; **11:**185, 295, 438, 475, 488–89, 525–26, 534

JUDE, LETTER OF
INTRODUCTION TO **12:**473–80; PLACE IN THE CANON **1:**8, 14–17, 19; **10:**370–71; RELATIONSHIP TO 2 PETER **12:**328–29

JUDGE
DEFINITION OF **2:**723, 1016

JUDGES, BOOK OF
ASIAN AMERICAN INTERPRETATION OF **1:**164; HISTORY OF ISRAEL AND **1:**258–59; INTRODUCTION TO **2:**723–29; LITERARY CONNECTION TO 1 AND 2 SAMUEL **2:**957; LITERARY STYLE OF **2:**524, 543, 545–50; PARALLELS TO JUDITH **3:**1090; PLACE IN THE CANON **1:**8, 10–11

JUDGMENT
AFTER DEATH **1:**288; IN APOCALYPTIC LITERATURE **7:**2–3, 10–14; DAY (*see* JUDGMENT DAY); IN THE GOSPEL OF JOHN **12:**516–17; IN ISRAELITE PROPHECY **6:**16;
IN LUKE **9:**152–53; IN MATTHEW **12:**426–58; ORACLES (*see under* ORACLE); PROPHECY OF (*see under* PROPHECY); IN REVELATION **12:**516–17, 710

JUDGMENT DAY
3:1002, 1179; **4:**510–11; **5:**474, 480, 484, 487, 559; **6:**210, 212, 214, 222, 228, 317, 335, 709, 767; **7:**115, 323, 326, 328, 334, 451, 664, 666, 682–83; **8:**531, 577, 595, 598, 631; **10:**247, 442, 613, 736, 829, 832, 834, 847, 886, 993; **11:**82, 335, 361, 469, 483, 516, 728, 856; **12:**121, 126, 158, 215, 291, 305, 311, 343, 348, 431–32, 488

JUSTICE
ABSALOM, DAVID, AND **2:**1319; IN AMOS **7:**346–47, 366–67, 388–97, 403, 416–17; IN APOCALYPTIC LITERATURE **8:**37–38; ASIAN AMERICAN INTERPRETATION AND **1:**165–66; BEING HUMAN AND **4:**534; BOUNDARY MARKERS AND **2:**486–87; THE CHURCH, MODERN SOCIETY, AND **2:**1021–22, 1031; **3:**555–56; **4:**138, 166; **5:**153–55, 176; **6:**832; **7:**77, 96, 184, 366–67, 396–97, 429, 458; **8:**628, 659–60, 714–15; **9:**86–87, 143–44, 379–80; **10:**605–7, 723; **11:**660; IN COLOSSIANS **11:**609–11, 658, 660; IN 1 CORINTHIANS **10:**815, 855, 956; IN 2 CORINTHI

JUSTICE *(continued)*
ANS **11:**75–76, 96, 130; COVENANT CODE AND **1:**869–70, 874–75; DAVID'S KINGSHIP AND **2:**1260, 1268, 1292, 1319, 1371–72; **3:**544, 556; THE DESTRUCTION OF SODOM AND GOMORRAH AND **1:**468–69, 473, 476–79; DEUTERONOMIC THEOLOGY AND **2:**405, 419–20, 422–23, 505, 582, 696, 727, 1016–18, 1048; DIVINE **2:**1341–42, 1370; **3:**985; **4:**335–36, 507–14; **5:**2, 5, 7–8, 25, 70, 119; **6:**763, 914, 1056–59, 1140, 1219–20, 1263–66, 1450–52; **7:**346, 441, 501, 544, 550, 561, 576, 581–83, 589, 597, 631–44, 679–80, 697, 703, 867–74; **8:**37–38; **10:**404–5, 413, 425–27, 438–44, 473, 476–79, 482, 492, 506, 515, 522, 695, 714; **12:**616, 660–62, 701–2; AND THE ENVIRONMENT **2:**129; IN EZEKIEL **6:**1140, 1219–20, 1263–66, 1529, 1582; AS FOUNDATION OF REALITY **4:**483–84;
IN GALATIANS **11:**238, 313; GOD'S GRACE AND MERCY AND **2:**727; **3:**582–83, 1003–4, 1019; **4:**420; **7:**483–85; GOD'S SOVEREIGNTY AND **2:**671; GOD'S VENGEANCE AND **2:**1170; THE GREEK GODDESS **10:**356; IN HABBAKUK **7:**624–27, 631–44, 648, 654–55; HISPANIC AMERICAN INTERPRETATION AND **1:**170–71; IN ISAIAH **6:**39–40, 56–59, 62–67, 68–69, 79, 86–96, 123–24, 128, 141–43, 167–70, 221–23, 228–29, 237–40, 247, 264–67, 272, 278–79, 468–69, 478, 485–86, 498–504, 521–22, 600, 606; JEHOSAPHAT'S REFORMS AND **3:**555–56; IN JEREMIAH **6:**618–19, 639, 641, 665, 739–46, 767, 840–41, 892, 914; IN 1 JOHN **12:**410; IN JONAH **7:**483–85, 501; JUSTIFICATION AND **10:**459, 465, 473, 815; **11:**75–76, 96, 130; IN LAMENTATIONS **6:**1056–59; LEVITICAL CODE AND **1:**1035–37, 1042, 1136, 1175; IN LUKE **9:**53–54, 247–48, 335–40; IN MALACHI **7:**861, 867–74; MANDATED FOR RULERS, JUDGES, AND COMMUNITY LEADERS **2:**419–25, 430–32, 723, 727, 1019–102, 1027, 1029; **3:**415, 544, 556; **5:**89, 148; IN MATTHEW **8:**179, 196, 200, 211, 281, 393; MERCY AND **8:**179; IN MICAH **7:**544, 550, 561, 569, 581–83, 589; MOSES AND **1:**705, 729–30, 827–30; MURDER AND **2:**265, 435–36, 447–48, 696; IN NAHUM **7:**597; IN OBADIAH **7:**441, 458; AS PART OF GOD'S NATURE **4:**400, 420; IN THE PROPHETIC LITERATURE **6:**20–21; IN PROVERBS **5:**56–57, 153–55, 158–61, 164, 176, 187–88, 234–47; IN THE PSALMS **4:**668–70, 674, 829–31, 907–10, 939–41, 961–65, 975–78, 1005–8, 1055–60, 1063–67, 1067–70, 1071–73, 1075–76, 1080–84, 1089–93, 1126–27, 1238–41, 1262–65, 1275–77; RETRIBUTIVE **1:**829; **2:**1093; **3:**926, 932; **4:**336, 364; **6:**89–90, 1292; **11:**749; IN REVELATION **12:**594, 616, 660–62, 701–2; AND RIGHTEOUSNESS (*see under* RIGHTEOUS); IN ROMANS **10:**399–400, 404–5, 413, 425–27, 438–44, 476–79, 492, 506, 515, 522, 607, 714, 718, 723; SALVATION AND **2:**1055–58; SAMUEL'S ADMINISTRATION OF **2:**1016, 1026–28; IN SIRACH **5:**627; AND SLAVERY IN EARLY CHRISTIAN COMMUNITIES **11:**658, 660; SOLOMON AND **3:**45–48, 87–88; IN 2 THESSALONIANS **11:**748–51; THOSE OUTSIDE THE JUDEO-CHRISTIAN COMMUNITY AND **1:**483; IN TITUS **11:**864, 871; AND UNJUST ACCUSATIONS **4:**479–81; IN WISDOM **5:**437, 439–42, 446, 451–92, 527–600; WOMEN AND **1:**184, 604–7; **2:**108, 471, 932, 1306, 1314; **3:**45–48, 873; **4:**1264; **9:**335–40, 627–30; **10:**110–15; IN ZECHARIAH **7:**774–76, 800–801; IN ZEPHANIAH **7:**683, 693–94, 697, 703. *See also* JUDGMENT; RIGHTEOUSNESS

JUSTIFY (*OR* JUSTIFIED, JUSTIFICATION, *ETC.*)
IN ACTS **10:**193; IN 2 CHRONICLES **3:**503, 540; IN 1 CORINTHIANS **10:**747, 749, 811, 815, 974; IN 2 CORINTHIANS **11:**27, 54, 75–76, 87, 95–98, 105, 109–10; IN EPHESIANS **11:**356, 392–93; IN GALATIANS **11:**183–84, 194–95, 236–38, 241, 256, 275, 313, 337; IN ISAIAH **6:**272; IN JAMES **11:**177; IN 1 JOHN **12:**177, 456, 462; IN LEVITICUS **1:**1101; IN LUKE **9:**312–13; IN LUTHER'S INTERPRETATION OF SCRIPTURE **1:**190, 193; **12:**456; IN THE PSALMS **4:**674–75, 731, 807, 887–88, 1252; IN ROMANS **10:**403–4, 420, 425–28, 438, 458–59, 463–74, 478–92, 494–95, 497–500, 502–6, 509–10, 512–21, 529, 540, 543, 548, 564, 585, 590, 601, 603–4, 606, 609–10, 613, 615, 655–56, 658, 661, 664–65, 700, 707, 722, 725, 733; IN 2 SAMUEL **2:**1255, 1258–59; IN SIRACH **5:**724; IN TITUS **11:**877. *See also* JUDGMENT; RIGHTEOUSNESS

K

KEEPER
BROTHER'S **1:**374, 1139; LEADER/MANAGER **2:**1141; **3:**451, 1159; **5:**314; **6:**15, 809; **7:**42; **8:**346; **9:**702; **10:**273; PROMISE **1:**543; **3:**497, 813; **4:**736, 1182; **12:**136

KERYGMA
1:191, 311; **4:**843; **8:**220, 731; **9:**9, 201, 319, 446, 468, 475, 481, 486; **10:**21, 74, 80, 84, 109, 382; **11:**244, 507, 858; **12:**375, 427–28, 441

KEYS, POWER OF
8:293, 345–46

KID
GOAT/YOUNG ANIMAL **1:**872; **2:**398, 842, 846; **3:**647; **6:**141; **9:**476. *See also* GOAT

KIDNAP, KIDNAPPING
1:615, 863, 1173; **2:**334, 405, 468, 835, 864, 886–87; **3:**886; **6:**774

KIDNEYS
1:1025, 1040, 1066; **3:**647; **4:**459, 737; **5:**60. *See also* HEART

KINDNESS
1:475, 483, 510–11, 611, 615, 659, 1142; **2:**125, 681, 894, 899–900, 904, 908, 911, 920–21, 925, 930, 932, 945–46, 1133–34, 1212, 1273, 1276; **3:**202, 592, 681, 782, 1005; **4:**383, 1125–26, 1244; **5:**63, 142, 144, 181, 188, 245, 262, 294, 536, 564, 626–27, 659–60, 664–65, 732, 789, 797, 832–33; **6:**596, 1340; **7:**161, 227, 580–81; **8:**34, 172, 210; **9:**84, 147, 248, 327–28, 393; **10:**355, 642, 686; **11:**51, 88, 345, 647, 790, 838, 876; **12:**92, 170, 337

KING, KINGSHIP
IN ANCIENT NEAR EAST **1:**297; **2:**416, 816, 1247–48; **4:**395, 689, 1062; **5:**5, 91–92, 112, 144; **6:**744; **7:**763, 774; DIVINE **2:**426, 534, 961, 1022, 1030, 1050, 1063, 1091, 1176, 1212–13, 1247–48; **3:**39, 70, 381, 400, 402, 657; **4:**792; **5:**125; **7:**763, 840; **8:**142; **12:**555; EARLY MONARCHY IN ISRAEL **1:**164, 248, 256–58, 312; **2:**308, 556–58, 865, 1023; **3:**48; EVIL (*see under* EVIL); GARMENTS OF (*see under* GARMENT); GREAT (*see under* GREAT); AND NEW YEAR FESTIVAL **4:**648–49; **7:**202; AND ROLE IN BATTLE **2:**606, 830, 1361; **3:**365, 403, 430, 486, 552, 560, 1178; AND ROLE OF JUSTICE **1:**260, 828; **2:**88, 142, 298, 419, 430–31, 538, 895, 960, 1027–31, 1048, 1053, 1060, 1242, 1268, 1292, 1314, 1319, 1371; **3:**43, 46–48, 87, 512, 555, 1144; **4:**223, 480, 540, 668, 963–64, 1006, 1073–75, 1082–83; **5:**91–94, 153, 158–61, 196, 205, 213–15, 242, 437, 497; **6:**21, 99, 124, 141, 143, 247, 264–65, 363, 739–46, 840, 1582; **7:**77, 428, 801, 827; **8:**659; **9:**364, 445–46; **10:**404, 524, 718; ROYAL SUCCESSION OF **2:**585, 763, 963, 1038, 1223, 1354; **3:**421, 469, 522, 573; **9:**93

KINGDOM, KINGDOMS
1:248, 262; **2:**165, 1229; **3:**95. *See also* GOVERNMENT; REIGN

KINGDOM OF GOD/OF HEAVEN
IN THE OT **2:**871–72; **3:**409, 960; **4:**501, 774, 882, 1070; **5:**291, 323, 343; **7:**10, 178, 458; IN MATTHEW **8:**107, 114, 142, 154, 156, 159, 162, 167–68, 288–94, 308, 311, 314, 346, 387, 394, 417, 450, 455, 472–73, 537; IN MARK **8:**512, 536–38, 541, 557, 564, 568, 570–72, 576–79, 588, 627–28, 643, 647–48, 678–79, 704, 707, 725–26; IN LUKE/ACTS **9:**20, 22, 143, 202, 222, 244, 272, 275–76, 313, 315, 329, 334, 344–45, 357, 370, 387, 408, 419, 459, 464, 479; **10:**14, 41–42, 45–46, 64, 72–73, 77, 82, 130, 138–40, 182, 192, 200, 266–67, 281–85, 361, 366–68; IN JOHN **9:**130, 493, 549–52, 634, 741; IN 1 AND 2 CORINTHIANS **10:**841–42, 855–56, 974, 982, 984, 988, 993–94; **11:**76–77; IN ROMANS **10:**411, 441, 518, 524, 528, 533, 541, 560, 568, 664, 703, 728, 736–41; IN THE OTHER EPISTLES **11:**224, 278, 327, 340, 384, 436, 463, 571, 596, 666, 690, 701, 718–19, 746–48, 855; **12:**159, 181, 192–95, 217, 261, 330, 337–38, 428; IN REVELATION **12:**527–28, 541, 563, 569, 615, 626, 643, 650, 666, 703–4, 708–13, 724, 729. *See also* HEAVEN: KINGDOM OF

KINSHIP
1:258, 324–25, 329, 353, 518, 781, 1024; **2:**33, 40, 267, 343, 349, 405, 420, 454–55, 459, 466–67, 471–72, 475, 558, 725, 921, 926, 930, 1233, 1240; **3:**986, 1009, 1016; **4:**143–44, 443, 541; **5:**77, 363, 428, 654–55; **6:**1358; **7:**206, 208, 277, 362, 451; **8:**192, 262; **9:**93; **11:**688; **12:**180, 409, 429

KISS (*OR* KISSES, *ETC.*)
2:1319; **8:**136, 196; **11:**450; BETRAYAL **5:**230; **9:**435; EROTIC **5:**374, 379–80, 397, 429; AS GREETING/HOMAGE **1:**535; **2:**1348, 1352; **3:**144, 956; **4:**554; **5:**775; **8:**477, 709; **9:**18, 172, 435–36, 439; **10:**763, 1002; **11:**179, 556, 735–36; AS RECONCILIATION **1:**572; **2:**1135, 1313–17; **9:**217, 302; **11:**451; THE SON **1:**29

KITCHEN, KITCHENS
1:224, 614; **8:**332; **9:**226, 490

KNEADING
See DOUGH

KNEEL (*OR* KNEELS, *ETC.*)
IN HOMAGE **3:**73; **4:**737, 783, 814, 1065, 1078, 1217, 1220; **8:**336, 488, 502, 544, 584; **9:**28, 433, 690; **10:**288; **11:**414, 424; SEXUALLY **4:**553; WHILE WARY **2:**802

KNOWLEDGE
DIVINE **4:**442; **5:**149, 647, 664, 699, 725, 757; **6:**248; **9:**367; **12:**515; OF GOD **1:**75–76, 350, 365, 442, 594; **2:**138, 194, 346, 601; **4:**219, 429, 578, 844, 940; **5:**34–35, 44, 49, 51, 126, 237, 250, 463, 503, 506, 558, 563, 797; **6:**144, 395–96, 402, 432, 600, 614, 1169; **7:**236–38, 245, 263, 289, 313; **8:**19–20, 24; **9:**60, 76, 181, 225, 249, 646, 670, 767; **10:**434, 641; **11:**106, 138, 287, 385, 415, 427, 527, 866; **12:**389, 553, 579; HUMAN **1:**354; **4:**1175; **5:**33, 49, 239, 250–51, 254, 256, 506, 516, 518–19, 627, 663; **6:**15; **8:**19, 410; **9:**550; **11:**385

KOSHER
2:13; **3:**866, 871, 888, 1089, 1147, 1157–58, 1161–62; **4:**39, 270, 286; **8:**332, 552, 607–8; **10:**162–63, 168, 735, 750; **11:**232

L

LABOR (*OR* LABORS, *ETC.*)
1:217–21, 349, 815, 846, 1017, 1020–21, 1159–61, 1166, 1173–74, 1187–88; **2:**50, 54, 470, 918; **3:**432, 522, 576, 695, 782, 788, 846,

LABOR *(continued)*
850, 1057; **4:**970, 1045, 1097–98, 1199, 1201; **5:**107, 114, 120, 134–35, 139, 186, 280, 293, 298, 319, 371, 416, 476, 511, 517, 685, 692–94, 758, 780, 813–14; **6:**184, 528, 544, 601, 712, 745, 969, 1057, 1410; **7:**30, 57, 111, 206, 226, 286, 664, 680, 694, 700, 709–10; **8:**61, 277, 658; **9:**307, 332; **10:**256, 272, 602, 667, 757, 904–5, 977, 983–84, 990–94, 1000; **11:**19, 76, 151, 242, 288, 296, 337, 339, 429, 432, 454, 484, 491, 660, 688, 691, 700, 711, 730; **12:**52, 140, 636, 661–62, 687; BIRTHING/PAINS **1:**699; **2:**1002; **5:**377, 416, 419; **6:**222, 318, 544, 547, 628, 685, 805, 897; **7:**571; **8:**442; **9:**779–80; **10:**597–98, 728, 888; **11:**29, 183, 296, 726, 802; **12:**648–49; CORVEE/FORCED/SLAVE **1:**251, 262, 694–96, 699, 702, 704–5, 723, 727, 730; **2:**50, 441, 570, 589, 595, 609, 794–96, 1300, 1354, 1380; **3:**50, 52–55, 58, 84, 87, 102, 477–79, 722, 779; **4:**393, 436, 442; **5:**128, 383, 850; **6:**261, 742, 1069–70; **7:**45, 560, 631

LADDER, LADDERS
1:277, 541; **5:**222, 524; **6:**630, 1551; **7:**810; **9:**197, 261, 532, 544; **10:**446, 655, 782; **11:**339, 825; **12:**457

LAMB, LAMBS
1:87, 91–93, 189, 491–92, 495–99, 777, 902, 913, 963, 1009, 1012, 1019, 1021, 1035–36, 1040, 1044, 1066, 1085, 1098–99, 1150, 1157–58; **2:**51, 65, 78, 87, 90, 126, 229–33, 411, 594, 1018, 1088, 1111, 1292–93; **3:**14, 18, 612, 617–18, 622, 646–47, 691, 712–13, 730, 928, 1143; **4:**312, 609; **5:**593, 715; **6:**88–89, 120, 141, 337, 552, 673–74, 1380, 1464, 1466, 1528, 1564, 1586–91, 1593; **7:**10, 112, 151–52, 242, 309, 468–69; **8:**33, 468, 659, 697, 702; **9:**69–70, 219–20, 222, 296, 399, 414–16, 418–19, 499, 528, 542, 719, 823, 833–34, 837, 860; **10:**391, 778, 848, 851; **11:**503; **12:**256, 258–59, 282–83, 287, 467, 513, 516–17, 525–26, 530, 548, 551, 562–63, 566, 576, 579, 583, 587, 589–94, 600–614, 618, 621, 624–26, 629, 632–34, 638, 642, 649–53, 656–60, 663–75, 681–87, 694–99, 702–3, 707, 714–15, 720–25, 729, 733; OF GOD (*see under* JESUS THE CHRIST, NAMES FOR/TITLES OF *in PERSONS IN THE BIBLE*); PASCHAL (*see under* JESUS THE CHRIST, NAMES FOR/TITLES OF *in PERSONS IN THE BIBLE*)

LAME, LAMENESS
1:26, 574, 782, 1148; **2:**1236–38, 1273–74, 1347; **3:**427; **4:**538, 1140; **6:**281, 283, 809, 1593; **7:**703; **8:**406; **9:**22, 26, 106, 113, 161, 287, 290, 316, 434, 503, 704; **10:**72, 75–86, 97, 188, 198; **12:**9

LAMENT (*OR* LAMENTS, *ETC.*)
1:133, 376, 394, 398, 444, 489, 519, 521, 536, 537, 544, 560, 600, 616, 636; **2:**112, 162, 166, 631–32, 748, 756, 798, 804, 833, 1203–9, 1225, 1289, 1326; **3:**498, 797, 931, 1001, 1174; **4:**20, 34, 36, 43, 63, 96, 110, 163, 366, 369–72, 387–88, 412, 415–16, 439, 457–61, 468, 474–77, 551, 569–70, 663–64, 705, 719–20, 762, 912, 1033, 1074; **5:**112, 121, 125, 463, 470–71, 485–86, 543, 579, 591, 809; **6:**16, 59, 158, 293, 355, 431, 436–37, 539–42, 573, 582, 613, 628, 639–40, 642–65, 666–67, 673–76, 679, 685, 696–99, 707–10, 716–18, 726–30, 741, 805–8, 810, 851, 891, 939, 971, 974–76, 980, 1011–72, 1140, 1177, 1266–74, 1354, 1358, 1367–68, 1371, 1382–84, 1390–95, 1425, 1429, 1434, 1439–40, 1501–3; **7:**122, 308, 312, 314, 322, 384–86, 398, 421–22, 517, 535, 541, 545–48, 555, 577, 584–86, 624, 630, 632–36, 638–39, 690–93, 752, 856; **8:**428, 437–38, 492, 650, 653, 707–8, 713, 717, 722–24, 726; **9:**209, 220, 232, 247, 318, 347–48, 372–75, 378, 395–96, 405, 451–53, 478, 704–5, 834; **10:**571, 599, 692; **11:**107, 251, 377, 703, 707–8, 860; **12:**30, 569, 659, 684, 693–97; COMMUNAL **1:**133; **3:**400, 497, 560–61, 773; **4:**64, 647–49, 724, 852, 856, 908, 915–16, 968, 972, 998, 1040–41, 1057, 1110, 1187, 1192, 1202; **6:**167–68, 202–3, 270, 472, 498–503, 524–26, 599, 654, 690–93, 727, 948, 1017–23, 1066–67; **8:**179; INDIVIDUAL **1:**563; **2:**633; **3:**446; **4:**369, 458, 464, 570, 644–46, 651, 724, 726, 818, 822, 847, 884, 894, 897, 901, 905, 908, 919, 926, 930, 958, 968, 983, 1027, 1086, 1088, 1124, 1167–68, 1178, 1202, 1204, 1239, 1243, 1246, 1250; **6:**212, 301, 1066–67; SONG(S) OF (*see under* SONG)

LAMENTATION, LAMENTATIONS
1:359; **2:**1221–22, 1297, 1305; **4:**37, 159; **5:**355, 809; **6:**5, 10, 167–68, 195, 202, 301, 348–49, 525, 642, 810, 933, 1016, 1024, 1034, 1044, 1066, 1358, 1367–68, 1371, 1373, 1391, 1425, 1432–34, 1437–40, 1530, 1578; **7:**10, 303, 307–11, 318, 362, 385, 392, 417, 547, 632, 752, 792; **8:**147, 205, 492; **9:**465, 779; **10:**132, 162; **11:**708; **12:**639

LAMENTATIONS, BOOK OF
2:501, 504–5, 514; **4:**458; **6:**431, 436, 449, 524, 948, 973, 976, 1013, 1023, 1034, 1044–45; **7:**441, 555, 697, 702

LAMP, LAMPS
1:888, 893, 898–902, 1067, 1157, 1163; **2:**80, 992, 1097, 1361, 1365, 1367; **3:**95, 97, 228, 485, 568, 570; **4:**23, 257, 468, 748, 1212–13; **5:**61–62, 80, 152, 187–88, 192, 261, 355, 630, 659, 700; **6:**551, 762, 996, 1008, 1435; **7:**422,

679–80, 769–71; **8:**182, 210, 450–51, 568, 575; **9:**180–81, 244–45, 263, 298, 542, 586, 675; **10:**277, 676; **12:**104, 342–43, 567–68, 592, 603, 694

LAMPSTAND, LAMPSTANDS
1:889–90, 892–93, 901, 960, 972, 1017, 1163, 1166; **2:**52–55, 80; **3:**485–87, 531; **4:**34; **5:**630; **7:**736, 739, 748, 766, 768–73, 782; **9:**180, 245, 542, 632; **12:**103, 566–68, 574–75, 642–43, 677

LANCE
2:631; **4:**624

LAND
INHERITANCE OF **2:**8, 153, 169, 202, 213, 217, 221, 249, 254, 263–64, 266, 365, 673, 853, 870, 928; **5:**621; **6:**1188, 1590; **7:**541; OF MILK AND HONEY **1:**430, 528, 1018; **2:**576, 612, 757; **5:**846; OWNERSHIP **1:**223, 785, 871, 950, 1115, 1133, 1138, 1166–75; **2:**127, 147, 153, 467, 471–72, 575, 594–95, 712, 915, 1274; **3:**667; **5:**145, 261, 862; **6:**93, 96, 854, 1196, 1452; **7:**417, 550, 710, 834; **8:**60, 392–93, 413–14; **9:**219, 307; **10:**97–98

LANDMARK, LANDMARKS
2:436, 487–88; **3:**18; **7:**247–48

LANE, LANES
9:22, 290; **10:**346, 355

LANGUAGE, LANGUAGES
OF THE ANCIENT NEAR EAST **1:**129, 229, 232, 411; **7:**19, 62; OF THE BIBLE **1:**22–32, 63, 99, 101, 104, 109, 123, 129–30, 159, 174–75, 196, 201, 229, 232, 234, 267, 292–93, 296, 299, 301–3, 411, 414; **3:**718, 899, 979; **4:**311, 611; **5:**27–28, 60, 645, 652, 725; **6:**190, 930–31; **7:**32, 62, 72; **8:**2–5, 7, 13, 91, 107; **9:**830; **10:**54–55, 57, 63, 112, 231, 944, 959; **11:**290; **12:**553, 735; SEMITIC **1:**31, 303–4, 1013; **2:**614, 910; **3:**44, 947; **5:**270; **6:**642; **7:**19, 156

LANTERN, LANTERNS
5:324; **6:**618; **7:**666; **9:**802

LAPIS AZULI
4:530; **6:**1116, 1392–93

LASHES, FORTY LESS ONE
2:471; **4:**210; **5:**167; **11:**22, 157

LAST DAY, DAYS/LATTER DAYS
1:13, 1160; **3:**259–95; **4:**401, 403, 636; **5:**708; **6:**67, 156, 207, 226, 228, 230, 451–52, 521, 743–74, 768–69, 797, 814, 842–77, 918, 1519; **7:**232, 428; **8:**29–30, 44–45, 144, 160, 167, 270, 272, 286, 310, 391, 396, 457, 480, 504, 526, 625, 713; **9:**200, 220, 312, 602–4, 608, 620, 622, 688, 719, 803, 824–25; **10:**15, 21, 24, 28, 40, 59, 64, 69, 81–85, 91, 99, 121, 123, 142, 152, 176, 203, 207, 209, 218, 305, 309, 431, 438, 441, 468, 521, 529, 575, 580, 830–31; **11:**23, 27, 46, 82, 88, 212, 361, 375, 463, 527, 534, 613, 811–12, 849, 852, 855–56, 865; **12:**21–22, 99, 116, 129, 145, 155, 216–17, 241, 250–51, 253, 275, 277, 296, 316, 328, 344, 348, 355, 403, 413, 476, 484, 487, 492, 494–98, 527, 530–33, 676–77, 704, 720, 727

LAST SUPPER, THE
1:776, 836; **4:**1139; **6:**1564; **7:**811; **8:**74, 81, 370, 398, 400–401, 468, 477, 659, 695, 702, 705; **9:**12, 197, 288, 415, 417–21, 445, 480, 495, 702, 704–5, 719, 722, 729, 731; **10:**353

LATIN LANGUAGE/TRANSLATIONS
1:5, 12, 15, 28, 75–76, 94, 101, 205, 269, 292, 301–4, 460, 598, 985, 987, 989, 1008; **2:**284, 391, 474, 641, 737, 904, 909–10, 1199; **3:**4, 1103, 1148, 1154; **4:**32, 39, 72, 107, 206, 242, 249, 378, 1099, 1181, 1205, 1267; **5:**8, 23, 175, 345, 448, 606–7, 635, 672, 715, 730, 837; **6:**930, 985; **7:**3, 522, 666; **8:**4–8, 13, 176, 369, 422, 490, 722; **9:**97, 386, 388, 830; **10:**17, 121, 215, 297, 481, 491, 593, 774, 777, 798, 860, 957; **11:**79, 470–71, 625, 859; **12:**15, 152, 533, 659

LATTICE
6:1555

LAVER
3:485; **6:**1547

LAW
BODIES OF **1:**65, 68, 861; **2:**927; BOOK OF THE **1:**9, 37, 40, 42, 65, 305; **2:**278–79, 487, 518, 520–21; **3:**279–80, 284, 645–46, 667, 715–16, 800–802, 806; **4:**40, 197, 684; **5:**555; **6:**562, 839–40; **7:**662; **11:**258, 313; CEREMONIAL **1:**1082, 1121, 1127, 1131, 1152; **8:**136, 278, 424; CIVIL (*see under* CIVIL); CODE (*see under* CODE); COURT(S) OF (*see under* COURT); IN FIRST-CENTURY JUDAISM **1:**11, 45, 285–86, 314; **8:**32, 246, 277, 363, 468; **9:**122, 449, 742; **10:**479; **12:**180–81; MOSAIC **1:**38–39, 41–42, 44–45, 88, 286, 305, 770, 1027, 1114; **2:**112, 275, 284, 310, 427, 488, 500–501, 510, 515–22, 562–5, 568, 570, 573–74, 584–85, 589, 599, 603–6, 634–35, 639–42, 711; **3:**260, 285, 691, 717–18, 976, 980, 1039; **4:**6, 9, 16, 1206; **5:**48, 80, 205, 234, 244, 562, 606, 623, 625, 627, 632, 643, 650, 758, 793, 828; **6:**962, 968, 1258; **7:**25, 177, 183, 873; **8:**45, 134, 191, 217, 547; **9:**58, 98, 219, 264, 284, 301, 386, 389, 523, 619, 628, 659; **10:**188, 191, 193, 292, 294, 361, 402, 552, 561, 570; **11:**185, 206, 213, 222, 224, 232, 258–59, 266, 302, 314, 329, 337–38, 437, 625; **12:**9, 87, 90, 123, 475–76, 489–90, 492, 596; IN THE NT **1:**305; **2:**221, 488–89, 569–70, 603, 609, 616, 642; **3:**348, 395, 464, 501, 556; **5:**12, 14, 808; **6:**244–45, 969; **8:**190, 195–96, 545, 592, 642–65; **9:**580, 586; **10:**311, 321, 479, 586, 878; **11:**188, 210, 259, 277–78,

LAW *(continued)*
307, 329–30, 434, 438, 791, 836; **12:**94, 179, 181, 559–60; AND THE PROPHETS **1:**10, 29, 43, 45, 188, 305, 315; **3:**348, 370, 395, 512–13, 647, 659, 926; **5:**2, 155, 642; **6:**22–23, 827, 931; **7:**254; **8:**172, 185–86, 213, 363, 424–25, 632; **9:**206, 312–15, 318; **10:**191, 361, 469, 512, 768; **11:**308

LAWLESS ONE, ONES
4:119; **5:**742; **9:**793; **11:**755–60; **12:**403, 700, 703

LAWSUIT, LAWSUITS
CAPITAL **2:**493; COVENANT **6:**596, 598, 607, 697, 715; **7:**577–78; WITH GOD **4:**363, 409–11, 439, 460, 629; LEGAL DISPUTE (*Heb.:* rîb) **4:**413; **5:**55, 697; **7:**237–38; **10:**233, 855; PROPHETIC **1:**931–32; **2:**526–27, 831; **6:**16, 19, 46–47, 52, 56, 64, 583, 585, 599; **7:**237, 535–36, 850; TESTIMONY IN (*see* TESTIMONY: IN LEGAL DISPUTE); OF YAHWEH **6:**76, 78, 600, 697, 766; **10:**400, 454. *See also* rîb *in BIBLICAL LANGUAGES: HEBREW*

LAWYER, LAWYERS
1:59; **2:**349; **5:**56, 155, 246; **6:**630, 658, 832; **7:**178, 561; **8:**16, 424, 430, 688; **9:**12, 20, 128, 164, 226–33, 245–51, 284, 286–87, 290, 345–46, 378, 399; **10:**88, 317, 521; **11:**878

LAYING ON OF HANDS
1:667, 1011, 1017, 1024–25, 1049; **2:**81, 162, 220; **3:**609; **6:**457; **8:**23; **9:**111, 273; **10:**297, 356; **11:**223, 779, 814, 833, 864; **12:**70–71

LAZY/SLOTH
5:74–75, 105, 107, 142, 186; **8:**308; **12:**35, 74, 127. *See also* SLUGGARD

LEADER (*OR* LEADERS, LEADERSHIP, *ETC.*)
CHURCH **1:**23, 94, 1150; **2:**906, 1065–66, 1227; **3:**418, 738; **4:**243; **7:**576; **8:**48, 104, 287, 375, 448; **9:**263, 310, 382, 425, 847; **10:**24, 168, 188–89, 206, 259, 263, 285, 292, 767, 968; **11:**193, 229, 425, 493, 516, 701, 704, 707–8, 727, 731, 792, 806, 809, 875, 893; **12:**68, 182, 314–17, 340, 398; MILITARY **1:**264, 438, 441; **2:**35, 219–20, 519, 551, 756, 772, 788, 792, 797, 809, 825, 842, 960, 1043, 1070, 1233–34, 1284, 1376; **3:**337, 522, 1078; **4:**645; **6:**141, 164, 858, 1079, 1081; **7:**29, 815; **8:**442; RELIGIOUS **1:**44, 66, 276, 442, 852, 961, 964, 1146; **2:**193, 430, 518, 732, 792, 809, 878, 994, 1136, 1141; **3:**734, 738, 751, 1163; **4:**122, 224, 270, 431–32; **5:**668, 798, 859–60; **6:**79, 183, 239, 490, 587, 600, 613, 627, 691, 694, 709, 750, 755–56, 773, 784–85, 826, 1059, 1063, 1314, 1316; **7:**72, 238–39, 245, 552, 589, 823; **8:**69, 125, 128–29, 142–34, 187, 241, 309, 427, 464, 484, 531, 540, 557, 596, 625, 628, 636, 660, 664, 668, 672, 710; **9:**4, 18, 21, 23, 28, 144, 249, 280, 296, 351, 374, 376, 379, 382–85, 392, 447, 449, 528, 699, 766, 815, 823–27; **10:**74, 106, 114, 192, 206, 235, 587; **11:**412; SYNAGOGUE (*see* ARCHISYNAGOGOS)

LEATHER
1:294, 300, 302, 1099; **2:**53, 344, 718; **3:**171; **6:**1228, 1507; **7:**424; **8:**170, 431, 487, 532; **9:**81; **10:**251; **11:**461, 675

LEAVEN (*OR* LEAVENS, *ETC.*)
1:90, 777, 1018, 1021, 1051, 1159; **2:**78, 127, 345, 412; **3:**713; **6:**455–56, 1496, 1558, 1596; **7:**256, 380; **8:**309, 468, 616–18, 697; **9:**275–76, 414–15, 542; **10:**778, 847–48, 851–52, 877; **11:**315

LECTIONARY, LECTIONARIES
1:128, 185, 188, 190, 195, 198–99, 202, 207, 212; **2:**12, 69, 578, 714, 1259; **3:**6, 41, 130, 144, 299, 1162; **5:**266, 350, 408; **6:**105, 148, 160, 1129, 1240, 1497; **7:**219, 253, 280, 572, 596, 620, 623, 641, 643, 846, 862, 867, 873–74; **8:**3–5, 109, 362, 395; **9:**11–12, 214, 494, 526, 540, 612, 847; **10:**3; **11:**279, 329, 595, 609, 617, 630, 639, 646, 658; **12:**4, 64, 262, 276, 286, 297, 377, 415, 438, 455, 510, 539

LEDGE, LEDGES
6:1547, 1551, 1566, 1568, 1585, 1592

LEE, LEES
6:891; **7:**679; **10:**346

LEEKS
1:218

LEFT HAND
See under HAND

LEGEND, LEGENDS
1:11, 253, 258, 273, 290, 300, 311, 335, 408, 624, 701; **2:**16, 177–78, 673, 905–6; **3:**17, 46, 82, 185, 192, 869, 978, 1080, 1132; **4:**362; **5:**524, 564, 654, 853; **6:**13–14, 17, 23, 300, 1360, 1512, 1516; **7:**21, 52, 62, 66, 82, 106–7, 118, 129, 150, 175, 467, 528, 847; **8:**92, 147, 155, 321, 395, 535, 598–99, 710, 717, 730; **9:**11, 100, 171, 281, 316–17, 476, 538; **10:**43, 150, 232, 234, 372, 755; **11:**904; **12:**133, 145–46, 493, 658

LEGION, LEGIONS
4:1131; **6:**1516; **7:**76, 145, 150; **8:**477, 579, 584–85, 684; **9:**186–88, 290, 333, 404; **12:**528

LEND
2:976–77; **4:**431, 829; **8:**23, 147; **12:**277

LENTIL, LENTILS
1:217–18, 522

LEOPARD, LEOPARDS
5:407, 715; **6:**141, 619; **7:**101–2; **12:**656

LEPROSY (*OR* LEPER *ETC.*)
1:91, 818, 877, 1060, 1062, 1094–96, 1098,

1100–1101, 1106, 1149; **2:**26, 60, 63, 81, 108, 110–11, 151, 469; **3:**207–9, 245, 590–92, 1052; **4:**71, 387, 453, 472, 833, 1131; **5:**339; **6:**647, 1063, 1342; **8:**60, 223–25, 237–38, 407, 466, 525, 544–49, 559, 585–89, 607, 699; **9:**12, 22–23, 29, 108, 114, 119–22, 132, 161, 169, 199, 206, 209, 290, 324–29, 338, 345, 355, 473; **10:**817; **11:**88, 165

LETTER
OF THE ALPHABET **2:**96; **4:**555, 684, 716, 718, 776–77, 813, 1132, 1166; **6:**1017, 1046, 1179; **7:**601, 686; **8:**187; OF THE LAW **1:**285; **2:**336, 1314; **3:**34–35, 997; **5:**798; **7:**88; **8:**134, 138; **9:**313, 409; **10:**448

LEVIATHAN
3:948, 1026; **4:**337, 368, 411, 530, 596–97, 615–27, 631, 974, 1098; **5:**11, 99, 322, 536, 678; **6:**206, 225–26, 228; **7:**101, 192; **9:**196; **12:**493, 632, 710. *See also* MONSTER

LEVIRATE LAW/MARRIAGE
1:1124; **2:**211–12, 214, 222, 265, 474–75, 629, 683–84, 904, 921, 928, 931, 933, 936–38, 941; **3:**330, 691, 1133, 1143; **4:**470; **5:**72; **6:**1223; **7:**216, 715; **8:**131, 422, 675–76; **9:**388, 567

LEVITE, LEVITES
1:878, 933–34, 985, 1011–12, 1026, 1173, 1190; **2:**36–55, 63, 69–84, 92, 99, 135, 138, 142, 147–49, 202–3, 213–14, 220, 247, 263–64, 364–67, 387, 403–4, 427–28, 547, 665–67, 687, 698–702, 741–42, 863, 870–88, 899, 973, 1012; **3:**300, 306, 344–48, 363–64, 386, 393–96, 436, 441–42, 433–47, 450, 452, 494, 498–99, 547, 556, 574, 607–10, 617–18, 624–25, 644–51, 686–88, 692, 712–13, 726–33, 743–46, 768–70, 797, 800–801, 804, 806, 816–17, 820, 824–26, 828–29, 830–39, 842, 846–51, 971, 993–94; **4:**32, 64, 281, 737, 1170; **5:**412–13, 633, 696; **6:**338, 546, 549, 826, 1110, 1167, 1284, 1491, 1573–78, 1581–82, 1604–5; **7:**267, 275, 829, 853, 859–60, 870, 873; **8:**435; **9:**69, 229, 326; **10:**97, 189; **11:**222; **12:**6, 11, 46, 87–90, 92, 114, 123; AND SINGING (*see under* MUSICIAN)

LEVITICAL CITIES/TOWNS
1:1173; **2:**9, 11, 180, 202, 262–64, 268, 428, 579, 616, 695–96, 700–701; **3:**346–47, 452, 838, 993; **6:**575; **9:**119

LEVITICUS
1:8, 12, 25, 67, 69, 79, 81, 85–86, 281, 307, 316, 365, 678, 870, 889, 900, 907, 913, 916; **2:**5–6, 10–11, 12–13, 25, 32, 47, 49, 60–61, 77–79, 126–27, 185, 198, 218, 230–33, 236, 266–67, 397, 453, 469, 876, 930; **3:**302, 609, 647, 733, 801–2, 936, 993, 1018; **4:**19, 39, 71, 107, 933, 1006, 1046, 1111; **5:**46, 407; **6:**467, 628, 831, 1152, 1154, 1206–7, 1238, 1321, 1397, 1472, 1484, 1489, 1534, 1537, 1546, 1569, 1578–79, 1601; **7:**128, 346, 380, 727, 822, 833; **8:**32, 151, 192, 195, 224, 238, 544; **9:**106, 119, 133, 229, 616, 677; **10:**219–20, 467, 474, 476, 658–60, 670; **11:**190, 260, 322; **12:**167, 193, 215, 217, 247, 256, 258–61, 387, 489

LIBATION, LIBATIONS
1:1160; **3:**378, 959; **4:**34; **6:**491, 639, 873, 1290, 1584; **7:**81, 309, 779; **8:**33; **9:**542, 616, 622, 653; **11:**513–14, 517, 856

LIBERATION
1:83, 165, 169–73, 175, 184, 190, 195, 438–42, 536, 678–86, 690–804, 807, 830, 834, 838–41, 843–47, 863–64, 869–73, 889–91, 914, 920–22, 926, 937, 949–50, 961; **2:**10–11, 129, 256, 346, 555, 590, 594, 666, 1057, 1267; **3:**96, 295, 526, 658, 1078; **4:**612, 848, 937, 1173, 1264; **5:**153, 341, 441, 470, 520, 525–30, 545; **6:**399–401, 449, 601, 669, 1255, 1264, 1402, 1418; **7:**91–93, 163–64, 262, 605, 643, 683; **8:**25, 64, 249, 463–64, 531, 654, 704; **9:**106, 108, 542, 675; **10:**105, 398, 467, 480, 508, 516, 547–48, 576, 589, 604, 610, 614, 618, 785; **11:**276, 292, 304, 451, 571, 596, 626, 628, 702; **12:**240, 287, 412, 527–28, 602, 604, 609, 662, 704; EXEGESIS **1:**183; **7:**121–22; MOVEMENT(S) **1:**335, 767; **3:**105; **7:**639, 648; **8:**293; **10:**547; THEOLOGY (*see under* THEOLOGY)

LIBERTINE, LIBERTINES
1:133; **10:**992; **11:**337, 438, 475–76; **12:**485

LIBERTY
1:1172, 1175; **2:**33; **3:**376; **5:**246, 597; **6:**831, 1537, 1590; **7:**907; **9:**81, 106, 387; **10:**617, 730, 900, 924; **11:**222, 310, 455, 798, 812, 815; **12:**181, 189, 194, 205

LICE
1:26

LICENTIOUS, LICENTIOUSNESS
1:685; **3:**501; **5:**549; **7:**211, 230–31, 234, 238, 240–41, 244, 267–68; **8:**608; **9:**301; **10:**729, 750; **12:**285, 305, 316, 345, 348, 350, 352, 485, 494

LIES, LYING
1:42, 376, 427, 477, 535, 848–49, 851, 1033, 1038, 1133; **2:**187–88, 549, 723, 858, 907, 1126–27, 1139, 1179, 1203, 1331; **3:**34, 164, 167, 197, 553, 789, 1075–76, 1119, 1148, 1150, 1153–54, 1159; **4:**296, 332, 356, 390, 424, 433, 454, 523, 700, 702, 847, 908, 924, 1082, 1125, 1178; **5:**5, 76–77, 97, 111, 127, 167, 192, 219, 225, 243, 253, 312, 455, 558–59, 674, 678, 739, 760, 793; **6:**49, 127, 237, 254, 336, 389, 500, 573, 598, 613, 619–21, 627, 635–39, 654, 657,

LIES, LYING *(continued)*
691–92, 703, 724, 726, 750–55, 783, 794, 858, 865–66, 1035, 1043–44, 1201, 1208, 1304, 1315, 1459; **7:**5, 142, 182, 194, 236, 262, 275, 282–83, 287, 363, 408, 581, 700–701, 813, 831; **8:**247, 481, 715; **9:**642–43, 646; **10:**395, 627; **11:**217, 377–78, 429–32, 643, 758; **12:**206, 286, 386, 403, 405, 414, 432, 585, 724

LIEUTENANT, LIEUTENANTS
2:585, 630; **3:**1147; **4:**113; **5:**846; **11:**790

LIFE
BOOK OF **5:**343; **6:**84; **9:**224, 658; **10:**969; **11:**590; **12:**571, 583, 601, 654, 657, 682, 715, 724, 730, 734; ETERNAL (*see* ETERNAL LIFE); EVERLASTING (*see* EVERLASTING LIFE); HUMAN **1:**6, 189, 213–15, 326, 329, 335, 351, 363, 368–69, 376, 381–84, 399–401, 425, 560, 722, 785, 838–39, 848–52, 863, 872–73, 893, 955, 1014, 1100, 1119–20; **2:**194, 220, 235, 255, 311, 315, 323, 327, 356–57, 376, 399, 408, 448, 488, 826, 1022; **3:**370, 926, 997–98, 1005; **4:**16, 241, 264, 360, 384, 397, 402, 423, 440–44, 604, 630–31, 670, 717–18, 727, 752–53, 766, 807, 835–39, 852–54, 877, 899, 903, 909, 927, 1006–7, 1041–44, 1087, 1119, 1122, 1150–51, 1172, 1175, 1198, 1205, 1236–37, 1255, 1263, 1279; **5:**6, 9–11, 21, 24, 93, 132, 138, 141, 190, 229, 232–34, 264, 278, 303, 327, 333, 340, 360, 451, 456, 459–65, 471, 480, 492, 497–99, 512, 567, 731; **6:**22, 49, 69, 272, 345, 631, 649, 677, 708, 746, 755, 786, 875, 982, 1044, 1265; **7:**7–8, 96, 102, 291, 357, 367, 431, 580, 606, 620, 638; **8:**31, 90, 137, 164–66, 197, 207, 210, 599, 623, 648, 694, 725; **9:**53, 99, 113, 118, 153, 252–54, 259, 348, 353, 390, 405, 411, 473, 555, 576, 691, 836; **10:**22, 69, 92, 244, 247, 274, 343, 430, 501, 544, 567, 581, 850, 901; **11:**23, 83, 122, 139, 282, 320, 378, 385, 392, 431, 481, 510, 530, 538, 570, 627, 635, 722, 880; **12:**42, 54, 179, 205, 216, 356, 525, 605; PRAYER **1:**201, 205; **3:**1075; **6:**58; **8:**202, 212; **9:**339; **10:**606; **11:**377, 590; **12:**57, 64, 285–88, 358; SOURCE OF **1:**180, 489, 742–43, 748; **2:**13, 139, 945, 1103, 1371; **3:**126, 1026; **4:**468, 673, 685–87, 752, 764, 778, 815, 823, 842, 847, 891, 946, 1048, 1051, 1100–1101, 1201, 1260–61; **5:**59, 69, 574–75, 644; **6:**359, 599, 711; **7:**336; **9:**173, 389, 525, 558, 597, 608, 834, 837, 858; **10:**526, 575, 815, 911; **11:**130; SPIRITUAL **1:**50, 1066; **2:**343, 442; **3:**367, 389, 538, 620, 632, 637, 1181; **5:**407, 690, 788; **6:**970, 982, 1043; **7:**419; **9:**584; **10:**41, 133; **12:**337, 340, 351, 353, 476, 479, 490, 493

LIGHT
CHILDREN OF THE **3:**757; **5:**12; **8:**195; **9:**309, 713–14; **11:**433–40, 443, 727; AND DARKNESS **1:**287, 289, 343–44, 766–68, 890–93, 902; **2:**178, 321, 1367; **3:**43, 97, 167, 554, 757, 982, 984, 992, 1061; **4:**250, 310, 367, 415, 422, 464–65, 468, 511, 518, 529–30, 537, 547, 598, 601–3, 787, 823–24, 903, 1070, 1236; **5:**59, 76, 300, 302, 353–56, 583–86, 598, 670; **6:**72–73, 94, 123, 156, 188, 228, 364, 438, 478, 505, 508–10, 1435, 1438; **7:**15, 321, 392–93, 558, 679, 872; **8:**195, 210; **9:**60, 65, 244–45, 252, 371, 460, 463, 506, 520, 524–25, 553, 602, 632, 643, 663–65, 686, 713, 730, 802–4, 824–26, 857; **10:**21, 334, 339, 434, 445, 629, 701, 728–29; **11:**75, 289, 377, 381, 384, 422, 434–43, 513, 593–96, 726–27; **12:**75, 189, 212, 267–69, 369, 374, 381, 385–87, 393–96, 400, 426, 436, 516–17, 615, 665, 676, 701, 723; IMAGES/SYMBOLS OF **1:**343, 901, 1166; **3:**982; **4:**517, 537, 1069; **5:**188, 353, 504, 786–87; **6:**515; **7:**148, 393, 872; **9:**632; **11:**726; OF THE WORLD (*see under* JESUS THE CHRIST, NAMES FOR/TITLES OF *in PERSONS IN THE BIBLE*)

LIGHTNING
1:240, 274, 400, 836, 854; **2:**88, 534, 790, 1018, 1367; **4:**351, 583, 589–93, 598, 605, 747, 792, 1069, 1097, 1105, 1220; **5:**486, 504, 578, 784, 834; **6:**627, 1007, 1129, 1131, 1289, 1304–5, 1576; **7:**136, 168, 352, 610, 654; **8:**443; **9:**331, 333, 434, 468; **10:**486, 711; **12:**561, 591–92, 597–99, 630, 724

LILY, LILIES
3:88; **4:**656; **5:**327, 389–90, 394, 547, 818, 859; **7:**296; **8:**211; **9:**259; **11:**709; OF THE FIELD **3:**88; **5:**327, 547; OF THE VALLEY **5:**389, 394

LIME, LIMESTONE
1:215, 218, 222; **2:**178; **7:**362

LINEN
1:90, 909, 1044, 1060, 1110, 1112–14; **2:**220, 454, 987, 1249; **3:**692, 914, 1158; **5:**262, 461; **6:**988, 1009, 1172, 1178–83, 1214, 1230, 1360, 1374–75, 1378, 1538, 1560, 1578, 1596; **7:**136–37, 148–49; **8:**494–95, 710, 726; **9:**316, 337, 465, 471–73, 836–37, 841; **12:**498, 561, 598–99, 619, 631, 672, 694–95, 699; FINE **5:**461; **6:**1378; **9:**316, 337, 465; **12:**694–95; GARMENT(S) (*see under* GARMENT)

LINTEL, LINTELS
1:1157; **6:**1260, 1586; **8:**724; **9:**833

LION (*OR* LIONS, LIONESS, *ETC.*)
1:193, 285, 665, 667, 1075, 1179; **2:**188, 190, 364, 536, 767, 842–43, 849–50, 853, 1111, 1207; **3:**108, 152, 257, 299, 871, 959; **4:**51, 55, 377, 384, 415, 442, 530, 597–98, 608–9, 626, 820, 908, 980; **5:**67, 118, 179, 199, 225, 237, 239, 255, 312, 340–42, 407, 463, 675, 715, 741–42, 764, 768,

849; **6:**98, 141, 198, 260, 282, 301, 766, 866, 896, 915, 1049, 1084, 1115, 1131, 1176, 1266–74, 1314, 1371, 1388, 1418, 1434, 1485, 1523, 1554, 1566, 1593; **7:**12, 53, 75, 85–96, 101–5, 180, 192–93, 248, 250, 262, 278–80, 352, 371–72, 574, 611–14, 667, 694, 817–18; **8:**15; **9:**282; **11:**858; **12:**143–44, 300, 316–17, 521, 526–27, 566, 576, 592, 598, 601–6, 609, 624, 631–32, 656; DEN OF **1:**285; **3:**871; **4:**51; **5:**118; **7:**89, 91, 93–95, 180, 192–93, 612; **12:**521

LITERATURE

ANCIENT (*see by title in ANCIENT LITERATURE*); OF ANCIENT NEAR EAST **1:**228–43, 323, 403; **2:**430–31, 763; **3:**26; **4:**378, 872; **5:**3–16, 332, 603–6; **6:**9–16, 23, 107, 343, 1019, 1099, 1152, 1595; **7:**114, 150; **10:**380; **12:**179; BIBLICAL/CHRISTIAN/ RELIGIOUS **1:**6, 22, 34, 87, 115–16, 125, 135, 163, 188, 213–14, 219, 226, 229–30, 234, 311; **2:**90, 98, 124, 187, 213, 222, 246, 264, 275, 311, 315, 431, 505, 539, 834; **3:**932, 982, 1089, 1102, 1107; **4:**288, 326, 378, 463, 553, 608; **5:**1, 381, 398, 532, 619, 625, 670, 695, 787; **6:**1, 23, 39, 59, 139, 208, 555, 935, 1082, 1197, 1210, 1245, 1260, 1290, 1349; **7:**28–29, 39, 43, 52, 54, 122, 636; **8:**1, 44, 46; **9:**3, 296, 333, 516, 787; **10:**385, 575; **11:**553, 654, 759, 864, 891; **12:**105, 172, 231, 250, 269, 290, 296, 324, 335, 484–85, 489, 575; MIDRASH **1:**66–71; **2:**7; **4:**241; **5:**523, 692; **7:**175, 472; **8:**109; **10:**16, 124; NARRATIVE **1:**240, 331; **2:**539–53; **8:**56–71; **10:**30; PROPHETIC **1:**31, 48, 81, 237, 986; **2:**221, 455, 461; **3:**389; **4:**576; **5:**474, 523, 613, 644, 752; **6:**1–23, 34–35, 52–53, 57, 81, 85, 87, 92, 126, 143, 158, 162–63, 182, 206–7, 225, 228, 230, 239, 252, 260, 265, 313, 327–28, 599, 1098, 1138, 1396, 1429; **7:**15, 50, 162, 178, 181, 302, 435, 465, 481, 548, 601, 624, 650, 659, 686, 691, 701, 708, 715, 740, 759, 772, 849 **11:**237; **12:**519, 542; RABBINIC **1:**68–69, 73–78, 82, 296; **3:**1114; **4:**241; **5:**479, 659–60, 688, 693, 716, 772, 808; **7:**472; **8:**188, 417; **9:**349; **12:**85; WISDOM **1:**18, 147, 232; **2:**121, 527, 893, 1370–71; **3:**513, 870, 916, 1014; **4:**303, 326–27, 345, 400, 449, 468, 524, 531, 552, 650, 683, 729, 813, 990, 1083; **5:**1–16, 69, 145, 183, 204, 238, 253, 269, 274, 303, 332, 358, 522–23, 603–6, 618, 620, 628, 651, 655, 682, 687, 700, 705, 708, 725, 752, 754, 765, 772, 800; **6:**2, 18, 53, 56, 141, 190, 221, 265, 708, 957, 960–63, 966–68; **7:**76, 161, 178, 182, 188, 249, 354, 371, 375; **8:**31; **9:**225, 271, 333, 506, 519; **11:**430, 828; **12:**24, 105, 179–80, 189, 521

LITTER

5:400, 419–20; **6:**1269

LITURGY, LITURGIES

1:28, 53, 78, 199, 200–212, 297, 302, 341, 539, 684, 691–95, 722, 762, 781, 796, 799, 803–4, 853, 893, 951–52, 976, 1066; **2:**69, 78, 83, 96, 130, 152, 267, 477–84, 613, 651, 1239, 1247; **3:**88, 453, 700, 801, 993, 1002, 1065, 1173, 1182; **4:**72, 119, 303, 378, 534, 650–51, 689, 732–34, 757, 772–73, 781, 787, 823, 854, 868, 870, 968, 1024, 1035, 1046, 1060–61, 1065, 1099, 1110, 1117, 1126, 1134, 1146, 1149, 1166, 1180, 1182, 1199, 1221, 1223, 1254, 1265, 1279–80; **5:**36, 50, 377, 438, 757; **6:**58, 232, 267–72, 635, 649, 690, 697, 1013, 1017, 1129, 1260; **7:**246, 321, 380, 437, 529, 536–37, 577, 579, 586–89, 601, 627, 666, 721; **8:**29, 100, 190, 202–4, 336, 339, 658; **9:**418, 468, 504, 606, 657, 665, 708–9, 754, 811, 823; **10:**189, 263, 485–86, 529, 547, 573–47, 589, 810, 935, 945, 1002; **11:**272, 345, 611; **12:**4, 13, 21, 24, 29, 31, 35, 48, 59, 110, 113, 126, 161, 173, 189, 200, 260, 358, 457, 569, 593, 596, 617, 725, 727, 734

LIVER, LIVERS

1:913, 1025, 1040, 1066; **3:**1026, 1029, 1033, 1040, 1050; **4:**539; **5:**793; **6:**74, 120, 1301–2; **7:**526, 558

LIVING CREATURE, CREATURES

See under CREATURE

LIZARD, LIZARDS

4:530; **5:**255

LOAF, LOAVES

1:102, 294, 816, 1018, 1159, 1163–64; **2:**1139; **3:**112, 819; **5:**303, 819; **7:**779; **8:**69, 163, 165, 324, 326, 471, 601, 614, 617, 619; **9:**26–27, 99, 118, 133, 195, 206, 209, 420, 486, 593, 597, 610, 613; **10:**918, 920; **12:**103. *See also* BREAD

LOCK, LOCKS

2:772; **5:**411–12; **6:**1174–75, 1420, 1538; **7:**64; **8:**293; **9:**352; **10:**104, 577; **11:**268–69, 295; **12:**707

LOCUST, LOCUSTS

1:760–65, 1081; **2:**182, 795, 803; **3:**205, 500, 1102, 1105–6; **4:**592, 611–12, 992, 1105; **5:**255, 529, 540, 573, 688, 834; **6:**883, 1140; **7:**302, 305–12, 314, 316, 323–24, 334, 380, 405–6, 618, 701, 870; **8:**156, 532; **9:**81, 282; **12:**538, 566, 619, 631, 634, 668; CUTTING **7:**307–8

LODGE, LODGES

2:907, 1010; **4:**475, 488, 913; **5:**616; **7:**775

LOG, LOGS

3:693; **4:**283; **5:**348; **6:**1335, 1337; **8:**212; **9:**150–52; **11:**107

LOGIA

8:92; **10:**453

LOGOS
1:192, 291; **5:**2, 15, 438, 505, 510, 759, 835; **8:**19, 41, 501; **9:**176, 463, 506, 517–19, 522, 587, 604, 629, 634, 637, 641, 643, 717, 742, 745, 775, 784, 787, 790, 796, 798, 802, 844; **10:**84, 191, 196, 207–8, 668, 705, 810–11; **11:**189, 324, 559–60, 598–99, 605; **12:**23, 54, 59, 67, 264, 371, 382, 532, 584, 593, 605, 625, 705, 725

LOINS
3:102, 217; **4:**477, 596, 618, 623; **5:**255, 261, 415, 777; **6:**11, 395, 585, 805, 1117, 1406, 1596; **7:**309, 312; **9:**262–63, 336; **11:**459–60; **12:**88, 95, 257, 598

LONG-SUFFERING
4:635; **5:**678; **6:**697, 1199; **7:**319, 553; **8:**670; **10:**641; **11:**593; **12:**221

LOOKING GLASS
See MIRROR

LOOM
1:1097; **4:**394; **6:**301

LOOPS
1:896

LORD
CHRIST **1:**208; **7:**67, 325; **9:**65, 267; **10:**166, 549, 574, 807; **11:**471, 476, 510, 513–14, 527, 537, 571, 574, 593, 620–21, 628, 654–62, 894; **12:**268, 276, 291, 298, 479, 486, 500, 669; OF HOSTS *(see under* GOD, NAMES FOR/TITLES OF *in PERSONS IN THE BIBLE*); NAME OF THE **1:**206, 209, 376, 435, 1152, 1164, 1166; **2:**65, 331, 369, 375, 391–92, 487, 834, 1112, 1126, 1134–37, 1168, 1175, 1188, 1212, 1230, 1248–49, 1314; **3:**19, 32, 37, 72, 86–88, 126, 164, 178, 194, 198, 656, 915; **4:**711, 754–56, 759, 773, 945, 1155, 1184, 1269–73; **5:**96, 474; **6:**74, 102, 132–33, 175, 212, 248, 256–57, 438–39, 665, 680, 697–98, 727, 774, 794, 864, 1198, 1455; **7:**324–28, 402, 699; **8:**403, 438; **9:**282, 353, 361, 364, 369, 372, 707–8; **10:**59, 64–65, 68–69, 72, 81, 99, 107, 139, 144, 152, 154, 195, 206, 263, 268–69, 639, 665–67, 798, 807, 844, 855–56; **11:**105, 441, 657, 746, 750, 847; **12:**221–22, 621

LORD'S
DAY **12:**248, 566, 569; PRAYER **3:**540; **11:**285, 430, 439, 443; **12:**194, 291, 589; SUPPER **3:**700; **11:**7, 11, 75, 92, 123, 175, 225, 234; **12:**166, 180, 264, 287, 310, 566

LOTS
1:32, 906, 1061, 1111; **2:**182, 213, 220, 686–90, 1047–48, 1098, 1183, 1211, 1243; **3:**442–43, 447, 451, 824–25, 828, 896, 938, 969; **4:**389; **5:**160; **6:**74, 1336, 1601; **7:**451, 467, 497–98, 502–3, 526, 550; **8:**24, 722; **9:**46, 454–55, 698, 799, 829, 831; **10:**51, 282

LOTUS
1:225; **4:**618; **7:**769

LOVE
COMMANDMENT **8:**74, 80, 193, 195, 217, 426, 455–56, 666, 678; **9:**635, 703, 720, 726, 731–34, 739, 758–59, 767, 837; **10:**115; **11:**190, 420; **12:**377, 393–96, 422; DIVINE **1:**1184; **2:**345–46, 350, 369, 494, 843, 854; **3:**500, 612, 658, 736; **5:**391, 430, 434, 512; **6:**1492; **7:**518, 855; **10:**171, 521; **11:**547; **12:**389, 419, 430, 432, 441, 589; FEAST(S) **5:**389; **6:**1329; **12:**350, 359, 475, 482, 492; OF GOD **1:**74, 563, 577; **2:**345–46, 513, 826, 854, 893, 932, 945–46, 975; **3:**88, 96, 427, 474, 502, 510, 512; **4:**234, 383, 398, 423, 451, 514, 592, 823–24, 830, 857, 859, 890–91, 981, 995, 997, 1034, 1091, 1125, 1151, 1224–25, 1252; **5:**142, 193, 323, 395, 492, 542, 547, 562; **6:**57, 302, 371, 381, 502, 550, 816, 827, 1345; **7:**227, 233, 277, 383, 553, 569, 597, 603, 854–55, 868, 872; **8:**293, 581; **9:**78, 108, 148–49, 162, 173, 239, 254, 283, 305, 324, 327, 345, 384, 390, 411, 417, 421, 552–55, 605, 663, 671, 673, 679, 694, 714–15, 727, 734, 744, 746, 749, 752, 781–83, 795–98, 837, 845, 860; **10:**38, 416, 471, 484, 508, 514, 517–25, 589, 601, 609–10, 614–19, 787, 827, 878, 883, 897, 954–56, 994; **11:**79, 92, 99, 129–30, 159, 179–80, 247, 348, 391, 400, 404, 414–15, 435, 439–40, 486, 761; **12:**96, 338, 358, 377, 388, 395, 399, 411, 417, 419, 429–33, 436–37, 441, 479, 481–83, 488, 497, 728; HUMAN **1:**554, 559–60; **5:**14, 254, 371, 377, 391, 430, 434, 512; **10:**519, 603, 605; **11:**645; **12:**389, 430, 440; OF JESUS **5:**377; **8:**649; **9:**496, 500, 671, 686, 708, 714, 720–21, 727–29, 732, 734, 748, 758, 760, 763, 776, 784, 790, 795, 798, 811, 837, 852, 862, 865; **11:**244, 451

LOVING-KINDNESS
1:1142; **2:**21, 125, 895, 904, 911–12, 932, 945–46, 1133; **5:**294; **7:**581; **8:**172, 210; **9:**84, 798; **11:**345, 790, 876, 880

LOWLAND, LOWLANDS
1:224–25, 247, 251, 255, 258–59; **2:**572, 595, 616, 637, 652, 662, 677, 680, 685, 787–88; **6:**1081

LUKE, GOSPEL OF
1:14, 46, 85; **3:**576, 1018, 1043; **4:**20, 34; **5:**567; **7:**169, 188, 526; **8:**97; **9:**1–31, 52, 56, 60, 76, 90–91, 103, 112, 123, 161, 286, 326, 388, 432; **10:**7, 40, 48; **12:**528–29, 588–89, 651, 704

LUMBER
1:215, 972; **3:**478–79, 692; **6:**1506

LUST, LUSTS
1:809, 909, 1142; **2:**1208, 1285, 1288, 1303–4; **3:**1041, 1159; **4:**914; **5:**185, 230, 232, 312, 397,

407, 422, 681, 695, 700, 735–36, 740, 748–49, 752, 773, 828; **6:**601, 1233–34, 1321, 1325, 1331, 1459; **7:**95, 176–82, 197, 243, 261, 292, 333; **8:**165, 197, 374–57, 425; **9:**312, 314, 394; **10:**313, 433, 554, 891; **11:**219, 337, 431, 635, 642, 799, 845–46, 871, 873, 876; **12:**77, 336–38, 345, 348, 352, 355, 401, 489, 493–97, 646, 694

LUSTRATION, LUSTRATIONS
5:797; **6:**1183

LUTES
3:840

LUZ
1:277, 659; **2:**743

LYE
6:60

LYING
See LIES

M

MACCABEAN
REVOLT **1:**10, 270, 284–85, 288; **3:**977, 1125, 1131, 1162; **5:**611, 651; **6:**6, 25; **9:**201, 214; **12:**726; WARRIOR(S) **4:**47, 80, 95, 174, 204, 276

MACCABEES
4:2–25

MADNESS
OF ANTIOCHUS **3:**193; OF DAVID **2:**1143; OF HEROD **5:**772; OF JOB **4:**467; OF NEBUCHADNEZZAR **7:**71; AS OPPOSITE OF WISDOM **5:**295–96, 664; **6:**1442; OF SAUL **2:**1103, 1123–29, 1138, 1147–49, 1156

MAGI
2:920; **3:**332, 512, 679; **5:**793; **8:**140–48, 167, 237; **9:**65–66, 526; **11:**850; **12:**97

MAGIC, MAGICIAN
1:188–89; **2:**195, 330, 428; **3:**199, 1040; **4:**368; **5:**90, 272, 585, 591, 715; **6:**411–12, 433, 966, 1203, 1298–99; **7:**44; **8:**22–23, 140, 238, 543–54, 563, 565; **10:**271; **11:**206, 361–62, 394, 415, 561, 564, 567; AND CURSING **2:**502; AND DIVINATION **3:**27; **6:**120, 176, 1002; AND IDOLATRY **6:**73–74, 77; AND MIRACLES **8:**613; **9:** 188, 191, 238, 401, 654, 162; **10:**188, 190, 267–69, 273–74, 293; AND RITUAL **2:**462; **5:**114; AND SIGN ACTS **6:**1143–44; TRIAL BY ORDEAL **2:**67–68

MAGISTRATE, MAGISTRATES
1:628, 697; **4:**105; **5:**213; **6:**1138; **9:**346

MAGNIFICAT
1:205; **2:**983, 1259; **3:**714, 1145; **4:**1139; **9:**55, 81, 105, 144, 211; **12:**239

MAID, MAIDEN
ABIGAIL **2:**1164; BILHAH **3:**319, 457; BLACK-SKINNED **5:**367–73, 380, 387–99, 403–33; OF DAVID **3:**14; OF EDNA **3:**1041; HAGAR **1:**490; ISRAEL **6:**158, 1222; OF JUDITH **3:**1075, 1084–87, 1093, 1102, 1130, 1147–48, 1154–81; RUTH **2:**918

MAMMON
3:761; **4:**784; **5:**176, 676, 780; **8:**210; **9:**100, 309–14, 320; **10:**270, 435; **11:**645–46; **12:**589, 681, 716

MAN AND WOMAN
AND FAMILY AND HOUSEHOLD **5:**259–60; **10:**234, 928; **11:**451, 802; IN THE GARDEN **1:**350, 352–54; IN LOVE **1:**553; **2:**1122; **5:**341, 363–71, 401; **8:**191; MALE VIOLENCE **1:**557, 867; **2:**456; **7:**78, 232 (*see also* CITIES: OF REFUGE); SEXUAL RELATIONS **1:**1104, 1126, 1134; **2:**197–99, 246, 349, 445, 492–93, 629, 752, 875, 928, 941; **3:**1133, 1158; **5:**71, 85, 254, 720; **8:**190–92; **9:**314, 628–29; **10:**869–76; **11:**654; THE TEMPTATION **1:**359–64, 369, 372; **12:**614; WOMAN AS PROPERTY OF MAN **1:**848; **2:**67–68; **3:**1014; **7:**208–9, 220; **9:**390; **10:**929, 970; WOMAN FOLLY/WOMAN WISDOM AND THE YOUNG MAN **5:**4, 11, 31, 36, 46

MANDRAKE, MANDRAKES
1:555; **5:**427

MANGER
8:140; **9:**62–63, 65–66, 274, 284, 526; **11:**78, 159

MANICHAEISM
1:93; **11:**393

MANIFESTATION
AS AN EPIPHANY OF GOD **2:**55; **3:**140; **4:**209–10, 263, 276, 287, 794, 960, 965, 1052, 1067, 1223; **6:**501, 508, 513; **7:**393, 602; **8:**64–65, 145, 510, 603–4, 630–31; **9:**184, 508, 539–40, 591, 712, 586, 856–58; **10:**150, 179, 227, 306, 966; **11:**58, 759, 829, 831, 836, 855

MANNA
1:809–16, 845, 963; **4:**486, 1004, 1043, 1098, 1111; **5:**578–79, 598; **8:**325; **9:**99, 594; **12:**580, 710; AND THE LORD'S SUPPER **1:**209–10, 688, 805, 815–16; **9:**594, 606; AND THE MULTIPLE LOAVES **9:**613

MAN OF LAWLESSNESS
11:758–59; **12:**703–4

MANTLE
OF DIVINE WARRIOR **5:**486; OF ELIJAH **2:**602; **3:**142–44, 173, 176–78, 215; OF EZRA **3:**733; OF HANNAH **9:**52; AS AN INHERITANCE **2:**446; OF A KING **7:**818; OF A PROPHET **3:**171; **7:**832, 877; OF SHINAR **2:**351, 393; WOMAN'S HAIR AS A **10:**929

MANUSCRIPTS
OF THE OT **1:**292–304; OF THE NT **1:**1–11. *See also by name in* ANCIENT LITERATURE

MARANATHA
10:1002; **12:**531, 734

MARBLE
6:988; **12:**597
MARCIONISM
1:14, 46–47, 84–85; **9:**5–6; **10:**685
MARGINALIZATION
1:147, 151, 168, 171; **2:**1023; **7:**70; **10:**750; **11:**609, 646; **12:**194–95
MARINER, MARINERS
1:392; **6:**1371; **10:**353. *See also* SAILOR
MARK
OF CAIN **1:**364; **5:**523; **6:**795; **10:**571; OF CROSS ON FOREHEAD **6:**1179
MARK, GOSPEL OF
IN THE CANON **1:**13–18; COMPARISON OF PSALM 62 TO JESUS' CALL IN **4:**924; LUKE'S EDITING OF **9:**195, 398, 461; MATTHEW'S EDITING OF **8:**95–96, 114, 304, 400; ROLE OF ELIJAH IN **2:**718; ROLE OF ZECHARIAH IN **7:**840
MARKETPLACE
1:223; **9:**202; CHILDREN IN **9:**166–67; DISHONESTY IN **1:**1135; **3:**205; **5:**117; **7:**417; **9:**149, 250; **10:**232–33, 606; MISSIONARY ACTIVITY IN **10:**244, 249, 375; **11:**662; SLAVERY IN **2:**505; **10:**867
MARRIAGE
BETROTHAL **10:**889; CEREMONY **1:**1142; **3:**975, 1138, 1401, 1403; **5:**36, 400–402, 409, 829; **8:**63, 235, 449, 555; **9:**51; **10:**957; AS COVENANT, LITERAL AND METAPHORICAL **1:**277, 1084; **2:**841, 893, 928–29; **3:**158, 568, 1040; **5:**44, 85, 401, 521; **6:**477, 609, 641, 809, 1224, 1228, 1239, 1242, 1321, 1331, 1471; **7:**197–98, 206, 209–10, 216, 224, 226–27, 229, 580, 850; **11:**455; EXOGAMY *(mixed)* **1:**580; **2:**901, 923; **3:**115, 156, 214, 733, 735, 740–43, 849; **5:**44, 632; **6:**1223; **10:**226–27, 683; FORCED, RESULT OF CAPTURE **2:**445, 1224; LEVIRATE (*see* LEVIRATE LAW/MARRIAGE); MATRIARCHAL **1:**512; **7:**223; MATRILINEAL **5:**429; MONOGAMY **2:**974; **3:**522; **5:**753; **9:**390; **12:**277; PATRIARCHAL **1:**527; **2:**537, 628; **4:**538; **6:**813–14; **8:**129; POLYGAMY **2:**446; **3:**522; **4:**470; **8:**82, 386, 642; **9:**313; **11:**805; PROPOSAL **1:**578, 1174; **2:**468, 928–29, 1118; **9:**88; WIFE PURCHASED AS PROPERTY **1:**848–49; **2:**336, 452; **5:**629; **6:**1309; **9:**628; **11:**451
MARTYR, MARTYRS
3:68, 582; **4:**202, 242; **5:**651; **6:**460; **7:**66, 188; **8:**46, 52, 264, 270, 437, 488, 628, 654, 723; **9:**27, 30, 98, 281, 433, 455, 461, 488, 862, 864–65; **10:**131, 337, 475; **11:**411, 458, 472; **12:**148, 315, 517, 522, 624
MARTYRDOM
OF ISAIAH **5:**853; **8:**29, 348; **9:**433; OF MATTHEW **8:**348; OF POLYCARP **4:**243; **9:**433; **11:**403
MASKIL
2:657
MASON, MASONS
2:1242; **3:**429, 431, 692, 704; **8:**588; **10:**603. *See also* STONECUTTERS
MASSORAH, MASSORETES
1:76, 78, 297; **3:**663
MASTER, MASTERS
1:509–12, 599, 609–10, 703, 725, 770, 772, 780, 834, 862–63, 1134, 1174; **2:**374, 448, 452, 566, 716, 928, 1164, 1193; **3:**179; **4:**30, 106, 202, 1078, 1187, 1240; **5:**5, 94, 133, 159, 852; **6:**196–97, 211, 403; **9:**21, 262–64; **11:**870; **12:**292. *See also under* GOD, METAPHORS FOR *in PERSONS IN THE BIBLE*; JESUS THE CHRIST, METAPHORS FOR *in PERSONS IN THE BIBLE*
MASTIC
5:757; **6:**1379; **7:**182
MATERIALISM
2:757; **3:**474; **9:**149, 261, 309; **10:**249; **11:**289, 627–28, 635, 645; **12:**402, 486
MATRIARCH, MATRIARCHS
1:512; **2:**900; **3:**735; **4:**1105, 1203; **6:**447; **7:**177, 224; **8:**147; **10:**636, 869–70
MAW
OF HELL/SHEOL **5:**322; **7:**508
MEAL
BOTTOMLESS JAR OF **3:**128; **9:**118, 336; LEAVENED **2:**412; **6:**1580; OFFERING (*see* CEREAL; OFFERING: GRAIN; OFFERING: MEAL)
MEAL, MEALS
AGAPE **12:**492–93; BREAD GAINED BY DECEIT **5:**187; BIRTHRIGHT **1:**535–39; **2:**846; **12:**154; COVENANT/TREATY **1:**529, 881, 990–91, 1018, 1062; **3:**137, 380, 1040; DAILY/FAMILY **2:**230; **3:**610; **4:**635, 1224, 1226; **7:**400; **10:**277, 352; EUCHARISTIC/POST-RESURRECTION **2:**1276; **3:**1065; **8:**44, 323–25, 702–6, 709, 729; **9:**197, 321, 417–22, 476–81, 486, 858; **10:**233, 918, 934; **11:**234; **12:**71, 166–67, 587; FAREWELL **9:**509, 613–14, 701, 720–30, 787, 789, 797, 799, 810; FASTING (*see* FASTING); FELLOWSHIP **1:**1133; **8:**25, 472; **9:**127, 421, 481; **12:**492, 493; FUNERARY **6:**1342; HEALING **8:**543, 546, 553; **8:**557; MARTHA'S **9:**231–32; MIRACLE **8:**601; **9:**549, 701, 864; MURDEROUS **6:**858; PASSOVER **1:**777, 781; **2:**90, 619; **3:**648; **4:**1149; **5:**591; **6:**455; **8:**468, 472–73, 687, 701; **9:**139, 415–18, 542, 719, 814; **10:**534; **11:**377; (*see also* PASSOVER AND FEAST OF UNLEAVENED BREAD); PHARISEES AT TABLE WITH JESUS **9:**247, 283–89; REUNION **1:**635; RITUAL/SACRIFICIAL **1:**440, 1010, 1014, 1024–28, 1053, 1119; **2:**387–88, 975; **3:**468, 1001; **4:**647, 764, 769, 813, 926, 933; **6:**216, 638, 1528; **10:**893, 917, 922–23; SALVATION **10:**352–53; SEX AFTER **5:**85, 721, 1001; PREPARED BY SINGING CHEFS **6:**1335; SINNERS AT TABLE

WITH JESUS **8:**59, 237; **9:**26, 127, 166, 169. *See also* BANQUET
MEASURES
See WEIGHTS AND MEASURES
MEAT
See FOOD
MEDIATOR (*OR* MEDIATORS, MEDIATION, *ETC.*)
ABRAHAM AS **1:**419, 509; ANGEL AS **4:**568–70; **7:**750, 753; AVENGER/REDEEMER **4:**460; CLOUDS AND FIRE AS **1:**789; DANIEL AS **7:**8, 105; DAVID AS **2:**1193–94; **3:**93–94; DEBORAH AS **2:**723; HOLY SPIRIT AS **7:**777; **10:**41, 154, 282, 949; JEREMIAH AS **6:**666; JESUS AS **1:**1072; **8:**64; **9:**781; **10:**175; **11:**372–73, 598, 798–99; **12:**12, 81, 100, 109–10, 124, 158, 388; JOSEPH AS **1:**655; JUDITH AS **3:**1138; LAW/TORAH **1:**39, 890; LOGOS **8:**41; MOSES AS **1:**679, 853–55, 1008–9, 1060; **2:**11, 109, 271, 283, 324, 337–39, 538, 865; **6:**363, 1289; **11:**267, 279; RAPHAEL AS **3:**985, 1010, 1056; SAMUEL AS **2:**960, 976, 1016–19, 1026, 1040–41, 1047, 1061–63; TEMPLE **1:**281
MEDICINE, MEDICINES
1:600, 1148; **3:**1040, 1050; **5:**160, 779; KNOWLEDGE OF **5:**506, 519, 813; **11:**444, 516; MAGIC AS **6:**966; PRACTICE OF **1:**1148; **3:**1040, 1049–50; **5:**779 (*see also* PHYSICIAN); SPIRITUAL **2:**66–67, 141, 167–68; **5:**574, 683; **6:**1501; **9:**610
MEDIUM, MEDIUMS
DISCERNMENT IN SELECTING **1:**1135; **2:**1182–84, 1191–92; **3:**370, 389; **6:**826–27, 1203, 1445; **7:**720; **10:**190
MEEKNESS
IN THE BEATITUDES **4:**672, 975; **8:**179–81, 848, 975; OF THE DEFENSELESS **4:**669, 672, 679, 717, 718, 719, 732, 828–30, 848, 980; **6:**141, 143, 247, 249; **11:**658; **12:**526, 700; IN ESSENE WRITINGS **11:**443; OF JESUS, SERVANT-KING **8:**125, 150, 158, 161, 178–79, 244, 268–69, 275, 281–82, 292, 309, 357, 361, 370, 403, 459–60, 487; AS A QUALITY/VIRTUE **12:**189, 205–6; OF RULERS **2:**682; **7:**76
MEMBER, MEMBERS
OF THE BODY/IN COMMUNITY **2:**54, 745, 790, 818; **5:**15, 75; **7:**96; **8:**378; **9:**761; **10:**709–10, 809, 863–66, 936–39, 941, 945–49; **11:**29, 86, 105, 229, 338, 357–58, 413, 422–25, 429–30, 443, 450, 456, 458, 633, 637, 642; **12:**287
MEMORIAL, MEMORY
CRY OF LAMENT/SONG/WAIL **2:**78, 1205–6; **4:**955; **5:**301; DAY/FESTIVAL **1:**786; **2:**911–12; **3:**969; **6:**70; THE EUCHARIST **1:**787, 1021; **3:**612; **4:**1229; **8:**470–73; **9:**420–21, 613–14; **10:**935–39; EULOGY FOR HERO/RACE **3:**1180–82; **5:**697, 824; **6:**971, 974, 981; OF GOD'S ACTIVITY/CHARACTER **1:**683, 773, 783; **4:**1260; **12:**128; OF GOD'S NAME **1:**861; **4:**1087; OFFERING (*see under* OFFERING); OF THE SABBATH **1:**845; **10:**277; AS SYMBOL OF PAST CONFLICT/CONQUEST **1:**906; **2:**135, 486, 601, 608, 707, 748, 1209; **4:**1196; AS VINDICATION OF RIGHTEOUS/HOPE FOR THE FUTURE **7:**846, 872. *See also* REMEMBRANCE
MENE, MENE, TEKEL, AND PARSIN
7:83–84, 149
MENORAH, MENORAHS
1:1017; **2:**69, 79–80; **3:**1162, 1167; **5:**765; **7:**769; **11:**364; **12:**103
MENSTRUATION
1:557, 1075, 1105; **2:**151, 455; **5:**416; **6:**999, 1488
MERCY
DIVINE **1:**940; **2:**727, 1381–83; **5:**564, 628; **6:**521, 867; **8:**179, 656; **9:**326, 459; **10:**645, 694; **11:**345–46; **12:**41–42, 288; HUMAN **2:**1013; **6:**521, 867; **8:**179, 656; **9:**326; **12:**194, 482, 498
MERCY SEAT
1:889–93, 897, 913, 960, 972, 998, 1012, 1111, 1113–14; **2:**2, 79; **3:**359; **6:**1118; **10:**474–76; **12:**41, 59, 104, 106, 113, 116, 167, 247–48
MERIT
TO EARN **1:**30, 449; **2:**893, 896, 932, 946, 1368; **4:**674, 882–83, 992, 1017, 1038, 1088, 1101; **5:**563, 867; **6:**699, 766; **9:**298, 303, 305; **10:**440, 459, 479, 529, 868; **11:**76; **12:**89
MESSENGER, MESSENGERS
APOSTLES AS **10:**196, 201, 360; **11:**294, 298, 520; BATTLEFIELD **2:**1002, 1201–2, 1287, 1323; **3:**21; **6:**293; COMMISSIONING OF **1:**509; FORMULA **2:**988, 1047, 1085, 1087, 1256; **6:**596–97, 1152; **7:**790–91; ISRAEL AS GOD'S **10:**629; JESUS AS **8:**274, 354; **9:**842; **10:**416; **12:**35; TO JOB **4:**351–52, 366; JOHN THE BAPTIST AS **8:**269, 530–31; **9:**15, 163–64, 215; TO JOSEPH **1:**671; MOSES THE **1:**735; A PROPHET AS **1:**42; **2:**994; **6:**101–4, 337, 370, 575, 582, 752, 1249; **7:**53, 445, 518, 525, 583, 667, 678, 693, 720, 847, 852, 861, 868–73; OF SATAN **11:**164–65; STATUS AND ROLE OF **5:**208; SUFFERING SERVANT AS **6:**456–57 (*see also under* SERVANT); OF YAHWEH **2:**179–84, 193–94; **7:**606. *See also* ANGEL
MESSIAH, THE
See JESUS THE CHRIST, NAMES FOR/TITLES OF *in PERSONS IN THE BIBLE*
MESSIAH, MESSIAHS
1:289–90; **2:**702, 1039, 1055; **4:**71–72; **7:**27–29, 709; **8:**142, 146–47, 353–54, 514, 712; **9:**97; DAVIDIC **1:**289; **2:** 603, 736, 895, 941–46, 983, 1258–59, 1368; **3:**576; **4:**689–90, 765, 965, 1037–38, 1063, 1130–31,1156; **5:**161; **6:**129, 264, 1252, 1269; **7:**570–71, 739, 763–68, 788,

MESSIAH, MESSIAHS *(continued)*
807, 814, 876; **8:**353–54, 656, 680; **9:**391; **10:**153, 191, 193, 219, 537, 748; **11:**264, 843; **12:**525–27, 602
MESSIANIC
1:289–90, 668, 686, 1174–75; **2:**190, 1039, 1042, 1255, 1259; **3:**179, 691, 704, 785, 787; **4:**650, 746, 861, 871, 1129–31, 1156; **5:**161, 256, 463, 617, 805, 855–56; **6:**38, 46, 100, 112, 137, 145, 158, 167–70, 239, 264, 464, 1531; **7:**7, 39, 141, 428–31, 568, 570–71, 739, 763, 768, 770, 780, 788, 805, 840; **8:**66, 97, 116, 126, 142, 146–47, 149, 156, 163, 169, 189, 224, 249, 519, 526, 572; **9:**97, 391, 565, 620, 624; **10:**14, 62–63, 122–23, 376, 417–18, 625, 650, 746–48; **11:**614; **12:**525–27, 582, 602–3, 636 FEAST (*see under* FEASTS/FESTIVALS); SECRET **8:**66, 110, 160, 225, 238–39, 281, 304, 336, 347, 356, 364, 369–70, 459, 519, 521, 572, 623; **9:**461, 690
METALLURGY
1:218, 224, 375; **5:**469; **6:**1306, 1312
METAPHOR, METAPHORS
FOR GOD (*see* GOD, METAPHORS FOR *in PERSONS IN THE BIBLE*); FOR JESUS (*see* JESUS THE CHRIST, METAPHORS FOR *in PERSONS IN THE BIBLE*); FOR THEOLOGY (*see under* THEOLOGY); USED AS FIGURATIVE LANGUAGE **1:**28, 115, 193, 352, 360, 796, 799, 1021; **2:**15, 97, 106, 190, 536, 685, 741, 872, 878, 918, 924, 928, 981, 1114, 1168, 1243; **3:**14, 135, 155, 164, 301, 364, 424, 497; **4:**106, 311–14, 336, 349, 352, 370, 402, 410, 501, 510, 512, 532, 749, 768, 920, 977, 980, 1000, 1092, 1182, 1236; **5:**36–37, 95, 107, 112, 119, 132, 230–31, 368–70, 401, 405, 469, 475, 489–90, 504–5, 512, 546–47, 597–98, 787, 851; **6:**56–57, 78, 127–28, 157, 203, 221, 227, 236, 254, 260, 277, 601, 1019, 1051, 1058, 1166, 1188, 1202, 1211, 1220, 1224–25, 1228, 1241–42, 1333–34, 1370–71, 1408, 1446, 1463–65; **7:**91, 95, 197–98, 226–29, 256, 618–19, 804, 820; **8:**60, 157–58, 275, 287, 299, 308, 447, 563, 575, 609, 617, 624, 653; **9:**117–18, 130, 177, 219–20, 247, 261, 271, 282, 408, 488, 528, 549–50, 567, 572, 605, 612–13, 625, 653, 670–71, 686, 713, 742, 748, 755–58, 779, 803, 817, 842; **10:**7, 44, 54, 68, 82, 89, 178, 190, 194–95, 205, 337, 457, 471, 490–92, 516, 533–34, 538, 571, 581, 597, 663, 676, 681, 683, 710, 724–25, 728, 754–55, 776, 812, 827–28, 862–63, 893, 899–901, 945–47; **11:**23, 81, 138, 187, 238, 260, 265, 267, 291, 293, 296, 386, 403–4, 455, 460, 496, 513, 544, 568–88, 623, 698–700, 795; **12:**22, 46, 70, 75, 81, 92, 102, 107, 120, 123, 148–49, 172, 236, 280, 286, 300, 339, 351–52, 390, 414, 435, 461, 484–85, 491–93, 506, 583, 602, 619, 648, 664, 673, 735
MIDRASH, MIDRASHIC
1:66–82, 438; **3:**45–46, 333; **4:**241, 659; **5:**99, 102, 305, 441, 523, 528–29, 622, 689; **6:**1016, 1052; **7:**50, 175, 192, 466–67, 472–74; **8:**31, 94–95, 97, 104, 109, 129, 359; **9:**600, 636, 653, 697; **10:**16, 62, 65, 191; **11:**63–64, 262, 267, 304–5; **12:**30, 49, 152, 579; LITERATURE (*see under* LITERATURE)
MIDWIFE, MIDWIVES
1:297–99, 476, 538, 585, 695–701; GOD AS **4:**602; **5:**12; **7:**293; LEGAL PERMIT FOR **9:**285; OF RACHEL **1:**585
MIGHTY MEN
See WARRIOR; NEPHILIM *in PERSONS IN THE BIBLE*
MIGHTY WORKS
APOSTOLIC WORKS **10:**38, 168; **11:**253; BIBLICAL THEOLOGY MOVEMENT **1:**197–98; OF GOD **2:**753; **4:**625, 1050, 1101–6, 1226; **5:**283, 570–71; **7:**855; **9:**21–22, 107, 584; **11:**255; OF JESUS **8:**171, 317; **9:**22, 110, 112–13, 116, 118, 120, 156, 173, 195, 199, 221, 225, 241, 278, 386, 656, 660, 663, 679, 693, 746; LORD OF CREATION **1:**721–22; **4:**589; **8:**229; LORD OF HISTORY **6:**1085, 1169, 1357, 1421, 1431, 1597; **7:**442
MILDEW
1:1097–99; **4:**592; **10:**659
MILK
AND HONEY **1:**164–65, 210, 430, 528, 1018, 1143; **2:**123, 136–37, 342, 374, 576, 608, 612, 748, 757; **4:**485; **5:**405, 846; **6:**671, 1277, 1491; **12:**264; AS HOSPITALITY **4:**538; A KID IN ITS MOTHER'S **2:**398; SPIRITUAL **2:**141; **10:**825, 837, 841; **12:**68–69, 263–64
MILL, MILLSTONE
1:1020, 1163; **8:**446; AS INSTRUMENT OF DEATH **2:**502, 634, 791, 816, 818, 1287; **3:**1090; **8:**375; **9:**202, 321–22; **12:**694; AS PERSONAL PROPERTY **2:**472, 858–60
MILLENNIUM
12:708–13; IN APOCALYPTIC GROUPS **7:**149; **10:**673; **12:**31, 507, 513, 517, 527, 532–36, 539–41, 544, 547, 686, 706, 716
MILLET
6:1379
MIND
BRING TO GOD'S **6:**1302; CHANGE OF GOD'S **1:**932; **2:**188, 825–26, 1090; **4:**1092; **6:**614, 638, 648, 691, 715, 717, 772, 774, 796, 865; **8:**59; **10:**402; **12:**5; CHANGE OF MIND AS REPENTANCE **1:**179, 788; **4:**629, 713; **6:**1279; **7:**514; **10:**67; **12:**154, 633; OF CHRIST **10:**806–7, 821–22; CONTRASTING FLESH AND **10:**572, 705–7; HEART, TRANSLATED AS **2:**1039; **3:**55; **4:**1208; **5:**301; **6:**674; KNOWLEDGE AND THE **5:**504, 671; LOVE WITH ALL YOUR **6:**606–7; OF ONE **11:**496–99,

546; OUT OF ONE'S **11:**90–91; RIGHT/SOUND **8:**584; **9:**187; **11:**91, 870; **12:**303; UNDERSTANDING **5:**498
MINE, MINING
OF METALS **4:**529; UNCOVERING HIDDEN TREASURES AS FIGURATIVE LANGUAGE **4:**529–33; **9:**481
MINISTER, MINISTERS
3:727, 1042–43; **5:**668; **6:**1464–65; JESUS AS MINISTER/OVERSEER/SERVANT **8:**251, 543; **9:**671–72; **12:**283; AS SHEPHERD **6:**1464; **9:**394; **11:**812–13. *See also* PASTOR
MINISTER IN THE OLD TESTAMENT
AS AGENT OF KING/RULER **1:**224, 620–22; **3:**49, 58, 102; **4:**135, 260, 268; AS SERVANT *(e.g., altar priests/Levites)* **1:**1024, 1049, 1063; **2:**83; **3:**344, 394; **5:**656; **6:**1568; **12:**116
MINISTER IN THE NEW TESTAMENT
9:379, 671; **11:**2, 14, 20, 156–57, 165, 466, 812; **12:**60, 307
MINISTRY, CHRISTIAN
APOSTOLIC **11:**661–62; EMERGENCE OF BISHOP AND ELDER **8:**103–4; **9:**310; **11:**454, 482, 775, 778–79, 805–6, 822, 864, 867; HUNGER **8:**577; JESUS COMMISSIONS **8:**561–62, 600; **9:**193, 487; **10:**38, 667; **11:**133; JESUS' PROPHETIC **10:**166; PAUL AS MODEL FOR **11:**58, 149, 482, 617; ROLE OF PROPHETS/TEACHERS *(sometimes false)* **8:**49, 169; **9:**402; **10:**189, 284; **11:**359–60, 409, 422–24, 822; **12:**325, 329, 343–45, 360, 475, 485, 489, 491, 495–96, 522; AS SERVANT **8:**432; **10:**761–62; **11:**591–92, 884; **12:**384; SPIRITUAL DISCERNMENT IN SELECTING **10:**201. *See also* DEACON; DEACONESS
MIRACLE, MIRACLES
1:56, 76, 104, 110, 133, 194, 241, 696–98, 794–96; **2:**108, 307, 538; **3:**129, 178, 183–84, 193, 202, 498, 1112; **4:**51, 511; **5:**597; **6:**122, 302; **7:**762; **8:**76, 148, 166, 171, 242, 246–51; **9:**113, 502–3, 597, 676, 738; **10:**140, 198
MIRROR, MIRRORS
1:943; **4:**591; **5:**504, 715; **10:**624, 634, 649, 954; **11:**70; **12:**545
MISSION, MISSIONS
GENTILE **6:**423, 429; **8:**46, 52, 54; **9:**106–7, 197, 794; **10:**32, 160–61, 174–75, 188, 204, 214–15, 270, 339, 390; **11:**229, 305; AND MONEY **2:**180; **4:**222–24; **6:**361, 423–24, 428, 514; **11:**120–27
MISSIONARY, MISSIONARIES
8:46, 102, 246, 255–59, 263, 417–18, 456, 595, 600; **10:**9, 175, 181, 211–12, 235, 239, 311, 935; **11:**184–88, 203–7, 249–51, 254–57, 263–64, 287–88, 305–6, 313–16, 337–38, 346–47, 462–63; MOVEMENTS **8:**45–47; **9:**197; **10:**31, 175, 214; **11:**229; RIVAL **11:**185–86, 189–90, 204–7, 218, 227, 249, 255, 294–95, 299–300, 306–7, 311, 313–17, 324–25, 329, 333–34, 343
MIST
AS A CREATIVE FORCE **5:**621, 757; AS DIVINE BLESSING/POWER **1:**536; **2:**87; **7:**288; **9:**410; AS EVANESCENCE OF LIFE **5:**460, 579; **12:**216; AS FRAGRANCE OF INCENSE **5:**504
MOABITE STONE
1:1189; **2:**182; **3:**123; **6:**1348, 1353, 1489; **7:**363
MOCK (*OR* MOCKING, *ETC.*)
CAPTIVES **7:**550; GOD **6:**293, 1459; JESUS **8:**488, 528, 591, 652, 723, 726; **9:**351, 376, 440–41, 456–57, 463, 822; JOB **4:**331, 419, 462, 491, 547; THE POOR **4:**170, 412, 664; RULERS **3:**629, 761; **6:**454; **7:**188; **8:**528; **11:**526; ZION **6:**1041
MOMENT
DECISIVE **1:**211; **2:**1326; **3:**252, 266; **4:**485, 595; **11:**130; **12:**516, 712. *See also* TIME
MONARCH, MONARCHY
See KING, KINGSHIP
MONEY
1:629, 634, 638, 917–18; **2:**33; **3:**897; **4:**925; **5:**327, 525; **6:**662, 944; **7:**778; **8:**453, 467, 483, 595; **9:**311; **10:**49, 759, 883; **11:**171; **12:**163; PIECE OF **4:**635. *See also* COIN; TITHE: COLLECTION OF MONEY/OFFERING/TITHES
MONEY CHANGERS
AND JESUS **8:**405–6, 483, 661, 663, 673; **9:**373, 543; **11:**319; **12:**727
MONOTHEISM
1:276, 841; **2:**280, 287, 329, 503; **3:**1125, 1154; **5:**9, 759, 788; **6:**413, 1010; **7:**200, 202, 241, 347, 357; **8:**179, 458; **10:**93, 665, 748, 778; **11:**364, 608, 798, 831; **12:**80; PLURALIZING **10:**32, 390, 580–81; AND SONG OF MOSES **2:**529–30
MONSTER
CHAOS/DRAGON/SEA **1:**232, 274, 344, 739, 800–801; **3:**1026, 1029, 1032; **4:**368, 411, 487, 518, 597, 617, 621–23, 974, 1098; **6:**448, 1401, 1404, 1425, 1429, 1434–37; **7:**192, 421, 509; **8:**328, 580, 584; **9:**243; **12:**493 (*see also under* SEA); "THE MONSTER IN THE BRIDAL CHAMBER" **3:**979–82, 1008; MOT **1:**236. *See also* BEHEMOTH; DRAGON; LEVIATHAN
MONTH
1:218, 228–34; **5:**497; **6:**939, 1454, 1536–37; **7:**715; **8:**400–401; **9:**52, 93, 675, 815. *See also* CALENDAR
MONUMENT
TO ABSOLAM **2:**1337; **7:**386; AT CARMEL **2:**1008; AS EUPHEMISM FOR PENIS **6:**485; AT GILGAL **2:**609; FOR JONATHAN THE MACCABEE **2:**152; IN MANASSAH **2:**706; AT MT. EBAL **2:**486–88; VIETNAM **2:**1209; WASHINGTON **9:**387; WASTED **6:**198

MOON
AS CREATION **4:**395, 1224, 1271; **5:**818, 834; **10:**596, 987; **11:**372, 376; **12:**357; AS A DEITY **2:**569–70; **3:**757; **4:**1098; **5:**556; **6:**213, 1130, 1589; **7:**62, 168; **10:**282; **11:**390–91; IN JOSEPH'S DREAM **1:**599; AS LIGHT/WITNESS **1:**902; **4:**517, 520, 554, 1036, 1272; **5:**326, 354, 419; LUNACY/MOONSTRUCK **4:**1181; **8:**368; LUNAR CALENDAR **2:**229, 332; **3:**441; **5:**834; **10:**288; NEW **1:**1156; **2:**230–32, 332, 647, 1135; **3:**691, 1133; **4:**1003; **5:**85; **6:**56, 539, 549, 1584, 1588–89; **7:**205, 244, 416; **11:**288, 631; AS REFERENCE TO TIME **1:**236; **2:**235, 647; **4:**305, 308; **5:**10; AS SIGN OF JUDGMENT **6:**228, 255, 277, 412, 509, 640, 1007, 1429; **7:**244, 328; **8:**444; **9:**407, 460; **10:**401, 571; **11:**421; **12:**614, 631, 648, 723; AS SOURCE OF POWER **2:**316; **4:**518

MORNING STAR
1:31; **3:**570; **7:**113; **12:**582

MORTAR
AND PESTLE **5:**231; A WALL WITHOUT **6:**1202

MOST HIGH
See under GOD, NAMES FOR/TITLES OF *in PERSONS IN THE BIBLE*

MOST HOLY PLACE
See HOLY: PLACE(S)

MOTE
6:753

MOTH, MOTHS
3:1018, 1162; **4:**312, 524; **6:**451, 453, 988, 1383; **7:**248; **8:**210; **10:**571; **12:**216, 250

MOTHER, MOTHERS
DANIEL AND THE QUEEN **7:**82; DETERMINED BY SOLOMON **3:**42–48; OF A FAMILY **4:**1215; OF ISRAEL **1:**559, 652, 696; **2:**551, 728, 940–42, 975, 1242; **3:**44–45; **5:**19, 108; **6:**1040, 1062; OF JESUS **8:**566; **9:**348–49, 536, 832; OF JOHN MARK **10:**180, 225; "LIKE MOTHER, LIKE DAUGHTER" **6:**1236, 1272; IN PRAISE OF A GREAT **4:**257–64; ROLE AT A WEDDING **5:**400; **9:**536; OF SEVEN MARTYRS **3:**240–42; WISDOM COMPARED TO **5:**498; ZION **4:**1024–25, 1208; **6:**238. *See also* NAMED WOMEN OF THE BIBLE *and* UNNAMED WOMEN OF THE BIBLE *in REFERENCE LISTS*

MOTHER-IN-LAW
AND INCEST **1:**1141; OF PETER **8:**228, 539, 543–46, 553; **9:**24, 103, 111, 114; OF RUTH **2:**477, 905–13, 924, 931; **3:**1168

MOUNT, MOUNTAIN, MOUNTAINS
OF ASSEMBLY **4:**518; **6:**159, 1114; OF GOD **7:**55; HOLY MOUNTAIN OF ZION **6:**144; LOCATION FOR JERUSALEM **4:**872; LOCATION OF EDEN **6:**1394; MANY **1:**41, 245, 274, 278, 359, 392, 460; **2:**13; **4:**618, 823; **6:**1427, 1435, 1474, 1480, 1482–83; **7:**782–83; MOSES AND THE COMMANDMENTS **1:**880, 948–60; POST-RESURRECTION **8:**502; SACRED HIGH PLACE **3:**39, 80, 472–73; **6:**1285; TEMPTATION OF JESUS **9:**97; THEOPHANY AT MT. HOREB **2:**14; TRANSFIGURATION OF JESUS **9:**205. *See also* HILL: MOUNTAINS AND

MOUNT, SERMON ON THE
See SERMON ON THE MOUNT

MOURNING
2:162; **3:**1142; **4:**63, 208, 355, 459, 547, 611, 1196; **5:**306; **6:**168–69, 202, 217, 293, 702, 859, 980, 1000, 1070, 1339, 1343, 1429, 1439–40; **7:**325; **8:**179, 444, 555; **9:**130, 779, 841

MULE
OF ABSOLOM **2:**1336; OF ADONIJAH **3:**20; OF DAVID **3:**20; PERSIAN **7:**71. *See also* ASS

MULTITUDE, MULTITUDES
OF ANGELS **9:**66; **12:**620–26, 695; OF DISCIPLES **9:**26, 195–96, 369; GREAT (*see under* GREAT); MIXED **1:**781; **4:**276; OF NATIONS **1:**457–59, 515; **2:**608, 1121; **3:**810, 1101; **6:**156; **7:**124, 137, 140, 792; **12:**598, 621–26, 700, 722; OF PEOPLE GATHERED **4:**269–70; **6:**94, 144, 1497; **8:**561; OF SINS **5:**619; **12:**304, 306; OF WORSHIPERS **4:**1272; **9:**46, 367, 369; **12:**591, 618, 620–26, 664, 666, 672, 695, 722

MURDER, MURDERS
1:847–48; **2:**266, 333, 432, 842, 872, 886, 1309, 1317, 1350–52; **3:**27; **6:**528, 1457; **8:**41, 150, 189, 390, 414, 608, 670; **9:**249, 383–84, 448; **10:**106, 130, 150–53, 570, 725; **11:**791; **12:**123, 193, 209, 211–19, 385, 418–20, 443, 606, 633

MURMUR
1:805, 98–100, 104–6; **2:**121–28, 135–37, 140, 160–64, 169, 254; **3:**1004; **9:**295, 298; **11:**512

MUSIC
AFRICAN AMERICAN **1:**156; DIVINE **5:**598; LAMENT **6:**1022–23; LYRICS IN SONG OF SONGS **5:**367, 377; MUSICAL MODES **3:**394; **4:**656; IN THE PSALMS **4:**656, 862, 946, 1014, 1227–28, 1279–80; SINGING PSALMS AND HYMNS **3:**447–48; **11:**444; TRANCE **3:**183; WINE AND **6:**211

MUSICIAN, MUSICIANS
2:787, 1094; **3:**300; **4:**602; DAVID AS **2:**1094, 1101–3, 1108, 1113, 1115, 1121, 1126–27; **5:**377; SINGING LEVITES **3:**306, 327, 345–46, 394, 399–400, 445–47, 499, 575, 609, 645–48, 838, 847

MUSICAL INSTRUMENTS
1:375; **2:**89, 1102–4, 1109, 1232; **3:**445, 447; **4:**309, 331, 960, 1268; **5:**597; **6:**1330, 1362; **7:**63, 650; **9:**952; **12:**1204. *See also by type of instrument*

MUSTARD SEED
6:1596; **8:**60, 308–11, 369, 568–69, 575–78; **9:**12, 179, 275–77, 332–33, 338, 340

MUTILATE (*OR* MUTILIATED, MUTILATION, *ETC.*)
1:1095, 1165; **2:**475, 1198; **4:**42, 467; **6:**1223, 1235, 1242, 1317, 1326; **9:**836; **11:**524–26
MYRRH
1:920, 1061; **3:**512, 889; **5:**388, 403, 405–6, 462, 757, 1230; **8:**143, 490, 722, 730; **9:**454
MYRTLE
1:1160; **3:**802, 886; **6:**482, 485; **7:**750–51, 756; **9:**542
MYSTERY, MYSTERIES
OF CHRIST/SALVATION **8:**304; **11:**357, 360, 374, 407; **12:**213, 298, 515, 518; CULTS/RELIGIONS **5:**496; **6:**176; **8:**25–26; **9:**177–78; **10:**374, 533; **11:**532, 561, 567, 653, 807; **12:**204; OF GOD'S WAYS **4:**422, 430; **6:**812; **9:**177–78; **10:**768; **11:**357, 807; **12:**206, 515, 530, 563, 638, 657; KNOWLEDGE OF **5:**699, 834; **6:**1388; **11:**618
MYTH, MYTHOLOGY
1:335; BAAL **1:**274; **2:**600; **5:**397; **7:**101, 136, 202; CREATION/EDEN/PARADISE **4:**449, 518, 619, 621; **6:**142, 1385, 1423; **7:**758; DIVINE WARRIOR **7:**601; HERO **3:**1086; ISHTAR **4:**603; **6:**1438; IN THE NT **8:**248, 291–92, 585; **9:**502; **10:**232; **11:**385, 400, 501, 604; **12:**114, 329, 341–44, 507–10, 547, 550, 644–45, 678; PROMISED LAND **2:**559, 586; SACRED MOUNTAIN **1:**278; **6:**1595; UGARITIC **4:**368, 469, 486, 622, 624; **6:**1114–15, 1387; **7:**602

N

NAHUM, BOOK OF
1:266; **3:**1069; **6:**7, 13, 18, 20, 313, 581, 1307, 1320, 1336; **7:**351, 482, 526, 661, 670–71, 691–92, 815; **12:**629, 678
NAIL, NAILS
3:484, 736; **4:**513; **6:**1116; **7:**193; **8:**722; **9:**485, 830; **11:**207, 572, 625–26, 628. *See also* TENT: PEG(S)
NAKEDNESS
1:336, 354, 359, 361–62, 364–65, 368, 404–5, 628, 861, 1060, 1124–25; **2:**559, 670, 879, 926–27, 1126, 1128, 1135; **3:**191, 598, 699, 733, 882, 995, 998, 1016, 1018; **4:**32, 352, 354, 445, 518, 1244; **5:**319, 374, 401, 425, 736, 823; **6:**12, 36, 81, 102, 149, 182–83, 376, 411, 918, 1030, 1065, 1086, 1141, 1145, 1150, 1227–28, 1230, 1234, 1259, 1309, 1316, 1327, 1392; **7:**180, 209, 220, 224, 248, 546, 614, 647; **8:**194, 197, 710; **9:**318, 455; **10:**269; **11:**84, 272, 643; **12:**54, 529, 587, 613, 614, 624, 652, 654, 667, 682, 693, 700, 704, 717, 728
NAME CHANGES
1:457, 459–60, 541, 566–68, 584–85, 843; **2:**95, 371, 487, 660, 739, 792, 798, 870; **3:**331, 810, 1132; **4:**217, 232; **5:**673; **6:**22, 277, 375, 515–16, 538, 544, 559, 722, 981, 1078, 1526, 1607; **7:**31–32, 39, 50, 82, 283, 788, 795; **8:**4, 345, 347, 526; **10:**97, 190, 213, 217; **12:**268, 585
NAMES OF GOD
See GOD, NAMES FOR/TITLES OF *in PERSONS IN THE BIBLE*
NAPHTHA
4:197–98
NARCISSISM
1:849–50, 892, 908, 925; **4:**914; **5:**525; **11:**710; **12:**428, 696
NARD
5:387; **9:**169
NARRATIVE
CRITICISM (*see under* CRITICISM); LITERATURE (*see under* LITERATURE)
NARRATOLOGY
2:540–42, 544, 552; **8:**108
NATIONALITY, NATIONALITIES
1:166, 1083; **2:**575; **3:**96, 130; **4:**1151; **5:**597, 620, 862; **7:**118, 129, 458; **9:**108; **10:**142, 165, 230, 298; **11:**611
NATIONS
See ORACLE: AGAINST THE NATIONS
NATURAL PHENOMENA
1:795; **2:**182, 316; **3:**1143; **4:**312, 441, 486, 591, 1220; **5:**274, 350, 536, 546, 571, 578, 580, 586, 784, 833; **6:**73, 211, 256, 660, 1382, 1414; **7:**382, 474, 545, 655; **8:**142; **10:**312
NAVE
3:62, 484, 486, 491; **6:**1106, 1548–52, 1554–55, 1557. *See also* PORCH; PORTICO; VESTIBULE
NAVEL
5:49, 370, 425–26; **6:**1595; **7:**528, 699; **8:**24
NECK
1:605, 665, 1119; **2:**445, 502, 905, 1002; **3:**46, 432, 656, 962, 1177; **4:**459, 624, 952, 1190; **5:**48, 54, 80, 239, 370, 387, 402, 426, 512, 526, 688–89, 730; **6:**117, 327, 375–76, 782, 866, 1033, 1228, 1431, 1530, 1596; **7:**220, 226, 275, 506, 527–28, 731; **8:**32; **9:**202, 302, 321, 830; **11:**361; **12:**285; STIFF **3:**656; **5:**239
NECKLACE, NECKLACES
3:484, 1080; **5:**54; **9:**310
NECROMANCY
1:1131, 1135, 1139; **2:**606, 1182–84; **6:**118
NECTAR
5:405
NEEDLE, EYE OF A/THE
7:801; **8:**391, 395, 650; **9:**151, 202, 348, 350, 359–60

NEEDLEWORK
1:901; **5:**357
NEHEMIAH, BOOK OF
1:39, 252, 268–69, 294, 303; **2:**897, 902, 942; **3:**657, 978, 987, 1016; **4:**196, 485, 1188; **5:**273; **6:**5, 315, 946; **7:**28, 121
NEHUSHTAN
2:8, 164
NEIGHBOR, NEIGHBORS
1:88, 234, 236–37, 239, 259, 276, 285, 460, 464, 517, 570, 581, 605, 688, 814, 839–40, 846, 848–49, 852, 865–67, 870, 872–75, 941, 949–51, 954, 989, 1040–41, 1051, 1104, 1131, 1134, 1189; **2:**26, 61, 201, 335, 380, 404, 423, 434, 436, 443, 452, 467, 469, 471–72, 492, 494, 510, 536, 562, 616, 632, 694, 758–59, 779, 865, 942, 1022, 1029–30, 1085, 1090, 1120, 1157, 1185, 1240, 1293, 1331; **3:**49, 75, 135, 157, 186, 211, 241, 245, 523, 529, 569, 597, 678, 680, 691, 694, 698, 700, 997, 1002, 1016, 1041, 1108, 1117–18; **4:**25, 47, 52, 73, 77, 83, 148, 258, 271, 283, 326, 347, 472, 504, 510, 519, 553, 700, 702, 732–33, 773, 848, 898, 916; **5:**5, 13, 16, 23, 36, 38, 43, 45–46, 54–56, 60–61, 64, 71, 74, 76–77, 80–81, 117–18, 128–29, 131, 144, 148, 162, 168, 193, 200, 205, 214, 219, 225, 230–31, 241–42, 314, 558, 614, 617, 638, 701, 730–31, 779, 849, 862; **6:**6, 12, 127, 218, 272–73, 276–77, 503, 519, 606, 618, 620, 637, 641, 654–55, 679–80, 721, 753, 778, 826, 832, 878, 890–91, 894, 896, 965, 966, 971, 974–76, 978–79, 1115, 1143, 1232, 1253, 1258, 1310, 1347–49, 1356, 1358–61, 1363, 1369, 1395–96, 1396–97, 1408, 1415, 1419, 1444, 1458, 1475, 1480, 1485; **7:**75, 355, 361–62, 371, 375, 390, 424, 428, 457, 574, 594–95, 606, 660–62, 670, 672, 676, 684–86, 688, 690, 692, 700, 767, 774, 838, 861, 877; **8:**32, 40–41, 148, 197, 214, 363, 608, 651; **9:**27, 35, 58–59, 84, 125, 133, 150, 153, 226, 229–30, 232, 235–39, 278, 287, 292, 294, 296, 298, 311, 316, 318, 336–37, 370, 538, 571, 654, 656; **10:**109, 222, 256, 447, 461, 548, 623, 644, 649, 661, 714, 731, 789, 893, 917–18; **11:**19, 41, 98, 239, 333–34, 405, 682–83, 696, 703, 741, 799, 810, 872, 876, 879; **12:**181, 205, 209, 215, 218, 222, 234, 236, 241, 254, 265, 270, 273, 277, 281, 286, 303, 311, 340, 347–48, 636; LOVE OF **1:**50, 998, 1133, 1136, 1173–74; **2:**286, 409, 887, 1057, 1161; **3:**547, 821, 987, 1018; **4:**83, 773, 835, 848; **5:**56, 92, 118, 219, 772; **7:**321, 776; **8:**193, 195, 213–14, 380, 390, 424–26, 466, 674, 678–79; **9:**35, 74, 84, 135–36, 148, 226–33, 248, 733; **10:**342, 387, 724–26, 745, 911, 924; **11:**54, 177, 322–24, 332–33, 338–39, 500, 595; **12:**179, 193, 195, 215, 223, 369, 395–96
NEO-ORTHODOXY
1:1, 104, 108, 195, 197; **6:**375
NEPHTHAR
See NAPHTHA
NEST, NESTS
1:1081, 1098; **3:**967; **4:**313, 442, 524, 539, 612, 898, 1013; **5:**104, 120, 230, 630, 651, 719–21; **6:**261, 708, 1252–53, 1425; **7:**258, 447; **8:**311, 577; **9:**91, 179, 217, 275–76, 369; **10:**586; TO FEATHER ONE'S **6:**1315, 1598; **11:**170
NET, NETS
1:207; **4:**234, 469, 475, 779, 800, 819, 905, 924, 1243; **5:**38, 193, 198, 242, 689, 701; **6:**7, 180, 762, 795, 1033, 1194, 1269, 1364, 1366, 1435, 1456, 1596; **7:**244, 258, 263, 267, 628; **8:**22, 169, 301, 313–15, 539; **9:**115–17, 858, 864; **10:**677; **11:**329, 332. *See also* SNARE; TRAP
NETTLE, NETTLES
3:967; **5:**326; **6:**277; **7:**285; **10:**570
NEW
BIRTH (*see under* BIRTH); COVENANT (*see under* COVENANT); CREATION (*see under* CREATION); EARTH/HEAVEN (*see under* EARTH; HEAVEN); HUMANITY **1:**191, 199, 316; **3:**480; **4:**723; **5:**61, 176; **6:**630; **10:**419, 524; **11:**242, 344, 400, 403, 411, 414, 422, 570–72, 574, 629, 643–44, 647–50; MAN **11:**429; MOON (*see under* MOON); YEAR **1:**275, 311, 392–93, 976, 1159; **2:**33, 412; **3:**69, 691, 751, 800, 860, 948; **4:**649, 868, 1053, 1061, 1064; **5:**266; **6:**946, 1107, 1536–37, 1570, 1585; **7:**76, 80, 202, 393, 683; **8:**205; **11:**649; YEAR *(Babylonian, Akitu)* **3:**860, 948; **6:**1536–38, 1570; **7:**76, 80, 715
NEW JERUSALEM
2:38, 1238–39; **3:**363, 475, 1026, 1061–62, 1065–66; **4:**866; **5:**343; **6:**808, 814; **7:**3, 10, 431; **8:**34, 36, 472; **11:**415; **12:**515, 521, 533, 535, 540–41, 558, 576, 578, 584–85, 591, 593–94, 612–13, 630, 641, 649, 656, 664–65, 668, 672, 676–77, 681, 686–87, 693–95, 701, 710, 718–25, 729–30, 734
NEW TESTAMENT
CANON **1:**4–5, 8, 13–22, 44–45, 46–49, 86, 161, 168–69, 188–89; **2:**609, 899; **3:**1079; **4:**641–42; **5:**273, 438, 553; **6:**310; **7:**2, 352; **8:**6, 72, 89, 106; **9:**6, 504, 589; **10:**3, 14, 26–27, 32, 281, 304, 369–70, 384, 387–89, 391; **11:** 277, 330, 354, 582, 775–77, 839, 883, 886; **12:**3, 4, 70, 161, 329, 455,466, 468, 519–20, 536, 546; CHRONOLOGY **8:**80–81, 110–11, 159, 319, 323, 336, 400–403, 430, 439, 463, 478, 494, 496–97, 737; **9:**62, 72, 80, 415, 451, 493, 543, 674, 704–5, 707, 719, 799, 823, 867; **10:**10, 14, 25, 40, 42, 275, 330, 372–73; **11:**163, 193, 221; **12:**90, 94, 96,

105, 367, 410, 505, 570; LANGUAGE **8:**1–11; TEXT **8:**1–11, 91, 517–18; **9:**4–10, 498–507; **10:**789–90; **11:**777–82, 883–84; **12:**6–10, 177–79, 230–36, 323–24, 365–66, 473–74

NEW ZION
2:38; **12:**722

NICANOR, DAY OF
3:859, 1167

NICENE CREED
See under CREED

NIGHT, NIGHTS
1:141, 206, 241–42, 286, 344, 391, 423, 474, 541, 555, 565–66, 568–69, 614, 652, 718, 748, 771, 773, 780, 783–84, 789, 865, 868–69, 882, 887, 913, 916, 930, 979, 1044, 1049, 1066, 1163, 1179; **2:**34, 54, 86, 88–89, 91, 126, 178, 182–83, 194, 232, 235, 252, 412, 470, 547, 584, 588, 601, 614, 619, 781, 797, 802–3, 830, 840, 854, 858, 860, 876, 877–78, 930, 991, 992–93, 1039, 1042, 1080, 1088, 1127–28, 1135, 1166, 1174, 1185–86, 1192, 1198, 1202, 1217, 1230, 1254, 1256, 1285, 1297, 1331, 1340, 1359; **3:**43–44, 142, 269, 363, 494, 563, 568, 576, 752, 776–77, 786, 813, 838, 885, 889–90, 908, 913, 915, 945, 975, 979, 984, 1008, 1024, 1026, 1028–29, 1031–33, 1040–41, 1049, 1056, 1069, 1141, 1148, 1153, 1160, 1189; **4:**16, 66, 77, 145, 197, 233, 247, 277, 305–7, 311, 358, 366–69, 371, 377–78, 393, 415, 416, 463, 508, 510–11, 520, 546, 548, 561, 569, 577, 581, 587, 593, 602–4, 614, 626, 684, 690, 694–95, 697, 711, 740, 752, 769, 805, 815, 853, 905, 913, 926–27, 929, 983, 1041–42, 1047, 1051–52, 1181, 1217, 1237, 1250, 1275; **5:**84, 261, 274–75, 300–301, 303, 324, 328, 350, 395, 396, 402, 409, 412, 441, 505, 525, 567, 583–85, 670, 797, 812, 814, 823, 834; **6:**10, 84, 93, 187–88, 213, 222, 329, 345, 414, 520, 600, 625, 653, 762, 826, 840, 1029, 1042, 1044, 1071–72, 1194, 1232, 1287, 1343, 1453, 1472, 1586; **7:**8, 81, 100, 122, 257, 287, 312, 389, 448, 501, 504–5, 509, 522–23, 526, 548, 618, 750, 764, 783–84, 836–37; **8:**22, 146, 148, 163, 308, 328, 451, 472–73, 475, 481, 583, 595, 659, 702, 707, 712; **9:**21, 25, 27, 51, 63, 73, 115–16, 137, 236, 238–39, 243, 256, 263, 316, 331–32, 336, 338–39, 355, 373, 401–2, 412, 418, 420, 428, 436, 440, 459–61, 476, 542, 548, 553, 555, 595, 632, 653, 667, 686, 730, 802, 833, 835, 857; **10:**104, 108, 161, 179, 227, 230, 239, 255, 284, 335, 352, 401, 534, 556, 610, 676, 727–29, 934, 1003; **11:**157, 288, 429, 457, 699, 726–28, 819, 857; **12:**43, 199, 356, 597, 603, 625, 635–36, 650, 667, 687, 724; DREAM(S)/VISION(S) **1:**242, 541, 614, 652; **2:**178, 991; **4:**377–78, 569; **5:**441; **6:**10, 329, 1453; **7:**8, 100, 750, 764, 783–84; **9:**401; **10:**227, 255; **11:**457; **12:**603; VIGIL/WATCH(S) **1:**206, 783–84, 1044; **2:**781, 1297, 1359–60; **3:**979, 1114; **4:**905, 926, 1041, 1073, 1126, 1252; **5:**441, 607; **6:**187, 520, 1497; **8:**328, 475, 495, 498, 707; **9:**263, 667, 833; **12:**356, 687; WEDDING (*see under* WEDDING)

NIGHTJAR
6:277

NIGHTMARE, NIGHTMARES
1:568; **2:**505; **5:**815, 823, 825; **7:**113; **9:**371; **12:**634

NINURTA
6:1499

NISAN
(month in Jewish calendar) **1:**1157–58; **2:**87; **3:**608, 616, 751, 755, 860, 896, 899, 925, 948, 956; **4:**297; **5:**1536–37; **8:**468, 470, 697, 702; **9:**414–15, 418, 542, 814, 823

NOAHIC COVENANT
See COVENANT: WITH NOAH

NOB, PRIESTS OF
2:966, 988, 1139, 1141, 1145, 1148–49, 1156, 1183, 1193, 1268; **3:**33

NOMAD (*OR* NOMADS, NOMADISM, *ETC.*)
1:215, 219–21, 225, 227, 246, 255, 258, 266, 310, 433, 453, 514, 590; **2:**191–92, 557, 581, 1087–88, 1179; **3:**537; **4:**78, 118; **5:**383; **6:**157, 834, 899, 1319, 1326, 1351, 1353, 1379; **8:**376–77

NORTH
ENEMY (ENEMIES) FROM THE **2:**779; **3:**773, 894, 1095; **6:**136–37, 163, 573, 584, 614, 625, 647, 696, 883, 913, 1296, 1523, 1531–32; **7:**302, 316, 323, 360, 691, 784

NORTHEASTER, THE
10:348

NORTHERNER
7:323

NOSE RING, RINGS
3:1040; **5:**119; **6:**1228, 1329

NOT MY PEOPLE
See NOT MY PEOPLE *in PERSONS IN THE BIBLE*

NOT PITIED
See NOT PITIED *in PERSONS IN THE BIBLE*

NUMBERS
RHETORICAL USE OF **1:**445; **3:**431, 467, 525, 530, 598, 858, 1102; **4:**228; **5:**260; **11:**157, 232; UNLUCKY **3:**899; VERSE NUMBERING **1:**297, 307; **7:**211. *See also individual numbers by name*

NUMBERS, BOOK OF
1:85, 307, 313, 678, 801, 805, 996, 1132; **2:**291–92, 309, 322, 342, 394, 479, 529, 555,

NUMBERS, BOOK OF *(continued)*
560, 580, 683, 701, 752–53; **3:**820; **4:**74, 945; **5:**14, 441, 443, 532, 573, 592; **6:**355, 408, 1589; **11:**214
NUMERICAL PROVERB
1:240; **5:**30, 77, 257, 639, 641, 647, 752, 759–61, 767, 861–63
NUN
(Hebrew letter) **2:**96; **4:**718, 1259; **5:**230; **7:**601
NUNC DIMITTIS
1:205–6; **4:**672; **9:**21, 70–71; **12:**518
NUNS
2:833; **8:**222; **9:**482, 865; **11:**417
NURSE, NURSES
1:511, 586, 700; **2:**106, 511–12, 877, 1317; **3:**14, 43, 228, 573, 1024; **4:**234; **5:**95, 401, 428, 497, 499, 779; **6:**141, 337, 509, 551, 658, 974, 1061; **9:**283, 404, 452, 571, 865; **11:**699, 705, 715
NUT, NUTS
See ALMOND

O

OAK, OAKS
1:584, 586; **2:**547, 796, 816, 1336; **4:**656; **6:**62–63, 73, 387, 447, 514, 1374; **7:**182, 817; **9:**475
OAK OF THE PILLAR
2:816
OATH, OATHS
1:276, 399, 440, 442, 446, 448–49, 491–92, 498, 510, 522, 529, 628, 658–59, 667, 669, 706, 789, 830–31, 835, 837, 866, 880–82, 889, 934, 1036, 1041, 1047, 1063, 1166, 1190; **2:**62–63, 124, 249–50, 330, 334, 359, 369, 480, 563, 568, 593, 641, 907, 945, 1078, 1080–82, 1090, 1093, 1126, 1127, 1134–35, 1159, 1188, 1223–24, 1230, 1237, 1314, 1347, 1357; **3:**18–20, 22–23, 28, 34, 44, 126, 128, 133, 497, 538–39, 656, 741, 780, 788, 797, 811, 817, 842, 849, 1139; **4:**91, 95–96, 107, 282, 341, 364, 390, 497, 522–24, 548–58, 576, 613, 707–8, 1081, 1083, 1212, 1237; **5:**2, 93, 147, 188, 245, 334, 339, 430, 559, 592, 629, 733, 750, 828, 842; **6:**74, 159, 271, 402, 549, 606, 619–21, 669, 671, 745, 805, 864, 1103, 1153, 1228, 1236, 1240, 1242, 1248–50, 1253, 1258, 1276–78, 1281–82, 1285–88, 1301–2, 1322, 1326, 1446, 1450, 1458, 1464, 1471, 1476–77, 1483, 1491; **7:**272, 377, 381, 401, 416–19, 774–76, 779, 810; **8:**187, 193, 321–22, 435, 457, 480–81, 599, 616, 715; **9:**45, 658; **10:**312, 498; **11:**32, 49, 52, 160, 204, 217, 403, 699, 856; **12:**19, 48, 51, 79–81, 83, 87, 91–94, 163, 195, 205, 222, 224, 601, 638; FALSE **1:**866, 1036, 1041; **2:**330; **6:**619–20; **7:**774–76, 779; **8:**193; FORMULA **2:**907; **3:**126, 128, 133; **4:**390, 522, 553, 576, 708; **6:**159, 1153, 1258, 1287, 1476; **7:**381; **8:**616; **9:**658. *See also* COVENANT; VOW
OBADIAH, BOOK OF
1:93, 573; **2:**162; **4:**31, 1228; **6:**13, 18, 20–21, 581, 1354; **7:**301, 336, 340, 351, 493, 596, 707
OBEISANCE
1:459, 599, 635, 653, 671; **2:**612, 1006, 1168, 1274; **3:**132, 196; **4:**1275; **6:**403, 408, 508–9; **7:**43; **10:**967; **12:**567, 585, 593, 604
OBELISK
See STELE
OBLATION, OBLATIONS
1:1051; **7:**254. *See also* OFFERING
OBSOLETE TERMS
FOR ANCIENT WRITERS **3:**61, 484; IN ENGLISH TRANSLATIONS **1:**1097
OCCUPATION, OCCUPATIONS
OF LAND **1:**41, 215, 248, 251–54, 308, 311–12, 1017, 1060; **2:**229, 299–300, 461, 615, 648, 718, 1207; **3:**346, 365, 560, 598, 802; **4:**95; **6:**529, 585, 868, 1069; **7:**20, 23, 26–27, 30, 156, 161, 169, 175, 189, 203, 437, 640, 690; **8:**478; **10:**181, 297; **12:**642; OR VOCATION **1:**246, 372–73, 653, 1055; **2:**192, 1111; **3:**1003; **4:**548; **5:**327, 604, 625, 636, 688, 812–14; **6:**205, 586–87, 966; **7:**341, 351, 410–11, 437, 498, 515, 629, 832; **8:**170, 539–40, 552–53, 566, 592, 650, 679; **9:**65, 575; **10:**254; **11:**675
ODOR, ODORS
1:393, 742, 818, 920, 1010, 1018; **2:**126–27, 229; **3:**1040; **5:**346; **6:**1230, 1285, 1290; **7:**72; **9:**691; **10:**162
OFFERING, OFFERINGS
ATONING **1:**1003, 1028; AND BLOOD **1:**777, 912, 916, 986, 999, 1005, 1010, 1012–13, 1024–27, 1033–37, 1040, 1043, 1048–49, 1061–62, 1066, 1072, 1085, 1099, 1101, 1111–12, 1135; **2:**151, 1376; **3:**346, 608–9, 612, 617–18, 647, 959; **6:**1546, 1564, 1568–69; **8:**720; **9:**833; **10:**474; **11:**435; **12:**74, 104, 106–8, 118, 120, 142, 155, 158, 387; BURNT/WHOLE **1:**32, 84, 393, 495, 880, 900, 912–13, 915, 931, 960, 972, 976, 989–91, 1003, 1005–7, 1009–21, 1023–28, 1035–36, 1039, 1043–46, 1049, 1061–62, 1065–67, 1072, 1084–86, 1098–99, 1105–6, 1110–11, 1113, 1119, 1158; **2:**52–54, 65, 78, 81–83, 126–27, 147, 229–30, 232, 236, 383, 386, 388, 487, 830–34, 846, 886, 1017–18, 1071, 1249; **3:**40, 136, 195, 346, 399, 421, 424–25, 437, 446, 468, 473, 477, 498, 510, 580, 608–12, 617, 622, 647–48, 691, 708, 710, 713, 730, 819, 1133, 1178; **4:**11, 39–40, 71–72, 190, 198, 243; **5:**469, 471, 611, 797, 859;

6:56, 379–80, 549, 639, 945, 1285, 1526, 1546–47, 1555, 1566, 1568–69, 1577, 1579, 1584, 1586, 1588–89; **7:**113, 162, 263, 320; **8:**33, 678; **9:**543; **11:**513; CEREAL **1:**1017; **2:**229; **3:**721, 846–47; **6:**1558, 1588–89; **8:**33, 617; COLLECTION OF MONEY/OFFERING/TITHES (*see under* TITHES); DRINK/ LIBATION **1:**585, 913, 1158, 1160; **2:**63, 65, 126, 149, 228–30, 232, 1376; **3:**611, 721, 959; **4:**39; **5:**779, 859; **6:**873, 1285, 1584; **7:**84, 309, 779; **8:**33; **9:**542; **11:**513–14, 856; ELEVATION **1:**913, 1054, 1099, 1158; **2:**81; EVENING **1:**1044, 1157; **2:**229; **3:**399, 691, 733, 735, 819, 821, 1143; **4:**1243, 1245; **6:**1589; **8:**33; AND FAT **1:**373, 1024–27, 1035–36, 1040, 1052–53, 1066–67, 1113; **2:**148, 1207; **3:**610–11, 647–48, 1178; **4:**198; **5:**849; **6:**277, 379, 1528, 1574, 1578; **9:**396; FELLOWSHIP **1:**1023, 1043; **2:**1071; **3:**40, 610, 647; **5:**85; OF FOOD **1:**1011, 1017; **2:**149; **6:**1160; **7:**860; **10:**181, 204; FREEWILL **1:**972, 1010, 1023, 1025–26, 1051; **2:**78, **3:**687, 721, 729, 1133; **4:**895; **6:**400, 569; **8:**682; GRAIN **1:**913, 991, 1003, 1005, 1015–23, 1028, 1036, 1043, 1045–47, 1049, 1065–66, 1072, 1098–99, 1158, 1166; **2:**62–63, 65, 77–78, 126, 229–30, 232–33, 842; **3:**346, 363, 424, 624, 819; **4:**39; **6:**549, 945, 1558, 1569, 1584, 1586, 1589, 1591; GUILT **1:**990, 999, 1003, 1005, 1009, 1013, 1019, 1027–28, 1032–33, 1037–43, 1045, 1048–49, 1098–99, 1134; **2:**62, 65, 78, 147, 1011–12; **3:**232, 346, 451, 624, 745; **6:**1546, 1558; **7:**839; HEAVE **1:**1054; **10:**683; INCENSE **2:**137; **3:**1114, 1143; **4:**257; **5:**859; **6:**943, 945; **7:**779; **9:**45, 436; JEALOUSY **1:**1018; **2:**62–63; OF MEAL **1:**1017; **2:**63; **3:**708, 710; **5:**707; MEMORIAL **1:**1018–20, 1045, 1164; **2:**62–63; **4:**833; **8:**170; PEACE **1:**25, 913, 990, 1003, 1005, 1009, 1016, 1019, 1022–28, 1034–36, 1039, 1043, 1049–54, 1061–62, 1065–66, 1072, 1098, 1132–33, 1158; **2:**78; **4:**154; **6:**1584; PLATE(S) **1:**1019–20; **2:**77, 135, 139–40; PURIFICATION **1:**281, 1033; **2:**78, 151, 248; **3:**609, 612; **4:**71, 198; **6:**1546, 1568–69, 1579, 1584, 1586, 1591; REMEMBRANCE **1:**1018, 1021; **2:**62–63; REPARATION **1:**1038–39, 1042, 1049, 1099; **2:**1010–12; **3:**745; **4:**277; **6:**1546–47, 1558, 1580, 1591; FOR THE SAINTS **10:**756, 995–96; **11:**113–14, 227; SIN **1:**18, 281, 912–13, 986, 999, 1003, 1005, 1009–13, 1018–19, 1027–28, 1032–37, 1039–43, 1045–49, 1052, 1060–62, 1065–66, 1072, 1084–86, 1098–99, 1105–6, 1110–14, 1158; **2:**65, 78, 81, 83, 127, 230, 232–33; **3:**232, 346, 451, 606, 608–9, 624, 712, 714, 730, 819, 1178; **4:**199; **6:**945, 1546, 1568; **7:**839; **9:**376; **10:**474, 553, 579; **11:**323, 392, 435; **12:**60, 107; THANK **1:**1050; 1152; **2:**483–84; **3:**722, 1001, 1174; **4:**764, 782, 813, 901, 1153; TRESPASS **1:**1038–40; VOLUNTARY **1:**1003, 1006, 1026, 1050; **3:**232, 678; VOTIVE **1:**1050–51, 1187; **2:**78, 228; **3:**691, 721, 723, 1161, 1180; **4:**199, 218; **9:**399; **10:**96; VOW **1:**1023, 1026–27, 1033, 1051, 1151; **2:**64, 233–34, 391, 830–37, 870, 885–87; **6:**1569; WAVE **1:**1054, 1062, 1079; **2:**81; WELL-BEING **1:**25, 1023; **2:**78, 228; **4:**198, 211; **6:**1584. *See also* CONTRIBUTION

OFFICER, OFFICERS
1:209, 223, 241, 727, 783, 972; **2:**247, 336, 430, 431–32, 470, 584, 586, 600, 602, 962, 966–67, 1038, 1050, 1268, 1285, 1288, 1314, 1354; **3:**27, 49, 84, 150, 205, 208, 210, 212, 217–18, 221, 224, 265, 293, 336, 342, 376, 378, 422, 433, 441, 445, 452, 547, 549, 556, 574, 624, 698, 775, 780, 826, 1101, 1105, 1151; **4:**44, 47, 80, 95, 236, 436; **5:**204, 544; **6:**79, 90, 95, 133, 261, 842, 858, 1241, 1326, 1386; **7:**33, 67, 130, 150, 162–63, 497, 663, 677, 709; **8:**121, 225–27, 726; **9:**46, 201, 215, 269, 310, 394, 415, 435–36, 801–3, 810, 817; **10:**177, 352; **11:**454, 777, 805, 842; **12:**326, 476. *See also under* COURT

OIL, OILS
5:380; **9:**316, 465; ANOINTING **1:**688, 919–20, 1061, 1071, 1101, 1148; **7:**771; OLIVE **1:**215, 222, 224–25, 901, 1017, 1036, 1163; **4:**110, 538; **5:**66, 166, 380; **6:**14, 1584; **7:**770–71; **9:**308; **12:**612; PRESS **1:**214, 224, 1017, 1163

OINTMENT
3:1147; **4:**625; **5:**325–6, 345–6, 415, 757; **6:**1266; **8:**698–700; **9:**169–170; **12:**587

OLD TESTAMENT
CANON **1:**4–5, 7–13, 16–22, 29, 37, 40–47, 51–53, 60, 65, 82, 94, 188, 132, 134–35, 292, 298; **2:**273–75, 291, 893, 1024; **3:**469, 663, 855, 896, 972, 997; **4:**1156; **5:**27, 125, 207, 244, 271, 273, 278, 281, 359, 364, 391, 438, 448, 483, 663–64; **6:**22–23, 48, 49, 190, 310, 932, 936, 986, 1240; **7:**2, 22, 148, 156, 175, 352, 408, 435–36; **8:**28, 94, 186; **9:**249, 486, 707; **11:**194, 227; **12:**238, 494, 519, 546; CHRONOLOGY **1:**54, 56, 102, 250, 253, 257, 262, 265, 284, 306, 314, 321, 336, 381, 389, 391–92, 1057; **2:**32, 77, 87, 278, 300, 378, 546–47, 1071, 1265, 1358; **3:**101, 538, 690, 698, 702, 751, 796, 833–34, 1186; **4:**18–19, 114, 160, 191, 216, 227–28, 230, 1281; **6:**99, 201, 560, 569, 932, 939–40, 942, 1326, 1536–37; **7:**121, 404, 436; **8:**130; LANGUAGE **1:**292–304, 1192; TEXT **1:**131–32, 292–304

OLIVE TREE, TREES
1:1017, 1163; **2:**471; **4:**110, 891; **5:**859; **6:**174, 670, 1360; **7:**769–71; **10:**11, 680, 683–84, 686; **11:**114, 284; **12:**642; WILD **3:**802; **10:**684–88; **11:**284, 404

OMEN, OMENS
1:237, 1135; **2:**189, 402, 483, 647, 914, 948; **5:**4, 793; **6:**9, 120, 393, 660, 1031–32, 1208, 1302, 1356; **7:**558, 618, 765–66; **8:**690; **9:**10, 42, 63, 280, 460; **11:**168, 497. *See also* PORTENT

ONE
FAITH **9:**792–93, 670–71; **10:**945–48; **11:**358, 383–84, 419–20; WITH THE FATHER **9:**676–77, 792–93; FLESH *(marriage)* **1:**353; **8:**386, 645; FROM ONE MAN *(Adam)* **1:**345, 379–80; **10:**247, 523–27 (*see also* ADAM *in PERSONS IN THE BIBLE*); WITH A PROSTITUTE **10:**863

ONENESS OF GOD
2:280, 343; **6:**377, 387; **6:**401–2; **8:**678; **10:**895–98; **11:**419–20, 798–99; **12:**198

ONIONS
1:218

ONLY BEGOTTEN
See under JESUS THE CHRIST, NAMES FOR/TITLES OF *in PERSONS IN THE BIBLE*

ONOMASTICA
5:833

ONUS
1:511; **2:**637; **3:**304, 656; **5:**345; **6:**1452; **9:**70, 376, 620

ONYCHA
5:757

ONYX
2:220; **5:**592; **6:**965, 1392; **12:**723

ORACLE, ORACLES
AGAINST ISRAEL **7:**349, 355, 357, 363–64; AGAINST JERUSALEM/JUDAH **4:**36; **6:**18, 1102, 1141; **7:**353, 536, 669, 673, 683, 693, 696; AGAINST THE NATIONS **1:**401, 476; **2:**178, 186, 190–92, 256; **6:**12, 18, 20, 43, 66, 147, 149–50, 156–57, 159–60, 162, 168, 173–75, 180, 186–89, 194, 201, 216, 218, 235, 273–74, 342, 376, 389, 410, 454, 567–68, 572, 580–81, 612, 731, 761, 766, 839, 878–921, 1085, 1088–89, 1104, 1304, 1347–1446, 1452, 1474–75, 1480, 1515, 1598, 1609; **7:**303, 336, 344, 347, 353–54, 357, 363, 395, 424, 435, 437, 439–40, 447, 472, 660–66, 669, 683, 686, 688–93, 696, 699, 737, 756–57, 761, 803, 805; **8:**272; OF BALAAM **1:**242, 665; **2:**8, 178–79, 184–95, 256, 910, 1370; **4:**30; **5:**251; **6:**9–10, 1159; **7:**660; **10:**453; **12:**579; AT DELPHI **6:**108; **8:**24; **10:**232, 453; DIVINE **1:**126–28; DYNASTIC **2:**953, 967, 1165, 1168, 1234, 1236, 1240, 1246, 1255, 1261–62; **3:**407–8, 461, 498; **6:**122–23; FORMULA **6:**173, 180, 195; **7:**708, 737, 790, 803, 833; JUDGMENT **2:**167, 986, 993, 1085, 1087, 1090, 1284, 1292–93; **3:**370, 511, 521–22, 564, 569, 630, 646, 649; **6:**16–17, 20, 376, 491, 548, 676, 685–86, 831, 838, 864, 1085, 1125, 1158, 1169, 1208, 1217, 1257, 1259, 1306–7, 1333, 1356, 1386, 1391, 1427, 1455, 1460, 1463, 1474, 1477, 1495, 1521, 1578; **7:**345, 375, 406, 421, 423, 435, 437, 482, 536, 548, 563, 595, 662–64, 694, 870; **8:**595, 640, 661, 685, 714; **9:**72, 372; OF NATHAN **2:**967, 1165, 1168, 1234, 1236, 1240, 1254–56, 1258, 1261–62, 1284, 1292–93, 1297, 1331; **3:**19, 26, 32, 35, 58, 95, 406, 408, 430; **4:**689; **9:**85; PROPHETIC **1:**127, 237, 453; **2:**184, 870–71, 1370; **3:**164, 649, 656; **6:**11, 14–16, 108, 149–50, 201, 561, 585–87, 677, 684, 698, 739, 744, 753, 785, 792, 830, 899, 1160, 1205, 1221, 1251–52, 1267, 1304–6, 1312, 1314, 1317, 1334, 1358, 1410, 1509, 1515, 1517, 1531; **7:**3–5, 235, 242, 244, 275; **8:**24, 684; **12:**101; RESTORATION **6:**1085, 1101, 1191, 1364, 1492; SALVATION (*see under* SALVATION); SIBYLINE **1:**290; **7:**3–4; **8:**24; WOE **1:**283; **2:**192; **6:**16, 18, 30, 92, 174, 230–31, 1199, 1333, 1414, 1461, 1463; **7:**385, 392, 398, 399, 468, 595–96, 612–13, 688, 690; **8:**271–72, 436; **12:**491

ORAL TRADITION
1:47, 67, 77, 132, 157, 231, 241, 297, 310–12; **3:**1087, 1091, 1171; **4:**328, 333; **5:**22; **6:**34, 46, 243, 280; **7:**81; **8:**27, 75, 92, 94, 169, 187, 220, 277, 332, 333–34, 392, 422, 510, 547, 595, 663; **9:**8, 40, 127, 388, 501–3, 509, 574, 593, 595–96, 684, 711, 726; **10:**745; **11:**354, 568; **12:**352, 519. *See also* CRITICISM: FORM

ORATORY
1:140; **2:**1332; **6:**1087, 1305; **8:**16; **10:**188, 305, 315, 317, 379, 818; **11:**134, 150, 189, 191, 310, 458, 493; **12:**15, 45, 353

ORCHARD, ORCHARDS
1:82, 223, 871; **2:**668, 670; **4:**510; **5:**421; **6:**1582, 1590; **7:**225, 585

ORDINANCE, ORDINANCES
1:38–39, 209, 862, 1026, 1110, 1117, 1156, 1163–64, 1183; **2:**12, 218, 272, 315, 323, 373, 378, 384, 714, 1194, 1367; **3:**26, 718, 723, 752, 802, 953; **4:**45, 50, 96, 164, 188, 605, 748, 752, 1166, 1168, 1171–73, 1269; **5:**72, 564, 798; **6:**549, 646–47, 955, 1086, 1152, 1186, 1188, 1258–61, 1264–65, 1278, 1280–84, 1326, 1487, 1491–92, 1502, 1510, 1562, 1568, 1573, 1589; **7:**122, 853, 860, 875–76; **8:**30–31; **10:**448, 450; **11:**77, 242, 277, 344, 356, 362, 364, 398–400, 403, 701; **12:**103, 457, 734

ORDINATION
1:181, 307, 316, 689, 907, 909–15, 1043, 1056, 1062–63, 1065, 1073, 1099; **2:**47, 54, 64, 141, 163, 220–21, 237; **3:**143–44; **6:**1101, 1111, 1124–26, 1569; **7:**227–28; **9:**581; **10:**240; **11:**278, 814, 823, 829; **12:**60, 71

ORE
1:215; **4:**529; **5:**688; **6:**1312; **9:**481
ORGAN, ORGANS
1:581, 718, 962, 1026, 1094, 1104–5, 1119; **2:**460, 1237; **3:**985; **4:**335, 391, 450, 459, 694, 701, 887, 927; **5:**60, 61, 64, 66–67, 76, 111, 113, 131, 142, 152, 173–74, 179, 186, 193, 219, 317, 328, 354, 415, 570; **6:**113, 1188, 1325; **7:**243, 505, 717; **10:**668; **11:**159, 317. *See also by name (e.g., heart)*
ORGIES
6:472, 1065, 1330; **7:**202; **10:**750; **11:**442
ORIGINAL SIN
1:196, 367, 737, 934; **4:**885; **8:**137, 213; **10:**531–32, 618; **11:**391, 393. *See also* SIN
ORIGINAL TEXT
1:17, 28, 54, 86, 101–2, 131, 146, 293, 1075; **2:**378; **3:**67, 424, 510, 810, 939, 1181; **4:**20, 562; **5:**687; **6:**660, 955, 1092–93, 1128, 1182, 1272, 1546, 1565, 1581; **7:**375, 442, 599; **8:**1–2, 5, 9, 91, 130, 369, 414; **10:**366, 646; **11:**106, 500, 634, 642; **12:**413
ORION, CONSTELLATION OF
4:605
ORNAMENT, ORNAMENTS
1:900, 906–7, 937–38, 941, 1110; **2:**163, 1207; **3:**483–84, 487, 1134, 1159; **5:**54, 80, 119, 400, 426, 600, 689, 745, 765; **6:**431, 456, 925, 1107, 1167–68, 1227, 1329, 1549, 1553–55; **7:**333, 725; **11:**801
ORPHAN (*OR* ORPHANS, ORPHANED, *ETC.*)
1:422, 829, 868, 1135; **2:**149, 369, 412, 470, 474, 481, 835, 915; **3:**128, 820, 857, 884, 886–87, 905, 909, 993, 1133; **4:**82, 207, 249–50, 389, 478, 500, 503, 510, 513, 538–39, 553, 719, 947, 1006, 1265; **5:**71, 144, 155, 205–6, 246, 462–63, 664, 798; **6:**20, 56, 60, 63, 82, 127–28, 630, 647, 745–46, 754, 1001, 1069, 1309, 1467, 1601; **7:**161, 263, 268, 295, 357, 406, 793, 846, 861, 868, 874; **8:**682; **9:**159, 336, 339, 397, 514, 738–39, 748, 751, 753, 776, 798, 884; **10:**111, 399; **11:**707, 820, 825; **12:**181, 195, 197, 201, 694, 725
ORTHODOXY
1:1, 14–15, 20–21, 35, 44, 48, 51–52, 55, 61, 103–4, 113, 194–95, 197, 201, 212, 288, 310, 681, 722, 951; **2:**352, 429, 1182; **3:**514, 526, 530, 581; **4:**492, 494; **5:**302, 798; **6:**58, 1218; **8:**425; **9:**125–26, 265, 581, 658, 679; **10:**122, 309, 321, 335, 337, 698; **11:**318, 620, 776; **12:**201, 405, 464
ORTHOPRAXIS
1:288; **5:**798; **6:**58; **11:**620
OSSUARY, OSSUARIES
4:462; **8:**606
OSTRACAN, OSTRACA
1:224, 249; **2:**683; **3:**52; **12:**249
OSTRICH, OSTRICHES
4:547, 598, 607, 610–12, 624; **6:**378; **7:**546
OUTCAST, OUTCASTS
1:454, 490, 695–96; **2:**825, 827, 1049, 1051, 1095, 1144–45, 1188, 1315–17; **3:**197, 209, 753, 1071; **4:**367, 472, 545, 547, 557, 604, 610, 632, 766, 1267; **5:**474; **6:**145, 168, 376, 431, 485–86; **7:**254, 703; **8:**60, 81, 235, 237, 316, 552; **9:**4, 9, 14, 21–23, 26, 30, 34, 56, 65, 98, 108, 126–29, 131–33, 139, 143, 166, 197, 288, 290, 294–96, 306, 327, 332, 345, 355–56, 359, 371, 374, 406, 421, 458, 466, 472, 647–48; **10:**35, 78, 134–46, 378, 390, 815–16; **12:**588, 626
OVEN, OVENS
1:224, 745, 1017, 1019, 1049, 1082, 1181; **3:**768, 839; **5:**395, 547; **7:**256–57; **9:**236; **11:**452
OVERLAY
FIGURATIVE **1:**260; **4:**591; **5:**150; **6:**1182; **9:**405; MATERIAL **1:**900; **6:**988
OVERSEER, OVERSEERS
1:306, 612, 621, 703; **2:**482; **3:**50, 479, 730, 825–26, 839, 921; **4:**10; **6:**509; **7:**279; **9:**171; **10:**52, 283, 285; **11:**480–81, 778, 804–7, 809, 813, 822, 863–64, 867, 869, 884, 886; **12:**283, 315, 454
OWL, OWLS
1:365; **2:**967; **4:**547, 610–11; **6:**277; **7:**546
OX, OXEN
1:217, 238, 492, 864–65, 869, 871–74, 924, 1034, 1080–81, 1118, 1134; **2:**77–78, 181, 188, 247, 452–53, 471, 878, 1054–55, 1061, 1249, 1381; **3:**144, 424, 712, 782, 820; **4:**218, 224, 256, 351, 387, 471, 510–11, 598, 608, 610, 618, 763; **5:**85, 139, 150, 282, 688–89, 765, 768, 791; **6:**9, 53, 93, 141, 266, 337, 601, 640, 782, 1131, 1184; **7:**403, 567; **9:**63, 273, 284, 289, 358; **10:**198, 904; **11:**103, 822; **12:**592, 598; WILD **2:**188; **4:**387, 598, 608, 610, 763
OXGOAD
2:772, 782, 841, 853

P

PAGAN, PAGANS
1:12, 49, 86, 88, 197, 242, 290, 1018, 1021, 1024, 1026–27, 1095, 1110, 1118–19, 1121, 1124, 1127, 1131–32, 1134–35, 1138, 1143, 1147, 1160, 1166, 1181; **2:**791–92, 809, 834, 860, 1028; **3:**525, 536, 539, 564, 569, 581, 607–8, 617, 619, 630, 635, 644, 733, 859, 869,

PAGAN, PAGANS *(continued)*
883, 959, 1041, 1124, 1155; **4:**11–12, 25, 37, 48, 185, 230, 232–33, 257; **5:**44, 417, 544–45, 597; **6:**1076, 1213, 1302, 1570, 1579; **7:**26, 40, 54, 67, 113, 116, 128, 189, 331, 376, 419, 528, 543–44, 575, 588, 662, 674, 678, 860, 864, 872; **8:**12–14, 20–22, 94, 97, 140, 142–43, 169, 176, 194–95, 197, 201, 210, 212, 214, 216, 257, 343, 360, 386–87, 420, 583, 651, 663, 673, 690, 712; **9:**52, 188, 252, 292, 313, 538; **10:**8–9, 80, 85, 96, 126, 146, 188, 197–99, 204, 214, 219–20, 222, 230, 232–34, 237, 240, 243, 247, 249, 252–53, 260, 269–73, 276, 285, 293–95, 298–99, 308, 314, 321, 329–30, 333, 336, 343, 349–50, 352–53, 363, 374–75, 377, 389, 398, 400–401, 405, 413–15, 418, 422, 424, 426, 428–29, 431, 433, 435, 437–39, 441–42, 443, 445, 447–48, 450–51, 453–54, 456, 460–61, 469, 475, 480, 492, 498, 503, 505, 519–20, 530, 553–54, 590, 597, 611, 622, 624, 626, 631, 637, 639, 648–50, 661, 665, 699, 710–11, 714, 718–20, 723, 726, 733, 736, 741, 750–51, 756, 918, 921, 941; **11:**183–84, 207, 213–14, 228, 253, 269, 271, 280, 282–83, 287, 289, 291, 353, 358, 361, 363–65, 403, 428–31, 435, 438, 442, 452, 460, 475, 496, 513, 524, 541, 548, 561, 563–64, 566, 608; **12:**71, 236–37, 239, 241, 246, 258, 265–66, 271–73, 275–78, 280, 287, 294, 301, 303, 305–6, 310–11, 325, 345, 347, 352, 369, 463, 522, 543, 553, 581, 712, 729

PAINT
3:1080; **4:**63; **5:**550, 557; **6:**661, 1325; **10:**310; **11:**405

PAINTINGS, THE BIBLE IN
1:499; **2:**1103–4, 1276; **3:**46, 347, 1051–52, 1092, 1147–48, 1162–63; **5:**291; **6:**143, 1023; **8:**367; **10:**471, 957; **12:**551, 699

PALACE, PALACES
1:222–23, 225, 233, 237, 248, 265, 284, 620, 622, 627, 745, 759, 978; **2:**426, 736, 771, 816, 1237, 1242, 1244, 1251, 1254, 1284–85, 1287, 1289, 1293, 1331, 1376; **3:**18, 21, 37, 40, 49, 50, 55, 58, 62, 67–68, 72, 80, 83–84, 86, 93, 118, 123, 132, 137, 139, 155, 221, 230, 242, 264–65, 275, 277, 290, 405–7, 452, 460–61, 477, 479, 486, 510, 524, 526, 569, 574, 576, 580, 581, 587, 630, 655–56, 699, 769, 858, 867, 878, 879–80, 882, 885, 888–89, 892, 894, 902, 903–904, 908, 911, 918, 932, 948, 1003, 1098, 1151, 1159; **4:**93, 156, 1199, 1232; **5:**4, 6, 95, 101–2, 138, 255, 363, 383, 425; **6:**10, 123–24, 197, 216, 221, 265, 294, 304–5, 443, 584, 655, 740, 742–43, 746, 839, 841, 925, 1015, 1038, 1077, 1079, 1114, 1131, 1233, 1245, 1295, 1330, 1360, 1366, 1373, 1387, 1418, 1533, 1550, 1555, 1561, 1574; **7:**39, 42, 72, 141, 179, 333, 561, 594, 610, 612, 662, 675, 678, 834; **8:**150, 267, 270, 319, 427, 466, 717; **9:**163, 405; **11:**488; **12:**140, 145, 261, 269; COUP/INTRIGUE **1:**233, 265; **2:**1376; **3:**21, 574, 581, 882, 889, 892, 904; **5:**363; **6:**1077; **7:**256, 662, 675, 678; OF SOLOMON **2:**736; **3:**37, 40, 55, 58, 62, 67–68, 80, 83–84, 86, 407, 461, 477, 479, 510; **4:**1199; **5:**95, 383; **6:**584, 742, 1245, 1550, 1555, 1561; TREASURE (*see under* TREASURE)

PALLET
8:549; **9:**124–25, 579

PALM
OF DEBORAH **2:**779, 796; TREE **1:**1159; **2:**190; **3:**802; **5:**426, 757; **6:**1543, 1554–55; **7:**273; **9:**171, 271

PALM SUNDAY
5:346; **8:**402, 658; **9:**707–9; **10:**357

PALMER WORM
See LOCUST

PAN
GREEK GOD **1:**1118; **8:**343

PAN, PANS
1:1001, 1017–20, 1049; **2:**137; **3:**679; **4:**240. *See also* POT

PANTHEISM
4:1272; **5:**834; **10:**247, 435, 615

PANTHEON, PANTHEONS
1:273, 328; **2:**315–16, 374, 527, 755, 1005; **3:**276; **4:**792; **5:**759; **6:**600, 638, 1170, 1213, 1387; **7:**500; **8:**21; **10:**232, 245, 271; TEMPLE **10:**894

PAPACY
8:345; **12:**538, 540–41, 543. *See also* POPE

PAPER
8:4–5; **12:**455

PAPYRUS, PAPYRI
1:234, 250, 267, 270, 294, 300, 302; **3:**710, 741, 751, 757, 833–34, 977, 1022; **4:**121, 202; **5:**4, 207, 334, 604, 625, 636, 643, 682, 708, 731, 808, 827; **6:**181, 941, 1144, 1398, 1416; **7:**24, 112, 124, 866; **8:**4–5, 8–11, 417, 564, 742; **9:**74, 151, 234, 316, 504, 574, 874; **10:**370, 380, 800, 875, 877; **11:**563, 583, 913; **12:**6, 9, 260, 448, 455, 638, 747

PARABLE, PARABLES
1:69, 75–76, 96, 115, 163, 277, 773, 1026, 1041–42, 1196; **2:**129, 186, 221, 357, 539, 872, 891, 893–94, 897, 902, 911, 920, 923, 946, 973, 1064, 1170, 1195, 1292–24, 1313–14, 1316–17; **3:**14, 88, 152, 273, 307, 370, 540, 562, 570, 576, 600–601, 636–37, 654, 658, 1102–3, 1110; **4:**360, 636, 878, 990, 999; **5:**20, 32, 55–56, 64, 93, 112, 118, 180, 222, 255, 261, 270, 303, 345,

401, 492, 544, 565; **6:**43, 53, 88–89, 226, 229, 232, 235, 237–38, 244, 389, 647–48, 684, 715, 721, 866, 1104, 1142, 1193, 1197, 1242, 1244–45, 1247–48, 1252, 1274, 1295, 1332–38, 1341, 1452, 1592, 1596; **7:**83, 93, 286, 467–69, 474, 800, 834; **8:**30, 36, 50–51, 56, 60–62, 69–70, 74, 77, 80–81, 89, 92, 109, 112–13, 122–23, 179, 181, 218, 268, 290, 294, 298–301, 303–6, 308–17, 348, 369, 372, 374–76, 380–84, 389–94, 396, 400–401, 407–9, 411, 413–14, 416–18, 428, 444–45, 447–49, 451, 453, 455, 497, 510, 518, 521–23, 538, 564, 567–80, 593, 607, 616–17, 627, 640, 668–72, 676, 683, 693–94; **9:**11–12, 14, 16–18, 22–24, 26–28, 34–36, 45, 56, 84, 91, 98, 116, 131, 141, 149–53, 158, 165, 169–70, 173–83, 214, 219, 227, 229–31, 233, 235–39, 242, 250, 255–58, 262–65, 270–72, 275–76, 278–79, 283, 285–86, 288–90, 292–98, 300–21, 323–27, 332, 335–43, 345, 347, 349, 353–54, 357–58, 360–64, 366–67, 369–70, 378–86, 389, 395–97, 408–10, 414, 425, 440, 458, 462, 473, 482, 493, 557–58, 565, 570–71, 584, 638, 666–68, 684, 704–705, 711, 740, 752, 757, 779–82, 861, 869; **10:**85, 89, 376, 642, 655, 827, 829, 904, 919; **11:**87, 125, 281–83, 439, 527, 595, 646, 838, 846; **12:**105, 138, 169, 194, 357, 523, 705, 708. *See also under* JESUS THE CHRIST *in PERSONS IN THE BIBLE*

PARABOLIC
2:896, 902; **3:**1109; **6:**714, 1145; **8:**81, 190, 294, 299, 304, 312, 314, 317, 372, 382, 391–93, 413, 419, 440, 572; **9:**17, 86, 262, 268, 277, 279, 570, 584, 727

PARACLETE
8:259; **9:**428, 497, 499, 548, 580, 617, 635, 709, 738–39, 747–51, 753, 759, 762–65, 770–78, 781–82, 796, 841, 847–48, 851, 853, 863, 869, 871; **11:**490; **12:**367, 423, 435, 449, 562, 705

PARADISE
See also PARADISE *in PLACES IN THE BIBLE*

PARADOX
1:115, 120, 122, 124, 171; **2:**107, 151, 167, 255, 349, 389; **3:**226–27, 236, 258, 331, 469, 502, 552, 681, 737, 753, 812–13, 1005, 1103; **4:**240, 299, 371, 396, 400, 415, 435, 465, 477, 485, 513, 523, 525, 534, 604, 674, 695, 803, 815, 840, 845, 858, 874, 974, 1001, 1105, 1188, 1207; **5:**11, 13, 30, 41, 50, 64, 81, 104, 114, 119, 124–25, 132–33, 135, 141, 145, 150, 153–54, 159, 172, 187–88, 195, 228–30, 232, 237, 240, 255, 437, 476–77, 492, 505–6, 575, 597–99, 739; **6:**377, 395, 430, 451, 459, 530, 532, 587, 589, 621, 795, 796, 808, 850, 958, 970, 978, 1042, 1119, 1239, 1302, 1305, 1496–97; **7:**76, 227, 291, 293, 373, 504, 647; **8:**229, 349, 355, 474, 546, 550, 616, 632, 696, 705–6, 713, 732; **9:**60, 108, 125, 128, 202, 267, 277, 343, 350, 382, 384, 403–4, 422, 436–37, 443, 522, 568, 638, 676, 698, 717, 726, 803–4; **10:**398, 402, 428, 441, 448, 468, 482–83, 516–17, 545–46, 555, 557, 563, 565, 567, 570–71, 577, 583, 586, 602–3, 616, 621, 631–32, 649, 657, 666, 705, 738, 826, 833; **11:**3, 80, 166–67, 176, 260, 267, 287, 293, 298, 310, 318, 321–22, 334, 340, 344, 348, 480, 487–88, 492, 509, 544, 547, 597, 609, 616, 628, 775; **12:**187, 216, 257, 286, 414, 416, 446, 505, 531, 546, 687

PARALIPSIS
11:719, 726

PARALLELISM
1:24, 29, 78, 89, 231–32, 343, 375, 869; **2:**186, 188–89, 909–10, 1121; **3:**318, 336, 401, 484, 500, 632, 889, 918, 928, 1144, 1177; **4:**34, 36, 43, 303–11, 313–15, 348, 352, 368, 402, 411, 414, 427, 477, 530, 569, 590, 652–53, 684, 690, 718; **5:**8, 16, 40, 46, 53, 64, 75, 84, 101, 103, 113, 135, 150, 161, 167, 186, 207, 219, 254, 300, 346, 437, 563, 590, 593–94, 673–74, 720, 823, 866; **6:**140, 190, 364, 808, 961, 1166, 1198, 1216, 1242–43, 1251, 1273, 1386, 1517; **7:**224, 238, 248, 258, 283, 449, 451, 522, 525, 535, 614; **8:**31, 61, 80, 156, 180, 195, 275, 365, 403, 471, 536, 624; **9:**71, 133, 163, 238, 264, 303, 421, 518–20, 641, 667, 676, 711, 758, 763, 831, 861; **10:**99, 142, 179, 198, 263, 270, 275, 282, 288, 312, 359, 504, 1009; **11:**97, 261, 265, 270, 291, 382, 434, 501, 509, 603; **12:**149, 333, 372, 445, 609; ANTITHETIC **2:**909; **4:**304, 307, 652; **5:**8, 300, 346; **9:**520, 667, 711, 758, 763, 861; INVERTED **10:**142; **12:**149; STAIR-STEP **4:**653; **9:**71, 163; SYNONYMOUS **2:**186, 188; **4:**304, 307, 652, 684; **5:**8, 673; **6:**190, 1166, 1198, 1216; **7:**535; **8:**194; **9:**71, 831; **11:**261, 270; SYNTHETIC **4:**304, 307, 652; **5:**8. *See also* CHIASM

PARALYSIS
1:737; **2:**1232, 1298, 1316; **5:**585; **6:**1086, 1167; **8:**223, 227, 234; **9:**124, 126, 355; **11:**455; **12:**388

PARALYTIC
1:1196; **8:**234, 521, 548–49, 551, 558, 588; **9:**29, 114, 122–24, 127, 172, 209, 322, 326, 360, 579; **10:**160–61

PARAPET
2:453; **4:**101; **6:**1541

PARCHMENT, PARCHMENTS
1:302; **2:**63; **3:**1022; **8:**4–5; **9:**863; **11:**857

PARENT, PARENTS
1:24, 85, 161, 164, 202, 216, 239–40, 306, 354,

PARENT, PARENTS *(continued)*
404, 454, 459, 464, 486, 517, 520–22, 534, 537, 599, 763, 778, 847, 849–50, 1009, 1131–32, 1135, 1141, 1173, 1181, 1190; **2:**33, 50, 125–26, 332–33, 416, 741, 1144; **3:**531–32, 670, 975–76, 986, 1014–15, 1070–71; **4:**368, 463–64; **5:**12, 19, 47–48, 79–80, 84, 107, 182, 187, 253–54, 658–60, 695, 777; **6:**605, 675, 957, 1257–58; **7:**177, 180, 198, 277–78, 583; **8:**32, 137–38, 148, 332–33, 337, 589–90; **9:**47, 70, 76–78, 147, 238, 653, 656–57; **10:**606; **11:**434, 446, 452–53, 652–54, 849; **12:**151–52, 180, 434, 649

PARK, PARKS
2:1306; **4:**548; **5:**297; **11:**386, 425

PAROUSIA OF CHRIST
See JESUS THE CHRIST: APOCALYPSE/PAROUSIA/SECOND COMING OF *in PERSONS IN THE BIBLE*

PARSIN
See MENE, MENE, TEKEL, AND PARSIN

PARTITION, PARTITIONS
1:898; **12:**82. *See also* CURTAIN

PASCHAL LAMB
See under JESUS THE CHRIST, NAMES FOR/TITLES OF *in PERSONS IN THE BIBLE*

PASS
THROUGH FIRE **1:**1138; **2:**247, 428; **6:**381, 1230, 1283–84, 1286; TOPOGRAPHICAL **2:**1070; **3:**286, 1075, 1104; **6:**1403; **7:**141

PASSION OF CHRIST, THE
2:90, 97–98, 235–36; **4:**673, 762–63, 765, 802, 830, 951, 960, 1038, 1128, 1156; **6:**223; **7:**743, 811, 824; **8:**50, 52, 66, 69, 79, 81–82, 122–23, 137, 140, 142, 254, 258–59, 281, 296, 331, 333, 341, 348–49, 352, 363, 366, 369–71, 383–84, 396, 404, 414, 459–60, 463–66, 470, 474, 477, 481–82, 491–92, 495–97, 512, 518, 520, 523, 525, 528, 540, 550, 556, 568, 572, 603, 618, 621, 623–25, 628, 630–31, 634–37, 652–56, 658, 660, 665, 669, 671, 685, 695–96, 700, 703–708, 710, 714, 722, 724, 728, 730–31, 735; **9:**8, 10, 12, 18–19, 22, 28, 32, 36, 40, 98, 198–201, 206–7, 210, 331, 335, 350–53, 366–67, 376, 391, 413–16, 419, 422, 437–38, 440, 447, 453, 456, 460, 462, 468–69, 476–78, 486, 498, 502, 532, 537, 543–44, 552, 613, 635, 675, 685, 701, 707, 709, 713–14, 753, 787, 799, 811, 816, 840; **10:**41, 45, 50, 72, 81, 282, 312, 340, 387, 973; **11:**247, 250, 294, 516, 829, 847; **12:**62, 270, 280–82, 285, 292, 296–97, 313, 319, 441, 516, 533, 607, 711, 727. *See also* JESUS THE CHRIST: CRUCIFIXION, RESURRECTION, AND ASCENSION OF *in PERSONS IN THE BIBLE*

PASSOVER AND FEAST OF UNLEAVENED BREAD
1:67, 74, 91, 209, 275, 311, 316, 318, 683–85, 688, 691, 693, 696–98, 712, 722, 773–74, 777, 782–87, 803, 836, 1012, 1018, 1021, 1072, 1098, 1113, 1156–59, 1161, 1196; **2:**4, 23, 32, 34, 51, 54, 69, 77, 84, 86–87, 90, 94, 127–28, 217, 229–30, 232, 236, 252, 411–14, 573–74, 578, 581, 586, 588–90, 592–94, 599, 601–5, 607, 609, 612, 619, 893; **3:**285, 305, 311, 389, 608, 613, 615–18, 622, 646–48, 651, 668, 670, 672, 691, 710, 713–14, 718, 730, 747, 802, 896, 899, 905, 948, 993, 1001, 1092, 1143; **4:**276, 795, 1138, 1141, 1148–49, 1153, 1155–56; **5:**366, 377, 591, 643, 655; **6:**222, 455, 1076–77, 1496–97, 1586, 1592; **7:**93, 136, 150, 190, 674; **8:**29, 33, 81, 124, 401, 403, 436, 463, 468–72, 472, 474, 492, 494, 523, 617, 658–60, 697–98, 701–3; **9:**12, 36, 76, 93, 102, 139, 169, 263, 276, 369, 413–16, 418–21, 436, 446, 448, 451, 460, 476, 493, 507, 528, 542–43, 578, 594, 616, 698, 700–701, 704–5, 707, 710, 719, 721, 802, 814–15, 818, 823, 833–34, 837; **10:**53–54, 179, 181–82, 276–78, 457, 471, 534, 537, 585, 610, 776, 831, 847–52; **11:**288, 377; **12:**140, 142, 493, 563, 602, 726

PASTOR, PASTORS
1:1, 3, 56, 173, 190, 198, 309; AS SHEPHERD **6:**1464; **9:**394; **11:**812–13. *See also* MINISTER

PASTORAL LETTERS, THE
8:22, 48–49, 54; **9:**336, 338, 359; **10:**24, 115, 225, 285, 370, 789, 969–71; **11:**218, 330, 353, 480, 577, 580, 659, 664, 667, 775–77, 785–86, 797, 832, 835, 862, 877; **12:**234, 271, 278, 285, 454, 573

PASTURE (*OR* PASTURES, PASTURING, *ETC.*)
1:215–19, 255, 433, 653, 801; **2:**561, 582, 698; **3:**346; **4:**510, 767; **5:**385, 394; **6:**183, 625, 828, 1351, 1466, 1582; **7:**314, 352, 588

PATH, PATHS
1:65, 93, 167, 169, 211, 221, 377, 794, 980; **2:**18, 183, 194, 298, 346, 351, 369, 437, 442, 484, 488–89, 491, 510, 761, 987, 1028, 1039, 1045, 1082, 1093, 1128–29, 1182, 1218, 1284, 1310, 1383; **3:**5, 101, 197, 214, 275, 303, 313, 382, 395, 503, 532–33, 551, 570, 632, 681, 898, 949, 1095, 1108, 1118; **4:**44, 314, 370, 475, 501, 530, 532, 597, 684, 830; **5:**19, 37, 44–45, 53, 59–62, 64, 67, 70, 80, 89–90, 92, 104, 111, 133, 135, 140–41, 149, 151, 154, 160–61, 211, 238, 274, 390, 395, 454, 504, 560, 600, 608, 616, 639, 655, 669–70, 688, 741, 768; **6:**68, 77, 101, 129, 282, 312, 433, 450, 456, 478, 601, 628, 645, 649, 653, 722, 729, 766, 850, 853, 961–62,

965, 967, 1049, 1096, 1118, 1132, 1135, 1295, 1324, 1327, 1408, 1451–52, 1496; **7:**129, 142, 279, 547, 602, 679, 693, 695, 771, 861; **8:**31, 32, 85, 162, 164, 169, 216, 351, 375, 537, 570; **9:**101, 152, 176–78, 207, 291, 367, 378, 383, 596; **10:**78, 143, 275, 320, 441, 461, 575, 577, 585, 594, 617, 625, 631, 644, 686, 693, 702, 706, 812, 833, 847, 897, 938, 969; **11:**308, 314, 348, 378, 400, 437, 443, 455, 462, 709, 844, 846; **12:**16, 26, 39, 43, 123, 152–53, 223, 282, 317, 390, 498, 504, 597, 612, 701

PATIENCE, PATIENT
1:396, 469, 612, 716, 767, 951; **2:**415, 596, 727, 796, 824, 888, 912, 1176; **3:**258, 592, 811, 612, 670, 916, 941, 998, 1001; **4:**319, 585, 701, 837, 845; **5:**6, 219, 242, 326, 378, 398, 574, 616, 619, 654, 678; **6:**521, 912, 980, 1140; **7:**125, 144, 408, 552, 561, 633; **8:**29, 311, 417, 545, 590, 660, 670, 671, 687; **9:**178–79, 338–39, 402; **10:**410, 439, 475, 515–17, 521, 595, 597–98, 616, 641–42, 686, 731, 744–46, 953, 968; **11:**51, 88, 97, 168, 253, 273, 419–20, 593, 647, 701, 705, 731, 733, 794, 828, 850, 855, 869; **12:**6, 64, 77–80, 147–48, 173, 221, 295, 356–59, 524, 563, 565, 567, 646, 657, 687

PATRIARCH, PATRIARCHS
1:253–55, 259, 273, 336, 381, 432, 527, 907–8, 1181; **2:**148, 292, 343, 352, 364, 466, 544, 570, 628, 630, 910; **3:**300, 304, 328, 381, 400–402, 408, 456, 468, 470, 735, 1080, 1138; **4:**188, 377, 402, 635, 1105, 1203; **5:**45, 113, 516, 541, 591, 605, 623, 698, 790, 862; **6:**93, 930, 957, 1238; **7:**3, 144, 162, 287, 365, 369; **8:**226, 294, 676; **9:**22, 278, 389, 619, 737, 787; **10:**126, 138, 398, 402, 637, 639, 680, 684, 746–47; **11:**28, 95, 243, 614; **12:**81, 136, 545, 725

PATRIARCHY
1:35, 62, 182, 363, 430, 538, 580; **2:**741; **4:**557; **5:**423; **6:**528, 1223; **9:**946; **10:**24; **11:**659; **12:**287, 550, 687

PAUL, LETTERS OF/PAULINE LETTERS
1:13, 15, 19, 85, 114, 129–30, 134, 156, 191–92; **2:**587, 641, 1250; **4:**143, 188, 728, 888; **8:**3, 39–40, 46, 48, 82, 95, 106; **10:**7, 11, 14, 27, 31–32, 63, 147, 153, 177, 215, 225, 238, 249, 252, 280–81, 284, 304, 318, 355, 370–91, 779, 789, 811, 854, 969–70; **11:**32–33, 41, 54, 70, 96, 109, 117, 140, 151, 202, 270, 282, 353–56, 369–72, 376, 380, 409–11, 444, 458, 522, 535, 553, 571–72, 577–79, 587–90, 599–601, 632, 668, 776–80, 789, 814, 841–42; **12:**231–32, 328, 704, 734

PAVEMENT
1:881; **6:**1542; **8:**720

PAVILLION
6:1374

PEACE
1:7, 109, 158, 170–71, 180, 204, 206, 208, 274, 393, 400, 425, 433, 435–36, 441, 447, 492, 529–30, 534, 556, 558, 568, 578, 579, 635–36, 639, 656, 818, 850, 878, 1010, 1021, 1023, 1036, 1179; **2:**65–66, 68–69, 195, 200, 256–57, 306–7, 311, 357, 386, 476, 494, 501, 506, 534, 566, 571, 617, 647, 697, 719, 731, 749, 759, 763–64, 766, 768, 781–83, 790, 796–97, 804, 810, 831, 838, 841, 870, 886, 976, 1017–19, 1030, 1049, 1057, 1062, 1066, 1114, 1136, 1160, 1166, 1169–71, 1176, 1188, 1209, 1217–18, 1224–25, 1236, 1238–40, 1256, 1280, 1286, 1298, 1319, 1352; **3:**49, 55, 58, 114, 146, 160–61, 167–68, 191, 196, 198, 201, 219, 221, 272, 274, 282, 355, 379, 382, 416–17, 426, 430, 432, 474, 486, 536, 538–39, 542, 547, 551–53, 576, 680–81, 693, 698–99, 701, 704, 714, 720, 723, 731, 813, 863–64, 883, 953, 966, 996, 1009, 1014, 1017, 1055, 1065, 1084–85, 1099, 1108, 1112, 1120, 1182; **4:**7, 21, 30–31, 52, 58, 68, 78, 91–92, 95–97, 104, 118–19, 137, 152, 156–57, 159, 165, 182, 186, 188–89, 205–6, 214, 222, 259–60, 264, 266, 268, 270, 275, 280–82, 285–87, 289, 308, 310–11, 381, 427, 445, 451, 492, 502, 516, 534, 594, 619, 632, 636–37, 641–42, 668, 670, 680–81, 694–98, 734, 749, 767, 787, 793–94, 813–14, 824, 828, 830, 833, 848, 853, 866–67, 870, 899, 903, 923–25, 927, 940, 961, 963, 965, 968–70, 980–81, 999–1000, 1011, 1016–18, 1021, 1052, 1063, 1105, 1140, 1174, 1177–79, 1182, 1184–86, 1188, 1192–94, 1201–1202, 1208, 1241, 1261, 1268, 1273, 1277; **5:**5, 30, 36, 53, 92, 107–8, 118, 127, 150, 153, 159, 164, 243, 300, 303, 305–7, 323, 337, 343, 357, 360, 440, 469–70, 474, 511, 558–60, 616, 682, 765, 828, 843, 849; **6:**39–40, 46, 65–70, 77, 79, 83, 85, 99–100, 122–24, 127, 134, 139–44, 147, 168–69, 181, 216, 221–22, 226, 229, 237, 249, 264, 266–67, 278, 293, 305, 325, 414, 421, 457, 477–78, 482, 486, 489–91, 493, 500, 509, 528, 547, 550–51, 613, 627, 643, 647, 691, 694, 698, 702, 704, 728, 750, 752–55, 776, 782, 784–85, 788, 792–93, 795, 807, 809, 811, 854, 884, 935, 962–63, 969, 972, 977, 980–82, 1049, 1105, 1168, 1199, 1202, 1208, 1210, 1266, 1305, 1315, 1370, 1400, 1461–62, 1470–73, 1510, 1607; **7:**7, 29, 55–56, 72, 74, 77, 96, 106–108, 125, 130, 140, 142, 161, 164, 218–19, 226, 312–13, 327, 336, 342, 358, 367, 370, 403, 425, 428–29, 533, 539, 554, 560, 563–65, 569, 571, 574, 606, 612, 664–65, 701–702, 724–25, 739, 753, 762, 766–67, 787, 799, 801–802,

PEACE *(continued)*
807–809, 811, 816, 822–23, 860–61; **8:**65, 176, 180–81, 258, 448, 537, 596, 628, 641, 659, 674; **9:**29, 47, 59–61, 63, 65, 67, 71–72, 86–87, 171–72, 187, 203, 213, 220, 222, 261, 266–67, 276, 291, 333, 352, 367, 369, 371–75, 379, 402, 406, 408, 431, 445, 484–85, 751, 771, 783–85, 846, 848; **10:**58, 107, 109, 154, 166, 181, 221, 237, 258, 298–99, 318, 322, 380, 410, 421, 426, 438, 440, 458, 463, 514–16, 521–22, 524, 554, 581–82, 589, 596, 604, 712, 714, 720, 723, 736, 741, 744, 749, 757, 763, 765, 768, 798, 831, 841, 877–78, 966, 968, 1003; **11:**27, 29, 38–39, 51, 75, 88, 98, 132, 138–39, 179–80, 202, 205, 208, 214, 242, 327, 330, 332, 344, 345–46, 348, 352, 365, 369–70, 396, 398–400, 405, 420, 424, 459, 461–62, 465–66, 481, 541, 547–48, 556, 570, 572, 575, 585, 588, 600, 603, 609–11, 627, 647–48, 650, 677, 688, 690, 692, 709, 726, 728, 730, 735, 751–53, 770–72, 790, 846, 862, 892; **12:**4, 12, 86, 143, 152–53, 169, 172, 178, 182, 200, 225, 247–48, 250, 282, 290, 318–19, 333–35, 353, 357, 359, 391, 450, 461, 466–67, 481–83, 530, 534, 554, 557, 579, 598, 612, 616, 636, 661, 670, 704, 710, 712; MAKER(S) **2:**1170; **4:**264, 981, 1179; **6:**67; **8:**180, 451; **9:**147; OFFERING (*see under* OFFERING); PROPHECY OF (*see under* PROPHECY)

PEACOCKS
3:82

PEARL, PEARLS
3:1080; **8:**143, 179, 212, 293, 301, 313–14; **10:**861; **11:**527, 801; **12:**123, 681, 694, 723

PEASANT, PEASANTS
REVOLT **1:**175, 226, 255, 725, 758, 840, 877–78, 897, 949

PEDDLER, PEDDLERS
1:217; **11:**849

PEDESTAL, PEDESTALS
2:364, 1001, 1248; **3:**104, 993; **5:**765; **6:**661; **11:**452; **12:**588

PEDIMENT
See LAVER; PILLAR

PEG, PEGS
1:896; **3:**736; **6:**1547. *See also under* TENT

PEN, PENS
"FALSE PEN OF THE SCRIBES" **6:**646, 650; FOR WRITING **6:**707; **9:**863; **12:**466

PENANCE
1:282; **2:**1017, 1325, 1345; **3:**424, 797, 806; **7:**482, 513–14, 523; **8:**555, 557; **9:**130, 305, 724, 847; **12:**444

PENITENCE
2:1018; **3:**159, 167, 715, 1079, 1086–87, 1113–14, 1141, 1145; **4:**704, 706, 780, 805, 1110, 1252; **5:**242; **6:**499, 517, 604, 631, 840; **7:**111, 122–23, 125, 312, 321; **9:**29, 458; **10:**727. *See also* REPENTANCE

PENITENT, PENITENTIAL
1:179, 207, 1001; **2:**1295, 1325; **3:**286, 497, 503, 645, 1086–87, 1142, 1144–45; **4:**568, 805, 834, 1088, 1110, 1206; **5:**238; **6:**501, 517, 840, 949; **7:**114, 160, 295, 500, 513, 528–29 665; **8:**35; **9:**28, 322, 450, 454–55, 457–58, 463, 472, 478; **10:**453

PENNY
9:269

PENTATEUCH
1:2, 9, 38–41, 44–45, 56–57, 65, 69–74, 77–82, 129, 170, 255, 282, 285, 305–19, 322, 330–22, 335, 347, 422, 444, 515, 593, 635, 677–78, 884, 985, 993, 997, 1002, 1008, 1080, 1109, 1143, 1178, 1196; **2:**5, 7, 10, 12, 32, 35, 48–49, 107, 109, 120, 123, 162, 178, 180, 192, 199, 215, 218, 221, 262, 271, 273–75, 278, 284, 288, 292, 325–26, 346, 365, 371, 425, 427, 518, 520–21, 527, 529, 538, 542–43, 557–58, 560, 951, 958; **3:**300, 344, 393, 396, 399, 616, 645, 647, 667, 678, 712, 716, 718, 721, 723, 725, 733, 736, 741, 757, 800, 802–3, 809, 819, 844, 936, 993–94, 1015–16, 1062; **4:**95, 671, 684–85, 704, 730, 754, 964, 1040–41, 1043, 1050, 1106, 1167–68, 1224; **5:**2, 244, 620; **6:**5, 8, 22, 33, 52, 84, 344, 608, 821, 968, 1146, 1207, 1279, 1309, 1589; **7:**90, 345, 394, 583; **8:**30, 32, 41, 112, 185, 422; **9:**568, 737; **10:**496, 660, 696; **11:**69, 512, 780, 791

PENTECOST
1:67, 207, 275, 414, 838, 1157–61; **2:**55, 232, 236, 412, 893, 1045; **3:**937, 1001, 1028, 1069; **4:**276, 674, 738, 1025, 1100; **5:**256; **6:**1497; **7:**301, 327, 674, 700; **8:**33, 158, 351; **9:**76, 86, 90–91, 202, 374, 434, 487, 542, 578, 616, 847–48; **10:**3, 14, 16, 18, 22–23, 25, 28, 35, 38, 40, 42, 44, 46, 52–54, 57–60, 62, 64–68, 72, 74, 76, 78–79, 81–83, 89–90, 97, 100, 105, 107, 112, 160, 167–70, 191, 203, 206, 208–9, 224, 275–78, 287–88, 291, 297, 305, 320, 335, 360, 625, 666, 776, 997, 1007; **11:**11, 291, 442, 877; **12:**4, 254, 262, 522, 614

PENTECOSTALISM
1:203; **7:**137; **10:**1011; **11:**248; **12:**407

PEOPLE
OF THE EAST **3:**792, 795; **4:**349, 369; **5:**272; **6:**1351–53; OF GOD **1:**38, 43, 67, 163, 170–71, 190, 324–25, 429, 435, 441, 447, 449, 454–55, 476, 484, 489, 500, 524, 581, 587, 592, 601, 606, 612, 623, 636, 654–55, 673–74, 752, 1021, 1100, 1118, 1136, 1138–39, 1143, 1161, 1179,

1183; **2:**11, 16, 26, 38–39, 49, 82, 86, 91, 97, 104, 111, 120, 168, 177, 221, 255–57, 273, 285, 602, 641–42, 752, 758, 760, 773, 783, 788, 790, 797, 838, 847, 855, 865, 892–93, 900, 911, 941, 946, 1028, 1045, 1315; **3:**115, 179, 243, 273, 305, 313, 319, 336–37, 347, 355–56, 358, 364, 366–67, 370, 376, 386, 401, 421, 432, 453, 457–58, 497, 510, 522, 525, 530–31, 576, 601, 603, 618, 645, 681, 688, 695, 794, 1008; **4:**163, 661, 665, 669, 702, 725, 736, 755, 766, 802–803, 805, 845, 854, 857, 871, 920, 929, 954, 972–74, 983, 985, 993, 996, 999, 1001, 1005, 1011, 1017, 1047, 1052, 1059, 1063, 1072–73, 1083, 1088, 1104, 1106, 1122, 1140–41, 1146, 1169, 1175, 1179, 1188, 1192–93, 1195–96, 1203, 1207, 1214–16, 1241, 1243, 1252, 1256, 1272, 1277; **5:**244, 561, 578, 730–31, 800; **6:**38–39, 52, 73–74, 78, 84, 113, 124, 138, 148, 157, 160, 164, 175, 191, 207, 212, 222, 228, 266, 273, 278, 283, 424, 454, 477, 485, 763, 813, 823, 864, 912, 982, 1369, 1395; **7:**95, 162, 168, 330, 348, 363, 366, 415, 550, 692, 756; **8:**27, 39, 55, 98–102, 135, 157, 175, 178–80, 182, 205, 211, 223, 252–53, 258, 277, 292, 323–25, 331–32, 335, 345, 376, 379, 405, 409, 416, 418, 431, 441–42, 447, 474, 496, 501, 503–4, 526, 671, 692; **9:**92, 136, 374, 419, 447, 532, 754, 757, 779; **10:**32, 51, 55, 71, 74, 99, 109, 125, 298, 390, 402, 405, 409, 413, 421, 429, 449, 461, 464, 468, 473, 480–82, 484, 487–88, 505–6, 517, 535, 550–51, 555–56, 581, 584, 586–87, 601, 604, 614, 616, 662, 684, 690, 723, 747, 778, 832, 850, 967, 983; **11:**73, 114–15, 186, 205, 224, 228, 233, 244–46, 267, 269, 272, 274, 304, 313, 345, 347, 351, 423, 461, 480, 512, 524–25, 529, 534, 537, 614, 647–48, 691, 714, 749, 769, 810; **12:**18, 47, 145–46, 163, 168, 170, 483, 490, 500, 528, 534, 543, 549, 566, 649, 651, 727; OF THE LAND **1:**286, 503, 526, 528, 581, 1138; **2:**109, 281, 688, 738; **3:**288, 574, 643, 655, 668, 695, 702, 713, 746, 927; **5:**859; **6:**586, 741, 944, 1079, 1150, 1196, 1270, 1314–15, 1415, 1589; **7:**424, 662, 723

PERDITION
2:1366; **5:**76, 692; **11:**610; **12:**524, 684, 713

PERFECTION
1:75, 170, 280–81, 346, 559, 655, 672, 1051, 1063; **2:**1232, 1315; **3:**429, 707; **4:**243, 345, 357–58, 709, 1014, 1082, 1168, 1171; **5:**102, 256, 307–8, 325, 327, 331, 479, 503; **6:**1041, 1391, 1394, 1405, 1511, 1563; **8:**189, 195–96, 222, 391; **9:**795; **10:**82, 554; **11:**159, 238, 252, 312, 370, 376, 417, 420, 422, 431, 438, 443, 452, 532, 537, 574, 599, 616, 648, 716, 763; **12:**39, 63, 69–71, 89, 94, 96, 115–16, 149, 158, 187, 198, 203–4, 258, 305, 381, 431, 509, 554, 620, 649, 659, 712–13, 716, 729

PERFUME, PERFUMES
1:920, 1103, 1105; **3:**511, 889, 1087, 1142, 1147; **5:**85, 365, 380, 461–62, 485, 757; **6:**1230, 1497; **8:**466; **9:**170, 691, 701, 836. *See also* FRAGRANCE

PERFUMER
2:1029; **3:**769–70

PERSECUTE (*OR* PERSECUTES, PERSECUTION, *ETC.*)
1:686; **2:**395, 617, 855; **3:**543, 840, 859, 861–62, 890, 941, 970, 977, 1076, 1125, 1145; **4:**8–12, 19, 24, 29, 36, 45, 82, 97, 181, 185, 190, 218, 229–30, 232–35, 240–41, 257, 268–70, 276, 286, 291, 445, 474, 479, 645, 687, 708, 749, 786, 801, 818, 919, 930, 953, 1067, 1070–71, 1087,1126, 1168, 1188, 1281; **5:**78, 291, 343, 449, 464; **6:**321, 442, 542, 550, 727, 1502; **7:**6–10, 20, 24–26, 143–44, 146, 149–50, 168, 267, 643, 729, 752, 776; **8:**15, 45, 51–52, 82, 99, 147, 180, 205, 258–61, 263, 328, 392, 436, 442–43, 474, 514–15, 551, 555, 565, 571, 573–75, 581, 627–28, 640–41, 651–52, 675, 687–88, 690–91, 693, 716, 720; **9:**12, 35–36, 145–47, 150, 178, 202, 235, 241, 250, 252–53, 331, 365, 375, 397–98, 400–403, 407–10, 429–30, 497, 505, 580, 648, 650, 657, 659, 704, 762–63, 765–66, 770, 780, 783–85, 793, 811, 846, 855, 863, 865; **10:**130–32, 140, 146, 150, 175–76, 196–98, 200, 282, 290, 306, 309, 333, 336–37, 450, 713, 717–18, 739, 841, 977; **11:**83, 167, 207, 213–14, 234, 252, 293–94, 305–6, 316, 342, 346, 492, 495, 497, 526, 549, 673, 694, 695, 698, 704, 708, 711–12, 714, 745, 747, 758, 760, 811, 851–52; **12:**9, 42, 66, 77, 92, 121, 125, 127, 144, 154, 162, 164, 234, 242, 251, 255, 259, 291, 310, 312, 316, 509, 514, 522, 533, 535, 538, 540, 547–48, 565, 568, 588, 614, 624, 639, 642, 649, 651, 684–85, 711

PERSIAN
COURT **3:**678, 718, 751, 856, 858–59, 862–63, 866, 878, 882, 885, 889–90, 903, 923, 929, 951, 955–56; **4:**348; **7:**20, 32, 88; EMPIRE **1:**247, 267, 269; **3:**319, 654, 665, 671–72, 674-76, 680, 723, 747, 752, 780, 782, 785, 855–56, 858–59, 877–79, 887, 897, 899, 913, 941, 951, 966, 1077–78, 1106, 1187; **4:**4, 30, 197, 253; **6:**8, 37, 945, 1366, 1443; **7:**20, 23–24, 29–33, 51, 72, 111–12, 137, 187, 301, 709–10, 731, 760, 779, 847–48, 866, 868; OLD **1:**267; **2:**687. *See also* PERSIA *in PLACES IN THE BIBLE*

PERVERSE, PERVERSION
1:51, 59, 62, 403, 848, 870, 932, 933; **2:**863, 876, 884, 1026; **3:**536, 553, 953; **4:**36, 330, 332,

PERVERSE, PERVERSION *(continued)*
370, 400, 411, 570, 708, 1083; **5:**55, 113, 140–41, 172, 178, 198, 237, 313, 412, 454–55, 558, 768; **6:**379–80, 466, 490, 501, 614, 627, 640, 708, 750, 753, 1064, 1166, 1229; **7:**178, 213, 235, 237, 396, 560, 630, 775–76, 824; **8:**164, 201, 217, 241, 333, 366, 368–69, 501; **9:**208, 312, 402, 445; **10:**433; **11:**184, 207–8, 274, 512–13, 531; **12:**173, 200, 325, 327, 361, 415, 444, 489, 507, 653

PESTILENCE
1:753, 876, 877, 1181; **2:**503, 530, 1380–81; **3:**423–24, 996; **4:**78, 524, 1047; **5:**540, 542, 656, 692, 818; **6:**412, 450, 655, 690, 831, 867, 1153, 1161, 1167, 1194, 1210, 1214, 1296, 1397, 1458, 1522; **7:**310, 312, 345, 380–81, 383, 582, 833; **8:**15; **9:**404; **12:**693

PESTLE
5:231

PETER, LETTERS OF
1 PETER **1:**8, 13, 15–16, 19, 1196; **2:**141; **8:**517; **9:**420; **10:**63, 72, 377, 379, 381, 390, 816; **11:**446, 454, 653, 718, 721; **12:**10, 146, 171, 323–25, 327–28, 355, 365, 398, 744; 2 PETER **1:**8, 14–16, 1196; **9:**410; **10:**63, 371, 377–78; **11:**835; **12:**229, 312, 365, 375, 474, 480, 489, 705

PHARAOH
1:165, 246–48, 257, 298, 306, 383, 427, 428–31, 469, 488, 555, 560, 593–95, 600–601, 609, 611, 614–16, 620–23, 628, 640, 643–46, 651–55, 669–72, 680, 682–84, 686, 688, 691–92, 694–95, 697, 698–701, 703–4, 707, 713–15, 717–23, 725–31, 735–48, 750–52, 754–55, 757–60, 762–64, 766–74, 778, 780–82, 785, 789, 792–96, 799–802, 804–6, 808, 812–13, 816, 825, 834, 841, 843, 882, 892, 923, 924–25, 933, 949, 953, 973, 1124, 1149, 1173, 1196; **2:**99, 164, 177, 182, 195, 200, 253, 414, 422, 461, 538, 547, 613, 619, 737, 752, 758, 781, 804, 809, 855, 1011; **3:**67, 81, 87, 90, 93, 102, 132, 233, 561, 575, 651, 654, 737, 811, 886, 897, 927, 980, 1081, 1144, 1173; **4:**66, 230, 264, 295, 592, 862, 934, 1104, 1142, 1220, 1225; **5:**5, 40, 72, 78, 160, 182, 239, 253, 316, 386, 497, 522, 525, 529, 534, 586, 591, 593, 596, 604, 627, 633, 664, 724, 726; **6:**122–23, 315, 335, 400, 421, 432, 527–29, 685, 693, 809, 882, 885, 1104–5, 1249, 1278, 1343, 1356, 1366, 1388, 1396–97, 1400–1408, 1412, 1415, 1418, 1419–24, 1427, 1429–30, 1432–40, 1442, 1444–45, 1516, 1530; **7:**34, 39, 40–41, 50, 73, 111, 179, 189, 192, 293, 355, 357, 372, 480, 481, 616, 668, 671, 675, 691, 752; **8:**147, 150, 537; **9:**458, 537; **10:**124, 126, 181, 267, 457, 525, 548, 638–42, 677, 680; **11:**166, 582, 696; **12:**140–41, 146, 592, 661, 672. *See also by name in* PERSONS IN THE BIBLE

PHARISEE, PHARISEES
1:44, 285, 287–89, 291, 1009, 1106, 1160; **2:**1013, 1141; **3:**1079, 1114, 1134; **4:**47; **5:**627, 629, 709; **6:**244, 1316, 1338; **7:**175, 253–54, 509; **8:**35, 39, 42, 59, 70, 78, 81, 99, 110, 115, 122, 142, 147, 151, 157, 162, 180–81, 187–89, 217, 224, 234–36, 240, 246, 271, 275, 278–80, 283, 285–87, 295–97, 300, 308, 311, 315, 317, 330–36, 340–42, 359, 371, 385–86, 406, 408–9, 412, 414–15, 417, 419–24, 426–28, 430–31, 434–36, 438, 457, 464, 474, 497, 501, 522, 540–41, 547–48, 552, 555–56, 559, 565, 567, 572, 588, 590, 597, 605–8, 614–18, 621, 639, 642–43, 645–46, 656–57, 668, 673–74, 678, 681, 683, 687; **9:**13, 20, 23, 26, 29, 32, 35, 72, 74, 76, 83, 114, 122–30, 133–36, 153, 155, 164, 166, 169, 172, 194, 211, 245, 247–51, 268, 273, 276, 280–81, 284–88, 290, 294–96, 298, 304, 306–7, 311–12, 318, 321, 329–31, 333, 341, 346, 348, 355–56, 358–59, 369, 376, 378, 385, 388, 392–93, 399, 436, 445–46, 505–6, 528, 541, 560, 569, 574, 624, 628–30, 633, 649, 651, 653–54, 656, 658, 661–70, 696, 700, 704, 708, 710, 720, 801, 813, 817; **10:**89, 104, 108, 206–7, 209, 306, 309–12, 315, 335–37, 718; **11:**224, 397, 438, 526; **12:**306, 621, 632, 726–27, 729

PHENOMENOLOGY
1:122, 198; **6:**926; **11:**275, 291

PHILEMON, LETTER TO
1:8, 13–14, 772, 873, 1196; **8:**14, 517; **9:**4; **10:**370, 373, 379, 730, 758, 779, 825, 885, 889, 969, 998; **11:**70, 92, 197, 202, 278, 365, 406, 453, 462–63, 479, 577, 579–80, 583, 587, 664–68; **12:**460

PHILIPPIANS, LETTER TO THE
1:8, 13, 182, 209, 1196; **6:**1266; **9:**523, 790; **10:**230, 370, 373, 461, 552, 690, 708, 717, 719, 761, 779, 789, 791, 825, 830, 880, 924, 975, 977, 984, 988; **11:**21, 24, 58, 70, 85, 94, 112, 123, 134, 145, 153, 196–97, 214, 369, 416, 462, 577, 587, 668, 675, 695, 704, 762, 865, 883, 888; **12:**232, 297, 300, 565

PHILOSOPHY (*OR* PHILOSOPHER, *ETC.*)
1:18, 50, 52, 54, 76, 88, 107, 109–11, 116–17, 122–24, 178, 192, 196–97, 287–88, 290–91, 310, 1139; **4:**216, 241, 453, 878, 914; **5:**8, 269, 275, 277, 290, 317, 439, 449, 460, 498, 502–3, 505–6, 518, 543, 546–47, 562, 597, 624–25, 647, 730, 834; **6:**223, 662; **7:**27, 147, 718; **8:**16–19, 21, 23, 26, 41, 48, 181; **9:**129, 506, 519, 742, 758; **10:**71, 243, 246, 374, 382, 437–38, 700; **11:**122, 293, 297, 316, 321, 358, 446, 452–53,

541, 553, 555–57, 559–62, 564–68, 571, 574–76, 579, 584, 592–94, 596, 600, 606, 613, 619–20, 622–26, 629–38, 640–44, 648, 652–53, 661–63, 675, 700, 751, 814, 864; **12:**17, 114, 136, 179, 199, 213, 336, 503, 553; SCHOOLS OF **1:**287–88

PHOENIX
4:539; **5:**808

PHYLACTERIES
2:344; **4:**555; **8:**431–32

PHYSICIAN, PHYSICIANS
1:669, 1027; **3:**543–44, 782, 1003, 1005, 1052; **4:**433; **5:**90, 305, 609, 624, 640, 705, 733, 779, 806–9; **6:**807; **7:**253–54; **8:**16, 59, 376, 553; **9:**4, 6, 9–10, 128–29, 190; **11:**437, 903; **12:**390; JESUS AS **7:**253–54; **8:**376; LUKE AS **3:**544; **5:**808; **9:**4, 6, 9–10, 190; **11:**903. *See also* DOCTOR

PIEOUS, PIETY
1:18, 21, 52–53, 103, 189, 194–95, 291, 404, 719, 787, 942, 977, 1072; **2:**14, 377, 551, 569, 656, 715, 718, 871, 912, 913, 924, 958, 961–62, 994, 1050, 1078–79, 1081–82, 1193, 1247, 1258, 1262, 1280–81, 1293, 1299, 1324–25, 1327, 1371, 1381–82; **3:**5, 35, 274, 581–82, 611, 624, 700, 747, 752, 871, 959, 966, 987, 992, 1080–81, 1132–34, 1138, 1143, 1145, 1180, 1182; **4:**34, 115, 205, 214, 229, 275–77, 319–20, 324, 326, 331, 334–35, 337, 343–45, 349, 351, 353–54, 359, 361, 364, 375–76, 384, 388–89, 396, 401, 410–11, 435, 442, 449, 457, 463, 468, 477, 479, 492, 494, 500, 502, 509, 529, 533–35, 548, 564, 571, 586, 601, 634, 636, 929, 1167, 1174–75; **5:**62, 149, 166, 176, 205, 234, 238, 250, 257, 263, 267, 274, 280, 293, 331–32, 339, 512, 606, 610, 617, 623–24, 626, 628, 650, 652, 655–56, 659, 663, 668, 674, 720, 761, 786, 808, 813, 824; **6:**58, 94, 105, 141, 148, 204, 244, 248, 262, 272, 294, 300–301, 304–5, 469, 548, 582, 1165, 1213, 1261, 1316, 1412, 1467; **7:**8, 122, 124, 147, 179, 253, 419, 465, 470–71, 502, 506–7, 509, 528, 537, 580, 582–83, 751; **8:**33, 41–42, 44, 51, 187, 200, 206, 278, 346, 395, 431, 494, 549, 554–55, 606, 618, 649, 681, 699; **9:**45, 48, 58, 70, 72, 86, 88, 130–31, 136, 144, 186, 197, 207, 217, 234, 247–51, 334, 336, 341–42, 346, 374, 393–96, 417, 540, 660, 671, 688, 691; **10:**24, 72, 77, 79, 133, 142–43, 163, 246, 294, 304, 322, 335, 378, 483, 506, 541, 552, 767, 852, 886, 962–63, 984; **11:**146, 214, 227, 363, 378, 399, 436, 446, 493, 509, 561, 584, 610, 686, 777, 797–99, 805, 808, 819, 827–28, 831, 833, 845, 849, 862, 871; **12:**110, 133, 200, 296, 336, 416, 440, 581

PIGEON, PIGEONS
1:1009, 1013, 1025, 1036, 1086, 1099, 1105; **2:**65; **8:**661; **9:**69–70

PILGRIM (*OR* PILGRIMS, PILGRIMAGE, *ETC.*)
1:275, 285, 426, 804, 950, 1113, 1156–57; **2:**148–49, 251, 413, 974; **3:**451, 473, 499, 521, 616–18, 643, 659, 678, 840, 993, 1001, 1180; **4:**301, 649, 852, 871–72, 868, 1012–14, 1176–77, 1180, 1183–84, 1186–88, 1195, 1198–99, 1201, 1203, 1210–17; **5:**721; **6:**67, 83, 221, 281, 414, 457, 635, 759, 813, 859, 943, 1316; **7:**205, 266, 285, 419, 528, 565, 568, 580, 655, 663, 665, 674, 707, 838–39; **8:**41, 33, 144, 226, 363, 407, 436, 457, 490, 493, 658–60; **9:**63, 76, 215, 282, 304, 369, 412, 473, 542–43, 545, 578, 616, 675, 710; **10:**36, 53, 65, 135, 142–47, 257–58, 270–71, 275–78, 287–89, 320–21, 357, 378, 513, 692, 754, 756, 954; **11:**87; **12:**10–13, 32, 47, 55–56, 63–64, 70, 72, 81, 99, 102, 135–39, 139, 145, 153–58, 257, 270–74, 288

PILLAR, PILLARS
AS BUILDING SUPPORTS **1:**216, 224, 277, 279, 344, 475, 542, 585, 587, 896, 951; **2:**53, 178, 385, 420, 486–87, 841, 854–55, 859, 861, 915–16, 1336; **3:**115, 180, 429, 484–85, 1134; **4:**165, 218, 371, 518, 865; **5:**93, 102, 125, 282, 446, 450, 524, 580, 585–86, 621, 630, 667, 757–58; **6:**586, 925, 1007, 1131, 1159, 1360, 1366, 1368, 1431, 1442, 1549–50; **7:**202–3, 206, 232, 272, 527, 575, 769–70; **8:**345; **9:**332; **11:**808, 810; OF CLOUD/OF FIRE **1:**688, 788, 938, 1066, 1179; **2:**108, 110, 126; **3:**811; **4:**197, 1075; **5:**517, 585, 621, 757–58; **6:**1510; **9:**632; **10:**513, 556, 581, 593; AS A METAPHOR FOR IDEAS OR PEOPLE **1:**519, 540, 565; **2:**603, 915–16, 923, 931, 942, 1236, 1255; **3:**514, 1056, 1058; **4:**214, 431; **5:**282; **6:**959, 1082, 1131; **7:**118, 556; **8:**172, 209; **10:**386, 389, 1000; **11:**19, 113–14, 194, 221, 225, 227–29, 245, 312, 316, 783, 808, 810; **12:**81, 585, 654, 729; OF SALT **1:**475; **5:**524; **9:**332

PILLOW, PILLOWS
1:542; **3:**19; **8:**229; **9:**170

PILOT, PILOTS
5:269; **6:**296; **7:**502, 527; **10:**346; **12:**203

PIN
2:841, 858

PINE TREE
6:1374; **7:**609

PINNACLE
4:1048; **8:**164, 405; **9:**97, 99–100

PIONEER, PIONEERS
1:368; **2:**97; **3:**382, 487; **6:**1125; **7:**117; **10:**422, 470; **12:**11, 13, 39, 42–43, 63–64, 93, 120, 149, 523, 531

PIPE, PIPES
DRAINAGE **7:**771; FOR MUSIC **1:**1163; **4:**1279; **7:**63; **9:**366 (*see also* MUSICAL INSTRUMENTS)

PIT
1:610; **2:**356; **3:**916; **4:**96, 264, 463, 531, 570, 737, 789, 796; **5:**12, 135, 207, 238–39, 270, 348, 354, 525, 715, 772; **6:**159, 449, 717, 729, 850, 892, 1104, 1358, 1427–28, 1439–40, 1442–45, 1516; **7:**6, 36, 85, 90, 93, 244, 478, 506; **8:**277; **9:**150, 221, 282, 284, 318, 380; **11:**165, 437; **12:**631, 682, 684, 707; AS ABODE OF THE DEAD **4:**570, 737, 789, 796, 842, 1028; **5:**45; **6:**212, 1369, 1388, 1445; OF DESPAIR **1:**616, 628; **4:**463, 1028, 1058, 1092; **5:**45, 350; **6:**1056–57; **7:**90; OF DESTRUCTION **2:**356; **4:**463; **9:**641; FOR OVEN/STORAGE **1:**216, 1019; **4:**264; AS A TRAP **1:**600, 621; **4:**533, 819, 842, 905; **5:**350; **6:**212, 1056, 1269; **7:**810. *See also* SHEOL *in PLACES IN THE BIBLE*

PITCH, RESINOUS
1:699, 1012; **6:**277; **7:**192

PITCHER, PITCHERS
1:511, 1160; **3:**136; **5:**355–57; **11:**855. *See also* POTTERY

PITFALL, PITFALLS
1:42, 163; **3:**905, 1019; **4:**1059; **5:**543, 683; **10:**101; **11:**302

PITY
3: 920; **4:**632, 953; **5:**618, 715, 772; **6:**127, 693, 976, 1029, 1038, 1061, 1153, 1166, 1170, 1177, 1179, 1258, 1281, 1334, 1338, 1345, 1543; **7:**218, 226, 320, 323, 325, 473, 483, 487–88, 500, 537, 611, 800; **8:**544, 634; **9:**310, 460, 819, 823; **11:**150, 809, 823; **12:**123, 268, 455; AS COMPASSION **2:**301, 393,1128, 1292; **3:**813; **4:**356, 1091, 1111; **5:**618; **6:**531, 956, 1023–24, 1042; **7:**471, 525; **10:**50; **11:**20, 41–42, 150; **12:**694; TO HAVE/SHOW **1:**700; **2:**628, 756; **3:**776, 810, 814; **4:**242, 477, 487; **5:**772; **6:**73; **7:**522–23, 821; **8:**44, 634; **10:**50; SELF-PITY (*see* SELF-PITY)

PLAGUE, PLAGUES
1:329, 428–29, 431, 473, 477, 934, 1096, 1099–1100, 1181; **2:**82, 141, 197–200, 202, 207, 247–48, 826, 960, 1005–7, 1102–3, 1149, 1380–83; **3:**76, 79, 864, 1106; **4:**44, 168, 469, 524, 612, 853, 992, 1104–5, 1133, 1220; **5:**430, 441, 445–46, 450, 470, 528–30, 533–36, 540–42, 571, 573–75, 577–80, 583–86, 590–93, 596, 598, 818, 853; **6:**113, 295, 655, 792, 883, 1167, 1215, 1278, 1341, 1485; **7:**291–92, 302, 304–9, 311–12, 314, 316, 318, 374, 380–82, 401–2, 405–6, 728, 838–39; **8:**247; **9:**282, 319, 400, 402; **11:**213; **12:**537–38, 612, 616, 630, 632–34, 636, 644, 656, 672, 675–78, 680, 693, 721, 732, 734; IN EXODUS **1:**298, 428–29, 473, 688, 715, 722–23, 729, 738–76, 780, 893, 948, 1196; **2:**50–51, 89, 91, 140, 182, 481, 543, 613, 737, 795, 834, 1001, 1010; **3:**184, 811; **4:**210, 358, 992, 1104–5, 1133, 1220; **5:**40, 72, 78, 149, 239, 494, 528–29, 596, 598, 842; **6:**1341, 1435, 1437, 1586; **7:**345–46, 355, 380–82; **12:**158, 642

PLAIN
AS A GEOGRAPHICAL LOCATION **1:**218, 245, 268, 278, 666; **2:**611, 717, 739–40, 744–45, 1000; **3:**150, 336, 357, 784, 932, 1023, 1098, 1109, 1113; **4:**57, 73, 81, 100, 111, 115, 129–30, 140, 146–47, 151–52, 156, 174–76, 281–82; **5:**445, 524, 593; **6:**43, 149, 185, 188–89, 369, 1136, 1143, 1152, 1349, 1442, 1499, 1502, 1512; **7:**61, 218, 331, 447, 542, 626, 828, 837; **8:**174–75; **9:**8, 23, 102, 137, 140, 196, 869; **10:**161, 643; **11:**470; **12:**669; MEANING/SENSE **1:**48, 51, 55, 66, 72, 74, 76–77, 81–82, 192–93; **2:**335, 678, 833; **6:**313, 331, 334, 337, 366, 541, 549; **10:**191, 238, 284, 309, 361

PLANE TREE
5:757; **6:**1426

PLANKS
6:1373

PLANT, PLANTS
AS A NOUN **4:**402–3, 427; **5:**355; **7:**483, 486–87, 521–22, 524; PLEASANT **6:**78, 89, 174; AS A VERB **4:**314; **6:**238, 583, 792

PLANTATION, PLANTATIONS
1:155–56, 164; **2:**595; **7:**198, 214, 264, 294–96

PLASTER
1:1019, 1099–1100; **2:**178, 486, 636; **4:**264, 433; **6:**10, 12; **7:**362; **9:**369

PLATE, PLATES
1:1148; **5:**150; **9:**399; OF ARMOR/GARMENT **1:**888; **3:**553 (*see also* BREASTPIECE/BREASTPLATE); OFFERING (*see under* OFFERING)

PLATTER
7:779

PLEDGE, PLEDGES
1:605–6, 634, 747, 835, 853, 882, 1010, 1021, 1106; **2:**64, 82, 234, 468, 470–72, 547, 585, 749, 825, 832, 899, 911, 931, 937, 945, 1113, 1115, 1324; **3:**102, 161, 217, 223, 251, 305, 364, 366, 376, 379, 381, 407, 475, 503, 539, 562, 574–75, 580, 607–8, 610, 643, 645–46, 725, 745, 779–80, 783, 797–98, 815, 819, 849, 1050; **4:**82, 461, 500, 510, 570, 670, 1081; **5:**205, 373, 401, 430, 747, 805; **6:**249, 361, 363, 433, 626, 656, 813, 1261, 1450; **7:**225, 290, 365, 416, 578, 641; **8:**471; **9:**25, 85, 230, 358–59, 393, 422–23, 438, 852; **10:**293, 320, 831, 920, 942, 957; **11:**26, 101, 124, 145, 150, 158, 285, 375–76, 609, 678, 689, 708, 732, 821, 872, 899; **12:**110, 200, 295–96, 298. *See also* COVENANT; DEBT, SURETY; VOW

PLEIADES
4:605

PLEROMA
11:384, 422, 450
PLOW (*OR* PLOWS, *ETC.*)
AS A NOUN **1:**218, 1134; **2:**718; **3:**145; **7:**54, 605; **8:**570; **10:**756; AS A VERB **1:**1113; **2:**410, 453, 850, 1053; **3:**144; **4:**332, 1203, 1244; **5:**127, 185, 687–88, 761, 765; **6:**238; **7:**234, 275–76, 403, 430, 560; **8:**58, 303, 539, 570; **9:**176–77, 217, 323, 542
PLOWMAN, PLOWMEN
1:1179; **7:**30; **8:**313; **11:**533
PLOW OXEN
1:217, 1134; **2:**453; **3:**144; **5:**688; **7:**403. *See also* OX
PLOWSHARE, PLOWSHARES
2:759, 1161; **4:**119; **6:**23, 42, 65, 68–69, 1305; **7:**332, 533, 574, 612
PLUMB LINE, LINES
4:601; **6:**237, 629, 655, 718, 746, 1140; **7:**406–7
PLURALSIM
1:4, 34, 48, 61, 159, 180, 196, 202, 410, 1139; **2:**194, 196, 587, 681; **3:**1125; **4:**941; **5:**245, 247; **6:**95, 239, 970, 1010; **7:**224, 457, 459; **8:**27, 335, 431, 557, 679; **9:**222, 379, 743; **10:**3, 32, 93, 222, 249, 390; **11:**186, 361, 423, 611, 815, 873; **12:**277, 486
POD, PODS
3:204; **8:**156; **9:**302
POET, POETS, POETRY
BIBLICAL AND GENERAL **1:**63, 111, 213, 236, 665–67, 747; **2:**376, 528–30, 600, 602, 789, 982, 1113, 1365, 1371; **3:**693, 812, 1077; **4:**302, 305, 307, 314, 428, 441, 443, 531–33, 535, 540, 597, 602, 609, 618, 624, 627, 642, 762, 765, 861–63, 892, 964, 1020, 1093, 1099, 1105, 1110, 1118, 1142, 1214, 1236, 1259; **5:**4, 6–7, 22, 43–45, 77, 103, 252, 254, 257, 312, 354, 367, 369–71, 380–81, 391, 395, 405, 409, 411, 434, 835; **7:**376, 593, 596–97, 599, 609–13, 618, 620, 653–54, 692, 702, 815; **9:**184; **10:**247; **11:**247; **12:**85, 514, 551, 678; HEBREW **1:**231–32; **2:**8, 789; **4:**301–15, 644–58; **5:**366; **6:**12, 15; NONBIBLICAL AND SPECIFIC **1:**156, 194; **2:**449, 840; **4:**339, 463, 604; **5:**27, 312, 346; **9:**324; **10:**486; **11:**378, 696, 734
POISON (*OR* POISONS, POISONING, *ETC.*)
1:614, 837; **2:**142, 513; **3:**190–91, 1032, 1081; **4:**31, 177, 391, 485, 487, 702, 1127, 1221; **5:**72, 329, 456, 570, 599; **6:**647–48, 655, 684, 1065, 1319, 1327, 1607; **7:**140, 272, 403; **8:**157; **9:**291, 642; **10:**197, 458, 631; **11:**643; **12:**204, 218, 450, 634, 724
POLEMICS
1:18, 20, 66, 71, 73, 76–77, 79, 87, 99–102, 276, 285, 328, 341, 344, 395, 494, 541, 616, 760, 799, 840, 844, 880, 893, 896, 916, 920, 927, 931, 949, 950, 955, 991; **2:**37, 50, 316–17, 329–30, 351–52, 364, 391, 420, 529, 530, 602, 642, 711, 864; **3:**75, 96, 135; **4:**9, 12, 183, 278, 397, 751, 792–94, 934–35, 945–47, 1098, 1144–46, 1219–21, 1232, 1268; **5:**276, 279, 368, 541–43, 597, 643, 647; **6:**9, 21, 277, 378–79, 385–87, 399, 401, 406, 599, 660–61, 750, 913, 933–34, 985–87, 989, 993, 1006, 1008, 1010, 1132, 1160, 1561, 1570; **7:**12, 52, 83, 169, 175, 193, 202–3, 241, 245, 488, 606, 820; **8:**17, 19, 24, 27, 30, 39, 49–50, 53–54, 102, 144, 182, 257, 275, 278, 287, 292, 333–34, 347, 371, 425, 431, 435–36, 487, 642; **9:**135, 225, 378, 382, 520, 529, 637, 642, 757, 783, 834; **10:**8, 31, 79, 129, 204–5, 209, 247, 271, 308, 318, 390, 413, 429, 442, 447, 484–86, 488, 501, 553, 690, 719, 764, 969; **11:**184, 194, 238, 277, 287, 300, 314, 318, 321, 333, 336–37, 362, 364, 397, 399–400, 402, 416, 463, 530, 562, 564, 573, 575–77, 584, 619, 623, 625, 635, 642, 703–4, 718, 778, 790–91, 812, 866; **12:**9, 21, 23, 26, 28, 47, 166, 326, 343, 372, 405, 440, 522, 545, 588
POLICE
2:628, 696–97, 1227, 1382; **3:**451–52, 587; **4:**18, 166; **6:**1069, 1241; **7:**32, 62, 64, 403, 765; **8:**405, 477, 501, 700; **9:**245, 364, 624, 649, 801, 803, 806, 809–10, 817; **10:**78, 105, 234, 236, 245, 277, 297, 319, 706; **11:**246, 454
POLITICAL THEOLOGY
See under THEOLOGY
POLLUTE, POLLUTES
1:1076, 1082, 1104; **2:**60, 198, 247, 265–66; **3:**1144; **4:**555, 1111; **5:**142, 345; **6:**211, 213, 640, 1100, 1489, 1534, 1574; **7:**236; **12:**492, 631
POLLUTION
1:281–82, 374, 390, 586, 742, 873, 1010, 1013, 1080, 1082, 1084, 1104–5, 1112; **2:**15, 20, 59–60, 62, 65, 129, 149, 198–99, 201, 245, 247, 255–56, 265–67, 687; **3:**178, 430, 609, 730, 1144, 1147; **4:**8, 23, 164–65, 230, 236, 254, 258, 555, 705, 712, 783, 793, 1111; **5:**149, 220, 345; **6:**210–11, 213–14, 600, 603, 640, 703, 998, 1084, 1100, 1190, 1259, 1283, 1290, 1306–7, 1310, 1327, 1389, 1394, 1469, 1488–89, 1530, 1534, 1546–47, 1574, 1577; **7:**40, 205, 236–37, 548, 676, 850, 860; **8:**34, 36; **9:**101, 648; **10:**23, 220–22, 243, 247, 253, 269, 273, 276–77, 285, 294; **11:**390, 610; **12:**463, 492, 498, 631, 636, 654, 722
POLYGAMY
1:1126; **2:**446–47, 474, 476; **3:**522; **4:**470; **5:**97, 255, 761, 764; **6:**82; **7:**206; **8:**386, 642; **9:**313; **11:**805

POLYTHEISM
1:165, 272–73, 800, 843, 876; **2:**527, 1001; **3:**104, 137–38, 421, 1119, 1124–25, 1154; **4:**12, 1006–7, 1035, 1061; **6:**101, 345, 413, 608, 892, 1010; **8:**179, 291, 459, 679; **11:**831; **12:**80

POMEGRANATE, POMEGRANATES
1:218, 1060; **2:**356; **5:**402–3, 405, 418, 427, 843; **6:**1272; **7:**309, 769; **9:**310

POND
5:834

POOL, POOLS
1:249, 1160; **2:**1215–16, 1230; **3:**167, 759, 766, 768–69; **4:**156, 1014; **5:**297–98, 337, 618, 853; **6:**107, 218, 335, 709, 1246, 1595; **8:**157; **9:**270, 535, 542, 578, 594, 654; **12:**305

POOR
1:169–71, 186, 214, 265, 477, 698, 768, 868–72, 874, 897, 918, 1001, 1013, 1018, 1025, 1035–36, 1039, 1051, 1084–85, 1110, 1131, 1133, 1136, 1159, 1170–71, 1184, 1191; **2:**178, 366, 369, 403, 405, 470–72, 482, 569, 578, 590, 592–96, 609, 679, 682, 689, 696–97, 719, 758, 789, 855, 915, 920, 923, 980–83, 1013, 1051, 1057, 1160, 1292, 1382; **3:**109, 128–29, 191, 199, 779–81, 783, 819, 865, 880, 912, 937, 979, 993, 997, 1001–2, 1005, 1015, 1058, 1144; **4:**77, 166, 219, 327, 335, 343, 379, 412, 429, 444, 480, 484–85, 500–501, 510–11, 538, 541, 545, 547–48, 553, 577, 585, 594, 609, 669, 672, 674, 679, 717–20, 724, 730, 732–33, 764–66, 814, 819, 829, 835, 844–45, 847–49, 861, 877, 945, 953, 955, 963, 965, 974–75, 980, 1057, 1075, 1086, 1125–28, 1138–40, 1240–41, 1256, 1261; **5:**4–5, 8, 25, 30, 71, 76, 105, 119, 121, 125, 128, 131–32, 134, 142, 144, 152–53, 161, 164, 166, 170, 175–76, 178–81, 186, 197, 198–200, 204–6, 237–39, 241, 243, 253, 256, 259–60, 262, 319, 322, 345, 351, 447, 462–63, 467, 480, 613–14, 617, 638, 664, 695, 705, 715–17, 732, 741, 774–75, 780, 797, 823; **6:**8, 15, 78–79, 88, 128, 141, 143, 204, 216–17, 221, 388, 600, 602–3, 619, 621, 626, 630, 648, 692, 721, 724, 740, 742, 745–46, 755, 763, 767, 777, 826, 851, 853–54, 858, 926, 944, 999, 1165, 1237, 1259–61, 1266, 1274, 1315, 1412, 1467, 1558, 1583, 1601; **7:**7, 45, 50, 55, 57–58, 63, 67, 75–76, 83, 129, 142–43, 161, 170, 188, 200, 268, 287, 293, 328, 345–46, 365, 376, 378, 383, 390, 395–96, 400, 406, 416–17, 425, 448, 457, 533–34, 553, 606, 631–33, 638–39, 680, 710, 725, 793, 848; **8:**31, 58, 76, 84, 104, 151, 170, 176, 178–79, 200, 204, 210, 264, 267, 277–78, 313, 391, 395–96, 458, 466–67, 553, 576, 611, 649–50, 663, 682–83, 698–99, 714; **9:**12, 22, 24–27, 31, 34–36, 43, 49, 56, 67, 70, 81, 84, 105–108, 121, 131–32, 139, 142–46, 149, 152, 161–62, 166–67, 171, 194, 196–97, 199, 213, 235, 254, 276, 287, 290, 296, 312, 315–19, 332, 334–38, 345, 347–50, 354, 357–59, 362, 364, 367, 371, 374, 395–97, 406, 457–59, 463, 472, 684, 702; **10:**10, 63, 72, 77, 97, 100, 111, 127, 142, 170, 256, 259, 271, 283, 285–86, 376, 378, 387, 506, 756, 759, 777, 814, 995; **11:**7, 21–22, 25, 96–97, 113–15, 123, 131, 194, 227, 230, 247, 342, 392, 446, 455, 459, 502, 504, 547–48, 645, 658, 709, 761, 825, 828, 886; **12:**24, 40, 178, 181–82, 187–88, 192–95, 197, 199, 200–201, 203, 217, 219, 221, 224–25, 254, 509, 511, 549, 568–69, 587–88, 614, 626, 700; "PREFERENTIAL OPTION FOR THE POOR" **1:**698; **6:**141, 204; **9:**145; **10:**142; **12:**192; IN SOUL **1:**941; **4:**764; IN SPEECH **1:**720, 735; IN SPIRIT **4:**975; **5:**161; **8:**76, 84, 104, 178–79; **9:**25, 144

POPE
1:14, 16, 19, 51, 796; **2:**1031; **3:**1019; **8:**6; **10:**621; **11:**394, 432; **12:**535–37, 713. *See also* PAPACY

POPLAR TREE
4:618

POPULAR RELIGION
See under RELIGION

PORCH
2:772; **3:**62, 451; **6:**1177, 1555; **7:**320; **9:**46, 390. *See also* NAVE; PORTICO; VESTIBULE

PORTENT, PORTENTS
1:767; **2:**503; **3:**1098; **4:**227–28, 959; **5:**364; **6:**9, 12, 42, 57, 114, 116, 118–19, 182, 478, 660, 1208; **7:**220, 354, 405, 765, 820; **8:**494; **9:**243, 382, 399–400, 407–8, 539; **10:**69, 666; **11:**168; **12:**403, 516, 575, 589, 658, 672. *See also* OMEN

PORTER, PORTERS
3:437. *See also* DOORKEEPER; LEVITE; PRIEST; WATCHMAN

PORTICO, PORTICOES
3:61–62, 484; **6:**1542; **9:**675; **10:**89, 99, 101. *See also* NAVE; PORCH; VESTIBULE

POSSESSION
See DEMON: POSSESSED BY

POST-EASTER
See under EASTER

POSTMODERN
1:34, 60, 124, 147, 354, 681; **2:**540, 552; **5:**20, 227; **10:**3, 436, 443, 463, 486, 548, 621, 697, 726; **11:**609, 627, 825

POT, POTS
1:1017, 1020; **2:**434, 812, 1001, 1024, 1048, 1082, 1098; **3:**10, 185, 190, 914; **4:**355, 625; **5:**126, 135, 226, 326, 591, 715, 746, 801;

6:247–48, 254, 461, 549, 579, 584, 714, 718, 721–22, 866, 996, 1061, 1104, 1130, 1186, 1190, 1332–38, 1457; **7:**55, 377, 393, 839; **8:**334; **11:**718, 845; **12:**104. *See also* COOKING: UTENSILS/VESSELS; EARTHENWARE; FRYING PAN; GRIDDLE; PAN; VESSEL

POTSHERD, POTSHERDS
1:224, 250; **4:**624; **5:**614; **6:**400, 406. *See also* SHARDS/SHERDS

POTTAGE
1:524

POTTERY
1:217, 224, 249–51, 1082; **2:**635, 688; **3:**331, 768; **4:**315; **5:**812; **10:**773; **11:**841, 845–46

POVERTY
1:190, 215, 818, 820, 838, 851, 868, 892, 908, 1015, 1099, 1191; **2:**333, 357, 404–5, 414, 468, 470, 569, 578, 589–90, 592, 608–9, 619, 666, 918, 921, 933, 1031, 1341; **3:**469, 996; **4:**381, 391, 513, 544–45, 547, 731, 931, 940, 974, 1248; **5:**25, 29, 70, 75, 80, 107, 111, 125, 128, 132–33, 142, 145, 150, 153, 164, 178–79, 207, 237, 239, 245, 250, 253, 614–15, 664, 716, 750, 765, 767, 780, 860; **6:**14, 81, 90, 105, 143, 981, 1034, 1066, 1223, 1486; **7:**54, 76, 400, 417, 647; **8:**150, 178, 214, 256, 263, 391, 683, 698; **9:**25, 87, 127, 141, 143–44, 149, 181, 255, 257, 301, 317, 348, 363, 396, 406; **10:**21, 100, 142, 377, 435, 659, 756; **11:**25–26, 119–20, 123, 289, 438, 452, 515–16, 548, 640, 752; **12:**144, 187–88, 200, 216, 313, 343, 535, 568, 577, 670, 708

POWER OF GOD/DIVINE POWER
1:279, 283, 464, 569, 697–98, 748, 768, 796, 803–4, 818, 842, 883, 892–93, 922–23, 941; **2:**35, 40, 50, 53, 67–69, 80, 82–83, 87, 91, 96, 98, 113, 120, 124, 127, 129, 139, 142, 168, 188, 193–95, 215, 236, 256, 283, 308, 316, 321, 349, 352, 363, 365–66, 370, 385–86, 403, 406, 410, 440, 481, 483, 487, 503, 512–13, 527–28, 530, 534, 537–38, 578, 787, 811, 846, 959–61, 964, 980–83, 996, 1006–7, 1010, 1013, 1015, 1019, 1031, 1037, 1043–45, 1051, 1053, 1055, 1057, 1070, 1073, 1102, 1111, 1149, 1211, 1232, 1243, 1248, 1251, 1261, 1265, 1281, 1294, 1326, 1366, 1367, 1368, 1370, 1357; **3:**6, 130, 142, 191, 208, 542, 586, 591, 657, 1040, 1043, 1063, 1110, 1161; **4:**210–12, 242, 248, 250, 254, 258, 266, 340, 381, 384, 415, 435, 444, 487, 508, 514, 518, 568, 583, 608, 632, 691, 758, 874, 877, 879, 899–900, 953, 980–81, 992, 1045, 1048, 1075, 1101, 1119, 1137, 1142, 1190, 1248, 1252, 1271; **5:**127, 291, 469, 504, 562, 564, 574, 577, 725–26, 818; **6:**5, 204, 248, 260, 266, 300–301, 338, 358, 481, 515, 621, 658, 694, 786, 819, 822, 868, 883, 919, 981, 990, 1058; **7:**21, 42, 56, 83, 124, 160, 180, 335, 352, 454, 473, 485–87, 495, 579, 644, 653, 682; **8:**22–23, 62, 64–65, 109, 125, 137, 163, 234, 245, 249, 281–82, 285, 289, 356, 369, 408, 422, 480, 487, 493, 528–29, 548, 565, 580, 584, 588–89, 630, 651, 659–60, 677, 725, 733; **9:**29, 34, 46, 51, 103, 113, 127, 183–84, 224, 242, 253, 325, 348, 350, 355, 357, 375, 442–43, 488, 545, 665, 677, 694–95, 741, 802, 844; **10:**8, 46, 53, 79, 96, 104, 138, 175, 194, 233–34, 236, 418, 426, 477, 585, 754, 798, 808–9, 811–13, 818, 842, 845, 909, 974, 977, 990–91; **11:**23, 26, 31, 57, 81, 136, 138, 167, 186, 202, 211, 223, 252, 316, 318, 330, 367, 377, 382–86, 390–91, 394, 409, 412, 415–16, 457–60, 462, 529, 536, 595, 616–17, 625, 628–29, 682; **12:**217, 295–96, 312, 316, 336, 589, 594, 605, 621, 713

POWERLESS
1:168, 171, 355, 538, 690, 697, 704, 736, 739, 742, 753, 757, 760, 772, 782, 891, 896; **2:**280, 333, 392, 432, 470–71, 503–4, 512–13, 528–29, 631, 633, 689, 787, 790, 835, 923, 969, 983, 1002, 1006–8, 1010, 1021, 1114, 1128, 1185, 1193, 1223, 1294, 1304, 1366; **3:**127, 130, 538, 560, 630, 873, 886–87, 900, 909, 924; **4:**212, 312, 394, 475–76, 480, 517, 537–38, 540, 554, 560, 572, 591, 1007, 1145, 1148; **5:**205, 239, 423, 442, 561, 574, 583, 798; **6:**56, 60, 63, 79, 133, 229, 247, 346, 437, 602, 636, 639, 661, 670, 740, 745, 766, 851, 891, 913, 920, 956, 988, 1005, 1007, 1019, 1052, 1071, 1085, 1131, 1156, 1165, 1309, 1317; **7:**27, 31, 53, 57, 64, 66, 103–4, 112, 124–25, 178, 183, 258, 509, 516, 580, 589, 822; **8:**505, 696, 713, 722, 732; **9:**67, 336, 339, 345, 354, 441, 648, 699, 752, 784, 802, 825; **10:**17, 72, 100, 111, 142, 151, 181, 285, 310, 376, 378, 387, 539, 568, 572, 745, 812, 815, 870, 975, 983; **11:**68, 158, 244, 283, 288, 296, 333, 352, 411, 621, 658; **12:**296, 490, 602, 652

PRAETORIUM
8:488, 719; **10:**314, 330; **11:**473–74

PRAISE (*OR* PRAISES, *ETC.*)
1:41, 156, 160, 201, 207, 212, 286, 316, 341, 344, 428, 440, 555, 605, 624, 700–701, 745, 799, 802, 893, 1018, 1027, 1051, 1134, 1159–60, 1196; **2:**482, 526–29, 534, 538, 763, 775–76, 787, 803–4, 810, 945, 977–81, 1013, 1118, 1124, 1169, 1209, 1217–18, 1230, 1236, 1251, 1261–63, 1366–67; **3:**22, 226, 278, 300, 309–10, 365, 396, 400–403, 408–9, 427, 431, 433, 464, 467–68, 470, 478, 495, 497, 499–500, 523, 538, 560–62, 610, 613, 618, 643, 693, 723–24, 761, 809–10, 814, 826, 835, 838, 840,

PRAISE *(continued)*
842, 914, 920, 956, 975–76, 1008, 1017, 1043, 1052–53, 1056–57, 1061–66, 1165, 1176, 1179; **4:**7, 23, 26, 39, 51, 69, 97, 148, 158, 166, 204, 298, 303–4, 309, 311, 326, 329, 332, 340, 349, 375, 380, 398, 410–11, 414, 424, 429, 439, 501, 509, 560, 570, 572, 583, 589, 597, 602, 608, 622, 645–49, 657–58, 661, 664–65, 669, 671, 674, 678, 681–82, 687, 700–701, 705, 707, 710–11, 717–18, 726–29, 747–48, 758, 762, 764–66, 769, 786, 789, 792, 794–97, 802, 809–11, 813–14, 818, 822–23, 834, 838, 843, 853–54, 860–62, 868–69, 871, 880, 887, 890, 894, 901, 906, 913–14, 919, 926–28, 930–31, 933–35, 937, 940, 945, 951, 953–54, 958–61, 964, 970, 973, 976, 980–81, 984–85, 991, 995–96, 1003, 1013, 1027, 1035, 1044, 1051, 1060–61, 1064–66, 1071–72, 1074, 1077–80, 1086, 1090–91, 1093, 1099–1100, 1103–106, 1110–13, 1118, 1121–22, 1124–26, 1132–34, 1137–41, 1144–45, 1149–51, 1156, 1167–68, 1170, 1173–74, 1188, 1190, 1206, 1213–14, 1216–17, 1219–21, 1223–24, 1230–32, 1237, 1247–48, 1255, 1258–65, 1267, 1269–75, 1277–80; **5:**4, 6, 45, 53, 64, 79–80, 90, 117, 125, 158, 229, 231, 237, 254, 257, 260, 263–64, 276, 316–17, 326, 341, 346, 353, 370, 377, 389, 402, 404, 420–21, 442–43, 449, 493, 503, 506, 522, 525–26, 528, 534, 542, 552, 554, 561, 564, 573, 579, 583, 591, 593, 596, 598–99, 604, 606–607, 609–10, 612, 619–20, 625, 627, 630–31, 633, 636, 638–41, 644–45, 648, 650, 663, 666–67, 674–75, 716, 719, 721, 730–32, 754, 756–57, 765–66, 784, 798, 800, 805–806, 815, 817–19, 823, 826, 833–34, 837, 842–43, 849, 853, 858, 863, 866; **6:**5, 11, 16, 45, 67, 102, 122, 147–48, 169, 190, 205, 207, 210, 212, 216–17, 221, 228, 270, 272, 294, 301, 336, 355, 365, 378, 386, 388, 470, 515, 525, 550, 621, 661, 685, 704, 709, 726, 728, 730, 746, 808, 814, 868, 918, 948, 956–57, 962, 968, 982, 1034, 1070, 1083, 1217, 1268, 1352, 1425–27, 1434, 1455, 1495, 1501, 1503; **7:**42–43, 52, 72, 95, 158, 162, 167, 169, 324, 347, 352, 382, 394, 422, 585–86, 630, 699, 703, 718, 774, 803, 813, 824, 839, 855, 859, 861–62, 875–76; **8:**22, 32, 35, 39, 58, 63–64, 200, 206, 235, 247, 275, 315, 428, 530, 609, 613, 623, 676, 683, 694, 698, 708; **9:**29, 41, 43, 46, 52, 54–56, 59, 65, 71, 74, 76, 87, 103, 152, 155–56, 209, 224, 248–49, 284, 287, 308, 315, 326–27, 356–57, 363, 367, 369, 375, 382, 385, 395–96, 418, 424, 456, 488–89, 532, 542, 587–89, 787, 834, 865; **10:**72, 77–78, 85, 170, 208, 269, 295, 406, 411, 433, 449, 458, 590, 630, 669, 680, 695–96, 721, 725, 733, 744, 746–48, 759, 768–69, 779, 782, 784, 791, 834–35, 926, 928, 951, 953; **11:**30–32, 40, 121, 144, 173, 254, 309, 370, 372–73, 375–81, 383, 410, 413, 416, 419, 436, 441–43, 486, 494, 510, 557–59, 584, 589, 595–98, 601–2, 605–8, 610–11, 648–49, 651, 657, 688, 745–46, 794, 855; **12:**4, 12, 23, 29, 35, 37, 48, 53, 62, 67, 93–94, 130, 160, 165, 167–68, 170, 172, 222, 243, 249, 251–52, 254, 266–68, 277–78, 282, 307, 317, 327, 399, 537, 561, 563, 592–95, 597, 603–4, 609, 615, 619, 621, 624, 629, 643–44, 650, 676, 695; SONG(S) OF (*see under* SONG)

PRAXIS
1:33, 52, 68, 170, 186; **5:**34, 470, 862; **10:**32, 367, 383, 385, 388, 390, 865, 929, 959; **11:**778, 852, 876, 877

PRAYER (*OR* PRAYERS, *ETC.*)
1:12, 41, 67, 69, 72, 96, 103, 176, 179, 201–2, 204–9, 212, 239, 241, 467, 482–84, 510–13, 521–22, 562–64, 569, 572, 746, 751, 753, 815–16, 916, 939, 942, 960, 962–63, 981, 991–92, 1021, 1027, 1041, 1044, 1052, 1066–67, 1100, 1164, 1182, 1196; **2:**8, 14, 91, 100, 112, 139, 141, 163, 188, 283, 331, 351, 356, 363–64, 366–67, 386, 388–89, 403, 407, 427–29, 445, 482, 484–85, 534, 538, 631, 633, 636, 647, 681, 753, 759, 775, 789–90, 804, 840, 859, 896, 942, 960, 962, 964, 967, 973, 978–79, 1018, 1021, 1066, 1073, 1152, 1154, 1237, 1261–63, 1267, 1325–26, 1331–32, 1382–83; **3:**8, 22, 40–41, 55, 68, 72, 75–77, 79–81, 88, 137–38, 201, 236, 271, 273, 286, 300, 310, 313, 328, 332, 355, 380, 389, 396, 399–400, 405, 407–9, 417, 423–25, 430, 433, 464, 467–70, 473, 478, 496–500, 502–3, 506, 514, 527, 538, 540, 543, 552–53, 560–62, 581–82, 602, 618, 619, 628, 630–32, 636–37, 657, 669, 673, 710, 728, 734–38, 740–41, 750–53, 755–56, 758, 773, 775–77, 782, 786, 789, 797, 806, 809–13, 815, 826, 835, 847, 850–51, 865–66, 871, 904, 946, 955–60, 962, 976, 980, 983–89, 998, 1003–10, 1015, 1024, 1026, 1031, 1039–43, 1049–52, 1055–58, 1061–65, 1069, 1075, 1079–80, 1086, 1089, 1093, 1110, 1114, 1130, 1132–33, 1137, 1139–43, 1145–47, 1158, 1161, 1165, 1176–78; **4:**8, 41, 57, 63–64, 66–67, 69, 72–73, 78, 80, 85, 96, 99–100, 122, 144, 184, 188, 197–98, 202, 229, 247, 249–50, 254, 257, 266, 276, 281, 289–90, 292, 296, 334–36, 355, 359, 387, 391, 394, 396, 398, 413, 421, 439, 450–51, 463–64, 468, 474, 477, 497, 502–3, 507–9, 511, 519, 534, 568, 570, 581–82, 586, 636–37, 642, 644–45, 647, 649, 657, 660, 663, 669–70, 677, 681, 693–97, 700, 702–3, 705, 707, 709, 717, 720–21, 724, 727–29, 736–37, 740, 742, 755,

758, 762, 765, 777, 779–82, 785–86, 788–90, 793, 795–96, 799–800, 802, 806, 809, 811, 818–23, 832–33, 842, 846–47, 852, 854, 857, 874, 880, 884, 887, 890, 894–95, 897, 899–902, 905, 908–9, 912, 916–20, 922, 925–28, 930, 933, 938–39, 944, 948, 952–53, 958, 963–65, 975, 983, 996, 999, 1001, 1008–11, 1016–17, 1019, 1022, 1027–29, 1041, 1043, 1057, 1067, 1081, 1084, 1086–88, 1110, 1112, 1117, 1124–28, 1146–47, 1149, 1155–56, 1167, 1171, 1175, 1178, 1180, 1184, 1187–89, 1192, 1196, 1203–4, 1207, 1211, 1217, 1226, 1228, 1230–31, 1237–41, 1243–46, 1250–53, 1273, 1279; **5:**2, 4, 12, 45, 61, 70, 118, 140, 149, 152, 188, 213–14, 224, 251, 253, 317, 323, 331, 339, 363, 441, 444–45, 450, 463, 494, 498, 500, 513, 515–19, 522, 526, 534, 540, 550, 553, 563, 579, 606, 608–10, 612, 616–17, 623–24, 629, 634–35, 639, 641, 655, 659, 671, 677, 693, 718, 741, 745, 748–49, 780, 798–801, 806–8, 829, 853, 863, 866; **6:**18, 56, 58, 72–74, 103, 105, 123, 137, 148, 159, 190, 202, 207, 220–23, 257, 270–71, 277, 284, 291, 293–95, 299–302, 327, 338, 357–58, 386, 394, 407, 456, 471, 503, 532, 546, 571, 581, 599, 613, 638, 649, 664–67, 674–77, 686, 690–93, 697, 699, 709, 716–18, 726–30, 733–34, 792–93, 796, 807–8, 810, 820–21, 827, 864, 930–34, 937, 939, 941, 945–46, 948–49, 952–53, 955–58, 960–61, 971, 973, 977–78, 980, 1026, 1034, 1044, 1055, 1058, 1066–67, 1070, 1109, 1140, 1209, 1306, 1313, 1530, 1537, 1570, 1592; **7:**21, 31, 41, 51–53, 72, 92, 94, 122–23, 125–29, 137, 157–58, 160–61, 163, 181, 194, 270, 304, 311–14, 320, 322, 381, 408, 418, 457, 471, 473, 485, 492, 499–500, 502, 504–7, 509, 517–19, 522, 535, 632, 653, 694–95, 699, 759, 860, 883, 885; **8:**17, 34–35, 60, 89, 100, 122, 148, 150, 161, 172, 182, 196, 200–208, 212, 214, 239, 245, 247, 250, 252, 272–74, 328, 336–37, 349, 369–70, 379, 403, 406, 408, 431, 471, 476–77, 480, 492, 523, 544, 546–47, 555, 561, 589, 602–3, 623, 625–26, 634–35, 650, 653, 656–57, 661, 663–67, 673, 695, 706–9; **9:**12, 27–28, 35, 46–47, 49–50, 55, 74, 79, 90, 100, 111–12, 120, 130, 137, 156, 179, 196, 199, 205, 207, 222, 224, 233–39, 250, 260, 263, 273, 324, 335–42, 345, 373, 393–94, 409–10, 428, 431–34, 455, 461, 463, 494, 509, 514, 657–58, 691–92, 704–5, 712, 719, 721, 735, 758–59, 780–81, 785, 787–92, 794–98, 810, 846, 853, 855, 863; **10:**28, 40, 44–46, 52, 71, 73, 77, 91–93, 113, 133, 139, 143, 163, 175, 178, 180, 182, 200–201, 227, 230–31, 233, 235, 277, 288, 356, 381–82, 420–22, 427, 453, 457–59, 485–86, 498, 517, 531, 544, 547–48, 572, 591, 593–94, 597–601, 605–7, 624, 627–29, 631–32, 653, 662, 664–66, 669–70, 672, 675, 682, 695–97, 712–13, 730, 746, 753, 757–58, 762, 769, 778, 821, 857, 872, 963, 969, 1002; **11:**43, 177, 201–2, 223, 241, 285, 345, 347, 352, 359, 361, 367, 370–71, 377–78, 380–81, 384, 386, 406, 411, 413–17, 430, 436, 439, 443–44, 458, 462–63, 471, 479, 482, 484–85, 540–51, 554, 556, 558–59, 575, 584, 589–90, 592–94, 616, 620, 654, 661–63, 667, 682, 684, 689, 692, 713–14, 717, 732–33, 735–36, 741, 744, 746–47, 752–54, 761–66, 771, 789, 797, 800–801, 811–12, 819, 832–33, 838, 851, 858, 860, 879, 892–93, 895, 904; **12:**46, 57, 62, 64, 91, 163, 169, 171–72, 178, 187–88, 194, 211, 213, 222–23, 225, 247, 253, 269, 276, 285–88, 291, 303, 307, 358, 380, 408, 422, 424, 428, 441–46, 459, 461, 486, 497, 539, 571, 589, 660, 687, 725, 734; LORD'S (*see under* LORD'S); PLACE OF **10:**231, 235, 471. *See also* THANKSGIVING

PREACHER, PREACHERS
See MINISTER; PASTOR

PREACHING
1:2, 21, 27, 45, 47, 55, 82, 84, 87, 97, 98, 100, 150, 160, 188–201, 330, 842, 887, 1114; **2:**12, 22, 38, 53–54, 69, 82–83, 90, 97–98, 111–12, 129–30, 141, 167, 195, 201–2, 215, 222, 236–37, 275, 277, 315, 366, 392, 514, 578, 581, 789, 896, 946, 989, 995, 1064, 1092, 1239, 1316, 1340, 1381; **3:**7, 299, 607, 619, 821, 1193; **4:**565, 672, 811, 830, 854, 882, 920, 924, 947, 1005, 1059, 1067, 1091, 1130, 1265; **5:**118, 285, 293, 316, 359, 395, 434, 499; **6:**41, 322, 521, 560, 562–63, 569–70, 573, 579, 588, 620, 634, 650, 694, 702, 704, 709, 721, 723, 727, 731, 768, 772–73, 866, 872, 1017, 1066, 1100, 1126, 1144, 1408, 1455, 1609; **7:**35, 302, 410, 419, 443, 458, 470, 481, 516, 538–39, 548, 557, 561, 583, 643, 660–61, 664, 685, 688, 735–36, 743, 747, 755, 790–91, 850, 873–74; **8:**29, 32–33, 35, 45–46, 78, 80–81, 90, 92, 111, 121, 138, 144, 149, 154, 157, 166, 168, 174, 180, 207, 220–21, 241, 245, 265, 266–67, 270, 274, 289, 293, 296, 299–300, 303, 311, 315, 334, 347, 351, 354, 366, 374, 410, 513, 522, 527–28, 530–32, 535–36, 538–39, 542–44, 553, 565–67, 570–72, 575, 578, 592–94, 596, 602, 616, 628, 631, 636, 640, 643, 675, 685, 690; **9:**11, 21, 25, 31, 33–34, 41, 47, 78–87, 90, 103–104, 112, 116–17, 128, 135–36, 159–60, 166, 174, 178, 194, 197, 207, 219–20, 230, 234, 243–45, 249, 253, 290, 304, 333, 377, 410, 463, 468, 481, 486–87, 490, 494, 501, 503, 539, 561, 662, 754, 778, 799, 838, 847, 853; **10:**41, 58, 62–63, 68, 93, 113, 115, 140, 142, 150, 167, 532, 1011; **11:**186, 190, 218, 222, 247, 276, 289–90, 298, 309, 339, 363, 372,

PREACHING *(continued)*
381, 408, 411, 461–62, 594, 606, 611, 618, 651, 664, 678, 685, 701, 812, 815, 822, 855, 859, 862, 870; **12:**6, 15, 18, 24, 28, 43, 49, 55, 70, 76, 78, 125, 127, 161, 164, 192, 200, 206, 238, 243, 248, 255, 261–62, 266, 286, 293–94, 297, 329, 331, 335, 340–41, 344, 348, 358, 378, 383–84, 426–27, 437, 482, 485–86, 490, 496, 538, 607, 713; APOSTOLIC **1:**47; **10:**389; **11:**411, 616; **12:**71, 329, 331, 335, 341, 485–86, 490; CHRISTIAN (*see under* CHRISTIAN); OF PAUL **1:**160; **3:**487, 571, 1181; **4:**978, 1079; **8:**14, 35, 40, 46–47; **9:**5–6; **10:**167, 189, 194–95, 198, 200–201, 205, 230–31, 238–40, 253, 256, 258, 283, 286, 321–22, 339, 361, 364, 367–68, 372, 374, 382, 537, 603, 619, 666, 668, 720, 758, 768, 775–76, 808, 810–11, 813, 815, 828, 840, 906, 910, 912, 973, 975, 977, 979–81; **11:**7, 16–17, 45, 55, 90, 108, 134, 144, 148–49, 168, 183, 193, 205–7, 210, 217, 222–23, 225, 227, 230, 234–35, 242, 248–51, 287–88, 291, 294–95, 302, 307, 310, 314–16, 346–47, 374–75, 410, 458, 469, 488–89, 614, 616, 618, 681, 877; **12:**155, 297

PRECIOUS STONES
See GEM; JEWELS AND PRECIOUS STONES

PREDESTINATION
4:1237; **5:**164, 284, 303, 752; **6:**134, 203–4, 580; **8:**315; **9:**717; **10:**196, 241, 602, 620, 677, 716; **11:**366, 373, 393, 410; **12:**266, 632

PRE-EXISTENCE
OF GOD'S LAW/WISDOM **10:**575, 663; OF THE SON/THE WORD **7:**571; **8:**41, 150, 275, 529; **9:**516, 518, 520, 523–24, 528–29, 646, 790, 796; **10:**663; **11:**283, 502–4, 507, 608, 808, 836; **12:**7, 12, 21–24, 29, 42, 61–62, 99, 155, 253, 382, 446, 515, 586, 657; OF SOULS **1:**18; **5:**511–12; **12:**53

PREFECT, PREFECTS
3:52; **8:**482, 712, 717–19

PRESBYTER
11:864, 867; **12:**449, 460

PRESENCE
BREAD OF THE *(see under* BREAD); OF GOD **1:**189, 199, 282–83, 318, 343, 367, 374, 376, 464, 475, 586, 612, 679, 685, 712, 802, 813, 835, 854, 861, 880, 882–84, 888–89, 892, 901–2, 905–7, 913–14, 925, 937, 942, 955, 961, 974, 976, 978–79, 981, 999–1000, 1005, 1024, 1035, 1066–67, 1070, 1075, 1097, 1101, 1103, 1106, 1111, 1179; **2:**14, 20, 25, 34, 38–39, 79–81, 83, 87–88, 90–91, 96, 107, 110, 125, 235–36, 338, 365, 386–87, 389, 796, 798, 980, 983, 987, 995, 1002–3, 1012, 1041, 1063, 1072, 1182, 1240, 1257, 1324; **3:**62, 71–72, 77–78, 144, 332, 344, 386, 396, 723, 949, 1018; **4:**299, 354, 360, 423, 445, 534, 573, 632, 668, 673, 787, 853, 866, 886, 970, 1015, 1055, 1075, 1119, 1141, 1144, 1212; **5:**50, 53, 92, 135, 158, 180, 316, 467, 484, 689; **6:**68, 84–85, 98, 104–5, 271–72, 457, 527, 531, 546, 586, 1058, 1119, 1567; **7:**13, 65, 150, 164, 246, 421, 481, 561, 678, 680, 682, 721, 723, 727, 762, 769, 771, 782, 784; **8:**250, 259, 271, 312, 327–28, 364, 376–77, 439, 476, 584, 588, 630, 632; **9:**51, 74–75, 113, 205–6, 329, 394, 434, 461, 482, 494, 505, 522, 545, 548, 552, 568, 576, 587, 613, 637, 661, 678, 680, 694, 699, 708, 712, 732, 743–44, 746, 749–50, 754, 764, 821, 824, 837, 853; **10:**18, 83, 110, 133, 192, 286, 358, 422, 474, 509, 513–14, 534, 546, 550, 575, 593, 604, 606, 616; **11:**58, 63, 189, 330, 512, 867; **12:**52–53, 69, 82, 91, 94, 96, 104, 106–7, 113, 145, 149, 158, 160, 294, 500, 523, 619, 630, 673, 678 (*see also* GOD, NAMES FOR/TITLES OF: DIVINE PRESENCE *in PERSONS IN THE BIBLE*)

PRESIDENT, PRESIDENTS
IN ANCIENT SOCIETIES **7:**88; **10:**310; MODERN POLITICIAN(S) **2:**595, 1013, 1065–66, 1073, 1114, 1186, 1208, 1214, 1227, 1251, 1290, 1346; **3:**110; **4:**981; **5:**155; **6:**745; **7:**117; **9:**387; **12:**414

PRESUMPTION
See PRIDE

PRETERIST INTERPRETATION
12:505, 544

PRIDE
1:157, 240, 366, 896, 906, 932, 1077, 1181; **2:**308, 359, 395, 414, 659, 838, 981, 1207, 1352; **3:**23, 198, 332, 402, 423, 514, 526, 546, 577, 591, 601, 630–31, 783, 836, 855, 890, 902, 912, 915, 956, 1058; **4:**43, 230, 369, 503, 530, 569–70, 581, 616, 623–24, 791, 869, 887, 913, 978, 1057, 1188, 1197, 1208; **5:**12, 21, 49, 91, 117, 121, 132, 139, 151, 161, 159, 170, 194, 211, 231, 253, 382, 564–65, 608, 617, 624, 626, 638, 642, 662–63, 674, 703, 705, 749, 814, 818, 842; **6:**73, 82, 94, 127, 133–34, 150, 157, 169, 189, 201–205, 218, 236, 414, 478, 550, 684–85, 892, 894, 896, 914, 918, 920, 980, 1104, 1166–67, 1217, 1237, 1269, 1274, 1339, 1343, 1356, 1361, 1383–84, 1386, 1389, 1395, 1400–1401, 1408, 1422, 1425, 1431–32, 1436, 1598; **7:**62, 66, 75–76, 112, 244–45, 257, 263, 362, 401, 416–17, 447–48, 451, 549, 609, 676, 691, 804–5, 808, 815, 817–18, 856; **8:**212, 227, 275, 428, 432, 516, 608; **9:**145, 152, 304, 341, 343, 385; **10:**211, 439, 480, 520, 554, 855; **11:**31, 51, 274–75, 295, 321, 332, 344, 348, 404,

524, 526, 530, 635, 806, 842; **12:**181, 211; OF AUTHORSHIP **5:**608, 624, 818; OF JACOB **4:**869; **7:**401, 416–17, 609, 856; OF PLACE **1:**168, 279, 305, 1132, 1157; **2:**18, 23, 49, 104, 106, 109, 232, 257, 285, 302, 309, 344–48, 362–63, 380, 386, 394, 399, 415–16, 437–43, 446, 451, 456, 485, 494, 496, 498, 522, 531, 547, 556, 574, 576, 591, 607–11, 616–19, 623–25, 645–48, 664, 671, 673, 678, 686–88, 691–93, 710, 712–13, 717–18, 721–22, 725, 727–28, 730–33, 735, 741–42, 745, 759, 768–70, 780, 787, 797, 801, 812, 815–17, 820, 824–26, 829–39, 842, 844, 846–47, 849–50, 994, 1113, 1134, 1154, 1187; **3:**100, 309, 382, 464, 506, 556, 608, 925; **4:**632; **5:**301, 620; **6:**1115; **9:**760, 863; **10:**840; **11:**48, 126

PRIEST, PRIESTS

1:65, 205, 211, 223, 265, 281–83, 289, 309, 316, 425, 541, 654, 682, 689, 723, 828, 834, 837, 880–81, 883–84, 897, 901, 905, 907–9, 912, 914, 918, 920, 935, 945, 954, 964, 985–87, 995, 1003, 1006, 1011–14, 1017–20, 1023–24, 1026, 1028, 1034, 1040, 1042–44, 1047–54, 1056–57, 1059–63, 1070–73, 1076, 1080–81, 1084, 1110–12, 1115, 1124, 1146–51, 1156, 1160, 1163, 1166, 1187, 1189, 1196; **2:**4, 12–13, 21, 25–26, 31, 37–38, 47–50, 52–54, 62, 64, 66, 69, 80–81, 83, 89, 92, 112, 134, 136–42, 147–51, 153, 193, 200, 220, 228–33, 236, 245, 247, 255, 263, 268, 281, 289, 297, 300, 324, 349, 366, 379, 387–88, 420, 423, 425, 427–29, 431–32, 436, 440, 469, 518, 520, 551, 569–71, 579–80, 589, 599–601, 608, 613, 687, 701–2, 729, 809, 834, 863, 867, 871, 887, 902, 966, 986–87, 987–88, 1006, 1010–12, 1139–41, 1145, 1148–49, 1152, 1156, 1193, 1237, 1268, 1324–25, 1332, 1346, 1354; **4:**6–8, 32, 39, 42, 51, 64, 71–72, 81, 93, 96, 99, 116, 122, 125, 143, 154, 163–65, 182, 184, 193, 197–98, 204, 243, 253, 257–58, 281, 289–90, 296–97, 737, 772, 781–82, 890, 1012, 1145, 1170, 1172, 1214, 1217, 1221; **5:**49, 72, 159, 213, 415, 612, 629, 638, 668, 670, 673, 695–96, 787, 793, 843, 859; **6:**5, 8, 67, 77, 102, 119, 120, 203–4, 235–39, 243–44, 272, 293, 338, 443, 453, 455–56, 514, 525–26, 546, 549, 556, 575, 577, 586, 599–600, 621–22, 646, 675, 694, 716, 721, 724, 750, 768, 773–75, 784–85, 826, 860, 913, 939–40, 942–43, 952, 990, 995, 998, 1000, 1002, 1004–5, 1008, 1043, 1063–64, 1106, 1110–11, 1168, 1177, 1183, 1206, 1228, 1254, 1257, 1260, 1284, 1306, 1314–15, 1392, 1491, 1527, 1532–34, 1544, 1547–48, 1557–58, 1564, 1568–70, 1574–82, 1584, 1588–93, 1597, 1604–5; **7:**25, 40, 52, 167–68, 188–90, 205, 232, 234, 239, 243–45, 252–53, 256–57, 260–61, 263, 272, 301, 304, 309, 311–14, 318, 320–21, 327, 417, 539, 541, 556, 559–60, 632, 674, 693–94, 727, 739, 761, 765–66, 788, 792, 800, 822, 834, 839, 843, 851, 853, 857, 859–62, 864, 869–70, 873; **8:**16, 22, 33–34, 99, 138, 140, 142–43, 151, 153, 162, 222, 278, 296, 332, 349, 353, 359, 371, 403, 405–6, 409–11, 413–15, 420, 431, 463–64, 467–70, 477, 480, 483–84, 491, 501, 505, 544–45, 652, 656–57, 663, 669, 673, 681, 695, 700, 712, 714, 719, 726; **9:**14, 45–46, 58, 74, 111, 120, 133, 201, 229, 281, 287, 326, 331, 351, 376–77, 380–83, 385, 388, 390, 393, 414–15, 422–23, 430, 435–36, 440, 442, 445–48, 451, 464, 469, 477–78, 505, 542, 696, 700, 801, 806, 816, 820, 823–24, 830, 865, 869; **10:**74, 83, 88, 114, 198, 312, 320, 325, 329–30, 336–37, 798; **11:**272, 301, 524–26, 631; **12:**60, 82, 84, 87, 89–90, 94, 97, 103–4, 107, 109, 115–17, 265, 405, 530, 539, 563, 602, 604, 707–8, 713, 724, 726; CHIEF **3:**230, 363, 556, 573; **5:**642; **6:**575, 627, 675, 694, 724, 860, 1079, 1491; **7:**715; **8:**138, 140, 142–43, 153, 406, 410–11, 413–14, 416, 420, 463–64, 467, 469–70, 477, 480, 483, 491, 501, 505, 652, 656–57, 663, 669, 673, 695, 700, 710, 712, 714, 726; **9:**14, 111, 201, 281, 331, 351, 376–77, 380–83, 385, 388, 390, 393, 414–15, 422–23, 430, 435–36, 440, 442, 445–48, 451, 464, 469, 477–78, 696, 700, 801, 816, 820, 823–24, 830; **10:**312, 329–30, 336–37; CODE **1:**282; **7:**859, 866; DAUGHTER OF A **1:**1148; **3:**687; **9:**45; **12:**682; AND ELDERS (*see under* ELDERS); GARMENTS OF **1:**906; **2:**1079; **3:**729; **6:**1228; HIGH **1:**270, 280, 285, 289, 908, 999, 1017, 1032–35, 1043, 1046–47, 1056–57, 1060, 1063, 1065–66, 1068, 1070, 1099, 1110–12, 1114–15, 1147–48, 1159, 1163, 1166, 1191; **2:**91, 152, 162–63, 191, 202, 219–20, 245, 265–66, 389, 567, 697, 988, 1268; **3:**33–34, 50, 280–81, 295, 344, 363, 422, 441, 469, 486, 590–91, 609, 666, 669, 685–86, 690, 692–93, 706, 716, 741, 768–70, 803, 825–26, 830, 832–35, 846, 849, 896, 1078, 1112–14, 1118, 1120, 1123, 1151, 1158, 1173, 1180; **4:**6–10, 21, 36, 52, 68, 72, 85, 93–97, 109, 112, 116–17, 119, 122, 125, 129, 140, 143, 151, 154–55, 160, 164–65, 168, 178, 182, 189–90, 197, 205–8, 211, 213–14, 216, 223, 229, 232, 258, 281, 285–87, 289–90, 348, 460, 1014, 1130; **5:**160, 593, 611–12, 641, 696, 836, 843, 856, 858–59; **6:**109, 414, 942–43, 1166–67, 1386, 1391–92, 1534, 1537, 1578; **7:**24–25, 113, 128, 136, 141–43, 671, 678, 703, 708, 715–16, 719, 737–39, 744, 763–67, 786, 788, 839, 873; **8:**23, 36–37, 66, 344, 351, 405, 420, 466, 477, 479–81, 526, 528,

PRIEST, PRIESTS *(continued)*
532, 696, 709, 711–14, 716, 718; **9:**80–81, 171, 366, 376, 388, 436, 438, 489, 675, 697–98, 705, 803, 806, 808, 810, 831; **10:**88, 104–6, 108–9, 268, 306, 309–10, 318–19, 719, 757; **11:**810; **12:**60, 62, 66, 79, 94, 104, 106–7, 112–13, 116, 120, 167, 490; HIGH PRIEST AS MEDIATOR **1:**1046–47, 1191; **6:**414; AND SACRAMENTS AS MEDIATORS **2:**141, 152, 229, 995

PRIESTHOOD
1:127, 211, 281, 285, 306, 314, 316, 440, 442, 682, 686, 716, 854, 888, 905–8, 912–14, 918, 926, 933, 973, 976, 986, 994, 997, 1001, 1004, 1021, 1047, 1049, 1056, 1060, 1063, 1071, 1076, 1082, 1115, 1124, 1144, 1147–48; **2:**10–11, 15, 21, 25, 47–50, 52–54, 66, 77–78, 81, 83, 94, 136, 138–41, 147–49, 197, 214, 229, 247, 281, 324, 376, 386, 403, 416–17, 427–28, 579, 687, 689, 702, 988, 1019, 1139, 1148, 1268; **3:**306, 344, 363, 415, 425, 437, 441, 456–57, 467, 522, 591, 664, 676, 686, 717, 731, 741, 757, 834, 836, 993, 1079, 1154; **4:**7–8, 22, 44, 51, 97, 122, 124, 135, 151, 160, 163–64, 185, 198, 214, 222, 228, 265, 286, 1212; **5:**7, 473, 612, 628–29, 842–43, 867; **6:**77, 205, 464, 586, 943, 1086, 1314, 1392, 1532, 1536, 1574, 1576, 1602; **7:**11, 62, 114, 136–37, 146, 213, 227–28, 235, 237, 239, 245, 252, 301, 411, 679, 761, 763, 765–67, 771, 846, 851, 859–63; **8:**34, 42, 359, 435; **9:**80, 697–98, 806; **10:**73, 133, 245, 759; **11:**132, 214, 364, 869; **12:**6, 17, 19, 30, 36, 41, 46, 60–61, 64, 67, 84–92, 97, 100, 114, 159, 166, 241, 265, 267–69, 312, 497, 726

PRIESTLY WRITER, WRITERS
(also known as P) **1:**282, 309–16, 340, 398, 592, 733, 736, 996, 1190; **2:**38, 40, 53, 59, 79, 82, 87, 121–22, 236, 528–29, 580, 606–7, 641, 684, 700–701; **3:**608, 716; **5:**314; **6:**366, 1090, 1146; HISTORY **2:**5, 7–11, 19, 32, 48–49, 51, 55, 87, 91, 94–97, 108, 128, 159, 165–66, 169–70, 180–81, 186, 207, 212, 219, 229, 232, 248, 250, 254–55, 267

PRINCE, PRINCES
1:222, 241, 249, 268, 274, 289, 438, 459, 503, 515, 700, 720, 1057; **2:**106, 135, 142, 179, 230, 521, 600, 617, 807, 982, 1071, 1136, 1164, 1168, 1205, 1222, 1226, 1234, 1250, 1279, 1303, 1306, 1309, 1315, 1319; **3:**17, 23, 39, 93, 126, 170, 184, 223, 457–58, 551, 570, 608, 681, 705, 899, 914, 925, 931, 1058, 1081, 1117, 1143–44; **4:**51, 163, 253, 281, 369, 538, 613, 981, 1139, 1169, 1263, 1265, 1276; **5:**4, 14, 38, 76, 215, 237, 243–44, 349, 420, 425, 604; **6:**8, 60, 76–78, 99, 112, 121–24, 180, 205, 265, 277, 330, 332, 343, 355, 400, 433, 444, 586, 733, 900, 943–44, 1061, 1070, 1103, 1168, 1174, 1194–95, 1232, 1245, 1266, 1268–69, 1271, 1273, 1292, 1299, 1301, 1303–04, 1306–08, 1314–15, 1358, 1367–68, 1371, 1379, 1384, 1386–89, 1391, 1417, 1427, 1438, 1444–45, 1463, 1469–70, 1507, 1509, 1512, 1516, 1528, 1570, 1582–84, 1586, 1588–90, 1593, 1601, 1604–5; **7:**9, 94, 107, 113, 117, 138, 142, 151, 232, 247–48, 260–61, 417, 678, 731, 776, 828–29; **8:**285, 428; **9:**177, 241, 424, 775; **11:**390, 436, 459–61; **12:**61, 516, 538

PRINCESS, PRINCESSES
1:459, 700–701; **2:**1305–1306; **3:**37, 40–41, 124, 128, 139, 214, 221, 227–28, 234, 328, 573, 863, 979, 1008; **4:**168, 352, 860; **5:**13; **6:**1020, 1029, 1228; **9:**52; **12:**30

PRINCIPALITY, PRINCIPALITIES
2:289, 862, 1115; **3:**563; **4:**1007; **10:**427, 524, 589, 615, 617, 720, 739; **11:**282, 288, 565, 623, 626–27; **12:**31, 40, 112, 293, 548, 716

PRISON, PRISONS
1:18, 84, 191, 609–11, 614–15, 620, 628, 1042; **2:**265, 858, 861, 1114; **3:**12, 287, 294, 543, 887; **4:**674, 1247; **5:**51, 121, 136, 291, 316, 337, 525, 584, 586; **6:**364, 369–70, 449, 819, 825, 849, 925–26, 944, 994, 1023, 1081, 1452; **7:**5–6, 41, 89–92, 95, 144, 160–61, 169, 267, 527, 632, 801; **8:**64, 166, 266, 270, 382; **9:**113, 160, 268–69, 271, 398, 400–401, 428, 439; **10:**65, 74, 84, 104, 108, 131, 146, 175, 179–80, 208, 218, 230, 233–34, 289–90, 311, 322–23, 370, 694, 717–18, 757, 762; **11:**85, 157, 275, 284–85, 355, 411–12, 416, 417–18, 424, 438, 462, 469, 473–74, 476, 484–86, 488–89, 495, 519–21, 542, 547, 623, 857, 887, 892, 902; **12:**107, 125, 144, 163, 173, 293–94, 297, 420, 434, 539, 577, 702, 714; GATE **8:**230

PRISONER, PRISONERS
1:186, 557, 614, 616, 1148, 1172; **2:**349, 405, 446, 454, 879, 1192; **3:**152, 379, 597–98, 600, 998; **4:**104, 151, 156, 264, 388, 416, 430, 700, 947, 996, 1087, 1118, 1264–65; **5:**790; **6:**128, 159, 182, 195, 243, 284, 294, 378, 391, 430, 449, 503, 930, 944, 974, 985, 996, 1052, 1156; **7:**6, 30, 40, 51, 75, 82, 89–91, 95, 168, 377, 502, 809–11; **8:**486, 488, 719, 723, 726; **9:**113, 318, 448–49, 458; **10:**105, 180, 230, 233–34, 291, 308–9, 314, 324, 329–30, 345–46, 351, 353–54, 356–57, 359–60, 366, 368, 571; **11:**9, 268, 279, 367, 406–7, 411–12, 418, 420, 424, 458–59, 462–63, 473, 479, 520, 666–68, 835, 837, 847, 856, 891–92, 903; **12:**163, 646

PRIZE
10:909–10; **11:**533, 537

PROCONSUL
8:23; **10:**190, 252, 255, 776; **11:**403, 681; **12:**565
PROCURATOR, PROCURATORS
3:994; **9:**80, 85, 814–15, 819–20; **10:**309, 313, 317, 323–26, 328
PRODIGAL
CHILDREN **1:**1026; **2:**1316–17, 1342; **3:**500, 531, 571, 600, 731; **5:**75, 239; **6:**1452; **7:**525; **8:**60–61; **9:**12, 23, 36, 298, 300, 302–3, 305–7, 316, 318–19, 337, 425; **10:**50, 698; **11:**809; SON **1:**1026; **2:**1316–17, 1342; **3:**600–601; **5:**75, 239; **6:**1452; **7:**525; **8:**60–61; **9:**12, 300–305, 425; **10:**50, 698; **11:**809
PROFANE (*OR* PROFANES, *ETC.*)
1:54, 282, 285, 685, 836–37, 839, 861, 885, 914–15, 917, 923, 954–55, 964, 977, 979–80, 985, 987–89, 999–1000, 1071, 1126–27, 1133, 1138–39, 1147–49, 1152; **2:**15, 25, 32, 34, 38–40, 49, 59, 65, 82, 126, 151, 235–36, 268, 383, 388, 396–97, 834, 1086, 1139–40, 1141; **3:**156, 574, 850, 1112; **4:**3, 9, 11, 38–40, 106, 116, 183, 208, 228, 934; **5:**9, 118, 431; **6:**4, 386, 400, 411, 413, 486, 1203, 1278–81, 1290, 1309, 1311, 1315, 1329, 1339, 1343, 1349, 1351, 1363, 1389, 1394, 1487, 1489–92, 1495, 1523, 1559, 1575, 1578–79, 1605; **7:**143, 272, 400, 665, 728, 836, 839, 864; **8:**212, 277, 405, 689; **10:**46, 143, 163, 165, 171, 206, 319–20, 339; **11:**317, 659, 688, 791, 813, 830, 841, 844; **12:**9, 123, 127, 154, 222, 353, 570, 724, 726
PROLEPSIS
8:492–93
PROMISE (*OR* PROMISES, *ETC.*)
1:283, 316; **2:**1370; **3:**568, 576, 612, 752; **6:**502, 812; **10:**471; **11:**64, 199, 262–64, 276; FULFILLMENT OF **1:**13, 160, 165–66, 239, 306–8, 317–18, 404–5, 418–20, 423–24, 426, 430, 436, 445–49, 453, 458, 467, 486, 488, 500, 515, 524, 530, 567, 581, 659, 731; **2:**180–81, 215, 221, 234, 249–50, 262, 467, 482, 510, 580, 648, 706, 1261; **3:**24, 33, 35–36, 234, 381, 406, 408, 474, 498, 576, 617, 636, 671, 677, 810; **4:**964, 1179, 1212–13, 1256; **6:**140, 327, 336, 339, 356, 358–59, 363, 424, 441, 443, 457, 463, 465, 470–71, 505, 509, 515, 521, 544, 547–48, 551, 958, 1282, 1411, 1447, 1454, 1471, 1531, 1569; **7:**324–25, 328, 330, 643, 663, 762, 767; **8:**29, 36, 63, 67, 131–33, 135, 144, 271, 356, 473, 529, 538; **9:**41, 55–56, 59, 69–71, 106–8, 110, 160–61, 167, 200, 203, 352, 401, 420, 426, 445, 459, 478, 486, 488, 568, 585, 608, 648, 671–72, 688, 699, 707, 710, 716, 748, 793, 803, 841, 843, 846, 848, 855, 857–58, 861; **10:**41–42, 46, 57, 81–82, 83, 125–27, 132, 196, 255, 339–40, 361, 372, 398, 405, 411, 413, 464–65, 471, 505, 525, 624, 629, 632, 634–35, 649, 654–55, 672, 756, 994; **11:**28, 94–95, 264, 268–69, 273, 276, 304, 324, 357, 374, 862; **12:**77, 138, 297, 336–37, 356, 411, 428, 534, 646. *See also* COVENANT
PROMISED LAND
1:164–65, 175, 210, 306, 315, 433–35, 439, 441, 503, 518, 530, 565–67, 577, 583, 585–86, 601, 611, 713; **2:**4, 16, 18–20, 34, 61, 70, 92, 94, 97, 99–100, 106, 120–22, 124–25, 127, 130, 136, 141, 152, 159, 161–63, 167, 169, 198, 202, 214–15, 218, 246, 249–50, 255–56, 262–63, 267–68, 272, 275, 294, 306, 310, 319, 356, 367, 510, 528, 535, 555, 564, 589, 606, 619, 706, 727, 731, 739, 747, 752, 756–57, 759, 826, 830, 853, 865, 899, 919; **3:**35, 127, 155, 177, 265, 277, 306, 313, 332, 386, 408, 424, 463, 468, 560, 659, 730, 811, 1119, 1171–72; **4:**36, 50–51, 55, 57, 78, 81, 157, 198, 200, 748, 1041, 1111, 1141, 1181; **5:**542, 560; **6:**157, 174, 335, 378, 424, 442–43, 453, 456, 467, 476, 529, 813, 852, 957, 1190, 1504; **7:**346, 348, 395, 401, 417, 431, 438, 456, 553, 579, 582, 660, 663, 683, 699; **8:**150, 178–79, 323, 325; **9:**278, 738; **10:**97, 125, 457, 471, 496, 511, 517, 534, 585, 608; **11:**276, 593; **12:**49, 258, 264, 267
PROPHECY, PROPHECIES
1:10, 13, 42–45, 56, 69, 75–76, 86–88, 90–92, 95, 98, 118, 127–28, 193, 228, 234, 237, 283, 289, 317–18, 380, 601, 667, 1035, 1181; **2:**8, 106–7, 110, 112, 189, 214, 272, 275, 316, 365, 392, 429–31, 503–4, 514, 535, 551, 571, 687–88, 1165, 1184, 1186, 1331; **3:**9–10, 18, 98, 102, 106, 109, 112–13, 120, 152, 160, 162, 167, 173, 183, 203, 208–10, 215, 217, 220–21, 223, 237, 280, 282, 284, 286, 303, 364, 379, 432, 446–47, 512, 515–16, 520, 538, 552, 561, 586, 598, 635, 645, 668, 676–77, 693, 728, 915, 1078, 1119–20, 1123–24, 1155; **4:**63, 88, 149, 189, 315, 1203; **5:**96, 160, 244, 381, 621, 647, 655, 700, 758, 793, 800, 813–14; **6:**6, 8, 10, 19, 22–23; **7:**2–5, 9, 55, 63, 84, 88, 121, 128, 147, 162, 193; **8:**23–24, 29–30, 32, 37–39, 50, 146, 153, 156, 177, 217, 246, 268, 286, 310, 333, 356, 403, 437, 477–78, 481, 512, 515–16, 526, 530, 535, 619, 625, 631, 654, 659, 663, 665, 681, 684–93, 714; **9:**9, 15, 42, 59, 73, 85, 87, 351, 359, 382, 401–3, 410, 440, 446, 514, 543, 621, 634–35, 698, 708, 710, 717, 720, 731, 733, 737, 773, 783, 808, 820, 851; **10:**11–14, 16, 20, 22–25, 35, 37–38, 40–42, 46, 49, 51–55, 57, 59–60, 62, 64–66, 68–69, 71–72, 77, 81, 83, 89–90, 92, 99, 121, 128, 131, 134–35, 142–47,

PROPHECY, PROPHECIES *(continued)*
150, 152–53, 165–67, 169–70, 175, 177, 181, 189, 190–98, 200–201, 203–4, 207–10, 213, 217–19, 221, 226, 230, 232–34, 240–41, 252, 254–55, 261–63, 269, 273, 276, 282–84, 288–89, 297–98, 307–12, 330, 334, 338, 340–41, 346, 351–53, 359–64, 367–68, 415–16, 447–48, 450, 605, 624, 666–67, 669, 673, 692–93, 710–11, 769, 949, 954, 958–60, 962, 967, 969, 972; **11:**63–64, 259, 304, 309, 335, 422, 430, 730, 732, 755, 795, 814; **12:**28, 30, 101, 139, 253, 255, 260–61, 267, 307, 325–30, 332, 340, 342–44, 347, 355–56, 360; OF DOOM **2:**430; **3:**113, 284; **6:**1199; **7:**563; ESCHATOLOGICAL **3:**586, 668; **4:**1203; **6:**32, 43, 66–67, 175, 206–7, 225, 227–28, 230, 273–74, 320; **7:**2, 5, 63, 454, 830, 852; **8:**37–39, 50, 153, 156, 268, 403, 512; **9:**87, 783; **10:**24–25, 64, 144, 196, 209, 219; **11:**259; **12:**325, 329, 347, 497, 505, 513, 528, 538–39, 543–44, 548, 566, 599, 625, 646, 684, 701, 732; FALSE **2:**381, 430; **3:**164; **6:**9, 48, 570, 585, 694, 743, 752, 755, 773, 777, 782, 785, 792, 805, 1102, 1191, 1210, 1411; **7:**833–34; **8:**217, 690; **11:**812, 815; **12:**343–44, 427, 531, 588, 650, 658; OF JUDGMENT **6:**42, 45, 59, 67, 81, 83, 159, 174, 236, 253, 273, 276, 635, 694, 1355; **12:**477; MESSIANIC **1:**13, 87, 193; **6:**46, 143, 265; **7:**428–29, 538, 568; **8:**146, 153, 310, 481, 514, 631, 663, 681, 714; **9:**85; **10:**20, 59, 62–63, 77, 89, 193, 195, 219, 240, 254, 262, 333–34, 340, 341, 361–62, 416, 450, 748; **11:**259; OF PEACE **3:**167, 282, 432; **6:**46, 65–66, 144, 147, 694, 750, 752, 782, 784–85, 792, 1210; **7:**55, 429, 533; **8:**659; OF SALVATION **6:**42, 45, 67, 83, 174, 248, 252, 271, 1461; **8:**62, 530; **10:**66

PROPHET, PROPHETS
OF BAAL **1:**1067; **2:**797; **3:**135–36, 139, 162, 184; **6:**9; **10:**676, 214; FALSE **1:**42; **2:**392, 538, 872, 1093; **3:**108–9, 164, 755, 785, 842, 1123; **6:**48–49, 490, 563, 582, 613, 694, 698, 702, 709, 716, 731, 750–55, 774, 778, 782–83, 785, 791, 793–94, 826–27, 838, 854, 952, 1102, 1199, 1201–2, 1208, 1210; **7:**373, 410, 528, 539, 544, 551, 586, 831; **8:**51, 121, 216–17, 246, 410, 442, 514–15, 526, 529, 663, 683, 687, 689–90, 692; **9:**144, 151, 153, 282, 399–400, 402, 404, 407–8, 410, 460; **10:**190, 201, 284; **11:**423; **12:**329, 342–45, 373, 403, 425, 427, 489, 491, 496, 533, 573, 575, 581, 609, 626, 650, 658, 677, 687, 697, 699–700, 702–3, 714–15, 724, 733, 735; FORMER **2:**274–75, 291–92, 520, 893, 952; **3:**4, 469, 512, 651; **5:**634; **6:**2; **7:**735–36, 746–47, 790, 793–94, 796–98; **8:**185; OF ISRAEL **6:**4–9; LATTER **1:**303, 305, 1034; **5:**281; **7:**212; **8:**28–29, 186; MINOR **1:**8, 65, 95, 294, 300, 1178, 1194, 1196; **5:**555; **6:**18, 20; **7:**212, 303, 435, 493, 533, 735, 743, 848–49; **8:**29; SONS OF **3:**152; **6:**3; **8:**359; TRUE **1:**283; **2:**381, 392, 420, 430, 538; **3:**164, 167; **5:**793; **6:**49, 582, 752–54, 773, 786, 805, 838, 1204, 1208, 1210, 1218, 1249, 1412; **7:**458, 538, 544, 554, 560, 585–86; **8:**116, 270, 318–19, 348, 410, 436, 685; **9:**163; **10:**190, 201; **12:**343, 345, 575, 581, 646

PROPHETESS, PROPHETESSES
2:1016; **3:**282, 294; **5:**81; **6:**116–17; **7:**679; **8:**24; **12:**573

PROPHETIC
CALL NARRATIVE **1:**692; **2:**991–92, 1036–37, 1040–41; **6:**4, 12–13, 19, 319, 330–31, 420, 573–74, 579, 587, 596, 878, 1121; **7:**138, 204, 219; **10:**15, 109; **11:**190, 215 (*see also under* CALL); LAWSUIT (*see under* LAWSUIT); LITERATURE (*see under* LITERATURE); ORACLE (*see under* ORACLE)

PROPITIATION
1:1010, 1025, 1066, 1111–12; **2:**718; **3:**609, 612; **8:**34; **10:**476; **12:**42, 388

PROSELYTE (*OR* PROSELYTIZE, *ETC.*)
1:301, 1120, 1164, 1173; **2:**908; **3:**618, 713; **4:**1145; **6:**454; **7:**528; **8:**42, 157, 213, 435; **9:**81, 710; **10:**25, 56, 113, 142–43, 145, 162, 194–96, 205, 207, 219, 233, 292, 413, 440, 460, 490, 513, 550, 552, 558, 655; **11:**186, 228, 249, 364, 525 26, 865; **12:**199

PROSTITUTE (*OR* PROSTITUTES, PROSTITUTION, *ETC.*)
1:605–7, 896, 1075, 1118, 1131, 1135, 1139, 1148; **2:**211, 246, 334, 462, 589–90, 592–96, 619, 631, 729, 764, 808, 810, 824–25, 827, 836, 840–41, 854–55, 860, 875, 930, 943, 1100; **3:**42–43, 46, 118, 167–68, 569, 1089, 1159; **4:**11, 232, 548, 586, 1111, 1131; **5:**11, 70–71, 80, 84–85, 101, 207, 242, 386, 397, 412, 481, 700, 759, 765, 828; **6:**183, 203, 205, 601–4, 615, 620, 685, 990, 995, 1002–3, 1160, 1203, 1222–24, 1230, 1232–33, 1242, 1316, 1319, 1321, 1325, 1327, 1329–30, 1362, 1579; **7:**5, 200, 202–3, 209, 215–16, 224, 226, 231, 241, 245, 261, 265, 365, 544, 598, 612, 614–15, 620; **8:**412; **9:**303, 840; **10:**220, 816, 858, 862–63, 865–66, 922; **11:**88, 105, 435, 452, 642; **12:**142, 405, 579, 682

PROTESTANT (*OR* PROTESTANTISM, *ETC.*)
1:8, 12, 16, 23, 34, 52–55, 100, 201, 209, 883, 920; **2:**587; **5:**407, 448; **8:**202, 347; **9:**832; **10:**485, 671; **11:**339; **12:**457; CHURCH (*see under* CHURCH); REFORMATION **1:**33, 51–55, 99–100, 103, 108, 202–3, 205, 207; **2:**702; **4:**867; **7:**717; **8:**30; **10:**485; **12:**149, 537

PROVERB, PROVERBS
1:220, 232, 237, 239–40, 991; **2:**125, 186, 1128; **3:**148, 266, 386, 761, 777, 1017, 1056; **4:**377, 379, 386, 402–4, 419, 421, 454, 462, 477, 485, 553, 575, 630, 876; **5:**2–3, 7–8, 20, 23, 25–26, 28–29, 32, 55, 63, 70–71, 111–12, 114, 143, 162, 175, 217, 229, 232, 252, 295–96, 300, 312, 316, 322, 326, 340, 345, 351, 613, 641, 674, 689, 701, 714–15, 752, 760, 767–68, 777, 813, 861; **6:**57, 69, 647, 708, 811, 1103, 1197–99, 1219–20, 1236, 1240, 1254–55, 1257–58, 1262, 1265, 1334, 1395, 1411, 1463, 1501; **7:**468, 615, 672; **8:**31–32, 235, 298, 552–53, 571, 575–76, 592, 638, 640, 693; **9:**107, 128, 150, 165–67, 181, 230, 276, 333, 362, 569–70, 574, 667–68, 781; **10:**837; **11:**315, 335, 337, 768; **12:**56, 74, 179, 315–16, 352–53

PROVERBS, BOOK OF
1:8, 9, 11, 28, 31, 43, 65, 72, 76, 239–40, 1196; **2:**351, 462, 476, 1367; **3:**396, 474, 870; **4:**172, 210, 303, 326, 377, 380–81, 412, 429, 469, 485, 502, 531, 552, 683, 813, 828; **5:**1–2, 4–5, 10–13, 15, 272–74, 276, 278, 281, 286, 406, 422, 430, 454, 496, 498, 502–3, 509, 517, 603–6, 608–10, 613–14, 620, 625, 636, 644, 646, 648, 650–51, 658, 664, 674, 688, 692, 708, 745, 752, 758, 765, 768, 774, 783, 800, 813, 849, 862; **6:**18, 190, 962, 966; **7:**468, 647; **8:**29; **9:**286, 505, 667; **10:**661, 715; **11:**597, 780; **12:**203, 315–16, 587

PROVIDENCE
1:18, 75, 85, 98, 196, 318, 510, 601, 647, 661, 699, 701, 734, 814–15, 852, 1179; **2:**18, 21, 82, 99–100, 105, 107, 111, 128, 165, 194, 320, 355–57, 374, 479, 481, 484, 512, 519, 527, 775, 922, 952, 955, 958, 961, 963, 965, 973, 980–81, 1078–79, 1104, 1119, 1135, 1154, 1158, 1170–71, 1174–76, 1298, 1324, 1326–27, 1333, 1341, 1366, 1383; **3:**144–45, 301, 332, 388–89, 396, 423, 426, 468, 474, 523, 525, 536, 539, 542, 552–54, 569–70, 575, 579, 585–88, 598, 628–30, 636–37, 643, 655, 680, 718, 723, 727–28, 730, 809–11, 844, 868, 873, 905–6, 913, 915, 978, 985, 989, 1024, 1050, 1055, 1158; **4:**183, 257, 414, 442, 560, 590, 597, 770, 828, 920, 959–60, 1097–98, 1180, 1224; **5:**114, 141, 281, 295, 305–7, 351, 446, 470, 479, 505, 516, 525–26, 528, 536, 552–54, 561, 577, 591, 610, 624, 639, 702, 754, 784, 786, 788; **6:**346, 359, 366, 381, 462, 465, 468, 521, 527, 597, 607, 614, 646, 860, 1206; **8:**211, 214, 578, 666; **9:**21, 112, 171, 197, 201, 252, 254, 259–61, 327, 339, 400, 421, 429, 434, 478, 486, 773; **10:**38, 49, 57, 66, 92, 99, 104, 108, 124, 192, 201, 244, 247, 252, 283, 318, 327, 350, 352, 355, 475, 600, 758; **11:**374, 377, 466, 900; **12:**48, 50, 55, 117, 266, 290, 310, 312–13, 326, 342, 355, 375, 541, 594, 630, 657

PROVINCE, PROVINCES
1:9, 244, 250, 263–65, 267–68, 270–71, 277, 284, 314; **2:**575, 586, 701; **3:**253, 313, 320, 337, 347, 379, 409, 505, 636, 654, 667–69, 685, 691, 699, 721–22, 732, 734, 742, 747, 765, 770, 773, 781–82, 785, 793, 825, 827, 830, 850, 856, 858, 861, 878, 899, 925, 927, 931–32, 935, 939, 953, 966, 1099, 1112–13, 1131; **4:**20, 60, 63, 95, 104, 107, 135, 140, 143, 157, 206, 249; **5:**93, 370; **6:**8, 556, 573, 851, 1076, 1250, 1269, 1360–61, 1380; **7:**66, 111, 709, 738, 760, 765, 779, 822, 826, 853; **8:**16, 25, 420, 515, 712, 717, 719; **9:**52, 67; **10:**13, 59, 105, 147, 197, 325, 755, 774–45, 996, 1001; **11:**12, 16, 38, 42, 108, 114–16, 135, 191–92, 202, 401, 488, 674, 695, 838, 884; **12:**76, 125, 247, 571

PRUDENCE
1:578, 758, 961; **2:**681, 1136; **5:**43, 54, 66, 285, 305, 307, 348, 510; **6:**788, 691, 963, 966, 698; **8:**198; **9:**255; **10:**108; **11:**779, 864; **12:**259, 285, 288. *See also* DISCRETION

PRUNING HOOK, HOOKS
1:1171; **2:**759; **4:**119; **6:**23, 68–70; **7:**332, 612

PSALM HEADINGS/TITLES
1:1018; **2:**1206; **3:**328, 400–401, 415, 446, 561; **4:**657, 938, 1061, 1176, 1182, 1259, 1268; **5:**32; **6:**650. *See also* SUPERSCRIPTIONS

PSALMODY
2:385; **3:**1178; **4:**519, 650, 655; **7:**601; **12:**726

PSALMS, BOOK OF
1:8, 11, 17, 28–31, 43, 45, 65, 70, 72, 74, 76, 78–79, 94–95, 100, 188, 201, 205–6, 208, 212, 234, 239, 294, 302, 1196; **2:**66, 211, 893; **3:**299, 346, 400, 540, 562, 840, 1057, 1178; **4:**303, 345, 380–81, 461, 469, 554, 622; **5:**2, 20, 33, 62, 159, 234, 273, 459, 606, 634, 834; **6:**22, 168, 190, 469, 477, 555, 676, 1019, 1430, 1501; **7:**6, 187, 250, 625; **8:**28–29, 33, 36, 130, 151, 178–79, 703; **9:**98, 105, 391, 486; **10:**744; **11:**524, 602

PSALTER
1:28, 75, 97, 205, 212, 239, 644; **2:**980, 1263, 1365; **3:**390, 446, 498, 512, 560, 610, 692; **4:**642–44, 647, 649–50, 655–59, 661–72, 675–77, 683–88, 690, 693–94, 700, 710, 736, 746–47, 753, 755, 765, 769, 778, 781, 783, 793, 800, 802, 805, 809, 811, 821, 823, 842, 843, 847, 856, 861, 868–69, 881, 884–85, 887, 893–94, 901, 905, 912, 914, 918, 924, 926, 931, 934, 945, 947, 960, 963–65, 967–68, 974, 976, 978, 984–85, 1011, 1013, 1023–24, 1034, 1036–37, 1040–41, 1047, 1051, 1053, 1055,

PSALTER *(continued)*
1062, 1067–69, 1073–74, 1078, 1091, 1096, 1099–1100, 1104, 1111–12, 1116–18, 1122, 1124–27, 1130–31, 1134, 1167, 1178, 1181, 1184, 1192–93, 1203, 1205, 1211, 1219, 1223, 1227, 1232, 1238, 1241, 1247, 1252, 1254–56, 1258, 1261–64, 1267, 1270–72, 1274, 1278–80; **5:**143, 800; **6:**147, 212, 216, 270, 300, 377, 396, 436, 525–26, 666, 697, 1279; **7:**347, 382, 585, 624, 627, 679; **9:**542, 834; **10:**66, 130, 193, 227, 748; **12:**29

PSALTERY
See MUSICAL INSTRUMENTS

PSEUDEPIGRAPHA
1:10, 18, 231; **2:**1387; **3:**1192–93; **4:**1286; **5:**874; **6:**223, 936, 990; **7:**16; **8:**744; **11:**582. *See also by individual title in* ANCIENT LITERATURE

PSEUDONYMOUS
1:70; **3:**1023; **5:**625; **6:**324, 933; **7:**2–3, 197; **10:**391; **11:**351, 366, 577, 580, 582–84, 587, 613, 661, 664, 668, 683, 686, 776, 779–81; **12:**183, 186, 232–24, 323–24, 328, 473–75, 519, 521, 546

PUBLICAN, PUBLICANS
8:107, 324, 391, 393; **9:**370

PULPIT, PULPITS
1:2, 159–60, 164, 190–91, 195; **5:**434; **6:**694, 1240, 1412; **7:**561; **9:**221; **11:**721, 756; **12:**78, 83, 118, 170, 207, 420, 456, 482

PULSE, PULSES
1:399; **7:**40

PUNISHMENT, PUNISHMENTS
1:48, 68, 72, 240, 336, 369, 374, 412–13, 469, 475, 477, 629–30, 665, 739, 754, 842, 863–64, 867–68, 873, 923, 934, 948, 986, 1027, 1100, 1105, 1124, 1137–38, 1144, 1148, 1165, 1180, 1189; **2:**64, 104, 106, 108, 125–26, 128, 130, 139, 160, 163–64, 197, 199–201, 211, 250, 265, 286, 300, 306, 309, 319, 328, 332–33, 335, 339, 345–46, 352, 355, 359, 370, 379–80, 392–93, 394, 421–22, 434–37, 447–48, 455–56, 469–71, 475, 490, 492, 500, 503, 505, 511, 520, 527–28, 546, 602, 613, 626–28, 630–33, 666, 706, 726–27, 729, 731, 737, 741, 749, 754, 757–58, 773, 780, 790, 824, 827, 851, 853–54, 885, 900, 1017, 1055, 1071–72, 1087, 1090, 1114, 1160, 1293, 1298, 1310, 1341, 1358; **3:**95–96, 109, 112–13, 152–53, 178, 208, 277, 289, 313, 358, 370, 407, 421–24, 426, 497, 500, 525, 536, 538, 542, 551–52, 568–69, 582, 586–87, 588, 592, 598, 602, 607, 618, 630, 635–36, 654–55, 657, 699, 710, 722, 737, 738, 742, 773, 804, 810, 812–14, 849, 892, 932, 995, 997, 1003, 1063, 1071, 1102, 1113, 1137–38, 1172, 1177, 1179; **4:**31, 40, 63, 82, 113, 150, 154, 165, 182, 185, 210, 218, 228, 233–34, 241–43, 248, 250, 254, 256, 277, 281, 297, 334, 367–68, 376–77, 397, 404, 420, 429, 439, 452, 458, 460, 462–64, 483, 485–86, 491–93, 495, 500, 503, 512, 525, 553–54, 557, 571, 577, 591–93, 604, 607–8, 610, 612, 630, 671, 684–86, 721, 742, 752, 820–21, 833, 835, 837–39, 847–48, 856, 891, 898, 938, 952, 954, 959, 970, 990–91, 995, 997, 1029, 1036, 1042, 1059, 1088, 1126–27, 1154, 1170–71, 1201, 1228, 1244, 1260; **5:**12, 59, 69, 111–12, 122, 135–36, 167, 173, 175, 180, 182, 186–87, 194, 198–99, 207, 220, 224, 244, 254, 277, 280, 305, 330, 339, 430, 445, 446, 455, 469–71, 476, 486–87, 498, 525, 528–29, 531–35, 540–44, 549, 559–60, 562, 565, 567, 570, 573–75, 577–78, 580, 583–86, 590–94, 596, 598, 609, 627, 656, 677–78, 692–93, 716, 724–25, 750, 752, 777, 779, 798, 807–8, 825; **6:**7, 17, 21, 39–40, 47, 54, 56–64, 69, 72, 77–78, 81–82, 88–89, 92–93, 95, 97–98, 104, 116–17, 127–29, 132–33, 136–37, 149–50, 156–57, 174, 180, 195, 207, 210, 213, 216–17, 222–23, 226–27, 236–37, 243–44, 253–58, 265–66, 270, 294, 297, 300, 317, 334, 371, 380, 391, 411, 413, 418, 420, 436–37, 439–40, 450–51, 454, 462, 467, 490, 492, 527, 530, 532, 543–44, 548–50, 564, 566, 585, 602, 606, 608–9, 614, 619–20, 647, 664–65, 675, 677, 686, 691, 694, 699, 717, 722–23, 733, 740, 743, 750, 758–59, 766, 768, 778, 784, 786, 791, 792–93, 795, 805, 807–8, 810, 822, 826, 831, 854, 860, 865, 872, 874, 891–92, 894, 911–13, 925, 939–40, 946, 948–50, 952–53, 955–56, 958, 974, 978, 980, 982, 1033, 1052, 1062, 1066, 1069, 1080, 1085, 1102, 1104–5, 1117, 1123, 1130, 1139–41, 1145–47, 1149–50, 1152–53, 1155–59, 1165–66, 1168, 1170–71, 1188, 1194, 1199, 1202, 1207, 1209–11, 1213–15, 1217, 1221, 1234, 1238, 1241, 1251, 1253–54, 1258, 1264–65, 1275, 1281, 1283, 1291–92, 1300, 1302–3, 1305–6, 1308, 1311–12, 1317, 1320–22, 1324, 1327, 1331, 1335, 1343, 1346, 1348–53, 1355–58, 1363–64, 1366, 1369, 1382, 1384, 1386, 1388–89, 1391, 1394, 1396–97, 1399–1401, 1406–9, 1417–18, 1420–21, 1425–27, 1431–32, 1436–37, 1445–46, 1450, 1458, 1461, 1464, 1466, 1472, 1474, 1476–78, 1480–83, 1487, 1493–96, 1503, 1512, 1518, 1521–23, 1574–77, 1598, 1609; **7:**5–6, 11–15, 30, 42, 51, 62–63, 67, 75, 81, 89–90, 93–95, 115–16, 122, 125, 142, 144, 148, 180, 184, 190, 192, 194, 207–11, 219, 224–25, 227, 229, 234, 244, 247, 262–63, 266, 275, 281, 283, 286, 293–94, 333, 353–55, 357, 363, 365, 368–69, 382–83, 391, 441, 446–47, 449, 454,

484, 486, 516, 528, 536, 541, 544–45, 548–55, 557–61, 563–64, 569, 574–78, 580–85, 589, 597, 631–32, 635–36, 639–40, 663–64, 671, 677–78, 680, 692, 696, 718, 741, 752, 755–56, 766, 778, 839, 875; **8:**16, 30–31, 34, 36, 62, 134, 190, 258, 346, 406, 438, 448, 453, 482, 487, 627, 640, 653, 684, 688; **9:**45, 123, 126, 263, 264–65, 314, 337, 363–64, 393, 405, 446, 448, 451, 628, 646, 819; **10:**308, 310, 337, 356, 399, 429, 431, 433–34, 473, 475–76, 575, 579, 639, 646, 652–53, 714–15, 718, 723, 813; **11:**6, 22, 53–54, 87, 157, 214, 258, 260, 393, 420, 437, 453–54, 456, 462, 509, 621, 749, 763, 802, 823; **12:**9, 34, 74, 76, 123–24, 126, 151, 159, 277–78, 283, 291, 306, 311, 326, 347–48, 401, 432, 488, 491–92, 497. *See also* CAPITAL: EXECUTION/PUNISHMENT; ETERNAL PUNISHMENT

PURIFY, PURIFIES
1:278, 580, 976, 1100, 1111; **2:**15, 81, 99, 150–51; **3:**178, 430, 846, 1180; **4:**277; **6:**47, 55, 60, 104, 454, 1487, 1509, 1526, 1546, 1578; **8:**33, 36, 158; **9:**46, 97; **10:**112, 122, 219; **12:**112, 212, 247, 252, 255, 259

PURIFICATION
1:9, 281, 584, 920, 986, 996, 999, 1033, 1045, 1060, 1084–85, 1099–1100, 1105, 1113; **2:**47, 61, 65, 78, 80–82, 99, 108, 127, 151–52, 219, 245, 247–48, 255, 440, 570, 607, 760; **3:**389, 609, 612, 713, 837–38, 842, 848, 1002, 1142, 1158, 1189; **4:**3, 19, 62, 69, 71, 85, 122, 184–85, 191, 196, 198, 213, 242, 249–50, 253, 256–57, 277, 281, 288, 290, 1046; **5:**381, 469, 471, 496, 536, 809; **6:**56, 58, 83–85, 102–4, 455, 544, 547–48, 606, 1107, 1526, 1534, 1546, 1558, 1565, 1568–69, 1579–80, 1584–86, 1591; **7:**673, 678, 699, 727–28, 744, 765, 824–25, 868–69; **8:**33, 158, 181, 332, 522, 531–32, 544–46, 588, 604–5, 607–8, 661; **9:**68–70, 74, 81, 86, 537–38, 557, 662, 700, 723; **10:**23, 72, 123, 128, 209, 214, 219, 291, 293–95, 315, 321, 367, 461, 475, 829; **11:**233, 375, 801; **12:**12, 23, 26, 35, 107, 110, 121, 209, 387, 410. *See also* IMPURITY, RITUAL

PURIM, FESTIVAL OF
See under FEASTS/FESTIVALS

PURPLE
1:896, 1060; **2:**53, 55; **4:**67, 102, 105, 122, 130, 148, 165, 223; **5:**262, 400, 689, 823; **6:**988, 1009, 1360, 1374, 1378–79; **7:**3, 82, 84; **8:**488; **9:**316–17, 337, 822; **10:**231–32; **12:**599, 648, 681, 694

PURPOSE OF GOD/DIVINE PURPOSE
1:44, 49, 324, 327, 347, 349, 355–56, 364, 366, 368, 447, 454, 465, 468, 484–85, 486, 489, 497, 505, 517–18, 522–23, 538, 559, 569, 574, 581, 594, 601, 635–36, 654, 673, 692, 721, 837, 906; **2:**297, 350, 359, 480–81, 775, 783, 790, 818, 827, 826, 888, 945, 958, 1007, 1021, 1081, 1091, 1119, 1153, 1226; **3:**3, 23, 129, 167, 380, 461, 464, 486, 498, 518, 568, 654, 656, 868, 873, 909, 970; **4:**591, 894, 963, 979, 1010–11, 1024, 1149, 1168, 1183, 1185–86, 1271; **5:**2, 51, 63, 464, 490, 496, 542, 558, 575, 802; **6:**332, 362, 400, 469–70, 681, 703, 729, 763, 783, 787, 796, 814, 853, 868, 878, 912, 1154, 1291, 1358, 1505; **7:**307, 367, 395, 483, 486, 712, 731, 797; **8:**67, 69, 132, 144, 306, 337, 464; **9:**9, 20–21, 31–32, 48, 59, 101, 437, 445, 456; **10:**14, 20, 45, 49, 89, 96, 105, 109, 132, 137, 139, 164–65, 196, 202, 208, 304–5, 314, 326, 349, 353, 402, 405–6, 424, 429, 446, 530, 539, 551, 565, 580, 614, 625, 634–38, 643, 651, 687, 695, 897, 939, 977, 994; **11:**22, 68, 269, 377, 408, 451, 512, 569, 608, 610–11, 636, 799, 807, 836, 862, 871–72; **12:**53, 106, 145–46, 151, 159, 329, 519, 524–25, 528–29, 682, 705, 709, 712, 716

PURSE, PURSES
3:582; **4:**440; **5:**12, 740; **9:**37, 220, 260, 422, 429–30, 702; **12:**170

PYRE
8:730

PYTHON
5:777; **8:**24; **10:**232. *See also* SNAKE

Q

Q COMMUNITY
8:51, 100, 102, 162, 180, 202, 256, 269, 272, 274, 284, 287, 354, 391

QERE
1:297; **3:**505, 793, 842; **4:**434; **5:**126, 181, 187, 195, 204; **6:**1337, 1352; **7:**261

QUAIL, QUAILS
1:688, 809, 812–13; **2:**108, 112, 357, 527; **4:**1111; **5:**446, 450, 536, 540, 573

QUARRY
6:628, 1458; **9:**84

QUART
1:1036, 1098–99, 1158; **3:**204; **6:**1149; **12:**612

QUARTER, SECOND
3:767; **7:**679

QUARTERMASTER
2:1110; **6:**941; **7:**804

QUEEN, QUEENS
1:239; **3:**14, 23, 32, 81–82, 86–88, 93, 112–13, 118, 138–39, 157, 221, 223, 227, 458, 510, 512–13, 570, 573–74, 582, 756, 857, 859, 867, 870, 874, 877, 879, 883–85, 887, 889–92, 894, 903–5, 908, 911, 914, 916, 918–20, 921, 923, 939–40, 950, 959, 1081, 1142, 1163; **4:**172, 469,

QUEEN, QUEENS *(continued)*
861, 862; **5:**3, 84, 129, 257–28, 264, 272, 297, 419, 421, 425, 511, 700, 849; **6:**411, 431–32, 509, 559, 685, 944, 1103, 1272, 1362, 1373, 1380, 1439; **7:**82, 175, 754, 779; **8:**130, 296, 598, 615, 699; **9:**52, 243, 245, 248, 259, 311; **10:**143, 328, 330; **11:**361; OF HEAVEN **3:**364; **6:**584, 635, 638–40, 642, 872–75, 1175, 1290; **7:**231, 779; MOTHER **3:**32, 118, 223, 227, 570, 574, 889; **5:**84, 129, 257–58, 264, 700; **6:**411, 559, 685, 944, 1272; **7:**82, 175

QUIVER
5:630, 765; **6:**1301

QUOTATION, QUOTATIONS
1:27, 72–73, 91, 99, 114, 203, 207, 209, 296–97, 301–3, 799, 990, 1056; **2:**106, 125, 207, 285, 733, 739, 1371; **3:**399, 446, 498, 569, 643, 657, 704, 708, 750–51, 773, 841, 1075, 1133; **4:**189–90, 240, 419, 426, 457, 568, 580–81, 621, 623, 627–28, 666, 673, 675, 698, 802, 890, 946, 956, 958, 977, 1004, 1024, 1121, 1125, 1202; **5:**33, 37, 55, 251–52, 277, 312, 345, 393–94; **6:**94, 237, 247, 255, 402, 613, 674, 698, 774, 794, 896, 915, 956, 1049, 1051, 1098, 1255, 1262, 1287, 1295, 1304, 1329, 1358, 1387, 1401, 1446, 1451, 1457, 1478, 1482, 1493, 1501; **7:**183, 387, 410, 423, 747, 793, 796, 808; **8:**2–4, 6–8, 82, 94, 96, 104, 111, 120, 135, 143, 146–47, 151–52, 161, 164, 167, 189, 211, 228, 235, 281, 305, 310, 333, 358, 361, 365, 378, 403, 414, 484, 530, 538, 606; **9:**3, 22, 47, 70, 80–81, 97–100, 105, 163, 177, 227, 248, 366–67, 369, 390–91, 430, 439, 461, 498, 501, 544, 548, 558, 600, 623, 630, 667, 716–17, 726, 742, 764, 833–34; **10:**128, 144, 409, 417, 423, 425–26, 439, 447, 456–58, 491, 493, 497, 500, 505, 508, 556, 573, 610–11, 634, 636–38, 641–43, 647, 650, 660, 665–69, 672, 675, 677, 680, 687, 691, 696, 703, 725, 731, 733, 738, 742, 745, 747–48, 833, 837, 865, 929; **11:**82, 106, 190, 230, 255, 260, 271, 279, 300, 302, 304, 306, 323–24, 366, 395, 413, 451, 490, 511, 543, 822, 839, 843, 845, 865; **12:**13, 25, 28–31, 33, 37, 40, 47, 50, 61, 64, 80, 90, 100–101, 104, 114–15, 126, 151, 159–60, 164, 236–38, 254, 258–60, 266, 290–91, 312, 315–16, 329, 342, 494, 518, 528–29, 545

R

RABBI, RABBIS
1:9, 38, 50, 66–68, 70–71, 73–82, 99, 121, 190, 290–91, 303, 881, 1010, 1019, 1085, 1109, 1160, 1165, 1189; **2:**77, 128, 202, 908, 909, 923, 934, 1288–89; **3:**46, 859, 866, 882, 886, 888, 890, 909, 914, 1182; **4:**138, 232, 234, 411, 421, 434, 1063; **5:**14, 120, 134, 172, 273, 366, 471, 553, 556, 606, 634, 642, 645, 664, 678, 694, 700, 715, 724, 781, 813; **6:**1129, 1131, 1189; **7:**57, 145, 148, 175, 495; **8:**18, 103, 129, 162, 169–70, 187–88, 197, 213, 224, 229, 247, 254, 274, 277, 299, 333, 361, 363, 374, 424, 431–32, 457, 470, 477, 547, 558, 742; **9:**74, 91, 110, 127, 173, 274, 296, 302, 310, 377, 423, 528, 531–33, 542, 549, 557, 628, 657, 842, 863; **10:**231, 399, 439, 650, 690, 704; **11:**211, 323, 493, 544; **12:**28, 98, 520, 596

RABBINIC LITERATURE
See under LITERATURE

RACE
AS ATHLETIC ENDEAVOR **3:**138, 310, 339, 382, 577; **5:**132, 341, 343; **6:**1446; **8:**14, 41; **9:**278; **10:**909; **11:**314, 533, 537, 856; **12:**148, 152–53; CAUCASIAN **1:**2–3, 105, 154, 156–59, 182–83, 186, 195, 197; **2:**595, 656, 690, 696, 711; **3:**873; **4:**391, 548, 1011; **5:**170, 227; **6:**183, 723; **7:**76, 95, 246, 701; **10:**484; **11:**278, 457; **12:**434; OF PEOPLE **1:**91, 105, 154, 158, 160, 165, 186–87, 346, 357, 364, 408–9, 623, 1106; **2:**67, 120, 122–23, 359, 371, 575, 601, 655, 711, 727, 978, 1100, 1137; **3:**95, 319, 895–96, 1088, 1124, 1167; **4:**36, 67, 82, 87, 229, 332, 449, 592, 920, 1151; **5:**8, 10–11, 16, 61, 93, 121, 176, 291, 370, 396, 404, 479, 505, 628, 860; **6:**82, 754, 767, 1044; **7:**77, 118, 268, 327, 569, 606, 620, 672, 676, 687, 701, 704; **8:**99, 145, 679; **9:**108, 229–30, 571; **10:**244, 247, 426, 431, 433–34, 438, 450, 463, 471–72, 511–13, 518–21, 524–27, 531, 547, 554, 566, 568, 587, 595–96, 601, 615, 623, 629, 631, 634, 647, 650, 662, 672–73, 682, 687, 689, 694, 697, 708, 747; **11:**231, 248, 254, 274, 279, 310, 414, 457, 525–26, 530, 611, 885, 905; **12:**88, 146, 194, 241, 269, 276, 298, 620

RACISM
1:35, 118, 157–58, 162, 164, 169, 186, 755; **2:**67, 130, 656, 1007, 1031, 1051, 1137, 1209; **4:**1112; **5:**825; **6:**105, 723; **7:**58, 262, 279, 457, 676, 681, 701, 729; **8:**102, 337–38, 716; **10:**485, 644; **11:**404; **12:**317

RAFT
7:467; **8:**248

RAHAB
DRAGON **1:**274; **4:**411, 518, 621, 1035; **5:**834; **6:**254, 448; **7:**101

RAIMENT
9:827; **12:**385. *See also* CLOTHES, CLOTHING

RAIN (*OR* RAINS, *ETC.*)
1:124, 217, 240, 274, 344, 349–50, 391–92, 419, 425, 477, 536, 600, 666, 840, 878, 1113, 1179–80; **2:**374, 755, 787–89, 1005, 1063, 1206, 1371; **3:**126–28, 131, 136–37, 140, 142–44, 155,

183, 403, 500, 742, 1129, 1137–38, 1154; **4:**51, 197, 380, 471, 485–86, 510–11, 518, 532–34, 539–40, 583, 589–93, 598, 604–5, 609, 626, 632, 721, 933–34, 945–46, 1014, 1099, 1195, 1268–69; **5:**54, 68, 75, 161, 180, 193, 219–20, 223, 237, 307, 350, 393, 446, 529, 553, 577–79, 598, 647, 757; **6:**84, 89, 138, 255, 386–87, 482, 600, 661, 692, 1005, 1202, 1383, 1442, 1462, 1471, 1473; **7:**11, 200, 202, 224, 250, 252, 276, 296, 309, 324, 389, 394, 422, 555, 574, 576, 655, 813, 816, 839; **8:**15, 218; **9:**107, 152, 268; **10:**199, 606, 665; **12:**76, 492, 636

RAINBOW, RAINBOWS
1:399–401, 417, 459; **2:**989; **3:**356–57, 403, 630; **4:**258; **5:**671, 834, 842, 859; **6:**214, 335, 548, 1117, 1131; **12:**592, 599, 611, 638, 713

RAM, RAMS
(animal) **1:**495–96, 498, 912–13, 963, 1039–40, 1042, 1062, 1065–66, 1110, 1134, 1158; **2:**78, 126, 185, 187, 189, 230, 232–33; **3:**691, 709, 712, 730, 745; **4:**312, 635; **5:**593; **6:**915, 1380, 1461, 1528, 1568–69, 1586, 1588–89; **7:**36, 110–13, 116–17, 139, 579–80, 814; BATTERING **6:**195, 242, 1143, 1302, 1366; HORN *(shophar)* **1:**91, 1171–72; **2:**89, 91, 656, 1319; **3:**20; **7:**112, 316; LEADER(S) **6:**1248, 1417, 1427–28, 1442, 1461, 1528; **7:**117, 814; FOR THE ORDINATION **1:**1062; **6:**1569

RAMPART, RAMPARTS
3:840; **4:**872–73; **6:**1429; **7:**691, 805; **9:**404; **11:**138, 459

RANSOM (*OR* RANSOMS, *ETC.*)
1:238, 787, 808, 865, 918, 998–99, 1010, 1012, 1111, 1119–20, 1134, 1142, 1165; **2:**80, 82, 84, 245, 247–48, 264, 266, 921, 1011, 1078; **3:**609, 612, 819, 979; **4:**78, 163, 264, 570, 587, 877, 879; **5:**132, 194, 430, 460; **6:**62, 281–83, 335, 375–76, 381, 391, 448, 469; **7:**291–92; **8:**399, 654, 696, 707, 720; **9:**201, 457, 714–15; **10:**342, 475, 864; **11:**596, 797–99, 873; **12:**238, 254, 603, 665

RAPE (*OR* RAPES, *ETC.*)
1:333, 474, 574, 577–81, 867, 872, 1165; **2:**379, 455–57, 548, 723, 742, 781, 788–89, 835, 863, 865, 872–73, 876–78, 884–87, 899, 963, 967, 970, 1170, 1217, 1232, 1270, 1284–85, 1289, 1293, 1302–1306, 1308–10, 1313, 1317, 1355; **3:**17, 890, 901, 919, 1081, 1119, 1132, 1143–44, 1161–62; **4:**21, 32, 63, 305, 436, 513, 552; **5:**193, 381, 408, 412–13, 419, 423, 692; **6:**615, 685–86, 850, 853, 1033, 1070, 1241, 1309–10, 1318, 1325, 1345; **7:**176–79, 183, 253, 262, 267, 275, 501, 618, 836, 839; **9:**85; **12:**489–90, 636

RAVEN, RAVENS
1:392–93; **2:**803; **3:**9, 125–29, 132; **4:**598, 608–9, 612, 626; **5:**382; **6:**1523; **7:**481; **9:**21, 177, 259

RAZOR
2:845, 859; **6:**113, 1150

REAP (*OR* REAPS, *ETC.*)
AS AN AGRICULTURAL ACTIVITY **2:**410, 913, 915; **4:**1195; **5:**119, 185, 350, 687, 692; **7:**275, 406, 448; **8:**211, 303, 556; **9:**133, 180–81, 259; AS A METAPHOR **1:**369, 424, 428, 482, 524, 528, 538, 541, 558, 581, 630, 673, 1128; **2:**737; **3:**313, 354, 370, 503, 514, 540, 552, 554, 582, 888; **4:**332, 377, 383, 1168, 1195; **5:**25, 41, 68, 105, 107, 119, 122, 131, 144, 185, 198–99, 331, 350, 692; **6:**57, 77, 213, 1400; **7:**261, 275–76; **8:**306; **9:**180–81, 259, 302, 372; **10:**413, 422, 433, 441, 919, 987; **11:**34, 129, 131, 336–37, 339–40; **12:**288, 668

REAPER, REAPERS
1:1179; **2:**916, 918, 923; **3:**189; **5:**824; **6:**174; **7:**193; **8:**578; **9:**570

REASON
AGE OF **1:**113; **2:**671; AND FAITH **1:**50, 52, 56, 117; **4:**243, 1225; **5:**34; **6:**245; **9:**259, 693; **10:**742; **12:**413–14

RECONCILE (*OR* RECONCILES, *ETC.*)
1:51–52, 102, 119, 190, 208, 272, 321, 389, 573, 656, 671, 875, 906, 953, 1035, 1144; **2:**339, 633, 647, 854, 981, 1024, 1050, 1325; **3:**7, 44, 125, 688, 700, 883, 905, 931, 1145; **4:**82, 154, 184, 188, 193, 298, 322, 583, 632, 697, 770, 886, 888–89, 1010; **5:**16, 447, 655; **6:**11, 39, 1171, 1183, 1238, 1275, 1344, 1409, 1453–54, 1564; **7:**197, 225, 232, 373, 583, 588, 866, 877; **8:**131, 645; **9:**212, 215, 308, 309, 313, 329, 334, 447, 575, 714, 831; **10:**127, 292, 514, 519–20, 721, 811, 876, 969, 974; **11:**23, 54, 92, 95–96, 98, 109–10, 116, 242, 344, 398, 400, 403, 504, 570, 575, 600–601, 603, 606, 608, 611, 623, 635, 640, 646, 707, 886, 902; **12:**359–60, 396, 424, 446, 708

RECONCILIATION
1:75, 330, 334, 452, 492, 518, 563, 571–74, 593–95, 601, 630, 635–36, 640–41, 643–45, 647, 651, 658, 670–71, 673, 891–92, 945, 1061, 1120; **2:**546, 660, 680, 759, 818, 1123, 1138, 1313–15, 1383; **3:**417, 424–26, 514, 777; **4:**154, 157, 184, 189, 270, 359, 445, 514, 568–70, 634–35, 637, 641, 886, 888, 1179; **5:**383, 484, 562, 700, 734; **6:**130, 137, 145, 216, 604, 1022, 1035, 1140, 1171, 1188, 1207, 1221, 1370; **7:**85, 198, 225, 227, 321, 694, 877; **8:**167, 180, 190, 500–501, 533, 608, 631, 645–46, 679; **9:**48, 60,

RECONCILIATION *(continued)*
117, 197, 266–67, 270, 303–4, 334, 447, 481, 714–15, 741; **10:**8, 114, 211, 258, 291, 513–15, 519–22, 525, 609, 635, 644, 651, 681–82, 791, 876–88; **11:**3, 8, 14, 23, 28–29, 34, 39, 53, 57, 72, 88–89, 91, 95–98, 118, 130–31, 179, 202, 278, 338, 348, 356, 370, 396, 398–400, 405, 515, 553–54, 556, 565, 570, 572–74, 589, 598–600, 605–7, 609–11, 614, 635, 646, 648, 650, 663, 858, 883, 885–86, 888, 898; **12:**287, 319, 386–88, 391–92, 414, 444, 661

RECORDER, RECORDERS
AS A MUSICAL INSTRUMENT **5:**348–49; AS AN OFFICER **2:**1268; **3:**49–51, 265; **6:**293; **10:**330

RED
1:521–22; **2:**55, 150, 588, 594; **3:**184; **5:**220, 382, 416; **6:**56, 520, 919, 1325, 1442, 1476; **7:**437, 609, 751, 783–84; **8:**488; **9:**282; **10:**423; **12:**610

REDACTOR, REDACTORS
1:79, 318, 322, 327, 340, 377–78, 391, 403, 418, 427, 457, 467, 485, 516, 592, 599, 656, 993; **3:**306, 437, 441, 457, 860, 931, 935, 938, 945–46, 949–51, 953–54, 960, 962–63, 967, 969–70, 978; **4:**642, 658; **5:**22, 206, 359; **6:**117, 232, 1090, 1092, 1094, 1146, 1317, 1329, 1487, 1505, 1521; **7:**168, 199–200, 204, 206, 219, 232, 234–35, 242, 249, 341, 384, 541, 553–54, 571, 604, 609, 736, 849, 852–53, 872; **9:**503, 560, 585, 803, 854, 862–63; **10:**951, 970; **11:**8, 106; **12:**233, 545

REDEEM (*OR* REDEEMS, *ETC.*)
1:62–63, 183–85, 194, 206, 272, 277, 661, 734, 786–87, 801, 808, 918, 1048, 1152, 1158, 1173–74, 1182, 1188–89; **2:**34, 40, 51–52, 54, 148–49, 391, 578, 590, 596, 599, 602, 619, 834–35, 861, 892–93, 895, 911, 924, 926, 933–35, 937–38, 1050, 1051, 1078–79, 1232, 1241, 1317; **3:**286, 386, 457, 501, 527, 568, 582, 632, 643, 746, 752–53, 779–80, 820, 868; **4:**341, 367–68, 480, 503, 511, 565, 570, 584, 675, 679, 779, 781, 800, 802, 858, 874, 877, 899, 927, 964, 973, 984, 1043, 1045, 1092, 1116–17, 1205–1207, 1217, 1224, 1272; **5:**16, 132, 189, 194, 387, 405, 412, 430, 519; **6:**40, 42, 59, 62, 247–48, 281–83, 339, 346, 359, 371, 381, 388, 411, 420, 433, 436, 439, 441, 448, 478–79, 485, 504, 514, 520, 585, 607, 619, 669, 671, 703–4, 711, 758, 763, 809, 815, 820, 826, 868, 884, 1056, 1106, 1139, 1284, 1353, 1488; **7:**43, 101, 156, 280–81, 291–92, 295, 415, 431, 567, 667, 702–3, 815, 822, 823; **8:**37, 50, 273, 365, 392, 459, 529, 531, 541, 716; **9:**49, 51, 55, 60, 69–70, 82, 84, 96, 101, 145, 158, 282, 334, 370, 371, 441, 443, 457, 664; **10:**41, 343, 405, 424, 502, 504, 511, 514, 585, 591, 596, 597–98, 604, 611, 635, 650, 665, 680, 699, 722, 815, 866, 877, 925, 936, 989; **11:**54, 57, 190, 224, 260–62, 275, 281, 283–84, 286, 289, 296, 373, 377, 394, 442, 610, 872; **12:**32, 69, 109, 250, 259, 261–62, 291, 319, 330, 346, 509, 591, 602, 616, 624, 664–65, 670, 721

REDEEMER, REDEEMERS
1:208, 442, 1173; **2:**265, 696, 892, 904, 921, 926–28, 930, 933–37, 940, 945–46; **3:**332, 754, 1138, 1143; **4:**460, 477, 479, 556–57, 753, 953, 1263; **5:**49, 206, 553, 599, 825, 867; **6:**393, 414, 432, 498, 501, 505, 508, 711, 807; **8:**264, 315, 537; **9:**478, 490, 502, 528, 558, 823; **10:**458, 692–93; **11:**358, 361, 374, 376, 384, 501, 604, 663; **12:**24, 58, 69, 252, 269, 283, 400, 519, 527, 734

REDEMPTION
1:61, 74, 85, 92, 101–2, 184, 209, 321, 326, 329, 355, 419, 425, 434, 464, 494, 498–99, 661, 666, 720, 786, 865, 869, 950, 986, 988, 1014, 1048, 1159, 1170, 1172, 1174, 1189; **2:**48, 50–52, 54, 147, 218, 268, 363, 602, 696, 783, 892–93, 895–97, 911, 919, 921, 926, 928–33, 935–42, 946, 1269; **3:**408, 997; **4:**449, 503, 570, 586, 627, 695, 731, 746, 754, 877, 1121, 1134, 1140, 1206, 1269; **5:**10, 16, 21, 49, 74, 599; **6:**42, 47, 61–62, 217–18, 248, 266, 283, 347, 381, 420, 443, 448, 459, 478, 485, 501, 509, 517, 519, 577, 640, 671, 710, 745, 768, 806–8, 810, 814, 820–22, 957, 971, 1284, 1595; **7:**310, 340, 346, 353, 567, 818, 833, 877; **8:**12, 51, 132, 365, 474; **9:**9, 43, 49, 52, 54–56, 59–60, 67, 69, 71, 73, 106, 143, 161, 206, 266, 334, 360, 382, 408–9, 411, 420, 423, 437, 445, 462–64, 475, 478, 490, 533, 664; **10:**15, 19, 82, 234, 424, 426, 447, 470–71, 501–2, 511–12, 534, 560, 591, 594, 597–601, 607, 615, 693, 696, 699, 786, 811, 813, 815, 823, 829, 866, 923, 935, 937, 953, 989, 994; **11:**69, 88, 92–94, 166, 191, 261, 277, 283–84, 289, 292, 298, 314, 326, 345, 355, 360, 366, 372–73, 376–77, 385, 394, 398, 430, 565, 571, 584, 596–98, 603–4, 606, 608, 610, 613, 639, 644, 678, 796; **12:**10–11, 22, 35, 39, 107, 239, 241, 251, 254, 288, 292, 333–35, 345, 602, 649, 668, 697, 709

REED, REEDS
1:7, 699, 701; **3:**113, 265; **4:**312, 618, 946; **5:**823; **6:**293, 365, 1104, 1232, 1401–1402, 1405–1406, 1408, 1538, 1540–41, 1559, 1596; **7:**292; **8:**267, 281, 488; **9:**123, 163–64; **12:**466

REFUGE
1:95, 215, 306, 557, 766, 900, 1075; **2:**480, 504,

520, 592, 680, 689, 774, 782, 816, 918, 1054, 1060, 1070, 1138, 1144, 1175, 1178, 1180, 1243, 1265, 1309, 1332, 1352, 1366; **3:**34, 209, 294, 337, 804, 1090; **4:**130, 175, 189, 228, 230, 261, 276, 314, 363, 442, 545, 554, 582, 665–68, 670, 679, 689–91, 693, 698, 701–2, 709, 717, 721–22, 730–32, 734, 736–37, 740–41, 747–49, 759, 779, 785, 790, 797, 800, 802, 814–15, 823–24, 830–31, 843, 848, 863–65, 872, 891, 893–94, 898, 905, 913, 919, 922–24, 930–31, 958, 968, 970, 1014, 1041, 1046–47, 1059, 1154, 1192, 1236, 1243–44, 1246–48, 1251, 1255–56; **5:**143–44, 158, 256, 609, 719, 815; **6:**109, 167–69, 174, 176–77, 216–17, 237, 265, 413, 491, 493, 710, 1357, 1431; **7:**140, 188, 250, 328–29, 334, 455, 602, 612, 690; **8:**147, 406, 410, 688; **9:**186, 363, 374; **10:**352; **11:**248, 884–85, 898, 900; **12:**200, 613; CITIES OF (*see under* CITY)

REGENERATION
1:57, 1061, 1110; **2:**406; **3:**632; **4:**441, 444–45, 475, 487, 568–69, 575; **5:**397; **6:**441; **9:**555; **10:**481; **11:**877

REGISTER, REGISTERATION, REGISTRY
1:918; **2:**33–35, 107, 254; **3:**48, 51–52, 333, 337, 353, 456, 624–25; **6:**1202; **7:**699; **9:**62–63, 460; **10:**527; **11:**540, 819–20; **12:**158

REIGN (*OR* REIGNS, *ETC.*)
DIVINE **1:**1111; **4:**672, 675, 690, 700, 793, 867, 944, 1044, 1059, 1270; **12:**643–44; FIGURATIVE **10:**528, 549; HUMAN **1:**264–65; **3:**119, 209–10, 247–48, 260, 280, 365, 468, 544, 654, 878; **7:**594; **9:**62; **10:**523–24, 980; **12:**683, 708. *See also* KING; KINGDOM

REINS
6:601; **11:**763

REJOICE (*OR* REJOICES, *ETC.*)
1:28, 182, 486, 488–89, 645, 782, 825, 1051, 1156, 1158, 1160; **2:**88, 110, 386, 407, 471, 536, 651, 745, 790, 817, 981, 994, 1010, 1012, 1055, 1056, 1126, 1206–7; **3:**104, 230, 400, 402, 407, 433, 462, 469, 498–99, 502, 523, 693, 700, 713–14, 802, 804, 839–40, 844, 857, 909, 927, 932, 935, 980, 1018, 1051, 1062, 1065, 1069–70; **4:**20, 72, 85, 156, 204, 234, 312, 368, 463, 502, 554, 611, 681, 701, 718, 727, 789, 796, 800–801, 809, 834, 930–31, 945, 1067–70, 1100, 1118, 1122, 1195; **5:**41, 69, 95, 99, 118, 140, 144, 152, 238, 274, 327, 353, 356–57, 379–80, 406, 422, 463, 473, 498, 501, 505, 681, 687, 720, 731, 801; **6:**122, 163–64, 217, 256, 281–82, 336, 339, 371, 456–57, 470, 517, 521, 545, 820, 914, 980–81, 1065, 1084, 1105, 1166, 1299, 1351, 1382, 1452, 1479, 1485, 1537; **7:**40, 103, 169, 265, 267, 269, 309, 324, 439, 451, 454, 482, 606, 638, 664, 667, 671, 702–4, 709, 742, 759, 761, 770, 806–7, 818; **8:**32, 180, 500, 658; **9:**19, 55–56, 58, 144–45, 224, 274, 294–96, 298, 304–5, 342, 357–58, 367, 396, 436, 526, 542, 558, 560, 586, 646, 675, 690, 707, 740, 751–52, 771, 779–80, 825, 841, 843, 846, 849; **10:**109, 142, 196, 221, 234, 407, 516, 520, 590, 604, 631, 665, 712, 775, 816, 839, 849, 888, 1000; **11:**21, 25, 44, 53, 99, 110–11, 118, 121, 178, 234, 308, 469, 483, 488–90, 513–14, 520, 522, 524, 540–43, 546–47, 554, 559, 613–14, 617–18, 730, 732–33; **12:**229, 251–52, 254–55, 261, 291–92, 310, 379–80, 448, 450–51, 459–61, 500, 617, 625, 638, 642, 644, 650, 692, 694, 695, 711

RELIGION
1:15, 20, 46, 54, 57, 60, 66, 85, 101, 116–17, 154–58, 160, 166, 173, 183–84, 194–95, 303, 327, 578, 679, 682, 747, 760, 819, 821, 836, 839–40, 861, 872, 878, 885, 897–98, 951, 963, 977, 990–92, 1037, 1074, 1132, 1136, 1174, 1180, 1182, 1195; **2:**12–15, 22, 32, 39–40, 66, 194, 236, 277, 285–86, 293, 310, 315, 330, 346, 349, 352–53, 366–67, 375, 377, 385, 392, 395, 410, 414, 432, 441–42, 445, 514, 521, 528, 564, 615, 716, 727, 771, 811, 819, 827, 870, 907, 920, 954, 977, 1003, 1013, 1145, 1258, 1359, 1387; **3:**48, 104, 130, 137–38, 226, 257, 344, 347–48, 473, 526, 532–33, 551, 576, 608, 613, 631, 850, 866, 869, 883, 1105, 1125, 1154, 1168, 1179, 1192; **4:**3, 12, 19, 23, 39, 40, 58, 73, 182, 198, 212, 219, 233, 258, 269, 283, 325, 334, 336, 358, 363, 383–84, 442, 446, 449, 451, 453, 457, 465, 500, 510, 519, 541, 578–79, 595, 787, 793, 883, 928, 1007–1008, 1286–87; **5:**2, 33–34, 48, 50, 72, 113, 118, 139, 145, 150, 159, 176, 317, 343, 381, 391, 626, 650, 654, 656, 660, 668, 670, 701, 731, 825, 874; **6:**8, 23, 69, 73–74, 109, 169, 176, 223, 244–45, 255, 262, 318, 345, 407, 421, 433, 503, 542, 549, 639, 641, 660, 828, 897, 946, 994, 1034, 1203, 1274, 1291, 1455, 1511, 1609; **7:**2, 29, 35, 89, 106–8, 143, 147, 169, 202, 260–61, 263, 339–40, 349, 368, 370, 375, 378, 395, 418, 553, 558–59, 632–33, 676, 687, 690, 710, 717, 861, 874; **8:**17, 21–22, 26, 31, 40, 53, 99, 182, 264, 275, 408, 420, 496, 529, 557, 574, 579, 611, 629, 664, 716, 743–44; **9:**28, 48, 78, 86, 97, 101, 159, 229–30, 336, 343, 386, 402, 472, 554, 650, 744–45, 814, 816, 875; **10:**11, 70, 93, 126, 145, 154, 206, 239, 243–47, 255, 270–72, 274, 294, 311, 329, 335–36, 341, 387, 409, 462, 464, 469, 485, 505–6, 586, 604, 615, 716, 735, 750, 922, 963, 1010–11; **11:**152, 161, 196, 198, 215,

RELIGION *(continued)*
218–19, 228, 239, 277, 283, 288–89, 316, 342, 344, 348, 363, 377, 380, 425, 432, 482, 493, 517, 521, 526–27, 537, 561, 564, 653, 659, 677, 722, 792, 798, 800–801, 808, 815, 820, 831, 833–34, 836, 859, 866, 874, 879, 913; **12:**71, 100, 114, 117, 127, 164, 181, 184, 187, 189, 192, 195–97, 200, 203–4, 240, 278, 282, 355, 496, 505, 538, 540, 542–43, 547–48, 554, 556–57, 575, 581, 607, 633, 654, 658, 661, 687, 701, 726–28; ANCIENT NEAR EASTERN **2:**483; **6:**67; OF THE BOOK **1:**20, 157; **5:**244; OF CANAAN **1:**273, 275, 931, 1018; **2:**344, 374, 399, 1198; **3:**126–27, 546, 569; **4:**1006; **5:**667; **7:**200, 269; OF EGYPT **2:**164, 493; OF ISRAEL **1:**81, 87, 272–83, 309, 313, 316, 1075; **2:**22, 50, 77, 88, 200, 287, 385, 398, 429; **4:**232, 325, 372, 409, 519, 548; **5:**44; **6:**176, 314, 1175; **7:**5, 201–3, 339–40; **8:**41–42; **11:**834; JEWISH **1:**284–91; **3:**1167; **4:**41, 165, 217; **7:**5, 146; **8:**30, 169; **10:**305; **12:**520, 725; PAGAN **3:**538; **10:**219, 230, 260, 285, 293, 363, 374; **11:**282, 291, 361; **12:**553 (*see also* PAGAN); POPULAR **1:**760, 885; **6:**638, 1203; **7:**370

REMEMBRANCE, REMEMBRANCES
1:187, 189, 388, 396, 560, 616, 683, 773, 783, 786–87, 845, 861, 906, 1018, 1021, 1109, 1135; **2:**62–63, 748, 820, 912, 1087, 1243, 1246, 1262; **3:**612, 701, 750, 850–51, 865, 913, 1182; **4:**443, 694, 796, 983–84, 1070, 1073, 1087, 1126, 1145, 1170, 1196, 1229–30, 1260; **5:**293–94, 301, 454, 525; **6:**981, 1021, 1051, 1056, 1302; **7:**75, 111, 190, 846, 872; **8:**52, 471, 509, 514, 518; **9:**98, 420, 544, 613, 708–9; **10:**43, 935; **11:**483, 689, 711–12, 714–15; **12:**116, 128, 295, 419, 456

REMISSION
1:988, 999; **2:**404–5, 566–69, 578, 589–90, 593, 626, 630, 670, 711, 1110; **5:**772; **6:**603; **12:**444

REMNANT, REMNANTS
1:236, 394, 473, 644, 654, 1183; **2:**324, 370, 689, 701, 788, 886–87, 942, 1139, 1148, 1205, 1212, 1233, 1276; **3:**145, 236, 269, 278, 294, 576, 600, 644, 678, 688, 713, 735–38, 751; **4:**205, 296; **5:**842, 849; **6:**17, 21, 42, 55, 84, 106–8, 119, 129–30, 136, 138, 145–46, 164, 174, 235–36, 295, 317, 390, 406, 411, 418, 421, 431, 433, 471, 478, 482, 484, 513–14, 540, 548, 572–73, 584, 626, 660, 758, 809, 842, 852, 854, 858–59, 860, 864–67, 874, 877, 974, 1080, 1180, 1187–88, 1326, 1345, 1466; **7:**91, 164, 328, 347, 349, 375, 386, 391, 417, 424, 426–28, 439, 455–56, 539, 574, 663–66, 669, 684, 690, 698–700, 716, 719–20, 723, 795, 805, 807, 833; **8:**178, 418, 531, 633; **10:**11, 19, 25, 99, 132, 362, 624, 634, 637, 640, 643, 645, 648, 655, 675–77, 681, 683–84, 688, 748; **11:**363, 373; **12:**134, 190, 427, 517, 527, 620

REPENTANCE (*OR* REPENT, *ETC.*)
1:16, 179–80, 191, 207, 282–83, 314, 380, 568, 646, 691, 758, 852, 991, 1044, 1073, 1110, 1113, 1159, 1181–82; **2:**511, 767, 821, 824–27, 892, 899, 963, 1016–17, 1021–22, 1031, 1062, 1091, 1123, 1289, 1292–95, 1380, 1383; **3:**76, 79, 236, 244, 276, 286, 303, 311, 328, 332, 338, 423, 425, 427, 497, 500–503, 526–27, 532, 543, 581, 587, 591, 601, 615, 617, 619, 628, 632–34, 636–37, 643, 649, 654, 658, 673, 721, 738, 753, 797, 805–6, 812, 902, 960, 1091, 1113, 1158; **4:**40, 63, 67, 85, 234, 254, 281, 497, 501–3, 507, 526, 568–70, 586–87, 835, 910, 999–1000, 1002, 1004, 1042, 1092, 1252, 1261; **5:**159, 479, 541–42, 573, 585, 659, 674, 678, 724, 730, 734, 842; **6:**47, 56, 64, 97, 103–5, 107–8, 110, 127, 181, 242–43, 255, 257, 472, 478, 482–83, 499, 513, 532, 540, 564, 570, 573, 589, 596, 603–6, 612–14, 627, 643, 649, 655, 666, 698, 700, 710, 717, 731, 758, 761, 768–69, 772, 774, 810, 838–41, 852–53, 930–31, 933, 934–35, 937, 939, 945–46, 948–50, 953, 955, 957–60, 969, 971, 980, 982, 1022, 1053–54, 1069, 1105, 1126, 1140–41, 1154, 1161, 1188, 1207, 1255, 1264, 1266, 1412, 1446–47, 1451–52, 1491, 1495; **7:**160, 198, 205–6, 209, 210–11, 214–15, 220, 225, 229, 232, 234–35, 244, 246, 249, 252–53, 258, 263, 278, 281, 284–85, 287, 294, 303–4, 307, 312–13, 318–21, 327, 334, 336, 381, 387, 406, 408–9, 467–68, 470, 472, 482–84, 486–91, 510, 514–16, 524–26, 528, 538, 541, 548, 560, 589, 735–36, 746–48; **8:**30–31, 34, 36, 157, 167, 189, 206, 220, 271, 273, 286, 378, 380, 436, 444, 483–84, 531–34, 536–37, 547, 555, 598–99, 670, 686, 716; **9:**9, 22–23, 35, 47–48, 56, 60, 81–88, 90, 92, 128–29, 144–45, 166, 221, 243, 250, 253, 269–71, 296, 298, 302–3, 304, 318–19, 322, 341–42, 348–51, 358–59, 374–75, 405–6, 428, 440, 452–53, 469, 486–87, 529, 847; **10:**22, 48, 67–68, 70, 81–83, 85, 89, 99, 106–7, 109, 124–25, 133, 139, 149, 161, 169, 192, 196, 208, 247, 250, 269, 282, 314, 339, 361, 364, 383, 453, 638, 662, 686; **11:**55, 102, 109–10, 112, 178, 257, 846; **12:**50, 66, 70, 73–74, 76–78, 124, 133–34, 154, 209, 212, 216, 235, 295, 301–2, 305, 312, 347–48, 356–57, 358–59, 399, 456, 556, 575, 578, 579–80, 632–33, 643, 676, 730, 735

REPTILE, REPTILES
1:1081; **5:**502, 570; **10:**433; **12:**205. *See also by indvidual species name*

RESERVOIR, RESERVOIRS
4:590; **5:**298; **6:**1353; **7:**610

RESH
7:496, 498
RESIDENT ALIEN, ALIENS
See under ALIEN
REST, RESTING
1:380, 392, 474, 504, 871, 891, 924–25, 939, 1010–11; **2:**89, 106, 190, 376, 386, 415, 764, 768, 782, 807, 820, 822, 838, 841, 878, 903–4, 925–26, 1145, 1230, 1257; **3:**278, 394, 406, 430–31, 437, 460, 497, 518, 536, 539–40, 562, 576, 630, 637, 730, 842, 937, 953, 967, 1088, 1090, 1109, 1173; **4:**369–70, 393, 593, 694, 769, 853, 927, 1062–63, 1261; **5:**15, 61, 224, 321, 360, 385, 469, 511, 513, 578, 663, 689, 716; **6:**40, 158, 203, 237, 254–55, 411, 489, 517, 531, 628, 647, 678, 762, 807, 811, 891, 1442–44, 1466; **7:**129, 242, 553, 748, 752–53, 762, 782, 784, 803, 811; **8:**600; **9:**207, 255–56, 311, 458, 837; **10:**55, 446, 459, 645, 884, 1003; **11:**55, 109, 119, 344, 712, 749, 771; **12:**11, 18, 48–49, 51–52, 55–57, 75, 77, 100, 401, 613, 728; DAY OF/SABBATH; **1:**286, 814,845, 871, 924–95, 1156–57, 1161, 1171; **2:**129, 235, 332, 768; **3:**302, 801; **4:**295; **5:**138; **6:**710; **7:**416; **8:**275, 277, 279, 558, 616, 622; **9:**135, 622; **12:**52–53, 118, 532, 534 (*see also* SABBATH); "THE LAND HAD REST" **2:**546, 655, 674, 764, 766, 768, 777, 789; **3:**1182; **4:**30, 101, 117, 159; PLACE OF **1:**278; **2:**97, 925, 1248; **3:**287, 645, 967; **4:**1211–12; **5:**757; **9:**318; "REST COMPLACENTLY ON THEIR DREGS" **6:**891; **7:**422, 679
RESTITUTION
1:579, 733, 863, 865–67, 872–74, 1033, 1040–41, 1149, 1165, 1173; **2:**9, 61–62, 1292, 1306; **4:**401, 554, 636; **6:**301, 379, 431, 476, 478, 1409, 1547; **7:**75, 77, 85; **8:**124, 482; **9:**144, 305, 358–59
RESTORATION (*OR* RESTORES, *ETC.*)
1:9, 18, 67, 240, 268, 270, 274, 289, 392, 689, 808, 845, 927, 945, 1098, 1156–57, 1178; **2:**61, 67, 279, 380, 384, 412, 512, 567, 603, 702, 892, 894, 930, 967, 1126, 1186, 1274, 1276, 1313, 1319, 1350; **3:**106, 191, 197–98, 228, 233, 276, 301–3, 305, 307, 309, 311, 313, 319, 327, 347, 359, 361, 364–66, 377, 381, 386, 390, 402–3, 457, 462, 497–98, 500–501, 505, 514, 518, 538, 565, 575–76, 580, 602–3, 607, 610–11, 616, 630, 634, 636–37, 643, 652, 654, 657, 659, 664, 668–69, 671, 678–80, 685, 691, 696, 705, 716, 725, 731, 736, 753, 788, 794, 832, 834–35, 844, 1064, 1069, 1085, 1120, 1133, 1137; **4:**52, 71–72, 119, 164, 236, 241, 260, 269, 287–88, 311, 329, 401, 403, 442, 497, 499, 503, 568–70, 578, 634–36, 690, 704, 730, 736, 795, 797, 845, 887, 930, 965, 990, 992, 1000–1001, 1016–17, 1037, 1046, 1081–82, 1086, 1129, 1167, 1195, 1212–13; **5:**5, 243, 463, 474, 530, 631, 675; **6:**5–6, 8, 17, 21–22, 61, 157–58, 207, 216, 318–19, 335, 378, 380, 423, 444, 462, 478, 493, 500, 517, 572, 603, 680, 694, 703, 710, 744, 783, 791, 797, 804–5, 807–12, 814, 821, 823, 825–28, 860, 878, 884, 892–93, 900, 911–12, 915, 917–18, 926, 933–34, 946, 950, 955–57, 981–82, 1026, 1044, 1057, 1067, 1070, 1085, 1088–89, 1099, 1101, 1104–6, 1191, 1213, 1237, 1251–52, 1351, 1335–37, 1364, 1370, 1396, 1399–1401, 1407, 1409, 1411, 1446, 1453–54, 1461–62, 1469, 1477, 1480, 1486–87, 1492, 1494–96, 1504, 1527, 1577, 1597–98; **7:**11, 42, 62, 88, 93, 128, 183, 206, 220, 223, 246, 253, 294, 304, 322, 324, 326, 348, 358, 362, 367, 396, 409, 428, 430, 454–56, 493, 567, 635, 703, 708, 711, 715, 717–18, 721, 725, 740–42, 744, 748, 754–55, 757, 763, 767, 772, 775, 782, 795, 802, 807, 809–14, 816, 820, 822–23, 859, 869, 877; **8:**2, 11, 29–30, 36–37, 357, 364–65, 379, 585, 622, 705; **9:**48, 70, 106, 186, 207, 272–73, 285, 300, 426, 428, 440, 454, 698, 714, 779; **10:**11, 16, 20–22, 24–25, 28, 40–42, 47–48, 57, 65, 67–69, 72, 77–79, 81–86, 99, 106, 123–24, 130, 135, 140, 152, 161, 176, 213, 218–19, 247, 252, 254, 267, 305, 339–41, 355, 360, 362, 364–65, 398, 524, 602, 625, 640–43, 659, 660–63, 667, 700, 869, 989; **11:**54, 95, 98, 110, 177, 261–62, 276, 304, 332, 335, 400, 504, 506, 536, 635, 770, 872; **12:**5, 74, 101, 105, 124, 224, 386, 402, 436, 498, 710, 726
RESURRECTED, RESURRECTION
1:13, 17, 37, 76, 84, 85, 91, 160, 169, 189, 191–92, 196, 199, 204, 208–10, 229–30, 288–89, 495, 500, 671, 799, 804, 836, 838, 954–55, 1020, 1022, 1063, 1121, 1159, 1161, 1196; **2:**90, 152, 235, 804, 847, 1008, 1209, 1232, 1299, 1353; **3:**9–10, 68, 78, 128, 130–31, 137, 185, 188, 210–11, 214, 234, 238, 512, 738, 977, 997–98, 1004–1005, 1071, 1181; **4:**240–41, 277, 442, 445, 477–78, 669, 673–74, 685, 728, 737–38, 742, 754, 765–66, 802, 830, 870, 874, 877, 879, 895, 903, 920, 924, 931, 938, 948, 954, 970, 1001, 1022, 1045, 1048, 1073, 1089, 1119, 1131, 1143, 1149, 1156, 1169, 1196, 1216, 1226, 1229–30, 1248, 1252, 1280; **5:**15, 128, 285, 301, 303, 313–14, 341, 343, 447, 449, 486, 717, 721, 825; **6:**198, 206, 218, 222–23, 469, 734, 810, 1171, 1395, 1462, 1502; **7:**2, 4–5, 8–10, 15, 67, 93, 95, 148–50, 249–50, 317, 328, 340, 348, 383, 415, 509, 655, 785, 877; **8:**20, 30, 36–37, 39–40, 50, 52, 64–66, 71, 73, 81–82, 95, 102, 110–12, 119, 122–25, 138, 149, 156, 168,

RESURRECTED, RESURRECTION *(continued)* 174, 188, 198, 224, 238, 245, 249, 251, 254, 258, 264, 279, 294, 295–97, 319, 325, 328, 341, 348–49, 351, 355–56, 360, 364, 366, 400–401, 409, 414, 419, 421–23, 439, 457, 459–60, 463, 471, 474, 476, 478, 480, 492–95, 497, 499–505, 511, 519, 523, 527, 529, 562, 590–91, 618, 624, 627, 630–32, 634–36, 657, 671, 673, 675–78, 698, 704–5, 707, 728–33, 735; **9:**6, 8, 10, 12–13, 16, 18, 21–22, 30–31, 36–37, 52, 77, 91, 94, 116–17, 137, 159, 190–91, 197, 200–201, 205–8, 210, 214–15, 220, 223, 225, 278, 288, 318–19, 331, 346, 351, 353–54, 387–91, 413, 439, 457, 459–60, 463–64, 466, 468–70, 472–73, 476, 478, 482, 484–90, 497, 509, 514, 523, 533, 537, 539–40, 544–45, 551–53, 585, 602–4, 608, 610–11, 616, 623–24, 633–35, 671, 681, 686, 688, 690–95, 699, 704–5, 708–11, 714–15, 718–19, 721–22, 726, 732–33, 735, 738, 741, 746, 748–49, 751, 753, 766, 770–72, 774, 776, 778, 780–81, 784–85, 787, 789, 794, 799–800, 804, 832–33, 837–38, 841–45, 847–49, 851–54, 856, 864, 869; **10:**3, 10, 20–21, 23–25, 28, 30, 40, 42–46, 48, 50, 58, 62–63, 72–74, 79–81, 84, 88–89, 91, 96, 100–101, 104, 106, 111, 125, 140, 151, 162, 166, 170, 177, 180, 189, 192–93, 238, 240, 242–43, 245, 247, 249–50, 253, 256, 262, 277–78, 281, 294, 310–12, 315, 318–21, 329, 333, 335–36, 340–43, 372, 375–76, 382, 387, 401–2, 407, 416–19, 424, 427–28, 432, 457, 467, 477–78, 488, 501–5, 507, 509, 512–13, 519–21, 524, 528, 534–35, 537–41, 545–49, 555–57, 574, 577–78, 580–85, 587, 591–92, 595–98, 601, 603–8, 613, 615, 617, 625–26, 638, 646, 655, 661, 663–64, 669, 681–84, 686, 690, 693–94, 696, 700–702, 706–7, 710, 715, 717, 727, 729, 733, 736–38, 744, 748, 753, 762, 786, 791, 794, 808, 811–12, 822, 842, 851, 865–66, 869, 935, 973–84, 986–94, 1002; **11:**23, 25–26, 57, 69, 81–82, 85–86, 88, 92–93, 99, 101, 138, 176, 202, 205, 208, 217–19, 228, 243, 246–49, 274–75, 283, 285, 308, 313, 317, 322, 326, 336–37, 344, 374, 382–84, 389, 392, 409, 429, 480, 491–92, 494, 497, 502, 504, 528–29, 532–33, 536, 538, 572–73, 591, 599–600, 603, 608–10, 614, 617, 623–25, 628–29, 633, 636–40, 643, 646, 678, 689, 715, 723–25, 727, 734, 767, 783, 795, 836, 843–45, 847, 849, 852; **12:**28–31, 40, 42, 61–62, 64, 70–71, 90, 93, 121, 139, 144, 155, 172, 180, 213, 223, 229, 231, 237–38, 240–41, 246, 250–52, 254–55, 259–60, 262, 292–93, 295–99, 302, 319, 360, 404, 441, 473, 525, 527, 531, 532, 543–44, 587, 589, 643, 662, 677, 703, 708–9, 711–13, 716; OF THE BODY **1:**160, 288; **3:**1004; **4:**241, 477–78; **5:**447, 486; **7:**249; **8:**37; **9:**711; **10:**343, 419, 507, 538, 555, 581, 866; **11:**86, 337–38, 374, 528, 573; **12:**712; OF THE DEAD **1:**76, 1161; **2:**152; **3:**9, 128, 130, 211, 238, 977, 1004; **4:**277; **5:**303, 341; **6:**206, 223; **7:**877; **8:**37, 39, 224, 422, 523, 675–76; **9:**346, 388–89, 391, 482, 688; **10:**84, 88, 310, 315, 318–19, 321, 375, 419, 664, 684, 744, 753, 791, 794, 973–74, 978–84, 986–87; **11:**338, 502, 529, 532, 573, 599, 723, 795, 843; **12:**70, 250, 703, 712, 716. *See also* JESUS THE CHRIST: CRUCIFIXION, RESURRECTION, AND ASCENSION OF *in PERSONS IN THE BIBLE*

RETRIBUTION
1:375, 377, 478, 594, 610, 671, 829, 864–65, 867, 1143; **2:**126, 300, 501–5, 728, 741, 808, 817, 853–54, 888, 1293, 1313, 1365; **3:**217, 236, 253, 264, 303, 527, 543, 569, 581, 643, 664, 736, 934, 985, 989, 994–95, 997, 1003–1004, 1009, 1015–17, 1039, 1056, 1061, 1064, 1068–69, 1071, 1189; **4:**44, 119, 204, 250, 281, 331, 363, 446, 451, 497, 499, 508, 547, 572, 593, 671, 705, 789, 835, 848, 931, 952, 1091, 1170; **5:**2, 9, 12, 76, 134, 254, 275, 287, 310, 335, 359, 536, 664, 677, 680, 701, 718, 729–30, 768, 771–72, 788; **6:**89–90, 160, 204, 277, 281, 542, 550, 613, 675, 697, 729, 758, 864–65, 883, 914, 1139, 1153, 1210, 1252, 1254, 1257, 1262–63, 1265, 1474; **7:**227, 229, 248, 262, 293, 486, 488, 537, 551, 560–61, 576, 612, 616, 620; **9:**271, 364, 375; **10:**65, 434, 641, 718; **11:**658, 729, 731, 733, 744, 746, 749, 751; **12:**540, 625, 676

REVELATION, REVELATIONS
1:20, 35, 37, 39, 41, 43–50, 52, 56, 62, 64–67, 69–72, 74, 79, 81, 84–86, 88, 95, 98, 102, 110, 121–22, 124, 126–32, 135, 147, 160, 178, 185, 189, 190, 195–97, 199, 273, 280, 286, 288–89, 306, 312, 315, 337, 373, 481, 541, 556, 559, 562, 594, 621, 659, 661, 733, 824, 852, 854, 1008, 1110, 1135, 1165; **2:**4, 10–11, 16, 25, 63, 69, 79–80, 83, 86, 89–91, 95–96, 98–100, 106, 108, 112, 120–21, 124–25, 128, 139, 177, 182, 188, 190, 193–94, 197, 202, 217–18, 222, 229, 254, 271, 273, 291–93, 297, 300, 309–10, 315, 319, 322, 325, 338, 431, 480–81, 487, 506, 512, 518–19, 521, 534, 616, 748, 753, 821, 892–93, 896, 923, 926, 992, 1040, 1065, 1089; **3:**8, 38, 41, 79–81, 83, 88, 332, 348, 364–65, 370, 380–82, 390, 395–96, 402, 407–9, 425, 432, 462, 464–65, 477, 480, 483, 486, 494, 496–99, 501, 506, 512, 515, 518, 547, 576, 602–3, 610, 618, 635, 645, 647, 649, 651, 657, 723, 983, 988, 1022–23, 1033, 1053, 1056–57; **4:**335, 377, 411, 426, 453–54, 569, 577, 627–28, 665–66, 671, 673–74, 684–85, 697, 704, 752, 754, 768, 778–80, 787, 800–801, 872, 874, 886, 913,

983–84, 1005, 1015, 1020, 1028, 1076, 1078, 1083, 1091–92, 1133, 1150, 1166–69, 1171–76, 1178, 1186, 1205, 1232, 1250, 1260, 1264; **5:**14, 43, 113, 119, 160, 244, 247, 251–53, 381, 383, 408, 416, 455, 471, 494, 496, 556, 609, 620, 625, 643–44, 647, 754, 768, 773, 793, 842, 853; **6:**10, 48, 66–67, 74, 102, 112, 118, 120, 155, 186, 206–7, 243, 245, 254, 256, 260, 281, 320, 324, 338–39, 381, 526, 545, 548, 579, 655, 673, 690, 745, 752–53, 811, 814, 827, 935, 958, 963, 970, 1109, 1130–31, 1277–78, 1280, 1338–39, 1513, 1573; **7:**1–4, 6, 8–15, 22, 95, 122, 181, 189–90, 210, 217, 228, 232, 283, 285–86, 302, 305, 326, 370, 444–45, 458, 487, 542, 544, 556, 558, 599, 633, 641, 737, 748, 762, 786, 790, 793, 803, 860, 876–77; **8:**37–39, 64, 67, 90, 103–4, 130, 134, 140, 143–47, 154, 175, 186, 203, 211, 218–19, 248, 264, 270–71, 274–75, 291, 310, 332, 344–45, 347–48, 350, 352, 357, 362, 363, 366–67, 398, 423, 425–26, 459, 486, 519, 532, 534, 561, 572, 584, 603, 613, 621, 630–32, 636, 676, 689, 694, 732; **9:**4, 22, 44, 47, 60, 66, 72–73, 91, 130, 153, 162, 197, 207, 225, 267, 351, 383, 463, 478, 482, 495–97, 502, 507–8, 519–20, 523–25, 531–34, 537, 539–40, 545, 567, 569, 572–73, 576, 580, 587, 592, 594, 596–98, 601, 603, 606, 612, 614, 616–17, 621, 625–26, 632, 635, 646, 653, 656, 659–61, 663–64, 668–70, 672, 686–87, 690, 693, 712, 727, 743–45, 748, 752, 764, 767, 771–77, 781, 782, 789–92, 794–95, 808, 816, 821, 824–26, 835, 844–45, 847, 852–53; **10:**32, 127, 172, 226, 282–83, 289, 311, 322, 338, 371, 376, 390, 405–6, 424–26, 428, 431–32, 437, 442–43, 455, 457, 462, 465, 469–70, 478, 480–82, 484, 486, 492, 497, 499, 502–3, 511, 516, 586, 595–96, 603–4, 612, 615, 668–70, 688–90, 695, 768–69, 787, 799, 804, 823, 962, 967, 970, 999; **11:**15, 17, 91, 113, 149, 162–67, 186, 206, 210–12, 215, 218–19, 221–23, 230, 267, 270, 276, 279, 282, 295, 307, 348, 357, 359, 374, 380, 385, 402, 404, 407–11, 413, 416, 421, 460, 488, 491, 494, 515, 527, 535, 545, 563, 572–74, 579, 582, 584, 608, 613, 615, 618, 639–41, 662, 674, 741, 744, 750, 758, 760, 771, 807, 871; **12:**6, 12, 22, 24, 33, 71, 76, 155, 181, 238, 253, 256, 257–58, 260, 303, 323, 328–29, 340, 342–43, 358, 360, 394, 414, 465, 475, 489–90, 503–6, 514–20, 522–23, 529–31, 533, 539, 553, 559–60, 567–69, 589, 705, 732

REVELATION, BOOK OF
1:15–16, 19–20, 48, 51, 88, 135, 188–89, 201, 203, 289, 893, 981, 1196; **2:**38, 91; **3:**447, 588, 928, 1057, 1065; **4:**463, 675, 1277; **5:**102, 552; **6:**185, 206–7, 214, 226, 521, 551, 814, 918, 982, 1384, 1531; **7:**1–11, 13–16, 63, 103, 107, 128–29, 147–48, 151, 228, 333–34, 762; **8:**34, 448, 487, 688; **9:**138, 431, 499–500; **10:**109, 299, 370, 390–91, 919, 1002; **11:**106, 397, 812; **12:**97, 234–35, 239, 276, 343, 366, 390, 399, 403, 465, 493, 502

REVENGE
1:374–75, 579, 584, 594, 630, 671–72, 1075, 1142; **2:**200, 333, 422, 432, 435–37, 446, 563, 578–79, 629, 696, 737, 763, 797, 807–8, 810, 817, 820, 841, 843, 851–54, 859, 878, 884–88, 921, 1164, 1167, 1218, 1270, 1273, 1293, 1303, 1305–1306, 1308–10; **3:**869, 895, 911, 913, 934, 1088, 1099, 1119, 1124, 1143–44, 1162, 1167, 1171–72; **4:**52, 275, 488, 645, 789, 848, 895, 902, 908–9, 913, 953, 996, 1124, 1127, 1227–29, 1237, 1240–41, 1252; **5:**159, 543, 764, 800; **6:**60, 90, 160, 278–79, 675, 718, 919, 1022, 1080–81, 1150, 1257–58, 1349, 1354–55, 1357, 1421, 1431, 1438, 1479; **7:**140, 291–92, 576, 588, 601; **8:**193–94, 487, 670; **9:**148; **10:**701; **12:**158, 418

REVERE, REVERENCE
1:9, 52, 70, 79, 100, 277, 280, 316, 848, 1048, 1106, 1121, 1131–33, 1135, 1139; **2:**124, 136, 139, 369, 1252; **3:**469, 611, 753, 800, 804, 1017, 1023, 1103, 1118, 1124–25, 1182; **4:**198, 334–35, 337, 563, 687, 701, 814, 824, 939; **5:**6, 24, 152, 159, 198, 264; **6:**141, 541, 957, 994, 1002, 1093, 1109, 1120–21, 1124, 1177, 1309; **7:**149, 188, 859; **8:**35, 136, 262, 289, 368, 500, 516; **9:**252, 314, 337, 349, 393, 434, 476, 8353–6; **10:**101, 274, 529, 832, 899; **11:**225, 442, 452–53, 798, 801, 869; **12:**23, 62, 64, 76, 156, 159–61, 168, 172, 238–39, 258, 284, 291, 492

REVILE, REVILED
1:869; **3:**1062, 1064; **4:**218, 698, 973; **6:**386; **8:**286–87; **9:**144, 401, 659; **10:**254, 841; **12:**76, 291, 305, 310, 345

REWARD (*OR* REWARDS, *ETC.*)
1:444–45, 448, 462, 554, 815, 923, 1172; **2:**82, 184, 190, 351, 427, 471, 825, 893–94, 923, 932, 945, 945–46, 1110–11, 1122, 1147, 1159, 1176, 1201–1203, 1212, 1229–30, 1244, 1277, 1336, 1339; **3:**226, 286, 406, 592, 631, 868, 873, 888, 892, 911–13, 941, 985–86, 989, 944–45, 997–98, 1003–1004, 1009, 1015–17, 1033, 1053, 1057, 1068, 1070, 1085, 1120, 1124; **4:**51, 84, 156, 236, 242, 277, 393, 445, 525, 540–41, 552, 667, 671, 685, 738, 741–42, 770, 778, 802, 824, 909, 924–25, 961, 969, 1014, 1048, 1059, 1133, 1136, 1170, 1173, 1198, 1244, 1260; **5:**48, 53, 55, 114, 126, 153, 198, 211, 220, 231, 233, 238,

REWARD *(continued)*
297–98, 302, 307, 319–20, 323, 332, 345, 351, 359, 407, 433, 454, 469, 476, 478, 486–87, 527, 535, 616, 623–24, 628, 656, 663, 665, 667, 675, 687, 709, 720, 746, 798, 813, 818, 824, 843, 867; **6:**337, 400, 407, 468, 472, 485, 521, 550, 694, 746, 810, 876–77, 913, 1100, 1240, 1259–61, 1291, 1309, 1410, 1601; **7:**51, 82, 84, 143, 148–49, 194, 552, 558, 643; **8:**177, 195, 200–201, 210, 245, 249, 263, 304, 391–92, 395, 398, 429, 639, 651, 699, 726; **9:**53, 129, 143–44, 181, 227, 230, 255, 262, 264, 288, 317, 323, 348–49, 362–63, 393, 424, 425–27; **10:**49, 171, 429, 433, 441, 715, 749, 829–32, 835, 840, 881, 906, 909, 924; **11:**337, 364, 411, 453, 456, 491, 494, 516, 521, 531, 573, 621, 650, 655, 657–58, 763, 898; **12:**34, 125–26, 133, 141–42, 146, 149, 188, 190, 194, 219, 221, 252, 256, 291, 348–49, 351, 365, 411, 453, 486, 491, 555, 611, 644, 708, 710, 733; JUST **1:**30; **3:**916; **5:**331; **7:**12, 182; **12:**605, 644; AND PUNISHMENT **1:**72, 469, 986; **3:**986, 1004, 1071; **4:**40, 495, 593, 604, 684, 752, 839, 891, 970, 1201; **5:**9, 277, 280, 339, 471, 476, 565, 664, 718, 730, 768, 788; **6:**223, 759, 1139, 1252, 1531; **7:**2, 4–5, 13–15, 229, 640; **8:**28, 31–32, 351; **9:**263, 265, 364, 393; **10:**356; **11:**87; **12:**280, 326, 342

RHETORIC
ANCIENT **10:**40, 334, 382, 553, 791, 831; **11:**352, 365, 408, 556; **12:**15, 178, 187; ASIATIC **1:**192; **12:**324; GRECO-ROMAN **1:**140, 192; **3:**953; **4:**236, 313; **5:**606, 632, 642, 793; **7:**62; **9:**863; **10:**34, 63, 261, 298, 310, 374, 377, 999; **11:**32, 196, 363, 543; **12:**7, 15, 22, 130, 324, 331, 480

RHETORICAL
CRITICISM (*see under* CRITICISM); QUESTION **1:**240, 465, 482, 557, 599, 716, 793, 800, 817; **2:**106, 107–8, 319, 904, 1041, 1147, 1224–25; **3:**75, 144, 560, 581, 846, 849, 851; **4:**313–14, 326, 349, 369–70, 376, 378–79, 387, 389, 395, 400, 409, 420, 434–35, 442, 462, 475, 491–92, 500, 512, 517, 528, 531, 563–64, 576, 580, 583, 589, 591, 596, 598, 601, 603, 608–10, 622, 625; **5:**69, 80, 173, 185, 205, 230, 250–51, 253, 256, 260, 270, 292–93, 321, 323, 332, 518, 616, 631, 647, 654–55, 695, 731, 736, 780, 784; **7:**371–72, 374, 394, 399, 402, 423, 448–49, 589, 612, 747, 790, 792, 795, 864; **8:**59, 181, 267, 333, 426–27; **9:**686, 696; **10:**167, 190, 209, 298, 437, 609, 611–12, 666, 737, 812, 854–55, 861, 904, 929, 949, 982; **11:**103, 156, 158, 171, 251, 706; **12:**28, 30, 33, 50, 89, 143, 145, 192, 196–98, 205, 209–10, 215, 355

RICH, THE
See WEALTH, WEALTHY

RICHES
1:225, 323, 359, 430, 941; **3:**39, 83, 87, 388, 457, 469, 473–74, 522, 546, 551, 882, 1055, 1068, 1173; **4:**66, 483, 485, 528–29, 531, 759, 877, 925; **5:**53, 119–20, 173, 210, 232–33, 312, 319–20, 322, 326, 341, 343, 437, 498, 509–10, 515, 639, 651, 663, 678, 714, 716, 779–80; **6:**72, 254–55, 396, 551, 656, 1314, 1383; **7:**13, 54, 88, 147, 188, 285–86, 293, 400, 516, 533, 610; **8:**574, 640; **9:**25, 101, 178–79, 231, 255, 259, 409, 511; **10:**635, 642, 665, 680–81, 695–96, 703, 943; **11:**25–26, 373, 381, 385, 389, 392, 414, 416, 545, 548, 572, 594, 615–16, 618, 827, 830–31; **12:**188, 419, 669, 685

RIDDLE, RIDDLES
2:110, 729, 773, 840–41, 843, 847, 850, 858–59; **4:**876–78, 992; **5:**33, 69, 206, 208, 251, 281, 297, 394, 398, 510, 687, 689, 698, 813, 849; **6:**1242, 1270, 1274, 1295, 1525; **7:**82, 88, 647, 864; **8:**298, 564, 571–72, 574; **9:**165–66, 169–70, 172, 382, 408, 528, 668, 755, 781; **12:**46

RIGHTEOUS, RIGHTEOUSNESS
1:23, 97, 230, 281, 393, 439, 448–49, 469–70, 538, 586, 607, 758, 841, 909, 1099, 1101, 1143, 1174; **2:**346, 359, 369, 502, 551, 603, 1176–77, 1365–68; **3:**40, 88, 117, 169, 278, 286–87, 389, 577, 587, 594, 809–10, 980–91, 984, 989, 993, 997, 1003, 1015, 1028, 1058, 1063–64, 1069, 1179; **4:**47, 50, 52, 60, 164, 309, 328–29, 333, 346, 378, 460, 485, 492, 500, 503, 523, 548, 557, 559, 570, 576, 581, 585, 592, 667, 679–80, 684, 687, 697, 700–702, 707, 709, 719, 721–23, 731, 742, 747–48, 752, 764, 769, 774, 800, 806–7, 815, 821, 824, 830, 843–44, 859, 861–63, 881, 885, 890, 934, 945, 960–61, 1017–18, 1037, 1052, 1068–69, 1071, 1092, 1130, 1133–35, 1171, 1173, 1179, 1203, 1250, 1260; **5:**2, 46, 50, 55, 89, 105, 107, 117, 119–20, 125, 127–28, 131, 146, 149, 152–55, 162, 188–89, 194, 197, 210, 218, 232, 331, 336–37, 340–41, 357, 449, 452–54, 461, 475–76, 501, 523–26, 552, 554, 615, 652, 674, 692, 843; **6:**47, 60, 92, 271, 300, 370, 380, 395–96, 402–3, 407, 414, 417, 438, 440–43, 447–48, 451, 457, 477, 490–91, 493, 499–500, 503–5, 509, 515–16, 520, 539, 547, 598, 602, 636, 674, 742, 744–45, 935, 952, 958, 972, 981–82, 1135, 1167, 1191–92, 1213–14, 1219, 1258, 1260, 1263, 1265, 1408, 1446, 1452, 1458; **7:**13, 128, 148, 261, 264, 276, 312, 324, 639, 643, 685, 791, 795; **8:**30–32, 35, 37, 76, 84, 104, 121, 136, 145, 160, 178, 180–81, 185, 187–88, 190–91, 198, 215, 217, 221, 249, 251, 383, 408, 496, 532, 692; **9:**59, 84, 90, 144, 153, 288, 296, 303, 319, 322, 341–43, 345–46, 349, 357, 772, 775, 796; **10:**190, 247,

323, 397–401, 403, 406, 410–11, 414, 423–26, 428–29, 445, 450, 452–55, 457–61, 463–64, 466–80, 482, 484–85, 486–88, 490–91, 493–95, 500–503, 508, 511, 513, 523–25, 528–30, 533, 535, 541–46, 549–50, 552, 555–57, 561, 567, 574, 579, 583–84, 596, 613, 622, 625, 635, 638, 643–44, 646–49, 651–52, 654–58, 660–64, 666, 669–71, 675–76, 680–81, 690, 692, 695, 720, 725, 729, 738, 741, 747, 768–69, 815, 841, 936; **11:**57, 65–66, 69, 72–73, 75, 95–96, 98, 131, 146, 151, 166, 198, 212, 214, 220, 237–38, 241, 243–44, 246, 255, 257, 260, 265, 268, 271–72, 275, 277, 279, 307–8, 314, 318, 321, 335, 356, 362, 391, 398, 400, 409, 428–29, 435, 436, 459, 461, 480, 485–86, 525–26, 527–29, 531, 695, 828, 836, 844, 846, 856, 876; **12:**30, 68, 86, 134, 177, 187, 189, 197, 204, 266, 281, 283, 291–92, 300, 330–31, 334, 336–37, 345, 348, 352, 357–58, 369, 374, 390, 399–400, 412, 418, 426, 436, 505, 522, 634, 636, 646, 699–702, 704; AND JUSTICE **1:**76, 166, 391, 445, 447, 450, 467–69, 477; **2:**88, 110, 346, 359, 376, 417, 423, 538, 620, 1170, 1176, 1242, 1294–95; **3:**87–88, 512; **4:**46, 72, 82, 400, 412, 480, 483–84, 496, 534, 538–40, 576, 592, 594, 641–42, 653, 668–69, 673, 708–9, 717, 734, 740, 742, 783, 810, 820, 823, 871, 873, 908–9, 940, 953, 959, 963, 695, 1006, 1008, 1010–11, 1035, 1037–38, 1054, 1058, 1065–66, 1069–70, 1072–73, 1075–76, 1092, 1105, 1110, 1127, 1133–34, 1168, 1174, 1213, 1250, 1252, 1276–77; **5:**25, 33–34, 43, 45–46, 49, 63, 90–92, 159–60, 176, 186, 196, 205, 212, 214, 243, 246, 310, 327, 454, 456, 510, 562–63, 598–99; **6:**20–21, 23, 39, 57–58, 61–64, 69, 88–90, 94–95, 110, 122–24, 141–43, 148, 221, 223, 229, 237, 239–40, 265–66, 270, 272, 408, 448, 450–51, 461–62, 478, 485–86, 492, 498–504, 514–15, 521, 580, 588, 606, 639, 656, 676, 680–81, 708, 728, 739–42, 744, 754, 763, 826, 919, 948, 956, 981, 1171, 1211, 1213, 1220, 1263, 1450, 1452, 1582–83; **7:**77, 103, 226, 355, 388, 394, 403, 580, 582, 643, 685, 693, 861, 873–74; **8:**39, 179, 182, 196, 200, 211, 294, 395; **9:**60, 757; **10:**322, 399–401, 404–5, 413–14, 425–26, 455, 459, 465, 469–70, 472–73, 476–77, 492, 503, 511, 590, 639–40, 654, 658, 700, 702, 815, 855, 997; **11:**75–76, 96, 130, 132, 238, 313, 393, 658, 748; **12:**143, 333–34, 388, 410, 412, 662; SELF-RIGHTEOUSNESS (*see* SELF-RIGHTEOUSNESS); TEACHER OF **4:**72; **5:**332; **7:**15; **8:**38–39, 432; **9:**642; **11:**421; WORKS **8:**145, 217, 249; **10:**485–86, 583, 654–55, 660, 675; **12:**197; AND WORKS (*see under* WORKS). *See also* JUSTICE

RIGHT HAND
See under HAND

RIGHT HAND OF GOD
See HAND: GOD'S RIGHT

RING, RINGS
AS JEWELRY **1:**605, 622, 937; **2:**189, 1001; **3:**897, 899, 918, 920, 923, 925, 1147; **4:**635; **5:**119, 218, 430, 730, 855; **6:**743, 1168, 1228, 1329, 1391; **7:**225, 713, 730–32; **9:**301, 303; **12:**194

RITUAL, RITUALS
CLEANNESS/CLEANSING/WASHING **1:**836, 918, 1051, 1106; **2:**147, 151; **3:**1002, 1086; **4:**277, 752; **5:**793; **6:**84, 103, 464, 1491, 1526; **8:**26, 156, 332, 495, 606–7; **9:**247, 537, 724; **12:**71, 105, 664; MEAL (*see* MEAL: RITUAL/SACRIFICIAL); UNCLEANNESS **1:**9, 1104–1105; **2:**62; **3:**129, 452, 592, 786, 847, 902, 959, 1002; **5:**67, 273; **6:**281, 1030, 1033, 1063, 1309; **7:**727; **8:**32, 237–38, 332–33, 436, 466; **9:**121, 815. *See also* CLEAN; IMPURITY, RITUAL

RIVER, RIVERS
1:233, 246, 250, 266, 269, 274, 293, 351, 388, 416, 565, 699, 742; **2:**63, 91, 164–65, 181, 184, 190, 600–601, 614, 668, 708, 750, 1266, 1280; **3:**82, 194, 253, 337, 379, 726, 949, 969, 1028, 1065; **4:**78, 132–33, 145, 275, 330, 444, 530, 569, 621, 823, 866, 964, 1000; **5:**356, 590, 593, 616, 674, 758, 818; **6:**10, 113, 117, 180, 214, 271, 375–76, 411, 478, 509, 599, 683, 882, 900, 916, 942–43, 1042, 1075, 1077, 1081, 1217, 1246, 1326, 1348, 1353, 1380, 1404, 1435, 1503, 1595–99, 1607; **7:**12, 58, 111, 114, 124, 136, 148, 526, 593, 602, 610, 616, 668, 807, 837; **8:**531; **9:**152, 271, 367; **10:**231; **12:**591, 598, 630, 651, 724; ORDEAL **2:**63

ROAD, ROADS
1:178, 222, 233, 271, 567; **2:**18, 124–25, 158, 163, 183, 253, 494, 634, 646, 787, 850, 1090, 1309, 1347, 1352; **3:**105, 555, 984, 995, 1023, 1049–50, 1108; **4:**57, 110, 130, 156, 275–76, 475, 494, 510; **5:**29, 31, 67, 84–85, 99, 124, 161, 163, 169, 394, 721, 742, 787; **6:**281–82, 603, 716, 978, 981, 1030, 1129, 1293, 1301, 1304, 1347, 1380, 1410, 1438, 1472; **7:**89, 252; **8:**12–13, 14, 216, 343, 656, 658–59, 705, 728, 731; **9:**22, 66–67, 155, 203, 217, 222, 229–30, 290, 302, 304, 325–26, 348, 351, 354, 356, 367, 370, 427, 451, 455, 482, 487; **10:**41, 142–43, 174, 196, 204, 237–38, 581, 594, 614, 697, 755, 761, 807, 894; **11:**405; **12:**4. *See also by name in* *PLACES IN THE BIBLE*

ROBBER, ROBBERS/ROBBERY
1:1041; **2:**426; **4:**370, 925; **5:**12, 63, 75, 85, 182, 264, 670, 716, 767, 805; **6:**626, 996, 1009, 1261, 1315, 1450; **7:**141, 256, 375–76, 448, 552; **8:**406, 491–92, 661, 663, 671, 710; **9:**373–74, 543, 841; **10:**273, 447, 850; **11:**150; **12:**633

ROBE, ROBES
1:586, 598, 600, 905–7, 973, 1060–61, 1110–11, 1113–14; **2:**162, 987, 1089, 1120, 1156–59, 1184; **3:**495, 914, 927; **4:**122, 223, 286, 352, 358, 601, 1053; **5:**341, 411, 592–93, 689; **6:**81, 102, 105, 196, 972, 977, 980–82, 996, 1061, 1151, 1157, 1228, 1368, 1430; **7:**64, 82, 103, 125, 514, 818; **8:**267, 433, 488, 681, 731; **9:**148, 163–64, 206, 301–2, 316–17, 393–94, 431, 446, 822; **10:**43, 485; **12:**523, 548, 561, 567, 583, 585, 587, 599, 613, 618, 624–26, 642, 651, 654, 667, 677, 681, 699, 730, 733–35

ROCK, ROCKS
1:176, 180, 215, 222, 249, 688, 805, 816–18; **2:**61, 99, 160–61, 527–28, 791, 796–97, 842, 853, 872, 1154; **3:**142, 581, 773, 811, 860, 931, 1171, 1178; **4:**39, 197, 403, 467–68, 470, 478, 538, 545, 577, 605, 991, 1004, 1244; **5:**68, 127, 185, 254, 422, 524, 531, 585, 745, 746–47, 768, 771, 775, 787; **6:**160, 196, 198, 421–22, 432, 664, 753, 755, 919, 1200, 1336–37, 1358–60, 1364, 1366, 1596; **7:**56, 92, 403, 437, 447; **8:**218, 345, 493–94, 726; **9:**152–53, 176–77, 372, 465, 601; **10:**352, 446, 484, 504, 516, 576, 914–15; **11:**69, 302, 701; **12:**305, 500, 614 (*see also* STONE); AS A METAPHOR FOR GOD/PERSON **1:**92, 207, 666; **2:**34, 528, 753, 981–82, 1366; **4:**50, 416, 510, 679, 747, 749, 753, 786, 789, 800, 842, 853, 918–20, 922–23, 958, 969, 1051, 1057, 1059, 1061, 1192; **5:**463, 867; **6:**174, 176, 265, 387, 408, 586, 628, 1458; **7:**55, 250–51, 317; **8:**122, 157, 343, 345–46, 349, 414, 562; **9:**84; **10:**915; **12:**141, 245, 268, 291

ROCK BADGER
1:1080; **4:**597

ROD, RODS
1:240, 556; **2:**160–61; **3:**176, 1124; **4:**210, 413, 768, 1193; **5:**108, 182, 198–99, 207, 224; **6:**36, 39, 113, 122, 132–33, 137, 141, 161, 163, 181, 204, 237, 293, 353, 386, 394, 579, 583–84, 604, 733, 757, 886, 1048, 1052, 1082–83, 1166, 1168, 1218, 1299, 1506, 1576; **7:**202, 240, 597, 661; **10:**233, 709; **11:**22, 136, 157, 806; **12:**104, 641, 649, 651, 694, 699–700, 703, 722–24. *See also* SCEPTER; STAFF

ROE, ROEBUCK
1:1081; **3:**782. *See also* DEER

ROLL
CALL/MUSTER **1:**735; **2:**1079, 1149, 1194; **3:**336, 376, 813; **4:**1024, 1128; **6:**314; **9:**81; **12:**127, 131–33, 144, 253, 602; MEMBERSHIP **6:**1202; **10:**8, 19, 115, 135, 189, 224, 294; PAPYRUS **4:**202; **6:**941 (*see also* PAPYRUS)

ROMAN, ROMANS
CENTURIAN **1:**1018; **6:**860; **7:**67; **8:**688; **10:**80, 146, 352, 354; CHRISTIANS **8:**514; **10:**357, 367, 406–8, 420, 701, 761; CHURCH (*see under* CHURCH); CITIZENS **10:**234–35, 308; **11:**157, 470; COURT **9:**442, 820; **10:**256, 289, 614; CULTURE (*see under* CULTURE); EMPIRE **1:**9, 83, 94–95, 166, 196, 200, 269–71, 284–85, 289, 291, 306, 992, 1040; **2:**192, 256, 510; **3:**932, 1076, 1124; **4:**5, 7, 12, 21–23, 26, 30–31, 35, 40–41, 102–7, 142–43, 153, 157, 160–61, 164, 169, 183, 206, 216, 228–29, 240, 266, 268, 270–71, 297, 873, 1131, 1277; **5:**490, 497, 542, 556, 567, 597, 612, 721, 742; **6:**164, 933, 973, 980, 1016; **7:**3–4, 7–8, 10, 141, 644; **8:**5, 15–16, 21–23, 52, 135, 142, 164, 166, 180, 420, 442–43, 480, 488, 490, 516, 560, 637, 663, 673, 684, 712, 718; **9:**28, 32, 52, 62, 80, 84–85, 127, 147, 155, 171, 199, 263, 316, 357, 363, 370, 372, 385, 405, 448–49, 452, 455, 465, 478, 543, 638, 658, 697, 814, 816, 823, 830; **10:**121, 147, 170, 189, 197, 202, 237–38, 255, 261, 266, 329, 333, 336, 348, 360, 366–67, 372, 376–77, 409, 423, 515, 550, 553, 624, 717–18, 721, 736, 755, 774, 763, 782, 997, 1007; **11:**139, 157, 205, 231, 342, 365, 377, 383, 470–71, 510, 535, 591, 653, 674–75, 677, 684, 703, 705, 726, 751, 771–72, 792, 885, 900; **12:**125, 144, 284, 287, 485, 493, 514, 533, 538, 547, 641, 678, 683, 685, 703, 726, 728, 744; GOVERNMENT **4:**22; **8:**371; **9:**801, 816, 825; **11:**677, 705, 771; GOVERNOR(S) **8:**15, 464, 482, 680, 685, 719; **9:**697, 801–2; **10:**311, 333–34; **11:**488; **12:**163; OFFICIALS **9:**801–2, 815; **10:**162, 313, 333, 774; RELIGION **1:**1105; **3:**1124–25, 1182; **4:**11; **5:**557, 696; **7:**10; **8:**15–16, 21–22; **10:**230, 271, 329, 374, 404, 409, 515, 718–19, 739, 774; **11:**205, 365, 383, 470–71, 510, 535, 653, 677; **12:**658, 685

ROMAN CATHOLIC
1:1, 5, 8, 10, 18, 20, 23, 26, 28, 31–34, 44, 50, 52–55, 58, 61, 63–64, 99–101, 106, 108, 119, 126–27, 162, 193, 198, 203, 205, 208, 212, 300, 303, 305, 309, 1194; **2:**153, 719, 950; **3:**861, 1092, 1173; **4:**72, 677, 1276; **5:**374, 407, 635, 788; **6:**244, 985; **7:**253, 227, 675, 873; **8:**6, 136, 202, 318, 347, 395; **9:**63, 101, 540, 606, 613, 832; **10:**396, 409, 485–86; **11:**197, 207, 238, 366, 721, 775; **12:**116, 444, 537–38; CHURCH (*see* CHURCH: CATHOLIC/ROMAN CATHOLIC). *See also* CATHOLIC

ROMANS, LETTER TO THE
1:8, 13, 16, 19, 86, 105, 110, 160, 1196; **2:**489, 609; **3:**382, 612; **4:**888, 1237; **5:**264; **6:**402, 423, 516, 656, 710, 815, 935; **7:**353, 623, 640, 643; **8:**13, 19, 29, 97, 514, 632; **9:**391, 434, 716;

10:10–11, 31, 109, 208–9, 322, 364–65, 369–70, 373, 379, 381, 386, 856, 869, 877, 889, 921, 949, 969, 972; **11:**27, 37, 41, 70–71, 76, 87, 94–95, 114, 124, 135, 141, 144, 166, 168, 193, 243, 259, 268–69, 277, 286, 343, 346, 354, 420, 423, 429, 473, 480, 528, 568, 603, 674, 695, 797, 883; **12:**4, 6, 87, 173, 182–83, 231, 236, 266, 274–75, 301–2, 466, 524, 530, 560, 573

ROOF, ROOFS
2:453, 547, 593, 804, 859, 876, 1284–85, 1289, 1293, 1331; **3:**429, 703, 768, 914, 1075, 1084, 1132–33; **5:**180, 193, 220, 614; **6:**995, 1551; **7:**71–72, 179; **8:**64, 164, 547, 549; **9:**123; CHAMBER **2:**771–72; OF THE MOUTH **2:**1238; **4:**1227; **6:**1061, 1137, 1454; TOP **2:**453; **5:**499; **9:**404; **10:**163

ROOM, ROOMS
FOUR-ROOM HOUSE **1:**216, 224; THRONE **1:**278–79, 897; **2:**771, 773; **3:**908; **6:**101, 124, 329, 1131, 1557, 1560; **7:**3, 5, 10, 13, 92, 103; **8:**680; **12:**519; THE UPPER **3:**486, 497, 770; **7:**91; **8:**468, 659; **9:**719; **10:**277. *See also* CHAMBER

ROOT, ROOTS
OF JESSE **6:**145; **7:**811; **10:**684, 748; **12:**602; LINGUISTIC **1:**380, 1063, 1065, 1071; **2:**63, 614, 901, 921, 927, 10051011; **3:**215; **4:**74, 309, 657, 671, 810, 820, 1066; **5:**92; IN PLANT/TREE IMAGERY **4:**31, 470; **5:**563; **6:**163; **8:**570, 573; **9:**84; **10:**683, 685

ROPE, ROPES
1:129; **2:**841, 853, 858; **3:**46, 151; **4:**586, 622; **5:**355; **6:**81, 477, 850, 1137, 1374, 1377; **7:**377, 477; **8:**395; **9:**348; **10:**348, 353; **11:**44, 160

ROSE, ROSES
5:389, 476; **10:**759; BUD(S) **5:**461, 716

ROSETTE
1:905, 907–8, 912, 973; **7:**766

ROSH HA-SHANAH
See under FEASTS/FESTIVALS

RUBIES
5:260; **6:**1378

RUDDER
1:391; **5:**787; **10:**353; **12:**203

RUDDY
1:521; **2:**1099, 1112; **5:**382–83, 416, 708; **6:**1061

RUE
9:247

RUG, RUGS
1:219; **2:**781; **6:**1380

RULER, RULERS
OF THE CITY **1:**222–23, 247, 250, 255, 259; **2:**307, 637, 678; **3:**765, 768, 770, 793, 825, 1114; **4:**178; **6:**1349, 1384, 1386, 1391, 1393, 1402; **7:**694, 805; **10:**230, 237, 239; OF THE SYNAGOGUE **7:**253; **8:**69, 237, 274, 332, 341, 431, 464, 540, 588; **9:**155, 190, 273–74, 809; **10:**191–92, 196, 254, 312, 359–60, 775, 777 (*see also* ARCHISYNAGOGOS). *See also* LEADER

RUNNER, RUNNERS
2:1339; **3:**575; **5:**219; **7:**641; ATHELETE **4:**312; **5:**341; **11:**314; **12:**82, 148, 150, 152

RUSHES
See BULRUSHES

RUST
5:565, 775; **6:**988, 995, 1336, 1383; **8:**210; **9:**260; **11:**88; **12:**216–17, 250

RUTH, BOOK OF
1:8, 11, 29, 43, 65, 241, 252, 592, 1196; **2:**65, 291, 461, 468, 477, 543, 761, 952, 1145; **3:**13, 507, 747, 959, 1016; **4:**20, 30, 510; **5:**273, 284, 364, 687; **7:**145, 620; **8:**28, 41

S

SABBATH, SABBATHS
1:55, 67, 69, 71, 82, 189, 278, 286, 291, 298, 316–17, 341, 346–47, 459, 607, 689, 743, 805, 812–15, 844–46, 852, 863, 871, 922–26, 950, 960, 1065, 1086, 1113, 1131–32, 1138, 1155–61, 1163, 1166, 1170–72, 1174, 1178–79, 1183, 1196; **2:**18, 77, 128–29, 217, 229–30, 232, 235, 325, 329, 331–32, 380, 393, 402–3, 406–8, 412–13, 415, 820, 1139, 1141; **3:**302, 574, 657, 666, 691, 712, 743, 797, 811, 813, 819, 847–48, 850–51, 1018, 1132; **4:**11, 36, 39, 46–48, 66, 115, 125, 182, 229, 233, 249, 277, 295, 496, 555, 939, 1050, 1052, 1061; **5:**45, 95, 101–2, 138, 260, 366, 474, 798; **6:**477, 486, 498, 500, 539, 549, 572, 707, 710, 712, 828, 1280–84, 1309, 1315, 1329, 1463, 1491, 1497, 1578–79, 1584, 1588–89; **7:**416, 785; **8:**15, 22, 33, 35, 39, 59, 63, 78, 97, 122, 196, 228, 234, 272, 275–80, 282, 332, 443, 497–98, 515, 521, 547–50, 554–59, 577, 624, 663–64, 678, 697, 725–26, 730; **9:**16, 18, 34, 110–11, 114, 122, 132–36, 211, 272–74, 280, 284–86, 355, 392, 465, 468, 542, 576, 578–81, 583–84, 588, 619–20, 654, 656, 659–60, 663, 705, 833, 836, 849; **10:**44, 143, 146, 152, 191–92, 194, 220, 223, 226, 230–31, 237–38, 240, 252, 254–55, 277, 293, 461, 481, 596, 661, 736, 778, 996; **11:**185, 213, 239, 251, 288, 313, 323, 362, 364–65, 631; **12:**52–53, 118, 532, 534, 566, 596, 711–12, 728

SABBATH DAY'S JOURNEY
10:44

SABBATICAL YEAR
1:870–71, 1113, 1132, 1156–57, 1170–71, 1174, 1180; **3:**718, 993; **4:**90–91, 178; **7:**128; **8:**577

SACKCLOTH
1:1082, 1113; **2:**1225; **3:**151, 796, 805, 901–3, 914, 927, 959–60, 962, 1086, 1091, 1113–14, 1134, 1139, 1142, 1147; **4:**43, 63, 208, 263, 459; **6:**81, 168, 195, 293, 977, 980, 1167, 1382, 1579; **7:**122, 124–25, 309, 312, 470–71, 483, 513–14; **8:**205–6; **9:**84, 221; **12:**642; AND ASHES **3:**902, 959–60, 1113, 1142; **4:**63; **8:**205–6; **9:**84, 221

SACRAMENT, SACRAMENTS
1:199, 204–5, 209–12, 539, 543, 685, 783–84, 846, 977, 1184; **2:**15, 40, 54, 67–68, 83, 112, 141–42, 152, 168, 194, 1376; **3:**395, 688, 731; **4:**854, 1243; **6:**710, 816; **7:**228; **8:**197, 325; **9:**606, 614, 834, 847; **10:**72, 236; **11:**451, 646, 651; **12:**128, 222, 229, 264, 298, 444

SACRIFICE, SACRIFICES
1:69, 279–82, 373, 391, 393, 729, 750–51, 767, 881, 900, 913, 989–95, 1024–26, 1034, 1051–52; **2:**14–15, 62–64, 77–78, 81–84, 126–27, 147, 151, 184–85, 228–33, 255–56, 386–87, 411–12, 606, 796–97, 825, 1071, 1088–89, 1340; **3:**40, 47–48, 425, 427, 498–99, 610–13, 691, 708, 710, 1178–79; **4:**39, 41, 197–99, 218, 240–41, 257, 277, 345–46, 359, 734, 753, 843, 845, 877, 881–83, 887–89, 1243; **5:**149, 166, 591, 696, 793, 795–98, 808; **6:**56, 276–77, 378–80, 639, 691, 940, 944, 1545–47, 1564, 1569, 1588–89, 1593; **7:**56, 143, 162, 241, 254, 380, 394, 477, 502, 507, 513, 666, 678, 680, 859–62; **8:**33–34, 179, 278–79, 627, 640; **9:**203, 457, 528, 543, 714, 734, 837; **10:**128, 294, 475–76, 579, 704–7, 769, 862, 918; **11:**58, 61, 170, 177, 439–40, 503, 514, 656; **12:**12, 42, 74, 104–5, 110, 158, 269; HUMAN **1:**494, 495, 785, 950, 1119, 1126, 1127, 1138–39; **2:**50, 391, 428, 570, 619, 724, 729, 821, 830–36, 842; **3:**184, 250, 255, 276, 598, 635, 1174; **4:**82, 243, 1111; **5:**542, 629; **6:**256, 635, 640, 721, 1230, 1284, 1286, 1290, 1325; **7:**288, 385, 485, 499–500, 580, 828; JESUS AS **1:**91, 93, 499, 914, 998, 999, 1015, 1114, 1120, 1152; **2:**83, 834; **3:**612; **4:**845, 1149, 1229; **6:**382, 1154, 1564; **8:**42, 471–72, 683, 702, 704–5, 720; **9:**714, 719, 794, 837; **10:**20, 339, 474, 519, 553, 610; **11:**187, 202, 261, 400; **12:**12, 43, 59–61, 64, 94, 96, 101, 106–8, 112–15, 118, 123, 145, 166–67, 259–60, 338, 387–88, 419, 423, 441, 523, 531. *See also* OFFERING

SACRILEGE
2:61–62, 67; **3:**441, 733; **4:**9, 11, 34, 39–40, 71, 206, 223, 232, 281; **8:**429, 442–43, 445, 516, 556, 657, 689, 693, 730; **9:**6, 393, 704; **10:**273, 319. *See also* DESOLATING SACRILEGE

SADDLE
1:557, 1104; **2:**1347

SADDLECLOTHS
6:1377

SADDUCEE, SADDUCEES
1:44, 287–88, 291, 1160; **3:**1004, 1079; **5:**316, 341, 627–28, 634, 651; **7:**175; **8:**37, 99, 122, 142, 147, 151, 157, 162, 223, 340–42, 371, 412, 421–23, 657, 675–76, 729; **9:**83, 346, 376, 388–89, 393, 399, 658, 688; **10:**77, 83–84, 86, 89, 104–5, 107–8, 126, 310–12, 315, 318–20, 330, 979

SAFFRON
5:462

SAGA
1:311, 324, 331, 335, 806; **2:**543, 674, 840, 847, 855, 860, 980; **3:**364, 576; **6:**1349; **7:**467; **10:**916, 978

SAGE, SAGES
AS AN HERB **1:**1098; AS A PERSON **1:**67, 73, 78–79, 318; **2:**351, 423, 446, 453, 462, 476, 1313; **3:**55, 859, 980, 1032, 1144; **4:**327, 333, 375–77, 389, 419, 448, 451, 559, 612; **5:**2, 7–12, 15–16, 20–22, 27, 33, 149, 162–64, 174, 176, 212, 244–45, 250, 272–73, 275, 280–81, 293, 300, 303, 312, 316–17, 325–26, 328, 331, 334, 337, 345, 358, 365, 373, 390, 422, 430, 437, 449, 451, 490–93, 495, 502, 510, 518, 526, 605–6, 628–29, 632, 637, 644, 655, 659, 663–64, 667, 669, 674–75, 683, 693, 702, 739–40, 745, 757, 766, 771–72, 787–89, 793 94, 823, 828, 837, 862; **6:**2, 8, 180, 265, 656, 1137, 1223, 1257; **7:**400, 449, 640; **8:**31–32, 38, 104, 248, 437; **9:**10, 66, 231, 148, 259, 286, 301, 337, 565, 742; **10:**695, 802, 808, 812, 820; **11:**81, 111, 150, 153, 382, 415, 431, 460, 607, 654, 659, 768, 796, 847, 853, 913; **12:**141, 203–4, 317

SAIL, SAILS
ON A SHIP **1:**92, 391; **6:**1374; **10:**348; **12:**127. *See also* FORESAIL

SAILING
1:233, 597; **3:**28; **4:**160, 243; **5:**394; **6:**1360, 1416; **7:**502; **8:**13, 340; **9:**116, 362; **10:**36, 191, 258, 276, 278, 288, 344–46, 348, 350, 617, 932; **11:**807. *See also* BOAT; SHIP

SAILOR, SAILORS
1:236; **4:**313, 1118; **5:**550, 553, 561, 568, 570; **6:**205, 1371, 1382–84; **7:**463, 467, 470–71, 473–79, 482–83, 485–86, 488, 491–92, 495–503, 505, 507, 513–14, 516–18, 521, 523, 527–28; **9:**296; **10:**348–49, 351–53, 773, 775; **12:**692–93, 697. *See also* MARINER; SEAFARER

SAINT, SAINTS
1:534, 538, 909, 1182; **2:**88, 152, 551, 564, 571, 574, 628, 694, 717–19, 827, 911–12, 1113, 1180, 1226; **3:**382, 513, 522–23, 536, 611, 631,

1041, 1182; **4:**319, 736, 765, 802, 891, 1030, 1156, 1274, 1277; **5:**284, 341, 345, 485, 606; **6:**358, 468, 470, 1531; **7:**321; **8:**3, 147, 391, 493, 632, 649; **9:**145, 207, 290, 394, 431, 459, 463, 490; **10:**161–62, 333, 336, 395, 401, 421, 485, 528, 588, 599, 756, 763, 798, 815, 831, 854–55, 916, 968, 995–96, 1000–1001; **11:**3, 5–6, 8, 10, 12, 15, 20, 37–39, 96, 111–15, 117–19, 122, 130–31, 134, 135, 170, 175, 179, 202, 227, 284, 298, 359–62, 369–70, 374, 382, 386, 402, 409–410, 415–16, 419, 431, 435, 440, 462–63, 476, 480–81, 546, 549, 587, 590, 593, 615, 658, 714, 750–51, 820, 836, 853, 855, 894–96; **12:**10, 12, 46, 77, 82, 92, 156, 173, 317, 377, 390, 454, 477–78, 484–85, 505, 533, 537, 541, 565–66, 583–84, 589, 593, 603–4, 611, 613, 619, 626, 630–31, 644, 650–52, 657, 667–68, 672–73, 676–77, 680–81, 684, 686, 694–95, 702, 710–12, 714, 734

SALT
1:1018–19; **2:**512, 817; **3:**178, 241, 453, 710, 722, 1029; **4:**125, 391, 470, 610; **5:**176, 326, 818; **6:**891, 1558, 1596–97; **8:**121, 181–83, 640–41; **9:**116, 292–93, 486; **11:**662; **12:**123, 556, 636; PILLAR OF **1:**475; **5:**524; **9:**332

SALUTATION, SALUTATIONS
5:664; **7:**82, 483, 514; **10:**92, 309, 380, 779, 792, 797, 800; **11:**34, 38, 40, 71, 101, 188, 199, 201–3, 587, 687–89; **12:**45, 231, 241–42, 245, 247–48, 272, 281, 370, 380–81, 430, 448–51, 459–60, 612

SALVATION
HISTORY **1:**47, 54, 126, 128, 152, 328, 418, 454; **2:**16, 48–49, 55, 139, 182–83, 188, 194, 219, 252, 256, 262, 267, 983, 1262; **3:**169, 723, 982; **5:**441, 516, 536, 605; **6:**272, 599, 786, 1274–75; **7:**265, 348, 396, 579, 684; **8:**160, 166, 186, 268, 337, 417–18, 530, 655, 670; **9:**56, 568, 716–17; **10:**38, 40, 49, 51, 57, 62–64, 69, 71, 82–83, 85–86, 109, 123, 132, 176, 191–92, 196, 207, 255, 283, 305, 309, 322, 375–76, 451, 472, 551, 626, 692; **11:**262, 639; **12:**54, 98, 139, 143, 145–46, 335, 533–35, 604, 713; ORACLE/PROPHECY **1:**444, 489, 644, 671, 793, 807, 948; **2:**1274; **3:**379, 381, 561, 649, 1155; **4:**645, 729, 768, 968; **6:**23, 46, 108, 137, 174, 222, 271, 291, 294, 300, 348, 352, 354–55, 369, 374, 385, 395, 401, 436, 476, 514, 582, 585–86, 621, 677, 690, 696, 698, 728, 744, 762, 768, 784–85, 788, 806–7, 814, 842, 864–65, 867–68, 876, 884, 971, 973, 1191, 1198, 1205, 1275, 1461, 1480, 1487, 1497, 1505–5, 1509, 1513, 1517, 1527, 1531, 1570; **7:**303–4, 323–25, 535, 554, 604–5, 665, 683, 720; **8:**67; **9:**596, 794; **10:**64, 234, 334. *See also* SAVIOR

SALVE, SALVES
4:443; **7:**106; **10:**85, 168; **12:**573

SAVE, SAVED
1:230; **2:**1055–56; **3:**232; **4:**204, 1100, 1155; **5:**518; **6:**293, 401, 1135, 1214; **7:**537, 807; **8:**491, 590, 650, 688; **9:**19, 454, 456, 553; **10:**90, 171, 348, 353, 624, 690–91; **12:**223

SAMARITAN, THE GOOD
2:878, 892, 902; **3:**601; **5:**56; **9:**12, 23, 35, 227–32, 255, 289, 325–27, 381, 571; **10:**50

SAMUEL, I AND II
1:8, 11, 25, 28–29, 237, 241, 252–53, 260, 296, 301–2, 764, 996, 1196; **2:**6, 166, 247, 274, 291, 432, 519, 541, 543, 246, 548, 551–52, 723, 727, 736, 768, 845, 863, 866, 886, 893–94, 943, 1385; **3:**4, 13, 299, 307–8, 329, 368, 370, 377–79, 384, 386–89, 393–95, 399, 407, 413–17, 422–26, 427, 430, 469, 505, 1191; **4:**20–21, 30, 199, 643–44; **5:**284, 634; **6:**2, 6, 15, 38, 88, 140, 181, 258, 261, 362, 543, 546, 574–75, 739, 752, 891, 1001, 1118, 1138, 1150, 1203, 1268–69, 1274, 1285, 1287, 1299; **7:**204, 344; **8:**28–29; **9:**51, 70; **10:**675; **12:**28

SANCTIFY (*OR* SANCTIFIES, SANCTIFICATION, *ETC.*)
1:833, 836, 992, 2020; **2:**11, 235, 411; **4:**465; **5:**85; **6:**65, 83, 85, 516, 710, 1117, 1280, 1283, 1495; **7:**123, 312, 320; **8:**376; **9:**234, 792–794; **10:**509–10, 546, 657, 798, 815, 831, 877–78; **11:**104, 201, 398, 678–79, 700–701, 716, 718–19, 736, 747, 762; **12:**115, 163, 291, 361, 598. *See also* HOLINESS; HOLY

SANCTUARY, SANCTUARIES
1:232, 241, 267, 278, 282, 306, 311, 315–16, 364, 424–25, 434, 504, 521, 541–43, 585, 801, 841, 884, 888–89, 892, 896–97, 978, 986, 995, 999, 1010, 1019, 1026, 1033–35, 1039–40, 1042, 1044, 1049, 1054, 1060–62, 1070–72, 1074, 1084–85, 1098–99, 1106, 1112–13, 1118, 1131, 1135, 1138–39, 1147–49, 1152, 1156–58, 1163, 1178–79, 1181, 1183, 1186–89; **2:**11, 14–15, 20–21, 25–26, 32–34, 36–37, 52–54, 65, 69–70, 78, 81–83, 88–89, 137, 147–50, 152, 200, 220, 233–34, 236, 246, 257, 264, 268, 276, 278, 281, 289, 310, 316, 321, 343, 345, 348, 352, 363–64, 381, 383–89, 391, 403, 407, 410, 412–14, 420–21, 427, 435, 453, 462–63, 467, 470, 479–81, 484, 487, 491, 519–20, 600, 614, 834, 871, 973–75, 978, 987, 992, 995, 1001, 1048, 1113, 1140–41, 1239, 1249, 1251, 1256; **3:**5, 22, 33–34, 37, 62–63, 70, 78, 81, 84, 94, 104, 109, 113, 168, 178, 225, 241, 250, 252, 255, 257–58, 260, 265, 276, 285, 304, 313, 345, 347, 389, 400, 407, 425, 464, 470, 473–74, 483–84,

SANCTUARY, SANCTUARIES *(continued)*
494–97, 502, 523, 525, 551, 569, 580, 583, 602, 608–12, 616, 618, 625, 635, 644, 646–47, 655–56, 696, 714, 723, 726, 802, 820, 993, 1002, 1144; **4:**34, 38–39, 52, 60, 64, 71–72, 92–93, 99, 146, 156, 159, 164–65, 193, 257, 378, 651, 741, 755, 769, 772, 901, 920, 944, 946, 969, 972–73, 1047, 1142, 1279; **5:**4, 242, 328, 621, 849–50, 859, 862; **6:**65, 74, 83, 102, 105, 176, 228, 285, 379–80, 388–89, 396, 400, 406, 411–14, 455–56, 474, 509, 525, 529, 559, 580, 637, 640–41, 654, 702, 724, 750, 772, 972, 1030, 1043, 1118, 1129, 1146, 1159–60, 1168, 1179, 1188, 1259, 1292, 1295, 1309, 1314, 1319, 1329, 1343, 1349, 1351, 1394, 1489, 1505, 1510, 1511, 1534, 1546, 1551, 1554–55, 1566, 1568, 1570, 1574, 1576, 1578, 1582, 1585, 1597, 1604–1605; **7:**3, 11, 113–14, 192, 202, 205, 241–42, 260, 270, 272–73, 286, 349, 352, 376, 378, 380, 387, 391, 394, 407, 410–11, 417–19, 421, 552, 690, 710, 748, 754, 763, 765, 778, 787, 806, 816, 822, 834; **8:**405, 556, 655, 661, 664, 683, 685, 689, 712, 723; **9:**40, 45–49, 70, 249, 387, 461, 675; **10:**650, 813, 831; **11:**440, 733; **12:**19, 82–84, 96–98, 100–104, 106–7, 112, 120, 131, 166–67, 247, 391, 523, 531, 723

SANDAL, SANDALS
1:712, 1000, 1060; **2:**475, 938; **3:**1147; **4:**917; **6:**182, 1228, 1330, 1342–43, 1583; **7:**365, 416; **8:**158, 256, 532–33, 595; **9:**85–86, 220, 303, 388, 429–30, 528; **11:**459, 461

SANHEDRIN
GOVERNING BODY **1:**84, 1035; **2:**106; **3:**533, 1114; **4:**105; **5:**664; **8:**66, 100, 190, 401, 483–84, 491, 494, 523, 623, 712, 714, 717–19, 723, 726; **9:**12, 30, 37, 201, 376–77, 441–42, 445–46, 464–65, 675, 696–99, 701, 704–5, 805–6, 808, 816, 835, 851; **10:**35, 86, 88–89, 91–93, 95, 101–2, 104–7, 120–23, 125, 169, 179, 305–6, 309–12, 315, 326, 329–30, 337, 341; TEXT **1:**126, 1195; **4:**1286; **5:**674, 682, 874; **8:**742; **9:**874; **10:**1010; **12:**747

SAPPHIRE
1:881; **5:**415; **6:**965, 1116, 1183, 1392; **12:**599, 632, 723

SASH
1:1060, 1110; **2:**162; **5:**262; **6:**196; **9:**263; **12:**561, 567

SATIRE
1:291; **2:**185, 194, 449, 767, 770, 773, 1333; **3:**877, 881, 1078, 1103, 1114, 1144, 1155, 1168; **4:**415, 426, 428–29, 451, 508, 522, 546, 575, 581, 596; **5:**6, 604, 606–7, 625, 705, 812; **6:**158, 385–89, 391, 406, 743, 985, 996, 1398, 1425, 1429; **7:**103, 118, 467, 469–72, 474, 524; **8:**18, 23–24, 309; **10:**437; **11:**154, 287, 298

SATISFY (*OR* SATISFIES, SATISFACTION, *ETC.*)
1:204, 787, 1026, 1040–42, 1099; **2:**1285; **4:**740, 927–28, 1044, 1116, 1193; **5:**69, 127, 174, 322; **6:**810, 1299–1300, 1233; **8:**178; **11:**545

SATRAP, SATRAPY
1:250, 267, 314; **3:**685, 698–99, 703, 709, 722, 730, 756, 768, 780, 878, 899, 925, 931; **4:**30, 59, 68, 84, 93, 103, 110, 129, 248, 253, 269; **7:**87–88, 94, 709, 738

SAVIOR, SAVIORS
1:85, 124, 208, 289, 329, 337, 441, 705, 820, 1015, 1063; **2:**54, 70, 139, 159, 190, 575, 646, 706, 758, 1366; **3:**93, 236–38, 244, 401, 812, 909, 949, 966, 1144; **4:**21, 199, 741, 869, 976; **5:**291, 516, 574; **6:**232, 382, 394, 400–401, 432–33, 469–70, 516, 525, 530, 1305; **7:**125, 176, 289–90, 292–93, 509–10, 537, 680; **8:**16, 30, 36, 135, 170, 234, 266, 274, 288, 414, 442, 608, 623, 627; **9:**4, 15–20, 56, 63, 65–66, 69, 98, 103, 129, 196, 242, 360, 445–49, 462–63, 469, 479, 489–90, 570, 572, 707–8, 823, 830; **10:**12, 20–21, 70, 77, 107, 132, 137–38, 192–93, 213, 247, 255, 357, 424, 515, 697, 730; **11:**421, 450–51, 535, 677, 772, 784, 790, 798, 813, 836, 862, 870–72, 874, 876–77; **12:**58, 275, 306, 330–31, 333, 353, 374, 392, 395, 431, 479, 500

SCABBARD
6:1293, 1296, 1304

SCALES, SCALY
1:149; **2:**834, 838; **3:**630; **4:**386, 391, 553; **5:**541, 660, 676, 748, 765, 772, 827; **6:**89, 1077, 1452, 1583; **7:**285, 681, 778; **9:**358; **10:**850; **12:**612; CROCODILES/LEVIATHAN **4:**624; **6:**1401, 1405, 1434; FISH WITHOUT **1:**1081; **2:**398; **9:**116; SKIN AFFLICTION (*see* DISEASE; LEPROSY); FOR WEIGHING **2:**838; **4:**386, 391, 553; **5:**541, 660, 676, 748, 765, 827; **6:**89, 627, 1452, 1583; **7:**285, 778; **12:**612. *See also* BALANCE; WEIGHTS AND MEASURES

SCALL
1:1096

SCAPEGOAT, SCAPEGOATS
1:282, 376, 1098, 1112; **2:**617, 632, 1288–89; **3:**204, 1158; **4:**339; **6:**959, 1034, 1146; **7:**830; **8:**515; **10:**716; **12:**606–7, 678

SCARAB
7:731

SCARECROW, SCARECROWS
6:986–87, 1009

SCARLET
1:1098, 1100; **5:**143; **6:**56; **7:**609; **12:**110, 680–81, 694

SCEPTER, SCEPTERS
1:607, 665; **2:**191, 594; **3:**908, 923, 962; **4:**690, 768, 862, 917, 1130, 1193; **5:**53, 93; **6:**158, 891, 1271–73, 1299, 1415, 1506–1507; **7:**752, 815; **8:**488, 674; **9:**367; **11:**361

SCHISM, SCHISMS
3:380, 676; **6:**6, 1509; **7:**376, 426; **9:**563, 656, 671; **10:**210, 802–4, 806, 822, 825, 837, 840, 943; **12:**375, 403–4, 426–27, 444, 452, 492

SCHOOL, SCHOOLS
AS PLACE OF LEARNING **1:**31, 59, 96–97, 106, 159, 202, 211, 231, 925, 1114; **2:**83, 426, 540, 1073, 1100, 1185, 1195, 1307; **3:**987; **4:**41, 108, 219, 287, 327, 430, 444, 494, 546, 691, 722, 914, 1007; **5:**3, 6–7, 15, 22, 93, 145, 167, 246, 269, 296, 584, 597–98, 604, 654, 670, 689, 777, 825; **6:**404, 776; **7:**118, 418, 663; **8:**13–14, 16–18, 57, 191, 537, 672; **9:**74, 149, 277, 397; **10:**267; **11:**269, 365, 386, 405, 431–32, 454–55, 560, 685, 751, 851; **12:**213, 288, 401, 428, 573; AS INTELLECTUAL ORIENTATION **1:**9, 13–14, 38, 49–50, 58, 94, 110, 112, 114–15, 131, 193, 197, 287, 311, 313, 316–17, 1028, 1080, 1113, 1170, 1190; **2:**5, 288, 299; **3:**987; **4:**304; **5:**377, 584, 597–98, 689; **6:**945, 1088, 1092, 1113, 1156, 1272, 1317, 1329, 1334, 1359, 1408, 1413, 1453, 1481, 1512, 1573; **8:**12, 17, 24, 48, 120, 153, 191; **10:**244, 306, 319, 789; **11:**105, 204, 446, 451, 560, 573, 582, 584, 701; **12:**344, 369, 405, 503, 545

SCIENCE, SCIENCES
1:49, 54–59, 81, 95, 104, 111, 116–17, 122, 237, 257, 337, 344, 354, 356; **2:**182, 541, 548; **3:**723, 1193; **4:**256, 314, 735, 793, 811, 1099, 1287; **5:**34, 294, 333, 497, 502, 506, 597, 875; **6:**302, 412, 946, 969–70, 1130; **7:**50, 314, 694; **8:**2; **9:**540, 699, 875; **10:**526, 606, 999, 1011; **11:**378–79, 516, 756; **12:**513, 523; FICTION **9:**333; **11:**380; SOCIAL **1:**109, 153, 182, 838; **5:**314; **8:**513; **9:**32–33; **10:**377; **12:**206, 331, 480, 547

SCOFF
THOSE WHO ARE MOCKED **2:**753; **4:**113, 973; **6:**239; **7:**635; **9:**19, 312, 454; **10:**193, 206, 520; **12:**326, 352, 707; THOSE WHO MOCK **4:**254, 667, 684; **5:**41, 103, 132, 134, 149, 243; **6:**238–39, 246–47, 249, 1137; **7:**696, 697; **10:**63, 247; **12:**324, 355, 358, 496

SCORPION, SCORPIONS
3:102; **5:**765, 818; **6:**1123–24, 1451; **9:**99, 224, 238, 282; **12:**631, 634

SCOURGE, SCOURGES
2:469; **3:**102, 1107; **4:**210; **5:**749; **6:**237, 493; **8:**34, 79, 652, 695, 714, 719; **9:**352, 818

SCREEN
See CURTAIN

SCRIBE, SCRIBES
1:39–40, 76, 131, 223, 231–32, 234, 237, 248–49, 286, 290–99, 301, 309, 382, 468, 1055; **2:**96, 106–7, 112, 275, 426, 492, 521, 560, 576, 586, 614, 660, 678, 697, 904, 1013, 1213, 1236, 1268; **3:**50, 330, 666, 692, 698, 715, 718, 720, 793, 797, 803, 815, 832, 838, 847, 863, 899, 925; **4:**12, 92, 95, 182, 236, 268, 330, 346, 358, 428, 562, 861; **5:**3–4, 6–7, 94, 121, 161, 205, 271, 273, 300, 365, 604, 607, 612, 623, 625–26, 633, 636–37, 642, 695, 702, 720, 739, 784, 812–13, 818; **6:**3, 16–17, 31, 47–48, 50, 205, 231, 244, 301, 560–61, 568, 600, 646–47, 650, 731, 761, 838–42, 860, 866, 876–77, 929, 933, 941, 1178, 1342, 1546; **7:**3, 12, 204, 374, 384, 509, 618, 852, 860; **8:**3, 8–10, 31–32, 38, 59, 64, 70, 97, 99, 104, 107, 115, 130, 138, 140, 142–44, 151, 153, 162, 170, 183, 187–88, 201, 216, 219–20, 223, 229, 231, 234–35, 265, 274–75, 283, 285, 295, 314–15, 331, 349, 403, 406, 408, 410, 420, 424, 427, 430–31, 435, 437–38, 464, 491, 523, 525, 540–41, 543, 545, 547–49, 551–52, 558–59, 563–65, 567, 572, 589–90, 605–8, 621, 631, 633, 638–39, 642, 645, 652, 656–57, 663, 667–69, 673–74, 677–82, 682–83, 695, 700, 710, 712, 714, 725–26, 728; **9:**13–14, 23–24, 28–29, 36, 72, 76, 111–12, 114, 122–25, 128, 134–36, 153, 178, 182, 184, 194, 201, 211, 226–27, 248–49, 280–81, 284, 295–96, 298, 304, 331, 348, 351, 355, 358, 363, 365, 375–77, 380–83, 385, 388–90, 392–96, 399, 414, 418, 422, 430, 436, 440, 442, 445–46, 455, 469, 471, 477, 559, 615, 627–30, 696, 702, 704–5, 806; **10:**17, 88, 120, 144, 273, 379, 572, 576, 599, 694, 757–58, 1001; **11:**302, 341–42, 369, 480, 546, 634, 667, 892; **12:**9, 38, 47, 66, 156, 161, 179, 232–33, 292, 306, 318, 413, 453, 566, 571, 583, 606, 632, 646, 727

SCRIPTURE, SCRIPTURES
AUTHORITY OF **1:**8–9, 14, 20–21, 33–65, 85–86, 98–99, 101–3, 108, 119, 163, 188–90, 193–94, 197; **3:**395, 513; **4:**1167; **5:**246; **6:**48; **7:**10; **8:**94, 187, 332, 422; **9:**21, 378–79, 386, 486, 853; **10:**16, 49, 51, 145, 166, 240–41, 383–84, 386, 744, 812; **11:**83, 279, 454, 457, 851; **12:**13, 238

SCROLL, SCROLLS
1:9–11, 26, 29–30, 65, 67, 69, 287, 292, 294–96, 299, 302, 307, 1175; **2:**271, 344, 520–21, 576, 687, 893, 950; **3:**377, 707, 800–801, 856, 863, 874, 938; **4:**11, 40, 258, 270, 478, 843; **5:**267, 623, 635, 637, 824, 867; **6:**47–48, 109, 118, 247, 285, 563–64, 580, 731, 761, 769, 775, 838–42, 857, 876, 916–17, 941, 946, 956, 1016, 1087,

SCROLL, SCROLLS *(continued)*
1089–92, 1098, 1100, 1110–11, 1114, 1124–25, 1127, 1132, 1144, 1170, 1207, 1213, 1296, 1318–19, 1325, 1335, 1339, 1349, 1359, 1364–65, 1369, 1412–13, 1422, 1430, 1439, 1454–55, 1457, 1481, 1487, 1494, 1496, 1499, 1504, 1507, 1512–13, 1530–31, 1573; **7:**10, 737, 744, 772–76, 778, 848, 867; **8:**3, 29–30, 35, 39, 666; **9:**105–6; **10:**460, 660; **11:**405, 857; **12:**115, 401, 512, 557, 600–602, 604–5, 611, 615, 630, 638–39, 646, 664, 702, 729; DEAD SEA/QUMRAN **1:**4, 6, 10, 12, 18, 24–25, 27–29, 286, 287–91, 293, 295–96, 1194; **2:**950, 1053–54, 1386; **3:**1075, 1191–92; **4:**6, 325, 379, 559, 1285–86; **5:**271, 332, 867, 873; **6:**223, 942, 949, 961, 1010, 1609; **7:**14, 21, 50, 53, 72, 105–6, 112, 115, 667, 848, 885–86; **8:**27, 30, 35, 38–39, 178, 666, 742; **9:**65, 85, 117, 224, 309, 873; **10:**460, 524, 660, 850, 931, 1010; **11:**238, 332, 374, 392, 421, 913; **12:**368, 395, 428, 546, 665, 705, 747 (*see also* DEAD SEA SCROLLS *and* QUMRAN SCROLLS *in ANCIENT LITERATURE*; QUMRAN KHIRBET *in PLACES IN THE BIBLE*); TEMPLE (*see* TEMPLE SCROLL *in ANCIENT LITERATURE*); WAR (*see* WAR SCROLL *in ANCIENT LITERATURE*)

SCULPTURE, SCULPTURES
2:1276; **3:**46; **5:**557; **6:**1119, 1176, 1193, 1245; **11:**801

SCYTHE
7:333

SEA, SEAS
1:274, 279; **2:**253, 600, 607, 677; **4:**368, 395, 518, 590, 602, 621, 872, 1142; **5:**590, 593; **6:**1364, 1525, 1596–97; **7:**101, 421, 499, 502; **8:**327–28; **9:**184; **10:**345; **12:**720; COAST(S) **2:**788; **3:**1093, 1107–1110, 1123, 1139; **4:**77, 127; **5:**862; **6:**1355; **7:**690 (*see also* COAST); CREATURE(S) (*see* CREATURE: SEA/WATER); OF GLASS/GLASSY **12:**558, 591–92, 663, 671–72, 723; MOLTEN **1:**279; **3:**429, 485; MONSTER(S) **1:**232, 344, 739, 800; **3:**1026; **4:**395, 518, 621, 1271; **6:**1404, 1429, 1434, 1436; **7:**193, 421, 509; **8:**580; **9:**243 (*see also* LEVIATHAN)

SEAFARER (*OR* SEAFARING, *ETC.*)
4:153; **5:**261; **6:**201, 1371, 1384; **7:**477, 500; **9:**184; **10:**348; **12:**15, 694. *See also* SAILOR

SEAH
3:136

SEAL, SEALS
AS A NOUN **1:**224, 248, 268, 605, 808; **3:**156, 496, 630, 667, 815, 863; **4:**555, 603, 1089; **5:**430, 730, 748, 812; **6:**243, 478, 743, 839, 941, 1391; **7:**10, 189, 731, 843; **9:**559, 599, 732, 741, 772, 844; **10:**261, 494–95, 757, 904, 1002; **11:**49, 51, 99, 316, 335, 381, 438, 592, 716, 845–47; **12:**530, 533, 535, 538–39, 544, 557–58, 562, 592–93, 601–2, 605, 608–14, 618–21, 625, 627, 629, 631–35, 638, 646, 659, 664, 667, 675, 677, 694, 707, 721, 744 (*see also* RING); AS A VERB **1:**535, 567; **2:**648; **3:**84, 156, 376, 407, 923; **5:**118; **6:**421, 743, 842, 1228, 1503; **7:**9, 92, 117, 128, 140, 148, 189; **8:**296, 471; **11:**122, 160, 629; **12:**638, 707, 733

SEASON, SEASONS
1:67, 128, 199, 205–6, 208, 212, 217–18, 220, 275, 344, 394, 698, 778, 871, 914, 961, 1156, 1158–61, 1179–80; **2:**32, 55, 121, 229, 386, 399, 402–4, 407, 410–14, 600, 893, 926, 1098, 1217, 1232, 1259; **3:**131, 183, 416, 939, 1005; **4:**311, 380, 453, 534, 593, 605, 609, 636, 780, 794, 797, 829, 889, 920, 938, 948, 960–61, 965, 1001, 1003, 1018, 1021, 1048, 1070, 1073, 1120, 1186, 1196, 1216, 1233, 1269, 1273, 1280; **5:**5, 53–54, 75, 114, 131, 185, 225, 234, 277, 284, 305, 307–8, 314, 350, 393, 425, 502, 509, 667, 672, 687, 716; **6:**15, 198, 213, 386, 414, 521, 621, 646, 711, 939, 946, 949, 1383, 1589; **7:**52, 103, 105, 108, 202, 250, 319, 538, 570, 813, 816; **8:**218, 249, 407, 413, 533, 537, 577, 641, 659–60, 692, 698; **9:**66–67, 169, 219, 280, 406, 481, 494, 526, 540; **10:**11, 24, 42, 45, 53, 58, 66, 77, 82, 90–91, 150, 178, 210, 267, 364, 378, 736; **11:**283, 288, 631, 635, 663, 696, 709, 726; **12:**4, 6, 262, 524, 704. *See also* SPRING; SUMMER; WINTER

SEAT, SEATS
OF AUTHORITY/POWER **1:**246, 266–67, 1111; **2:**417, 771, 1002, 1340; **3:**70, 556, 768, 1114; **4:**307, 538, 992, 1081, 1139; **5:**102; **6:**184, 627, 745, 808, 1119, 1316, 1329–30, 1595; **7:**313, 594, 785, 826; **8:**46, 431, 681; **9:**26, 67, 248, 250, 343, 393–94, 822–23; **10:**325, 459, 830, 999; **11:**86, 758, 838; **12:**149, 597, 656, 712 (*see also* MERCY SEAT); OF EMOTIONS/THOUGHT **1:**1025; **2:**1039; **5:**5, 301, 322, 664; **6:**1386; **7:**74, 318, 447; **9:**319; **11:**381, 428, 484; **12:**117, 387, 391, 422; OF MOSES **8:**431

SECOND
ADAM (*see under* JESUS THE CHRIST, NAMES FOR/TITLES OF *in PERSONS IN THE BIBLE*); COMING **1:**95; **4:**1018, 1185–86; **7:**429, 571–72, 655; **8:**222, 443, 448; **9:**410, 741, 862; **10:**43, 673, 689; **11:**383, 547, 696, 836, 852, 855; **12:**29, 31, 113, 323, 342–43, 409, 539–41, 702, 711; QUARTER **3:**767; **7:**679

SECRETARY, SECRETARIES
2:1268, 1354; **3:**50, 55, 265, 280, 293, 703, 718, 815; **4:**641; **5:**5; **6:**197, 293, 839–40; **8:**142; **9:**397; **10:**379–80; **11:**230, 577–78, 857; **12:**14

SECULAR
1:55, 66, 199, 201–2, 229, 238, 280, 324, 492, 594, 607, 862, 885, 917, 922, 941–42, 964, 988, 1000, 1054, 1070, 1073, 1082, 1121, 1152; **2:**38, 61, 273, 285, 321, 336, 349–50, 383, 387, 394, 415, 431, 448–49, 500, 514, 617, 768, 892, 911, 920, 1031, 1050–51, 1093, 1139, 1213, 1226, 1231, 1359, 1383; **3:**123–25, 310, 362, 436, 438, 448, 452, 456–57, 556, 563, 597, 665, 706, 728–29, 742, 838, 860, 868, 870, 927, 935, 962, 1005, 1156; **4:**480, 675, 695, 725, 753, 767, 769, 779, 787, 811, 861, 920, 1001, 1011, 1137, 1199, 1201, 1265; **5:**5, 34, 101, 114, 150, 264, 274, 333, 344, 350, 363–64, 366, 369–70, 547–48, 668, 730, 750, 788, 790, 801; **6:**257, 642, 763, 826, 852, 946, 1216, 1253, 1257, 1315, 1335; **7:**77, 113, 164, 516, 529, 632; **8:**3, 14, 27, 166, 289–90, 299, 335, 346, 420, 448, 557, 590; **9:**41, 45, 56, 74, 82, 179, 379, 406, 792, 821; **10:**8, 12, 50, 85, 124, 130, 147, 177–79, 181, 222, 233, 236–37, 239, 243, 247, 249–50, 285, 299, 304, 307, 313, 322, 329–30, 336, 340–41, 343, 346, 443, 451, 531–32, 689, 791, 834, 842, 942, 963; **11:**229, 289, 370, 372, 374, 385, 401, 444, 481, 492, 548, 866, 893; **12:**271, 277, 287, 411, 428, 460, 508, 551, 673, 728

SEED, SEEDS
1:391, 524, 1134; **2:**736, 744, 746, 774, 931, 967, 1123, 1318; **3:**136, 370, 599; **4:**258, 555, 789, 931, 1059, 1195; **5:**436, 471, 560, 580, 593; **6:**238, 331, 421, 450, 603, 861, 1253; **7:**40, 44, 177, 261, 276, 648–49, 776; **8:**304, 309, 522, 576–78; **9:**98, 180, 182, 275, 520, 569, 699, 711, 754; **10:**512, 515, 531, 631, 987, 989, 993; **11:**219, 340; **12:**535, 710

SEEDTIME
4:368, 603; **8:**569

SEER, SEERS
1:237, 242, 306, 981; **2:**22, 177–80, 182–83, 185, 193–94, 196, 201, 1036, 1038–39, 1097; **3:**255, 445–46, 636, 647, 865; **4:**377, 604, 635; **5:**61, 271; **6:**2, 4, 10, 13, 185–86, 241, 243, 253–54, 256; **7:**2–3, 5–6, 8–10, 12, 105, 121, 142, 405, 410, 558, 660, 738, 852; **8:**550; **9:**642; **11:**372, 409, 615; **12:**505, 515, 525, 527, 530, 562, 603, 646, 705, 716, 724, 729

SELAH
4:657, 869, 894, 1023, 1239; **5:**650

SELF-CONTROL
1:1075; **2:**422; **4:**706, 883; **5:**70, 127, 221, 510, 574, 639, 650–51, 734–35, 748, 783; **7:**178; **9:**829; **10:**322–23, 866, 869, 872, 874, 888, 890, 892, 902, 909, 967; **11:**51, 88, 105, 328, 849, 871; **12:**155, 199, 204, 337–38

SELF-DENIAL
1:569, 1075, 1113; **2:**233–34; **3:**928, 1048, 1213; **4:**70, 81, 715; **5:**70, 81, 715; **6:**499; **8:**352, 654; **9:**98, 255, 734; **10:**706; **11:**844

SELF-DISCIPLINE
3:1058; **5:**81, 153, 651, 690, 718, 765; **8:**19, 22; **10:**357, 889, 910, 938, 961, 967; **11:**328, 813; **12:**148

SELF-PITY
1:630; **2:**514; **4:**416, 970; **7:**471, 481, 502; **11:**88

SELF-RIGHTEOUSNESS
2:350, 633, 681, 757; **4:**472, 526, 687, 709, 783, 1174, 1203–4; **5:**543; **6:**138, 146, 517; **8:**222, 257; **9:**324, 341, 630; **10:**655; **12:**646

SEMEN
1:605, 1105, 1149; **2:**61, 67; **4:**414; **5:**497

SENATE
3:1114; **4:**5, 93, 102–3, 105, 107, 121, 143, 192, 254, 269, 281, 283; **5:**612; **9:**171, 362; **10:**404, 774

SENATOR, SENATORS
2:1214; **4:**105, 224

SENTINEL, SENTINELS
2:1339; **3:**219; **4:**524; **5:**396, 412, 806; **6:**187, 191, 325, 455, 457, 494, 498–99, 505, 515, 518, 520, 1105, 1446–48; **7:**266; **12:**168

SENTRY, SENTRIES
3:363, 525; **5:**400, 748; **6:**186, 613; **7:**316, 806

SEPULCHRE
6:724; **10:**457; HOLY **8:**490

SERAPHIM
1:278; **2:**164, 167; **6:**102, 331, 334, 432, 751, 1120; **12:**592

SERMON ON THE MOUNT
1:103, 815; **2:**437; **3:**452, 474, 658; **4:**734, 774–75, 882, 1030; **5:**307; **8:**34, 84, 112, 118, 120–21, 136, 144–45, 171–72, 174–75, 177–80, 183, 192, 196–97, 199, 201–3, 206, 217–22, 256, 261, 272, 280, 287, 342, 342, 425, 428–29, 435, 448, 450–51, 504, 665, 735; **9:**8, 105, 137, 140–41, 147, 154, 235, 278, 734, 869; **10:**100, 450, 715; **11:**429, 830; **12:**274, 291

SERMON ON THE PLAIN
8:175; **9:**8, 23, 102, 137, 140, 196, 869

SERPENT, SERPENTS
1:85, 350, 352, 359–63, 365–66, 373, 405, 1173; **2:**9, 100, 158, 163–64, 167, 183, 746, 804; **3:**260, 757, 979, 1008, 1026; **4:**96, 256, 368, 519, 621; **5:**350–51, 446, 465, 529, 536, 570, 573–75, 592, 605, 627, 737, 741–42; **6:**102, 163, 225, 544–45, 1176, 1404; **7:**192–93, 422, 780, 827; **8:**729; **9:**224, 282, 552, 642–43; **10:**291, 315, 390, 433, 563, 764, 767, 857, 919; **11:**147;

SERPENT, SERPENTS *(continued)*
12:632, 651, 653, 707; BRAZEN **5:**446, 529, 536, 573, 592; BRONZE **2:**164, 167; **3:**260; **5:**574; **7:**780; FIERY **2:**9, 100, 158, 163–64; **6:**163. *See also* ASP; PYTHON; SNAKE; VIPER
SERVANT, SERVANTS
HERITAGE OF THE **1:**325, 347, 424, 430, 444, 474, 476; OF A LANDOWNER, ETC. **1:**512, 610; **2:**1167, 1274; **3:**194–95, 863; **4:**393, 1078; **5:**145; **8:**382, 453; **9:**363; OF SOLOMON **3:**22, 58, 90, 94, 664, 686–87, 722, 727, 745, 824; **6:**1574; TABLE **11:**240. *See also* SLAVE, SLAVES, SLAVERY
SERVANT, SUFFERING
See under SUFFERING
SERVANT OF THE LORD, THE
1:1042, 1061, 1173; **2:**316, 752, 797, 932; **3:**127, 217, 225, 580, 752; **4:**823, 1216; **6:**300, 347, 424, 430, 442, 444, 476, 630, 678, 762, 763, 782, 787–88, 912; **7:**498; **8:**281, 361, 366; **9:**52, 66, 352; **10:**503, 613, 712
SEVEN
1:341, 621, 1156, 1180; **2:**212, 233, 613, 979, 981, 1358; **3:**76, 882, 982, 985, 1008, 1038, 1107; **4:**152, 635, 792, 1036, 1235; **5:**102, 503; **6:**1396; **10:**113; **12:**533, 562, 620; CHURCHES (*see under* CHURCH); DAYS (*see under* DAY)
SEVENTH DAY
See under DAY
SEVENTY
1:290, 306, 321, 409, 652, 654, 669, 694, 880–81; **2:**5, 105–8, 219, 298, 634, 763, 790–92, 810, 816–17, 1012, 1234; **3:**14, 137, 223, 301–3, 656–57, 677, 726, 840, 925; **4:**199; **5:**801; **6:**18, 203–4, 762, 792–93, 795–96, 989, 994, 1176, 1185, 1330, 1362, 1538, 1552; **7:**12, 39, 44, 121, 124, 127–29, 437, 660–61, 752–53, 792; **8:**29, 274; **9:** 322, 398, 462; **10:**447; ELDERS (*see under* ELDERS)
SEVENTY, THE
2:790; **9:**29, 98, 193, 219–25, 231, 429; **12:**529
SEW (*OR* SEWS, *ETC.*)
1:294; **2:**128; **4:**414, 459; **5:**306; **8:**236
SEX, SEXES
1:186, 1085, 1143; **2:**457, 1289; **4:**256; **5:**28, 108, 121, 263–64, 332, 368–70, 379, 389, 397, 652, 669, 700; **6:**82; **7:**676; **10:**882, 928; **11:**273, 718. *See also* GENDER
SEXUALITY, SEXUAL BEHAVIOR
1:182, 345, 363, 477, 580, 604–5, 609–10, 612, 836, 844, 848, 862, 872, 925, 1004, 1086, 1103, 1105–1106, 1110, 1115, 1122–25, 1127; **2:**247, 451, 454–57, 463, 467–68, 473, 657, 723, 788, 897, 924, 1100, 1165, 1185, 1232, 1285; **3:**592, 1080, 1087, 1089, 1158; **4:**405, 565, 612, 885; **5:**26, 63, 67–70, 72, 74, 78, 81–82, 85–86, 103, 232, 254, 263, 298, 327, 364, 366, 368–69, 371, 374, 377, 380–81, 385, 394, 397, 407–8, 416–17, 419, 423, 430–31, 652, 681, 720, 753, 765, 825; **6:**82, 543, 1241–42, 1309, 1317, 1319, 1331; **7:**200, 202, 206, 208–9, 211, 216, 231, 233, 239, 255, 240–41, 243, 261, 269, 292, 612, 615, 620; **8:**132, 137, 190, 197, 375; **9:**164, 389, 571, 630; **10:**145, 433, 435, 849, 859, 869–70, 872–74, 879–80, 882, 885, 891, 969, 971; **11:**330, 339, 440, 452, 635, 645, 718, 793; **12:**163, 170, 277, 347, 401, 475, 488, 490
SHADE (*OR* SHADES, *ETC.*)
2:106, 816; **3:**402; **4:**240–41, 393, 511, 517, 608, 691, 748; **5:**45, 341, 720, 758; **6:**158–59, 212, 217, 222–23, 265, 1216, 1246, 1425, 1430, 1503; **7:**73, 75, 251, 296–97, 471, 483, 486, 506, 520–21, 524, 527; **8:**577
SHADOW, SHADOWS
1:206; **3:**271, 274, 1085, 1099; **4:**367, 393, 402, 430, 440, 443, 459, 511, 529, 601, 741, 768, 823, 838, 840, 905, 923, 1047, 1087, 1117, 1126, 1181; **5:**279, 285, 313, 324, 340, 389, 394, 460, 485, 550, 715, 793, 846, 853; **6:**60; **8:**587; **11:**734; **12:**11
SHADOW, VALLEY OF THE
1:467, 501; **4:**768, 923; **6:**1169, 1218, 1467; **7:**767; **10:**615
SHALEM
2:1236
SHALOM
1:61, 599–600, 621, 634, 636, 639, 865, 874, 893, 940, 1023; **2:**1022; **4:**698, 793, 820, 829, 833, 923, 963, 1184; **5:**55, 107; **6:**754, 814, 852, 1370, 1471; **7:**72, 366, 724–25, 797; **9:**172, 336, 369; **10:**150, 343, 798; **11:**38, 132; **12:**248
SHAME (*OR* SHAMED, *ETC.*)
1:31, 206, 241, 289, 336, 362, 364, 404, 428, 451, 486, 523, 539, 557, 644, 822, 844, 955, 1035, 1126, 1179; **2:**63, 110, 448, 452, 454, 475, 514, 589, 607–8, 630, 818, 877, 901, 983, 1110, 1133, 1135, 1230, 1250, 1274, 1279, 1293, 1304–1305, 1326; **3:**302, 402, 421, 576, 620, 735, 761, 780, 918, 1090, 1124, 1133, 1137, 1145, 1154, 1165, 1167, 1178, 1180; **4:**16, 30, 69, 111, 212, 379, 389, 436, 472, 491, 525, 562, 697, 705, 731, 777, 779, 800–801, 819, 951–52, 959, 997, 1036, 1069, 1126; **5:**74, 77, 131, 181, 220, 238, 464, 467, 469, 476, 480, 484, 489, 534, 586, 591, 597, 609, 625, 638, 641, 671–75, 758, 815, 826–30, 861; **6:**53, 77, 82, 182, 217, 248, 253, 358, 389, 401, 440, 451, 455, 472, 477, 514, 538, 596, 602, 605–606, 637, 640, 655, 685–86, 690, 699, 709–10, 805, 853, 882–83, 891, 913–14, 918,

920, 939, 990, 1002, 1020–21, 1023, 1033, 1036, 1044, 1049, 1057, 1065–66, 1103, 1194, 1220–21, 1232, 1237, 1240, 1242, 1275, 1291, 1291, 1321, 1327, 1411, 1443–45, 1488, 1492, 1502, 1562, 1577; **7:**63, 81, 161–63, 242, 253, 419, 546, 551, 553, 558, 564, 614, 814, 832; **8:**66, 198, 325; **9:**35, 134, 147, 166, 191, 231, 233, 235, 238, 248, 252, 304, 317, 334, 346, 369, 405, 439, 454, 850; **10:**64, 105, 318, 424, 433, 443, 450, 517, 526, 531–32, 546, 611, 616, 650, 657, 665–66, 715, 718, 745, 811, 814, 840–41, 854, 916, 929, 931, 934, 970, 974, 983; **11:**7, 26, 32, 57, 74, 79, 88, 134, 151, 157, 180, 237, 297, 490, 494, 498, 509, 534–35, 537, 549, 626, 629–30, 643, 681, 698, 768, 802, 837, 865, 870, 892; **12:**42, 76, 83, 123, 137, 140–41, 149–51, 155, 167, 204–5, 241, 265, 275, 291, 295–97, 301, 305, 351, 410, 469, 492, 529–30, 613, 624, 728; AND HONOR **2:**762, 775, 1213; **3:**874, 1099, 1113, 1123, 1144, 1170; **4:**43, 361, 461, 475, 483, 544, 547–48, 554–55, 595, 613; **5:**48, 125, 142, 172, 182, 185, 189, 197, 222, 226, 231, 651–52, 673, 675, 680, 693, 720, 740, 827; **6:**150, 189, 20–23, 205, 952–53, 958, 1009–1010, 1030, 1167, 1223, 1239, 1438; **7:**206–9, 225, 239, 241, 243, 269, 272, 647; **8:**18, 533, 545, 559, 565, 592; **9:**124, 128, 172, 236, 274, 287, 347, 378, 584, 645; **10:**234, 782–83, 835–36, 928; **11:**31, 97, 128, 141, 169, 173, 503, 734, 838–39, 843; **12:**10–11, 124, 192, 266, 345–46, 360, 485

SHARDS/SHERDS
6:254, 1090, 1327; **7:**498. *See also* POTSHERD

SHAVE (*OR* SHAVES, *ETC.*)
1:621, 1098, 1135, 1147, 1171; **2:**65, 81, 726, 841–42, 858–61, 1279; **3:**733, 838; **4:**352; **6:**195, 899, 990, 1000, 1102, 1150, 1154, 1167, 1578–79; **9:**119; **10:**293, 928, 931

SHEATH, SHEATHS
2:1382; **3:**423; **6:**886, 1304

SHEEP
1:87–88, 92, 217–20, 245, 492, 552, 556, 666, 703, 711, 777, 786, 789, 801, 865, 869, 950, 1000, 1009, 1013–14, 1024–26, 1039–41, 1051, 1076, 1080–81, 1118, 1152; **2:**148, 219, 247, 411–12, 452, 589, 606, 788, 802–3, 832, 879, 961, 1080, 1088–89, 1099–100, 1103, 1110–11, 1113, 1166, 1234–35, 1238; **3:**320, 424, 514, 647, 709, 712, 766, 782, 1003, 1155; **4:**345, 351, 471, 539, 609–10, 679, 767–68, 770–71, 854, 857–58, 877, 973, 1062, 1078–79, 1168; **5:**112, 150, 345, 386, 561, 740; **6:**74, 113, 141, 337, 625, 640, 673, 675–76, 756, 896, 913, 915, 1257, 1269, 1289, 1377, 1461–64, 1466–70, 1472–73, 1492, 1546, 1584, 1592–93; **7:**112, 118, 148, 193, 286, 314, 351, 406, 411, 571, 574, 741–42, 745, 811, 813–14, 820–23, 832–34; **8:**61–62, 217, 226, 252, 256, 258, 286, 324, 336, 376, 455, 474, 601, 609, 618, 670, 672; **9:**12, 23–24, 35, 153, 195, 242, 282, 294–96, 298, 303, 323, 358, 361, 428, 439, 543, 647, 666–73, 676, 678, 689, 702–3, 734, 755, 783, 802, 817–18, 842, 845, 852, 860–62, 864; **10:**135, 390, 610–11, 615, 642; **11:**87; **12:**4, 172, 282–83, 287, 315, 413, 699, 704, 717; AND GOAT(S) (*see under* GOAT)

SHEEPFOLD, SHEEPFOLDS
2:1113; **7:**814; **8:**61–62; **9:**666–67, 669, 755; **12:**283

SHEEPSHEARING
2:1166, 1308; **7:**406

SHEKEL
See under COIN; WEIGHTS AND MEASURES

SHEKINAH
1:1007, 1035, 1179; **6:**1511; **8:**79, 364, 366; **10:**556, 575, 580–81, 583

SHEMA, THE
2:343; **3:**801; **4:**881, 1004; **5:**512; **6:**176, 597, 601, 604, 641, 656, 848, 1260; **7:**837; **8:**291, 364, 424, 459, 678; **9:**100, 105, 227, 309; **10:**420, 482–83, 517, 601, 629, 707, 769, 897–98; **11:**267, 300, 798, 831

SHEOL
See SHEOL *in PLACES IN THE BIBLE*

SHEPHERD, SHEPHERDS
1:67, 206, 372–73, 552, 598, 612, 653, 655, 661, 666, 703–4, 712, 789, 1025; **2:**219, 550, 982, 1095, 1099–1012, 1115, 1166–67, 1233–34, 1250, 1252, 1262–63; **3:**24, 164, 407, 424, 1038, 1155; **4:**314, 332, 460, 539, 544, 609–10, 690, 768–71, 790, 984, 998–1000, 1062, 1079; **5:**112, 150, 233–34, 359, 366, 370, 375, 385–87, 393–94, 396, 402–6, 408–9, 411, 415–22, 424–26, 428–31, 433, 584, 628, 720, 731; **6:**157, 183, 337, 378, 391, 444, 490, 498, 527, 575, 605, 625, 664, 679, 709, 744, 756, 766, 809, 811, 896, 915, 1105, 1176, 1201, 1269, 1289, 1461–67, 1469–70, 1506, 1509–10, 1593; **7:**242, 340, 351, 375, 411, 539, 554, 573, 588, 619, 741–42, 744–45, 811, 813–14, 817–24, 829–30, 832–34; **8:**61–62, 140, 150, 252, 324, 376, 455, 467, 474, 512, 601, 603, 606, 618, 670, 672; **9:**11, 19, 24, 29, 62–63, 65–67, 174, 195, 295–96, 337, 369, 462, 513, 665–73, 676, 698, 817, 827, 861; **10:**91, 283, 615, 904; **11:**169, 422–23, 515, 809; **12:**4, 283, 287, 315, 492, 625, 699; THE GOOD (*see* GOD, METAPHORS FOR: SHEPHERD *in PERSONS IN THE BIBLE*; JESUS THE CHRIST, METAPHORS FOR: SHEPHERD *in PERSONS IN THE BIBLE*)

SHEWBREAD
10:474
SHIBBOLETH
2:821, 838
SHIELD, SHIELDS
1:223, 444; **2:**787, 1112, 1207, 1266, 1366; **3:**116, 510, 526, 540, 591; **4:**89, 130, 161, 163, 169, 171, 624, 693, 708–9, 747–48, 789, 811, 819, 867, 869, 1014, 1035, 1047, 1145, 1172; **5:**403, 486, 592, 867; **6:**68, 295, 636, 1374, 1443, 1516, 1524; **7:**145, 242–43, 250, 377, 609–10, 827; **9:**88; **10:**404; **11:**15, 459, 461; **12:**434, 645
SHIP, SHIPS
1:92, 233; **2:**192, 788, 1006; **3:**168, 510–11; **4:**30, 152–53, 218, 228, 597; **5:**61, 111, 131, 254, 261, 422, 552–53; **6:**73, 202–3, 271, 509, 1360–61, 1371–76, 1378, 1380, 1382–84, 1391, 1398, 1415–16; **7:**143, 147, 467, 470–71, 477–80, 492, 495–500, 502, 506, 518–19, 527; **10:**214, 285, 288, 345–49, 351–55, 357, 761; **12:**492, 694. *See also* BOAT; FLEET: OF SHIPS; HARBOR, GALLEYS; SAILOR
SHIPMASTERS
6:1384; **12:**692
SHOES
See SANDLE
SHOFAR-CHESTS
9:395
SHOPHAR
See RAM: HORN
SHOULDER, SHOULDERS
1:488, 660, 1026, 1054, 1061; **2:**1048; **3:**393; **4:**555; **5:**590; **6:**406, 454, 1335, 1353, 1406, 1410; **7:**699; **8:**24, 431; **9:**398; **12:**598
SHOWBREAD
2:52–54; **3:**819; **4:**34, 190, 257; **6:**1555; TABLE OF **6:**1555; **10:**912, 918, 919
SHRINE, SHRINES
1:277–79, 282, 285, 841, 861, 871, 919, 954, 957, 996; **2:**79, 220, 365, 384, 564–74, 579, 587, 589–90, 606–7, 612, 614, 635, 688, 694, 718–19, 744, 870–71, 899, 991, 1038–39, 1042, 1141, 1240, 1320; **3:**33, 115, 257, 285, 355, 603, 729, 1108–1109; **4:**38–39, 289, 583; **6:**4, 457, 575, 1185, 1229–30, 1534, 1537–38; **7:**53, 778, 780; **8:**23–24, 431, 589; **9:**563; **10:**246, 271, 273, 378, 453, 863, 894; **11:**682; **12:**81–82, 121, 523, 531, 725
SHROUD, SHROUDS
2:1184; **4:**208, 263; **6:**217; **8:**494, 726
SHUTTLE
1:1097; **4:**394, 444
SIBBOLETH
2:821, 838
SIBLINGS
1:377, 455, 530, 553, 1126; **2:**200, 592; **4:**345; **8:**136; **9:**348, 688. *See also* BROTHER; SISTER
SIBYLLINE ORACLES
See under ORACLE
SICK (*OR* SICKNESS, *ETC.*)
1:239, 241–42, 606, 877, 1051; **2:**142, 514, 1102, 1127; **3:**76, 79, 271, 543–44, 569, 628, 630–31, 694, 755, 998, 1005, 1024; **4:**31, 242, 395, 645–46, 703–6, 727, 795–97, 801, 818, 832–38, 847–48, 922, 984, 1027, 1086–87, 1118–19, 1148; **5:**11, 67, 135, 173, 219, 305, 412, 462, 466, 471, 574, 579, 609, 655, 733–34, 778–79, 806–8; **6:**15, 54, 133, 271, 281, 301, 465–66, 626–27, 631, 648, 664, 698–99, 709, 776, 807–8, 883, 1070, 1233, 1239, 1336, 1466–67, 1593; **7:**90, 220, 248–49, 253–54, 257, 262–63, 400, 403, 515, 546, 859; **8:**223, 228, 237, 245, 296, 323, 456, 491, 546, 590, 705–6, 729; **9:**31, 56, 108–13, 128–29, 135–36, 139, 160, 189, 191–96, 220, 230, 273, 281, 576, 578; **10:**21, 65, 78, 85, 89, 170, 268–69, 336, 362, 445, 572, 598, 659, 939; **11:**662, 827; **12:**40, 180, 181, 222–25, 390, 407, 636, 730. *See also* DISEASE
SICKLE
1:217; **7:**333; **9:**133; **12:**668
SIEGE, SIEGES
1:222, 239, 250, 265, 1171, 1181; **2:**280, 406, 501–5, 607, 611, 677, 1053–55, 1152–53, 1212, 1237, 1279–80, 1283–87, 1300, 1352; **3:**202–10, 253, 265, 270, 293, 591, 628–29, 992, 996, 1075, 1103–1129; **4:**7, 35, 87–90, 118, 134–35, 140, 156, 168–69, 172, 178, 216, 218, 261–64, 276, 282, 476; **5:**68, 345, 543, 564–65; **6:**37, 54, 194–97, 241–42, 271–72, 284–85, 291–95, 584–86, 1065, 1078–81, 1142–50, 1153, 1334–36, 1358–61, 1365–66, 1410, 1420, 1454–55; **7:**53, 138, 141, 270, 554, 609–10, 618, 626, 635, 683, 691, 810, 822, 826–27; **8:**20, 52, 343; **9:**404; **10:**138; **12:**545, 641. *See also* BATTLE; WAR
SIEVE, SIEVES
1:1017; **5:**768; **6:**256; **7:**424–25
SIGN, SIGNS
1:13, 42, 115, 400–401, 460, 448, 718–19, 721, 762, 777; **2:**229, 343, 356, 402, 753, 804, 847, 994, 1041; **3:**114, 142, 680, 813, 978; **4:**227–28, 997; **5:**506, 586, 721, 834; **6:**114–20, 123, 182, 229, 295, 300, 660–61, 694, 877–75, 1008, 1504–1507, 1341; **7:**106, 326–28, 367, 758; **8:**24, 62, 76, 297, 441, 444, 615–16, 687–88, 693, 709, 723–24; **9:**65, 241–43, 329, 333–34, 398–400, 406–9, 502–3, 539, 545–46, 549, 576,

593–94, 599, 704, 851–52; **10:**69, 140, 201, 531, 606, 928, 950; **12:**648–54, 678

SIGNAL, SIGNALS
1:246, 412, 418, 512, 528, 593, 622, 671, 758, 907, 1010, 1061–62, 1182; **2:**10, 35, 87, 91, 106,166, 180–81, 201, 631, 802, 1135, 1257, 1293; **3:**22, 78, 178, 219, 389, 857, 880, 1105; **4:**119, 138, 218, 612, 657, 917, 1003, 1073, 1210; **5:**64, 253, 647, 689, 834; **6:**98, 132, 145, 156, 376, 411, 431, 519, 615, 972, 1116, 1124–25, 1206, 1310, 1321; **7:**32, 795, 811; **8:**147, 442, 709; **9:**46, 229, 242, 399, 435, 447, 734; **10:**38, 42, 64, 176, 199, 217, 219, 683; **11:**43, 118, 688, 692–93, 708, 847; **12:**77, 313, 630

SIGNATURE
1:605, 622; **3:**710; **4:**555; **10:**379, 382; **12:**14

SILENCE, SILENCED
1:62, 185–86, 190, 430, 434, 475, 495–97, 499, 510, 580, 599, 610, 643, 672, 706–7, 726, 772, 881; **2:**771, 906, 908, 1198, 1302, 1305–1306; **3:**142–46, 212, 733, 867, 904, 913, 1049; **4:**165, 358, 366, 371, 375, 378, 438, 464, 491, 510, 561–63, 572, 577, 623, 797, 805–7, 837–39, 908, 933, 1229; **5:**111, 121, 128, 160, 255, 306, 404, 415, 526, 631, 644, 651, 737–40; **6:**118, 347, 367, 411, 542, 674, 885–86, 1051, 1129, 1139, 1149, 1366, 1382, 1453; **7:**55, 390, 557, 678; **8:**25, 281, 485, 543, 559, 572, 584, 589–91, 636, 655–56, 713, 729, 732–33; **9:**76, 110, 135, 284–85, 369, 386, 388, 428, 446, 821; **10:**104, 308, 458, 906, 956, 968–70; **11:**150, 268, 721; **12:**203–4, 283–84, 525, 629, 633–34

SILK
3:1080; **4:**440; **5:**143

SILVER
1:90, 224, 238–39, 251, 629, 638–40, 715, 770, 782, 849, 861, 864, 888, 961, 972, 1039, 1138, 1160, 1165, 1187, 1189; **2:**35, 65, 77, 89, 393, 454, 456, 467, 469, 576, 629, 760, 792, 809, 858, 869–70, 1011, 1037, 1266; **3:**82, 264, 416, 424, 432, 462, 474, 487, 679, 687, 692, 708, 721–22, 728–29, 780, 819, 897, 995, 1132; **4:**67, 104, 216, 218, 222, 369, 434, 502, 524, 529, 531; **5:**43, 91, 111–12, 226, 271, 297, 355, 400, 433, 446, 536, 550, 566–67, 585, 611, 630, 687, 765, 775, 825, 849, 859; **6:**60, 71–72, 74, 407, 509, 629, 662, 943–44, 965–66, 969, 988, 990, 994, 1167, 1220, 1224, 1230, 1306, 1311–1313, 1325, 1337, 1360, 1371, 1377–78, 1393, 1518, 1583; **7:**21–22, 54–55, 81, 83, 140–41, 146–47, 194, 231, 235, 260, 288, 346, 365, 407, 416, 679, 724, 735, 779, 787–88, 805, 822, 824, 839; **8:**382, 467, 673; **9:**46, 69, 145, 171, 193–94, 245, 256, 296, 363, 386, 396, 415, 804; **10:**269–70; **11:**17, 56, 845; **12:**87, 261, 633, 693

SILVERSMITH
2:870; **10:**270–71; **11:**857

SIMEON, SONG OF
See NUNC DIMITTIS

SIMPLICITY
1:293, 861, 873; **2:**340, 385, 437, 479; **3:**47; **4:**224; **5:**461, 505, 861; **9:**234; **10:**286, 471; **11:**828; **12:**213, 222–23

SIN, SINS
CONSEQUENCES OF **1:**329, 363, 369, 398, 478–79, 481, 484, 1033; **2:**139, 826, 836, 989, 1091, 1258, 1291–95, 1326–27; **3:**112–13, 257–58, 655; **4:**404, 475, 807, 835, 885; **5:**59, 85, 111, 114, 154, 536, 560, 681, 691–94, 828; **6:**57, 371, 493, 545, 708, 920, 959, 1153, 1170, 1219, 1331, 1488–89; **7:**267, 333, 537; **9:**322, 324, 634; **10:**140, 504, 618, 864; **11:**260, 624, 627–28, 646, 823; **12:**302, 351–52, 376, 415; AND EVIL (*see under* EVIL); FORGIVENESS OF (*see under* FORGIVENESS); FREEDOM FROM (*see under* FREEDOM); INNOCENCE FROM (*see under* INNOCENCE); MORTAL **1:**369, 988; **2:**1299; **3:**370; **5:**764; **9:**384; **10:**468, 477, 530, 544, 546, 557, 565, 580, 984; **11:**92, 628; **12:**74, 213, 300, 338, 443; MULTITUDE OF **5:**619; **12:**304, 306; OFFERING (*see under* OFFERING); OF OMISSION **3:**609; **5:**55–56, 60, 131, 245; **6:**380, 1461, 1463, 1466; **12:**216; ORIGINAL **1:**196, 376, 737, 934; **5:**885; **8:**137, 213; **10:**531–32, 618; **11:**391, 393; UNFORGIVABLE/UNPARDONABLE **1:**1034; **8:**286–88, 564; **9:**253–54, 634; **10:**579; **12:**443–44; WAGES OF **1:**1012; **3:**328, 370, 587, 654; **5:**111, 337; **6:**622–32; **10:**546; **11:**87, 629

SINCERITY
1:1021; **2:**715, 908; **3:**987; **5:**610; **6:**243–45; **10:**848–49; **11:**46; **12:**410

SINEW, SINEWS
1:618; **5:**425; **6:**1089, 1497–1500; **11:**633

SING (*OR* SINGS, *ETC.*)
1:203–4, 207, 802–3, 954, 1160; **2:**108, 208, 214, 389, 427, 762, 834, 983, 989, 1104, 1108, 1121, 1123–24, 1133, 1193, 1207–10, 1217–18, 1225, 1370; **3:**300, 306, 345, 363, 396, 399–401, 407, 445, 447, 498–99, 608–9, 612, 826, 835, 840, 1144, 1173, 1177, 1223; **4:**304, 309, 601, 644, 656–57, 665, 672, 675, 810, 934, 1073–74, 1223, 1154–56, 1223, 1227–28, 1265, 1279–80; **5:**254, 377, 393, 525–26, 607–8, 623, 700, 859; **6:**18, 123, 147–48, 158, 203, 367, 1298; **7:**10, 160–61, 169, 414, 697; **8:**33, 472; **9:**81, 225, 237, 345, 542; **10:**616, 961–63; **11:**417, 441,

SING *(continued)*
444, 697, 728; **12:**4, 42–43, 53, 595, 598, 713; SINGING LEVITES **3:**306, 327, 345–46, 394, 399–400, 445–47, 499, 575, 609, 645–48, 838, 847. *See also* SONG

SINNER, SINNERS
1:16, 62, 190, 1041–42, 1085, 1097, 1182; **2:**827, 1051; **3:**88, 105, 238, 244, 514, 554, 658, 997, 1017; **4:**48, 219, 404, 480, 503, 512, 593, 684–85, 731, 783, 806–7, 885–88; **5:**37–38, 44–45, 63, 133–34, 144, 207, 302, 304–5, 532, 627, 664, 677–78, 720–21, 724–25, 787, 808; **6:**61–64, 77–78, 93, 1254, 1260, 1265; **7:**253–54, 321, 333, 408–9, 666; **8:**35, 213, 235, 288, 379, 551–53, 557, 708; **9:**22–23, 26, 29, 83–84, 121, 127–29, 147, 170, 270–71, 296, 305, 317, 341–42, 462, 469, 659–60, 663–64; **10:**206, 438, 440–41, 465–66, 471–72, 514, 518–20, 527–29, 544, 575–76, 641; **11:**119, 236–41, 794; **12:**292, 297, 306, 327, 347, 388, 391–92, 414, 444, 479, 488–89

SISTER, SISTERS
IN THE FAITH **1:**169, 182, 186; **3:**1077; **9:**182; **12:**40, 45, 162; AS FIGURATIVE LANGUAGE **3:**1077; **6:**1237–38, 1329; SISTERS-IN-LAW **5:**428. *See also* BROTHER; SIBLINGS

SIVAN
(month in Jewish calendar) **3:**925

SIX HUNDRED AND SIXTY-SIX (666)
1:88, 262; **3:**431; **12:**533, 538, 562, 659

SKIFFS
4:312

SKIN
1:986, 1009, 1013–14, 1035, 1049, 1074–75, 1086, 1094–1101, 1104–1105, 1149; **2:**53, 59–60, 67, 104, 110, 147, 151, 233, 469, 656; **3:**192, 245, 251, 592, 895; **4:**303, 331, 354–55, 391, 393, 401, 414, 436, 459, 469, 477–79, 538, 547, 624; **5:**122, 368, 382, 384, 404, 408, 416, 765, 801; **6:**685, 1034, 1061, 1069–70, 1089–90, 1186, 1466, 1497–1500, 1503, 1511; **7:**501, 618, 672, 681; **8:**33, 224, 544; **9:**119–20, 153; **10:**268; **11:**64, 702; DISEASE (*see also* DISEASE: HANSEN'S DISEASE/SCALE/SKIN; LEPROSY)

SKIRT, SKIRTS
2:1158; **4:**602; **6:**39, 724, 1030; **7:**242–43, 614, 843

SKULL
2:634, 791–92, 818; **3:**1165; **8:**490, 722; **10:**526

SKY
1:88, 124, 344, 356, 445, 978, 1180; **3:**137, 155, 176, 347, 735; **4:**395, 471, 518–19, 591, 604, 711, 865, 1036; **5:**93, 254, 422, 469, 618; **6:**213, 277, 344, 1005, 1007, 1114, 1432; **8:**142, 229, 341, 495; **9:**333, 408; **10:**44, 596; **11:**288; **12:**358, 492, 614, 713

SLANDER (*OR* SLANDERS, *ETC.*)
1:10, 586; **2:**123, 129–30, 457, 1055–56, 1135, 1347; **4:**214, 290, 356, 381, 433, 474, 504, 645, 697, 700, 733, 789, 1240; **5:**226, 331, 455, 609, 617, 680, 683, 740, 765, 771–73; **6:**654, 657, 716, 728, 1480; **8:**15, 197, 454; **10:**454, 841, 865; **11:**97, 398, 430–31, 643, 653, 806, 873; **12:**180, 195, 203–6, 215–16, 218, 223–24, 229, 234–36, 241–42, 252, 263–64, 269, 273–76, 282–83, 290–92, 297, 301, 303, 309–10, 350, 405, 489–90, 577

SLAVE, SLAVES, SLAVERY
1:35, 151, 155–57, 184, 186, 226–27, 318, 405, 490, 600–601, 609–12, 614–15, 639, 654–55, 691, 694–95, 702, 706–7, 712–15, 726–27, 735, 737, 800, 862–65, 872, 923, 1131, 1134, 1173–74; **2:**16, 53, 99, 265, 405–8, 411, 414, 461–62, 470, 501, 506, 543, 560, 588–90, 595, 608–9, 626; **3:**523, 736, 780, 812, 814, 918, 1108, 1119; **4:**82, 105–6, 248, 367, 393, 404, 476, 478, 582, 753; **5:**135, 596–97, 791; **6:**14, 21, 62, 119, 282, 297, 601, 628, 669, 809, 1069, 1081, 1278, 1361, 1495; **7:**25, 31, 144, 179, 190, 220, 279, 293, 333, 361, 633, 822; **8:**20, 210, 654, 720; **9:**637–38; **10:**126, 128, 457, 511–12, 533–34, 542–48, 551, 560, 572, 593, 596, 815, 880–81, 884, 902, 906–10; **11:**76, 154, 195, 225, 249, 260, 273, 278, 282–93, 302–8, 321–22, 424, 454, 457, 462, 508, 657–60, 695–96, 825, 885–87, 900–901; **12:**107, 156, 240, 278, 286–87, 330–31, 333, 345, 612. *See also* SERVANT

SLEDGE, SLEDGES
THRESHING **4:**625; **6:**355; **7:**360

SLING
2:1165, 1168; **3:**1108, 1112; **6:**664; STONES **7:**810

SLUGGARD, SLUGGARDS
5:78, 128, 131, 150–51, 181, 194, 199, 213–15, 225, 237, 262, 745. *See also* LAZY/SLOTH

SMELL, SMELLS
1:393, 535–36, 728–29, 742–44, 912, 920, 1010–1011, 1013; **2:**127, 772; **4:**416, 612; **5:**61, 346, 369, 388, 393, 406, 415, 426, 429, 550, 730; **6:**277, 648; **7:**64, 861; **8:**585; **9:**319; **11:**88; **12:**594, 700

SMELT (*OR* SMELTER, SMELTING, *ETC.*)
5:166, 217; **6:**60, 408, 629, 669, 1304, 1306, 1311–13, 1337, 1393; **7:**146

SMITH, SMITHS
2:738, 781; **3:**67; **5:**142, 218, 625, 812; **6:**388, 944; **7:**756

SMOKE
1:446, 836, 854, 1013, 1015, 1035, 1111; **2:**78,

321, 651, 1367; **4:**305, 310, 312, 623–24, 945, 973, 999, 1087; **5:**460, 485; **6:**84, 102–4, 163, 543, 885, 996, 1501, 1521; **7:**64, 93, 288, 328, 875; **8:**281; **9:**410; **12:**630–32, 672–73, 694, 700

SNAILS
3:178

SNAKE, SNAKES
1:85, 359–60, 363, 666–67, 716, 739, 1135; **2:**12, 164, 167, 1055; **3:**1058; **4:**485, 530, 1240; **5:**254, 348–50, 422, 573, 708, 741, 764; **6:**141, 163, 647–48, 866, 883, 1404; **7:**192; **8:**157, 213; **9:**83, 99, 238; **10:**147, 356, 913; **11:**850; CHARMER(S)/CHARMING **5:**348–49, 351, 715; POISONOUS **1:**356, 666; **2:**163; **5:**570, 573; **6:**141; **9:**83; **10:**147, 291, 356. *See also* ASP; PYTHON; SERPENT; VIPER

SNARE, SNARES
1:949; **2:**254, 256, 747–48, 750, 757, 808, 1366; **4:**36, 74, 469, 501, 621, 931, 1190, 1243; **5:**135, 198, 242–43, 381, 553, 558–59, 701; **6:**118, 212, 717, 1055, 1194, 1285, 1404, 1434; **7:**244, 266–67, 638; **10:**677, 832; **11:**828, 846–47; **12:**254, 306, 351, 669. *See also* NET; TRAP

SNOW
1:1100; **2:**110, 600; **3:**1057; **4:**314, 512, 590, 598, 1268–69; **5:**219, 262, 577–78, 618, 834; **6:**1061; **12:**561, 597, 599

SOCIETY
ANCIENT ISRAELITE **1:**213, 221, 255, 275; **2:**234, 379, 405, 416, 420, 456–57, 472, 566, 783, 923; **5:**189; **6:**5, 8, 16, 143, 638, 1223, 1239, 1241, 1592; **7:**206, 210, 395; **12:**726; MODERN WESTERN **1:**182, 200, 202, 730, 941, 1105, 1139, 1184; **2:**67–68, 111, 194, 267, 422, 835, 1031; **3:**46, 880; **5:**23, 36, 48, 55, 136, 147; **6:**109, 642, 657, 662, 745–46, 795, 982, 1010, 1315; **7:**57, 176, 378, 396, 418, 561, 680; **9:**25–26, 121, 792; **10:**506, 521, 726; **11:**660, 802; **12:**271, 396, 415, 661

SOCKETS
3:486

SOJOURNER, SOJOURNERS
1:419, 449, 504, 734, 779, 783, 868, 1175; **2:**127, 783, 876, 900, 916, 1202; **3:**713; **4:**1182, 1265; **5:**462, 544, 664, 705; **6:**454; **7:**129, 258, 358; **12:**135, 146, 230, 238, 270, 305

SOLDIER, SOLDIERS
1:223; **2:**37, 97, 247–48, 439, 718, 802–3, 807, 833, 838; **3:**376, 378, 424, 1105; **4:**12, 58, 60, 277, 287, 290, 1025, 1277; **5:**341, 708, 805; **6:**133, 1046, 1232, 1356, 1374, 1410, 1415, 1442; **7:**28, 33, 64, 67, 330, 362, 502, 653–55, 827; **8:**195, 355, 405, 477, 488, 491–92, 495–97, 499, 501, 505, 515, 658, 719–24; **9:**19, 84–85, 156, 289, 292, 316, 359, 440, 446, 451, 454–57, 801–2, 810, 818–19, 825, 829–33; **10:**179–80, 296–98, 308, 311, 313, 345, 349–54, 357, 904; **11:**137, 165, 169, 326, 458–63, 520, 668, 842, 846–47, 892, 903

SON OF GOD
See under JESUS THE CHRIST, NAMES FOR/TITLES OF *in PERSONS IN THE BIBLE*

SON OF MAN
IN APOCALYPTIC LITERATURE **1:**288–89; **7:**8–10, 13–15, 35, 840; **8:**30, 36; **10:**401, 723; **11:**37; **12:**524, 561; CHRISTOLOGICAL TITLES IN MATTHEW **8:**353–61; CHRISTOLOGICAL TITLES IN LUKE **9:**13–19, 192–97, 199–204, 391, 442; CHRISTOLOGICAL TITLES IN JOHN **9:**532, 548; AS DIVINE JUDGE **5:**345; **7:**104–7, 113, 317; **8:**99, 229, 234, 258, 280, 282, 296, 300, 308–10, 314, 391–92, 396; **9:**216, 250, 252–54, 263, 349, 434–36, 484, 635, 660–61, 665, 826; **11:**696; **12:**517–19, 533, 557, 571, 578, 580, 587, 603, 605, 633, 650, 668, 704–5, 707, 721, 731–33; AS OF THE KINGDOM **8:**290; **11:**383; JESUS SELF-IDENTIFIES **2:**91; **8:**344, 353–61; **9:**199–204, 551, 599, 608, 610, 834; **12:**695; KEY TO ETERNAL LIFE **2:**167; **8:**102; **9:**532–33; **12:**515; AS LORD OF SABBATH **2:**1141; **8:**287; AS A MORTAL **6:**1121, 1217; **8:**229, 286; AS REDEEMER **1:**787; **5:**381; **8:**50, 64, 260; **9:**457; AS SIGN OF FORGIVENESS **2:**803; **7:**509, 516; **9:**243, 460; AS A SUFFERING, VINDICATED, RESURRECTED GOD **4:**713; **7:**509, 516; **8:**40, 122, 281, 347–52, 364, 366, 368, 370, 384; **9:**217, 282, 331–34, 401–10, 469, 552, 732, 765, 819; **10:**131; **11:**421; **12:**564–70, 611. *See also under* JESUS THE CHRIST, NAMES FOR/TITLES OF *in PERSONS IN THE BIBLE*

SONG, SONGS
OF DEBORAH **2:**558, 585, 724, 762, 772, 774–76, 784–90, 792, 805, 873; **3:**1090, 1165, 1176; **4:**945; FUNERAL DIRGE(S)/SONG(S) **4:**352; **6:**158, 170, 805, 1019, 1021; **7:**344, 349, 385, 414, 595, 601; OF HANNAH **2:**958–59, 961, 964, 970, 975, 979–83, 994, 1252, 1259–60, 1365, 1369–71; **3:**1063, 1145; **4:**1138–39, 1233; **9:**55; OF JUDITH **3:**1089–90, 1162, 1173, 1176–79; OF LAMENT **2:**1203, 1205, 1208–9; **6:**212, 270; MARY'S MAGNIFICAT **1:**205; **2:**983, 1259; **3:**714, 1145; **4:**1139; **9:**55, 81, 105, 144, 211; **12:**239; OF MIRIAM **1:**774, 798–99, 802–3; **2:**108–9, 983; **3:**714, 1173–74; **4:**1065, 1268; **5:**525, 593 (*see also* SONG OF THE SEA); OF MOSES **1:**272, 798–99; **2:**47, 191, 515, 518, 520, 526–30, 758, 774, 861; **3:**714, 1062; **4:**57, 240, 689, 1043; **5:**526, 593; **6:**39, 147, 973; **9:**209, 787; **10:**669; **11:**258; **12:**29, 672 (*see also* SONG OF THE SEA); OF PRAISE **2:**979, 1013; **3:**976; **4:**648, 710, 860, 926, 933, 976, 1003, 1060, 1064, 1072, 1074, 1077, 1090,

SONG, SONGS *(continued)*
1103, 1110, 1132, 1138, 1141, 1150, 1219, 1231 1263, 1267, 1271, 1274; **5:**404, 525–26; **6:**102, 216, 726, 728; **7:**52; **9:**55, 65; **12:**222; OF SIMEON (*see* NUNC DIMITTIS); SPIRITUALS **1:**156–57, 203; **7:**701; **9:**402; **10:**924; **11:**728; OF THE SUFFERING SERVANT (*see under* SUFFERING); TAUNT (*see* TAUNT: SONG TYPE); OF THANKSGIVING (*see* THANKSGIVING: PSALMS/SONGS OF); OF VICTORY **1:**799, 802; **2:**8, 108–9, 159, 600, 1367; **3:**1090, 1144, 1177; **4:**57, 946; **6:**207; **7:**665, 667, 701–4; OF WAR **2:**8, 255; **6:**915; **7:**573. *See also* BALLAD; HYMN; SING

SONG OF SOLOMON
1:43; **4:**1172; **5:**272, 363, 366, 377; **7:**376; **10:**359

SONG OF SONGS
1:8–9, 11, 29, 31, 45, 65, 70, 74, 94, 96; **4:**303, 312; **5:**1, 13, 20, 69, 82, 272–73, 290, 297–98, 361–434, 509, 629, 765; **8:**29; **11:**147, 450; **12:**687

SONG OF THE SEA
1:318; **2:**161, 253; **3:**1090, 1144, 1174, 1176–77; **4:**790, 868, 872, 973, 1053, 1110–11, 1275; **7:**589

SONS OF GOD
1:382–83, 759; **5:**256, 381; **6:**10, 1443; **7:**65, 751; **8:**41, 104, 178, 180, 360; **9:**389; **10:**643, 854; **11:**271, 281, 284, 286, 290, 305, 504; **12:**29, 151, 293, 664

SONS OF PROPHETS
See under PROPHET

SONS OF THUNDER
See BOANERGES *in PERSONS IN THE BIBLE;* SONS OF THUNDER *in PERSONS IN THE BIBLE*

SOOTHSAYER, SOOTHSAYERS
1:1157; **2:**431, 1185; **6:**72

SORCERER, SORCERY
1:739, 867, 1131, 1135, 1157; **2:**63, 68, 187–88, 1082; **3:**635; **5:**542; **6:**411–13, 491, 1124, 1203, 1222; **7:**50, 575–76, 614; **8:**140; **11:**206, 640, 851–52; **12:**633, 668, 694, 722

SORE, SORES
1:1025, 1096–97, 1152; **2:**678; **4:**355; **7:**248, 262; **9:**316, 319–20; **10:**767; **12:**676, 678

SORREL
12:610

SORROW
1:380, 389, 395, 489, 585–86, 630, 645, 1073, 1110, 1113, 1159; **2:**750, 756, 1092, 1208, 1324; **3:**151, 159, 205, 693, 813, 821, 984–85, 992, 1004, 1028, 1039, 1063; **4:**635, 726–27, 801, 899, 1167–69; **5:**105, 107, 112, 140–41, 259, 280, 291, 295, 328, 354, 412, 459, 779; **6:**164, 168–69, 265, 281–83, 465, 648, 664, 785, 971, 975–80, 1022–23, 1033, 1055, 1059, 1327, 1371, 1501; **7:**253, 266, 457, 583, 701; **8:**17, 370, 391, 444, 480; **9:**762, 771, 778–80, 785; **10:**124, 453, 485, 563, 621, 628, 636; **11:**25, 50, 54, 99, 109, 493–94, 520–21, 707, 709; **12:**211, 218, 616, 694–95, 697

SOTERIOLOGY, SOTERIOLOGICAL
1:84, 369, 1158; **8:**315, 704, 720; **9:**525, 552, 584–85, 626, 632, 664, 689, 695, 713–14, 717–18, 789, 852–53; **10:**41, 167, 169, 207, 293, 387, 572, 665, 682; **11:**239, 382, 385, 390, 408, 420–21, 571; **12:**197, 286, 446, 531

SOUL, SOULS
1:49, 69, 94, 96, 126, 206, 287–88, 568, 924, 941, 998, 1034, 1075, 1111, 113; **2:**369, 442, 513, 1120, 1135–36, 1342; **3:**90, 431, 501, 909, 1004, 1062, 1179; **4:**228, 241, 311, 349, 395, 704, 767, 773, 777, 852–54, 938, 1029, 1106; **5:**33, 64, 74, 120, 140, 193, 232–33, 322, 340, 351, 355–56, 377, 396, 401, 407, 454–55, 460, 475, 498, 511–13, 536–37, 558, 574, 579, 682, 765; **6:**56, 221, 223, 551, 606, 956–57, 1049, 1071, 1325, 1500; **7:**5, 11, 253, 287, 642, 681, 725; **8:**17, 32, 160, 298, 351, 531; **9:**72, 100–101, 179, 227, 245, 255–56, 320, 346, 357, 388, 406, 434, 634, 640–41; **10:**72, 100–101, 111, 720, 823, 866, 924; **11:**277, 301, 362, 372, 376, 385, 411, 450–52, 457–58, 460, 463, 504, 566–67, 623, 632, 657, 709; **12:**54, 121, 126–27, 137, 211, 223, 239, 272–73, 336, 461, 468, 505, 599, 613, 694, 700, 707, 716; AND BODY (*see under* BODY)

SOW (*OR* SOWING, SOWER, *ETC.*)
1:217–18, 224, 654, 1084, 1113, 1134, 1188; **2:**410, 614, 817; **3:**355, 370, 503, 540; **4:**332, 377, 789, 931, 1195; **5:**25, 41, 68, 76–77, 105, 114, 119, 122, 131, 185, 198–99, 308, 350, 687, 692, 765; **6:**57, 213, 266, 1148, 1484; **7:**164, 198, 218, 223, 226, 261, 264, 276, 296, 815–16; **8:**60, 62, 170, 211, 300–301, 303–10, 568–80, 607, 627, 640; **9:**98, 173, 176–78, 180–81, 219, 259, 409, 570, 711; **10:**716, 987; **11:**129–33, 224, 316, 337, 339–40

SPARROW, SPARROWS
1:1174; **5:**206; **8:**214, 264; **9:**21, 171, 252, 254

SPEAR, SPEARS
2:197, 199, 759, 787, 1070, 1103–1104, 1108, 1110, 1112, 1114, 1121, 1123, 1127, 1147, 1174–76, 1202, 1217, 1336, 1361; **3:**378, 775–76; **4:**119, 622, 624, 819, 867, 1203; **6:**23, 68–69, 1305, 1524; **7:**55, 332, 609, 612–13, 653; **8:**492, 495; **9:**431, 485; **11:**213, 461; **12:**700

SPECK, SPECKS
4:283; **5:**345, 541; **8:**212; **9:**150, 152, 348

SPELT
TYPE OF WHEAT **1:**759
SPICE, SPICES
1:515, 916, 920, 1061; **3:**82, 511, 543; **5:**365, 405–6, 415, 433, 461, 757; **6:**1377, 1380; **9:**465, 468, 472–73, 836
SPIDER, SPIDERS
4:402–3; **5:**70, 72
SPIKENARD
See OIL
SPIN, SPINNING
3:1003; **4:**440; **5:**72, 327, 547; **8:**211
SPINDLE
1:216; **2:**1225; **5:**262; **6:**1006
SPIRIT, SPIRITS
EVIL (*see under* EVIL); FAMILIAR **6:**118, 120, 389; HOLY (*see* HOLY SPIRIT *in PERSONS IN THE BIBLE*); HUMAN **1:**89, 383, 1075; **3:**176, 1024; **4:**395; **5:**135, 173, 188, 313, 567, 570; **6:**1115, 1500; **7:**382; **8:**525; **10:**418, 566, 823, 866, 989; **11:**415; **12:**210; IN PRISON **10:**234; **12:**293–94, 297
SPIRITUAL
BODY **1:**288; **10:**987; **11:**536; GIFTS **1:**414, 922; **3:**179; **6:**140–41, 1131; **7:**304, 326–28; **8:**264, 535; **9:**509, 559, 566, 597, 623, 708, 753, 771, 774, 800, 833, 846–48, 851; **10:**48, 55, 59, 68, 71, 74, 169, 210, 219, 422, 448, 556, 574, 576, 607, 615, 710, 768, 778, 794, 799, 926, 940–41, 943–44, 949–51, 959, 989; **11:**121, 142–43, 179, 201, 404, 420, 425, 500, 579, 877; **12:**35, 304, 450, 575
SPIRITUALITY
1:49, 185, 288, 291, 701, 883, 902; **2:**343, 345, 389, 587, 601, 1269; **3:**299, 338, 370, 418, 427, 431–32, 469, 474, 500, 540–46, 570, 582, 592, 597, 606–7, 628, 630, 643, 646, 650–51, 1133, 1142, 1145–46, 1174; **4:**648, 704; **5:**78, 391, 499, 513, 669, 671; **6:**532, 958, 970; **7:**576, 632; **8:**178, 557; **9:**482, 490; **10:**101, 343, 451, 615, 632, 959, 962; **11:**218, 291–92, 493, 610, 635–36, 640, 659; **12:**646, 669, 687, 697
SPIT (*OR* SPITS, *ETC.*)
2:110, 164, 475, 629–30, 938, 1142; **4:**396, 462, 472, 546; **5:**41, 772; **7:**94, 611; **8:**79, 480, 488, 652, 695, 714, 719; **9:**351–52, 388, 469, 654; **11:**294
SPOIL, SPOILED
5:8, 207, 346; **6:**629, 714, 718, 1130; **7:**94, 679; **10:**640; **11:**806; **12:**250
SPOILS OF WAR
See under WAR
SPONGE
12:43
SPOONS
1:1164
SPRING
OF LIFE/LIVING WATER **5:**69; **6:**608; **9:**566, 623; **12:**1230; RAIN **2:**374; **4:**540; **5:**161, 223, 393; **7:**250, 276, 813, 816; SEASON OF **1:**275, 1155–59; **2:**50, 87, 230, 236, 411–12; **3:**61, 713, 751, 860, 878, 948; **4:**18–19, 30, 87, 189, 218, 453, 1024; **5:**393; **6:**217, 943, 1363, 1395, 1536–38; **7:**405, 813; **8:**303, 445, 570; **10:**526; **11:**11–12, 424; SOURCE/WATER **1:**15, 222, 249, 278, 473, 666, 1082, 1098; **2:**151, 165, 377, 607, 611, 678, 738, 741–42, 853, 877, 1237; **3:**20, 178, 628, 759, 768–69, 800, 949, 969; **4:**330, 441, 530, 603, 1014, 1024, 1098, 1100; **5:**68, 97, 144, 220, 388, 406, 610, 745, 853; **6:**117, 335, 711, 1246, 1387, 1596; **7:**12, 276, 293; **8:**189, 343; **9:**242, 250, 317; **10:**486, 773; **12:**347, 351, 489, 573, 630–31, 635, 676, 721, 734
SPY, SPIES
1:629–30; **2:**19–20, 33–34, 37, 120–24, 198–99, 201–2, 262–63, 298, 306, 561–62, 586, 592–94, 627–28, 630, 739, 743, 1174, 1279, 1284, 1325, 1332; **3:**379, 1089; **4:**51, 1111; **5:**560, 719; **6:**1147, 1175, 1216, 1279, 1485, 1490; **7:**73; **9:**385–86; **11:**225; **12:**49, 488
SQUAD, SQUADS
3:173; **8:**491, 493, 628, 726; **10:**179, 645; **11:**871
SQUARE, SQUARES
PUBLIC **2:**876; **3:**607, 629, 742, 800, 870, 904, 1134; **4:**11; **5:**40, 85, 396; **6:**168, 501; **7:**220, 610, 794; **8:**13–14, 148; **9:**220; **10:**153, 222, 262, 375, 382; SCRIPT **1:**294, 298; **3:**698; SHAPE **1:**1061; **2:**38, 268, 540, 668; **6:**1115, 1533, 1540, 1542, 1547–49, 1555, 1566, 1582, 1605–1607
STABLE, STABLES
2:1100; **3:**132; **7:**231; **8:**150
STADIA
4:266; **8:**327; **9:**475
STAFF, STAFFS
1:605, 607, 665, 716–17, 739–40, 817, 820; **2:**99, 135, 140, 631, 796–97, 804, 1080, 1112; **3:**144, 189; **4:**328; **5:**517; **6:**76, 133, 158, 293, 455, 891, 1006–1007, 1149, 1166, 1207, 1218, 1232, 1289, 1402, 1406, 1506; **7:**240, 605, 752, 820–23; **8:**256, 595; **9:**171, 194, 197, 220, 367; **11:**78; **12:**139, 599
STAG
5:85, 394, 433. *See also* DEER
STAIRS
3:769, 806, 839; **4:**1176, 1178; **6:**1557

STALLS
1:218, 223; **3:**54, 511, 821; **7:**872; **8:**405; **9:**64
STANDARD
2:95, 98; **4:**249, 282; **6:**256
STAR, STARS
1:31, 88, 288, 344, 445, 599; **2:**32, 191, 229, 235, 569–70, 647, 788–89; **3:**479, 570, 776, 810, 886; **4:**313, 395, 410, 469, 517, 520, 592, 601, 605, 626, 1269, 1271; **5:**9, 61, 354, 357, 419, 469, 546–47, 556, 584, 672, 834, 859; **6:**159, 204, 277, 342–44, 411, 413, 827, 962, 967–68, 1007, 1130, 1392, 1429, 1435, 1570, 1589; **7:**2, 9, 113, 147–48, 162, 168, 447, 618; **8:**24, 142–46, 444, 724; **9:**65–66, 399, 407, 460; **10:**348, 401, 490, 498, 500, 987; **11:**264, 282, 288, 372, 390, 415, 457, 513, 563, 565–66; **12:**43, 80, 343, 357, 492, 567, 579, 582, 597, 614, 630–31, 635, 648–49, 668
STATUE, STATUES
1:285; **2:**79, 83; **3:**226, 484, 679, 1109, 1182; **4:**38–39, 51, 60, 212, 218, 292, 577, 945; **5:**550, 556–57, 564, 569, 611; **6:**210, 866, 986–90, 994–96, 998, 1001–1002, 1004–10, 1090, 1119, 1175, 1182–83, 1280, 1417; **7:**50, 53–55, 57, 61–67, 81, 128, 137, 143, 160, 188, 527, 756; **8:**25, 684, 689; **9:**382; **10:**607, 623, 894; **11:**78, 412, 677, 759, 838; **12:**76, 505, 658, 707
STEADFAST, STEADFASTNESS
1:41, 564; **2:**276, 1065; **3:**527; **4:**211; **5:**113, 291; **6:**606; **7:**250, 642, 866; **9:**421, 427, 437, 760; **10:**990–91; **11:**40, 97, 497, 588, 688–89, 691, 703, 712, 715, 747, 765, 849–51
STEADFAST LOVE
1:510; **2:**741, 1257; **3:**407, 495, 498, 723, 736; **4:**663–64, 671, 741, 748, 758, 778, 800–801, 809, 872, 891, 912–13, 922–23, 927, 938, 952, 983, 1043, 1121, 1127, 1206, 1225, 1255; **7:**276. *See also* LOVING-KINDNESS
STEAL (*OR* STEALS, *ETC.*)
1:42, 557, 638, 639, 848, 851, 863, 1027, 1033, 1133, 1139; **2:**61, 62, 65, 467, 609, 789, 795, 810, 830, 851–22, 865, 869, 871, 1319; **3:**729, 1005, 1085; **4:**377, 495, 548, 882, 952; **5:**81, 105, 147, 253, 558; **6:**88, 753, 990, 995, 998, 1000, 1259–60, 1327, 1383, 1518; **7:**236, 400, 403, 448, 548, 581; **8:**494, 497, 587; **9:**133, 260, 310, 394; **10:**445, 447; **11:**263, 429, 432, 453; **12:**43
STEEDS
5:346; **7:**783
STEEL
1:218; **5:**291; **7:**609
STELE, STELES
2:182; **4:**46; **6:**20, 1561; **7:**61
STEPPE
2:190; **4:**603; **7:**314
STEWARD, STEWARDS, STEWARDSHIP
1:224, 241, 629, 633–39, 917–18, 962–64; **2:**1045, 1195; **3:**50, 132, 348, 468, 539, 624, 630, 657, 756, 821; **4:**605, 1272; **5:**147, 233; **6:**93, 196, 330, 344, 469, 1469; **7:**309; **8:**61, 649; **9:**175, 306–12, 314, 318, 345, 354, 362, 364, 382–84, 538–40; **10:**24, 97, 596, 721, 798, 829, 831, 833, 835, 865–66, 957, 996; **11:**99, 105, 139, 281, 569, 615, 617, 864, 867; **12:**169, 584; OF GOD **3:**468; **6:**96, 1465; **7:**309, 325; **9:**310; **10:**721, 834; **11:**281, 357, 408, 615, 763; **12:**304; OF THE KING **3:**456, 460; OF LAND **1:**1133; **9:**310, 406
STIFF-NECKED
1:937, 941, 948, 951, 953, 955, 961; **2:**511; **3:**602, 617; **4:**1062; **5:**242; **6:**1168; **10:**124–25, 129
STOCKS
3:543; **5:**689, 792; **6:**722, 724; **10:**233
STOICISM, STOICS
1:291; **5:**90, 441, 460, 498, 503–6, 510, 545–46, 562, 579, 584, 624, 647, 730, 834; **8:**17–24, 392; **9:**519; **10:**72, 244, 246–47, 441–42, 516, 705, 783, 848, 870, 880–81, 892, 896, 910; **11:**85, 111, 213, 377, 382, 391, 414, 446, 458, 544, 548, 643, 698, 828, 831; **12:**278, 413
STOMACH, STOMACHS
1:1080; **2:**197, 1225, 1230; **5:**319, 337; **6:**1033, 1405, 1489; **7:**504; **9:**599; **10:**199, 860, 862; **11:**534, 823; **12:**639
STONE, STONES
1:276, 424, 542, 558, 861, 1017, 1019–20, 1061, 1099–1100; **2:**220, 254, 486–88, 589, 599, 601, 607, 625, 627, 634–36, 648, 771, 1112, 1326, 1336; **3:**115, 136, 432, 691, 704, 772, 776, 896, 1017, 1161; **4:**71, 152, 381, 388, 403, 443, 471–72; **5:**147, 291, 305, 348, 474, 592, 679, 742, 766, 779, 837; **6:**127, 367, 432, 657, 866, 1001, 1049, 1366, 1392, 1394; **7:**56–57, 117, 232, 725, 770, 810–11, 834; **8:**133, 163, 165, 213, 671; **9:**84, 98, 177, 321, 355, 369, 380, 398–99, 591; **12:**237, 264–65, 571, 722, 727 (*see also* ROCK); BOUNDARY **2:**635; **5:**93, 105, 205; FIGURED **2:**254; HEAP OF **2:**625, 627; 1336, **4:**471; **7:**725; PRECIOUS **1:**359, 906; **3:**467, 487, 1062, 1065, 1152; **4:**530; **5:**387, 498, 593, 843, 859; **6:**1061, 1360, 1377, 1380, 1391–94; **7:**147, 766; **12:**648, 681, 693–94, 723 (*see also* GEM; JEWELS AND PRECIOUS STONES; *by individual type*)
STONECUTTERS
3:429
STONED, STONING
1:84, 238, 987, 1138, 1142, 1148, 1165; **2:**392,

447, 455, 562–63, 629, 631, 688, 1192; **3:**102, 156, 479; **4:**471; **5:**207; **6:**1330; **7:**208, 224, 278; **8:**14, 269; **9:**282, 352, 381, 628, 646–47, 677, 816, 820; **10:**105, 133, 199, 308; **11:**214, 294; **12:**158, 728
STORK
4:597, 611; **6:**1425
STORM, STORMS
1:194, 232–33, 236, 283, 398, 836; **2:**198, 316, 356, 534, 1063; **3:**142, 196, 1058; **4:**51, 313, 525, 583, 589–90, 593–94, 600, 792, 881, 1118–19; **5:**40, 112, 193, 220, 354–55, 485–86, 575–80, 598, 787; **6:**180, 217, 242, 265, 752, 1089, 1109, 1113, 1118–19, 1129, 1202, 1257, 1517; **7:**101, 310, 463, 467, 469–71, 473–75, 482, 485, 492–93, 495–96, 499–500, 502, 518, 653–54, 828; **8:**64, 84, 218, 223, 228–30, 235, 247, 327–28, 510, 579–84, 593, 603; **9:**153, 183–84, 322, 460, 596; **10:**348–49, 353, 773; **11:**381; **12:**351, 700
STRANGER, STRANGERS
1:85, 462–64, 475–77, 484, 504, 580, 599, 628, 635, 748, 1120, 1136, 1173; **2:**127, 369, 740, 783, 863, 876–79, 886, 913, 918–19, 923; **3:**43, 723, 813, 882, 979, 993, 996, 998, 1008, 1039, 1055; **4:**36, 87, 228, 232, 476, 479, 504, 538, 554, 742, 770, 894, 1025, 1105; **5:**44, 55, 67–69, 71–72, 74, 85, 92, 145, 220, 229, 321, 400, 406, 544, 596–97, 699, 715; **6:**382, 601–2, 745–46, 976, 1069, 1167, 1203, 1233, 1388–89; **7:**162, 265, 268, 425, 451; **8:**489, 658; **9:**320, 339, 347, 388, 416, 477, 480, 482–83, 667–68; **10:**22, 50, 143, 378; **11:**220, 284, 358, 396, 402, 820, 825; **12:**12, 66, 125, 135, 137, 146, 162, 170, 236–38, 246, 254, 277, 287, 454, 462–63, 468–69, 704
STRANGLED, STRANGLING
1:1121; **3:**1001; **4:**395; **8:**573; **9:**101; **10:**220; **11:**194, 225
STRAW
1:16, 102, 727, 729, 800; **4:**440; **6:**141, 753, 1200; **7:**685; **9:**135; **10:**829
STREAM, STREAMS
1:349, 1098, 1119, 1160; **2:**838; **3:**628; **4:**82, 174, 306, 311, 388, 484–85, 712, 854, 1131, 1195; **5:**69, 172, 293, 406, 475, 625, 745, 765, 818; **6:**23, 117, 256, 266, 271, 280–81, 335, 342, 386, 708, 1246, 1404, 1413, 1434, 1436, 1532, 1595–99, 1607; **7:**394, 437, 685, 701, 836–37; **9:**458; **11:**261; **12:**526, 597, 700, 724
STREETS
1:191, 216, 222–23; **2:**184, 1185, 1232; **3:**475, 1065; **4:**18, 40, 43, 159, 208; **5:**88, 121, 328, 394, 396, 400, 406, 454, 509; **6:**8, 36, 367, 638, 655, 723, 825, 873, 1009, 1071, 1167, 1170, 1233, 1330, 1362, 1437; **7:**220, 262, 403, 610, 794, 805; **8:**13–14, 649, 672, 694; **9:**22, 149, 220, 278, 542; **10:**31, 297; **11:**769; **12:**201, 420, 723
STRIPE, STRIPES
1:155, 864; **4:**105; **6:**465
STRONGHOLD, STRONGHOLDS
2:739, 1080, 1145, 1159, 1237, 1243, 1366; **3:**52, 376, 967; **4:**36, 125, 134, 147, 154, 168, 249, 261, 276, 511, 666, 717, 747, 785, 790, 830, 913; **5:**126; **6:**294, 1038, 1222, 1269, 1320, 1382, 1418, 1458; **7:**250, 262, 275, 334, 353, 355, 401, 602, 618, 809; **9:**88, 373; **11:**138, 141
STRUCTURALISM
1:109, 112, 115, 122, 140–43, 145; **2:**539–40, 548
STUBBLE
1:800; **3:**487; **5:**469; **6:**95, 271; **7:**605
STUFF
1:521–22; **2:**454; **4:**728; **6:**432–33
STUMBLING BLOCK
1:49; **4:**674, 874, 1029; **6:**1135, 1167, 1205–1207, 1576; **8:**270, 371–72, 375; **9:**149, 384, 679, 686, 743; **10:**650–51, 677, 811, 896; **11:**316–17, 319; **12:**237, 268, 394, 578, 605
SUFFER (*OR* SUFFERED, SUFFERING, *ETC.*)
1:18, 72, 366, 449; **2:**98, 649, 666, 739, 748, 798, 825, 827, 878, 1057; **3:**81, 426–27, 984, 997–98, 1005, 1056; **4:**234, 241–43, 329, 334–36, 371–72, 382–84, 416, 422–23, 435–36, 464–65, 471–72, 520, 535, 571–73, 646, 691, 705–6, 713, 834–35; **5:**466, 499, 534–36, 734; **6:**98, 170, 204, 222, 301, 685, 699, 813, 852, 1021, 1024, 1051; **7:**114–16, 262, 383, 509, 560; **8:**34, 52, 348–49, 354, 362, 397–98, 442, 459, 495, 529–30, 625–26, 707–8; **9:**24, 162, 352, 370, 402, 453, 478, 799; **10:**109, 152, 289–90, 521, 595, 607; **11:**41–43, 408, 497–98, 517, 614–18, 713, 747–48, 842, 847; **12:**39, 64, 155, 280–82, 292, 295, 308, 310, 313; OF CHRIST (*see under* JESUS THE CHRIST *in PERSONS IN THE BIBLE*); CHRISTIAN **9:**292; **10:**109; **11:**42; **12:**296–97, 281–82, 310, 313; AND EVIL **1:**72, 396; **2:**739, 760, 798; **3:**426; **4:**234, 375, 451, 471–72, 503, 535, 544, 571–73, 581, 821, 974–75, 996–97, 1054–55; **5:**13, 764, 817; **6:**98, 493, 498, 673, 813, 982, 1057–58, 1431; **7:**93, 129, 145, 333, 551, 553, 576, 581; **8:**64, 197–98, 357, 460, 529–30, 546, 652, 688, 696, 709, 732; **10:**311, 342–43, 378, 541, 701; **11:**417, 497–98, 761; **12:**152, 190, 242, 252, 281–82, 290–91, 296–97, 312, 350, 636; HUMAN **1:**478; **3:**543; **5:**467, 599; **6:**1262, 1483; **7:**411; OF ISRAEL **2:**826–27, 835; **3:**336, 423; **4:**240; **7:**560; SERVANT **1:**367, 1042;

SUFFER *(continued)*
2:752; **4:**241, 243, 436, 663, 691, 713, 858, 954, 1022, 1167, 1171, 1173, 1175, 1191, 1221, 1251; **5:**441, 463, 485–86, 562; **6:**360–67, 423–70, 471–552; **7:**90, 145; **8:**52, 158, 160, 166, 228, 349, 356, 366–67, 480, 535, 654, 707, 710, 717–18; **9:**200–201, 430, 479, 486; **10:**63, 80, 129–30, 144; **11:**449, 569, 614–15, 617; **12:**113, 237, 280

SUICIDE, SUICIDES
1:269; **2:**666, 723, 1024, 1102, 1198, 1330–31, 1333; **3:**123, 457, 1005, 1008–1009; **4:**5, 46, 207, 292, 444, 1185; **5:**311, 323, 351, 567; **6:**729; **7:**648; **8:**482–84, 546; **9:**634, 704; **10:**763; **11:**444, 696

SUKKOT
See FEASTS/FESTIVALS: OF BOOTHS/SUKKOT/TABERNACLES

SULFUR, SULPHUR
1:473; **2:**512; **4:**470; **6:**277, 1311, 1522; **9:**330, 332; **11:**88; **12:**489, 632–33

SUMMER
1:217–18, 275; **2:**412, 480; **3:**706–7; **4:**60, 121, 127, 176, 311, 368, 388, 463, 603; **5:**54, 68, 107, 161, 185, 219, 823; **6:**848, 1079, 1176; **7:**265, 376, 407, 414, 715; **8:**445, 693; **9:**52, 408; **10:**776–77; **11:**12

SUN
1:88, 217, 232–33, 236, 285, 343–44, 599, 622, 1157; **2:**87–88, 198, 229, 570, 646–47, 789, 1371; **3:**184, 271, 969; **4:**178, 197, 218, 410, 422, 518, 554, 591, 597, 751–52, 926, 1036, 1098, 1181, 1272; **5:**5, 62, 75, 292–94, 335, 353–54, 371, 383, 416, 504, 556, 579, 585, 647, 720, 787, 833–34, 846; **6:**84, 213, 277, 300, 396, 640, 1114, 1129, 1176–77, 1179, 1435, 1549; **7:**250, 328, 417, 471, 521–22, 609–10, 770, 774–75, 782–83, 872–73; **8:**366, 444, 570–71, 723–24; **9:**399, 407, 460, 829; **10:**337, 348, 987; **11:**282, 288, 390, 415; **12:**357, 507, 612, 625, 630–31, 638, 648, 651–52, 676, 699; HORSES DEDICATED TO **6:**1177; **7:**783

SUNDIAL
3:271; **6:**300

SUPERSCRIPTIONS
2:1102; **4:**301, 643–44, 655–57, 1050; **5:**377–78; **6:**11, 18, 33, 47, 300–301, 574–75, 1110; **7:**351, 650. *See also* PSALM HEADINGS/TITLES

SUPERSTITION, SUPERSTITIONS
1:778; **3:**464; **4:**295; **6:**72, 176, 244–45, 1066; **8:**22, 331; **9:**74, 113, 191; **10:**249, 268–69, 329, 335, 355; **12:**98, 273

SUPPER, THE LAST
See *LAST SUPPER, THE*

SUPPER, THE LORD'S
See under LORD'S

SUPPLIANT, SUPPLIANTS/SUPPLICANT, SUPPLICANTS
1:745; **2:**602, 633, 1365–67; **4:**547, 597, 895, 959; **5:**4, 172, 866; **6:**1191; **7:**702; **8:**238, 544, 584; **10:**294, 336; **11:**414; **12:**715, 603

SURETY
4:461–62, 570; **5:**3, 187, 205, 775; **6:**454, 826; **10:**19, 132, 201, 232, 297, 992; **12:**92

SURGERY, SURGERIES
1:353; **7:**115, 575

SURNAME, SURNAMES
4:42–43; **6:**394

SWADDLING
4:602; **5:**497, 499; **12:**457

SWALLOW, SWALLOWS
1:800–801, 804; **2:**138, 771; **3:**985, 1026, 1029; **4:**396, 485, 631, 1190; **5:**38, 66–67, 182, 187, 241, 322; **6:**217, 762, 1038, 1218, 1401, 1576; **7:**261, 467, 470–71, 481–83, 504–5, 507, 509, 526–27; **9:**202, 278, 348; **12:**651

SWAMPS
6:1597

SWARMING CREATURES
See under CREATURE

SWARTHY
5:382

SWEAR (*OR* SWEARS, *ETC.*)
1:442, 446–49, 510, 512, 522, 592, 659, 866, 1033, 1041, 1133, 1166; **2:**593, 1090, 1127, 1134–35, 1158, 1188, 1273, 1361; **3:**19, 28, 230, 741; **4:**522, 928, 1211; **5:**339, 558–59, 750; **6:**74, 181, 221, 403, 680–81, 864, 1250, 1253, 1276, 1279, 1491, 1601; **7:**236, 376, 416, 419, 775–76, 778; **8:**457; **9:**282, 476; **10:**738; **11:**52, 403; **12:**49, 80, 90, 92, 139, 222. *See also* COVENANT; OATH

SWEAT
1:816, 897; **6:**1578; **9:**370, 433; **11:**816

SWEET CANE
See CANE: FRAGRANT

SWINE
4:39; **8:**212, 231–32, 583–84; **9:**186–87, 302, 304; **12:**123

SWORD, SWORDS
1:365, 1181; **2:**671, 707, 771, 1104, 1112, 1114, 1217, 1381–82; **3:**423–24, 553, 560, 598, 775–76; **4:**296–97, 441, 486, 619, 621, 829, 913, 931, 1277; **5:**67, 127, 194, 231, 253, 425, 486, 592, 742, 772, 818; **6:**23, 55, 68–69, 261, 276–77, 358, 412, 691, 693, 766, 886, 915, 919, 1292–1306, 1393; **7:**144–45, 151, 332, 380, 576,

612–13, 833–34; **8:**261, 477, 709–10; **9:**19, 72, 399, 429–31, 435–37; **10:**235, 614, 720; **11:**214, 459, 462; **12:**41, 54, 513, 533, 540, 566–67, 578, 636, 645, 657, 699–703; FALL BY THE (*see under* FALL)

SYCAMORE TREE
3:82, 756; **6:**127; **7:**340–42, 411, 644; **9:**322, 357; DRESSER OF **7:**411

SYMBOLISM
1:53, 184, 278, 901, 977, 1049, 1060, 1062, 1098, 1166; **2:**80, 88, 98, 188, 316–17, 330, 364, 385, 493, 613, 1013, 1251; **3:**18, 351, 407, 948, 1102, 1142, 1161; **4:**122, 441, 854, 1083, 1088; **5:**37, 43, 71, 85, 95, 161, 219, 242, 257, 383, 583, 683, 690, 745; **6:**226, 260, 722, 1563; **7:**6, 67, 91, 101, 143, 228, 551, 768; **8:**67, 253, 327, 339, 450, 532, 535, 658, 704; **9:**184, 196, 460–61, 494, 519, 528, 538–39, 565, 596, 601, 613, 620, 632, 719, 756, 759, 780, 857–58; **10:**50, 54, 67, 538; **11:**274, 343; **12:**194, 211, 504–5, 509–10, 515, 523, 525, 530, 545, 567, 604, 615, 653, 697. *See also* SIGN

SYNAGOGUE, SYNAGOGUES
1:37, 39, 41, 43, 65, 68–70, 77, 80–82, 188, 191–92, 205, 285, 291–92, 296, 302, 317, 986, 992, 995, 1109–10, 1113, 1156, 1160; **2:**33, 893, 1295; **3:**33, 893, 1295; **4:**576, 800–801, 1133–34; **5:**266, 269, 341, 439–40, 629, 635, 781, 801; **6:**285, 759, 860, 1316; **7:**228, 245, 620, 860, 876; **8:**14, 34–35, 42, 69–70, 97–102, 174, 188, 200–203, 237, 274, 279, 318, 323, 334, 431, 488, 501, 540–41, 558–59, 565, 588, 650, 685; **9:**103, 105–6, 110–11, 248, 273–74, 339, 393, 400, 504–10, 647–48, 657–58, 663, 809; **10:**27–28, 120–21, 170, 188, 194–97, 220–24, 231–35, 239–40, 252, 254–55, 360, 364, 440–41; **11:**22, 78, 214, 274, 363–64, 397, 405, 561, 567–68, 682, 696, 865; **12:**71, 125, 128, 138, 164, 192, 577, 585, 588, 657, 727; RULER OF (*see under* RULER); WORSHIP (*see under* WORSHIP)

SYNCRETISM
1:276, 624, 900; **3:**3, 37, 257, 278, 734, 849; **4:**1111; **6:**843; **7:**660, 663, 674–76, 679; **8:**22; **10:**260; **11:**576, 600, 831

SYNOPTIC PROBLEM
1:132–34; **8:**71–75, 91–96, 285, 401, 465–66, 509–13, 703–4; **9:**4–10, 140. *See also* CRITICISM: SOURCE/SOURCE CRITICAL

T

TABERNACLE
1:884, 960, 961, 976, 978, 1007, 1008; **2:**3, 11, 13, 15, 24–26, 32, 35, 36, 50, 60, 69, 70, 77, 79, 80, 88, 90, 412; **3:**345, 346, 399, 462, 473, 484; **4:**198; **6:**1228, 1575; **7:**769; **12:**98, 102, 103, 104, 114, 116, 721; TO DWELL/RESIDE **3:**70, 78. *See also* BOOTH; TENT

TABERNACLES, FEAST OF
See FEAST/FESTIVALS: OF BOOTHS/SUKKOT/TABERNACLES

TABLE, TABLES
1:192, 208–9, 224, 279, 890, 1026, 1163; **2:**547, 1274, 1276; **3:**28, 485, 608; **4:**766, 1015; **5:**683, 1330; **6:**184, 1540, 1546, 1547, 1555; **7:**41, 61, 400, 557; **8:**406, 663, 699; **9:**26, 128, 232, 316, 373, 416, 422–23, 426, 479, 480, 490, 543, 545; **10:**74, 113–15, 279, 677, 919; **11:**199, 230–32, 234, 235, 240, 245, 348, 353, 806; **12:**104, 166; CHRONOLOGICAL **1:**7; OF DEMONS **10:**912; OF DUTIES (*see* TABLE: LISTS); FELLOWSHIP **1:**890, 892; **8:**608, 609; **9:**25–27, 128, 278, 480; **10:**168, 278, 677; **11:**231, 232, 234, 235, 245; LISTS **1:**7; **11:**303, 355; **12:**278, 290, 744; OF THE LORD **4:**1015; **9:**289, 480; **10:**918, 919; **11:**234; SERVANTS **11:**240; OF SHOWBREAD **6:**1555; **10:**912, 918, 919; TURNING THE *(i.e., reversal)* **1:**556, 580, 628; **2:**620, 627, 651, 688, 773; **3:**580, 930; **4:**1126; **6:**914, 956, 978, 1482; **8:**391, 564, 642; **9:**25, 232, 816; **11:**176, 244, 638

TABLET, TABLETS
1:39, 218, 306, 839, 844, 846–49, 880, 889, 924, 932, 945, 946, 956; **2:**96, 107, 254, 277, 314, 320, 324, 328, 339, 363, 364, 470, 486, 538, 543, 614, 648, 755, 1001; **3:**70, 72, 494, 495, 707; **4:**18, 107, 157, 160, 163, 165, 198, 328, 329, 478; **5:**3, 4, 6, 48, 561, 730; **6:**10, 11, 12, 116, 247, 377, 1143, 1411, 1474, 1507, 1515; **7:**11, 202, 641, 774, 775; **8:**39, 247; **9:**59; **10:**123, 380, 561, 741; **11:**63, 64, 67, 77, 536; **12:**104, 560

TACKLE
AS IN FISHING EQUIPMENT/A SHIP'S RIGGING **7:**502; **10:**348, 352; AS A VERB **1:**86; **6:**1272, 1486; **11:**37

TALENT, TALENTS
ABILITY/CAPACITY/SKILL **1:**204, 230, 442, 623, 964, 1042, 1152; **2:**805, 1044, 1109; **4:**166; **5:**140, 208, 417, 502; **6:**210, 371, 581; **7:**8, 9, 141; **8:**453; **10:**24, 55, 92, 113, 115, 177, 246, 253, 268, 318, 329; **11:**412, 805; **12:**697; AS A MEASURING STONE/STANDARD **12:**678; AS A MONETARY UNIT (*see under* COIN)

TALISMAN
7:778, 779; **8:**74; **10:**440, 448, 950; **12:**725

TALITHA KUMI
9:190

TALMUD
1:66, 68, 70, 73, 75, 79, 82, 228, 284, 1057, 1126; **2:**950; **4:**357, 389, 525, 1261; **5:**14, 101, 102, 224, 355, 553, 634, 720, 758; **6:**277, 949; **7:**407, 436, 877; **8:**31, 32, 197, 299, 359, 417;

TALMUD *(continued)*
9:653, 659, 687, 697, 748, 863; **10:**447; **11:**506; **12:**579, 636; BABYLONIAN **1:**11, 65, 69; **3:**1191; **4:**1285; **5:**101, 674, 689, 732; **6:**1148; **7:**472; **8:**490, 742; **9:**874; **12:**657; JERUSALEM **8:**742; **9:**874

TAMARISK TREE
2:1147, 1198, 1359; **6:**1246

TAMBOURINE, TAMBOURINES
2:1173–74, 1108; **3:**1139, 1173, 1177; **4:**1275

TANNER, TANNING
2:83, 1114; **10:**162, 164

TAPESTRY, TAPESTRIES
3:332, 628, 1089; **5:**437; **6:**566, 570; **9:**434; **11:**64, 66, 609; **12:**35, 266, 551

TARGET, TARGETS
1:57, 59, 363, 374, 796; **2:**468, 476, 502, 547, 573, 593; **3:**33, 166, 487, 581, 646, 898, 1049; **4:**40, 60, 426, 459, 592, 668, 1112, 1126; **5:**167, 187, 461, 462; **6:**82, 238, 414, 435, 1293, 1301, 1305, 1331, 1348, 1374, 1486–1515; **7:**258, 470, 471, 501, 616; **8:**18; **9:**127; **10:**106, 371, 372, 382, 484, 485, 496, 506, 681, 728, 755, 915; **11:**59, 67, 103, 300, 707, 790, 791; **12:**163, 182, 218, 490; AUDIENCE **7:**439; CORRECT/ON TARGET **1:**428, 482, 489; **6:**344, 653, 1455; **10:**221; **11:**684; **12:**66, 420; LANGUAGE **1:**23, 24, 30; **5:**642; AS A VERB **2:**748; **4:**729; **5:**276; **6:**1314; **7:**502; **11:**853

TASKMASTER
2:167, 506; **3:**102; **4:**369, 916; **5:** 536, 627

TASSEL, TASSELS
2:128, 454; **8:**431; **9:**190, 191

TATTOO (*OR* TATTOOED, *ETC.*)
1:374, 1131, 1135

TAU
(Hebrew letter) **6:**1179

TAUNT (*OR* TAUNTS, TAUNTED, *ETC.*)
ACT OF **2:**807, 973, 975, 979, 981, 1079; **3:**377; **6:**727, 853, 882; **8:**722, 723, 724; **9:**166, 440, 454, 455, 544, 820; AS A NOUN **2:**166, 186, 817, 837, 1110, 1236, 1237; **3:**178, 266, 773, 783, 1008; **4:**129, 130, 197, 241, 264, 290, 546, 763, 852, 853, 901, 995, 996, 1038, 1088; **5:**433; **6:**158, 410–12, 661, 697, 709, 710, 727, 783, 808, 813, 853, 882, 891, 892, 920, 1056, 1304, 1384, 1418, 1493, 1494, 1598; **7:**75, 587, 647; **8:**491; **9:**441, 454, 456–58, 463, 469, 818, 820, 823; **10:**994; **11:**664; **12:**125; THE ONE(S) SUBJECTED TO **3:**773; **9:**14; PERSON(S) DOING THE **4:**852; **12:**283; SONG TYPE **1:**375; **4:**852; **5:**32; **6:**155, 157–59, 163, 167; **7:**550, 559; AS A VERB **2:**841, 973, 975, 1079, 1110, 1112, 1175, 1226, 1236; **3:**135, 911; **4:**204, 295, 554, 853, 858, 952, 973, 1036, 1170; **6:**545, 614, 709, 727, 808, 963, 1293, 1304, 1411, 1450, 1478; **7:**647, 690; **8:**543, 723; **9:**373, 440, 441, 446, 457–59, 463, 659, 819, 822

TAX, TAXES, TAXATION
1:36, 222, 224, 225, 262, 878; **2:**148, 247, 403, 566, 589, 659, 669, 681, 771, 923, 1110, 1194, 1268, 1380, 1382; **3:**51, 52, 53, 54, 55, 58, 232, 258, 452, 556, 642, 666, 669, 685, 699, 700, 709, 721, 722, 779–83, 812, 819, 844, 889, 941; **4:**125, 136, 138, 151, 154, 159, 165, 168, 205, 254, 265; **5:**128, 200, 242, 318, 439, 597, 612, 790; **6:**305, 559, 650, 745, 1584, 1593; **7:**24, 40–42, 54, 57, 81, 138, 141, 144, 390, 406, 560, 779, 822; **8:**33, 107, 123, 165, 371, 372, 381, 382, 401, 419, 420, 514, 523, 552, 642, 663, 672, 673; **9:**28, 60, 62, 66, 84, 126, 353, 357–59, 364, 370, 374, 385, 386, 445, 447, 705; **10:**231, 720, 721, 724, 774; **11:**470; **12:**219, 514; CENSUS/POLL **1:**972; **4:**125, 548, 783, 1131; **5:**439; **8:**420, 673; **9:**84, 126, 171, 386; FISCUS IUDAICUS **12:**684; HEROD'S TAX **9:**171; SANCTUARY/TABERNACLE/TEMPLE **1:**285, 314; **2:**33, 35, 82, 148, 149; **3:**580, 582, 819, 844; **8:**15, 33, 41, 122, 370, 371, 682; **9:**171, 543; AS A VERB **1:**918; **2:**816; **5:**693; **12:**507, 560

TAX COLLECTION
1:222; **2:**33, 149; **3:**452; **7:**738; **9:**62

TAX COLLECTOR, COLLECTORS
(incl. tax agent[s] and tax farmer[s]) **1:**224, 226; **2:**149, 659; **3:**600; **4:**6; **5:**307, 334, 481, 585; **7:**118, 141, 142, 253, 254; **8:**59, 61, 79, 81, 107, 170, 195, 235, 237, 376, 377, 378, 412, 473, 503, 513, 547, 552, 699, 726; **9:**12, 22, 23, 25, 26, 28, 36, 45, 56, 83–85, 98, 114, 126–29, 131, 138, 164, 167, 170, 280, 295, 296, 304, 335, 338, 340, 341, 34–45, 349, 350, 353, 355, 356–59, 360, 362, 392, 426, 462, 472; **10:**817; **11:**88

TEACHER, TEACHERS
1:3, 21, 36, 49, 58, 59, 65, 66, 69, 75, 76, 82, 84, 89, 93, 94, 99, 100, 109, 110, 120, 192, 202, 286, 483, 497, 1034, 1037, 1150; **2:**10, 54, 153, 256, 365, 366, 437, 536, 540, 548, 876, 888, 919, 923, 931, 946, 1288, 1313, 1377; **3:**546, 647, 726, 727, 1005; **4:**6, 22, 41, 72, 172, 199, 563, 589, 591, 593, 676, 677, 809, 886, 990, 1063, 1167, 1169, 1171, 1172, 1175; **5:**6, 13, 14, 19, 24, 56, 58, 68, 97, 112, 132–33, 145, 233, 269, 271, 281, 287, 293, 295, 298, 336, 345, 389, 395, 398, 407, 506, 604, 608, 610, 613–14, 623, 632, 642, 644, 651–52, 654–55, 659, 664–65, 670, 672, 683, 688–89, 690, 692; **6:**67, 69, 89, 255, 377, 420, 437, 600, 650, 933, 940, 963, 1137, 1299, 1465; **7:**15, 129, 181, 194, 245,

509, 525, 539, 560, 562, 662, 664, 674, 852, 862; **8:**30, 34, 37, 39, 47–48, 119, 142, 144, 157, 169, 171, 174–75, 183, 189, 200, 214, 229–30, 260, 264, 295, 299, 304–5, 308, 310, 314, 342, 346, 354–55, 361, 368, 371, 379, 386–87, 390, 408, 410, 420, 423–24, 427; **9:**31, 76, 77, 117, 123, 125, 128, 129, 150, 153, 184, 232, 248, 284, 334, 346, 347, 377, 389, 397, 399, 402, 416, 430, 449, 511, 531, 533, 541, 549, 551, 557, 565, 568, 628, 642, 660, 668, 725, 726, 774, 775, 777, 842–44, 853, 863; **10:**9, 64, 101, 107, 145, 149, 155, 188, 189, 191, 194, 211, 219, 253, 255, 258, 261, 263, 266, 284, 299, 306, 342, 363, 371, 374, 381, 447, 450, 478, 599, 701, 710, 711, 722, 758, 803, 812; **11:**185, 230, 243, 269, 293, 295, 319, 331, 335–36, 353, 360, 374–75, 390, 392, 409–10, 422–23, 431–32, 438, 544, 557, 560–61, 575–76, 582, 591, 594, 616–18, 651, 654, 659, 663, 695, 701, 710, 718, 745, 782, 786–87, 789; **12:**9, 31, 32, 55, 68, 78, 84, 109, 116, 145, 155, 164, 169, 170, 186, 203, 205, 206, 209, 384, 395, 404, 449, 466, 468, 475, 492, 596; FALSE (*see under* FALSE); OF THE LAW/TORAH **8:**39, 142, 567; **9:**122; **11:**783; OF RIGHTEOUSNESS **1:**289; **4:**72; **5:**332; **7:**15; **8:**38, 39, 432; **9:**178, 642; **11:**410, 420; TEACHER-KING **5:**271–72, 295–300

TEACHING
IN THE EARLY CHURCH **1:**15, 48, 191–92, 315; **3:**501, 1018; **5:**15, 717; **8:**21, 80, 203, 300, 514, 596; **9:**861; **10:**3, 266, 370, 713, 779; **11:**335, 423, 582, 775, 811, 815, 891–92; **12:**24, 324, 344, 454; FALSE (*see under* FALSE); OF JESUS (*see under* JESUS THE CHRIST *in PERSONS IN THE BIBLE*)

TEETH
See TOOTH

TEMPERANCE
3:610; **11:**805, 864

TEMPLE, TEMPLES
1:278; **2:**14, 288; **3:**452; **4:**60, 193, 232, 253, 369; **5:**95; **6:**73, 176, 995, 1000–1003, 1260, 1315, 1360; **7:**717, 860; **8:**16, 34; **10:**219–22, 243, 447, 604, 732, 773, 832, 964; **11:**405; **12:**98, 325; AND ATONEMENT (*see under* ATONEMENT); AND PAUL (*see under* JERUSALEM TEMPLE *in PLACES IN THE BIBLE*). *See also* JERUSALEM TEMPLE *and other temples by name in PLACES IN THE BIBLE*

TEMPTATION, TEMPTATIONS
1:516, 523, 580, 816, 819, 842–44, 872, 878, 914, 942, 950, 1014, 1041; **2:**342, 345; IN DAVID'S LIFE **2:**1156, 1160, 1164, 1176, 1231, 1267, 1288–95, 1370, 1381; **3:**794, 891; ENTICEMENT (TO SIN) **1:**62, 206, 306, 359–63, 365, 366, 372, 373, 376, 378, 815; **2:**111, 280, 289, 310, 314–16, 321–22, 332–33, 335, 339, 343, 348–49, 351, 355–57; **3:**426; **4:**1243–45; **5:**70, 677; **7:**169; **8:**205; **9:**100, 235; **10:**322; **12:**415, 491, 498; OF JESUS (*see under* JESUS THE CHRIST *in PERSONS IN THE BIBLE*)

TENANT, TENANTS
1:773, 1020, 1172, 1174; **2:**218, 221–22, 384; **3:**156, 468; **4:**838; **8:**69, 413–14, 568, 670–71, 676; **9:**14, 91, 307, 379–85, 393, 414, 440; **10:**655, 757; **11:**283

TEN COMMANDMENTS
1:207, 277, 281, 298, 306, 678–79, 688, 830, 839, 853–54, 949, 1000, 1124, 1131–32, 1137, 1178; **2:**96, 98, 271, 273, 288, 314, 316, 322–28, 335, 336–40, 342–43, 349, 350, 355, 359, 363–64, 369, 373–74, 380, 416, 423, 463, 484, 486, 490–91, 810, 864; **3:**494, 501; **4:**732, 774, 885, 1221; **5:**45, 54, 70, 80, 127, 644; **6:**19, 176, 214, 641, 987, 1189, 1206, 1219; **7:**321; **8:**33, 277, 608, 645; **10:**725; **11:**791; **12:**164, 193

TENT, TENTS
1:219, 403, 434, 512, 893, 938, 941, 1008; **2:**107, 151, 197, 199, 356, 384, 547, 559, 774, 778, 781, 782, 788, 841, 878, 922, 1113, 1249, 1256, 1331; **3:**20, 33, 394, 406, 445, 565, 735, 1002, 1075, 1084, 1088, 1090, 1106, 1123, 1124, 1132, 1133, 1137, 1147, 1151, 1161, 1165, 1167, 1173, 1180, 1181; **4:**44, 198, 241, 421, 452, 468–71, 476, 502, 538, 733, 786, 1014, 1097; **5:**15, 140, 616, 668, 720, 757; **6:**68, 271, 301, 476, 543, 614, 664, 834, 848, 1038, 1110, 1118, 1228, 1259, 1319, 1510; **7:**427, 691, 701, 827, 865; **8:**598; **10:**125, 128; **11:**23, 84, 106, 675; **12:**97, 192, 104, 105, 106, 113, 117, 136, 138, 145, 728; OF THE BODY **12:**339; OF DAVID **7:**427; **10:**147, 213, 219, 252; TO DWELL **11:**167; **12:**650; (*see also* TABERNACLE: TO DWELL/RESIDE); DYNASTY **6:**167; EARTHLY **11:**81, 84, 137, 167; **12:**97, 166, 399; HEAVENLY **12:**613; OF ISRAEL **1:**404, 433, 557; **2:**36, 105, 136, 138, 190, 679; **3:**78; **5:**303, 668, 687; **6:**1319; OF MEETING **1:**279, 907, 913, 918, 938, 960, 978, 995, 999, 1007, 1008, 1010, 1012, 1034–35, 1048, 1055–57, 1060, 1098, 1111, 1113, 1117, 1134; **2:**9, 11, 14, 25, 31–33, 35–37, 47, 50, 59, 65–66, 78–81, 89, 106–8, 110, 124–25, 135, 138, 140, 147–49, 151, 160–61, 163, 193, 199, 217, 219, 228–29, 384, 519, 658, 686; **3:**39, 69, 393, 437, 473, 494; **4:**198, 290; **5:**516–17; **6:**84, 1139, 1510, 1534, 1575–76, 1579; **7:**286; **8:**631; **12:**58, 97, 116; OF MOLOCH **10:**128; OF NOMADS/SHEPHERDS **5:**383, 385, 721; **6:**625, 1464; PEG(S) **2:**781–82, 858, 878; **3:**735, 738, 920, 1090; **5:**616, 721, 765, 768; **6:**196; **7:**814; TABERNACLE/BOOTH **1:**893; **7:**266, 285–86; **9:**522; **12:**103, 116, 166 (*see also*

TENT, TENTS (continued)

BOOTH; TABERNACLE); OF TESTIMONY/WITNESSES **1**:686; **10**:128; **12**:672

TENTMAKER (OR TENTMAKING, ETC.)

8:12, 170; **10**:147, 213, 252–54, 256, 258, 762; PAUL AS **10**:753; **11**:675

TEN WORDS

1:39, 854, 950; **5**:219

TEREBINTH

4:656; **5**:757

TEST/TEMPT

4:1048; **8**:162, 341; **9**:241; GIDEON TESTING GOD **2**:759–60, 797–803; GOD TESTING ABRAHAM **1**:420, 462, 489, 495–500, 568, 628; **2**:759; **3**:1138; **4**:241; **5**:670, 842; **10**:835; **12**:138; GOD TESTING CHRISTIANS **10**:914–16; **11**:309, 701; **12**:188, 255, 282; GOD TESTING HEZEKIAH **3**:630–31; GOD TESTING ISRAEL **1**:494, 813, 818; **2**:138, 345, 748, 757–60; **3**:631, 1138; **4**:991; **6**:1208, 1218; **9**:100; **10**:914; GOD TESTING JOB **4**:320, 329, 344, 355–61

TESTIMONY

ARK OF **2**:79, 140, 1001; **6**:1118; OF THE BIBLE **1**:33–64, 354; **6**:317; EYEWITNESS **2**:753; **6**:296; **8**:106, 502, 505; **9**:41, 470, 500, 835, 851, 863; **10**:15, 43, 63, 100; **12**:342–43, 382; FALSE (see under FALSE); GOD TESTIFIES TO JESUS **12**:438–40, 461, 465, 562, 565, 584; OF THE HOLY SPIRIT **1**:51; ISAIAH'S OF GOD'S JUDGMENT **6**:347–452, 470, 1455; OF JESUS **11**:220, 346, 724, 796, 856; **12**:652, 687, 696, 715, 773; AT JESUS' TRIAL **9**: 825–26; OF JOHN THE BAPTIST **9**:527–29, 556–60, 570, 586–87, 678; IN LEGAL DISPUTE(S) **1**:874, 889–90; **2**:380, 1060; **3**:230; **4**:820, 1125; **5**:77, 126–27, 150, 161, 174, 179, 194, 213, 219, 245, 736; **6**:118; **7**:774–75; **8**:480, 712–13, 723; **9**:30, 219, 443; **10**:124, 208, 211; **12**:123; OF MIRACLES **8**:225, 259, 543–45, 561, 621; **10**:15, 66, 79; **12**:35; OF PAUL **11**:835–40, 855–60; SCRIPTURES TESTIFY TO JESUS **9**:588; **10**:166, 192, 218; TENT OF **1**:688; **10**:128

TETA

5:748; **7**:290, 498; **10**:630

TETRAGRAMMATON

(incl. "I am who I am") **1**:290, 714; **2**:747; **5**:294, 748; **7**:290, 498; **10**:630; **11**:510; **12**:562

TETRARCH, TETRARCHY

6:1094; **8**:319, 321, 622; **9**:80, 88, 194, 199, 281, 363

TETRATEUCH

1:307, 312, 313, 317; **2**:6, 7, 165, 559–61, 568, 569, 573, 579, 580, 589, 593, 599, 606, 636, 655, 666, 673, 683, 701, 714

TETTER

1:1097. See also DISEASE: HANSEN'S/SCALE/SKIN

TEXTUAL

CORRECTION (see under CORRECTION); CORRUPTION (see under CORRUPTION); CRITICISM (see under CRITICISM)

THANK OFFERING

See under OFFERING

THANKSGIVING

6:122, 147, 216, 301, 808; **7**:280, 470, 505–9, 518; **9**:691–92; **10**:799; **11**:43, 371, 380, 436, 548, 554, 703; HYMN(S) OF (see under HYMN); PRAYER IN THE NT **8**:274; **9**:341, 394, 691; **10**:91, 380–81, 544; **11**:201, 367, 371, 377; **12**:380–81, 384–86, 436, 479, 482, 485, 541, 558, 584, 589, 593–94, 661–63, 682, 692, 714, 732, 744, 753, 762, 789, 812; PSALM 18 **4**:746; PSALM 28 **4**:788; PSALM 30 **4**:795; PSALM 32 **4**:805; PSALM 34 **4**:813; **9**:834; PSALM 40 **4**:842; PSALM 41 **4**:846; PSALM 50 **4**:879; PSALM 65–68 **4**:933–46; PSALM 92 **4**:1050; PSALM 103 **4**:1090; PSALM 107 **4**:1117; PSALM 116 **4**:1147; PSALM 118 **4**:1153; **9**:707; PSALM 126 **4**:1194; PSALM 138 **4**:1230; PSALMS/SONGS OF **1**:236, 239, 511, 560, 616, 1015; **2**:963, 968, 979–81, 1354, 1365; **3**:347, 400, 470, 498, 561, 637, 1016, 1176; **4**:51, 303, 329, 569, 570, 585, 586, 647–48, 717–19, 746–47, 749, 764, 789, 795, 805, 813, 842–43, 847, 901, 926, 933, 937, 939, 940, 944, 968, 1050, 1090, 1117, 1147, 1149, 1153, 1178, 1194, 1202, 1231, 1248; **5**:144; **6**:46, 122, 123, 147, 148, 269, 299, 301, 428; **7**:470, 505, 518; **8**:642, 707, 834; **11**:132. See also THANKSGIVING HYMNS in ANCIENT LITERATURE

THEATER

6:1144; **7**:375; **8**:719; **9**:718; **10**:272–73, 894

THEFT

2:467, 471; **4**:349; **5**:253, 774, 778; **6**:406, 990; **7**:552, 775–78; **8**:588, 608; **9**:85; **10**: 445, 447; **11**:429, 432; OF GODS **1**:559; OF LAND **4**:510; OF AN OX **1**:865; ROBBERY **1**:1041, 1173; OF A "SELF" **1**:851; **2**:334–35; **5**:81

THEOCRACY

2:148, 257, 417, 426, 431, 534; **3**:407; **6**:64, 109; **7**:442, 742; **8**:673; **10**:405, 509, 713; **12**:713

THEODICY

1:72, 477; **2**:503, 504, 670, 798, 1093; **3**:426; **4**:379, 383, 384, 486, 493, 494, 577, 630, 830, 839; **5**:164, 274, 310, 328, 626, 677, 709, 724, 786, 817, 818, 833; **6**:620, 675, 676, 685, 820, 913, 1058, 1139, 1170, 1213, 1257, 1282; **7**:485, 502, 583, 633, 636; **8**:708; **9**:653; **10**:25, 60, 372, 377, 378, 641; **12**:313, 594, 615, 676, 701; BABYLONIAN **4**:329, 330, 332, 333, 362, 400, 492; **5**:3, 604

THEOLOGIAN, THEOLOGIANS

1:35, 42, 49; **2**:256, 670; **3**:1134, 1163; **9**:510;

10:673; **11:**211; **12:**546; CHURCH **1:**58; **9:**498, 737, 861

THEOLOGY

APOCALYPTIC **10:**431, 561; **11:**759; BIBLICAL THEOLOGY MOVEMENT **1:**197–98 (*see also* MIGHTY WORKS); CHRISTIAN **1:**7–8, 48, 105, 152, 169, 315, 367, 752, 822, 1121; **2:**152, 194, 834; **3:**1065; **4:**557, 1093; **5:**77; **6:**143, 221, 272, 609, 681; **7:**148, 370; **8:**2, 161, 473, 481, 674; **9:**664; **10:**31, 211, 384, 553; **11:**183, 290, 307, 393, 432, 619, 781, 874; **12:**200, 268, 377, 391, 457, 508; COMMON (*see under* COMMON); COVENANT **2:**350, 1254; **3:**77, 94, 1040; **6:**671; **7:**395; **10:**399, 449, 472, 494, 560–61, 671; **11:**844; **12:**127; CREATION **1:**355; **5:**218, 519, 523; **7:**772, 816; OF THE CROSS **4:**728; **9:**552; **10:**20, 284, 531, 643, 715; **11:**450; AND EXILE **2:**389, 504; **3:**192, 408, 1102, 1113, 1119–20; **4:**994; **6:**273, 293, 304, 621, 934, 940, 949, 955–56, 982, 1010, 1431; **7:**115–16, 122, 182, 346, 396, 441; **9:**375; **10:**698; **12:**615; GOD (*see* GOD, NAMES FOR/TITLES OF *in PERSONS IN THE BIBLE*); OF GRACE **2:**932; **3:**408, 425, 503; **10:**96; **11:**575, 577; LIBERATION **1:**112, 121, 147–48, 165, 168, 182, 255–56, 536, 684, 723, 740; **2:**1057; **3:**104; **4:**82; **5:**319; **7:**151, 396, 457, 632; **9:**145; **10:**485; **12:**200, 219, 547, 549–50, 554–55; METAPHORS IN **1:**177, 196, 822; **2:**256, 321; **4:**416, 556–57; **6:**1222; **7:**209–10; **8:**60; **9:**756; **10:**533; **12:**236, 715–16; NARRATIVE **1:**737; **8:**424, 608; NATURAL **2:**616; **4:**753; **8:**18–19; **10:**432; **12:**553; POLITICAL **7:**116; **12:**554, 712; SACRAMENTAL **2:**26; **9:**606; SYSTEMATIC **1:**58, 78, 272; **4:**465; **5:**141; **7:**874; **10:**395, 404, 510; **12:**555

THEOPHANY

1:444, 458, 636, 838–39; **4:**501, 591, 746, 792; **5:**504; **6:**529, 1119, 1121; **7:**382, 543, 602, 723; **8:**499; **9:**468, 475, 707; **11:**506; **12:**21; AMOS **7:**381; BAPTISM **8:**535; DANIEL **7:**122; ELIJAH **3:**142, 144, 146; **4:**378; HABAKKUK **7:**653; ISAIAH **7:**544; **9:**717; JOB **4:**560, 583, 591, 600; JOEL **7:**317; JOSEPH **1:**594, 644, 671; LUKE-ACTS **2:**90; MALACHI **7:**872; MICAH **7:**543; MOSES/SINAI **1:**679, 684, 692, 711–12, 830–33, 837–41, 854, 937, 946; **2:**11, 25, 49, 69, 80, 86, 88, 95, 125, 135, 140, 316, 338, 534; **9:**587; **10:**127; **12:**156–59, 531, 591, 616, 630, 664; NAHUM **7:**600; PSALM 18 **4:**748; PSALM 50 **4:**881; PSALM 63 **4:**926; PSALM 80 **4:**999; PSALM 94 **4:**1057; PSALM 97 **4:**1068; PSALM 104 **4:**1099; PSALM 133 **4:**313; SAMUEL **2:**991, 1063; SOLOMON **3:**470–73, 494, 499; TRANSFIGURATION **8:**364; WALKING ON WATER **9:**596; ZEPHANIAH **7:**683

THIEF, THIEVES

1:865–66; **4:**545; **6:**1383; **7:**448, 775; **8:**406; **9:**310, 669

THIGH, THIGHS

1:90, 566, 659, 913, 1053–54, 1062; **2:**771, 853, 926; **5:**370, 415, 425–26, 736; **6:**1299, 1335; **12:**699; OF CHRIST **12:**699; OF JACOB **1:**566, 659; RIGHT **1:**1053–54, 1062; **2:**771; STRIKE THE **6:**1299

THIRD DAY

PEACE OFFERING **1:**1023–27, 1051, 1133; **6:**1149; RESURRECTION **6:**223; **8:**322, 348–49, 729–30; **9:**18, 201, 206, 281, 351–52, 419, 468–69, 478, 481, 486, 536, 687; **10:**976; **12:**62; SANCTIFICATION **1:**836; **6:**250. *See also under* DAY

THISTLE/THORNS

1:363, 393; **2:**182, 747–48, 1371; **3:**967; **4:**380; **5:**151, 198, 207–8, 326, 433; CROWN OF **8:**488; **9:**822; AS DIVINE JUDGMENT **6:**89, 133, 226, 265, 277, 378, 482, 544, 1123, 1397, 1451; **7:**231, 272, 277, 282, 296, 585; **8:**570–73; **9:**151, 176–80, 231–32, 347, 409; **10:**596; **12:**76

THONG

See SANDAL

THORNS

See THISTLE/THORNS

THREAD

CONTRASTED WITH HOPE **1:**440; **4:**394, 444

THREE

1:8, 16, 1076; **2:**436, 658; **4:**362; **5:**643, 654; **8:**203, 481; **11:**776–77

THREE DAYS

See under DAY

THRESHING

1:1179; **2:**410, 796; **4:**624; **5:**188; **6:**227, 335, 544, 1517; **7:**360; FLOOR **1:**670; **2:**149, 802, 909, 924, 926–32, 935, 941, 968, 1152, 1248–49, 1380–82; **3:**162, 164, 204, 236, 421, 423, 424, 427; **4:**636, 685; 7:265, 267, 288, 360, 424; **8:**158; **9:**86, 160; SLEDGE(S) **4:**625; **6:**355; **7:**360

THRESHOLD

1:694, 764, 853, 1071; **2:**215, 221, 877, 906, 1006, 1195; **3:**645, 1085–87, 1130, 1143, 1148, 1165; **4:**1014; **5:**31–32, 37, 67, 412, 630; **6:**1179, 1182–84, 1540–41, 1547, 1561, 1588, 1595; **7:**826, 837

THRONE

ASCENT TO **2:**1228, 1240, 1248; **3:**905; **8:**691; OF CHRIST **5:**345; **8:**392, 397–98, 427, 455, 503; **12:**30, 707; OF DAVID **1:**1142; **2:**264, 280, 446, 502, 549, 562, 895, 951–52, 962, 965, 981, 1071, 1091, 1094–95, 1120, 1165, 1199, 1223, 1226, 1233–36, 1254, 1257, 1259, 1269, 1302, 1308, 1314, 1319, 1345, 1375; **3:**4–7, 13–14, 19, 23–26, 31, 33, 39, 58, 87, 94, 168–69, 227, 234, 244, 377, 409; **4:**1034, 1036, 1210; **5:**186; **6:**38, 107, 123–24, 141, 169, 744, 1082–83, 1116, 1214; **7:**569, 731, 770, 788; **8:**130–31, 427, 680;

THRONE *(continued)*
9:14, 51, 67, 134, 354, 381, 426, 456; **11:**76, 392; OF GOD **1:**278–79, 288, 801–2, 889, 893, 897, 1143; **2:**79, 88, 96, 164, 365, 1001; **3:**70, 409, 469, 478, 501, 540, 1056, 1065; **4:**307, 400, 480, 496, 518, 590, 721, 773, 865–66, 869, 904, 964, 999, 1013, 1035, 1054, 1075, 1130, 1180, 1279; **5:**161, 186, 412, 494, 517, 594; **6:**22, 101–2, 294, 329, 605, 692, 708, 751–52, 766, 772, 867, 900, 1116–19, 1131, 1172, 1182–84, 1214, 1244, 1394, 1534, 1538, 1557, 1560–61; **7:**3, 9–10, 13, 103, 150, 167; **8:**33, 550, 624, 680, 691, 714, 732; **9:**334; **10:**129, 528, 611, 723; **11:**39, 285, 372, 382, 392, 401, 415; **12:**30, 34, 57, 97, 104, 149, 159, 294, 500, 512, 515–17, 519, 558, 562–63, 566, 567, 578, 582–83, 587, 591–93, 596–605, 610–11, 621, 624, 629–31, 634, 638, 650, 656, 664–66, 672, 677, 687, 694–96, 699, 704, 706–7, 715, 720–22, 724, 729–30; NAME **3:**288, 290, 529, 569, 654; **4:**733; **6:**122–23, 743, 981; OF A RULER **1:**27, 250–70, 306, 679, 770, 1142; **2:**264, 281, 417, 426, 511, 628, 688, 771–73, 982, 1043, 1048, 1068, 1120, 1156–58, 1180, 1212–13, 1223, 1332; **3:**87, 90, 113–14, 119–20, 184, 213, 221–26, 288, 290, 461, 569, 629, 654, 865, 878, 905, 1155; **4:**5, 12; **5:**78, 96, 128, 160–61, 186, 217–18, 243, 255, 272, 334, 702, 823; **6:**20, 37, 122, 199, 204, 411, 559, 575, 584, 685, 739, 741, 743, 745, 848, 851, 866, 883, 1076–78, 1248–49, 1270, 1384–87; **7:**7, 10, 21, 24, 32, 68–75, 87–88, 92, 102, 113, 116, 121, 140, 200, 342, 513, 594, 660–61, 675, 715, 738; **8:**404, 658; **9:**203, 243, 362, 366; **10:**192, 423, 516, 717; **11:**401, 734, 856; **12:**514, 538, 551, 578, 661, 676; THRONE-CHARIOT **6:**1116–17, 1119, 1172, 1538; **12:**520, 591–92, 596–97; WHITE **12:**558, 699, 706, 715–17. *See also* ENTHRONEMENT

THUMMIM
See URIM AND THUMMIM

THUNDER
AND LIGHTNING **1:**836, 854; **2:**88, 374, 534, 1018; **4:**520, 583, 590, 592, 611, 792–93, 945, 1069; **7:**136, 875; **8:**537; **12:**610, 630, 724; SONS OF (*see* SONS OF THUNDER *in PERSONS IN THE BIBLE*)

TILES
6:1245; **9:**123

TIMBER
1:214, 262; **3:**431, 755–56, 758; **5:**415; **6:**1245, 1360, 1366, 1373–75, 1506

TIMBRELS
2:833; **6:**256

TIME
BEGINNING OF **1:** 279, 336, 342, 417; **5:**197; **7:**578; **9:**249; **12:**258, 312; CONCEPTS OF **1:**41, 69–70, 123, 177–78, 275, 336, 354, 615; **2:**414–15; **5:**305–8; **7:**115–16; **8:**401, 460–62, 468; **9:**542; **10:**81; **12:**311, 610, 638; OF CORRECTIONS **12:**105–6; DURATION OF **2:**15–16, 158, 231; **3:**119, 130–31, 302, 523, 656; **4:**14–15, 443, 483, 523, 923; **5:**305, 316; **6:**793–94, 932; **7:**115–16; **8:**401, 460–61, 468; **9:**92, 522, 542; **10:**81, 367; **11:**157; **12:**404, 610; END OF **1:**288, 893; **4:**648; **6:**67, 84; **7:**10, 15, 115, 327; **8:**30, 82, 144, 157, 187, 361, 526, 731; **9:**200, 202–3, 404; **10:**20, 131, 363, 660–61, 669, 719, 936; **12:**259, 312, 544 (*see also under* END, THE); GOD AND **1:**279, 342–47, 417, 729, 845–46, 874–75, 889, 923, 1132; **2:**84, 229, 235–36, 747; **3:**656; **4:**1041, 1043; **5:**305, 307, 800; **6:**382, 387, 510; **8:**526, 654, 690, 692; **9:**616; **11:**281, 758; **12:**105, 330, 610; HUMANITY AND **1:** 137–38, 253–54, 275; **2:**231; **4:**14–15, 18; **5:**305–8, 672; **7:**115–16; **8:**468; **9:**542; PERPETUITY OF **1:**369, 436, 820, 916, 924; **4:**973; **5:**306; **6:**1151; **9:**552; **11:**63, 75–76; **12:**404; SACRED **1:**178, 275, 347, 845–46, 874–75, 884, 923, 1156–57; **2:**228–35, 331, 337, 400–404, 409, 413–15; **3:**1142, 1180; **4:**39; **5:**9; **6:**710; **8:**468, 535; **9:**49, 133, 616, 542; **10:**28, 936; **12:**566. *See also* CHRONOLOGY; DAY; ESCHATOLOGY; FEASTS/FESTIVALS; HOUR; IMMORTALITY; WATCH; WEEK

TIN
REFINED IN THE FIRE **1:**1138; **6:**1306, 1312; WALL OF **7:**406–7

TITHE, TITHES
COLLECTION OF MONEY/OFFERING/TITHES **3:**613, 826; **8:**664; **10:**259, 291–92, 294, 322, 612, 697, 753, 756, 759, 781, 794, 995–96; **11:**3, 5–10, 12, 15, 20, 22, 24, 37, 48, 96, 110–24, 126, 129–31, 134–35, 143, 170–71, 173, 175, 227; AS FESTIVE MEAL FOR THE LEVITES OR TITHE GIVER **2:**386–87, 403–4, 428; **3:**624, 821, 847; **4:**64; **8:**435; FOR LEVITES GUARDING THE SANCTUARY **2:**148–49, 262; **4:**64; **7:**870; OF ONE'S LIFE, FOR THE GOSPEL **9:**906–7; AS THE PROPERTY OF GOD **1:**1040, 1187–91; AS SPOILS, FOR MELCHIZADEK **1:**440, 442; **9:**86–88, 94–95; FOR SUPPORTING THE CLERGY **2:**153; **3:**842, 994; **4:**64; FOR SUPPORTING THE GOVERNMENT OF JERUSALEM, THE HOLY CITY **3:**825, 993; **7:**41; FOR THE TEMPLE AS GIVEN BY THE PHARISEES **9:**247, 250, 342; FOR THE WIDOWS AND ORPHANS **2:**149, 481–83

TITLE
APOSTLE **9:**137; THE BAPTIST **9:**166; BROTHER **4:**122; DISCIPLE **8:**731; FRIEND OF THE KING **3:**50, 457; **4:**242; **9:**822; GOD OF HEAVEN **3:**678; GOD'S PERSON **11:**828; GOD'S SLAVE **11:**861; **12:**481; GOVERNER **7:**719; KING OF PERSIA **3:**677; KING'S EUNUCH **3:**885; MOST EXCELLENT **9:**40; MY SERVANT **11:**503; PUBLIC PROSECUTOR **6:**1302; RAB-MAG **7:**792; RABSHAKEH

6:292; SCRIBE **3:**715, 718; SHEPHERD **7:**352. *See also* GOD, NAMES FOR/TITLES OF *in PERSONS IN THE BIBLE*; JESUS THE CHRIST, NAMES FOR/TITLES OF *in PERSONS IN THE BIBLE*

TITTLE
8:187

TOMB, TOMBS
OF ABSALOM **2:**1337; OF ASAHEL **2:**1217; EXTRAVAGANT/WASTEFUL **6:**196–99; OF ISHBOSHETH **2:**1230; OF JACOB **1:**669; OF JESUS **2:**846, 1232; **5:**340; **7:**92; **8:**65, 69, 71, 401, 459, 493–94, 496–500, 505, 512, 520, 636, 671, 724–26, 728–33; **9:**13, 52, 159, 243, 367, 465–74, 478, 482–83, 486, 514, 704–5, 832, 836–44, 851; **10:**42–43, 72, 261, 342; **12:**634; OF JONATHAN **4:**26, 152; OF JOSHUA **1:**557, 564; **2:**694, 717–18; OF JUDITH **3:**1182; OF LAZARUS **9:**459, 691–93, 701; OF RACHEL **8:**147; OF SAMSON **2:**859; OF SAUL, SON OF KISH **2:**1359; **4:**228; WHITEWASHED **8:**436; **9:**186

TONGUE, TONGUES
CONFESSING/SINGING **4:**855, 887; **10:**738, 509, 513, 516, 536; CONFUSED **5:**174; CONTROLLED **5:**122, 348, 740; **12:**178, 189, 197–208, 290; CUT OUT THE **3:**240, 297; DECEPTIVE/WICKED **3:**1153, 1159; **4:**390–91, 484, 701, 733, 890, 930, 1178; **5:**77, 113, 160, 192, 220, 455, 674, 736, 749; **7:**142; **10:**457; **12:**178; OF FIRE **10:**54; **12:**522, 597; FLATTERING **4:**701; GOLDEN **5:**111; HEALING **5:**126; PARALYZED **4:**1228; PARCHED **9:**317; SHARP/VIOLENT/WOUNDING **1:**1164; **3:**989, 1049; **4:**1240; **5:**14, 76, 127, 141, 219; **6:**653–54, 657, 716; **7:**258; **10:**729; TONGUE-TIED **6:**1137, 1140, 1454; **9:**58–59

TONGUES, GIFT OF
2:1045; **3:**1370; **10:**10, 55, 57, 167, 599, 944, 950–52, 960–62, 967; **11:**142

TOOTH, TEETH
1:88, 239, 656, 787, 1164; **2:**108, 111, 125, 530; **3:**569, 650, 914; **4:**404, 434, 458, 463, 477, 624, 626, 820, 829, 908; **5:**112, 253, 354, 402, 404, 415, 418, 422, 741, 777; **6:**355, 1049, 1201, 1219, 1254, 1257; **7:**107, 178, 308, 360, 381, 805; **8:**226, 311, 314, 418; **9:**278; **10:**130, 436, 520, 726; **11:**81; **12:**631, 632; ANGRY/GNASHING/GRIEVING **4:**458, 463; **6:**1049; **10:**130; "BY THE SKIN OF MY TEETH" **4:**477; SET ON EDGE **1:**239; **2:**125, 530; **3:**650; **4:**404; **6:**1257; SNARLING **4:**624, 741; "A TOOTH FOR A TOOTH" **1:**864; **2:**436; **4:**541, 791; **6:**1483; **8:**148

TOPAZ
12:723

TORAH
1:9–10, 38–44, 65–67, 71, 75–79, 126, 286, 305, 678, 890, 935, 1164; **2:**429, 521, 535, 687; **4:**11, 63, 159, 166, 232, 684, 751–54, 1167; **5:**99, 246, 492, 522, 525, 564, 623, 627; **6:**22, 460, 543, 628, 646, 827, 1281; **7:**3, 876–77; **8:**30–31; **10:**400, 440, 448–49, 458–60, 480–83, 490, 551–52, 586–87, 649, 657–58, 725

TORTURE
1:31; **4:**16, 236, 240, 248, 388; **6:**1052, 1061, 1066; **7:**334, 360, 526; **8:**487–88, 714; **9:**318, 818; **10:**315; **11:**165, 462; **12:**9, 144, 146, 631

TOUCH
HOLY THINGS **3:**393; **5:**72; INTIMACY **10:**970; SENSORY **1:**535; **5:**570, 730; **11:**233

TOWER
CITY TOWER/ZIGGURAT **1:**411–13, 541; COST OF A **3:**757; **9:**292; STRONG **4:**919; **5:**173, 245; **7:**251; **11:**459; TEMPLE **3:**484, 756, 768–70, 839; WATCH **3:**770; **5:**806; **7:**567; **8:**413; **9:**380. *See also individual towers by name in PLACES IN THE BIBLE*

TOWN, TOWNS
1:29, 223, 215, 258; **2:**393, 441, 588, 594, 627, 631, 634, 646, 654–55, 648, 660–62, 677–78, 684, 694, 696–97, 700–701, 1161; **3:**346–47, 827; **4:**16; **6:**684, 1161; **7:**95, 547; **8:**593, 595; **9:**174, 220–21; CLERK **10:**273. *See also* CITY; VILLAGE

TRADE AND COMMERCE
1:214–25, 245, 261, 1172–73; **2:**161, 308, 357, 467, 472, 570, 658, 662, 711, 957, 1242–44; **3:**245, 848, 966; **5:**351; **6:**1246, 1356, 1360–63, 1369, 1377, 1380, 1388, 1391, 1394, 1464; **7:**362; **8:**12–15; **10:**367, 803; **11:**405, 675, 885; **12:**694–96

TRADER
2:475, 576; **5:**262; **10:**376

TRADES
5:1081, 1377, 1379; DESPISED **9:**296; FOUR **5:**625, 812; SATIRE OF THE **1:**6; **5:**604–7, 625, 812

TRADITION
CRITICISM (*see under* CRITICISM); HISTORY (*see under* CRITICISM; HISTORY); ORAL (*see* ORAL TRADITION)

TRAIN
OF A GARMENT **8:**33

TRANCE
2:190; **3:**183; **4:**378; **6:**4, 11, 1111, 1499; **7:**115, 497; **8:**25; **10:**163; **12:**598

TRANSCENDENCE
1:343–45, 355, 543, 924, 1000–1001; **2:**321, 340, 386; **3:**72, 75, 497; **4:**411, 414, 501, 520, 559, 1075–76, 1092, 1140, 1145; **5:**50, 506, 511, 551, 562, 608, 644; **6:**752, 1510; **7:**2; **8:**362, 457; **9:**74, 482, 693; **10:**128, 182; **11:**420, 608; **12:**206, 326, 505, 543

TRANSFIGURATION
1:838, 883, 955; **2:**90, 718; **3:**179, 928; **4:**673,

TRANSFIGURATION *(continued)*
691, 1005, 1076; **7:**877; **8:**64, 351, 366, 370, 476, 503, 522, 527, 572, 589–90, 621, 627–32, 707, 724, 729–33; **9:**14–15, 27, 35, 51, 90–91, 137, 153, 190, 192, 195, 202, 204–10, 233, 318–19, 381, 409–10, 414, 432, 434, 442, 456, 468, 477, 479, 539; **10:**43, 123, 227; **11:**328, 342–43, 567, 598

TRANSGRESSION
1:23, 359, 947, 1114; **2:**127, 627, 1089; **4:**805, 822, 933; **5:**160; **6:**78, 379, 385, 491, 502, 1450; **10:**459, 496, 527, 629; **11:**238, 242, 266–67; **12:**413; OF ABRAHAM **2:**495–500, 513; **10:**496

TRAP, TRAPS
1:633–34; **2:**934, 936, 1351; **3:**208, 525, 755, 757, 909, 913–14; **4:**74, 115, 141, 469, 1243; **5:**12, 126, 198, 348, 771–72; **6:**717, 1388; **7:**371; **8:**412, 565, 673; **9:**12, 170, 229, 281, 365, 385–86, 409–10; **10:**677, 681, 811; **11:**165. *See also* NET; SNARE

TREASURE, TREASURES, TREASURY
3:1018; **8:**314; **9:**260; HEAVENLY/SPIRITUAL **5:**74, 84, 565; **7:**1383; **8:**209–10, 313–14; **9:**144, 179, 260, 312, 347; **11:**27, 83, 170, 575, 590, 601, 613, 636, 649; **12:**141; HIDDEN **3:**1026; **4:**34, 486, 529; **5:**43–44, 134, 232, 740, 824; **8:**301, 313–14; PALACE **3:**82, 118; **6:**399, 1325; **7:**24, 38, 141, 822; **8:**484, 657, 663, 682, 698, 718; **9:**270, 395–96, 633–34; **10:**143; TEMPLE (*see under* JERUSALEM TEMPLE *in PLACES IN THE BIBLE*)

TREASURER
1:55; **3:**679; **9:**310; **10:**777, 814; **11:**374

TREE, TREES
ALLEGORY/FABLE OF **2:**816; **6:**1425–28; GOD RULES THE **1:**350; **4:**1006, 1098–1100; OF KNOWLEDGE/LIFE **1:**335, 350–51, 360, 383; **6:**545; TO MAKE BOOTHS **3:**801–2; WISDOM LIKE A **5:**757. *See also individual types by name*

TRIAL OF JESUS
See under JESUS THE CHRIST *in PERSONS IN THE BIBLE*

TRIBE, TRIBES
OF ISRAEL **1:**258–59, 666, 1164; **2:**37, 212–13, 250, 263, 266, 535–36, 558, 561, 638, 671, 744, 755, 763, 803, 822, 863–65, 870, 872, 887; **3:**34, 95, 336, 346, 356–57, 422, 561, 671, 1134; **6:**1506, 1606; **12:**182, 186, 620–21, 642–43, 707, 722; TERRITORIES OF **2:**657; **6:**1600. *See individual tribes by name in PERSONS IN THE BIBLE*

TRIBULATION, TRIBULATIONS
4:113, 728, 1128; **5:**442; **6:**667, 851; **8:**205, 261, 441–48, 690; **9:**780; **10:**276, 440, 597, 888, 893, 1002; **11:**99, 494, 579, 613–14; **12:**282, 348, 522, 528, 535, 543, 563, 565, 609, 613, 633–36, 639, 704

TRIBUNAL
1:866; **7:**179; **10:**83, 88, 122, 255, 309, 325, 719, 737–38, 857; **11:**28, 87, 90, 173

TRIBUNE
10:296–312; **11:**130

TRIBUTE
2:1226; **3:**251, 512, 600, 699; **4:**14, 31, 248; **6:**175, 1076, 1232, 1348, 1360; **7:**200, 275, 661; **8:**673; EXACTING **2:**771, 1226; **3:**524; **6:**1360; **7:**594

TRIGON
7:63. *See also* MUSICAL INSTRUMENTS

TRINITY, THE
See TRINITY, THE *in PERSONS IN THE BIBLE*

TRIUMPHAL ENTRY
OF EXILES **6:**335–37; OF JESUS (*see under* JESUS THE CHRIST *in PERSONS IN THE BIBLE*); OF YAHWEH **1:**802

TROUGH
9:63, 67. *See also* MANGER

TRUMPET, TRUMPETS
BLAST(S) **1:**90, 836, 854, 1159, 1160; **2:**32, 69, 70, 86, 88, 89, 91, 198, 229, 246, 742, 803, 1070, 1217; **3:**386, 393, 399, 531, 532, 561, 562, 610, 618, 692, 801, 838, 840, 1120; **4:**64, 71, 78, 100, 174, 612, 691, 869, 1003; **5:**859; **6:**206, 227, 498, 612, 625, 972, 1448, 1537; **7:**156, 260, 316, 320, 371, 666, 682, 683; **8:**200, 537; **9:**395; **10:**989; **11:**289, 728; **12:**156, 302, 532, 534, 538, 539, 544, 557, 562, 566, 591, 592, 605, 609, 616, 620, 629, 630–32, 634, 635, 638, 643, 659, 675, 676, 677, 682, 683, 694, 703; FEAST OF (*see* FEASTS/FESTIVALS: OF ROSH HASHANAH/TRUMPETS)

TRUSTEE, TRUSTEES
OF THE LAW/TORAH **2:**589, 696; **11:**281, 283; OF PROPERTY **4:**636; **6:**93, 96. *See also* CUSTODIAN; GUARDIAN; STEWARD; TREASURER

TRUTH
2:39, 589, 696; **4:**636; **6:**93, 96, 413; **11:**281, 283

TUMOR, TUMORS
2:1005–6, 1010–12, 1015

TUNIC, TUNICS
1:905, 907, 973, 1060, 1070; **2:**1005, 1006, 1010, 1011, 1012, 1015; **4:**105, 212; **9:**94, 831; **12:**498

TURBAN, TURBANS
1:907, 1061, 1110; **2:**162, 1103; **3:**927; **5:**843; **6:**1303, 1325, 1342, 1343, 1578; **7:**64, 765, 787, 839

TURQUOISE
6:1378, 1392; **12:**723

TURTLEDOVE, TURTLEDOVES
1:1009; **4:**304; **5:**393; **9:**69, 70

TUTOR
3:457; **4:**192; **5:**269; **9:**69, 70; **11:**281
TWELVE
1:1057; **2:**178, 615; **3:**712, 725, 730–31
TWELVE, THE
APOSTLES **8:**102–3, 253–54; **9:**136–37; **10:**49; **12:**707, 722; TRIBES OF ISRAEL **1:**664–68; **2:**37, 207–11, 534–36; **3:**136, 457; **12:**186, 618–20; MINOR PROPHETS **1:**8, 11, 65, 294; **6:**18, 20, 22
TWINS, TWIN BROTHERS
1:48, 521, 606; **2:**211, 741, 941; **5:**418; **7:**326, 438, 833; **9:**687; **10:**357
TYPOLOGY
1:46, 86, 91–95, 98, 210, 369, 1020, 1174; **3:**464; **6:**525; **7:**14; **8:**58, 147, 175, 223, 252, 274, 295, 363, 366, 573; **10:**15, 54, 72, 127, 192, 338, 369, 512, 759, 913, 981–82, 988; **11:**690; **12:**237

U

ULCER, ULCERS
1:1094–96; **12:**211
UMPIRE
4:413; **6:**1138; **10:**722; **11:**632
UNBELIEF
1:448, 465, 1143; **2:**798; **3:**1181; **4:**695, 1140; **8:**239–41, 251, 318, 337, 621, 634; **9:**266, 319, 485, 553, 559, 586–88, 591, 605, 610–11, 642–43, 690, 717–18, 850; **10:**78, 267, 481, 504, 622, 624, 627, 643, 680, 685–86, 693, 709, 742; **11:**207, 247; **12:**49–50, 60, 142, 146, 274, 488, 611, 712
UNCIRCUMCISED, UNCIRCUMCISION
See under CIRCUMCISION
UNCLEAN, UNCLEANNESS
1:9, 96, 282, 316, 344, 391, 399, 836, 986–88, 999–1000, 1013, 1033, 1036, 1052, 1074–77, 1080–86, 1095–1101, 1104–6, 1112, 1120, 1126–27, 1135, 1139, 1147–49, 1187–89; **2:**13, 62, 87, 148, 152, 397–400, 482, 767, 832–33, 842, 845, 849–51, 1135; **3:**127, 129, 430, 451–52, 507, 592, 602, 609, 616, 713, 731, 847, 903, 959, 994, 1002, 1158; **4:**39–40, 157, 206, 242, 297, 377, 440–41, 609, 995, 1111; **5:**67, 273, 793; **6:**13, 103–4, 211, 213, 281, 439, 454–56, 463, 467, 529, 640, 1030, 1033, 1063, 1148–49, 1167, 1176, 1206, 1226, 1260, 1307, 1309–10, 1314, 1499, 1526, 1528, 1578–79; **7:**102, 265, 553, 727–29, 829, 831; **8:**32–33, 59, 62–64, 195, 224, 237–38, 244, 311, 331–33, 436, 466, 484, 525, 541, 582–84, 607; **9:**20, 24, 69, 99, 103, 110–11, 113, 119–23, 128, 142, 155, 170, 186–87, 191, 229, 241–42, 248, 276, 284, 358, 724, 815; **10:**138, 162, 163–65, 167–69, 171, 189, 297, 546, 740, 742; **11:**103, 105–6, 232–33, 247, 428, 442, 524, 866; **12:**110, 352, 529, 654, 664, 677, 681, 692, 697. *See also* CLEAN
UNGODLY
4:55, 58, 87, 159, 205, 234; **5:**455, 460, 466, 476, 479, 524, 534, 568–69, 577–80, 590, 824; **6:**750; **9:**410–11; **10:**429, 473, 491–92, 506, 518–19; **11:**92; **12:**330, 347–48, 350, 356–57, 476–78, 484–85, 487–91, 494–97, 500
UNITY
BIBLE/SCRIPTURE **1:**27, 41, 65, 68, 86–81, 89, 96, 108, 197; CHRISTIAN/IN CHRIST **1:**19; **4:**1215; **9:**797, 831; **10:**203, 210–11, 450, 703–4, 739, 804, 806–7, 809, 918, 922, 949, 995; **11:**218, 271, 273, 278, 290, 359, 372, 395–405, 431, 546; **12:**319, 405; CHURCH **1:**19, 414; **3:**700; **10:**505, 525, 702, 726; **11:**190, 228, 248, 370, 424; COMMUNITY/SOCIAL **1:**369; **2:**403, 415, 762, 776, 831–32, 837, 953–54; **5:**255; **8:**27, 660; **9:**760; **10:**23, 73, 750, 788, 818; **11:**6, 248, 278, 420, 423–24, 646; **12:**319; FATHER-SON/JESUS-GOD **9:**646, 676–79, 693, 699, 723, 740, 743, 747, 764, 788, 790, 792, 794–95, 836; **11:**450; **12:**409; STAFF **7:**821–22
UNIVERSALISM
1:159, 413; **3:**93, 931; **4:**941; **5:**290, 301, 541, 702, 757, 759; **6:**1169, 1597; **7:**488, 860; **9:**22; **10:**93, 340–41, 355, 521, 529, 673; **11:**338, 571, 798–99, 813
UNIVERSE
1:56, 76, 160, 176, 189, 288, 291, 321, 342, 401; **2:**321, 530, 1368; **3:**401, 417; **4:**240, 288, 514, 534–35, 654, 711, 752–54, 793, 811–12, 823–24, 865, 905–6, 974, 1017, 1069, 1073, 1097, 1220–21, 1225, 1269; **5:**2, 9, 11, 23, 31, 54, 62, 85, 90, 93–95, 98, 327, 333, 441, 466, 502, 506–7, 541, 546–49, 554, 577–78, 593, 599, 618, 624, 627–28, 648, 663, 678, 724–25, 729–30, 757, 801–2, 818–19, 833–34; **6:**74, 302, 345, 380, 621, 812, 966–67, 970, 1072, 1095, 1257; **7:**6, 11, 62, 565, 731; **8:**17, 19, 23, 37, 250, 294, 471; **9:**519, 542; **10:**319, 359, 986, 989; **11:**92, 218, 318, 372, 376–79, 383–86, 390, 410–12, 415, 421, 440, 460, 565–67, 570, 631–33, 636–37, 640, 722; **12:**23, 30, 46, 133, 159, 391, 476, 517, 569, 605, 645, 696
UNKNOWN GOD, ALTAR TO AN
10:246
UNLEAVENED BREADS, FEAST OF
See FEASTS/FESTIVALS: OF PASSOVER/UNLEAVENED BREAD; PASSOVER AND FEAST OF UNLEAVENED BREAD
UNPARDONABLE SIN
See SIN: UNFORGIVABLE/UNPARDONABLE

UNWRITTEN SAYINGS
11:724
UPPER ROOM, THE
3:486, 497, 770; **7:**91; **8:**468, 659; **9:**719; **10:**277
UPRIGHT
1:521, 991; **2:**1206; **3:**1039; **4:**332, 345, 376–77, 457, 468, 570, 669, 708, 720–22, 806, 809–10, 877, 1051, 1057–58, 1068–69, 1118, 1133, 1193, 1241; **5:**2, 43, 55, 140, 149–50, 161, 182, 243, 332, 426; **6:**699, 1213, 1260; **7:**297, 585, 642; **8:**708; **11:**377, 443, 531; **12:**241, 346, 418
URIM AND THUMMIM
1:906, 908, 1035, 1061, 1063, 1111; **2:**47, 162, 220, 536, 1047, 1079–80, 1183; **3:**687, 896; **4:**72; **5:**160, 787, 843; **9:**698
URN
5:346; **6:**1095
USURY
2:467; **9:**306, 308, 312
UTENSILS
1:278, 900–901, 1160; **2:**52–55, 83, 147, 468; **3:**363, 608; **5:**550, 567; **6:**1377, 1547, 1575; **7:**41; **12:**105, 108. *See also* COOKING: UTENSILS/VESSELS

V

VAIN
1:285, 1067; **2:**1112; **3:**56, 88, 522, 1123; **4:**354, 383, 572, 697–98, 923, 1045, 1198–99; **5:**139, 279, 294, 460, 818; **6:**198, 428–29, 435, 550, 743, 1065; **7:**146; **8:**675; **9:**472; **10:**321, 973–75, 977, 983, 990–93; **11:**57, 96, 99, 112–14, 119, 149, 223, 242, 252, 288–89, 513, 895; **12:**210, 357; TAKING THE LORD'S NAME IN **1:**1133; **2:**865; **5:**188; **6:**257, 606
VALIANT
MAN/SOLDIER **1:**1179; **2:**915, 1048, 1081, 1198, 1207; **3:**826, 1137; **4:**122; **5:**341; **6:**94; WOMEN **3:**1137; **5:**34–35, 91, 259–64
VALLEY
See by name in SUBJECTS AND THEMES, PLACES IN THE BIBLE, and PLACES OUTSIDE THE BIBLE
VALOR, MAN OF
2:915, 1102, 1178; **4:**122
VANITY
1:312, 932; **2:**1315; **3:**68, 88, 855, 858; **4:**178, 697, 838; **5:**132, 278–79, 283, 290–91, 294–95, 297–98, 316–17, 321–22, 342, 346, 350, 354–56, 364, 384, 549, 557; **6:**521, 969; **7:**248; **11:**298, 343
VAT, VATS
1:224; **3:**205; **5:**49–50; **7:**267, 324, 334; **9:**380
VATICAN COUNCIL, SECOND
See COUNCIL: SECOND VATICAN COUNCIL
VAULT, VAULTS
4:314; **5:**757; **12:**720
VEGETABLE, VEGETABLES
1:85, 217–18; **3:**155, 1147; **5:**153; **6:**742, 745, 1148; **7:**40, 177, 405–6; **8:**436; **10:**735
VEIL, VEILS
1:512, 605, 953–55; **3:**512; **5:**386, 553; **6:**1203; **9:**463; **10:**431, 769; **11:**64–65, 68–69, 73, 451; **12:**530–31; OF THE TEMPLE (*see under* JERUSALEM TEMPLE *in PLACES IN THE BIBLE*)
VENGEANCE
1:240, 374–75, 578, 848, 864, 873; **2:**268, 320, 333, 435, 470, 763–64, 790, 808, 817–19, 853–54, 872, 888, 1055, 1158–60, 1167–69, 1171, 1225–26, 1230, 1263, 1313–14, 1316, 1326, 1357–58; **3:**28, 135, 869, 1171; **4:**52, 92, 95, 101, 669; **5:**764; **6:**160, 520, 1349, 1354–55, 1357; **7:**96, 138, 140, 333, 563, 567, 569; **8:**380, 537, 670; **9:**146, 362, 364; **10:**714–15, 718, 723; **11:**645; **12:**133; DIVINE **2:**246, 528, 1169–70; **3:**430, 787, 1178; **4:**100, 240, 909, 916, 1009, 1011, 1057, 1059, 1125–27, 1229, 1237, 1276; **5:**220, 678, 771–72; **6:**273, 276–78, 281, 413, 521–22, 674–75, 912, 914, 919, 1336–37, 1354–55, 1357; **7:**96, 484–85, 575–76, 810; **9:**88, 105, 147, 336, 404; **10:**712; **11:**695, 719–20, 722, 749–50, 757–58; **12:**528, 547, 613, 617, 646
VESSEL, VESSELS
1:1019–20, 1100, 1104; **2:**62, 127, 151; **3:**191, 285, 1002; **5:**567, 768, 787, 859; **6:**14, 254, 549, 714, 718, 722, 891–92, 1079, 1083, 1130, 1186, 1242, 1291–92, 1307, 1327, 1336–38, 1360, 1378; **8:**663; **9:**26, 180, 247, 538; **10:**640–41; BROKEN/CRACKED **4:**349, 801; **6:**722; **10:**818; **11:**818; HUMAN/USED BY GOD **1:**1067; **2:**1099, 1140; **5:**186; **6:**105, 582; **7:**192, 767; **10:**591, 642, 648, 680, 818, 939; **11:**718; **12:**285; OCEAN/RIVER **3:**511; **5:**545, 550; **6:**1371, 1380, 1382–83, 1416; **7:**511 (*see also* BOAT; SHIP); SACRED/TEMPLE (*see under* JERUSALEM TEMPLE *in PLACES IN THE BIBLE*); OF SOUL/SPIRIT **1:**93; **5:**682; TREASURE IN EARTHEN **10:**817; **11:**81, 84, 86–87, 137, 164, 166–67; **12:**234. *See also* EARTHENWARE; POT
VESTIBULE, VESTIBULES
2:772; **3:**62, 484–85; **6:**1541, 1543–47, 1549–51, 1554–55, 1557, 1570, 1588; **7:**320, 774, 787; **9:**40. *See also* NAVE; PORCH; PORTICO
VESTMENT, VESTMENTS
1:279, 905, 913, 960, 1114; **2:**162, 219; **3:**692; **4:**64, 122; **5:**842–43, 859, 861; **6:**1228, 1391, 1558, 1578, 1591; **11:**84

VIAL, VIALS
3:889; **8:**698
VICE, VICES
1:12, 1077; **3:**514; **5:**77, 108, 153, 162, 164, 253, 558, 652, 765; **6:**1481; **8:**18–20, 23, 29, 41, 334, 608, 640; **10:**190, 255, 382, 431, 433–34, 441, 784, 823, 842, 844, 848–52, 855–58, 860, 868, 913, 981; **11:**172–73, 175, 327, 330, 419–20, 426–30, 432–39, 442, 555, 572, 593, 628, 641–47, 698, 813, 849, 866, 869; **12:**72, 164, 204, 209–10, 218, 263, 269, 273, 301, 336, 351, 530, 675
VICTORY
BOOTY/SPOILS **2:**563, 615, 969, 1191–92, 1266; **3:**152, 561, 586, 932; **4:**249, 945; **6:**337, 1410; **7:**454; OVER DEATH/EVIL **1:**204; **2:**755; **4:**722; **5:**513; **7:**4–8, 12, 335, 626; **8:**654; **9:**497, 671, 851; **10:**723; **11:**628; **12:**252, 293–94, 297, 399, 427, 436, 549; OF GOD/JESUS **1:**441; **2:**98, 1022; **3:**416, 576, 1179; **4:**749, 857; **6:**339; **7:**653; **8:**162, 205, 234, 286, 348, 352, 397, 429, 473, 680; **9:**274, 413, 497, 738, 770, 783–85, 804, 844, 851; **10:**717, 765; **11:**57, 166; **12:**293, 313; MILITARY **1:**249, 441–42, 852; **2:**255, 293, 439–40, 723, 731, 741, 763–64, 772, 791–92, 810, 830, 833, 1243, 1248; **3:**378, 413–14, 591, 594, 1178; **4:**749; **6:**145, 343, 413, 430, 515, 519, 899; **7:**4, 112; **11:**205, 626; **12:**144, 611; SONG **1:**799, 802; **2:**8, 108–9, 159, 600, 1367; **3:**1090, 1144, 1177; **4:**57, 946; **6:**207; **7:**665, 667, 701–4; SYMBOL **2:**98; **12:**621
VILLAGE, VILLAGES
1:29, 215–21, 225–27, 246–48, 251, 258–59, 845, 1173; **2:**38, 148–49, 250, 557, 629, 658–59, 667–70, 678, 688, 718, 765, 775, 1011–12, 1149, 1179; **3:**336, 414, 671, 784, 826–27, 847, 935, 969,1095; **4:**16, 390, 460, 478–79, 497, 509, 523, 554, 557, 625; **5:**93, 108, 199, 670, 813; **6:**345, 729, 914, 919, 952, 1518; **7:**95, 576, 655, 676, 758; **8:**44, 49, 51, 105, 566, 592–93, 597, 651; **9:**23, 103, 122–23, 127, 174, 181, 193–94, 214–15, 219–21, 236, 252, 292, 303, 321, 371; **10:**549; **11:**439, 726, 824; **12:**303; WALLS OF (*see* WALL: CITY/VILLAGE)
VINDICATE, VINDICATION
1:867, 1165; **2:**137, 527, 613, 861, 1060,1159, 1176; **3:**136, 969–79; **4:**457, 479, 523, 853, 894; **5:**155; **6:**437, 440, 519, 676, 697, 728, 785, 1282, 1495; **7:**3, 204, 215, 458, 583, 683, 696; **8:**30, 348, 423, 467, 550, 625, 675; **9:**19, 124, 167, 336, 338–39, 349; **10:**375, 389, 400–401, 623, 735–36; **11:**237, 340, 768, 772; **12:**221, 303, 504
VINE (*OR* VINEYARD, *ETC.*)
1:89, 218, 226, 403, 615, 866, 1133; **2:**166, 221, 356, 439, 453, 467, 471, 614, 816, 849; **3:**153, 155–58, 736, 1099; **4:**159, 165, 349, 452, 1000–1001; **5:**69, 77, 95, 187, 261, 327, 365, 373, 383, 386, 392, 416, 427, 432–33, 475, 746, 757, 768; **6:**39, 46, 54, 69, 78, 86–89, 92–93, 169, 211, 225–26, 265, 293, 482, 490, 544, 602, 807, 1211, 1215–19, 1219–20, 1244–48, 1252, 1266, 1268, 1270–74, 1371, 1379, 1394, 1423, 1452, 1506, 1582; **7:**73, 226, 234, 244, 263, 270–73, 296, 308, 333, 448, 468–69, 521, 550, 585, 767, 834; **8:**61, 153, 392, 412–14, 417, 471, 668–72, 674, 678; **9:**14, 84, 271, 289, 380–84, 418–19, 463, 602, 739, 755–60; **10:**89, 904; **11:**283, 399; **12:**76, 468, 668, 710
VINEDRESSERS
7:80
VINEGAR
5:112, 162, 219; **8:**492; **9:**832–33
VIOLENCE
BEGETS VIOLENCE/CYCLE OF **1:**581, 704–5, 873; **2:**695–96, 887, 1156, 1159–60, 1307, 1309–10, 1314, 1316; **4:**626, 1228, 1241; **5:**55; **7:**229; **9:**147, 216; **11:**609; **12:**286, 607; IN COMMUNITY/CULTURE/SOCIETY **1:**581, 586, 594, 704–5, 787, 868, 873; **2:**67, 98, 335, 437, 494, 552, 579, 617, 749, 759, 783, 873, 1156, 1227, 1306–7, 1316, 1341; **3:**723, 773, 850, 934; **4:**58, 429, 471, 593, 626–27, 731, 1241; **5:**37–38, 108, 189, 247, 790; **6:**626, 631, 665, 754, 1084, 1177, 1180, 1190, 1309, 1421; **7:**25–26, 32–33, 110, 262, 378, 742, 840; **8:**311, 363, 596, 667, 672, 711, 720; **9:**149, 406, 441; **10:**713; **11:**628; **12:**213, 508, 606–7, 616–17, 678; DIVINE/OF GOD **1:**787, 803; **3:**1172; **4:**387, 410, 415, 446, 458–60, 463–65, 578; **6:**1038; **8:**554–45; DOMESTIC/FAMILY/AGAINST CHILDREN **1:**377, 576–77, 581; **2:**47, 749, 834–35, 963, 1177, 1226, 1232, 1283, 1306, 1316, 1342; **3:**931, 1005, 1171; **4:**465; **5:**170; **6:**1024, 1241, 1331; **7:**211, 226–28, 262; **9:**374, 441, 453; **11:**455, 645; **12:**213, 420; EVIL/SIN/THE WICKED AND **1:**375, 377, 383–84, 398; **2:**888, 899, 1160, 1293–94, 1298; **3:**159; **4:**472, 603, 709, 722, 740, 749, 898, 908–9, 1240; **5:**111, 193, 350, 436, 452, 459, 461, 464–67, 481, 484–87, 499–500, 523; **6:**1306, 1394; **7:**484, 486, 514; **8:**197; **9:**195, 381; **11:**627–28; **12:**213, 489, 701, 737; SEXUAL/AGAINST WOMEN **1:**474; **2:**552, 725, 749, 781, 872, 878, 888, 1232, 1284, 1289, 1304–7; **4:**554; **5:**108, 412–13; **6:**20, 1024, 1220, 1241–42, 1309, 1317–18, 1331; **7:**176–77, 206, 226–28, 245, 262, 525, 614–15; **9:**374, 453; **11:**455, 645; **12:**490
VIOLET
2:55; **3:**356

VIPER, VIPERS
5:818; **8:**157; **9:**83; **10:**355–56. *See also* SERPENT; SNAKE

VIRGIN, VIRGINS
1:27, 30, 577, 867, 1148, 1165; **2:**245–47, 282, 454–55, 629, 833–34, 877, 886, 1055, 1303, 1305; **3:**14, 32, 849, 885, 891, 1133,1161; **4:**304–5, 552; **5:**261, 425, 692; **6:**112, 294, 691, 715, 811, 1041, 1070, 1319, 1579; **7:**308–9, 385–86; **8:**135, 197, 450; **9:**50–52, 95, 278; **10:**271, 869, 879, 884; **11:**148; BIRTH **1:**87; **6:**432; **7:**571; **8:**4, 132, 135, 137–38; **9:**8, 14, 50, 71, 76, 78, 95; **10:**813; **11:**283; **12:**62, 155

VIRTUES
1:18, 88, 1174; **2:**377, 442, 879, 1136; **3:**417, 513, 547, 556, 813, 941, 984, 986, 1003, 1016, 1038, 1069, 1086, 1145, 1162; **5:**91, 122, 125, 166, 188, 305, 307, 316, 325, 502, 510, 512, 849; **6:**486, 658; **7:**458; **8:**20, 22, 29, 68, 514–15, 608, 678; **9:**98; **10:**318, 355, 404, 848, 951, 954–56; **11:**252, 353, 374, 386, 419–20, 422–31, 435, 438, 455, 458–61, 541, 548, 575, 641–49, 653, 779, 828, 864–65, 871; **12:**16, 155, 273, 289, 330, 336–38, 340, 361, 401, 482

VISION, VISIONS
APOCALYPTIC **1:**43, 166, 289, 838; **2:**91, 1238; **3:**949; **4:**675; **6:**13, 83, 206, 228, 931, 956, 1513–14; **7:**1, 5, 9, 12, 19, 22–23, 97–152, 654–55, 820; **8:**356, 363–65, 391–92, 516, 519, 535, 550, 577, 654, 671–72; **10:**822–23, 854, 999; **11:**219, 296, 376, 385, 409, 415, 463, 715, 728; **12:**59, 85, 342–43, 412, 518–28, 552, 560–61, 569, 593, 596–99, 610, 622–23, 635–36, 645, 659, 668, 672, 688, 692–96, 701–5, 707–17, 720–24; OF PROPHETS **1:**42–43, 91, 240–42, 278, 444, 601; **2:**80, 910, 1092; **3:**164, 201–2, 552, 631, 1069; **4:**377, 1016; **6:**4–5, 9–11, 13, 18–19, 48–49, 66, 99–104, 183, 186, 236–37, 257, 280, 293, 320, 456, 583–84, 752–55, 778, 784–85, 1039, 1041, 1110–11, 1113–21, 1172, 1174–77, 1182–87, 1497–1504, 1532–1607; **7:**5, 106–7, 128, 138, 286, 351, 358, 405–8, 435, 444, 542–44, 558, 572, 599, 641–42, 653–54, 735–36, 755–56, 796, 832; **9:**106, 717; **10:**124, 150, 164, 224, 227, 305–8, 425–26; **12:**22, 46, 325, 329–30, 343, 560, 565–67, 571–73, 680–84, 692–96, 725–26, 734, 739–43

VISION, VALLEY OF
6:149, 194

VOCATION
AS A CALL **1:**719, 722; **2:**797–98, 1044; **4:**1272; **6:**101, 104–5, 238–39, 319, 420, 428–29, 580, 582, 629, 666, 750; **9:**101, 117, 294; **10:**109, 415, 602, 606, 798; **11:**614, 675; **12:**281–82, 565–67, 646

VOTIVE OFFERING
See under OFFERING

VOW, VOWS
1:238–39, 241, 440, 537, 542–44, 584–85, 835, 837–38, 1042, 1186–90; **2:**163, 236–37, 254, 265, 369, 467, 615, 738, 748–49, 830–37, 872, 907, 959, 973, 1047, 1064, 1134, 1167–68, 1223, 1274, 1319; **3:**232, 393, 797, 1139, 1154; **4:**254, 502–3, 764, 789, 919–20, 933, 1124–25, 1149, 1211; **5:**85, 127, 188, 317, 339, 401, 697, 733; **6:**18–19, 82, 138, 243, 1002, 1154, 1290, 1474–75; **7:**477, 500, 502, 575, 606, 630; **8:**25, 193, 333, 435, 598, 606–7; **9:**75, 312, 358, 401, 418–19; **10:**547; **11:**40, 799; OF DESTRUCTION **1:**1187, 1189; **4:**74, 82; LAY **2:**64, 202, 228; MARRIAGE/WEDDING **2:**234, 237; **5:**401, 431; **6:**184, 477, 1242; **7:**215, 226; **8:**295; **9:**314; **12:**163, 433; NAZIRITE **1:**281, 1033; **2:**60, 64–68, 233–34, 762, 767, 842, 845–46, 849–53, 858–59, 975–76; **4:**64; **7:**365; **9:**354; **10:**258, 291, 293–94, 306, 312, 320; **11:**631; OFFERING (*see under* OFFERING); PRAISE **4:**570, 645, 762, 818, 894

VULTURE, VULTURES
2:398; **4:**451, 598, 612; **5:**254; **6:**1499, 1523; **7:**260, 547; **8:**443; **9:**333

W

WAFER, WAFERS
1:912–13, 1047

WAGE, WAGES
1:164, 556, 1133, 1136; **2:**149, 470, 595, 1195; **3:**478, 568, 1003, 1016, 1023, 1028, 1053, 1055; **4:**166, 555, 586; **5:**119, 464, 558, 797; **6:**203, 1410, 1412; **7:**44, 544, 821–22, 824, 861; **8:**61, 382, 453, 467, 601; **9:**171, 230, 296, 386, 570, 702; **10:**269, 490–91, 806, 827, 829–30, 834, 906–7; **11:**137; **12:**216–17, 351 OF SIN (*see under* SIN)

WAGON, WAGONS
2:77; **4:**115, 157, 236; **7:**366

WAIL (*OR* WAILS, WAILER, *ETC.*)
2:107, 748; **3:**1049, 1065, 1113; **4:**331; **5:**328, 355; **6:**82, 156, 163, 168, 202, 655, 734, 885, 890, 892, 1057, 1292, 1299, 1382, 1414, 1425, 1438–40; **7:**258, 308–9, 312, 392, 407, 546, 679, 690, 817–18; **8:**238, 439, 686; **9:**166, 451, 453; **12:**212, 216, 405, 643, 693

WAIST
6:1178; **8:**532; **9:**81, 263; **12:**561, 598

WAIT, WAITING
ON GOD/THE LORD **1:**453, 707, 729, 893; **2:**983, 1004, 1259, 1327, 1333; **3:**208, 409, 562; **4:**310, 388, 487, 663–65, 700–702, 720, 777, 779, 787, 802–3, 811, 828–29, 834, 837–38, 842, 844–45, 891, 902, 922–23, 952–54, 960, 984, 1022,

1037, 1167, 1173, 1205–7, 1256, 1268; **5:**187, 617, 730; **6:**118, 216–17, 229, 255, 329, 343, 363, 370, 432, 479, 483, 503, 648, 957, 1051, 1486; **7:**106, 129, 266, 281, 287, 545, 565, 572, 585, 644; **8:**181, 207, 494, 533, 578; **9:**13, 43, 48–49, 56, 106, 239, 250, 488, 497, 572, 738; **10:**40–42, 44–46, 53, 69, 109, 233, 595–96; **11:**314, 491, 685, 694, 708, 715–16; **12:**12, 116, 148, 223, 258, 357, 615, 649, 652, 667

WALL, WALLS

CHURCH **2:**193; **3:**355; **9:**382; **11:**248; **12:**396, 418–19; CITY/VILLAGE **1:**215, 221–23, 239, 277, 1101, 1173, 1181; **2:**183, 701, 791, 871, 1168, 1198, 1239, 1287, 1352, 1359; **3:**37, 150, 221, 293, 505, 607, 628, 635, 1076, 1098; **4:**105, 125, 193, 228, 233, 243, 292, 472, 548, 981, 1183; **6:**218, 775, 792, 1038, 1175, 1232, 1358, 1360, 1364, 1366–67, 1374–75, 1442, 1521, 1606; **7:**82, 316, 610, 679, 810; **8:**15; **9:**348; DIVIDING/SEPARATING **1:**159; **3:**355, 380; **4:**1025; **6:**381; **8:**145; **9:**461; **11:**234, 242, 248, 398–99, 405; OF FIRE **7:**758, 774–75; HOUSE/BUILDING **1:**216, 224, 1097; **2:**594; **3:**889; **5:**720; **6:**1023, 1086; **11:**285; **12:**597; IMAGERY/METAPHOR/PARABLE **2:**505, 1166, 1168; **3:**736; **4:**214, 459, 546; **5:**173, 433, 616, 759, 788; **6:**73, 254, 503, 586, 718, 866, 1047, 1049, 1140, 1143, 1186, 1189, 1201–2, 1315, 1597; **7:**406–7; **8:**20, 247; **9:**369; **10:**310, 502, 719; **11:**458–59; **12:**526; INSCRIPTIONS/PAINTINGS **5:**93, 275, 298, 341, 696–97, 781; **6:**294, 1176; **7:**29, 612; **8:**16; **12:**722; TEMPLE (*see under* JERUSALEM TEMPLE *in PLACES IN THE BIBLE*); OF WATER **1:**794, 800; **2:**599; **6:**691; WRITING ON THE **7:**81, 83–84, 149. *See also by name in PLACES IN THE BIBLE*

WAR

HOLY/JUST **1:**823, 1105; **2:**19–21, 23, 69–70, 89, 91–92, 94–99, 107, 120, 124–25, 129, 148, 151, 158, 161–63, 165–66, 169, 179–80, 183, 190, 199–200, 202, 214, 220, 237, 244–50, 252, 254, 256, 266, 307, 311, 351, 393, 440–42, 461, 736, 739, 743, 745–47, 749, 756–59, 787, 841, 863, 870–71, 885, 1001, 1007, 1016, 1018, 1023, 1055, 1062, 1071–72, 1078, 1085, 1087, 1092–93, 1140, 1158, 1179, 1185, 1193, 1243, 1247–49, 1300; **3:**150–53, 156–57, 176, 202, 238, 329, 497, 529, 532, 538, 547, 553–54, 559–63, 628–29, 742, 775–77, 895, 926, 932, 1106, 1123, 1171–72; **4:**17, 52–53, 55, 230, 264, 471, 758, 857, 917, 1130, 1276; **6:**55, 60, 69, 72–73, 84, 108, 137, 156, 161, 194, 242, 249, 253, 256, 261, 294, 337, 625, 1352, 1355, 1410, 1419, 1580; **7:**312, 344, 349, 352–55, 357–58, 362, 366, 370, 381, 393, 441, 449, 455, 558, 567, 660–61, 683, 688, 703, 730; **8:**671; **9:**289, 430; **10:**720, 723; **12:**664, 702, 713–14; HORSE **4:**598, 610, 612, 624; **6:**646; **7:**807, 814; **8:**309, 403; **9:**367; IMPLEMENTS OF **4:**811, 980; **6:**1305; METHODS/STRATEGY/TACTICS **2:**441, 613, 885, 1180, 1243, 1331–32; **3:**532; **4:**97, 178, 296; SONG(S) OF (*see under* SONG); OF THE SONS OF LIGHT AND THE SONS OF DARKNESS **4:**78; **6:**72–73, 228; **12:**665; SPOILS OF **1:**260, 440, 444–46, 579, 800, 821; **2:**245, 247, 351, 393, 441, 563, 613–14, 625, 630, 651, 789, 969, 996, 1088–89, 1179, 1185, 1191–94, 1211, 1216; **3:**184, 415, 452, 598, 935, 1143, 1171–72; **4:**78, 82, 87, 249–50, 298, 945; **5:**245; **6:**78, 116, 119, 122, 132, 337, 1351, 1410, 1518; **7:**142, 567, 709, 760, 836; **11:**137; **12:**87. *See also* BATTLE

WARDROBE

3:863–64; **6:**1228

WARES

4:483; **5:**812; **6:**481, 1374, 1377; **7:**471, 499

WARRIOR, WARRIORS

2:123, 151, 306, 461, 528, 906, 1048; **3:**769, 825–26; **4:**459, 1130; **5:**194; **6:**82, 805, 851, 882–83, 1033, 1442, 1499, 1528; **7:**275, 449, 810; ANCIENT HEROES *(perhaps angelic in some texts)* **1:**382–84, 408; **2:**1206–7; **5:**381; **6:**1443–45; **7:**332–33, 783, 811; OF DAVID **2:**1216, 1332, 1336, 1340, 1361, 1375–76; **3:**18, 376, 456; **6:**1245; OF DEBORAH **2:**779–80; DIVINE (*see under* GOD, METAPHORS FOR *in PERSONS IN THE BIBLE*); OF GIDEON **2:**802–803; **5:**196; HOLY **2:**151, 245–49, 255; **6:**156; OF JUDITH **3:**1090, 1144, 1180; LEFT-HANDED BENJAMINITE **2:**771, 885; MACCABEAN **4:**47, 80, 95, 174, 204, 276; PHILISTINE **2:**767

WASH, WASHING

1:9, 281, 389, 586, 665–66, 836, 976, 1048, 1060–61, 1063, 1074, 1082, 1096, 1100, 1104–5, 1110, 1120; **2:**81, 151–52, 926, 1286, 1295; **3:**194, 838, 1002; **4:**412, 773, 781, 886; **5:**403; **6:**56, 58, 244, 710, 1491, 1546, 1577, 1579; **7:**526; **8:**25–26, 136, 196, 205–6, 331–33, 335, 486, 531, 595, 606–7; **9:**26, 81, 116, 119–20, 170, 172, 247, 251, 326, 425–26, 509, 557, 701–3, 711, 719–29, 732–33, 741, 758–59, 763, 803; **10:**847; **11:**105, 440, 450–51, 699, 820, 877; **12:**121, 295, 298, 468, 548, 583, 618, 624–25, 677, 730, 733–35

WASPS

5:542; **7:**411

WATCH (*OR* WATCHES, *ETC.*)

1:206, 558, 783, 794, 865, 1173; **2:**36, 316, 448, 529, 687, 781, 1175; **3:**274, 574, 794, 979, 1028, 1112; **4:**395, 494, 537, 609–10, 686, 1082, 1199, 1205; **5:**80, 179, 316, 318, 335, 433, 436, 667, 672–73, 714, 750, 787; **6:**11, 186, 456, 544, 583–84, 755, 777, 994, 1010, 1410, 1467,

WATCH *(continued)*
1503–4, 1576; **7:**112, 163, 178, 183, 576, 635, 729; **8:**328, 419, 451, 475, 495, 547, 618, 630, 657, 681, 707, 723; **9:**71, 263, 265, 269, 410, 432; **10:**283, 285, 357, 644, 764–65, 829, 914, 999; **11:**332, 402, 524, 734; **12:**33, 159, 168, 356, 447, 489, 583, 615, 652
WATCHMAN, WATCHMEN
2:1309; **3:**687; **6:**186–87, 472, 490, 515, 520, 1133–35, 1199, 1203, 1374, 1446, 1448; **7:**73, 303, 371, 585; **9:**71. *See also* DOORKEEPER; LEVITE; PORTER; PRIEST
WATCHTOWER
3:770; **5:**806; **7:**567; **8:**413; **9:**380
WATCHER, WATCHERS
2:187; **4:**396, 895; **5:**787; **7:**2, 5–6, 11, 73, 105; **12:**347, 351, 356, 488–90, 492, 497, 646
WATER, WATERS
OF BITTERNESS **2:**63, 68; CLEANSING/PURIFYING **1:**394, 1060, 1100; **2:**81, 151–52, 247; **3:**838, 1002; **6:**1491, 1579; **7:**829, 831; **8:**332, 532; **9:**81, 537–38, 622, 723–24; **11:**442; **12:**107, 121; COURSE **2:**599; FLOOD (*see under* FLOOD); LIVING **1:**1160; **2:**151; **4:**824; **5:**68, 405; **6:**600, 608, 698, 709; **7:**837; **9:**4, 463, 499, 566–67, 569, 572, 599, 605, 613, 623, 626, 694, 833–34, 857; **10:**137; **12:**317, 439, 591, 630, 724; MANY **6:**1246; **12:**561, 664, 680, 682, 695; RIGHTS **1:**528, 552, 873; **2:**678; SHAFT **1:**222; **2:**1237; **5:**194; SKINS **4:**518, 605; SYSTEM/WORKS **1:**222–23, 265; **5:**298; **6:**1404; WALKING ON **1:**398; **2:**91; **8:**64, 165, 247–48, 327–30, 602–4; **9:**113, 184, 503, 591, 595–97
WAVE OFFERING
See under OFFERING
WAX
4:945; **5:**730; **6:**244; **10:**527
WAY
OF THE CROSS **4:**1119; **6:**550, 795; **8:**281, 350; **9:**352; **10:**809; **11:**207, 628; JESUS AS THE **5:**674, 936; **9:**742–43, 773; **10:**707; **12:**381, 390; OF LIFE **1:**178, 284, 324, 586, 909; **2:**339, 488; **3:**303, 339, 453, 497, 501, 582, 1015; **4:**9, 13, 213–34, 281, 287, 669, 777, 797, 806, 845, 849, 1119; **5:**2, 12, 63, 80, 145, 462–64, 477, 489–91; **6:**439, 619, 627, 635, 734, 970, 1034; **7:**493, 729; **8:**18, 211, 217, 384, 399, 418, 431, 553; **9:**86, 145, 293, 318, 404, 406, 672, 742; **10:**122, 271, 335, 340, 450, 536, 581, 592, 701, 725; **11:**247, 274, 293, 312, 337, 363, 378, 393–95, 426–32, 443, 456, 499, 593, 620, 643, 689, 692–734, 843; **12:**225, 345–46, 381, 451, 525, 595, 611, 634, 667, 673, 727; OF THE LORD **1:**467, 469, 476, 1099; **2:**757; **3:**26, 35, 138, 145, 158; **4:**689; **5:**113; **6:**335, 338–39, 455, 491, 580, 588, 599, 756, 758, 786, 1155, 1264, 1446, 1451–52; **7:**565; **8:**156, 531, 533, 537; **9:**163–64; **10:**57, 261, 263
WAYFARER
2:600
WAYSIDE
8:216; **10:**638
WAYWARD, WAYWARDNESS
1:934; **4:**299; **6:**52, 1189; **7:**215, 279, 672, 674, 685; **10:**503; **12:**11, 60
WEAKNESS, WEAKNESSES
1:49, 62, 124, 529, 672, 706, 757; **2:**82, 311, 344, 376, 446, 461, 477, 528, 542, 552, 681, 787–89, 796–98, 858, 980, 1288; **3:**145, 378–79, 381–82, 409, 417, 422, 576, 776, 962, 966, 1024, 1139; **4:**13, 256, 307, 376–77, 388, 440, 454, 674, 687, 690, 718, 749, 812, 909, 924, 946, 997, 1037, 1073, 1093, 1119, 1207, 1248; **5:**67, 153, 451, 461–62, 464, 466, 473–77, 499, 516–19, 544, 559, 594, 599–600, 849; **6:**370–71, 656, 929–30, 959, 1130, 1219, 1418, 1445; **7:**55, 115, 138, 544, 587, 678, 721, 725, 781; **8:**19, 165, 179, 206, 344, 476–77, 581, 654, 705, 708–9; **9:**55, 163, 273–74, 525, 730; **10:**151, 545, 598, 600, 657, 745, 809, 812, 817, 939, 957, 987; **11:**3, 16, 26–27, 81, 137–39, 153–54, 157–60, 163, 166–67, 176–77, 288, 293–94, 298, 333, 492, 515, 525–26, 536, 645–48, 815, 823, 860; **12:**58, 60, 94, 130, 144, 223–25, 296–97, 361, 583, 587–88, 606, 687, 705
WEALTH, WEALTHY
1:14, 164–65, 213, 225, 233, 246, 259–62, 265, 285, 287, 428, 512–13, 527–28, 556–57, 730, 846, 888, 896, 905–6, 963, 1132, 1174; **2:**82, 356–57, 404–5, 414, 467, 472–75, 566, 594–95, 697, 712, 871, 915, 945, 982, 1048–49, 1166, 1169–71, 1244, 1256; **3:**28, 39, 54–55, 84–89, 138, 144, 186–89, 209–10, 272–73, 300, 461, 468, 473–74, 509–10, 525, 868–69, 879–80, 911, 921, 979, 1002, 1004, 1017, 1055–56, 1068, 1080–81, 1132–33, 1144, 1147, 1159, 1181; **4:**6–8, 138, 153, 163–66, 172, 217, 228, 331–32, 345, 484, 513, 524, 547–48, 554, 586, 634–35, 829, 876–79, 890–91, 925, 1198, 1248; **5:**4, 8, 13–14, 34, 37–38, 48–50, 53, 102–3, 111–12, 118–22, 125–26, 128–29, 131–35, 142–43, 145, 150, 153, 155, 158–59, 166, 172–76, 178–79, 194, 197–200, 206, 225–27, 230, 237–39, 246, 253, 262–64, 298–300, 318–23, 345–46, 445, 485, 498, 510–12, 623, 676–78, 713–17, 764, 776, 780–81, 789, 823–25; **6:**74, 81–82, 93–95, 278, 509–10, 621, 630, 656–58, 708–9, 745, 777, 914, 965–66, 1061, 1219, 1342, 1371, 1383–84,

1388–89; **7:**13–14, 26, 40–41, 81, 91, 142, 188, 208, 284–85, 362, 365, 376–78, 399–400, 416–17, 534, 617–18, 631–32, 647–49, 678–80, 723–24, 804–5, 838–39; **8:**32, 104–5, 210, 390–96, 453, 494–95, 552–53, 627, 648–52, 664, 681–83, 685, 688, 726; **9:**25–27, 52, 127, 141, 144, 149, 163–64, 170, 179, 197, 202–3, 255–56, 259–61, 306–9, 314–16, 347–50, 357, 362–64, 397, 836; **10:**10, 84, 100–101, 270–71, 775, 777, 788, 808, 853–54; **11:**11, 21, 25–26, 123, 134, 348, 377, 407, 418, 432, 547–48, 611, 826–31; **12:**141, 187–88, 195, 216–17, 493, 587, 605, 652–53, 693–97

WEAPON, WEAPONS
1:250; **2:**265, 437, 771–73, 782, 1103, 1160, 1227, 1237, 1307; **3:**511, 775–76, 1130, 1144, 1161; **4:**168, 332, 419, 424, 483, 486, 612, 624, 811, 819, 908, 930, 965, 1245; **5:**77, 92, 127, 225, 312, 462, 486, 525, 675, 818, 825; **6:**161, 194, 239, 716, 1298–1300, 1357, 1443, 1479, 1524; **7:**145–46, 151, 179, 192, 194; **9:**430–31, 436–37, 449, 649, 743, 802; **10:**715, 728–29; **11:**138, 459, 801; **12:**29, 78, 303, 665; BIBLE AS A **1:**35, 151, 169, 171; **2:**759; **11:**462; DIVINE **1:**400; **4:**519, 590, 604; **6:**156, 915, 1038, 1076, 1296, 1304–5, 1414–15, 1435, 1522; **7:**101, 112; **12:**700; OF WAR **1:**357, 740; **2:**982, 1070, 1205, 1208; **3:**230, 591; **4:**53, 85, 156, 867; **5:**127; **6:**67–68, 98, 733, 853, 920, 1169, 1395; **7:**57, 145–46, 151, 218, 236, 332; **11:**461, 645; **12:**634, 652, 665. *See also* ARMS: AS WEAPONRY

WEATHER
2:755; **3:**669, 742, 1070; **4:**152, 560, 590–92, 604, 792, 1268; **5:**140, 180, 218, 220, 426, 660, 683, 742; **6:**84, 120, 175, 302; **9:**268–69, 329; **10:**345–50, 352, 807

WEAVE (*OR* WEAVING, WEAVER, *ETC.*)
1:1134; **2:**858, 1108, 1361; **3:**332, 1003; **4:**394, 414, 1236; **7:**779; **11:**64; **12:**658

WEDDING, WEDDINGS
1:1142; **2:**842, 850, 926, 1195; **3:**975, 977, 979, 985, 987, 1008, 1026, 1028–29, 1031, 1033, 1038–45, 1050–51; **4:**115, 127, 303, 312, 649, 860–62; **5:**36, 80, 365, 399–402, 405, 425, 431, 829; **6:**184, 602, 762, 825, 828, 1230; **8:**79, 269, 359, 449–51; **9:**51, 74, 130–31, 265, 558, 565; **10:**957; **11:**451; **12:**445, 721; BANQUET/FEAST **1:**1026; **2:**859; **3:**975, 985, 987, 1028, 1033, 1042, 1044–45, 1048, 1051, 1055; **5:**366, 401; **7:**40; **8:**204, 235–36, 324–25, 417–18, 473, 555, 601, 603, 704; **9:**234, 263–64, 289–90, 536, 565; **12:**603, 721; AT CANA **5:**298; **9:**503, 535–40, 727, 832, 856; CHAMBER (*see under* BRIDAL); NIGHT **3:**975, 979, 1008, 1028–29, 1031, 1040, 1056, 1069, 1141; **5:**402, 409; **9:**51; VOWS (*see* VOW: MARRIAGE/WEDDING); WINE (*see under* WINE)

WEEDS
1:141, 218; **3:**599; **4:**555; **5:**544; **7:**266, 272, 431, 506; **8:**308–15; **9:**293; **10:**592, 716

WEEK
1:316, 346, 380, 553, 1065, 1084–86, 1095–96, 1098, 1104–6, 1158–60, 1163–64, 1191; **2:**202, 233, 235; **3:**441, 499, 608, 718, 742; **4:**1050; **5:**827; **6:**1588; **7:**525; **8:**35, 73, 81, 545, 555; **9:**45, 51, 102, 119, 205, 311, 476, 490, 701, 707, 840, 856; **10:**276–77, 963; **11:**115, 127, 217, 348; **12:**64, 532, 543; HOLY (*see under* HOLY)

WEEKS, FEAST/FESTIVAL OF
See FEASTS/FESTIVALS: OF FIRSTFRUITS/PENTECOST/WEEKS; PENTECOST

WEEP (*OR* WEEPS, WEEPING, *ETC.*)
1:553, 572, 587, 629–30, 635, 643, 669, 671, 773; **2:**178, 199, 748–49, 773, 885, 905, 988, 1055, 1135, 1148, 1159, 1192, 1202, 1207, 1224, 1250, 1305, 1309, 1324–25, 1341; **3:**212, 237, 668–69, 804, 923–24, 1024, 1028, 1039, 1049, 1069; **4:**281, 358, 395, 459, 461, 555, 705, 796, 1087, 1195, 1227; **5:**140, 809; **6:**168, 194–95, 202, 380, 605, 648, 654–55, 658, 664–65, 685, 717, 723, 734, 741, 810, 815, 858, 943, 975, 980, 1016, 1019–20, 1029, 1033, 1041, 1055, 1072, 1140, 1177, 1343, 1382, 1425; **7:**12, 125, 188, 283–84, 308, 312, 547; **8:**147, 176, 226, 311, 314, 418, 716, 731; **9:**11–12, 24, 26, 143–44, 158, 166, 278, 367, 371–75, 452, 779–80, 834, 841–42; **10:**162, 170, 285, 290, 753; **11:**50; **12:**154, 216, 602, 606, 681, 692–94

WEIGHTS AND MEASURES
1:1127, 1136; **2:**475; **5:**160; BATH *(volume)* **6:**1583–84; **7:**308; BEKA *(weight)* **3:**510; COR *(volume)* **12:**710; CUBIT *(length)* **1:**391; **2:**79; **3:**484, 708; **6:**1540–41, 1547, 1553, 1557, 1556–57; **9:**259; EPHAH *(volume)* **1:**1098–99, 1136, 1188; **2:**126, 229–30, 232–333; **3:**329; **4:**228; **6:**93, 1583–84, 1586, 1588–89; **7:**737, 774, 757, 772, 774, 776–81; FOOT *(length)* **1:**1019; **2:**123; **10:**125; HANDBREADTH *(length)* **3:**484; **6:**1540, 1547; HIN *(volume)* **6:**126, 229–30, 1149, 1186, 1188, 1589; HOMER *(volume)* **1:**1188; **6:**93, 1583–84; **7:**231; KAB *(volume)* **4:**204; LAWS FOR **1:**1127, 1135–36; **2:**475; **5:**160, 827; **6:**1583; OMER *(volume)* **1:**1158; SEAH *(volume)* **7:**136; SHEKEL *(weight)* **1:**314, 918, 1039, 1042, 1136, 1187–89; **2:**35, 1037; **3:**580, 721, 798, 819; **6:**1583; **8:**33, 371; **9:**171; SPAN *(length)* **2:**1110; **6:**1541; YARD *(length)* **2:**36; **3:**494, 768; **5:**859; **6:**1559; **9:**116. *See also* BALANCE; SCALE

WELL, WELLS
1:222, 433, 485, 528–30, 552, 703, 1160; **2:**165, 1376; **3:**378, 813, 1037; **4:**379, 796; **5:**68, 185, 199, 355, 405; **6:**608, 626; **8:**67; **9:**284, 565–66, 569; **11:**697

WHALE, WHALES
1:180; **5:**322; **7:**505, 509

WHEAT
1:217–18, 275, 759, 1017, 1019–20, 1158; **2:**356, 910, 1063, 1139, 1230; **3:**58, 424, 710, 722, 1001; **4:**1004; **5:**63, 188, 544; **6:**20, 579, 753, 1003, 1200, 1360, 1377–79, 1400, 1583–84; **7:**309, 430, 502; **8:**61, 158, 308, 577; **9:**160, 171, 264, 307–8, 438; **10:**353, 716; **12:**416, 612, 710; HARVEST (*see* HARVEST: BARLEY/GRAIN/WHEAT). *See also* SPELT

WHEEL, WHEELS
1:1025; **3:**538, 813; **4:**236; **5:**188, 218, 355–57, 787; **6:**98, 886, 1109, 1113, 1116, 1119, 1128, 1130, 1182–84; **7:**613; **10:**785, 808; **12:**144, 435, 591–92, 597–98

WHELP, WHELPS
2:536; **6:**1273, 1371

WHIP, WHIPS
3:102; **4:**210; **5:**749; **7:**31, 279, 613; **8:**487; **9:**543, 545

WHIRLWIND
1:816; **2:**165; **3:**175; **4:**51, 319–20, 323, 333–37, 378, 410, 519, 583, 595–97, 600, 631; **5:**93, 536; **6:**57, 186, 213, 342, 1114; **7:**261, 602; **10:**43, 842, 950; **12:**85

WHITE
1:666, 851, 883, 909, 1096–97, 1110, 1114; **2:**55, 110, 987; **3:**495, 1080; **4:**368, 625; **5:**340–41, 355, 415; **6:**1379; **7:**13, 103, 257, 308; **8:**630, 731; **9:**205–6; **10:**43, 310, 539; **11:**272; **12:**263, 548, 561, 571, 580, 583, 587, 592, 597, 611, 613, 618–19, 621, 624–25, 642, 651, 667–68, 681, 699, 710, 730; GARMENT(S) (*see under* GARMENT); HORSE (*see under* HORSE); THRONE (*see under* THRONE)

WHORE, WHORES
1:579–80; **2:**547; **3:**46; **4:**1111; **5:**419; **6:**60–61, 334, 345, 442, 601–2, 628, 1230, 1232, 1234, 1241; **7:**211, 215–16, 225, 614, 781; **12:**536, 680–81, 686, 725

WICK
6:365, 1435; **7:**769; **8:**281

WIDOW, WIDOWS
1:74, 249, 605, 830, 868, 1015, 1124, 1135; **2:**149, 211, 234, 369, 412, 426, 468, 474–75, 481, 629, 683–84, 835, 904, 907, 915, 919, 922–23, 933, 935–38, 978, 1313–14; **3:**67, 94, 127–29, 138, 186–87, 191, 330, 820, 1075, 1080–81, 1112, 1132–33, 1144–45; **4:**12, 82, 207, 249–50, 382, 436, 478, 500, 511–13, 524, 538, 947, 1265; **5:**71–72, 92, 105, 144, 151, 205–206, 384, 419, 462–63, 467, 798; **6:**14, 20, 60, 82, 127–28, 431, 693, 745–46, 975–76, 1029, 1069, 1222–23, 1269, 1309, 1579; **7:**161, 216, 357, 846, 874; **8:**58, 400, 657, 670, 681–83, 698; **9:**12, 15, 24–25, 51, 72–73, 156–59, 171, 178, 237, 335–40, 350, 393–97, 726; **10:**110–11, 114, 161–62, 170, 869, 874, 886; **11:**802, 805, 818–21, 825, 830, 869; **12:**144, 181, 195, 197, 201, 694, 725–27

WIFE, WIVES
1:185–86, 363–64, 430, 452–54, 475, 483, 489–90, 501, 509–11, 527, 537, 609–10, 824–25, 862, 1086, 1125–26, 1147; **2:**62–63, 67–68, 213, 234, 760, 845–46, 850, 852–53, 858, 974, 1081, 1169, 1223, 1250, 1284, 1286, 1289; **3:**14, 32, 40, 112, 117, 156, 228, 328–30, 352–53, 357, 522, 687, 882–86, 1016, 1084–85, 1133, 1138; **4:**69–71, 356, 552–53, 476–77, 545, 557, 569, 572; **5:**80, 82, 96, 125, 129, 180, 193, 220, 257, 260–61, 341, 509, 524–25, 695, 753, 764–65; **6:**10, 82, 104, 112, 198, 596, 603–4, 608–9, 811, 1086, 1223, 1342–43, 1345; **7:**196–98, 210–11, 215–16, 224–33, 244, 276–77, 286–87, 294, 297, 865; **8:**129–30, 132, 134, 190–92, 247, 319–20, 386, 546, 642–45, 673; **9:**313–14, 332, 348–49, 388, 476, 628, 831; **10:**872, 875–78, 885, 891, 928, 932, 980; **11:**452, 718–19, 801–2, 804–5, 820–21, 869–70, 892; **12:**211, 285, 287, 461, 581, 633; FOREIGN (*see under* FOREIGN); AND HUSBAND(S) (*see under* HUSBAND)

WILDERNESS
1:39, 41, 70, 210, 253–54, 275, 306, 312, 316, 433–34, 452–53, 806–9, 812–14, 817, 991–92, 995, 1066, 1112; **2:**4–5, 16–20, 25–26, 31–33, 86, 92, 94–100, 103–11, 120–28, 134–40, 157–67, 169–70, 177, 197, 244–45, 254, 262, 291–93, 305–10; 752–53, 795, 807, 826, 853, 861, 865, 871, 885, 901, 906, 1001, 1049, 1153, 1157–59, 1166, 1179, 1324–25; **3:**140, 143–44, 306, 313, 363–64, 370, 376, 540, 580, 671, 691, 811, 813, 829, 842, 1133, 1139; **4:**46, 48, 81, 114, 190, 198, 230, 313, 430, 486, 520, 548, 607, 898, 926, 944–45, 991–92, 1004, 1043–44, 1062, 1076, 1098, 1105, 1111–12, 1117, 1119, 1133, 1141–43, 1224; **5:**50, 429, 531–34, 536, 560, 573, 578, 584, 599, 621–22, 757, 807; **6:**84, 113, 184–86, 281–83, 335–39, 378, 382, 420–21, 430, 447, 455–56, 461, 467, 526–27, 531–32, 597–602, 614, 1275, 1283–84, 1288–89, 1405, 1491, 1516; **7:**225, 235, 264–66, 268–70, 273, 277–79, 282, 285–90, 292–93, 317, 346, 365, 394; **8:**33, 63, 111, 147, 156, 159, 162–63,

267–68, 323–25, 525, 530–33, 535–37, 542, 546, 601, 615–16, 671; **9:**79–81, 84, 95, 97–99, 102, 114, 120, 163–64, 195–97, 206, 234–35, 302, 542, 552, 599, 605, 612–13, 632; **10:**128–29, 142–43, 192, 298, 405, 432–33, 511–14, 517, 534, 555–56, 581, 593–94, 617, 914–15, 937; **11:**138, 216, 266, 512; **12:**5, 7, 52, 55, 59, 118, 141, 156, 247, 258, 266–67, 488–90, 494–95, 579, 588, 649, 651–52, 680

WILL, FREE
See FREE CHOICE/FREE WILL

WILL OF GOD
1:33, 39–41, 44, 58, 61–62, 74, 84, 103, 126–27, 131, 137, 156, 210, 286, 351, 355–56, 365, 376–77, 396, 398, 401, 413–14, 452, 469, 486, 501, 529, 606, 611, 646, 679, 684–85, 694, 697, 722–23, 742, 820, 828, 831, 852, 887, 906, 908, 1008, 1042, 1054, 1056, 1063, 1072–75, 1099, 1128, 1134, 1143, 1184; **2:**111, 186–87, 213, 300, 319, 324, 329, 392, 426, 453, 492, 529–30, 604, 617, 620, 631, 702, 739, 741, 747, 749, 759, 783, 789, 804–5, 811, 818, 827, 847, 851, 855, 864, 879, 888, 892, 912, 958–59, 970, 981, 987, 993–96, 1002, 1038, 1047, 1058, 1072–73, 1078–79, 1082, 1092–94, 1145, 1154, 1165, 1168, 1262–63, 1267, 1324, 1333, 1341, 1355; **3:**3–4, 7, 23–26, 35–36, 87–88, 93–98, 102–5, 117, 125, 144–45, 150, 167, 169, 185, 191–92, 197, 202, 215, 226–27, 233, 271, 273, 339, 389–90, 395–96, 408–9, 426, 432, 497, 518, 520, 523, 560, 580, 620, 624, 649, 721–24, 731, 761, 794, 828, 868, 940, 960, 1004, 1065–66, 1137–38; **4:**101, 110, 188, 296, 332, 382, 442, 641–42, 669–70, 673, 702, 712, 733, 749, 756, 810–11, 820–21, 823, 843–45, 848, 861–63, 866–67, 882–83, 888–89, 895, 909–10, 917, 937, 953, 963–65, 977–78, 1004–5, 1008, 1011–12, 1021–22, 1030, 1037–38, 1054–55, 1069, 1092–93, 1127–28, 1174–75, 1199, 1206–7, 1215, 1225, 1250–52, 1265, 1269; **5:**9, 14–15, 51, 72, 97–98, 283–84, 302–3, 307–8, 353, 620, 652, 656, 674, 814; **6:**74, 98, 109, 124, 133–34, 161, 297, 342, 363, 401, 432, 483, 485–86, 605, 626–27, 641, 656, 729, 766, 787–88, 796, 808, 868, 1218, 1252, 1412, 1496; **7:**117, 129, 220, 240, 335–36, 347, 354, 366–67, 372, 395, 431, 458, 482, 558, 569, 572, 580, 662, 664, 681, 696, 720–21; **8:**25, 31, 134, 150, 158–59, 160–64, 179, 186–92, 196–97, 202–4, 211–12, 217–19, 222, 225, 246, 275, 278, 291–94, 298, 322, 386, 408, 411–13, 420, 455–56, 464, 477, 529, 543–48, 563, 566–68, 626–27, 642–43, 653, 677–78, 694, 708–9, 733; **9:**27, 145, 153, 201, 203, 234–35, 239, 437, 497, 552, 569, 602–3, 664, 671, 679, 693, 712, 742, 763, 795; **10:**38, 51–52, 130, 171, 189, 207–12, 218–19, 256, 276, 288, 299, 307, 311, 314, 337, 339, 386–87, 447, 555, 572, 581, 586, 600, 706, 723, 757, 930; **11:**202, 207–8, 240, 242, 357, 369–70, 372, 443, 515, 530, 587, 667, 680, 718, 730–31, 832, 834, 836; **12:**11–12, 35, 74, 89, 117, 120, 126, 172, 205, 216, 270, 275, 300–301, 305–6, 313, 316, 336–37, 400–402, 442–44, 499, 538, 562, 594, 707

WILLOW, WILLOWS
1:1159–60; **3:**802; **6:**386–87; **9:**542

WIND
1:80, 342–43, 356, 392, 620, 794, 800, 804, 812, 922, 962; **2:**108, 1243, 1367; **3:**88, 183, 236, 255; **4:**110, 209–10, 330, 332, 351, 377–78, 389, 394, 400, 484, 519, 524–25, 532–34, 546, 591–92, 598, 604, 747, 913, 1220, 1268–69, 1272; **5:**41, 54, 97, 120, 150, 220, 252, 270, 278–79, 293, 311, 335, 350, 426, 475, 485, 525, 546, 583, 680, 708, 746, 768, 793; **6:**57, 213, 222, 236, 265, 355–56, 376, 613, 756, 915, 920, 1007, 1115–16, 1119, 1153, 1177, 1202, 1224, 1245, 1271–72, 1361, 1382–83, 1500–1502; **7:**164, 167, 193, 261, 282, 292–93, 352, 474–75, 481–86, 495, 500–502, 783–84; **8:**64, 158, 218, 267, 580–81; **9:**85–86, 91, 163–64, 184, 187, 268, 550; **10:**54, 68, 348, 353, 355, 419, 575, 891; **11:**463, 566, 791; **12:**29, 31, 33, 158, 351, 492, 614, 619

WINDOW, WINDOWS
1:225, 344, 356, 392; **2:**55, 83, 547, 647, 788, 1127, 1250, 1276; **3:**180, 221, 237–38, 497, 624, 1008; **5:**84, 354–55, 616, 720, 829; **6:**212, 214, 655, 742, 1023, 1541, 1543, 1554–55; **7:**91–92, 94, 288, 528, 870; **8:**210; **9:**298; **10:**277, 502; **11:**160, 846; **12:**441, 507, 551, 694

WINE
1:90, 208, 210, 215, 223–25, 249, 380, 403, 440, 539, 585, 614, 666, 1026, 1071, 1158, 1160; **2:**64–65, 68, 126–27, 147–49, 229–30, 233–34, 589, 683, 845, 849–50, 927, 975–76, 1169, 1309; **3:**128, 205, 224, 265, 358, 452, 710, 722, 751, 755–56, 782, 820, 846–47, 881, 918, 959, 1017, 1019, 1076, 1154, 1160; **4:**40, 177, 233, 351, 511, 564, 1098, 1149; **5:**49, 63–64, 102–3, 152, 183–88, 194, 230, 263–64, 297, 303, 340, 343, 351, 379–80, 389, 405–6, 462, 558, 624, 699, 701, 720, 736, 783–84, 818–19, 825; **6:**60, 93, 169, 211, 236–37, 481–82, 684, 765–66, 815, 834–35, 891, 1079, 1216, 1327, 1379, 1579, 1589; **7:**39–40, 44–45, 81, 190, 231, 256–58, 265–67, 296, 308–9, 323, 330, 335–36, 365, 400, 430, 552, 710, 772, 862; **8:**79, 248, 435, 471–72, 490, 492, 532, 552, 601, 653, 658, 670, 705, 722–23; **9:**46, 48, 165–66, 230, 286, 380,

WINE *(continued)*
418–19, 454, 456, 572, 608, 832–33; **10:**742, 934; **11:**232, 234, 470, 513, 631, 635, 805–6, 823, 869; **12:**86, 598, 612, 614, 666–68, 692–94, 699, 710, 717; NEW **3:**501, 601; **5:**613; **6:**490; **7:**240, 265, 308, 679, 771, 811; **8:**236, 555, 705; **9:**131–32, 136, 538; **10:**62, 469; PRESS **2:**149, 796; **5:**787; **6:**892, 1033, 1400; **7:**265, 308, 314, 329, 333–34; **8:**413; **9:**380; **12:**668, 699; SKIN(S) **2:**1169; **3:**358; **4:**564; **6:**1330; **8:**79, 236, 555; **9:**131–32, 136; VAT(S) **3:**205; **5:**49–50; **7:**267, 324; **9:**380; WEDDING **2:**842; **6:**27; **8:**63; **9:**503, 508, 536–40, 575–76, 591, 599, 613, 833, 857, 864

WING, WINGS
1:206, 569, 1013; **2:**79, 918, 922, 924, 926, 928, 930–31, 1004; **3:**70; **4:**109–11, 174, 282, 310, 611, 741, 823, 905, 927, 1047, 1099, 1181; **5:**206, 317; **6:**117, 253, 260–61, 1109, 1115–16, 1118–20, 1128, 1130–31, 1183–84, 1228, 1244–45, 1252, 1560; **7:**102, 112, 242, 748, 873; **8:**17; **9:**282–83, 371–72; **12:**267, 526, 592, 597–98, 631, 651–52

WINNOW, WINNOWING
5:188, 680; **6:**355, 516; **7:**756; **9:**86

WINTER
1:217, 275; **2:**600, 670; **3:**137, 139, 155, 751; **4:**30, 152, 160, 176, 311, 368, 453, 583, 590, 593, 675, 865; **5:**742, 823; **6:**840; **7:**376, 750; **8:**445; **9:**52, 404, 675, 801; **10:**346, 348, 355, 776–77, 997; **11:**11–12, 857, 859, 878

WISDOM
AND COSMOS (*see under* COSMOS); PERSONIFIED **4:**313, 402, 429, 450, 602; **5:**5, 13–15, 35, 40, 43, 84, 89, 94–96, 138, 454, 475, 490, 492–93, 496–509, 517, 522, 527–31, 546, 558, 562–63, 578, 580, 594, 606, 615–16, 619, 626–27, 629, 646–48, 651, 667–70, 687–89, 719–21, 754, 756–58, 867; **6:**961; **7:**14; **8:**274, 356; **10:**915; **11:**570, 607; PROVERBIAL/SPECULATION **2:**437, 502, 682; **4:**277, 371; **5:**23, 102, 160, 626, 663, 669, 689, 842; **6:**238; **7:**5, 111; **8:**30, 38, 41, 183, 210, 260, 567; **10:**802; **11:**337, 451, 599–600, 605; **12:**521

WISE MAN, MEN
1:739, 1166; **2:**1136; **3:**34, 882, 884, 916, 953, 996, 1017, 1119; **4:**330, 575; **5:**11, 94, 218, 225, 243, 272, 322, 343, 345, 358, 607, 690, 705, 716; **6:**600, 1374; **7:**44, 53, 449, 570; **8:**140, 547; **9:**76; **10:**780; **11:**458–59, 515; **12:**521. *See also* MAGI

WIT, WITTY
2:1136; **3:**934; **4:**348, 462, 480; **5:**351, 624, 644, 689; **7:**194, 469; **8:**57; **9:**131, 170, 284, 388; **10:**17, 268–69, 341; **11:**315, 435, 618, 662, 901

WITCH, WITCHCRAFT
2:395, 1183; **3:**370, 576, 635; **4:**58, 504; **6:**827, 1203, 1222; **7:**468; **11:**250, 636

WITHER, WITHERED
1:240, 621; **2:**374; **4:**110, 402–3, 468, 1087; **5:**459, 461, 716; **6:**63, 168, 183, 211, 331–32, 1176, 1245, 1271, 1273, 1429; **7:**309, 314, 415, 478, 520–25, 602, 805; **9:**178, 409, 426; **11:**816; **12:**273, 729; FIG TREE **8:**401, 407–8, 661, 663–65, 672; **9:**373, 704; HAND **2:**771, 1238; **3:**106, 108, 1171; **4:**1228; **8:**59, 63, 247, 558; **9:**114, 134, 209, 211, 284, 355

WITNESS (*OR* WITNESSED, *ETC.*)
1:152, 834, 846; **2:**369, 1028, 1062; **3:**179, 723; **4:**436, 460, 806, 843, 953; **6:**315, 433, 1044, 1131, 1179, 1250, 1279, 1489, 1523, 1529; **7:**641; **8:**630, 651; **9:**30, 488, 523, 528–30, 533, 551, 557–61, 569–70, 586, 590, 633, 765, 826–27; **10:**54, 78, 199, 307, 338; **12:**46, 90, 438, 562, 626, 733; CLOUD OF (*see under* CLOUD); FALSE (*see under* FALSE)

WIZARD, WIZARDS
2:574, 1183–84; **6:**118, 827, 1203

WOLF, WOLVES
1:667; **2:**803; **5:**715; **6:**141, 552, 1315; **7:**667, 694; **8:**212, 217, 258; **9:**153, 219, 222, 282, 668; **10:**284, 286, 315, 390, 712, 764; **11:**216, 218; **12:**413

WOMAN, WOMEN
IN THE BIBLE/PORTRAYAL OF **1:**149, 182–87; **2:**782, 860; **3:**920, 994, 1156; **4:**862; **5:**19–20, 70, 129, 364, 368, 413, 629; **7:**175; **9:**24–25, 571–72; **11:**800–803, 821; **12:**652, 686–87; AS DISCIPLES/PROPHETS **1:**182, 186; **8:**493, 567, 731; FOREIGN (*see under* FOREIGN: WIVES/WOMAN/WOMEN); AS A MINORITY **1:**2, 151, 182–87; **3:**872–73, 940; **4:**278, 931; **5:**82; **11:**43; ROLE OF **1:**181, 223, 226, 242, 323–24, 335, 354, 518; **2:**234, 245, 551–52, 1304; **3:**295, 883, 920; **4:**565; **5:**365; **6:**81; **8:**138; **9:**43, 94; **11:**783, 800–803; VALIANT **3:**1137; **5:**34–35, 91, 259–64; VIOLENCE AGAINST (*see* VIOLENCE: SEXUAL/AGAINST WOMEN). *See also* NAMED WOMEN OF THE BIBLE *and* UNNAMED WOMEN OF THE BIBLE *in REFERENCE LISTS FROM THE BIBLE*

WONDERS AND SIGNS
1:718, 739, 740; **2:**319, 481, 503; **4:**992; **5:**510, 525, 584, 621, 800; **6:**112, 1278; **7:**65, 72; **8:**62, 246, 632; **9:**212, 401, 487, 575; **10:**14–15, 23, 59, 63–66, 71, 76–78, 91–92, 99, 101, 112–13, 121, 124, 127, 130, 132, 135, 139, 146, 162, 175, 188–89, 197, 210, 225; **11:**15, 168–69, 253, 758; **12:**34–35, 75, 703

WOOD
1:233, 889–90, 1009, 1013, 1024, 1035, 1082,

1098, 1100; **2:**128, 151, 198, 265, 321, 363, 1012, 1248, 1381; **3:**82, 136, 178, 199, 269, 484, 666, 703–4, 708, 710, 756, 800, 819–21, 936; **4:**197, 402, 513–14; **5:**405, 523, 526, 550–54, 558, 742, 772, 807; **6:**342, 357, 662, 786, 996, 998, 1001, 1007, 1069, 1217, 1269, 1334–35, 1506–7, 1524, 1555, 1574; **7:**21, 67, 83, 168, 194, 240, 272, 360, 609, 717; **8:**592–93; **9:**74, 321, 452–53; **11:**461, 845; **12:**635, 694

WOOL
1:92, 218–20, 225, 1040; **2:**220, 454, 802–3; **3:**1003; **4:**312; **6:**1360, 1377, 1379, 1442, 1463–64, 1578, 1593; **7:**13; **10:**182; **12:**110, 561

WORDPLAY
2:707, 910, 1169; **3:**76, 184, 225, 328, 332, 379, 386, 389, 430, 483, 486, 524, 538, 555, 561; **5:**54, 69, 111, 117, 133–34, 172, 187, 193, 715, 853; **6:**108, 583–84, 599, 614, 621, 722, 744–45, 753, 894, 1062, 1285, 1319, 1526, 1566, 1607; **7:**84, 182, 218, 223, 231–32, 256–58, 260, 265, 270, 275, 283, 286, 290, 407, 414, 478, 666; **10:**128, 179, 326, 334, 434, 569, 862; **11:**130, 143, 245; **12:**109, 284

WORKS
OF GOD **2:**753; **3:**1040, 1056, 1058; **4:**625, 1137; **5:**283, 563, 570–71; **7:**855; **8:**21–22, 107, 584, 656, 660, 663, 679; **12:**595; GOOD **2:**931; **3:**501, 1003; **5:**320, 678, 730, 867; **8:**183, 201, 408; **9:**73, 83, 279; **10:**161, 166, 199, 339, 420, 446, 725; **11:**30, 119, 130, 239, 337, 356, 393–95, 531, 593, 805, 870, 874–80; **12:**9, 121, 128, 274, 337, 444; AND RIGHTEOUSNESS **1:**450, 1099; **3:**287; **4:**1092, 1133–34; **8:**145, 217, 249; **9:**153; **10:**460, 479–80, 485–86, 493, 543, 555, 583, 654–58, 660–61, 675–76, 725; **11:**151, 237–38, 241, 356, 362, 391, 393, 836, 876–77; **12:**177, 197

WORLD
CREATION OF **1:**38, 67, 74, 232, 278, 289, 355, 357, 365, 845, 884; **2:**546; **4:**411, 608, 631, 1078, 1099, 1224, 1279; **5:**94, 442, 506, 523, 578; **6:**190, 1537; **7:**528; **9:**519; END OF THE (*see under* END, THE); INHABITED **5:**10, 95, 505; **6:**354; **10:**247; NETHER **4:**603; **5:**45, 397; **6:**411, 1358, 1368, 1388, 1438, 1444–45, 1566; **7:**463, 475, 504, 506

WORM, WORMS
1:231, 814, 1081; **2:**106; **3:**1178–79; **4:**254, 393–94, 512, 517; **5:**26, 180, 241, 252, 692; **6:**159, 355, 451, 453; **7:**467, 471, 473–74, 486–87, 520–21, 525; **8:**210, 640; **9:**594; **10:**181–82; **11:**389, 849, 880

WORMWOOD
5:67; **6:**655; **7:**388, 417; **12:**630

WORSHIP
CHRISTIAN **1:**189, 204, 209, 778; **2:**69, 83, 98, 235, 1251; **3:**479; **4:**672, 677, 736; **5:**656; **6:**113; **7:**623; **8:**328, 336, 428; **9:**196, 555; **10:**72, 704, 724; **11:**444, 567, 641, 833; **12:**160, 262, 510; COMMON **1:**1156; **10:**73, 406–7, 746; COMMUNAL/CONGREGATIONAL/PUBLIC **1:**26, 43, 47, 96, 200–212, 683, 813; **2:**15, 40, 69, 294, 427, 429, 490, 1013; **3:**400, 447, 501–2, 539, 609–13, 1134; **4:**11, 41, 64, 72, 777, 1154, 1223; **5:**269, 623, 859; **6:**272, 1017, 1044, 1592; **7:**586, 623, 632; **8:**95, 109, 200, 205, 602; **9:**86–87, 489; **10:**28, 99, 133, 191, 201, 256, 295, 967; **11:**494, 636, 640, 648; **12:**160–61, 168, 669, 728; FALSE (*see under* FALSE); JEWISH **1:**285; **2:**194, 519; **3:**956, 1078, 1125, 1134; **4:**18–19, 672, 857, 868; **7:**63–64, 860; **8:**15, 34–35, 200; **9:**567–68, 766; **10:**28, 191, 213, 220, 407, 704, 733; **11:**22, 224, 417, 529, 861; **12:**727; SYNAGOGUE **1:**80; **8:**148, 200; **9:**106; **11:**22; **12:**164, 727; TEMPLE (*see under* JERUSALEM TEMPLE *in PLACES IN THE BIBLE*); TRUE **1:**988, 1073; **2:**277, 757; **3:**632; **5:**628; **6:**542, 640; **9:**396, 568; **10:**125–26, 629, 708; **12:**585

WRATH OF GOD
1:356, 1010, 1045, 1066, 1119; **2:**40, 534, 1170; **3:**286, 292, 427, 630, 650, 731; **4:**40, 212, 671, 703, 1042, 1104; **5:**574–75, 592, 594, 818; **6:**189, 612, 629, 670, 718, 812–13; **7:**115, 402, 702; **9:**561; **10:**431, 476, 519, 936; **11:**257, 391, 434, 572–73, 610, 642, 646, 678, 693, 703–4, 708; **12:**50, 518, 529, 566, 595, 607, 612, 630, 633, 643–44, 651, 656, 666, 672, 675, 677–78, 681, 692, 699

WREATH, WREATHS
1:212; **3:**1078, 1174; **4:**202; **5:**624, 784; **10:**909; **11:**708, 813

WRESTLE (*OR* WRESTLES, WRESTLING, *ETC.*)
1:335, 543, 555, 564–70, 748, 1178; **2:**91, 741, 758, 797–98, 846; **3:**1023, 1056; **4:**97, 216, 637, 900; **5:**524; **6:**1511; **7:**501; **8:**206; **10:**599, 757, 982, 991–93

WRITING, WRITINGS
BIBLICAL **1:**2, 79, 129–36, 140, 147, 193, 197, 229, 293; **2:**429, 441, 541; **5:**1, 7, 479, 549; **10:**8, 371, 384, 398; **12:**81, 159; BOARDS **6:**1507; CASE **6:**1178; MATERIALS **8:**2, 4–5

Y

YAHWEH, NAME OF
See under GOD, NAMES FOR/TITLES OF *in PERSONS IN THE BIBLE*

YAHWIST, YAHWISTS
(also known as J) **1:**308, 311, 313, 322, 340, 367,

YAHWIST, YAHWISTS *(continued)*
993; **2:**5–6, 179, 201, 954; **3:**678; **4:**964; **5:**567; **6:**22, 255, 277, 556; **7:**860; **12:**418

YARN
1:1060, 1097–98, 1100; **5:**261

YEAR
AGRICULTURAL/FARMING **2:**407, 410–14; **4:**934; **6:**176; OF FREEDOM **1:**1172; GREAT **1:**308, 1156; JUBILEE/OF LIBERTY **1:**1156, 1170–75, 1188–89; **2:**937; **6:**831, 1109–110, 1537, 1590; **9:**106; **10:**72; **12:**85; LITURGICAL/CHURCH/CHRISTIAN **1:**96, 189, 206, 212, 875, 1109; **2:**32–33, 55, 89, 230, 233, 235–36, 912; **7:**873; **8:**3; **9:**847; **10:**278; NEW (*see under* NEW); OF RELEASE **1:**770, 1174; **2:**404, 407–8; SABBATICAL (*see* SABBATICAL YEAR); SOLAR **1:**380, 392; OF THE TITHE **2:**149

YEAST
1:785, 1018, 1021, 1047, 1157, 1159; **6:**1338; **8:**298, 309, 311–12, 315, 342, 468, 617–18, 681; **9:**12, 24, 251, 275–77, 281; **10:**831, 847–51, 877

YELLOW
1:1097, 1157; **6:**1466; **7:**136

YOKE, YOKES
1:368, 536, 1180; **2:**151, 166, 656, 680, 1012; **3:**470, 518, 525, 723; **4:**32, 106, 154–56, 165, 189, 332, 464; **5:**15, 627, 688–90, 765, 772, 777, 823; **6:**9, 93, 159, 195, 242, 437, 454, 601, 619, 778–88, 806, 849, 866, 1051, 1054, 1069, 1143, 1249, 1361, 1418, 1442; **7:**220, 275, 550, 605; **8:**32, 274–76, 291–92, 416, 431, 433; **9:**318; **10:**548, 554, 887, 997; **11:**249, 306–7, 320, 798, 887; **12:**612, 644, 712, 716

YOKEFELLOW
11:540

YOM KIPPUR
See ATONEMENT, DAY OF; FEASTS/FESTIVALS: ATONEMENT/YOM KIPPUR

YOUTH, YOUTHS
1:29, 93, 218, 393, 490, 598, 684, 1020; **2:**16, 192, 537, 674, 688–89, 916, 992, 1036, 1061, 1100, 1108, 1159; **3:**39, 94, 233, 429, 885, 983, 993, 997, 1031, 1062; **4:**43, 67, 216, 310, 313, 327, 440, 544, 562–63, 586, 959; **5:**37, 44, 67, 69, 85, 93, 188, 198, 207, 230, 271, 316, 353–56, 406, 411, 461, 467, 477–81, 489, 497, 509–10, 652, 658, 685, 720, 760, 773, 849, 867; **6:**411, 477, 574, 582, 597, 606, 614, 693, 1221, 1238, 1266, 1319, 1321–22, 1325, 1471; **7:**142, 180, 183, 185, 225, 382, 516, 832, 864–65; **8:**68, 390, 394, 539, 560, 628, 694, 731; **9:**10, 347, 425, 861; **10:**335, 374, 607; **11:**61, 454, 763, 813–14, 818; **12:**315–16, 399, 652

Z

ZEAL, ZEALOUS
1:286, 979; **2:**21, 220, 311, 392, 420, 430; **3:**142, 223–25, 287, 522, 530, 570; **4:**9, 47, 50–51, 58, 873, 1173; **5:**74, 178, 182, 205, 239, 259, 302, 390, 397, 486, 843, 861; **6:**122, 127, 221, 379–80, 550, 600, 646, 919, 978, 1153, 1348, 1530; **7:**107, 322–23, 481, 753, 789, 876; **8:**2, 46, 435; **9:**270, 823–24; **10:**123, 150, 170, 292–94, 296–97, 306, 309, 400, 567, 587, 649, 653–54, 722, 956, 960–61, 972, 995–96; **11:**5–6, 9, 15, 37, 53, 110–11, 116–18, 121, 123, 125–28, 131, 149, 213–14, 216, 219, 243, 295, 316, 342–43, 453, 531, 695, 874; **12:**127, 151, 271, 277, 290, 538, 581, 673, 708

ZEALOT, ZEALOTS
1:287; **2:**200, 395; **4:**9; **8:**99, 217, 254, 420, 516, 663, 690; **9:**84, 138, 196, 430, 658; **10:**150, 154, 756; **11:**214, 232–33, 342; **12:**212

ZION, DAUGHTER OF, DAUGHTERS OF
1:30; **3:**1147; **6:**54, 65, 81–84, 294, 410, 413, 423, 431, 454, 547, 615, 913, 1020–21, 1023, 1027, 1029–30, 1032–36, 1038–46, 1065–66, 1069; **7:**702, 761, 808; **8:**704; **9:**367

ZION TRADITION
1:438; **2:**1238; **3:**630; **5:**619; **6:**19, 66–67, 133, 137, 140, 145, 163, 231–32, 242, 261–62, 314, 476, 1020, 1063, 1115, 1118–20, 1254; **7:**660, 739, 742

ZOROASTRIAN, ZOROASTRIANISM
3:966; **5:**570; **7:**89

ANCIENT LITERATURE

A

ABOT
1:68, 1017; **2:**195; **5:**111, 128, 134, 153, 172, 306, 326, 327; **7:**181, 340; **8:**79, 129, 172, 187, 194, 254, 332, 374, 379, 431–32; **9:**74, 93, 127, 227, 231, 565, 640–41; **11:**211, 306. See also *PIRQE (ABOT (PIRKE AVOT/ABOTH)*

ABRAHAM, TESTAMENT OF
See *TESTAMENT OF ABRAHAM*

ACTS OF ANDREW AND MATTHIAS
7:526, 528

ACTS OF JOHN
8:13, 491; **12:**336

ACTS OF PAUL
Or *Acts of Paul and Thecla* **1:**15; **3:**1143; **10:**372; **11:**780, 838, 857

ACTS OF THOMAS
8:232; **9:**687

ADAM AND EVE, LIFE OF
See *LIFE OF ADAM AND EVE*

ADAM, APOCALYPSE OF
See *APOCALYPSE OF ADAM*

ADDITIONS TO DANIEL
1:5, 292, 300; **3:**1083, 1176; **4:**563; **7:**64, 72, 113, 126, 153, 155–57, 175

ADDITIONS TO ESTHER
1:8; **3:**943, 945–46, 1083, 1086, 1098, 1114, 1119, 1142, 1159; **5:**634; **11:**233

ADMONITIONS OF IPU-WER
5:6

AESCHYLUS
4:229, 243; **5:**708; **11:**701; **12:**646

AGGADAH
1:66, 68–69, 76–77

AHIKAR (AHIQAR)
SAYINGS OF/WORDS OF **5:**207, 604, 625, 674, 748, 777; STORY OF **1:**233–34, 240–41; **3:**977, 979–82, 996, 1017, 1051, 1068–69, 1118; **5:**1, 6

ALEPPO CODEX
1:296

ALEXANDER POLYHISTOR
1:270; **4:**102

ALPHA TEXT
3:860–61, 894, 929

AMARNA LETTERS
1:247; **2:**637, 1236; **3:**37; **6:**1223

AMBROSE
1:93, 201; **2:**256; **4:**243; **5:**552; **6:**451, 551; **9:**623; **12:**711

AMBROSIASTER
11:252, 603

ANDREW AND MATTHIAS (MATTHEW), ACTS OF
See *ACTS OF ANDREW AND MATTHIAS*

ANIMAL APOCALYPSE
In *1 Enoch* **7:**6–7

ANTIOCHUS SOTER
4:369

APOCALYPSE, ANIMAL
See *ANIMAL APOCALYPSE*

APOCALYPSE OF ABRAHAM
Or *Apoc.-Ab.* **7:**2–3, 6–7, 11–12; **8:**418; **10:**1010; **11:**563, 565, 913; **12:**545, 598

APOCALYPSE OF ADAM
Or *Apoc. Adam* **10:**1010; **11:**390, 400, 913

APOCALYPSE OF BARUCH
Or *Apoc. Bar.* **5:**558; **10:**1010; **11:**913; **12:**527, 632, 636, 709, 746

2 APOCALYPSE OF BARUCH
Or *2 Apoc. Bar.*; *Syriac Apocalypse of Baruch* **11:**203, 296, 304, 345, 374, 582; **12:**328, 356–57, 401, 527, 632, 636, 709

APOCALYPSE OF ELIJAH
7:122

APOCALYPSE OF ENOCH
Or *Enoch Apocalypse* **12:**519, 546, 645

APOCALYPSE OF EZRA
Or *2 Esdras* **1:**314; **7:**122

APOCALYPSE OF JOHN
1:8; **6:**206; **12:**96

APOCALYPSE OF MOSES
Or *Apoc. Mos.* **8:**530; **11:**163, 373, 913

APOCALYPSE OF PAUL
Or *Apoc. Paul* **11:**625

APOCALYPSE OF PETER
1:15; **8:**103; **12:**324

APOCALYPSE OF WEEKS
In *1 Enoch* **7:**6

APOCALYPSE OF ZEPHANIAH
Or *Apoc. Zeph.* **7:**7; **11:**625

APOCRYPHA
1:5, 8, 12–13, 16, 18, 269, 1194; **3:**861, 869, 945, 1075; **5:**1, 635; **6:**929; **7:**340; **8:**95

APOCRYPHA, NEW TESTAMENT
1:5, 20–21; **8:**51, 107; **9:**433

APOCRYPHON OF JEREMIAH
6:942, 994

APOCRYPHON OF JOHN
Or *Ap. John* **11:**384, 414, 438, 451
APOLLODORUS
8:328; **10:**273
APPIAN
4:84, 157, 193, 216, 260
APPU AND HIS TWO SONS
1:241
APULEIUS
8:13, 25, 565; **11:**69
AQHAT
1:233, 240–42; **3:**1091; **4:**328–29, 500; **5:**13; **6:**1213–14, 1388
AQUILA'S VERSION
1:11, 301, 304; **6:**454; **12:**343
ARABIC VERSIONS
1:70–73, 75–76, 1112; **3:**979; **6:**930, 985
ARAMAIC LEVI DOCUMENT
7:846, 862
ARAMAIC TEXTS
1:237, 249; **3:**699, 708, 761, 1017; **5:**94, 332; **6:**1250; **7:**21, 39, 50, 73, 163, 750; **8:**204
ARAMAIC VERSION(S)
2:613, 930; **3:**955, 976; **6:**1016; **7:**72, 653; **8:**6; See also *SYRIAC VERSION(S)*
ARISTEAS, LETTER/EPISTLE OF
See *LETTER OF ARISTEAS*
ARISTOBULUS, LETTER OF
See *LETTER OF ARISTOBULUS*
ARISTOTLE
1:75–76, 142, 1085; **3:**1023; **5:**56, 117, 120, 232, 244, 331, 443, 497–98, 505, 598; **7:**118; **8:**17, 20, 197; **9:**477, 479, 758; **10:**100, 382, 432, 439, 442, 553–54, 587; **11:**189, 303, 333, 420, 435, 446, 557, 559, 653, 658, 688, 744–46; **12:**130, 198, 211, 278
ARMENIAN VERSION
3:979; **4:**206; **6:**930; **8:**6, 395
ARSINOUS
1:15
ARTAPANUS
3:1080; **4:**198
ASCENSION OF ISAIAH
Or *Ascen. Isa.* **5:**853; **11:**105, 383, 913; **12:**58, 144, 545, 592, 722
ASSUMPTION OF MOSES
Or *As. Mos.* **8:**232, 249, 444, 531, 741; **9:**489, 873; **10:**189; **11:**163
ASSYRIAN TEXTS
1:250, 252; **6:**11, 17, 23, 54, 292, 295, 620, 1366, 1435, 1516; **7:**360–61, 804
ASTRONOMICAL BOOK
From *1 Enoch* **7:**5, 11
ASTRONOMICAL DIARIES
4:34
ATHENAEUS
6:1379
ATRAHASIS MYTH
1:232, 246, 341, 388; **5:**1; **6:**1213
AUGUSTINE
1:12–13, 16, 50, 93–96, 126, 128, 140, 193, 196, 200, 1190; **2:**256, 513, 1341–42; **4:**243, 292, 355, 807, 853–54, 1206, 1215, 1252, 1261; **5:**61, 104, 112, 264, 438, 448, 634; **6:**366, 451, 551, 1131; **7:**8, 76, 426, 516, 606; **8:**171, 180, 220, 298, 345, 351, 418; **9:**623, 630, 723, 778, 841, 858; **10:**266, 370, 425, 479, 620, 707, 728, 861, 884; **11:**76, 183, 284, 290, 293, 377, 393, 486; **12:**6, 377, 396, 398, 403, 414, 430, 433, 439, 443, 534, 536, 551, 555, 711–12
AUTHORIZED VERSION
Or King James Version **1:**5; **2:**1387

B

BAAL CYCLE/EPIC/MYTH
1:274; **2:**600; **4:**485, 602, 621; **5:**95; **6:**1434; **7:**654
BABA BATHRA
Or *B. Bat.*; *Baba Batra* **1:**11, 65, 68, 79, 305; **4:**357, 389, 411, 525; **5:**664, 732, 734, 775, 825, 855; **8:**200; **9:**301, 691
BABA METZI'A
1:68; **5:**797; **8:**247
BABA QAMMA
Or *B. Qam.* **1:**68; **5:**808; **9:**302
BABYLONIAN JOB
4:329; **5:**4. See also *I WILL PRAISE THE LORD OF WISDOM*
BABYLONIAN TEXTS
1:262; **3:**1099; **4:**228, 329; **5:**6, 604; **6:**1301, 1366; **7:**792
BABYLONIAN THEODICY
4:329–33, 362, 400, 492; **5:**3, 8, 604
BARAITA
1:11; **8:**197
BARNABAS, EPISTLE OF
See *EPISTLE OF BARNABAS*
BARTHOLOMEW, GOSPEL (QUESTIONS) OF
See *GOSPEL OF BARTHOLOMEW*
2 BARUCH
Or *2 Bar.* **1:**289; **3:**948; **4:**197, 198, 214; **6:**942; **7:**2, 7, 11–12, 14, 122; **8:**38, 129, 235, 252, 263, 324–25, 442, 601, 630, 676, 690; **9:**55, 97, 177, 196, 787; **10:**403, 432, 445, 495, 498, 524, 695; **11:**563, 565, 614, 616, 748, 877; **12:**318, 710
3 BARUCH
Or *3 Bar.* **5:**558; **6:**929; **7:**7, 11, 13; **8:**34

4 BARUCH
Or *4 Bar.* **6:**929, 942
BARUCH, APOCALYPSE OF
See *APOCALYPSE OF BARUCH*
BARUCH, BOOK OF
Or *Bar.* **1:**8, 12, 17–18; **3:**710, 722, 750, 809, 948, 986, 1086, 1113, 1144; **4:**531, 705; **5:**13–15, 90, 95–96, 99, 252, 281, 332–33, 549–50, 623, 634, 647; **6:**3, 10, 468, 560, 561, 563, 564, 572, 731, 761, 769, 775, 820, 838–42, 866, 875–77, 985, 1009, 1016, 1415, 1418, 1609; **7:**3, 121, 125–26, 162, 182, 796; **8:**34, 36, 41, 274; **10:**645–46, 659, 661–63, 718, 917; **11:**798; **12:**449
BASILIDES, GOSPEL OF
See *GOSPEL OF BASILIDES*
BEL AND THE DRAGON
3:1123; **4:**52, 193; **5:**634, 779; **6:**987; **7:**64, 72, 156–57, 175, 185, 187, 193–94; **8:**29, 33
BERAKOT
Or *Ber.* **1:**70; **4:**1261; **8:**201, 247, 379, 393, 637; **9:**177, 211, 419
BEROSSUS
1:388, 411
BEZAE, CODEX
8:5; **9:**29, 419; **10:**17
BLESSINGS (APPENDIX B TO 1QS)
Or 1QSb **11:**372, 563
BODMER PAPYRI
8:8
BOHAIRIC VERSION
1:304; **8:**6
BOOK OF JASHAR
See *JASHAR, BOOK OF*
BOOK OF JUBILEES
See *JUBILEES*
BOOK OF REMEMBRANCE
7:846, 872
BOOK OF THE ACTS OF SOLOMON
3:6; **4:**111
BOOK OF THE ANNALS OF THE KINGS OF ISRAEL
3:6; **6:**2
BOOK OF THE ANNALS OF THE KINGS OF JUDAH
3:6, 113
BOOK OF THE COVENANT (*OR* COVENANT CODE, *ETC.*)
1:37, 76, 286, 860–61, 870, 880, 1115, 1156; **2:**128, 273, 277, 379–80, 386, 420, 493; **3:**285, 646, 747; **4:**881; **5:**12, 14; **6:**962, 968
BOOK OF THE DEAD
1:233; **5:**672
BOOK OF THE LAW
1:9, 37, 39–40, 42, 65, 305; **2:**12, 278, 487, 518, 520–21; **3:**12, 279–80, 284, 645–46, 667, 715–16, 800, 802, 806; **4:**40, 197, 684; **5:**555; **6:**562, 839–40, 1258; **7:**662; **11:**258, 313
BOOK OF THE WARS OF THE LORD/YAHWEH
2:8, 165, 184
BOOK OF THE WATCHERS
7:2, 5–6, 11

C

CALLISTHENES
Or *Pseudo-Callisthenes* **4:**31, 250; **11:**566, 655
CHESTER BEATTY PAPYRI
8:8, 91; **10:**370; **12:**6
CHRYSOSTOM
1:49–50, 94, 193; **3:**932; **4:**243, 355, 929; **8:**13–14, 16, 19–20; **9:**574, 623, 690; **10:**213, 442, 560, 835, 860; **11:**73, 293, 337, 419, 437, 446, 459, 604, 698–99, 768, 892; **12:**189, 203, 223
CICERO
4:297; **5:**510, 546; **8:**13, 23–25, 142, 197; **10:**243; **11:**30, 135, 150, 156, 383, 446, 688, 745–46
CLEMENT
1:89, 93, 192; **3:**1077; **5:**438, 635; **8:**363; **9:**501; **10:**247; **11:**135, 173, 438, 471, 540; **12:**6–8, 10, 67, 69, 168, 171, 449, 475. See also *1 CLEMENT*; *2 CLEMENT*
1 CLEMENT
Or *1 Clem.*; *First Clement* **1:**7, 15, 19; **3:**1114, 1138, 1162; **8:**19, 515, 728; **9:**861; **10:**720, 775; **11:**135, 173, 227, 821; **12:**130, 133–35, 152, 154, 168, 177, 290, 315, 328, 356, 492
2 CLEMENT
Or *2 Clem.* **1:**15; **9:**151; **11:**375; **12:**328, 356, 357
CLEODEMUS MALCHUS
4:143–44, 228
CLEOMENES
4:297
CODE OF HAMMURABI
1:1188; **2:**63, 461, 468, 486; **4:**965; **5:**92, 144, 258, 541; **6:**10, 20–21, 1226, 1463; **9:**148
CODEX ALEXANDRINUS
5:772
CODEX BEZAE
8:5; **9:**29, 419, 874; **10:**17
CODEX EPHRAEMI
Or C; C2 **5:**636; **8:**164
CODEX KORIDETHI
8:8
CODEX SINAITICUS
1:28, 302; **5:**735; **8:**7–8; **9:**874

CODEX VATICANUS
1:299, 302, 304; **3:**377; **5:**719, 778; **8:**8
CODEX WASHINGTONIANUS
8:5, 8
COFFIN TEXTS
1:233; **5:**90
COMMUNITY RULE
See *RULE OF THE COMMUNITY*
COPTIC VERSIONS
1:292, 304; **6:**930, 985; **8:**5–6, 341, 368–69, 490; **11:**625
CORINTHIANS, THIRD EPISTLE TO THE
1:14
CORPUS HERMETICUM
11:69, 567, 599, 410
COUNSELS OF SHUBE'AWILIM
5:6
COUNSELS TO A PRINCE
5:604
COVERDALE'S VERSION
8:202
CYPRIAN
5:635; **8:**7, 205; **9:**831
CYRIL OF ALEXANDRIA
9:737, 752, 787, 858
CYRUS CYLINDER
1:267; **3:**678, 680, 710; **6:**394, 406; **7:**29, 62, 81, 187, 709

D

DAMASCUS DOCUMENT
Or CD **1:**10, 285–86, 289; **4:**8, 46, 72, 205, 501; **6:**934, 949; **7:**426, 867; **8:**31, 33–34, 39, 193, 277, 532, 544, 643; **9:**284; **10:**470, 524; **11:**105, 373, 399, 421–22, 429–30, 451, 461, 850; **12:**395, 413, 488
DANEL
1:230, 233, 242, 273; **6:**1213–14
DANIEL, ADDITIONS TO
See *ADDITIONS TO DANIEL*
DEAD SEA SCROLLS
Or DSS **1:**4, 6, 12, 18, 24–25, 27–29, 286–91, 293–95, 298–99, 302–3, 1194; **2:**1053; **3:**1075; **4:**6, 325, 379, 559; **5:**271, 332; **6:**223, 331, 942, 949, 961, 1010; **7:**14, 21, 50, 53, 72–73, 105, 112, 115, 667; **8:**27, 178; **9:**117, 309; **10:**460, 660, 850, 931; **11:**238, 332, 374; **12:**368, 395, 428, 546, 665, 705. *See also* QUMRAN SCROLLS; QUMRAN, KHIRBET *in PLACES IN THE BIBLE* and *PLACES OUTSIDE THE BIBLE*
DEMETRIUS OF PHALERUM
10:784
DIADORUS SICULUS
1:269
DIALOGUE OF A MASTER AND HIS SLAVE
5:604–5
DIALOGUE OF PESSIMISM
5:45, 207, 252
DIATESSARON
Of Tatian **1:**47; **8:**5–6, 240
DIDACHE
1:19, 315; **4:**586; **5:**635; **8:**13, 103–6, 212, 220–21, 257, 264; **9:**130, 194, 201, 278, 342, 792; **11:**811–12; **12:**162, 369, 413, 454, 531, 573, 575, 734
DIO CASSIUS
8:214; **11:**458; **12:**514, 684
DIOGNETUS, LETTER/EPISTLE TO
7:129; **11:**163
DIONYSIUS
4:266; **5:**740; **9:**80, 366; **10:**247; **11:**653; **12:**297, 366, 514, 545, 562, 711
DIOSCORIDES
4:197; **5:**642
DISPUTE BETWEEN A MAN AND HIS BA
5:8
DOCTRINA CHRISTIANA
Of Augustine **1:**193; **5:**104, 448
DOCTRINA SAPIENTIA
5:686
DOOMED PRINCE, THE
1:241

E

EBIONITES, GOSPEL OF THE
See *GOSPEL OF THE EBIONITES*
ECCLESIASTICUS
1:10; **5:**275, 603, 606; **6:**931, 934. *See also* SIRACH
EGERTON PAPYRUS
See PAPYRUS EGERTON
EGYPTIAN TEXTS
1:231, 246–47; **4:**689; **5:**368–69, 372, 405, 607, 625, 680, 731; **6:**1260; **7:**670
EGYPTIAN VERSIONS
5:493
ELEPHANTINE PAPYRI
1:234, 250, 267–68, 285; **2:**413, 935; **3:**708, 710, 726, 733, 741, 747, 751, 757, 780, 833–34, 871, 897, 899, 951, 977, 979, 1017, 1040, 1118; **4:**555; **5:**643; **6:**181, 546, 1408; **7:**28, 125, 792, 860, 866; **8:**34
ELIJAH, APOCALYPSE OF
See *APOCALYPSE OF ELIJAH*
1 ENOCH
1:8; **3:**1038, 1057; **4:**6, 8, 33, 47, 197, 205, 241, 281, 488, 516, 570, 591, 604, 618; **5:**15, 430, 757,

833; **6:**223, 930, 966; **7:**2–3, 5–7, 11, 13–14, 23, 73, 101, 103, 113, 115, 128, 146, 148, 150, 429; **8:**29–30, 33–34, 36–41, 95, 232, 235, 258–59, 286, 296, 343, 363, 391, 418, 541, 572, 622, 630, 676, 690, 704, 713; **9:**18, 47–48, 125, 196, 200, 255–56, 317, 458; **10:**43, 692, 854; **11:**203, 259, 288, 296, 304, 345, 383, 460, 565–66, 582, 598, 614–15, 625, 726, 749, 759, 779, 823; **12:**36, 58, 82, 294, 329, 347, 356–57, 386, 388, 394, 474, 476, 478, 480, 485, 488, 492–94, 514, 521, 523, 546, 560, 571, 592, 597, 601, 603–4, 631, 645–46, 672, 702, 704, 715, 724, 726, 732. *See also* ENOCH, BOOK OF

2 ENOCH
Or *Slavonic Enoch* **1:**380, 384; **5:**252; **7:**7; **8:**36, 137, 214, 216, 363; **9:**458; **11:**163, 373, 383, 563–64, 566, 598, 625; **12:**40, 133, 726

ENOCH, BOOK OF
1:5, 288–89, 326, 379, 1112; **5:**465, 725; **6:**213; **7:**13–14; **8:**20, 152; **9:**316, 620, 660, 741; **12:**146, 159, 520, 704. See also *1 ENOCH*

ENOCH, EPISTLE OF
See *EPISTLE OF ENOCH*

ENOCH, ETHIOPIC
See ENOCH, BOOK OF

ENOCH, SIMILITUDES OF
See *SIMILITUDES OF ENOCH*

ENOCH, SLAVONIC
See *2 ENOCH*

ENUMA ELISH
1:232, 341; **2:**600; **4:**296, 395, 532, 597, 602, 622, 624; **6:**1537, 1579; **7:**101, 193, 654

EPHRAEMI SYRI, CODEX
Or C; C2 **5:**636

EPIC OF KIRTA
1:273; **6:**1398

EPICTETUS
4:16; **5:**546; **7:**169; **8:**18–21, 610; **10:**432, 437, 553–54, 587, 705, 929; **11:**31, 322, 437, 695, 698, 700, 768; **12:**68, 189, 199

EPIPHANIUS
8:100, 318; **12:**710

EPISTLE OF ARISTEAS
See *LETTER OF ARISTEAS*

EPISTLE OF BARNABAS
1:89, 93; **5:**635, 675; **9:**861; **12:**69, 386

EPISTLE OF BARUCH
11:582

EPISTLE OF ENOCH
7:13; **11:**582

EPISTLE OF JEREMIAH
See JEREMIAH, LETTER OF

EPISTLE OF JEREMY
See JEREMY, EPISTLE OF

EPISTLE TO DIOGNETUS
7:129; **11:**163

EPISTLE/LETTER TO THE LAODICEANS
Or *Ep. Lao.* **1:**14–15, 19; **11:**668; **12:**588

EPISTLES OF IGNATIUS
See IGNATIUS, EPISTLES OF

ERRA EPIC
4:412; **6:**1185, 1296, 1422, 1537–38

ERUBIN
5:689, 767, 772; **6:**1148; **8:**197

1 ESDRAS
Or *1 Esdr.* **3:**679, 684–85, 687–88, 691–92, 694, 704, 709, 712, 715–16, 720, 725, 733, 742, 745–46, 755, 796, 800, 817, 878; **4:**99; **5:**629, 642, 687–88, 730, 784; **7:**21, 53, 111, 161, 731; **11:**718

2 ESDRAS
Or *2 Esdr.* **1:**8, 25, 314, 343, 367; **4:**618; **5:**70, 93, 220, 252, 341, 349, 430, 611, 628, 634–35, 833; **7:**11, 44, 54, 103; **8:**34, 577, 713; **9:**489, 620; **10:**854; **11:**203, 304, 409, 437, 724; **12:**524, 546, 635. See also *4 EZRA*

ESTHER, ADDITIONS TO
See *ADDITIONS TO ESTHER*

ETHIOPIC ENOCH
See ENOCH, BOOK OF

ETHIOPIC VERSION
1:304

EUPOLEMUS
Includes Pseudo-Eupolemus **1:**270; **4:**102, 116, 198–99, 217–18, 298; **5:**626

EURIPIDES
4:16; **8:**16; **10:**104, 273; **12:**198, 410

EXEGESIS OF THE SOUL
11:450

1 EZRA
7:436

3 EZRA
See *1 ESDRAS*

4 EZRA
1:11, 289; **4:**199; **6:**975; **7:**3, 7–8, 11–12, 14, 752; **8:**252, 258, 303, 324, 360, 363, 442–43, 573, 601, 622, 687; **9:**91, 196, 200, 252, 278, 318; **10:**400, 402–3, 524, 563, 622–23, 659, 661; **11:**271, 296, 335, 345, 374, 563, 566, 614–15, 759; **12:**318, 336, 343, 357, 401, 503, 504–5, 520, 523–28, 567, 603, 629, 635, 639, 646, 665, 693, 700, 702–4, 710, 723. See also *2 ESDRAS*

EZRA, APOCALYPSE OF
See *APOCALYPSE OF EZRA*

F

FLAVIUS JOSEPHUS
Or Josephus **1:**8, 10–12, 38, 44–45, 248, 253, 270, 285–88, 290–91, 296, 300, 305, 412, 1112,

FLAVIUS JOSEPHUS *(continued)*
1157, 1159, 1171, 1181; **2:**89, 950, 1006, 1012, 1026, 1053, 1070, 1148, 1336; **3:**17, 45, 86, 116, 192, 201, 204, 212, 228, 245, 512, 530, 573, 678, 679, 742, 756–57, 759, 788, 832–33, 849, 861, 866–67, 878, 882, 884, 888, 891, 894–95, 898, 904, 908, 913–14, 919, 945, 950–51, 955, 959, 966–67, 994, 996, 1002, 1040, 1080, 1114; **4:**6, 8, 13, 22, 30, 34, 47, 56, 74, 78, 89, 91–92, 98, 102, 105, 110–11, 116, 125, 132–33, 135, 137–38, 140, 143, 169, 174, 176–78, 188–89, 192, 202, 205–7, 210–11, 216, 219, 222–23, 228–29, 232–33, 240–41, 248, 254–55, 269, 281–82, 285, 292, 1131; **5:**160, 334, 339, 503, 511, 524–26, 553, 567, 578, 612, 642, 643, 555, 859; **6:**942, 952, 1348, 1361, 1398; **7:**25, 30, 33, 40, 55, 64, 83, 88, 128, 141, 270; **8:**23, 33, 35, 38, 135, 156, 193, 286, 319, 321, 343, 363, 371, 406, 417, 421, 442, 468, 478, 482, 491, 516, 519, 526, 531–32, 595, 597–98, 630, 659, 663, 668, 675–76, 682, 684–85, 690, 696–97, 710, 712, 717–20, 724–25, 729; **9:**9, 15, 39, 47, 62, 76, 85, 88, 93, 116, 122, 215, 242, 270, 281, 308, 333, 362–63, 366–67, 372–73, 388, 395–96, 398–400, 404–5, 448, 451, 460, 542, 565, 586, 634, 676, 696–98, 700, 802, 806, 815–16, 818, 831; **10:**44, 66, 78, 90, 97, 105, 107, 114, 122, 124, 150, 165, 174, 178, 181, 268, 298, 306, 310, 322, 325, 333, 447, 665, 718–19, 979; **11:**22, 157, 163, 224, 231–32, 235, 269, 283, 320, 364, 374, 396–99, 411, 422, 490, 564, 582, 631, 644, 652–53, 655, 688, 703, 736, 759; **12:**141, 182, 278, 328, 348, 405, 407, 418, 489, 491, 673, 680, 694, 723

FLORILEGIUM
Or 4QFlor **7:**426; **8:**656; **10:**676; **12:**702

G

GENESIS APOCRYPHON
1:10; **3:**886, 978, 1007, 1151

GENEVA BIBLE
12:537–39, 549, 713

GEORGIAN VERSION
8:6

GEZER CALENDAR
5:185

GILGAMESH EPIC
1:231–32, 236, 242, 246, 323, 350, 388, 391; **2:**126–27; **4:**351, 420, 443, 518, 568, 603, 618; **5:**1, 4, 13, 252, 274, 605; **6:**1444; **7:**74; **8:**328

GITTIN
Or *B. Git*; *M. Git*; *T. Git.* **3:**996; **8:**191; **9:**229

GOSPEL OF BARTHOLOMEW
8:106

GOSPEL OF BASILIDES
8:491

GOSPEL OF PETER
Or *Gos. Pet.* **8:**82, 444, 491, 497, 505; **9:**263, 468, 822

GOSPEL OF PHILIP
Or *Gos. Phil.* **8:**72, 106, 450–51; **11:**643, 845

GOSPEL OF THE EBIONITES
1:14, 47

GOSPEL OF THE HEBREWS
1:15; **8:**72; **12:**104, 110, 565

GOSPEL OF THE NAZARENES
8:160, 204, 453, 724

GOSPEL OF THOMAS
Or *Gos. Thom.* **1:**14, 18–19, 48; **5:**15; **8:**72, 82–83, 106–7, 147, 200, 305, 309, 313, 376, 416–18, 555, 564, 568, 573, 575, 577, 626, 665, 670; **9:**11, 150–51, 176, 263, 266, 275–76, 289–90, 296, 380, 385, 452, 498, 574, 742; **10:**661; **11:**643; **12:**53, 69

GOSPEL OF TRUTH
Or *Gos. Truth* **8:**72; **11:**384, 600, 626; **12:**69

GOTHIC VERSION
8:6–7

GREEK VERSION(S)
1:5, 46; **3:**3, 61, 862, 866, 886, 923, 945, 949, 959, 969–71; **4:**22; **5:**448, 479, 765; **6:**180, 654, 696, 826, 839, 930–31, 968; **7:**27, 62, 74, 83, 88, 149, 155–56, 174; **10:**64; **11:**72, 512; **12:**230, 233, 518

H

HABAKKUK COMMENTARY/PESHER
Or 1QpHab **4:**30; **8:**38; **9:**178, 642; **10:**676, 854; **11:**374, 397, 421; **12:**356, 369

HAGIGAH
6:1131; **12:**520, 596

HAGIOGRAPHA
1:45, 65, 70–72

HALAKAH/HALAKHAH
1:68–69, 288; **5:**609–10; **8:**183, 278, 334, 346, 386; **10:**89, 122, 131, 206, 208, 213, 218–20, 254, 538; **11:**701, 816

HALAKHIC LETTER
Or 4QMMT **1:**286; **4:**8; **10:**453, 466, 487, 493, 622–23, 645–46, 660–62; **11:**239, 399

HAMMURABI, CODE OF
See CODE OF HAMMURABI

HEBREWS, GOSPEL OF
See *GOSPEL OF THE HEBREWS*

HECATAEUS OF ABDERA
1:270; **4:**6–7, 12, 144, 228, 241

HERACLEON
9:498, 504, 506

HERACLITUS
5:550; **8:**20
HERMAS, SHEPHERD OF
See SHEPHERD OF HERMAS
HERMOGENES
10:442; **11:**838
HERODIAN
10:273
HERODOTUS
1:267, 313, 1071; **2:**668; **3:**22, 722, 755, 780, 878–79, 882–83, 885, 892, 904, 908, 911, 913–14, 920, 1099, 1102, 1106; **4:**89, 144, 204, 218, 223, 229, 254, 263; **5:**642, 708, 853; **6:**295, 995, 1003, 1360, 1389, 1404, 1444, 1515; **7:**44, 61, 65, 73, 81–83, 88, 138, 187, 203, 771, 779; **10:**124; **11:**138
HESIOD
1:88; **4:**192, 263, 604; **5:**78; **7:**54; **8:**216
HEXAPLA
1:90, 301, 303; **6:**985
HIPPOCRATES
1:1085; **5:**642; **8:**390; **12:**398
HIPPOLYTUS
1:210; **7:**61; **9:**623; **11:**631, 643; **12:**522, 532, 711
HITTITE TEXTS
1:228, 232–33, 238, 241, 276, 1019; **6:**1250, 1257, 1398; **9:**388
HURRIAN TEXTS
1:228, 232, 241
HYMN TO THE ATON
4:602

I

IBN EZRA, ABRAHAM
1:73, 76–77, 308, 1010; **3:**940; **4:**394, 413, 518; **5:**327; **7:**406
IGNATIUS, EPISTLES OF
11:213, 838; **12:**278, 373, 454, 575, 582. See also *LETTER TO POLYCARP* and individual letters to the Ephesians, Magnesians, Philadelphians, and Smyrnaeans
ILIAD, THE
2:1109; **3:**801; **4:**18, 263, 296; **5:**624, 681; **6:**1376
INFANCY GOSPEL OF THOMAS
8:147; **9:**11, 76
INFANCY GOSPELS
8:147, 529; **9:**11, 76
INSINGER PAPYRUS
See PAPYRUS INSINGER
INSTRUCTION FOR DUAUF
See *TEACHING FOR DUAUF*
INSTRUCTION OF AMENEMOPE
1:240; **5:**24, 143, 201, 205, 275, 604, 683, 783; **7:**826
INSTRUCTION OF ANI
5:206–7, 275, 604, 606
INSTRUCTION OF ANKHSHESHANKY
5:604, 606, 708, 740, 768
INSTRUCTION OF PRINCE HARDJEDEF
5:4
INSTRUCTION OF PTAH-HOTEP
5:604
INSTRUCTIONS OF SURUPPAK
5:3, 654
IRENAEUS
1:7, 47–48, 50, 91, 93, 192–93, 368; **5:**438; **6:**551, 1131; **8:**7, 16, 286; **9:**5, 498, 504; **10:**51, 144; **11:**211, 775, 859; **12:**515, 532, 534, 659, 684, 710
ISAIAH, MARTYRDOM OF
See *MARTYRDOM OF ISAIAH*
I WILL PRAISE THE LORD OF WISDOM
4:329; **5:**4, 6, 252, 604

J

JAMES, PROTEVANGELIUM OF
See *PROTEVANGELIUM OF JAMES*
JANNES AND JAMBRES
11:849–52
JASHAR, BOOK OF
2:1205
JEREMIAH, APOCRYPHON OF
See *APOCRYPHON OF JEREMIAH*
JEREMIAH, EPISTLE OF
See JEREMIAH, LETTER OF
JEREMIAH, LETTER OF
1:294; **3:**1123; **4:**198; **5:**634–35, 779; **6:**1, 929, 983, 985–91, 993–1010; **7:**190; **11:**582
JEREMIAH, PARALEIPOMENA OF
4:214; **6:**929, 942
JEREMY, EPISTLE OF
6:986, 988–89
JEROME
1:5, 12–13, 15, 51, 68, 93–95, 99, 131, 193, 200, 301, 303–4, 1190; **2:**950; **3:**663, 679, 976–77, 1080, 1133; **4:**39, 691, 763, 802, 996; **5:**1, 20, 294, 350, 438, 448, 606, 634–35; **7:**376, 407, 436, 523; **8:**6, 19, 72, 100, 318; **9:**623; **11:**266; **12:**6, 532, 537
JESUS, WISDOM OF
See SIRACH
JOHN, ACTS OF
See *ACTS OF JOHN*
JOHN, APOCRYPHON OF
See *APOCRYPHON OF JOHN*
JONATHAN
See TARGUM: TARGUM JONATHAN

JOSEPH AND ASENETH
3:1081, 1086–87, 1114, 1141–43, 1150, 1159; **8:**33, 37, 666; **11:**233; **12:**518, 599
JOSEPH, PRAYER OF
See *PRAYER OF JOSEPH*
JOSEPHUS, FLAVIUS
See FLAVIUS JOSEPHUS
JUBILEES
Or *Jub.* **1:**8, 10, 380, 384, 1085, 1171; **3:**951, 1016, 1132, 1143; **4:**8, 19, 30, 33, 47, 50, 74; **5:**590; **6:**223, 934, 987; **7:**14, 40, 128, 137, 846, 861; **8:**29–33, 36–39, 41, 137, 232, 286, 296, 556, 570, 641, 687, 697, 713; **9:**84, 133, 177, 646, 737, 787; **10:**54, 495–96; **11:**105, 233, 271, 288, 300–301, 345, 397, 460, 566, 658; **12:**33, 53, 347, 410, 489, 504, 571, 636, 721
JUDITH, BOOK OF
Or *Jdt.* **1:**8, 12, 17–18, 28, 286; **2:**935; **3:**856, 859, 866, 870–72, 882–83, 889, 918, 920, 947, 951, 960, 962, 966, 978, 985, 1008; **4:**47–48, 52, 57, 64, 96, 101, 177, 193, 254, 297, 1208; **5:**119, 326, 562, 630, 634–35, 648, 809, 833, 838; **6:**943, 965; **7:**40–41, 53–54, 62, 81, 122, 125, 160, 177, 179, 181–82, 188, 513; **8:**29, 598, 640; **9:**55, 72, 224; **10:**653; **11:**233, 460, 708; **12:**138
JUSTIN MARTYR
1:11, 87–88, 91–93, 192; **4:**60, 127, 157, 193; **6:**451, 551, 1131; **8:**17, 21, 100, 153, 286, 305, 438; **9:**385, 433, 617, 623, 636, 822; **10:**763; **11:**381, 812, 878; **12:**513, 531, 710
JUVENAL
1:291; **8:**13, 17, 24

K

KERET
See *KIRTU*
KETUBOT
Or *Ketub.* **9:**586, 633
KIRTU
Or *Keret*; *Kirta* **1:**233, 239, 241–42, 273, 1018, 1023; **2:**586, 613; **3:**17; **4:**470, 500; **5:**77; **6:**1398

L

LACTANTIUS
12:711
LATIN VERSIONS, OLD
See OLD LATIN VERSIONS
LENINGRAD CODEX
1:296
LETTER OF ARISTEAS
Or *Ep. Aris.*; *Epistle of Aristeas* **1:**11, 1077; **4:**125, 199, 241; **5:**439, 545, 642; **6:**961, 1415; **7:**44, 155; **8:**37, 41, 42, 214, 607; **9:**219, 476; **10:**432; **11:**233, 242, 269, 399, 428–29, 450
LETTER OF JEREMIAH
See JEREMIAH, LETTER OF
LETTER OF/TO ARISTOBULUS
4:185, 192
LETTER TO POLYCARP
Or Ign. *Pol.* **10:**745; **11:**824; **12:**278
LETTER TO THE EPHESIANS
Or Ign. *Eph.* **8:**103; **9:**151; **12:**356, 475, 629
LETTER TO THE LAODICEANS
See *EPISTLE/LETTER TO THE LAODICEANS*
LETTER TO THE MAGNESIANS
Or Ign. *Magn.* **8:**181; **11:**829; **12:**562, 573
LETTER TO THE PHILADELPHIANS
Or Ign. *Phld.* **10:**737; **12:**573, 588
LETTER TO THE PHILIPPIANS
Or Pol. *Phil* **10:**737; **11:**472, 522, 824; **12:**229, 368, 403
LETTER TO THE SMYRNAEANS/SMYRNEANS
Or Ign. *Smyrn.* **9:**486; **11:**821, 829; **12:**123
LETTERS OF IGNATIUS
See EPISTLES OF IGNATIUS
LEVI DOCUMENT, ARAMAIC
See ARAMAIC LEVI DOCUMENT
LEVI, TESTAMENT OF
See *TESTAMENT OF LEVI*
LIFE OF ADAM AND EVE
5:464, 523; **10:**470
LIVES OF THE PROPHETS
4:198; **7:**853; **8:**436
LUCIAN
1:94, 300, 301; **4:**202; **5:**461; **8:**13, 18–19, 23, 247; **9:**63; **11:**294, 429, 806; **12:**199
LUCRETIUS
5:567, 584; **10:**987; **12:**347

M

1 MACCABEES
Or *1 Macc.* **1:**10, 17, 44, 286; **2:**192, 1005; **3:**691, 710, 718, 756–57, 819, 831, 856, 936, 1078, 1107, 1112–14, 1117–18, 1132, 1154, 1167, 1171; **4:**181–85, 189–90, 193, 198–99, 206, 212, 216–18, 222–23, 226–30, 232–33, 236, 242, 247–49, 253–55, 257, 260–67, 269–70, 275–77, 280–83, 285–89, 291, 295–98, 369, 972–73, 994; **5:**262, 523, 527, 611, 619, 673, 838; **6:**942; **7:**25–26, 32, 102–3, 114, 124, 128, 143, 147, 182, 456; **8:**29, 32, 35, 37–38, 246, 403, 405, 556, 663, 690; **9:**15, 303, 675, 707; **10:**50, 205, 653, 718, 746; **11:**214, 798, 812, 815, 858, 866; **12:**135, 138, 154, 164, 403, 521, 726
2 MACCABEES
Or *2 Macc.* **1:**8, 10–12, 17–18, 28, 269, 270, 356; **2:**588; **3:**757, 802, 842, 935–36, 953, 1004, 1008, 1078, 1080, 1112–13, 1123, 1129, 1132,

1138, 1155, 1158, 1167, 1170, 1174, 1179; **4:**3, 7–12, 16–19, 21, 33–34, 36, 39–40, 42, 46–47, 52, 55–56, 60, 62–64, 68–69, 72, 74, 78, 80–81, 84–86, 88–89, 91–94, 98, 100–101, 105–6, 122, 141, 150–51, 154, 165, 795; **5:**446, 462, 469, 497, 611, 612, 626, 634, 658, 673, 693, 784, 806, 809, 843, 859; **6:**988; **7:**40, 66, 103, 124, 180–81, 183; **8:**29–30, 34–38, 246, 264, 403, 405, 443, 556, 658, 663, 730; **9:**317, 389, 399, 468, 480, 675, 707; **10:**50, 90, 181, 310, 474–75, 563, 614, 639, 677, 691, 713, 725; **11:**204, 213, 338, 458, 582, 598, 644, 703, 708, 755, 795, 829, 871; **12:**144, 152, 160, 387, 485, 621

3 MACCABEES
Or *3 Macc.* **1:**8, 1135; **3:**900, 953, 967, 971, 1080, 1113, 1129, 1170, 1174; **4:**34, 209, 211, 282, 286; **7:**51, 53–54, 102, 140, 143, 179–80, 188; **8:**666; **9:**224, 234, 331; **10:**191; **11:**271, 535, 708; **12:**403, 488

4 MACCABEES
Or *4 Macc.* **1:**8, 12, 44; **2:**200; **4:**236, 243, 292; **5:**469, 497, 510; **7:**178, 180, 183, 188; **8:**29, 32, 34, 37, 41, 95, 264, 488; **9:**201, 388–89, 433; **10:**467, 475, 562; **11:**213–14, 243, 564, 718; **12:**138, 148, 151, 336, 376

MAIMONIDES
1:75–76, 992, 1075; **6:**1141

MAN AND HIS GOD
5:329

MANASSEH, PRAYER OF
1:8, 12; **3:**809, 1086; **4:**85, 503, 568; **5:**634–35; **8:**34

MANUAL OF DISCIPLINE
1:10; **3:**1158; **5:**690. *See also* 1QS

MARCION, GOSPEL OF
1:47, 192; **9:**21

MARI LETTERS
2:614, 630–31

MARK, SECRET GOSPEL OF
See *SECRET GOSPEL OF MARK*

MARTYRDOM OF ISAIAH
5:853; **8:**29, 348, 398; **9:**433

MARTYRDOM OF POLYCARP
4:243; **9:**433; **11:**403

MASORETIC TEXT
1:27, 79, 103, 292, 296; **2:**3, 738, 914, 950, 1012, 1079; **3:**307, 494, 766, 860, 894, 918, 929; **5:**300; **6:**561, 564, 567–68, 626, 878, 1016, 1048, 1092, 1373, 1384, 1467; **7:**72, 375, 437, 442, 456, 596, 667, 864; **8:**29, 147; **9:**227; MT **1:**28, 30, 292–93, 295–99, 301–3, 308, 863, 1011, 1028, 1032, 1034, 1039, 1043, 1080; **2:**61, 96, 139, 192, 207, 228, 487, 576, 594, 608, 613–14, 636, 655, 658, 678, 687, 697, 738, 973–74, 979, 981, 1006, 1012, 1069, 1109–10, 1122, 1153, 1370; **3:**318, 330, 332, 336, 347, 368, 378, 386, 389, 394, 401–2, 406, 415–16, 421, 424, 425, 446, 451–52, 484–85, 496, 500, 506, 510, 516, 524–25, 530, 538, 556, 559–60, 564, 570, 575, 581, 598, 600, 619, 624, 628, 644, 646–47, 679, 695, 708, 712, 717, 720, 728, 730, 740, 746, 751, 766, 768–69, 774, 794, 796, 838, 848, 860–62, 866, 871, 886, 904, 913, 918, 921–22, 928–29, 932, 945–46, 948–51, 953–59, 962–63, 966–67, 969–72, 1098, 1119; **4:**77, 402, 440, 451, 452, 497, 508–9, 531, 658; **5:**133, 144, 157, 182, 186, 204, 206, 409, 428; **6:**17, 331, 336, 343, 356, 379, 387, 390, 400, 405, 567–68, 1016, 1093, 1110, 1116, 1122, 1128, 1133, 1145–46, 1151, 1161, 1174, 1177, 1182, 1194, 1232, 1238, 1251, 1261, 1263, 1269, 1272–73, 1312, 1337, 1366, 1374–75, 1378–79, 1382, 1389, 1391, 1393–94, 1415, 1417–18, 1422, 1425, 1427–29, 1434–35, 1439–40, 1443–44, 1454, 1459, 1463, 1467–68, 1473, 1476, 1478–79, 1485, 1487, 1504–5, 1508–9, 1519–20, 1523, 1525–26, 1530, 1540, 1546–49, 1551–52, 1554–55, 1557–58, 1560, 1570, 1581–84, 1591, 1596, 1601, 1604–5; **7:**92, 218–19, 225, 230–31, 237–40, 242, 247, 249, 252–53, 255–58, 260–61, 266, 270, 272, 275, 277–78, 284, 288–89, 296, 352, 357, 362, 386, 403, 406, 414, 427–28, 602, 605–6, 609, 667, 690, 724, 771, 779, 788, 792, 815, 821–22, 824, 828, 832, 839; **8:**160, 281, 333, 349, 375, 390, 403, 474, 673; **9:**163, 543, 834; **10:**218–19, 668, 692, 725, 745; **11:**241, 258; **12:**265, 328

MATTHEW'S BIBLE
8:119, 125–26

MATTHIAS (MATTHEW), ACTS OF ANDREW AND
See *ACTS OF ANDREW AND MATTHIAS*

MAXIMUS OF TYRE
11:700, 768

MEGILLA
1:67, 70; **3:**856, 882, 886, 915, 996; **6:**942, 1240

MEKILTA/MEKHILTA
1:69; **4:**233–34; **7:**57

MELCHIZEDEK TEXT
Or 11QMelch **8:**36, 680; **12:**85

MELITO OF SARDIS
1:93, 192; **5:**273; **9:**504; **11:**364; **12:**513

MEMPHITIC VERSION
See BOHAIRIC VERSION

MENAHOT
Or *Menah.* **2:**3; **5:**745; **8:**201

MENANDER
5:479; **6:**1398; **8:**16–17; **10:**983; **11:**656

MERNEPTAH INSCRIPTION
1:249, 251–53, 258, 558
MESHA STELE
See MOABITE STONE
MIDRASH
Or Midrashim **1:**66, 68–71, 74–76, 79, 438; **3:**45–46, 332; **4:**241, 659; **5:**99, 102, 305, 405, 441, 443, 523, 528–29, 532, 534, 622, 689, 720, 729; **6:**1052; **7:**50, 175, 192, 467, 472–74, 528; **8:**31, 94, 109, 359; **9:**600, 636, 678, 757; **10:**16, 62, 65–66, 68, 79, 91–92, 123, 127, 191, 193, 220, 375, 381, 506; **11:**63, 262; **12:**30, 49, 89, 114, 152
MINUSCULES
1:302; **8:**4–5, 7, 91, 164, 205, 743; **9:**874
MISHNA
8:702
MOABITE STONE
Or Mesha Stele **1:**1189; **2:**182, 248; **3:**123; **4:**46; **6:**1348, 1353, 1489; **7:**362–63
MO'ED QATAN
Or *MO'ED QAT.* **9:**691
MOSES, ASSUMPTION OF
See *ASSUMPTION OF MOSES*
MOSES, TESTAMENT OF
See *TESTAMENT OF MOSES*
MURATORIAN CANON
1:15; **5:**438; **9:**6, 504; **10:**370
MURATORIAN FRAGMENT
1:15; **9:**6; **11:**775, 883
MUSONIUS RUFUS
10:929

N

NACHMANIDES
1:77, 81, 992; **2:**833
NAG HAMMADI TEXTS
1:14, 18, 20–21; **8:**36, 72, 82, 103; **9:**498, 517; **11:**384, 568; **12:**418, 520, 649
NAHUM PESHER
Or 4QpNah **8:**39; **11:**260
NAZARENES, GOSPEL OF THE
See *GOSPEL OF THE NAZARENES*
NAZIR
9:229; **10:**258
NEDARIM
Or *Ned.* **8:**606; **9:**619; **11:**252
NEOFITI
Or *Tg. Neof.*; *Targum Neofiti. See* TARGUM: NEOFITI

O

ODES OF SOLOMON
5:272, 849; **8:**274; **9:**517; **11:**599; **12:**430, 705
ODYSSEY, THE
2:612, 668; **3:**801; **4:**263, 296, 470; **5:**13; **8:**328; **9:**722; **10:**345; **11:**701
OLD GREEK VERSIONS
Or OG **1:**300–304; **2:**1109; **7:**72, 83–84, 91, 156, 180
OLD LATIN VERSIONS
Or OL **1:**200, 302–4, 1194; **2:**1386; **3:**630, 861–62, 902, 937, 949, 950, 959, 962, 976, 994, 1003, 1008, 1014, 1016–17, 1031, 1041–42, 1045, 1049–50, 1055–56, 1064–65, 1068, 1070, 1191; **4:**1285; **5:**114, 636, 873; **6:**985, 1069, 1487; **7:**275, 277, 885; **8:**6–7, 130, 205, 240, 365, 743; **9:**418, 452, 470, 873; **10:**1009; **11:**452, 913; **12:**746
ONKELOS (ONQELOS)
Or *Tg. Onq.*; *Targum Onkelos. See* TARGUM: ONKELOS/ONQELOS
ORACLES, SIBYLLINE
See *SIBYLLINE ORACLES*
ORIGEN
1:12, 37, 49–50, 68, 88–94, 96, 121, 128, 131, 192–93, 301–3, 1112; **2:**833; **3:**663; **4:**23, 242; **5:**438, 552, 636; **6:**551; **8:**7, 21, 100, 103, 231, 345, 363, 437, 486; **9:**40, 186, 205, 348, 504, 574, 623, 641, 697, 723, 752; **10:**683; **11:**604, 850; **12:**6, 69, 177, 197, 366, 475, 532, 534, 565, 571, 711
OSTRACA OF SAMARIA
1:224, 249; **2:**683, 688; **3:**52
OVID
10:199, 404, 553
OXYRHYNCHUS PAPYRI
Or *POxy* **5:**503; **8:**8; **9:**74, 150–51, 574; **11:**453

P

PAPIAS
8:76, 483, 517–18; **9:**5; **12:**366, 513, 533, 710
PAPYRUS/PAPYRI
1:234, 250, 267, 293–94, 300, 302, 314; **3:**833, 951, 1017, 1022; **4:**202; **5:**808; **6:**181, 941, 1144, 1398, 1416, 1487; **7:**28, 112, 124–25, 866; **8:**4–5, 8–10, 91, 204, 345, 417, 564; **9:**74, 150–51, 234, 316, 385, 504, 574; **10:**370, 380, 800, 875, 877; **11:**415, 563; **12:**6, 9, 245, 260, 448, 455, 638
PAPYRUS ANASTASI I
6:1398
PAPYRUS EGERTON
Or P. Egerton **9:**151, 385
PAPYRUS INSINGER
5:4, 207, 220, 604, 606, 625, 682, 708, 731, 792
PARALEIPOMENA OF JEREMIAH
See JEREMIAH, PARALEIPOMENA OF

PAUL AND THECLA, ACTS OF
See *ACTS OF PAUL*
PAUL, ACTS OF
See *ACTS OF PAUL*
PAUSANIUS
8:248
PEDAMUS
5:642
PENTATEUCH, SAMARITAN
See SAMARITAN PENTATEUCH
PESAHIM
Or *Pesa.* **8:**468, 658; **9:**418, 823
PESHITTA
1:303, 1147; **4:**512; **5:**636, 779; **8:**6
PETER, APOCALYPSE OF
See *APOCALYPSE OF PETER*
PETER, GOSPEL OF
See *GOSPEL OF PETER*
PETRONIUS
3:1017
PHILIP, GOSPEL OF
See *GOSPEL OF PHILIP*
PHILO
1:12, 49, 88, 93, 128, 192, 285, 287, 290–91, 300, 305, 1001, 1053, 1075, 1165; **3:**1133; **4:**292; **5:**438–40, 498, 503–5, 510–11, 517, 530, 545–46, 553, 557–58, 567, 570, 574, 578–79, 586, 593, 597, 626, 643, 758; **6:**966; **7:**39; **8:**21, 38, 41, 137, 150, 193, 363, 371, 390, 424, 519, 588, 625, 641, 684, 717, 719, 725; **9:**39, 76, 331, 347, 506, 517, 519, 551, 600, 605, 632, 646, 740, 815, 820, 863; **10:**43, 54–55, 143, 261, 432, 660, 683, 705, 915; **11:**103, 105, 163, 267, 279, 283, 301, 383, 385, 390, 397–98, 411, 414–15, 420–21, 423, 429, 435–36, 506, 535, 563, 565–66, 597–98, 603, 605, 631, 642, 652–53, 655–56, 688, 703, 718, 736, 745, 768, 795, 851; **12:**10, 36, 46, 53–54, 59, 68, 80, 85, 90, 98, 116, 123, 133, 135–37, 141, 164, 199, 203, 211, 278, 328, 343, 348, 385, 398, 401, 413, 418, 436, 489, 491
PHILOPATRIS
11:163
PHILOSTRATUS
8:248; **9:**157
PHOCHYLIDES
Or Pseudo-Phochylides **11:**446
PHOENICIAN TEXTS
1:228, 233, 236, 239, 990; **3:**49, 698; **6:**638; **7:**465, 792
PILATE, ACTS OF
8:486
PIRQE 'ABOT (PIRKE AVOT/ABOTH)
Or *Sayings of the Fathers* **4:**138; **5:**14, 58, 623, 656, 659, 683, 688–89, 694, 698–99, 745, 781, 813, 867; **7:**877; **10:**122; **12:**203
PLATO
1:123; **2:**668–69; **3:**1103; **4:**233, 292; **5:**167, 475, 505, 510, 518, 523, 541, 550, 557, 564, 598, 669; **7:**63; **8:**21, 137, 677; **9:**737, 758; **10:**90, 710; **11:**85, 383, 414, 420, 490, 653, 675, 724, 865; **12:**98, 116, 137, 210–11, 216, 278, 347, 395
PLINY
1:287; **3:**1050, 1159; **4:**227–28; **8:**15–16, 22, 619, 723; **9:**286; **10:**762; **11:**807; **12:**76, 163, 235, 311
PLUTARCH
2:185; **3:**1082; **4:**31, 101, 197, 203, 266, 297; **5:**479, 584, 740; **8:**15–16, 18, 20, 22, 24, 104; **9:**366, 476, 489; **10:**54, 710, 860; **11:**20, 46, 50, 102–3, 156, 162, 298, 383, 390, 429, 451–53, 567, 655, 662, 699–700, 725, 771, 801; **12:**189, 203–4, 211, 216, 351, 405
POEM OF ERRA
See ERRA EPIC
POLYBIUS
1:269; **3:**1098; **4:**34, 60, 67, 84, 89, 93, 98, 102, 104, 121, 169–70, 193, 203, 223, 228–29, 240, 248, 253, 270, 283; **5:**642; **7:**143; **10:**62; **11:**458, 460–61
POLYCARP, MARTYRDOM OF
See *MARTYRDOM OF POLYCARP*
POLYCRATES
9:504
PRAYER OF AZARIAH
3:1080, 1142, 1176; **4:**96; **5:**800; **6:**948; **7:**53, 64, 126, 157–58, 160; **8:**34
PRAYER OF JOSEPH
12:571
PRAYER OF MANASSEH
See MANASSEH, PRAYER OF
PRAYER OF NABONIDUS
Or 4QPrNab **4:**355; **7:**21, 50–51, 72–73, 81–82, 84
PROTESTS OF THE ELOQUENT PEASANT
5:6, 8
PROTEVANGELIUM OF JAMES
8:147, 318; **9:**249
PSALMS SCROLL
Or 11QPsa **5:**636, 800, 867; **6:**973; **8:**36, 38–39, 556, 680
PSALMS OF SOLOMON
Or *Ps. Sol.*; *Pss. Sol.* **1:**12, 15, 290; **4:**197; **5:**272, 801, 849; **6:**931–32, 961, 972–73, 981; **8:**34–36, 38, 359, 391, 622, 665; **9:**48, 85, 97, 200, 391, 458; **10:**403, 438, 563, 660, 692,

PSALMS OF SOLOMON *(continued)*
738; **11:**163, 271, 338, 345, 724, 748, 755, 759; **12:**527, 602, 702–3
PSEUDO-DANIEL
Or 4QPsDan **7:**39
PSEUDO-JONATHAN
Or *Tg. Ps.-J.*; *Targum Pseudo-Jonathan. See* TARGUM: (PSEUDO) JONATHAN
PSEUDO-JOSEPHUS
1:8
PSEUDO-PHILO
4:50; **8:**175; **10:**54, 659; **12:**356
PSEUDO-PHOCYLIDES
11:453; **12:**179
PSEUDO-PLUTARCH
8:16, 18; **11:**453
PUNIC TEXTS
1:239, 990, 1009
PYRAMID TEXTS
1:233

Q

Q (QUELLE)
Or Sayings Source **1:**2, 13, 19, 32; **5:**15; **8:**50–51, 75–77, 79–80, 84, 91, 93, 95–96, 100, 102, 104–7, 111, 113–15, 118–19, 151–52, 154–59, 162–63, 171–72, 174, 176, 178–82, 185, 187, 190, 192–96, 199–200, 202, 204–5, 210–11, 213–15, 217–18, 222, 226, 229, 235, 240–41, 246, 251, 255–58, 260–63, 265–66, 268–69, 271–74, 278–79, 284–87, 289, 292, 295–96, 300–301, 305, 308–9, 311, 314, 317, 319, 332–34, 341–42, 354, 356, 358, 360–61, 368, 372, 374–76, 378, 380, 383–84, 389, 391, 400, 405, 416–18, 429, 435–37, 439, 441, 443–49, 453, 457, 490, 509, 512, 515, 517, 519, 530, 532–33, 535, 564, 577, 595, 615, 641, 666, 678, 681; **9:**7–8, 40, 81, 83, 85, 99, 140, 163, 165, 176, 180, 214, 224–25, 234, 243, 422; **11:**696; **12:**352
1Q28b
See *RULE OF THE BLESSINGS*
1QH
See *THANKSGIVING HYMNS*
1QM
See *WAR SCROLL*
1QpHab
See *HABAKKUK COMMENTARY/PESHER*
1QS
Qumran scroll including both the *Manual of Discipline* and the *Rule of the Community* **4:**71, 243, 440; **5:**160, 339; **6:**949; **7:**126; **8:**34, 36, 39, 126, 193–95, 216, 378, 526, 531–33, 572, 622; **9:**85, 97, 134, 147, 391, 528, 713; **10:**403, 470, 524, 552, 640, 650, 676; **11:**238, 327, 332, 345, 373–75, 381–82, 389–90, 393, 397–98, 408, 410, 419–21, 423, 426, 428–29, 435–37, 442–43, 499, 525, 593, 596, 615, 641, 726; **12:**369, 385, 395, 405, 412–13, 423, 447, 604, 702. See also *MANUAL OF DISCIPLINE*; *RULE OF THE COMMUNITY*
1QSb
See *BLESSINGS (APPENDIX B TO 1QS)*
1Q*
All citations of Qumran scrolls from Cave 1 not cited individually in this index **6:**356; **9:**225; **10:**665
4Q171
10:524
4QFlor
See *FLORILEGIUM*
4QMMT
See *HALAKHIC LETTER*
4QpNah
See *NAHUM PESHER*
4QPrNab
See *PRAYER OF NABONIDUS*
4QpsDan
See *PSEUDO-DANIEL*
4QTALES OF THE PERSIAN COURT
3:862, 866, 894, 913, 929, 951, 955, 959
4QTestim
See *TESTIMONIA TEXT*
4Q*
Qumran scrolls from Cave 4 not otherwise cited individually in this index **1:**289, 294–96, 298–99, 302; **2:**634, 950, 982, 1053, 1370; **3:**308, 377, 386, 394, 415–16, 421, 423–25, 862, 864–65, 936, 979, 1008, 1014, 1031, 1039, 1050–51, 1057, 1064–65, 1068; **4:**71; **5:**553; **6:**942–43, 948–49, 961, 994; **7:**73, 105, 848, 865–66, 875–76; **8:**526, 588, 666; **9:**234; **10:**195, 416, 460, 470, 665; **11:**392, 399, 415, 446, 451–52; **12:**28, 597
11QMelch
See *MELCHIZEDEK TEXT*
11QPsa
See *PSALMS SCROLL*
11QTemple
See *TEMPLE SCROLL*
11Q*
Qumran scrolls from Cave 11 not otherwise cited individually in this index **1:**303; **8:**406; **10:**106
QIDDUSHIN
5:660, 694, 752, 767; **9:**228
QIMHI
7:406

QUINTILLIAN
10:54; **11:**66, 150, 688
QUMRAN SCROLLS
6:73; **8:**39, 666, 691; **9:**65, 85; **10:**524; **11:**421. *See also* DEAD SEA SCROLLS; QUMRAN, KHIRBET *in PLACES IN THE BIBLE and PLACES OUTSIDE THE BIBLE*

R

RABBAH
Or *Rab. (rabbinic works related to scripture [e.g., Exodus Rabbah or Exod. Rab.])* **1:**69, 126; **2:**195, 894, 908, 923, 931; **3:**332; **5:**94, 99, 102, 305, 405; **6:**393, 942; **8:**450, 709; **9:**646, 687, 697, 757; **10:**399, 470, 563, 638; **11:**506; **12:**199, 351
RASHI
1:68, 74–75, 77, 79, 81; **2:**833, 908, 934; **3:**424, 937; **5:**113, 126, 158, 172, 182, 199; **6:**551, 1270, 1272; **7:**406
RAS SHAMRA TABLETS
1:990; **7:**202
RULE OF THE BLESSINGS
Or 1Q28b **11:**460
RULE OF THE COMMUNITY
1:287, 289; **3:**969; **4:**46; **6:**949; **8:**38–39, 531, 533; **11:**332, 430, 442. *See also* 1QS

S

SABBAT
Or *Sabb.* **1:**998; **5:**207, 818; **8:**194, 277; **9:**465; **11:**324
SAHIDIC VERSION
1:304; **8:**6, 743
SAMARITAN PENTATEUCH
Or SP **1:**292, 295, 298–99, 305, 308, 1012, 1106, 1194; **2:**487
SANHEDRIN
Or *Sanh.* **1:**126, 1126; **2:**195; **4:**105, 539, 1063; **5:**101, 634, 674, 682, 779; **6:**1240; **7:**436; **8:**422, 490; **9:**123, 465, 617, 628, 677, 820; **12:**351
SATIRE ON/OF THE TRADES
5:6, 604, 606–7, 625, 812
SAYINGS OF THE FATHERS
See *PIRQUE 'ABOT* (PIRKE AVOT/ABOTH)
SAYINGS SOURCE/Q
See Q (QUELLE)
SECRET BOOK OF JOHN
See *APOCRYPHON OF JOHN*
SECRET GOSPEL OF MARK
8:710
SEFIRE
3:1017; **6:**831
SENECA
5:564, 584; **8:**13, 17, 20; **9:**454; **10:**443, 554, 860, 987; **11:**31, 138, 151, 384, 436, 446, 453, 459, 643, 675, 707, 731, 736, 768; **12:**40, 187, 189, 203, 216
SEPTUAGINT
Or LXX **1:**12, 27, 29, 32, 45, 94, 292, 297–304, 308, 341–42, 383, 671, 751, 898, 953, 1012, 1023, 1075, 1111–12, 1147–49, 1164; **2:**3, 33, 166, 190–92, 271, 586, 594, 608, 612–14, 619, 631, 634, 636, 646–47, 655, 658, 666, 678, 694, 697, 707, 718, 899, 950–51, 982, 993, 1007, 1012, 1062, 1069, 1079–80, 1109–10, 1119, 1122, 1134, 1140, 1148, 1166, 1188; **3:**318, 332, 336, 357, 363, 384, 389, 402, 406, 415, 424, 446–47, 451, 487, 500, 505, 511, 524–25, 530, 546, 553, 556, 559, 570, 586, 591, 600, 622, 630, 655, 657, 671, 794, 848, 860–62, 865–67, 871, 878, 879, 884–88, 891–97, 901–4, 913–14, 925–27, 930–31, 935, 938, 945–50, 953–63, 966, 969–72, 992, 1038, 1147, 1171, 1176; **5:**21, 41–43, 55, 74, 84, 88, 98, 108–10, 114, 118, 141–44, 151, 157, 188, 193–94, 199, 204, 207–8, 212–13, 230, 233, 250–57, 297, 337, 382, 419–20, 448, 463, 465, 469, 479, 542, 553, 558, 658–59, 669, 673, 730, 846; **6:**17–18, 67, 78, 84, 122, 239, 331, 379, 567–68, 613, 930, 948, 952, 985, 988, 997, 1016, 1048, 1092, 1115–17, 1122, 1151, 1164, 1174, 1232, 1237, 1261, 1272, 1294, 1336–37, 1342, 1352–55, 1374, 1378, 1389, 1392–94, 1415–18, 1427–29, 1434, 1439, 1443–44, 1454, 1463, 1467, 1472–73, 1476–79, 1485, 1519–20, 1531, 1540, 1545, 1547–49, 1551–52, 1554–55, 1557–58, 1581–82, 1585, 1591, 1596, 1600–1601, 1604–5; **7:**55, 156, 160, 175, 177–81, 183, 187, 189–90, 192, 231, 240, 289, 314, 374, 407, 427–28, 667, 778, 808, 815, 822, 828, 830; **8:**29–30, 94, 107, 126–28, 134–35, 147, 152, 156, 160, 166, 176, 196, 201, 228, 252, 258, 281, 296, 298–99, 333, 346, 348–49, 358, 364, 390, 399, 403, 407, 413–14, 424–25, 474, 476, 492, 577, 606, 612, 631; **9:**76, 91, 105, 227, 367, 380–81, 405, 407, 419, 454, 505, 519, 522, 543, 596, 603–4, 634, 667–68, 690, 707, 712, 716, 773, 793, 802, 831–32, 834; **10:**15–16, 50, 59, 64, 66, 80, 82–83, 89, 113, 123–29, 142, 150, 165, 189–91, 193, 199, 205–6, 218–19, 282, 338, 361–62, 374, 417, 419–20, 425, 439, 453, 459, 474–75, 487, 492, 503, 511, 516, 570, 579, 611, 625, 630, 642–43, 647, 665–68, 675–77, 692, 696, 725, 738, 745, 747–48, 821, 988, 999; **11:**63, 68–69, 75, 82, 95, 105–6, 126, 129–30, 202, 205, 215, 235, 241, 258–63, 302, 304, 324, 372–73, 376, 381, 384, 393, 398, 402, 428, 437, 452, 459–60, 490, 503–4, 510, 533, 563, 593, 596–99, 604–6, 613, 624, 631, 647–49, 693, 700, 727, 746, 750, 762–64, 808, 812; **12:**13, 28–29, 33–42, 46–88,

SEPTUAGINT *(continued)*
52, 63–64, 81–82, 92–93, 98, 101, 105, 115, 123, 126, 131–33, 138–42, 151, 154, 159–60, 164, 172, 178, 193, 210, 221–23, 237, 265–67, 291, 312, 315, 328, 343–45, 348, 351–52, 355–57, 481, 489, 579, 614, 632
SHEPHERD OF HERMAS
Or Herm. **1:**7, 15; **5:**635; **11:**375, 562, 819; **12:**76, 169, 172, 177, 328, 336, 356, 489, 522
SIBYLLINE ORACLES
Or *Sib. Or.* **1:**285; **6:**1512; **7:**3–4, 103; **8:**24, 42, 531; **9:**252; **11:**105, 163, 428; **12:**347, 659, 683, 702
SIFRA/SIFRE
1:69; **2:**77; **5:**720, 730, 734, 772; **9:**228
SILOAM INSCRIPTION
1:249; **5:**298
SIMILITUDES OF ENOCH
1:289; **7:**7, 13–14; **8:**92; **9:**332; **12:**704
SINAITICUS
See CODEX SINAITICUS
SIRACH
Or Ecclesiasticus; Wisdom of Jesus Ben Sira; Wisdom of Jesus Son of Sirach **1:**8, 10–12, 17–18, 286, 292, 294, 303, 1113; **2:**1108; **3:**986, 1056; **4:**7, 22, 48, 50–51, 57, 113, 172, 188, 199, 202, 234, 327, 367, 377, 531, 562, 601; **5:**1–2, 10–15, 96, 119, 164, 219–20, 243–45, 257, 271, 275–76, 281, 437, 441, 447, 465, 479, 493, 496, 502, 504, 509, 517, 523, 527, 532; **6:**931, 934, 961–62, 968; **7:**14, 177–78, 180, 181, 189, 731, 875; **8:**41, 152, 304, 328, 374; **9:**255, 301, 336, 505, 519, 668; **10:**496, 498, 556, 580, 669, 724; **11:**415, 443, 453, 502; **12:**203, 388, 521
SLAVONIC ENOCH
See *2 ENOCH*
SLAVONIC VERSIONS
3:979; **5:**625; **8:**6–7
SOLOMON, ODES OF
See *ODES OF SOLOMON*
SOLOMON, PSALMS OF
See *PSALMS OF SOLOMON*
SOLOMON, TESTAMENT OF
See *TESTAMENT OF SOLOMON*
SOLOMON, WISDOM OF
See *WISDOM OF SOLOMON*
SOLON
2:566, 669, 688; **5:**331, 708
SONG OF THE HARPER
5:6
SONG OF THE THREE JEWS
Or *Song of the Three Young Men* **3:**1080, 1176; **5:**634; **7:**64, 156–58, 164, 175, 179, 181
SOPHOCLES
5:525, 660, 708; **12:**395
SOTA
2:195; **4:**434; **7:**877; **8:**262, 363, 381
STRABO
4:60, 84, 197, 202; **6:**1378–79, 1398; **7:**203; **8:**24; **10:**775
SUETONIUS
8:22–23, 625; **9:**830; **10:**253, 717; **11:**57; **12:**273, 658, 683
SUKKA
Or *Sukk.* **5:**660; **9:**616, 622, 632, 653
SUMERIAN KING LIST
6:1176, 1463; **7:**5
SUMERIAN TEXTS
1:228, 232, 246, 340, 388; **2:**614; **3:**446; **4:**329; **5:**3, 8–9, 94, 604, 610, 654, 730, 777; **6:**1176, 1221, 1309, 1376, 1463, 1512, 1566; **7:**5, 62, 90
SUSANNA
3:978, 1080, 1086, 1102, 1132, 1141–42, 1158–59; **4:**563; **5:**77, 119, 126, 480, 622, 629, 634, 760–61; **7:**116; **8:**29; **10:**492
SYMMACHUS
1:301, 304; **4:**622; **10:**503
SYRIAC VERSION(S)
Or *Sy.*; *Syr.*; *Sys.* **1:**292, 303, 1106; **3:**979; **4:**822; **5:**118, 144, 178, 193, 198, 204, 208, 303; **6:**930, 985; **7:**667; **8:**6, 414, 429, 435, 472, 486. *See also* ARAMAIC VERSION(S)

T

TA'ANIT
Or *Ta'an.* **1:**290; **4:**270; **7:**340; **8:**247
TACITUS
3:1017; **4:**143, 227; **5:**558, 562–63; **8:**15, 22–23, 482, 515, 684, 718; **9:**653, 815; **10:**313, 717, 721; **11:**138, 233, 383, 396–97, 580, 655, 703; **12:**273
TALE OF TWO BROTHERS
1:609
TALES OF THE PERSIAN COURT
See 4QTALES OF THE PERSIAN COURT
TALMUD
JERUSALEM TALMUD **1:**66, 68, 70, 73–74, 76, 79, 228, 284, 1057, 1126; **2:**950; **4:**357, 389, 1261; **5:**14, 102, 207, 355, 634; **6:**277, 949; **7:**407, 436; **8:**31–32, 197, 299, 359; **11:**506; BABYLONIAN TALMUD **1:**11, 65, 69; **4:**525; **5:**101, 553, 674, 689, 720, 732, 758; **6:**1148; **8:**490; **12:**657
TAMID
5:859; **9:**46–47
TARGUM
Or *Targums/Targumim* **1:**70–71, 298, 302–3, 1007, 1112; **2:**191, 212, 739, 772, 833; **3:**192,

205, 245, 330, 331, 406, 801, 861, 866, 892, 894, 904, 911, 953, 966; **4:**325, 467, 497, 559, 635, 901, 1040; **5:**94, 144, 193, 198, 204, 371, 405, 730; **6:**84, 986, 1016, 1110, 1240, 1330, 1507, 1592; **7:**331, 376, 840, 852, 866–67; **8:**29, 143, 147, 210, 228, 281, 398, 463; **9:**566, 742; **10:**650; **12:**351, 571; TO ESTHER **3:**861, 892, 904, 966; TO ISAIAH **10:**650; OF JOB **1:**1194; **4:**467, 497, 559, 635; NEOFITI ON THE PENTATEUCH **1:**70, 303, 1095; **5:**94; **8:**463; **10:**1001; PALESTINIAN **8:**398; **9:**566, 742; OF THE PROPHETS **1:**70; (PSEUDO) JONATHAN **1:**70, 303; **5:**574, 730; **7:**852; **12:**571; TARGUM JONATHAN **1:**303; **7:**852; TARGUM NEOFITI **1:**70, 303; **8:**463; **10:**638; TARGUM OF THE ONGELOS **1:**70, 1112; TARGUM ONKELOS/ONQELOS **1:**70–71, 303; **2:**191; **5:**574; TARGUM YERUSALMI **1:**70, 1007; **5:**574; TO ZECHARIAH **7:**840. *See also* ARAMAIC VERSION(S); PROPHETS

TATIAN
1:47; **8:**5–6, 19; **9:**504, 723. See also *DIATESSARON*

TEACHING FOR DUAUF
Or *INSTRUCTION FOR DUAUF* **5:**604, 607, 625, 812

TEACHING OF THE APOSTLES
1:15

TEMPLE SCROLL
Or 11QTemple **1:**10, 286; **3:**451, 800; **4:**19, 125, 206, 281; **6:**1541; **7:**867; **8:**31, 192, 641, 643, 713; **10:**106; **11:**260; **12:**642

TERTULLIAN
1:12, 85; **3:**1134; **4:**243; **7:**334, 843; **8:**14–15, 24, 205, 318, 486; **9:**5–6, 723; **11:**562, 780; **12:**6, 76, 78, 366, 443, 513, 711

TESTAMENT OF ABRAHAM
Or *T. Abr.* **3:**1080; **7:**7; **10:**854; **11:**565–66, 625

TESTAMENT OF BENJAMIN
Or *T. Benj.* **8:**678; **10:**689; **11:**381

TESTAMENT OF DAN
Or *T. Dan* **4:**570; **9:**227; **11:**105, 429, 643

TESTAMENT OF DANIEL
8:678

TESTAMENT OF ISSACHAR
Or *T. Iss.*; *T. Issachar* **8:**677; **9:**227; **10:**725; **11:**381, 435; **12:**403

TESTAMENT OF JOB
Or *T. Job* **3:**1080, 1179; **4:**356; **8:**29, 41, 707; **9:**244; **11:**563; **12:**221

TESTAMENT OF JOSEPH
Or *T. Jos.* **3:**1080; **7:**82, 125, 145, 169; **8:**41, 710; **11:**41

TESTAMENT OF JUDAH
Or *T. Jud.*; *T. Judah* **3:**328; **11:**435–36, 441, 642; **12:**427, 451

TESTAMENT OF LEVI
Or *T. Levi* **3:**1143; **4:**570; **5:**524, 862; **7:**3, 429, 846, 861; **8:**34, 36, 232, 531–32, 630; **9:**458; **11:**66, 163, 373, 383, 435, 565, 598; **12:**41, 82, 385, 394, 412, 702

TESTAMENT OF MOSES
Or *T. Mos.* **4:**46; **7:**3; **8:**30, 32, 36–38; **10:**659; **12:**329, 474, 476, 489

TESTAMENT OF NAPHTALI
Or *T. Naph.* **7:**429; **9:**331; **10:**640; **11:**437

TESTAMENT OF REUBEN
Or *T. Reub.* **11:**105, 435, 642

TESTAMENT OF SIMEON
Or *T. Sim.* **11:**66, 460

TESTAMENT OF SOLOMON
5:272; **11:**566; **12:**222

TESTAMENT(S) OF THE TWELVE PATRIARCHS, THE
3:328, 1080; **5:**541, 623, 772, 787, 790, 862; **6:**930; **7:**3, 144; **8:**29, 34, 424, 438; **9:**737; **12:**545

TESTIMONIA TEXT
Or 4QTest **8:**36; **10:**82

TEXTUS RECEPTUS
8:7–8, 190; **10:**311, 560; **12:**638

THANKSGIVING HYMNS
Or *Hodayot*; 1QH **1:**10; **4:**379, 440; **5:**108, 160, 164, 745; **8:**30, 37, 39, 532; **9:**65, 117, 341, 642; **10:**524, 571, 640, 650, 676, 695; **11:**296, 345, 373–74, 389, 398, 410, 438, 461, 490, 563, 593, 596, 615, 625; **12:**395, 705

THECLA, ACTS OF PAUL AND
See *ACTS OF PAUL*

THEODOTION
1:11, 301; **7:**52, 92, 156, 163, 167, 179, 180–81, 183, 187

THEOPHRASTUS
8:22, 25

THOMAS, ACTS OF
See *ACTS OF THOMAS*

THOMAS, GOSPEL OF
See *GOSPEL OF THOMAS*

THOMAS, INFANCY GOSPEL OF
See *INFANCY GOSPEL OF THOMAS*

THUCYDIDES
1:267; **3:**22; **4:**207, 275; **5:**642; **9:**147; **10:**62, 124; **11:**461, 767

TIMAEUS
4:202; **5:**505, 523, 550; **11:**384, 414; **12:**210, 347

TOBIT, BOOK OF
Or *Tob.* **1:**8, 12, 17–18, 28, 294, 300, 511; **3:**937, 1081, 1086, 1091, 1095, 1098, 1102–3, 1115, 1118, 1132, 1141, 1154, 1158–59, 1167–68, 1176, 1189; **4:**64, 174, 207, 369, 553, 635; **5:**1,

TOBIT, BOOK OF *(continued)*
6, 24, 84, 151, 355, 574, 578, 623, 630, 634, 659, 697, 779, 797; **6:**943, 973, 994; **7:**40, 53–54, 161, 177, 340, 386, 429, 526; **8:**29, 31–36, 38, 41, 126, 210, 213, 230, 286, 393, 422, 494, 555, 585, 610; **9:**47, 51, 130, 147, 190, 217, 224, 256, 301, 405, 476–77, 480, 485–86, 742; **10:**498, 518; **11:**233, 364; **12:**162, 386, 492, 629–30; 4QTOB **3:**976–77, 1191

TOSEPHTA/TOSEPTA/TOSEFTA
3:800; **5:**366, 526; **9:**177; **12:**596. *See also individual tractates (e.g., Gittin and Megilla)*

TRADITION OF THE ELDERS
8:606; **11:**399

TRIPARTITE TRACTATE
11:415, 422, 450, 600

TYCONIUS
12:534, 551, 711

TYNDALE'S VERSION
1:24–25, 1042, 1112; **8:**202

U

UGARITIC TEXTS
1:231, 233, 236, 239–42, 273, 509, 990, 1009, 1011, 1018, 1023, 1081, 1112, 1125; **2:**231, 306, 364, 586, 600, 613, 755, 904, 1005–6, 1028, 1223, 1236; **3:**32, 126, 171, 178, 1091; **4:**305, 328–29, 368, 395, 469–70, 485–86, 500, 518–19, 530, 539, 618, 621–22, 624; **5:**6, 77, 90, 95, 389, 397, 604, 670, 725, 752; **6:**159, 180, 1175, 1213, 1368, 1387, 1398, 1515, 1525, 1561, 1595; **7:**65, 351, 400, 602, 654; **9:**388

UNCIAL(S)
1:302; **5:**636; **8:**3–5, 7, 9–10; **10:**389; **11:**883

V

VALENTINUS
1:15; **8:**630; **9:**498, 506

VEGETIUS
3:249

VERSIONS, ENGLISH
Includes modern English versions **1:**22–24, 26, 30–31, 292, 1164; **2:**330, 453, 910, 912, 926; **3:**383, 416, 425, 510, 526, 772; **5:**279, 289; **6:**988; **7:**303, 452; **10:**415, 434, 473; **11:**255; **12:**398, 453

VICTORINUS
6:1131; **11:**252; **12:**532–34, 538, 562, 592–93, 611, 652, 711

VIRGIL
4:605; **5:**583; **8:**328, 723; **9:**460; **10:**345

VULGATE
Or Vg **1:**5, 8, 12, 17, 28, 52–53, 74, 99–101, 297, 303–4, 307, 383, 1023, 1094, 1149; **2:**3, 772, 950, 1006, 1042; **3:**101, 630, 679, 861, 947, 952, 955, 957, 961, 964, 968, 970, 976–77, 1001, 1017, 1041, 1051, 1170; **4:**512, 938, 1147; **5:**20, 193, 195, 204, 208, 297, 326, 406, 437, 453, 603, 606, 634, 636, 658, 686, 725, 749, 772, 775, 779, 787, 809, 813, 834; **6:**929, 985, 1041, 1375, 1584; **7:**91, 407, 437, 521, 682, 724, 815, 855, 866–67; **8:**6–7, 190, 202, 205, 285; **9:**316; **10:**370; **11:**452; **12:**524

W

WAR SCROLL
Or 1QM **1:**10, 289; **3:**559, 969; **4:**30, 64, 66, 78, 249, 277, 282, 516; **5:**699; **7:**4, 105; **8:**126, 142, 178, 691; **9:**713; **10:**403; **11:**389, 593, 596, 615; **12:**413, 664–65, 714

WISDOM, BOOK OF
See WISDOM OF SOLOMON

WISDOM OF JESUS BEN SIRA
See SIRACH

WISDOM OF JESUS SON OF SIRACH
See SIRACH

WISDOM OF SIRACH
See SIRACH

WISDOM OF SOLOMON
Or Book of Wisdom; (Book of) Wisdom **1:**8, 12, 15, 17–18, 290, 300; **3:**1032, 1063, 1084, 1144; **4:**210, 234, 241; **5:**1–2, 7–8, 10–16, 20, 32–33, 95–96, 272, 275–76, 281, 313, 331, 340–41, 606, 611, 619, 622–23, 625, 634, 643, 758, 779, 788, 817, 849, 871; **6:**961–62, 968; **7:**55, 188; **8:**19, 30, 37, 41, 425, 676–77; **9:**410, 505, 643; **10:**429, 433, 438–39, 622–23, 640; **11:**391, 437, 460, 566; **12:**10, 585; Or *Wis.; Wisd. Sol.* **1:**360, 367, 475; **3:**948–49, 1004, 1032, 1063, 1123, 1133, 1138, 1144; **4:**46, 234, 241, 248, 378, 414, 531; **5:**10, 12, 14–15, 93, 95–97, 112–13, 129, 239, 254, 281, 313, 331, 340–41, 622, 651, 654, 669, 680, 696, 716, 725, 758, 787, 817, 833, 838, 842; **6:**961, 966, 968, 985, 987, 989, 1006; **7:**55, 188; **8:**152, 274, 296, 360, 418, 491–92, 538, 676, 722, 724; **9:**63, 76, 331, 388, 407, 411, 505, 519, 632, 661, 773, 846; **10:**403, 429, 432, 439, 498, 524, 556, 593, 604, 639, 641, 649, 661, 663, 694, 718, 721, 802, 854, 913, 984; **11:**70, 283, 285, 287, 384, 428, 436–37, 459–60, 502, 566, 597, 599–600, 605, 641–42, 703, 718, 726, 805, 829, 856; **12:**23, 25, 54, 105, 130, 133–35, 151, 154, 158, 303, 336, 347, 401, 579, 625, 633, 649, 699

WORDS OF THE HEAVENLY LIGHTS
8:34

WORDS OF THE LUMINARIES
Or 4Q504–506 **6:**948

WYCLIFFE'S VERSION
8:202; **9:**51

X

XENOPHON
1:267; **3:**1081, 1115; **4:**249, 297; **7:**81–82, 771; **10:**487; **11:**333, 446, 458, 657, 767

Y

YEBAM
2:908

YERUSALMI
Or *TARGUM YERUSALMI*. *See* TARGUM: YERUSALMI

YOMA
1:1111; **2:**3; **5:**734, 859; **8:**277, 378; **9:**47, 134, 274

Z

ZENO
3:757; **5:**334; **8:**19; **10:**929

ZENO(N) PAPYRUS/PAPYRI
1:270; **3:**757; **4:**121; **5:**334, 643, 827–28; **7:**24

ZEPHANIAH, APOCALYPSE OF
See *APOCALYPSE OF ZEHPANIAH*

PERSONS

In the Bible

A

AARON
1:75, 289, 306, 315, 442, 682–83, 686, 691–92, 716–20, 725–30, 733, 735–40, 742, 744–48, 750, 754, 763, 780, 782, 812–13, 825, 828, 834, 867, 880–82, 901, 905–8, 912–14, 916, 921, 927, 930–35, 938, 941, 945, 947, 949–51, 954, 956, 961, 973, 976, 986–87, 995, 999, 1005, 1008, 1011–12, 1017, 1019, 1023, 1034, 1043, 1045, 1047, 1056–57, 1059–63, 1065–73, 1080, 1095, 1110–15, 1117, 1147–48, 1152; **2:**3–4, 10, 25–26, 31, 36, 47–50, 53, 61, 66, 80–81, 87, 99–100, 104, 108–13, 123–24, 126, 134–42, 146–49, 151, 157–63, 198–99, 202, 207, 213–14, 219, 222, 250, 252, 254, 363, 546, 579–80, 599, 687, 701–2, 714, 809, 870, 887, 988, 1062, 1140; **3:**137, 344, 441, 457, 669, 678, 681, 687, 717, 725, 733, 931, 1139; **4:**44, 50, 71–72, 81, 164–65, 198–99, 281, 862, 1074–76, 1214; **5:**72, 517, 525, 529, 532, 584, 590, 592, 595, 620–21, 631, 836, 842–43; **6:**582, 1110–11, 1147, 1166–68, 1176, 1207, 1278, 1284, 1397, 1533, 1558, 1569, 1575–76, 1579; **7:**579, 861; **8:**354, 359, 366, 526, 537; **9:**46, 48, 133, 145, 489; **10:**127, 474, 563; **11:**64, 214; **12:**46–47, 57, 60–61, 64, 90, 247, 269

AARONITES
2:147; **5:**843; **7:**727, 859, 870

ABBA (NAME OF GOD)
See under GOD, NAMES FOR/TITLES OF

ABBIR YA'AQOB
1:273

ABDA
3:826, 832

ABDIAS
7:437

ABDON
1:259; **2:**762, 764–65, 819, 839–40

ABEDNEGO
4:51; **6:**164; **7:**39

ABEL
1:76, 93, 220, 372–77, 400, 1005, 1017, 1120; **2:**192, 250, 266; **3:**583; **4:**247, 345, 460; **5:**56, 161, 278, 523, 527, 536, 622; **6:**205, 469, 529, 649, 1336; **7:**832; **8:**437; **9:**249, 300; **11:**56, 855, 866; **12:**133, 136, 145, 158, 418–19, 603

ABIATHAR
1:311, 905; **2:**688–89, 988, 1138, 1148–49, 1152–53, 1183, 1192–93, 1268, 1323–25, 1332, 1346, 1354; **3:**18–19, 21, 23, 32–34, 49, 415, 725; **5:**696; **6:**5, 575; **9:**133

ABIDAN
2:95

ABIEZER
3:379, 382

ABIGAIL
2:549–50, 673, 949, 958, 962, 1126, 1138, 1157, 1164–71, 1174, 1176–79, 1192, 1211, 1219, 1229, 1257, 1352; **5:**102, 119, 133, 153, 261, 264, 682; **9:**722

ABIHAIL
3:337, 889

ABIHU
1:880–81, 905, 986–87, 1057, 1060, 1069–73, 1110; **2:**25, 49, 54, 137–38, 214, 229; **3:**441, 725; **4:**281, 387; **6:**1397; **8:**366

ABIJAH
1:263; **2:**1026; **3:**112–14, 116–18, 120, 329, 442, 529, 531–33, 602, 607, 649, 657; **9:**45

ABIMELECH
1:259–61, 419, 481–85, 491–92, 517, 526–30, 578; **2:**62, 109, 634–35, 726, 737, 762–64, 776, 791–92, 797, 810–11, 815–21, 825, 831, 873, 879, 1287; **3:**100, 415, 649, 1090, 1144; **4:**78, 569; **5:**38, 238; **6:**396

ABINADAB
2:1012, 1081, 1099, 1197, 1247–49; **3:**51

ABIRAM
1:1070; **2:**10, 19, 99, 134–39, 142, 146, 158–60, 211, 370; **5:**592, 631, 725, 843; **6:**1533–34, 1573; **11:**845

ABISHAG
2:1223; **3:**14, 18, 32–33, 885

ABISHAI
2:949, 1174–75, 1177, 1216–17, 1225, 1280, 1326, 1335–36, 1346, 1351, 1361, 1376; **3:**415, 456; **4:**63

ABIUD
8:128, 130

ABNER
2:432, 549, 562, 949, 962, 1081, 1095, 1113, 1174–75, 1199, 1202, 1211–18, 1221–27, 1229–30, 1232–33, 1250, 1252, 1273, 1326, 1335, 1346, 1350–51, 1359, 1376; **3:**27, 32, 34; **4:**43, 129

ABRAHAM
1:32, 68, 165, 241, 248, 254, 257–58, 273, 306, 308, 316–18, 322, 325, 328–29, 351, 375–77, 381, 391, 401, 403, 408–9, 411–12, 415–20, 422–27, 432, 434–35, 438, 444, 447, 449–51, 454, 457–60, 462–65, 467–70, 473–79, 481–86, 488–92, 494–501, 503–4, 509–18, 520, 522–23, 526–29, 536–37, 539, 541, 558–60, 563, 567–69, 577–78, 580–81, 583–86, 590–94, 600, 604, 612, 616, 622, 628, 652, 660–61, 667, 674, 703, 706, 854, 988, 1005, 1009, 1010, 1065, 1084, 1118, 1139, 1181–82, 1190; **2:**6, 20, 49, 109, 162, 182, 271, 273, 277, 297, 310, 359, 510, 542–44, 546–50, 552, 555, 601, 603, 608, 670, 709, 714, 737, 755, 759, 783, 792, 802, 810, 826, 834–36, 846, 879, 896, 932, 943, 974, 1236; **3:**47, 317–18, 332, 401, 468, 483, 560, 615, 664, 671, 809–13, 886, 932, 956–57, 986, 994, 1007, 1016, 1038–39, 1042, 1062, 1089, 1119, 1138, 1165, 1168, 1171–72; **4:**50–51, 66, 143–44, 164, 188, 228, 232, 241, 343, 361, 378, 423, 465, 470, 503, 569, 582, 733, 807, 869–70, 940, 964, 1024, 1104–5, 1169, 1182; **5:**2, 51, 55, 125, 172, 174, 186, 189, 199, 232, 428, 445, 502, 516, 522–24, 527, 605, 621–22, 631, 670, 725, 787, 836, 842, 855, 867; **6:**5, 13, 247–48, 353–56, 358, 361–64, 366, 375, 377, 386, 402, 432, 441–43, 447, 477, 516, 525–28, 530, 580, 588, 606, 619, 628, 638, 669, 877, 980, 1015, 1154, 1214, 1219, 1238, 1240, 1278, 1282, 1296, 1347, 1379, 1447, 1457–58, 1510, 1531; **7:**3, 12, 39, 162, 188, 284, 287, 330, 355, 357, 369, 382, 419, 429, 574, 580, 597, 751, 828, 864–65; **8:**41–42, 126–29, 131–33, 139–40, 144, 149, 157, 345, 356, 358–59, 363, 423, 504, 570, 665; **9:**8, 20–21, 25, 45, 47, 59, 71, 83–84, 86, 91, 94–95, 98, 143, 145, 235, 273–74, 313, 315–19, 326, 346, 355, 357, 359, 369, 381, 389, 475, 482, 485, 602, 636, 638–41, 644–46, 648, 669, 678, 717, 823; **10:**19, 79–80, 82–83, 125–27, 131–32, 151, 171, 205, 376, 399, 405, 413–14, 416, 451, 453, 464–66, 471–72, 478, 482–84, 487–508, 511, 513–15, 517, 520, 524–25, 530–31, 534–35, 543, 550, 555–57, 561, 574, 585–86, 591, 593, 596, 602, 604, 610–12, 616, 622, 624–26, 629, 634–36, 638, 642–44, 646–47, 649, 654–55, 657, 663, 669–70, 673, 675–76, 681–85, 687–90, 693, 696, 698–99, 732, 736, 742, 769, 835, 913; **11:**23, 28, 49, 76–77, 145, 156, 186, 189–90, 202, 227, 243, 249, 252, 255–59, 261–65, 267–71, 273–77, 279–80, 283–84, 289, 300–302, 304–306, 309, 314, 319, 324, 333, 346, 375, 404, 524, 528, 866, 877; **12:**41, 76–81, 83–88, 95, 110, 134–42, 145, 162, 167, 182–84, 187, 189, 194, 197–99, 201, 211, 237, 246, 253, 285, 519, 536, 599, 649

ABRAHAM, CHILDREN OF
1:165, 419, 463, 468, 488, 490, 514–15; **3:**1171–72; **6:**432; **8:**133; **9:**20, 84, 273, 315, 369, 639–41, 644; **10:**413, 490, 494, 505–6, 611, 636, 688; **11:**202, 255–56, 309, 333, 346; **12:**41, 81, 285

ABRAM
1:306, 336, 422–35, 438–42, 444–49, 451–55, 457–59, 567, 937; **2:**35, 94, 148, 190–91, 194, 215, 542, 547, 559; **3:**100, 318–19, 810, 1165, 1171; **4:**1198; **5:**294, 326, 454, 523–24, 547, 591; **6:**354, 363, 366, 376, 1380; **7:**39, 330; **8:**29, 345; **10:**487

ABSALOM
1:585, 924, 1186; **2:**549, 552, 949, 963, 1037, 1211, 1213, 1219, 1223, 1229, 1269–70, 1273, 1285, 1287, 1291, 1293, 1302–3, 1305–6, 1308–10, 1313–20, 1323–26, 1330–33, 1335–37, 1339–42, 1345–48, 1350–53, 1355, 1359; **3:**17–18, 27–28, 32–33, 522, 687, 901; **4:**141, 150, 193, 269, 345, 443, 694, 898; **5:**78, 107–8, 122, 174, 182, 433; **6:**181; **7:**386, 670; **9:**302

ABUBUS
4:176

ACHAICUS
10:777; **11:**135

ACHAN
1:579, 1182, 1189; **2:**351, 393–94, 470, 562–63, 577, 589, 606, 613, 619, 625–27, 630–32, 706–7, 1047; **3:**135, 153, 328; **4:**55, 82, 471; **5:**484; **6:**212, 1257; **7:**142

ACHIOR
3:1076, 1078, 1082, 1088–90, 1095, 1102, 1104, 1117, 1119–20, 1123–24, 1127, 1132, 1139, 1154–55, 1167–69

ACHISH
2:550, 962, 1142, 1175, 1178–80, 1187–89, 1192, 1206; **3:**34; **4:**814

ACHSAH
2:678, 736–38, 741–42, 749, 757, 766, 782, 835, 841, 853, 872, 877; **3:**330

ADAM
1:47, 88, 92, 191, 252, 325, 329, 335–36, 345, 351, 353, 364, 367, 369, 372, 375, 379–82, 398, 403, 405, 408, 428, 434, 604, 716, 1085; **2:**49, 191, 551, 746, 887; **3:**318, 332, 464, 480, 1041, 1043; **4:**449, 554; **5:**56, 72, 101, 301, 314, 422, 445, 494, 497, 518, 522–23, 525–26, 567, 584, 620–22, 631, 633, 693, 716, 758, 764, 805, 823, 836, 838, 842, 856; **6:**375, 528–29, 551, 795, 1121–22, 1391–92, 1394; **7:**55, 115, 252; **8:**128–29, 221, 363, 535, 537; **9:**9, 94–95; **10:**247, 399, 402, 405, 420, 433, 470, 472, 508,

512, 516, 523–530, 533, 535–36, 539, 541–44, 547, 550, 552–54, 558–60, 562–63, 565–66, 568, 570–72, 574, 586, 622, 624, 629, 635, 638, 680–82, 684, 694, 742, 765, 981–82, 988; **11:**79, 159, 377, 390, 393, 400, 429, 450–51, 503–6, 508–9, 510, 515, 536, 597, 798, 800–801, 866; **12:**37, 40, 206, 494, 532, 535, 574
ADIN
3:725, 817
ADONAI/ADONAY
See under GOD, NAMES FOR/TITLES OF
ADONI-BEZEK
2:646, 726, 735–37, 741, 749, 757, 853
ADONIJAH
2:136, 264, 1219, 1223, 1319; **3:**17–24, 31–34, 94, 100, 817; **6:**5, 575
ADONIKAM
3:725, 817
ADONIRAM
2:1268; **3:**49, 58
ADONI-ZEDEK
1:439; **2:**646, 736
ADORAM
2:1354; **3:**49, 102
AENEAS
10:160–62
AGABUS
10:175, 177, 181, 288–89, 297
AGAG
2:190, 606, 1088–90, 1092, 1153, 1193; **3:**894, 932, 951
AGAGITE
3:893–95, 916, 919, 923, 927, 938, 951, 1118
AGRIPPA
1:271; **3:**364; **8:**653; **9:**88, 363, 401, 451; **10:**178, 181, 321, 323, 325, 328–30, 333–36, 338–43
AGUR
5:21, 33, 250–52, 256, 780
AHAB
1:225, 249–51, 262, 264–65, 1172, 1189; **2:**221, 376, 422, 575, 612, 614, 619–20, 810, 1072, 1087, 1294; **3:**7, 118–19, 123–28, 130–32, 135–40, 146–47, 150–53, 155–71, 175, 180–81, 183, 209, 214–17, 219–21, 223–28, 230, 234, 238, 274, 276, 280, 328, 422, 544, 546, 551–53, 564–65, 568–70, 573, 576, 586, 649, 959; **4:**32, 51, 55, 63, 290, 555, 592, 861; **5:**122, 187, 205, 326, 851; **6:**134, 613, 742, 745, 794–95, 1111, 1198–99, 1208, 1348, 1360, 1463, 1582, 1590; **7:**5, 362, 436, 480, 558, 582, 677; **8:**319, 598; **12:**581
AHARAH
3:342
AHASUERUS
3:698, 855, 857–59, 868, 869, 871, 877–78, 880, 883, 885–86, 890, 892, 897–900, 905, 908–11, 913, 918–20, 923, 925, 935, 938, 940–41; **5:**425; **7:**121
AHAZ
1:282–83, 1138; **2:**181, 391, 570; **3:**250–51, 253, 259–60, 271, 276, 285, 302, 353, 367, 593, 597–600, 606, 608, 635, 637, 654; **4:**31, 759, 872; **5:**670; **6:**30, 35–36, 38, 40, 99, 106–8, 111–12, 116–17, 136, 146, 149, 162–64, 174, 237, 284, 295, 481–82, 640, 867, 1076, 1160, 1178, 1232, 1286, 1324–25, 1526; **7:**248, 533, 859; **12:**255
AHAZIAH
1:264; **2:**567; **3:**4, 123, 159, 167, 169, 171, 173, 175, 180, 209–10, 212, 214–15, 219–20, 223, 227, 233–34, 242, 250, 544, 564–65, 569–71, 587; **8:**130
AHER
3:342
AHIEZER
3:379, 382
AHIJAH
1:257; **2:**543, 574, 1079, 1090, 1139, 1148; **3:**94–95, 98, 100, 102, 109, 112, 120–21, 357, 452, 512, 520, 718, 785; **6:**6, 1143, 1509
AHIKAM
2:688; **3:**293; **6:**6, 842, 857, 942, 1079
AHIKAR
3:979, 1118–19, 1167–68; **9:**271
AHILUD
3:49–51
AHIMAAZ
1:311; **2:**1332, 1339; **3:**51, 717
AHIMAN
2:122; **3:**826
AHIMELECH
2:962, 1138–41, 1143, 1147–48, 1174, 1268; **3:**415–16, 441; **6:**1257; **9:**133
AHINOAM
2:1081, 1169–70, 1179, 1192, 1211
AHIO
2:1248; **3:**357
AHIRA
2:95
AHIRAM
3:58, 70, 342
AHISHAR
3:50
AHITHOPHEL
2:549, 1320, 1325, 1330–33, 1352; **3:**457, 1008; **4:**898; **6:**181

AHITUB
2:1139; **3:**363, 415, 717
AHLAI
3:329
AHOAH
3:357
AHOLIAB
3:478
AHURA MAZDA
7:89
AKKUB
3:826, 835
ALCIMUS
4:8, 21, 92–99, 101, 109, 114, 116–19, 127, 177, 182, 205, 214, 282, 285–87, 289–91, 298
ALEXANDER (SON OF SIMON CYRENE)
8:489, 722
ALEXANDER BALAS/EPIPHANES
4:121–23, 125, 127, 129–30, 132–33, 135, 137, 140, 145, 147, 168; **5:**867
ALEXANDER OF EPHESUS
10:272; **11:**857
ALEXANDER THE GREAT
1:11, 247, 267, 269–70; **3:**676, 832, 834, 878, 894, 951, 966, 1099; **4:**4–5, 19, 30–32, 34, 36, 39, 49–50, 63, 85, 102, 104, 176–77, 218–19, 282; **5:**21, 271, 634, 824; **6:**208, 1361, 1389, 1398, 1410, 1512, 1515; **7:**11, 24, 26, 103, 105, 111–12, 116, 139–40, 147, 150, 155, 169, 333, 810; **8:**13, 17, 21, 57; **9:**366; **12:**573
ALMIGHTY
See under GOD, NAMES FOR/TITLES OF
ALPHAEUS
8:562; **9:**127, 138; **11:**217
AMALEK/AMALEKITE
1:590, 820–21; **2:**178, 190–91, 475–76, 548, 770, 773, 802, 871, 1085, 1087–90, 1092, 1179, 1185, 1191, 1192–94, 1197, 1201–3, 1211, 1222, 1225, 1228–30, 1266; **3:**379, 894, 1118; **4:**1010; **5:**525, 531
AMARIAH
3:556, 717, 825
AMASA
2:1332, 1346, 1350–52; **3:**27, 34
AMASAI
3:379
AMASHSAI
3:826
AMAZIAH (KING)
1:265; **2:**470; **3:**234, 241–42, 245, 250, 526, 586–88, 590, 630; **6:**1258; **8:**130
AMAZIAH (PRIEST)
2:142; **6:**420, 627, 675, 694, 724; **7:**404, 407–8, 410–12, 552, 834
AMITTAI
3:243; **7:**463, 466, 470, 472, 474, 493, 513
AMMI
7:223, 238–44, 253, 264, 277–78, 295
AMMIHUD
2:95
AMMINADAB
2:95; **3:**345; **9:**94
AMMINADIB
5:420
AMMISHADDAI
2:95
AMMON/AMMONITES
1:245, 248, 259, 261, 274, 419, 432, 476, 989–90, 1084, 1126; **2:**165–67, 305–6, 461, 547, 551, 770, 773, 821, 824–25, 827, 830–34, 836–38, 841–42, 885, 901, 1032, 1053–55, 1061–62, 1070, 1081, 1099, 1198, 1212, 1266, 1278–80, 1283–84, 1293, 1300, 1332; **3:**115, 416, 559, 581, 591, 594, 733, 737, 757–58, 770, 773, 819, 842–43, 848, 850, 1089, 1099, 1117–19, 1123–24, 1139, 1167–68; **4:**74, 263, 1010; **5:**849; **6:**559–60, 782, 857–59, 878–79, 894, 917–18, 920, 1078, 1080, 1249, 1270, 1293, 1301, 1304, 1325, 1347–53, 1355–56, 1358, 1363, 1369, 1378, 1396, 1400, 1403, 1408, 1419, 1482; **7:**50, 142, 147, 353, 355, 360, 362, 663, 690, 696, 699
AMNON
2:949, 963, 1170, 1219, 1269–70, 1285, 1302–6, 1308–10, 1313–15, 1317, 1355; **3:**17, 901; **4:**345, 694; **5:**78, 107, 122, 193, 263, 622, 737; **6:**1033
AMOK
3:816, 831
AMON (EGYPTIAN GOD)
6:1398, 1418; **7:**616
AMON (KING)
1:266, 1126, 1138; **2:**567, 688; **3:**275, 277–78, 280, 602, 632, 636, 643–44, 650, 656; **6:**1077, 1561; **7:**662, 674–75; **8:**130
AMORITES
1:164–65, 236, 408, 439, 446, 660; **2:**5, 21, 123, 165–67, 181, 198, 248, 250, 293, 300, 571, 576, 589, 607, 627, 637, 647, 689, 714, 744–45, 830–31, 870, 1019, 1358; **3:**733, 819; **4:**80; **5:**560; **6:**1282, 1496
AMOS
1:2, 118, 225, 262, 265, 870, 992, 1136, 1179; **2:**142, 221, 332, 408, 430, 855, 1016, 1043; **3:**22, 96, 769, 809, 819, 848, 1002, 1069, 1098; **4:**36, 63, 80, 513, 592, 892, 1111; **5:**692, 716,

752, 797, 851; **6:**2–3, 6–8, 12–13, 16, 18, 20–21, 23, 49, 58, 60, 72, 82, 84, 97, 108–9, 126–27, 156, 158–59, 183, 194, 212, 235, 239, 249, 293, 420, 580–81, 613–14, 627, 637, 647–48, 656, 675, 709, 724, 734, 740, 746, 812, 841, 866, 1090, 1140, 1144, 1164–65, 1179, 1290, 1296, 1303, 1315, 1366, 1412–13, 1451; **7:**41, 267–68, 312, 339–48, 351–55, 357–58, 360–63, 365–78, 380–83, 385–97, 399–419, 421–28, 430–31, 435–36, 440, 456, 481, 580, 635, 660, 663–64, 666, 680, 683, 685, 688, 692, 699, 707, 832, 834, 849, 853, 855, 861; **8:**130–31; **9:**45, 408, 545; **10:**128, 147, 207, 213, 215, 217–19, 221, 230–31, 234, 252, 255, 269, 284, 367, 445; **11:**75, 152, 617; **12:**216, 287, 639

AMOZ
6:3, 17, 19, 30, 33, 36, 48, 155; **7:**702

AMPLIATUS
10:762

AMRAM
2:213; **3:**344–45, 452

ANAIAH
3:800

ANAK
2:21, 122–23, 739

ANAN
3:817

ANANIAH
9:367

ANANIAS (HEALER OF PAUL)
9:118; **10:**151–52, 163, 201, 226, 305, 307, 314, 337

ANANIAS (HIGH PRIEST)
10:309–10, 318

ANANIAS (HUSBAND OF SAPPHIRA)
3:332, 464; **9:**425; **10:**74, 95, 97–101, 111, 140

ANATH
2:772

ANCIENT OF DAYS
See under GOD, NAMES FOR/TITLES OF

ANDREW
1:14; **7:**526–28; **8:**167, 169–70, 539, 543, 553, 567, 636; **9:**111, 139, 531, 594, 685, 710

ANDRONICUS
4:182, 222–24, 229; **9:**137; **10:**762

ANNA (PROPHET)
9:23, 69–70, 72–75, 174, 336, 338, 341, 393, 395, 464, 478, 489; **11:**819; **12:**687

ANNA (WIFE OF TOBIT)
3:976, 983, 986, 989, 1001, 1003–5, 1007, 1011, 1014, 1024–25, 1028, 1039, 1048–50, 1052, 1069; **5:**630

ANNAS
9:80, 800, 803, 805–6, 808–11, 824; **10:**88

ANTICHRIST
12:372, 375, 403–4, 426–27, 452, 467, 493, 518, 532–40, 544, 605, 659, 661, 703, 711–12

ANTIOCHIANS
4:217

ANTIOCHUS III (THE GREAT)
1:269; **3:**1158; **4:**5–7, 10–11, 30–31, 60, 104–6, 125, 143, 169, 192–93, 204–6, 217, 222–23, 232, 248, 255, 269; **5:**612, 705, 800, 824, 859; **7:**24, 55, 61, 102, 140–41; **11:**567

ANTIOCHUS IV (EPIPHANES)
1:268–70, 285–86, 288; **2:**229; **3:**840, 951, 967, 977, 1078, 1179; **4:**3, 5–12, 18–20, 30–31, 34–36, 38–41, 47–48, 50, 52, 54, 59–61, 63, 67–69, 72, 74, 77–78, 84–86, 88, 91, 93–94, 99, 102, 104, 121, 133–34, 151, 159, 163, 165, 168, 177, 181–82, 184, 190–91, 193, 202, 204, 207, 213, 216–19, 222–23, 226–33, 240–42, 244, 247–48, 253–60, 265, 268–70, 280–83, 295, 795, 994; **5:**611–12, 656, 673, 702, 843; **6:**933, 973, 1213, 1502; **7:**4, 6, 8–10, 20, 24–26, 28, 61, 63, 94, 100, 102–3, 105, 113–14, 116–17, 122, 128, 139, 141–43, 146–47, 149, 151; **8:**30, 33, 35, 442, 663, 690; **9:**107, 675; **10:**181; **11:**204, 214, 759; **12:**493, 521, 726

ANTIOCHUS V (EUPATOR)
4:39, 60, 69, 84, 86, 88, 93–96, 255, 260, 265, 268–69, 280–83, 286–87, 289; **6:**1512

ANTIOCHUS VI (SON OF BALAS)
4:137, 140–41, 143, 147, 154–57, 168, 189

ANTIOCHUS VII (SIDETES)
4:5, 12–13, 38, 167–69, 171–73, 176–78

ANTIPAS
See HEROD ANTIPAS

ANTIPATER
4:144; **9:**362

APELLES
10:762–63

APOLLONIUS
4:10, 36, 42, 55–57, 129–30, 174, 206, 218, 227, 229, 247, 260, 275; **8:**248–49

APOLLOS
2:768; **3:**409, 432; **9:**477; **10:**252–53, 258, 260–63, 719, 762, 777–78, 780, 801–5, 807, 825–29, 831, 833–37, 840–41, 868, 993, 998; **11:**16, 295, 357, 409, 592, 615, 802, 878; **12:**6

APOLLYON
12:632

APPHIA
10:969; **11:**891–92, 902

AQUILA
8:13; **10:**251–54, 258, 260–63, 361, 732, 761–63, 774, 777–78, 827, 1001; **11:**858
ARABS
1:591; **2:**649, 660, 1307; **3:**761; **4:**137; **6:**188, 899, 1347–48, 1379; **7:**438; **9:**116; **10:**484; **11:**302
ARAH
3:788
ARAM
1:516; **8:**129
ARAMEANS
2:1266, 1278–80; **3:**96, 118, 150, 152, 161, 166, 181, 192, 196, 198, 201–3, 207–9, 214, 233, 236, 238, 244, 251, 329, 551; **4:**62, 129, 344; **6:**1270; **7:**354, 361, 403, 424, 699
ARAUNAH
2:1381
ARCHELAUS
See HEROD ARCHELAUS
ARCHIPPUS
11:556, 666, 668, 891–92
ARCHITE
2:1323
AREOPAGITE
12:297
ARETAS
9:88; **11:**138, 160, 216
ARIARATHES
4:117, 170
ARIEL
3:378; **6:**241–42
ARIOCH
7:51–53, 82
ARISTARCHUS
10:272–73, 345, 353; **11:**666–67, 903
ARISTOBULUS
1:270, 290; **3:**1118; **4:**13, 191–92; **9:**87; **10:**763
ARIUS
4:143–44; **9:**752
ARPACHSHAD
1:408, 416; **6:**1442
ARPHAXAD
3:1075–76, 1095, 1098–1100, 1131
ARSACES
4:104, 157, 170; **9:**171
ARTAXERXES I
1:268, 286; **3:**665–66, 668–69, 694, 696, 698–701, 712, 715, 717–18, 720–23, 726, 736, 742, 750–51, 753, 755–57, 761, 765, 782, 788, 796, 819, 846, 878, 948, 951, 953, 959, 966; **6:**443; **7:**102, 139, 331
ARTAXERXES II
3:666, 715, 741, 751, 834, 892
ARTAXERXES III
3:833, 878, 1077, 1101, 1106; **6:**1398
ARTEMAS
11:878
ARTEMIS
4:40, 60, 84–85, 193, 222, 243; **8:**22; **10:**270–74; **11:**361, 460, 792, 808; **12:**571
ARTIFICER
6:1131
ASA
1:257, 264; **2:**149; **3:**5, 114, 118–19, 168–69, 214, 217, 233, 278, 332, 388, 505, 536, 538, 541–44, 546–47, 552, 559–60, 562, 564, 580–81, 628, 657; **4:**30, 71; **5:**807, 853; **6:**859; **7:**770; **8:**130
ASAHEL
2:1174, 1216–18, 1225–26, 1376; **3:**456; **4:**129
ASAIAH
3:345, 825
ASAPH
3:300, 345, 363, 394, 401, 445–46, 451, 610, 648, 686, 692–93, 756, 826, 838, 842; **4:**656, 658, 852, 881, 972, 1013, 1104; **6:**293; **8:**130
ASENATH
1:622, 624, 659
ASHER (PERSONAL NAME)
1:555, 598; **2:**212; **3:**351, 353, 457; **4:**538; **12:**620
ASHER (TRIBE)
2:34, 37, 208, 212–13, 263, 536, 744, 788, 802–3; **3:**52, 320, 351, 353, 457; **4:**538; **6:**1605–6
ASHERAH
1:233, 239; **2:**277, 286, 420, 569–70, 687, 766, 797; **3:**115, 118, 124, 135, 139, 162, 276, 1108; **6:**1175–76; **7:**224, 226, 240, 272, 779
ASHHUR
3:329–30
ASHPENAZ
7:42, 44–45
ASHTORETH
3:96
ASHUR
2:586; **6:**1442; **7:**606
ASMODEUS
3:989, 1008, 1010–11, 1026–27, 1029, 1031, 1033, 1039–40, 1051; **6:**585
ASRIEL
2:683; **3:**342
ASSIR
3:345

ASSUR
6:11, 1361
ASSYRIANS
1:248, 256, 265–67, 408; **2:**311, 319, 461, 568–69, 572–73, 635–36, 859–60, 864; **3:**5, 113, 123, 251, 257–58, 260–61, 264–65, 272, 286, 505, 613, 636, 680, 710, 773, 848, 992, 1075–76, 1078, 1081, 1095, 1097–99, 1102, 1104, 1106, 1109, 1111, 1117, 1120, 1127, 1137, 1144, 1150, 1154–55, 1165, 1168, 1170–71; **4:**100, 204, 990, 999; **5:**113; **6:**7, 36–37, 40, 89, 108, 117, 127, 129, 133, 137, 164, 186, 188–89, 196, 227, 232, 237, 248, 253, 260–61, 266, 291–92, 294, 303–5, 376, 454, 915, 1076–77, 1232, 1317, 1322, 1325–26, 1361, 1422, 1442, 1466, 1484, 1501, 1511, 1516, 1521, 1605; **7:**90, 106, 200, 203, 219, 270, 279, 342, 361, 378, 395, 399, 403, 563, 576, 595, 597, 612, 618, 626, 792
ASTARTE
1:1135; **2:**569–70, 755, 757, 1017, 1198; **4:**80, 276, 945; **6:**345, 638, 1360, 1392; **7:**779
ASTYAGES
1:267; **7:**73, 187
ATARGATIS
4:80, 193, 276
ATER
3:817
ATHAIAH
3:825
ATHALIAH
1:264–65; **3:**214–15, 227–28, 230, 234, 280, 551, 565, 570, 573–76, 581, 600; **6:**943; **8:**130
ATHENOBIUS
4:171–72
ATTALUS
4:170
AUGUSTUS
4:170; **5:**493–94, 597; **8:**16, 343, 420; **9:**60, 62–63, 65, 67, 80, 386, 460; **10:**404, 515, 624; **11:**191, 205, 401, 677, 771; **12:**683
AURANUS
4:223; **5:**658
AUTHOR OF LIFE
See under JESUS THE CHRIST, NAMES FOR/TITLES OF
AVVIM
2:306, 662
AZAL
3:358
AZARIAH
3:50, 52, 242, 245, 250, 251, 344, 538, 541, 547, 590, 685, 717–18, 816, 825, 832, 838, 941, 1023, 1080, 1142, 1176; **4:**78, 81, 89, 96, 249, 261, 276; **5:**800, 853; **7:**20, 39, 63, 67, 78, 158, 160, 167, 170, 179, 183, 188–89
AZAZEL
1:1111–12
AZBUK
3:769
AZEL
3:368
AZGAD
3:817
AZZUR
3:817; **6:**1186

B

BAAL
1:233, 236, 239, 274–76, 840, 1067, 1147, 1181; **2:**189, 198, 277, 286, 306, 364, 374, 399, 480, 534, 569, 570, 600, 755, 757, 766, 772, 791–92, 797, 802, 810, 841, 1005, 1017–18, 1029, 1062, 1212–13, 1230, 1274; **3:**21, 124–28, 130–31, 133, 135–36, 138–39, 142–43, 145–46, 150, 156, 158, 162, 170, 178, 180, 183–84, 214–15, 224–26, 228, 230, 234, 276, 285, 357, 575, 582, 598, 635; **4:**51, 197, 290, 395, 469, 485–86, 518, 592, 621–22, 792–93, 934, 945–47, 1097, 1220, 1268; **5:**36, 71, 227, 397, 430, 622, 667, 673, 800; **6:**9, 21, 159, 180, 217, 597, 599–601, 607, 640, 655, 670, 679, 707, 721, 750, 913, 1002, 1213, 1224, 1360–61, 1387, 1393, 1434; **7:**101, 105, 113, 167–68, 188–89, 200, 202–3, 206, 224–26, 234–35, 239, 244, 258, 264, 269, 288, 602, 717, 779, 828; **8:**343, 580; **10:**676; **11:**214; **12:**581, 725
BAAL (KING OF TYRE)
6:1361, 1367
BAAL I (KING)
6:1361
BAAL II (KING)
6:1361
BAAL-BERITH
2:635
BAAL-HADAD
3:21, 678; **6:**1114
BAAL-HAZOR
2:198
BAAL-HERMON
2:198
BAALIS
6:1080, 1348
BAAL-MALAGEC
6:1361
BAAL OF PEOR
2:159, 197–98, 348, 715, 907; **4:**32; **7:**269, 272, 288; **12:**578. *See also* BAAL-PEOR *in PLACES IN THE BIBLE*

BAAL-SAPHON
6:1361
BAAL-SHAMAYIM/SHAMAYN/SHAMEM/SHAMEN
1:237; **6:**1360–61; **7:**25, 114, 143
BAAL-ZEBUB/BAAL-ZEBUL/BEELZEBUL
3:170, 173, 212, 1117; **4:**88; **8:**59, 115, 117, 163, 261–62, 284–87, 296, 564; **9:**98, 182, 241–43, 245. *See also* LUCIFER; SATAN
BAANA
3:51, 768
BAANAH
2:1230; **3:**817
BAASHA
1:264; **3:**118–22, 125, 536, 542, 564
BACCHIDES
4:95–98, 109–11, 113–19, 121, 125, 140–41, 146, 150–52, 156, 249, 286, 298
BACENOR
4:276
BAEAN
4:74
BAGOAS
1:268; **3:**685, 1077, 1101–2, 1106, 1147, 1158–59, 1161, 1170
BAKBUKIAH
3:826, 832, 835
BALAAM
1:234, 242, 249, 365, 440, 665, 821; **2:**5–6, 8, 22, 96, 169–70, 177–98, 201–2, 245–46, 256, 461, 599, 607, 665–67, 910, 1090, 1370; **3:**424, 842, 844, 1119–20; **4:**30, 635; **5:**251–52, 622, 668; **6:**9–10, 1159, 1348; **7:**579, 583, 660; **8:**425; **9:**641; **10:**453; **11:**796; **12:**351–52, 491–92, 546, 578–79, 581, 589, 687, 697, 734
BALAK
1:242; **2:**5, 96, 169–70, 177, 179–91, 193–95, 197, 245–46, 256–57, 599; **3:**842; **4:**306; **5:**668; **6:**1159; **7:**579; **12:**351, 491, 579
BANI
3:769, 801, 817
BANNAS
3:832
BARABBAS
1:26; **8:**438, 485–86, 491, 718–20; **9:**448–49, 799, 818–19
BARAK
2:547, 724, 726, 745, 759, 762, 774–77, 779–83, 787–90, 792, 795, 805, 820–21, 831, 873, 1062; **3:**904, 1090, 1138; **12:**143
BAR-JESUS
8:23; **10:**190, 201
BAR JONAH/BARJONA
10:97, 161
BARNABAS
1:1011; **3:**364; **8:**567, 595; **9:**99, 137, 139, 219, 349; **10:**10, 59, 95, 97–98, 100, 153–54, 175–77, 182, 188–91, 194, 196–201, 203–7, 210–11, 217–19, 221–22, 224–27, 258, 266, 288, 292, 735, 756; **11:**113, 191, 193, 221–23, 225–29, 234, 241, 245, 579, 667, 814; **12:**6
BARSABBAS
10:221
BARTHOLOMEW
8:253
BARTIMAEUS
1:178, 707; **8:**63, 239, 619, 621, 655–56, 665; **9:**354, 356
BARUCH
3:766, 769, 816, 825; **4:**214, 705; **6:**3, 10, 468, 560, 561, 563–64, 731, 761, 769, 775, 820, 838–42, 866, 876–77, 929–35, 939–47, 949–50, 952, 955–66, 968–71, 973–74, 978, 980–82, 985, 1009, 1016, 1415, 1418; **7:**3, 13, 121, 125–26, 796
BARZILLAI
2:1345, 1347–48, 1353, 1359; **3:**28, 687
BATHSHEBA
1:118, 383, 428, 606; **2:**247, 541–42, 547, 551, 746, 949, 963–64, 1140, 1158, 1165, 1169, 1229, 1231, 1242, 1252, 1256, 1269–71, 1279, 1283–89, 1292–95, 1297–98, 1300, 1302–4, 1306, 1309, 1317, 1331, 1367; **3:**14, 18–20, 23–24, 31–33, 43, 94, 117, 152, 330–32, 414, 421, 1158; **4:**643, 885; **5:**85, 109, 122, 129, 139, 263, 422, 466, 622, 849; **6:**6, 88, 258, 300, 1274; **7:**93, 179; **8:**144; **10:**453; **11:**56
BATH-SHUA
3:330, 332, 421
BAVVAI
3:769
BEBAI
3:817
BECORATH
2:1351
BEDAN
2:1062
BEELZEBUB/BEELZEBUL
See BAAL-ZEBUB/BAAL-ZEBUL/BEELZEBUL
BEERAH
3:337
BEERI
7:200, 217

BEL (DEITY)
3:680, 710, 1123; **4:**52, 193; **5:**4, 612, 634, 779; **6:**11, 345, 405–6, 413, 912, 987, 995, 1002, 1537; **7:**64, 72, 80, 141, 156–57, 175, 185, 188–90, 192–94, 606; **8:**29
BELA
3:357
BELOVED DISCIPLE
8:103; **9:**416, 466–67, 471–72, 498–501, 514, 686, 705, 729–30, 808, 829, 832, 834, 840–41, 843–44, 855, 857, 859–60, 862–65; **11:**227; **12:**438, 465. *See also* JOHN THE EVANGELIST
BELSHAZZAR
4:577; **5:**765; **6:**939, 945; **7:**21, 40, 42, 80–85, 100, 103, 111, 121, 149; **12:**521
BELTESHAZZAR
7:39, 73, 136
BEN-ABINADAB
3:51
BENAIAH
2:1268, 1376; **3:**18–20, 24, 32–34, 49–50, 456; **6:**1186, 1345
BEN-AMMI
6:1347
BEN-DEKER
3:51
BEN-GEBER
3:51
BEN-HADAD
1:265; **3:**146–48, 150–53, 156–57, 161, 203, 212, 215, 236; **6:**134
BEN-HESED
3:51
BEN-HUR
3:51
BEN-IMLAH
See IMLAH
BENINU
3:817
BENJAMIN (PERSONAL NAME)
1:259, 552, 554, 585–86, 627–30, 633–36, 638–40, 644–45, 667, 864; **2:**536, 660, 845; **3:**319, 745, 769, 838; **4:**461; **5:**122, 411; **6:**810, 1606; **12:**620
BENJAMIN/BENJAMINITES (TRIBE)
1:164, 259, 261, 1164; **2:**34, 37, 213, 247, 263, 536, 563, 627, 646, 659, 660–61, 672, 678, 681, 687, 694, 726, 736–37, 739–41, 762, 765, 770–71, 776, 788, 803, 835, 842, 863–64, 876, 884–88, 1016, 1037–38, 1047, 1055, 1145, 1147, 1216–17, 1224, 1230, 1233, 1346, 1350–51; **3:**28, 33–34, 39, 52, 95, 102, 320, 342, 351–52, 356–58, 363, 367, 378–80, 422, 456, 678, 684, 686, 694–95, 712, 742, 825, 865, 886, 981, 1079; **4:**32, 63, 206, 946; **6:**1508, 1526, 1605; **7:**123, 247, 465; **8:**147; **10:**675; **11:**214, 526
BENO
3:442
BEN-ONI
1:585
BEOR
1:234, 242; **2:**178, 181, 189, 191, 246; **5:**252; **6:**9–10, 1348; **12:**351
BERECHIAH
1:67; **3:**363, 701, 766, 788, 834; **6:**5; **7:**739–40
BERIAH
3:353
BERNICE
9:87; **10:**328–30, 333, 341
BETHEL (DEITY)
2:565, 572, 687; **7:**792
BETHUEL
1:511–13; **7:**305
BEZAI
3:817
BEZALEL
1:921–22, 961–62; **3:**329, 473, 478, 484–85
BICHRI
2:1351; **4:**193
BIGTHAN
3:892, 950
BIGVAI
3:685–86, 726, 817
BILDAD
1:236; **4:**399–402, 404, 468–70, 474, 483, 516–18
BILGAH
3:816; **4:**8, 206, 222–23
BILGAI
3:816
BILHAH
1:553–54, 664–65; **2:**918; **3:**319, 342, 457; **6:**1605–6
BINNUI
3:692, 769, 817, 832
BISHLAM
3:698
BLASTUS
10:181
BOANERGES
8:562; **9:**215
BOAZ
1:1173; **2:**65, 265, 541, 760, 899, 905, 908–9, 913–19, 921–40, 942–43, 945–46, 1100; **4:**510; **5:**125, 282, 687; **6:**1549; **8:**130

BOSOR
12:351
BUNNI
3:817, 826
BUZ
3:337
BUZI
6:1075, 1086, 1110

C

CAIAPHAS
3:1120; **8:**464, 479, 481, 483, 717; **9:**80, 549, 621, 697–99, 708, 806, 808, 810, 816, 820–21, 823, 851; **10:**150
CAIN
1:220, 325–26, 367, 372–78, 380, 382, 400, 403, 408, 428, 434, 515, 1005, 1017, 1120; **2:**124, 192, 250, 266, 697, 738, 808; **4:**345; **5:**56, 232, 278, 328, 445, 522–23, 526, 584, 622, 805; **6:**205, 649, 795; **7:**832; **9:**300, 643; **10:**570–71; **11:**56; **12:**50, 158, 418–19, 491, 603, 631, 694
CALCOL
3:328
CALEB
1:962; **2:**21, 120–26, 214, 249, 263, 298, 561, 646, 655, 671, 673–74, 677–78, 701, 735, 737–41, 749, 753, 757, 765–66, 782, 877, 900; **3:**327–30, 332; **4:**50–51; **5:**631, 836, 846; **6:**371, 424, 442, 468; **12:**50, 53, 488
CALLISTHENES
4:250
CANAAN
1:403–5, 409, 503; **2:**182, 559–60, 601, 608, 626, 681; **6:**1398; **7:**182
CANAANITES
1:74, 164–66, 175, 273, 279, 308, 404–5, 408, 424, 433, 442, 446, 492, 503, 510, 577, 579–81, 584, 590, 593, 604, 666, 669–70, 734, 801, 820, 878, 1125–27, 1143; **2:**123, 163, 181, 297, 300, 352, 442, 547, 555, 559–60, 562, 571–72, 575–77, 589, 593–95, 608–9, 616–19, 625–26, 631, 635, 637, 649, 655, 658, 662, 668, 670, 681, 685, 689, 731, 736, 738, 740, 743–50, 756–57, 759–60, 766, 773, 776–77, 779–83, 787–90, 795, 805, 807, 816, 853, 878, 885, 1236; **3:**136, 183, 635, 733, 811, 819, 983, 1016, 1117–18; **4:**792–93, 872, 934, 1268; **5:**262, 536, 542, 759, 787, 862; **6:**604, 733, 1226, 1282, 1491; **7:**168, 202, 355, 357, 456, 877; **10:**429, 640
CANDACE
10:143
CARITES
3:230; **6:**1574
CARMI
3:328, 330
CARPUS
11:857
CENDEBEUS
4:173–75, 178
CEPHAS
3:364; **8:**562, 731; **9:**481; **10:**801, 804, 806–7, 833; **11:**113, 163, 194, 217, 225–28, 230–31, 316; **12:**230, 245
CHAEREAS
11:682
CHALPHI
4:141
CHELUBAI
3:327, 329
CHEMOSH
1:274, 1189; **2:**166, 198, 830–31, 907; **3:**96, 184; **6:**890–92, 894, 920, 1489
CHENAANAH
3:162
CHENANI
3:817
CHERETHITES
2:1268, 1324; **6:**1355; **7:**690, 700
CHILEAB
2:1170, 1219, 1303; **3:**17
CHILION
2:901, 940; **3:**733
CHILMAD
6:1380
CHIMHAM
2:1348
CHLOE
10:803, 807, 969; **11:**135
CHRIST
See JESUS THE CHRIST
CHUZA
9:175
CLAUDIA
11:859
CLAUDIUS
1:291; **5:**440, 597; **8:**16; **10:**177–78, 253, 361, 406, 422, 623, 719, 732, 739, 761–63, 774, 1001; **11:**57, 677
CLAUDIUS FELIX
10:313
CLAUDIUS LYSIAS
10:297–99, 305, 308–9, 311–15, 322
CLEMENT
11:471, 540
CLEOPAS
9:475–78, 482; **10:**43

CLEOPATRA I
1:269, 271; **2:**1289; **3:**970; **4:**5, 35, 219; **5:**461; **7:**55, 141–42; **9:**362
CLEOPATRA II
4:188–89
CLEOPATRA THEA
4:127, 140, 168
CLOPAS
9:477, 831
COL-HOZEH
3:768, 824–25
CONIAH
6:743, 1391; **8:**130
CORNELIUS
1:1018, 1083; **7:**700; **8:**595; **9:**137, 155, 220, 316, 337; **10:**15, 146, 160–71, 188, 191, 203, 206–9, 211, 218, 226, 231, 363; **11:**233, 251; **12:**98, 522
COZBI
2:200, 246
CRATES
4:275; **8:**19
CRESCENS THE CYNIC
8:19; **11:**857
CRISPUS
10:252, 254, 807
CUSHAN-RISHATHAIM
2:546, 767
CUSHI
6:659–61, 663–67, 670–72, 674–76, 678–82, 685–86, 688, 692–94, 697, 699–701, 703–4
CYRUS
1:65, 247, 266–68, 900; **2:**602; **3:**657, 665–66, 668, 675, 677–80, 685, 690–92, 694–96, 700, 702, 704–8, 710, 712–13, 717, 721, 770, 878, 899, 913, 925, 1108; **4:**661; **6:**37, 186, 313, 315, 318, 348–49, 352–54, 356–58, 361–62, 375–76, 385, 388, 390–91, 393–96, 399–402, 406–8, 410–11, 413, 417–19, 423, 429–30, 437, 444, 455, 460, 513–14, 520, 763, 939–40, 943, 945, 1513; **7:**23, 26, 28–29, 44, 54, 62, 65, 73, 80–81, 84, 87, 89, 93, 102, 105, 112, 116, 121, 136–39, 150, 169, 187, 330, 709, 715, 731, 738; **9:**698; **12:**573

D

DAGON
2:840–41, 854–55, 859–60, 960, 997, 1005–8, 1010, 1013, 1015, 1029, 1198; **3:**368; **4:**130, 371; **5:**556
DAMARIS
10:247; **12:**297
DAN (PERSONAL NAME)
1:585, 598, 664; **3:**319, 342, 457; **12:**620
DAN/DANITES (TRIBE)
1:666, 1164; **2:**34, 37, 95, 213, 263, 536, 694, 743–45, 765, 788, 845, 863, 865, 870–72, 885, 899; **3:**347, 351, 478, 617; **5:**54; **6:**1379, 1604–6; **12:**537
DANIEL
1:230, 240–41, 268, 288–90, 1182; **2:**392, 855, 1170; **3:**497, 725, 816, 865, 868, 870–71, 873, 888, 946, 948–49, 959, 966, 1138, 1147, 1154; **4:**40, 46, 51, 72, 296, 328, 343, 377, 430, 503, 563; **5:**6, 118, 231, 271, 274, 281, 334, 480, 511, 527, 740; **6:**13, 260, 520, 547, 550, 989, 1210, 1213–14, 1258, 1388; **7:**3, 8–9, 12, 20–22, 31, 39–40, 42–45, 49–54, 56–57, 62–64, 72–76, 78, 82–84, 88–95, 100–101, 103, 105–6, 111–17, 121–22, 126–29, 136–39, 141–42, 144–45, 148–52, 156, 158, 174–76, 178–85, 187–90, 192–94, 408; **8:**66, 246, 692; **9:**47, 206, 382; **10:**398, 401, 640; **11:**858; **12:**143–44, 505, 512, 521, 527, 532, 561, 567, 598, 639, 682, 733
DARDA
3:328
DARIUS I
1:247, 267–68, 314; **3:**665–66, 668, 675, 690–91, 695–96, 698, 700–702, 704–7, 709–13, 720, 782, 819, 863, 882, 913, 925, 1081, 1109, 1137; **4:**51, 125; **5:**731; **6:**444, 1443; **7:**28–29, 32, 44, 54, 72, 87–89, 91–94, 102, 121, 136, 138–39, 187, 193–94, 708–9, 714–15, 718, 731, 738, 747, 750, 779, 788–89, 791
DARIUS II
3:722, 834–35
DARIUS III
3:832–35, 1100; **4:**30; **7:**139
DARIUS THE MEDE
3:1081; **7:**84, 87–88, 121, 139, 187
DATHAN
1:1070; **2:**10, 19, 99, 135–39, 142, 146, 158–60, 211, 370; **5:**592, 631, 725, 843; **6:**1534, 1573; **11:**845
DAVID
1:17, 74, 93, 95, 118, 164, 218, 225, 236, 240, 242, 245–46, 248, 252–53, 255–57, 260–63, 278, 289–90, 298, 308–9, 383, 412, 419, 426, 428, 438–39, 441–42, 445–47, 455, 458, 476, 479, 590–91, 599, 604, 606, 612, 665, 700, 821–22, 924, 960, 963, 989, 1009, 1014, 1061, 1063, 1072, 1134, 1152, 1166, 1179, 1182; **2:**5, 123, 147, 191, 200, 219, 230, 247–48, 264, 279, 283, 286–87, 300, 365, 426–27, 432, 440, 446, 518, 535–36, 541, 543, 546–52, 556–72, 574–77, 579, 584–86, 589–90, 601–3, 606, 609, 612, 614, 619–20, 625–26, 630–31, 634–35, 637, 639, 641, 646, 655, 660, 662, 666, 671, 673, 678, 680,

DAVID *(continued)*
682, 687–89, 696, 701–2, 711, 715, 717, 723, 736–37, 739–40, 746, 752, 810, 826, 833, 845, 864–65, 886–87, 891–92, 894–95, 900, 915, 933, 943, 945–46, 949, 951–54, 956–64, 969–70, 974, 977, 980–82, 987–88, 995–96, 1000, 1002, 1012, 1017, 1019, 1023–24, 1027, 1030–32, 1037–38, 1042–45, 1049, 1060, 1064–66, 1069–73, 1079–81, 1085, 1087–95, 1097–1104, 1108–15, 1118–24, 1126–29, 1132–45, 1147–49, 1152–54, 1156–61, 1164–71, 1174–80, 1182–85, 1187–89, 1191–95, 1197–99, 1201–3, 1205–19, 1221–44, 1246–52, 1254–63, 1265–71, 1273–81, 1283–95, 1297–1300, 1302–10, 1313–20, 1323–27, 1330–33, 1335–36, 1339–42, 1345–48, 1350–61, 1365–72, 1375–77, 1379–83; **3:**4–5, 13–14, 17–24, 26–28, 31–37, 39–40, 43, 49–50, 58, 62, 69, 72, 77, 80, 87, 90, 93–97, 100, 102, 106, 109, 114, 117, 119, 152, 168–70, 214, 227–28, 230, 233–34, 241–42, 244, 250, 260, 269, 271, 279, 286–87, 295, 304, 306, 313, 317, 319, 327–28, 332–33, 336, 344–45, 348, 351–53, 355, 357, 362–66, 368, 370, 376–86, 388–90, 393–96, 399–403, 405–9, 413–18, 421–27, 429–33, 436–38, 441–42, 446–47, 450, 452, 456–58, 460–64, 467–69, 472–74, 477–79, 483, 485–87, 494–500, 502, 505–6, 511, 512, 514, 518, 522, 524, 529, 531, 544, 546–47, 556, 562, 565, 568–70, 573–76, 587, 598, 602–3, 606–7, 610–11, 622, 644, 647–48, 651, 654, 657, 667, 680, 686–87, 691–93, 699–700, 712, 725, 727, 747, 756, 759, 769, 785, 794, 826, 835, 839, 842, 885–86, 901, 909, 911, 914, 993, 1014, 1016, 1091, 1112–13, 1137, 1155, 1161, 1173; **4:**21, 36, 43, 46, 49–51, 56, 58, 62–63, 66, 69, 77–78, 81, 93, 101, 111, 129, 164, 171, 188, 193, 199, 217, 228, 230, 254, 264, 276, 297, 309–10, 343, 348, 439, 539, 556, 562, 613, 643–44, 655–60, 663, 689, 694, 733, 746–49, 823, 838, 861, 885–88, 890–92, 894, 898, 901, 905, 912, 916, 926–27, 979, 990, 992, 994, 1019, 1034–36, 1040, 1064, 1081, 1104, 1112, 1129, 1156, 1176, 1183, 1199, 1211–13, 1246, 1255, 1261; **5:**2, 11, 20, 32, 59, 61, 74, 102, 107, 109, 122, 138–39, 143–44, 153, 164, 166, 168–70, 174, 180, 186–87, 189, 194–96, 206, 220, 252, 256, 263, 268, 272, 282, 289, 300, 377, 403, 416, 422, 466, 510, 517, 606, 620, 622, 631–33, 656–57, 682, 708, 724, 757, 836, 843, 846, 849, 852–53, 855, 867; **6:**2, 5–8, 22, 35–36, 38, 40, 61, 88–89, 107–9, 119, 121, 123–24, 139–41, 143, 145, 147–48, 163, 167, 169–70, 181, 194, 218, 237, 242, 258, 262, 271, 284, 295, 300–301, 304, 314, 336, 344, 377, 395–96, 399, 402, 413, 443–44, 464, 481–83, 527–28, 530, 575, 733–34, 739–40, 742–44, 763, 826, 858, 874, 877, 926, 1015, 1080, 1082, 1084, 1086, 1119, 1138, 1152, 1245, 1252–54, 1266, 1268, 1272–74, 1280, 1299, 1319–20, 1325, 1347–49, 1352, 1360, 1386, 1411, 1461–64, 1469–70, 1473, 1506, 1509–10, 1561, 1578, 1593; **7:**82–83, 93, 121, 147, 164, 179, 206, 232, 348, 361–62, 425–28, 437–38, 469, 547, 558, 567–68, 570–72, 588, 667, 670, 699, 732, 737, 739, 741–42, 766, 770, 807–8, 811, 814, 816, 823, 825–31, 833–34; **8:**94, 126–27, 129–32, 134–35, 137–38, 140, 144, 148–50, 161, 167, 223, 239, 244, 246, 278–79, 281–82, 284–85, 290, 317, 336–37, 344, 354–59, 363, 383, 399–400, 403–4, 406, 426–27, 455, 484, 515, 526–28, 530, 538, 556, 621, 655–57, 659, 673, 680–81, 696, 712–13, 718; **9:**8, 14–19, 51, 59, 63, 65, 67, 85, 93–95, 133–34, 139, 167, 200, 302, 326, 341, 353–57, 360, 362, 366, 369, 381, 388, 390–92, 426, 442, 445–46, 595, 668, 713, 722, 737, 834; **10:**49, 63, 66, 92, 147, 192–93, 219, 252, 398, 416–18, 453, 492–95, 511, 537, 549, 556–57, 598, 629–30, 660, 663, 710, 748; **11:**40, 56, 76, 93, 106, 159, 264, 319, 404, 421, 480, 526, 582, 728, 780; **12:**22, 29, 52, 61, 143–44, 158, 343, 527, 531, 536, 567, 584, 602, 702, 721; DYNASTY of **2:**1257; **3:**26, 95; **4:**111, 164, 1034–36, 1183, 1199, 1211; **5:**849, 852–53; **6:**107, 122–23, 242, 742–45, 826, 1469–70; **7:**828–30; **8:**126, 129–33, 239, 403–4, 656, 659; **9:**51, 63, 67; **10:**66, 92, 192–93; **12:**584, 602, 734; GOD'S COVENANT WITH **2:**1254–63; **3:**95; **4:**600, 1034–36, 1211; **5:**853; **6:**743–44, 1470; **8:**129; **9:**59; **10:**192; PSALMS OF **1:**17; **3:**567–70; **4:**199, 309, 643–44, 655–59, 689, 694, 746–49, 838, 885–89, 894, 916, 990, 1019, 1156, 1246; **5:**849; **10:**193

DEBORAH (JUDGE AND PROPHET)
1:186, 242, 258; **2:**108, 551, 558, 585, 637, 651, 723–24, 726, 745, 759, 762–63, 765, 767, 772, 774–83, 787–92, 795–96, 805, 820–21, 827, 829, 831, 835, 872–73, 983, 1016, 1062; **3:**136, 1077, 1090, 1113, 1138, 1148, 1165, 1176; **4:**945; **5:**81, 620, 629; **6:**2, 5, 117; **9:**72; **12:**144

DEBORAH (REBEKAH'S NURSE)
1:511, 584, 586

DEBORAH (TOBIT'S GRANDMOTHER)
3:986, 994, 1014

DELAIAH
1:268; **3:**687, 708, 757, 786; **6:**775

DELILAH
2:738, 782, 821, 824, 840–43, 850, 853, 858, 860, 869; **6:**726

DEMAS
11:667, 857–58, 903–4

DEMETRIUS I SOTER
4:31, 93–95, 98, 101–3, 107, 109–10, 116–17, 119–21, 123–25, 127, 129–30, 136–38, 140, 143, 145, 154, 167–68, 173, 181, 202, 248–49, 283, 286, 296; **7:**102, 140
DEMETRIUS II NICATOR
4:125, 129–30, 132–38, 140, 143, 147, 152, 154, 157, 160, 164–65, 167–71, 173, 189
DEMETRIUS III EUCAERUS
4:5, 17, 20
DEMETRIUS THE SILVERSMITH
10:247, 266, 270–74; **11:**857; **12:**461, 463, 465, 467–69
DEMOPHON
4:275
DEUEL
2:95
DIBLAIM
7:217–18, 231
DINAH
1:518, 539, 555, 576–81, 584–85, 600, 652; **2:**47, 876; **3:**1119, 1132, 1143–44; **5:**422, 433
DIONYSIUS
10:247; **12:**297
DIONYSUS
1:1135; **4:**11, 39, 233, 257, 290; **8:**248; **11:**58, 653, 677
DIOTREPHES
12:464–68
DIVES
9:316, 319–20; **12:**194
DOEG
2:1140, 1147–48; **4:**890
DORCAS
9:336; **10:**160–61
DORYMENES
4:223, 233, 247, 253, 260, 268
DOSITHEUS
3:971; **4:**125, 276
DRUSILLA
8:16; **10:**320–21, 328

E

EBED
3:725
EBED-MELECH
6:6, 468, 842, 849–50, 852, 876–77; **7:**670, 685
EBER
1:408–9; **2:**192; **3:**834; **4:**30
EBIASAPH
3:345, 451
EDNA
3:975, 981, 986, 989, 1038–42, 1050, 1069
EDOM/EDOMITES
1:248, 261, 458, 516, 521, 534, 536, 539, 570–71, 573, 590–91, 593, 598, 801, 1084; **2:**5, 157, 162, 178, 191, 255, 257, 306, 461, 535, 737, 830, 1140, 1266; **3:**90, 93, 96, 168, 170, 183, 214, 241–42, 251, 319, 332, 586, 597–98, 691, 1118, 1127; **4:**31, 89, 313, 357, 453, 916–17, 1010, 1122, 1125, 1228; **5:**849, 862; **6:**20, 273, 276–78, 472, 505, 518–20, 525–26, 559, 581, 782, 857, 878–79, 896, 920, 1065–66, 1245, 1249, 1347–50, 1352, 1354–56, 1358, 1363, 1369, 1377–78, 1380, 1396, 1400, 1403, 1408, 1438, 1444, 1474, 1476–86; **7:**50, 147, 336, 346, 353, 355, 361–63, 426–28, 435–42, 444–49, 451–52, 454–58, 493, 587, 818, 847, 855–56, 868, 872; **10:**219, 637
EGLON
1:26; **2:**726, 770–73, 782, 829, 841, 1062; **3:**1090; **4:**1276; **6:**1405
EGYPTIAN, THE
10:298
EHUD
1:26, 258–59; **2:**726, 745, 762–63, 765, 767, 770–74, 776, 779, 782, 791–92, 804, 820–21, 827, 830–31, 838, 841, 1062; **3:**357, 1090; **4:**30, 1276; **6:**1405
EL
See under GOD, NAMES FOR/TITLES OF
ELA
3:18
ELAH
1:264; **3:**118–19, 122, 125, 252, 825; **4:**177
ELAMITES
1:408; **6:**194, 900, 1443
ELASAH
2:687
EL BERITH
See under GOD, NAMES FOR/TITLES OF
ELDAD
2:105, 107, 110, 113
ELEAD
3:353
ELEAZAR BEN SIRA
1:10; **4:**562; **5:**607–8
ELEAZAR (FATHER OF JASON)
4:106
ELEAZAR (PRIEST)
2:1010, 1012–13
ELEAZAR (PRIEST, SON OF AARON)
1:905, 1060, 1071–72; **2:**49, 52, 139, 151, 162, 199, 202, 207, 217, 219–20, 228, 245–50, 263, 546, 555, 580, 630, 657, 683, 686, 701, 707, 718; **3:**363, 441, 725; **5:**843; **6:**430, 456; **11:**214

ELEAZAR (SCRIBE)
4:182
ELEAZAR (SUPPORTER OF DAVID)
2:1375; **3:**379, 382
ELEAZAR (WARRIOR/PRIEST/MARTYR)
4:16, 23, 89, 212, 223, 236, 240, 242–43, 248–49, 277, 282, 291, 296; **7:**188; **9:**389, 433, 475
ELECT LADY
12:449–50, 452–53, 456, 460
EL ELOHE ISRAEL
See under GOD, NAMES FOR/TITLES OF
EL ELYON/ELYON
See under GOD, NAMES FOR/TITLES OF
ELHANAN
2:958, 1108, 1361; **3:**417
ELI
1:1024, 1060; **2:**233, 688, 949, 960, 969–70, 973–76, 978, 986–89, 991–97, 999, 1002, 1004, 1010, 1013, 1015–17, 1019, 1023, 1026, 1045, 1049–50, 1079, 1092, 1097, 1139, 1148, 1167, 1201, 1246, 1371, 1382; **3:**33, 725; **4:**77, 388; **5:**76, 107, 187; **6:**575; **7:**411; **8:**359; **9:**70; **12:**444
ELIAB
2:95, 135, 1098, 1111, 1144
ELIAKIM
3:265, 288, 839; **4:**555; **6:**196–98, 293, 559, 1077, 1326, 1403; **7:**814; **8:**131; **12:**584
ELIAM
2:1284
ELIAS
8:492
ELIASHIB
3:716–17, 741–42, 768–70, 832–34, 836, 846, 849–50
ELIEZER
1:445, 509, 825; **3:**23, 564, 730; **5:**792
ELIHOREPH
3:718
ELIHU
3:329, 457; **4:**320–23, 325–26, 417, 428, 460, 478, 558–65, 567–72, 575–78, 580–83, 585–87, 589–95; **5:**479, 622, 687; **6:**600, 1114
ELIJAH
1:95, 265, 275–76, 380, 838, 849, 1067; **2:**90, 106, 564, 573–74, 602–3, 606–7, 718–19, 792, 797, 811, 860, 1040, 1063, 1206, 1294; **3:**6, 125–33, 135–40, 142–46, 153, 156, 158, 160, 162, 166–67, 169, 171–79, 183–84, 186, 189, 197–98, 201, 209, 212, 215–17, 219–21, 223, 225, 237, 328, 425, 569, 959, 1004; **4:**51, 55, 63, 197, 230, 369, 378, 411, 562, 592, 609, 737, 821, 877, 894, 927, 969, 1063, 1175; **5:**219, 394, 622, 631, 836, 851–52; **6:**2, 4, 9, 22, 107, 317, 563, 676–77, 913, 1111, 1144, 1302; **7:**65, 122, 188–89, 194, 436, 480–81, 582, 753, 832, 846, 869, 873, 875–77; **8:**129, 156, 158–59, 169, 230, 246–47, 267–68, 319, 324, 344, 362–65, 367, 432, 492, 530, 532, 539, 589, 597–98, 601, 622, 630–32, 636, 665, 683, 707, 723–24, 729–30; **9:**15, 22, 46–48, 81, 107–8, 113, 118, 127, 157–61, 164, 195, 198–99, 204–7, 215–17, 316, 319, 336, 440, 479, 489, 527–28, 565, 621; **10:**43–44, 137, 142, 145, 675–76, 843, 950; **11:**214, 216; **12:**58, 85, 144, 187, 189, 223, 532–33, 540, 543, 581, 642, 658, 712
ELIMELECH
2:899, 901, 913–14, 920, 930–31, 933–38, 940, 943; **3:**733
ELIOENAI
3:342, 839
ELIPHAZ
3:318; **4:**328, 330, 332, 362–64, 375–84, 386–87, 389–91, 395, 401, 409, 411, 415, 418, 429–30, 444–46, 448–53, 457, 459–60, 463, 467–68, 482–83, 491–92, 496–97, 499–504, 507–8, 516–17, 523–24, 530, 539, 553, 564, 569, 576, 580–81, 585, 636; **5:**252; **6:**966; **7:**449; **9:**323
ELISHA
1:265; **2:**230, 549, 564, 573–74, 602–3, 606–7, 935, 1040, 1206; **3:**6, 14, 143–45, 162, 173–81, 183–87, 189–92, 194–205, 208–12, 214–17, 219, 234, 236–39, 244, 570, 785, 1049; **4:**50, 211; **5:**631, 836, 846, 851–52; **6:**2–5, 12, 14, 17, 182–83, 317, 1111, 1137, 1144, 1174–75, 1374–75, 1378; **7:**528; **8:**169, 230, 246, 324, 432, 539, 589, 601; **9:**15, 22, 107–8, 113, 118–20, 127, 157, 161, 195–98, 200, 206, 217, 326, 480; **10:**715
ELISHAMA
2:95; **3:**329–30
ELISHUA
3:330
ELIZABETH
1:186; **5:**253; **8:**131; **9:**11, 16, 23, 29, 42, 44–45, 47–52, 54–56, 58–59, 62, 69–70, 72, 174, 224, 337, 341, 464, 477
ELIZAPHAN
3:394
ELIZUR
2:34, 95
ELKANAH
2:548, 970, 973–76, 978, 986; **3:**345; **9:**45
ELNATHAN
3:782; **6:**775; **7:**770
ELOAH
See under GOD, NAMES FOR/TITLES OF

ELOHE
See under GOD, NAMES FOR/TITLES OF
ELOHIM
See under GOD, NAMES FOR/TITLES OF
EL OLAM
See under GOD, NAMES FOR/TITLES OF
ELON
1:259; **2:**762, 764–65, 819, 839
ELPAAL
3:357
EL-ROI
See under GOD, NAMES FOR/TITLES OF
EL SHADDAI/SHADDAI
See under GOD, NAMES FOR/TITLES OF
ELYMAS
8:23; **9:**401; **10:**188, 190, 194, 201
ELYON
See GOD, NAMES FOR/TITLES OF: EL ELYON/ELYON
ELZAPHAN
1:1070
EMIM
2:306, 654
EMMANUEL
See under JESUS THE CHRIST, NAMES FOR/TITLES OF
ENAN
2:95
ENOCH
1:288–89, 326, 379–80; **3:**179; **4:**50, 402, 604, 737, 877, 969; **5:**252, 479, 494, 527, 620–21, 631, 633, 836, 842, 856; **7:**3, 5, 11, 13–14, 861; **8:**39, 630, 729; **9:**95, 489; **10:**43; **11:**779, 791, 855, 866; **12:**58, 85, 133, 136, 146, 485, 494, 519, 532, 537, 560, 571, 597, 646
ENOSH
1:375, 380; **5:**631, 836, 856
EPAENETUS
10:762
EPAPHRAS
11:558–59, 569, 590–92, 618, 665, 667–68, 894, 903–4
EPAPHRODITUS
10:631, 939; **11:**58, 94, 472, 474–75, 518–21, 540, 542–43, 545, 674
EPHAH
3:329; **4:**228
EPHER
4:228
EPHRAIM (SON OF JOSEPH)
1:259, 622, 656, 659–61; **2:**34, 212, 680, 683; **3:**337, 353; **5:**668; **6:**809–11, 1508, 1600, 1605; **7:**281, 292, 810; **8:**354; **12:**139, 620
EPHRAIM/EPHRAIMITES (TRIBE)
1:258–59, 261–62, 264, 660–61; **2:**37, 95, 212–13, 220, 263, 282, 535–36, 556, 561, 563–64, 647, 660–61, 665, 680–81, 684, 687, 715, 717, 739–40, 743–44, 763, 765, 776, 788, 803, 807, 821–22, 826, 834, 837–38, 841, 873, 877, 887, 941, 973; **3:**52, 94, 98, 337, 345, 347, 351–53, 358, 363, 598, 616, 825, 1117, 1123; **4:**313, 917, 998; **5:**153, 633; **6:**108, 127, 137, 174, 235–36, 336, 809–11, 1169, 1171, 1232, 1422, 1466, 1478, 1505–8, 1604–6; **7:**234, 239, 242, 244–48, 251–53, 256–58, 261–62, 265–67, 269–70, 272, 275, 277–79, 281–83, 285–88, 291–93, 296–97, 456, 493, 802, 804, 809–10, 814–16; **8:**147, 354
EPHRATHITE
2:900, 905; **3:**94
EPICUREANS
5:461, 510, 584; **8:**15, 18, 24; **10:**244, 246; **11:**720, 731; **12:**326, 341, 355
EPIPHANES
See ALEXANDER BALAS/EPIPHANES; ANTIOCHUS IV (EPHIPHANES); PTOLEMY V (EPIPHANES) *in PERSONS OUTSIDE THE BIBLE*
ER
1:604–6, 652; **2:**211; **3:**328, 332; **8:**129
ERASTUS
10:270, 766, 777, 814; **11:**135, 858–59
ESARHADDON
1:237, 250; **3:**695, 979, 996, 1070; **6:**11, 295, 1077, 1245, 1361, 1366, 1398, 1499; **7:**51, 594–95
ESAU
1:216, 325, 329, 377, 408, 433, 503, 514, 516–23, 526, 534–39, 552–54, 558, 562–69, 571–74, 584–85, 590–91, 593, 598, 601, 606, 628, 636, 812, 1016; **2:**49, 65, 161–62, 305, 461, 549–50, 741, 845, 1167; **3:**24, 317–18, 1118, 1127; **4:**74, 81; **5:**78, 445, 522, 524, 622, 659, 668; **6:**386, 1347, 1474, 1476, 1478; **7:**283–85, 362, 412, 444, 448, 455, 832, 849, 855–56, 868; **8:**484; **9:**54, 300, 302–3, 653; **10:**637–38; **11:**796; **12:**5, 9, 139, 154
ESDRIS
4:277
ESHBAAL
2:1212; **3:**368
ESTHER
1:241, 284; **3:**856–57, 859–62, 865–73, 877, 880, 883–92, 894–95, 897, 899, 901, 903–6, 908–16, 918–29, 931–36, 938–41, 946, 949–51, 958–60, 962–63, 966, 969–70, 972, 1081, 1087, 1102, 1113–14, 1132, 1141–43, 1147, 1167; **5:**189, 291, 334; **7:**21, 41, 43, 50, 56, 124, 156; **8:**66, 598
ETHAN
3:328, 345, 394, 445; **4:**655

ETHBAAL
1:264; **6:**1360, 1398
ETHIOPIAN EUNUCH
3:1168; **9:**150; **10:**28, 35, 134–35, 140, 142–43, 145
EUBULUS
8:859
EUERGETES
See PTOLEMY III (EUERGETES); PTOLEMY VIII (PHYSKON EUERGETES II)
EUMENES II OF PERGAMUM
4:104, 270
EUNICE
10:226
EUODIA
10:969; **11:**471, 481, 483, 495, 539–40, 546, 668
EUPATOR
See ANTIOCHUS V (EUPATOR)
EUPOLEMUS
1:270; **4:**7, 102, 106, 116, 198–99, 217–18, 298; **5:**626
EUTYCHUS
10:276–78
EVE
1:92, 350–52, 360, 364, 367, 372, 375, 381–83, 428, 434, 604, 1085; **2:**191, 551, 746, 887; **3:**1041, 1043; **4:**256; **5:**56, 71, 422, 523, 567, 584, 621, 693, 716, 758, 764, 805, 823, 825; **6:**528, 795, 1169, 1391–92, 1394; **7:**115, 781, 832; **8:**537; **9:**537; **10:**247, 433, 525–26, 765; **11:**147, 159, 390, 400, 450–51, 800; **12:**574
EVI
2:246
EVIL-MERODACH
3:294
EZEKIEL
1:96, 229–30, 278, 282–83, 290, 734, 838, 881, 993, 1010, 1028, 1034, 1138, 1180–81; **2:**38, 89, 149, 182, 229, 264, 316, 355, 504, 860, 1002, 1238, 1262; **3:**70, 362–63, 462, 502, 514, 587, 656, 658, 679, 687, 735, 1069; **4:**157, 214, 256, 314, 328–29, 346, 404, 503, 591, 898, 975; **5:**46, 381, 401, 544, 631, 634, 647, 663, 800, 818, 836, 855; **6:**5, 7–8, 12–13, 15, 18–19, 101, 103, 183, 186, 222, 257, 310, 320, 444, 464, 467, 492, 576, 579, 581, 629, 638, 702, 794, 812, 942–43, 945, 1075–76, 1078, 1080, 1082, 1084–93, 1095, 1099–100, 1109–11, 1113–32, 1134–61, 1164–72, 1174–77, 1179–80, 1182–1234, 1236–55, 1257–71, 1273–88, 1290–92, 1294–99, 1301–22, 1324–27, 1329–31, 1333–47, 1350–60, 1362–71, 1373–78, 1380, 1382–84, 1386–93, 1395–97, 1399–1402, 1404–32, 1435–40, 1442–84, 1486–92, 1494–97, 1499–1534, 1536–43, 1545–55, 1557–65, 1567–70, 1573–79, 1581–83, 1585–86, 1588–93, 1595–1602, 1605–7; **7:**5, 111, 138, 162, 179, 189, 268, 302, 312, 323, 339, 348, 375, 382, 386, 428, 430–31, 440, 472, 489, 544, 548, 693, 727, 756, 775, 780, 804, 807, 817, 820, 822–23, 831, 833, 837, 846; **8:**601; **9:**93; **10:**145, 150, 447–49, 451, 831; **12:**283, 512, 515, 520–21, 560–61, 566, 569, 591–92, 595–96, 598, 603, 639, 641, 681, 685–86, 711, 714, 721–24, 727
EZER
3:373, 379, 766, 769, 839
EZRA
1:9, 39, 65, 250, 268–69, 285–86, 306, 309, 314; **2:**544, 760, 894, 902, 923, 926, 942; **3:**95, 305, 328, 355, 511, 518, 547, 554, 615, 664–71, 676, 679, 685–86, 690–91, 699, 704, 712–13, 715–18, 720–23, 725–38, 740–43, 746–47, 751, 756, 768, 770, 794, 796–97, 800–805, 813, 816, 824, 826, 830, 832–33, 835–36, 838, 840, 842, 846–47, 849, 1069; **4:**71, 77, 119, 122, 199, 249, 1243; **5:**37, 44, 607, 632–34, 642, 669, 759, 801, 855–56, 862; **6:**243, 318, 400, 527, 942–43; **7:**3, 11–12, 21, 29, 31, 40, 43–44, 52, 111, 113, 138, 163, 178, 182, 488, 723, 738–39, 763, 770, 786–88, 847, 852, 864, 866; **8:**36, 248; **9:**489; **12:**519, 524–25, 639, 726
EZRAHITE
3:328

F

FEAR OF ISAAC
See under GOD, NAMES FOR/TITLES OF
FELIX
9:401; **10:**311, 313–14, 317–26, 329–30
FESTUS
9:401; **10:**322, 324–30, 333–35, 340–43, 737, 757
FORTUNATUS
10:777; **11:**135

G

GAAL
2:817
GABAEL
3:975, 987, 996, 1011, 1014, 1017, 1022, 1033, 1044–45, 1049
GABATHA
3:950
GABBAI
3:825
GABRIEL
2:1259; **3:**1057; **6:**1240; **7:**4, 9, 114–15, 122,

126–27, 129, 136–39, 148–49; **8:**36; **9:**14, 20, 47–48, 50–52, 59, 413, 468; **12:**646
GAD (PROPHET)
2:1138, 1145, 1380–81; **3:**423, 469, 609–10; **6:**2, 6
GAD (SON OF JACOB)
1:555, 598; **3:**337–38, 457; **6:**1605; **12:**620
GAD/GADITES (TRIBE)
1:666; **2:**34, 37, 213, 244, 248–50, 254, 263, 308, 512, 536, 665, 707, 745, 807, 1054; **3:**337–38, 351, 379, 457; **4:**36; **6:**894, 1347, 1601, 1605; **7:**360
GAIUS
4:102; **8:**16; **10:**178, 272–73, 623, 766, 777, 807, 814; **11:**135, 759–60; **12:**460–61, 463–67, 469
GALILEANS
1:169; **8:**44, 167, 169; **9:**23, 270–71, 278, 319, 446, 574; **10:**55, 58
GALLIO
10:252–53, 255–56, 258, 262, 272–73, 304, 330, 775–76; **11:**681
GAMALIEL
2:95; **5:**813; **8:**247; **9:**122, 377; **10:**104, 106–9, 189, 226, 273, 306, 310
GAREB
6:813
GASHMU
3:761, 785
GAULS
4:104, 204, 263
GEBER
3:52
GEDALIAH
1:267; **2:**306, 504, 688; **3:**293–94, 768; **6:**560, 582, 842, 857–60, 864, 925, 942–43, 994, 1079–80, 1348, 1415, 1418; **7:**90, 792, 828
GEHAZI
1:1095; **3:**189, 192, 197–98, 211, 219; **6:**3
GEMARIAH
2:687; **6:**839
GENNAEUS
4:56
GERA
3:28, 357
GERON
4:10, 232, 281
GERSHOM
1:825; **2:**96; **3:**344–45, 363, 394, 451, 645, 725; **7:**829
GERSHON
1:736; **2:**47, 51, 213; **3:**344–45, 436, 442
GESHEM
3:757, 761, 768, 773, 784–85, 788–89
GESHURITES
2:665, 1179
GIBLITES
4:1010
GIDEON
1:259, 440–42, 465, 713, 738, 896, 1179; **2:**246, 613, 726, 745, 762–65, 767–68, 770, 776, 791–92, 795–98, 802–5, 807–11, 816–22, 824, 827, 830–31, 837–38, 841–42, 873, 884, 888, 1022, 1040–41, 1043–44, 1050, 1055, 1062; **3:**260, 407, 775, 1106; **4:**57, 78, 111, 290, 562, 1010; **5:**153, 196, 846; **6:**101, 579, 582, 599, 1400, 1522; **7:**138, 570; **9:**139, 475; **12:**143, 713
GIDEONI
2:95
GILEAD/GILEADITES
2:212, 788, 821–22, 824–25, 827, 830–31, 836–38, 1347; **3:**28
GINNETHOI
3:816
GINNETHON
3:816
GIRZITES
2:1179
GISHPA
3:826
GITTITES
2:1108, 1249, 1323–24, 1335; **3:**394, 451
GOD, METAPHORS FOR
AVENGER/REDEEMER **4:**478, 753, 1236; **5:**553; **6:**432–33; BIRD *(e.g., mother hen)* **1:**184, 206; **2:**918; **4:**741, 823, 905, 1047; **7:**251, 918; **9:**282–83; BUILDER/POTTER **1:**341–42, 349, 353, 1174; **4:**414, 601, 1236; **5:**94, 102, 232, 567, 679, 787; **6:**247, 249, 400, 528, 629, 714–18, 759, 813, 1130; **10:**429, 622, 640, 670, 677; **11:**847; **12:**136–37, 142; CHEESEMAKER **4:**414; CLOUD **1:**938, 1179; **2:**90, 108, 110, 126; **3:**78, 811; **4:**1075; **5:**517, 585, 621, 757–58; **6:**1510; **10:**513, 556, 593; CREATOR/SUSTAINER **1:**174, 179, 338, 349, 354–55, 395, 409, 442, 455, 490, 512, 539, 556, 760, 844, 926, 997; **2:**221, 527, 981–82; **3:**269–73, 402; **4:**414, 465, 487, 519, 556, 581, 589, 596–612, 619, 810, 934, 1061, 1072, 1094–1100, 1236, 1263–64; **7:**168–69, 414, 816, 839; **10:**520 (*see also* CREATOR *in SUBJECTS AND THEMES*); DIVINE GLORY **1:**1066; **2:**38, 90, 386; **3:**429, 432, 487; **6:**548, 981, 1131; **8:**691; **11:**872–73; **12:**104, 593, 597, 604, 611, 614, 657, 705, 723, 727; DIVINE WARRIOR **1:**774, 804; **2:**600, 613, 747, 749, 758, 774, 781, 787–90, 1247–49; **3:**238, 1178; **4:**52, 57, 69, 71, 80, 193,

GOD, METAPHORS FOR *(continued)*
197, 200, 297, 410, 459, 501, 516–18, 590, 595, 616, 667–88, 945, 947, 980, 1011, 1054, 1072, 1097; **5:**486; **6:**365, 369, 472, 501, 733, 751, 808, 883, 886, 900, 915, 919, 1038, 1084, 1121, 1153, 1167, 1512, 1523; **7:**3, 5, 11, 167, 349, 351–53, 355, 367, 376, 598, 600–603, 612, 620, 654–55, 660, 664, 674, 683, 688, 696, 703, 840; **8:**533, 584, 707; **9:**367, 462, 669; **12:**699; FATHER **5:**553; **6:**528, 1579; **7:**250; **8:**60; **9:**433, 671, 738, 842; **10:**284; **11:**290–91, 588; FIRE **2:**15, 90, 321; **5:**851; **8:**158; **9:**85–86, 266; **10:**54, 513, 581; HUSBAND OF ISRAEL/ZION **1:**277; **6:**515, 1240; **7:**206–10, 226–27, 250; JUDGE **1:**442; **2:**980; **4:**512; **6:**57, 78; **7:**198, 537, 544; **8:**157; **10:**473, 492 (*see also* JUSTICE: DIVINE *in SUBJECTS AND THEMES*); KING **1:**177; **2:**671, 899, 1027–28; **3:**693, 1062–64, 1118; **4:**360, 664, 668, 711, 783, 796, 866, 868–69, 973, 1003, 1061, 1255, 1259, 1274, 1276, 1279; **5:**95; **6:**377, **7:**103, 660, 665, 667, 703, 807; **8:**60, 455, 471, 824; **12:**672 (*see also* KING, KINGSHIP *in SUBJECTS AND THEMES*); LIBERATOR **1:**442; LIGHT **1:**768, 893, 902; **2:**1367; **4:**517, 537, 853, 1035, 1236; **5:**504; **12:**385, 385, 395, 423; LION **4:**415, 609, 980; **5:**340; **6:**301, 766, 1566; **7:**12, 248–50, 262, 278–80, 352, 371–72; LOVE **4:**416, 753, 824; **9:**837; **12:**431; MAGGOTS/ROTTENNESS **7:**248; MASTER **1:**1242; **4:**1139, 1209; **5:**552, 617, 748; **6:**812; **7:**389, 578; **12:**406; MIDWIFE **4:**602; **5:**12; **7:**293; MOTHER **4:**416; **7:**198, 206, 279; **10:**840; PARENT **1:**741; **4:**463; **7:**198, 209, 234, 238, 277, 281; **11:**588; ROCK **4:**748–49, 753, 789, 853, 920, 1061, 1192 (*see also* ROCK: AS METAPHOR FOR GOD/PERSON *in SUBJECTS AND THEMES*); SAVIOR **1:**337; **2:**54, 70, 139, 190, 1366; **3:**401, 909; **4:**199, 741, 976; **5:**516, 574; **6:**382, 394, 400–401, 432, 530, 1305; **7:**289, 292–93, 509, 537; **11:**790, 798, 813 (*see also* SAVIOR *in SUBJECTS AND THEMES*); SHADOW **1:**206; **4:**741, 840, 905, 1181; **6:**443, 449; **7:**296; SHEPHERD **4:**767, 769, 857; **6:**744, 1105, 1461–66, 1473; **7:**571, 833; **8:**376; **9:**668 (*see also under* GOD, NAMES FOR/TITLES OF); **12:**283; SMELLER OF ODORS **1:**393; **5:**469; SPEAKER **1:**343; WEAVER **4:**1236.
See also GOD, NAMES FOR/TITLES OF

GOD, NAMES FOR/TITLES OF
1:87, 183, 328, 349, 401, 439, 453, 460, 566, 611, 861, 946, 1126–27, 1147, 1164, 1178; **2:**139, 180, 182, 190, 375, 389, 397, 431, 484, 506, 519, 521, 671, 747, 1094, 1237, 1267; **3:**59, 72, 179, 443, 704, 945, 956, 1052; **4:**234, 752, 755, 768, 881, 891, 913, 917, 1149; **5:**250, 334, 422; **6:**355, 390, 393, 550, 690, 753, 979, 1083; **7:**55, 268, 402, 831; **8:**193, 289, 682; **9:**496, 677, 791; **10:**448, 450, 459; **11:**508, 510, 825; **12:**585, 618, 625, 644, 657, 664, 676, 705, 724–25; ABBA **5:**533; **8:**202–3, 666; **9:**234, 302, 433; **10:**470, 593–94, 603, 606, 857; **11:**63, 202, 285–86, 290–91, 305; ADONAI/ADONAY **1:**297, 1164; **2:**1261; **4:**533; **6:**436, 1036, 1038, 1042–43, 1052, 1123; **7:**377, 444; **9:**224; ALMIGHTY **1:**273, 458, 460, 666, 991, 999, 1000, 1017, 1051, 1163, 1166; **2:**180, 190–91, 910; **3:**1177; **4:**332, 576, 578, 935; **5:**9, 15, 330, 350, 504, 506; **6:**9, 38, 957, 1116–17; **7:**376, 501, 717; **9:**200, 323; **10:**391, 475, 614; **11:**105–6; **12:**444, 507, 565, 592–93, 661, 672, 677, 695, 699, 723, 725; ALPHA AND OMEGA **6:**387; **10:**798; **12:**276, 567, 721, 733; ANCIENT OF DAYS **4:**428; **7:**9, 13, 103, 105, 150; **9:**206; **10:**401, 528, 723; BEGINNING AND END (*see* GOD, NAMES FOR/TITLES OF: ALPHA AND OMEGA); COMFORTER **4:**458, 540; **6:**441, 476, 1030, 1044; **9:**747; **10:**58; **12:**569, 575; CREATOR (*see under* CREATOR *in SUBJECTS AND THEMES*); DELIVERER **1:**160, 569; **2:**400, 760, 810, 1366; **4:**410, 477, 1264; **6:**1309; **7:**505–6; **9:**823; **10:**692; **11:**596; DIVINE PRESENCE **1:**37, 42, 63, 277–78, 281, 316, 362, 364, 418, 517, 542–43, 562–63, 611–12, 881, 981, 1001, 1007, 1035, 1114; **2:**18, 65, 80, 83, 88, 216, 364–65, 388, 461, 491, 552, 820, 992, 995, 1095, 1134, 1259, 1281; **3:**20, 59, 61, 68–69, 72, 75–76, 78, 81, 88, 143, 269, 378, 462, 484, 494, 498, 502, 544, 547, 556, 559, 562, 591, 629, 649, 659, 738; **4:**434, 519, 591, 733, 981; **5:**9, 14, 462, 466, 526, 610, 647, 842; **6:**84, 140, 349, 355, 390, 457, 526, 540, 579, 641, 692, 994, 1188, 1190, 1511, 1595; **7:**480, 485, 498, 501, 718, 720, 744, 763, 770, 772; **8:**135, 259, 328–29, 367, 411; **9:**74, 747–49; **10:**580, 584; **11:**64, 71, 377, 566, 599, 632; **12:**523, 604, 625, 630, 653, 665, 672, 721, 723, 727, 729 (*see also* PRESENCE: OF GOD *in SUBJECTS AND THEMES*); EL **1:**233, 241–42, 273–74, 276–77, 328, 439, 440, 492, 566, 577, 1018; **2:**34, 139, 180, 190–91, 194, 364, 586, 817, 1001; **3:**922; **4:**380, 394, 400, 530, 558, 600, 621, 862, 881, 1006; **5:**33, 818; **6:**10, 702, 1122, 1213, 1387, 1393, 1566; **7:**103–4, 105, 200, 226, 279, 602; EL BERITH **2:**635, 817; EL ELOHE ISRAEL **1:**273, 577; EL ELYON/ELYON **1:**273–74, 439–40, 442; **2:**180, 191, 194; **5:**690, 837, 846; ELOAH **4:**367, 370, 600; ELOHE **1:**577; ELHOIM **1:**309, 349, 487; **2:**179–80, 552, 907, 1184; **4:**380, 600, 658, 862, 881; **5:**9, 730; **6:**528, 551, 1503; **7:**464, 513; EL OLAM **1:**273, 492; EL-ROI **1:**453, 458; **4:**394; EL SHADDAI/SHADDAI **1:**273, 458, 635, 659, 666, 733; **2:**34, 178, 180, 190–91, 194, 311, 901, 910; **4:**400, 420, 502, 510, 524, 529, 600; **6:**1278, 1560; FATHER **1:**47, 169, 192; **3:**319, 1063; **4:**1007; **5:**99, 553, 628, 748; **6:**403, 528, 531–32, 552; **8:**61, 202–3, 221, 290, 567, 637, 666; **9:**92, 145, 159, 234–35, 238–39, 260, 324, 336, 420, 448,

455, 496, 580, 599, 634, 691, 743–44, 787, 789, 791, 798, 845; **10:**383, 421, 696, 737, 746, 798, 898; **11:**40, 106, 201–2, 208, 240, 290–91, 360, 370, 372, 377–78, 414, 416, 465, 481, 510, 513, 545, 588, 678, 688–89, 744, 892; **12:**231, 247–48, 258, 374–75, 435, 450, 481–82; FATHER IN HEAVEN **1:**926, 1136; **4:**882; **5:**307, 574, 790; **7:**56; **8:**195, 217, 372, 374; **9:**147, 237–38, 260, 263, 302, 488; **12:**274, 290, 391, 424, 626, 664; FEAR OF ISAAC **1:**558; **5:**239, 696; FINGER OF **1:**39, 924–25; **2:**362; **3:**963; **5:**584; **8:**286; **9:**20, 242, 245; GOD OF GODS **1:**442; **2:**369, 706; **3:**752; **5:**377; **7:**146; GOD OF HOSTS **2:**959, 962, 1095, 1199, 1235, 1237; **4:**913, 1000, 1035; **5:**251; **6:**196, 812, 833; **7:**347, 376, 382, 783; **11:**214; **12:**291; GOD OF THE COVENANT **2:**635, 817; **3:**479, 496; **5:**557; **12:**616; HOLY GOD **1:**574, 679, 830, 836–39, 844, 890, 893, 906, 913, 972, 977, 986–88, 997, 1000, 1022, 1072–73, 1098, 1127–28; **2:**4, 15, 20, 23, 25, 62, 1012–13; **4:**1075; **6:**635, 723, 1206, 1578, 1592; **7:**82, 576; **8:**65; **10:**206, 474, 641; **11:**277, 480, 646; **12:**257–58, 298, 500, 591; HOLY NAME **1:**846, 1041, 1139, 1149; **4:**1104, 1112; **5:**818; **6:**414, 526, 1106, 1290, 1487, 1489–90, 1522–23, 1530, 1561; HOLY ONE *(also sometimes refers to Jesus)* **1:**27, 685, 718, 721, 836, 854, 880–81, 896, 916, 994, 1027, 1131, 1143; **2:**95, 339, 981; **3:**269; **4:**36, 388, 525, 1076, 1265; **5:**101–2, 251, 532, 621, 668, 787, 818, 834, 853; **6:**29, 38–40, 53–54, 94, 105, 133, 147, 174, 247–49, 254, 281, 338, 342, 344, 346, 352, 355–59, 361, 363, 367, 369, 377, 402, 411–14, 421, 433, 492, 527–28, 532, 541–42, 552, 588, 640, 980, 1199, 1232, 1411, 1523; **7:**56, 132, 229, 241, 278–79, 282, 804; **8:**147, 203–4, 206, 525, 541, 545, 564, 566, 572, 583; **9:**110, 463, 611, 613, 678; **10:**193, 832; **11:**481; **12:**376, 404, 453, 570, 584, 597, 601, 676, 682; HOLY PRESENCE **1:**834, 891, 893, 897, 905–6, 908, 1149; **2:**25, 1063, 1251; **3:**344; **6:**320, 531, 1564, 1592; "I AM WHO I AM" **1:**290, 714; **2:**747; **5:**294; **7:**290; **10:**977; **11:**510; **12:**562; JEHOVAH **1:**84–85, 183; JUDGE **1:**468–69, 478, 528; **5:**628; **6:**532, 1296; **12:**330, 391, 422; KING OF KINGS **3:**386, 563; **4:**281; **7:**61; **9:**171; **12:**566, 614; AND LAST **6:**354, 387, 412, 418; **12:**567; LIVING GOD **1:**809, 1015, 1027, 1060, 1063, 1085, 1118, 1121, 1132, 1135, 1139, 1178; **2:**413, 461, 599, 1111, 1114–15; **3:**9, 125, 396, 427, 592, 1061, 1063; **4:**1013–14, 1106; **5:**550, 644, 861; **6:**293, 493, 661, 1332; **7:**93, 181, 188, 219, 334; **8:**76, 137, 344, 360; **10:**199, 245, 247, 363, 433, 436, 505, 513, 521, 604, 704; **11:**28, 63, 72, 103, 105–7, 224, 247, 271, 625, 783, 808, 813; **12:**5, 108, 118, 120, 123, 158, 181, 213, 245, 447, 619; LORD OF HOSTS **1:**1131; **2:**974–75, 1001, 1006, 1087, 1112, 1248–49, 1261; **3:**75, 176, 406, 472, 890, 1179; **4:**312, 773, 865, 935, 1013; **6:**49, 54–55, 60, 72, 78, 88, 93, 102, 118, 122, 127, 137, 150, 156, 159, 180–81, 186, 189, 201, 213, 403, 414, 681, 784, 883–84, 892, 894, 900, 913, 1118, 1120, 1492; **7:**13, 161, 612, 717–18, 720–21, 723, 731, 736, 751, 753–54, 772, 833, 849, 852, 865, 873; **9:**278, 543; **12:**181, 222–23, 246, 298, 592; LORD OF LORDS **2:**369; **3:**752; **5:**377; **12:**566, 682, 699, 702; MIGHTY ONE **1:**666; **5:**846, 867; **6:**60, 432; **12:**636; MOST HIGH **1:**273, 286, 289, 439–50, 444; **2:**104, 180, 191, 527, 529, 830, 1108, 1259; **3:**68, 864, 1003, 1165; **4:**355, 568, 680, 708, 865, 1024, 1045, 1069–70; **5:**12, 14–15, 252, 486, 490, 617, 642, 690, 757, 798, 824, 833, 837, 846, 853; **6:**159, 336, 343, 477, 962, 968, 1052, 1595; **7:**3, 65, 72, 74–75, 93, 105, 143, 258, 261, 277, 579; **8:**526, 713; **9:**14–15, 51, 90–91, 147, 157, 163, 187–88, 373, 381, 489, 677; **10:**133, 230, 232, 235, 244, 401, 498, 528; **11:**301, 382; **12:**86, 94, 524, 527, 599, 635, 646, 704, 727; MOST HOLY **1:**280, 897, 916, 976, 986, 1019, 1021, 1033, 1045, 1048–49, 1062, 1070–72, 1110–11, 1114, 1148–49, 1161; **2:**48, 52–54, 147, 614; **3:**346, 437, 484, 576, 624; **4:**39, 198, 233; **6:**102, 1528, 1549–50; **7:**128, 787; **8:**493; **9:**133; **12:**82, 103, 106, 113, 116, 120, 497, 597; ROCK OF ISAAC **5:**867; SHIELD OF ABRAHAM **5:**867; SHEPHERD **1:**206, 661; **4:**767–68, 769, 857, 998–1000; **5:**359, 628; **6:**1105, 1461, 1465–67, 1473; **7:**571, 588, 833–34; **8:**376–77; **9:**668–69 (*see also under* GOD, METAPHORS FOR); YAH/JAH **4:**1138–39; **7:**330, 660, 671; YAHWEH **1:**32, 260, 306, 309, 328, 349, 372–73, 376, 425, 442, 453, 483, 492, 541, 690, 714–19, 723, 733–37, 748, 757, 793, 795, 799, 803, 842, 940, 946, 1124, 1138–39, 1164; **2:**34, 65–66, 89–91, 139, 179–80, 182, 185–86, 568, 671, 687–89, 747, 974, 982, 1111–12, 1126, 1168, 1248, 1262; **3:**677, 711, 752–53, 769, 811, 956; **4:**352, 428, 523, 600, 658, 752, 768, 792, 881, 895, 913, 945, 1000, 1048, 1050, 1087, 1139, 1235; **5:**2, 9, 27, 96, 119, 159, 173, 251, 253, 256, 283, 617, 621, 656, 688, 856, 859; **6:**256, 394, 774, 1036, 1085, 1203, 1208, 1274, 1277–79, 1290, 1487–90, 1495–96, 1523, 1530, 1561; **7:**285, 289–90, 381–82, 388, 428, 437, 464, 513, 753–54, 774, 831, 836–39; **8:**135, 358, 423; **9:**596; YAHWEH OF HOSTS **7:**753–54, 760, 783, 790, 826, 839; YHWH **1:**273–76, 297–99, 309; **2:**11, 15, 25, 49, 51, 79, 88–89, 91–93, 124, 135, 139–40, 179, 384, 552, 870, 907, 1001, 1261; **3:**20, 710, 1023, 1101; **4:**881, 1078; **5:**251, 626, 668, 748; **6:**141, 319, 354, 403, 423, 436, 478, 514, 526, 811, 1041, 1051, 1117, 1120, 1123, 1154, 1160, 1212, 1239, 1250, 1275, 1287, 1405, 1451, 1607; **7:**277, 377, 444, 475, 489, 493, 498, 522, 554, 601–2, 605,

GOD, NAMES FOR/TITLES OF *(continued)*
612, 615, 717; **8:**328; **10:**398, 400, 420, 447–48, 458, 517, 529, 601, 659, 662, 669–70, 677, 690, 692, 715, 738, 758; **11:**688, 746, 750; **12:**562. *See also* GOD, METAPHORS FOR

GOG
2:190; **6:**1086, 1106, 1443, 1512–32, 1540; **7:**323; **8:**671; **12:**534, 699, 702, 706, 714. *See also* MAGOG *in PLACES IN THE BIBLE*

GOIIM
2:655

GOLIATH
2:123, 440, 550, 958, 1103–4, 1108–15, 1120, 1122, 1126, 1140, 1148, 1165, 1168, 1198, 1206, 1216, 1361; **3:**368, 378, 417, 1091, 1161, 1167, 1173, 1180; **4:**51, 56, 66, 101, 129, 254, 264, 295, 297, 624; **5:**196, 849; **6:**1464; **11:**159; **12:**144

GOMER
5:413; **6:**1143, 1378, 1516; **7:**198, 203, 211, 215–18, 220, 224–25, 230–33

GORGIAS
4:62, 64, 66, 78, 85, 110, 145, 152, 247–48, 253, 261, 264, 268, 276–77, 282, 286

H

HAAHASHTARI
3:330

HABAKKUK
3:554; **4:**977; **6:**3, 13, 20, 142, 395, 1140, 1218; **7:**187, 192–94, 340, 623–27, 629–44, 646–48, 650, 652–55, 661, 667, 678, 707; **8:**38–39; **9:**369; **10:**193–94, 254, 426; **11:**314

HACALIAH
3:750; **4:**196

HADAD
1:590; **3:**93, 96, 319; **4:**276

HADADEZER
2:1266, 1279–80; **3:**93, 414, 416

HADAD-RIMMON
3:196; **7:**828

HADAR
1:590

HADASSAH
3:886

HADORAM
3:520

HADRACH
7:803–4

HAGAR
1:95, 186, 330, 353, 418–20, 428, 451–55, 460, 485, 487–91, 495, 515, 554, 580; **2:**18, 94, 540, 905, 918, 975; **3:**23; **4:**394, 423; **5:**199, 255, 412; **6:**355, 966; **7:**150, 164, 179, 181; **10:**500, 636; **11:**76, 190, 249, 300–306, 309; **12:**156, 649, 652

HAGGAI
1:274, 1045–46, 1149; **3:**668, 690–91, 693, 701, 705–6, 708, 711, 785, 1069; **4:**113, 116, 1016, 1267; **6:**2, 8, 18, 20, 826; **7:**650, 707–12, 715–21, 723–25, 727–32, 736–39, 747, 750, 760, 763–65, 770, 788–89, 796, 803, 807, 847–48, 852, 855; **12:**726

HAGGI
7:707

HAGGIAH
7:707

HAGGITH
3:17–18, 32, 94; **7:**707

HAGRITE/HAGRITES
1:455; **4:**1010

HAKKOZ
3:687, 730, 768; **4:**7–8, 106

HALLOHESH
3:768, 817

HAM
1:403–5, 408–9; **2:**559, 576, 670, 691, 700–701

HAMAN
1:284–85, 896; **3:**857–59, 862–63, 865–69, 872, 892–901, 904–5, 908–16, 918–35, 938, 950–51, 953, 956, 959, 966–67, 969, 1098, 1118–19, 1124, 1171; **5:**118; **7:**43

HAMATHITES
2:571

HAMITES
1:404

HAMOR
1:577–80; **2:**816–17

HAMUL
2:211

HAMUTAL
6:1269–70, 1272

HANAMEL
6:820

HANAN
3:801, 817, 847

HANANI
3:542–43, 751, 776, 793–94, 825, 839

HANANIAH
2:392, 430; **3:**330, 766, 768, 770, 793, 817, 839, 1023; **6:**9, 743, 782, 784–88, 792, 794–95, 806, 866, 925, 1143, 1199, 1276; **7:**20, 39, 63, 67, 78, 158, 170, 179, 183, 188–89

HANANIEL
3:992

HANNAH
1:186, 216, 241, 768, 1182, 1186; **2:**233, 236,

548, 832, 845, 949, 958–59, 961, 964, 970, 973–83, 986–87, 994, 997, 1006, 1010, 1019, 1021, 1045, 1049, 1099, 1156, 1160, 1167, 1184, 1193, 1237, 1239, 1252, 1259–60, 1356, 1365, 1369–71, 1382–83; **3:**1004, 1049, 1061, 1063, 1145; **4:**23, 703, 1138–39, 1233; **5:**76, 128, 140, 253, 255, 258, 620; **9:**45, 47, 51–52, 55, 70–71, 458; **11:**442

HANUN
2:1279; **3:**766, 768, 770

HAREPH
3:330

HARIM
3:686, 745, 768, 816, 826, 832

HARIPH
3:817

HAROEH
3:330

HARUMAPH
3:768

HASADIAH
6:941

HASHABIAH
3:718, 727–29, 817, 832

HASHABNAH
3:817

HASHABNEIAH
3:817

HASHUM
3:817

HASIDEANS
4:8, 19, 47, 52, 92, 95–96, 118–19, 127, 268, 286

HASSENAAH
3:768

HASSENUAH
3:825

HASSHUB
3:766, 769, 817

HASSOPHERETH
5:268

HATHACH
3:903–4

HATTUSH
3:330, 725, 768, 834

HAZAEL
1:265; **3:**143–44, 203, 209–10, 212, 215, 233, 236

HEBER
2:738, 780–81, 788

HEBREWS
1:75, 158, 297, 306, 408–9, 439, 683, 690, 695–98, 701, 703–4, 706, 714–15, 725–26, 730, 742, 749–54, 757–60, 762–64, 772–73, 781, 812, 830, 891–92, 1040; **2:**137, 192, 977, 1001, 1070, 1079, 1188; **3:**1119, 1151; **4:**30, 202, 242, 268, 298; **5:**60, 446, 525–27, 532, 591, 596–97; **6:**697, 809, 1147, 1402, 1420, 1463, 1491, 1496, 1537; **7:**23, 472, 801; **9:**184; **10:**25, 74, 110–12, 115, 121, 130–31, 139, 374; **11:**17, 156, 159, 214, 526, 887, 904; **12:**4, 6, 9.
See also ISRAEL (PEOPLE); JEWS

HEBRON/HEBRONITES
1:261; **2:**47, 213; **3:**394, 442, 452

HEGAI
3:885, 888–89, 905, 908, 935, 940

HEGEMONIDES
4:282

HELDAI
7:787–88

HELI
8:130–31; **9:**94

HELIODORUS
4:181–82, 206–8, 211–12, 216, 250, 254, 258, 268, 281, 289, 691; **7:**141

HELLENISTS
3:1163; **5:**456, 608, 828, 862; **7:**118, 139; **9:**336, 382; **10:**25, 74, 110–15, 120–21, 131–32, 134, 139, 150, 154–55, 162, 255, 289, 309, 337

HELON
2:95

HEMAN
2:981; **3:**300, 328, 345, 394, 445–47, 561; **4:**635, 655–56; **7:**671

HENADAD
3:692, 769

HEPHER
2:683

HERCULES
8:249

HERMES
4:218; **10:**198

HERMOGENES
11:838

HEROD ANTIPAS
1:271; **8:**156, 167, 291, 319, 323, 385, 531–32, 536, 559, 598, 643–45, 674, 696, 712; **9:**80, 87–88, 155, 215, 363; **10:**178, 189; **11:**578, 589

HEROD ARCHELAUS
1:271; **4:**107; **8:**147, 289; **9:**73, 80, 363

HERODIAN FAMILY
8:319, 643; **10:**328; **11:**364

HERODIANS
1:251; **2:**603; **3:**484; **6:**933; **8:**35, 267, 319, 321, 341, 420, 439, 547, 559, 567, 589, 597–98, 617, 643, 646, 657, 673–74, 685, 700; **9:**135, 385; **10:**328; **11:**364

HERODIAS
8:319, 321, 598, 645, 699, 720; **9:**87–88, 363
HERODION
10:762–63
HEROD PHILIP
1:271; **8:**343, 592, 598, 622; **9:**80, 88, 215
HEROD THE GREAT
1:251, 271; **3:**1127; **4:**107; **5:**772; **6:**978; **7:**438; **8:**142, 147, 291, 319, 343, 382, 671, 710, 712, 717–19; **9:**63, 80, 87, 93, 363, 446, 544; **10:**178; **12:**144
HEZEKIAH
1:79, 222, 249, 262, 265–66, 1012, 1018, 1072; **2:**87, 164, 556–57, 559–61, 568, 573, 599–600, 606, 615, 657, 660, 673, 677, 680–82, 689, 717, 725, 752, 865; **3:**4–6, 75, 118, 259–61, 264–66, 269–74, 276–79, 286, 301, 303, 306, 342, 353, 389, 456, 474, 477, 509, 536, 592, 600, 602–3, 606–7, 610–11, 616, 618–19, 622, 624, 628–31, 644–45, 649, 651, 654, 657, 691, 713–14, 802, 941, 996; **4:**50, 72, 77, 82, 99, 172, 204, 222, 394, 759, 990; **5:**21, 32, 48, 217, 219, 298, 459, 574, 620, 631, 836, 853, 855, 858; **6:**14, 27, 30, 32, 35, 37, 48, 121, 123, 133, 140, 150, 195, 197, 230–31, 242, 247, 253, 260–62, 284–85, 291–95, 299–305, 317, 327, 329, 357, 394, 439, 443, 547, 636, 670, 762, 774, 850, 1076–77, 1135, 1199, 1232–33, 1326, 1386, 1402, 1406; **7:**533–34, 547, 560, 594, 659–61, 670–71, 675, 678, 691–92, 780; **12:**725
HEZRON
2:211; **3:**327, 329–30; **9:**94
HIEL
2:575, 612, 619–20, 625, 634–35, 639
HIERONYMUS
4:275
HILKIAH
1:309; **2:**567–68, 687–88; **3:**280, 826; **4:**555; **6:**196, 941, 943–44; **7:**764; **9:**45; **12:**584
HIRAM
1:262, 900; **2:**1242; **3:**53, 58, 61, 67–68, 70, 81, 83–84, 87, 93, 388, 430, 477–78; **4:**218; **6:**176, 1360; **7:**362; **11:**582
HITTITES
1:164–65, 232, 239–40, 408, 503–4, 667; **2:**21, 123, 557, 571, 576; **3:**90, 207, 733, 819; **8:**358; **12:**237, 246
HIVITES
1:164–65, 251, 408, 577; **2:**563, 571, 576, 625, 642, 759; **3:**819
HOBAB
2:22, 95–97, 738, 780
HODAVIAH
3:692, 832
HODIAH
3:801, 817
HOLOFERNES
3:871, 920, 1075–78, 1082–85, 1087–90, 1095, 1099, 1101–11, 1113–14, 1117–20, 1123–25, 1127, 1130, 1132–33, 1137–39, 1143–44, 1147–51, 1153–55, 1157–63, 1165, 1167, 1170–71, 1173, 1177–78, 1180; **4:**48, 57, 96, 101, 177, 193, 297; **7:**41; **8:**598
HOLY GHOST
1:954; **10:**606. *See also* HOLY SPIRIT
HOLY SPIRIT
1:45, 51, 52, 54–55, 58, 60–61, 74, 87–88, 91, 103, 119, 126, 211, 686, 1034, 1061, 1063, 1101, 1114, 1159, 1163, 1166; **2:**90, 236, 681, 1295; **3:**179, 358, 409, 470, 1043; **4:**687, 886, 1079, 1100, 1176, **5:**22, 102, 480; **6:**339, 366, 472, 527, 531–32, 550–52, 1191; **7:**326–27; **8:**23, 73, 80, 134, 137, 158, 161, 259, 287, 504, 525, 532, 534, 541, 563–65, 688–89, 696; **9:**17, 30, 48, 51–52, 54–55, 59, 69–70, 85–86, 91, 103, 153, 160, 207, 224, 238, 253, 266, 398, 401, 434, 441, 469, 484, 487–89, 529, 544, 634, 723, 751, 775, 792, 833, 846–48, 849; **10:**14, 17, 21–25, 29–30, 37–38, 41–49, 53–58, 62, 68, 73, 78, 89–90, 92, 95–97, 100, 107, 112–13, 121, 127, 129–31, 138–40, 152, 154, 167–69, 176, 189–90, 196–97, 201, 208, 210–11, 221, 260–63, 282–83, 285, 288, 307, 363, 419, 453, 552, 555, 581, 594, 600, 624–27, 696, 744, 820–22, 825, 843–46, 856, 863–65, 909, 941, 950, 961–63; **11:**11, 18, 23, 49, 51, 58, 63, 65, 73, 78, 84, 86, 89, 105, 179, 184, 211, 223, 229, 251–54, 261, 265, 271, 285, 286, 309, 318, 322, 335, 375–76, 381, 430, 442, 469, 496, 529, 678–79, 689, 708–9, 716, 719–20, 722, 732, 746, 877; **12:**11–13, 24, 34–35, 37, 47–48, 50, 52, 54–55, 62, 71, 74–75, 104, 108, 116, 118, 123, 126, 180, 237, 253, 304, 330, 343, 376, 388, 407, 414, 449, 479, 497, 533, 535–36, 539, 541, 611, 728
HOPHNI
2:974, 986–89, 996, 1001–1002, 1004, 1026
HOPHRA
6:872, 874–75, 883, 1079, 1249, 1403–1404, 1411, 1420
HORITES
1:590; **6:**1474
HORONITE
3:757, 849
HOSAH
3:451
HOSEA
1:68, 73, 265, 276, 679, 937, 1182; **2:**89, 99, 142, 187, 264, 343, 355, 468, 1050, 1056; **3:**226,

522, 542; **4:**36; **5:**45, 113, 237, 381, 401, 512, 798, 851; **6:**6–7, 18, 21, 45, 49, 62, 119, 183, 227, 313, 491, 596, 614, 630, 653, 656, 702, 1143–44, 1169, 1216, 1221, 1224, 1228, 1232, 1320, 1339, 1341, 1471, 1589; **7:**198–200, 202–7, 209–11, 215–20, 223–27, 230–37, 239–41, 245–46, 248–50, 252–54, 256–58, 260–70, 272–75, 279, 281, 283, 285–88, 290, 292–94, 297, 346, 380, 396, 417, 419, 544, 548, 779, 864; **8:**537; **9:**183; **11:**75, 844; **12:**256, 267–69, 389, 614

HOSHAIAH
3:838

HOSHEA
1:250, 265; **2:**122; **3:**248, 252–53, 257, 260; **6:**117, 1322, 1402; **7:**217, 248, 270

HULDAH
1:242; **2:**574; **3:**282, 286, 294; **5:**81, 620; **7:**679; **9:**72

HUPPIM
3:342

HUR
1:881; **2:**246; **3:**328–30, 768

HURAM/HURAM-ABI
3:417, 429, 477–78, 480, 486–87, 692

HUSHAI
2:1323, 1325, 1330–33, 1336, 1352; **3:**50–51, 457, 554

HUSHIM
3:342

HYMENAEUS
11:794–96, 845, 847

HYRCANUS
1:270, 287; **3:**1078, 1107, 1112–13, 1118–19, 1125, 1127; **4:**5–6, 12–13, 22, 51, 207, 222, 276, 281; **5:**160, 862; **7:**24; **9:**388, 698

I

IBNEIAH
3:825

IBZAN
1:259; **2:**762, 764–65, 819, 839

ICHABOD
2:1002; **9:**272

IDDO
3:51, 512, 532, 701, 726–27, 816, 831, 834; **6:**5; **7:**472, 739–40

ILLYRICUM
10:339, 374, 754; **11:**144, 674, 857

IMALKUE
4:137

IMLAH
3:162; **6:**101, 1198, 1463; **7:**5, 542, 558

IMMANUEL
See under JESUS THE CHRIST, NAMES FOR/TITLES OF

IMMER
3:363, 745, 770, 826, 832

IMRI
3:825

IR
3:342

IRA
2:1268, 1354

IRAD
1:380

IRI
3:342

ISAAC
1:32, 68, 93, 248, 254, 257–58, 273, 318, 325, 328, 377, 404, 416, 418–20, 422, 427, 429, 455, 459–60, 464, 468, 481, 485–86, 488–92, 494–501, 503, 509–23, 526–30, 534–39, 541, 553, 557–60, 567, 577, 584–86, 592–94, 598, 600, 604, 652, 660–61, 666, 674, 706, 1010, 1065, 1139, 1181; **2:**49–50, 65, 162, 182, 271, 277, 359, 510, 540, 543, 546, 549–50, 555, 755, 759, 834–36, 845, 1159; **3:**23, 47, 317, 468, 483, 615, 994, 1016, 1038, 1042, 1089, 1138; **4:**50, 66, 164, 174, 188, 345, 361, 582, 1105; **5:**170, 239, 429, 516, 523–24, 605, 622, 629, 631, 654, 659, 670, 696, 734, 836, 842, 867; **6:**363, 366, 386, 669, 980, 1154, 1238, 1278, 1531; **7:**40, 283–84, 295, 407, 419, 811, 828, 832; **8:**29, 65, 137–38, 358, 423, 476; **9:**42, 45, 73, 91, 300, 381, 389, 565, 638, 646; **10:**416, 451, 498, 500, 505, 593, 610, 612, 635–37, 693, 769; **11:**76, 227, 243, 300–301, 304–5, 307, 309, 346; **12:**80, 83, 135–39, 142, 146, 154, 182, 198–99, 213

ISAIAH
1:87, 96, 226, 237, 262, 266, 278, 282–83, 679, 838, 1131; **2:**16, 38, 89, 164, 221, 408, 430, 440, 503, 511, 573, 602, 1063; **3:**75, 140, 164, 265–66, 269–71, 274, 278, 362, 432, 522, 542, 561, 592, 631, 657, 659, 677, 680, 693, 992, 1098, 1155; **4:**99, 759, 1275; **5:**96, 303, 463, 473, 631, 634, 670, 836, 853; **6:**2–3, 7–8, 10–14, 17–19, 22, 28, 30, 32–40, 45–49, 52, 54, 58, 62–64, 66, 77, 79, 87–89, 95, 99, 101–13, 116–21, 136, 140, 143, 146, 148–50, 155, 162, 180–83, 186, 189, 194, 196–98, 201, 206, 230–32, 235, 237–39, 242–44, 246–47, 252–55, 259, 261–62, 270, 273, 280, 284–86, 291–93, 295, 299–300, 303–4, 309, 311–15, 317, 319–22, 327–31, 334–35, 337–38, 353, 358–59, 364–65, 370, 375–77, 395, 403, 414, 421, 423–24, 429, 431, 434, 437, 439, 441–43, 451, 457, 467–68,

ISAIAH *(continued)*
473, 478, 485, 489, 491, 502, 504–5, 515, 519–21, 541, 544–45, 547–48, 550–51, 579, 601–2, 629, 656, 702, 746, 784–85, 867, 874, 1045, 1063, 1090, 1129, 1135, 1141, 1144–45, 1150, 1199, 1218, 1221, 1232, 1303, 1320, 1324, 1339, 1341, 1357, 1362, 1402, 1411, 1442, 1458, 1471, 1481, 1486, 1521, 1532; **7:**5, 10, 41, 54, 90, 138, 182, 220, 339, 357, 394, 407, 412, 481, 533–34, 546, 564, 574, 623, 641, 654, 660–61, 670, 675, 690–93, 740, 752, 755, 761, 803, 846, 852; **8:**36–37, 156, 333, 480, 530–31, 535, 572, 665, 672; **9:**15, 66, 72, 80–81, 105–7, 113, 119, 244, 281, 318, 374, 478, 698; **10:**42, 72, 97, 129, 143–44, 193, 195, 218, 307–8, 334, 337–38, 361–63, 447–48, 451, 469, 640, 668–69, 675, 677, 692, 696, 769; **11:**75, 190, 215, 261, 304, 844; **12:**216, 255, 260–61, 510, 512, 515, 519, 566, 588, 614, 726

ISHBAAL
2:962, 1069, 1081, 1095, 1199, 1212, 1222, 1229, 1274

ISHBOSHETH
2:1199, 1211–13, 1216, 1221–33, 1273, 1326, 1359; **5:**673

ISHMAEL
1:325, 329, 377, 408, 418–20, 432, 451, 453–55, 457–61, 485, 487–92, 495, 497, 501, 514–15, 518, 537, 539, 590–91, 593, 601, 1084; **2:**49, 94, 162, 541, 546, 905; **3:**23, 294, 317; **4:**423, 610; **5:**199; **6:**366, 560, 842, 858–59, 864, 966, 1080, 1348, 1379; **7:**829; **9:**42, 300, 638; **10:**500, 636–37; **11:**300–302, 305–7, 309

ISHMAELITES
1:451, 455, 458, 598–600, 609; **4:**1010; **6:**1379

ISHVI
2:1081

ISRAEL (PEOPLE)
1:1, 9–10, 17–18, 20, 27, 37–41, 43, 45, 47, 65–70, 74–76, 78–79, 81, 83–84, 86–87, 92–93, 95, 126, 128–29, 131–33, 135–36, 151, 165–66, 175, 184–85, 189, 191, 206, 208–10, 213, 215, 218, 221, 225–27, 229–30, 234–39, 242, 244–50, 252–62, 264–66, 268–69, 272–77, 281, 284, 290–91, 656, 664–67, 694, 706, 723, 734, 777, 781, 785, 788–90, 799–803, 830–40, 860–61, 880–82, 957, 997–1000, 1170, 1178; **2:**3–12, 14–16, 18–22, 25–26, 31–41, 47–49, 51–55, 59, 61, 66, 68–70, 77, 79–83, 86–92, 94–100, 104–6, 109–12, 120–21, 124–29, 134–42, 146–53, 158–70, 177–95, 197–202, 213–15, 218–22, 228–30, 232–33, 235–36, 244–46, 248–50, 252–57, 262–64, 266–68, 271–72, 274–83, 285–86, 291–94, 297–300, 305–12, 314–17, 319–20, 322–30, 333–34, 336–40, 342–45, 348–53, 355–59, 363–67, 369–71, 373–77, 379–81, 383–89, 391–98, 403–5, 408–14, 416–17, 420, 422, 425–32, 435, 439–43, 445–46, 449, 452, 454–57, 459–63, 466–68, 470, 472, 476–89, 491–92, 494, 500–506, 510–13, 515, 518–21, 526–30, 534–38, 540–49, 551, 555–59, 589–90, 594, 599–608, 612–13, 618–19, 626, 630–31, 634–38, 646–48, 651, 656, 659–62, 670, 689, 706–7, 711, 715, 717, 723–27, 731–34, 736–52, 755–68, 770–83, 787–92, 795–98, 802–5, 807–11, 816–22, 824–27, 830–43, 845–47, 849–51, 853–55, 858–66, 869–73, 875–79, 884–88, 892–96, 899–900, 902, 904–5, 907, 913, 918–19, 921, 931, 935, 939, 941–43, 945–46; **3:**556, 693, 718, 753–54; **8:**29–31, 33–37, 39, 41–42, 44, 63, 66–67, 99, 100, 117, 129, 131–35, 144, 146–47, 149–50, 158, 163, 168–69, 178, 180, 182, 189, 215, 224, 226, 240, 251–53, 256–59, 271, 281, 286, 291–97, 300, 308, 316, 318–19, 332, 336, 339, 342–43, 346–48, 356, 359–60, 368, 371, 375–77, 391–92, 398, 405–6, 408, 410, 413–20, 436, 438–39, 444–45, 450, 459, 474, 492–93, 501, 503, 516, 526, 528, 530, 535, 537, 562, 585, 598, 603, 606, 608–9, 616, 624, 642, 657, 660, 666, 670–72, 696, 698, 704, 723; **9:**4, 9, 15, 18, 21–22, 41–43, 45–49, 51, 54–56, 58–60, 63, 65, 69–73, 76–77, 81, 83–86, 91, 94–100, 106–8, 120, 123, 133, 136–37, 139, 143–45, 156, 158, 177, 179, 195–96, 200–201, 206–7, 209, 212, 219–20, 235, 237, 243, 249, 267, 271, 278, 282, 296, 300, 302, 309, 322, 326, 335, 338, 345, 347, 349, 370, 372, 374–76, 378, 380–83, 385, 391, 405, 408–9, 414, 419–21, 426, 442, 445, 453–54, 456–57, 460, 464, 469, 475, 478, 487, 518, 521–22, 524, 528, 532–34, 551, 558, 560, 565, 568, 594, 596, 601, 612, 616, 632, 638, 668, 670, 672, 675, 677, 698, 707, 716, 738, 751, 754, 757, 817, 823; **10:**9–16, 18–25, 27–28, 38, 40–43, 45–50, 53–57, 59–60, 63–69, 72–74, 77–85, 88–92, 96–97, 99, 103–9, 111–14, 121–30, 132–35, 137–40, 142–47, 152–53, 155, 160–61, 163–67, 169–71, 176, 178, 180–81, 188–89, 192–93, 195–98, 200, 203, 205–6, 208–10, 213–15, 217–20, 230, 232, 234, 237–40, 247, 252–56, 258, 262, 267–69, 276, 278, 281, 283–84, 294–96, 304–5, 307–15, 318–20, 322, 324–25, 327, 333–41, 343, 346, 360–65, 367, 372, 374–75, 377–78, 398–408, 413, 415–16, 418–21, 424–26, 428–29, 432–33, 438–40, 445–65, 467, 470–72, 474–78, 480–82, 486, 488, 495–96, 499–500, 502–5, 511–13, 515–18, 524–25, 528–31, 534, 537, 547, 549–58, 560–72, 575, 578–81, 585–87, 590, 593, 596, 601, 604, 608, 610–11, 616, 620–25, 627–29, 631–32, 634–52, 654–62, 665–67, 669–73,

675–94, 696–700, 702, 704, 710, 715, 718, 725, 731, 738, 744–48, 750–51, 778, 809, 829, 833, 848, 863, 890, 893, 897–98, 902, 910, 913–16, 918, 935, 937, 979, 996; **11:**40, 67–68, 75–76, 78–79, 106, 147–48, 185, 187, 193, 195, 213–15, 223–25, 232, 236, 242, 257–62, 266–69, 271, 276, 279, 282, 284, 287, 290, 300, 303–4, 307, 309, 319, 323, 332, 337, 345–46, 348, 357, 359, 362–64, 370, 373, 396–99, 402–4, 428, 440, 456, 503, 512–13, 524, 526, 608, 617, 647, 688, 808–10, 819, 822, 825, 834, 836, 843, 847, 867, 872, 874; **12:**7, 11–13, 15, 29, 32, 34, 46–53, 55, 59–60, 64, 71, 80, 87, 89, 95, 97, 99–101, 108, 110, 117–18, 139, 142, 159, 172, 182, 211, 221–22, 236–37, 246–47, 258, 264, 266–67, 273, 277, 334, 342, 344, 351, 387, 481, 483, 491, 505, 509, 520–21, 535, 543, 563, 569, 578–79, 581, 585, 588, 591–92, 602, 614, 620–21, 629, 639, 673, 681, 704, 707, 714, 722–23, 726, 734. *See also* HEBREWS; JEWS *in PERSONS IN THE BIBLE*; ISRAEL (KINGDOM/TERRITORY) *in PLACES IN THE BIBLE*

ISRAEL (PERSONAL NAME)
1:93, 253, 259, 306, 308, 318, 329, 381, 424, 429, 458, 516, 536, 565–67, 569, 574, 577, 580–81, 585–86, 590, 593, 598, 600, 627, 633–34, 645, 654–55, 674, 694, 906; **2:**186, 191, 461, 667, 680, 792, 939; **3:**332, 358, 468, 615; **6:**355, 380, 386–87, 390, 396, 413, 423, 429–33, 439, 447, 513, 527, 605, 960; **12:**620

ISSACHAR (PERSONAL NAME)
1:555, 666; **6:**1606; **12:**620

ISSACHAR (TRIBE)
1:666; **2:**34, 37, 213, 263, 536, 765, 788; **3:**52, 120, 320, 351–52, 882; **6:**1605–6

ISSHIAH
3:442

ITHAMAR
1:905, 972–73, 1060, 1071–72; **2:**49, 52; **3:**344, 441, 725

ITHIEL
5:251

ITHREAM
2:1219

ITTAI
2:1323–25, 1335–36

IZHAR
2:135; **3:**345, 452

IZRAHIAH
3:342, 838

J

JAAZANIAH
6:1176, 1186

JAAZIAH
3:442

JABESH
3:248

JABEZ
3:331–32

JABIN
1:258; **2:**547, 651, 726, 774, 779, 781–82, 878, 1062; **3:**1090; **4:**1010; **6:**1463

JACHIN
3:336

JACOB
1:91, 93, 216, 241, 248, 253–54, 257–59, 273, 277–78, 306, 308, 318, 321–22, 325, 328, 335, 375, 377, 404, 414, 416–17, 422, 424, 427, 432, 434, 440, 446, 453, 458–59, 489, 501, 503–4, 509–10, 514, 516–23, 526–29, 534–44, 552–60, 562–81, 583–87, 590–95, 598–601, 604–7, 611, 627–30, 633–36, 639–41, 643–45, 651–56, 658–61, 664–71, 674, 693–94, 703, 706, 712, 718, 735, 748, 780, 1005, 1016, 1023, 1063, 1139, 1181, 1186, 1190; **2:**47, 49, 65, 91, 106, 148, 161–62, 182, 186, 188, 191, 212, 234, 271, 277, 305, 359, 374, 461, 480, 491–92, 510, 534–36, 540–43, 546–47, 549–50, 552, 665, 680, 706, 736, 740–41, 755, 758, 792, 796–97, 804, 807, 810, 816, 826, 830, 832, 845–46, 939, 941, 974, 1043, 1062, 1099–1100, 1159, 1167, 1259; **3:**24, 26, 103–4, 317, 319, 332, 358, 401, 457, 468, 473, 525, 664, 747, 894, 901, 994, 996, 1014, 1016, 1023, 1038, 1042, 1056, 1089, 1127, 1138, 1143; **4:**21, 34, 43, 49–52, 55, 66, 74, 87, 111, 188, 234, 354, 439, 563, 582, 609, 755, 774, 869, 1013, 1105; **5:**33, 48, 78, 170, 251, 422, 428–29, 445, 516, 522, 524, 596, 605, 621–23, 631, 633, 659, 668, 750, 757, 764, 836, 842, 849, 867; **6:**16, 22, 65, 67–68, 72–73, 136, 155, 173–74, 225–27, 246–48, 344, 347, 354–55, 361–63, 375–76, 379–80, 386–88, 390, 393, 396, 400–401, 406, 413, 417–18, 420, 423, 429–33, 439, 447, 461, 498, 500–502, 513–14, 527, 596, 598, 654, 661, 669, 708, 763, 806, 808–10, 813, 827, 960, 962, 968, 980, 1138, 1140, 1154, 1186, 1238, 1240, 1266, 1277–78, 1299, 1303, 1347, 1399, 1401, 1474, 1476, 1510–11, 1530–31, 1574, 1600–1601; **7:**164, 183, 275, 281, 283–87, 291, 295, 297, 362, 401, 406, 408, 411, 416–17, 424, 444, 451, 455, 501, 525, 548, 609, 750, 760, 804, 807, 811, 832, 849, 855–56, 860–61, 865, 868, 870, 875, 877; **8:**67, 128, 130–31, 142, 423; **9:**45, 51, 54, 71, 94, 143, 300, 302–3, 310, 354, 381, 389, 413, 426, 532, 544, 565–66, 645, 648, 653, 737; **10:**128, 416, 451, 495, 505, 593, 599, 635, 637–38, 661, 692–93, 769; **11:**215, 227, 243,

JACOB *(continued)*
319, 372; **12:**136–37, 139, 154, 343, 571, 579, 620, 624
JADDUA
3:717, 817, 832–36
JADON
3:768
JAEL
1:186, 242; **2:**547, 738, 740, 759, 762, 774–77, 779, 781–83, 787–90, 804–5, 827, 830, 835, 841, 858, 872, 878; **3:**920, 1090, 1109, 1138, 1165; **9:**55
JAHATH
3:345, 442
JAHAZIEL
3:560–61
JAHZEIAH
3:743
JAIR
1:259; **2:**250, 309, 762, 764, 791, 819–20, 839; **3:**864, 886
JAIRITE, THE
2:1268, 1354
JAIRUS
1:1106; **4:**787, 903; **8:**63, 237, 587–91, 612, 619, 630, 634, 707, 729; **9:**24, 155, 158, 175, 187, 189–91, 200, 205, 346, 415, 432, 486, 684; **10:**540
JAKEH
5:251
JAKIM
4:8
JAMBRES
11:849–52
JAMES
1:15, 1037, 1073; **3:**173, 364, 587, 631; **5:**127; **8:**29, 41, 44, 58, 72, 103–5, 193, 362–63, 366, 368, 398, 493, 539, 562–67, 589, 621, 628, 630, 636, 653–54, 665, 684, 705, 707, 709, 724, 729, 732; **9:**100, 111, 117, 127, 138–39, 151, 159, 190, 205, 212, 215, 217, 353, 355, 384, 401–2, 415, 431–32, 465; **10:**8, 20, 24, 31, 44, 100, 130, 133, 175, 178–80, 203–4, 207–8, 211–15, 217–24, 226, 231, 233, 237, 243, 247, 252–54, 269, 276, 284–85, 291–95, 304, 322, 336, 362, 367, 370, 386–87, 735; **11:**113, 163, 194, 217, 225–26, 228, 232–35, 245, 256, 579, 704, 830; **12:**180–83, 186–90, 192–206, 209–13, 215–19, 221–25, 287, 342, 396, 473–74, 481–82
JANNES
11:849–52
JAPHETH
1:91, 403–5, 408–9; **4:**30; **6:**1378, 1516
JARIB
3:336, 726
JASON
4:7–8, 10, 12, 36, 85, 93, 106, 153, 182, 189–90, 205, 213, 216–19, 222, 228, 230, 248, 254–55, 258, 265, 269, 277, 280–81, 287; **5:**611–12; **7:**24–25, 128, 142–43; **10:**238–39, 766
JAVAN/JAVANITES
6:1378–79, 1516; **7:**810
JEATHERAI
3:335
JEBUSITES
1:164–65, 251, 408, 441; **2:**21, 123, 571, 576, 678, 736–37, 739–40, 876, 879, 1235–38, 1381–82; **3:**377, 733, 819; **4:**264; **6:**242, 1320; **7:**805
JECHONIAH/JECONIAH
2:1012; **3:**330, 886; **6:**940, 943; **7:**715; **8:**130
JEDAIAH
3:745, 768, 815, 831–32; **7:**787–88
JEDIDAH
3:849
JEDIDIAH
2:1298
JEDUTHUN
3:300, 363, 394, 445–46, 826; **4:**655–56
JEHDEIAH
3:442
JEHIEL
3:437, 452, 741
JEHIELI
3:452
JEHOAHAZ
1:250, 265–66; **3:**146, 173, 234, 236, 239, 244, 287–88, 290, 330, 569, 654; **6:**559, 739, 741, 743, 1077, 1269–70, 1272, 1326, 1403
JEHOASH
1:1187; **2:**567–68; **3:**173, 228, 234, 236–39, 241–45, 278, 280, 768; **4:**31; **7:**764, 766; **8:**130
JEHOHANAN
3:716, 741–42, 757, 768, 788, 833
JEHOIACHIN
1:250, 266; **2:**502, 504, 547, 1276; **3:**3, 287, 290, 294–95, 330, 654–55, 679, 886; **4:**1167; **6:**14, 443, 559, 685, 731, 739, 743–44, 783–84, 848, 925–26, 942–43, 1075, 1078, 1081, 1110, 1174, 1246, 1248, 1270, 1272–73, 1275–76, 1326, 1363, 1391, 1410, 1412, 1420, 1424, 1434, 1439, 1454, 1536, 1538; **7:**32, 38, 41, 90, 121, 638, 715, 731; **8:**130

JEHOIADA
3:19, 228, 230, 233, 285, 574–75, 579, 581, 622, 832, 849; **6:**943; **7:**764–66
JEHOIAKIM
1:266; **2:**419, 505, 687, 1294; **3:**287–90, 294, 330, 654–55, 700; **4:**40; **6:**559, 563–64, 566, 576, 634–35, 690, 708, 731, 739, 741–46, 757, 761, 768–69, 772, 774, 782, 838–40, 848–49, 853, 876, 925, 943, 956, 1077–78, 1270, 1272, 1326, 1342, 1348, 1403; **7:**38–39, 626, 631, 633, 638, 670; **9:**45
JEHOIARIB
4:42–43
JEHONADAB
3:224
JEHORAM
1:249, 264; **3:**159, 170, 173, 180–81, 183, 185, 192, 204–5, 209, 214, 227, 250, 551, 565, 568–70, 573, 594; **6:**1348
JEHOSHABEATH
3:573, 576
JEHOSHAPHAT
1:264–65, 828–29; **2:**1268; **3:**5, 49–51, 160–62, 164, 166–70, 181, 183, 214, 217, 227, 233, 241, 278, 332, 338, 388–89, 474, 514, 542, 544, 546–47, 551–56, 560–62, 564–65, 568, 570, 582, 594, 624, 628–30, 644, 657; **4:**212; **5:**853; **6:**1348; **7:**124, 330, 766; **9:**336
JEHOSHEBA
3:228, 573
JEHOVAH
See under GOD, NAMES FOR/TITLES OF
JEHOZADAK
3:690, 717; **6:**943; **7:**715, 765, 787
JEHU
1:249–50, 252, 265; **2:**106, 547, 1040; **3:**121, 143, 173, 210, 215–17, 219–21, 223–26, 228, 234, 236, 238, 241–43, 248, 542, 564, 570, 573, 785; **4:**11; **5:**80; **6:**1322; **7:**218, 804; **8:**403, 658; **12:**677
JEHUDI
7:670
JEIEL
3:357
JEMIMAH
4:635
JEPHTHAH
1:259–60, 274, 1186; **2:**165, 726, 738, 745–46, 762–65, 767–68, 770, 776, 791, 802, 816, 818, 820–22, 824–25, 827, 830–42, 846, 863, 873, 884, 886, 888, 1055, 1062, 1080; **3:**1174; **4:**21, 77; **5:**127, 629; **6:**1347; **7:**828; **12:**143
JEPHTHAH'S DAUGHTER
2:551, 724, 741, 748, 782, 833–35, 860, 872; **5:**412; **7:**385–86; **8:**598
JEPHUNNEH
2:124
JERAHMEEL
3:327–29, 442; **8:**839
JERED
1:380
JEREMIAH
1:96, 237, 262, 283, 289, 679, 748, 1034, 1138; **2:**142, 221, 275, 282, 355, 365, 391–92, 406, 430, 504, 511, 514, 574, 687–88, 731, 825–26, 860, 1016, 1294; **3:**33, 292–94, 364, 543, 655–56, 668, 677, 680, 701, 789, 812, 1069; **4:**198, 214, 296, 314, 410, 526, 564, 1167; **5:**46, 93, 381, 401, 634, 643, 687, 692, 793, 798, 855; **6:**2–3, 5–10, 13–19, 21–22, 49, 66, 101, 103, 109, 118, 148, 183, 186, 313, 320–21, 353, 358, 412, 428, 442–44, 448, 451, 464, 468, 555–56, 559–66, 573–89, 596, 598–99, 602–4, 609, 613–15, 618–21, 626–29, 634–35, 637–39, 641, 643, 648, 654, 665–67, 669, 673–78, 680, 684, 690–91, 694, 696–99, 702–4, 707–10, 712, 714–18, 721–24, 726–28, 730–31, 733, 750–51, 753–55, 758, 761, 763, 766–69, 772–78, 782–88, 791–94, 797, 804–5, 807, 811–13, 819–20, 826, 838–42, 848–52, 857–58, 866–67, 872–74, 876–79, 882, 891, 911–12, 916–17, 925, 929, 933, 941, 943, 945, 952, 956, 985–88, 1015–16, 1023, 1065, 1084, 1091, 1124, 1126, 1128, 1140, 1143–44, 1166, 1170, 1199–1201, 1208, 1214, 1221, 1233, 1253, 1295–96, 1315, 1317, 1320, 1339, 1341, 1411, 1442, 1455, 1463, 1505, 1517, 1521, 1526, 1532; **7:**74, 90, 121, 128, 181–82, 220, 227, 267, 302, 316, 341, 357, 372, 408, 412, 430, 440–41, 480–81, 489, 515, 534, 544, 548, 560, 574, 585, 623–24, 627, 631–32, 637, 641, 660–62, 670, 735, 747, 760, 779, 796, 820, 831, 846, 864; **8:**29, 406, 438; **9:**45, 372, 374, 404, 420, 545; **10:**209, 218, 307, 640; **11:**63–64, 215; **12:**101, 117, 139, 344, 389, 639, 641, 697, 701, 726
JEREMOTH
3:357
JERIMOTH
3:446
JEROBOAM I
1:257, 264, 931; **2:**142, 363, 376, 557, 562, 565, 571, 574–75, 634, 646, 683, 687, 706, 717, 792, 816, 855, 871, 915, 987, 1090, 1350–52; **3:**5–6, 90, 94–95, 98, 100–106, 108–16, 118–25, 180–81, 226, 234, 236, 244, 247, 252–53, 255, 257–58, 274, 277–78, 285, 512, 516, 518, 522,

JEROBOAM I *(continued)*
527, 529–32, 649, 785, 993; **4:**21, 32; **5:**419, 631, 836, 849–50; **6:**6, 74, 751, 1386, 1509; **7:**205, 260–61, 265, 272, 352, 376, 407, 410, 426, 834; **10:**660
JEROBOAM II
1:265; **3:**236, 243, 248; **6:**841, 1143, 1165, 1412; **7:**200, 217, 256, 342–43, 355, 360, 362, 403, 410, 466, 493
JEROHAM
3:357
JERUBBAAL
2:797–98, 809–10, 817, 1062; **3:**100
JESHAIAH
3:718, 727
JESHUA
1:268; **3:**665–66, 685–86, 690–95, 702, 704, 706, 716–17, 745, 769, 801–2, 817, 826, 830–35, 850; **4:**197, 199; **5:**607, 631, 642, 836, 855–56, 867; **6:**823, 943; **7:**715. *See also* JOSHUA (HIGH PRIEST)
JESSE
1:218; **2:**943, 1086, 1098–1100, 1102–3, 1110–11, 1113, 1135, 1144, 1147, 1167, 1175, 1259; **3:**329; **5:**256; **6:**140, 147; **7:**811; **9:**354; **10:**416, 537, 684, 748
JESUS THE CHRIST
ANGUISH OF **8:**492, 707; **9:**433, 461; APOCALYPSE/PAROUSIA/SECOND COMING OF **1:**47, 95, 166, 191; **2:**91; **4:**445, 1018, 1186; **6:**119; **7:**4, 8, 15–16, 145, 148–49, 429, 571–72, 655; **8:**34, 38, 40, 51–52, 68, 92, 125, 157–58, 187, 205, 222, 232, 249, 254, 258–62, 287, 290, 303, 309–10, 345, 349–51, 356, 363–64, 366, 370, 391, 392, 414, 417, 428, 438–41, 443–48, 450–51, 453, 455–59, 471, 474, 476, 492, 512, 514, 516–19, 525, 528, 535, 537–38, 550–51, 571–72, 577, 627–28, 630–32, 653–54, 659, 663, 671, 684, 687–90, 694, 700, 704, 723, 728, 732; **9:**18–19, 90–91, 124–25, 167, 200–202, 223–24, 263–64, 288, 329, 331, 398–400, 410, 458, 499, 528, 552, 741, 748, 752, 778–79, 793, 862; **10:**20, 24–25, 28, 42–43, 63–64, 376, 401, 424, 431, 449, 621, 663–64, 666, 672, 673, 677, 691–92, 695, 768, 786, 822, 870, 886, 938, 980, 982, 984, 988, 992–93, 1002; **11:**82–83, 88, 149, 202–3, 218–19, 296, 314, 343, 385, 491–92, 511, 547, 556, 579, 614, 618, 639–40, 654, 677–79, 686, 690, 692, 695, 706–8, 713–15, 716, 719, 721, 723–27, 732, 735, 741, 746, 750–51, 754–55, 758–59, 784, 811–12, 829, 836, 852, 855; **12:**30, 58–59, 85, 113, 121, 126, 221, 258, 276, 323–27, 329–32, 336, 338, 341–45, 347–48, 351–52, 354–60, 375, 403, 409, 476–77, 479, 482, 488–89, 494–95, 497–99, 499, 504, 506, 515–17, 519, 522, 525, 529–31, 532, 543, 546, 560, 562–63, 568, 575, 584–85, 588, 596, 602, 614, 625–26, 643, 649, 653, 702–5, 708, 734, 744; BAPTISM AND TEMPTATION OF **1:**210, 838; **2:**285, 356, 602–4, 609, 1045; **4:**673, 691, 794, 1048; **6:**365, 1497; **7:**101, 562; **8:**110–11, 115, 117, 150, 156, 159–66, 169–71, 270, 274–75, 281, 341, 344, 364, 366, 385, 405, 504, 513, 525, 527–28, 534–36, 541–43, 616, 621, 631–32, 724; **9:**8, 11, 14, 27, 78–79, 85, 87, 90–95, 97–103, 105, 111, 114, 130, 160, 205–7, 241, 266, 378, 381, 413, 415, 425–26, 432, 434, 442, 529, 559, 624; **10:**50, 262, 534, 603; **11:**600; **12:**11, 28–29, 61, 64, 439, 533, 569, 625, 651, 727; BIRTH AND GENEALOGY OF **1:**85, 87, 476, 587, 606, 671, 838, 954; **2:**32, 861, 1100, 1284; **3:**24, 331–32, 1132; **4:**673, 794, 965, 1001, 1018, 1067, 1070, 1073, 1186, 1196, 1233, 1273; **6:**113, 124, 339, 432; **7:**568, 571–72, 731, 771; **8:**4, 64, 67, 69, 89, 102, 110, 113, 126–33, 135–40, 142–43, 149–50, 152, 160, 169, 175, 234, 289, 297, 310, 319, 355, 359, 385, 402, 422, 464, 486, 519, 529, 592, 675; **9:**8–11, 13–14, 16–17, 19, 24, 29–30, 33, 42, 49, 50–51, 55, 58, 60, 62–63, 65, 68–71, 73, 76–78, 83, 85, 87, 90–91, 93–96, 98–99, 101, 103, 111–12, 114, 116, 200, 313, 315, 337, 354, 369, 378, 391, 413, 426, 442, 445, 456, 460, 462, 464, 479, 494, 516, 603, 624; **10:**362, 535; **11:**180, 283, 515; **12:**29, 42, 58, 61, 535; AND CALL OF DISCIPLES **4:**815, 928, 1252, 1277; **8:**66, 103, 115, 169–71, 175, 178, 182–83, 193, 195–98, 215–17, 220, 228, 230, 234–35, 251, 256, 275, 281, 286, 288, 300, 322, 335, 349–52, 363, 383, 391, 395–96, 398–400, 499–500, 503, 537, 539–40, 547, 552–53, 562, 567, 571, 574–75, 594–95, 626–27, 641, 648–49, 656, 671, 687, 694, 709, 733; **9:**27, 90, 98, 111, 114–18, 126–29, 133, 136–37, 139–40, 142, 152–53, 160, 187, 193, 197, 202, 217–18, 222, 226, 233, 291–93, 309, 334, 348, 402–3, 426–27, 430, 432, 439, 469, 531, 533–34, 557, 611, 703, 710–11, 727, 733, 751, 857, 860–61, 864–65; **10:**109, 111; **11:**140, 149, 162, 809; **12:**167, 170, 230, 245; CRUCIFIXION, RESURRECTION, AND ASCENSION OF **1:**13, 83–85, 91, 160, 169, 189–92, 199, 204, 208–10, 671, 799, 836, 838, 898, 954–55, 1121; **2:**90, 98, 152, 235, 447, 798, 804, 847, 1100, 1143, 1231–32; **3:**68, 78, 130, 179, 512, 612, 738, 928, 997, 1004, 1057, 1143, 1181; **4:**278, 445, 673–74, 728, 738, 742, 754, 765–66, 802, 830, 849, 870, 874, 879, 903, 920, 924, 938, 947, 954, 956, 970, 1001, 1022, 1048, 1073, 1089, 1119, 1131, 1143, 1149, 1156, 1196, 1216, 1226, 1248, 1252, 1280; **5:**15, 303, 313, 343, 717, 721, 825; **6:**223, 440, 468–69, 1072, 1504; **7:**15, 67, 76, 148, 317, 328, 415, 510, 569, 655, 687, 830; **8:**37, 39–40, 50, 52, 64–66, 71–73, 81–82, 95, 102, 110, 112, 125, 138, 140,

149–50, 156, 163, 168, 174, 188, 198, 215, 224, 238, 245, 249, 251, 254, 258, 267–69, 295–96, 312, 319, 322, 325, 328–29, 341, 344, 348–49, 351, 354–56, 364–66, 396, 400, 402–3, 405, 414, 419, 422–23, 437–39, 447, 457, 459–60, 463–64, 466–67, 470–71, 474, 476, 478, 480, 486, 488, 491–97, 499–505, 511, 519–20, 527–28, 539, 543, 562, 590–91, 618, 623–24, 627, 630–32, 634–36, 657, 673, 675–78, 680, 696–98, 703–5, 707, 710, 713, 717, 719–20, 722–24, 726, 728–33; **9:**4, 6, 8, 13, 16–19, 21, 28, 30–31, 52, 77, 91, 94, 116–17, 137, 159, 174, 191, 197, 200–203, 205–8, 210, 214–15, 220, 223, 225, 278, 313, 319, 331, 346, 351–52, 354, 369, 376, 381–82, 388–91, 407, 412, 429–30, 439, 448–57, 459–64, 466, 468–70, 472–73, 477–78, 484–90, 493, 497, 509, 523, 528, 533, 537, 539–40, 544–45, 551–53, 585, 595, 602–4, 608, 610–11, 616–17, 623–24, 633–35, 671, 681, 686, 688, 690–95, 699, 708–11, 713–15, 718–19, 721–22, 726, 732–33, 735, 738, 741, 746, 748–49, 751, 753, 766, 770–72, 774, 776, 778, 780–81, 784–85, 787, 789, 794, 799–800, 804, 811, 816, 818, 820–21, 823–25, 827, 829–33, 836–38, 841–45, 847–49, 851–54, 856, 864; **10:**12, 14, 19–21, 23–24, 25, 30, 37, 40–46, 48, 50, 52, 58, 62, 65–66, 79–81, 84, 88–89, 91, 96, 100, 104, 106, 121, 125, 140, 146, 151, 162, 166, 170, 180, 189, 192–93, 240, 242–43, 249–50, 256, 262, 277–78, 281, 310–12, 315, 330, 333–36, 338–43, 375–76, 378, 387, 401–2, 416–19, 423–24, 427–28, 432, 457, 465, 467, 474, 477–78, 480, 488, 501–5, 507, 509, 513, 519–21, 524, 530, 534–35, 537–41, 546–49, 557, 559, 578, 580, 584–85, 587, 591, 596, 598, 603–5, 607–8, 613, 617, 625–26, 645–46, 650, 655, 663–64, 669, 677–78, 686, 690, 694, 696, 700–702, 706–7, 710, 715, 717, 719, 727, 729, 733, 736–38, 745, 748, 753, 808, 811, 817–18, 828, 842, 870, 973, 976–77, 983–84; **11:**57, 81–82, 85, 88, 138, 167, 184, 202, 205, 208, 217–19, 242–44, 228, 246–51, 255, 260–61, 274–76, 283, 285, 293, 298, 308, 313, 317, 319, 322, 328, 339, 343–44, 346–48, 374, 382, 384, 412, 480, 486, 502, 509, 515, 600, 607–9, 617, 628, 640, 678–79, 689, 696, 715, 723–25, 727, 837, 851–52; **12:**28–29, 40, 42–43, 46, 58, 61–62, 64, 71, 90, 97, 107, 121, 155, 172, 180, 213, 223, 231, 246, 250, 254–55, 259, 293, 294, 296–99, 384, 404, 439, 441, 473, 530, 560, 569, 611, 643–44, 662, 708, 713, 716; DIVINITY OF **1:**46; **2:**1369; **8:**64, 137, 356, 520, 562, 580, 630, 632; **9:**92, 95, 111, 184, 206, 367, 378, 569; **10:**416, 418, 520, 630, 823; **11:**476, 607; **12:**12; OF GALILEE **1:**169; **2:**1100; **8:**45, 714–17, 724; **9:**113, 161, 438, 446, 808; **10:**696; **12:**474; HEALINGS AND MIRACLES OF **1:**178, 192, 465, 809, 818, 1105; **2:**67, 152, 753, 804; **3:**1117; **4:**1119, 1265; **6:**432; **7:**115, 253–54; **8:**52, 58–59, 62–64, 76, 95, 111–12, 137, 149, 163, 165–66, 169–71, 174–75, 217, 222–30, 232, 234–35, 237–41, 244–46, 248–51, 256, 266, 273, 280–81, 285–87, 295, 300, 317–18, 323–25, 329, 331, 336–37, 339, 348, 352, 363, 367–68, 372, 383–85, 400, 404, 406–7, 410, 492, 500, 505, 510–12, 518, 520, 525–26, 528–29, 539, 541–51, 553, 555–56, 558–61, 565–66, 570, 579–80, 585, 587–96, 600–605, 608–9, 611–21, 623, 625–26, 628, 630, 632–35, 646, 650–51, 654–56, 660, 665, 696, 706, 708–9, 713, 729, 733; **9:**8, 12, 23–24, 27, 29, 47, 50, 56, 76, 103, 108, 110–26, 128, 133–35, 142, 154–57, 160–61, 172–75, 178, 184, 189–96, 199, 204, 208, 210–12, 220, 223, 241, 244, 272–74, 281, 283–86, 325–27, 335, 344, 353–57, 360, 369, 391–92, 401, 430, 434, 436, 446, 462, 473, 487, 503, 508, 535–40, 543, 546, 557, 566, 574–76, 578–81, 584, 586, 591–97, 599–600, 603, 606, 612, 614, 616, 619–21, 629, 636, 651–54, 656–61, 663, 665–66, 669, 671, 676, 680, 686–88, 690–93, 696, 698–99, 701–2, 708, 727, 764, 803, 849, 851–52, 856–59, 864; **10:**12, 21, 41, 47, 74, 76–78, 80–81, 84–85, 88–89, 91, 99, 151, 160–62, 166, 170, 198, 230, 232, 267–69, 273, 277–78, 307, 336, 356, 365, 451, 505; **11:**607; **12:**64, 223, 283; AND THE HOLY SPIRIT **1:**1061; **3:**179; **7:**327; **8:**137, 158, 161, 259, 287, 504, 525, 532, 534, 541, 563–65, 688–89, 696; **9:**17, 30, 52, 59, 68–69, 85, 103, 153, 207, 224, 253, 266, 398, 401, 434, 441, 469, 484, 488, 529, 544, 723, 751, 833, 846–47, 849; **10:**14, 18, 21, 23, 30, 37–38, 41–42, 46, 53–54, 58, 92, 106, 121, 127, 130, 139, 142, 154, 166–67, 169, 176, 189, 210, 227, 261, 263, 419, 512–13, 521, 696, 720, 857, 941; **11:**18, 322; **12:**11–12, 62, 74, 376, 388, 407, 449; IMPRISONMENT OF **8:**714; **10:**262; AND THE JEWS **1:**45–46, 83–84, 86–87, 91, 169, 686, 697, 955; **2:**603–4; **3:**533, 601, 932–33; **4:**191, 278, 672, 965, 1025, 1037–38, 1131; **7:**145, 396, 570, 643; **8:**34, 39–42, 44–46, 99, 102, 115, 132–33, 153, 158, 167, 182, 202, 221, 292, 330, 332, 336, 339, 371–72, 391, 405–6, 460, 481–82, 486–87, 479, 516, 554–55, 558, 607, 673–74, 688, 712–14, 717, 720; **9:**229–30, 383, 449, 505, 527, 543–44, 579–81, 586–91, 603, 605–7, 610, 617, 621, 634, 636, 638–51, 653, 657, 662, 674–78, 686–91, 696, 698, 702, 732–33, 803, 809–10, 815–27, 830; **10:**11–13, 19, 55–57, 166, 240, 310–11, 413–14, 450–51; **11:**703; AND JOHN THE BAPTIST **1:**988; **2:**603, 718; **7:**15, 847, 873; **8:**38, 67, 81–82, 115–16, 154–56, 159, 166–67, 204, 220, 234–36, 258, 265, 267–68, 270–71, 275, 280, 348, 354, 365, 385–87, 410, 436–37, 494–95, 505, 512, 520, 525, 527, 530–37, 539, 543, 548, 555–56, 559, 593,

JESUS THE CHRIST *(continued)*
597–600, 622, 625, 631, 643–45, 668–69, 671, 699–700, 707, 712, 720, 723, 725–26; **9:**8, 11, 18, 20–21, 49, 52, 58, 60, 69, 79, 83–84, 87, 90, 102, 116–17, 123, 128, 130, 157–58, 160, 165–66, 184, 194–95, 199, 219, 248–49, 272, 281, 302, 313, 315, 319, 352, 359, 369, 378, 401, 434, 455–56, 465, 478, 487, 508, 515–16, 518, 520, 524–25, 528–29, 533, 549, 551, 557–61, 565, 570, 586–87, 589, 591, 640, 660–61, 675–76, 678, 681, 751–52, 764–65, 826, 834; **10:**41, 53, 67–68, 192, 261–63, 451–52; **12:**438, 562; AND THE MARGINALIZED **1:**169–70; **2:**1145; **4:**766, 1215; **8:**223, 237, 316, 377, 406, 472; **9:**30, 98, 108, 129, 131–32, 139, 231, 290, 332, 345, 354, 359, 406, 421, 472, 565, 648; **10:**72, 135, 144, 390, 816; **12:**194, 569, 588, 728; AND MOSES (*see under* MOSES); PARABLES OF **1:**115, 1041; **2:**1316; **3:**1102; **4:**636; **5:**64; **6:**1452; **7:**469; **8:**50–51, 61, 69, 74, 77, 80–81, 268, 298–300, 303–5, 310–16, 348, 376, 381, 396, 409, 411, 413, 416–17, 455, 497, 518, 538, 564, 567–69, 572, 574–76, 578–79, 593, 616, 640, 669–70, 683; **9:**12, 16, 18, 22–24, 27, 56, 84, 116, 151, 158, 173–74, 176–80, 214, 229, 236, 239, 250, 256, 262, 272, 275, 283, 292–96, 298, 300–301, 304, 306, 310–11, 316, 319, 323, 335, 337, 358, 396–97, 473, 493, 638, 684, 711, 779; **10:**85, 376, 827, 829, 920; **11:**125, 281; **12:**708; PASSION OF (*see* PASSION OF CHRIST, THE *in SUBJECTS AND THEMES*); PERSON OF **1:**194; **8:**160, 220, 353; **11:**570, 594; **12:**533; AND PRAYER **1:**102, 815, 842; **2:**91; **3:**380, 506, 540, 582, 777, 1052; **4:**402, 790, 793, 820–21, 895, 909, 965, 1008, 1011, 1244; **5:**317, 693; **6:**796; **8:**161, 196, 200–207, 212, 239, 245, 260, 272, 274, 328, 336–37, 349, 368, 403, 406, 408, 431, 471, 476–77, 480–81, 492, 544, 546, 555, 561, 589, 602–3, 623, 625–26, 634–35, 650, 653, 656–57, 651, 661, 663–67, 673, 695, 707–9; **9:**12, 27–28, 79, 90, 100, 111–12, 120, 130, 137, 156, 179, 199, 205, 207, 222, 224, 233–35, 238–39, 250, 260, 263, 273, 336–39, 342, 345, 393, 428, 431–34, 437, 439, 448, 450, 454–55, 461–63, 494, 509, 688, 691–92, 712, 719, 721, 735, 746, 758–59, 780–81, 787–92, 794–98, 810, 846, 855, 863; **10:**40, 44–45, 51, 77, 133, 591, 593–94, 607, 713, 730, 757, 857; **11:**285, 414, 439, 490, 541; **12:**11, 62, 64, 223, 287–88, 422, 442–43, 734; AND PROPHECY OF **1:**13, 87–88, 92; **5:**96; **6:**113, 143, 451; **7:**428, 538, 572, 771; **8:**38, 50, 62, 146–47, 153, 156, 176–77, 217, 267–68, 286, 310, 333, 344, 356, 391, 403, 437, 477–78, 481, 512, 514–16, 530, 535, 619, 625, 631, 654, 659, 663, 665, 681, 684–85, 687–89, 691, 693, 714; **9:**9, 15, 42, 73, 87, 351, 359, 382, 401–3, 410, 440, 446, 543, 621, 634–35, 698, 708, 710, 717, 720, 733, 773, 783, 808, 820, 851; **10:**11–14, 16, 20, 22, 24–25, 37–38, 40–42, 46, 51, 53–55, 57, 59, 64–66, 68–69, 71–72, 77, 81, 89, 92, 99, 107, 121, 127, 131, 134–35, 143–44, 147, 150, 153, 166, 169, 175, 189, 191–93, 195–96, 198, 200, 203, 208–10, 213, 226, 232–34, 240, 254–55, 261–63, 282–84, 288–89, 307–8, 330, 334, 338, 341, 359–62, 367–68, 415, 450, 605, 667, 692, 748, 769, 972; **11:**259, 730, 815; **12:**28, 255, 267, 327, 342, 344, 355, 477, 485, 494–95, 498–99, 506, 517, 528, 535, 560, 575, 584, 588, 643, 658, 665, 696, 727, 733–35; AND THE SCRIBES AND PHARISEES **1:**1106; **2:**1013, 1141; **3:**1114; **5:**709; **6:**244, 860, 1316, 1338; **7:**253–54, 509; **8:**39, 59, 64, 70, 78, 81, 99, 104, 110, 115, 130, 138, 140, 142–44, 147, 151, 153, 157, 162, 170, 180, 189, 217, 219–20, 223–24, 229, 234–36, 240, 265, 271, 274–75, 278–80, 283, 285–87, 295–97, 300, 308, 311, 314–15, 317, 330–36, 341–42, 349, 371, 385–86, 403, 406, 408–10, 412, 414, 419–24, 426–28, 430–31, 434–38, 457, 464, 474, 491, 497, 525, 540–41, 543, 545, 547–49, 551–52, 555–56, 558, 563–65, 557, 572, 588, 590, 597–98, 605–8, 616–18, 621, 631, 633, 638–39, 642–43, 645–46, 652, 656–57, 667–69, 673–74, 678, 680–83, 687, 695, 700, 710, 712, 714, 726, 728; **9:**13–14, 20, 23–24, 26, 28–29, 72, 74, 76, 111–12, 114, 122–30, 133–36, 153, 155, 164, 166, 169, 172, 178, 182, 184, 194, 201, 211, 247–49, 251, 268, 273, 276, 280–81, 284–88, 290, 294–96, 298, 304, 306–7, 311–12, 318, 321, 329, 331, 333, 341, 348, 351, 355–56, 358–59, 363, 365, 369, 375–78, 380–83, 385, 388–90, 392–96, 399, 414, 422, 430, 436, 440, 442, 445–46, 455, 477, 528, 541, 559–60, 569, 574, 624, 627–30, 633, 651, 653, 656, 661–70, 696, 700, 708, 710, 720, 801, 806, 813, 817; **10:**104, 108, 120, 144, 209, 309, 311–12, 315, 336; **11:**397; **12:**306, 621, 632, 726–27; SERMONS OF **1:**133, 815; **3:**129, 452; **4:**774, 882; **5:**307; **6:**1383; **8:**34, 84, 112, 136, 144–45, 171–72, 174–75, 177–78, 182–83, 188, 192, 196–97, 202–3, 207, 211, 214, 217–22, 226, 256, 261, 267, 272, 287, 342, 425, 428, 435, 504, 665; **9:**8, 23, 102, 105, 137, 140–43, 147–49, 151–54, 157, 159–60, 193, 196, 235, 278, 374, 536, 662, 734, 799; **10:**14, 16, 62, 66–67, 79–80, 100, 195, 715; **11:**830; **12:**254, 297, 391; SUFFERING OF **8:**631; **9:**418; **10:**290; **11:**503; **12:**27, 62, 149, 252, 282–83, 288, 292, 297, 299, 310; TEACHING OF **8:**73, 80, 174–75, 525, 504, 525, 606; **9:**103, 110, 365, 377, 436, 614, 779–80, 809; **10:**122, 876; **12:**454; IN THE TEMPLE **8:**667, 710, 719; TEMPTATION OF **2:**285, 356; **9:**97–101; TRANSFIGURATION

OF **1:**838, 883, 955; **2:**90, 718; **3:**179, 928; **4:**673, 691, 1005, 1076; **5:**341; **8:**64, 351, 363, 366–67, 370, 476, 503, 511, 527, 572, 589–90, 621, 627–28, 630–33, 707, 724, 729–33; **9:**14–15, 27, 90–91, 137, 153, 190, 192, 195, 202, 204–10, 233, 319, 381, 409, 432, 434, 442, 456, 468, 478–79, 539; **10:**43; **11:**227; **12:**342, 567; TRIAL OF **8:**478–86, 711–19; **9:**441–49, 805–19; TRIUMPHAL ENTRY OF **3:**512; **7:**808; **8:**153, 400, 402, 438, 659; **9:**366, 370, 704–6; **11:**856; **12:**621, 624; AND WOMEN **1:**182, 184, 186, 606, 799; **2:**805, 846–47, 1008; **3:**129–30, 746, 1132; **4:**1131, 1209, 1215; **5:**700, 745–46; **7:**227–28; **8:**129, 132, 138, 143, 191, 196, 223, 238, 386–87, 405, 466, 493–95, 500–502, 512, 520, 529, 546, 567, 588, 636–37, 643, 645, 647, 698–99, 724, 726, 729–33; **9:**13, 22–25, 70, 94, 98, 111, 114, 173–75, 182–83, 229, 232, 273–74, 313, 333, 345, 370, 389, 393, 416, 450–54, 462, 464–70, 472, 478, 490, 496, 535–36, 571–72, 628, 630, 829, 831, 840, 843, 859; **10:**43–44, 106, 180, 230, 235, 238, 263, 342, 875–76; **11:**655; **12:**287, 687, 728

JESUS THE CHRIST, METAPHORS FOR

ATTORNEY/JUDGE **1:**14; **8:**260, 354, 393, 550, 624; **9:**125, 253, 591, 718, 796, 814, 817; **10:**20, 166, 738; **11:**855; **12:**400, 517, 734; BRIDEGROOM **5:**407; **7:**227–28; **8:**79, 450, 555; **9:**130–31, 538, 558, 570, 751; **11:**147; BUILDER **8:**345; **12:**46; CREATOR **1:**14; DIVINE GLORY **8:**691; **11:**872–73; **12:**609, 611, 614, 657; KING **8:**357–58, 503; **9:**824; LAMB **1:**91–92, 988, 1072; **2:**90; **3:**612, 928; **6:**1564; **8:**697, 702; **9:**70, 391, 415, 419, 431, 457, 463, 499, 528–30, 533, 719, 823, 833–34, 837; **11:**503; **12:**283, 516–17, 530, 562, 602, 605–6, 611, 621, 624–26, 650–51, 659, 665, 668, 694, 696, 703, 715 (*see also* LAMB *in SUBJECTS AND THEMES*); LIGHT **10:**341; **12:**374; LION **12:**527, 602, 604, 606, 624; SAVIOR **1:**208; **8:**234, 274; **9:**4, 16–20, 56, 65–66, 103, 196, 360, 445, 456–57, 463, 490, 572; **10:**20–21, 107, 137, 192, 255, 515; **11:**535, 784, 790, 836, 862, 872, 874, 876; **12:**275, 333, 479, 500 (*see also* SAVIOR *in SUBJECTS AND THEMES*); SHEPHERD **2:**1235; **4:**770–71; **6:**1467; **7:**571, 834; **8:**376–77; **9:**602, 651, 668–73, 677, 727, 733, 742, 776, 783, 793, 802, 817–19, 827, 842, 851, 860, 862; **12:**283; VINE **9:**739 (*see also under* JESUS THE CHRIST, NAMES FOR/TITLES OF); WISDOM **5:**96–98; **11:**608. *See also* JESUS THE CHRIST, NAMES FOR/TITLES OF

JESUS THE CHRIST, NAMES FOR/TITLES OF

THE ANOINTED ONE **1:**27, 289, 1061; **2:**602, 895, 958, 980, 982–83, 988, 1037, 1039, 1041, 1045, 1072, 1089, 1091–92, 1097, 1099–1102, 1128, 1143, 1147, 1156–58, 1168–69, 1174–75, 1197, 1201–3, 1207, 1217, 1231, 1234, 1259, 1332, 1347, 1366–68, 137–71; **4:**660, 756, 765, 1034, 1037, 1130, 1211; **5:**254; **6:**140, 169, 394–95, 399, 402, 455, 1059, 1065; **7:**128; **8:**30, 177, 353, 359, 427; **9:**17, 197, 199, 200; **12:**141, 375, 406–7, 587, 644, 710; APOSTLE **12:**45; AUTHOR OF LIFE **2:**340; **5:**497; **10:**80; DELIVERER **9:**53, 65; **11:**688, 696; EMMANUEL **4:**771, 866, 1238; **9:**51, 486; HIGH PRIEST **12:**95–96; HOLY ONE OF GOD **9:**611; IMMANUEL **3:**659; **5:**96, 251; **6:**42, 110–13, 116–17, 375, 823; **8:**135; **12:**728; KING **2:**946; **3:**24, 479, 486, 512; **4:**690, 692, 749, 759, 863, 866, 965, 1001, 1037–38, 1073, 1156; **6:**124, 143; **7:**67, 428, 571–72, 808, 840; **8:**115–17, 125, 130–34, 139–40, 142–43, 147, 149–50, 158, 167–68, 178, 186, 189, 223, 236, 268, 282, 285–86, 289–90, 292, 294, 309, 312, 323, 354–55, 357, 360, 403, 427, 455–56, 460, 474, 487–88, 492, 503, 526, 528, 535, 622, 655–59, 664, 680, 696, 698–99, 704, 714, 718–19, 723; **9:**17–19, 70, 91, 131, 200, 345, 353, 361–64, 366–67, 369–70, 373, 379, 391, 440, 445–47, 452, 454, 456, 460, 463–64, 532, 594–95, 597, 697, 707, 814, 816, 818–20, 822–24, 827, 829–30, 834; **10:**66, 192, 239, 404, 415, 537, 718, 725, 750, 768; **11:**609, 677; **12:**23, 28, 61, 95–96, 193, 342, 621; KING OF KINGS **12:**682, 699, 702; LAMB OF GOD **1:**91, 207, 495, 988, 1053, 1072; **6:**338; **9:**391, 431, 457, 463, 528, 533; **12:**283, 526, 602, 612; LIGHT OF THE WORLD **1:**892, 1166; **3:**453; **4:**824, 903; **6:**506–10; **8:**183; **9:**52, 534, 602, 632, 660–61, 686, 730, 802, 824, 826; **10:**435, 445–47, 450, 453, 455, 467, 629; **12:**272, 385; LIVING BREAD/BREAD OF LIFE **1:**209, 813, 1022; **4:**824; **5:**15; **9:**4, 513, 592, 598, 600–608, 611–14, 694; LORD **8:**224, 328; **9:**16–17, 151, 158; MASTER **3:**1105; **8:**361; **9:**19, 183–84, 189–90, 308–9, 326; **10:**415, 736; **11:**657, 861; **12:**330, 345–46, 485; MESSIAH/CHRIST **1:**13, 83–84, 87, 419, 606, 686, 988, 1042, 1061, 1106; **2:**91, 603, 798, 946, 983, 1045, 1100, 1143, 1231, 1259, 1368; **3:**332, 576; **4:**278, 691, 756, 759, 765, 965, 1037–38, 1063, 1073, 1130–31, 1156; **5:**14–16, 35–36, 46, 98–99, 104, 114, 129, 183, 189, 208, 254, 256, 370, 401, 463, 492, 507, 552, 565, 801, 852; **6:**124, 143, 239; **7:**328, 429, 538, 570, 571, 724, 768, 788, 840, 876; **8:**42, 44–45, 66, 90, 97, 98–99, 102, 112, 116, 126–27, 129, 131–32, 135, 137–38, 140, 142–44, 147, 149–50, 153, 156–59, 162–67, 169, 174, 186–87, 189, 222, 225–26, 236, 240–41, 248–49, 251–52, 266–67, 270, 281, 286, 292, 304, 310, 317, 336, 339, 343–44, 349, 353, 354, 358–60, 362, 364–65, 377, 399, 426–27, 438, 442–43, 455, 459, 463–64, 480–81, 486–87,

JESUS THE CHRIST, NAMES *(continued)*
493, 496, 511, 514, 519, 526, 528–29, 535, 572, 580, 613, 619, 621–24, 627, 630–31, 663, 673, 680–81, 687, 690–91, 693, 696, 706, 713–14, 718, 723; **9:**13, 15–19, 27–28, 42–43, 63, 70–71, 85–86, 91, 94, 97, 112, 118–19, 123, 125, 137, 140, 153, 160, 164, 192, 194, 198–201, 204, 211, 243, 312, 356, 360, 365, 391, 419, 442–43, 445, 454, 456–57, 463, 478, 486, 527, 531, 533, 557, 565, 568–70, 572, 580, 620–21, 624–25, 657, 660, 675–77, 689, 713, 780, 852; **10:**11, 14, 19–21, 23, 30, 37–38, 40–44, 46–50, 53–54, 57, 62–63, 65–67, 77, 81–82, 85, 97, 104, 108, 122–28, 130, 132, 137–38, 151, 153, 155, 166, 176, 188, 191–93, 195, 205, 209–10, 227, 232, 237–40, 245, 250, 252, 254–56, 262, 276–78, 281, 296, 304–5, 311–12, 319, 330, 333–37, 340, 360–62, 364–65, 376, 401–2, 404–6, 408, 413–15, 417–29, 431, 437–38, 443–45, 449–50, 459, 464, 466–72, 478, 480, 482, 484, 496, 502–5, 509–10, 512–14, 516–21, 524–25, 527–29, 534–35, 537–41, 545–46, 548–51, 554, 557, 559, 566, 571, 576–80, 583, 585–89, 594, 602–4, 607, 609–11, 613–16, 619, 621, 624–26, 629–32, 642, 644–46, 650–53, 655, 660, 662–68, 670–73, 677–78, 680, 685, 687, 690, 692, 695–97, 699–702, 706, 709–10, 715, 718–20, 722, 729–31, 733, 735, 737–38, 741, 745–49, 753–55, 757, 764, 768–69; **11:**185, 190, 260, 298, 375, 397, 404, 790, 810, 834, 843, 865; **12:**61, 342–43, 388, 403, 427–28, 457, 473, 525–27, 531, 569, 602, 606, 649, 652, 665, 693, 705, 716; MORNING STAR **12:**343; NAZAREAN **2:**861; NAZARENE **8:**147; **9:**354, 477; **10:**66; ONLY BEGOTTEN **5:**99, 308, 463; **6:**1083, 1386; **8:**526; **9:**206; **11:**301, 303, 305; **12:**22, 29, 61, 263, 376, 410–11, 414, 416, 427, 430, 435–36, 445–46; PASCHAL LAMB **1:**91, 93, 1019, 1157; **2:**90; **6:**1564; **8:**702; **9:**419, 528, 542, 719; **10:**778, 848, 851; RABBI **8:**431–32; **9:**399; THE RIGHTEOUS ONE **10:**129; **11:**259; SAVIOR (*see* SAVIOR *in SUBJECTS AND THEMES*); SECOND ADAM **1:**336; **5:**856; **8:**221; **9:**95; **11:**504; **12:**37; SERVANT **12:**333; SHEPHERD **2:**1235; **4:**770–71; **9:**602, 651, 668–73, 667, 727, 733, 742, 776, 783, 793, 802, 817–19, 827, 842, 851, 860, 862 (*see also* JESUS THE CHRIST, METAPHORS FOR); SON OF DAVID **8:**403, 427, 696; **9:**18–19, 124; SON OF GOD **1:**169, 289–91; **2:**55, 426, 1259; **3:**381, 409; **4:**673, 759, 863; **5:**256, 258, 463, 553; **6:**346, 440, 935, 1131; **7:**65, 383, 396; **8:**76, 115, 126, 133–34, 137–38, 149–50, 160–65, 177, 232, 281, 328, 344, 351, 354–68, 455, 459, 480, 491–93, 496, 504, 511–12, 520, 526–30, 534–36, 543, 561, 580–81, 621–24, 627; **9:**9, 14–15, 17–18, 30, 43, 51, 76–79, 91, 95–100, 106–7, 111–12, 114, 196, 203, 225, 243, 391, 411, 442–43, 448, 456, 461, 477, 529, 532–34, 555, 585, 603, 675, 678, 686, 689–90, 694, 743, 752, 775, 787, 798, 820, 837, 852; **10:**153, 342, 416–19, 422, 424, 478, 520, 549, 575, 580, 591, 594, 602, 629–30; **11:**215, 244–45, 247, 260, 275, 282, 284, 314, 318, 323, 339, 370, 375, 422, 502–8, 515, 696; **12:**7, 9, 22, 29–30, 57, 61, 75–76, 86, 123, 127, 138, 353, 372–73, 375, 384, 413–14, 424, 435, 437, 439–43, 446–47, 453, 581–82; SON OF MAN **1:**288–89, 787; **2:**91, 167, 804, 1141; **4:**713; **5:**345; **6:**381, 1122, 1217; **7:**8–10, 13–15, 103, 105, 107, 113, 317, 509–10, 840; **8:**30, 36, 40, 50–51, 58, 64, 77, 81, 102, 229, 234, 258–59, 276–82, 286–87, 290, 292–93, 296, 308, 314, 344, 348–52, 354–70, 375, 383–84, 391–92, 396–98, 440–47, 450–51, 455, 459, 470, 480, 503, 512, 519, 550–51, 556, 623–27, 630–31, 691–93, 695–96, 707–8, 713–14, 728–32; **9:**16–19, 72, 133–34, 144, 160, 166, 200–204, 206, 217, 252–54, 281–82, 329–39, 349–51, 359, 391, 398–401, 407–11, 423, 435–36, 442–43, 456–57, 460, 469, 477, 532–33, 544, 548, 551–52, 585, 599–600, 607–8, 610, 635, 660–61, 713, 732, 819–20, 843; **10:**131, 401, 723; **11:**383, 421, 696; **12:**37, 515–19, 524, 533, 561, 566–68, 571, 581, 587, 603–5, 611, 633, 650, 664, 668, 693–96, 699, 702, 704–7, 732–33. *See also* JESUS THE CHRIST, METAPHORS FOR

JETHRO
1:711, 717–18, 805, 824–29, 1005, 1023; **2:**22, 95–96, 106, 190, 195, 198, 738; **4:**64, 1220

JEUEL
3:825

JEWS (*OR* JEWESS, *ETC.*)
AND CHRISTIANS **1:**11–13, 45–46, 83–84, 127, 292, 300, 304, 685–86, 779, 977; **2:**521; **3:**873, 890, 949, 954, 1145; **4:**965, 1025; **6:**1409; **7:**732; **8:**15, 27, 42, 99, 391, 487, 515–16, 555, 560, 660, 675, 688; **9:**455, 505, 507, 579, 587, 637, 645–50, 679, 809; **10:**28, 86, 176, 406–7, 450–51, 484, 489, 623, 626, 671, 683–87, 698, 714, 756; **11:**219, 225, 232, 235, 245, 342, 404; AND GENTILES **1:**291; **2:**603–4; **3:**869, 899–900, 932, 935, 947, 954, 967, 969; **4:**11, 74, 77–80, 87, 182, 211, 222, 233, 276, 965; **8:**40–42, 46, 99, 102, 182, 226, 336, 339, 408, 493, 496, 516, 610; **9:**71, 229; **10:**32, 59, 146, 152–53, 168–71, 174–75, 213–14, 294–95, 305, 364–65, 400, 406–7, 437, 440, 457, 461, 484, 624, 626, 643, 653, 667, 680–81, 684–87, 697, 756, 907; **11:**113, 186, 195, 213, 224, 232–33, 235–37, 241–42, 245, 291, 342, 364, 396–99, 524, 682, 865; **12:**300, 405; AND JESUS (*see* JESUS THE CHRIST:

and the Jews); and Samaritans **1:**267, 299; **2:**487; **3:**533, 1112; **4:**10, 229, 232; **5:**612, 862; **6:**227; **8:**298; **9:**23, 229–30, 270, 326, 563, 565–74, 644–45; **10:**23, 25, 135, 137–38. *See also* hebrews; israel (people)
JEZEBEL
1:264, 1172; **2:**106, 547, 1294; **3:**124, 126, 128, 132, 138–40, 142–43, 156, 158, 169, 180, 214–15, 217, 219–21, 223, 226, 228, 551, 959, 1004; **4:**230, 555, 861; **5:**76, 80; **6:**1322, 1360; **7:**112; **8:**319, 598; **12:**543, 545, 567, 573, 581, 589, 650, 686–87, 722, 735
JEZRAHIAH
3:839
JEZREEL
7:218, 223, 226, 276
JOAB
2:264, 432, 547, 549, 949, 1174–75, 1215–18, 1221–22, 1224–27, 1229, 1237, 1268, 1278, 1280–81, 1283–87, 1293, 1300, 1309, 1313–16, 1326, 1332, 1335–36, 1339–40, 1346, 1350–52, 1355, 1361, 1376, 1380; **3:**18–19, 27–28, 32–34, 376–77, 415–16, 422, 456–57, 725; **4:**63, 193; **5:**143; **6:**858, 1347
JOACHIM
7:176
JOAH
3:265
JOAHAZ
3:236
JOAKIM
3:1112–13, 1173, 1180; **4:**940, 943; **7:**176–78, 180
JOANNA
9:175, 470
JOARIB
4:42–43
JOASH
1:25, 250, 265; **2:**796; **3:**5, 228, 230, 232–34, 236–37, 241, 250, 573–74, 580–82, 590, 649, 691, 819; **5:**853; **6:**183, 943; **7:**217
JOB
1:96, 934, 1028; **2:**671; **3:**571, 751, 1001; **4:**241, 314, 324, 328, 330–32, 334, 336–37, 343–45, 347–64, 366–72, 375–77, 379–84, 387–405, 409–24, 426–36, 440–46, 448–54, 457–62, 464–65, 467–68, 474–80, 482–86, 488, 491–97, 499–504, 507–14, 516–17, 519–20, 522–26, 534–35, 537–42, 544–48, 552–57, 559–60, 564, 567–69, 571–72, 575–83, 585–87, 589, 591–92, 594–98, 600–5, 608–17, 621, 623, 625–32, 634–36, 705, 708, 733, 819, 821, 838–39, 952–54, 1029; **5:**3, 9–12, 50, 93, 112, 125, 149, 155, 160, 173, 206, 238, 311, 320–22, 326, 335, 337, 382, 459, 476, 618, 631, 655, 678, 787, 823; **6:**336, 358, 367, 439, 585, 600, 676, 755, 813, 919, 962, 965, 982, 1057–58, 1139–40, 1210, 1214, 1252, 1257–58, 1336, 1346; **7:**40, 83, 262, 485, 509, 525, 633, 640; **9:**235, 323, 346, 389, 427, 458, 482; **10:**699; **11:**165, 490; **12:**187, 189, 631–32
JOB'S WIFE
1:869, 1164; **3:**1001, 1068
JOCHEBED
2:213–14
JOEL
2:1016, 1026; **3:**337, 825; **5:**647, 798, 800; **7:**302, 305–12, 314, 316–20, 324–29, 331, 334–36, 810; **8:**143; **10:**15–16, 59, 64–66, 68–69, 71, 81, 83, 89–90, 92, 107, 121, 152, 167, 169, 175, 192–93, 195, 197, 203, 206, 209–10, 213, 218, 368, 666–67, 690
JOEZER
3:379, 382
JOHANAN
3:330, 717, 741, 832–35; **6:**1080. *See also* jonathan (high priest)
JOHN (SON OF ZEBEDEE)
1:15; **3:**173, 364, 587; **8:**44, 58, 72, 362–63, 366, 368, 398, 493, 539, 567, 589, 621, 628, 630, 636, 653–54, 684, 705, 707, 709, 729, 732; **9:**111, 117, 139, 190, 205, 212, 215, 217, 353, 355, 415–16, 431–32, 465, 498–99, 857, 865; **10:**31, 304, 370; **11:**194, 225–28, 579, 704; **12:**342, 366, 396, 515
JOHN MARK
10:180, 190–91, 225; **11:**903
JOHN OF PATMOS
12:235, 366, 370, 552, 574, 736
JOHN THE BAPTIST
1:988, 1081; **2:**603, 718; **3:**442, 1043, 1158; **4:**42; **6:**338; **7:**15, 847, 869, 873, 876; **8:**38–39, 67, 81–82, 115–16, 154–56, 159, 166–67, 204, 220, 234–36, 258, 265, 268, 270–71, 275, 291, 348, 354, 365, 385–87, 410, 436–37, 494, 504–5, 512, 520, 525, 527, 530–34, 536–37, 539, 543, 548, 555–56, 559, 593, 597–600, 622, 625, 631, 643–45, 668–69, 671, 699–700, 707, 712, 720, 723, 725, 726; **9:**8, 11, 18, 20–21, 29, 47, 49, 52, 58, 60, 69, 71, 79, 83–84, 87–88, 90, 102, 116–17, 123, 128, 130, 157–58, 160, 165, 166, 184, 194–95, 199, 219, 248, 272, 281, 302, 313, 315, 319, 352, 358–59, 369, 378, 401, 434, 445, 456, 465, 478, 487, 508, 515–18, 520, 524–25, 528–29, 533, 549, 551, 557–61, 565, 570, 586–87, 589, 591, 640, 661, 675–76, 678, 752, 764–65, 826; **10:**41, 53, 67–68, 192, 261–62, 451; **11:**55; **12:**39, 71, 438, 562, 571, 638;

JOHN THE BAPTIST *(continued)*
"THE BAPTIST" FOR JOHN THE BAPTIST **8:**156, 531–32, 534–36, 539, 669, 726; **9:**84, 88, 166, 520; BIRTH OF **3:**442; **9:**11, 29, 33, 43, 46, 48, 50, 55, 57–58, 69, 71, 85, 478, 487; IMPRISONMENT OF **8:**266, 270–71, 319, 531; **9:**11, 87, 102, 160; AND JESUS (*see under* JESUS THE CHRIST)

JOHN THE EVANGELIST
1:13, 1166; **3:**380, 506; **6:**1131; **7:**808; **8:**74, 81, 85, 615; **9:**97, 137, 478, 497, 500–503, 505, 507, 515–19, 521–25, 528–29, 531–32, 534, 536–38, 541, 543–44, 546, 548, 550, 552–53, 555, 557–58, 560, 566, 571, 574–77, 579, 581, 583, 535, 585–86, 590, 596, 602–3, 605–6, 608, 611–14, 617–20, 623, 625–26, 632–33, 636–37, 642–43, 645, 647–52, 654, 657–58, 661–64, 667–68, 675, 679, 684–86, 689, 691–93, 696–98, 701–3, 709, 711–13, 716–22, 724, 729, 736–38, 742–45, 747, 750–51, 757, 762, 765, 772, 774, 777–78, 782, 785, 787, 789–90, 792, 797, 799–804, 806, 808–9, 811, 813–15, 818–19, 823–25, 829, 831–32, 834, 836, 838, 840–46, 849, 851, 853–54, 858, 860; **11:**515, 780; **12:**367, 374, 385, 395–96, 416, 443, 515, 561, 724

JOIADA
3:717, 768, 832–34

JOIAKIM
3:441, 717, 830–36, 850

JOIARIB
3:726, 815, 831

JOKSHAN
6:1379

JOKTAN
1:409

JONADAB
2:1303, 1309; **5:**105, 108, 737; **6:**769, 828, 834–35

JONAH
2:106, 860, 1050; **3:**1004, 1069; **4:**63, 1118; **5:**322, 341, 394, 725; **6:**57, 204, 257, 300, 355, 587, 717, 1126; **7:**145, 192, 470–71, 473–88, 493–515, 517–29; **8:**129, 273, 296–97, 444, 580; **9:**72, 243–45, 319, 399, 469, 624; **10:**160–62, 167, 169–70, 349; **12:**245, 646

JONATHAN (HIGH PRIEST)
3:717, 725, 741, 743, 832–34, 836. *See also* JOHANAN

JONATHAN (SON OF ABIATHAR)
3:21–22

JONATHAN (SON OF SAUL)
1:260–61; **2:**220, 230, 547, 550, 630, 949, 961–62, 981, 1038, 1047, 1066, 1068–71, 1078–82, 1103, 1115, 1118, 1120, 1123–24, 1126–29, 1132–37, 1143, 1147, 1153, 1156–57, 1159, 1183–84, 1197–99, 1202–3, 1205–8, 1212–13, 1217, 1224–25, 1230, 1232, 1273–74, 1276–77, 1279, 1289, 1292, 1314, 1325–26, 1332, 1340, 1347, 1357–59; **3:**736; **4:**57, 69, 78, 228; **5:**127–28, 160, 168, 322; **6:**202, 1245, 1268, 1349; **7:**547

JONATHAN THE MACCABEE
1:270; **2:**1005; **3:**830, 1113; **4:**3, 17–21, 36, 51–52, 78, 93, 97, 102, 104, 109, 111–19, 121–25, 127, 129–32, 134–36, 138, 140–52, 154, 156, 159–61, 163–65, 168–69, 171–72, 174–75, 178, 189, 197, 249, 265, 269, 275–76, 297, 309; **5:**867

JORAM
2:1266; **3:**123, 180, 214, 216–17, 219–21, 233–34, 241; **7:**436, 804

JOSEPH (BARNABAS)
10:97

JOSEPH (HUSBAND OF MARY)
5:793; **7:**873; **8:**65, 130–31, 134–36, 138, 143, 146–48, 150, 179, 196, 317–18, 358, 592–93; **9:**8, 23–24, 42, 51, 63, 65–66, 68–69, 71, 73–77, 94, 106–7, 111, 174, 339, 354, 391, 401, 464, 531–33; **12:**97

JOSEPH (SON OF JACOB AND RACHEL)
1:93, 241, 248, 259, 329–30, 364, 377, 417, 422, 503, 509, 516, 518, 536, 539, 541, 554–55, 560, 571–72, 577, 580–81, 583, 591–95, 598–601, 604–5, 609–12, 614–16, 620–24, 627–30, 633–36, 638–41, 643–46, 651–56, 658–60, 664–74, 694, 700, 712, 789–90, 1017; **2:**34, 124, 200, 211–12, 543, 547, 549–50, 552, 635, 667, 680, 683, 718, 752, 760, 845, 941, 950, 1037, 1044, 1050, 1099; **3:**44, 319, 337, 733, 745, 835, 870, 894, 897, 901, 927–28, 941, 946, 948–49, 981–82, 996, 1016, 1050, 1062, 1081, 1138, 1143, 1150; **4:**43, 50–51, 343, 563, 842, 1000, 1105; **5:**1, 5–6, 50, 75, 111, 120, 122, 159, 170, 179, 182, 231, 253, 271, 276, 316, 322, 334, 445, 511, 522, 524–25, 527, 596–97, 622, 631, 633, 654, 705, 715, 740, 753, 792, 801, 836, 842, 856; **6:**335, 752, 809–10, 926, 1336, 1379, 1401–2, 1508, 1600, 1606; **7:**5, 21, 50, 56–57, 82, 89–90, 125, 144, 156, 169, 178, 292, 516, 569, 810; **8:**41, 66, 666, 710; **9:**255, 300, 310, 458, 537; **10:**124, 126; **11:**372, 696; **12:**139, 521, 620

JOSEPH (SON OF MARY)
8:493

JOSEPH/JOSEPHITES (TRIBES)
1:22, 79, 166, 206, 656, 665; **2:**263, 535–36, 660–61, 681, 685, 689, 711, 715, 718, 732–33, 743–48, 1232, 1346; **3:**351, 479; **6:**1466, 1505–8, 1606; **7:**347, 400, 455, 810, 814–16; **8:**354

JOSEPH OF ARIMATHEA
8:105, 494, 538, 725–26, 730; **9:**29, 45, 341, 443, 450, 464–65, 468, 799, 808, 835–36; **10:**132

JOSEPH THE PRIEST
4:81, 89, 248–49, 261, 276; **7:**170
JOSEPH THE TOBIAD
4:7; **7:**142
JOSES
8:493, 724, 726
JOSHEB-BASSHEBETH
2:1375
JOSHUA (HIGH PRIEST)
1:1017, 1060; **3:**690; **7:**113, 715–16, 719–20, 723, 727, 737–38, 740, 763–67, 771, 786–88, 861; **10:**829. *See also* JESHUA
JOSHUA (SON OF NUN)
1:248, 253, 306–8, 436, 584, 820, 881–82, 905, 908, 932–33, 938, 1011, 1060, 1160, 1179; **2:**19, 21, 107–8, 110, 112–13, 122–24, 126, 140, 202, 214, 217, 219–20, 245, 248–50, 254, 263, 272, 294, 310, 389, 504, 511, 514, 519, 538, 541, 543–44, 559–65, 569–71, 573, 578, 580, 584–89, 593–95, 599–607, 609, 612–15, 617–20, 625–28, 630–39, 641–42, 646–49, 651–52, 655, 657–62, 666–69, 673–74, 680, 684–85, 689, 694–95, 701, 707, 709–11, 714–15, 718–19, 736–37, 739, 747, 752–53, 816, 1012, 1216, 1358; **3:**35, 144, 177, 286, 353, 432, 464, 469, 669, 675, 686, 730, 740–41, 802, 804, 811, 830, 835, 938; **4:**36, 49–52, 55, 77–78, 84, 136, 157, 275, 295; **5:**620, 846; **6:**174, 253, 371, 430, 442, 456–57, 460, 467–68, 1491, 1496, 1574; **7:**550, 752, 814, 877; **8:**129, 134–35, 178, 246, 252; **11:**159, 211, 728; **12:**47, 50, 52–53, 60, 64
JOSIAH
1:9, 37, 39, 226, 253, 266, 285, 309, 996, 1012, 1127, 1138; **2:**5, 87, 265, 278–83, 366, 381, 383–84, 387, 412, 417, 426, 441, 460, 556, 559–60, 565–80, 585–86, 588–90, 592–94, 599–600, 603, 605–6, 609, 612–15, 619–20, 625–31, 634–35, 637, 639, 641, 648–49, 654–55, 657–62, 665–72, 674, 677, 681–82, 684, 687–89, 694–97, 711, 714, 717–19, 725, 865; **3:**4, 6, 40, 106, 118, 277–80, 282, 284–88, 292–93, 329–30, 536, 602, 607, 610, 616, 622, 632, 636, 643–47, 649–51, 654, 656, 686, 713–14, 801–2, 824; **4:**40, 50, 52, 82, 121, 156, 751; **5:**620, 631, 655, 836, 853, 855–56, 858; **6:**28, 32, 37, 137, 140, 201, 264, 266, 284, 555–56, 559, 561–63, 566, 575–77, 598, 604–5, 634, 640, 669–70, 707, 739, 741–42, 746, 762, 772, 774, 839, 857, 859, 873, 943, 1077, 1083, 1110, 1159–60, 1175, 1177, 1199, 1286, 1326, 1380, 1403, 1575, 1592; **7:**199, 205–6, 272, 659–62, 670–71, 674–75, 678–79, 690, 703, 764, 779, 787, 828–29; **8:**130; **9:**45; **12:**677, 725–26
JOTHAM
1:265; **2:**543, 726, 815–17; **3:**245, 248, 250–51, 594, 769; **5:**255; **6:**107, 1076, 1378; **7:**468, 533
JOZABAD
3:730, 824, 826
JOZADAK
3:686; **6:**943; **7:**715
JUDAH (SON OF JACOB AND LEAH)
1:476, 536, 539, 577, 580, 590, 592–93, 595, 598–600, 604–7, 624, 627, 629, 633–34, 638–41, 643, 652, 656, 664–65, 667–68; **2:**211, 214, 333, 535, 549, 660, 673, 680, 904, 932–33, 939, 941–43, 1159; **3:**327–29, 332–33, 356, 745, 825, 832, 838, 864–65, 981; **4:**461, 556; **5:**122, 386, 430; **6:**1605; **8:**129; **10:**449; **12:**620, 624
JUDAH/JUDAHITES (PEOPLE/TRIBE)
1:262, 267, 656, 665, 1138, 1164; **2:**34, 37, 77, 95, 208, 211, 213, 263, 352, 388, 501, 536, 561–63, 569–70, 577, 602, 634, 646–47, 660, 671, 673–74, 678, 681, 732–33, 735–40, 743–45, 750, 765–66, 776, 826, 841, 843, 853, 861, 865, 873, 885, 887, 1166, 1169–70, 1179, 1187–88, 1205–6, 1233, 1236, 1320, 1345, 1348, 1350–51; **3:**6, 18–19, 95, 97, 102, 304, 320, 328–29, 332–33, 336–37, 343–44, 351, 363, 379–80, 422, 424, 457, 461, 478, 486, 501, 524, 556, 563, 565, 575, 594, 602, 608, 678, 712–13, 742, 768, 824–25, 827, 847, 886, 959, 1167; **6:**6, 8, 15, 17, 68, 72, 78, 87–88, 112, 182, 221, 295, 559, 627–28, 634–35, 637–38, 661, 679, 684–85, 716, 721, 777, 859, 874, 1082, 1157, 1170, 1280, 1313, 1574, 1578, 1605; **7:**326, 376, 436–37, 441–42, 445, 449, 451, 454–55, 457, 547, 595–96, 670, 683, 708–10, 715–16, 727, 739, 780, 789, 805, 807, 810, 813–14, 826–27; **8:**131, 147, 354, 406; **9:**94, 367, 420, 757; **12:**89, 318, 601–2, 606, 609, 620. *See also* JUDAH (KINGDOM/TERRITORY) *in* PLACES IN THE BIBLE
JUDAH THE MACCABEE
3:840, 1078, 1131. *See also* JUDAS THE MACCABEE
JUDAS ISCARIOT
2:753; **4:**848–49, 1128; **7:**824; **8:**66, 147, 166, 254, 262, 361, 370, 432, 464, 467–70, 477, 481, 483–85, 487, 500, 562, 695, 697, 699–700, 703, 707, 709; **9:**18, 137–38, 179, 210, 225, 351, 401, 414–16, 422–23, 426–28, 432, 435–37, 439, 449, 469, 611, 619, 701–3, 722, 724, 727, 730, 733, 748–49, 753, 757, 793, 799, 801–4, 809–10, 821, 833; **10:**44, 48–51, 67, 107, 178, 282; **11:**56; **12:**81, 351, 516, 649
JUDAS THE MACCABEE
1:10, 18, 270; **3:**859, 936, 1118, 1131, 1167, 1170; **4:**3–4, 19–22, 31, 40, 45, 47, 57–59, 62, 66–69, 74, 77–78, 81–82, 84–85, 87, 92–95, 98,

JUDAS THE MACCABEE *(continued)*
100, 102, 104–5, 110–13, 116, 119, 122, 129, 142–43, 149, 156, 163, 165, 169, 174–75, 178, 182–84, 187, 191, 193, 196, 198, 217–18, 230, 247–50, 257, 261–66, 268–69, 275–77, 281–83, 285–90, 295–99; **7:**122, 823; **8:**33, 403; **9:**675; **10:**50. *See also* JUDAH THE MACCABEE

JUDE
1:14–15, 17; **8:**593; **10:**44; **12:**473–76, 478–79, 481–83, 485–95, 497–98, 500

JUDEANS
1:213–15, 221, 223, 245, 250, 252–53, 256–57, 262, 265–67, 278, 282–83; **2:**413, 504, 547, 712, 942, 1346; **3:**18–20, 32, 52, 58, 94, 100, 108, 117, 119, 160, 167–68, 181, 209, 226, 241, 245, 248, 251, 255, 265, 269, 272, 287, 292, 294, 305, 317, 332, 357, 380, 402, 510, 514, 523, 526, 530, 532, 538, 553, 597–98, 601, 607, 610, 617, 629, 644, 656–57, 680, 698, 714, 747, 773, 776, 837, 1107, 1112, 1120; **4:**40, 47, 95, 138, 233, 254, 328, 649, 661, 690–91, 747, 860, 862, 1034, 1129, 1228; **5:**670, 730, 798; **6:**36, 73, 121, 163, 175, 185, 188, 191, 202, 227, 236, 276, 280, 284, 291–94, 560, 563, 581, 584, 596, 635, 642, 654, 657, 660, 703, 733–34, 743, 751, 757, 759, 774–76, 778, 783–84, 791–93, 795, 809–11, 813, 815, 819, 831, 835, 839, 851, 857–58, 860–61, 866, 868, 872–74, 878, 883, 885, 912, 925–26, 934, 945–46, 949, 952, 957, 982, 985, 989, 993, 1009–10, 1045, 1075, 1077–80, 1082–85, 1098, 1141, 1150, 1155, 1161, 1164, 1167–68, 1177–78, 1180, 1185, 1191, 1196, 1217–18, 1241, 1285, 1293, 1302, 1313, 1336, 1348–49, 1356, 1378, 1403, 1412, 1415, 1418, 1421, 1430, 1445, 1455–58, 1460, 1464, 1466, 1474, 1489, 1492, 1513, 1526, 1531, 1536; **7:**141, 199, 205–6, 217, 248, 253, 307, 312, 316, 318–19, 321, 326–27, 340, 352, 361–62, 396, 426, 428, 533, 593–94, 624, 626–27, 630–32, 634–36, 638, 775, 787, 789, 805, 810; **8:**130, 167; **9:**278, 404, 574; **10:**63, 65, 84, 137, 206; **11:**205, 232, 342

JUDITH
1:186; **3:**920, 960, 1075–76, 1079–81, 1083, 1085–87, 1089–90, 1095, 1098–99, 1101–4, 1106, 1108–14, 1119–20, 1123–25, 1127, 1129–30, 1132–33, 1137–40, 1142–44, 1147–49, 1151, 1154–63, 1165, 1167–68, 1170–71, 1173, 1177–80, 1182–83; **4:**52, 57, 177, 297; **5:**119, 335; **7:**53, 181; **8:**598; **9:**55, 72

JULIA
10:763

JULIUS (CENTURION)
10:345–46, 353–54, 357

JUNIA
9:137; **10:**762

JUSTUS
10:51, 252, 254, 256; **11:**665, 667

K

KADMIEL
3:817, 832

KAIWAN
7:394

KAREAH
6:842

KARTAH
3:347

KELITA
3:801

KENAN
1:380

KENAZ
2:737, 768

KENITES
2:178, 191–92, 735–36, 738, 740, 780–81, 1088, 1179; **3:**224, 330

KENIZZITE
2:735, 737, 739–40; **3:**332

KEREN-HAPPUCH
4:635

KETURAH
1:419, 434, 515, 601; **3:**317; **4:**228; **6:**1379

KEZIAH
4:635

KISH
2:915, 1037, 1043, 1047, 1081, 1099, 1359; **3:**358, 436, 886; **6:**1463

KOA
6:1326

KOHATH
1:736; **2:**47, 51, 134–35, 213–14; **3:**344–45, 363, 394, 436, 442, 450, 645; **9:**93

KOHELETH
5:278, 300, 316, 321, 335, 341, 353, 355; **6:**198. *See also* QOHELET/QOHELETH

KORAH
1:1070; **2:**10, 94, 99–100, 134–42, 146, 160–61, 211, 217, 219, 370; **3:**345, 450; **4:**81, 656, 852, 881, 898, 1013, 1019, 1111; **5:**525, 592, 631, 725, 843; **6:**1258, 1533–34, 1573, 1576; **11:**845; **12:**60, 491–92, 497, 700

KOZ
3:331

L

LABAN
1:511–13, 516–17, 519, 537, 552–60, 577, 1023;

2:941; **3:**1038, 1138; **4:**354, 439; **5:**522, 524; **6:**654, 1138; **7:**286
LACEDAEMONIANS
4:228
LADAN
4:436, 452
LAHMI
2:1108, 1361
LAMECH
1:372, 375, 377, 380, 403; **2:**192, 543, 808, 853; **8:**380
LAPPIDOTH
2:779
LASTHENES
4:135–36
LAZARUS (DIVES)
9:316, 320; **12:**194
LAZARUS (POOR MAN)
5:118, 142; **7:**118; **9:**25–26, 56, 143, 306, 309, 312–21, 326, 337, 357, 389, 458, 482; **12:**194
LAZARUS OF BETHANY
6:432; **8:**74, 407; **9:**169, 319, 366, 459, 503, 575, 585, 681, 684–94, 696, 698–99, 701–3, 708, 710, 712, 727, 730, 741, 743, 758, 841; **10:**42, 540
LEAH
1:186, 372, 452–53, 503, 517–19, 552–57, 559–60, 572, 577, 664, 667; **2:**47, 491, 939–43, 975; **3:**328, 457, 1038; **5:**383, 428, 764; **6:**1531, 1605–6; **10:**505, 693
LEGION
8:584–85; **9:**186–87; **12:**528
LEMUEL
4:177; **5:**21, 185, 251, 258, 262, 664, 700
LEVI (DISCIPLE)
8:107, 235, 253, 552–53, 556, 562, 593, 699, 726; **9:**26, 114, 126–28, 133, 136, 247
LEVI (SON OF JACOB AND LEAH)
1:555, 576–77, 579, 581, 584, 604, 660, 664–65, 667–68, 736, 905–6, 933; **2:**47, 49, 135, 213–14, 535–36; **3:**135, 328, 436, 441, 450–51, 731, 747, 834, 1119, 1143–44; **4:**1063; **6:**1574, 1578; **7:**829, 846, 860–64, 868, 873; **8:**354, 532; **12:**88–90, 94–95, 620
LEVI/LEVITES (TRIBE)
1:281, 682, 878, 933–35, 973, 985–87, 1011–12, 1017, 1060, 1062, 1066, 1173, 1187, 1190; **2:**4, 12, 15, 21, 25–26, 31, 36–40, 47–54, 59, 63, 69, 77, 79–84, 89, 92, 135, 137–38, 140, 142, 147–49, 151, 153, 197, 202–3, 207, 211, 213–14, 220, 245, 247, 254, 262–64, 268, 363–67, 387, 395, 403–4, 420, 427–28, 481–82, 520, 561, 563, 570, 589, 599, 634, 661, 665–67, 687, 689, 696, 701–2, 834, 870, 876, 887, 988, 1012, 1252; **3:**33, 300, 302, 304–6, 320, 343–48, 351, 356, 362–64, 379–80, 386, 393–96, 399, 422, 433, 436–38, 441–43, 445–46, 450, 452, 456–57, 485, 494, 498–99, 522, 547, 556, 574, 576, 607–10, 617–18, 624–25, 644–49, 651, 671, 678, 686–88, 692, 712–13, 718, 721, 726–28, 730–33, 736, 741, 743, 745, 769–70, 793, 797, 800–801, 804, 806, 811, 816–17, 820, 824–26, 828, 830, 832, 834–35, 837–39, 842, 844, 846–47, 849–51, 993–94; **4:**46, 64, 281, 737, 1170, 1172; **5:**633, 696, 843; **6:**338, 546, 549, 826, 1167, 1284, 1491, 1573–78, 1581–82, 1591–92, 1600, 1604–6; **7:**829, 850, 853, 859–60, 870, 873; **8:**435; **9:**69; **12:**87, 89–90, 92, 114, 123
LIBNI
3:345, 436
LILITH
3:967; **4:**611; **6:**277
LO-AMMI
7:218–19, 223–24, 290
LOIS
10:226
LORD OF HOSTS
See under GOD, NAMES FOR/TITLES OF
LO-RUHAMAH
7:218, 223, 295
LOT
1:419, 422–24, 430, 432–35, 438–42, 462, 467, 469, 473–76, 479, 491, 515, 522, 584, 590, 601; **2:**542, 549, 877, 896, 927, 933; **3:**1171; **5:**172, 445, 522, 524, 596, 621–23, 1214, 1347–48, 1352, 1380; **7:**774; **9:**331–33, 335, 408; **10:**643; **12:**86, 348, 489, 633
LOTAN
4:368, 621; **7:**101
LUCIFER
6:159; **11:**507–8; **12:**669. *See also* BAAL-ZEBUB/BAAL-ZEBUL/BEELZEBUL; SATAN
LUCIUS
4:105, 169; **10:**766
LUKE THE EVANGELIST
1:13; **3:**332; **6:**432, 1131, 1497; **8:**23, 75, 83–85, 150–51, 203, 207, 509–10; **9:**5–10, 78, 83, 94, 97, 136–37, 176, 369, 456, 460, 463, 478, 484, 487, 518, 835, 838; **10:**5–6, 8, 68, 70, 82, 113, 145, 198, 289; **11:**515
LYDIA
4:188; **10:**230–35, 254; **12:**571
LYSANIAS
9:80
LYSIAS
4:18, 38, 59–60, 62, 68–69, 85, 88–89, 91–93, 95, 98, 110, 121, 141, 150, 152, 247, 253, 255, 260, 265–66, 268–70, 276–77, 280–83, 286

LYSIAS, CLAUDIUS
See CLAUDIUS LYSIAS
LYSIMACHUS
1:269; **3:**971; **4:**7, 206, 223, 228; **7:**111

M

MAACAH
3:34, 117, 352–53, 522, 530
MAADIAH
3:816
MAASEIAH
3:800, 825, 839
MAAZIAH
3:816
MACCABEUS
See JUDAS THE MACCABEE; SIMON THE MACCABEE
MACHIR
2:212, 250, 309, 683, 788, 1273; **3:**352–53
MACRON
See PTOLEMY MACRON
MADAI
6:1516
MAGBISH
3:686, 817
MAGDALENE
See MARY MAGDALENE
MAGPIASH
3:817
MAHALALEL
1:380
MAHER-SHALAL-HASH-BAZ
6:116
MAHLI
3:345, 727
MAHLON
2:901, 930, 937, 940, 943; **3:**733
MAHSEIAH
6:941
MALACHI
1:1009, 1014, 1042, 1151; **3:**427, 746, 847; **4:**64, 113; **6:**826, 1481, 1593; **7:**312, 740, 803, 847, 852–53, 856, 858, 860–68, 870, 873; **8:**597; **9:**46, 85, 160, 300
MALCHIJAH
3:768, 770, 816
MALCHISHUA
2:1081, 1197
MALCHUS
9:803
MALLUCH
3:816–17
MANAHATHITES
3:330
MANASSEH (HUSBAND OF JUDITH)
3:1132–33, 1181–82
MANASSEH (IN JERUSALEM)
3:825, 833
MANASSEH (KING)
1:266, 1126–27, 1138; **2:**391, 570, 575, 612, 660, 688, 1294; **3:**6, 250, 274, 276–78, 280, 285–86, 289, 294, 301, 600, 602, 616, 632, 634–37, 643–46, 649–50, 654–56, 737, 766; **4:**503, 568; **6:**2, 640, 693, 1077, 1175, 1177, 1257, 1286, 1526, 1561; **7:**594, 662, 674–75, 679; **9:**281
MANASSEH (SON OF JOSEPH)
1:259, 622, 656, 659–61; **2:**34, 212, 214, 309, 683; **3:**337, 353, 358, 745; **5:**668; **6:**1508, 1600, 1605; **12:**139, 620
MANASSEH/MANASSITES (TRIBE)
1:259, 660; **2:**37, 208, 212–14, 217, 244, 248, 250, 263, 266, 308–9, 512, 535–36, 563, 586, 647, 661, 665, 680–81, 683–84, 696, 715, 718, 743–45, 788, 796, 802–3, 941, 1054; **3:**329, 337–38, 351–52, 358, 363, 379, 457; **4:**998; **5:**663; **6:**127, 1508, 1601, 1605–6; **7:**360
MANOAH
2:845–47; **5:**629; **9:**45, 476
MARA
2:909
MARESHAH
3:329
MARK THE EVANGELIST
1:13; **6:**365, 1131; **8:**75, 84–85, 93, 95, 490–91, 509–14, 518–20, 525, 534, 541, 548, 550, 559, 565, 603, 607–9, 614–16, 619, 640, 644, 683, 724, 731–32; **9:**5, 137, 176, 460, 579, 675, 701–2, 729, 799, 803, 808, 819, 838
MARTHA OF BETHANY
1:186; **8:**58, 407; **9:**12, 24, 169, 175, 179, 226, 231–32, 319, 345, 568, 676, 684–85, 687–89, 691, 694–95, 701, 718; **10:**598
MARY (MOTHER OF JAMES AND JOSEPH/JOSES)
8:493, 724, 726
MARY (MOTHER OF JESUS)
1:184, 186, 205, 464–65, 1013, 1085; **2:**846, 983, 987, 1043–44, 1259, 1369; **3:**909, 1145, 1162, 1165, 1173; **4:**672, 1073, 1139, 1233; **5:**48, 128; **6:**113, 822; **7:**52, 169, 571, 830, 873; **8:**65, 67, 130–32, 134, 136–38, 143, 147–48, 150, 297, 318, 493, 566, 592–93; **9:**8, 11, 19–20, 23, 25, 42, 47–48, 50–56, 58–59, 62–63, 65–66, 68, 70–72, 73–78, 81, 94, 174, 182, 224, 242, 281, 315, 413, 464, 536–37, 831; **10:**44; **12:**4, 43, 62, 155, 652, 687
MARY (MOTHER OF JOHN MARK)
10:180, 762

MARY (WIFE OF CLOPAS)
9:831
MARY MAGDALENE
1:186; **8:**493, 724, 726, 728; **9:**175, 467, 470, 485, 487–88, 780, 831, 838, 840–46, 849, 852, 859; **10:**762
MARY OF BETHANY
1:186; **8:**58, 407; **9:**12, 24, 169, 175, 179, 187, 231–32, 319, 345, 684–90, 701–3, 710, 836; **10:**598; **11:**617
MATTAN
3:230; **6:**1361
MATTANIAH
3:290, 826, 832, 835, 839, 847; **4:**197; **6:**1078, 1248
MATTATHIAS
3:1143; **4:**3, 19, 21, 40, 42–55, 57, 85, 87, 93, 97, 111–13, 122, 141, 147–50, 163, 165, 174, 177–78, 230, 242, 269, 295, 369; **5:**527; **11:**214
MATTHAN
8:131; **9:**94
MATTHAT
9:94
MATTHEW THE DISCIPLE
1:15; **8:**106–7, 235, 253, 391; **9:**127
MATTHEW THE EVANGELIST
1:13; **2:**325; **3:**332; **6:**432, 1131; **7:**808, 824; **8:**75, 83–84, 93–95, 100, 107, 150, 172, 203, 207, 258, 264, 308, 314, 490–91, 509–10, 732; **9:**94, 97, 118, 137, 518, 531, 702, 729, 803, 808, 819, 831, 838; **11:**515; **12:**416
MATTHIAS
3:831; **7:**503, 526–28; **9:**137, 426; **10:**48–49, 51–52
MEDAD
2:105, 107, 110, 113
MEDES
1:266–67; **3:**253, 904, 921–22, 925, 966, 994–95, 1075–76, 1095, 1098, 1177–78; **6:**156–57, 353, 356, 399, 407, 413, 556, 911, 913, 1077, 1305, 1443; **7:**73, 84, 94, 112, 116, 595, 597, 735
MEHUJAEL
1:380
MELATIAH
3:768
MELCHIZEDEK/MELCHIZEDECH
1:439–42, 444, 1152, 1190; **2:**148, 191, 1236; **3:**486, 1165; **4:**1130; **6:**354; **9:**391; **12:**5, 30–31, 41, 57, 61, 64, 66–67, 71, 79–80, 82, 84–91, 93–94, 159
MEMUCAN
3:882–83, 897
MENAHEM
1:250, 265; **3:**248; **6:**1232; **7:**217, 248
MENELAUS
2:1109; **4:**7, 10, 12, 68, 93, 116, 182, 189, 205–6, 213–14, 222–23, 228–30, 232, 248, 258, 261–62, 266, 268–71, 280–81, 285, 287; **5:**611–12; **7:**24–25, 143
MENESTHEUS
4:55, 218, 260
MENUHOTH
3:330
MEPHIBOSHETH
2:547, 949, 1132, 1135, 1212, 1230, 1273–74, 1276, 1279, 1325, 1345–47, 1353, 1357–59; **5:**174, 186, 673; **7:**827
MERAB
2:550, 1081, 1118–19, 1121–23, 1359
MERAIOTH
3:717, 816, 826
MERARI
1:736; **2:**47, 51, 213; **3:**344–45, 363, 394, 436, 442, 450, 645, 727, 826
MERARITES
2:38, 48, 52–53, 77, 213; **3:**345
MEREMOTH
3:730–31, 768, 816
MERIBBAAL
2:1230; **5:**673
MERODACH-BALADAN
6:37, 304, 1326
MEROZ
2:788
MESHA (KING OF MOAB)
1:249, 1040, 1126, 1189; **2:**182, 614; **3:**181, 329, 357; **4:**46; **6:**1348, 1353; **7:**351, 362, 828
MESHACH
4:51, 363; **6:**164
MESHELEMIAH
3:450–51
MESHEZABEL
3:817
MESHULLAM
3:330, 743, 766, 768, 770, 788, 800, 816–17, 825, 835, 838, 846
METHUSELAH
1:380
METHUSHAEL
1:380
MEUNIM
3:336
MICA
2:1273; **3:**817

MICAH THE EPHRAIMITE
1:259; **2:**792, 869–71
MICAH THE PROPHET
1:266, 1028; **2:**601; **4:**71, 159, 981, 1203; **5:**586; **6:**2, 7, 9, 11, 656, 774–75, 807, 1154, 1186, 1295, 1336; **7:**431, 493, 533–34, 536–38, 541–48, 550–62, 565, 568–69, 571–73, 575–76, 580, 582, 584–86, 589, 660, 674–75, 693, 767; **11:**75
MICAIAH
1:240, 242; **3:**162–64, 167, 530, 552, 839; **5:**122; **6:**101, 752, 1198, 1463; **7:**5, 542, 558, 677, 751
MICHAEL
1:287–89; **3:**1057; **7:**4, 9–10, 13, 15, 65, 105, 107, 113–14, 117, 127, 137–39, 148, 151; **8:**36; **11:**463; **12:**350, 488–90, 642, 646, 648–49, 651, 657
MICHAL
2:546–47, 550–51, 949, 962, 1081, 1115, 1118, 1120, 1122–24, 1126–27, 1129, 1143, 1170, 1208, 1222, 1224, 1233, 1246, 1248–52; **3:**368, 395–96, 399; **4:**613
MIJAMIN
3:816, 838–39
MILCAH
1:501
MILCOM
1:1126; **2:**830, 1300; **3:**96, 115, 416; **6:**894; **7:**675, 766
MINIAMIN
3:816, 832, 838–39
MIRIAM
1:186, 242, 315, 774, 798–99, 802–3, 932, 1095, 1100; **2:**4, 10, 47, 60, 99, 104, 108–13, 157–60, 162, 198, 214, 219, 222, 254, 469, 551, 599, 637, 833, 983; **3:**344, 714, 733, 931, 1173–74, 1176–77; **4:**264, 387, 1065, 1268; **5:**404, 525, 532, 593; **6:**5, 117; **7:**501, 579, 670; **9:**72
MISHAEL
1:1070; **2:**20, 39, 63, 67, 78, 170, 179, 183, 188–89
MITHREDATH
3:679, 698
MNASON
10:290
MOAB (SON OF LOT)
1:419, 479; **2:**901, 945
MOABITES
1:432, 476; **2:**166, 184, 195, 773, 901, 1265; **3:**184, 238, 733, 1117–18; **6:**167, 218, 892, 919–20, 1347
MOADIAH
3:816
MOLECH/MOLOCH
1:1126–27, 1137–39; **2:**127, 391, 830, 834; **3:**250; **5:**542; **6:**256, 345, 1526; **10:**128
MORDECAI/MORDECHAI
1:241, 284, 897; **3:**856–57, 859–65, 867–70, 872, 884, 886–90, 892, 894–97, 901–6, 908, 910–11, 913–16, 919–21, 923–29, 931–32, 934, 936–41, 945–46, 948–51, 953, 956–57, 959, 966, 969–70, 972, 1098, 1124, 1142, 1182; **4:**297; **5:**118, 334, 341, 740
MOSES
AND AARON **1:**75, 306, 682, 691–92, 716–18, 720, 725–30, 735–39, 742, 745, 813, 834, 882, 901, 930–35, 976, 987, 1056–57, 1060, 1062, 1065–67, 1072, 1110; **2:**4, 25, 48–50, 99–100, 104, 108–13, 125, 135–42, 146, 159–62, 218–19, 222, 596, 687; **3:**137, 344, 733; **4:**81, 198–99, 862, 1076; **5:**525, 529, 532, 592, 621, 842–43; **6:**582, 1147, 1167, 1533; **7:**366; **8:**537; **10:**127; **11:**64; **12:**46–47, 57, 61; AND JESUS **1:**686–87, 705, 737, 765, 799, 818, 855, 880, 955–56, 977, 980, 1072; **2:**83, 90, 130, 167, 222, 325, 521, 603, 718, 804, 855, 1013; **3:**575; **4:**188, 927, 1005, 1076, 1206; **6:**852; **8:**126, 134, 137–38, 147–50, 163–64, 174–75, 223, 249, 252, 274–75, 295, 356, 361–67, 403, 463, 519, 530, 601, 630–32, 643, 707, 724, 729–30; **9:**15, 97, 113, 118, 160, 184, 199, 204–7, 209, 242, 255, 295, 310, 313, 319, 359, 385, 389, 443, 477, 479, 486, 489, 551–52, 588, 594, 599–600, 619–21, 624, 636, 648, 659, 669, 809; **10:**43–44, 54, 82–83, 121–24, 126–27, 129, 191, 222–23, 340, 534, 587, 662; **11:**185, 267, 510; **12:**46, 57, 141, 163, 167, 172, 730; AND JETHRO **1:**711, 717–18, 805, 823–28, 1005, 1023; **2:**22, 95–96, 106, 190, 198, 738; **3:**64; AND JOSHUA **1:**306–7, 314–15, 820, 881–82, 1011; **2:**10, 107–8, 110, 112–13, 120, 126, 140, 202, 218–20, 248–49, 310, 511, 514, 518–21, 543–45, 560–69, 580, 584–90, 599, 602–4, 609, 612–13, 673, 710–13, 752–53; **3:**431; **4:**50–52; **6:**442, 457; **8:**252; **11:**211; AND MIRIAM **1:**242, 314–15, 691, 774, 797–99, 932, 1095; **2:**4, 10, 47, 60–61, 98–99, 104, 108–13, 157–59, 162, 213, 219, 222, 254, 469, 599; **3:**714, 733, 931, 1174, 1176–77; **4:**1065; **5:**404, 525, 532, 593; **6:**5; **7:**501, 579, 670; AND PHARAOH **1:**429, 560, 692, 701–4, 707, 713–14, 717–20, 724–30, 735, 737–39, 741–42, 744–54, 757–59, 762–74, 780, 782, 792–96, 825, 933, 973; **2:**99, 200, 538, 737, 752, 804, 855; **3:**93, 233, 1144; **4:**230, 295, 862; **5:**40, 522, 525, 534, 591; **6:**432, 527–28, 1278, 1402; **7:**50, 480; **8:**147, 150, 537; **9:**26, 638–39; **12:**140–41, 672; AND YAHWEH **1:**306, 309, 328, 376, 681, 684, 690, 692, 712–21, 725–30, 734–55, 757–59, 762–66, 766–74, 780, 792–96, 802, 806–7, 812–13, 817, 820, 824–25, 830–39, 854, 880–82, 884, 887, 917, 930–34, 937–40,

945–48, 976; **2:**14, 18–21, 25, 47, 61, 80, 89–91, 95, 99, 107, 110–11, 124–26, 129–30, 136–40, 160, 182, 197, 219, 562–68, 574, 580, 584–85, 588–89, 599, 609, 612, 627, 665, 706, 711, 1001; **3:**811; **4:**4; **5:**623, 647, 655; **6:**364, 468, 1118, 1120, 1141, 1167–68, 1201, 1208, 1279, 1288–89, 1490–91, 1533–34; **7:**480–81, 501, 662, 747, 798, 809; **11:**11; AND ZIPPORAH **1:**509, 718; **2:**96, 109, 181

MOST HIGH
See under GOD, NAMES FOR/TITLES OF

MUSHI
3:345

N

NAAMAH
1:375; **3:**115

NAAMAN
1:1095; **2:**549, 915; **3:**192–99, 201–2, 212, 214, 219, 502, 1119; **4:**254; **5:**792; **6:**585; **9:**108, 113, 119–20, 174, 320, 325–26

NAAMATHITE
4:328

NABAL
2:549, 673, 1138, 1157, 1164–71, 1174–75, 1211, 1229, 1304; **5:**102, 153, 159, 187, 255

NABATEANS
3:848; **4:**78, 115, 118, 275; **8:**321; **9:**88; **11:**160, 216

NABOTH
1:226, 1164, 1172; **2:**221, 334, 436; **3:**153, 155–58, 215, 217, 219–21, 223; **4:**555; **5:**76–77, 187, 205; **6:**742, 745, 1582, 1590; **9:**282

NADAB
1:264, 880–81, 905, 986, 987, 1057, 1060, 1069–73, 1110; **2:**25, 49, 54, 137–38, 214, 229; **3:**113–14, 118–21, 125, 358, 441, 725; **4:**281, 387; **6:**1397; **8:**366

NAHAMANI
3:685

NAHASH
2:1053–55, 1057, 1061–62, 1198, 1212, 1279

NAHOR
1:416, 501, 509, 511, 558; **6:**1278

NAHSHON
2:95

NAHUM
3:1069; **6:**313, 1307, 1320, 1336; **7:**482, 526, 593, 595–97, 599, 601–3, 605–7, 610–12, 615–16, 618, 620, 661, 691–92, 815; **12:**629

NANEA
4:193

NAOMI
1:241; **2:**477, 891–93, 896, 899, 901, 903–19, 921–22, 924–35, 940–42, 945–46, 1324; **3:**1155, 1168; **4:**423; **7:**501

NAPHTALI (SON OF JACOB AND BILHAH)
1:555, 585, 598, 664, 666; **3:**352, 457; **6:**1606; **12:**620

NAPHTALI (TRIBE)
2:34, 37, 213, 263, 536, 677, 694, 701, 744–45, 779, 788, 802–3; **3:**52, 67, 352, 478, 978, 992; **6:**1604–6

NARCISSUS
10:763

NATHAN
1:311; **2:**811, 891–92, 949, 953, 962–63, 1027, 1071, 1097, 1165, 1168, 1234, 1236, 1240, 1251, 1254–56, 1258, 1261–62, 1269, 1283–84, 1288, 1290–95, 1297–98, 1300, 1303, 1313–14, 1317, 1319, 1331, 1340, 1355, 1381; **3:**18–20, 23, 31–32, 50, 52, 152, 408, 461, 469, 512, 609–10, 726, 785; **4:**116, 343, 689, 885, 1035, 1211; **5:**180, 631, 836, 849; **6:**2, 6, 8, 38, 88–89, 258, 300, 1082, 1274; **7:**82–83, 468–69, 558, 829; **8:**131; **9:**51, 85, 94

NATHANAEL
4:866; **8:**253; **9:**531–32, 534, 546, 567, 578, 707, 710, 850, 857, 865

NAZAREAN
2:861; **8:**147; **9:**354; **10:**306

NAZAREES
8:147

NAZARENE
8:147; **9:**354, 477; **10:**66

NAZIRITES
1:281, 1033, 1106, 1149, 1171; **2:**9, 21, 26, 60, 64–66, 68, 81, 223, 234, 762, 767, 842–43, 845–46, 849–50, 853, 858–59, 861, 975–76; **4:**64; **5:**67; **7:**365; **8:**147; **9:**46, 354; **10:**258, 293–95, 306, 312, 631

NEBAI
3:817

NEBAT
3:90, 94, 98, 100, 102, 181, 236, 243, 247, 253, 255, 257–58, 277–78, 285; **6:**1143; **7:**272; **10:**660

NEBO
3:710; **6:**345, 405–6, 413; **7:**606

NEBUCHADNEZZAR/NEBUCHADREZZAR
1:250, 263–64, 266–67; **2:**441, 688; **3:**289–90, 293–94, 657, 668, 679, 705–6, 708, 717, 720–21, 871, 886, 1075–78, 1081–82, 1084, 1089, 1091, 1095, 1097–102, 1104, 1106, 1108–10, 1117, 1120, 1123, 1125, 1131, 1139, 1147, 1153–55, 1159–60, 1168, 1170, 1177, 1179; **4:**38, 40, 51, 193, 254, 256, 281, 363, 503, 568–69, 608; **6:**37, 164, 406, 444, 455, 550, 559, 761–63, 768, 782–83, 788, 794, 806, 866–67, 874, 879,

NEBUCHADNEZZAR *(continued)*
882–83, 885, 892, 899, 912, 939, 942, 944–45, 980, 994, 1075–79, 1081, 1088, 1161, 1186, 1190, 1246, 1248–50, 1253, 1270–71, 1275–76, 1293, 1296, 1301–2, 1304–5, 1312, 1325–26, 1334–35, 1338–39, 1347–49, 1353, 1355–56, 1358–59, 1361–62, 1365–67, 1369, 1379–80, 1383, 1388, 1395, 1400, 1403, 1408, 1410–13, 1416, 1420–21, 1423, 1427, 1431, 1436–37, 1442, 1454–55, 1458, 1460, 1489, 1494, 1515, 1521, 1532, 1538; **7:**21–22, 30–32, 38–39, 44, 49–56, 58, 61–67, 71–77, 80–84, 90, 92–93, 100, 102, 114, 116, 121, 136–37, 144, 150, 160, 163, 168–69, 180, 183, 188–89, 192–93, 357, 451, 626, 636, 731, 765, 787, 810, 821, 855; **8:**147, 205; **9:**275, 382; **10:**718; **12:**521, 726

NEBUZARADAN
6:851, 859–60, 925–26, 994, 1079, 1150, 1454, 1456

NECHO/NECO
1:266; **3:**286, 288, 649, 654, 722; **6:**37, 556, 559, 741, 882, 1077–78, 1270, 1326, 1402–4, 1415; **7:**828

NEHEMIAH
1:247, 268, 286; **2:**332, 356, 393, 760, 894, 902, 923; **3:**305, 328, 355, 511, 554, 615, 665–69, 671, 679–80, 684–87, 699–700, 715–16, 718, 722, 728, 730, 736, 741–42, 746–59, 762, 764–66, 768–73, 775–77, 779–89, 793–94, 796–97, 800–801, 814–15, 818–20, 824, 827–30, 832, 834, 838–42, 844, 846–51, 994; **4:**71–72, 77, 119, 184, 196, 198–200; **5:**44, 620, 631, 633, 669, 801, 836, 855–56, 858, 862; **6:**546, 975; **7:**21, 27, 29, 41–44, 113, 175, 599, 742, 786–87, 810, 826, 870; **8:**36; **9:**458; **12:**726

NEHUSHTAN
2:8, 164

NEKODA
3:687

NEO-ASSYRIANS
6:6–7, 20

NEPHILIM
1:336, 382–84; **2:**21, 123, 129–30; **6:**1443

NER
2:549, 1081, 1221; **3:**358

NEREUS
10:763

NERGAL
6:1174, 1439; **7:**606, 792

NERGAL-SHAREZER/RAB-MAG
7:792

NERIAH
2:687; **6:**941

NETHANEL
2:95

NETHANIAH
6:1080

NETHINIM
3:727, 731, 745, 770, 826; **6:**1574

NICANOR
3:859, 1078, 1132, 1167; **4:**4, 62–63, 78, 85, 98–101, 109–11, 119, 142, 169, 176, 181–84, 193, 202, 247–50, 253–54, 259, 265–66, 268, 275, 277, 282–83, 286–92, 295–99

NICODEMUS
2:167–68; **9:**508, 530, 535, 541, 544, 546, 548–51, 553–55, 559, 564, 566–69, 578, 613, 624, 634, 656, 659, 661, 691, 717, 782, 808, 835–36, 862; **12:**276, 515

NICOLAITANS
12:538, 545, 567, 575, 578–79

NICOLAUS
10:113

NIMROD
1:326, 408–10; **2:**109; **6:**1444; **7:**482, 573

NIMSHI
3:217

NISROCH
3:269; **6:**330, 345, 394

NOADIAH
3:787; **6:**117

NOAH
1:47, 56, 230, 257, 306, 316, 325–26, 328–29, 336, 356, 370, 377, 379–81, 388–94, 396, 398, 400, 403–5, 407, 415, 417–18, 446, 458, 616, 941, 1005, 1009, 1119; **2:**49, 64, 127, 182, 559, 601, 626, 989; **3:**317–18, 1004, 1016; **4:**50, 328–29, 345, 503, 608, 733, 1272; **5:**3, 55, 445, 522–23, 526, 552–54, 621–22, 631, 836, 842, 855; **6:**211–12, 214, 278, 477–78, 481, 528, 530, 548, 630, 1177, 1210, 1213–14, 1258, 1516; **7:**633, 665, 674–75, 692, 696, 861; **8:**446; **9:**91, 331, 333, 335, 408; **10:**999; **11:**76, 728; **12:**133–34, 136, 160, 293–95, 347–48, 536, 592, 604, 633

NOT MY PEOPLE
6:119; **7:**226, 290; **10:**643; **12:**267

NOT PITIED
6:119; **7:**218, 226; **12:**267

NUMENIUS
4:144, 161, 169

NUN
2:124, 250; **3:**802; **4:**51

NYMPHA
11:659, 665, 668, 802

O

OBADIAH (IN AHAB'S COURT)
3:132–33, 135, 138, 142, 162, 177
OBADIAH (LEVITE/PRIEST)
3:816, 832, 835
OBADIAH THE PROPHET
2:162; **3:**586; **4:**31; **6:**21; **7:**336, 436–37, 441–42, 444–47, 451–52, 454, 456–59, 493, 707
OBED
2:933, 940–41, 943; **7:**437
OBED-EDOM
2:1249; **3:**386, 394, 400, 451, 618
OCHRAN
2:95
ODED
3:538, 598
OG
2:21, 123, 158, 165–67, 180, 207, 248, 250, 255, 257, 293, 305, 307–9, 440, 512, 593, 638, 641, 655, 665; **3:**811; **4:**1220, 1225
OHOLAH
6:1316–17, 1319, 1321–22, 1324, 1327, 1329–31, 1459; **7:**184
OHOLIAB
1:921–22, 961–62, 973
OHOLIBAH
6:1316–17, 1319–20, 1324–27, 1329–31, 1459; **7:**184
OLYMPAS
10:763
OMRI
1:249, 251, 256–57, 262, 264–65; **2:**614; **3:**7, 118–19, 123–25, 181, 209, 214, 217, 221; **5:**419; **6:**1348, 1489; **7:**218, 375, 582
OMRIDES
1:264–65; **3:**158, 209–10, 223, 227–28; **5:**851; **6:**1322
ONAN
1:604–6, 652; **2:**211; **3:**328
ONESIMUS
10:758, 825, 886; **11:**92, 556, 569, 665, 667, 884–87, 894–95, 897–902, 904
ONESIPHORUS
11:838, 858
ONIAS
1:285; **4:**6–7, 125, 143–44, 182, 189, 205–7, 213–14, 222–23, 229, 254, 258, 268, 281, 286, 289, 291, 296–97; **5:**527, 611–12, 632–33, 643, 859; **7:**24, 128, 141–42
OREB
2:803
ORPAH
2:903–8, 945
OSNAPPAR
3:699
OTHNIEL
1:258; **2:**647, 673, 678, 726, 735–38, 741, 745, 762–68, 770, 774, 779, 782, 791, 802, 817, 821, 830–31, 841–42, 853, 863, 1055; **3:**332; **4:**30

P

PAGIEL
2:95
PAHATH-MOAB
3:686, 725, 768, 817
PALAL
3:769
PALESTINE
1:68–69, 94, 213–27, 231, 244–51, 254–255, 259; **2:**557, 718; **7:**24, 29; **8:**50
PALTI
2:1170, 1224, 1250–51
PALTIEL
2:1224, 1252
PAROSH
3:725, 769, 817
PARTHIANS
4:59, 140, 157, 168, 170, 178; **9:**171, 362; **12:**658
PASEAH
3:768
PASHHUR
3:686, 745, 816, 826, 832; **6:**722, 724, 727, 733, 1386
PAUL THE APOSTLE
AND CIRCUMCISION **1:**89, 460, 603, 609; **4:**32, 674, 656; **10:**205–9, 226, 446–48, 494–98, 580, 585, 788, 880; **11:**207–8, 221–336, 239, 249, 251–53, 255–56, 259, 272–74, 277, 305, 311–14, 316–19, 321–23, 327–28, 337–39, 342–45, 347–48, 524–25, 568, 623, 644, 865; CALL/CONVERSION OF **9:**118; **10:**70, 146, 149–55, 188, 190, 207, 226, 293, 306–9, 314, 333–34, 337–38, 342–43, 373, 415, 604, 718; **11:**163, 193, 215, 220, 412, 531; **12:**518, 522; AND IMPRISONMENT **8:**688; **9:**4, 9, 230; **10:**230, 282, 297–98, 314, 326, 368, 373, 379; **11:**278, 355, 365, 369, 406–7, 411–14, 438, 459, 462–66, 473–74, 478, 484–85, 487–89, 492–95, 525, 546, 558–59, 569, 661–68, 843, 856, 884–85, 902–3; AND JERUSALEM **1:**815; **3:**418, 469, 582, 625; **8:**46, 565; **9:**137, 480; **10:**97, 147, 153, 175, 193–95, 198, 202–11, 214, 217, 257–59, 274–313, 319–30, 337, 339, 359–63, 373, 701, 753, 756, 758, 781, 995–96; **11:**113–19, 193–94, 205, 210, 214–17, 221–36, 304; LETTERS OF **1:**8, 13–16, 130, 192, 1196;

PAUL THE APOSTLE *(continued)*
2:1259; **4:**143, 188; **8:**17, 46–48, 82, 95; **9:**8; **10:**24, 30–31, 147, 188–89, 215, 238, 243, 249, 252–53, 259, 266, 280–81, 292, 370–82, 388–90, 702, 768, 776–79, 788–89, 797–98, 825, 923–24, 969–70, 984, 1002; **11:**3, 19, 29, 54, 62–63, 82, 110–11, 140–43, 178–79, 201–3, 354, 466, 472–74, 479, 481, 522, 673–75, 682–84, 776–72, 883–84; **12:**2, 232; AND MISSION **8:**35, 44–50; **9:**21, 487; **10:**83, 146–49, 153, 187–91, 194–206, 214–15, 219–48, 250–63, 265–72, 280–85, 291–96, 307–25, 333–34, 338–40, 358–67, 372–77, 389, 667–68, 697; **11:**113–17, 215, 222–30, 408. *See also* SAUL OF TARSUS

PEDAHZUR
2:34, 95

PEDAIAH
3:330, 691, 769, 847; **6:**1270

PEKAH
1:250, 265; **3:**248; **6:**36, 107, 117, 174, 1324; **7:**217, 246, 256

PEKAHIAH
1:265; **7:**217

PEKOD
6:1326

PELAIAH
3:801

PELATIAH
3:817; **6:**1186–87, 1345

PELEG
1:408

PELETH
2:135–36

PELETHITES
2:1268, 1324

PENINNAH
1:216; **2:**973–75, 979, 981

PEREZ
1:606; **2:**211, 933, 939, 941–43; **3:**327–28, 330, 363, 825; **9:**54

PEREZ-UZZAH
3:382, 388

PERIZZITES
1:164–65, 581; **2:**571, 576, 740; **3:**733, 819

PERSEUS
4:5, 30, 35, 104, 106

PERSIANS
1:9, 248, 250, 256, 266–67; **3:**606, 665–66, 680, 698–99, 701, 706–8, 710, 715, 718, 722, 728, 731, 735–36, 746, 749, 752, 756, 780, 785, 812, 821, 834, 882–83, 921–22, 925, 949, 951, 966–67, 1099, 1177–78; **4:**196, 263, 297; **6:**155, 520, 911, 913, 1443; **7:**24, 26–34, 62, 73, 81, 84, 88–89, 92, 94, 105, 111–12, 116, 136, 138, 739, 754, 826; **8:**195

PERSIS
4:157; **10:**763

PETER
1:14, 84, 179; **4:**674, 783; **5:**256; **7:**92, 327–28, 834; **8:**66, 77, 95, 102–3, 170, 254, 328–29, 343–51, 363–68, 371–72, 380, 474–75, 478–81, 483–84, 517, 525–27, 539, 546, 562, 619–25, 630, 705–9, 712, 715–16, 731; **9:**5, 111–12, 116–18, 138, 198–200, 203, 205–6, 262–65, 348, 427–29, 438–40, 466–67, 472, 481, 531, 611, 723–24, 731–34, 774, 803, 808–11, 840–41, 857–58, 860–65; **10:**24, 49–50, 60–70, 77–85, 88–92, 98–99, 101, 105–6, 109, 139–40, 160–71, 178–82, 198, 208–10, 217–18, 247; **11:**217, 226, 230–35, 241–42, 245; **12:**230–36, 315, 323–24, 339–40. *See also* SIMEON PETER; SIMON PETER

PETHAHIAH
3:826

PETHUEL
7:305

PETRA
3:560

PHARISEES
1:44, 285, 287, 1160; **3:**1079; **4:**47; **5:**709; **6:**244, 1316; **7:**253–54; **8:**39, 142, 157, 217, 224, 240, 278–80, 285–87, 330–35, 340–42, 385–86, 420–37, 547, 559, 565, 606, 615–18, 642–43, 673; **9:**23, 26, 122–36, 211, 245–51, 280–81, 284–90, 295–98, 311–12, 329–41, 369, 392–93, 528, 624, 628–30, 633, 656, 658, 661–70, 696, 708; **10:**104, 206–9, 310–12; **11:**526; **12:**306, 726–27

PHICOL
1:492

PHILEMON
10:373, 779, 825, 886, 998; **11:**92, 665, 884–87, 892, 894–96, 898–905

PHILETUS
11:845, 847

PHILIP
1:14; **9:**743; **10:**134–46, 160–61, 175, 288–89

PHILIP (FRIEND OF ANTIOCHUS)
4:255

PHILIPPIANS
1:103; **10:**830, 924, 975, 977, 988; **11:**21, 58, 85, 94, 145, 153, 462, 480, 483–85, 490–91, 495–99, 506–7, 510–14, 519–21, 525, 527–29, 532, 534–37, 541, 543–48, 675, 704; **12:**297, 565

PHILISTINES
1:404, 492, 528; **2:**615, 662, 739, 772, 840–44, 852–55, 858–60, 969, 995–1001, 1003–16,

1018–19, 1020–21, 1023, 1036, 1071, 1078–1081, 1183, 1188, 1198, 1215–16, 1243, 1249, 1265, 1361; **3:**389, 413–16, 599; **4:**57–58, 69; **5:**862; **6:**163, 1349, 1355; **7:**424

PHILOLOGUS
10:763

PHINEHAS (SON OF ELEAZAR)
2:159, 197, 199–202, 245–46, 546, 707; **3:**725; **4:**21, 44, 50–51, 53; **5:**620, 631, 836, 842–43, 859, 862; **7:**860–61; **11:**213–14

PHINEHAS (SON OF ELI)
2:974, 986–89, 996–97, 1001–2, 1004, 1026; **7:**272

PHOEBE
3:382; **10:**761–62, 766, 969; **11:**38, 135, 151, 480, 802

PHOENICIANS
1:248; **2:**662; **3:**53, 58, 90, 429, 692; **6:**201–3, 205, 1230, 1360, 1389, 1398, 1438, 1442, 1444; **7:**333, 362; **10:**181

PHYGELUS
11:838

PILATE
8:482–88, 497, 716–20; **9:**12–13, 28, 80, 270, 351, 445–50, 461, 465, 807, 811–27, 830; **10:**90. *See also* PONTIUS PILATE

PILTAI
3:832

POCHERETH-HAZZEBAIM
5:268

PONTIUS PILATE
8:717; **9:**80; **11:**829; **12:**43, 62, 155, 606. *See also* PILATE

PORCIUS FESTUS
See FESTUS

POTIPHAR
1:600, 609–12, 614, 622, 635; **5:**5, 525, 753; **9:**310

POTIPHAR'S WIFE
1:594, 609–10, 612; **4:**50; **5:**253, 445, 522, 524–25, 753; **7:**125; **8:**710

POTIPHERA
1:622

PREACHER, THE
5:232, 268–69, 278, 364, 461, 498, 518; **6:**337

PRISCA/PRISCILLA
8:13; **10:**24, 28, 235, 251–54, 258, 260–63, 361, 732, 761–63, 774, 777–78, 827, 969, 1001; **11:**802, 858; **12:**6

PTOLEMY MACRON
4:68, 253, 260, 264, 268, 282, 289

PTOLEMY III (EUERGETES)
4:6; **5:**502, 610, 645; **7:**140, 143

PTOLEMY VI PHILOMETOR
4:34, 121, 218, 228, 255, 260; **7:**142–43

PTOLEMY VIII (PHYSKON EUERGETES II)
4:35, 169, 188–89; **5:**610, 643

PUAH
1:297, 696–97

PUBLIUS
10:356

PUDENS
11:859

PUL
3:248; **7:**594

Q

QOHELET/QOHELETH
1:43; **2:**453, 476, 544; **5:**1–2, 7, 10, 267, 268–70, 272, 275, 279–81, 283–85, 290, 293–301, 303, 305, 307–14, 317, 319–20, 322–33, 335–37, 339–43, 345–46, 349–50, 353, 356–58, 390, 460–61, 476, 479, 510, 663, 670, 680, 698, 708, 715–16, 720, 725, 772, 779, 787, 793, 818; **6:**337; **12:**216. *See also* KOHELETH

QUARTUS
10:766, 777

QUEEN OF HEAVEN
3:364; **6:**584, 635, 638–40, 642, 872–75, 1175, 1290; **7:**231, 779

QUEEN OF SHEBA
3:81–82, 86–88, 510, 512; **4:**172; **5:**272, 297, 511, 849; **6:**1380; **8:**296, 615; **9:**243, 245, 248, 259

QUEEN OF THE SOUTH
8:296; **9:**243

QUIRINIUS
9:62

R

RAB-MAG
See NERGAL-SHAREZER

RAB-SARIS
3:265

RABSHAKEH
2:440; **3:**265, 268; **5:**853; **6:**14, 133, 291–94, 330, 357, 394, 1232, 1402, 1406

RACHEL
1:198, 372, 452, 517–18, 552–60, 585, 587, 599, 652, 659; **2:**939, 941–42; **6:**810, 815, 978; **8:**147; **9:**47

RAGUEL
3:977, 981–82, 986, 1033–43, 1050, 1057, 1062–63, 1069; **9:**486

RAHAB (PERSON)
1:606; **2:**550, 562, 577, 588–90, 592–96, 606–7, 613, 618–19, 625–27, 630, 641–42, 656, 706–7,

RAHAB (PERSON) *(continued)*
743–44, 775, 855, 943, 945–46, 1100; **3:**1089–90, 1119; **5:**170, 384; **6:**860; **8:**130, 132; **12:**142, 187, 189, 194, 198–99, 201, 579

RAM
3:327; **4:**562

RAPHA
2:1361

RAPHAEL
3:975–76, 983–85, 987, 989, 992, 1008, 1010–11, 1014, 1022–26, 1029, 1031, 1033, 1038–40, 1042, 1044, 1048–50, 1053, 1055–58, 1063, 1069; **5:**623; **8:**36; **9:**476

RAZIS
3:1008; **4:**16, 286, 291–92, 296, 299

REAIAH
3:330

REBA
2:246

REBEKAH
1:501–3, 509–13, 518, 520–23, 527, 535–38, 586; **2:**549–51; **6:**386; **9:**54

RECAH
3:332

RECHAB
2:1230; **3:**224, 332, 768

RECHABITES
3:224, 332; **6:**769, 828, 834–35

REGEM-MELECH
7:792

REHOBOAM
1:223, 257, 262–64; **2:**634, 816; **3:**98, 100–103, 114–18, 511, 518, 522–26, 530–32, 591, 594; **5:**118, 849–50

REHUM
3:675, 698, 700, 704, 718, 751, 769, 785, 815–17

REI
3:18

REKEM
2:246

REMALIAH
3:248; **6:**107–8, 111

REPHAIAH
3:768

REPHAIM
2:123, 167, 306, 309, 654–55, 662, 1361; **3:**416; **6:**1444

REUBEN
1:585, 599–600, 629–30, 664–65; **2:**34–35, 37, 211, 535–36; **3:**337; **12:**620

REUEL
1:703–4, 711; **2:**95, 738; **3:**982, 1038

REUMAH
1:501

REZIN
3:251; **6:**36, 107–8, 111, 174, 1324

REZON
3:93–94, 96

RHODA
10:180

RIMMON
2:1229; **3:**196; **7:**828

RIZPAH
2:1213, 1222–23, 1226, 1359–60

RODANIM
6:1378

RUFUS
8:489, 722; **10:**763, 929

RUHAMAH
7:223

RUTH
1:476; **2:**477, 892–93, 899–900, 903–8, 910–13, 915–33, 936–46, 1101, 1324; **3:**332, 909, 1155, 1168; **4:**125; **5:**282; **8:**130, 132

S

SABEANS
4:351, 453; **7:**333

SADDUCEES
1:44, 287–88; **3:**1004; **5:**628; **8:**99, 142, 157, 341–42, 371, 412, 421–22, 675–76; **9:**346, 376, 388–89, 399, 688; **10:**77, 83–84, 86, 89, 104–5, 310–12, 315, 318–20

SAKKUTH
7:394

SALAMIEL
3:1132

SALATHIEL
8:131

SALLAI
3:825

SALLU
3:825

SALMA
2:943; **3:**330

SALOME
1:270; **8:**321, 398, 493, 724, 726; **9:**88

SALU
2:200; **11:**214

SAMARITANS
1:267–68, 270, 298–99, 1157; **2:**487, 902; **3:**173, 258, 532, 757, 1112–13; **4:**10, 13, 229, 232, 548; **5:**519, 608, 612, 633, 730, 782; **6:**227; **7:**184, 727; **8:**67, 256, 298; **9:**22–23, 191, 214–17, 230, 232, 270, 326, 345, 370,

487, 563–67, 573–74, 644–45; **10:**23, 25, 135–39, 263

SAMSON
1:1067; **2:**64, 550, 662, 724, 726, 745–46, 762–64, 767–68, 773, 820–21, 831, 839–63, 865, 873, 888, 975; **5:**67; **9:**476

SAMUEL
1:241, 260, 821; **2:**233, 551, 606, 960, 969–74, 976–77, 986–87, 991–95, 1015–23, 1026–29, 1031–32, 1036–43, 1046–49, 1053–56, 1059–66, 1068–69, 1071–73, 1085–90, 1092–93, 1097–1100, 1126–28, 1157, 1165–66, 1182–85, 1193; **3:**94, 345, 364, 648; **4:**63, 164, 388, 1074–75; **5:**61, 107, 527, 836, 846; **6:**692, 827, 1159, 1214, 1287, 1590; **7:**365, 411; **9:**45, 51, 70, 354; **10:**675

SANBALLAT
1:268; **3:**669, 714, 751, 755, 757–58, 761, 768, 770, 772, 773, 777, 782, 784–85, 787–89, 832–33, 842, 846, 848–50

SAPPHIRA
3:332, 464; **10:**74, 95, 97–101, 111

SARAH/SARAI
1:186, 427–30, 450–59, 462–65, 481–83, 486, 488–90, 500, 503, 515; **3:**813; **6:**1458; **8:**144, 309; **9:**45, 52, 550; **10:**500, 505, 636; **11:**76, 190, 249, 301, 303

SARAH (WIFE OF TOBIAH)
3:975, 989, 1007–11, 1026–29, 1031, 1033, 1037–43, 1050–51; **8:**422

SARASADAI
3:1132

SARGON II
1:250, 265; **2:**660; **3:**253, 264, 695, 773, 978, 993, 995, 1102; **6:**36–37, 130, 132, 137, 149, 180, 182, 231, 236, 1076, 1322, 1361, 1402; **7:**203, 342, 594, 805

SATAN
1:289, 363, 820, 1109; **2:**285, 759, 790, 861, 1289, 1380; **3:**421–23, 426, 794, 1109, 1117, 1162; **4:**206, 297, 320, 324–25, 334, 339, 343, 347–50, 353–56, 358, 360–61, 370, 460, 488, 523, 525, 547, 600, 627, 1125, 1283; **5:**465, 620, 724, 742, 764; **6:**226, 336, 751, 1445, 1531; **7:**3–4, 6, 8, 10, 15, 101, 161, 744, 763, 765, 767, 770; **8:**23, 114–18, 125, 162–65, 181, 194, 223–24, 228, 232, 234, 240, 244, 246, 249, 283–87, 292, 308, 310, 321, 329–30, 335, 342, 346, 349, 368, 385, 405, 420, 424, 435, 455, 525, 535–37, 541, 543, 553, 563–66, 573–74, 580, 584–85, 624, 708; **9:**27, 28, 97–101, 210, 224–25, 241–42, 244, 274, 282, 413–17, 422, 427–31, 435, 437–38, 642, 690, 722, 730, 804; **10:**98, 339, 422, 457, 524, 530, 588, 755, 765, 847–48, 851–52, 856, 872; **11:**23, 27, 51, 54, 65–66, 74, 87, 105, 139, 151, 164–66, 315, 356, 383, 397, 460, 680, 708, 711, 714, 758–59, 762, 765, 795, 806, 821; **12:**35, 112, 272, 300–301, 316, 350, 415, 446, 516, 529, 532, 538, 558, 577–78, 581, 585, 591, 609, 611, 619, 632, 635, 642, 648–51, 653, 656–58, 661, 669, 675, 680, 682, 694, 695, 702, 706–7, 712–14, 716; THE ACCUSER **3:**422; **4:**347–50, 353–54, 511, 1125–26; **6:**336; **7:**765, 767; **8:**163; **12:**650; THE ADVERSARY **2:**183–84, 758; **3:**1380; **4:**347–48, 354, 1125; **5:**465, 557; **6:**751; **8:**194; "THE EVIL ONE" **4:**895; **5:**339; **6:**339; **8:**157, 163, 194, 205, 310; **9:**793, 797; **10:**191, 342; **11:**443, 462, 765; **12:**317, 418, 427, 445–46; FALL OF **2:**790; **9:**98–99, 225; **11:**806; **12:**529. *See also* BAAL-ZEBUB/BAAL-ZEBUL/BEELZEBUL; LUCIFER

SAUL (KING OF ISRAEL)
1:28, 164, 240, 245, 248, 252, 255–63, 590, 665, 764, 821, 1010, 1061, 1139, 1181; **2:**107, 190, 192, 198, 213, 229, 535–36, 541, 548–51, 562, 574–75, 584, 589, 606, 626, 630–31, 641, 723, 736, 738, 767, 864, 878, 887, 894, 945, 949–51, 953–54, 957, 561, 963, 966–67, 973, 976–77, 780–81, 1002, 1018–19, 1022–25, 1028, 1032, 1036–61, 1066–99, 1101–4, 1108–13, 1115–1136, 1138–40, 1144–60, 1164–88, 1191–94, 1197–1208, 1210–13, 1216–18, 1222–25, 1230, 1234, 1238, 1250, 1270, 1273, 1279, 1293, 1325–26, 1346–47, 1357–59; **3:**94–95, 358, 366–70, 376–78, 381, 388, 396, 687, 886; **4:**101, 111, 210, 228, 297, 556, 890, 912, 926; **5:**160, 206, 633, 827; **7:**312; **10:**675. *See also* SAUL (SON OF KISH)

SAUL (SON OF KISH)
2:1037, 1043, 1047, 1081, 1099, 1359; **3:**886. *See also* SAUL (KING OF ISRAEL)

SAUL OF TARSUS
6:1129; **10:**151, 154, 175–76, 224–25, 446, 462, 676. *See also* PAUL THE APOSTLE

SCEVA
8:23; **10:**266, 268–69

SCYTHIANS
1:266; **4:**223; **6:**1443, 1516; **11:**644

SELEUCUS
7:24, 31, 102, 111, 139–40, 216, 223, 255, 281, 283, 289

SENNACHERIB
3:265, 996; **4:**100, 204; **5:**853; **6:**7, 14, 37, 195–96, 231, 242, 260, 284, 291–92, 294–95, 1076–77, 1232, 1402, 1499; **7:**62, 534, 547, 594

SERAH
2:212, 214

SERAIAH
2:1268, 1354; **3:**685, 690, 717–18, 825; **6:**916, 1079; **7:**715, 765, 787

SERGIUS PAULUS
10:188, 190, 194, 201
SERON
4:56–58, 81, 87, 100, 110, 247
SERUG
1:416
SETH (SON OF ADAM AND EVE)
1:345, 372, 375–76, 379, 381–82, 415; **2:**191; **5:**631, 633, 836, 856; **6:**528–29; **11:**400
SHABBETHAI
3:743, 824, 826
SHADDAI
See GOD, NAMES FOR/TITLES OF: EL SHADDAI/SHADDAI
SHADRACH
4:51, 363; **6:**164; **7:**39
SHAHARAIM
3:357
SHALLUM
1:265; **3:**247–48, 330, 363, 450, 768, 825–26, 835; **4:**165; **6:**739, 741, 743, 1077; **7:**217
SHALMAN
7:275
SHALMANESER
1:250, 265; **3:**253, 995, 1070; **6:**1076, 1322, 1360–61, 1380, 1402, 1442; **7:**248, 270, 594
SHAMGAR
2:762, 764, 772, 774, 779, 782, 787, 819–20, 839, 841, 853, 1062
SHAMIR
3:442
SHAMMAH
2:1099, 1375
SHAPHAN
2:687–88; **3:**280, 293; **6:**6, 857, 1176, 1186
SHARON
5:389; **6:**281; **10:**161
SHASHAK
3:357
SHEALTIEL
3:691; **7:**715; **9:**94–95
SHEAR-JASHUB
6:107–8, 116, 295
SHEBA (BROTHER OF DEDAN)
6:1379–80
SHEBA THE BENJAMINITE
2:1345, 1348, 1350–53, 1357; **3:**102; **4:**193
SHEBANIAH
3:816–17
SHEBNA
3:265; **6:**150, 196–98, 293; **12:**584
SHEBUEL
3:442, 452
SHECANIAH
3:330, 725, 740–41, 788, 816
SHECHEM
1:517, 539, 577–80, 584; **2:**47, 546, 817; **3:**1119, 1143–44; **5:**422
SHEDEUR
2:34, 95
SHEERAH
2:353, 355
SHE IS NOT PITIED
7:218, 226
SHELAH
1:605; **2:**211, 904; **3:**327–28, 332, 363, 825
SHELEMIAH
1:268; **3:**450, 847; **7:**670
SHELOMITH
3:725; **7:**770
SHELOMOTH
3:725
SHELUMIEL
2:95
SHEM
1:325, 336–37, 381, 403–5, 407–9, 412, 415–16; **2:**182, 559, 576; **5:**631, 633, 836, 856; **6:**1442
SHEMA
3:357
SHEMAIAH (FALSE PROPHET/PRIEST TO NEHEMIAH)
3:786–87, 842, 846
SHEMAIAH (FALSE PROPHET TO JEREMIAH)
6:794–95, 805
SHEMAIAH (PRIESTLY FAMILY WITH NEHEMIAH)
3:816, 831, 838
SHEMAIAH (PROPHET TO REHOBOAM)
3:98, 102, 516, 520, 525–26; **6:**22
SHEMED
3:357; **6:**795, 805
SHEMER
1:251
SHEMIDA
3:353
SHENAZZAR
3:679
SHEPHATIAH
2:1219; **3:**725
SHEREBIAH
3:727–28, 801, 832
SHESHAI
2:122
SHESHAN
3:329

SHESHBAZZAR
3:705–6, 782, 899
SHETHAR-BOZENAI
3:703
SHEVA
2:1354
SHILONITE
3:94, 98, 100, 109, 120; **6:**6
SHIMEL
3:446
SHIMSHAI
3:698, 700, 703, 718, 815
SHIPHRAH
1:297, 696–97
SHISHA
3:50
SHISHAK
1:249, 257, 264; **3:**118, 526, 656, 736
SHOA
6:1326
SHOBACH
2:1280
SHOBAL
3:330
SHUBAEL
3:442
SHUHITE
4:328
SHULAMMITE
5:371, 375, 383, 421, 423, 426, 429
SHUNEM
2:1183; **3:**14, 189, 209
SHUPPIM
3:342, 451
SHUTHELAH
3:353
SIHON
2:165–67, 180, 207, 248, 250, 254, 257, 293, 305, 307, 309, 440, 512, 665, 830; **3:**811; **4:**1220, 1225
SILAS
7:160, 169, 170; **9:**219, 401; **10:**221, 224–26, 230, 232–35, 239–40, 252, 254, 256, 260, 324; **11:**48–49, 471, 540, 707; **12:**6. *See also* SILVANUS
SILVANUS
8:517; **10:**379; **11:**19, 48–49, 202, 577; **12:**232–33, 318–19. *See also* SILAS
SIMEON (SON OF JACOB AND LEAH)
1:576–77, 579, 581, 584, 604, 629–30, 633–34, 652, 659–60, 664–65, 667, 736; **2:**47; **3:**135, 328, 745, 747, 1089, 1119, 1132, 1143–44, 1177; **11:**620
SIMEON (TRIBE)
1:581; **2:**34, 37, 200, 213, 263, 535, 694, 701, 735–36, 739–40; **3:**336–37, 351, 357, 379–80, 1143; **6:**1605–6
SIMEON BEN ELEAZAR BEN SIRA
5:607, 611, 619, 867
SIMEON PETER
10:213–14, 217–18; **11:**323, 333. *See also* PETER; SIMON PETER
SIMEON THE MACCABEE
See SIMON THE MACCABEE
SIMEON THE PROPHET
1:205–6; **4:**672; **6:**339; **8:**67; **9:**17, 19, 21, 23, 29, 45, 60, 69–75, 77, 174, 267, 341, 359, 382, 413, 445, 456, 464, 478, 489; **10:**311; **11:**98, 518
SIMON (SON OF ONASIAS)
4:7
SIMON MAGUS
See SIMON THE GREAT
SIMON PETER
3:634; **8:**63, 170, 254, 344, 345, 481, 562, 636; **9:**115–17, 138, 427, 481, 484, 531, 611, 685, 729, 734, 803, 857, 860; **10:**164; **11:**230, 234, 245, 333; **12:**230, 234. *See also* PETER; SIMEON PETER
SIMON THE CANANEAN
8:253
SIMON THE DISCIPLE
8:169, 345, 543
SIMON THE GREAT
10:134, 138–39, 190, 263, 268
SIMON THE MACCABEE
1:270; **3:**1113; **4:**3, 7, 12, 17, 19, 21–22, 51, 82, 84, 88, 102, 104, 111–12, 140, 143, 149, 151–52, 154–57, 163–65, 167, 169, 171, 174, 176–78, 189, 214, 223, 261–64, 275–76, 286–87, 289, 297; **5:**527, 611–12, 631–33, 696, 836, 842, 858–59; **6:**37, 403
SIRACH, SON OF
1:10; **4:**562; **5:**603, 606–8, 866
SISERA
2:778–83, 787–90, 804, 818, 830, 841, 858, 878, 1062; **3:**920, 1090, 1109, 1165; **4:**945, 1010
SODOMITES
1:435, 442, 474, 478, 481; **10:**858–59; **12:**494
SOLOMON
1:74, 164, 251–52, 256–57, 260–64, 277; **2:**5, 14, 264, 279, 384, 549, 570, 659, 687–88, 988, 1227, 1237, 1242, 1255, 1298, 1347, 1350, 1355; **3:**3–5, 18–43, 46–62, 67–75, 77–98, 100–102, 168, 205, 278, 304–5, 365, 396, 407–9, 421, 429–33, 460–64, 467–79, 485, 496–506, 509–14,

SOLOMON *(continued)*
536, 849; **4:**72, 102, 190, 196, 198–200, 218, 963, 1199; **5:**20, 32, 53, 272, 289, 291, 297, 363, 365, 377, 400, 433, 437, 493–503, 509–19, 558, 563, 849–50, 546; **7:**40, 362, 722, 779; **8:**403; **9:**94, 243–45, 259; **10:**128; **11:**40; **12:**727
SONS OF THUNDER
8:562; **9:**138, 215. *See also* BOANERGES; ZEBEDEE, SONS OF
SOPATER
10:766
SOSIPATER
4:276; **10:**766
SOSTHENES
10:252, 254–56, 379, 775, 777–78, 797; **11:**38, 202; **12:**232
SOSTRATUS
4:222
STACHYS
10:762
STEPHANAS
10:762, 777, 807, 1000–1001; **11:**135
STEPHEN
1:84, 868, 1164; **3:**68, 582; **8:**45; **9:**28, 99, 253, 281, 331, 373, 401, 455, 461, 465; **10:**14, 74, 112, 113, 120–134, 146, 191–92, 308; **11:**214
SUSANNA
3:1080, 1086, 1102, 1132, 1141–42, 1159; **4:**563; **5:**77, 119, 126, 480, 511, 629, 634, 760–61; **7:**156, 175–85, 189; **8:**29; **9:**175; **10:**492
SYNTYCHE
10:969; **11:**471, 481, 483, 495, 539–40, 546, 668

T

TABEEL
3:698; **6:**108, 1076, 1324
TABITHA
10:160–62, 170
TABRIMMON
3:161
TAHATH
3:345
TALMAI
2:122, 1309
TALMON
3:826, 835
TAMAR (DAUGHTER-IN-LAW OF JUDAH)
1:364, 476, 538, 604–7, 610, 641; **2:**211, 546, 904, 932, 937, 939, 941–46, 1100, 1159; **3:**328, 332; **4:**556; **5:**380, 383, 386, 430; **6:**603; **8:**129–30, 132, 422; **9:**567
TAMAR (SISTER OF ABSALOM)
1:27; **2:**949, 963, 1170, 1270, 1285, 1302–6, 1308–10, 1313, 1315, 1317, 1355; **3:**317, 901; **4:**694; **5:**193, 263, 433, 622; **6:**1033, 1325
TAMMUZ
1:1135; **4:**38; **6:**1000, 1110, 1176–77, 1454; **7:**146
TARTAN
3:264
TATTENAI
3:675, 703–6, 709, 711, 899; **7:**709
TEMANITE
4:328; **6:**966
TERAH
1:325, 336, 381, 415, 417, 422; **5:**523; **6:**1278, 1380
TERESH
3:892, 950
TERTIUS
10:379, 766; **11:**342
TERTULLUS
10:314, 317–21, 335
THADDAEUS
9:138
THEOPHILUS
9:8–9, 28, 39–41; **10:**5, 7–10, 37, 260
THEUDAS
10:107
THOMAS
2:753, 804, 847; **6:**469; **9:**138, 473, 476, 484–85, 687, 742, 848–53, 855; **12:**254
TIBERIUS
8:16, 343, 420, 718; **9:**80, 88, 386; **10:**774
TIGLATH-PILESER III
1:247, 250, 264–65; **3:**248, 251, 253, 617, 922, 978, 995; **6:**6, 36, 102, 107, 117, 122, 174, 664, 1076, 1233, 1360–61, 1379; **7:**169, 200, 248, 342, 361, 377, 399, 534, 594, 804
TIGLATH-PILNESER
3:337
TIMNA
3:318
TIMOTHY
10:11, 224–27, 803, 840, 998; **11:**11, 19, 38, 48–49, 135, 465, 479–80, 482, 518–21, 577, 587, 591–92, 664, 668, 707, 710, 714, 781–82, 790, 794–95, 813–15, 823, 833, 841, 845, 855–56; **12:**8, 173
TIMOTHY (AMMORITE RULER)
4:74, 78, 80, 249, 253–54, 262–64, 275–76
TIRAS
6:1516

TIRHAKAH
3:268, 996; **6:**1361, 1402, 1406; **7:**671, 691
TIRZAH
2:212
TITUS
10:11, 998; **11:**6, 12, 37, 53, 55–56, 110–13, 115–17, 121, 125–26, 171, 222, 781–82, 862, 864, 870
TITIUS JUSTUS
10:252, 254, 256, 262
TOBIAH (GOVERNOR OF AMMON)
3:687, 757, 770, 783, 787–89, 842, 846–50
TOBIAH (SON OF TOBIT)
3:975–76, 979, 980–81, 983–92, 1001–1002, 1008, 1010–11, 1014–19, 1022–24, 1026–58, 1068–70
TOBIAS
3:1011, 1041; **4:**8, 207; **7:**24, 526; **9:**217, 476, 486
TOBIEL
3:992
TOBIJAH
7:787–88
TOGARMAH
6:1378, 1516
TOI
2:1266
TOLA
1:259; **2:**762, 764–65, 791, 819–20, 839; **3:**342
TOU
3:414–15, 417
TOUBIANI
4:276
TRINITY, THE
6:105; **8:**161, 504, 274; **9:**490; **10:**22, 57, 556; **12:**248
TROPHIMUS
10:297; **11:**859
TRYPHENA
10:763
TRYPHO
4:138, 140, 147, 150–52, 154, 157, 168, 172–73
TRYPHOSA
10:763
TUBAL
6:1378
TYCHICUS
11:369–70, 465, 556, 569, 592, 665, 667, 857, 878, 884

U

UCAL
5:251
URBANUS
10:762
URI
3:52
URIAH
1:118; **2:**247, 432, 459, 547, 673, 746, 810, 963–64, 1122, 1129, 1140, 1158, 1165, 1169, 1217, 1231, 1269–71, 1279, 1283–89, 1291–93, 1297–98, 1300, 1303, 1306, 1309, 1317, 1331, 1335, 1339, 1350, 1366–67, 1375–76; **3:**14, 117, 332, 378, 421, 423, 730; **4:**885, 887; **5:**122, 138, 849; **6:**88, 258, 300, 774, 1274; **7:**93; **8:**130
URIEL
3:1057
UTHAI
3:726, 825
UZZAH
2:1012, 1247–49, 1251–52; **3:**382, 388–89, 393; **4:**387; **6:**1533
UZZI
3:342, 826, 839
UZZIAH
1:263, 265–66, 281, 706; **3:**11, 101, 244–45, 250–51, 522, 525–26, 588–92, 594, 630, 768, 787, 1087, 1089, 1129, 1138–39, 1148, 1165, 1167
UZZIEL
1:1070; **3:**394, 452, 768

V

VASHTI
3:857, 861, 869, 877–85, 889–90, 895, 897, 899, 904, 908, 910, 927, 938; **5:**425; **6:**27, 36, 48, 99, 102, 107, 1348; **7:**342, 352, 361, 426, 788; **9:**45

W

WIDOW OF ZAREPHATH
3:132, 140, 186, 189, 197; **5:**851; **9:**113, 157, 159, 174, 395; **12:**144
WISE WOMAN OF TEKOA
1:242; **2:**1313–14, 1319, 1352; **3:**152, 911, 1138; **5:**11, 160; **7:**468–69

Y

YAH/JAH
See under GOD, NAMES FOR/TITLES OF
YAHWEH
See under GOD, NAMES FOR/TITLES OF
YHWH
See under GOD, NAMES FOR/TITLES OF

Z

ZABAD
3:353

ZABADEANS
4:145
ZABBAI
3:769
ZABBUD
3:726
ZABDI
3:328
ZABDIEL
3:826; **4:**145
ZACCAI
3:769
ZACCHAEUS
9:356–60, 362, 478–79
ZACCUR
3:726, 768, 817
ZADOK
1:439, 905; **2:**687, 688, 988, 1268, 1323–25, 1332, 1339, 1346, 1354; **3:**18–20, 23, 32–34, 49–50, 416, 441, 457, 469, 717, 769, 815, 817, 847; **4:**8; **7:**28, 861; **8:**422; **9:**388
ZALMUNNA
2:807–8
ZAMZUMMIM
2:306, 654
ZAPHENATH-PANEAH
1:622
ZATTU
3:817
ZEBAH
2:807–8
ZEBEDEE, SONS OF
8:398; 400, 493, 512, 562, 627; **9:**138, 401, 470, 498–99, 857, 865; **11:**217, 226; **12:**365–66, 515.
See also BOANERGES; SONS OF THUNDER
ZEBIDAH
6:1270; **8:**398, 400, 493, 513, 562, 567, 627; **9:**138, 401, 470, 498–99, 857, 865; **11:**217, 226; **12:**366, 515
ZEBUL
2:817
ZEBULON/ZEBULUN (PERSONAL NAME)
2:492; **6:**1606; **12:**620
ZEBULUN (TRIBE)
2:34, 37, 213, 263, 536, 744, 765, 779, 788, 802–3; **3:**351, 617; **6:**1606; **8:**167
ZECHARIAH (FATHER OF JOHN THE BAPTIST)
3:442, 1043; **4:**42; **9:**11, 15, 20–21, 29, 44–55, 58–60, 72
ZECHARIAH (PROPHET)
1:265; **3:**101, 248, 300, 581, 583, 834; **6:**5, 8, 329; **7:**708, 735–43, 846; **8:**65, 131; **9:**249, 281, 367, 783, 834
ZEDEKIAH (KING OF ISRAEL)
1:263, 266–67; **2:**511, 826; **3:**12, 101, 164, 287, 291–95, 330, 552, 602, 655; **6:**443, 559–60, 732–33, 745, 782, 819, 830–31, 849–53, 944, 1078–79, 1161, 1194–95, 1248–51, 1253, 1273; **7:**39, 671; **8:**403, 437, 484, 658, 704
ZEDEKIAH (SON OF CHENAANAH)
3:162
ZEEB
2:803
ZELOPHEHAD
2:49, 128, 169, 202, 212, 222, 262, 265–66, 683–84, 928; **3:**352–53, 1039
ZENAS
11:878
ZEPHANIAH
2:689; **6:**733, 1079; **7:**422, 482, 659–662; **9:**304, 707–8
ZERAH (PERSONAL NAME)
1:606; **2:**211; **3:**327–28, 363, 559, 825–26; **9:**54
ZERAHITES (TRIBE)
3:328
ZERESH
3:857, 867, 911, 916
ZERUAH
3:94
ZERUBBABEL
1:95, 250, 268–69, 1017; **2:**752; **3:**295, 330, 657, 665–69, 675–76, 679, 685, 690–91, 693–95, 702, 704–6, 709, 711, 716, 725, 757, 782, 832, 842, 844, 847; **4:**196–97, 199; **5:**626, 631, 836, 855–56; **6:**444, 743, 1391; **7:**21, 39, 44, 88, 113, 709, 715, 719–20, 727, 730–32, 737–38, 740, 763, 765, 769–72, 788, 807, 814; **8:**128, 130–31; **9:**94
ZERUIAH
2:1174, 1216, 1225, 1326, 1346, 1351, 1361; **3:**27, 415
ZIBA
2:1273–74, 1323, 1325, 1346–47, 1353; **5:**174
ZIBIAH
3:232
ZICHRI
3:825
ZIHA
3:826
ZIKLAG
2:1142, 1179, 1187–88, 1191–93, 1195, 1201, 1211, 1224, 1234, 1268; **3:**376, 379, 827
ZILPAH
1:553–54, 664; **2:**918; **3:**457; **6:**1605–6
ZIMMAH
3:345

ZIMRI
1:264; **2:**200, 246; **3:**118–19, 123, 221, 328, 1008; **6:**1322; **11:**214
ZINA
3:437
ZIPHITES
2:1153, 1174
ZIPPOR
2:181, 183, 187
ZIPPORAH
1:509, 718; **2:**96, 109, 181
ZIZA/ZIZAH
3:437
ZOPHAR
4:320–21, 328, 330, 332, 362–63, 418–27, 433–34, 467–68, 482–89, 492, 496–97, 499, 507, 512, 516, 522, 524, 528–29, 552, 564
ZUAR
2:95
ZUPH
2:973
ZUR
2:200, 246
ZURISHADDAI
2:95

OUTSIDE THE BIBLE

A

AARONIDES
1:682, 880, 906, 916; **3:**725
AELIUS ARISTIDES
8:22, 24–25
AEMILIUS PAULLUS
4:104
AENEAS
4:227
AESCHYLUS
4:243; **5:**708; **11:**701
AGATHOCLES
7:140
AKIBA, RABBI
1:68, 78, 121, 290; **4:**234; **5:**273, 634; **9:**228
ALEXANDER JANNAEUS/JANNEUS
1:270; **3:**1078, 1107; **4:**13; **9:**448
ALEXANDER OF ABONOTEICHOS
8:13
ALEXANDRA
1:270
AMBROSE
1:93, 201; **2:**256; **4:**243; **5:**552; **6:**451, 551; **9:**623; **12:**711
ANANIAS
4:254; **9:**399
ANTAIOS
4:227
ANTIGONUS
1:269; **4:**31, 254; **7:**140; **9:**362–63
ANTIOCHUS I (SOTER)
3:966; **4:**248; **7:**140
ANTIOCHUS II (THEOS)
7:140
ANTIOCHUS IX (CYZICENUS)
4:5, 13
ANTIOCHUS HIERAX
4:248
APHRAHAT
4:243
APULEIUS
8:25
AQUILA
1:11, 301, 304; **6:**454
AREUS
4:143
ARISTEAS
4:241; **5:**642; **9:**476
ARISTOTLE
1:75–76, 142, 1085; **5:**117, 120, 232, 331, 497–98; **7:**118; **8:**17; **9:**479, 758; **10:**100, 382, 553–54, 587; **11:**558–59, 658; **12:**130, 211, 278
ARTEMIDORUS
7:49, 54; **8:**24–25
ASHURBANIPAL/ASSURBANIPAL
1:237, 250, 265–66; **2:**572; **6:**1077, 1366, 1380, 1410, 1422, 1443; **7:**593–95, 612, 691
ATHANASIUS
1:1, 7, 12, 15; **5:**99; **6:**404; **9:**752; **11:**597
AUGUSTINE
1:12–13, 16, 50, 93–96, 128, 140, 193, 196, 200, 1190; **2:**256, 513, 1341; **4:**243, 355, 807, 853–54, 1206, 1215, 1252, 1261; **5:**61, 104, 112, 264, 438, 448, 634; **6:**451, 551; **7:**8, 76, 606; **8:**220, 298; **9:**623, 630, 723, 752, 778, 841, 858; **10:**266, 370, 479, 620, 707, 728, 861, 884; **11:**76, 183, 284, 290, 377, 393, 486; **12:**6, 377, 396, 403, 414, 433, 443, 534, 536, 551, 555, 709, 711–12

B

BACCHUS
1:843
BALTHASAR
11:850
BAR KOCHBA, SIMON
1:290; **2:**191; **8:**142
BELIAL
1:287, 289; **3:**969; **4:**488; **11:**105, 442, 596
BEL-MARDUK
6:406, 1537; **7:**190
BEL-SHAR-USUR
7:80
BEN ELEAZAR, RABBI SIMON
7:56
BEN HANNANIAH, RABBI JOSHUA
5:797; **8:**247
BEN HYRCANUS, RABBI ELIEZER
8:197
BEN LEVI, RABBI YOSHUA
4:1063
BEN ZAKKAI, RABBI JOHANAN
5:797; **6:**1189, 1240; **9:**863
BERENICE
7:55, 140
BESSUS
4:30
BETHEL-SHAREZER
7:792
BEZA, THEODORE
4:929, 1206
BONHOEFFER, DIETRICH
3:619; **5:**51, 129, 136; **6:**681; **11:**417–18; **12:**508

C

CALIGULA
1:285; **4:**292; **5:**439–40, 597, 626; **8:**16, 684, 689–90; **11:**759
CALVIN, JOHN
1:51–52, 102–3, 193, 699, 726, 747, 758, 814, 847, 850, 870; **4:**355, 687, 802, 856, 1001, 1079, 1188, 1236, 1277; **5:**227, 238, 635; **6:**244–45, 485, 673, 785, 866; **7:**94, 376, 767–68, 781; **8:**172; **10:**620; **12:**197, 371, 391, 406, 443, 537
CAMBYSES
3:691, 701, 878; **7:**44, 88, 138–40, 709, 715, 738
CASSANDER
7:111; **11:**675
CASTOR
10:357
CELSUS
8:21; **11:**850
CERINTHUS
12:545, 709
CHRYSOSTOM, JOHN
1:49–50, 94, 193; **3:**932; **4:**243, 355, 929; **9:**623, 690; **11:**337, 892
CICERO
8:23–24; **11:**30, 156
CIMMERIANS
6:1516
CLEANTHES THE STOIC
8:17
CLEISTHENES
2:669
CLEMENT OF ALEXANDRIA
1:7, 89, 93, 192; **5:**438, 635; **9:**501; **11:**438; **12:**6, 67, 69, 475
CLEMENT OF ROME
1:7; **3:**1077; **11:**135, 173; **12:**6–8, 10, 168
CLEODEMUS MALCHUS
4:143–44, 227
CYNICS
8:18–20, 595; **10:**833; **11:**459, 544, 698–99, 828, 831
CYPRIAN
4:248; **5:**635; **8:**7
CYRIL OF ALEXANDRIA
9:737, 752, 858

D

DANAOS
4:144
DAN'EL
4:328–29, 470, 503, 555
DECIUS
8:15
DEMETRIUS OF PHALERUM
10:784
DEMOSTHENES
4:40, 101
DIANA
8:22; **10:**271; **11:**361
DIODORUS SICULUS
4:7, 31, 38, 133, 138, 193; **7:**89
DIOGENES
3:1144; **6:**618, 630; **8:**16, 18; **9:**476
DIONYSIUS
5:740; **9:**80, 366; **11:**653; **12:**366, 514, 545
DOMITIAN
1:271; **7:**7, 10; **8:**16; **12:**234, 514, 544, 683–85

DRACO
2:566, 688, 696

E

EBIONITES
1:14, 47
ELEAZAR FROM ADIABENE
4:254; **11:**224
ELEAZAR THE EXORCIST
3:1040; **9:**242
ELIEZER, RABBI
4:234; **5:**642; **6:**1240; **8:**197, 247
ENLIL
4:204; **6:**1463
EPICTETUS
8:18–21; **10:**437, 554, 587, 929; **11:**31, 322, 700; **12:**199
EPICURUS
5:303, 441, 461; **8:**17–18; **11:**675
EPIMENIDES
8:17; **11:**865
ESHMUNAZAR
7:757
ESHNUNNA
1:238
ESSENES
1:10, 44, 287–88; **4:**47; **5:**339; **8:**50, 277, 308, 526, 529, 531–32, 552, 643, 646; **9:**81, 84, 147, 178, 346, 388; **10:**451; **11:**363, 372, 375, 389–90, 398, 400, 403, 408, 410, 419, 423, 430, 437–38, 441–42, 451
EULAEUS
7:142
EURIPIDES
4:16; **8:**16
EUSEBIUS
1:7, 15, 270; **4:**152, 192, 218; **7:**71, 700; **8:**414, 509, 517; **11:**580; **12:**318, 474, 513, 534

F

FLAMINIUS
4:104
FRANCIS OF ASSISI
4:1272; **8:**649; **12:**535–36

G

GASPAR
11:850
GRACCHUS, T. SEMPRONIUS
4:270
GREGORY OF NAZIANZOS
4:243
GREGORY OF NYSSA
1:94
GREGORY THE GREAT
1:96
GUDEA
4:378; **5:**517; **6:**1376

H

HADES
11:390; **12:**567
HADRIAN
1:271; **5:**557
HAMILCAR BARCA
4:104
HAMMURABI/HAMMURAPI
1:238, 246, 266; **2:**293, 461, 468, 486; **5:**91–92, 144; **6:**10, 20–21, 1226, 1463; **7:**774; **9:**148
HANNIBAL
4:104
HASDRUBAL
4:104
HASIDIM
3:501; **4:**285–86; **7:**24; **8:**38; **10:**325
HASMONEANS
1:284; **3:**756, 1077–78, 1105, 1118, 1132; **4:**3, 8, 20–22, 47, 51, 86–87, 92, 104, 111, 140, 153, 163, 165, 171, 174, 178, 230, 295, 297; **8:**353; **9:**122; **12:**61
HECATAEUS OF ABDERA
1:270; **4:**6–7, 12, 144, 227, 241
HERACLES
4:143–44, 218, 227, 277
HERACLIDES
4:93
HERMAS
12:76, 78, 169
HERODOTUS
1:267, 313; **2:**668; **3:**22, 722, 755, 780, 878–79, 892, 904, 1099, 1102, 1106; **4:**144, 204, 218; **5:**642, 853; **6:**295, 995, 1003, 1360, 1389, 1404, 1444; **7:**61, 73, 81–82, 187, 203; **10:**124
HESIOD
1:88; **4:**192, 604; **5:**78; **7:**54
HILLEL, RABBI
1:998; **4:**138; **5:**172, 326, 689; **8:**191, 213–14; **9:**147, 228
HIPPOLYTUS
7:61; **9:**623; **12:**532
HOMER
1:88; **2:**639; **4:**192, 296; **6:**1376; **11:**301, 701
HOR
4:35
HURRIANS
1:232, 590

HYKSOS
1:246, 254, 257

I

IBN EZRA, RABBI ABRAHAM
1:73, 76–77, 308, 1010; **4:**394, 413; **5:**327; **7:**406
IGNATIUS OF ANTIOCH
8:103, 105–6, 137, 432; **9:**311, 504, 610; **11:**213, 781, 838; **12:**373, 454, 562, 573–74, 582
IGNATIUS OF LOYOLA
1:99, 101; **11:**395, 440; **12:**569, 669
IRENAEUS
1:7, 47–48, 50, 91, 93, 192–93, 368; **5:**438; **6:**551, 1131; **8:**7; **9:**5, 498, 504; **10:**51; **11:**211, 859; **12:**366, 531–32, 534, 658, 710
ISHTAR
3:886; **4:**603, 618; **5:**4, 397; **6:**11, 1003, 1438, 1530; **7:**606, 610, 612, 614
ISIS
3:1125; **4:**622; **5:**90, 496, 511, 667, 757; **8:**13, 15, 25–26; **11:**58, 361, 653, 677, 792
IZATES OF ADIABENE
4:254; **11:**224

J

JANNEUS
See ALEXANDER JANNAEUS/JANNEUS
JASON OF CYRENE
3:183, 202
JEROME
1:5, 12–13, 15, 51–52, 68, 93–95, 99, 131, 193, 200, 301, 303–4, 1190; **2:**950; **3:**663, 679, 976–77, 1080, 1133; **4:**691, 763, 802, 996; **5:**1, 20, 294, 350, 438, 448, 606, 634–35; **7:**376, 436; **8:**6, 72, 318; **9:**623; **11:**266; **12:**6, 532, 537
JOSE, RABBI
4:234; **5:**781; **9:**301
JOSEPHUS, FLAVIUS
1:10–12, 38, 248, 253, 270, 286–88, 290–91, 296, 300, 305, 412, 1112, 1157, 1159, 1171; **2:**89, 1012, 1026, 1053, 1070, 1148, 1336; **3:**45, 212, 512, 530, 573, 678–79, 759, 788, 832–33, 861, 866–67, 878, 882, 884, 888, 891, 894–95, 898, 904, 908, 913–14, 945, 950, 955, 959, 966–67, 994, 996, 1002, 1040, 1080, 1114; **4:**6, 8, 13, 22, 30, 56, 74, 91, 102, 110–11, 116, 133, 135, 138, 176, 178, 189, 202, 207, 211, 228, 248, 254–55, 281, 292, 1131; **5:**160, 334, 339, 503, 511, 525, 553, 567, 578, 612, 642–43, 855, 859; **6:**942, 1348, 1361; **7:**25, 30, 33, 40, 55, 83, 270; **8:**35, 38, 135, 156, 319, 343, 371, 417, 478, 491, 516, 519, 531–32, 597–98, 659, 668, 684–85, 710, 712, 718–20; **9:**9, 62, 85, 88, 116, 122, 242, 270, 281, 308, 333, 362–63, 366, 372–73, 388, 395–96, 398–400, 404, 448, 460, 565, 697–98, 700, 806, 816, 818, 831; **10:**124, 178, 268, 306, 322; **11:**22, 157, 163, 224, 231–32, 397–99, 411, 564, 582, 644, 652–53, 703; **12:**278, 328, 405, 407, 418, 673, 694
JULIUS AFRICANUS
8:131
JULIUS CAESAR
5:502; **8:**723; **9:**460; **10:**775; **12:**683
JUPITER
8:22, 142, 371. *See also* ZEUS
JUSTIN MARTYR
1:11, 87, 91, 192; **6:**451; **8:**17, 19, 21, 153; **9:**433; **10:**763
JUVENAL
1:291; **8:**17

K

KADMOS
4:144
KERET, KING
1:233, 1018, 1023; **2:**586, 613; **3:**17; **4:**470, 500
KIERKEGAARD, SØREN
1:494; **4:**361; **8:**179; **12:**138
KIMCHI
1:76, 78; **2:**833; **5:**113, 134. *See also* QIMHI
KING, MARTIN LUTHER, JR.
1:18, 195; **2:**587, 1031, 1057, 1209; **4:**17, 212, 738; **5:**635; **6:**119, 183, 724; **7:**694; **8:**159; **9:**734, 865; **10:**46; **11:**348, 394, 412, 728, 751, 761, 768; **12:**278, 297, 433
KNOX, JOHN
4:802, 948, 1079; **11:**898
KUTURNAḪḪUNTE, KING OF ELAM
4:204

L

LAODICE
7:140
LENAEUS
7:142
LIPIT ISHTAR
6:1309
LUTHER, MARTIN
1:12, 16, 23, 96, 101; **2:**513, 652, 834, 1006; **3:**448, 533, 868, 931, 972, 1077; **4:**709, 727, 802, 864–65, 1156, 1206, 1252; **5:**21, 448; **7:**156, 419, 717, 762, 781; **9:**434; **10:**403, 621; **11:**183, 194–95, 207, 222, 238; **12:**177, 378, 390, 414

M

MARCION
1:14–15, 17, 19, 46–47, 49, 84–87, 192; **7:**334; **9:**5–6; **10:**370, 483, 623, 758; **11:**78, 830; **12:**513
MARCUS AURELIUS
10:782, 866
MARDUK
1:232; **3:**678–79, 886; **4:**395, 518, 624; **5:**4, 6, 92; **6:**226, 394, 406, 912, 1002, 1085, 1155, 1170, 1185, 1338, 1366, 1379, 1435, 1465, 1489, 1537–38, 1560, 1570, 1607; **7:**62, 72, 76, 81, 89, 101, 187, 190, 193; **8:**580
MARDUK-APAL-IDDIN
6:1326
MASTEMA
4:488; **9:**177
MATI'EL
6:831
MEGASTHENES
7:71
MELCHIOR
8:850
MENAHEM
1:290
MENANDER
6:1398; **8:**16–17; **10:**983
MERNEPTAH
1:249, 251–54, 258; **2:**615
MOLON
4:248

N

NABONIDUS
1:266; **4:**355; **6:**519, 939, 945; **7:**21–22, 50–51, 62, 71–73, 80, 84, 90, 855
NABOPOLASSAR
1:266; **6:**406, 556; **7:**595, 597, 626
NACHMANIDES
1:77, 81; **2:**833
NATHAN, RABBI
4:232; **5:**14; **8:**247; **9:**271
NAUSITHOOS
2:668
NEBUCHADNEZZAR II
6:1075–77; **7:**62, 626
NERO
1:270; **8:**16, 514–15, 651; **9:**404; **10:**324, 326, 367, 406, 717, 732; **11:**234; **12:**234, 493, 514, 533, 658–59, 678, 683–85
NICIAS
4:101
NINURTA
6:1499

O

OCTAVIUS
4:270, 286, 296
ORIGEN OF ALEXANDRIA
1:49, 89, 121; **2:**833; **4:**23; **8:**7, 21
OROPHERNES
4:117
OSIRIS
4:483; **5:**496, 511

P

PABIL
2:586, 613
PAN
1:1118; **8:**343
PAPIAS
8:76, 517–18; **9:**5; **12:**366, 513, 534, 710
PASHA, IBRAHIM
2:718–19
PEREGRINUS
8:19
PHILO OF ALEXANDRIA
1:12, 49, 88, 93, 128, 192, 285, 290, 1075; **5:**440; **8:**21, 38, 41; **10:**261
PLATO
1:291; **2:**668–69; **3:**1103; **4:**233, 292; **5:**475, 510, 550, 557, 564, 669; **7:**63; **8:**21, 677; **9:**737, 758; **11:**675; **12:**98, 116, 136, 278
POLLUX
10:357
POLYCARP
9:311; **10:**720; **11:**403, 472, 522; **12:**229, 368
POMPEY
1:269–70, 290; **4:**5, 107, 183; **6:**932; **7:**26; **11:**759
POPILIUS
7:25
PSEUDO-CALLISTHENES
4:31; **11:**566
PSEUDO-PHILO
4:50; **10:**54
PTOLEMAUS
4:93
PTOLEMY I
4:202, 254; **5:**439; **7:**111, 139, 140
PTOLEMY II (PHILADELPHUS)
1:300; **7:**140, 155
PTOLEMY V (EPIPHANES)
5:349

Q

QIMHI
7:406. *See also* KIMCHI
QUINTILIAN/QUINTILLIAN
10:54, 861; **11:**735; **12:**138

R

RA/RE
1:622; **5:**5, 90, 94, 833
RAMESES II
1:254, 257, 1124; **6:**1402
RAMESES III
1:248, 695
RAMESES VI
1:248, 695
RASHI
1:74–75, 77, 79, 81; **2:**833, 934; **3:**424, 937; **5:**113, 126, 158, 172, 182, 199; **6:**551; **7:**406

S

SARGON I
1:246
SCIPIO AEMILIANUS
4:169
SCIPIO AFRICANUS
4:104
SCOPAS
7:141
SEA PEOPLES
1:247; **2:**557, 615, 1000, 1109; **3:**52
SENECA
8:20; **9:**454; **10:**255, 322, 443, 554; **11:**31, 446, 675; **12:**203
SESOSTRIS
2:668–69
SETH (EGYPTIAN DEITY)
4:618
SHALEM
2:1236
SHAMMAI, RABBI
5:689; **8:**191, 213
SOCRATES
3:1088; **5:**61, 167, 220, 301; **7:**95; **8:**519; **9:**118, 737; **10:**243–46, 249; **11:**223, 701; **12:**127, 211, 317
SOLON
2:566, 669, 688; **5:**331, 708
SOPHERIM
1:297–98
SOURON
4:102, 218
STRABO
4:84, 202; **6:**1379, 1398; **7:**203
SULLA
4:105, 202
SYMMACHUS
1:301, 304; **4:**622

T

TATIAN
1:47; **8:**5–6; **9:**504
TERTULLIAN
1:12, 85; **3:**1134; **7:**334, 843; **8:**15, 24, 318; **9:**5–6; **12:**6, 76, 78, 443, 513, 711
THEODOTION
1:11, 301; **7:**92, 156, 163, 180–81, 183, 331
THEON
8:57
THEOPHILUS
1:93; **4:**218
THOMAS À KEMPIS
4:929, 1017; **12:**260, 401
THOMAS OF HARKEL
8:6
THUTMOSE III
1:246–47; **6:**1404, 1434
TIAMAT
1:342, 356; **2:**600; **4:**395, 411, 518, 532, 622, 624; **5:**833; **6:**226, 1425, 1435, 1537; **7:**101, 193; **8:**580
TIMAEUS
4:202; **5:**550
TIMARCHUS
4:93, 95, 103, 110
TISCHENDORF, CONSTANTIN VON
8:7, 10
TRAJAN
1:271; **5:**440; **12:**76, 163, 235, 311
TUKULTI-NINURTA
5:95

U

USHTANI
7:709

V

VALENTINUS
1:15; **9:**498, 506
VAPHRES
4:102
VESPASIAN
4:1131; **8:**16, 23, 247, 343, 659; **9:**242, 404

W

WEN-AMON
6:1398

WESLEY, JOHN
1:102; **2:**1051; **3:**348; **4:**1206; **6:**1346, 1412; **9:**434, 483; **10:**63, 464; **11:**482, 537; **12:**365, 440, 542

X

XERXES
1:247; **3:**675, 685, 696, 698, 855, 859, 863, 868, 878–79, 889, 892, 914, 948, 951, 1081; **4:**204, 227, 229; **6:**1398; **7:**102, 121, 138–39, 190

Z

ZADOKITES
1:935; **5:**843, 867; **6:**5, 1578–79, 1582, 1605

ZAKKUR
1:237; **3:**236

ZENO
5:334; **8:**19; **10:**929

ZEUS
1:760; **3:**1144; **4:**11, 38–39, 60, 193, 218, 229, 232, 254, 263; **5:**611; **7:**25, 61, 114, 128, 143; **8:**22, 24; **10:**88, 198, 201, 220, 232–33, 357; **11:**414, 598, 865. *See also* JUPITER

ZIMRI-LIM
6:10

PLACES

IN THE BIBLE

A

ABANA
3:194
ABARIM MOUNTAINS
1:315; **2:**164, 218; **6:**742, 1525
ABARIM VALLEY
6:1525
ABEL
2:1352–53; **3:**1138, 1165
ABEL-BETH-MAACAH
3:542; **4:**193
ABEL-MAIM
3:542
ABEL-MEHOLAH
3:144
ABEL-MIZRAIM
1:670
ABEL-SHITTIM
2:198
ABILENE
9:80
ABRONAH
2:251, 254
ACACIAS VALLEY
7:336
ACCO
4:78, 233
ACHAIA
4:105; **10:**252, 255, 261, 270, 774, 935; **11:**6, 12, 37, 38, 114, 116–17, 135, 150, 674, 690, 694–95, 746
ACHAR/ACHOR, VALLEY OF
2:631; **3:**328
ACHZIB
7:547
ACRE
4:78
ADAM (CITY)
2:600; **7:**252
ADASA
4:100, 296
ADIDA
4:146–47, 150–51, 171, 174; **9:**404
ADMAH
2:512; **7:**278
ADORA
4:13, 79, 152
ADRAMYTTIUM
10:345
ADRIA
10:351
ADULLAM
2:655, 1144, 1376; **3:**379; **4:**277
AHAVA
3:726; **6:**943; **7:**111, 124
AI
1:216, 217, 219, 253–54, 433; **2:**351, 393, 559, 562–63, 589, 600, 606, 613, 615–16, 625–27, 630–31, 634, 636, 640–41, 651, 686, 706, 885; **3:**686; **4:**78; **6:**1491
AIJALON
2:646–47, 1078; **3:**357, 525; **4:**63, 174
AIJALON, VALLEY OF
2:646; **4:**63
AIN
2:262
AKRA
4:48, 71–72; **7:**25, 147
AKRABATTENE
4:74, 140
AKRABBIM/AKRABBIN
2:262; **4:**74
ALEMA
4:78
ALEXANDRIA
1:8, 11, 18, 46, 88, 89, 93, 127, 192–93, 269, 290–91, 300; **3:**898, 971; **4:**35, 169, 183–84, 199, 228, 255; **5:**439–40, 441, 461, 543, 597, 626, 643, 824; **6:**931, 1413; **7:**155, 700; **8:**15, 28–29, 105, 684; **9:**362, 506; **10:**261; **11:**231, 675; **12:**6, 8, 98
ALMON-DIBLATHAIM
2:164
ALUSH
2:253–54
AMANA
5:403
AMAW
2:179, 181

AMMON
1:245, 248, 259, 990, 1126; **2:**166, 305–6, 770; **3:**416; **4:**74, 228, 263; **6:**10, 857, 859, 894, 1080, 1304, 1347–48, 1396, 1403; **7:**360, 690
AMPHIPOLIS
10:238
ANAB
2:654
ANATHOTH
2:574, 579, 687–89, 701; **3:**33, 686, 817; **6:**5, 8, 575, 675–76, 684, 716, 819–20, 1166; **12:**139
ANGLE, THE (JERUSALEM WALL)
3:1048
ANTI-LEBANON
1:245; **2:**662, 1266; **6:**1379
ANTIOCH (AT JERUSALEM)
4:10, 60, 217–18, 232, 255
ANTIOCH (PISIDIAN)
10:14, 188, 191, 194–95, 197, 201–2, 206, 254, 359
ANTIOCH (SYRIAN)
1:49, 94, 127, 192–93, 269, 270, 291, 300; **4:**11, 17, 23, 69, 93, 117, 120–21, 129, 132–33, 137, 138, 140, 147, 183, 214, 217, 222–23, 230, 240, 243, 255, 257, 268, 270, 282; **5:**271, 824; **7:**24; **8:**46, 49, 52, 95, 103, 105, 107, 137, 567; **9:**6, 9, 506; **10:**59, 60, 113, 175–78, 181–82, 188–89, 191, 196, 199–200, 203–7, 211, 218–22, 225, 257–59, 270, 294, 376, 407, 735, 754, 756, 776; **11:**163, 193, 205, 217, 221–25, 227, 230–36, 241–42, 245, 248, 256, 293, 295, 312, 324, 343, 814; **12:**186, 454, 574
ANTIPATRIS
10:313
ANTONIA (FORTRESS)
3:756, 768
APHEK
1:247; **2:**655, 662, 717, 1000, 1018, 1183, 1188, 1193; **3:**238
APOLLONIA
10:238
APPIAN WAY
10:355, 357
AR
2:164–65, 184
ARABAH
2:677; **3:**243; **6:**1194, 1474, 1595; **7:**362, 837
ARABAH, SEA OF THE
3:243
ARABIA
1:214, 262, 271, 408, 989, 1018, 1135; **2:**161; **3:**82, 590; **4:**104, 133, 562; **5:**695; **6:**187, 520, 966, 1360, 1377, 1379–80, 1415; **7:**362; **8:**46; **9:**243; **11:**216, 302–3
ARABIAN DESERT
1:214–15, 245; **3:**878; **6:**187, 1296, 1379
ARAD
1:224, 253–54; **2:**98, 158, 163, 252, 254–57, 616, 655
ARADUS
4:147, 170
ARAH
2:662
ARAM
2:186, 824, 830–31; **3:**82, 143, 146–47, 160, 176, 192, 201–3, 212, 215, 233, 238–39, 251, 529, 536, 542, 560, 597–99, 607; **4:**63; **5:**326; **6:**108, 174, 183, 878, 897, 1076, 1208, 1237, 1324, 1360, 1378, 1442; **7:**286
ARAM-NAHARAIM
1:510; **2:**767
ARARAT
1:392
ARBA
2:654
ARBATTA
4:78
ARBELA
3:995; **4:**110; **6:**11
AREOPAGUS
8:14; **10:**242, 245–46, 247, 271; **12:**297. *See also* MARS HILL
ARIMATHEA
8:105, 494, 538, 725; **9:**29, 45, 341, 443, 450, 464–65, 468, 799, 808, 835; **10:**132
ARMAGEDDON
12:543–44, 677
ARNON
1:261; **2:**158, 164–66, 184, 248, 308; **6:**1348, 1353
AROER
2:250
ARPAD
6:897
ARTISANS, VALLEY OF
3:828
ARUBBOTH
3:48
ARVAD
6:1361, 1374–75
ASCALON
3:1107
ASHDOD
1:248; **2:**123, 616, 660, 1005–7; **3:**337, 848, 1107; **4:**66, 111, 130, 175; **6:**36, 180, 182, 885,

1232, 1349, 1355, 1398, 1416; **7:**361, 374–76, 686, 805
ASHER
1:666; **2:**263, 660, 677, 694, 743, 802–3; **3:**320, 351; **6:**1604–5
ASHER GATE
6:1606
ASHKELON
1:248–49; **2:**739, 850–51, 1206; **3:**1107; **6:**885, 1077, 1349, 1355; **7:**361, 686, 805
ASHKENAZ
1:74
ASHTAROTH
3:368
ASHTEROTH-KARNAIM
4:80
ASHTORETH
3:96
ASHUR
1:246
ASIA
1:13, 47, 88, 161, 232, 245, 266–67, 269, 408, 822, 1166; **2:**595; **3:**42, 82, 409, 1101, 1108; **4:**4–5, 30–31, 40, 60, 104–5, 120, 154, 170, 192, 222, 229, 248; **5:**612; **6:**1233, 1378, 1443, 1516; **7:**10, 111, 140–41, 456, 639, 648, 661, 672, 690, 810; **8:**16, 44, 46, 48, 49; **9:**498, 504, 571; **10:**121, 147, 188, 214, 224, 226–27, 230–31, 267, 270, 271–72, 276, 281, 283, 296–97, 318, 345, 374, 390, 686, 754, 762, 1001; **11:**11–12, 20, 42, 55, 108, 115, 160, 184, 191–92, 205, 222, 361, 363–65, 376, 397, 399, 401, 411, 422, 465, 469, 474, 564, 582, 616, 665, 674, 838, 857, 884; **12:**232–38, 240, 246–48, 251, 259, 260–62, 270, 274, 277, 280, 287, 292, 295, 299, 301–2, 306, 311–12, 315, 318, 325, 368, 370, 475, 515, 545, 562, 565, 573, 658, 684–85, 710, 733
ASKALON
4:130, 140
ASSHUR
2:178, 192; **3:**995; **4:**30; **6:**556; **7:**595
ASSOS
10:277
ASSUR
6:1380
ASSYRIA
1:237, 247–48, 250, 264–66, 283, 351, 408; **2:**281–82, 440, 528, 565, 572–73, 574, 638, 658, 662, 688, 859; **3:**248, 251, 260–61, 265, 269, 272, 302, 522, 542, 597–98, 629–30, 649, 677, 699, 713–14, 865, 871, 976–77, 992–93, 994–96, 1050, 1069–70, 1078, 1095, 1097–99, 1112, 1124, 1144; **4:**32, 159, 204, 229, 1009–1010; **5:**174, 274, 544, 674; **6:**20, 36, 39, 61, 98, 102, 112–13, 116–17, 119, 124, 129, 132–34, 136–37, 145–46, 149, 155, 159, 161, 175, 181–82, 185, 196, 204, 227, 230–32, 237, 239, 252–53, 255–56, 259, 261–62, 276, 291–93, 295, 300, 304, 314–15, 327, 330, 334, 342–43, 353, 357, 375–76, 380, 386, 394, 400, 403, 411, 436, 439, 454, 478, 481, 547, 556, 559, 562, 581, 601–2, 684, 762, 797, 807, 886, 917–18, 1069, 1076–77, 1114, 1150, 1159, 1203, 1220, 1232, 1245, 1250, 1253, 1296, 1304–5, 1316, 1321–22, 1324, 1326, 1348–49, 1360, 1369, 1378–80, 1398, 1402, 1406, 1408, 1410, 1416, 1422–30, 1434–35, 1438–39, 1442–44, 1499, 1505, 1508, 1515–16, 1522, 1595; **7:**50, 62, 184, 200, 234, 246, 248, 257–58, 261, 265, 267, 269–70, 272, 275, 278, 282, 295, 330, 343, 357–58, 374–75, 377, 395–96, 425, 465, 493, 534, 542, 547, 550, 568, 571, 573, 576, 582, 593–97, 601, 604–6, 612, 614–16, 618–19, 661–62, 664, 675, 690–91, 696, 741, 753, 779, 815, 817–18; **8:**577; **12:**298
ATAD
1:670
ATAROTH
2:250
ATHENS
1:247; **2:**566, 669, 696, 753; **4:**10, 60, 216, 228–29, 232, 254; **6:**414; **8:**14, 17, 19–20, 23; **9:**85; **10:**147, 240, 242–46, 250, 271, 755, 773–75; **11:**675, 681, 707; **12:**277
ATROTH-SHOPHAN
2:250
AVEN, VALLEY OF
7:361
AZAZ
1:1112
AZEKAH
2:646; **3:**827
AZMAVETH
3:686, 838
AZMON
2:262
AZOTUS
3:1107; **4:**66, 130, 132, 175; **10:**144. *See also* ASHDOD
AZOTUS, MOUNT
4:111

B

BAALAH
2:1248
BAALAH OF JUDAH
2:1248

BAALATH
3:505
BAALE-JUDAH
2:1248
BAAL-HAMON
5:433
BAAL-MEON
2:250; **6:**1353
BAAL-PEOR
2:5, 8–9, 11, 169–70, 181, 195, 197–98, 199, 202, 207, 244–46, 310, 312, 316, 321, 348, 907; **7:**269, 288; **12:**578. *See also* BAAL OF PEOR *in PERSONS IN THE BIBLE*
BAAL-PERAZIM
2:1243; **3:**382, 388
BAAL-ZEPHON
2:253
BABEL
1:336, 408, 410–13, 415, 422; **2:**818; **4:**256, 484, 898; **5:**294, 325, 445, 506, 523; **6:**548, 814, 1126; **7:**39, 73, 699, 778; **8:**132
BABEL, TOWER OF
1:336, 422; **2:**818; **4:**256, 484; **5:**294, 325, 523; **6:**548, 814, 1126; **7:**39, 73, 699; **8:**132
BABYLON (OT)
1:9, 31, 68, 83, 209, 221, 232, 237, 246–248, 250, 264, 266–69, 291, 295, 297, 303, 365, 388, 411, 412, 422, 438, 680, 736, 770, 900, 1182; **2:**311, 319, 406, 417, 440, 502–4, 520, 528, 547, 572–73, 600, 602, 687, 723, 725, 731, 736, 861, 932, 996, 1024, 1209, 1258, 1276; **3:**272, 274, 286, 287, 289, 290, 293, 294, 630, 635, 636, 654–55, 656, 665, 666, 667, 669, 677, 678, 679, 681, 684, 685, 687, 690, 698–99, 703, 705–8, 710, 714, 718, 721–22, 725, 728, 730, 737, 743, 762, 768, 773, 777, 796, 813, 834, 846, 859, 871, 878, 890, 948, 1081, 1097, 1099, 1102, 1120, 1124, 1171; **4:**30–31, 34, 40, 61, 84–85, 157, 197, 228, 254, 256, 442, 661, 856, 1009, 1024, 1072, 1125, 1190, 1195, 1207, 1224, 1227–28; **5:**45, 78, 91, 92, 174, 198, 271, 274, 480; **6:**10, 14, 17, 20, 37, 66, 149, 155–61, 163, 167, 185–86, 188–89, 204, 208, 214, 221, 231, 248, 270–71, 280–82, 284–85, 297, 303–5, 313, 316, 327, 329–30, 334–35, 342–44, 348, 353, 356, 377–78, 390–91, 394, 399, 406–8, 410–13, 417–19, 423, 431, 436, 439–40, 443–44, 449, 454, 472, 482, 489–91, 498, 520, 556, 559–60, 562, 564, 567–68, 576, 580, 582, 585, 620, 723, 731, 733, 743, 757–58, 762–63, 766, 768, 778, 782–84, 786, 791–97, 805–7, 815, 819, 830, 838, 848–49, 851–52, 858–59, 861, 866–67, 868, 874, 878–79, 882–84, 911–20, 925, 939, 941–46, 952, 974–75, 980, 985, 988, 993–94, 1015, 1045, 1065, 1075, 1078–79, 1085, 1114, 1130, 1143, 1147, 1155, 1157, 1161, 1176, 1185, 1194–95, 1219, 1222, 1233, 1248–52, 1266, 1269–70, 1273, 1286, 1296, 1301, 1304, 1325–26, 1330, 1338, 1362, 1364, 1366, 1369, 1383–84, 1388, 1398, 1413, 1416, 1420–21, 1427, 1429, 1432, 1435–36, 1456–57, 1464, 1489, 1537–38; **7:**5, 21, 23–24, 26, 28, 30, 34, 39, 44, 50, 61–62, 65–66, 71–73, 80–82, 84, 89–90, 111, 113, 121, 139, 140, 176, 187, 190, 192, 194, 356, 414, 451, 547, 563, 567–68, 571–73, 575–76, 582, 587, 594–95, 626, 646–47, 661, 699, 709, 715, 717, 719, 725, 737–38, 747, 754, 759–61, 765, 775, 778, 784, 786–87, 804, 818
BABYLON (NT)
8:34–35, 131, 147, 272–73, 303, 517; **9:**94, 221, 372, 404; **10:**109, 128, 299, 401, 415, 424, 718; **11:**106, 806; **12:**235–37, 246, 318, 509–10, 513, 519, 521, 529, 533, 535–36, 548–49, 551, 565–66, 569, 574, 577, 579, 587, 589, 591, 594, 596, 602, 606, 609, 612–14, 621, 624, 626, 630, 633–34, 644, 646, 648–53, 656, 659–60, 663, 666–67, 669, 675, 677–78, 680–87, 692–97, 699–700, 702, 707, 715–17, 720–25, 730, 734
BABYLONIA
1:68–69, 408, 411, 422, 996; **3:**654, 699; **4:**18, 93, 183, 197, 248, 253, 297; **5:**798, 801, 993, 1075–77; **6:**1078, 1080–81, 1086–87, 1088, 1089, 1091, 1092, 1098, 1108, 1114, 1120–21, 1136, 1140, 1141, 1155, 1166, 1172, 1185, 1189, 1199, 1203, 1215, 1220, 1246, 1249, 1250, 1253, 1271, 1292–93, 1296, 1302, 1304, 1305, 1325, 1326, 1344, 1348–50, 1355, 1361, 1365, 1369, 1403, 1410, 1415, 1421, 1427, 1436–37, 1443, 1446–47, 1453–54, 1458, 1460, 1466, 1480, 1515, 1522, 1530–31, 1536–37, 1555; **7:**6, 31, 184, 193, 330, 396, 435–37, 454–55, 595, 601
BACA
4:1013
BAHURIM
2:1326; **3:**34
BAKERS' STREET
1:223
BALQUIDDER VALLEY
9:462
BAMOTH
2:164
BAMOTH-BAAL
2:185
BASHAN
1:308; **2:**21, 123, 165–67, 248, 293, 307–9, 512, 536, 683; **3:**338; **4:**944–45; **6:**82, 742, 1374–75, 1528; **7:**374, 376, 588, 602, 817

BASKAMA
4:152
BATH-RABBIM
5:426
BEALOTH
3:48
BEAUTIFUL GATE
10:77
BEER
2:164–65
BEEROTH
2:1230; **3:**686
BEER-SHEBA
1:219, 221–22, 224, 491–92, 528–29, 541, 652, 828; **2:**570, 694, 993, 1026, 1223, 1332, 1380; **3:**140, 232, 285, 336, 616, 827; **4:**282; **6:**1294, 1407; **7:**394, 419, 455, 481
BEKKA VALLEY
1:245
BENE-JAAKAN
2:254
BEN-HINNOM
See HINNOM, VALLEY OF
BENJAMIN (TOWN)
2:701
BENJAMIN/BENJAMINITE (TERRITORY)
2:547, 556, 562–63, 574, 600, 646, 648, 659, 677–78, 681, 687, 691, 694, 737, 740, 745, 876, 884–85, 973, 1016, 1018, 1068–69, 1216; **3:**18, 33, 39, 520, 684, 686, 824–25, 828, 838, 1079; **4:**228; **6:**575, 1526, 1605; **7:**247–48; **8:**147
BENJAMIN GATE
3:768; **6:**1606
BERACAH, VALLEY OF
3:559; **7:**330
BEREA
4:110
BEROEA
4:281; **10:**237, 239–40; **11:**115, 707
BEROTHAH
6:1601
BEROTHAI
3:415
BETHANY
1:186; **8:**407, 474, 659, 699; **9:**169, 353, 367, 373, 488, 528, 681, 685, 701, 804
BETH-ARABAH
2:678
BETH-ARBEL
7:273, 275
BETH-AVEN
2:630; **7:**242, 247, 272, 779
BETH-AZMAVETH
3:686
BETH-BAAL-MEON
6:1353
BETHBASI
4:118
BETH-EDEN
2:594; **7:**361
BETH-EKED
3:223
BETHEL (CITY)
1:254, 259, 277–78, 424, 432–33, 516, 519, 541, 557, 565, 567, 584–85, 659, 718, 1164, 1186; **2:**148, 234, 278, 363, 559, 561–62, 565, 571–72, 574–75, 579, 606, 612, 615, 626, 631, 634, 636, 646–47, 655, 681, 687, 717, 743–45, 748, 864, 871, 885, 1019; **3:**5, 22, 104, 106, 108, 110, 174, 176–78, 226, 252, 257–58, 530, 532, 686, 767, 993; **4:**111; **5:**524, 850; **6:**15, 724, 891, 1118, 1208, 1290, 1316, 1509; **7:**205, 242, 247, 260–61, 265, 272, 275, 284, 287–88, 357, 376, 380, 388, 394, 410, 419, 421, 552, 792, 798–99; **11:**871
BETHEL (SANCTUARY/SHRINE)
1:541, 584–85; **2:**234, 278, 565, 571, 579; **3:**5, 22, 104, 178, 252, 257–58; **5:**850; **6:**724; **7:**205, 242, 260, 272, 376, 380, 410, 421, 552
BETH EL, MOUNT
4:110
BETHESDA
1:1160; **3:**766
BETH-EZEL
7:547
BETH-GILGAL
3:838; **4:**110
BETH-HACCHEREM
3:765, 768
BETH-HAGGAN
3:220
BETH-HARAN
2:250
BETH-HORON
4:57, 63, 100, 150, 281, 295
BETH-JESHIMOTH
6:1353
BETH-LEAPHRAH
7:547
BETHLEHEM
1:87, 585, 587, 605; **2:**678, 765, 863, 870, 875, 892, 899–901, 908, 911, 913, 920, 922–23, 932, 939–42, 945, 1098–99, 1108, 1110, 1134–35, 1217, 1376; **3:**378, 686, 838; **4:**118, 306, 1212; **6:**396, 414, 815, 978, 1080; **7:**351, 533, 538,

BETHLEHEM *(continued)*
567, 570, 572–73; **8:**111, 129, 139–40, 142–44, 147–50, 251; **9:**8, 42, 63, 65–68, 72–73, 462, 624; **11:**417
BETH-MAACAH
2:1352; **3:**542; **4:**193
BETH-MILLO
2:816–17
BETH-NIMRAH
2:250
BETH-OPHRAH
7:547
BETH-PEOR
2:310; **7:**269
BETHPHAGE
9:367
BETH-REHOB
2:1266, 1279; **3:**416
BETHSAIDA
8:272, 275, 594, 619; **9:**195, 219–21, 243, 319, 578
BETH-SHAN
2:1198, 1212, 1359; **4:**80, 101, 147, 228, 276, 297
BETH-SHEMESH
2:694, 1010, 1012–14, 1249; **3:**48, 242
BETH-TOGARMAH
6:1377–78, 1516
BETHULIA
3:1075, 1082, 1085–89, 1099, 1104, 1112–13, 1115, 1124, 1127, 1129–30, 1132, 1137, 1139, 1148, 1154–55, 1159, 1161–62, 1165, 1167, 1171, 1173, 1178, 1180–81; **4:**101, 297; **5:**630
BETH-ZAITH
4:96
BETHZATHA
9:578
BETH-ZECHARIAH
4:63, 88–89, 110, 129, 281–82
BETH-ZUR
1:1170; **3:**765, 769; **4:**17, 63, 69, 87–90, 96, 115, 121, 140, 146–47, 152, 156, 164, 196, 266, 282
BEYOND THE JORDAN
1:670; **2:**293, 607, 1198, 1213; **6:**1574; **7:**690; **8:**385
BEYOND THE RIVER
1:9, 250, 267, 1118; **2:**859, 1280; **3:**685, 699, 703, 709, 721–22, 730, 756, 768, 780, 899; **4:**249; **6:**1496; **7:**709, 738
BEZEK
2:736, 1055
BEZER
2:265
BITHYNIA
3:409; **4:**4; **8:**15; **11:**469; **12:**76, 163, 325
BOCHIM
2:647, 747–48
BOZRAH
4:77; **6:**277; **7:**362, 855
BROAD WALL
3:768, 839
BUZ
4:562

C

CABUL
3:84
CAESAREA
1:15, 94, 301; **4:**13, 78, 152, 210; **7:**700; **8:**105, 464, 717; **9:**270; **10:**137, 145, 162, 164, 174, 181, 258, 288–90, 305, 311, 313–14, 317–18, 324–26, 330, 361, 737, 776; **11:**474–75, 884; **12:**534
CAESAREA PHILIPPI
8:76, 342–43, 526, 622, 630, 635, 719; **9:**90, 199, 205, 353, 611; **12:**245
CALAH
3:995; **5:**95
CALNEH
7:399
CALVARY
4:858; **5:**377; **6:**461, 469; **8:**490, 722; **10:**477, 539, 578, 671; **11:**531
CANA
5:298; **6:**27, 70; **9:**502–3, 508, 536, 538–39, 543, 546, 575–76, 584, 591, 599, 601, 613, 653, 727, 832–33, 856–58, 864
CANAAN
1:41, 91, 165–66, 232–33, 248–49, 253–55, 273–76, 306–8, 316, 388, 404–5, 408, 416, 422, 424–27, 433, 438, 441, 451, 481, 491, 503–4, 513, 515, 518, 541, 552–53, 557–58, 562–63, 573, 590, 593, 598, 600, 622, 627, 629, 634, 638–39, 644–45, 652, 654, 659–60, 665–66, 669–70, 674, 949, 995, 1124, 1138, 1143, 1171, 1173, 1179; **2:**4–5, 10–11, 16, 18, 20–21, 35, 37, 47, 51, 69, 87, 89, 92, 100, 121–23, 129, 136–37, 148, 159, 163, 169, 180, 182, 191, 198, 202, 211, 215, 218–19, 221, 230, 244, 248, 252, 254–55, 262–68, 374, 547, 555–56, 564, 567, 571, 573, 575–77, 588, 594, 601, 607–8, 613, 616, 619, 625, 634, 636–37, 639, 642, 646–47, 649, 651, 659, 667, 670–71, 673, 677, 695–96, 714, 718, 723–24, 726, 731–33, 735–37, 739–40, 745–50, 752–53, 755, 759–60, 765–66, 772, 774, 779, 781–82, 787–89, 795–97, 803, 807, 816, 824, 826, 830–31, 837–38, 858, 863, 865, 870, 878, 885, 901, 1361; **3:**4, 50, 70, 224, 400, 869, 1090,

1115, 1119, 1172; **4:**115, 485, 945, 992, 1220; **5:**6, 11, 113, 174, 388, 543–44; **6:**181, 625, 865, 966, 1147, 1160, 1168, 1216, 1244, 1246, 1275, 1278–79, 1282, 1285, 1290, 1380, 1437, 1458, 1463, 1466, 1485, 1489–90, 1530, 1600–1601; **7:**51, 203, 264, 269, 277, 357, 437, 455–56, 550, 601; **10:**490, 514; **12:**52, 136–37, 139, 488, 725

CANNEH
6:1380

CAPERNAUM
8:62, 111, 167, 226, 228, 234, 272–73, 275, 317, 371, 374, 513, 525, 539–40, 542–43, 547, 558, 563, 566, 591, 603, 636, 642, 651; **9:**23, 103, 107, 110–14, 116, 120, 155, 219–21, 321, 409, 575, 596, 599, 608, 809; **10:**232

CAPHAR-SALAMA
4:98, 289

CAPHTOR
2:306; **7:**424, 699

CAPPADOCIA
4:4, 117, 120, 170

CARCHEMISH
1:266; **2:**181; **3:**286, 289, 649; **6:**559, 761, 882–83, 1077, 1326, 1348, 1361, 1403, 1415; **7:**39, 424, 626

CARIA
4:170

CARMEL
2:1166, 1169, 1211; **5:**426; **6:**281, 1111; **7:**352, 602

CARMEL, MOUNT
1:1067; **2:**792, 797, 1088; **3:**6, 130, 135, 137–40, 142–43, 162, 169, 173, 177–78, 189, 225; **4:**78; **6:**9, 183, 913; **7:**188, 421, 481

CARNAIM
4:78, 80–81, 249, 276

CASIPHIA
3:727

CASPIN
4:275–76

CAUDA
10:348

CENCHREAE
10:761, 766, 773, 969; **11:**38, 135, 151

CHALDEA
1:422; **4:**50; **6:**413, 1233, 1246, 1325; **7:**810

CHAPHENATHA
4:146

CHASPHO
4:275

CHEBAR
6:943, 1075, 1081, 1109–10, 1120, 1129, 1136, 1175, 1182, 1184, 1503, 1529, 1560; **7:**111

CHEPHIRAH
3:686

CHINNERETH
2:262; **3:**338

CHINNERETH, SEA OF
2:262; **3:**338

CHIOS
10:278

CHOBA
3:1171

CHORAZIN
8:272, 275; **9:**219–21, 243, 319

CILICIA
3:82; **4:**133, 140, 248; **6:**1374; **8:**45–46; **10:**225, 305, 374; **11:**163, 217, 222; **12:**186

CITY OF MOAB
2:184

CITY OF THE SUN-GOD
6:1418. *See also* HELIOPOLIS

CNIDUS
4:170; **10:**346

COELE-SYRIA
1:269; **4:**4–5, 12, 55, 62, 129, 133, 145–46, 205–6, 214, 223, 233, 260; **6:**1348

COLOSSAE
11:567, 580, 588, 590, 665, 667–68, 674, 884, 892, 898, 902–3; **12:**27, 41, 522, 577, 586

CORINTH
1:192, 1073; **2:**768; **3:**395, 487, 544; **4:**105, 170; **8:**13–14, 20, 73, 562; **9:**292, 313; **10:**147, 215, 220, 252–58, 261–62, 267, 272–73, 283, 396, 718, 732, 739, 742, 755, 761–62, 766, 773–77, 781, 787–88, 801, 803–4, 807–8, 811, 814–15, 817–18, 828, 832, 838, 840–41, 844, 846, 849, 855, 864–65, 869, 875, 880–81, 893, 895–97, 899, 905, 909, 913, 917, 923, 927, 931, 934, 937, 940–41, 943–44, 947, 954, 959, 964, 967, 969–71, 979–80, 982, 984, 988, 998, 1000; **11:**3, 5–6, 11–15, 17–19, 21, 32, 37–38, 48–50, 55, 59, 63, 74–75, 102, 112, 114–17, 121, 126, 128, 134–35, 141, 145, 148, 151, 169–70, 172–76, 179, 189, 202, 222, 273–74, 294–95, 327, 409, 439, 451, 543, 674, 681–82, 707, 715, 790, 812, 842, 858, 878; **12:**7

CORINTH, TEMPLE AT
10:894

CORNER GATE
3:759, 767, 802, 839

COS
4:102, 170

COURT OF THE GENTILES
3:502; **8:**405; **10:**297

COURT OF THE GUARD
3:769, 839; **6:**849, 1016

CRETE
1:408; **2:**192, 306; **4:**135, 143, 170; **6:**1349, 1355; **7:**424, 690; **10:**346, 348, 351; **11:**465, 781, 857, 864, 872, 874
CUN
3:415
CUSH
1:351, 408; **2:**109; **3:**268, 538; **4:**707, 946; **6:**175, 376, 882, 1361, 1379, 1402, 1407, 1415–16, 1517; **7:**147, 424–25, 573, 616, 661, 671, 690–92, 699–701
CUTH
2:573
CYPRUS
4:30, 35, 121, 127, 170, 222, 260, 275; **5:**564; **6:**203, 600, 638, 1361, 1374–75; **10:**97, 175, 189, 191, 225, 290, 346; **11:**222
CYRENE
4:170, 183, 202; **6:**850; **8:**489, 722, 724; **9:**13, 450–51, 454, 461, 829; **10:**175, 189, 755, 763

D

DAMASCUS
1:248, 265, 285–87, 289, 439, 445; **2:**181, 1266; **3:**93–94, 96, 143–44, 151, 192, 194, 197, 203, 212, 251, 599, 703, 756, 1171; **4:**133, 137, 140, 145; **5:**270, 394, 426; **6:**36, 107–8, 111, 116–17, 149, 173–75, 354, 878, 896–97, 919, 1076, 1129, 1324, 1360, 1377–80, 1601; **7:**342, 353, 355, 358, 360–62, 375, 395, 399, 804, 844; **8:**565; **9:**284, 427, 487; **10:**52, 128, 146, 149–51, 153–55, 176, 227, 304–7, 336–39, 376, 401, 415, 417, 567; **11:**20, 27, 138, 158, 160–61, 163, 214–16
DAMASCUS ROAD
5:394; **6:**1129; **9:**427, 487; **10:**52, 149–50, 153, 176, 227, 304–5, 307, 336–38, 376, 401, 415, 417, 567; **11:**214–15
DAMASCUS, WALL OF
11:159–61
DAN
2:363, 574, 646–47, 677, 697, 726, 743, 864–65, 871, 993, 1223, 1332, 1352, 1380; **3:**5, 104, 140, 226, 252, 257–58, 616, 993; **5:**850; **6:**647, 1407, 1509, 1604, 1606; **7:**205, 260–61, 376, 419
DAPHNE
4:222
DATHEMA
4:77–78
DAVID, CITY OF
(*or* DAVID'S CITY) **2:**563, 740, 1113, 1235–39, 1247, 1249, 1251, 1256, 1324; **3:**20, 37, 40, 69, 169, 377, 384, 494, 505, 587, 759, 769, 839; **4:**36, 46, 171, 217, 1176, 1183; **5:**757; **6:**148, 194, 1561; **7:**147, 427, 567; **8:**148; **9:**16–17, 19, 63, 65, 341, 360
DAVID, TOWER OF
5:403
DEAD SEA
1:245, 278, 285, 287, 289, 293–94, 438–39, 473, 565, 665; **2:**122, 164, 218, 262–63, 612, 648, 677, 691, 1154; **3:**337, 538, 559; **4:**74, 115, 325; **5:**273, 524, 634, 668; **6:**168, 890, 1348, 1364, 1474, 1525, 1595–96, 1598, 1601, 1605, 1607; **7:**323, 336, 352, 381, 437, 690, 837; **8:**598; **9:**293; **11:**799; **12:**347, 489, 665
DEBIR
2:646, 648, 654, 671, 673–74, 678, 701, 737–38; **3:**332
DECAPOLIS
1:271; **8:**174, 339, 582–83, 585, 592; **9:**102, 186–88
DECISION/VERDICT, VALLEY OF
7:334
DEDAN
4:562; **6:**1354, 1377–79, 1518
DELOS
4:60, 277
DERBE
10:197, 200, 225; **11:**191
DESSAU
4:287
DIBON
1:249; **2:**164, 166, 250, 254; **3:**827; **6:**168
DOK
4:176, 178
DOPHKAH
2:253
DOR
2:655; **4:**9, 168–69, 172
DOTHAN
1:599; **2:**683; **3:**201, 1109
DOTHAN VALLEY
2:683
DRAGON'S SPRING
3:759
DUMAH
6:149, 185, 187–88, 520
DUNG GATE
3:759, 767–68, 838
DURA
5:341; **7:**61

E

EASTERN SEA
6:1601

EAST GATE
3:363, 451, 767, 770; **6:**1172, 1182, 1184, 1186, 1541–43, 1545, 1548, 1557, 1559–60, 1570, 1573, 1588–89, 1595
EBAL, MOUNT
2:486–88, 491, 634, 636; **3:**691
EBENEZER
2:1000, 1018; **6:**1349
ECBATANA
3:706–7, 859, 878, 987, 989, 993, 1007–8, 1011, 1022–23, 1026–28, 1031, 1033, 1038, 1045, 1048, 1052, 1069, 1098, 1100; **4:**30, 193, 253; **6:**399; **7:**29
EDEN, GARDEN OF
1:76, 88, 278, 329, 336, 350–51, 359, 365–66, 375, 398, 405, 417, 434, 516, 558, 1085; **2:**80, 183, 748, 887; **4:**256, 1100; **5:**53, 103, 314, 364, 369, 412, 427, 693, 758; **6:**335, 441–42, 447, 1086, 1106, 1380, 1391–95, 1423, 1426, 1429–30, 1432, 1487, 1493, 1531, 1538, 1595, 1597–99; **7:**177, 317, 750; **9:**167, 458; **10:**563, 571; **12:**50, 145, 574, 614, 723. *See also* PARADISE *in PLACES IN THE BIBLE*; GARDEN: THE GARDEN *in SUBJECTS AND THEMES*
EDEN-HARRAN-ASSUR
6:1377
EDER
1:585
EDOM
1:245, 248, 250, 259, 563, 990; **2:**158, 161–64, 166, 190–91, 252, 262, 305, 309, 677, 787; **3:**184, 318, 414, 559–60, 568, 591, 598; **4:**80, 89, 916–17; **6:**187, 277–78, 520, 857, 966, 1294, 1347–48, 1352, 1354, 1427, 1474, 1479; **7:**336, 361–63, 426–28, 437; **10:**219
EDREI
2:167
EGLON
2:646, 648
EGYPT
1:10, 14, 18, 75, 83, 87, 93, 151, 155, 209, 214–15, 230–33, 235, 245–49, 253–55, 257, 266–72, 285, 295, 299–300, 304, 306–8, 311–12, 314, 317–18, 365, 405, 419, 424, 427–29, 432–34, 446–47, 451–54, 468, 473, 504, 527, 560, 579–80, 592–93, 595, 598–600, 604, 612, 614–16, 620–22, 624, 627–28, 633–35, 638–39, 643–46, 651–56, 659, 669–70, 672, 674, 679–80, 690, 692, 694–96, 700, 702–5, 713–15, 717, 719–21, 725–26, 728, 735, 739, 742–43, 746, 748–49, 752, 754–55, 757–59, 763, 766, 768, 770–73, 777–78, 780–82, 785–86, 788–90, 793–96, 799–802, 806–7, 809, 812–15, 818, 824–25, 834, 868–69, 887, 889, 931, 937–38, 949, 973, 991–92, 995–96, 1005, 1008, 1017, 1044, 1084, 1118, 1124–25, 1132, 1135–36, 1152, 1157–58, 1164, 1171, 1174, 1180–81; **2:**10–11, 16, 19, 32, 34–35, 39, 51, 54, 86, 94, 96, 99, 105, 107, 109, 120, 123–24, 127, 129, 135–37, 141, 159–64, 177, 181–82, 188, 192, 195, 200, 207, 219, 221, 250, 252–53, 256, 262, 271, 281, 283, 306, 308, 329, 342, 345, 359, 362, 369–70, 374, 406, 408, 411–14, 417, 422, 426, 461–62, 470, 480–81, 501, 503–4, 506, 510, 543–44, 546–48, 552, 555, 570, 574, 576, 588–90, 594, 599–600, 602, 607–8, 612, 616, 619, 626, 638, 648, 662, 668, 688, 740, 747, 752–53, 755–56, 781, 783, 792, 795–97, 804, 809, 819, 830, 833, 853, 865, 876, 878, 901, 977, 988, 1001, 1003, 1010–11, 1027, 1047, 1050, 1062, 1085, 1087, 1256; **3:**37, 39–40, 49–50, 53, 72, 82, 89–90, 93, 95–96, 101, 104, 132, 155, 184, 253, 265, 286–89, 293–94, 353, 386, 408, 499, 591, 629, 649, 654, 670, 680, 698–99, 708, 710, 713, 721–22, 735, 747, 756, 761, 782, 785, 809, 811–12, 846, 860, 878, 941, 956, 970–71, 977, 980, 983, 1001, 1004, 1018, 1040, 1050, 1077, 1099, 1101, 1106, 1118, 1124–25, 1137; **4:**3–5, 9–10, 12, 30–31, 34–36, 40–41, 50, 66, 95, 102, 104, 107, 122, 127, 133, 140, 144, 152, 188, 190–91, 197, 199, 206, 217–18, 226–29, 249, 255, 260, 270, 282, 329, 410, 513, 581, 604, 611, 857, 872, 916, 937, 946, 992, 1000, 1004, 1017, 1024, 1028, 1035, 1065, 1074, 1105, 1110, 1207, 1220, 1224–25, 1247, 1252, 1268; **5:**2–4, 6–7, 61, 96, 122, 135, 160, 170, 227, 257, 261, 271–73, 275, 322, 326, 334, 437, 439, 441, 445, 459, 461, 469, 496, 517, 525–26, 528–32, 534–36, 540, 542–44, 557, 560, 569–71, 573–74, 578, 584–85, 590, 596–98, 604, 606, 610, 612, 621–22, 643, 651, 654, 664, 672, 692, 695, 739, 757, 793, 812, 818, 828, 833, 856; **6:**8, 11–12, 15, 36–37, 62, 112–113, 145–46, 149, 157, 173, 175, 180–82, 202, 222, 226–27, 230–31, 237, 239, 247, 253–54, 259–62, 282, 284, 291, 293, 297, 342, 375–76, 378, 382, 389, 391, 394, 400, 403, 421, 432, 444, 454, 549, 555, 559–60, 567, 576, 584, 599, 601–2, 639, 669, 671, 677, 697, 733, 741, 743, 745, 762, 774, 795, 842, 848, 859, 861, 864–68, 872–74, 876, 878, 882–85, 890, 892, 917–19, 925, 931, 939, 941–42, 955, 989, 994, 1065, 1076–80, 1085, 1147, 1154, 1156, 1216, 1220, 1232–33, 1238, 1246, 1248–49, 1253, 1266, 1269, 1274–82, 1288–92, 1302, 1305, 1312–13, 1316, 1319–22, 1324–27, 1329, 1348–50, 1356, 1359, 1361–62, 1366, 1368, 1375, 1379–80, 1387–88, 1396, 1398, 1400–18, 1420–24, 1427, 1429–30, 1432, 1434–40, 1442–45, 1455, 1463,

EGYPT *(continued)*
1466, 1490–91, 1495, 1586, 1598, 1601–2; **7:**5, 24–25, 28, 50, 111, 140–43, 147, 184, 200, 205, 220, 225, 234–35, 257–58, 260–62, 264–67, 269, 273, 277–79, 281–82, 285–87, 289–90, 296, 336, 346–47, 355, 357–58, 365, 369, 374–76, 380–82, 392, 396, 406, 411, 424–25, 438, 467, 516, 546, 579, 582, 588–89, 594, 616, 661, 667, 670–72, 690–91, 699–700, 709, 717, 722, 730, 741, 792, 805, 810, 813, 815, 818, 839, 860; **8:**6, 34, 45, 49, 51, 105, 111, 130, 134, 144, 146, 148–50, 163, 175, 325, 492, 616; **9:**42, 63, 72–73, 170, 414, 420–21, 504, 542, 637, 691, 742; **10:**126–28, 192, 197, 261, 298, 398, 405, 424, 471, 511–12, 514, 534, 546, 548, 551, 553, 556, 566, 571, 576, 585, 588, 593, 596, 598, 604, 622, 638, 677, 755, 778, 910, 913–14, 916, 918, 935, 937; **11:**40, 64, 159, 166, 373, 566, 596, 792, 887; **12:**49, 81, 125, 136, 139–42, 158, 170, 203, 221, 267, 475, 518, 563, 602, 642, 649, 725

EGYPT, BROOK OF
1:447

EKRON
1:224, 248; **2:**694, 739, 1007, 1012, 1109; **3:**170–71, 212; **4:**78, 80, 130, 140, 171; **6:**885, 1232, 1349, 1402; **7:**361, 666, 686, 805

ELAM
3:677, 686, 698, 740–41, 817, 878; **4:**60, 84, 204; **6:**185, 878, 900, 917–18, 1438, 1442–43; **7:**111, 141, 361, 595

ELASA
4:110, 129, 174

ELATH
3:242, 251, 590; **7:**362

EL-BETHEL
1:584

ELEALEH
2:250

ELEUTHERUS
4:132, 145

ELIM
1:805–6, 808, 812; **2:**252–53

ELISHAH
6:1374–75, 1378

ELKOSH
7:599

ELON BETH-HANAN
3:48

ELOTH
3:590

ELYMAIS
4:84, 157, 193, 253; **5:**612; **7:**141

EMEQ-AVEN
2:594

EMMAUS
2:97, 847; **4:**63, 66–67, 100, 115, 1206; **9:**8, 13, 26, 196–97, 320, 352, 413, 457, 466, 475–76, 479–84, 486, 842; **10:**142

EMMAUS-NICOPOLIS
9:475

EMMAUS ROAD
2:97, 847; **4:**1206; **9:**8, 13, 37, 196–97, 320, 352, 413, 457, 466, 474–76, 479, 481, 483–84, 842; **10:**142

ENAIM
1:605

ENDOR
2:1184, 1192; **3:**370; **6:**827, 1203, 1445

EN-EGLAIM
6:1364, 1596

EN-GEDI
1:287; **2:**1154, 1157; **3:**379, 559; **5:**388, 395, 757; **6:**1364, 1596

EN-HAKKORE
2:853

EN-RIMMON
3:827

EN-ROGEL
3:18, 21, 100, 768

EPHESUS
1:301; **3:**395, 1081, 1115; **6:**1398; **8:**13, 23, 105; **9:**9, 366, 498, 506; **10:**147, 215, 220, 258, 260–62, 266–76, 278, 280–83, 285, 297, 341, 718, 739, 755, 758, 761–62, 776–77, 982–83, 991–93, 996–98, 1001; **11:**11–12, 38, 41, 48, 115, 174, 352, 361, 369, 458, 465, 474, 519, 674, 781, 790–92, 808, 822, 824, 838, 857–59, 864, 878, 884; **12:**515, 567, 571, 574–75, 581, 588

EPHESUS, TEMPLE TO ARTEMIS AT
10:271–73

EPHRAIM
1:261–62, 264, 660, 667, 828; **2:**37, 563, 660–61, 665, 680, 687, 691, 694, 696, 701, 715, 717–18, 743, 752, 779, 838, 863, 870, 875–76, 900, 1055, 1079; **3:**52, 100, 353, 839; **4:**917, 998; **6:**108, 127, 137, 174, 235–36, 1478, 1604; **7:**234, 242, 244–48, 251–53, 256–58, 261–62, 266–67, 269–70, 272, 275, 277–79, 281–83, 285–88, 291–93, 296–97, 456, 493, 802, 807, 809–10, 815; **9:**367, 698

EPHRAIM FOREST
2:1336

EPHRAIM GATE
3:767, 802, 839

EPHRATHAH
2:678, 900, 939; **3:**94; **4:**306, 1212; **7:**570
EPHRON
1:503–4; **4:**21, 80, 276
ERECH
1:232; **3:**698–99
ESAU, MOUNT
7:449, 456
ESDRAELON
1:666; **3:**286, 1109, 1113; **4:**147, 151
ESHTAOL
2:694
ETAM
2:678
ETHAM
2:252–53
ETHIOPIA
1:155, 408; **2:**109; **3:**268, 859, 878, 882, 925, 937, 966, 1099; **4:**1024; **6:**12, 149, 173, 175, 180–82, 294, 375–76, 382, 391, 394, 403, 1402, 1415; **7:**147, 170, 220, 424, 546, 616, 671, 690–91, 699–700; **10:**143
EUPHRATES
1:215, 237, 246, 250, 260–62, 267, 351, 388, 392, 416, 422, 447; **2:**179, 181, 186, 614, 1266, 1280; **3:**53, 113, 252–53, 337, 678, 699, 726, 1098; **4:**95, 140, 143, 206, 249, 260, 964, 1000, 1227; **5:**758, 818; **6:**10, 113, 117, 227, 601, 683–84, 866, 882, 916, 942, 1077, 1081, 1278, 1326, 1502; **7:**136, 424, 804, 807; **10:**498; **12:**632, 634, 677
EZION-GEBER
2:254; **3:**168, 511; **6:**1360

F

FAIR HAVENS
10:345–46, 348–49
FERTILE CRESCENT
1:166, 214, 268; **2:**600; **6:**556, 558, 787, 1076, 1114, 1156, 1296, 1366, 1442
FIELD OF BLOOD
8:484
FISH GATE
3:766–67, 839; **7:**679
FISH TOWER
9:175
FORUM OF APPIUS
10:357
FOUNTAIN GATE
3:759, 767–69, 839
FULLER'S FIELD
6:107

G

GABA
3:1109
GAD
1:666; **2:**745, 807
GADARA
1:270; **8:**231; **9:**186
GAD GATE
6:1606
GALATIA
4:248; **8:**593; **10:**197, 259, 756, 777, 880, 996; **11:**113, 183–85, 191–93, 202, 204–5, 207, 217, 221, 224–25, 227, 230, 232, 236, 239, 241–42, 245, 248–49, 268, 282, 285–86, 289, 294–95, 307–9, 313, 316, 324, 329, 335, 337, 341, 346–48, 438, 496, 631, 674, 857; **12:**325, 577
GALILEE
1:169, 245, 247, 261, 268; **2:**90, 492, 655, 696; **3:**978, 992, 1109, 1171; **4:**13, 73, 77, 78, 87, 90, 110, 140, 145, 147, 233, 276, 924; **6:**795, 1232; **7:**342, 352, 412, 732; **8:**33, 35, 45, 73, 85, 105, 110–11, 113, 134, 139, 147, 149–50, 159–60, 163, 167, 170, 190, 226, 263, 272, 279, 319, 328, 369, 383–85, 406, 474, 493, 500, 513–14, 520, 531, 535–37, 539, 542–44, 546, 560, 592, 597–98, 603, 609–10, 635–36, 640, 642–43, 656, 659, 674, 702, 705, 724, 728–32; **9:**8, 11, 13, 24, 51, 68, 73, 80, 88, 95, 97, 102–6, 110, 112, 116–17, 122, 155, 169, 177, 186, 195, 197, 199, 214, 220–22, 268, 276, 281, 288, 325, 363, 369, 374–75, 421, 446, 451, 462, 464–66, 468–70, 473, 479, 481–82, 489, 493, 508, 536, 565, 574, 591, 616, 624, 856–57; **10:**154, 166, 470, 623; **12:**183, 255, 323, 474
GALILEE, SEA OF
1:194, 245, 666; **2:**536, 1280; **3:**992; **4:**77; **6:**1601, 1605; **8:**231, 327, 339, 341, 343, 525, 568, 579, 593, 601, 612, 615, 622; **9:**110, 116–17, 175, 184, 186, 221, 321, 593, 856
GALLIM
2:678
GARDEN OF EDEN
See EDEN, GARDEN OF
GARDEN OF GETHSEMANE
1:501; **4:**854; **5:**693; **9:**100, 431, 690, 752; **11:**227
GATE BETWEEN THE TWO WALLS
6:1194
GATE OF SAMARIA
3:205
GATE OF SHALLECHETH
3:451

GATE OF THE GUARD
3:839
GATH
1:248; **2:**122, 1007, 1109, 1142, 1144, 1175, 1178–80, 1187, 1206, 1243, 1265, 1324, 1361; **3:**34, 353, 357, 378, 413–14; **4:**901; **6:**885, 1349; **7:**361, 399, 547
GATH-GITTAIM
3:357
GATH-HEPHER
7:463, 493
GAUGMELA
4:30
GAZA
1:248; **2:**122, 660, 677, 739, 854–55, 858, 860; **3:**336, 1107; **4:**140, 282; **6:**885, 1232, 1349, 1355, 1398; **7:**140, 353, 355, 361–62, 594, 666, 686, 805; **10:**142
GAZARA
4:17, 21, 66, 100, 115, 156, 164, 171–72, 174–75, 263–64
GEBA
2:570, 1069–71, 1079; **3:**285, 357, 389, 686, 838; **7:**837
GEBAL
2:662; **4:**1010; **6:**1374
GEDER
2:655
GEDOR
3:336
GEHENNA
1:1127; **5:**808; **8:**197, 359, 436; **9:**86, 252, 565, 641; **12:**204, 347, 488
GEHINNON, VALLEY OF
7:331
GELILOTH
2:707
GENNESARET, LAKE
4:140; **9:**116
GERAR
1:481–82, 527–28; **3:**336, 538, 591, 649
GERAR VALLEY
3:336
GERASA
1:270; **8:**231, 582; **9:**186, 369
GERIZIM
1:298–99; **4:**229, 232
GERIZIM, MOUNT
1:270, 295; **2:**487–88, 491, 634–35, 816; **3:**676, 1078, 1108, 1112, 1125, 1137; **4:**13; **5:**862; **9:**270, 563, 567; **10:**126
GERUTH CHIMHAM
6:1080
GESHUR
1:1186; **2:**662, 665, 1309, 1319; **3:**328
GETHSEMANE
1:880; **8:**204, 370, 398, 470–71, 477, 481, 495, 544, 589, 625, 630, 650, 695, 705, 707–8, 710, 722, 731; **9:**27, 137, 139, 190, 205–6, 233, 235, 410, 412, 431–32, 712, 752, 789, 801; **10:**593, 607, 745; **11:**414; **12:**62
GETHSEMANE, GARDEN OF
1:501; **4:**854; **5:**693; **9:**100, 431, 690, 736, 752; **11:**227
GEZER
1:218, 222, 247, 249, 251, 261; **2:**638, 646, 648, 655, 681; **3:**37, 81–82, 416, 505; **4:**21, 156, 174, 263; **5:**185; **6:**1540
GIBEAH
1:261; **2:**547, 627, 876–77, 884–85, 887, 894, 976, 1048, 1055, 1069–71, 1079, 1090, 1127, 1147, 1153, 1159, 1216, 1358; **4:**554; **7:**247, 264, 267, 273, 275
GIBEATH
2:1069
GIBEATH-ELOHIM
2:1069
GIBEON
1:222; **2:**562–63, 615–16, 625, 641, 646–48, 1205, 1215–16, 1352; **3:**39–42, 80, 345, 347, 357–58, 389, 399–400, 422, 425, 433, 445, 470, 473–74, 483, 485, 494, 499, 525, 686, 768, 770; **4:**101; **5:**498; **6:**237, 784, 1574
GIBEON VALLEY
3:389
GIHON RIVER
5:758
GIHON SPRING
1:249, 278, 351; **2:**1237; **3:**20, 100, 628, 768–69, 800; **5:**853; **6:**117
GILBOA
2:1183, 1206–7, 1213
GILBOA, MOUNT
1:261; **2:**1081, 1188, 1197, 1201–2, 1206, 1230; **3:**368, 379
GILEAD
1:245, 259, 261, 557; **2:**248–50, 264, 308–9, 683, 707, 765, 821–22, 824–25, 827, 830–31, 836–38, 1332; **3:**28, 126, 164, 338, 342, 353, 1171; **4:**16, 36, 77–78, 82, 87, 90, 152, 249–50, 275–76; **5:**402–3, 418; **6:**648, 650, 740, 826, 883, 1379; **7:**252, 286, 343, 360–62, 456, 588, 815, 817
GILGAL
1:311; **2:**460, 486, 488, 562–63, 578, 589, 593, 599, 601, 605–9, 612, 625, 627, 630, 655, 671, 686–87, 707, 718, 747, 771, 1053, 1056, 1060,

1068, 1071, 1088–89, 1345–48; **3:**176, 190; **4:**110, 937; **6:**546, 1290, 1316; **7:**205, 242, 264, 270, 273, 286, 380, 387, 394, 579; **9:**215
GILOH
1:219
GITTAIM
2:1230; **3:**353
GOAH
6:813
GOB
3:416
GOLAN
2:265
GOLGOTHA
1:1120; **2:**1217; **4:**874; **8:**489–90, 722, 726; **9:**454, 829; **10:**547; **12:**288, 391. *See also* PLACE OF THE SKULL
GOMORRAH
1:329, 420, 435, 438–39, 441, 449, 462, 467–68, 473, 477, 483, 494; **2:**512, 548, 802, 877; **4:**312, 452, 722; **5:**55, 125, 524, 621, 725, 818; **6:**46, 54–55, 157, 161, 277, 335, 412, 547, 550, 619, 630, 750, 896, 918, 1062, 1213–14, 1522–23; **7:**278, 381, 730; **8:**595; **9:**331–32; **10:**643; **12:**347–48, 356, 489–90
GOPHNA HILLS
4:45, 56–57, 63, 74, 98, 281, 295
GORTYNA
4:170
GOSHEN (IN EGYPT)
1:644, 651, 653, 659, 754, 758; **6:**1402
GOSHEN (NOT IN EGYPT)
2:648
GOZAN
3:253
GRAPE-CLUSTER VALLEY
2:122
GREAT SEA
2:262; **3:**865; **6:**1364, 1601; **7:**101
GREAT SYNAGOGUE, THE
11:211
GREECE
1:13, 247, 323, 408; **2:**566, 669, 688; **3:**680, 1108, 1124; **4:**5, 31, 143, 227, 248; **5:**189, 253, 264, 326, 688, 793; **7:**4, 111, 116, 139, 141, 147, 331, 456, 467, 809–10; **8:**17, 24, 44, 46, 49, 248, 303; **9:**174; **10:**147, 214, 255, 276, 398, 754, 773; **11:**656; **12:**504
GUDGODAH
2:254
GULLOTH (UPPER AND LOWER)
2:738
GUR-BAAL
3:591

H

HABOR
3:253
HADAD-RIMMON
7:828
HADES
1:1143; **3:**953, 1004, 1017, 1063; **4:**236, 240; **5:**341, 353, 456, 460, 574, 583; **6:**551; **7:**168; **8:**346, 676; **9:**317, 357, 410, 482, 634; **11:**390, 421, 438; **12:**302, 347, 567, 612. *See also* HELL
HADID
3:686
HADRACH
7:201, 803, 804
HALAH
7:456
HALICARNASSUS
4:170; **11:**653
HALL OF TYRANNUS
8:14, 267, 271
HAMATH
1:237; **2:**573, 1266; **3:**236, 414–15, 417, 505; **4:**145; **5:**270; **6:**851, 897, 1161; **7:**399, 804
HAMATH-ZOBAH
3:505
HAMONAH
6:1526
HAMON-GOG, VALLEY OF
6:1525–26
HANANEL, TOWER OF
3:756, 768, 839
HARADAH
2:251
HARAN
1:266, 416, 422, 426, 446, 509–10, 513, 518, 537, 541, 552, 558, 562–63, 573, 580, 584; **3:**100, 1038; **6:**248, 1380; **7:**845; **9:**566
HARMON
7:377
HASHMONAH
2:253
HAURAN, MOUNT
6:1601
HAVILAH
1:351
HAZAR-ADDAR
2:262
HAZAR-ENAN
2:262–63

HAZAZON-TAMAR
3:559
HAZER-HATTICON
6:1601
HAZEROTH
2:19, 94, 104, 111, 254
HAZOR
1:222, 224, 247, 251, 261, 265; **2:**563, 615–16, 639, 648, 651, 759, 779, 781; **3:**82; **4:**140; **6:**898–99, 1540; **7:**352
HEBRON
1:252, 261, 424, 432–34, 599, 652, 659, 670; **2:**121–22, 126, 561, 616, 646, 648, 654–55, 671, 673–74, 678, 696, 701, 736–37, 739–40, 854–55, 1144, 1153, 1166, 1168–69, 1194, 1211, 1213, 1215, 1218, 1224–25, 1229–30, 1233–34, 1242, 1319–20; **3:**17–18, 28, 100, 330, 347, 376–77, 379, 384, 388, 560, 768–69, 827; **4:**51, 81, 152; **7:**456
HEBRON, MOUNT
4:69
HELAM
2:1280
HELBON
6:1379
HELECH
6:1374
HELEK
2:683
HELIOPOLIS
1:622; **6:**1418
HELL
1:85; **3:**386, 658; **4:**469, 898; **5:**252, 291, 301, 304, 322, 341, 430, 716; **6:**212, 256, 277, 1345, 1445; **7:**2, 507–8, 611, 874; **8:**220, 359, 435, 641; **9:**99, 101, 252, 318; **10:**443, 644, 673; **11:**650; **12:**26, 204, 294, 347, 391, 525, 716.
See also HADES; SHEOL
HEPHER
2:655, 683; **3:**52
HEPHZIBAH (FOR JERUSALEM)
6:22
HERMON, MOUNT
2:308, 600, 694, 1266, 1279; **4:**946, 1035, 1214; **5:**403, 407, 757; **6:**1114, 1373; **9:**205
HESHBON
1:253; **2:**166–67, 184, 191, 250, 307, 512, 616; **4:**74, 222; **5:**426
HETHLON
6:1601
HIERAPOLIS
11:580, 667; **12:**710
HIGH GATE
5:159
HINNOM, VALLEY OF
1:1126; **2:**65, 391; **3:**598, 768, 827; **6:**721, 813, 1286, 1526; **8:**436; **9:**86, 145, 252
HOLY LAND
1:94, 1127; **2:**363; **4:**184, 189; **5:**759; **6:**297; **7:**761, 764, 780; **8:**257, 363, 443, 490; **10:**25, 220, 222, 329, 673, 680, 698
HOR, MOUNT
2:19, 157–58, 162–63, 219, 254, 262
HOREB, MOUNT
1:38–39, 41, 313, 316, 318, 711, 818; **2:**14, 120, 218, 271, 273, 277, 291–94, 297, 299, 306, 309, 314, 316–17, 321, 323–26, 338, 350, 358, 362, 367, 374, 463, 480–81, 510–12, 519, 534, 589, 612, 718; **3:**70, 142–44, 217; **4:**51; **5:**851; **6:**874, 1168; **7:**481, 853, 875–76; **9:**205; **11:**216
HORESH
2:1153
HORMAH
2:126, 158–59, 163, 168, 256, 561, 627, 655, 739
HORONAIM
3:757
HORSE GATE
3:767, 769

I

IAZER
See JAZER/IAZER
ICONIUM
10:188, 196–97, 199, 202, 224; **11:**191, 316
IDUMEA
3:337; **4:**13, 62–63, 69, 74, 87, 152, 248, 261, 277, 282; **7:**438, 456; **8:**560; **9:**142, 363
ILLYRICUM
10:339, 374, 754; **11:**144, 674, 857
INDIA
1:303, 1094; **3:**42, 590, 859, 878, 882, 925, 937, 966; **4:**104–5; **5:**612; **6:**119, 1378; **7:**112; **8:**529; **9:**277; **10:**755
IR
2:191
IR-MOAB
2:184
IR-SHEMESH
2:694
ISHTAR GATE
6:1176
ISRAEL (KINGDOM/TERRITORY)
1:9–11, 18, 67–68, 74, 215, 221, 245, 247–49, 251, 259, 261–62, 264, 274, 282, 284, 291, 308, 364, 404, 430, 441, 476; **2:**5, 136, 178–84, 186–87, 191, 246, 248, 266, 268, 279–83,

285–86, 290–92, 297, 300, 305, 307–11, 315, 324, 333–34, 336–37, 344–45, 350, 352–53, 355–57, 364–65, 367, 371, 374, 376, 380–81, 383–89, 391–92, 394–95, 403–5, 408, 410–11, 414, 416–17, 425–27, 432, 435, 440–42, 445–46; **3:**3–6, 14, 18–20, 22, 26, 32, 35, 39, 45, 48, 51–52, 54, 58, 61, 70–72, 76–80, 84, 87–90, 93–96, 100, 102–4, 109–10, 112–15, 118, 120, 123, 125–30, 132–33, 135–38, 142–43, 146–47, 150–51, 153, 155–61, 167–68, 170, 173, 176, 178, 181, 183–84, 193–95, 198–99, 201–3, 208, 212, 224–25, 232, 234, 238, 278, 305, 309, 313, 318, 338, 376–77, 385, 406, 414, 422, 457, 500, 520, 531, 598–99, 672, 678, 949, 993, 1078–79, 1095, 1098–99, 1117; **4:**22, 30–32, 36, 39, 51, 82, 129, 145, 147–48, 156, 159, 163, 171, 177, 193, 198, 313, 328, 343–44, 348, 372, 400–402, 410, 412, 449–50, 480, 492–93, 500, 523, 526, 539, 541, 547–48, 590, 594, 604, 610–11, 635, 642, 644, 649, 661–62, 668–69, 673, 700, 730, 748, 768, 866, 887, 964, 1143, 1150, 1178, 1275; **5:**2, 6–7, 9–14, 16, 19–21, 26–27, 33, 35–36, 44–46, 48–51, 54–55, 59, 61, 67, 69, 71, 77, 80–81, 89–90, 93–97, 108, 111–13, 117, 121, 125, 134–36, 138–39, 142–46, 149, 151–55, 158–60, 166, 168–70, 172–76, 179–80, 182–83, 185–86, 189, 192, 196–97, 199–200, 204–5, 207–8, 213, 219, 222, 231, 233, 237–39, 242, 251–53, 255–56, 261, 264, 270–74, 280–84, 293, 298, 339, 341, 363–65, 368, 370–71, 377, 381, 401, 408, 427–28, 430, 453, 463, 469, 474, 476, 478, 485, 490, 492–93, 497, 502, 505–6, 509, 511–12, 516–18, 522, 525, 528–32, 534–36, 540–44, 553, 561–63, 567, 569, 573–75, 579–80, 585–86, 590–94, 605–6, 618–24, 645, 651, 655, 658–59, 662, 665, 667–69, 673, 683, 688, 692, 708, 724, 730, 739, 748, 750, 754, 757–59, 764, 772, 777, 780, 787–88, 798, 800, 802, 805–7, 836–38, 842, 846, 851, 855, 858–59, 867; **6:**2–16, 19–23, 29, 35–36, 38–40, 49–50, 52–58, 60, 62, 67, 72–73, 78–79, 82–84, 88–89, 94, 96, 102–3, 108–9, 111, 116–17, 119–20, 122–23, 127–30, 132–34, 136–37, 140, 143, 145–47, 149–50, 155–58, 160–61, 163, 173–76, 181, 183, 201–2, 204–5, 207, 211–13, 217–18, 222–23, 226, 227–28, 321, 339, 344, 346, 347–48, 354–55, 357, 364, 371, 375–77, 400–401, 429–30, 459–62, 530, 574, 588, 597, 661, 811–12, 932–34, 957, 968, 1123, 1159, 1206, 1215–17, 1221–22, 1230, 1251–52, 1262–63, 1274–75, 1277–78, 1288, 1312, 1348, 1399, 1480, 1484, 1495, 1521, 1523, 1532–33, 1597–1601; **7:**8, 30, 43, 75, 90, 113, 122, 137–38, 182, 184, 193, 198, 200–201, 203, 205–7, 218–21, 223–38, 241–46, 248, 250, 252–53, 256–58, 260–65, 267–70, 272, 281–83, 294–95, 301, 309, 312, 330, 333, 342–44, 346–47, 349, 352–58, 360–67, 369, 372–77, 380–82, 385–86, 391, 393–95, 397, 399, 402, 407, 411, 417–18, 422, 424–25, 427–28, 430–31, 435, 437–38, 454–56, 465, 469, 472, 480–81, 493, 526, 534, 538, 542–43, 545–47, 550–51, 558, 565, 567, 570–71, 573–77, 582, 586, 588, 593–94, 606, 627, 632, 635–36, 661, 663, 683, 685–86, 688, 691–92, 699, 725, 744, 756, 784, 804, 807, 810–13, 815–17, 820–24, 826, 829–30, 836, 839, 843, 844–46, 855, 876; **8:**132, 134, 289; **9:**97, 207; **10:**46, 77, 192, 416, 578; 1402, 1451; **7:**203, 268, 546; FALL OF **1:**282; **2:**556, 858–59, 887; **3:**95, 102; **4:**32; **5:**270; **6:**127, 134, 173–74, 806, 1169, 1232, 1307, 1402, 1451; **7:**203, 268, 546; HOPE TO RESTORE **9:**97, 200, 207; **10:**46, 64, 82, 267. *See also* ISRAEL (PEOPLE) *in PERSONS IN THE BIBLE*

ISSACHAR (TERRITORY)
2:263, 536, 660, 677, 745; **6:**1605–6

ITALY
1:13, 73, 79; **4:**104, 153; **8:**303; **10:**345, 357, 754; **11:**469, 656; **12:**6, 10, 173

IYE-ABARIM
2:164–65, 254

J

JAAR
4:1212

JABBOK
1:313, 519, 565, 572, 636, 661; **2:**91, 165–66, 178, 308; **6:**1240, 1511; **7:**283, 501

JABESH-GILEAD
1:261; **2:**247, 741, 782, 886–87, 1032, 1037, 1042–43, 1048–49, 1051, 1053–58, 1198, 1211–12, 1214, 1217–18, 1273, 1279, 1359; **3:**369, 890; **4:**228; **7:**252

JABNEEL
2:677. *See also* JAMNIA/YAVNEH

JAHAZ
2:165–66

JAHZAH
2:166

JAMNIA/YAVNEH
1:8–9, 11, 306; **3:**1107; **4:**81, 129–30, 132, 174–75, 261, 275–77, 282, 296; **5:**634; **8:**98, 100–102, 152, 435, 684

JARMUTH
2:616

JAVAN
6:1377–79; **7:**810

JAZER/IAZER
2:166, 248–50; **3:**452; **4:**36, 74, 249, 263–64

JEBUS
2:547; **3:**377
JEHOSHAPHAT, VALLEY OF
7:330–32, 334
JERICHO
1:85, 178, 253, 270, 287, 995, 1160, 1189; **2:**164, 169, 177, 180, 215, 267, 300, 308, 367, 440–41, 562–63, 575, 586, 588–90, 593–94, 599–600, 606–7, 611–13, 615, 618–20, 625–27, 634, 636–38, 646, 681, 691, 738, 743, 747, 770, 775, 792, 803, 855, 870, 943, 1001, 1100, 1279; **3:**150, 174, 176–78, 190, 597–98, 686, 768, 770, 1089; **4:**55, 78, 110, 115, 175–76, 275; **5:**196, 757, 867; **6:**212, 1194, 1525, 1601; **7:**309; **8:**399, 619, 621; **9:**19, 29, 214, 229, 335, 353–54, 357, 363–64, 366, 369–70, 404, 462; **12:**140, 142
JERICHO, WALL OF
1:1160; **2:**588, 594, 792, 855; **11:**159
JERUSALEM
1:9–10, 18, 31, 74, 169, 184, 217, 221–23, 226, 230, 245–47, 249–52, 256, 259–64, 266–68, 270–71, 275–76, 278, 282–83, 285–87, 289–90, 295–96, 298, 306, 309, 314, 336, 369, 399, 411, 419, 438–39, 441, 445, 467, 477–78, 496, 585, 680, 801, 815, 823, 828, 884, 900, 931, 996, 1019, 1113, 1117, 1121, 1126, 1164, 1172, 1181, 1184, 1186; **2:**14, 65, 79, 87, 89–90, 97, 122, 148, 162, 164, 265, 278–83, 309, 316, 330, 332, 352, 363, 365, 383–88, 391–92, 406, 413, 417, 427, 481, 487, 501–2, 504–6, 534, 544–45, 547, 552, 563, 565, 567, 570–76, 579, 600, 602–3, 606, 612, 614, 625–26, 634–35, 641, 646–47, 660, 672, 677–79, 687–89, 691, 696, 701, 735–37, 739–40, 816, 826, 858, 860, 876, 879, 887, 952, 954, 957, 962–63, 988, 996, 1012, 1018, 1113, 1213, 1222, 1229, 1234–40, 1242–44, 1246–51, 1256, 1266, 1273, 1276, 1280, 1283–86, 1300, 1308–9, 1313, 1315–17, 1319–20, 1323–25, 1327, 1330–32, 1335, 1337, 1345–48, 1351–52, 1354–55, 1357, 1371, 1381–82; **3:**3, 5–6, 18, 28, 33–34, 37, 39–41, 58, 61, 67, 69, 75, 80, 82, 84, 86, 90, 93–96, 102, 104, 109, 114–15, 117–19, 135, 142, 168, 171, 220, 228, 233–34, 236, 242, 244–45, 251, 260, 264–65, 268–72, 274, 276, 278–79, 282, 285–87, 290, 292–95, 304, 306, 319–20, 332, 348, 377, 384, 556, 686, 756, 793, 1154; **4:**3–9, 11–12, 23, 25, 32, 34, 36–39, 42, 44, 46, 57, 60, 63–64, 66, 71–72, 88, 90, 95–96, 98–101, 109–11, 114–15, 117–19, 121, 124, 130, 136, 141, 145–47, 150–54, 156, 163, 168, 171–72, 174–78, 181–83, 185, 189–93, 196–97, 199, 204–7, 213–14, 217–19, 222–24, 226–32, 240, 247–50, 253–54, 257–58, 261, 264, 266, 269–70, 275, 281–82, 286–87, 289–90, 296, 297–98, 310, 647–49, 661, 668, 673, 681, 689, 694, 793, 865–66, 871–74, 887, 944–45, 947, 963–64, 972–73, 979, 981, 990, 992, 994–96, 1012–14, 1023–25, 1034, 1036, 1040, 1064–65, 1075–76, 1087, 1104, 1122, 1130, 1156, 1176–77, 1182–88, 1190, 1192, 1195, 1197–98, 1201–2, 1208, 1210–12, 1214, 1216–17, 1227–28, 1244, 1267–68, 1272, 1279; **5:**1, 7, 14–15, 48, 118, 174, 194, 243–44, 271, 273–74, 297–98, 300, 303, 346, 364, 368, 380, 386, 389–90, 396, 400, 406, 409, 412–19, 421–22, 424, 429, 448, 473–74, 516–17, 608–12, 621, 632–33, 651, 664, 687, 703, 724, 757, 759, 797–98, 849, 853, 855–56, 862; **6:**3, 5, 7–8, 14–15, 17, 21–22, 32–33, 36–40, 45–46, 48, 52, 54–55, 59–62, 64–69, 76–79, 81–85, 87–89, 92, 94, 98, 107–9, 117–18, 127, 129–30, 132–34, 136–37, 140–43, 145, 147, 149–50, 155, 163–64, 167–69, 173–76, 182, 186, 194–98, 201–2, 207, 210, 212, 214, 216, 221, 226–27, 230–31, 235–38, 241–44, 260–62, 284–86, 291–92, 304, 328, 596, 685, 693, 710, 741, 743, 813–14, 821, 839, 848, 857–59, 872–73, 891, 925, 933, 940–44, 950, 971, 974–78, 980–81, 1062–63, 1075–76, 1079–82, 1088, 1141–43, 1152, 1172, 1179, 1215, 1220–21, 1226, 1228, 1232, 1237, 1295, 1307, 1309, 1320, 1329–30, 1337, 1453; **7:**3, 5, 7, 10–12, 22–23, 25, 27, 29–30, 32, 38, 50, 54, 62, 72–73, 75, 89, 90, 92, 113–14, 116, 122–23, 126–27, 140–44, 161, 184, 193, 205, 220, 242, 265, 293, 301, 306, 308–9, 330, 336, 340, 351–52, 362, 376, 399, 421–22, 427, 430–31, 435–41, 451, 454–55, 479, 488–89, 528, 533–34, 536, 541–44, 546–47, 550, 554–56, 559–61, 565, 567, 569, 572–73, 582, 584, 587–88, 594, 623, 626, 660–67, 669, 671, 674–75, 677, 679, 682, 685, 691, 693–97, 698–703, 708–10, 715, 717, 725, 727, 729, 731, 736–40, 742, 744–45, 747–49, 751–54, 756–66, 770, 773–74, 779–80, 789, 791–92, 794–95, 797, 799–802, 804–11, 815, 817, 821–22, 825–29, 831, 833–40, 846, 855, 860; **8:**33–34, 36–37, 44–46, 49, 52, 54, 73–74, 77, 81, 104–5, 110, 112, 123, 140, 142, 144–45, 147–48, 150, 153, 178, 205, 285, 331, 341, 343, 345, 383–85, 395–96, 399–400, 402–3, 406–7, 409, 412, 414, 418, 431, 436–39, 442–43, 464, 468, 487, 493, 500, 502, 516, 520, 525, 528, 532–33, 540, 543, 556, 560, 562–67, 593–94, 603, 605–6, 621, 625, 635, 642, 651–53, 655–60, 663, 665, 678, 680–81, 683, 685, 687, 695–96, 698–99, 702, 704–5, 717–19, 725–26, 730–32; **9:**8–9, 11–13, 15–17, 22, 24, 30, 40, 47, 52, 55–56, 60, 65–66, 68–71, 73, 76–77, 88, 97, 100, 102, 108, 117–18, 122, 133, 137, 142, 145, 169,

182, 195, 204, 206–7, 212–17, 219, 229, 231, 252, 266, 270–72, 277, 280–82, 291–92, 319, 325, 331, 341, 350–57, 361–63, 365–67, 369–70, 372, 374–78, 381–83, 391, 393, 398–401, 403–10, 412, 414–16, 426, 428, 430, 440, 445–46, 450–53, 455–56, 464–66, 469, 475–82, 487–89, 493, 504–5, 528, 541, 543, 545–46, 563, 567, 571, 574, 578–79, 591, 616–17, 619–20, 628, 632, 644–45, 647–48, 658, 674–75, 678, 685, 687, 697, 706–8, 710, 779, 801, 809, 823, 834, 856–57; **10:**3, 8–13, 25, 32, 41–46, 53, 57, 59–60, 63, 65, 69, 71, 73–74, 76, 78, 81–82, 84, 88, 90–93, 95–97, 99, 101, 103–6, 110, 112–15, 120–21, 123, 125–27, 130, 132–35, 137, 139–40, 142–43, 146–47, 150, 153–55, 160–62, 165–69, 174–82, 188–94, 198, 203–12, 214, 217–19, 221–22, 224–26, 246, 252, 254–55, 257–59, 269–70, 272, 275–78, 282–83, 285, 287–97, 305–7, 309–13, 318–22, 324–26, 329–30, 335–39, 357, 359–62, 373–74, 376, 390, 396, 402, 415, 461, 510, 556, 575, 581, 583, 586, 598, 612, 614, 650, 666, 701, 704, 718, 753–54, 756–59, 776, 781, 995–96; **11:**3, 5–6, 8, 10, 12, 15, 17, 20, 22, 37, 40, 48–49, 55, 96, 111–19, 126, 130–31, 134–35, 144, 156, 163, 170, 175, 184, 186, 193–94, 205, 210, 213–14, 216–17, 221–36, 242, 245, 303–4, 306, 309, 312, 342, 365, 414, 417, 438, 525, 647, 759, 833, 859; **12:**10, 84, 101, 136, 156, 158, 182–83, 186, 246, 277, 449, 473, 481, 521, 528, 532, 539, 544–45, 569, 596, 621, 630, 642, 653, 669, 672, 704, 711, 720, 722, 725–26, 728

JERUSALEM TEMPLE

1:268, 900; **2:**79, 1237; **3:**384, 668, 720, 1114, 1134, 1154; **4:**22, 34, 64, 1196, 204; **6:**933, 940, 943–44; **7:**143, 564, 717; **8:**34, 659; **9:**372, 487, 543; **10:**83–84, 137, 319; **11:**303; **12:**641, 725–29; BURNING OF THE **3:**677; **4:**107, 455; **5:**643; **6:**455, 866, 925; CAPTAIN OF THE **9:**376; **10:**83, 105; CHOIR **2:**214; **3:**501, 847; **4:**657; **7:**665, 671; CODES **12:**725–27; COURT **3:**345, 442, 485, 495, 561, 575, 580–81, 599, 607–9, 647–48, 768; **4:**99; **6:**634, 722; 8:408, 439; **9:**542–43, 632; **11:**703; CURTAIN(S) **1:**689, 896–98, 1033–35, 1110–11, 1114; **2:**53, 77; **3:**484, 1151; **4:**34, 1097; **6:**1228; **8:**493; **9:**829; **12:**82, 103–4, 158; DESTRUCTION OF THE **1:**9, 66, 285; **2:**79, 280; **3:**80, 115, 655–56, 1120; **4:**107, 307, 937, 975; **6:**555, 637, 710, 774, 859, 929–33, 940; **7:**3, 72, 441; **8:**34, 54, 405, 429; **9:**373, 399, 403, 442, 543, 685, 687; **11:**703; **12:**523, 596, 725–29; GALLERY OF THE **6:**1551; GATE **3:**248, 251, 450–51, 580, 768, 1165; **4:**732, 772, 1061, 1083, 1155; **6:**710, 1259, 1577; **8:**719; **10:**77; GUARD **2:**211; **3:**848; **8:**479; **10:**180; OF HEROD **8:**142, 515, 663, 671; **9:**574; **10:**128, 181; AND HOLY OF HOLIES **1:**282, 290, 893, 898, 976, 999, 1033, 1034, 1067, 1070, 1110, 1112, 1147, 1163; **2:**52–54; **3:**269, 386, 429, 484, 496, 591, 1151; **4:**34, 211, 789; **5:**273, 290, 843, 859; **6:**1119, 1167, 1176, 1179–80, 1182–83, 1393, 1533, 1549–50, 1554–55, 1557, 1560–62, 1565, 1575; **8:**33, 405, 723; **9:**376; **12:**41, 58, 82, 103–6, 727; AND HOUSE OF THE FOREST **3:**67; **6:**194, 740, 1245, 1295, 1555; KITCHEN **6:**1591–92; MEDIATOR **1:**281; PAUL AND THE **10:**77, 292–98, 317–21, 418, 433, 461, 516, 581, 604, 662, 704, 831–32, 844–45, 849–51, 865–65, 909–10, 966; **11:**105–7, 422, 525, 866; **12:**703; ROOM **1:**277–78; 3:484, 486, 648, 770, 846, 850; **6:**843, 1119, 1541, 1549–52, 1554, 1557, 1560; **7:**320, 787; **8:**201, 468; SCREEN **1:**897, 901; **3:**484; OF SOLOMON **1:**260–62, 276–77, 900, 960, 1067; **2:**14, 384, 386, 565, 570, 590, 636, 736, 988, 1236–38, 1255–57, 1266, 1354; **3:**40–41, 59, 62, 67–68, 72, 344–46, 465, 428–33, 470–513, 536, 622, 648; **4:**71–73, 116, 188; **10:**1228; **11:**40; **12:**727; TABERNACLE/TEMPLE CULT **1:**67, 285; **2:**11, 15, 25, 86, 89, 96, 99, 177, 193; **3:**677, 729; **4:**206; **5:**469, 628–29, 631, 798; **6:**1261; **7:**113; **8:**33, 36, 45; **9:**541; **10:**422, 474–75, 704; **12:**726; TAXES (*see* TAXES: SANCTUARY/TABERNACLE/TEMPLE *in SUBJECTS AND THEMES*); TITHES GIVEN BY THE PHARISEES **9:**247, 250, 342; TREASURY **1:**900; **2:**462, 613; **3:**67, 233, 251, 451–52, 708, 768, 847; **4:**34, 60, 165, 193, 207, 222, 228, 289, 586; **5:**612; VEIL OF THE **1:**999, 1070, 1111, 1114, 1163; **2:**53; **3:**502; **6:**1534; **8:**405, 493, 628, 665, 723–24; **9:**373, 460–62; **12:**58–59, 61, 82, 120, 131, 523, 653, 727; VESSEL **1:**268, 890, 900; **2:**36, 246, 614; **3:**363, 393, 429, 432, 452, 462, 494, 580, 608, 611, 654–55, 679–81, 750–6, 721, 728, 846–47, 850, 1112; **4:**159, 184, 198, 222–23, 296; **5:**517; **6:**443, 453, 455–56, 782–84, 925, 944; **7:**38, 54, 81, 83–84; **8:**663; **9:**339; **12:**112; WALL **2:**178; **3:**429, 484, 703–4; **4:**7, 92; **6:**996, 1119, 1393, 1539–44, 1547, 1551–52, 1554–55, 1557–60, 1556–68; **9:**100, 399; WORSHIP **2:**14; **3:**348, 396, 436–37, 447, 479, 485, 501, 506, 514, 530–31, 536, 539, 560, 565, 610–11, 624, 649, 654, 657, 819; **4:**71–72, 93, 99, 197–98, 309; **6:**102; **7:**860; **8:**405; **9:**543, 545, 647; **10:**72, 214, 704; **12:**725; OF ZERUBBABEL **1:**268; **3:**295, 665–68, 675–76, 685, 690–95, 702–12, 842, 844; **4:**197–200; **5:**355; **7:**716, 731, 737–38, 763, 770–72, 786–88

JERUSALEM, GATE OF

3:348, 753, 793; **4:**189, 1180; **6:**330, 574, 584, 1063; **7:**546, 554

JERUSALEM, HOLY CITY
1:189; **2:**547, 1236, 1238; **3:**452, 669, 824–25, 840, 850, 1064; **4:**7, 193, 241, 289; **5:**555; **6:**46–47, 54, 84, 175, 217–18, 262, 284, 417–18, 454–56, 509, 733, 773, 813, 1061; **7:**127, 161, 560, 565; **8:**129, 164, 179, 402; **9:**353, 370, 459; **10:**8, 13, 19, 40, 57, 59, 95, 110, 114, 123, 130, 134, 145–47, 167, 178, 204, 214, 258, 270, 275–76, 287–91, 296, 306, 320, 359; **12:**136, 266, 579, 594, 642, 649, 702, 711, 720, 722, 726, 734

JERUSALEM, WALL OF
1:251; **3:**242, 759, 760, 766, 771, 788, 838; **8:**395

JESHANAH/JESHANAH GATE
3:767

JESHURUN
2:527, 534

JEZREEL
1:261; **2:**1169, 1188, 1211, 1230; **3:**137, 139, 153, 155, 158, 167, 210, 214, 216, 219, 223, 226, 228, 234, 1109; **6:**119, 1111; **7:**218, 223, 236

JEZREEL VALLEY
1:217; **2:**651, 684, 1183; **5:**261; **7:**218

JOGBEHAH
2:250

JOKNEAM
2:655; **3:**347

JOPPA
3:692; **4:**88, 130, 132, 146–47, 150–51, 153, 156, 159, 164, 171–72, 219, 255, 275, 277, 282, 468, 478–79, 495, 497, 506, 511; **7:**201, 468, 478–79, 494, 506, 511; **8:**141; **10:**160–64, 170

JORDAN PLAIN
2:612

JORDAN RIVER
1:38, 210, 215, 242, 261, 270, 274, 306–7, 557, 565, 573, 666, 670, 924, 995; **2:**123, 164, 169, 177–78, 180–81, 198, 248–50, 252, 254, 262–63, 265, 267, 271–72, 276, 291, 293, 305–9, 312, 320, 324, 338–40, 342, 358, 367, 371, 376, 389, 434–35, 486–88, 491, 510–12, 515, 520, 536, 555, 561, 564, 569, 573, 578, 580, 584–90, 593, 599–604, 606–7, 613, 619, 626, 634, 648–49, 655, 665–67, 673, 677, 683, 691, 694–96, 706–8, 718, 770, 772, 788, 805, 807–8, 822, 830–31, 837–38, 1055, 1198, 1213, 1326, 1332, 1345–48, 1351; **3:**6, 127, 176–77, 194, 198–99, 201, 226, 336, 338, 431, 452, 730, 1109; **4:**36, 73, 77, 80–81, 114–15, 152, 222, 263, 312–13, 609, 618–19, 853, 937, 977, 1141–42; **5:**492, 758; **6:**4, 443, 455–56, 648, 1378, 1525, 1574, 1582, 1596, 1601, 1605; **7:**252, 360, 380, 403, 579, 583, 817–18; **8:**111, 157, 159, 174, 267, 319, 385, 582, 643; **9:**80, 99, 120, 170, 221, 325–26; **10:**534, 810; **12:**569

JORDAN VALLEY
1:245, 249, 433; **2:**308, 356, 460, 535–36; **3:**144, 768–69; **4:**115, 118, 147; **7:**309, 411, 690; **8:**267

JOSEPH (TERRITORY)
2:685, 694, 743, 746

JOSEPH GATE
6:1606

JOTBATHAH
2:254

JUDAH (CITY)
2:701; **3:**587; **6:**1078

JUDAH (KINGDOM/TERRITORY)
1:213, 215, 221, 224–27, 236, 245–50, 256, 260, 262, 264–71, 284, 286, 314, 432, 491, 667, 747, 821, 1119, 1126, 1187; **2:**5, 279, 281–82, 308, 384, 388, 391, 394–95, 403, 432, 440, 443, 446, 461, 501–5, 512, 514, 542, 545, 552, 559, 565, 568, 570–72, 574–75, 582, 600, 616, 646, 654–55, 659–60, 662, 671–73, 677–79, 681, 684, 687, 691, 694, 701, 718, 736, 743, 745–48, 760, 765, 770, 816, 826, 841, 860–61, 863, 865, 870, 875, 887, 895, 899–900, 903, 941–42, 959, 962, 1087, 1094, 1109–10, 1118, 1127, 1144–45, 1152, 1166, 1170, 1178–79, 1189, 1192, 1194, 1199, 1211–13, 1215, 1218, 1223, 1228, 1233–34, 1236, 1243–44, 1248, 1258, 1286, 1293, 1319–20, 1346, 1348, 1351–52, 1358, 1376, 1380; **3:**3, 5–6, 18–20, 34, 50, 52, 72, 78, 104–6, 108–10, 114–16, 118, 132, 140, 160, 167–68, 170, 173, 183, 211, 214, 217, 219–20, 223, 227–28, 230, 232, 234, 236, 239, 241–42, 244–45, 250–53, 255, 261, 264–65, 269, 271–72, 274–79, 282, 284–87, 289–90, 292–95, 306, 317, 319, 332, 336, 338, 346–47, 358–59, 362, 364, 366, 370, 376–77, 379, 381–82, 395, 401–2, 417, 422, 477, 511, 514, 516, 518, 520, 522, 524–27, 530–33, 538, 546–47, 559–63, 569, 571, 574, 581–82, 586, 591, 597–602, 606–9, 615, 617, 619, 628–29, 634, 636, 644–45, 649, 654–56, 664–68, 679–81, 684–86, 688, 690–92, 694–95, 700, 705, 708, 721–22, 732, 735–36, 756–57, 765, 773–75, 779, 782–83, 785, 788, 793, 796, 819–20, 825–28, 838, 841, 844, 846, 848, 850, 886, 899, 993, 996, 1097, 1099, 1112, 1117, 1119; **4:**6, 31–32, 40, 48, 52, 55, 72, 77–78, 84–85, 107, 109, 276, 296, 305, 313, 423, 526, 642, 644, 649, 668, 673, 867, 917, 964, 981, 1069, 1142–43, 1150, 1196, 1227–28; **5:**7, 143, 160, 273, 275, 370, 702, 730, 759, 797–98, 801, 823, 828, 852–53, 855, 862; **6:**2, 4–9, 12, 14, 17–18, 20–22, 35–37, 39, 45–46, 48, 52, 65–67,

76–78, 81, 83, 89, 98, 102, 107–9, 112–13, 116–18, 124, 127–30, 132, 136–37, 140, 145, 147, 149, 163, 169, 173–75, 181, 185, 187, 189, 194–96, 205, 207, 216, 218, 220, 225–26, 230–31, 235–36, 238–39, 242; 472, 604, 635, 739, 750–51, 769, 778, 797, 851, 874, 1076, 1299, 1303, 1349, 1352, 1403, 1437, 1508; **7:**23, 32, 75, 90, 92, 182, 184, 203, 207, 210, 213, 218–19, 223, 242, 244–48, 251–53, 262, 268, 282–83, 302, 305–9, 311–12, 318–19, 321, 323, 325–26, 329–30, 334–36, 340–42, 350–55, 361–63, 369, 376–77, 399, 411–12, 414, 422, 428, 430, 436–39, 441–42, 444–45, 449, 451, 454–57, 465, 469, 533–34, 541–44, 546–47, 553–54, 571, 575, 582, 587, 594–96, 599–600, 604, 606, 623–26, 628, 631, 634–36, 638, 643–44, 646, 660–65, 669–70, 672–76, 678–80, 683–86, 688, 690–91, 696, 698–700, 703, 708–11, 715, 717–18, 725, 730–31, 736–40, 742, 744, 747–49, 752–53, 756–57, 759–60, 762, 765–66, 770–71, 775–76, 778–80, 783–84, 786–87, 792, 794, 805–7, 810–13, 816–17, 820–22, 826–29, 833, 836–40, 843, 846, 855, 872; **8:**130–31, 135, 289, 577; **9:**45; **10:**193, 445, 511; **11:**444, 492, 566, 576. *See also* JUDAH/JUDAHITES (PEOPLE/TRIBE) *in PERSONS IN THE BIBLE*

JUDAH GATE
6:1606

JUDEA/JUDAEA
1:274, 298; **3:**736, 859, 971, 1075, 1077–79, 1095, 1097, 1099, 1101, 1103, 1106–7, 1109, 1111–13, 1117–18, 1120, 1125, 1131–32, 1137; **4:**3, 5–10, 16, 24, 26, 38–40, 48, 53, 59–60, 63, 69, 78, 85, 87, 97, 99, 102, 107, 109, 114–19, 122, 125, 127, 130, 132, 135–36, 140, 143, 145–48, 150–54, 156, 159, 164–65, 167–68, 172, 174–78, 188–89, 190, 196–97, 204–5, 212, 216, 227, 231–33, 241, 249, 254, 259, 263–64, 268, 270, 275–76, 278, 280–81, 286–88, 298, 305; **5:**269–70, 273, 275, 705; **6:**945–46, 948, 952, 1294; **7:**41, 141, 147, 193, 200–201, 301, 444; **8:**111, 139, 142, 147, 149, 159, 341, 382–83, 385, 406, 420, 443, 482, 492, 500, 517, 532, 536, 560, 683, 690, 702, 712, 717–18, 730; **9:**45, 49, 54, 59–60, 62, 80–81, 103, 112, 116, 122, 142, 158, 268, 362–63, 385, 405, 415, 446, 469, 487, 493, 565, 574, 616–17, 678, 686–87, 808, 814–15, 820, 830; **10:**13, 42, 59, 132, 134, 143, 166, 177, 205–6, 292, 313, 324, 339, 361, 623, 757; **11:**12, 48, 115, 117–18, 193, 217, 220, 690, 693, 704; **12:**712, 726

JUDEAN DESERT
1:278, 293–95; **2:**600; **6:**567, 1079, 1596; **7:**14

JUDEAN HILLS
1:219; **2:**646; **4:**63, 66, 69, 110, 281; **5:**261; **7:**351, 718

JUTTAH
3:347

K

KADESH
1:439; **2:**19, 94, 121, 123, 157–62, 164, 198, 219, 252, 254, 306, 316, 371, 528; **4:**140, 145; **12:**48–51, 53, 494

KADESH-BARNEA
2:120, 158, 249, 262, 294

KAIN
2:192

KARNAIM
4:80; **7:**403

KEDAR
3:761; **4:**1178; **5:**383; **6:**188–89, 600, 898, 900, 917, 1377, 1379

KEDEMOTH
2:164

KEDESH
2:265, 696, 780

KEDRON
4:174–75

KEHELATHAH
2:251

KEILAH
2:1152–53; **3:**765, 769

KERIOTH
7:363; **9:**415

KHIRBET QUMRAN
See QUMRAN, KHIRBET

KIBROTH-HATTAAVAH
2:105, 108, 254

KIBROTH-HATTAAVEH
2:104

KIBROTH-HATTAVEH
2:94

KIDRON
3:34; **9:**801

KIDRON VALLEY
2:1324, 1336–37; **3:**18, 34, 608, 628, 759, 760, 769; **4:**146; **6:**1189; **7:**331, 336; **9:**341, 801. *See also* WADI KIDRON

KING'S GARDEN
3:768, 879

KING'S GATE
3:451, 892, 897

KING'S HIGHWAY
2:161, 166

KING'S POOL
3:759, 769
KING'S VALLEY
1:439; **2:**639
KIR
3:251; **7:**361, 424, 699
KIRIATHAIM
2:250; **6:**891, 1353
KIRIATH-ARBA
3:827
KIRIATHARIM
3:686
KIRIATH-BAAL
2:1248
KIRIATH-HUZOTH
2:184
KIRIATH-JEARIM
2:678, 691, 1010, 1248; **3:**384, 686; **4:**1212
KIRIATH-SEPHER
2:737, 766; **3:**330, 332
KISHON VALLEY
3:136
KITTIM
2:192; **3:**1076; **4:**30, 228; **6:**1375, 1378; **7:**143
KUE
3:82; **6:**1378

L

LACHISH
1:221–22, 224, 247, 1054; **2:**615–16, 648; **3:**242, 268, 591, 996; **6:**7, 294, 329, 584, 1193; **7:**547, 594, 810
LADDER OF TYRE
4:140, 145
LAISH
2:694, 863, 870–71, 885; **5:**54
LAODICEA
1:7; **4:**283; **11:**353, 556, 580, 616, 659, 666–68, 884; **12:**573–74, 584, 586–88, 626
LASHARON
2:655
LEBANON
1:215, 303, 883; **2:**662; **3:**67, 84, 692, 756; **5:**262, 403, 405, 407, 415, 426, 502, 757, 859; **6:**137, 247, 249, 281, 342, 740, 742–43, 1244–46, 1295, 1373, 1375, 1422–25, 1429, 1555; **7:**170, 376, 424, 602, 648, 813, 815, 817–18; **8:**577
LEBANON MOUNTAINS
1:245; **5:**262, 403; **6:**247, 1245, 1375
LEBANON, FOREST OF
3:67, 756; **6:**740, 1245, 1295, 1555; **7:**817
LEBANON, TOWER OF
7:376
LEBO-HAMATH
2:122, 262–63; **3:**243, 499; **6:**1601; **7:**356
LEHEM
3:331. *See also* BETHLEHEM
LESHEM
2:694, 870
LEVI GATE
6:1606
LIBNAH
2:648, 655; **3:**214, 268, 569; **6:**294, 1269
LIBYA
1:249, 408; **6:**1374, 1517; **7:**147, 616; **8:**489; **9:**451; **10:**755
LOD
3:357, 686
LO-DEBAR
2:1273; **7:**403
LUD/LUDIM
6:882, 1374–75, 1415, 1442
LUZ
1:277, 659; **2:**743
LYCIA
4:170
LYCUS VALLEY
11:353, 567, 580, 591, 665, 667–68, 884
LYDDA
4:42, 146, 281; **10:**160–61
LYDIA
1:267; **3:**677; **4:**105, 248; **6:**1374, 1415, 1516; **7:**456; **11:**567
LYSTRA
8:14; **10:**188, 197–99, 202, 220, 224–25, 243, 245; **11:**191, 316, 833
LYSTRA, TEMPLE OF ZEUS AT
10:199–201

M

MAACAH
2:665, 1280, 1352
MAAPHA
4:78
MACEDONIA
1:269; **3:**409, 966; **4:**5, 30, 104, 107, 143, 248; **7:**111, 141; **9:**174; **10:**147, 214, 224, 227, 230–31, 237, 254, 270, 272, 276, 754, 756, 775, 935, 997; **11:**5–6, 11–12, 48, 55, 108–11, 114–17, 120, 469–70, 474, 483, 544, 674, 690, 694–95, 717, 720, 746
MACHPELAH
1:503–4, 585, 659, 667; **2:**546–47; **3:**1182

MADON
2:638
MAGADAN
8:339
MAGDALA
1:186; **8:**339; **9:**175
MAGOG
6:1512–16, 1523, 1529–32; **8:**671; **12:**534, 699, 702, 706, 714. *See also* GOG *in PERSONS IN THE BIBLE*
MAHANAIM
1:562–63; **2:**1211–13, 1216, 1273, 1332, 1336; **3:**28
MAKAZ
3:48
MAKKEDAH
2:648, 655
MALLUS
4:222
MALTA
10:351–52, 355–57; **11:**864
MAMRE
1:434, 503, 584, 670; **2:**547; **9:**475
MANAHATH
2:678
MANASSEH (TERRITORY)
2:212, 308, 512, 563, 587, 634, 660, 680, 694, 701, 706, 715, 718, 743, 745, 831; **3:**51–52, 351–53, 379; **4:**998; **5:**633; **6:**1601, 1604
MAON
2:1153, 1166, 1169; **3:**336, 379
MARAH
1:805–6, 808; **2:**253, 607; **3:**178; **6:**378
MARDUK, TOWER OF
6:1606
MARESHAH
3:538
MARISA
4:13, 81, 277
MAROTH
7:547
MARS HILL
10:243, 245, 249. *See also* AREOPAGUS
MASSA
5:258
MASSAH
1:818; **2:**536; **4:**991, 1062
MATTANAH
2:164–65
MEDEBA
2:166; **3:**416; **4:**13, 114–15
MEDIA
3:677, 706, 989, 994–96, 1008, 1011, 1022–23, 1028, 1055, 1070, 1081; **4:**93, 103, 105, 110, 129, 157, 253, 270; **6:**185, 399, 1380; **7:**6, 456
MEDITERRANEAN
1:5, 9, 13, 73, 75, 88, 162, 166, 186, 213–15, 225, 244–45, 247–48, 266, 268–70, 308, 408, 1025; **2:**262–63, 576, 662, 668, 677, 711–12; **3:**511, 1040, 1099, 1103, 1109, 1159; **4:**4–5, 34, 85, 291, 792, 964, 1000, 1215; **5:**54, 380, 422, 426, 428, 673, 675, 827; **6:**202–3, 577, 966, 1213, 1221, 1356, 1358–60, 1364, 1370–71, 1377–78, 1384, 1410, 1523, 1525, 1582, 1596, 1601, 1604–5; **7:**8, 24, 101, 143, 323, 411, 421, 456, 502, 543, 655, 738, 742, 802, 805, 807, 837; **8:**13–14, 27, 40, 44–46, 56, 257, 314; **9:**268, 302, 362, 506, 519, 584, 629, 632, 645, 667, 697–98, 722, 737, 742, 744, 756, 787, 863; **10:**161, 308, 345–46, 348, 407, 415, 486, 623, 753, 755, 773; **11:**57, 62, 157, 164, 173, 179, 183, 297, 347, 674, 682, 710, 808, 838; **12:**10, 14, 124, 130, 137, 170, 180, 203, 485
MEGIDDO
1:221–22, 224, 232, 247, 251, 261, 265–66; **2:**616, 651, 655, 661, 788; **3:**48, 52, 70, 82, 220, 286, 649; **5:**185; **6:**559, 741, 1077, 1403, 1540; **7:**828; **12:**677
MEGIDDO VALLEY
6:1077
MELITA
10:355. *See also* MALTA
MEMPHIS
1:246; **6:**601, 883, 1415, 1417–18; **7:**138, 266
MERIBAH
1:818; **2:**160, 536; **4:**1004, 1062; **12:**48
MERIBATH-KADESH
2:218, 528; **6:**1601
MEROM
2:651
MEROM, WATERS OF
2:651
MERRAN
6:966
MESALOTH
4:110
MESHECH
4:1178; **6:**1377–78, 1438, 1443–44, 1512, 1516
MESHECH-TUBAL
6:1438, 1443–44, 1516
MESOPOTAMIA
1:166, 214–15, 230–32, 235, 237, 245–47, 266–69, 306, 344, 408, 411–12, 417, 512, 622, 989, 1018, 1094; **2:**281, 306, 503, 536, 662, 714, 767, 779; **3:**50, 70, 416, 695, 698, 751, 757, 846, 977, 994, 1003–4, 1138; **4:**4, 59, 95, 157, 328–29, 395, 401, 449–50, 463, 492, 604; **5:**2–3, 6–7, 13,

MESOPOTAMIA *(continued)*
90, 257–58, 604–5, 651, 672, 793, 833; **6:**8, 11, 74, 102, 120, 225, 660, 683, 878, 1076–77, 1156, 1177, 1203, 1221–22, 1305, 1348, 1360, 1366, 1377, 1379–80, 1432, 1530–31, 1605; **7:**5, 19, 24, 43, 50, 111, 140, 424, 573, 588, 709; **8:**40; **12:**137, 141
MICHMASH
2:1070, 1079; **4:**109, 119
MIDIAN
1:306, 702–5, 717, 721, 725, 825; **2:**5, 34, 89, 94–95, 179–80, 192, 200, 202, 219, 232, 245–48, 796, 803, 805, 807–10, 817, 819, 837, 1022; **3:**93, 430; **4:**1010; **6:**137, 966, 1416; **12:**141
MIGDOL
2:253; **6:**1407, 1415
MILETUS
7:29, 138; **9:**260, 737; **10:**277–78, 280–82, 288, 292, 341, 367; **12:**859
MINNITH
6:1378
MISHNEH GATE
3:766–68, 839
MITYLENE
10:278
MIZPAH/MIZPEH
1:267; **2:**213, 825, 884, 886, 1016, 1018–19, 1028, 1046–48, 1053, 1145; **3:**294, 539, 765, 768, 825, 839, 1154; **4:**63–64, 66–67, 78, 80; **6:**943, 944, 1079–80, 1348–49; **7:**123–24, 244
MOAB
1:38, 225, 245, 248–50, 259, 264, 306–7, 315, 990, 995, 1040, 1189; **2:**4, 10, 16, 99, 158, 163–67, 169–70, 177–84, 186, 188, 190–91, 197–98, 201–2, 207, 215, 245–46, 252, 254, 267, 272, 275–76, 305–6, 308–9, 384, 461, 481, 501, 510–11, 519, 535, 614, 665, 770–73, 779, 824, 830–31, 899–902, 910, 915–16, 920, 935, 938, 943, 945, 1062, 1138, 1144–45, 1265; **3:**170, 180–81, 183–85, 332, 357, 414, 559, 686, 757, 848, 1090; **4:**46, 74, 198, 243, 306, 917, 1010, 1276; **5:**564, 668; **6:**17, 66, 149, 167–70, 207, 216, 218, 559, 782, 857, 878–79, 890–92, 894, 896, 917–20, 1245, 1249, 1347–50, 1352–53, 1356, 1358, 1363, 1369, 1396, 1400, 1403, 1418, 1489, 1525; **7:**50, 269, 288, 351, 353, 355, 362–63, 437, 663–64, 690, 696, 699, 828; **8:**130; **9:**738
MODEIN
4:42, 45, 152, 163, 174, 281–82, 295
MOREH
1:424
MORESHETH
6:9; **7:**533, 542
MORIAH
1:496; **3:**483; **12:**138
MORIAH, MOUNT
3:483; **12:**138
MOSERAH
2:162, 254
MUSTER GATE
3:767, 770, 839
MYNDOS
4:170
MYRA
10:346

N

NACON
2:1249
NADABATH
4:115
NAHALIEL
2:164
NAIN
3:130; **9:**20, 29, 157–59, 174, 190, 208–9, 336, 345, 395, 462, 465; **10:**540
NAIOTH
2:1128
NAPHATH-DOR
3:48, 52
NAPHTALI (TERRITORY)
2:677, 694, 743, 745; **3:**992; **6:**1604; **8:**167
NAPHTALI GATE
6:1606
NARBATTA
4:78
NAZARETH
1:83, 87, 169, 186, 737, 988, 1061, 1114; **2:**521, 1043, 1161; **3:**909; **4:**643, 690, 863, 874, 1037, 1131, 1213; **5:**313, 553, 721; **6:**143, 365, 451, 852; **7:**148, 327, 732; **8:**40, 69, 71, 86, 90, 93, 110–11, 125, 139–40, 143–44, 147, 150, 154, 156, 160, 167, 170, 198, 297, 317–19, 323, 365, 459, 500, 549, 566, 592–93, 616, 651, 712, 731; **9:**8, 22, 25, 30, 42, 51, 56, 63, 68, 73, 77, 88, 98, 102–8, 110–13, 116, 119, 122, 143, 157, 159, 199, 205, 215, 236, 325, 336, 352, 354, 360, 409, 468, 477, 479, 487, 531–34, 536, 830; **10:**20, 59, 63, 65–66, 76, 78, 80, 84–85, 97, 122, 132, 142, 306, 336, 342, 376, 384, 405, 419, 450–51, 461, 535, 537, 671, 697, 754; **11:**607–8; **12:**64–65, 428, 515, 709
NEAPOLIS
11:469
NEBO
2:164, 250, 614; **3:**686, 817; **6:**891

NEBO, MOUNT
2:61, 218, 526, 528; **3:**362; **4:**198; **12:**137
NEEDLE'S EYE GATE (LEGENDARY)
8:395
NEGEB/NEGEV
1:245, 247, 261, 424, 439, 584; **2:**121–23, 163, 677, 737–38, 1087, 1179, 1193, 1268; **3:**329–30, 332, 336, 505, 827; **4:**311, 1195; **6:**150, 253–54, 1294–95; **7:**361, 436, 455–56
NETOPHAH
3:362, 686, 838
NICOPOLIS
9:475; **11:**878
NILE DELTA
3:761; **6:**866; **7:**700
NILE RIVER
1:215, 234, 250, 267, 447, 620, 623, 699, 716, 742–43, 745, 750, 795; **2:**374; **3:**386; **4:**605; **5:**531, 533–34, 590, 758, 818; **6:**180, 601, 882, 1364, 1401, 1403–4, 1407, 1413, 1416, 1419, 1422, 1432, 1434, 1436–37, 1516, 1601; **7:**111 417, 422, 424, 616, 670, 672, 691, 700, 813, 815, 839; **8:**15
NILE VALLEY
1:166, 214; **3:**1040; **4:**63; **6:**1435; **7:**670, 690, 699
NINEVEH
1:95, 221, 237, 266; **2:**572, 824, 860; **3:**253, 269, 636, 871, 901, 985, 989, 994–96, 1002, 1004, 1007–8, 1028, 1033, 1049, 1051, 1063, 1068–71, 1097–98; **4:**63; **5:**517, 655, 818; **6:**7, 11, 20, 204, 257, 292, 300, 556, 717, 1126, 1307, 1336, 1378, 1412, 1422; **7:**62, 456, 465, 468, 470–73, 475–76, 478–87, 489–90, 492–95, 499, 505–6, 510–19, 522–28, 593–97, 599, 602–6, 609–16, 618–19, 661, 691–92, 697, 758, 845; **9:**72, 243, 319, 372; **10:**161–62; **12:**646
NO/NO-AMON
6:1418; **7:**595
NOB
2:988, 1113, 1138–41, 1148–49, 1156, 1183, 1193, 1268; **4:**890; **9:**133
NOD
1:375
NOPH
6:1418
NORTHERN KINGDOM
See EPHRAIM; ISRAEL (KINGDOM/TERRITORY)

O

OBOTH
2:164, 254
OCINA
3:1107
ODOMERA
4:118
OHOLAH
6:1316–17, 1319, 1321–22, 1324, 1327, 1329–31, 1459; **7:**184
OHOLIBAH
6:1316–17, 1319–20, 1324–27, 1329–31, 1459; **7:**184
OLD GATE
3:766–67, 839
OLIVES, MOUNT OF
1:278; **2:**1324–25; **3:**90, 115; **4:**926; **6:**1154, 1189; **7:**836, 840; **8:**403, 439, 474, 657–59, 704, 707; **9:**28, 201, 322, 367, 412–13, 428, 431–32, 434, 461, 476, 628, 801
ON
1:622; **6:**1418
ONO
3:357, 686, 784
OPHEL
3:759, 766, 768–70, 826
OPHIR
3:81–82, 168; **4:**502; **5:**695; **6:**965, 1360; **7:**136
OPHRAH
2:796–97, 809–10; **7:**547
ORONTES VALLEY
4:145
ORTHOSIA
4:147, 173

P

PADDAN-ARAM
1:585; **3:**1138; **6:**1530; **7:**291
PALESTINE
1:28, 94, 148, 213–27, 231, 233, 245–59, 266, 269–71, 388, 404, 439, 473; **2:**306, 556–57, 569, 571–72, 574–76, 586, 615–16, 649, 659–60, 662–63, 666–68, 685, 694; **3:**654; **4:**661; **5:**68, 75, 220, 223; **6:**36, 558, 1076–78; **7:**23–26, 67, 121; **8:**50–54, 141, 303, 449, 513; **9:**64, 113, 116, 117, 296, 472, 507, 699; **10:**306, 324, 376; **12:**182
PAMPHYLIA
4:167, 170; **10:**191, 225
PANEAS
5:859; **8:**343
PAPHOS
10:188–90, 194
PARADISE
1:88, 164, 346, 349–50, 365–67, 396, 430, 475, 1196; **2:**137, 747–48; **4:**604; **5:**71, 135, 252, 301; **6:**142, 1385, 1391–95, 1426, 1437, 1595, 1597–98; **7:**62, 177, 527–28; **8:**533, 535;

PARADISE *(continued)*
9:317–18, 360, 457–58, 463; **10:**507; **11:**17, 20, 36, 91, 158, 161–63; **12:**41, 525, 576, 630, 724, 729–30. *See also* EDEN, GARDEN OF
PARAH
6:684
PARAN
2:19–20, 94–95, 98, 108, 111, 121, 123, 159, 1166; **3:**93
PARAN, MOUNT
2:95; **4:**517
PARAN, WILDERNESS OF
2:19, 94–95, 123, 1166
PARTHIA
4:4–5, 13, 59, 84, 104, 169–70; **9:**88
PATHROS
6:1401, 1407, 1415, 1418
PATMOS
9:499; **12:**235, 366, 370, 504, 552, 562, 565–66, 569, 574, 736
PELUSIUM
3:996; **4:**34, 282; **6:**1418
PENIEL
1:567, 585; **2:**91; **5:**524. *See also* PENUEL
PENUEL
1:567, 718; **2:**792, 797, 807–8, 817, 841, 873; **3:**103–4
PENUEL, TOWER OF
2:807, 817
PEOR
2:159, 185, 189, 198, 678, 707, 715; **4:**32; **7:**264, 272
PERAZIM, MOUNT
3:389
PEREA
1:271; **8:**33, 111, 319, 385, 536, 643; **9:**88
PEREZ-UZZAH
3:382, 388
PERGA
10:191
PERGAMUM
1:269; **4:**4,104, 170, 199, 270; **12:**571, 578, 587–88, 656
PERSEPOLIS
3:859; **4:**193, 253; **7:**29
PERSIA
1:267, 286, 680; **2:**528; **3:**526, 665, 677–78, 695, 699, 704, 713, 717, 722, 736, 761, 862, 865, 892, 914, 977, 1077, 1081, 1098, 1100–1101, 1108, 1124, 1137; **4:**30, 60–61, 84–88, 197, 248; **5:**271, 274; **6:**352, 376, 763, 1374, 1517; **7:**4, 6, 28, 73, 87–88, 111, 118, 138–39, 331, 709, 715, 738, 742, 754, 757; **10:**398. *See also* PERSIAN: EMPIRE *in* SUBJECTS AND THEMES
PETHOR
2:179, 181, 186; **6:**1348
PHARPAR
3:194
PHASELIS
4:170
PHASIRON
4:118
PHILADELPHIA
4:178; **12:**575, 587, 594, 626, 631–32, 657
PHILIPPI
5:824; **8:**24; **10:**215, 230–37, 244, 266, 270, 272, 276–78, 739, 754–55, 775; **11:**3, 48, 112, 114–15, 202, 361, 469–71, 474–75, 480–83, 485, 496, 498–99, 501, 510–11, 518–21, 525, 533, 535, 540, 543–44, 546, 674, 681–82, 698, 703, 707, 805
PHILISTIA
1:245, 266; **2:**594, 662, 824, 1005–6, 1012, 1152, 1243; **3:**150, 336, 597; **4:**917, 1010, 1024; **6:**149, 163, 182, 878, 885, 890, 917, 1077, 1347, 1350, 1355–56, 1363, 1369, 1396, 1400; **7:**301, 331, 361, 699, 802, 805
PHOENICIA
1:264, 278, 666, 990; **2:**662; **3:**95, 693; **4:**5, 56, 62, 102, 129, 170, 206, 214, 223, 233, 260; **5:**273; **6:**201–2, 316, 1076, 1360–61, 1366, 1398; **7:**143, 802, 806; **8:**382; **10:**288
PHOENIX
10:345–46, 348
PHRYGIA
4:248; **10:**259, 777; **11:**567, 580; **12:**710
PI-HAHIROTH
2:253
PIRATHON
2:765
PISGAH
2:164, 166, 185, 187
PISGAH, MOUNT
2:164–65, 185, 187, 310
PISHON
1:351; **5:**758
PITHOM
1:695
PLACE OF THE SKULL
9:454, 829. *See also* GOLGOTHA
PONTIUS
8:13
PONTUS
1:14, 192; **4:**4; **12:**76, 325

POTSHERD GATE
3:759; **6:**721
POTTER'S FIELD
8:484
PRAETORIUM
8:488, 719; **10:**314, 330; **11:**473–74
PTOLEMAIS
4:5, 77–78, 121, 125, 127, 129, 134, 147, 173, 233, 282–83; **7:**140
PUT
6:882, 1375, 1415, 1517; **7:**616
PUTEOLI
10:327

Q

QUMRAN, KHIRBET
1:10–11, 25, 87–88, 287, 289, 293, 295–96, 300, 304, 307, 1194; **2:**527, 950–51, 979, 1053–54, 1102, 1249, 1386; **3:**308, 451, 809, 859, 862, 936, 969, 971, 976–77, 987, 992, 1031, 1039, 1064, 1076, 1133, 1151, 1158, 1191; **4:**8, 20, 30, 46, 64, 66, 71–72, 78, 96, 123, 125, 197, 199, 205, 243, 249, 281, 355, 467, 497, 501, 658, 662, 1259, 1285–86; **5:**12, 160, 164, 244, 273, 332, 629, 634, 636, 673, 690, 699, 764, 800, 834, 867, 873, 875; **6:**73, 228, 454, 466, 567, 570, 660, 934, 942, 949, 973, 988, 994, 1541, 1547, 1609; **7:**3, 13–15, 150, 601, 667, 848, 867, 885–86; **8:**28–31, 34–39, 102, 152, 156–57, 178, 195–96, 345, 353, 371, 432, 458, 526, 531–33, 537, 545, 588, 666, 702, 742; **9:**65, 84–85, 147, 178, 196, 224, 287, 506, 527, 632, 641–42, 648, 713, 873; **10:**72, 82, 460, 466, 516, 524, 571, 663, 676, 785, 850, 931, 1010; **11:**259, 357, 363, 373–74, 377, 415, 421, 446, 459–60, 499, 532–33, 563, 593, 596, 615, 726, 799, 913; **12:**28, 59, 61, 71, 85, 98, 368–69, 395, 405, 519, 596, 726, 747. *See also* QUMRAN SCROLLS *in ANCIENT LITERATURE*

R

RAAMAH
6:1377, 1379–80
RABBAH
2:167, 1279–80, 1283–84, 1286, 1300; **3:**416; **6:**894, 1293, 1304, 1347–48, 1351, 1378; **7:**362
RAGAU
3:1098. *See also* RAGES
RAGES
3:1011, 1023, 1027–28, 1031, 1033, 1044, 1098–99
RAHAB
4:1024, 1035; **6:**254; **7:**699. *See also* EGYPT
RAMAH
1:585; **2:**973, 1017, 1019, 1027, 1047, 1090, 1099, 1127–28, 1133, 1145; **3:**536, 686; **6:**810, 815; **7:**247; **8:**147
RAMATH-LEHI
2:853
RAMESES
1:653, 695, 781; **2:**252–53; **4:**991
RAMOTH
2:265
RAMOTH-GILEAD
3:161–62, 164, 181, 192, 216–20, 248, 551, 570; **6:**1198, 1208; **7:**252
RAPHIA
5:612; **7:**140
RED SEA
1:209–10, 274, 343, 661; **2:**39, 99, 124–25, 158–59, 161, 163, 252–53, 753, 774, 833; **3:**168, 511, 1080, 1173; **5:**525, 527, 531, 591, 593; **6:**448, 1360, 1403–4; **8:**150, 169, 457, 471, 512, 588, 590; **12:**140, 142, 672–73
REED SEA
4:313; **6:**1245; **7:**101; **9:**596. *See also* RED SEA
REHOB
2:122, 262–63, 1266; **3:**817
REHOBOTH
1:528
REPHAIM, VALLEY OF
3:389
REPHIDIM
1:824; **2:**254, 1087; **5:**525
RHEGIUM
10:357
RHODES
4:167, 170; **6:**1378, 1380
RIBLAH
2:262; **3:**288, 293; **6:**1077, 1079, 1161, 1186, 1194–95, 1251, 1336
RIMMON
7:837
RITHMAH
2:253
ROME
1:14–15, 85, 95, 270–71, 287, 289–91, 796; **2:**191, 774; **3:**898, 1124, 1167, 1181; **4:**5, 11, 20, 31, 35, 39, 93, 98, 102, 104–8, 121, 133, 142–44, 148, 151, 158, 160, 163–64, 169–71, 198, 216–18, 233, 243, 248, 255, 270, 282, 298, 883, 996, 1277; **5:**189, 556, 612, 626; **6:**185, 214, 226, 1384; **7:**4, 10, 12, 25, 61, 74, 76, 103, 141, 143; **8:**12–13, 16, 44, 46, 49, 52, 105, 142, 180, 198, 350, 371, 420, 485, 487, 509, 514–17, 651, 659, 663, 668, 671, 683–85, 718; **9:**6, 49,

ROME *(continued)*
60, 80, 88, 156, 362–63, 386, 401, 460, 488, 665, 707, 814, 816, 818, 823, 830; **10:**3, 7, 9, 12–22, 25, 28, 31, 46, 80, 122, 126, 130, 147, 195, 203–4, 213–15, 235–37, 239, 252–53, 256, 261, 270, 272–73, 275–78, 283, 285, 288–89, 291–92, 297–99, 304–5, 310–14, 320–21, 324–27, 329–30, 333–34, 338, 340–42, 344–46, 349, 352, 355–57, 359–64, 366–68, 373–74, 396, 398, 404–8, 420–24, 437–39, 479, 504–5, 514, 524, 587, 593, 612, 614, 618, 623, 627, 629, 653, 664, 681, 683–84, 686, 699, 701, 710, 717–19, 731–32, 735, 737–39, 748, 750, 753, 755–58, 761–63, 765–66, 768–69, 773–75, 969, 997, 1001; **11:**58, 135, 144, 194, 202, 231, 303, 369, 379–80, 405, 417, 470, 473–75, 488–89, 519, 535, 546, 674–75, 703, 781, 838, 884, 898, 903; **12:**173, 233–35, 318, 324, 504, 524, 532–33, 538, 543–44, 551, 683–84, 705, 712

ROME, TEMPLE TO LUSTITIA/AUGUSTA AT
10:404

RUMAH
6:1270

S

SALAMIS
3:951; **10:**189

SALEM
1:439, 577; **2:**148, 191, 1236; **4:**504; **6:**354; **12:**86

SALT, VALLEY OF
3:241

SALT SEA
6:1595, 1599

SAMARIA (CITY)
1:221–22, 224–25, 249–52, 262, 264–65, 267–68, 270, 467, 477; **2:**560, 680; **3:**52, 124, 126, 147, 155, 158, 162, 167, 177–78, 192, 197–98, 201–2, 204–5, 210, 220, 223, 228, 234, 236, 242, 251–53, 255, 586, 601, 992, 1099; **5:**419; **6:**36, 107, 116–17, 174, 227, 236, 574, 647, 711, 943, 1076, 1202, 1221–22, 1224, 1232, 1236–38, 1307, 1316, 1319–22, 1324, 1329–30, 1402, 1459, 1605; **7:**224, 256, 260–61, 270, 272, 275, 293–94, 342, 374–75, 394, 399, 400, 419, 534, 536, 541–44, 546, 582, 584, 709, 753; **10:**138, 167, 182, 268

SAMARIA (TERRITORY)
1:250, 256, 262, 264, 467; **2:**319, 555, 568, 573, 586, 635–36, 660, 683, 810; **3:**3, 155, 251–52, 255, 258, 261, 264–65, 274, 276, 278, 285, 551, 554, 667, 679, 685, 695, 698–99, 708, 751, 757, 772, 1075, 1078, 1095, 1099, 1103, 1109, 1111–13, 1117; **4:**9–10, 13, 45, 56, 74, 115, 140, 147, 171, 229, 275, 295, 999; **5:**633, 801; **6:**16, 74, 82, 89, 108, 127–29, 132, 137, 227, 231, 235–36, 260, 865; **7:**184, 456; **8:**23, 67, 256, 382, 385; **9:**112, 214–15, 217, 268, 325, 372, 469, 487, 565, 570–71, 574; **10:**13, 42, 59, 126, 132, 134–35, 137–40, 142, 167

SAMARIA, MOUNT
3:1113; **7:**376, 399

SAMARIA, TEMPLE AT
10:137

SAMOS
4:170; **10:**278

SAMPSAMES (SAMSUN, AMISOS)
4:170

SARDIS
1:93, 192; **4:**270; **5:**273; **7:**456; **9:**504; **11:**364; **12:**513, 574, 582–83, 587–89, 626, 667, 725, 733

SAREPTA
3:128; **6:**1398. *See also* ZAREPHATH

SHECHEM, TOWER OF
2:817–18

SCYTHOPOLIS
3:1109; **4:**13, 80, 147, 182, 276

SEBA
1:409; **4:**964; **6:**375–76; **7:**331

SEIR
1:521, 563, 573, 590; **2:**191, 305, 461; **3:**317–18; **4:**517; **5:**862; **6:**187, 520

SEIR, MOUNT
2:158; **3:**559; **5:**407; **6:**1352, 1427, 1474–80, 1484

SELA
3:241; **7:**447

SELEUCIA
4:132, 140, 147, 157, 168; **7:**140

SENAAH
3:686, 768

SENIR
5:403; **6:**1373, 1375

SEPHARAD
7:456

SEPHARVAIM
2:573

SHALLECHETH GATE (WEST GATE)
3:451

SHAPHIR
7:547

SHARON
1:245; **5:**389; **6:**281; **10:**161

SHEBA
3:81–82, 86–88, 510, 512; **4:**172, 964; **5:**272, 297, 511, 849; **6:**1377, 1380, 1518; **8:**296, 615; **9:**243, 245, 248, 259

SHECHEM
1:260–62, 295, 298, 311, 424, 503, 516, 577, 581, 584, 599, 660, 665, 674; **2:**264–65, 486, 546–47, 563, 578, 607, 634–36, 641, 680, 683, 686, 696, 709, 714–15, 736, 752, 791, 810, 816–18, 876; **3:**100, 103–4, 347, 353, 518, 691, 1119; **4:**13, 50, 56, 248; **5:**862; **6:**943; **7:**252; **10:**126, 138

SHEEP GATE
3:766, 767, 770, 839

SHELAH, POOL OF
3:759, 768

SHEOL
1:31, 236, 447, 515, 600; **2:**65, 138, 162, 981, 1336; **3:**1004, 1061, 1063; **4:**236, 240–41, 306, 415, 420, 442, 444, 461–62, 485, 508, 512, 517–18, 529, 603, 704, 718, 737, 747–48, 789, 796, 842, 877, 898, 1028, 1058, 1148, 1236, 1244; **5:**38, 40, 45, 67–68, 76, 85, 89, 104, 149, 151, 194, 207, 231–32, 241, 253, 276, 285, 311, 322, 341, 353, 430, 459, 651, 716, 730, 757, 823, 824; **6:**94, 158–59, 212, 223, 342–43, 411, 691, 1105, 1114, 1388, 1422–23, 1428–30, 1438–40, 1442–45, 1534; **7:**2, 291–92, 421, 480, 506, 509, 527, 817; **8:**676; **9:**221, 346; **11:**625; **12:**254, 492, 632, 700. *See also* HELL

SHEPHALAH
7:542, 547

SHEPHAM
2:262

SHEPHELAH
1:218; **2:**638, 646, 677; **3:**336, 598, 756–57, 827; **4:**281; **7:**456

SHESHACH
6:766. *See also* BABYLON

SHIHOR
3:386

SHILOAH, POOL OF
See KING'S POOL

SHILOAH, WATERS OF
3:759; **6:**117, 411, 481

SHILOH
1:316, 665, 1186; **2:**233, 548, 563, 574, 582, 661, 667, 686–90, 694, 706, 715, 726, 782, 871, 886–87, 949, 960, 969–70, 973–76, 986–87, 991–93, 997, 999, 1001–2, 1007, 1010, 1012, 1014–16, 1019, 1090, 1139, 1184, 1240, 1247; **3:**33, 75, 94, 112, 363, 399, 725, 890; **4:**992; **6:**575, 637, 772, 943, 1118, 1143, 1349, 1509; **7:**550; **9:**70, 375

SHINAR
1:408, 411, 438; **2:**351, 393; **7:**39, 73, 777–80

SHITTIM
2:197–98, 599–601; **7:**244, 579

SHITTIM, VALLEY OF
7:335

SHUR
1:452

SHUR, WILDERNESS OF
2:253

SIBMAH
2:250

SIBRAIM
6:1601

SICYON
4:170

SIDE (IN PAMPHYLIA)
4:167, 170

SIDDIM, VALLEY OF
1:438–39

SIDON
1:236, 248, 264, 278, 666; **2:**536, 662, 824; **3:**139, 1107; **4:**77, 102, 147, 199, 233, 282; **5:**261; **6:**202–3, 559, 782, 1249, 1350, 1356, 1359–61, 1374–75, 1392, 1396–98, 1400, 1403–4; **7:**50, 141, 301, 331, 456, 757, 804, 810; **8:**105, 111, 174, 272, 336, 560, 610; **9:**22, 107, 221, 243, 336, 565; **10:**181, 346

SILOAM
1:249, 1160; **3:**273, 628, 630, 768; **5:**298, 853; **9:**270, 273, 653–54

SILOAM, POOL OF
1:249, 1160; **3:**768; **5:**853; **9:**270, 654

SILOAM, TOWER OF
9:270, 273

SIMEON (TERRITORY)
2:694, 701; **6:**1605

SIN, WILDERNESS OF
2:252–53

SINAI
1:37–38, 66–67, 245, 274–75, 280–81, 299, 306–7, 311–13, 316, 318, 490, 529–30, 678–79, 685–86, 711, 807, 830–31, 834–40, 860–61, 880, 882–83, 887, 891, 927, 932, 937–39, 949, 955, 962, 1062; **2:**5–6, 10, 12, 16, 19, 23, 33, 35, 65, 86–87, 92, 94–97, 99–100, 104–5, 125, 163, 170, 214–15, 229, 254, 316, 480, 677, 1087, 1238, 1258, 1262; **3:**718, 811, 1040; **4:**198, 774, 881, 944–45, 947, 990, 1004–5, 1135, 1142, 1220; **5:**33, 113, 132, 283, 363, 562, 730; **6:**19, 211, 444, 453, 529, 597, 639, 669, 734, 758, 831, 1075, 1082, 1084, 1129, 1245, 1254, 1274, 1280, 1461, 1470, 1472–73; **7:**309, 369, 660, 674–75, 683, 690, 722, 783, 837, 864, 876; **8:**36, 188, 291, 332, 346; **9:**469, 519, 522, 587, 738; **10:**53–54, 457, 536, 552, 562–63, 624, 628, 662, 692; **11:**211, 267, 303, 404; **12:**33, 101, 104, 110, 117, 159–60, 504, 530–31, 560, 591, 616, 664, 735

SINAI PENINSULA
2:95, 316, 662, 1179
SINAI, DESERT OF
1:245, 1043; **2:**677
SINAI, MOUNT
1:69, 71, 81, 278, 805, 861, 884, 891, 994–95, 1000, 1007–8, 1043, 1055–56, 1066, 1171, 1182, 1190; **2:**11, 14, 20, 25, 32, 77, 79–82, 86, 88–92, 94, 99–100, 106–7, 110, 120, 136, 197, 202, 252, 254, 267, 271, 273, 325, 484, 519, 534, 747, 753, 792, 809, 826, 887, 1001, 1013, 1022, 1057, 1255; **3:**142, 671, 1001, 1137; **5:**48, 99, 526; **6:**19, 38, 103, 190, 216, 676, 1154, 1167–68, 1280, 1289, 1466, 1538; **7:**250, 662, 674, 677, 876; **8:**175, 247, 364, 537; **9:**205–6; **10:**123, 440, 512, 550, 563, 631; **11:**64, 185, 216, 302–3, 440; **12:**156, 158, 592
SINAI, WILDERNESS OF
1:306, 1055; **2:**4, 12, 16, 32–33, 35, 94, 207, 214–15, 252, 254
SLAUGHTER, VALLEY OF
6:813, 1526. *See also* HINNOM, VALLEY OF
SMYRNA
4:104; **12:**569, 571, 575–76, 587–88, 626, 632, 708
SODOM
1:329, 419–20, 433–35, 438–42, 449, 462, 467–70, 473–79, 483, 494; **2:**512, 542, 547–49, 802, 877; **4:**312, 452, 503, 554, 722; **5:**55, 125, 172, 186, 524, 596–97, 621, 725, 818; **6:**46, 54–55, 157, 161, 277, 335, 354, 412, 441, 448, 541, 547, 550, 619, 630, 750, 896, 918, 1062, 1084, 1213–14, 1219, 1221, 1236–38, 1296, 1307, 1522–23; **7:**278, 381–82, 597, 730, 751; **8:**257, 272, 595; **9:**219–20, 231–32; **10:**643; **12:**86, 347–48, 356, 488–90, 633, 636, 642, 693
SODOM, SEA OF
12:636
SOLOMON'S PORTICO
9:675; **10:**89, 99, 101
SOREK
2:858; **4:**174
SOREK, VALLEY OF
2:858
SOUTHERN KINGDOM
See JUDAH (KINGDOM/TERRITORY)
SPAIN
1:71–73, 75–76, 99, 101; **3:**898; **4:**104, 964; **6:**202, 1378; **7:**456, 494; **9:**88; **10:**374, 396, 407, 612, 701, 753, 755, 757–59; **11:**144, 474, 674–75, 781
SPARTA
4:105, 143–44, 148, 160, 163
SUCCOTH
1:275, 573; **2:**230, 253, 807–8, 817, 841, 873, 1286
SUPHAH
2:165
SUR/SUR-RI/SOR
2:165; **3:**1107; **6:**1359. *See also* TYRE
SUSA
1:896; **2:**544; **3:**698–99, 751, 761, 782, 856–57, 859–61, 868, 878–79, 885–86, 888, 899, 901, 904–5, 926–27, 932, 934–35, 967, 1113; **6:**1443; **7:**111, 138
SYCHAR
3:533
SYENE
6:1407, 1415
SYRACUSE
4:275; **10:**357
SYRIA
1:214–15, 225, 231–33, 235, 237, 245–50, 254, 257, 259, 265–66, 269–70, 408, 1018, 1095, 1135; **2:**161, 181, 536, 557, 614, 660, 1266; **3:**82, 146, 160, 193, 288, 654, 695, 1078, 1099; **4:**4–5, 23, 31, 34–35, 63, 93, 95–96, 134, 140, 147, 168, 193, 217, 270, 276, 281, 328; **5:**271, 867; **6:**6–7, 11, 36, 102, 107, 137, 173–74, 225, 231, 253, 556, 559, 562, 782, 851, 897, 1114, 1213, 1233, 1245, 1348, 1360, 1379–80, 1398, 1402; **7:**24, 111, 140, 143, 202, 246, 257, 342, 424, 481, 612, 661, 709–10, 802–4, 806; **8:**44–46, 49–52, 54, 105, 174, 382, 515; **9:**22, 62, 80; **10:**146, 205, 225, 258, 276, 376, 398; **11:**163, 217, 222, 231, 397; **12:**186, 368, 475
SYRO-ARABIAN DESERT
1:515; **2:**600; **3:**505; **6:**1351
SYRTIS
10:348

T

TAANACH
2:655; **3:**48, 52
TABERAH
2:104
TABOR
2:808; **7:**244
TABOR, MOUNT
4:1035; **6:**1114; **9:**205
TADMOR
3:505
TAHPANHES
6:1080, 1415, 1418
TAMAR
3:505; **6:**1601

TANIS
6:1418. *See also* ZOAN
TAPPUAH
2:655
TARSHISH
3:511, 564; **4:**964; **5:**394; **6:**73, 202–3, 509, 548, 1360, 1376–80, 1382, 1518; **7:**468, 470, 473, 477, 479, 492, 494, 499, 517–18, 527
TARSUS
1:94, 288; **4:**55, 222; **6:**1129; **10:**151, 154, 175–76, 225, 298, 305, 308, 310, 314, 335, 374, 446, 462, 676; **11:**163, 217, 222
TEHAPHNEHES
6:1413, 1418
TEKOA
1:242; **2:**678, 1313, 1319, 1352; **3:**152, 329, 756, 769–70, 838, 911, 1138; **4:**114, 188, 152; **5:**11, 160; **6:**8; **7:**340, 351–52, 411, 468–69
TEL-ABIB
3:687; **6:**1081, 1086, 1088, 1111, 1128, 1132
TEMA
4:562; **6:**189, 191, 966
TEMAN
6:966, 1294–95, 1354; **7:**362, 449
THEBES
1:246, 249; **2:**637; **4:**144; **5:**93; **6:**1418, 1422; **7:**595, 597, 616, 661, 691–92
THEBEZ
2:634, 738, 817
THERA
7:111. *See also* AHAVA
THESSALONICA
10:215, 237–40, 754–55, 775, 964, 993; **11:**48, 112, 114–15, 161, 202, 470, 542, 544, 673–77, 680–82, 705, 707, 712, 715
THREE TAVERNS
10:357
THYATIRA
10:231; **12:**543, 571, 581, 588
TIBER
8:15
TIBERIAS
8:609; **9:**175, 186
TIBERIAS, SEA OF
9:509, 855–56
TIGRIS
1:215, 246, 269, 351, 388, 392; **3:**1028, 1031, 1098; **4:**157, 1227; **5:**758; **6:**900, 1326; **7:**136, 526, 593; **12:**598
TIGRIS-EUPHRATES VALLEY
1:351, 388, 416
TIMNAH
1:224, 605; **2:**694, 842, 849
TIMNATH-HERES
2:694
TIMNATH-SERAH
2:694, 717
TIPHSAH
3:248
TIRZAH
1:224, 262; **2:**212, 634, 680, 683; **5:**365, 419
TISHBE
3:126
TOB
2:825, 1280; **3:**416; **4:**77
TOPHETH
1:1126; **6:**721–22, 1286, 1526
TOWER OF THE FLOCK
7:567
TOWER OF THE HUNDRED
3:756, 767, 839
TOWER OF THE OVENS
3:768, 839
TRANSJORDAN
1:242, 245, 259, 261, 268, 270–71, 670; **2:**8–9, 16, 157–59, 164, 166–67, 169, 178, 202, 207, 244, 248–50, 255, 262–63, 265, 305, 307–9, 492, 655, 825, 830, 1212–13, 1273, 1280, 1332, 1336, 1347; **3:**161, 378–79, 414–15, 551, 594, 811; **4:**13, 74, 78, 114, 207, 263–64, 275, 1010; **5:**633; **6:**168, 1347–48, 1528; **7:**252, 342; **8:**105, 111, 560, 642; **9:**142, 186
TRAVELERS, VALLEY OF THE
6:1525
TRIPOLIS
4:93, 173, 283
TROAS
3:409; **10:**276–77; **11:**55–56, 60–61, 108–10, 115, 469
TUBAL
6:1377–78, 1512, 1516–17
TYRE
1:221, 248, 262, 359, 896, 900; **2:**536, 660, 1242; **3:**53, 58, 67, 83, 388–89, 417, 429, 478, 1107; **4:**30, 77, 102, 140, 145, 147, 199, 218, 222, 233, 256, 282, 861, 1010, 1024; **5:**261; **6:**149–50, 176, 189, 201–3, 509, 559, 782, 966, 1222, 1249, 1301, 1330, 1350, 1356, 1358–71, 1373–80, 1382–84, 1386–89, 1391–96, 1398, 1400, 1403–4, 1410–12, 1415, 1420, 1425–26, 1429, 1432, 1434, 1442–43, 1445, 1482, 1516–18, 1595–96; **7:**50, 140, 270, 301, 331, 353, 355, 362–63, 699, 752, 803–6, 808, 810, 818; **8:**34, 105, 111, 174, 272, 336, 560, 610, 612, 663; **9:**221, 243; **10:**181, 288; **11:**40, 806; **12:**30, 680–81, 693, 723

TYROPOEON VALLEY
3:451, 759, 768

U

ULAI
7:111, 114
UPHAZ
7:136; **12:**561, 598
UPPER GATE
3:248, 251, 575, 766
UPPER ROOM, THE
3:497, 770; **7:**91; **8:**468, 659; **9:**719; **10:**277
UR
1:246, 411, 422, 445, 1118; **3:**810; **6:**377, 381, 1380; **8:**144; **10:**492
UZ
3:13; **4:**319, 328, 344

V

VALLEY GATE
3:759, 767–68, 838–39
VIA DOLOROSA
9:352
VIA EGNATIA
10:237–38; **11:**469, 470, 675, 682
VIA SEBASTE
10:1197

W

WADI BESOR
2:1193
WADI CHERITH
3:127
WADI EL-HESA
2:164. *See also* WADI ZERED
WADI ESCHOL
2:120–22
WADI KIDRON
6:1175. *See also* KIDRON VALLEY
WADI KISHON
2:788
WADI ZERED
2:158, 164, 294; **6:**1348, 1474; **7:**437
WAHEB
2:165
WAILING/WESTERN WALL
8:439, 686
WATER GATE
1:1160; **3:**767, 769, 800, 802, 839; **9:**542

Y

YAHWEH, MOUNT
2:9–10, 14, 19, 94–96
YAVNEH
See JAMNIA/YAVNEH

Z

ZAANAN
7:547
ZALMON
4:945
ZANOAH
3:768, 770, 827
ZAPHON
4:872, 1035; **6:**1114
ZAPHON, MOUNT
4:518, 872; **6:**67, 159, 1114–15, 1118, 1387, 1393
ZAREPHATH
3:128, 132–33, 140, 186, 189, 197; **5:**851; **7:**456; **9:**107, 113, 157, 159, 174, 395; **12:**144
ZEBOIIM
2:512; **7:**278
ZEBULUN (TERRITORY)
1:666; **2:**677, 743; **6:**1605
ZEDAD
2:262–63; **6:**1601
ZEMARAIM, MOUNT
3:530
ZEPHATH
2:739, 743
ZERED BROOK/STREAM
See WADI ZERED
ZIN
2:94, 262
ZIN, DESERT/WILDERNESS OF
2:19, 122, 159, 217, 219, 252–54, 262; **6:**1601
ZION
1:279, 914, 1060; **2:**18, 38, 387, 602, 1246; **3:**69, 96, 659, 840, 865, 1171; **4:**73, 78, 80, 84, 241, 309, 313, 400, 458, 648, 649, 668, 680, 682, 730, 733, 755, 772, 864, 865, 871–72, 874, 887, 933–34, 944–46, 979–81, 992, 994, 1012–13, 1022–25, 1054, 1069, 1075–76, 1081, 1086–88, 1091, 1176, 1183–84, 1190, 1192, 1200–1203, 1209–14, 1216–17, 1219, 1221, 1227, 1264; **5:**343, 486, 621, 757, 800, 853; **6:**3, 15, 17, 20, 40, 47, 54, 62, 65, 67–69, 81–84, 136, 147–48, 163–64, 167–69, 183, 230, 237, 239, 255, 261, 270–71, 277–78, 280–82, 285, 292, 316, 318–20, 327–30, 334–37, 347, 349, 357, 363, 365, 377, 380, 391, 393–95, 399, 402, 406–8, 410, 412–14, 419, 423–24, 428, 430–37, 439–43, 447–51, 453–56, 460–61, 463, 465, 467, 471–72, 474, 476–79, 481–82, 485, 490–91, 493, 498, 505, 508–10, 513–20, 529–30, 540–45, 547–51, 605, 612, 615, 620, 635, 641, 664–65, 692, 774, 787, 808, 811, 860, 891, 913–14, 939,

973, 1015, 1020–21, 1023, 1027, 1029–30, 1032–36, 1038–46, 1059, 1061, 1063, 1065–67, 1069–71, 1222, 1472; **7:**12, 113, 321, 324, 328, 334, 336, 352, 399, 425, 454, 565, 660, 699, 702, 737, 739, 742, 744, 747, 749, 753–54, 758–63, 765, 767, 770, 783, 786, 789, 795, 802, 804, 806–11, 826, 837, 838, 839; **8:**33, 36–37, 533, 655, 659, 680; **9:**70, 367; **10:**448, 458, 651, 665, 692, 756; **11:**205, 402; **12:**159–60, 238, 260, 521, 613, 635, 677, 684, 693, 724, 726

ZION, MOUNT
2:14, 350, 388, 1236–38, 1255, 1266; **3:**407, 429, 1179; **4:**71, 84, 87, 163, 197, 689, 733, 773, 871–72, 973, 1079, 1180–81; **6:**37–38, 66–67, 73, 118, 137, 142, 175, 206–7, 210, 213, 216–17, 228, 260, 295, 1070, 1083–84, 1115, 1252, 1393, 1430, 1538, 1595; **7:**328, 439, 442, 454–56, 458, 795, 811; **8:**33, 339; **10:**666; **11:**227, 261; **12:**156, 158, 525, 603, 663–64, 704, 714, 722

ZIPH
2:1153; **3:**379

ZIPH, WILDERNESS OF
2:1153

ZIPHRON
2:262

ZOAN
4:991–92; **6:**180, 1418

ZOAR
1:435, 475–76, 479; **2:**547; **5:**524; **7:**774

ZOBAH
2:1266, 1279; **3:**93, 414–15, 505

ZOPHIM, FIELD OF
2:187

ZORAH
2:694; **3:**827

ZUPH
2:974; **6:**1159

OUTSIDE THE BIBLE

A

AEGEAN SEA REGION
1:408; **2:**557, 711; **7:**424; **10:**224, 231, 259, 278, 346, 775, 997; **11:**48, 55, 108, 781, 842

AKABA
2:254

AKHETATEN
2:637

AMARNA
1:232; **2:**637

ARAQ-EL-EMIR
4:222, 276; **8:**34

ARMENIA
1:408; **4:**270; **7:**361

B

BAALBECK
7:361

BERLIN WALL
2:1021, 1114; **8:**159; **11:**405

BETHER
2:678

BIRKET EL-HAMRA
3:769

BLACK SEA
1:14; **2:**668; **4:**170; **11:**644

BYBLOS
1:248; **2:**662; **4:**1010; **5:**261; **6:**1361, 1367, 1374–75, 1392, 1398

C

CAIRO GENIZAH
5:14, 300, 454, 635, 867

CAUCASUS
2:711

CULIACAN
2:719

D

DALMATIA
11:674, 857

DURA-EUROPOS
7:61

E

EL-AMARNA
1:232

ELEPHANTINE
1:234, 250, 267–68, 285; **2:**413, 935; **3:**708, 733, 747, 751, 780, 977, 979, 1040, 1118; **5:**643; **6:**181, 546, 1408; **7:**125, 792, 860, 866; **8:**34

EL-JIB
3:39

EL-QUBEIBEH
9:475

ET-TELL
1:253; **2:**627

H

HERODIUM
3:756; **8:**35, 267
HIERAPOLIS-BAMBYKE
4:193
HYRCANIA
4:157

I

IRAQ
1:822; **2:**614; **3:**994; **4:**30; **7:**593
ISSUS
1:269; **4:**30; **7:**111

J

JAFFA GATE
8:719
JEBEL MUSA
2:316
JERASH
8:231; **9:**186
JORDAN (MODERN)
1:234, 1126; **3:**28; **5:**334; **7:**170, 362

K

KEREM
2:678
KHIRBET EL TABEIQA
4:69
KHIRBET RADDANA
1:216
KOLOUN
2:678

L

LATIN AMERICA
1:1, 112, 121, 171, 203; **7:**151, 457, 639; **12:**549–50, 554–55

M

MARI
1:237, 246; **2:**614–15, 630–31, 1005; **6:**10–11, 1269
MASADA
1:293, 296; **5:**634–35, 824, 842; **8:**35, 267, 319
MEEROTH-BENE-JAAKEN
2:254
MIDDLE EAST
1:229, 234, 490, 822; **2:**659, 719, 1307; **4:**1185; **5:**271, 328; **7:**449; **9:**172, 571; **10:**697; **12:**544
MITANNI
1:246

N

NAG HAMMADI
1:14, 18, 20–21; **8:**72, 82, 103; **9:**517; **11:**568; **12:**520
NEAR EAST
1:214, 220, 230, 242, 246, 250, 267, 269, 308, 427, 860, 989, 1025; **2:**627, 662; **3:**265, 979; **4:**108, 441; **5:**255, 270; **6:**945, 990, 998, 1000, 1007; **7:**24, 26, 307; **8:**308; **12:**26
NIPPUR
1:246; **4:**204, 562; **6:**1081; **7:**28

P

PELLA
1:269–70; **4:**13, 30
PITRU
2:181
PUNJAB VALLEY
4:30

Q

QUMRAN, KHIRBET
1:10, 87–88, 293–96, 300, 307, 1194; **2:**527, 950–51, 1053–54, 1102, 1249, 1386; **3:**41, 809, 862, 936, 969, 976–77, 1039, 1064, 1133, 1158, 1191–92; **4:**8, 20, 71–72, 199, 281, 497, 501, 658, 662, 1285–86; **5:**273, 684, 867, 873; **6:**454, 994; **7:**7, 14–16, 885–86; **8:**29, 36, 38–39, 156–57, 178, 531–32, 742; **9:**506, 648, 873; **10:**460, 663, 1010; **11:**421, 459–60, 596, 615; **12:**368–69, 747

R

RAS SHAMRA
1:990; **7:**202

S

SINALOA
2:719
SORES
2:678
SUMER
5:604; **7:**62

T

TATAM
2:678
TEL AVIV
1:9; **2:**677, 1000; **3:**82
TEL SERA
2:616

TELL DEIR 'ALLA
1:234, 242, 249; **2:**178; **6:**10
TELL EL-FE'RAH
2:616
TELL EL-KHELEIFEH
7:855
TELL EL-MASKHUTA
3:761
TELL ES-SEBA
1:219
TELL JEZER
1:251
THRACE
4:104, 248
TYROPOEON VALLEY
3:451, 759, 768

U

UDUM
2:586
UGARIT
1:230–31, 233, 236, 239, 273, 383, 990, 1081; **2:**364, 755, 1005, 1028; **4:**329, 395; **5:**77; **6:**1213, 1388, 1398; **9:**388

W

WADI EL-ARISH
2:677; **3:**386
WADI EL-HESA
2:164
WADI EL-MUJIB
1:261

Y

YARMUK RIVER
2:248
YAVNE
2:677
YAVNEH/JAVNEH/JAMNIA
1:8–9, 11, 306; **3:**1107; **4:**174, 261, 275, 277; **5:**634; **8:**98–101, 684
YEHUD
1:250, 268; **2:**701; **3:**313, 320, 347, 667, 678, 685, 702, 722, 746–47, 764–65, 768, 770, 827; **7:**738, 846, 853, 855, 860

BIBLICAL LANGUAGES

Hebrew and Aramaic Transliteration

CONSONANTS

א	= ʾ	ט	=	ṭ	פ or ף	=	p
ב	= b	י	=	y	צ or ץ	=	ṣ
ג	= g	כ or ך	=	k	ק	=	q
ד	= d	ל	=	l	ר	=	r
ה	= h	מ or ם	=	m	שׂ	=	ś
ו	= w	נ or ן	=	n	שׁ	=	š
ז	= z	ס	=	s	ת	=	t
ח	= ḥ	ע	=	ʿ			

Masoretic Pointing

PURE-LONG		TONE-LONG		SHORT		COMPOSITE *SHEWA*	
ָה	= â	ָ	= ā	ַ	= a	ֲ	= ă
ֵי or ֶי	= ê	ֵ	= ē	ֶ	= e	ְ or ֱ	= ĕ
ִ or ִי	= î			ִ	= i		
ֹ or וֹ	= ô	ֹ	= ō	ָ	= o	ֳ	= ŏ
ֻ or וּ	= û			ֻ	= u		

Hebrew

Transliteration	Hebrew	English	Volume and Page
A			
ʾāb	אב	father, ancestor	**2:**1133, 1184; **3:**140; **5:**749, 866
ʾābad	אבד	to perish, be destroyed	**3:**225; **4:**443, 518, 684, 689, 701, 1010, 1168, 1174; **5:**240; **6:**1394, 1501; **7:**476, 500, 523
ʾābal	אבל	to mourn	**6:**1429; **7:**309, 422
ʾābaq	אבק	to wrestle	**1:**565
ʾābbāʾ	אבא (Aramaic)	father	**8:**202–3, 666; **9:**234, 302, 433
ʾābbir Yaʿaqob	אביר יעקוב	the Bull of Jacob	**1:**273
ʾābîb	אביב	Abib, the month of Passover	**3:**896
ʾăbîḥayil	אביחיל	Abihail, "my father is mighty"	**3:**889

Transliteration	Hebrew	English	Volume and Page
ʾābîkā hāriʾšôn	אביך הראשון	first ancestor	**6:**379
ʾābînû malkēnû	אבינו מלכנו	our Father, our King	**5:**749; **8:**203
ʾăbiyyônâ	אביונה	desire	**5:**355
ʾādām	אדם	human, humankind	**1:**335, 345, 353, 375, 380, 382, 716; **4:**380, 753, 1098–99, 1263; **5:**55, 231, 240, 300, 332, 856; **6:**400, 528, 530, 614, 1117, 1121–22, 1473; **7:**279, 427, 523, 666
ʾădāmâ	אדמה	ground, earth	**1:**350, 351, 372, 382, 861; **4:**380, 753, 1099, 1263; **6:**255, 786, 1165; **7:**324, 666
ʾadderet	אדרת	glory	**7:**817–18
ʾaddîr	אדיר	majestic	**4:**711, 980; **7:**817
ʾaddîrîm	אדירים	nobles	**3:**764
ʾadmat yiśrāʾēl	אדמת ישראל	the soil of Israel	**6:**1165
ʾădmônî	אדמוני	ruddy	**1:**521
ʾādôn	אדון	master, lord	**4:**1187; **7:**376
ʾādônʾereṣ	אדון ארץ	Lord of earth	**5:**800
ʾādôn hakkōl	אדון הכל	Lord of all	**5:**800
ādôn kōl hāʾāreṣ	אדון כל הארץ	Lord of all the earth	**5:**800
ʾădōnāy	אדני	the Lord	**1:**297, 1164; **3:**768; **4:**533; **6:**1036
ʾădōnāy YHWH	אדני יהוה	Lord God	**2:**1261; **6:**436, 1123; **7:**377, 444
ʾădummîm kaddām	אדמים כדם	red as blood	**3:**184
ʾăgāgî	אגגי	Agagite	**3:**894
ʾăgarṭāl	אגרטל	basins, dishes	**3:**679
ʾāhab	אהב	to love	**2:**1120, 1208; **3:**553, 889; **5:**341, 668; **6:**1340; **7:**230, 391, 580
ʾahăbâ	אהבה	love	**6:**597, 809
ʾăhāh	אהה	"Ah!," a cry of alarm	**6:**1295
ʾāhēb	אהב	friend	**5:**230
ʾāḥ	אח	brother	**2:**404, 426, 475, 935; **3:**417; **4:**174, 476; **5:**77
ʾaḥar	אחר	after, behind	**3:**479; **4:**403

Transliteration	Hebrew	English	Volume and Page
ʾaḥar haddābār hazzeh	אחר הדבר הזה	after this matter	**3:**109
ʾaḥărê	אחרי	end	**7:**115
ʾaḥărê-kēn	אחרי־כן	afterward	**3:**202; **7:**326
ʾaḥărît	אחרית	end, latter time	**4:**402–3, 636, 829; **5:**212, 651, 709; **6:**412; **7:**421
ʾaḥărîtēk	אחריתך	your survivors, "the after-part of you"	**6:**1327
ʾaḥărôn	אחרון	at the last	**4:**478; **6:**377, 387
ʾāḥaz	אחז	to grasp, take hold	**4:**403; **6:**1579
ʾaḥēr	אחר	other, another	**4:**403
ʾăḥî	אחי	brother of	**3:**417
ʾăḥuzzâ	אחזה	possession, property	**1:**504; **6:**1579, 1582
ʾak	אך	surely	**4:**544, 838, 968
ʾākal	אכל	to eat, consume	**5:**134; **6:**988; **7:**257, 870
ʾākal tāmîd	אכל תמיד	to eat continually	**2:**1276
ʾăkalû qarṣêhôn	אכלו קרציהון	to accuse (idiom), "they ate bits off"	**7:**63
ʾakzāb	אכזב	a deceiving brook	**7:**547
ʾakzîb	אכזיב	Achzib	**7:**547
ʾal	אל	no, not	**1:**869; **5:**692; **6:**638, 866; **7:**500
ʾal-māwet	אל־מות	no death	**5:**128
ʾal-nāʾ	אל־נא	do not let	**2:**111
ʾal-tašḥēt	אל־תשחת	"Do Not Destroy," musical tune	**4:**656
ʾal tîrāʾ	אל תירא	do not fear	**6:**974
ʾal tōmar	אל תאמר	do not say	**5:**724
ʾal-yēḥad	אל־יחד	not be included	**4:**368
ʾal-yiḥad	אל־יחד	let it not rejoice	**4:**368
ʾal-yiṭʿămû	אל־יטעמו	let them not taste	**7:**478
ʾālâ	אלה	to lament, wail	**7:**308
ʾālâ	אלה	oath	**5:**828; **6:**1248; **7:**774
ʾălêhem	אליהם	to/against them	**6:**1428
ʾālep	אלף	aleph	**4:**380, 777, 813, 1166; **5:**42, 607; **6:**1018
ʾallûp	אלוף	clan, chief	**3:**318
ʾalmānâ	אלמנה	widow	**6:**1269
ʾalyâ	אליה	tail fat of sheep	**1:**1025
ʾāmâ	אמה	maid-servant	**2:**928; **7:**610
ʾāmal	אמל	to be weak	**7:**602

Transliteration	Hebrew	English	Volume and Page
ʾāman	אמן	to believe in, confirm, support	**1:**795; **3:**408; **4:**1054, 1250; **6:**108; **7:**513
ʾămānâ	אמנה	firm agreement	**3:**815
ʾāmar	אמר	to say	**2:**48, 124; **4:**751, 1169; **5:**250, 724; **6:**331, 336, 402, 1373; **7:**492, 510
ʾāmēṣ	אמץ	to be strong, prevail	**3:**530
ʾāmēn	אמן	amen	**8:**187
ʾammâ	אמה	Ammah, cubit	**3:**414
ʾāmôn	אמון	master worker (?)	**5:**94–95, 102
ʾămuṣṣîm	אמצים	gray, strong (?)	**7:**783
ʾānaḥ	אנח	to groan, sigh	**1:**706; **6:**1296; **7:**407
ʾănām	אנך	plummet	**7:**406–7
ʾānan	אנן	to complain	**2:**104
ʾānam	אנק	to groan, sigh	**7:**407
ʾănāšîm	אנשים	people, "men"	**4:**590; **6:**1342; **7:**477
ʾănî	אני	I (pronoun)	**1:**771; **4:**558, 977, 1028; **6:**1048, 1373; **7:**289, 380, 507
ʾănî mārēʾ	אני ירא	I am fearing	**7:**498
ʾănî YHWH	אני יהוה	I am Yahweh	**2:**89
ʾānnâ	אנה	please	**7:**500, 517
ʾānōkî	אנכי	I (pronoun)	**4:**558, 977; **7:**285, 289
ʾānōkî lōʾ-ʾehyeh lākem	אנכי לא־אהיה לכם	I am not I AM to you	**7:**290
ʾanšê	אנשי	people of, "men of"	**4:**590
ʾanšê ḥesed	אנשי חסד	faithful men	**5:**609, 833, 837
ʾanšê rākîl	אנשי רכיל	slanderers, "merchant men"	**6:**1309
ʾap	אף	nose, anger	**4:**458, 563, 704, 833, 1042; **6:**1038; **7:**257
ʾap	אף	also	**4:**563
ʾāpâ	אפה	to bake	**7:**256–57
ʾăpēlâ	אפלה	darkness	**1:**766
ʾāpîq	אפיק	stream, ravine	**4:**311
ʾarâ	ארה	to burn	**6:**1566
ʾārab	ארב	to lie in wait	**5:**715; **7:**257
ʾărām	ארם	Syria	**4:**63
ʾărammî ʾōbēd	ארמי אבד	wandering Aramaean	**2:**480
ʾārar	ארר	to curse	**1:**393, 424
ʾărāyôt	אריות	lions	**6:**1268
ʾarbaʿ rûḥê šĕmayyāʾ	ארבע רוחי שמיא	four winds of heaven	**7:**101

Transliteration	Hebrew	English	Volume and Page
ʾarbeh	ארבה	swarming locust	**7:**307
ʾărîʾēl	אראיל	altar hearth, "lion of El"	**6:**1566
ʾarmôn	ארמון	citadel, fortress	**6:**1269
ʾărôn	ארון	ark	**3:**494
ʾărôn bĕrît	ארון ברית	the ark of the covenant	**2:**96
ʾărōn haʿēdut	ארן העדת	ark of the covenant/ Testimony	**2:**79
ʾarṣâ	ארצה	earth, country	**3:**238
ʾărubbôt	ארבות	lattices, windows	**5:**355
ʾārûr	ארור	cursed	**1:**363; **7:**690
ʾaryēh	אריה	lion	**7:**248, 278
ʾāsap	אסף	to gather	**2:**105, 108, 916; **7:**666, 674
ʾăsapsup	אספסף	rabble	**2:**105
ʾāsar	אסר	to bind, imprison	**7:**89, 258
ʾāsîp	אסיף	ingathering, harvest	**7:**674
ʾăsîrîm	אסירים	prisoners	**4:**1118
ʾāsôn	אסון	harm	**1:**864
ʾāsōp ʾāsēp	אסף אסף	I will utterly sweep away	**7:**666, 674
ʾāšam	אשם	to offend, be guilty	**6:**1547
ʾāšām	אשם	guilt, guilt offering	**1:**530, 629, 646, 990, 1028, 1038–39; **2:**1011; **6:**467, 1547
ʾāšar	אשר	to walk	**5:**103
ʾašdôd	אשדוד	Ashdod	**4:**111
ʾăšēdôt	אשדות	slopes	**4:**111
ʾăšer	אשר	who, which, that	**1:**1032; **2:**166, 832; **3:**886; **4:**303; **6:**438
ʾăšer-kĕnaʿănîm	אשר־כנענים	who are the Canaanites	**7:**456
ʾăšērâ	אשרה	sacred pole, Ashera pole	**3:**115, 124
ʾašrê	אשרי	happy	**4:**665, 666, 683–84, 1013; **5:**52, 103, 719; **8:**176
ʾaššap	אשף	enchanter	**7:**50
ʾaššûr	אשור	Assyria	**6:**1422
ʾātâ	אתה	he came	**2:**165
ʾatt	את	you	**6:**1392, 1393
ʾattâ	אתה	you	**4:**719, 736, 974, 1069, 1246; **6:**1146, 1440
ʾāwâ	אוה	to desire	**6:**709
ʾāwen	און	wickedness, sorrow	**4:**708, 823, 847; **6:**1342, 1418; **7:**286

Transliteration	Hebrew	English	Volume and Page
ʾayil	איל	ram	**6:**1417, 1427–28
ʾayin	אין	nothing, not	**4:**411
ʾāyōm	אים	terrible, dreadful	**5:**418
ʾayyēh	איה	where	**7:**290–91
ʾayyelet haššaḥar	אילת השחר	"The Doe of the Morning," musical tune	**4:**656
ʾāz	אז	then, now	**3:**42
ʾāzal	אזל	to go away	**1:**1112
ʾê	אי	where	**6:**546
ʾebyôn	אביון	needy	**4:**955, 1138; **7:**416
ʾēd	אד	mist, primordial waters	**4:**590
ʾêd	איד	disaster, calamity	**4:**469; **6:**1476
ʾêdām	אידם	calamity	**7:**452
ʾĕdôm	אדום	Edom, red, Idumea	**3:**184; **4:**63; **6:**1476; **7:**427, 437
ʾĕhî	אהי	where, I am (?)	**7:**290–92
ʾēhûd	אהוד	Ehud	**3:**357
ʾeḥad	אחד	one	**2:**655; **6:**1506, 1604; **7:**864
ʾēḥûd	אחוד	Ehud	**3:**357
ʾêk	איך	how	**6:**1268, 1368
ʾêkâ	איכה	how	**6:**59, 1023, 1029, 1036, 1046, 1061, 1268, 1368
ʾĕkol-šām leḥem	אכל־שם לחם	eat bread there	**7:**410
ʾel	אל	to	**7:**715, 727
ʾēl	אל	El, God	**1:**273, 274, 276, 440, 566, 577, 584; **2:**139, 180, 191; **3:**992; **4:**400, 862, 881; **5:**33, 674, 818; **6:**1122, 1387, 1428; **7:**279; **8:**492
ʾēl ʾānî	אל אני	"A god am I," or "El am I"	**6:**1387
ēl ʾerek ʾappayim hûʾ	אל ארך אפים הוא	God is long-suffering	**5:**678
ʾel-bêt ʾimmî	אל־בית אמי	to my mother's house	**5:**397
ʾēl ĕlōhê yiśrāēl	אל אלהי ישראל	El, the [patron] god of Israel	**1:**273
ʾēl ʿelyôn	אל עליון	El, the highest one	**1:**273, 439, 440; **5:**846
ʾel-kol-šĕʾēr bĕśārô	אל־כל־שאר בשרו	to all remainder of his flesh	**1:**1125
ʾēl nāʾ	אל נא	O God, please	**2:**111

Transliteration	Hebrew	English	Volume and Page
ʾēl ʿolām	אל עלם	El, the eternal one	**1:**273
ʾēl qannôʾ	אל קנוא	a jealous God	**7:**602
ʾēl šadday	אל שדי	El, the mountain-dwelling one	**1:**273, 458, 635, 659, 666, 733; **2:**910
ʾĕlāh ʾăbāhātî	אלה אבהתי	God of my ancestors	**7:**52
ʾĕlāh šĕmayyāʾ	אלה שמיא	God of heaven	**7:**52
ʾēlayik habbaytâ	אליך הביתה	inside the house	**2:**593
ʾēlê gibbôrîm	אלי גבורים	chief warriors	**6:**1443
ʾēlem	אלם	silence (?)	**4:**908
ʾelep	אלף	thousand, military division	**2:**34, 630, 802, 1000, 1055, 1087, 1280, 1331; **3:**422, 547
ʾēlî	אלי	my God	**8:**492
ʾēlî-ʿezer	אליעזר	help, "God is help"	**1:**825
ʾĕlîlîm	אלילים	worthless, scornful expression for foreign or false gods	**6:**180
ʾĕlîlîm	אלילם	nothings, idols	**1:**1178; **6:**1417
ʾêlîm	אילים	rams	**6:**1417
ʾĕlîšāʿ	אלישע	Elisha, "my God saves"	**3:**237
ʾēlleh	אלה	these	**1:**1080; **3:**484
ʾelleh tôlĕdôt	אלה תולדות	these are the generations	**1:**307–8
ʾĕlōâ	אלה	God	**5:**828
ʾĕlōah hakkōl	אלה הכל	God of all	**5:**800
ʾĕlōhê yiśrāʾēl	אלהי ישראל	God of Israel	**4:**913
ʾĕlōhênû	אלהינו	our God	**3:**776
ʾĕlōhîm	אלהים	God	**1:**568; **2:**180, 552, 907, 1184; **3:**772, 776; **4:**218, 532, 658, 693, 711, 862, 881; **5:**9, 33, 283, 674, 842, 846; **6:**1387; **7:**464, 488
ʾĕlōhîm ʾānî	אלהים אני	A god am I	**6:**1387
ʾĕlōhîm ṣĕbāʾôt	אלהים צבאות	God of hosts/armies	**4:**913
ʾelʿāzār	אלעזר	Eleazar, "help of God"	**4:**249
ʾēm bĕyiśrāʾēl	אם בישראל	mother in Israel	**2:**787
ʾêmâ	אימה	terror	**1:**877
ʾĕmet	אמת	faithfulness	**1:**511, 563, 659, 946; **2:**715; **4:**671, 886, 1021, 1134, 1150, 1232; **5:**669, 674;

Transliteration	Hebrew	English	Volume and Page
ʾĕmet *(continued)*			**6:**363, 773; **7:**236; **9:**523
ʾĕmûnâ	אמונה	faithfulness	**4:**1050–51, 1078, 1171; **5:**652; **6:**618; **7:**236, 642
ʾĕmûnôt	אמונות	righteous deeds	**4:**1028
ʾên ʾîš	אין איש	no man	**6:**502
ʾên ḥēqer	אין חקר	unsearchable	**4:**420, 533
ʾên kĕsût	אין כסות	without covering	**4:**518
ʾên mapgîaʿ	אין מפגיע	no one to intervene	**6:**502
ʾên mošlô	אין משלו	none can dominate him	**4:**625
ʾên mispār	אין מספר	innumerable	**4:**532
ʾēn-qôrēʾ	אן־קורא	there is no one who calls	**6:**529
ʾĕnôš	אנוש	human, mortal	**4:**718
ʾĕnôš šĕlômî	אנוש שלומי	close friend, one of my peace	**6:**728
ʾēper	אפר	ashes	**5:**705
ʾepes	אפס	cessation	**5:**824; **6:**454
ʾēpôd	אפוד	ephod	**1:**23
ʾeprayim	אפרים	Ephraim	**7:**261, 270, 292, 295
ʾeprātî	אפרתי	"Ephraimite" or "Ephrathite"	**3:**94
ʾerek ʾapayim	ארך אפים	slow to anger	**1:**946; **7:**319, 518
ʾereṣ	ארץ	earth, land	**1:**351, 430; **4:**427, 591, 869, 1068, 1082; **5:**45, 113, 237, 242, 702; **6:**363, 411, 1165; **7:**774, 777
ʾereṣ kĕnaʿan	ארץ כנען	land of "Canaan" or "trade"	**6:**1246
ʾereṣ yiśrāʾēl	ארץ ישראל	the land of Israel	**6:**1165
ʾĕsār	אסר (Aramaic)	decree	**7:**89
ʾesttēr	אסתר	Esther, star, "I will hide"	**3:**886
ʾēš	אש	fire	**1:**1011; **2:**166; **3:**173; **5:**700; **7:**314
ʾēš ʾĕlōhîm	אש אלהים	fire of God	**5:**851
ʾēš-ʾîš	אש איש	quarrelsome person	**5:**226
ʾēš zārâ	אש זרה	strange fire	**1:**1070; **2:**49
ʾēšet bĕrîtekā	אשת בריתך	your wife by covenant	**7:**865
ʾēšet ḥayil	אשת חיל	a woman of noble character	**2:**929
ʾēšet nĕʿûrêkā	אשת נעוריך	the wife of your youth	**7:**865

Transliteration	Hebrew	English	Volume and Page
ʾēšet zĕnûnîm	אשת זנונים	wife of whoredom	**7:**216
ʾeškārēk	אשכרך	product to be delivered	**6:**1378
ʾēškôl	אשכול	grape-cluster	**2:**122
ʾēššôhî	אשוהי	[its] burnt offerings	**3:**708
ʾēt	את	direct object marker	**2:**165; **3:**417; **4:**303; **6:**466
ʾet-gibbôrîm nōpĕlîm mēʿărēlîm	את־גבורים נפלים מערלים	the fallen warriors of the uncircumcised	**6:**1443
ʾet-wahēb bĕsûpâ	את והב בסופה	Waheb in Suphah	**2:**165
ʾet-laḥmî	את־לחמי	Lahmi	**3:**417
ʾêtān	איתן	ruin, hard (?)	**5:**133
ʾetnan	אתנן	harlot's hire, fee	**6:**1233
ʾĕwîl	אויל	fool, foolish	**4:**379; **5:**688
ʾezrāḥ	אזרח	a native (Israelite)	**2:**127, 636
ʾim	אם	if	**1:**1009, 1032, 1187; **4:**400; **6:**1477
ʾimrâ	אמרה	promise, utterance, word	**4:**1166, 1232
ʾissār	אסר	a pledge	**2:**234
ʾîš	איש	man	**1:**353, 372, 565; **2:**187; **3:**173, 510; **4:**590; **5:**162; **7:**279
ʾîš ʾĕlōhîm	איש אלהים	man of God	**5:**851
ʾîš ʾîš	איש איש	"man, man," no one	**1:**1125
ʾîš ʾîš mibbêt yiśrāʾēl	איש איש מבית ישראל	anyone of the house of Israel	**6:**1206
ʾîš baʿal śēʿār	איש בעל שער	"a man, a possessor of hair"	**3:**171
ʾîš bĕliyyaʿal	איש בליעל	a worthless person	**5:**715
ʾîš gādôl	איש גדול	great man	**3:**193
ʾîš hāʾĕlōhîm	איש האלהים	man of God	**6:**4
ʾîš habbĕliyyaʿal	איש הבליעל	a worthless man	**2:**1168
ʾîš-habbēnayim	איש־הבנים	a champion, "a man between the two"	**2:**1109
ʾîš-ḥămûdôt	איש־חמדות	one who is greatly beloved	**7:**137
ʾîš ḥayil	איש חיל	person of substance, wealthy man	**5:**767
ʾîš kî	איש כי	if anyone	**1:**1187
ʾîš lōʾ ʿāmad lipnêhem	איש לא עמד לפניהם	no one is able to withstand them	**3:**930

Transliteration	Hebrew	English	Volume and Page
ʾîš māgēn	איש מגן	armed robber, highwayman	**5:**75
ʾîš môkîaḥ	איש מוכיח	a reprover	**6:**1137, 1454
ʾîš nābûb yillābēb	איש נבוב ילבב	a stupid person will get understanding	**4:**421
ʾîš rîb	איש ריב	adversary at law	**4:**555
ʾîš zār	איש זר	stranger	**5:**72
ʾiššâ	אשה	woman	**1:**353; **5:**332, 700
ʾiššâ gĕdôlâ	אשה גדולה	great woman	**3:**193
ʾiššâ zārâ	אשה זרה	strange, loose woman	**5:**71, 669
ʾiššeh	אשה	burnt offering	**1:**1011
ʾittî	אתי	with me	**3:**544
ʾittô	אתו	him	**2:**78
ʾiwwelet	אולת	foolishness	**4:**833; **5:**142–43
ʾîzāl	איזל	Izalla	**6:**1379
ʾôb	אוב	spirit of a dead person, medium	**1:**1135; **2:**1184
ʾôhēb	אוהב	lover	**5:**682
ʾôhēb ʾĕmûnâ	אוהב אמונה	a faithful friend	**5:**683
ʾōhel	אהל	tent	**5:**720; **6:**1319; **7:**286
ʾōhel môʿēd	אהל מועד	tent of meeting	**2:**32; **6:**1319; **7:**286
ʾōmen	אמן	faithfulness	**4:**844
ʾôn	און	calamity, vigor, manhood	**4:**469; **7:**285–86
ʾŏnî	אני	ship	**6:**1373
ʾŏniyyâ	אניה	ship	**7:**479, 494
ʾôpān	אופן	wheel	**6:**1183
ʾôpeh	אפה	baker	**7:**256–57
ʾōr	אור	to become light, shine	**1:**1063; **4:**1173
ʾôr	אור	light	**3:**982; **4:**591, 785, 823, 980, 1172
ʾôr gôyim	אור גוים	light of the nations	**6:**364
ʾôrâ	אורה	light	**3:**927
ʾōraḥ	ארח	path, way	**4:**402
ʾôṣār	אוצר	treasure, treasury	**6:**394; **8:**484
ʾôṣĕrôt ḥōšek	אוצרות חשך	treasures of darkness	**6:**394
ʾôt	אות	sign	**4:**973; **6:**112, 1207, 1280, 1282
ʾôtāh	אותה	her	**6:**1440; **7:**242
ʾôtāh šokbû	אותה שכבו	they lay with her	**6:**1321
ʾōtî	אתי	my	**5:**688
ʾôyēb	אויב	enemy	**1:**800; **2:**191; **4:**1251
ʾûlām	אולם	but, however	**4:**443

Transliteration	Hebrew	English	Volume and Page
ʾûlāy	אולי	Ulai, "perhaps"	**7:**111, 496, 514, 685
ʾummōt	אמת	nations	**5:**669
ʾûṣ	אוץ	to make haste	**5:**192
ʾuššôhî	אשׁוהי	its foundations	**3:**708
ʾûzzal	אוזל	Uzal	**6:**1379
ʿāb	עב	uncertain architectural term	**6:**1555
ʿābad	עבד	to work, serve, worship	**1:**349, 351, 372, 559, 560, 694, 780; **3:**225; **4:**586, 964, 1078, 1088; **5:**126; **6:**601, 786; **7:**286
ʿābar	עבר	to pass by, over, to perish	**1:**777, 946, 1138; **2:**161, 249, 607; **4:**411, 586, 1041; **5:**179; **6:**1284, 1525; **7:**407
ʿābdôhî dî-ʾĕlāhāʾ	עבדוהי די־אלהא	most high God	**7:**65
ʿābîm	עבים	clouds, darkness	**6:**988
ʿăbōdâ	עבדה	service	**1:**280; **2:**14; **4:**1098
ʿăbūdâ	עבדה	service	**4:**351
ʿābûr	עבור	produce	**2:**607
ʿad	עד	until, up to	**3:**834; **4:**354; **6:**266, 377
ʿad-ʾānâ	עד־אנה	how long	**2:**124; **7:**630
ʿad-ʾargîʿâ	עד־ארגיעה	only a moment	**5:**127
ʿad-bōš	עד־בשׁ	until he was embarrased	**3:**212
ʿad hayyôm hazzeh	עד היום הזה	to this day	**2:**370
ʿad-kallēh	עד־כלה	unto completion	**3:**238
ʿad-mātay	עד־מתי	how long	**2:**124
ʿad ʿôlām	עד עולם	forever	**3:**304
ʿādar	עדר	to help	**3:**379–80
ʿădat bĕnê-yiśrāʾēl	עדת בני־ישׂראל	the congregation of the children of Israel	**2:**197
ʿădî	עדי	ornaments	**6:**1167–68
ʿāgab	עגב	to lust, have inordinate affection	**6:**1321
ʿăgābîm	עגבים	flattery, devotion	**6:**1459
ʿāakôr	עכור	Achor, trouble	**2:**631
ʿal	על	over, upon, against	**2:**136; **3:**834; **6:**878, 1511; **7:**493
ʿal-ʾopnāyw	על־אפניו	fitly (?)	**5:**218

Transliteration	Hebrew	English	Volume and Page
ʿal-dĕbār	על־דבר	concerning, about	**1:**991
ʿal haḥătûmîm	על החתומים	upon the sealed documents	**3:**815
ʿal-kēn	על־כן	therefore	**4:**500; **7:**236
ʿal-mâ	על־מה	why	**4:**434
ʿal-ʿawlâ	על־עולה	concerning iniquity	**4:**590
ʿal-ʿôleh	על־עולה	concerning the one who comes up	**4:**590
ʿal-pĕnê	על־פני	to the face of	**3:**90
ʿal-pĕnêkem	על־פניכם	to your face	**4:**390
ʿal-pî YHWH	על־פי יהוה	according to the word of the Lord	**2:**51
ʾal yĕhî lô zēker	אל יהי לו זכר	let his name not be mentioned	**5:**850
ʿālâ	עלה	to go up	**1:**433, 694, 713, 937, 939, 979; **2:**122, 136, 733, 747, 1211; **3:**678–79; **4:**869, 1069, 1176; **5:**224; **6:**1546; **7:**369, 478, 506, 579
ʿālâ ʿal	עלה על	to surpass (idiom)	**5:**263
ʿālal	עלל	to deal severly with	**6:**1043
ʿălāmôt	עלמות	young female singers (?)	**4:**656
ʿālas	עלס	to be glad, flap wildly	**4:**611
ʿālāy	עלי	with me	**4:**727
ʿālay mâ	עלי מה	upon me what may	**4:**434
ʿāleykā	עליך	about you	**3:**32
ʿălîlâ	עלילה	deed	**4:**893
ʿăliyyâ	עליה	upper chamber	**4:**1097; **6:**1551
ʿalmâ	עלמה	young woman	**6:**112; **8:**135
ʿam	עם	people	**2:**124, 197; **5:**850, 856; **6:**78, 364, 1008; **7:**618
ʿam hāʾāreṣ	עם הארץ	people of the land	**1:**1138; **2:**688; **5:**859; **7:**723
ʿam-qĕdōšîm	עם־קדשים	people of the holy ones	**7:**117
ʿam YHWH	עם יהוה	people of Yahweh	**2:**139–40
ʿāmad	עמד	to stand	**3:**195; **4:**684–85
ʿāmāl	עמל	toil, trouble	**4:**369, 393, 708–9, 719; **5:**280, 293
ʿāmas	עמס	to carry a load	**6:**405
ʿāmît	עמית	associate, fellow	**7:**833
ʿammîm	עמים	peoples	**6:**78

Transliteration	Hebrew	English	Volume and Page
ʿāmōq	עמק	deep	**5:**663
ʿānâ	ענה	to answer, sing	**3:**692; **4:**696, 755, 762, 899, 916, 1020, 1268
ʿānâ	ענה	to be occupied with, afflict, force	**1:**452, 454, 580, 624, 763, 868, 1113; **2:**1304; **3:**728; **4:**1057, 1211; **5:**319; **6:**1052, 1309; **7:**123
ʿānâ nepeš	ענה נפש	to afflict/deny one's self/soul	**1:**1113
ʿānān	ענן	cloud	**6:**1517
ʿānāw	ענו	poor, humble	**7:**685
ʿănāwâ	ענוה	humility	**5:**652; **7:**685
ʿănāyin	ענין (Aramaic)	poor, oppressed	**7:**75
ʿānî	עני	poor, afflicted	**1:**868; **4:**547, 585, 764, 814, 819, 829, 953, 1086; **7:**75, 416
ʿŏnî	עני	affliction, misery	**1:**560; **4:**1118; **6:**1049
ʿanôn	ענון	afflicted, oppressed	**1:**694; **6:**514
ʿāpal	עפל	to swell	**7:**642
ʿāpār	עפר	dust, dry earth	**4:**380; **5:**705; **6:**1366; **7:**547
ʿāpār wāʾēper	עפר ואפר	dust and ashes	**4:**628
ʿāqab	עקב	to supplant, deceive	**1:**521; **6:**654; **7:**283
ʿāqal	עקל	to bend, twist	**7:**630
ʿāqar	עקר	to pluck, uproot	**7:**666
ʿāqēb	עקב	heel	**1:**521
ʿāqōb	עקב	devious, deceitful	**6:**708
ʿārab	ערב	to pledge, give in pledge	**3:**779
ʿārab	ערב	to enter	**6:**1377
ʿărābâ	ערבה	Araba, southern desert-plain of Israel	**6:**1596
ʿāral	ערל	to be uncircumcised	**6:**1443
ʿărāpel	ערפל	dark cloud	**4:**501
ʿārēl	ערל	uncircumcised	**1:**1134
ʿărîsâ	עריסה	dough, dough vessel	**2:**127
ʿārîṣ	עריץ	ruthless, terrifying	**4:**894
ʿārîṣê gôyim	עריצי גוים	the most terrible of nations	**6:**1388
ʿārôm	ערום	naked	**4:**518
ʿārûm	ערום	crafty	**1:**359, 363; **5:**140, 149

Transliteration	Hebrew	English	Volume and Page
ʿărûmmîm	ערומים	naked	**1:**359
ʿāṣar	עצר	to keep in bounds	**2:**1039
ʿăṣeret	עצרת	closing assembly	**1:**1159–60; **6:**654
ʿāš	עשׁ	moth (?)	**4:**379, 524; **7:**248
ʿāšaq	עשׁק	to oppress	**5:**239
ʿāšar	עשׁר	to be rich	**5:**131
ʿāšat	עשׁת	to be smooth, to think	**7:**477
ʿāšēš	עשׁשׁ	to waste away	**4:**801
ʿāšîr	עשׁיר	rich	**4:**876; **5:**346
ʿāśâ	עשׂה	to make, do	**1:**342; **3:**478, 483; **4:**414, 508, 532, 619, 733, 789, 810, 1061–62, 1078, 1096, 1126, 1145, 1154, 1220, 1224, 1275; **5:**260; **6:**661; **7:**253, 260, 477, 500
ʿāśar	עשׂר	to confiscate one tenth	**2:**1029
ʿāṭap	עטף	to turn, cover oneself	**4:**508
ʿăṭārâ	עטרה	crown, turban	**3:**927
ʿātar	עתר	excessive (?)	**5:**230
ʿātēq	עתק	to proceed, transcribe (?)	**5:**217
ʿattâ	עתה	now	**2:**929, 1262; **3:**468, 555, 736; **4:**544; **6:**368, 370, 386, 419; **7:**288, 518, 605, 723, 728
ʿāwâ	עוה	to bend, distort	**4:**475
ʿāwel	עול	injustice, wrong deed	**4:**893
ʿawlâ	עולה	injustice, deceit	**4:**390, 523
ʿāwôn	עון	sin, guilt	**1:**374, 475, 646, 947; **2:**392; **4:**805, 833, 885, 912; **5:**673; **6:**1062, 1145–47, 1302, 1343, 1576; **7:**285–86, 295, 369, 765–66, 778
ʿawwâ	עוה	distortion	**6:**1303
ʿayin	עין	eye	**2:**913; **3:**704; **4:**822, 1082, 1187, 1208; **7:**523, 778
ʿayir	עיר	domesticated ass	**4:**421
ʿāzab	עזב	to leave, abandon	**2:**907, 913, 919; **3:**524, 581, 768, 772; **4:**762,

Transliteration	Hebrew	English	Volume and Page
			786, 829, 959; **6:**709, 1377; **7:**666
ʿāzar	עזר	to help	**1:**825; **3:**379; **4:**917, 1020; **6:**354
ʿăzārâ	עזרה	ledge	**6:**1566
ʿāzaz	עזז	to be strong	**4:**946
ʿazzâ ʿăzzûbâ	עזה עזובה	"Gaza shall be deserted"	**7:**666, 686
ʿebed	עבד	slave, servant	**1:**593, 639; **5:**145, 463, 675; **6:**354, 361; **7:**498, 731
ʿebrâ	עברה	wrath	**4:**1041; **5:**198
ʿēd	עד	witness	**4:**415; **5:**127
ʿēd bĕliyyaʿal	עד בליעל	worthless witness	**5:**182
ʿēdâ	עדה	congregation	**1:**813, 1035; **2:**33, 124, 139; **4:**686, 1133; **5:**664
ʿēdût	עדת	covenant, testimony	**1:**889–91; **2:**79, 140, 323; **3:**26, 230; **4:**1166; **6:**1118
ʿēgel	עגל	young bull, fatted calf	**2:**771
ʿeglâ mĕlummadâ	עגלה מלמדה	trained female calf, heifer	**7:**275
ʿeglôn	עגלון	Eglon	**2:**771
ʿelyôn	עליון	Most High	**2:**180, 191, 527; **4:**1024, 1069; **5:**846, 853
ʿēqeb	עקב	reward, consequence	**5:**198
ʿeqrôn teʿāqēr	עקרון תעקר	Ekron shall be uprooted	**7:**666, 686
ʿēr wĕʿōneh	ער וענה	"arousing or responding"	**7:**864
ʿēreb	ערב	mixed	**1:**781; **6:**1415
ʿērek	ערך	equivalent, estimate	**1:**1187
ʿerwâ	ערוה	nakedness	**2:**926
ʿēṣ	עץ	tree	**4:**685; **6:**1335, 1504, 1506–7; **7:**240
ʿēṣâ	עצה	counsel, plan	**4:**596, 598, 601, 686, 726; **5:**181; **6:**141, 412; **7:**662
ʿeṣem	עצם	bone	**4:**395; **6:**1335
ʿēt	עת	time	**3:**882; **5:**672, 673
ʿēz	עז	female goat	**1:**1025, 1112
ʿēzer	עזר	help, helper	**1:**352; **4:**1190
ʿî	עי	ruin	**4:**547

Transliteration	Hebrew	English	Volume and Page
ʿibrî	עברי	Hebrew	**2:**405, 1188; **7:**498
ʿibrî ʾānōkî	עברי אנכי	"I am a Hebrew"	**7:**477, 498
ʿilʿôlâ	עלעולה	storm	**4:**590
ʿim	עם	with	**3:**544; **4:**969, 1206; **5:**327
ʿimmāk	עמך	with you	**4:**969
ʿImmānû-ēl	עמנו אל	God is with us	**8:**135
ʿimmî	עמי	with me	**3:**544
ʿinyan	ענין	business, occupation	**5:**270
ʿiqqĕšût peh	עקשות פה	crooked speech, "a crooked mouth"	**5:**61
ʿîr dāmîm	עיר דמים	city of blood(shed)	**7:**613
ʿîr-hāʾĕmet	עיר־האמת	faithful city	**7:**795
ʿîr haqqōdeš	עיר הקדש	holy city	**3:**824
ʿizzābôn	עזבון	wares	**6:**1377
ʿizzûz	עזוז	strong	**4:**772
ʿōbadyâ	עבדיה	Obadiah	**7:**437
ʿôd	עוד	still, again, besides	**1:**962; **7:**512, 641
ʿôd zōʾt	עוד זאת	this too	**6:**1494
ʿōkēr	עכר	a troubler	**3:**135, 328
ʿōl	על	yoke	**7:**605
ʿōlâ	עלה	whole burnt offering	**1:**495, 992, 1009; **2:**78; **6:**56, 945, 1546, 1568
ʿôlâ kālîl	עולה כליל	whole burnt offering	**1:**1009
ʿōlâ hattāmîd	עלה התמיד	continual burnt offering	**8:**33
ʿôlām	עולם	forever	**2:**1261, 1262; **4:**483, 983; **5:**306–7, 663, 673, 720; **6:**369, 1443
ʿôlēl	עולל	child	**6:**1030, 1043
ʿōneš	ענש	toll, fine	**3:**510
ʿŏpālîm	עפלים	mounds, tumors	**2:**1006
ʿōpel	עפל	hill, mound, fort	**7:**567
ʿôperet	עופרת	lead	**6:**1312
ʿōrbîm	ערבים	crows, ravens	**6:**988
ʿorlâ	ערלה	foreskin	**1:**1134
ʿormâ	ערמה	craftiness	**5:**142
ʿōseq	עסק	trouble	**5:**823
ʿōṣeb	עצב	pain	**3:**331
ʿōśeh	עשה	maker	**4:**1275
ʿōz	עז	strength, might	**3:**401; **4:**772, 790, 865, 919, 922, 946, 959, 984, 1013, 1035, 1240, 1279

Transliteration	Hebrew	English	Volume and Page
ʿōzēr	עזר	helper	**4:**895
ʿûd	עוד	to give witness, compare	**2:**1028; **6:**1041
ʿūnôt	ענות	hardships	**4:**1211
ʿûq	עוק	to crush (?)	**7:**366
ʿûr	עור	to rouse, awaken	**3:**677; **6:**352, 437; **7:**256–57, 810

B

Transliteration	Hebrew	English	Volume and Page
bāʾaš	באשׁ	to grow foul, stink	**4:**833
baddîm	בדים	poles	**3:**393
bāgad	בגד	to betray, be treacherous	**4:**311; **7:**244, 252, 864
bagōhî	בגהי (Aramaic)	Bagohi	**3:**951
bāhal	בהל	to be terrified, confused	**1:**1180; **4:**704, 1010
bāḥan	בחן	to test, examine	**4:**708, 722
bāḥar	בחר	to choose	**3:**304, 461, 499, 810; **6:**386, 1277–78; **7:**369
bāḥărî-ʾap	בחרי־אף	burning anger, "hot of nose"	**6:**1038
bākâ	בכה	to weep	**3:**740; **6:**1029
bākāʾ	בכא	Baca (unknown valley?)	**4:**1013–14
bālâ	בלה	to become old, worn out	**6:**1330
bālag	בלג	to smile, gleam	**4:**839
bālal	בלל	to confuse	**1:**413
bālaʿ	בלע	to swallow	**4:**1190; **5:**182; **6:**1038, 1041; **7:**470, 483, 504
ballāhâ	בלהה	terror	**4:**469
bāmâ	במה	illicit cultic site, "high place"	**2:**1206; **6:**1157, 1159–60, 1230, 1285; **7:**407
bānâ	בנה	to build	**1:**353, 889; **3:**505, 765; **4:**789, 1198; **6:**431, 515; **7:**872
bānîm	בנים	children	**4:**1044, 1198
baʿad	בעד	behind, about, on behalf of	**1:**999, 1110; **4:**590, 693
baʿal	בעל	chief, lord, Baal (Canaanite god)	**1:**1147; **2:**1213, 1274; **3:**698; **5:**262; **6:**599; **7:**200, 261, 288, 675
baʿal hāmôn	בעל המון	Baal-hamon (unknown site), "possessor of abundance"	**5:**433
baʿal ḥēmâ	בעל חמה	a wrathful lord	**7:**602

Transliteration	Hebrew	English	Volume and Page
baʿal sôdekā	בעל סודך	lord of your counsel	**5:**682
baʿal zĕbûb	בעל זבוב	lord of the flies	**9:**241
bāʿar	בער	to burn	**1:**866, 1138; **7:**257
baʿar lōʾ yēdāʿ	בער לא ידע	the senseless man does not know	**5:**252
baʿar welōʾ ʾēdāʿ	בער ולא אדע	I was senseless and ignorant	**5:**252
bāʿat	בעת	to terrify, startle	**3:**919
bāʿēt hahîʾ	בעת ההוא	at that time	**2:**181
bāqaʿ	בקע	to split, force open	**4:**518, 530, 974
bāqaq	בקק	to empty, lay waste	**6:**721
bāqar	בקר	to enquire, seek	**6:**1466
bāqār	בקר	cattle, herd	**7:**403
bāqaš	בקש	to seek	**3:**303, 500, 521, 544, 559; **4:**1104; **5:**667, 668, 689
baqbuq	בקבק	clay flask	**6:**721
bar	בר (Aramaic)	son	**4:**690; **5:**258
bar-abbāʾ	בר־אבא (Aramaic)	son of the father	**8:**486; **9:**448
bar-ʾĕlāhîn	בר־אלהין (Aramaic)	son of God, one of the host of heaven	**7:**65
bar ʾĕnāš	בר אנש (Aramaic)	son of man	**7:**104; **8:**550
bar ʾĕnōš	בר אנש (Aramaic)	son of man	**8:**360
bar naša	בר נשא (Aramaic)	son of man	**8:**286
bārāʾ	ברא	to create, form	**1:**342, 948, 962; **4:**886, 1271; **5:**354, 730; **6:**84, 375, 386, 395, 1392, 1394
bāraḥ	ברח	to flee	**4:**1236; **7:**494
bārāq	ברק	lightning	**6:**1300
bārak	ברך	to bless	**3:**495; **4:**346, 352, 356, 366, 737, 1061, 1065, 1091, 1216–17, 1219
bārûk	ברוך	blessed	**4:**944; **6:**1128
barzel	ברזל	iron	**3:**28; **6:**1312
bassēter	בסתר	secret	**5:**663
bāšal	בשל	to boil, cook	**3:**647
bāšēl mĕbuššāl	בשל מבשל	boiled	**3:**647
bāśar	בשר	to bear news, publish	**1:**826; **3:**21; **4:**843, 1065; **6:**336, 513; **7:**606
bāśār	בשר	flesh	**1:**1104, 1119

Transliteration	Hebrew	English	Volume and Page
bāśār wĕdām	בשׂר ודם	flesh and blood	**5:**716
bāṭaḥ	בטח	to trust	**3:**265; **4:**727, 762, 786, 809, 902, 905, 923, 959, 1144, 1192; **5:**143, 219, 237
bat	בת	daughter	**5:**263, 630
bat-ʾēl nēkār	בת־אל נכר	daughter of a foreign god	**7:**865
bat-nādîb	בת־נדיב	queenly maiden	**5:**421
bat-ʿammî	בת־עמי	daughter of my people	**6:**1040
bat qôl	בת קול	daughter voice	**9:**91
bātal	בתל	to set apart, seclude	**1:**1148
bayin	בין	between, among	**6:**387
bayit	בית	house, temple	**2:**939, 1254, 1257; **3:**37, 405, 920; **4:**1012; **5:**44, 120, 138, 859; **6:**1540
bayyôm hahûʾ	ביום ההוא	on that day	**7:**730
bāzaz	בזז	to spoil, plunder	**6:**913; **7:**610
bĕ	ב	in, by, because of	**1:**1120; **2:**61–62; **5:**254, 659
bĕʾaḥărît haššānîm	באחרית השׁנים	in future years	**6:**1517
bĕ ʾaḥărîtô	באחריתו	at the end of his life	**5:**709
bĕʾašmat šōmĕrôn	באשׁמת שׁמרון	shame of Samaria	**7:**419
beʾĕmet	באמת	truly	**6:**773
bēʾēr	באר	to expound	**2:**293
bĕʾōš	באשׁ	bad smell	**1:**728
bĕdîl	בדיל	tin	**6:**1312
bĕhaʿăbîr bĕnêkem bāʾēš	בהעביר בניכם באשׁ	causing their children to pass through fire	**6:**1286
bĕhēmâ šeqeṣ	בהמה שׁקץ	loathsome animals	**6:**1176
bĕkî	בכי	tears	**4:**1014
bĕkōl-dôr wādôr	בכל־דור ודור	in all generations	**3:**938
bĕkôr	בכור	firstborn	**6:**1284
bĕkôr bāneykā	בכור בניך	the firstborn of your sons	**6:**1284
bĕkôr hāʾādām	בכור־האדם	firstborn of human beings	**6:**1284
bĕkōrâ	בכרה	birthright	**1:**535
bĕlayil	בליל	at night	**4:**510
bĕlēb šālēm	בלב שׁלם	single mind, wholeheartedness	**3:**467
bĕlî lô	בלי לו	not their own	**4:**510
bĕlî-mâ	בלי־מה	nothing, “without-what”	**4:**518

Transliteration	Hebrew	English	Volume and Page
bĕlîl	בליל	fodder	**4:**510
bĕliyyaʿal	בליעל	worthless, scoundrel	**2:**976, 986, 1049, 1371; **4:**510; **5:**76; **7:**605–6
bēn	בן	son	**3:**442, 701, 832; **4:**690, 1044, 1198; **5:**19, 185, 616, 655, 667, 686, 842; **6:**431, 515, 1030, 1121; **7:**659, 771; **8:**358, 360
ben-ʾādām	בן־אדם	son of a human	**2:**187; **4:**1000; **8:**360
ben-bĕliyyaʿal	בן־בליעל	a worthless man, a good-for-nothing	**2:**1167
bên hāʿarbāyim	בין הערבים	between the evenings	**1:**1157
ben-kûšî	בן־כושי	son of Cushi	**7:**670
ben-māwet	בן־מות	one who deserves to die, "a son of death"	**2:**1292
bēn-pārîṣ	בן־פריץ	violent son, shedder of blood	**6:**1261
bên ragleyhā	בין רגליה	between her feet/legs	**2:**788
ben-rēkāb	בן־רכב	associated with the Rechabite guild ("a chariotmaker," or the like)	**3:**224
ben-šāḥar	בן־שחר	Day Star, son of Dawn	**6:**344
bĕnê	בני	sons of	**7:**771
bĕnê bĕliyyaʿal	בני בליעל	worthless ones	**2:**1056; **3:**156
bĕnê bitnî	בני בתני	sons of my belly	**4:**476–77
bĕnê dĕdān	בני דדן	the Dedanites	**6:**1378
bĕnê gālût	בני גלות	sons of exile	**7:**53
bĕnê lēwî	בני לוי	sons of Levi	**3:**834
bĕnê-nēkār	בני־נכר	aliens, "sons of foreignness"	**4:**1255; **6:**1574
bĕnê rōdān	בני רדן	the Rhodians	**6:**1378
bĕnê taʿănûgāyik	בני תענוגיך	children of your delight	**7:**547
bĕnê-yiśrāʾēl	בני־ישראל	Israelites	**2:**33; **3:**317, 456
bĕʿēl-ṭĕʿēm	בעל־טעם	royal deputy	**3:**698
bĕʿērâ	בערה	burning	**2:**104
bĕqereb	בקרב	in the midst of	**2:**619, 665
bĕrākâ	ברכה	blessing	**1:**535, 564, 572; **3:**195, 265; **4:**1014; **5:**118, 667; **10:**381

Transliteration	Hebrew	English	Volume and Page
bĕrēʾšît bārāʾ ʾĕlōhîm	בראשית ברא אלהים	in the beginning God created	**5:**730
bĕrēkôt	ברכת	pools	**4:**1014
bĕrît	ברית	covenant	**1:**882; **2:**314; **4:**1212; **6:**361, 364, 471, 477, 481; **7:**361
bĕrît ʿām	ברית עם	covenant to the nations/ people	**6:**364, 430, 513
bĕrît ʿôlām	ברית עולם	everlasting covenant	**6:**362
bĕrît šālôm	ברית שלום	covenant of peace	**6:**1471
bĕrōʾš haššānâ	בראש השנה	at the beginning of the year	**6:**1536
bĕrōšîm	ברשים	cypress trees (?)	**7:**609
beṣaʿ	בצע	a cut, unjust gain	**6:**627, 1459
bĕšālôm	בשלום	in safety, peace	**3:**166, 553; **4:**899
beṭaḥ	בטח	security, safety	**4:**698, 737
beṭen	בטן	belly, womb	**7:**479–80, 506
bêt	ב	bet (Hebrew letter)	**4:**1166; **5:**667; **8:**187
bêt-ʾāb	בית אב	father's house	**1:**216; **2:**33, 592, 715; **5:**364, 397, 428
bêt ʾābôt	בית אבות	fathers' house	**3:**667, 685; **7:**710
bêt-ʾēl	בית אל	house of God	**1:**277–78, 542, 584
bêt ʾēm	בית אם	mother's house	**5:**364, 428
bêt ʾimmāh	בית אמה	mother's house	**2:**903
bêt haḥopšît	בית החפשית	the house of freedom	**3:**245
bêt haḥōrep	בית החרפ	winter house	**6:**840
bêt-hallaḥmî	ביתהלחמי	Bethlehemite	**3:**417
bêt keleʾ	בית כלא	prison, "house of confinement"	**7:**90
bêt-leḥem	בית־לחם	house of bread	**2:**903
bêt lĕʿaprâ	בית לעפרה	Beth-leaphrah	**7:**547
bêt marzēaḥ	בית מרזח	house of mourning	**6:**702
bêt midrāšh	בית מדרש	house of instruction	**5:**867
bêt mišteh	בית משתה	house of feasting, "drinking house"	**5:**326
bêt mûsār	בית מוסר	house of learning	**5:**867
bêt nĕtîbôt	בית נתיבות	crossroads, "house of ways"	**5:**89
bêt tipʾartî	בית תפארתי	glorious house	**6:**525
bĕtāmîm ûbeʾĕmet	בתמים ובאמת	with integrity and with faithfulness	**2:**715
bĕtûlâ	בתולה	virgin	**1:**1148; **3:**885, 891

Transliteration	Hebrew	English	Volume and Page
bĕyad	ביד	through, by the hand	**4:**590; **7:**716
bĕyad malʾākî	ביד מלאכי	by the hand of my messenger/Malachi	**7:**852
bĕyād rāmâ	ביד רמה	high-handed	**2:**127
bĕyôm	ביום	on the day, when	**2:**77, 88
bĕyôm ʾeḥad	ביום אחד	on the first day	**7:**766
bĕyôm higāmēl	ביום הגמל	day of weaning	**1:**68
bibrāʾ ʾēl	בברא אל	when God created	**5:**730
bîn	בין	to perceive, consider	**4:**420, 467, 533, 789, 878; **5:**195; **6:**53, 356
bînâ	בינה	understanding	**4:**531; **6:**141
binnûy	בנוי	Binnui	**3:**832
binyāmîn	בנימין	Benjamin, "son of the right hand"	**2:**771
binyān	בנין	structure, building	**6:**1552–53, 1557–58, 1561
biʿēr bātêhem	בער בתיהם	he destroyed their sanctuaries	**3:**644
biqʿâ	בקעה	valley, plain	**6:**1499
biqqōret	בקרת	due punishment	**1:**1134
bîrâ	בירה	fortress	**3:**467, 878
bišlām	בשלם	Bishlam, "in peace"	**3:**698
biṭṭāḥôn	בטחון	confidence, trust	**3:**265; **5:**340
bizzâ	בזה	spoil, booty	**7:**142
bôʾ	בוא	come, enter	**1:**735, 888; **2:**219; **3:**594, 923; **4:**370, 502, 531, 1155; **5:**76; **6:**1285; **7:**365, 380, 477, 494, 724
bōhaq	בהק	brightness	**1:**1097
bōkîm	בכים	Bochim, weepers	**2:**748
bôlēs šiqmîm	בולס שקמים	dresser of sycamore trees	**7:**411
bôqēr	בוקר	herdsman (?)	**7:**411
bôr	בור	pit, cistern	**4:**842, 1028; **6:**1388
bōser	בסר	sour grapes	**6:**1257
bôš	בוש	to be ashamed	**4:**389, 562, 705; **6:**1492
bōšet	בשת	shame	**1:**1126; **2:**1213, 1230, 1274; **4:**1211; **5:**828; **7:**269
bûqâ ûmĕbûqâ ûmĕbullāqâ	בוקה ומבוקה ומבלקה	devastation, desolation, and destruction	**7:**611

Transliteration	Hebrew	English	Volume and Page
bûs	בוס	to tread down, trample	**4:**857
bûṣ	בוץ	linen	**3:**692; **6:**1378
bûz	בוז	to despise	**5:**118
bûz	בוז	Buz	**4:**562

D

dābaq	דבק	to cling	**2:**905, 907, 913, 917; **3:**90, 260
dābar	דבר	to speak	**2:**48; **3:**500, 923; **6:**727, 1127; **7:**284, 286, 510
dābār	דבר	word, thing	**1:**753; **2:**343, 771; **3:**94, 125; **4:**810, 902, 1105, 1166, 1168; **5:**131, 162; **6:**66; **7:**291–92, 511, 662
dad	דד	breast	**5:**69, 380
dāg	דג	fish	**7:**480, 505
dākā᾽	דכא	to crush	**4:**1058; **6:**492
dakkā᾽	דכא	contrite	**6:**492
dakkā᾽	דכא	dust, something pulverized	**4:**1041
dal	דל	poor, weak	**1:**870; **4:**847; **5:**239; **7:**416
dālal	דלל	to hand, be low	**4:**530; **7:**602
dālap	דלף	to drip, be sleepless (?)	**4:**461
dālaq	דלק	to burn, hotly pursue	**5:**226
dalet	ד	dalet (Hebrew letter)	**6:**1467; **7:**258, 496, 498; **8:**129
dām	דם	blood	**6:**1476
dāmâ	דמה	to be like, resemble	**6:**1382; **7:**286
dāmâ	דמה	to cease, destroy	**7:**448
dāmam	דמם	to be silent, cease to move	**4:**697; **6:**1342
dāmîm	דמים	bloodshed, violence, guilt	**4:**887
dān	דן	Dan	**6:**1379
dā῾ak	דעך	to go out, be extinguished	**4:**468
da῾at	דעת	knowledge	**5:**295; **6:**141; **7:**148, 236
dāqar	דקר	to pierce	**7:**828
dāraš	דרש	to seek	**3:**303, 369, 383–84,

Transliteration	Hebrew	English	Volume and Page
dāraš *(continued)*			393, 400, 418, 425, 431, 461, 473, 536, 544, 551, 559, 586, 590, 643; **4:**1104; **5:**663, 668, 689; **6:**1276, 1290, 1464, 1466, 1494; **7:**390–91, 427, 472; **8:**31
dāt	דת	decree, edict	**3:**879, 882, 889, 899, 925, 937, 939
dāwid	דוד	David	**8:**129
day/dê	די	enough	**1:**962
dĕʾāgâ	דאגה	fearfulness	**6:**1196
dēaʿ	דע	knowledge	**4:**558
dĕbar YHWH	דבר יהוה	the word of the Lord	**7:**493, 715
dĕbarîm harbēh marbîm hābel	דברים הרבה מרבים הבל	the more words, the more vanity	**5:**322
dĕbēlâ	דבלה	figcakes	**7:**218
deber	דבר	pestilence	**1:**753
dĕbîr	דביר	rear room, inner sanctuary; "Holy of Holies"	**3:**484; **5:**859; **6:**1119, 1550
degel	דגל	standard	**2:**37
degel maḥănēh	דגל מחנה	regimental encampment	**2:**37, 95
dĕlîlâ	דלילה	Delilah, "flirtatious"	**2:**858
dĕmāmâ	דממה	silence	**3:**142; **4:**378
dĕmešeq	דמשק	Damascus (?)	**7:**375
dĕmût	דמות	likeness	**6:**1115, 1117
dĕmût kĕmarʾēh ʾādām	דמות כמראה אדם	the likeness of humanity	**6:**1117
deraš	דרש	homiletical meaning	**1:**66, 71, 77, 82
derek	דרך	way	**3:**143; **4:**370, 532, 684, 689, 777; **5:**37, 159, 198, 254; **6:**1047; **7:**514; **9:**742
derek bĕʾēr-šābaʿ	דרך באר־שבע	the way of Beersheba	**7:**419
derek ḥaṭṭāʾîm	דרך חטאים	way of sinners	**4:**684
dĕrôr	דרור	liberty, freedom	**1:**1172
dibbat hāʾāreṣ	דבת הארץ	bad report of the land	**2:**123
dikrônâ	דכרונה (Aramaic)	a record	**3:**707
dîn	דין	to judge	**4:**881, 963, 1066
dîn	דין	judgment, cause	**3:**882; **4:**1241
dôd	דוד	love, beloved	**5:**69, 380, 388; **6:**1228

Transliteration	Hebrew	English	Volume and Page
dôdî lî wa'ănî lô	דודי לי ואני לו	my lover is mine and I am his	**5:**393
dolĕqîm	דלקים	fervent, "burning"	**5:**226
dôr	דור	generation	**4:**983; **6:**466
dôr dôrîm	דור דורים	future generations	**6:**448
dōrôt 'ôlāmîm	דרות עולמים	generations of long ago	**6:**448

G

Transliteration	Hebrew	English	Volume and Page
gā'āh	גאה	to rise up	**4:**415
gā'al	גאל	to redeem	**1:**734, 801; **2:**892, 927, 933; **4:**367, 953; **6:**282; **7:**567
gā'al	גאל	to defile, pollute	**7:**40, 860
gā'ôn	גאון	high, proud	**4:**616, 1188; **5:**91, 161; **7:**401, 818
gab	גב	defense, reply, pit	**4:**434; **6:**1232
gābah	גבה	to be high, exalted	**6:**1551
gābar	גבר	to be strong, mighty	**4:**1150
gād	גד	Gad, troop	**1:**666
gādad	גדד	to cut	**7:**258
gādal	גדל	to grow, become great	**1:**702; **2:**986; **4:**396, 955, 1051, 1279; **7:**522
gādar	גדר	to wall in	**6:**1047, 1049
gādēr	גדר	wall	**3:**736; **6:**1552
gādōl	גדל	great	**1:**870; **4:**984, 1020, 1232, 1267; **7:**477, 522
gaga'	גגע	cackling	**5:**716
gal	גל	heap, fountain	**2:**627; **5:**406; **7:**286
gālâ	גלה	to uncover, reveal	**2:**924, 926, 997, 1002; **5:**158; **6:**411; **7:**272, 361, 387, 422, 430
gālal	גלל	to roll	**5:**158
gālāl	גלל	hill, excrement	**2:**678
gāla'	גלע	to expose, break out	**5:**172
galgal	גלגל	wheelwork	**6:**1182–83
galmûd	גלמוד	barrenness	**4:**368
gālût	גלות	exile	**6:**411
gam	גם	also, even	**2:**631; **3:**22; **6:**676; **7:**380
gāmal	גמל	to deal fully with, wean a child	**4:**1208

Transliteration	Hebrew	English	Volume and Page
gamlā	גמלא	camel	**8:**436
gan	גן	garden	**5:**406
gan yārāq	גן ירק	vegetable garden	**3:**155
gānab	גנב	to steal	**1:**863; **6:**1259
gaʿgaʿ	גע גע	ridiculing	**5:**716
gāʿal	געל	to loathe, abhor	**2:**817, 921, 924
gāraš	גרשׁ	to drive out	**1:**769; **2:**182; **7:**505
gārê bêtî	גרי ביתי	guests in my house (?)	**4:**476
gat	גת	Gath	**3:**414
gāwaʿ	גוע	to die, perish	**2:**161
gāzal	גזל	to tear away, seize	**6:**1259, 1450
gāzām	גזם	cutting locust	**7:**307
gāzar	גזר	to cut off	**4:**1028; **6:**1501; **10:**144
gê hāʿōbĕrîm	גי העברים	Valley of Abarim (?)	**6:**1525
gêʾ hinnom	גיא הנם	Valley of Hinnom	**8:**436
gēʾâ	גאה	pride	**5:**91
gēʾeh	גאה	pride (negative)	**4:**616, 1057
gĕʾôn yaʿăqōb	גאון יעקב	the pride of Jacob	**7:**609
gĕʾôn yiśrāʾēl	גאון ישׂראל	the pride of Israel	**7:**609
gēʾût	גאות	majesty	**4:**1053
gebaʿ	גבע	Geba	**2:**1069
geber	גבר	strong man, soldier	**6:**1046, 1051
gĕberet	גברת	lady, queen	**6:**411
gēbōrîm	גברים	mighty men	**2:**631
gĕbûl	גבול	border, boundary	**6:**1373, 1541, 1600
gĕbûrâ	גבורה	strength, might	**4:**1279; **6:**141
gĕderet	גדרת	wall	**6:**1552
gĕdôlâ	גדולה	great	**3:**839
gĕdûd	גדוד	bandits	**7:**256
gĕdûd yĕgûdennû	גדוד יגודנו	bands of raiders	**1:**666
gĕdûllâ	גדולה	honor	**4:**960
gēhâ	גהה	face (?)	**5:**169
gēl	גל	heap, excrement	**2:**678
gelālîm	גללים	dung pellets	**6:**1159
gĕlîlôt	גלילות	Geliloth, region near the Jordan	**2:**707
gemara	גמרא	Gemara	**1:**68
gĕmîr	גמיר (Aramaic)	complete, perfect	**3:**720
gĕmûl	גמול	benefit, recompence	**4:**1091
gĕʿārâ	גערה	rebuke	**5:**132
gepen	גפן	vine	**6:**1272

Transliteration	Hebrew	English	Volume and Page
gēr	גר	alien	**1:**653, 704, 718, 734, 783, 825, 1080; **2:**127, 916; **3:**468; **4:**476; **5:**705; **6:**1601
gēršōm	גרשׁם	foreigner	**1:**704, 825
gešem	גשׁם	rain, shower	**6:**1314
gēwâ	גוה	pride, a lifting up	**4:**503
gibbēn	גבן	hunchbacked	**1:**1148–49
gibbôr	גבור	mighty man	**2:**631, 915, 1207; **4:**908; **5:**194, 767; **7:**332
gibbôr ḥayil	גבור חיל	mighty man	**2:**915, 929, 1037; **3:**94; **5:**767
gibʿâ	גבעה	Gibeah, hill	**2:**1069; **7:**275
gidlê bāśār	גדלי בשׂר	big of flesh	**1:**1104
gilgāl	גלגל	Gilgal	**7:**387
gillāyôn	גליון	tablet	**6:**1507
gillûl	גלול	log, excrement	**2:**678
gillûlîm	גלולים	idols, dung pellets	**1:**1181; **6:**1159, 1205, 1417, 1575
ginâ	גנה	lament	**5:**809
gittît	גתית	a certain musical instrument	**4:**656
gizrâ	גזרה	restricted area	**6:**1552
gōbah	גבה	height, exaltation	**4:**616; **6:**1551
gōʾēl	גאל	redeemer, kinsman	**1:**661, 1173; **2:**265, 696, 915, 921, 926–29, 940; **3:**1143; **4:**477, 478, 508, 753
gōʾēl haddām	גאל הדם	the avenger of blood	**2:**435; **3:**1144
gôlâ	גולה	exiles	**2:**926, 942; **3:**679; **7:**786–88, 839
gōlem	גלם	unformed substance, embryo	**4:**1236
gôrāl	גורל	lot	**4:**736
gôy	גוי	nation	**1:**423, 482; **2:**655; **6:**364, 547, 1509
gôy ʾeḥād	גוי אחד	one nation	**6:**1509
gôy nābāl	גוי נבל	a foolish nation	**5:**862
gôyim rabbîm	גוים רבים	great nations	**6:**1425
gullâ	גלה	spring, bowl	**2:**678; **7:**769
gullōt	גלת	springs, bowls	**2:**678

Transliteration	Hebrew	English	Volume and Page
gullōt māyim	גלת מים	springs, basins of water, watery excrement	**2:**678, 738
gûmmāṣ	גומץ	pit	**5:**270
gûp	גוף	self, body	**8:**471
gûr	גור	to sojourn	**1:**429, 481; **2:**181; **4:**733; **7:**258
gûr	גור	cub, young	**6:**1269
H			
ha	ה	the	**4:**303
hāʾăsuppîm	האספים	gatherings, storehouse	**3:**451
hāʾĕlōhîm	האלהים	the god	**7:**476
hābal	הבל	to become vain	**4:**524
hādār	הדר	majesty, splendor	**4:**861, 1044
hădassâ	הדסה	Hadassah, "myrtle"	**3:**886
haddĕbārîm haʾēlleh	הדברים האלה	these words, things	**2:**343; **3:**937
hădōm roglayim	הדם רגלים	footstool	**4:**1130
hadrat-qōdeš	הדרת־קדש	holy splendor	**4:**792
hāgâ	הגה	to plot, meditate	**4:**689, 829, 960; **5:**719
haḥēl-hazzeh	החל־הזה	their hosts	**7:**456
hăkînôtî	הכינותי	I have provided	**3:**467
hakkōhănîm halwiyyim	הכהנים הלוים	Levitical priests	**2:**47
hakkōhēn haggādôl	הכהן הגדול	high priest, great priest	**7:**715
hālak	הלך	to go	**1:**429, 560, 700, 780, 937; **4:**348, 419, 684, 782; **7:**249, 365, 477, 493–94, 511, 580, 582, 757
hālal	הלל	to praise, boast	**4:**814, 1104, 1138, 1174, 1271, 1278; **5:**229, 257, 263
halĕlû-yāh	הללו־יה	"praise the Lord"	**4:**664, 1100, 1138–39, 1149, 1219, 1221, 1262–63, 1267, 1270, 1274
hāmâ	המה	to moan, growl	**4:**853, 865, 934; **5:**185
hāmam	המם	to throw into confusion or panic	**2:**1018; **3:**938
hammaśśāʾ hazzeh	המשא הזה	this oracle	**6:**1194
hammayim hārabbîm	המים הרבים	great waters	**6:**1369
hammiṣwâ	המצוה	the commandment	**2:**373
hammišneh	המשנה	Mishneh (gate)	**3:**766, 839

Transliteration	Hebrew	English	Volume and Page
hammitnaddĕbîm	המתנדבים	willingly offered	**3:**825
hammōrîm	המרים	rebels	**2:**160
hammōšēl ʾāmar	המשל אמר	the one who spoke in Proverbs	**5:**606
hāmôn	המון	multitude, noise, wealth	**5:**672; **6:**1415, 1440; **7:**334
hămôn nōʾ	המון נא	the horde of No	**6:**1418
hăniḥōtî ḥămātî	הנחותי חמתי	"I will satisfy my wrath"	**6:**1300
hannaḥ-lô	הנח־לו	"Let him alone"	**7:**242
hanniš ʾār	הנשאר	survivors	**3:**678
hāʿām	העם	the people	**2:**197
hāʿām hazzeh	העם הזה	this people	**7:**716
hāʿēdût	העדת	the testimony	**6:**1118
hāʿelem	העלם	forgetfulness	**5:**307
hāʿōlām	העלם	eternity, world	**5:**306–7, 663
ha-ʿōlām ha-bāʾ	העולם הבא	the coming age	**8:**157
hāpak	הפך	to turn, overturn	**3:**858, 930; **5:**125, 683, 689, 818; **7:**381, 389, 470, 511–12, 514
happĕruṣîm	הפרצים	gaps	**3:**773
haptarâ	הפטרה	prophetic lection	**1:**69
haqqōdeš	הקדש	the holy place	**3:**494
har	הר	mountain	**1:**1055; **3:**173
har ʾēl	הר אל	mountain of God	**6:**1566
har bêt-ʾēl	הר בית־אל	Mount Beth El	**4:**110
har haqqodeš	הר הקדש	holy mountain	**7:**795
hārag	הרג	to kill	**1:**703; **6:**1055
hārāpâ	הרפה	the Rephaim, giants	**2:**1361
harʾēl	הראל	hearth	**6:**1566
harbēh	הרבה	great	**4:**1206
hărēgâ	הרגה	slaughter	**7:**821
hāriš ʿâ	הרשעה	wickedness, wrongdoing	**7:**779
hāsâ	הסה	to be silent	**7:**414, 665, 678
hassôkēk	הסוכך	shielding, guardian (?)	**6:**1393
hăšālôm	השלום	"Is all well?"	**3:**215, 219
hăšîbēnû	השיבנו	restore us, "cause us to return"	**4:**999
haššēm	השם	the Name	**1:**1164
haššiqqûṣ mĕšômēm	השקוץ משומם	the desolating sacrilege	**4:**39; **7:**143
haššōʾăpîm ʿal-ʿăpar-ʾereṣ bĕrōʾš dallîm	השאפים על־עפר־ארץ בראש דלים	those who trample on the dust of the earth, on the head of the poor	**7:**365

Transliteration	Hebrew	English	Volume and Page
haśśāṭān	השׂטן	the accuser	**4:**347–48; **7:**765
hawwâ	הוה	destruction	**4:**890; **5:**107
hāyâ	היה	to be	**1:**714; **2:**747, 927–28; **3:**125; **6:**1133, 1374, 1377; **7:**290, 296, 492, 542
hāyâ qeṣep ʿal	היה קצף על	there was a wrath against	**3:**185
hăyēš-pōh ʾîš	היש־פה איש	"Is a man (anyone) here?"	**2:**781
hāyû bāk	היו בך	were within you	**6:**1374
hazenôtāh	הזונתה	religious prostitution	**1:**1135
hazkîr	הזכיר	memorial offering	**4:**955
heʾāḥ	האח	"Aha!," expression of joy	**5:**824
hēʾānēq dōm mētîm	האנק דם מתים	"moan in deathly stiffness"	**6:**1342
hebel	הבל	wind, puff, ephemeral	**3:**255; **4:**494, 524, 838; **5:**278–80, 290, 311, 354; **6:**692
heh	ה	heh (Hebrew letter)	**6:**1319
hêkāl	היכל	temple	**5:**859; **7:**331, 610, 787
hēkālôt	היכלות	temple chambers	**1:**279
hêmînû	הימינו	kept in his right hand	**3:**776
hēmmâ	המה	they, them	**6:**1578
hēn	הן	behold, see, if	**4:**434, 583; **6:**230, 264
hên ʿārēb	הין ערב	sweet palate	**5:**683
heʿîr hāʾĕlōhîm et-rûḥô	העיר האלהים אתרוחו	(those) whose spirit God had stirred	**3:**678
hēšîbû ʾeškārēk	השיבו אשכרך	rendered you tribute	**6:**1378
hîʾ yāšĕrâ bĕʿênāy	היא ישרה בעיני	she pleases me, "she is right in my eyes"	**2:**849
hîn	הין	hin (unit of measure, about a gallon)	**6:**1149
hinĕnî ʾălêkem	הנני אליכם	"see now, I am coming to/against you"	**6:**1484
hinĕnî ʾēlayik	הנני אליך	"see, I am against you"	**7:**612, 614
hinnāzēr	הנזר	mourning, devotion	**7:**792
hinnēh	הנה	behold, look	**3:**556; **6:**1182, 1420, 1499
hinnēh ʾaššûr	הנה אשור	"consider Assyria"	**6:**1422
hinnēh ʾeliyyāhû	הנה אליהו	"Elijah is here"	**3:**133
hinnēh hinnām	הנה הנם	"behold, behold them"	**6:**356
hinnēnî	הנני	"here I am"	**6:**454
hippaḥtem ʾôtô	הפחתם אותו	"you sniff at it"	**7:**860
hiqdîš	הקדיש	to sanctify	**2:**160

Transliteration	Hebrew	English	Volume and Page
hiqšîb	הקשב	to heed	**2:**1089
hirkîb	הרכיב	transporting	**3:**393
hišlîṭ	השליט	empowered	**5:**340
hiššāpēk nĕḥuštēk	השפך נחשתך	"you poured out your (lust ?)"	**6:**1234
hištaḥăwâ	השתחוה	prostrate oneself (in worship)	**4:**352
hitʿallēl	התעלל	to make fools	**2:**1011
hittammĕhû tĕmāhû	התמהו תמהו	be utterly amazed	**7:**635
hôd	הוד	authority, glory	**2:**220; **4:**711, 861, 1271
hôlēlôt	הוללות	madness	**5:**295
hōmiyyâ	המיה	loud	**5:**40, 84
hôn	הון	wealth, treasure	**5:**683; **6:**1388
hôsîʿâ nāʾ	הושיעה נא	Save, I/we beseech you	**8:**403
hōwâ	הוה	disaster	**6:**412
hôy	הוי	woe to, alas	**5:**655, 824; **6:**16, 53, 92, 264, 741, 1199, 1268, 1461; **7:**385, 392, 398–99, 613, 647, 686, 688, 690, 693, 759
hûʾ	הוא	he	**3:**378, 594; **4:**532; **6:**1302; **7:**257
hûʾ . . . wĕhûʾ	הוא . . . והוא	he . . . and he	**3:**594
hûsad	הוסד	measurement, foundation	**3:**484

Ḥ

Transliteration	Hebrew	English	Volume and Page
ḥābar	חבר	to unite, be joined	**4:**1184
ḥăberâ	חברה	companion	**7:**865
ḥăbûrôt	חבורות	associations concerning ritual cleanness	**9:**247
ḥādad	חדד	to be sharp	**6:**1298
ḥādaš	חדש	to renew	**5:**834
ḥamîšâ ḥûmšê hattôrâ	חמישה חומשי התורה	the five fifths of the Law	**1:**305
ḥādēl	חדל	fleeting, transient	**4:**838
ḥag	חג	festival	**1:**777, 780, 931; **6:**1585; **7:**606
ḥāgag	חגג	to make a pilgrimage	**7:**707
ḥaḥ	חח	a hook	**6:**1269
ḥākâ	חכה	to wait, wait for	**4:**811
ḥākām	חכם	wise, skillful person	**1:**960; **3:**916; **5:**280, 626

Transliteration	Hebrew	English	Volume and Page
ḥăkāmâ	חכמה	wise	**2:**1313
ḥālā᾿	חלא	to be sick, diseased	**6:**1336
ḥālal	חלל	to profane, make common	**1:**1152; **2:**198; **6:**998, 1329, 1389
ḥālal	חלל	to pierce, slay	**4:**612; **6:**1389; **7:**829
ḥālap	חלף	to move on, pass by	**4:**411, 420–21
ḥālaq	חלק	to divide, allocate	**1:**800; **5:**808
ḥālāq	חלק	smooth, slippery	**5:**226
ḥălaqlaqqôt	חלקלקות	slippery, smoothness	**4:**819
ḥālaṣ	חלץ	to take off, deliver, rescue	**1:**700; **2:**938
ḥalḥālâ	חלחלה	anguish, writhing	**6:**1415
ḥama᾿	חמא	Hama	**3:**863
ḥāmad	חמד	to desire, covet	**6:**1341; **7:**549–50
ḥāmal	חמל	to have pity	**1:**700; **2:**1153, 1292; **6:**1343, 1530
ḥamān	חמן	incense altar	**3:**536
ḥāmar	חמר	to boil	**5:**664
ḥāmās	חמס	violence	**1:**390; **4:**709; **5:**724; **6:**1166, 1177, 1394; **7:**631
ḥămušîm	חמשים	fifty	**1:**789
ḥămôr	חמור	donkey	**1:**1188
ḥămôt	חמות	mother-in-law	**2:**905
ḥāmûd	חמוד	desire, something desirable	**7:**724
ḥānâ	חנה	to decline, encamp	**7:**806
ḥānak	חנך	to dedicate	**5:**198
ḥānan	חנן	to be gracious, make supplication	**1:**635, 869; **3:**923; **4:**411, 476, 789, 801, 885, 1087, 1187, 1250; **7:**391
ḥannâ	חנה	Hannah, "charming, attractive"	**2:**974
ḥannûn	חנון	gracious	**1:**946; **4:**671, 983, 1133, 1136, 1148; **7:**319, 477
ḥannûn wĕraḥûm	חנון ורחום	gracious and merciful	**7:**518
ḥāpaś	חפש	to search for, plot	**4:**930; **7:**442
ḥāpēṣ	חפץ	to delight in, desire	**2:**1126; **3:**87; **4:**848; **5:**724
ḥāqaq	חקק	to cut, inscribe, decree	**5:**92, 94

Transliteration	Hebrew	English	Volume and Page
ḥāqar	חקר	to search	**4:**533; **5:**217, 238, 663, 689
ḥārâ	חרה	to be furious, kindled, burn	**4:**828; **7:**517
ḥārab	חרב	to lay waste, make desolate	**6:**1196
ḥāram	חרם	to utterly destroy, devote	**2:**1087–88; **3:**742; **7:**567
ḥārān	חרן	Haran, "road"	**6:**1380
ḥārap	חרף	to mock, insult	**3:**629; **4:**1036
ḥāraš	חרשׁ	to plow	**2:**453
ḥărê yônîm	חרי יונים	dove dung	**3:**204
ḥārēb	חרב	waste, desolate, ruined	**7:**716
ḥărîšît	חרישׁית	fierce, strong	**7:**477
ḥārôn	חרון	anger, fury	**1:**800
ḥarṭōm	חרטם	magician	**7:**50
ḥārum	חרם	disfigured	**1:**1148
ḥāsâ	חסה	to seek refuge	**4:**66–67, 690, 747, 905, 1243; **5:**144
ḥāsad	חסד	to be good, kind	**4:**748; **6:**1340
ḥăsar-lēb	חסר־לב	lacks sense/heart	**5:**111
ḥāsîd	חסיד	faithful	**4:**697, 806, 891, 1020; **5:**833
ḥăsîdayyāʾ	חסידיא (Aramaic)	Hasideans	**4:**47
ḥăsîdîm	חסידים	faithful, loyal ones	**3:**498; **4:**47, 95, 802
ḥāsîl	חסיל	destroying locust	**7:**307
ḥăṣar ʿam-ʾēl	חצר עם־אל	"the court of the people of God"	**4:**163
ḥāṣēr	חצר	court, enclosure	**6:**898
ḥāṣîr	חציר	grass	**6:**387
ḥăṣôṣĕrōt	חצוצרת	trumpets	**2:**89
ḥāšâ	חשׁה	to keep silence	**4:**837
ḥāšab	חשׁב	to think, plan	**1:**672; **4:**956; **6:**1038; **7:**477
ḥāšak	חשׁך	to grow dark	**4:**468; **6:**1418
ḥašmal	חשׁמל	electrum, glowing ember	**4:**591; **6:**1114, 1117
ḥāšaq	חשׁק	to love, be attached to	**4:**1048
ḥāśak	חשׂך	to withhold, refrain	**6:**1418
ḥāṭāʾ	חטא	to sin, miss the mark	**1:**435, 482, 646, 728, 758; **4:**885; **5:**178, 758; **6:**1450, 1546; **7:**261

Transliteration	Hebrew	English	Volume and Page
ḥaṭāʾâ	חטאה	sin	**1:**482; **4:**805
ḥaṭṭāʾîm	חטאים	sinners	**4:**684; **5:**37
ḥaṭṭāʾt	חטאת	sin, sin-offering	**1:**281; **2:**78, 151; **3:**609; **4:**833; **6:**498, 945, 1450, 1546; **7:**122
ḥātam	חתם	to seal, affix a seal	**3:**815; **7:**149
ḥātān	חתן	son-in-law, husband	**1:**1084
ḥātar	חתר	to dig, hollow out	**7:**477, 499
ḥātat	חתת	to be dismayed, shattered	**5:**111; **7:**861
ḥătîmâ	חתימה	conclusion	**1:**69
ḥătumîm	חתמים	sealed	**7:**149
ḥāwâ	חוה	to prostrate oneself (in worship)	**4:**352, 792
ḥay-ʾănî	חי־אני	"as I live"	**2:**124
ḥāyāh	חיה	to live, have life, restore to life	**3:**377; **4:**403, 1169; **7:**391
ḥayil	חיל	strength, might	**2:**915, 939, 1048; **4:**747; **5:**260, 263, 677; **6:**1388
ḥayyâ	חיה	life	**3:**736
ḥayyîm	חיים	life	**1:**350
ḥāzā	חזה	to see, look at	**4:**403; **6:**48, 66; **7:**405, 410, 542
ḥāzaq	חזק	to strengthen, harden, urge	**1:**781; **2:**877–78, 1303; **3:**765; **4:**523; **5:**689, 853; **6:**354, 1126; **7:**723
ḥāzĕqû ʿālay dibrêkem	חזקו עלי דבריכם	"your words were strong against me"	**7:**871–72
ḥāzôn	חזון	vision	**5:**244; **6:**48, 66; **7:**444
ḥebel	חבל	portion, cord	**2:**685
ḥebel middâ	חבל מדה	measuring line	**7:**773
ḥēk	חך	mouth, palate	**5:**66
ḥelʾātāh	חלאתה	rust, encrusted (?)	**6:**1336
ḥēleb	חלב	fat	**1:**1025
ḥeled	חלד	lifespan	**4:**422, 838
ḥēleq	חלק	portion, reward	**4:**736, 969, 1170; **5:**298, 319, 824; **6:**491
ḥemāʾâ	חמאה	cream, curds	**4:**538
ḥēmâ	חמה	anger, wrath	**3:**895; **4:**704, 828; **7:**602

Transliteration	Hebrew	English	Volume and Page
ḥēn	חן	grace, undeserved favor	**1:**390, 572, 715, 940; **4:**861; **5:**54, 118, 673
ḥēq	חיק	bosom, lap	**3:**14; **4:**509; **5:**66
ḥēqer	חקר	a search, investigation	**4:**420
ḥereb	חרב	sword	**5:**127; **6:**450, 1150, 1354
ḥērem	חרם	devoted, dedicated	**1:**867, 1019, 1189–90; **2:**147–48, 163, 255, 393, 562–63, 590, 606, 613–15, 625, 627, 630–31, 648, 651, 1085–90, 1148, 1179, 1300; **3:**1180; **6:**1580; **7:**619, 876
ḥerpâ	חרפה	reproach, scorn	**4:**952, 1036; **5:**683
ḥesed	חסד	graciousness, kindness	**1:**475, 483, 492, 510–11, 563, 611, 615, 659, 801, 842, 946, 1142; **2:**904, 925, 929, 932, 945, 1120, 1133–36, 1159, 1208, 1212, 1230, 1258, 1273–74, 1276–77, 1279, 1281, 1324, 1331; **3:**95, 304, 495, 498–99, 736; **4:**51, 388, 663, 670–71, 701, 748, 768, 844, 872, 885, 913, 983, 1020, 1034, 1078, 1082, 1091, 1116, 1121, 1126, 1150, 1171, 1232, 1255; **5:**181, 185; **6:**336, 597, 809, 1051; **7:**42–43, 163, 236, 252, 319, 507, 580; **8:**425; **9:**84, 523
ḥešbôn	חשבון	sum	**5:**270
ḥet	ח	khet (Hebrew letter)	**6:**1298
ḥēzeq	חזק	strength	**4:**747
ḥîdâ	חידה	riddle	**5:**698; **6:**1242
ḥilqiyyāhû	חלקיהו	Hilkiah, "Yahweh is my portion"	**2:**687

Transliteration	Hebrew	English	Volume and Page
ḥinnām	חנם	for nothing, without cause	**4:**349, 354, 411; **6:**454
ḥisōnîm	חסנים	outside	**5:**634
ḥiššĕbâ lĕhiššābēr	חשבה להשבר	"thought itself to break up"	**7:**478–79, 495
ḥizqiyyāhû	חזקיהו	Hezekiah	**5:**853
ḥizzāyôn	חזיון	vision	**4:**1035
ḥôaḥ	חוח	bramble, hook	**5:**224
ḥōbâ	חבה	debts	**8:**202
ḥōbēl	חבל	sailor	**7:**477
ḥōdeš	חדש	moon, month	**5:**834
ḥōkmâ	חכמה	wisdom	**3:**27; **4:**419, 531, 1098; **5:**12, 89, 94, 102, 105, 142, 280–81, 295, 652, 667, 674, 686; **6:**141
ḥokmôt	חכמות	wisdom	**5:**667
ḥōl	חל	profane, common	**1:**1127, 1152; **2:**1139; **6:**1605
ḥôl	חול	sand	**4:**539
ḥômâ	חומה	wall	**3:**505; **6:**1540
ḥômat ʾănāk	חומת אנך	a wall of plumb line	**7:**406
ḥōmer	חמר	dry measure equal to the load a donkey can carry	**1:**1188
ḥômeš happĕqûddîm	חומש הפקודים	the fifth of the census totals	**2:**3
ḥônēn	חונן	generous, gracious	**4:**829
ḥōq	חק	statute, ordinance, "groove"	**2:**323, 384; **3:**26; **4:**50, 509, 532, 1166, 1168; **5:**253, 261, 824; **6:**1280, 1282, 1589
ḥōq ûmišpāṭ	חק ומשפט	statutes and ordinances	**4:**50
ḥōr	חר	recess, hole	**6:**1175
ḥorbâ	חרבה	ruin, a place laid waste	**6:**455, 1354
ḥōreb	חרב	drought	**7:**716
ḥōrep	חרף	autumn, harvest time	**5:**185
ḥōrîm	חרים	nobles	**3:**759, 824
ḥōsen	חסן	treasure	**5:**149
ḥōšek	חשך	darkness	**3:**982; **4:**430, 1027, 1236
ḥôṭeʾ	חוטא	sinner, fool, bungler	**5:**302, 345
ḥôṭēʾ napšô	חוטא נפשו	forfeit, miss life	**5:**185
ḥōṭer	חטר	twig, shoot	**5:**139

Transliteration	Hebrew	English	Volume and Page
ḥôtām	חותם	seal, signet ring	**6:**1391; **7:**731
ḥôtēm tāknît	חותם תכנית	"you were a sealing of proportion"	**6:**1391
ḥōtēn	חתן	father-in-law	**1:**1084
ḥōzeh	חזה	seer	**6:**4; **7:**405, 410, 558
ḥûd ḥîdâ	חוד חידה	to propound a riddle	**6:**1242
ḥûl	חול	to twist, writhe	**3:**903; **4:**829, 1142; **6:**1415
ḥûmāš	חומש	the fivefold book	**1:**305
ḥuqqîm	חקים	ordinances	**2:**323, 384; **4:**1166, 1168
ḥuqqôt 'ôlām	חקות עולם	eternal ordinance	**6:**1589
ḥûs	חוס	to pity, look upon with compassion	**7:**321, 486–87, 522–24
ḥûš	חוש	to hasten	**4:**956

K

Transliteration	Hebrew	English	Volume and Page
kābâ	כבה	to snuff out	**6:**1435
kābaš	כבש	to subdue	**1:**346; **2:**1266
kabbîr	כביר	great, powerful one	**4:**576, 585
kābēd	כבד	to be heavy, honored	**1:**847, 863; **2:**1011; **5:**133, 187, 696; **6:**1117; **7:**717, 859
kābēd	כבד	heavy	**4:**613
kābôd	כבוד	glory, honor	**1:**316; **2:**997, 1002, 1005, 1011; **4:**693, 696, 708, 772, 792, 964, 1232; **5:**119, 223, 667, 673; **6:**1117, 1175; **7:**239, 269, 272, 724, 760
kaddorbānôt	כדרבנות	like goads	**1:**67
kaddur Banôt	כדר בנות	a girl's ball	**1:**67
kaggepen baddîm kî	כגפן בדים כי	"like a vine (full of) shoots because. . ."	**6:**1272
kāhâ	כהה	to restrain, grow weak	**2:**992
kāḥad	כחד	to hide, conceal	**4:**388
kāḥaš	כחש	to deceive, act deceptively	**6:**1208; **7:**832
kālâ	כלה	to finish, perish	**1:**973, 976, 978; **2:**901; **4:**1042
kālâ ya'ăśeh	כלה יעשה	"he will make an end"	**7:**602

Transliteration	Hebrew	English	Volume and Page
kālā'	כלא	to withhold	**4:**844
kālam	כלם	to insult, humiliate	**4:**475; **6:**1492
kālîl	כליל	whole offering	**1:**1009
kallâ	כלה	daughter-in-law	**2:**903
kānâ	כנה	to give a name	**6:**1391
kāna'	כנע	to be humble, brought into subjection	**3:**302, 403, 413, 600
kānāp	כנף	wing, cloak, corner of garment	**2:**918, 926, 928; **6:**1245
kānas	כנס	to gather, collect	**6:**1531
kā'as	כעס	to be angry	**7:**288
ka'aś	כעשׂ	grief, anguish	**4:**386
kāp	כ	kap (Hebrew letter)	**8:**187
kap	כף	flat of hand, sole of foot	**4:**568
kāpar	כפר	to cover, atone	**1:**563, 889, 892, 913, 918, 933, 998, 1111; **3:**609; **4:**933, 995; **5:**159, 194; **6:**1568
kapōret	כפרת	mercy seat, atonement cover	**1:**889, 998, 1111; **2:**79
kārar	כרר	to dance	**3:**394
kārat	כרת	to cut, cut off, make a covenant	**2:**127, 1134, 1157; **3:**500; **4:**829; **6:**1207, 1212; **7:**575
karbēl	כרבל	to put on a mantle, clothe	**3:**395
kāsâ	כסה	to conceal, cover	**5:**111; **6:**1429; **7:**478
kāsap	כסף	to long for	**4:**442
kāšal	כשל	to stumble, stagger	**6:**1485
kašrût	כשרות	kosher food law	**2:**13
kaśdîm	כשדים	Chaldean	**7:**44
kātab	כתב	to write	**6:**709
kātēp	כתף	shoulder	**6:**1353, 1547
kāzab	כזב	to lie	**2:**187, 188
kāzāb	כזב	lie, falsehood	**7:**282
kĕ'ayin	כאין	as nothing	**4:**838
kĕ'immâ bittâ	כאמה בתה	"like mother, like daughter"	**6:**1236
kĕbār	כבר	already	**5:**270, 340
kĕbôd YHWH	כבוד יהוה	"the glory of Yahweh"	**2:**11, 15, 25, 49, 79, 88, 124, 135; **6:**1117, 1120
kĕdumâ	כדמה	"like silence, like something destroyed"(?)	**6:**1382

Transliteration	Hebrew	English	Volume and Page
kĕlāyôt	כליות	belly, kidneys	**5:**60
keleb	כלב	dog	**2:**462, 673; **4:**544
kĕlî	כלי	objects	**2:**1011; **5:**218; **6:**892
kĕlî ʾādām	כלי אדם	someone's dish	**6:**988
kĕlî ʾădāmâ	כלי אדמה	earthen dish/vessel	**6:**988
kĕlimmâ	כלמה	shame	**6:**1577
-kem	־כם	your	**7:**635
kĕmô-ʾel	כמו־אל	like God	**4:**477
kēn	כן	right, thus	**5:**237, 842; **7:**605
kĕnāpôt	כנפות	skirts, edges of the earth	**4:**602
kĕʿan	כען	now	**3:**699
kêpaʾ	כיפא	Cepha, "rock"	**8:**345, 562
kĕpîr	כפיר	young lion	**6:**1269; **7:**248, 278
kĕrābîd	כרביד	encircling, "like a necklace"	**3:**484
keseh	כסה	full moon	**4:**518
kesep	כסף	silver, money	**1:**629, 864; **6:**1312
kesep napšôt ʿerkô	כסף נפשות ערכו	money from personal vows	**1:**1187
kĕsîl	כסיל	fool, Orion	**4:**605; **5:**106, 223
kešep	כשף	sorcery	**7:**614
kĕtîb	כתיב	what is written	**1:**29–30, 297
kĕtûbîm	כתובים	Writings	**1:**8, 16, 22, 29, 65, 69; **6:**2
kĕzābîm	כזבים	lies, deceptive things	**6:**1459
kĕzōʾt	כזאת	thus	**4:**478
kî	כי	for, because	**1:**802, 842, 881, 923, 1009, 1032; **3:**526; **4:**500, 648, 964, 1192; **5:**674; **6:**62, 72, 76, 122, 157, 167, 254, 260, 276, 417, 1124, 1209, 1217, 1351, 1358, 1365; **7:**275, 330, 333, 380, 493, 499, 500, 514, 685, 741, 870
kî-ʾāz	כי־אז	at that time, "for then"	**7:**699
kî ʾim	כי אם	but	**4:**684
kî-lĕkā	כי־לך	for you	**4:**834
kî ʿattâ	כי עתה	for now	**7:**272
kî pāʿălû šāqer	כי פעלו שקר	who deal falsely	**7:**256

Transliteration	Hebrew	English	Volume and Page
kî-śānē᾽ šallaḥ	כי־שׂנא שׁלח	for he hates divorce/ "sending away"	**7:**865
kî yaʿăśû mikkol-ḥaṭṭō᾽t hā᾽ādām	מכל־חטאת האדם־ כי יעשׂו	wrongs committed by/ against any human	**2:**61
kikkār	ככר	Jordan Valley, cover	**3:**769; **7:**778–79
kilmad	כלמד	Chilmad	**6:**1380
kilyâ	כליה	kidney	**4:**459
kîmâ	כימה	Pleides, "the herd"	**4:**605
kimrîrê yôm	כמרירי יום	blackness of the day	**4:**367
kiplayim	כפלים	doubled, complete, full	**6:**334, 436, 450
kis᾽ôt	כסאות	thrones	**4:**1184
kissē᾽	כסא	throne	**4:**518, 1184; **7:**478
kitbê qôdeš	כתבי קודשׁ	sacred writings	**1:**65
kiyyûn	כיון	an image (?)	**7:**394
kōaḥ	כח	power, strength	**4:**1133, 1268; **5:**677
koh ᾽āmar YHWH	כה אמר יהוה	"thus says the Lord"	**7:**605
kōhēn	כהן	priest	**3:**494; **6:**1578
kol	כל	all, every	**1:**579, 961; **3:**468; **4:**712, 940, 1090; **5:**157–58, 278, 307, 311
kol-bĕkôr	כל־בכור	every first-born	**6:**1284
kol-hā᾽āreṣ	כל־הארץ	all the land/earth	**6:**877
kol-hāʿēdâ	כל־העדה	the whole congregation	**2:**159
kol-peṭer rāḥam	כל־פטר רחם	first-born child, "every first womb issue"	**6:**1283, 1284, 1530
kol-rō᾽š	כל־ראשׁ	all the heads	**2:**36
kōper	כפר	ransom	**1:**865, 998, 1142; **4:**570; **5:**194
kûb	כוב	an unknown people	**6:**1415
kûl	כול	to seize, nourish	**3:**132
kûllānû	כלנו	all of us	**6:**529, 530, 543
kûn	כון	to be firm, provide	**3:**429, 467, 484; **4:**414, 533, 634, 945, 1054; **7:**381
kûr	כור	furnace	**6:**1312
kûš	כושׁ	Cush, Etheopia, Sudan	**7:**616, 691, 699
kûšî	כושׁי	Cushi, African	**7:**670

L

lā᾽â	לאה	to weary	**7:**579
lābab	לבב	to hearten, encourage	**5:**405

Transliteration	Hebrew	English	Volume and Page
lābaš	לבשׁ	to put on, wear	**4:**1053; **7:**513
lābaṭ	לבט	to thrust down, ruin	**5:**108
lābîʾ	לביא	lion	**7:**248
lahebet šalhebet	להבת שׁלהבת	blazing flame, "flame of flame"	**6:**1295
lāhem	להם	to/for them	**3:**772
lākad	לכד	to take, seize	**2:**1300
lākēn	לכן	therefore	**4:**627; **6:**454, 1152, 1250, 1321, 1327, 1336–37, 1350, 1363, 1388, 1420, 1457, 1464, 1468, 1476, 1478, 1481, 1485, 1490, 1519, 1530; **7:**288, 696
lākîš	לכישׁ	Lachish	**7:**547
lāḥam	לחם	to fight, do battle	**4:**819, 901
lāḥaṣ	לחץ	to oppress	**1:**713; **4:**902
laḥōreb bayyôm	לחרב ביום	to the heat by day	**6:**840
lāmad	למד	to teach, learn	**5:**667, 698; **6:**420, 437
lamed	ל	lamed	**5:**42
lāmmâ zeh	למה זה	why	**1:**566, 573
lamnaṣṣēaḥ	למנצח	to the leader	**4:**656
lāʿăbōd ʾet-ʿăbōdat	לעבד את־עבדת	to do the service	**2:**50
lāʿad	לעד	forever	**4:**478
lāʿag	לעג	to mock, deride	**4:**999; **5:**664
laʿag	לעג	mocking, ridicule	**7:**258
laʿăzāʾzēl	לעזאזל	for/to Azazel	**1:**1112
lāqaḥ	לקח	to take	**1:**429, 578–79, 734, 780, 1142; **2:**901, 940, 1029, 1061, 1242; **3:**67, 197, 655; **6:**1509; **7:**216, 787
lāqaḥ nĕpāšôt	לקח נפשׁות	to take lives	**5:**120
lāqaš	לקשׁ	to glean	**4:**510
lārekeš	לרכשׁ	to a team of horses	**7:**547
lārîb bāʾēš	לרב באשׁ	"judgment by fire"	**7:**406
lāšôn	לשׁון	tongue, language	**4:**930; **5:**111–12
lāwâ	לוה	to be joined	**2:**147
lĕ	ל	to	**6:**1507, 1547; **8:**308, 313
lĕʾôr gôyim	לאור גוים	"a light to the nations"	**7:**699
lēb	לב	heart	**1:**962; **2:**1039, 1043;

Transliteration	Hebrew	English	Volume and Page
lēb *(continued)*			**4:**450, 844, 930, 1136, 1208; **5:**60, 111, 150, 152, 724; **6:**1052
lēb ḥākām	לב חכם	a wise heart	**5:**664
lēb kābēd	לב כבד	a hard heart	**5:**664
lēb qāṭān	לב קטן	small of heart	**5:**716
lēbāb	לבב	heart	**4:**969, 1082; **5:**60, 724–25; **6:**656
lĕbab	לבב (Aramaic)	heart	**7:**74
lĕbiyyā'	לביא	lioness	**6:**1268
lĕbōnâ	לבנה	incense offering	**6:**945
lĕbônâ	לבונה	frankincense	**5:**403
lĕdabbēr 'al-libbâ	לדבר על־לבה	"to speak tenderly to her"	**2:**876
lĕdōr wādōr	לדר ודר	for all time, "to generation and generation"	**4:**983
lĕgallôt 'ervâ	לגלות ערוה	to uncover the nakedness	**1:**1124
lĕhazkîr	להזכיר	to invoke, make petition	**3:**400
lĕhit'annôt	להתענות	to humble oneself	**7:**123
lĕhôdôt	להודות	to throw, cast, praise	**3:**400
leḥem	לחם	bread, food	**2:**903; **3:**782; **4:**1098; **6:**1148; **7:**449
leḥem 'ônîm	לחם אונים	meal brought to the bereaved (?)	**6:**1342
lĕḥuqqat mišpāṭ	לחקת משפט	a statute and an ordinance	**2:**218
lēk šûb	לך שוב	"Go, return"	**3:**144
lēk šûb lĕdarkĕkā	לך שוב לדרכך	"Go, return to your way"	**3:**143
lekû lĕšālôm nōkaḥ YHWH darkĕkem	לכו לשלום נכח יהוה דרככם	"Go in peace. Your way way is in front of the Lord."	**2:**870–71
lĕma'an	למען	in order that	**6:**1427
lĕma'lâ	למעלה	highly	**3:**388
lĕmelek	למלך	belonging to the king	**1:**224
lĕpānēkā	לפניך	in your presence, "to your face"	**4:**848
leqaḥ	לקח	teaching, learning	**4:**419; **5:**58
lĕrābîb 'ēš	לרבב אש	"a shower of fire"	**7:**406
lēṣ	ליץ	scorner	**4:**461, 684; **5:**664
lēṣîm	לצים	scoffers	**4:**684
lĕšibtĕkā	לשבתך	to enthrone, reside	**3:**71
lĕšobê peša'	לשבי פשע	those who turn from transgression	**6:**498

Transliteration	Hebrew	English	Volume and Page
lĕšortô	לשרתו	in serving him	**3:**437
lēwî	לוי	Levi	**2:**147; **3:**494, 834
lĕyôm ʾeḥād	ליום אחד	each day	**3:**782
lî	לי	for me, on my side	**4:**1154
lî ʾāmar	לי אמר	it shall be said	**6:**402
limmudāy	למדי	those taught, disciples	**6:**420
limmûdê YHWH	למודי יהוה	taught by the Lord	**6:**478
limmûdîm	למודים	ones taught, disciples	**6:**420, 478
limʿāl-maʿal	למעל־מעל	acting faithlessly	**6:**1212
lîn	לין	to lodge	**4:**475, 913
liqsām qāsem	לקסם־קסם	to consult an omen	**6:**1301
lisdāqâ wĕhinnēh ṣĕʿāqâ	לצדקה והנה צעקה	"for righteousness, but behold a cry"	**4:**310
liškâ	לשכה	room, chamber	**6:**1542, 1552
lišrōšiw	לשרשו (Aramaic)	banishment	**3:**722
lô	לו	to him	**3:**212; **4:**434
lōʾ	לא	no, not	**1:**869; **3:**212; **4:**411, 434, 509, 531; **6:**417, 638, 866, 1369, 1477
lōʾ ʾăšîbennû	לא אשיבנו	"I will not turn it back"	**7:**354
lōʾ naʿăleh	לא־נעלה	"We will not go up"	**2:**136
lōʾ nûkal	לא נוכל	"We are not able"	**3:**773
lōʾ ʿāl	לא על	"not Most High"	**7:**258
lōʾ ʿammî	לא עמי	"not my people"	**7:**290
lōʾ šālawtî wĕlōʾ šāqaṭtî wĕlōʾ-nāḥĕtî wayyābōʾ rōgez	לא שלותי ולא שקטתי ולא־נחתי ויבא רגז	"I have no ease, no quiet, no rest— what comes is turmoil"	**4:**370
lōʾ tinḥāl	לא תנחל	"you shall not receive as a possession"	**6:**1579
lōʾ tîrāʾû	לא תיראו	"do not fear"	**6:**621
lōʾ yēšĕbû	לא ישבו	they shall not remain	**7:**265
lōʾ-yiggah	לא־יגה	does not shine	**4:**468
lōʾ yittākēn	לא יתכן	to be unfair	**6:**1263
lōʾ yirʾû	לא יראו	do not see	**6:**621
lōʿēz	לעז	strange language	**4:**1142
lû	לו	if only	**4:**509
lûaḥ	לוח	tablet	**6:**1507
lûb	לוב	Libyan	**6:**1415
lūḥōt hā ʿēdūt	לחת העדת	tablets of the testimony	**1:**924
luḥōtāyim	לחתים	ribs, planks	**6:**1373
lûlîm	לולים	enclosed shaft with steps (?)	**6:**1551

Transliteration	Hebrew	English	Volume and Page
M			
m	מ	place of, from	**6:**1516; **7:**477, 498
mâ	מה	how	**4:**711; **6:**1285; **7:**477, 498
maʾăkāl	מאכל	food, slaughter	**4:**858
māʾas	מאס	to reject	**2:**1027, 1047, 1089, 1098; **4:**578, 628; **6:**1299; **7:**270
mabbāṭ	מבט	hope	**7:**805
mabbûl	מבול	flood of waters	**1:**391; **4:**793
mādôn	מדון	strife, quarrel	**5:**77, 245; **7:**631
māgēn	מגן	shield	**1:**444; **4:**747, 789, 869, 1014, 1035
maggāl	מגל	sickle, pruning knife	**7:**333
maggēpâ	מגפה	blow, slaughter	**6:**1341
mahălak	מהלך	walk	**7:**511
māhar	מהר	to hasten	**2:**601
māḥâ	מחה	to blot out	**1:**934; **6:**386
māḥāʾ	מחא	to beat, clap	**3:**710; **6:**1351
maḥălāpîm	מחלפים	knives	**3:**679
māḥălat	מחלת	unknown musical term	**4:**656
māḥălat lĕ ʿānnôt	מחלה לענות	unknown musical title	**4:**656
maḥăneh	מחנה	encampment, company	**1:**572; **5:**425
māḥār	מחר	tomorrow	**1:**745
maḥēʾ	מחא (Aramaic)	to spare, let live	**7:**83
maḥlĕqôt	מחלקות	divisions	**3:**451
maḥmad	מחמד	desire	**6:**1341
maḥmal napšĕkem	מחמל נפשכם	the longing of your life	**6:**1343
maḥseh	מחסה	refuge, shelter	**4:**864, 919, 922, 958, 1047, 1059, 1247
maḥtôt	מחתות	censers	**2:**137
makʾôb	מכאוב	pain, suffering	**4:**834
mākar	מכר	to sell	**1:**646; **2:**935; **4:**858
makbēr	מכבר	a kind of woven material	**3:**212
makkat ḥereb	מכת־חרב	edge of the sword	**3:**931
mālak	מלך	to be king	**2:**1159; **3:**18, 472, 885; **4:**700, 764, 1258, 1275, 1279
mālal	מלל	to speak, utter, shuffle	**5:**76
mālaṭ	מלט	to deliver	**6:**405–6
malʾāk	מלאך	messenger, angel	**1:**565, 568, 661; **2:**161;

Transliteration	Hebrew	English	Volume and Page
			3:140, 171; **6:**393; **7:**720, 852, 869
mal'ak YHWH	מלאך יהוה	messenger of Yahweh	**2:**179
mal'ākî	מלאכי	Malachi, "my messenger"	**7:**720, 847, 852
mal'ăkût	מלאכות	message	**7:**720
mālē'	מלא	to fill, be full	**1:**800, 907; **3:**18–19; **4:**741
māle' yād	מלא יד	to consecrate oneself, one's service	**3:**610
malkâ	מלכה	queen, queen mother	**3:**756, 923; **7:**82
malkût	מלכות	kingship, royalty	**3:**29, 908; **4:**1258–59
mallāḥîm	מלחים	sailors	**7:**477
mamlākâ	ממלכה	kingdom, reign	**3:**29; **4:**1142
mammôn	ממון	wealth, riches	**5:**780–81; **8:**210
mān hû'	מן הוא	"What is it?"	**1:**813
mānâ	מנה	to count, reckon, assign	**7:**476–77, 520
mānâ	מנה	part, portion	**3:**935
mānôaḥ	מנוח	security, a resting place	**2:**925
mānôn	מנון	grief (?)	**5:**245
mānôs	מנוס	refuge	**4:**913, 1247
mā'ad	מעד	to slip, totter	**5:**219
mā'al	מעל	to break faith	**2:**61, 627; **3:**329, 524, 636, 753
ma'al	מעל	unfaithful, treacherous act	**1:**1182; **2:**62; **3:**329, 358, 369, 591, 598, 607; **4:**494; **6:**1251
mā'al ma'al	מעל מעל	to practice unfaithfulness, committ treachery	**3:**302–3, 329
ma'ălôt	מעלות	ascents	**4:**1176
ma'ămaqqîm	מעמקים	deep, depths	**4:**952, 1205
ma'ărāb	מערב	imports	**6:**1377
ma'ăśeh	מעשה	work, deed	**4:**925, 1132
mā 'ôn	מעון	dwelling place	**4:**1047
mā'ôz	מעוז	refuge, strength	**4:**790, 891
ma'yānôt	מעינות	springs	**4:**1024
mappelet	מפלת	ruin, downfall	**6:**1367
māqaq	מקק	to rot, fester	**4:**833; **6:**1343, 1450
māqôm	מקום	place, region, quarter	**3:**867; **4:**470, 529; **6:**1552; **7:**602
maqqēl	מקל	wooden staff	**6:**1006, 1506; **7:**240
mar	מר	bitter	**2:**63, 905; **4:**508

Transliteration	Hebrew	English	Volume and Page
mārâ	מרה	to rebel, be contentious	**2:**63; **4:**1111; **6:**1033
mārâ	מרה	bitter	**2:**909
mārar	מרר	to be bitter	**2:**63; **4:**1111
māraṭ	מרט	to polish, make smooth	**6:**1298
mar'eh	מראה	appearance	**5:**394; **6:**1115
mar'ôt 'ĕlōhîm	מראות אלהים	divine visions	**6:**1110, 1503
marbaddîm	מרבדים	coverings	**5:**262
margĕlôt	מרגלות	feet	**2:**924
mārôm	מרום	height	**4:**902
mārōr	מרר	bitter	**4:**459
mārôt	מרות	Maroth	**7:**547
marpē'	מרפא	healing, tranquil	**3:**656; **5:**148
marzēaḥ	מרזח	feast	**1:**225
māsāk	מסך	screen	**1:**901
māsas	מסס	to melt	**4:**628
masgēr	מסגר	smith	**6:**930, 944
massâ	מסה	trial	**5:**669
masweh	מסוה	a veil	**1:**953
māṣā'	מצא	to find	**3:**888; **4:**420, 529, 531; **5:**211, 667, 689, 720; **7:**270
māṣā'tî ḥēn	מצאתי חן	found favor	**3:**918
māṣôr	מצור	rampart	**7:**805
maṣṣâ	מצה	unleavened bread	**2:**50
maṣṣēbôt	מצבות	pillars, sacred stones	**3:**115
māšâ	משה	to draw	**1:**700
māšaḥ	משחâ	to anoint	**1:**907, 976; **6:**1393
māšāl	משל	to rule, speak a parable	**1:**344; **2:**808; **4:**712, 1091; **6:**1242, 1295; **7:**570
māšāl	משל	proverb, saying	**2:**186; **4:**434, 876, 990; **5:**32, 251, 377, 613, 616, 689; **6:**158, 1197–98, 1207, 1242–43, 1257–58, 1295; **7:**467–68, 647; **8:**298, 568; **9:**667–68, 755
mašîaḥ	משיח	an anointed one	**1:**289; **2:**895, 982, 1039, 1061, 1097; **4:**673, 756, 1014, 1104; **6:**391; **7:**571; **9:**531

Transliteration	Hebrew	English	Volume and Page
mašmîaʿ šālôm	משמיע שלום	"who proclaims peace"	**7:**606
mašmîm	משמים	desolate	**6:**1128
mašrôqîtāʾ	משרוקיתא	pipe, flute	**7:**63
maśkîl	משכיל	poem, wise, wise one	**4:**657; **7:**143, 390
māśôś	משוש	joy	**4:**403
maśśāʾ	משא	oracle, utterance, burden	**5:**251; **6:**150, 253, 405, 710, 753, 1194; **7:**599, 629, 741, 803, 852
maśṭēmâ	משטמה	animosity, enmity	**7:**267
maṭṭāʿ lĕšēm	מטע לשם	a planting of renown	**6:**1473
maṭṭāʿ šālōm	מטע שלם	a peaceful planting	**6:**1473
maṭṭaʿ YHWH	מטע יהוה	"God's own planting"	**6:**514
maṭṭeh	מטה	tribe, staff	**2:**37, 140, 580, 658; **6:**1166, 1418, 1506
mattānâ	מתנה	gift	**1:**989; **6:**1286
māwet	מות	death	**4:**946
mayim	מים	water	**3:**776; **4:**952; **5:**69; **6:**1425
mayim ḥayyîm	מים חיים	living water	**2:**151
mayim rabbîm	מים רבים	floods	**5:**430; **6:**1425
mayim qĕdošîm	מים קדשים	holy water	**2:**63
mazkîr	מזכיר	recorder, herald	**3:**50
mazkîr ʿāwōn	מזכיר עון	public prosecutor	**6:**1302
mazzārôt	מזרות	Mazzaroth	**4:**605
mê ḥaṭṭāʾt	מי חטאת	water of sin, sin-offering	**2:**81, 151
mê mĕrîbâ	מי מריבה	waters of Meribah	**2:**160
mê niddâ	מי נדה	water of cleansing	**2:**81, 151
mê rabâ	מי רבה	waters of Rabbah	**3:**416
mēʾarbaʿ rûḥôt	מארבע רוחות	the four winds	**6:**1500
mĕʾîrat	מאירת	giving light	**1:**1063
mĕʾōd	מאד	very	**3:**423; **6:**656
mĕbaśśēr	מבשר	tidings-bearer, messenger	**6:**336; **7:**606
mĕbaśśeret ṣiyyôn	מבשרת ציון	"O Zion, herald of good tidings" or "you who bring good tidings to Zion"	**6:**336
mĕbînîm	מבינים	wise, teachers	**3:**726
mĕgîḥān lĕyammāʾ	מגיחן לימא	stirring the sea	**7:**101
mĕgillâ	מגלה	scroll	**4:**843
mĕgillâ ʿapâ	מגלה עפה	flying scroll	**7:**773
mĕgillot	מגלת	Five Scrolls, "scrolls"	**2:**893; **5:**267; **6:**1016

Transliteration	Hebrew	English	Volume and Page
mĕhûmâ	מהומה	a panic, disorder	**2:**1007; **6:**1308
mĕḥittâ	מחתה	terror	**6:**709
mĕkaššēp	מכשף	sorcerer	**7:**50
mĕlāʾkâ	מלאכה	occupation, work	**5:**205; **7:**720
melek	מלך	king	**1:**1126; **2:**808, 1036, 1038, 1041, 1142; **3:**20, 416, 472, 923; **4:**1258, 1275; **5:**205, 749; **6:**1007, 1391, 1509; **7:**570, 702
melek-kûš	מלך־כוש	king of Nubia/Cush	**7:**671
melek yiśrāʾēl Yahweh	מלך ישׂראל יהוה	the king of Israel, the Lord	**7:**702
mēlîṣ	מליץ	an intermediary	**4:**460–61, 569
mĕlōʾ	מלא	fullness	**6:**1196
mĕlûkâ	מלוכה	dominion	**4:**764
mĕmaššēl mĕšālîm	ממשל משלים	a speaker of parables	**6:**1295
memšālâ	ממשלה	dominion	**4:**1142
mĕnôrâ	מנורה	lampstand	**2:**80
mĕnûḥâ	מנוחה	rest, security	**2:**903–4, 925; **7:**553, 804, 806
mēʿal ligĕbûl yiśrāʾēl	מעל לגבול ישׂראל	beyond the borders of Israel	**7:**855
mēʿālāyik	מעליך	from you	**7:**605
mĕʿārâ	מערה	cave	**3:**142
mēʿay dak	מעי דך	bowels of the oppressed	**5:**664
mēʿeh	מעה	heart, belly, inward parts	**4:**844; **5:**411, 415; **7:**479, 505
mĕʿîl	מעיל	robe	**2:**1184
mĕpakkîm	מפכים	trickling	**6:**1595
mĕpāraš	מפרשׁ (Aramaic)	translate extemporaneously	**3:**699
mēpîṣ	מפיץ	scatterer, disperser	**7:**609
mĕqûmāh	מקומה	opposition	**7:**603
mĕraḥēm	מרחם	merciful	**4:**1148
mērāḥôq	מרחוק	distant	**5:**663
mĕrappîm yĕdê	מרפים ידי	discouraged, "weakened the hands of"	**3:**695
mĕrēʿîm	מרעים	evildoers	**4:**828
mĕrērâ	מררה	gall	**4:**459
mĕrî	מרי	defiant, rebellious	**4:**508; **5:**167
mĕrîbâ	מריבה	strife, contention	**1:**433; **2:**528

Transliteration	Hebrew	English	Volume and Page
merkābâ	מרכבה	chariot	**6:**1119, 1129
mĕsārĕpô	מסרפו	one who burns him/it (?)	**7:**401
mĕsibbâ	מסבה	gallery	**6:**1551
mĕsillâ	מסלה	highway	**6:**335
mĕsillôt	מסלות	public roads	**4:**110
mĕsôs	מסוס	"withers"	**4:**403
mĕsûkâ	מסוכה	a covering (?)	**6:**1392
mēṣar	מצר	distress	**4:**1154
mĕṣôlōt	מצולת	depths	**1:**800; **4:**1028
mĕṣōrāʿ	מצרע	leprosy	**3:**592
mĕṣûdâ	מצודה	fortress, snare	**4:**747, 958, 1047; **6:**1194
mĕṣûlâ	מצולה	the depths	**4:**624; **7:**750
mêšārîm	מישרים	uprightness, equity	**5:**207
mĕšārtê mizbēaḥ	משרתי מזבח	"ministers of the altar"	**5:**668
mĕšārtê YHWH	משרתי יהוה	"ministers of Yahweh"	**5:**668
mēšîb	משיב	a restorer, one who causes to turn around	**2:**899
mĕšōl māšāl	משל משל	to proclaim a parable	**6:**1242, 1335
mĕšubâ	משבה	faithless, apostate	**6:**604
mĕtê	מתי	men	**6:**957
mêtê Yiśrāʾēl	מיתי ישראל	the dead of Israel	**6:**957
meteg	מתג	Metheg, bridle	**3:**414
meteq	מתק	sweetness, counsel	**5:**230
mēydĕbāʾ	מידבא	Medeba, water of rest	**3:**416
mēyuddāʿ	מידע	close friend, companion	**2:**914–15; **4:**476
mĕzimmâ	מזמה	prudence, discretion, plan	**5:**43; **6:**752
mî yĕšîbennû	מי ישיבנו	unhindered	**4:**420
mî–yittēn	מי־יתן	"oh that . . . ," "who will set"	**4:**478; **5:**748
mî yôdēaʿ	מי ידע	"who knows?"	**5:**655
mibbeṭen šĕʾôl	מבטן שאול	from the womb of Sheol	**7:**480
mibkî nĕhārôt	מבכי נהרות	sources of the rivers	**4:**530
mibṭāḥ	מבטח	trust	**4:**843
midbār	מדבר	desert, wilderness	**4:**604
midraš	מדרש	homilies	**1:**66, 70; **5:**443, 867; **7:**472–73; **8:**31; **10:**16, 375, 381
migdal-ʿōz	מגדל־עז	strong tower	**4:**919
migrāš	מגרש	common, open land	**6:**1605
miḥyâ	מחיה	sustenance	**3:**736

Transliteration	Hebrew	English	Volume and Page
mîkâ	מיכה	Micah, "Who is like the Lord?"	**2:**869
miktām	מכתם	unknown psalm title	**4:**657
mikšôl	מכשול	stumbling block, calamity	**6:**1135
milkōm	מלכם	Milcom	**3:**416
millēʾ	מלא	to confirm	**3:**18–19
millēʾ yād	מלא יד	to fill one's hand	**3:**467
millibô	מלבו	willingly, "from his heart"	**6:**1052
milluʾîm	מלאים	"fillings," ordination	**1:**1062
mimmiṣrayim	ממצרים	from Egypt	**2:**181
mimšaḥ	ממשח	anointed (?)	**6:**1393
min	מן	from, because of	**1:**999, 1110; **4:**580
min-hāʾēš	מן־האש	from the fire	**2:**147
minḥâ	מנחה	gift, grain offering	**1:**563, 572, 1016–17; **2:**77, 229; **6:**56, 945
minlām	מנלם	wealth (?)	**4:**452
minzār	מנזר	prince, guard (?)	**7:**618
mippĕnê kĕlimmātēk	מפני כלמתך	"on account of your humiliation"	**6:**1239
miqdāš	מקדש	sanctuary	**1:**888; **4:**969; **6:**1510, 1568
miqdāš mĕʿaṭ	מקדש מעט	a little sanctuary (?)	**6:**1188
miqlāṭ	מקלט	asylum	**2:**696
miqnēh ʾap	מקנה אף	indignant wrath	**4:**590
miqneh ʾap	מקנה אף	the cattle also	**4:**590
miqqereb ʾaḥeyka	מקרב אחיך	"one from among your brothers"	**2:**426
miqqōdeš haqqŏdāšîm	מקדש הקדשים	from the most holy	**2:**147
miqrāʾ	מקרא	what is read	**1:**65, 71, 74, 80
miqrāʾê qodeš	מקראי קדש	sacred assembly	**1:**1156
miqreh	מקרה	fate, chance	**5:**282, 319
miqwāʾôt	מקואות	ritual bathing pools	**4:**156
mirmâ	מרמה	treason, deceit	**3:**220; **6:**654; **7:**282, 283, 285
mirzaḥ	מרזח	revelry, feasting	**7:**399
mispār	מספר	number	**3:**447, 456
miṣrayim	מצרים	Egypt	**2:**181
miṣwâ	מצוה	commandment	**2:**373; **3:**26; **4:**1166; **5:**303, 787, 789; **6:**968
miškāb	משכב	couch, place of lying	**6:**489, 1443

Transliteration	Hebrew	English	Volume and Page
miškān	משכן	tabernacle, dwelling	**1:**884, 888, 981; **2:**32; **4:**470, 1013; **6:**1510–11
mišlê ben sirā'	משלי בן סרא	The Proverbs of the Son of Sira	**5:**606
mišlê [šĕlōmōh]	משלי [שלמה]	the Proverbs [of Solomon]	**5:**20
mišmār	משמר	custody, prison	**1:**1164
mišmeret	משמרת	service	**2:**36
mišnâ	משנה	teaching, repetition	**1:**67
mišneh	משנה	double, second	**3:**679
mîšôr	מישור	level, level ground	**4:**786
miš'ān	משען	a support	**3:**532
miš'enet	משענת	staff	**6:**1506
mišpaḥâ	משפחה	clan, family	**1:**216; **2:**33, 630, 918; **3:**938
mišpāṭ	משפט	justice	**1:**467, 469, 896; **2:**1027, 1048; **4:**400, 433, 475, 575, 580, 596, 616, 685, 708, 774, 829–30, 1082, 1134, 1172, 1241; **5:**125, 160, 242; **6:**88, 354–55, 362–64, 369, 386, 390, 412, 478, 485, 498, 618, 646, 892, 1529, 1582; **7:**388, 403, 484, 580, 868
mišpaṭ hammelek	משפט המלך	justice of the king	**2:**1028, 1048
mišpaṭ hammĕlukâ	משפט המלכה	rights and duties of the kingship	**2:**1048
mišpāṭ ûṣĕdāqâ	משפט וצדקה	justice and righteousness	**6:**1263
mišpāṭîm	משפטים	ordinances	**1:**862; **2:**323, 384; **3:**26; **4:**752, 963, 1104, 1166, 1168, 1269; **6:**1280
mišteh	משתה	feast	**2:**850; **7:**41
miśgāb	משגב	stronghold, fortress	**4:**747, 913, 1048
miśpāḥ	משפח	bloodshed	**6:**88
mizmôr	מזמור	psalm, song	**4:**301, 657
mizzeh . . . mizzeh	מזה . . . מזה	this side and the other	**7:**775
mô'āb	מואב	Moab	**2:**901

Transliteration	Hebrew	English	Volume and Page
mōdā‘	מודע	kinsman, relative	**2:**914–15
mōhar	מהר	bride price	**1:**867; **7:**231
môkîaḥ	מוכיח	arbitrator, reprover	**4:**413, 563; **6:**1137–38
mōledet	מלדת	kindred	**3:**923
mōlek	מלך	Molech	**1:**1126
mô‘ădîm	מועדים	time-markers	**4:**308
mô ‘ēd	מועד	appointed time, meeting place	**1:**1156; **2:**32, 229; **4:**973, 977; **7:**286
môpēt	מופת	miracle, portent (?)	**4:**959, 1104; **6:**1339, 1453
mōpĕtîm	מפתים	wonders	**1:**717
môqēš	מוקש	trap	**7:**371
mōrâ	מרה	bitter	**7:**547
môrāšâ	מורשה	possession	**6:**1482
môreh	מורה	teacher	**8:**432
mōrek	מרך	fearful	**1:**1181
mōṣ	מץ	chaff	**4:**685
mōšeh	משה	Moses	**1:**700
môšēl	מושל	ruler	**7:**570
môšîa‘	מושיע	savior	**3:**236, 237, 238
môṭ	מוט	to move, shake	**4:**732, 865, 916, 1066, 1180
môṭ	מוט	pole, carrying frame	**3:**393
mōṭēh	מטה	yoke, staff	**7:**605
mōṭôt miṣrayim	מטות מצרים	the bars of Egypt	**6:**1418
môt	מות	Mot (Canaanite god of death)	**4:**946
môt tāmût	מות תמות	"you shall surely die"	**6:**1134
môt yûmāt	מות יומת	"shall surely die"	**1:**836, 863, 923
mûg	מוג	to melt	**7:**610
mûl	מול	to cut off	**4:**1154
mûm	מום	blemish	**4:**421
munnāḥ	מנח	open space	**6:**1557
mûsār	מוסר	instruction, discipline	**5:**59, 620, 627, 652, 688, 867; **7:**244, 258, 664–65, 693, 696
mûsār bōšet	מוסר בשת	instruction concerning shame	**5:**828
muṣāq	מצק	cast, firm	**4:**422
muṭṭeh	מטה	perversion of law	**6:**1166
mût	מות	to die	**2:**1287; **5:**181; **7:**523

Transliteration	Hebrew	English	Volume and Page
mût labbēn	מות לבן	"The Death of the Son," musical tune	**4:**656

N

Transliteration	Hebrew	English	Volume and Page
naʾ	נא	"now, please"	**1:**495
nāʾap	נאף	to commit adultery	**6:**1224; **7:**256; **8:**191
nāʾwâ	נאוה	fitting, beautiful	**4:**1267; **5:**383
nābāʾ	נבא	to prophesy	**2:**1121; **7:**552
nābāl	נבל	fool, foolish, senseless	**2:**1166, 1169, 1304; **4:**545, 729, 886; **5:**167, 169, 862
nābaṭ	נבט	to see, consider	**2:**1098; **6:**1032–33, 1043, 1064, 1068; **7:**635
nābaʿ	נבע	to flow	**5:**729–30
nābîʾ	נביא	prophet	**2:**993, 1256; **6:**4, 319, 429, 443; **7:**558, 852
nād	נד	wanderer	**5:**805
nādâ	נדה	to cast off	**2:**151
nādab	נדב	to prompt, incite	**1:**888; **3:**825
nādāb	נדב	Nadab	**3:**358
nādîb	נדיב	generous, a noble	**1:**960; **4:**546, 886
nāgad	נגד	to make known	**2:**1039; **4:**960
nāgaʿ	נגע	to touch, reach, strike	**1:**429
nāgar	נגר	to pour, flood	**4:**486
nāgîd	נגיד	ruler, leader	**2:**1036, 1038–39, 1041, 1043, 1071, 1169, 1234; **3:**20, 826; **6:**1386, 1391
nāhâ	נהה	to wail, lament	**6:**1439
nahăpôk hûʾ	נהפוך הוא	"the reverse occurred"	**3:**858, 930
nāhār	נהר	river	**7:**602
nāḥâ	נחה	to lead	**1:**788
naḥal	נחל	dry river bed, wadi	**4:**530
naḥălâ	נחלה	inheritance, heritage	**1:**847; **2:**221, 658; **4:**945, 1172, 1198; **6:**1485, 1579, 1581, 1600; **7:**553
nāḥam	נחם	to be sorry, change one's mind	**1:**788, 932; **2:**187, 756, 1088, 1090–91; **4:**768, 953, 1043; **7:**406, 477, 514–15

Transliteration	Hebrew	English	Volume and Page
nāḥāš	נחש	snake	**2:**1054
naḥlat bêt-yiśrāʾel	נחלת בית־ישראל	"the inheritance of the house of Israel"	**6:**1479
nākâ	נכה	to attack, kill	**1:**702, 715; **2:**493; **3:**238–39, 414, 423; **4:**694, 1220; **7:**520–21
nākal	נכל	to be deceitful, crafty	**2:**200
nākar	נכר	to take notice	**2:**918; **4:**394; **5:**186
nākĕrî	נכרי	foreigner	**1:**704
nāʿ	נע	fugutive	**5:**805
naʿălāmîm	נעלמים	hypocrites, "those who conceal themselves"	**4:**782
naʿălêtā	נעלית	exalted	**4:**1069
naʿămān hāʾărammî hazzeh	נעמן הארמי הזה	Naaman, that Aramean	**3:**197
nāʾap	נאף	to commit adultery	**6:**1321, 1329
naʿar	נער	young man, servant	**2:**916, 986; **3:**884; **4:**351, 586; **5:**198, 349; **7:**758
naʿărâ	נערה	young woman, servant	**2:**916; **7:**365
nāʿēm	נעם	to be pleasant	**4:**1244; **5:**151
nāʿîm	נעים	gracious, charming	**2:**909, 1207–8; **4:**1267
nāpaḥ	נפח	to breathe, blow	**6:**1500; **7:**860
nāpal	נפל	to fall	**7:**386, 427
nāpaṣ	נפץ	to shatter, disperse	**1:**410
napšî	נפשי	my life, self	**1:**535
nāqâ	נקה	to be empty, clear	**1:**863, 947; **4:**753; **7:**774
nāqab	נקב	to pierce, curse, blaspheme	**1:**1164
nāqam	נקם	to avenge	**1:**864; **6:**697, 914, 1354–55, 1474
nāqām	נקם	vengeance	**6:**273
nāqî	נקי	innocence	**4:**773
nāsâ	נסה	to test	**1:**818; **2:**345; **4:**991; **5:**670
nāsaʿ	נסע	to journey	**1:**481, 794, 979; **4:**1000
nāsîk	נסיך	prince, anointed one	**6:**1444
nāṣal	נצל	to deliver, plunder	**1:**569, 700, 704, 712, 715, 728, 734, 736, 781, 825, 938; **3:**630,

Transliteration	Hebrew	English	Volume and Page
			730; **4:**763, 800, 1006; **7:**375, 471
nāṣar	נצר	to watch, guard	**4:**396; **5:**787
nāšâ	נשה	to forget	**6:**1530
nāšak	נשך	to bite	**6:**1259; **7:**647
nāšîm nokriyyôt	נשים נכריות	foreign women	**7:**865
nāšîm zōnôt	נשים זנות	women prostitutes	**3:**43
nāśāʾ	נשא	to lift, take, spare	**1:**469, 563, 946–48, 1072; **2:**901–2, 940; **3:**17, 385, 393, 888, 908; **4:**1076, 1251; **6:**405, 1530; **7:**629, 804; **9:**552
nāśāʾ ʿāwōn	נשא עון	to bear iniquity	**6:**1145–46, 1576
nāśāʾ ʾet-ʿăwōnah	נשא אתעונה	to bear iniquity	**2:**64
nāśag	נשג	to overtake	**1:**800
nāśĕʾâ ḥēn	נשאה חן	gained favor	**3:**918
nāśîʾ	נשיא	leader, prince	**1:**869, 1035; **2:**34; **3:**679; **6:**1168, 1194, 1417, 1470, 1509, 1570
nāṭâ	נטה	to slip, stretch out	**4:**1058
nāṭaʿ	נטע	to plant	**1:**350
nāṭap	נטף	to preach, drip	**6:**1294; **7:**552
nātak	נתך	to pour out, be smelted	**6:**1337; **7:**122
nātan	נתן	to give	**1:**346; **2:**50, 586; **3:**424; **5:**112, 174, 748; **6:**1369, 1377
nātan-lāh kĕyad	נתן־לה כיד	"he gave to her like the hand of"	**3:**510
nātaš	נתש	pluck up	**7:**430
nātaṣ	נתצ	to tear down	**6:**825
nātĕnâ bĕyad	נתנה ביד	"she gave into the hand of"	**3:**510
nāzâ	נזה	to sprinkle, spatter	**6:**463
nāzar	נזר	to dedicate, separate	**1:**1106, 1149; **2:**64; **7:**792
nāzîr	נזיר	Nazirite, separated one	**2:**845; **9:**354
nĕʾāqâ	נאקה	groaning	**1:**706; **2:**756
neʾĕlāḥ	נאלח	corrupt	**4:**450
neʾĕmānîm	נאמנים	trustworthy	**4:**1134
nĕʾum	נאם	oracle, utterance	**2:**189, 1370; **4:**822

Transliteration	Hebrew	English	Volume and Page
nĕbālâ	נבלה	an outrage, wicked thing, folly	**2:**455, 1168, 1304
nĕbālōt	נבלות	foolish women	**4:**356
nĕbîʾîm	נביאים	Prophets	**1:**8, 16, 22, 29, 65, 70; **6:**1
nĕdābâ	נדבה	freewill offering	**6:**1569
nēdeh	נדה	a gift	**6:**1233
neder	נדר	vow	**1:**1187; **2:**64, 234; **6:**1569; **7:**606; **8:**193
nĕdîbâ	נדיבה	nobility	**4:**546; **5:**169
negaʿ	נגע	plague, stroke	**1:**1096; **4:**838
negeb	נגב	Negeb, dry land in south	**6:**1294
neged	נגד	opposite, like, comparable to	**4:**63
nĕhî	נהי	wailing, lamentation, mourning song	**6:**1440
nĕḥaš nĕḥōšet	נחש נחשת	bronze serpent	**2:**164
neḥmād	נחמד	desire, covet	**1:**361
nĕḥōšet	נחשת	bronze	**6:**1312
nĕḥuštān	נחשתן	name later given to brass serpent of Moses	**3:**260
nĕkāsê šeqer	נכסי שקר	deceitful riches	**5:**678
nĕkōḥâ	נכחה	plain	**5:**688
nĕkônâ	נכונה	right, correct	**4:**634
nĕmālâ	נמלה	ant	**5:**74
nĕpal	נפל	to fall	**7:**63
nepeš	נפש	life	**1:**845, 924, 1032, 1075, 1119; **2:**892, 941, 1120; **4:**391, 395, 704, 927, 952, 1190, 1246, 1251; **5:**54, 119, 126, 131, 133, 152, 161–62, 173, 178–80, 205, 219, 220, 230, 322, 787; **6:**221, 656; **7:**401, 477, 506, 527
nepeš bĕ-nepeš	נפש בנפש	"a life in exchange for a life"	**1:**1120
nepeš ḥayyâ	נפש חיה	a living being	**1:**350; **6:**221
nepeš ʿazzâ	נפש עזה	insatiable desire	**5:**681
nepeš taḥat nāpeš	נפש תחת נפש	"a life in place of a life"	**1:**1120, 1165
nĕpilîm	נפלים	giants	**5:**725

Transliteration	Hebrew	English	Volume and Page
nĕqābeykā	נקביך	"your engravings" (?)	**6:**1392
nēr	נר	Ner, lamp	**3:**358; **7:**679
nēs	נס	something lifted up, sign	**6:**515, 1374; **7:**811
nĕsîkê qedem	נסיכי קדם	giants of old	**5:**725
neṣaḥ	נצח	perpetuity, ever	**4:**983
nēṣer	נצר	a shoot	**9:**354
nĕšāmâ	נשמה	breath	**4:**523, 563, 1279; **5:**188
nešek	נשך	interest, "something bitten off"	**1:**1173; **6:**1259
nešeq	נשק	weapons	**6:**1524
nešer	נשר	eagle	**6:**1245
nĕśîʾ rōʾš mešek wĕtūbāl	נשׂיא ראשׁ משך ותבל	[the] chief prince of Meshech and Tubal	**6:**1516
neteq	נתק	skin rash, scab	**1:**1096
neter	נתר	soda	**5:**219
nĕtibôt ʿôlām	נתבות עולם	ancient paths	**4:**501
nĕtînîm	נתינים	temple servants	**3:**664, 686, 718, 727
nēzer	נזר	branch, crown	**1:**1148; **8:**147
niddâ	נדה	impurity, menstruation, cleansing	**1:**1105; **2:**151; **3:**736; **6:**1030, 1033, 1167; **7:**831
niḥam	נחם	relief, comfort, rest; moved to pity (niphal)	**1:**380, 389; **2:**756, 1090–91; **6:**772
niḥām ʿal-hārāʿâ	נחם על־הרעה	repenting about the evil	**7:**518
nikmĕrû raḥămîm	נכמרו רחמים	emotions stirred up	**3:**44
nilḥam bĕ	נלחם ב	to fight against	**7:**838
nîn	נין	offspring	**2:**166
nînĕwēh hāyĕtâ	נינוה היתה	"Nineveh was"	**7:**465
niplāʾot	נפלאת	wonders	**1:**715; **4:**629, 977, 1020, 1133, 1223; **5:**663, 834
niqqāyôn	נקיון	innocence	**4:**969
niqrāʾ-šĕmî	נקרא־שמי	called by my name	**3:**500
nîr	ניר	yoke, freshly broken field	**2:**166; **5:**134
nistārôt	נסתרת	things hidden	**5:**663
niṣṣābîm	נצבים	one set in place, appointee	**3:**51
nišbār	נשבר	broken	**4:**887
nišbat	נשבת	vanished, shattered	**6:**1368
niśgāb	נשׂגב	high, safe	**5:**173
niṭṭĕšâ ʿal-ʾădmātāh	נטשה על־אדמתה	forsaken on her land	**7:**386

Transliteration	Hebrew	English	Volume and Page
nit'āb	נתעב	abhorrent	**4:**450
Nō' 'āmôn	נא אמון	Thebes	**7:**616, 691
nôgēś	נוגשׂ	ruler	**7:**814
nōgĕśîm	נגשׂים	taskmasters	**1:**725
nōḥam	נחם	sorrow	**7:**291
nōkḥâ	נכחה	obvious	**5:**688
nokrî	נכרי	foreigners	**1:**783; **5:**44, 705
nokriyyâ	נכריה	foreign woman	**2:**916, 918, 923, 928, 941; **5:**71, 669
nō'am	נעם	pleasant, favor, beauty	**2:**909; **4:**786
nōp	נף	Memphis	**6:**1417
nōqēd	נקד	sheep breeder	**7:**351, 411
nōqēm YHWH	נקם יהוה	"revengeful [is] Yahweh"	**7:**601
nôrā'	נורא	awesome	**4:**1134
nôrā' mĕ'ōd	נורא מאד	"exceedingly dreadful"	**5:**834
nôrā' mĕ'ōd wĕniplā'ôt	נורא מאד ונפלאות	"exceedingly terrifying and wondrous"	**5:**834
nōšĕkêkā	נשכיך	debtors, "those who pay interest"	**7:**647
nôtār	נותר	remainder	**6:**1605
nōzĕlîm	נזלים	"living water"	**5:**68
nûaḥ	נוח	to rest	**6:**1502; **7:**242, 784
nûaḥ	נוח	remnant	**5:**842
nûb	נוב	to bear fruit	**5:**113
nûd	נוד	to shake, lament	**4:**953
nûm	נום	to slumber	**4:**1181
nun	נ	nun	**4:**1259; **5:**230, 667; **6:**1477
nûp	נוף	to elevate	**1:**913
nûs	נוס	to flee, escape	**7:**610
P			
pā'ar	פאר	to beautify, glorify	**4:**1275; **6:**525
pādâ	פדה	to redeem, set free	**1:**786–87; **2:**54, 590; **4:**953; **6:**62, 282, 1284
pāga'	פגע	to encounter, meet	**2:**921
paḥ	פח	snare, trap	**7:**244, 371
pāḥad	פחד	to dread, be in awe	**5:**696
paḥad	פחד	terror, dread	**1:**828; **3:**927, 930; **4:**612, 893
paḥad yiṣḥāq	פחד יצחק	fear (or kinsman) of Isaac	**5:**696

Transliteration	Hebrew	English	Volume and Page
pak	פך	bottle	**6:**1595
pālâ	פלה	to set apart, be distinct	**1:**1187; **4:**697
pālāʾ	פלא	to do wondrously	**1:**1187; **2:**64; **4:**1155; **6:**821
pālas	פלס	to weigh, examine	**5:**61
pālaṭ	פלט	to deliver, escape	**4:**747, 800; **7:**504
pālēʾ	פלא	to be wonderful, to be hard/difficult	**1:**464
pālîṭ	פליט	fugitive, survivor	**2:**837; **6:**1453
pānâ	פנה	to turn	**4:**952
pānîm	פנים	face, presence	**1:**564–65; **2:**364; **4:**786, 848, 952, 1035; **6:**356
pannag	פנג	millet, confections (?)	**6:**1379
pāʿal	פעל	to make, do	**4:**733, 789, 1051, 1098; **7:**256
pāqad	פקד	to visit, attend to	**1:**486, 719, 934, 947; **2:**33; **4:**396; **6:**744; **7:**369
pāqaḥ	פקח	to open (eyes or ears)	**6:**449
pāqîd	פקיד	overseer, officer	**2:**34
pāqōd yipqōd	פקד יפקד	will surely come	**1:**789
par	פר	calf	**1:**1034
pārâ	פרה	to be fruitful, fertile	**2:**900; **7:**292
pārâ	פרה	heifer, cow	**7:**275
pārad	פרד	to separate, spread abroad	**1:**410
pāraḥ	פרח	to bud, sprout	**7:**295
pāraʿ	פרע	to lead, let loose, neglect	**1:**933, 1071
pārar	פרר	to break open	**4:**459
pāraṣ	פרצ	to spread abroad, burst forth	**1:**414, 837; **2:**1249; **3:**383–84, 388, 393, 773; **4:**349
pāraš	פרש	to make distinct, clarify	**3:**699, 801
pārāš	פרש	horseman	**7:**609
pāraś	פרשׂ	to spread out, scatter	**4:**590; **7:**759
parbār	פרבר	colonnade	**3:**451
pardēs	פרדס	garden, orchard, royal forest	**1:**77, 82; **3:**756
pārōket	פרכת	curtain	**1:**897–98
parsâ	פרסה	hoof	**1:**767
parwār	פרור	porch	**3:**451

Transliteration	Hebrew	English	Volume and Page
pāsaḥ	פסח	to hop, leap	**2:**412
pāṣaṣ	פצץ	to shatter	**4:**459
pāšaṭ	פשט	to raid, strip off	**7:**618
pāšaṭ gĕdûd baḥûṣ	פשט גדוד בחוץ	the bandits raid outside	**7:**256
pāšaʿ	פשע	to rebel, transgress	**6:**1450, 1509; **7:**380
pātâ	פתה	to be open	**3:**551
pātâ	פתה	to be enticed, deceived	**6:**726, 1208–9
pātaḥ	פתח	to open	**2:**821
pāzar	פזר	to scatter, disperse	**5:**119
pēʾâ	פאה	side, edge	**6:**1601
pĕʾēr	פאר	turban	**6:**1342
peger	פגר	corpse, monument	**6:**1561
peh	פה	mouth	**5:**131, 322
peh ʾel-peh	פה אלפה	"mouth to mouth"	**2:**110
peḥâ	פחה	governor	**7:**709, 715
pĕlādôt	פלדות	metal	**7:**609
pĕlaḥ	פלח	to serve, worship	**7:**63
peleʾ	פלא	wonder	**4:**984, 990–91; **5:**663
pelek	פלך	district, spindle	**3:**765; **6:**1006
pĕlêṭâ	פליטה	remnant	**3:**736
pĕlîʾâ	פליאה	wonderful	**5:**663
pĕlîṭê haggôyim	פליטי הגוים	"the nations' survivors"	**6:**401
pĕlōnî ʾalmōnî	פלני אלמני	such-and-such a person/ place	**2:**934
pen tōmar	פן תאמר	"lest you say"	**5:**724
pĕninnâ	פננה	Peninnah, "fertile, prolific"	**2:**974
pĕnû-bî	פנו־בי	face me	**4:**390
pĕquddâ	פקדה	oversight, overseer	**3:**575
pĕraq	פרק	to break off, tear away	**7:**75
pĕrāt	פרת	Euphrates, Parah (?)	**6:**683–84
pereʾ	פרא	wild ass	**4:**421; **7:**261, 292
pereṣ	פרץ	hole, breach	**6:**1315
pĕrî	פרי	fruit, reward	**4:**909; **7:**270, 295
perûš	פרוש	commentaries	**1:**66, 70–71
pesaḥ	פסח	Passover	**1:**777; **2:**412; **6:**1586
pesel	פסל	image, idol	**1:**842; **3:**644
pešaʿ	פשע	conscious violation	**1:**282, 1114; **4:**805, 885, 933; **5:**724; **6:**491, 498, 1302, 1450; **7:**354
pēšer	פשר	interpretation	**5:**270, 332, 808; **8:**152
pešhat	פשט	plain meaning	**1:**66, 77, 82

Transliteration	Hebrew	English	Volume and Page
petaḥ	פתח	door, entrance, opening	**3:**486; **5:**40, 89
pî-qāret	פי־קרת	city gate, "mouth of the town"	**5:**89
pidyōn	פדין	redemption	**1:**865
pigrê malkêhem bāmôtām	פגרי מלכיהם במותם	"the corpses of their kings at their high places"	**6:**1561
pîlegeš	פילגש	concubine	**3:**889
pinnâ	פנה	cornerstone	**7:**814
piqqûdîm	פקודים	precepts	**4:**1134, 1166, 1168
pisqôt	פסקות	short paragraphs	**1:**307
pitḥôn peh	פתחון פה	an opening of the mouth	**6:**1239
piyyût	פיוט	religious poetry	**1:**66
pōsĕḥîm ʿal-štê hassĕʿippîm	פסחים על־שתי הסעפים	"hobbling upon two branches"; straddle the issue	**3:**135
pōʿal	פעל	work, deed	**4:**1051
pōʿălê ʾāwen	פעלי און	doers of evil	**7:**256
pōtēr	פתר	dream interpreter	**1:**614
pōtôt	פתות	sockets	**3:**486
pûaḥ	פוח	to breathe, blow	**7:**641
pûr	פור	lot, stone	**1:**1061; **3:**896, 938
pûrayyāʾ	פוריא	possible Aramaic source of word "Purim"	**3:**860
pûṣ	פוץ	to scatter, be dispersed	**1:**410; **6:**1489

Q

qābaʿ	קבע	to rob, plunder	**5:**205; **7:**870
qābaṣ	קבץ	to gather, collect	**6:**1531
qādad	קדד	to bow down	**1:**635
qādar	קדר	to be dark, cause to mourn	**6:**1429
qādaš	קדש	to be holy	**1:**888, 907, 976, 1046; **2:**80, 160, 331, 614; **6:**740, 1510; **7:**312, 320, 558
qādaš hûʾ	קדש הוא	it is holy	**1:**912
qaddîšîn	קדישין	holy ones	**7:**105
qādîm	קדים	east wind	**7:**281
qādôš	קדוש	sacred, holy	**1:**1135; **2:**349, 614; **4:**1075; **5:**668, 818; **6:**29, 281, 355–56
qāhal	קהל	to assemble	**5:**268–69

Transliteration	Hebrew	English	Volume and Page
qāhāl	קהל	assembly	**1:**1035; **3:**740; **4:**77, 107, 782; **5:**268
qāhāl yahweh	קהל יהוה	"congregation of Yahweh"	**8:**346
qal	קל	swift, light	**4:**512
qālal	קלל	to lighten, curse, hold in contempt	**1:**393, 424, 452, 847, 863, 869, 1164; **2:**1011; **4:**346, 366, 512, 613; **5:**133, 187
qalmā'	קלמא	gnat	**8:**436
qālôn	קלון	shame	**7:**239
qāmîm	קמים	adversaries, "those who arise"	**4:**974
qānâ	קנה	to produce, acquire	**1:**372, 442, 801; **2:**933, 936, 938, 940; **4:**1236; **5:**92, 98, 683; **7:**832
qānā'	קנא	to be jealous, zealous	**2:**199; **7:**322, 753
qāneh	קנה	reed, stem, measuring stick	**1:**7; **2:**80
qannō' qinnē'tî	קנא קנאתי	zeal, jealousy	**3:**142
qāpā'	קפא	to thicken, congeal	**7:**679
qārâ	קרה	to set/lay beams	**4:**1097
qārā'	קרא	to call, proclaim	**1:**946, 986, 1156; **2:**940; **4:**696, 1027; **6:**334, 529, 727, 1492; **7:**277, 381, 428, 476, 478, 493, 499, 505, 513–14
qārā' šēm	קרא שם	to call a name	**2:**940
qārab	קרב	to draw near, approach	**2:**78; **4:**933
qāran	קרן	to shine	**1:**953
qārôb	קרוב	a near one	**2:**915, 921; **4:**476
qāsam	קסם	to practise divination	**6:**1301; **7:**558
qāṣar	קצר	to bear	**2:**824
qaṣār	קצר	impatient, short	**4:**491
qāṣar lēb	קצר לב	unintelligent	**5:**688
qāṣaṣ	קצץ	to cut off	**7:**414
qāṣeh	קצה	end, extremity	**4:**934
qaš	קש	straw	**7:**685
qāšâ	קשה	to be hard, heavy	**2:**1005; **4:**1062
qāšar	קשר	to bind together, conspire	**3:**773; **7:**410
qāṭar	קטר	to burn	**7:**380

Transliteration	Hebrew	English	Volume and Page
qāṭōn	קטן	small, least	**7:**447
qāw	קו	a measuring instrument	**6:**1596
qāwâ	קוה	to wait, hope	**4:**829, 838, 891, 902, 923, 952, 1205; **5:**688; **6:**1051
qāyin	קין	iron smith	**2:**738
qāyiṣ	קיץ	ripened, summer fruit	**6:**1165; **7:**407, 414; **9:**408
qaytĕrôs	קיתרוס	lyre, zither	**7:**63
qĕdēšâ	קדשה	cult prostitute	**1:**1135; **4:**586; **7:**241
qĕdôš Yiśrāʾēl	קדוש ישראל	"the Holy One of Israel"	**1:**1131
qēn	קן	nest	**5:**720
qēneṣ	קנץ	snare (?)	**4:**467
qênî	קיני	Kenite	**2:**738
qĕrāʾ bĕšēm Yahweh	קרא בשם יהוה	"call on the name of the Lord"	**7:**699
qĕrēʾ	קרא	what is read	**1:**297
qereb	קרב	midst, middle	**2:**619, 665
qeren	קרן	horn	**4:**1035
qĕrîʾâ	קריאה	proclamation, calling	**7:**477
qesem	קסם	divination, oracle	**2:**182; **5:**160; **6:**1301
qēṣ	קץ	end	**5:**800, 824; **6:**1165, 1303; **7:**407, 414; **9:**408
qĕṣar-ʾappayim	קצר־אפים	quick to anger	**5:**141
qĕṣēh hāʿām	קצה העם	the outer edge of the people	**2:**185
qeṣep	קצף	rage, anger	**2:**36; **3:**184, 722; **4:**833
qeṣep gādôl	קצף גדול	great wrath	**3:**184
qĕšat-rûaḥ	קשת־רוח	deeply troubled	**2:**976
qešer	קשר	conspiracy	**2:**1320
qešet	קשת	a bow	**2:**1205
qĕśîṭâ	קשיטה	a piece of money	**4:**635
qĕṭannôt	קטנות	small	**6:**1591
qĕṭōn	קטן	little one, little thing	**3:**102
qĕṭōreṭ	קטרת	incense	**2:**78, 137
qĕturôt	קתרות	joined	**6:**1591
qîʾ	קיא	to vomit	**7:**470, 483, 504
qînâ	קינה	dirge/lament for the dead, limping meter	**2:**1205, 1226; **4:**301, 308; **6:**1021, 1266, 1268, 1368, 1440; **7:**385

Transliteration	Hebrew	English	Volume and Page
qinʾâ	קנאה	zeal, envy, passion	**4:**1173; **5:**311, 430; **6:**1153
qîqāyôn	קיקיון	a certain plant	**7:**477, 520
qiryâ neʾĕmānâ	קריה נאמנה	faithful city	**7:**795
qiryat pōʿălê ʾāwen	קרית פעלי און	"city of evildoers"	**7:**286
qîṣ	קיץ	to awake	**4:**1237
qōdeš	קדש	holy	**1:**985; **2:**15, 147, 1139–40; **4:**984, 995, 1142; **5:**668; **7:**727
qōdeš-qodāšîm	קדש־קדשים	most holy	**2:**614; **6:**1549
qōhelet	קהלה	Qohelet, the assembler	**5:**268–69, 289, 332; **6:**337
qôl	קול	voice, sound	**1:**907; **4:**378, 792, 869, 1054; **5:**393, 411; **6:**329; **7:**478, 682, 693
qôl dĕmāmâ daqqâ	קול דממה דקה	"a sound of fine silence," a "still small voice"	**3:**142
qôl hămôn haggāšem	קול המון הגשם	"a sound of rushing rain"	**3:**142
qôl haqqôrēʾ	קול הקורא	"the voice that cries out"	**6:**334
qôl qôrēʾ	קול קורא	"a voice crying"	**6:**529
qôl Yahweh	קול יהוה	"the voice of the Lord"	**7:**682
qôlî ʾel-ʾĕlōhîm	קולי אל־אלהים	"my voice unto God"	**4:**983
qōp	ק	Qop (Hebrew letter)	**7:**477
qorbān	קרבן	a sacrifice, dedicated to the temple	**1:**989, 1005, 1009; **8:**606
qōsēm	קסם	diviner	**7:**558
qôṣ	קוץ	thorn	**6:**1397
qôṣê hāmmidbār	קוצי המדבר	thorns of the desert	**6:**1397
qubbâ	קבה	tent	**2:**199
qudšû	קדשו	holiness, perhaps an epithet for Ashera	**7:**779
qûm	קום	to arise	**1:**780, 800; **2:**96; **3:**911, 939; **4:**478, 685, 693, 974, 1169, 1212; **6:**952; **7:**476, 493, 603
qûṣ	קוץ	to be overcome with fear	**2:**181
R			
rāʾâ	ראה	to see	**1:**495, 560, 706, 719; **2:**1097–98, 1102; **3:**483; **4:**389, 414, 420,

Transliteration	Hebrew	English	Volume and Page
			592, 843, 930; **5:**690; **6:**356, 621, 1030, 1032–33, 1041, 1043, 1048, 1055, 1068, 1182; **7:**405, 542, 635, 764, 852
rab	רב	much, enough, great	**3:**140, 779; **4:**693, 872; **7:**143, 261
rab haḥōbēl	רב החבל	captain, "the chief of the ropes"	**7:**477
rab-ḥesed	רב־חסד	abounding in steadfast love	**1:**946; **7:**518
rab-lākem	רב־לכם	gone too far, enough	**2:**136, 138; **6:**1573
rab mimmĕkā haddārek	רב ממך הדרך	"the way is too much for you"	**3:**140
rābâ	רבה	to increase, become great	**6:**1259; **7:**261
rabbî	רבי	rabbi, "my great one"	**8:**374, 432
rabbîm	רבים	many, great	**6:**465, 468, 471, 477; **7:**143
rādâ	רדה	to have dominion	**1:**346; **4:**712
rādap	רדף	to pursue	**1:**800; **4:**768
rādam	רדם	to be in/fall into deep sleep	**7:**115, 496
rāgal	רגל	to slander	**4:**733
rāgan	רגן	to murmur, whisper	**5:**225
rāgaʿ	רגע	to disturb, stir up	**4:**518
rāḥab	רחב	to be wide, grow wide	**4:**697; **5:**850
rāḥāb	רחב	broad, wide	**4:**801
rāḥăbâ	רחבה	broadening	**6:**1551
rāḥam	רחם	to love, have compassion	**4:**1092; **7:**218, 295
raḥam	רחם	womb, compassion	**2:**789; **4:**1087, 1092; **6:**1530
raḥămānîyôt	רחמניות	compassionate women	**6:**1062
raḥămeyhā	רחמיה	her compassion	**3:**44
raḥămîm	רחמים	womb, compassion	**1:**635; **4:**778, 885, 983–84, 995
rāḥôq	רחוק	far	**4:**762; **5:**663
raḥûm	רחום	merciful, compassionate	**1:**946; **4:**671, 995, 1133; **5:**656, 678; **7:**319, 477, 518
rak	רך	tender, delicate	**6:**1252
rākab	רכב	to ride	**6:**834
rākal	רכל	to go about from one to another	**6:**1373, 1377, 1388

Transliteration	Hebrew	English	Volume and Page
rām	רם	lofty	**4:**562
rāmâ	רמה	lofty place	**6:**1232
rāmâ qarnî	רמה קרני	"my horn is raised"	**2:**981
rāmas	רמס	to trample	**7:**113
rānan	רנן	to give a ringing cry	**4:**1003; **5:**243
ra‘	רע	evil	**1:**435, 474, 640, 661, 672, 728, 768; **4:**768, 789, 885; **5:**80, 161, 193; **7:**148, 256
rā‘â	רעה	to shepherd, feed, rule	**4:**690, 1000; **5:**112; **6:**709, 744, 1463
rā‘â	רעה	evil, distress	**1:**646; **3:**353; **4:**847; **5:**54, 120, 133, 630, 724; **6:**412, 671, 709, 744, 750, 793, 850, 872–73; **7:**256, 372, 477, 493, 497, 514, 517, 596
rā‘āb	רעב	famine, hunger	**6:**450
rā‘a‘	רעע	to break, be evil	**1:**640; **4:**690, 847; **6:**850
rā‘aš	רעש	to quake	**4:**916; **6:**1196, 1367; **7:**723, 730
ra‘mâ	רעמה	thunder	**4:**611
ra‘yôn	רעיון	longing, striving	**5:**270
rāpâ	רפה	to sink down, abate	**3:**695; **4:**866, 1232
rāpa’	רפא	to heal	**1:**1096; **4:**796; **6:**1596
rāpō’ yĕrapē’	רפא ירפא	will fully heal	**1:**863
raq	רק	surely, only	**1:**483, 758; **2:**110; **3:**180
rāqa‘	רקע	to spread out	**4:**1224
rāqēb	רקב	to rot	**5:**716
rāqîa‘	רקיע	firmament, expanse	**4:**1279; **6:**1116
rāṣâ	רצה	to be pleased with, accept	**4:**441, 591, 857, 1016; **5:**340; **6:**691; **7:**717
rāṣâ	רצה	delight, favor	**5:**159, 419
rāṣaḥ	רצח	to murder	**1:**848; **2:**333; **4:**923
rāṣîm	רצים	runners, guards	**3:**575
rāṣôn	רצון	favor	**1:**907; **5:**120
rāš	רש	impoverished	**5:**705
rāša‘	רשע	to be guilty, wicked	**1:**866; **5:**168
rāšā‘	רשע	wicked, guilty, guilty one	**1:**703–4, 758; **4:**369, 576, 585, 616, 684,

Transliteration	Hebrew	English	Volume and Page
			822, 828, 1126; **5:**105, 168, 193; **7:**630, 638
rāšā‘ hû’	רשע הוא	he is wicked	**6:**1261
rātaḥ	רתח	to boil	**6:**1335
rāwâ	רוה	to be saturated, drenched	**4:**414; **5:**69
rāwaḥ	רוח	to be relieved	**2:**1103
rāz	רז	secret	**5:**699; **8:**571
rēa‘	רע	friend	**4:**461; **5:**54, 80, 168, 193, 230–31, 682
rē’šît	ראשית	first, best	**4:**618, 636; **5:**648
rĕbābâ	רבבה	multitude, ten thousand	**4:**693
rĕgaš	רגש (Aramaic)	to be/gather in tumult	**7:**88
regel	רגל	foot	**5:**85
reḥem	רחם	womb, compassion	**1:**946; **3:**44; **4:**671, 1087; **6:**1062; **7:**218, 518
rekeb	רכב	chariotry	**5:**386; **6:**1528
remeś	רמש	creeping things	**6:**1176
remez	רמז	allusion, allegory	**1:**82
rĕmiyyâ	רמיה	deceit	**4:**1083
rĕnānîm	רננים	screechers	**4:**610–11
rĕ‘ût	רעות	longing, striving	**5:**270
rē‘ût	רעות	woman friend	**2:**908
rĕpā’îm	רפאים	shades, inhabitants of the underworld	**4:**517; **6:**158
rêqā’	ריקא	airhead	**8:**190
rêqām	ריקם	empty-handed	**2:**931
rêqîm	ריקים	nothings, emptinesses	**5:**126
rĕṣāpîm	רצפים	hot coals	**3:**140
reš	ר	resh (Hebrew letter)	**6:**1467; **7:**258, 496, 498
rĕšā‘îm	רשעים	(the) wicked	**4:**684, 1263
rešet	רשת	a net	**6:**1194, 1269
rešet pĕrûśâ	רשת פרושה	net spread	**7:**244
rĕwāyâ	רויה	full-to-overflowing	**2:**908
ri’šôn	ראשון	former	**6:**387
rîb	ריב	to quarrel, contend	**3:**848; **5:**698; **6:**598, 675
rîb	ריב	complaint, dispute	**1:**817–18; **2:**160, 797; **4:**433, 553; **5:**55, 166; **6:**598, 675, 697, 1307; **7:**224, 236–37, 281, 283, 631

Transliteration	Hebrew	English	Volume and Page
rinnâ	רנה	a cry, song of deliverance	**4:**740, 806, 1195
rîq	ריק	to draw, emptiness	**1:**800; **4:**697
riqmâ	רקמה	embroidered cloth	**6:**1228, 1245, 1374
rîr	ריר	to flow (like slime)	**1:**1104
riṣpâ	רצפה	pavement	**6:**1542
rišyôn	רשיון	a grant	**3:**692
rō᾿š	ראש	first, head, before	**2:**34; **5:**730; **6:**356, 1516; **7:**272, 399, 421
ro᾿š haššānâ	ראש השנה	New Year's Day	**1:**1159
rō᾿šîm	ראשים	chiefs	**2:**198; **3:**223
rōgez	רגז	turmoil	**4:**370
rogzâ	רגזה	shaking, trembling	**6:**1196
rōḥab lēb	רחב לב	broadness of heart/ mind	**3:**55
rōkel	רכל	merchant, trader	**6:**1373; **7:**618
rômēmâ	רוממה	exalted	**4:**1154
rō᾿eh	ראה	seer	**6:**4; **7:**405, 852
rō῾ēh	רעה	a shepherd	**2:**1234; **4:**1000; **6:**709
rō῾î	רעי	shepherd	**4:**768
rûaḥ	רוח	wind, spirit	**1:**350, 383, 392, 394, 800, 804, 962; **2:**108, 976, 1101, 1120; **4:**378, 400, 563, 800, 886, 1099, 1236, 1268; **5:**150, 311; **6:**140, 1065, 1115, 1121, 1500, 1502; **7:**281; **9:**550; **10:**419
rûaḥ ᾿ĕlōhîm	רוח אלהים	"wind of God"	**1:**80, 343
rûaḥ kabbîr	רוח כביר	mighty wind	**4:**400
rûaḥ sĕ῾ārâ	רוח סערה	a tempestuous windstorm	**6:**1114
rûa῾	רוע	to shout	**4:**868, 917, 934, 937, 1003
rûd	רוד	to roam, wander restlessly	**7:**282
ruḥāmâ	רחמה	pitied	**7:**218
rûḥî zārâ	רוחי זרה	"my spirit is alien, my breath is repulsive"	**4:**476
rûm	רום	to rise, be exalted	**4:**786, 796, 866, 919, 976; **5:**118; **6:**1128, 1581
rûṣ	רוץ	to run	**3:**575; **5:**243
rûš	רוש	to be poor	**5:**131, 237

Transliteration	Hebrew	English	Volume and Page
S			
sābab	סבב	to turn, go around	**3:**369; **4:**1154
sābal	סבל	to bring, bear	**3:**708; **5:**355
sabbāl	סבל	burden bearer	**3:**773
sabbĕkāʾ	סבכא	trigon, triangular musical instrument	**7:**63
sābîb	סביב	round about	**4:**693
sāḥar	סחר	go around, travel about	**6:**1377
sākak	סכך	to overshadow, cover	**6:**1393
sākan	סכן	to be of service or benefit	**4:**502
sākar	סכר	to stop	**4:**928
sālaḥ	סלח	to pardon, forgive	**1:**948; **4:**1091; **7:**408
sālal	סלל	to lift up	**1:**757, 763
sāmak	סמך	to rest heavily on	**1:**1011; **4:**694
sanhedrîn	סנהדרין	Sanhedrin	**3:**1114, 1123
sanwērîm	סנורים	blindness, a blinding light	**3:**201
sāʿar	סער	scatter, hurl	**7:**759
sap	סף	cup, threshold	**7:**826
sāpad	ספד	to wail, lament	**7:**312
sāpan	ספן	to cover, panel	**7:**716
sāpar	ספר	to tell, recount	**1:**762, 826; **4:**533, 718, 873, 1268
sārab	סרב	rebel, liar	**5:**674
sāraḥ	סרח	to be unrestrained, lounge	**7:**399
sātam	סתם	to stop, close up	**7:**149
sātar	סתר	to hide	**4:**930; **5:**663
sēbel	סבל	burden, load	**4:**1004
sĕdārîm	סדרים	divisions	**1:**67, 307
sĕgad	סגד	to do homage	**7:**63
sĕgānîm	סגנים	officials, administrators	**3:**759, 824
sekel	סכל	folly	**5:**346
selâ	סלה	liturgical instruction (?)	**4:**657, 869, 894, 1023, 1239
selaʿ	סלע	rock	**4:**747, 958; **7:**447
sĕnāʾâ	סנאה	Senaah	**3:**686
sĕneh	סנה	bush	**1:**711
sēter	סתר	hiding place, shelter	**4:**806, 1047
sĕtumîm	סתמים	closed	**7:**149
sĕʿārâ	סערה	stormy wind, whirlwind	**4:**591, 600; **6:**1114
sepeq	ספק	scoffing	**4:**587
sēper	ספר	book, written account	**1:**380; **4:**555; **6:**1507

Transliteration	Hebrew	English	Volume and Page
Sēper ʾêkâ	ספר איכה	the book of how (Lamentations)	**6:**1023
sēper mûsār	ספר מוסר	the book of Discipline/ Instruction	**5:**606
sĕpînâ	ספינה	ship	**7:**477, 479
sĕpûnîm	ספונים	paneled	**7:**716
sikkût	סכות	tent (?)	**7:**394
siklût	סכלות	folly	**5:**295
sillôn	סלון	brier	**6:**1397
sîmānîm	סימנים	signs	**1:**307
sîr	סיר	pot	**5:**326; **6:**1335
sîrîm	סירים	thorns	**5:**326
sôd	סוד	council, counsel, intimacy	**1:**77, 82; **4:**778–79, 930, 1010; **5:**55
sōkenet	סכנת	companion, governess	**3:**14
sōlet	סלת	fine flour	**1:**1017; **6:**1228, 1589
sōmĕkê miṣrayim	סמכי מצרים	"the support[er]s of Egypt"	**6:**1415
sôp	סוף	end	**5:**709
sōpēr	ספר	scribe	**1:**297–98; **3:**718
sûg lēb	סוג לב	backslider	**5:**141
sukkâ	סכה	booth	**2:**233; **7:**427
sûmpōnyâ	סומפניה	wind instrument	**7:**63
sûp	סוף	reed	**1:**699
sûpâ	סופה	Suphah, whirlwind	**2:**165; **7:**602
sûr	סור	to turn aside	**3:**180; **5:**61, 688, 867; **6:**455; **7:**258
sûr mērāʿ	סור מרע	turning from evil	**4:**533
sûrû sûrû. . . ṭāmēʾ ʾal-tiggāʿû	סורו סורו . . . טמא אל־תגעו	turning aside from uncleanness	**6:**455
sûsâ	סוסה	mare	**5:**386
sût	סות	to entice	**3:**551; **4:**586
ṣaʾănān	צאנן	Zaanan	**7:**547
ṣābāʾ	צבא	war, warfare, service	**2:**34, 95; **3:**445; **4:**442, 773
ṣādaq	צדק	to be just, be justified	**1:**866; **4:**409, 419, 562, 616
ṣaddîq	צדיק	righteous person	**1:**390, 758; **3:**223; **4:**576, 585, 667, 708, 828, 1133, 1148, 1263; **5:**160, 842; **6:**1033; **7:**365, 630, 638, 642, 807

Transliteration	Hebrew	English	Volume and Page
ṣaddîq hûʾ	צדיק הוא	righteous is he	**6:**1259
ṣaddîq tāmîm	צדיק תמים	righteous and perfect	**4:**426
ṣādēq	צדק	to be just, righteous	**4:**580, 1173; **5:**168
ṣāḥaq	צחק	to laugh, play	**1:**474, 488, 931
ṣaḥar	צחר	wool	**6:**1379
ṣāḥōr	צחר	yellow	**1:**1097
ṣālaḥ	צלח	to advance, prosper	**6:**1248
ṣālēaḥ	צלח	to prosper, succeed	**3:**430, 509
ṣalmāwet	צלמות	deep darkness	**4:**430, 459
ṣāmāʾ	צמא	thirst	**7:**419
ṣāmad	צמד	to join, yoke	**2:**198
ṣāmaḥ	צמח	to sprout	**4:**380
ṣāmat	צמת	to be silenced, be destroyed	**4:**509
ṣammeret	צמרת	crown	**6:**1245
ṣānaḥ	צנח	to dismount, descend	**2:**678
ṣānaʿ	צנע	to preserve, be humble	**5:**729; **7:**580
ṣāʿaq	צעק	to cry out	**1:**728; **4:**1027, 1117; **5:**664; **6:**743
ṣāʿâ	צעה	to stoop, bend	**6:**449
ṣaʿrat	צרעת	leprosy	**8:**544
ṣāpan	צפן	to hide, store up	**4:**486; **5:**134; **7:**671
ṣāpôn	צפון	north, [Mt.] Zaphon	**4:**518, 872; **6:**1114; **7:**323
ṣappaḥat	צפחת	jar	**3:**140
ṣar	צר	narrow, small, distress	**4:**485, 586, 697, 801; **5:**211; **6:**1030
ṣārâ	צרה	rival, trouble	**2:**975; **5:**211
ṣāraʿat	צרעת	a skin disease	**1:**1094–95, 1097, 1099; **2:**60, 469
ṣārar	צרר	to be in great danger	**2:**1191
ṣāw	צו	idols	**7:**248
ṣāwâ	צוה	to command	**4:**1271
ṣĕʾû miššām	צאו משם	"go forth from there"	**6:**455
ṣĕbāʾôt	צבאות	companies, armies	**1:**783; **2:**1087; **4:**865; **7:**376
ṣĕbî	צבי	beauty, honor, gazelle	**2:**1206; **7:**113
ṣĕdāqâ	צדקה	righteousness	**1:**30, 445, 467, 556, 606–7; **4:**421, 576, 580, 593, 774, 953, 959; **5:**107; **6:**88, 95, 395, 478, 485, 498,

Transliteration	Hebrew	English	Volume and Page
ṣĕdāqâ *(continued)*			515, 599, 1263, 1582; **7:**324, 388, 403; **8:**179
ṣĕdāqôt	צדקות	mighty deeds, deeds of kindness	**5:**621, 660
ṣedeq	צדק	vindication, rightness	**4:**390, 400, 483, 667, 708, 722, 820, 843, 963, 1017, 1069, 1071, 1130, 1173; **5:**105, 168; **6:**95, 354, 520, 1583
ṣēl	צל	shade, shadow	**2:**816; **4:**1047; **6:**1425; **7:**471, 521
ṣelem	צלם	likeness, image	**4:**838
ṣĕlî	צלי	roasted	**3:**647
ṣemaḥ	צמח	a sprout, growth	**6:**1226
ṣĕmar	צמר	Zemar	**6:**1374
ṣĕʿāqâ	צעקה	a cry	**1:**771; **5:**664; **6:**88
ṣĕpan-yāh	צפניה	Zephaniah, "Yahweh protects"	**7:**659
ṣĕpirâ	צפרה	doom	**6:**1166
ṣĕrôr	צרור	hostility	**2:**200
ṣĕrôr	צרור	bundle, pebble	**5:**683; **7:**424
ṣĕrôr ḥayyîm	צרור חיים	the bag of the living	**5:**682
ṣidqôt	צדקות	mighty deeds	**5:**800
ṣîm	צים	ships	**6:**1416
ṣinnâ	צנה	hook, barb	**7:**377
ṣinnîm	צנים	thorns (?)	**5:**198
ṣinnôr	צנור	waterfall (?)	**2:**1237
ṣirʿâ	צרעה	pestilence	**1:**877
ṣiyyîm	ציים	beasts	**7:**143
ṣiyyîm kittîm	ציים כתים	beasts/ships of Kittim	**7:**143
ṣōpîm	צפים	watchers	**2:**187
ṣôr	צור	Tyre	**6:**1374
ṣŏrî	צרי	balm, salve	**5:**683
ṣûr	צור	to confine, beseige	**4:**1235–36
ṣûr	צור	rock	**2:**528; **4:**747, 919, 958; **6:**387
šāʾal	שאל	to ask, pray	**2:**976, 978, 987, 1048, 1148, 1183, 1185; **3:**388; **4:**1184; **5:**682
šāʾal šālôm	שאל שלום	to ask about one's well-being	**5:**682

Transliteration	Hebrew	English	Volume and Page
šā᾽ap	שׁאף	to trample	**4:**901; **6:**1482; **7:**416
šā᾽ar	שׁאר	to remain, be left over	**3:**678, 751
ša᾽ûl	שׁאול	Saul	**2:**976–77
šāba‘	שׁבע	to swear an oath	**3:**538; **6:**1238
šābar	שׁבר	to break	**4:**694; **6:**1418
šabbat	שׁבת	to cease, rest	**1:**1157
šabbat šabbātôn	שׁבת שׁבתון	"sabbath of complete rest"	**1:**1157
šābu‘ôt/šavu‘ôt	שׁבועות	weeks, Feast of Weeks	**2:**893; **3:**538; **10:**53
šad	שׁד	breast	**2:**910
šādad	שׁדד	to destroy, lay waste	**6:**890
šadday	שׁדי	Almighty	**2:**180, 191, 901, 910; **4:**400; **5:**9; **6:**1116
šāgâ	שׁגה	to err, go astray	**5:**69, 185, 317
šāgag	שׁגג	to err, go astray	**1:**1033
šāḥâ	שׁחה	to be bowed down, worship	**2:**1274; **4:**701, 964, 1061; **5:**44
šāḥaḥ	שׁחח	to bow down, cast down	**4:**852
šaḥal	שׁחל	lion	**4:**530; **7:**248, 278
šāḥar	שׁחר	to seek	**4:**928
šāḥar	שׁחר	to be black	**5:**382
šāḥat	שׁחת	to destroy, corrupt, kill	**1:**390–91, 1118
šāḥat	שׁחת	to ruin, destroy	**6:**684
šaḥat	שׁחת	a pit, destruction	**1:**435; **6:**1269, 1388; **7:**506
šaḥăṭâ	שׁחטה	pit	**7:**244
šāḥōr	שׁחר	black	**1:**1097
šākab	שׁכב	to lie down	**2:**924, 926, 1304; **4:**696; **6:**489; **7:**496
šākal	שׁכל	to be bereaved	**6:**1485
šākan	שׁכן	to tabernacle, dwell	**1:**882, 884, 888, 913–14, 978, 981; **2:**32; **3:**62, 70; **4:**1178; **5:**669; **6:**635
šālâ	שׁלה	to have peace	**4:**311
šālaḥ	שׁלח	to send, send away	**1:**428–29, 488, 560, 644, 738, 769; **2:**1041; **3:**93, 775; **6:**693; **7:**449
šālak	שׁלך	to throw, cast	**6:**840; **7:**505
šālal	שׁלל	to spoil, plunder	**6:**913
šālāl	שׁלל	booty, plunder	**6:**467; **7:**142
šālam	שׁלם	to be complete, sound	**1:**865–67, 874; **3:**215, 486; **4:**401, 925

Transliteration	Hebrew	English	Volume and Page
šālap	שׁלף	to pull off	**2:**938
šālēm	שׁלם	whole, sound	**1:**1023
šāliaḥ	שׁלח	agent	**8:**600
šālîšîm	שׁלישׁים	officers	**5:**204
šālôm	שׁלום	peace, well-being	**1:**61, 529, 553, 577, 579, 598–600, 621, 634, 636, 639, 767, 828, 873–74, 893, 1023; **2:**68, 200, 1022, 1166, 1171, 1224, 1236, 1286, 1298; **3:**166, 189, 215, 219, 220, 223, 226, 379, 430, 486, 553, 698; **4:**308, 310–11, 698, 793, 820, 833, 899, 923, 940, 963, 968, 1017, 1178, 1184; **5:**48, 53, 55, 107, 433, 682; **6:**68, 141, 395, 599, 647, 702, 751, 793, 795, 807, 850, 1168, 1370, 1471; **7:**72, 366, 607, 724–25, 797, 861; **8:**176; **9:**172, 336, 751
šālôm ʿălêkem	שׁלום עליכם	peace be with you	**9:**485
šālṭān	שׁלטן (Aramaic)	sovereignty	**7:**72, 102
šalwâ	שׁלוה	tranquility, security	**4:**308, 311, 1184
šām	שׁם	there	**1:**704; **4:**730, 1184; **6:**1290, 1538
šāmad	שׁמד	to be destroyed	**6:**1467
šāmaʿ	שׁמע	to hear	**1:**317, 560, 706, 834, 837; **2:**619, 1027, 1085, 1087–89; **3:**516, 804; **4:**628, 1004; **5:**152, 659, 669, 698–99; **6:**356, 465, 482, 621, 864, 1260; **7:**270, 555, 653, 719; **10:**420, 482–83
šāmar	שׁמר	to keep, protect	**1:**349, 351, 459; **2:**36; **4:**309, 395, 609,

Transliteration	Hebrew	English	Volume and Page
			1180–81; **5:**672, 787; **6:**485, 1467; **7:**284, 286–87, 861
šāmāyim	שמים	heavens, sky	**4:**358; **6:**1008
šāmēm	שמם	to be appalled, desolated	**6:**914, 1196, 1284, 1475
šāmēm	שמם	appalled, devastated	**4:**358
šamĕrû ʾet-mišmeret	שמרו את משמרת	to perform duties	**2:**50
šāmmâ	שמה	there	**4:**980
šammôt	שמות	desolate	**6:**1482
šāʿan	שען	to be at ease, rely, trust	**3:**527, 532, 537; **5:**677; **6:**891
šāʿar	שער	to calculate	**5:**206
šaʿar	שער	gate	**3:**892
šaʿărê ṣiyyôn	שערי ציון	gates of Zion	**4:**1024
šaʿărurit	שעררת	horrible thing	**6:**715
šaʿaṭnēz	שעטנז	mixed stuff	**2:**454
šāpaṭ	שפט	to judge	**2:**1016, 1027; **3:**39; **4:**708, 853, 963, 1006, 1066
šāpāt	שפת	hook, peg	**6:**1547
šāqâ	שקה	to give to drink	**4:**1098
šāqad	שקד	to watch, wake	**6:**583, 619, 873; **7:**406
šāqal	שקל	to weigh	**3:**729; **5:**729
šāqaṭ	שקט	to be quiet	**3:**536
šāqēd	שקד	almond tree	**6:**583; **7:**406
šāraṣ	שרץ	to swarm	**1:**746
šārat	שרת	to serve, minister	**3:**437; **5:**668; **6:**696, 1577
šāsâ	שסה	to spoil, plunder	**6:**913
šāt	שת	foundation	**4:**721
šātâ	שתה	to drink	**7:**454
šātal	שתל	to transplant	**6:**708
šātam	שתם	to be open	**2:**189
šātaq	שתק	to be quiet	**7:**477
šāwâ	שוה	to agree with, resemble	**3:**918
šāwʾ	שוא	empty, void, false	**2:**330; **4:**393; **7:**248
šāwaʿ	שוע	to cry out (for help)	**4:**789, 1027
šāwĕʾ	שוא	emptiness, nothingness	**4:**773
šāwʿâ	שועה	a cry	**1:**706; **4:**842
šĕʾār	שאר	remnant	**3:**735, 824; **6:**55
šĕʾēr	שאר	flesh, flesh relation	**1:**1124; **5:**119
šĕʾērît	שארית	remnant	**7:**719

Transliteration	Hebrew	English	Volume and Page
šĕʾērît yiśrāʾēl	שארית ישׂראל	remnant of Israel	**7:**700
šĕʾôl	שׁאול	Sheol	**4:**1028; **5:**38, 430; **6:**158
šĕbāṭîm	שׁבטים	rods	**5:**182
šeber	שׁבר	fracture, breaking	**6:**450, 1041, 1062
šēbeṭ	שׁבט	tribe, royal scepter	**2:**580; **5:**198; **6:**1299
šēbet	שׁבת	cessation, seat	**1:**863; **3:**76
šĕbî	שׁבי	captivity, captives	**6:**411; **7:**422
šĕbûʿâ	שׁבועה	oath	**8:**193
šēd	שׁד	demon	**7:**138
šĕgāgâ	שׁגגה	inadvertent sin	**1:**1033, 1149
šēgal	שׁגל	consort	**3:**756
šĕḥîn	שׁחין	boil, eruption	**4:**358
šĕḥôrâ	שׁחורה	black	**5:**382
šēkār	שׁכר	strong drink	**1:**1071; **6:**93
šĕkem	שׁכם	shoulder, ridge of land	**1:**660
šĕkem ʾeḥād	שׁכם אחד	one shoulder	**7:**699
šĕkôl	שׁכול	forlorn, bereavement	**4:**819
šĕlāmîm	שׁלמים	peace offerings	**1:**990, 1023; **2:**78; **3:**40, 610, 647; **6:**1569
šĕlēmîm	שׁלמים	at full strength	**7:**605
šĕlōmōh	שׁלמה	Solomon	**3:**430, 486
šĕlôšîm	שׁלושׁים	thirty	**5:**204
šēm	שׁם	name, memorial	**1:**412, 1164; **2:**386, 933, 937, 940; **3:**429; **4:**711, 976, 1112, 1148, 1219; **5:**824; **6:**485, 974, 1489
šēm haqqādôš	שׁם הקדושׁ	"his holy name"	**5:**818
šēm ʿôlām	שׁם עולם	"an everlasting name"	**5:**720
šēm qodšô	שׁם קדשׁו	"his holy name"	**4:**1104; **5:**818
šĕmāmâ	שׁממה	devastation, waste	**6:**1196
šĕmāmâ ûmĕšammâ	שׁממה ומשׁמה	a desolation and a waste	**6:**1475
šēmeṣ	שׁמץ	a fragment, whisper	**4:**377
šĕmînîṭ	שׁמינית	musical term, perhaps related to the number eight	**4:**656
šĕmûʾēl	שׁמואל	Samuel	**2:**976
šĕmûʿâ rāʿâ	שׁמועה רעה	bad news	**4:**1136
šēnāʾ	שׁנא	sleep	**4:**1198
šĕnayim	שׁנים	two, two parts	**3:**176
šēnît	שׁנית	again, a second time	**2:**608; **3:**891

Transliteration	Hebrew	English	Volume and Page
šĕpāṭîm	שְׁפָטִים	judgments	**5:**182
šeqer	שֶׁקֶר	false, lie	**1:**727; **4:**1178
šeqeṣ	שֶׁקֶץ	detestable thing, abomination	**7:**614
šerēṣ	שֶׁרֶץ	swarming things, small reptiles	**1:**1081
šĕrirût	שְׁרִרוּת	stubborness	**6:**715
šēš	שֵׁשׁ	fine linen, marble, alabaster	**6:**988, 1374, 1378
šibbōlet	שִׁבֹּלֶת	ear of corn, stream	**2:**838
šibṭê mōšĕlîm	שִׁבְטֵי מֹשְׁלִים	royal scepters	**6:**1299
šibʿānâ	שִׁבְעָנָה	seven (irregular form)	**4:**635
šiggāyôn	שִׁגָּיוֹן	song (?)	**4:**657
šîlōh	שִׁילֹה	Shiloh, a ruler, tribute	**1:**665
šilšôm	שִׁלְשׁוֹם	formerly, three days ago	**5:**204
šimʿû šāmayim wĕhaʾăzînî ʾereṣ	שִׁמְעוּ שָׁמַיִם וְהַאֲזִינִי אֶרֶץ	"Hear, O heavens, and listen, O earth"	**4:**310
šimmāmôn	שִׁמָּמוֹן	dismay	**6:**1196
šimʿû šāmôaʿ	שִׁמְעוּ שָׁמוֹעַ	listen carefully	**6:**482
šipḥâ	שִׁפְחָה	servant, maidservant	**2:**918, 928
šiptê ḥēn	שִׂפְתֵי חֵן	gracious lips	**5:**683
šiqqûṣîm	שִׁקּוּצִים	abomination, something repugnant	**6:**640
šiqqûṣîm mĕšōmēm	שִׁקּוּצִים מְשֹׁמֵם	desolating sacrilege	**4:**11
šîr	שִׁיר	to sing	**4:**1065
šîr	שִׁיר	song	**3:**842; **4:**301, 309, 657; **5:**326
šîr hammaʿălôt	שִׁיר הַמַּעֲלוֹת	pilgrimage song	**4:**301
šîr haššîrîm	שִׁיר הַשִּׁירִים	song of songs	**5:**365, 377
šîr haššîrîm ʾăšer lišlōmōh	שִׁר הַשִּׁירִים אֲשֶׁר לִשְׁלֹמֹה	the song of songs which belongs to Solomon	**5:**377
šîr ḥādāš	שִׁיר חָדָשׁ	new song	**4:**301
šîr ṣiyyôn	שִׁיר צִיּוֹן	Zion song	**4:**301
šîrâ	שִׁירָה	song (feminine)	**4:**301
šiššēʾtîkā	שִׁשֵּׁאתִיךָ	"and I will lead you" (?)	**6:**1523
šît	שִׁית	to put, set	**1:**375
šmiṭṭâ	שְׁמִטָּה	remission, release	**2:**404
šōʾâ	שֹׁאָה	waste, ruin, storm	**6:**1517
šôʾâ	שׁוֹאָה	ruin	**6:**412
šōʾâ ûmĕšōʾâ	שֹׁאָה וּמְשֹׁאָה	waste and desolate	**4:**604
šôaʿ	שׁוֹעַ	independent, noble	**4:**546
šōbnâ	שֹׁבְנָה	"go back!"	**2:**908

Transliteration	Hebrew	English	Volume and Page
šōd	שֹׁד	destruction	**2:**910; **4:**724; **6:**450; **7:**282, 631
šōḥad	שֹׁחַד	bribe	**5:**152
šōma'	שֹׁמַע	fame, "what was heard"	**2:**619
šômēr napšô	שׁוֹמֵר נַפְשׁוֹ	cautious, "one who guards his life"	**5:**198, 787
šōnôt	שֹׁנוֹת	various	**3:**891
šôpār	שׁוֹפָר	ram's horn, war trumpet	**1:**1172; **2:**89; **3:**20; **7:**316, 320
šōpēṭ	שֹׁפֵט	judge	**2:**723, 779; **4:**881; **6:**1315
šōqēd	שֹׁקֵד	watching	**7:**406
šôr	שׁוֹר	ox	**1:**1034
šôrēr	שׁוֹרֵר	watcher	**4:**895
šôrĕray	שׁוֹרְרַי	my enemies	**4:**701
šošannîm	שֹׁשַׁנִּים	"Lilies," musical tune	**4:**656
šošannîm 'ēdût	שֹׁשַׁנִּים עֵדוּת	"Lilies of the Covenant," musical tune	**4:**656
šōṭēr	שֹׁטֵר	officer, supervisor, scribe	**1:**725; **2:**106, 586
šûaḥ	שׁוּחַ	to sink down	**5:**45
šûb	שׁוּב	to return	**1:**179, 932; **2:**96, 899, 905, 908, 910, 941; **3:**76, 102, 105, 195, 556, 581, 600, 1064; **4:**708, 999, 1017, 1042; **5:**674; **6:**255, 356, 498, 596, 603, 645, 670, 698, 715, 810, 1071, 1377; **7:**198, 232, 244, 249, 253, 258, 265, 277, 278, 284, 294, 381, 477, 514–15, 746
šûb šĕbît	שׁוּב שְׁבִית	restored the fortunes	**4:**1016
šûb šĕbût	שׁוּב שְׁבוּת	restore the fortunes	**6:**797, 805
šûḥâ	שׁוּחָה	pit	**5:**45
šûmān	שׁוּמָן	fat	**1:**1025
šûšan 'ēdût	שׁוּשַׁן עֵדוּת	"Lily of the Covenant," musical tune	**4:**656
šûṭ	שׁוּט	to rove about, go to and fro	**4:**348
śāba'	שָׂבַע	to be satisfied	**5:**174
śāba'	שָׂבָע	fullness, satisfied	**4:**740

Transliteration	Hebrew	English	Volume and Page
śābar	שׂבר	to hope	**4:**1172
śābĕʿâ napšî bĕ-	שׂבעה נפשׁי ב	"my soul is satisfied with"	**4:**1028
śāday	שׂדי	field	**7:**286
śādeh	שׂדה	field, country	**2:**900–901, 910, 915; **6:**1295
śāgab	שׂגב	to be high, exalted	**4:**1271; **5:**173
śāḥaq	שׂחק	to play, contest, laugh	**2:**1216; **4:**612; **5:**112
śākal	שׂכל	to study, be careful	**4:**1082, 1110–11; **5:**161, 193; **6:**356; **7:**143
śākar	שׂכר	fare, wages	**7:**494
śākîr	שׂכיר	hired worker	**1:**1171
śāmaḥ	שׂמח	to rejoice	**5:**69, 720; **7:**521
śānēʾ	שׂנא	to hate	**1:**842; **4:**701; **5:**179, 724; **7:**391
śar	שׂר	ruler, prince, commander	**2:**137, 298; **3:**775, 824, 842; **5:**237; **6:**944, 1314–15; **7:**138
śar hammîssîm	שׂר המיסים	captain of the Mysians	**4:**36
śar hammûsîm	שׂר המוסים	chief collector of tribute	**4:**36
śar mĕnûḥâ	שׂר מנוחה	chief quartermaster	**6:**941
śar ʿam-ʾēl	שׂר עם־אל	"prince of the people of God"	**4:**163
śārâ	שׂרה	to struggle	**1:**565
śārap	שׂרף	to burn	**2:**163; **4:**175; **7:**402
śārar	שׂרר	to reign over	**2:**137
śārê-môʾāb	שׂרי־מואב	princes of Moab	**2:**179
śārîd	שׂריד	survivor, remnant	**2:**788; **4:**485; **6:**55
śāśôn	שׂשׂון	joy	**5:**720
śāṭâ	שׂטה	to go astray	**2:**62
śāṭān	שׂטן	adversary, Satan	**2:**183, 1380; **3:**422; **4:**320, 324–25, 334, 343, 347–50, 353–56, 358, 360–61, 370, 460, 525, 547, 600, 1125; **6:**336, 751; **7:**765
śaʿărâ	שׂערה	hair	**4:**378, 411
śātam	שׂתם	to be closed	**2:**189
śēaḥ	שׂח	thought, complaint	**5:**689; **7:**382
śĕʾēt pĕnê	שׂאת פני	to be partial, "to raise the face"	**5:**172

Transliteration	Hebrew	English	Volume and Page
śĕʾû-zimrâ	שְׂאוּ־זִמְרָה	raise a song	**4:**1003
śêbâ	שֵׂיבָה	old age, grey hair	**6:**405; **7:**257
śĕdēh ʾărām	שְׂדֵה אֲרָם	land of Aram	**7:**286
śĕdērâ	שְׂדֵרָה	row, rank of soldiers	**3:**574
śeh	שֶׂה	lamb	**1:**499
śekel	שֶׂכֶל	understanding, intellect, skilled person	**2:**1166; **3:**727
śēkel-ṭôb	שֵׂכֶל־טוֹב	good sense	**5:**48
śekwî	שֶׂכְוִי	a celestial appearance (?)	**4:**605
śēʿār	שֵׂעָר	hair, hairy	**1:**521; **5:**206
śĕʿārâ	שְׂעָרָה	whirlwind	**4:**378, 411
śĕʿîrîm	שְׂעִירִם	hairy ones, goat-gods	**1:**1118
śĕrāpîm	שְׂרָפִים	poisonous or fiery serpents	**2:**163
śîaḥ	שִׂיחַ	to speak, a plant	**4:**427
śîaḥ	שִׂיחַ	meditation, musing	**4:**1104, 1172; **5:**698
śîḥâ	שִׂיחָה	meditation	**5:**689
śîm	שִׂים	to make, put, establish	**1:**644; **4:**1000; **6:**356, 363
śîmḥâ	שִׂמְחָה	joy	**3:**843; **5:**151, 681
śîmû lĕbabĕkem	שִׂימוּ לְבַבְכֶם	give careful thought, "set your heart"	**7:**716
śin	שׂ	sin (Hebrew letter)	**6:**1477
śināʾâ	שְׂנֻאָה	hated one	**3:**686
śûk	שׂוּךְ	a hedge	**4:**349
śûm	שׂוּם	to determine	**2:**192
śûś	שׂוּשׂ	to rejoice	**4:**312

T

Transliteration	Hebrew	English	Volume and Page
ṭābaḥ	טָבַח	to slaughter, butcher	**6:**1299, 1300
ṭāhēr	טָהֵר	to be clean, purified	**1:**1096; **2:**81; **6:**1314, 1337, 1491, 1493, 1509
ṭāmēʾ	טָמֵא	to be unclean	**4:**1111; **6:**1286, 1329, 1488–89
ṭāmēʾ	טָמֵא	unclean, defilement	**1:**1096; **2:**62; **4:**995; **6:**281, 455
ṭaʿam	טַעַם	a command, decree	**3:**711–12; **7:**478, 514
ṭap	טַף	children	**1:**764
ṭārap	טָרַף	to tear, mangle	**1:**867; **4:**458, 467; **7:**613
ṭĕhôrâ	טְהוֹרָה	pure	**4:**752
ṭĕmēʾ-nepeš	טְמֵא־נֶפֶשׁ	defiled (by contact with a corpse)	**7:**727

Transliteration	Hebrew	English	Volume and Page
ṭerep	טרף	prey	**7:**613
ṭet	ט	tet (Hebrew letter)	**6:**1298
ṭĕʿēm	טעם (Aramaic)	a decree	**3:**711–12
ṭibḥâ	טבחה	something slaughtered	**4:**858
ṭimmēʾ	טמא	unclean, defiled	**3:**736
ṭipsār	טפסר	scribe, official (?)	**7:**618
ṭîṭ	טיט	mire, mud	**4:**624, 842
ṭîṭ hayāwen	טיט היון	mud of the mire	**4:**842
ṭôb	טוב	good	**1:**383, 640, 699, 940; **3:**788; **4:**502, 768, 778, 1014, 1078, 1110, 1170, 1201, 1214; **5:**150, 561; **6:**793, 810
ṭôb-ʿayin	טוב־עין	generous, "good of eye"	**5:**198
ṭôb šēm miššemen ṭôb	טוב שם משמן טוב	"a good name is better than good ointment"	**5:**325
ṭôbâ	טובה	goodness, bounty	**2:**1212; **4:**934
ṭôbî	טובי	Tobi	**3:**992
ṭôbiyyâ	טוביה	Tobiah	**3:**788
ṭohŏrâ	טהרה	pure, clean	**4:**197
ṭūḥôt	טחות	inward parts	**4:**605
ṭûl	טול	to hurl	**7:**476, 495, 505
ṭumʾâ	טמאה	uncleanness	**3:**713
ṭûr	טור	row	**6:**1592
taʾăwâ	תאוה	craving	**2:**105
tabʿērâ	תבערה	Taberah	**2:**104
tabnît	תבנית	pattern, plan	**1:**888–89; **3:**462
tahpukâ	תהפכה	perverse	**5:**113
tahpukôt	תהפכות	perverse things	**5:**44, 76
taḥănûn	תחנון	supplication	**4:**1205
taḥaš	תחש	fine leather	**6:**1228
taḥat	תחת	in place of, instead of	**1:**1165
taḥat ʾašer ʿinnāh	תחת אשר ענה	"in lieu of having forced her"	**1:**1165
taḥbulôt	תחבלות	advice, guidance	**5:**125
tākan	תכן	to regulate, measure	**6:**1263–64, 1391
taklît	תכלית	boundary, limit	**4:**420, 529
tāknît	תכנית	measurement, proportion	**6:**1391
tālāʾ	תלא	to hang	**2:**627
tālal	תלל	to deceive	**6:**654
talmûd	תלמוד	Talmud	**1:**68

Transliteration	Hebrew	English	Volume and Page
tām	תם	innocent, upright	**1:**521; **4:**345, 403, 412; **5:**837
tāmak	תמך	to support	**5:**239
tāmam	תמם	to be complete	**5:**117; **6:**1337
tāmîd	תמיד	continually, regular	**1:**901, 1044, 1047; **2:**229, 236; **3:**399–400; **5:**690
tāmîm	תמים	complete, whole, unblemished	**1:**390, 912, 1063; **2:**715; **4:**585, 733, 748, 1082–83; **5:**842; **6:**1568; **8:**196
tānâ	תנה	to recount, celebrate, extol	**5:**263
tanaḥ	תנך	Tanakh	**1:**65
tannîn	תנין	sea monster, serpent	**1:**344, 739; **4:**621–22; **6:**1404, 1434; **7:**192, 505
tāʿab	תעב	to be abhorred	**4:**701; **6:**1226
taʿar	תער	razor	**6:**1150
tāpaś	תפש	to lay hold of	**5:**720
tappûaḥ	תפוח	apple, apple tree	**5:**218; **7:**309
tāqaʿ	תקע	to drive, thrust	**2:**782, 841, 858
tarbît	תרבית	interest	**6:**1259
tardēmâ	תרדמה	a deep sleep	**4:**378
tarmît	תרמית	deceitfulness	**6:**646
taw	ת	taw	**6:**1018
tāw	תו	a mark	**4:**555
tĕʾaššûr	תאשור	cypress	**6:**1422
tĕʾûnîm helʾāt	תאנים הלאת	"has frustrated all efforts" (?)	**6:**1337
tēbâ	תבה	ark, basket	**1:**391, 699
tēbēl	תבל	world	**4:**772
tĕbûʾâ	תבואה	product, produce	**4:**502; **5:**149
tĕbûnâ	תבונה	understanding	**5:**89, 179, 674
tĕhillâ	תהלה	praise, song of praise	**4:**1259, 1261
tĕhillîm	תהלים	praises	**4:**657, 1278
tĕhôm	תהום	"[the] deep"	**1:**342, 392, 394, 800; **4:**624, 853; **5:**833; **6:**1369, 1422, 1425
tĕḥinnâ	תחנה	supplication	**4:**1174
tēl	תל	ruin, mound	**2:**626–27
tĕlāʾâ	תלאה	hardship	**3:**812

Transliteration	Hebrew	English	Volume and Page
tĕmîmâ	תמימה	whole, complete	**1:**1063; **2:**150
tĕmûnâ	תמונה	form, likeness	**4:**378, 741
tĕnû tôdâ	תנו תודה	give thanks	**3:**742
tĕnûpâ	תנופה	wave offering	**1:**1054
tĕʿālôt	תעלות	irrigation canals	**6:**1425
tĕpillâ	תפלה	prayer	**4:**511; **5:**149
tēqaʿ napšāh mēhem	תקע נפשה מהם	"her soul recoiled from them"	**6:**1325
tēqaʿ napšî mēʿāleyhā	תקע נפשי מעליה	"soul recoils from her"	**6:**1325
tĕrûmâ	תרומה	offering, heave offering	**1:**888, 1054; **5:**242; **6:**1580–81, 1584, 1604–5
tĕrûmâ laYHWH	תרומה ליהוה	"Yahweh's portion"	**6:**1581
tĕrûmat haqqōdeš	תרומת הקדש	"the holy portion"	**6:**1581
tĕrûʿâ	תרועה	shout, war cry	**2:**1001; **4:**810; **5:**764
tĕšallaḥ ḥărōnĕkā	תשלח חרנך	"you sent out your fury"	**4:**302
tĕšûʿātô	תשועתו	his saving deeds	**5:**818
tĕšûbâ	תשובה	return, an act of repentance	**5:**674
tĕšûqâ	תשוקה	desire	**5:**427
tĕšûʿâ	תשועה	victory, salvation	**3:**238, 498; **4:**916
tiklâ	תכלה	perfection, completeness	**4:**1171
tipʾeret	תפארת	glory	**3:**429
tipʾeret ʾādām	תפארת אדם	"the splendor of Adam"	**5:**856
tipʾeret ʿammô	תפארת עמו	"the splendor of his people"	**5:**856
tiplâ	תפלה	wrongdoing	**4:**353, 511
tiqwâ	תקוה	hope	**4:**381, 394, 402, 444
tiršātāʾ	תרשתא	governor	**3:**687, 782
titnaśśĕʾû	תתנשאו	to exalt yourselves	**2:**136
timʿol maʿal	תמעל מעל	commit a trespass	**1:**1038
tôdâ	תודה	thanksgiving, thanksgiving offering	**1:**1051; **4:**980, 1077; **6:**1569
tōhû	תהו	worthless thing, chaos	**2:**1064; **4:**518; **5:**824; **6:**211, 277, 342
tōhû wābōhû	תהו ובהו	formless void	**1:**342; **4:**518
tôḥelet	תוחלת	hope	**4:**838
tôk	תוך	midst, middle	**3:**422; **6:**1510
tôkaḥat	תוכחת	argument, reproof	**7:**639
tôlāʿ	תולע	worm	**7:**521
tôlaʿat	תולעת	worm	**7:**521

Transliteration	Hebrew	English	Volume and Page
tôlēdôt	תולדות	genealogy/generations, account/story	**1:**325–26, 349, 407; **2:**35, 48–49, 55; **6:**528; **8:**126
tôlēʿâ	תולעה	worm	**7:**521
tōm	תם	integrity, completeness	**4:**782
tôʿēbâ	תועבה	abhorrence, abomination	**2:**351, 397, 421, 475; **4:**701; **5:**77, 620, 724; **6:**1153, 1226, 1237, 1458, 1574; **7:**864
tôpēś tôrâ	תופש תורה	"the one who handles the law"	**5:**720
tōpet	תפת	fireplace	**6:**640
tôr	תור	dove	**4:**974
tôrâ	תורה	Torah, Law	**1:**8, 16, 22, 29, 38–39, 65, 70, 305, 786, 827, 985, 987, 1043, 1100; **2:**272, 284, 315, 323, 344; **3:**26, 278, 496; **4:**502, 650, 665–66, 671, 684–86, 751–54, 778, 845, 876, 1021, 1166–69, 1171–72, 1175, 1263; **5:**59, 80, 89, 132, 234, 237, 244, 620, 824; **6:**1, 38, 55, 67, 95, 118, 254, 363–64, 369–70, 471, 968; **7:**204, 238, 246, 260–61, 662, 693, 727; **8:**30; **10:**374–75
tôšāb	תושב	temporary resident	**1:**1171
tukkiyyîm	תכיים	baboons, peacocks (?)	**3:**82
tûmmâ	תמה	integrity	**4:**345, 354, 523
tuppeykā	תפיך	"your settings" (?)	**6:**1392
tûr	תור	to seek out, spy	**2:**96, 121–22, 124
tûšiyyâ	תושיה	wisdom, practical knowledge	**4:**419; **5:**43, 91, 172

U

ûbĕrōb gᵓĕônĕkā tahărōs qāmêkā	וברב גאונך תהרס קמיך	"in the greatness of your majesty you overthrew your adversaries"	**4:**302

Transliteration	Hebrew	English	Volume and Page
ûkĕḥakkê ʾîš gĕdûdîm	וכחכי איש גדודים	"as bandits lie in wait for someone"	**7:**256
ûkĕʿenet	וכענת	and now	**3:**699
ûmeteq rēʿēhû mēʿăṣat-nāpeš	ומתק רעהו מעצת־נפש	"a friend's counsel is better than one's own advice," uncertain	**5:**230

W

Transliteration	Hebrew	English	Volume and Page
watĕhî-lô lĕʾiššâ	ותהי־לו לאשה	"she became his wife"	**2:**940
waw	ו	waw (Hebrew letter)	**6:**1379, 1462; **8:**129
wāyayin ʾaḥar	ויין אחר	"and wine from them"	**3:**782
wayĕhî	ויהי	"and it came to pass"	**2:**927–28
wayĕqaw lĕmišpāṭ wĕhinnēh miśpāḥ	ויקו למשפט והנה משפח	"he expected justice, but saw bloodshed"	**4:**310
wayšārĕtēhû	וישרתהו	"and he attented to him"	**3:**144
wayyaḥšĕbehā lô ṣĕdāqâ	ויחשבה לו צדקה	"and he reckoned it to him righteousness"	**10:**487
wayyaʿălû	ויעלו	"and they went up"	**2:**122
wayyaʿaś	ויעש	"and he made"	**3:**478, 483–84
wayyinnāpaš	וינפש	catch one's breath	**1:**1157
wayyišlaḥ sĕpārîm	וישלח ספרים	"and he sent letters"	**3:**939
wāzār	וזר	guilty (?)	**5:**193
wĕ	ו	and, but	**6:**1530, 1578; **7:**318
wĕʾattâ ʾādām wĕloʾ-ʾel	ואתה אדם ולא־אל	"but you are a human and not a god"	**6:**1387
wĕʾim	ואם	and if	**1:**1187
wĕgam-ʾănî	וגם־אני	"but for my part"	**7:**380
wĕgam ʾănî lōʾ ʾeḥmôl	וגם אני לא אחמול	"I will have no pity"	**6:**1343
wĕhikratî ʾet-kĕretîm	והכרתי את־כרתים	"and I will cut off the Cherethites"	**6:**1355
wĕhinnēh	והנה	"and behold"	**3:**556
wĕhûʾ-mazkîr ʿāwōn	והוא־מזכיר עון	"and he will cause iniquity to be remembered"	**6:**1302
wĕkol-hāʿereb	וכל־הערב	"and all the mixed people"	**6:**1415
wĕlāʾăsuppîm	ולאספים	"and for the storehouses"	**3:**451
wĕliwyat	ולוית	garland	**5:**143
wĕniḥamtîʿal	ונחמתי על	"I repent on account of"; "I am consoled concerning"	**4:**628
wĕnittĕkâ bĕtôkāh ṭumʾātāh	ונתכה בתוכה טמאתה	"and her impurity will be X in her midst"	**6:**1337

Transliteration	Hebrew	English	Volume and Page
wĕʿattâ	ועתה	"and now"	**2:**929, 1262; **3:**468, 555, 736
wĕšillamtî	ושלמתי	"and I will repay"	**3:**215, 220
wîrēʾ ʾĕlōhîm	וירא אלהים	fears God	**4:**533
Y			
yābām	יבם	brother-in-law, sister-in-law	**2:**904
yabbōq	יבק	Jabbok	**1:**565
yābēš	יבש	to wither, be dried up	**7:**521
yābēš	יבש	dry, dry land	**2:**593; **7:**521
yād	יד	hand	**2:**1005; **4:**801, 1240; **5:**107; **6:**485, 1420
yādâ	ידה	to throw, cast, praise	**3:**400, 826; **4:**853, 940, 1121
yādaʿ	ידע	to know	**1:**351, 467, 706, 914, 939; **2:**752, 913, 924, 926, 1184; **4:**686, 872, 980, 990, 1048, 1235; **5:**43, 126, 296; **6:**356, 703; **7:**369, 476, 602
yādaʿ mĕbôʾô	ידע מבואו	knows its setting	**4:**308
yādîd	ידיד	beloved	**6:**87
yāgôn	יגון	sorrow	**4:**726
yāhad	יהד	to become a Jew	**3:**927
Yahweh	יהוה	YHWH	**1:**297, 528, 541, 713, 733; **2:**91, 179–80, 185–86, 552, 747, 907, 910; **3:**956; **4:**658, 792, 881, 1139; **5:**9, 251, 748, 846; **6:**1036; **7:**464, 498; **8:**328; **10:**419
Yahweh ʾĕlōhîm	יהוה אלהים	Lord God	**7:**464
Yahweh, Qadôš Hûʾ	יהוה קדוש הוא	"Yahweh, Holy is He"	**5:**251
Yahweh ṣĕbāʾôt	יהוה צבאות	"Lord of hosts"	**2:**1001; **6:**957, 1120; **7:**612, 717
Yahweh šammâ	יהוה שמה	"Yahweh is there"	**6:**1607
yāḥal	יחל	to wait, hope	**4:**434, 837, 960, 1172, 1206; **6:**1051; **7:**585
yaḥărîš bĕʾahăbātô	יחריש באהבתו	"he will be silent in his love"	**7:**703
yaḥdāw	יחדו	together	**6:**356

Transliteration	Hebrew	English	Volume and Page
yākaḥ	יכח	to judge, rebuke	**4:**833; **6:**1137–38
yākōl	יכל	to be able, prevail	**1:**748, 754; **6:**726–27
yālad	ילד	to bear	**1:**451, 453, 486
yālal	ילל	to howl, wail	**6:**454
yāleq	ילק	hopping locust	**7:**307
yām	ים	sea	**1:**279; **4:**368; **7:**403, 477
yam-sûp	ים סוף	Sea of Reeds	**1:**788
yāmîn	ימין	right hand	**4:**1130, 1154; **6:**1294
yānâ	ינה	to oppress	**7:**493
yānaq	ינק	to suckle, nurse	**1:**700
yāʿad	יעד	to meet, assemble	**1:**890, 1008; **2:**32–33; **4:**872; **7:**371
yāʿal	יעל	to profit, benefit	**6:**599
yaʿan	יען	because	**6:**514, 1386, 1388, 1401, 1468, 1476, 1478, 1481, 1485
yaʿan ʾăšer	יען אשׁר	because	**6:**1427
yaʿan kî	יען כי	because	**6:**81
yaʿănâ	יענה	ostrich, owl (?)	**4:**610–11
yaʿăqōb	יעקב	Jacob	**1:**521; **7:**283, 870
yaʿar	יער	forest	**6:**1295
yaʿar haśśādeh	יער השׂדה	the forest of the field	**6:**1294
yaʿar haśśādeh negeb	יער השׂדה נגב	the forest land in the Negeb	**6:**1295–96
yāʿaṣ	יעץ	to advise, counsel, plot	**2:**190; **3:**587; **4:**1010
yaʿbēṣ	יעבץ	Jabez, "he [God] inflicts pain"	**3:**331
yāʿēn	יען	ostrich	**4:**610–11
yāpaʿ	יפע	to shine forth	**4:**999
yāpeh	יפה	fair, suitable, beautiful	**5:**306, 418
yāqaʿ	יקע	to execute, be dislocated	**2:**1358; **6:**1325
yāqār	יקר	precious, costly	**4:**1149
yāqeh	יקה	Jakeh (unknown name)	**5:**251
yārâ	ירה	to teach, throw, cast	**2:**63; **3:**496; **4:**1021, 1169; **5:**76
yārad	ירד	to go down	**4:**1214; **6:**1442; **7:**478, 480, 494, 496, 506
yāraš	ירשׁ	to take possession, destroy	**1:**800; **3:**156; **4:**919; **5:**720; **6:**1478, 1482, 1492; **7:**427, 455

Transliteration	Hebrew	English	Volume and Page
yārē᾽	ירא	to fear	**2:**585, 715, 1119; **4:**389, 449, 500, 592, 785, 814, 843, 902, 979, 980, 1134, 1205; **6:**621; **7:**476, 495, 498, 500, 719, 859
yarkĕtê hassĕpînâ	ירכתי הספינה	the innards of the ship	**7:**479
yārōq yāraq	ירק ירק	"had but spit"	**2:**110
yārûm mimmennî	ירום ממני	"higher than I"	**4:**919
yāsad	יסד	to found, establish	**3:**484, 705, 718; **4:**772, 1098
yāsap	יסף	to add, do again	**1:**694; **3:**923
yāsar	יסר	to instruct, admonish	**4:**376, 737, 833, 1058; **5:**181; **7:**258
yāsûrû bî	יסורו בי	"they turn away from me"	**7:**258
yāṣā᾽	יצא	to go forth, come out	**1:**445, 473, 700, 713, 734–35, 748, 772, 777, 780, 914; **2:**34, 136, 181, 219, 1055, 1120, 1216; **3:**810; **4:**529, 945, 1142; **6:**363, 449, 455, 693; **7:**369, 547, 772, 778, 783
yāṣar	יצר	to form, fashion	**1:**349; **6:**375, 387
yāšab	ישב	to settle, dwell	**1:**593, 674, 888; **2:**594; **3:**62, 70–71, 76, 377, 556, 730; **4:**684, 717, 764, 782, 1139; **6:**405–6, 411–12, 1368; **7:**231–32, 265, 295, 519, 826
yāšam	ישם	to ruin, be desolate	**6:**1196
yāšān	ישן	old	**3:**766, 839
yāšaʿ	ישע	to save	**1:**703–4, 727, 794, 820; **2:**1053, 1056; **3:**236; **4:**693, 708, 747, 755, 757, 762, 774, 800, 810, 1020, 1071, 1110; **5:**800, 818; **6:**365, 441, 516, 520, 1509; **7:**456, 815

Transliteration	Hebrew	English	Volume and Page
yāšār	ישׁר	upright, just	**2:**1205–6; **4:**570, 1173
yāšēn	ישׁן	to sleep	**4:**696, 1181; **7:**257
yāṭab	יטב	to be good, pleasing	**5:**659
yātar	יתר	to be left over	**1:**962; **3:**824; **6:**1605
yātēd	יתד	tent peg	**7:**814
yāwān	יון	Javan	**6:**1379
yĕbûl	יבול	a flood, produce	**4:**486
yĕdîdôt	ידידות	lovely	**4:**1013
yĕgîaʿ kappekā	יגיע כפיך	"work of your hands"	**4:**414
yĕhab ʾuššayyāʾ	יהב אשׁיא	laid the foundations	**3:**705
yĕhāpēk lĕbab	יהפך לבב	"change his mind"	**1:**792
yĕhî ʾôr	יהי אור	"let it be light"	**4:**367
yĕhî ḥōšek	יהי חשׁך	"let it be darkness"	**4:**367
Yĕhôsūaʿ	יהושׁע	Joshua, "Yahweh saves"	**8:**134
yĕhûdâ	יהודה	Judah	**3:**1131
yĕhûdî	יהודי	a Jew	**3:**923
yĕḥallû pĕnê	יחלו פני	to seek the face of someone	**5:**179
yĕḥam lĕbābô	יחם לבבו	in hot anger	**2:**435
yĕḥezqēʾl	יחזקאל	Ezekiel, "God toughens"	**6:**1127
yeled	ילד	child, boy, youth	**3:**102
yĕqallēl ʾĕlōhāw	יקלל אלהיו	"curse God"	**4:**346
yĕrîʿâ	יריעה	tent, curtain of a tent	**4:**1097
yĕrîʿot	יריעת	curtains	**1:**897
yĕrûšālayim	ירושׁלים	Jerusalem	**6:**1607
yēṣer	יצר	inclination, plan	**1:**389; **5:**725; **6:**407
yēṣer hārāʿ	יצר הרע	evil inclination	**5:**724; **9:**417
yēṣer hāṭṭôb	יצר הטוב	good inclination	**5:**724; **9:**417
yēš	ישׁ	particle of existence, "there is"	**5:**615, 673, 683
yešaʿ	ישׁע	salvation, deliverance	**6:**395, 441, 516
yĕšaʿyāhû	ישׁעיהו	Isaiah	**6:**365, 395, 441
yĕšārîm	ישׁרים	"upright ones"	**4:**1133
yĕšûʿâ	ישׁועה	salvation, Jeshua, "he is saved"	**1:**666, 794; **4:**546, 758, 790, 819, 857, 1065, 1154; **6:**441; **8:**134–35
yeter	יתר	remnant, remainder	**3:**824
yiddĕʿōnî	ידעני	wizard, spiritist	**2:**1184
yiḥar-ʾap	יחר־אף	"anger burns hot"	**1:**932
yipʿâ	יפעה	splendor, radiance	**6:**1388
yiprĕṣēnî pereṣ ʿal-pĕnê-pāreṣ	יפרצני פרץ על־פני־פרץ	"he breaches me breach upon breach"	**4:**459

Transliteration	Hebrew	English	Volume and Page
yiptaḥ	יפתח	Jephthah, "he opens"	**2:**821
yir᾽â	יראה	fear	**4:**1134
yir᾽at ᾽ădōnāy	יראת אדני	"fear of the Lord"	**4:**533; **6:**141
yir᾽at ᾽ĕlōhîm	יראת אלהים	"fear of God"	**4:**449
yir᾽ê YHWH	יראי יהוה	"fear of the Lord"	**5:**626
yiṣhār	יצהר	oil	**7:**771
yiṣḥāq	יצחק	"he laughs," Isaac	**1:**459
yiśḥaq lĕpaḥad	ישׂחק לפחד	"laughs at fear"	**4:**612
yō᾽kĕlēmô kaqqaš	יאכלמו כקשׁ	"it consumed them like stubble"	**4:**302
yôbēl	יובל	ram, ram's horn	**1:**1171; **2:**89
yod	י	Yod (Hebrew letter)	**6:**1379; **8:**187
yōdēa᾿	ידע	friend	**4:**476
yôḥānān	יוחנן	Johanan	**3:**833
yôm	יום	day	**1:**346; **2:**77, 88; **3:**782; **4:**368; **7:**451, 666, 682
yôm᾽ap-Yahweh	יום אף־יהוה	"the day of the Lord's wrath"	**7:**685
yôm hakkippūrîm	יום הכפרים	"Day of Atonement"	**1:**1109
yôm-Yahweh	יום־יהוה	"the Day of the Lord"	**7:**664, 666, 677, 696
yôm yizrĕ᾿e᾽l	יום יזרעאל	"day of Jezreel"	**7:**223
yôm zā᾿am	יום זעם	"the day of indignation"	**6:**1314
yônat ᾽ēlem rĕḥōqîm	יונת אלם רחקים	"A Dove on Distant Oaks," musical tune	**4:**656
yônātān	יונתן	Jonathan	**3:**833
yôṣēr	יוצר	potter	**8:**484
yôšĕbîm	יושבים	inhabitants, "the ones who sit"	**2:**594
yyy	ווו	abbreviation for "Yahweh"	**5:**846

Z

Transliteration	Hebrew	English	Volume and Page
zābaḥ	זבח	to sacrifice	**1:**1118; **2:**1089; **6:**1527; **7:**678
zādôn	זדון	pride	**6:**1166
zāhar	זהר	to warn	**1:**1106
zāhîr	זהיר	estrange	**5:**715
zākâ	זכה	to be clean, pure	**4:**517
zākak	זכך	to be clean, bright	**4:**517
zākar	זכר	to remember	**1:**560, 706, 845, 932; **2:**331; **3:**400, 556, 748, 749; **4:**309, 755, 778,

Transliteration	Hebrew	English	Volume and Page
			796, 955, 960, 991, 1087, 1170, 1211; **5:**319; **6:**1049, 1068; **7:**579
zālal	זלל	to be light, worthless	**6:**1033
zāmam	זמם	to plan	**6:**1042; **7:**797
zamar	זמר	to sing, make music	**4:**304, 869
zānâ	זנה	to be a harlot, commit fornication	**1:**606, 1118; **2:**198, 841, 854, 875; **4:**1111; **6:**1224, 1286, 1321, 1329; **7:**216, 230, 256
zānāb	זנב	tail	**4:**618
zānaḥ	זנח	to spurn, reject	**4:**983, 1028
zānōh tizneh	זנה תזנה	to play the whore	**7:**216
zāʿam	זעם	to be indignant	**6:**1315
zaʿam	זעם	indignation, wrath	**7:**258, 602, 752, 753
zāʿap	זעף	to be enraged	**7:**477
zāʿaq	זעק	to cry out	**1:**706; **2:**767; **4:**1246; **6:**727; **7:**495, 499, 557, 647
zāqān	זקן	beard	**4:**1214
zāqēn	זקן	old, old man, elder	**7:**306, 320
zār	זר	stranger	**4:**894–95; **5:**72, 74, 699, 705, 715; **6:**1233, 1388, 1574; **7:**261
zārâ	זרה	to scatter	**6:**1489; **7:**756
zārâ	זרה	alien, strange	**1:**1070; **5:**44, 66, 69
zāraʿ	זרע	to sow, scatter seed	**7:**261
zāraq	זרק	to scatter, sprinkle	**4:**358; **6:**1183
zebaḥ	זבח	a sacrifice	**1:**990, 992; **3:**225; **6:**56, 1527–28
zēdîm	זדים	insolent	**4:**894
zĕdôn libbĕkā ḥiššîʾekā	זדון לבך השיאך	"your proud heart has deceived you"	**7:**447
zeh	זה	this (masculine)	**1:**1080; **4:**493; **6:**546
zĕker	זכר	name, "remembrance"	**4:**796, 1087, 1133
zĕmān	זמן	time, season	**5:**672
zĕmirôt	זמרות	strength, songs	**4:**581
zeraʿ	זרע	seed, offspring	**1:**375, 1104; **6:**477, 500, 513, 543; **7:**40
zĕraḥ haššemeš	זרח השמש	east, "rising of the sun"	**7:**783
zĕrôaʿ	זרוע	arm	**6:**1420

Transliteration	Hebrew	English	Volume and Page
zîd	זיד	to act insolently	**3:**811
zikkārôn	זכרון	maxim, remembrance	**4:**434
zimmâ	זמה	evil intent, crafty	**1:**992; **5:**125, 194, 211; **6:**1232, 1309, 1330, 1337; **7:**253
ziqnê midyān	זקני מדין	elders of Midian	**2:**179
ziqnê mô'āb	זקני מואב	elders of Moab	**2:**179
zō't	זאת	this (feminine)	**1:**1080; **3:**44; **4:**478
zôb	זוב	emission, discharge	**1:**1104; **2:**61
zôlēlâ	זוללה	worthless	**6:**1032
zônâ	זונה	prostitute	**1:**606; **2:**841, 854; **7:**216, 241
zûa'	זוע	to tremble, quake	**3:**911

Greek Transliteration

α	=	*a*	ι	=	*i*	ρ	=	*r*
β	=	*b*	κ	=	*k*	σ or ς	=	*s*
γ	=	*g*	λ	=	*l*	τ	=	*t*
δ	=	*d*	μ	=	*m*	υ	=	*y*
ε	=	*e*	ν	=	*n*	φ	=	*ph*
ζ	=	*z*	ξ	=	*x*	χ	=	*ch*
η	=	*ē*	ο	=	*o*	ψ	=	*ps*
θ	=	*th*	π	=	*p*	ω	=	*ō*

Greek

Transliteration	Greek	English	Volume and Page
A			
Abba ho Patēr	ἀββα ὁ πατήρ	Abba! Father!	**11:**63
Abdiou	Αβδιου	Obadiah	**7:**437
abyssos	ἄβυσσος	abyss	**12:**631
achreios	ἀχρεῖος	worthless, unworthy	**9:**323
achrēstos	ἄχρηστος	useless	**5:**476; **11:**898
achri	ἄχρι	until, as far as	**11:**143
adelphē	ἀδελφή	sister	**3:**1039
adelphoi	ἀδελφοί	brothers and sisters	**8:**363, 432, 456; **9:**182, 843; **10:**508–9, 628, 653, 806–7, 836, 840; **11:**42, 178, 202,

Transliteration	Greek	English	Volume and Page
			211, 331, 347, 353, 487, 688; **12:**418
adelphos	ἀδελφός	brother	**3:**962, 1039; **4:**122; **8:**102, 211, 378; **9:**843; **11:**126
adiakritos	ἀδιάκριτος	undivided, unwavering	**12:**209
adialeiptōs	ἀδιαλείπτως	constantly	**11:**689, 732
adiaphora	ἀδιάφορα	indifferent matters	**10:**407, 783, 870, 880–81; **11:**25, 85, 93, 97
adikēma	ἀδίκημα	crime, a wrong	**10:**214, 255, 321
adikia	ἀδικία	unrighteousness, injustice	**9:**308, 312; **10:**432, 439, 646, 855; **12:**386
adikos	ἄδικος	unrighteous	**5:**559; **9:**309, 312
adikōs	ἀδίκως	unrighteously	**5:**559
adokimos	ἀδόκιμος	disqualified	**10:**910, 938; **11:**123, 144, 176–77
adontes	ἄδοντες	singing	**11:**649
adynatos	ἀδύνατος	weak, powerless, impossible	**10:**745; **12:**74
agalliaō	ἀγαλλιάω	to rejoice	**12:**251
agamos	ἄγαμος	unmarried person	**10:**874–75
agapaō	ἀγαπάω	to love	**8:**425; **9:**671, 686, 739, 758, 860; **11:**244, 324, 466, 655, 878; **12:**259–60
agapē	ἀγάπη	love, charity	**8:**195–96, 425, 442; **10:**711; **11:**314, 391, 415, 420, 422–23, 894; **12:**287, 336, 338, 377, 389, 431, 433, 449, 460, 492, 589
agapē meta pisteōs	ἀγάπη μετά πίστεως	love with faith	**11:**465
agapētos	ἀγαπητός	beloved	**9:**91; **11:**892; **12:**310, 393, 425, 429
agathopoieō	ἀγαθοποιέω	to do good	**12:**312
agathos	ἀγαθός	good	**3:**984; **8:**390; **11:**87
agathotēs	ἀγαθότης	goodness	**5:**504
agelaious	ἀγελαίους	flocks, belonging to a herd	**4:**287

Transliteration	Greek	English	Volume and Page
ageledon	ἀγεληδόν	in a flock or herd	**4:**287
agnoia	ἄγνοια	ignorance	**9:**135; **10:**81, 248
Agnōstos Theos	Ἀγνώστος Θεός	unknown god	**10:**246
agō	ἄγω	to lead	**9:**773
agōn	ἀγών	a struggle, contest	**11:**498, 616, 813; **12:**148
agōnia	ἀγωνία	distress, anguish	**4:**208
agōnizomai	ἀγωνίζομαι	to contend, struggle	**4:**97; **11:**813
agora	ἀγορά	marketplace	**10:**233, 242, 244, 253
agorazō	ἀγοράζω	to buy, purchase	**10:**867; **12:**587
aichmalōsia	αἰχμαλωσία	captivity	**11:**421
aichmalōtoi	αἰχμαλώτοι	captives	**9:**105
aikia	αἰκία	torture	**4:**242
aineō	αἰνέω	to praise	**9:**29
aiōn	αἰών	forever, ages	**3:**1062; **4:**164; **11:**74, 389–90, 392, 411; **12:**23, 108
aiōnios	αἰώνιος	eternal, everlasting	**6:**971; **11:**83
aireō	αἵρεω	to choose, prefer	**11:**491
airō	αἶρω	to lift up, remove	**9:**757; **10:**144
aischrologia	αἰσχρολογία	foul language	**11:**643
aischynō	αἰσχύνω	to be ashamed	**11:**490
akakos	ἄκακος	blameless	**12:**93
akatakritos	ἀκατάκριτος	uncondemned	**10:**308
akatharsia	ἀκαθαρσία	impurity	**11:**428, 435, 642
akēdia	ἀκηδια	sloth, indifference	**12:**35, 127
akeraios	ἀκέραιος	pure, sincere	**10:**765
akmēn	ἀκμήν	still, yet	**8:**334
akoē	ἀκοή	the ability to hear	**10:**668; **11:**251–52
akoē pisteōs	ἀκοή πίστεως	the gospel message	**11:**254
akoloutheō	ἀκολουθέω	to follow	**9:**530, 632
akōlytōs	ἀκωλύτως	freely, without hindrance	**9:**212; **10:**368
akouō	ἀκούω	to hear	**9:**176, 604, 773; **10:**91, 420; **12:**71
akousatōsan autōn	ἀκουσάτωσαν αὐτῶν	Let them hear them!	**9:**318
akribeia	ἀκρίβεια	conformity, accuracy	**10:**306
akribestatēs	ἀκριβεστάτης	strictest	**10:**335
akribōs	ἀκριβῶς	accurately	**10:**261
akrobystia	ἀκροβυστία	uncircumcised	**10:**778

Transliteration	Greek	English	Volume and Page
alalētos	ἀλαλήτος	speechless	**10:**599
alazōn	ἀλαζών	know-it-all	**9:**477
alazoneia	ἀλαζονεία	arrogance	**12:**216, 401
alētheia	ἀλήθεια	truth, fidelity	**3:**984, 993, 1003, 1064; **5:**652; **9:**637, 742, 771; **10:**340, 849; **12:**421, 449, 460
alēthēs	ἀληθής	true, valid	**9:**633
alēthinos	ἀληθινός	truthful	**5:**652; **9:**633, 757; **12:**584
alēthōs	ἀληθῶς	truly	**9:**264
alla	ἀλλά	but	**10:**151, 220, 562, 814, 855; **11:**301, 729
alla pros to euschēmon	ἀλλὰ πρὸς τὸ εὔσχημον	but toward good order	**10:**887
allēgoreō	ἀλληγορέω	to explain allegorically	**11:**301
allēn parabolēn	ἄλλην παραβολήν	another parable	**8:**301
allotrios	ἀλλότριος	strange	**4:**87
allophylos	ἀλλόφυλος	foreigner, Gentile, Philistine	**4:**21, 69, 77
allos	ἄλλος	another	**9:**747
alogos	ἄλογος	unreasonable, illogical	**10:**330
alypoteros	ἀλυπότερος	less anxious, sorrowful	**11:**520
alysitelēs	ἀλυσιτελής	harmful, unprofitable	**12:**169
amarantos	ἀμάραντος	unfading	**5:**491
ameixias chronois	ἀμειξίας χρόνοις	times of separation	**4:**285
ametakinētos	ἀμετακίνητος	immovable	**10:**991
amemptos	ἄμεμπτος	blameless	**9:**45; **11:**700
amemptous en hagiōsynē	ἀμέμπτους ἐν ἁγιωσύνῃ	unblamable in holiness	**11:**700
amēn	ἀμήν	amen, truly	**8:**187, 226, 255, 257–58, 369, 374, 379, 391, 408, 411, 439, 450, 467, 470, 475; **9:**107, 264, 345, 409, 532
amēn, amēn	ἀμὴν ἀμήν	very truly	**9:**645–46, 726
amēn, amēn, legō	ἀμὴν ἀμὴν λέγω	very truly I say . . .	**9:**532, 549, 861
amiantos	ἀμίαντος	undefiled	**12:**93
amnos	ἀμνός	lamb	**12:**602
amōmos	ἄμωμος	without blame	**11:**512, 606
amphiblēstron	ἀμφίβληστρον	casting net	**9:**116

Transliteration	Greek	English	Volume and Page
ana meson	ἀνα μέσον	at the center	**12:**625
anabainō	ἀναβαίνω	to go up	**4:**71; **9:**617; **10:**259; **12:**619
anachōreō	ἀναχωρέω	to retire, withdraw	**8:**167, 280, 323, 336, 341
anagennaō	ἀναγεννάω	to be born again	**12:**250
anagkazō	ἀναγκάζω	to compel	**4:**268; **11:**224, 342
anagkē	ἀνάγκη	necessity, fate	**8:**349
anaideia	ἀναίδεια	shamelessness	**9:**236
anaireō	ἀναιρέω	to destroy, kill	**10:**336
anakainizō	ἀνακαινίζω	to renew	**12:**74
anakainōsis	ἀνακαίνωσις	renewal	**11:**877
anakeimai	ἀνάκειμαι	to take one's place, recline	**8:**324
anakrinō	ἀνακρίνω	to examine	**10:**239
analambanō	ἀναλαμβάνω	to lift up, take up	**9:**215
analēmpsis	ἀνάλημψις	a taking, receiving up	**9:**215
analogia	ἀναλογία	right relationship, comparison	**10:**711
analysis	ἀνάλυσις	departure, breaking up	**11:**856
anamartētos	ἀναμάρτητος	the one without sin	**9:**629
anamenō	ἀναμένω	to wait for, expect	**11:**694
anangellō	ἀναγγέλλω	to announce	**9:**580, 773–74, 781
anantirrētos . . . deon	ἀναντίρρητος . . . δέον	cannot be denied, "necessarily undeniable"	**10:**273
anapepautai	ἀναπέπαυται	to be refreshed, comforted	**11:**895
anaplēroō	ἀναπληρόω	to fulfill	**11:**333
anapsychō	ἀναψύχω	to refresh, cheer up	**11:**838
anasōzomenos	ἀνασωζόμενος	escaping	**10:**666
anastenazō	ἀναστενάζω	to sigh deeply	**8:**616
anastrephō	ἀναστρέφω	to conduct one's self	**11:**45; **12:**169, 273
anastrophē	ἀναστροφή	conduct, behavior	**12:**284
anathallō	ἀναθάλλω	to cause to bloom again	**11:**543
anathema	ἀνάθεμα	a curse, something cursed	**10:**628, 1002; **11:**206
anatithēmi	ἀνατίθημι	to declare, set before	**11:**223
anatrepō	ἀνατρέπω	to upset, overturn	**11:**865
anaxiōs	ἀναξίως	unworthily	**4:**291; **10:**937
andres	ἄνδρες	people, "males"	**8:**325
andres adelphoi	ἄνδρες ἀδελφοί	brothers	**10:**360
Andres Israēlitai	Ἄνδρες Ἰσραηλῖται	Israelites	**10:**191
andros	ἀνδρός	man, husband	**10:**928

Transliteration	Greek	English	Volume and Page
anechō	ἀνέχω	to bear with	**11:**149
anechomai	ἀνέχομαι	to endure	**11:**747
anegklētos	ἀνέγκλητος	blameless, irreproachable	**11:**606
anekdiēgētō dōrea	ἀνεκδιηγήτῳ δωρεα	indescribable gift	**11:**131
aneleēmonas	ἀνελεήμονας	ruthless, unmerciful	**10:**434
anepilēmptos	ἀνεπίλημπτος	blameless	**11:**805
anēr	ἀνήρ	man, husband	**11:**801
anēr dynatos	ἀνὴρ δυνατός	man of valor	**4:**122
anēr polemistēs	ἀνὴρ πολεμιστής	warrior	**5:**767
anesis	ἄνεσις	rest, relief	**11:**55, 109, 119
aneuriskō	ἀνευρίσκω	to discover	**10:**288
angelos	ἄγγελος	messenger, angel	**11:**165–66; **12:**26, 571
angelos kyriou	ἄγγελος κυρίου	angel of the Lord	**10:**104
angelos satana	ἄγγελος σατανᾶ	messenger/agent/ angel of Satan	**11:**164
aniēmi	ἀνίημι	to release	**5:**579
anistēmi	ἀνίστημι	to arise	**9:**127, 352; **10:**162
anō	ἄνω	above, heaven	**11:**637
anoia	ἄνοια	foolishness, fury	**9:**135
anoigō	ἀνοίγω	to open	**9:**238
anoikodomeō	ἀνοικοδομέω	to rebuild	**10:**213, 284
anoixas . . . to stoma autou	ἀνοίξας . . . τὸ στόμα αὐτοῦ	began to speak, "opening his mouth"	**10:**144
anomia	ἀνομία	wickedness, lawlessness	**7:**177; **8:**217; **12:**412, 413
anomos	ἄνομος	lawless	**9:**452
anōthen	ἄνωθεν	from above, again, anew	**9:**549–50, 552, 554–55, 559, 566, 578
antanaplēroō	ἀνταναπληρόω	to fill up, complete for someone else	**11:**613
antapodidōmi	ἀνταποδίδωμι	to give back, repay	**11:**749
anthrōpos	ἄνθρωπος	man, person	**3:**1029; **8:**215, 355, 386, 470, 477; **9:**275, 416; **10:**571; **12:**659, 678, 721
anthrōpos tis	ἄνθρωπός τις	a certain man	**9:**229, 294
anti	ἀντι	instead	**5:**529, 573; **12:**149
antichristos	ἀντίχριστος	counterchrist	**12:**403
antilambanomai	ἀντιλαμβάνομαι	to help, come to the aid of	**10:**745
antilegō	ἀντιλέγω	to reject, speak against	**9:**72

Transliteration	Greek	English	Volume and Page
antilogia	ἀντιλογία	hostility, controversy	**12:**150
antipsychon	ἀντίψυχον	ransom	**10:**475
antitassō	ἀντιτάσσω	to resist, oppose	**12:**217
antitypos	ἀντίτυπος	corresponding to	**12:**295
anypokritos	ἀνυπόκριτος	genuine, unhypocritical	**10:**726; **12:**259
anypotaktos	ἀνυπότακτος	undisciplined, insubordinate	**11:**865
aoratos	ἀόρατος	invisible	**11:**603; **12:**142
apagchomai	ἀπάγχομαι	to hang	**8:**484
apagō	ἀπάγω	to lead, bring	**6:**974; **9:**400
apaitousin	ἀπαιτοῦσιν	they will demand	**9:**256
apalgeō	ἀπαλγέω	to become callous, lose sensitivity	**11:**428
apangellō	ἀπαγγέλλω	to tell, proclaim	**8:**501; **9:**781; **12:**382
apantaō	ἀπαντάω	to meet	**4:**147; **8:**500
apantēsis	ἀπάντησις	meeting	**4:**135; **11:**677, 725
aparchē	ἀπαρχή	first fruits	**10:**981
apechō	ἀπέχω	to have back, receive in full payment	**11:**544
apeipon	ἀπεῖπον	to renounce, disown	**11:**73
apeitheō	ἀπειθέω	to disobey	**9:**559; **10:**267
apekdechomai	ἀπεκδέχομαι	to expect, eagerly await	**10:**598; **11:**313
apekdyomai	ἀπεκδύομαι	to undress, strip off	**11:**624
apēllotriōmenoi	ἀπηλλοτριωμένοι	alienated, being aliens	**11:**397
apestalken me	ἀπέσταλκέν με	he has sent me	**9:**105
aphaireō	ἀφαιρέω	to take off a garment	**4:**286
aphema	ἄφεμα	relief	**4:**154
aphesis	ἄφεσις	deliverance, release	**9:**105; **10:**15, 67
aphesis tōn hamartiōn hymōn	ἄφεσις τῶν ἁμαρτιῶν ὑμῶν	forgiveness of your sins	**10:**67
aphiēmi	ἀφίημι	to pardon, leave alone	**4:**154; **8:**333; **9:**751, 847; **10:**875–76
aphistēmi	ἀφίστημι	to withdraw from	**4:**190; **11:**812; **12:**75
aphomoion	ἀφομοιόν	like	**5:**643
aphorizō	ἀφορίζω	to set apart	**10:**189, 415, 602
aphormē	ἀφορμή	a starting point, base of operations	**11:**321
aphormēn	ἀφορμήν	opportunity	**5:**643
aphormēn tē sarki	ἀφορμήν τῇ σαρκί	an occasion to the flesh	**11:**321
aphrōn	ἄφρων	foolish	**9:**256; **10:**974; **11:**153
aphtharsia	ἀφθαρσία	incorruptibility	**5:**437
apisteō	ἀπιστέω	to disbelieve, distrust	**12:**50

Transliteration	Greek	English	Volume and Page
apistia	ἀπιστία	unbelief, disloyalty	**8:**318; **10:**685; **12:**49
apistos	ἄπιστος	unbelieving	**9:**850
apo	ἀπό	from	**11:**497
apo doxēs eis doxan	ἀπὸ δόξης εἰς δόξαν	from glory into glory	**11:**70
apo merous	ἀπὸ μέρους	in part, for awhile	**10:**688, 756
apo tote	ἀπὸ τότε	from that time	**8:**348
apo tote ērxato ho Iēsous	ἀπὸ τότε ἤρξατο ὁ Ἰησοῦς	from that time Jesus began to . . .	**8:**112
apodidōmi	ἀποδίδωμι	to give	**9:**209
apodokimazō	ἀποδοκιμάζω	to reject	**8:**671; **9:**382
apokalypsis	ἀποκάλυψις	revelation	**7:**1, 15; **10:**768; **11:**212, 220, 749–50; **12:**323, 515, 518, 560
apokalyptō	ἀποκαλύπτω	to reveal, uncover	**8:**345, 349; **10:**401, 768; **11:**212, 216, 269; **12:**518
apokatallassō	ἀποκαταλλάσσω	to reconcile	**11:**600
apokathistanō	ἀποκαθιστάνω	to restore	**10:**82
apokritheis	ἀποκριθείς	answered, responded	**8:**274
apōleia	ἀπώλεια	destruction	**11:**759
apōleian kai synteleian	ἀπώλειαν καὶ συντέλειαν	final destruction	**4:**63
apōleto to paidion mou	ἀπώλετο τὸ παιδίον μοῦ	my child has perished	**3:**983
apollymi	ἀπόλλυμι	to destroy, be lost	**8:**417; **9:**294, 599, 793; **10:**811, 825; **11:**759
apologeomai	ἀπολογέομαι	to defend oneself	**10:**334
apologia	ἀπολογία	reply, defense	**10:**904; **11:**858
apōlonto hypo tou olothreutou	ἀπώλοντο ὑπὸ τοῦ ὀλοθρευτοῦ	were destroyed by the destroyer	**12:**632
apolouō	ἀπολούω	to wash	**11:**105
apolyō	ἀπολύω	to set free, dismiss	**9:**71; **12:**173
apolytrōsis	ἀπολύτρωσις	redemption	**9:**408; **10:**815; **11:**373, 376, 596
apopheugō	ἀποφεύγω	to escape, flee	**12:**352
apophthengomai	ἀποφθέγγομαι	to speak out, declare	**10:**340–41
aporia	ἀπορία	distress	**9:**407

Transliteration	Greek	English	Volume and Page
aporphanizō	ἀπορφανίζω	to make an orphan, be separated from	**11:**707
apostasia	ἀποστασία	rebellion	**11:**758
apostasian didaskeis apo	ἀποστασίαν διδάσκεις ἀπό	teaching apostasy against	**10:**293
apostellō	ἀποστέλλω	to send	**8:**600; **9:**112, 552, 570, 678; **10:**38, 667; **12:**246
apostereō	ἀποστερέω	to defraud	**5:**664
apostolē	ἀποστολή	apostleship	**11:**226
apostoloi ekklēsiōn	ἀπόστολοι ἐκκλησιῶν	representatives of the churches	**11:**126
apostolos	ἀπόστολος	apostle	**8:**253; **10:**38; **11:**133, 149, 201, 359–60, 369, 402, 520; **12:**45, 333, 694
apostrephō	ἀποστρέφω	to mislead, turn away from	**9:**447; **11:**838
aposynagōgos	ἀποσυνάγωγος	put out of synagogue	**9:**657, 765
apotassomai	ἀποτάσσομαι	to give up, take leave of	**9:**293
apōtheomai	ἀπωθέομαι	to reject, push aside	**10:**194–95
apothnēskō	ἀποθνῄσκω	to die	**4:**87; **9:**688
apothnēskontes anthrōpoi	ἀποθνήσκοντες ἄνθρωποι	mortal, “dying men”	**12:**88
apotithēmi	ἀποτίθημι	to put off, get rid of	**12:**263
apotomōs	ἀποτόμως	sharply, harshly	**11:**177
apotropiasmos	ἀποτροπίασμος	the Averter	**1:**1112
aproskopos	ἀπρόσκοπος	clear, causing no trouble	**10:**320
ara	ἄρα	therefore	**10:**575
ara oun	ἄρα οὖν	so then	**10:**528, 592; **11:**727
archē	ἀρχή	beginning, ruler	**8:**527; **9:**539; **11:**460, 599, 605
archēgos	ἀρχηγός	leader	**12:**39
archēgos kai sōtēr	ἀρχηγὸς καὶ σωτήρ	Leader and Savior	**10:**107
archēgos kai teleiōtēs	ἀρχηγός καὶ τελειωτής	originator and completer	**11:**275
archiereus	ἀρχιερεύς	high priest	**12:**45
archisynagōgos	ἀρχισυνάγωγος	leader of a synagogue	**10:**775
architektōn	ἀρχιτέκτων	master builder	**11:**360
archōn	ἄρχων	ruler, official	**4:**160, 165; **6:**944; **7:**162; **11:**390

Transliteration	Greek	English	Volume and Page
archontes tou aiōnos toutou	ἄρχοντες τοῦ αἰῶνος τούτου	the rulers of this aeon	**10:**822, 825
areskō	ἀρέσκω	to be pleasing	**10:**704
aretē	ἀρετή	virtue, valor, excellence	**4:**236, 296; **8:**22; **12:**337
argos	ἀργός	inactive, idle	**12:**198
argyrion	ἀργύριον	silver	**9:**171
ariston	ἄριστον	meal	**9:**287
Arithmoi	ἀριθμοι	Numbers	**2:**3
arneomai	ἀρνέομαι	to deny, disown	**10:**80
arnion	ἀρνίον	sheep, lamb	**12:**602
arpazō	ἁρπάζω	to seize, take away	**11:**725
arrabōn	ἀρραβών	pledge, down payment	**11:**49, 84, 376
arsenokoitai	ἀρσενοκοῖται	homosexual offenders	**10:**858
arti	ἄρτι	now	**9:**783; **12:**643
artigennētos	ἀρτιγέννητος	newborn	**12:**263
artos	ἄρτος	bread	**9:**420, 858
asaleutos	ἀσάλευτος	firm, immovable	**12:**159
aschēmoneō	ἀσχημονέω	to behave improperly	**10:**889
asebēs	ἀσεβής	godless, ungodly	**4:**57; **5:**460; **12:**485
aselgeia	ἀσέλγεια	lustful indulgence	**12:**485
Asidaioi	Ἀσιδαῖοι	Hasideans	**4:**47
askeō	ἀσκέω	to strive	**10:**320
asōtōs	ἀσώτως	debauched living	**9:**301
asphaleia	ἀσφάλεια	security	**11:**677
aspis	ἀσπίς	small round shield	**11:**461
assarion	ἀσσάριον	penny, "assarion"	**9:**171; **11:**401
asthenēs	ἀσθενής	weak, ill	**10:**745; **11:**140, 730–31
astheneia	ἀσθένεια	weakness, illness	**9:**273; **11:**294
astheneō	ἀσθενέω	to be weak, powerless	**11:**154
astocheō	ἀστοχέω	to miss the mark, go astray	**11:**845
astorgous	ἀστόργους	heartless	**10:**434
asynetous	ἀσυνέτους	foolish, senseless	**10:**434
asynthetous	ἀσυνθέτους	faithless, untrustworthy	**10:**434
ataktos	ἄτακτος	unruly, lazy	**11:**730–31, 765, 767–68
athanasia	ἀθανασία	immortality	**5:**437, 454
athanatos	ἀθάνατός	immortal	**5:**454, 469
atheoi en tou kosmou	ἄθεοι ἐν τοῦ κόσμου	without God in the world	**11:**403

Transliteration	Greek	English	Volume and Page
atheos	ἄθεος	without God	**11:**398, 403–4, 417
atheteō	ἀθετέω	to annul	**11:**263
atimos	ἄτιμος	without honor	**9:**107
atmis	ἀτμίς	breath	**5:**504
atopos	ἄτοπος	wrong, out of place	**9:**458; **10:**325
aulē	αὐλή	courtyard, castle	**6:**996; **8:**481, 715; **9:**242
aulizomai	αὐλίζομαι	to spend the night	**9:**412
autarkeia	αὐτάρκεια	contentment, self-sufficiency	**11:**828
autarkēs	αὐτάρκης	content, self-sufficient	**11:**543–44
authairetoi	αὐθαίρετοι	of their own free will	**11:**121
authenteō	αὐθεντέω	to have authority, domineer	**11:**801
autoi	αὐτοί	they	**9:**815
autois	αὐτοῖς	them	**10:**495
automoleō	αὐτομολέω	to desert	**4:**96
autos	αὐτός	he, himself	**8:**364
autos egō	αὐτὸς ἐγώ	I of myself	**10:**572, 628
autou	αὐτοῦ	here, in this place	**8:**476
autous	αὐτούς	them	**8:**456
auxano	αὐξάνω	to grow, cause to grow	**11:**591, 745
auxō	αὔξω	to grow, increase	**11:**402, 422
axioi eisin	ἄξιοί εἰσιν	they are worthy	**12:**676
axiopistos	ἀξιόπιστος	reliable	**5:**652
axios	ἄξιος	worthy	**12:**593
axios estin	ἄξιός ἐστιν	he is worthy	**9:**155

B

Transliteration	Greek	English	Volume and Page
badizete	βαδίζετε	walk, march	**6:**977
ballō	βάλλω	to throw	**12:**593, 630
baptismos	βαπτισμός	baptism, washing	**12:**71
baptizō	βαπτίζω	to baptize	**8:**157, 653
Barabbas	Βαραββᾶς	Barabbas	**8:**486
barbaros	βάρβαρος	barbarian, non-Greek	**4:**202; **10:**355–56, 358
baros	βάρος	weight, burden	**11:**699–700; **12:**581
barys	βαρύς	weighty, burdensome	**11:**140–41
basanizō	βασανίζω	to be put to the test	**5:**670; **8:**327; **12:**648
basanos	βάσανος	torment	**9:**318
basileia	βασιλεία	kingdom	**8:**374; **9:**817; **10:**741
basileia tou theou	βασιλεία τοῦ θεοῦ	Kingdom of God	**1:**175–80; **10:**15

Transliteration	Greek	English	Volume and Page
basileuō	βασιλεύω	to rule	**8:**289; **10:**524, 741; **12:**644
basileus	βασιλεύς	king	**5:**490; **9:**445, 816
basilikos	βασιλικός	royal, relating to the king	**12:**193
baskainō	βασκαίνω	to bewitch	**11:**250
bastazō	βαστάζω	to bear, help	**9:**773; **10:**745; **11:**332, 334–35
bathmon kalon	βαθμόν καλόν	good or excellent standing	**11:**807
batos	βάτος	bath (unit of liquid measurement)	**9:**308
battalogeō	βατταλογέω	to babble (?)	**8:**201
bdelygma erēmōseōs	βδέλυγμα ἐρημώσεως	desolating sacrilege	**4:**11
bebaioō	βεβαιόω	to make firm, establish	**10:**799–800
bebaios	βέβαιος	valid, binding	**12:**33–34, 81
bebaioteron	βεβαιότερον	more certain	**12:**342
bebēloō	βεβηλόω	to profane, desecrate	**10:**319
Beliar	βελιάρ	Satan, "worthlessness"	**11:**105
bēma	βῆμα	tribunal, seat	**10:**255, 325, 737; **11:**86
biazō	βιάζω	to force	**8:**268
biblaridion	βιβλαρίδιον	small book, scroll	**12:**638
biblion	βιβλίον	book	**4:**40; **6:**941; **12:**638
biblos	βίβλος	book	**6:**941; **8:**125; **12:**601
biblos geneseōs	βίβλος γενέσεως	book of genesis	**8:**125
biblos logōn	βίβλος λόγων	the book of the deeds	**3:**992
bios	βίος	life	**9:**301, 303; **12:**401, 447
biōtika	βιωτικά	ordinary matters	**10:**854, 857
blasphēmeō	βλασφημέω	to blaspheme, deride	**8:**491; **9:**454, 458
blasphēmia	βλασφημία	blasphemy, slander	**8:**234; **11:**643; **12:**577
blepete ton Israēl kata sarka	βλέπετε τὸν Ισραὴλ κατὰ σάρκα	consider Israel according to the flesh	**10:**628
blepō	βλέπω	to see, see to it	**8:**694; **11:**524; **12:**49
Boanērges	Βοανηργές	sons of thunder	**8:**562; **9:**215
boaō	βοάω	to call, cry out	**9:**338
boētheō	βοηθέω	to help, rescue	**10:**227
Bosor	Βοσόρ	Bosor	**12:**351
Bougaion	Βουγαῖον	Bougaion	**3:**894, 951
boulē	βουλή	plan, purpose	**4:**118; **10:**283
boulēma	βούλημα	intention, purpose	**12:**300–301

Transliteration	Greek	English	Volume and Page
bouleuomai	βουλεύομαι	to consider, consult	**4**:118; **9**:698
boulomai	βούλομαι	to want, desire	**11**:48
brachyti	βραχύτι	a little	**12**:37
brephos	βρέφος	infant, child	**9**:344
brochos	βρόχος	yoke, noose	**10**:887
brō sis	βρῶσις	food, eating	**8**:210; **9**:569
byblos	βυβλός	papyrus	**6**:941

C

chaire	χαῖρε	greetings (a salutation)	**10**:380
chairein	χαίρειν	greetings (a salutation)	**11**:202, 522, 790; **12**:247
chairete	χαίρετε	greetings (a salutation)	**11**:522
chairō	χάιρω	to rejoice	**3**:1065; **8**:477, 500; **9**:357; **11**:178, 483, 514, 543; **12**:695
chalkos	χαλκός	copper	**9**:171
chara	χαρά	joy	**3**:1065; **11**:483, 536
charagma	χάραγμα	mark, stamp	**12**:658
charis	χάρις	grace	**5**:15, 673; **9**:73, 517, 523; **10**:96, 176, 326, 380, 612, 996; **11**:53, 57, 114, 118–19, 131, 202, 244, 266, 356, 370, 420, 497, 790, 794, 841; **12**:173, 247, 257, 281, 411, 450
charis megalē	χάρις μεγάλη	great grace	**10**:98
charis tou theou	χάρις τοῦ θεοῦ	grace of God	**10**:176
charisma	χάρισμα	gift	**2**:103, 111; **10**:524, 693, 710, 787, 799, 830, 940–41, 943–45, 949, 951; **11**:27, 43, 143
charismata ta meizona	χαρίσματα τὰ μείζονα	the greater gifts	**10**:949
chariti theou	χάριτι θεοῦ	by the grace of God	**12**:38
charizomai	χαρίζομαι	to give freely, hand over	**10**:326, 612; **11**:53, 265, 430, 497
cheir	χείρ	hand	**7**:188
cheirographon	χειρόγραφον	a written document	**11**:625
cheiropoiē tos	χειροποίητος	idol	**7**:188

Transliteration	**Greek**	**English**	**Volume and Page**
cheirotoneō	χειροτονέω	to elect by raising a hand	**11:**126
chērai	χῆραι	widows	**10:**874
chi	Χ	chi (Greek letter)	**3:**1084, 1104; **5:**607
chilia	χίλια	thousand	**12:**707, 709
chitōn	χιτών	tunic	**8:**194; **9:**831
chora	χώρα	country	**4:**113
chōreō	χωρέω	to permeate	**5:**504; **11:**101, 106
chōris ergōn nomou	χωρὶς ἔργων νόμου	apart from works of the law	**10:**658
chōris nomou	χωρὶς νόμου	apart from the law	**10:**495, 658
chōris theou	χωρὶς θεοῦ	apart from God	**12:**38
chōrizō	χωρίζω	to separate, part	**10:**875
chortazō	χορτάζω	to eat	**9:**316
chreia	χρεία	necessity, need	**5:**674; **8:**57, 169, 547; **11:**545
chrēmatismos	χρηματισμός	a dream oracle	**8:**25; **10:**676
chrēmatizō	χρηματίζω	to impart a revelation	**10:**164; **12:**97
chrēstos	χρηστός	kind	**5:**561
chrēstotēs	χρηστότης	kindness	**10:**642, 686
chriō	χρίω	to anoint	**8:**466; **12:**587
chrisma	χρῖσμα	an anointing	**12:**406–7
christianos	Χριστιανός	Christian	**8:**526; **12:**311
Christos	Χριστός	Christ, anointed one	**4:**673; **8:**46, 357; **9:**199, 445, 531; **10:**415, 535; **11:**264, 375, 490, 688; **12:**406, 435, 707
christos kyrios	χριστὸς κύριος	the Messiah, the Lord	**9:**17
Christos peri hamartiōn apethanen	Χριστὸς περι ἁμαρτιῶν απέθανεν	Christ died for sins	**12:**292
Christos peri hamartion epathen	Χριστὸς περι ἁμαρτιῶν ἔπαθεν	Christ suffered for sins	**12:**292
Christou einai	Χριστοῦ ἔιναι	to be of Christ	**11:**140
chronizō	χρονίζω	to delay	**9:**264
chronōn apokatastaseōs pantōn	χρόνων ἀποκαταστάσεως πάντων	time of universal restoration	**10:**82
chronos	χρόνος	time (ordinary)	**1:**179; **5:**672; **10:**82–83; **12:**105, 311, 638

Transliteration	Greek	English	Volume and Page
D			
daimōn	δαίμων	demonic	**9:**644
daimones	δαίμονες	demons, intermediate beings	**8:**23
daimonion	δαιμόνιον	demon	**9:**619; **11:**390
dapanaō	δαπανάω	to spend freely	**11:**170
dapanēma	δαπάνημα	money spent, expense	**4:**270
de	δέ	connective particle, and, now	**6:**987; **8:**134, 154; **9:**422; **10:**138, 584, 600; **12:**73, 100
dechomai	δέχομαι	to receive, accept	**10:**820; **11:**693
dei	δεῖ	it is necessary	**8:**349, 625, 688; **9:**20, 201, 331, 358, 558, 565; **10:**18, 49, 51, 90, 137, 152, 200, 207, 238, 270, 273, 285, 311, 349, 989; **11:**808
deiknymi	δείκνυμι	to show, teach	**3:**1064; **8:**349
deiknyō	δεικνύω	to show, teach	**8:**349
deilia	δειλία	cowardice	**8:**22
deiliatō	δειλιάτω	to be a coward	**9:**751
deipnon	δεῖπνον	dinner	**9:**701
deisidaimonesteros	δεισιδαιμονέστερος	extremely religious	**10:**246
deisidaimonia	δεισιδαιμονία	religiosity, superstition	**8:**22; **10:**329, 335
dekamēniaios	δεκαμηνιαῖος	pregnant, in the tenth month	**5:**497
dektos	δεκτός	accepted, welcome	**9:**107
dēmos	δῆμος	populace, citizens' assembly	**3:**1114; **4:**107, 163, 269–70; **10:**239
dēnarion	δηνάριον	denarius	**9:**171
deomai	δέομαι	to pray	**9:**410; **11:**137
deos	δέος	awe	**12:**160
derō	δέρω	to beat	**9:**381, 440
desmios	δέσμιος	prisoner	**11:**891
desmos	δέσμος	bond, fetter	**11:**420
desmōtēs	δεσμώτης	prisoner	**6:**944
Despota	Δέσποτα	Sovereign Lord	**10:**92
despotēs	δεσπότης	master	**3:**1009, 1042; **5:**659; **12:**280, 345, 485, 613
deuteran charin	δευτέραν χάριν	double favor	**11:**48
deuteron	δεύτερον	a second time	**12:**695

Transliteration	Greek	English	Volume and Page
dexion keras	δεξιὸν κέρας	the right wing, "the right horn"	**4:**109
di 'hypomonēs	δἰ ὑπομονῆς	through patience	**10:**598
dia	διά	through, because of	**10:**200, 268, 503, 613; **11:**97, 528
dia Iēsoun	διὰ Ἰησοῦν	for Jesus' sake	**11:**81
dia pantos	διὰ παντὸς	continually, forever	**10:**678
dia pisteōs Iēsou Christou	διὰ πίστεως Ἰησοῦ Χριστοῦ	through the faith of (or in) Jesus Christ	**11:**236, 239–40
dia ton laon	διὰ τὸν λαόν	because of the people	**10:**91
dia tou haimatos tou idiou	διὰ τοῦ αἵματος του ἰδίου	with his own blood	**10:**284
dia touto	διὰ τοῦτο	therefore, for this reason	**9:**258, 671; **10:**497, 523; **11:**73
diabolos	διάβολος	devil	**11:**356, 806–7; **12:**577, 650
diadochos	διάδοχος	deputy, substitute	**4:**289
diaginōskō	διαγινώσκω	to examine, determine	**10:**312
diagongyzō	διαγογγύζω	to murmur, grumble	**9:**295, 358
diaireō	διαιρέω	to distribute, divide	**10:**943
diairesis	διαίρεσις	division, allotment	**10:**943
diaitēma	διαίτημα	mode, rule of life	**4:**270
diakatelegchomai	διακατελέγχομαι	to powerfully refute	**10:**261
diakoneō	διακονέω	to serve, minister to	**8:**456; **9:**232, 425; **11:**63, 114; **12:**77
diakonia	διακονία	service, "table service"	**8:**45; **9:**231; **10:**292, 944, 1000–1001; **11:**63, 65–66, 114, 118, 131, 150, 156; **12:**581
diakonia tou thanatou	διακονία τοῦ θανάτου	that brought death	**11:**66
diakonoi Christou	διάκονοι Χριστοῦ	ministers of Christ	**11:**17, 156
diakonoi dikaiosynēs	διάκονοι δικαιοσύνης	ministers of righteousness	**11:**151
diakonos	διάκονος	deacon, servant, "table servant"	**8:**398, 432; **9:**425; **10:**719, 721, 761, 827–28; **11:**97, 151, 156, 241, 359, 409, 480–81, 592, 806, 812
diakrinō	διακρίνω	to decide between, hesitate	**10:**168, 209, 900; **12:**497

Transliteration	Greek	English	Volume and Page
diakrinōn to sōma	διακρίνων τὸ σῶμα	discerning the body	**10:**936
diakrisis	διάκρισις	discernment, judgment	**10:**735
dialegomai	διαλέγομαι	to argue	**10:**238, 244, 258, 277
dialogismos	διαλογισμός	debate, argument	**9:**211; **10:**735; **11:**512
dialogizomai	διαλογίζομαι	to debate	**9:**211
diamartyromai	διαμαρτύρομαι	to declare solemnly and emphatically	**10:**166; **11:**700, 719
dianoia	διάνοια	mind, intellect	**9:**227
dianoigō	διανοίγω	to open, explain	**9:**480, 486; **10:**238
diaphtheirō	διαφθείρω	to destroy, ruin	**11:**83; **12:**644
diaponeomai	διαπονέομαι	to be disturbed, annoyed	**10:**84
diaporeō	διαπορέω	to be perplexed	**10:**105
diasōzō	διασώζω	to save, rescue	**10:**353
diastrephō	διαστρέφω	to pervert	**9:**447
diatassō	διατάσσω	to arrange, order, direct	**11:**264, 267
diathēkē	διαθήκη	testament, covenant	**1:**17; **10:**646; **11:**263, 264; **12:**92, 109
diathēkēs hagias	διαθήκης ἁγίας	holy covenant	**4:**32
didachē	διδαχή	teaching	**7:**662; **8:**220; **9:**201; **12:**376, 454
didaskalia	διδασκαλία	teaching	**11:**850
didaskalos	διδάσκαλος	teacher	**9:**346, 531, 628; **11:**360, 422; **12:**68
didaskō	διδάσκω	to instruct, teach	**8:**501; **10:**367; **11:**801
didaskontes kai nouthetountes	διδάσκοντες καὶ νουθετοῦντες	teaching and admonishing	**11:**649
didōmi	δίδωμι	to give	**9:**386, 420, 552, 603; **10:**107, 193; **11:**125, 244, 269, 749; **12:**594, 657, 676
didrachmon	δίδραχμον	two drachma	**9:**171
Didymos	Δίδυμος	Thomas, "twin"	**9:**687
diecheirisasthe	διεχειρίσασθε	you had killed	**10:**106
dieilen ton laon	διεῖλεν τὸν λάον	he divided the people	**4:**174
diēkō	διήκω	to pervade	**5:**504
diermēneuō	διερμηνεύω	to interpret	**9:**480
dikaiōma	δικαίωμα	decree, righteous deed	**10:**434, 524, 529, 574, 577, 580

Transliteration	Greek	English	Volume and Page
dikaiōma tou nomou	δικαίωμα τοῦ νόμου	righteous verdict of the law	**10:**577
dikaioō	δικαιόω	to make right, justify	**9:**167, 312; **10:**459, 540; **11:**237–38, 241, 313
dikaios	δίκαιος	righteous	**3:**984; **4:**268; **8:**134, 393; **9:**29, 45, 458, 461, 477, 772; **10:**129, 647; **11:**238, 749, 871; **12:**223, 386, 388, 418, 422
dikaiōs	δικαίως	rightly	**9:**458; **10:**459; **11:**528
dikaiōsis	δικαίωσις	justification	**10:**459, 524, 529, 580
dikaiosynē	δικαιοσύνη	righteousness, justice	**3:**993, 1003, 1064; **5:**453, 469; **8:**179, 196, 200, 211; **9:**772; **10:**190, 322, 399, 404, 459, 524, 646–47, 654, 702, 815, 855; **11:**96, 130, 238, 241, 246, 313, 485, 528; **12:**410, 412
dikaiosynē tēs pisteōs	δικαιοσύνη τῆς πίστεως	righteousness of faith	**10:**700
dikaiosynē theou	δικαιοσύνη θεοῦ	the righteousness of God	**10:**398, 403, 453, 465, 482, 575, 621, 625, 638, 646, 652, 654–55
dikastai	δικασταί	judges	**5:**490
dikē	δίκη	just penalty	**5:**559; **11:**749
diktyon	δίκτυον	fishing net	**9:**116
dio	διό	therefore	**10:**219, 746; **11:**82, 83, 106, 167, 897
dio legei	διὸ λέγει	therefore it says	**11:**356
diodeuō	διοδεύω	to travel, go through	**9:**174
diōgmos	διωγμός	persecution	**10:**196; **11:**745
diōkō	διώκω	to persecute	**9:**400
dioper	διόπερ	therefore, for this reason	**10:**918
dioti	διότι	for, because	**10:**458, 582
dipsaō	διψάω	to be thirsty	**9:**832
distazō	διστάζω	to doubt, "have two minds"	**8:**180, 210, 328–29, 502

Transliteration	**Greek**	**English**	**Volume and Page**
dogma	δόγμα	decree, command	**11:**625
dokein	δοκεῖν	to seem	**12:**373
dokimazō	δοκιμάζω	to test	**11:**123, 176, 437
dokimē	δοκιμή	trial, ordeal	**11:**53, 123, 131, 175–76
dokimos	δόκιμος	genuine, reliable	**10:**937; **11:**97, 123, 144, 844
doloō	δολόω	to adulterate, falsify	**11:**73
dolos	δόλος	deceit	**10:**190
dōmen dexias	δῶμεν δεξιάς	let us come to terms, "give the right (i.e., good) hand"	**4:**91
dōrea	δωρεά	free gift	**5:**775; **10:**524; **11:**131, 245
dorean	δωρεάν	freely	**11:**150, 245
dōrēma	δώρημα	free gift	**10:**524
doulagōgeō	δουλαγωγέω	to enslave, bring into subjection	**10:**909
douleuō	δουλεύω	to serve as a slave	**10:**560; **11:**321, 519, 658, 694–96
douloi tēs phthoras	δοῦλοι τῆς φθορᾶς	slaves of corruption	**12:**352
doulos	δοῦlovς	slave, servant	**5:**463; **8:**398; **9:**264; **10:**80; **11:**74, 95, 207, 480, 503, 519, 695; **12:**186, 333, 481, 581, 619
doulos Christou	δοῦλος Χριστοῦ	servant of Christ	**11:**592
Doulos kyriou	Δοῦλος κυρίου	Servant of the Lord	**7:**498
doulos mou	δοῦλος μου	my servant	**10:**64
doxa	δόξα	glory	**5:**15, 504, 667, 673; **9:**287, 522, 790, 795; **11:**66–67, 118, 381, 411, 416, 499, 536; **12:**593, 724
doxazō	δοξάζω	to glorify	**9:**29, 462, 522, 732, 790; **10:**80
drachmē	δραχμή	drachma	**9:**171
drakōn	δράκων	dragon	**3:**948; **7:**192
drosos	δρόσος	dew	**7:**164
dynamai	δύναμαι	to be able	**10:**736
dynamis	δύναμις	power, mighty act	**5:**504; **8:**62, 246, 480;

Transliteration	Greek	English	Volume and Page
			9:227, 488; **10:**42, 96; **11:**168, 253, 383, 409; **12:**589, 594
dynamis tou theou	δύναμις τοῦ θεου	power of God	**10:**138
dynastēs	δυνάστης	sovereign	**4:**209
dynatoi	δυνατοί	nobles, "the powerful"	**6:**943
dynatos	δυνατός	powerful, mighty	**10:**814

E

Transliteration	Greek	English	Volume and Page
ē	ἤ	or	**9:**294
ean	ἐάν	if, when	**8:**378; **11:**206
ebrychon tous odontas	ἔβρυχον τοὺς ὀδόντας	ground their teeth	**10:**130
echei polyn ponon	ἔχει πολύν πόνον	he is working hard	**11:**667
echō	ἔχω	to have, hold	**10:**258, 515; **11:**50, 71, 373; **12:**166, 356
echōmen charin	ἔχωμεν χάριν	we give thanks	**12:**159
echomen tēn prosagōgēn	ἔχομεν τὴν προσαγωγὴν	we gain access	**11:**401
egeirō	ἐγείρω	to rise up	**8:**591; **9:**468, 481, 544; **10:**192
egenēthēte engys	ἐγενὴθητε ἐγγὺς	come near, approach	**11:**398–99
egeneto de	ἐγένετο δέ	and it came to pass	**9:**133, 137
eggiken	ἤγγικεν	has drawn near	**1:**179
egkainizō	ἐγκαινίζω	to dedicate, renew	**4:**71
egkataleipō	ἐγκαταλείπω	to forsake, abandon	**11:**857
egkrateia psychēs	ἐγκράτεια ψυχής	self-control of the disposition	**5:**735
egkrinō	ἐγκρίνω	to reckon, classify with	**11:**143
egō	ἐγώ	I	**8:**226
egō eimi	ἐγώ εἰμι	I am	**9:**399–400, 443, 527, 596, 601, 634–35, 646, 726, 742, 756, 802, 808
egō ouk eimi	ἐγὼ οὐκ εἰμι	I am not	**9:**527
ei	εἰ	if	**8:**163; **10:**973; **11:**206
ei de	εἰ δέ	but if	**10:**683
ei de tis lelypeken	εἰ δέ τις λελύπηκεν	if someone has caused pain	**11:**52
ei katechete	εἰ κατέχετε	if you remember, hold fast to	**10:**975
ei mē	εἰ μή	unless, except	**10:**973

Transliteration	Greek	English	Volume and Page
ei tis thelei opisō mou elthein	εἴ τις θέλει ὀπίσω μου ἐλθεῖν	if anyone would follow me	**8:**350
eidō	εἴδω	to know	**5:**563; **11:**84, 237, 436, 687, 730; **12:**442
eidōla	εἴδωλα	idols	**6:**1010
eidōlothytōs	εἰδωλόθυτος	sacrificed to an idol	**10:**221, 778, 893
eikē	εἰκῆ	at random, in vain	**11:**289
eikōn	εἰκών	likeness, form, stamp	**10:**988; **11:**70, 74, 429, 504, 597
eikōn tou theou	εἰκών τοῦ θεοῦ	image/reflection of God	**11:**74
eilikrineia	εἰλικρίνεια	sincerity, integrity	**10:**848; **11:**45, 59
eilikrinēs dianoia	εἰλικρινής διανοία	sincere intention	**12:**355
eimi	εἰμί	to be	**10:**582, 709; **11:**167, 602
eipen martyrēsas	εἶπεν μαρτυρήσας	provided testimony	**10:**192
eiper	εἴπερ	if after all	**10:**584; **11:**749
eirēnē	εἰρήνη	peace	**9:**71, 372, 751; **10:**380; **11:**202, 370, 396, 420, 790; **12:**247, 450, 612
eirēneuō	εἰρηνεύω	to live at peace, keep peace	**11:**179
eirēnikos	εἰρηνικός	peaceful	**1:**1023
eirēnopoieō	εἰρηνοποιέω	to make peace	**11:**600
eirōn	εἴρων	ignorance	**9:**477
eis	εἰς	for, to, into	**10:**68, 768; **11:**269–70, 392; **12:**264, 267
eis allēlous kai eis pantas	εἰς ἀλλήλους καί εἰς πάντας	for one another and for all	**11:**720, 731
eis andra telion	εἰς ἄνδρα τέλιον	maturity, perfect man	**11:**422
eis apantēsin	εἰς ἀπάντησιν	to meet	**8:**450
eis auton	εἰς αὐτόν	in him	**11:**373
eis cheimona	εἰς χειμῶνα	for the winter	**5:**742
eis chōma	εἰς χῶμα	for a tomb	**5:**742
eis diakonian	εἰς διακονίαν	to/for service	**10:**1000
eis dikaiosynēn	εἰς δικαιοσύνην	for vindication	**10:**665
eis hēmas	εἰς ἡμᾶς	toward us, into us	**10:**595
eis hēmas tous pisteuontas	εἰς ἡμάς τούς πιστεύοντας	for us who believe	**11:**382
eis hous	εἰς οὕς	to whom	**10:**338

Transliteration	Greek	English	Volume and Page
eis huious kai thygateras	εἰς υἱοὺς καὶ θυγατέρας	for/as sons and daughters	**11:**106
eis kenon	εἰς κενόν	in vain	**11:**96, 711
eis metanoian	εἰς μετάνοιαν	to repentance	**11:**109
eis psychēn zōsan	εἰς ψυχὴν ζῶσαν	a living being	**10:**988
eis Rōmē	εἰς Ῥώμη	into Rome	**10:**357
eis ta idia	εἰς τὰ ἴδια	to his own home	**9:**832
eis telos	εἰς τέλος	to the end, the full extent	**9:**721; **11:**704
eis tēn emēn anamnēsin	εἰς τὴν ἐμὴν ἀνάμνησιν	for my remembrance	**8:**471
eis tēn Rhōmēn	εἰς τὴν Ῥώμην	into Rome	**10:**357
eis ton aiōna	εἰς τὸν αἰῶνα	forever	**9:**638; **12:**450
eis ton esō anthrōpon	εἰς τὸν ἔσω ἄνθρωπον	inner being	**11:**414
eis tous ptōchous tōn hagiōn	εἰς τοὺς πτωχοὺς τῶν ἁγίων	the poor who are among the saints	**11:**114
eiserchomai	εἰσέρχομαι	to enter	**9:**801
eisodos	εἴσοδος	entrance, welcome	**11:**698
ek	ἐκ	out of, by means of	**9:**309; **11:**59, 256
ek pisteōs	ἐκ πίστεως	by faith	**11:**259, 268, 270–71, 314
ek pisteōs Iēsou Christou	ἐκ πίστεως Ἰησοῦ Χριστοῦ	through faith in/of Jesus Christ	**11:**269
ek tōn katō	ἐκ τῶν κάτω	from below	**9:**634
ek tou kosmou	ἐκ τοῦ κόσμου	of the world	**12:**427
ek tou spermatos tēs patrias hēmōn	ἐκ τοῦ σπέρματος τῆς πατριᾶς ἡμων	out of my family	**3:**1016
ekballō	ἐκβάλλω	to drive away, cast out	**8:**545; **9:**660; **12:**464
ekdapanaomai	ἐκδαπάνομαι	to be spent, give one self	**11:**170
ekdēmeō	ἐκδημέω	to leave one's country, be absent	**11:**85–86
ekdiēgeomai	ἐκδιηγέομαι	to tell, recount	**10:**193, 206
ekdikeō	ἐκδικέω	to avenge, get justice for	**10:**714
ekdikēsis	ἐκδίκησις	vengeance	**4:**92; **11:**749
ekkleiō	ἐκκλείω	to shut out, exclude	**10:**480; **11:**295
ekklēsia	ἐκκλησία	assembly, church	**4:**77; **5:**268; **8:**102, 346, 378; **11:**179, 358–59, 383, 575, 599, 688–89, 809; **12:**12, 180, 222, 449, 463, 585

Transliteration	Greek	English	Volume and Page
Ekklēsiastēs	Ἐκκλησιαστής	one who leads a congregation	**5:**268
ekklinō	ἐκκλίνω	to turn away	**4:**89
eklegomai	ἐκλέγομαι	to choose, elect	**9:**137, 611; **10:**208
ekleipō	ἐκλείπω	to fail	**9:**460
eklektos	ἐκλεκτός	chosen, elected	**8:**418; **9:**338; **12:**247, 682
eklogē	ἐκλογή	what is chosen	**10:**152, 676; **12:**337
ekmassō	ἐκμάσσω	to wipe	**9:**701
ekmyktērizō	ἐκμυκτηρίζω	to ridicule	**9:**312, 454–56
ekomisanto	ἐκομίσαντο	recover	**4:**257
ekpeirazō	ἐκπειράζω	to put to the test, tempt	**9:**227
ekplēssomai	ἐκπλήσσομαι	to be amazed	**8:**220
ekpneō	ἐκπνέω	to breathe out, expire	**9:**461
ekporeuomai	ἐκπορεύομαι	to go out from	**9:**764
ekptyō	ἐκπτύω	to spit	**11:**294
ekrina de emautō touto	ἔκρινα δὲ ἐμαυτῷ τοῦτο	I made up my mind	**11:**48
ekrizoō	ἐκριζόω	to uproot, raze	**4:**80
ekstasis	ἔκστασις	ecstacy, trance	**7:**496; **10:**78, 163
ektenesteron proseuchomai	ἐκτενέστερον προσεύχομαι	to pray earnestly	**9:**433
ektithēmi	ἐκτίθημι	to abandon, explain	**10:**168, 361
ektos	ἐκτός	besides, as well	**4:**280
ektrephō	ἐκτρέφω	to feed, nourish	**11:**451
ekzētēsai dikaia	ἐκζητῆσαι δίκαια	seek just peace terms	**4:**92
ekzētōn	ἐκζητῶν	watching over	**6:**994
elachistos	ἐλάχιστος	smallest least	**11:**409
elaphros	ἐλαφρός	slight, insignificant	**11:**83
eleēmōn	ἐλεήμων	charitable, merciful	**3:**984; **8:**179
eleēmosynē	ελεημοσυνη	charity, almsgiving	**3:**993, 995, 1003, 1015–16, 1064; **5:**660
eleeō	ἐλεέω	to have mercy	**3:**1064; **10:**639
elegchō	ἐλέγχω	to expose, convict	**9:**772; **11:**437, 823
elegchos	ἔλεγχος	a means of proof	**12:**131
elegmos	ἐλεγμός	schooling, reproof	**11:**852
elegxei . . . peri	ἐλέγξει . . . περὶ	will expose . . . concerning	**9:**772
eleos	ἔλεος	mercy	**4:**51, 174; **5:**654; **6:**956; **7:**163; **10:**639, 703; **11:**790, 876; **12:**450

Transliteration	Greek	English	Volume and Page
eleuthera	ἐλευθέρα	free woman	**11**:304
eleutheroō	ἐλευθερόω	to make free, liberate	**9**:637
ēli	ἠλί	my God (from Hebrew)	**8**:492
Elias	Ἠλίας	Elijah	**8**:492
ēlisgēsamen autous	ἠλισγησαμεν αὐτους	we polluted it	**7**:860
elpis	ἐλπίς	hope	**5**:654; **10**:335; **11**:385, 573
elpizō	ἐλπίζω	to hope	**11**:902; **12**:257
emathete ton Christon	ἐμάθετε τὸν Χριστόν	you learned Christ	**11**:428
embateuō	ἐμβατεύω	to step in, stand on	**11**:564
embrimaomai	ἐμβριμάομαι	to openly express anger	**8**:545; **9**:690–91
empaiktēs	ἐμπαίκτης	mocker, scoffer	**12**:355, 496
empaizō	ἐμπαίζω	to mock	**9**:454, 456
emperipateō	ἐμπεριπατέω	to walk about, live among	**11**:106
emphanizō kata	ἐμφάνιζω κατά	to make known against	**10**:325
emphobos	ἔμφοβος	afraid, frightened	**10**:322
emphysaō	ἐμφυσάω	to breathe	**9**:846
empimplēmi	ἐμπίμπλημι	to fill, satisfy, enjoy	**5**:485
en	ἐν	in	**4**:163; **8**:424; **10**:768; **11**:59, 97, 157, 392, 401, 590, 615, 689
en agapē	ἐν ἀγάπη	in love	**11**:373
en agōnia	ἐν ἀγωνιᾳ	in anguish	**9**:433
en alētheia	ἐν ἀληθεία	in truth	**11**:591
en aphtharsia	ἐν ἀφθαρσία	in incorruptibility	**11**:465
en autō	ἐν αὐτῶ	in him	**10**:247; **12**:389
en autō tō kairō	ἐν αὐτῶ τῶ καιρῶ	at that very time	**3**:1007
en cheiri angelou autou	ἐν χειρὶ ἀγγέλου αὐτοῦ	at the hand of his messenger	**7**:852
en Christō	ἐν Χριστῷ	in Christ	**11**:488
en ekeinō tō kairō	ἐν ἐκείνῳ τῳκαιρῷ	at that time	**8**:276
en emoi	ἐν ἐμοί	because of me, in me	**8**:474; **11**:215
en Ephesō	ἐν Εφέσω	in Ephesus	**11**:352, 369
en epignōsei	ἐν ἐπιγνώσει	come to know	**11**:380
en epithymiais sarkos aselgeiais	ἐν ἐπιθυμίαις σαρκὸς ἀσελγείαις	by licentious desires of the flesh	**12**:352
en heni pneumati	ἐν ἑνὶ πνεύματι	in one Spirit	**11**:401
en hō	ἐν ὧ	in whom	**11**:372, 624; **12**:293

Transliteration	Greek	English	Volume and Page
en hō krazomen abba ho patēr	ἐν ᾧ κράζομεν αββα ὁ πατήρ	whereby we cry, Abba, Father	**10:**593
en homoiōmati anthrōpōn	ἐν ὁμοιώματι ἀνθρώπων	in the likeness of humans	**10:**578; **11:**509
en hymin	ἐν ὑμῖν	in you, among you	**10:**844–46, 965–66; **11:**296, 507
en kainotēti zōēs	ἐν καινότητι ζωῆς	in newness of life	**11:**93
en kairō	ἐν καιρῷ	at the proper time	**9:**264
en kairō chreias dounai apokrisin	ἐν καιρῷ χρείας δοῦναι ἀπόκρισιν	to give answer in time of need	**5:**674
en lypē	ἐν λύπῃ	in pain	**11:**48, 50
en morphē theou	ἐν μορφῇ θεοῦ	in the form of God	**11:**504–6
en nomō	ἐν νόμῳ	in, by the Law	**11:**268
en ōsin	ἐν ὠσίν	with ears	**10:**63
en ouranois	ἐν οὐρανοῖς	in the heavens	**11:**356
en panti	ἐν παντὶ	in everything	**11:**109, 450
en panti pantote pasan	ἐν παντὶ πάντοτε πᾶσαν	all things in all times	**11:**130
en panti topō	ἐν παντὶ τόπω	in every place	**11:**57
en parabolais	ἐν παραβολαῖς	in parables	**8:**564
en parabolē	ἐν παραβολή	figuratively, "in a parable"	**12:**138
en pasē eulogia pneumatikē	ἐν πάσῃ εὐλογία πνευματικῇ	with every spiritual blessing	**11:**372
en plērophoria pollē	ἐν πληροφορία πολλῇ	with full conviction	**11:**698
en pneumati	ἐν πνεύματι	in the Spirit	**11:**396
en prosōpō Christou	ἐν προσώπῳ Χριστοῦ	in the face/presence of Christ	**11:**54, 75
en sarki	ἐν σαρκὶ	in the flesh	**11:**137, 397; **12:**426
en tais eisodois autēs	ἐν ταί εἴσοδοίς αυτής	in her entrances	**5:**719
en tais eschatais hēmerais	ἐν ταῖς ἐσχάταις ἡμέραις	in the last days	**10:**64
en tais kardiais hymōn	ἐν ταῖς καρδίαις ὑμῶν	in your hearts	**11:**414
en tē eschatē hēmera	ἐν τῇ ἐσχάτῃ ἡμέρᾳ	on the last day	**9:**688
en tē haplotēti hēmōn	ἐν τῇ ἁπλότητι ἡμῶν	in their innocence	**4:**46
en tē hēmera ekeinē	ἐν τῇ ἡμέρα ἐκείνῃ	on that day	**3:**1007; **10:**218

Transliteration	Greek	English	Volume and Page
en tē hēmera tautē	ἐν τῇ ἡμέρα ταύτῃ	on the same day	**3:**1007
en tē hēmera tē ponēra	ἐν τῇ ἡμέρα τῇ πονηρᾷ	that evil day	**11:**461
en tē hodō	ἐν τῇ ὁδῷ	on the way	**1:**178
en thlypsei pollē	ἐν θλίψει πολλῇ	in great persecution	**11:**698
en tō ēgapēmenō	ἐν τῷ ἠγαπημένω	in the Beloved	**11:**373
en tō hyiō	ἐν τῷ υἱω	in the Son	**12:**389
en tō kairō	ἐν τῷ καιρῷ	at the time when	**6:**942
en tō kosmō	ἐν τῷ κόσμω	in the world	**11:**45
en tō kosmō . . . phthoras	ἐν τῷ κόσμω . . . φθορᾶς	corruption in the world	**12:**352
en tō onomati tou Kyriou Iēsou	ἐν τῷ ὀνόματι τοῦ κυρίου Ἰησοῦ	in the name of the Lord Jesus	**10:**844, 856
en tō tritō etei	ἐν τῷ τρίτω ἔτει	the third year	**3:**994
en tois aiōsin tois eperchomenois	ἐν τοῖς αἰῶσιν τοῖς ἐπερχομένοις	in the ages to come	**11:**392
en tois epouraniois	ἐν τοῖς ἐπουρανίοις	in heavenly places	**11:**356
en tois Toubiou	ἐν τοῖς Τουβίου	land of Tobiani	**4:**276
en toutō	ἐν τούτω	by this	**12:**389
enantion	ἐναντίον	before, in the presence of	**9:**477
endeigma	ἔνδειγμα	evidence	**11:**748
endeiknymai	ἐνδείκνυμαι	to show	**11:**392
endeixis	ἔνδειξις	proof, evidence	**11:**126, 497
endēmeō	ἐνδημέω	to be at home, in one's own land	**11:**85
endēmēsai pros ton kyrion	ἐνδημῆσαι πρὸς τὸν κύριον	be at home with the Lord	**11:**86
endikos	ἔνδικος	fair, just	**12:**34
endyō	ἐνδύω	to clothe, put on	**11:**461, 648, 727
enedreuō	ἐνεδρεύω	to lie in wait, ambush	**5:**462
enedynamōthē tē pistei	ἐνεδυναμώθη τῇ πίστει	he grew strong in faith	**10:**742
enepyrisan	ἐνεπύριοαν	was burned	**4:**190
energeia	ἐνέργεια	action, operation, energy	**5:**504; **11:**423, 616
energēma	ἐνέργημα	activity, work	**10:**944; **11:**226
energeō	ἐνεργέω	to work, operate	**11:**226, 318, 512, 730
eneulogēthēsontai	ἐνευλογηθήσονται	will bless themselves	**10:**83
engizō	ἐγγίζω	to draw near	**9:**367
engyos	ἔγγυος	surety, guarantee	**12:**92

Transliteration	Greek	English	Volume and Page
engys sou to rhēma estin	ἐγγύς σου τὸ ῥῆμα ἐζτιν	the word is near you	**10:**668
eni sōmati	ἐνὶ σώματι	one body	**11:**400
enischyō	ἐνισχύω	to strengthen	**9:**433
enistēmi	ἐνίστημι	to be present, be imminent	**11:**755
enkakeō	ἐγκακέω	to lose heart, despair	**11:**81, 83
enkrateia	ἐγκράτεια	self-control	**10:**322; **11:**328; **12:**337
enoikeō	ἐνοικέω	to dwell	**11:**106
enōtizomai	ἐνωτίζομαι	to listen	**10:**63
entellomai	ἐντέλλομαι	to command, direct	**10:**195
enteuthen	ἐντεῦθεν	from here, on our way	**9:**753
entolē	ἐντολή	order, instruction	**4:**222; **9:**732, 746
entos	ἐντός	among	**9:**329
entromos	ἔντρομος	trembling	**10:**234
entygchanō	ἐντυγχάνω	to intercede	**10:**676; **12:**92
enybrizō	ἐνυβρίζω	to outrage	**12:**123
enypniazomai	ἐνυπνιάζομαι	to dream	**12:**489
epagonizomai	ἐπαγωνίζομαι	to contend	**12:**484
epainos	ἔπαινος	praise, approval, recognition	**10:**834; **11:**486
epaischynomai	ἐπαισχύνομαι	to be ashamed	**11:**838
epangelia	ἐπαγγελία	promise	**10:**335; **11:**269; **12:**126
epangelma	ἐπάγγελμα	promise	**12:**352
eparrēsiasametha	ἐπαρρησιασάμεθα	having courage	**11:**698
epataxen	ἐπάταξεν	struck down	**4:**118
epechō	ἐπέχω	to hold on to	**11:**513
epēgagen	ἐπήγαγεν	brought up	**6:**974
epeita	ἔπειτα	then	**11:**222, 725
epelexen	ἐπέλεξεν	he picked	**4:**174
epepesen phobos	ἐπέπεσεν φόβος	fear fell	**10:**269
eperchomai	ἐπέρχομαι	to come along, appe ar	**11:**392
eperōtēma	ἐπερώτημα	appeal, pledge	**12:**295
epesen epi tēn koitēn kai egnō hoti apothnēskei	ἔπεσεν ἐπὶ τὴν κοίτην καὶ ἔγνω ὅτι ἀποθνῄσκει	to fall sick, "to fall on his bed, perceive/realize that he was dying"	**4:**31
epetaxen	ἐπέταξεν	placed	**4:**118
eph' hō	ἐφ᾿ ᾧ	inasmuch, because	**10:**526–27; **11:**533
ephapax	ἐφάπαξ	once, at once	**10:**541
ephēbeion	ἐφηβεῖον	body of youth (?)	**4:**216

Transliteration	Greek	English	Volume and Page
ephyteusen ampelōna	ἐφύτευσεν ἀμπελῶνα	planted a vineyard	**9**:380
epi	ἐπί	on, upon	**8**:248; **11**:862
epi tē pistei tou onomatos autou	ἐπὶ τῇ πίστει τοῦ ὀνόματος αὐτοῦ	by faith in his name	**10**:81
epi tō onomati Iēsou Christou	ἐπὶ τῷ ὀνόματῖ ʼΙησοῦ Χριστου	in the name of Jesus Christ	**10**:68
epi tō onomati touto	ἐπὶ τῷ ὀνόματι τούτῳ	in this name	**10**:90
epi tōn adikōn	ἐπὶ τῶν ἀδίκων	before the unrighteous	**10**:854
epiballō	ἐπιβάλλω	to arrest, "lay hands on"	**9**:400
epibareō	ἐπιβαρέω	to burden	**11**:700
epidiatassomai	ἐπιδιατάσσομαι	to add to	**11**:264, 267
epidiorthoō	ἐπιδιορθόω	to set right	**11**:864
epidontes	ἐπιδόντες	appended below	**4**:269
epieikeia	ἐπιείκεια	kindness, fairness	**6**:956; **11**:136
epieikēs	ἐπιεικής	kind, gentle	**11**:540
epiginōskō	ἐπιγινώσκω	to recognize, perceive	**9**:477; **11**:176; **12**:336
epignōsei pantos agathou	ἐπιγνώσει παντὸς ἀγαθοῦ	to perceive all the good	**11**:895
epignōsis	ἐπίγνωσις	knowledge	**12**:334, 336, 352
epignōsis hamartias	ἐπίγνωσις ἁμαρτίας	the knowledge of sin	**10**:562
epikataratos	ἐπικατάρατος	cursed	**11**:260
epikranen	ἐπίκρανεν	embittered	**4**:55
epilambanomai	ἐπιλαμβάνομαι	to arrest, accompany	**10**:245
epilanthanomai	ἐπιλάνθανομαι	to forget	**12**:163
epilysis	ἐπίλυσις	interpretation	**12**:343
epimenō	ἐπιμένω	to remain	**11**:491
epimixia	ἐπιμιξία	dealings, mixing with others	**4**:285–86
ēpios	ἤπιος	gentle	**11**:699, 846
epiousios	ἐπιούσιος	essential, daily (?)	**8**:204; **9**:234
epiphainō	ἐπιφαίνω	to appear	**11**:876
epiphaneia	ἐπιφάνεια	manifestation, epiphany	**4**:202, 290; **11**:759, 829, 836, 855
epiphanes	ἐπιφανές	glorious, spendid	**4**:290
ʼEpiphanēs theos	ʼΕπιφανής θεός	god manifest	**4**:38
epipotheō	ἐπιποθέω	to long for	**11**:520
episkēnoō	ἐπισκηνόω	to take up residence	**11**:167
episkeptomai	ἐπισκέπτομαι	to select, look favorably on	**10**:113, 218
episkopē	ἐπισκοπή	overseer, bishop	**11**:805

Transliteration	Greek	English	Volume and Page
episkopeō	ἐπισκοπέω	to be watchful, look out for	**12:**154
episkopos	ἐπίσκοπος	overseer, bishop	**10:**283; **11:**480–81, 864; **12:**315
epistamai	ἐπίσταμαι	to understand	**10:**269
epistatēs	ἐπιστάτης	master	**9:**183, 189, 326
epistēmē	ἐπιστήμη	understanding, knowledge	**5:**648; **6:**961, 966
epistērizō	ἐπιστηρίζω	to strengthen	**10:**221
epistolē	ἐπιστολή	letter, epistle	**6:**941; **12:**14
epistrephō	ἐπιστρέφω	to turn	**6:**969; **11:**69, 287, 695–96
episynagō	ἐπισυνάγω	gather, assemble	**4:**20
episystrepsai	ἐπισυστρέψαι	convene	**4:**165
epiteinō	ἐπιτείνω	to exert	**5:**578
epiteleō	ἐπιτελέω	to complete, finish	**11:**121
epithymeō	ἐπιθυμέω	to desire, long for	**12:**77
epithymia	ἐπιθυμία	desire, longing	**7:**178; **8:**425; **10:**433, 542; **11:**325; **12:**301, 352, 355, 694
epithymia kakē	ἐπιθυμία κάκη	evil desire	**11:**642
epitimaō	ἐπιτιμάω	to order, rebuke	**8:**399, 623–24; **9:**111, 200, 354, 458; **11:**855
epitimia	ἐπιτιμία	punishment	**11:**53
eplēsthēsan thambous kai ekstaseōs	ἐπλήσθησαν θάμβους καὶ ἐκστάσεως	filled with wonder and amazement	**10:**78
eplēthynthē ta kaka	ἐπληθύνθη τὰ κακά	misfortunes had increased	**4:**63
epouranioi	ἐπουράνιοι	heavenly places	**11:**372
eprathēsan tou poiēsai to ponēron	ἐπράθησαν τοῦ ποιῆσαι τὸ πονηρόν	sold themselves to do evil	**4:**32
eraunaō	ἐραυνάω	to search	**9:**624
erchesthō pros me	ἐρχέσθω πρός με	come to me	**9:**623
erchomai	ἔρχομαι	to come, go	**8:**186; **11:**750; **12:**438, 611
erēmia	ἐρημία	wilderness	**5:**584–85
erēmos topos	ἔρημος τόπος	uninhabited place	**8:**600
erēmōsis	ἐρήμωσις	desolation	**9:**404
erga nomou	ἔργα νόμου	works of the Law	**11:**239
ergazomai	ἐργάζομαι	to work	**9:**599; **11:**730, 768
ergois agathois	ἔργοις ἀγαθοῖς	good works	**11:**356
ergon	ἔργον	deed, work	**8:**265; **9:**586, 653,

Transliteration	Greek	English	Volume and Page
			676; **10:**194, 991; **11:**356, 392, 512, 730; **12:**198
ergon kalon	ἔργον καλόν	a good work	**8:**467
erōtaō	ἐρωτάω	to ask	**9:**780, 795; **11:**729
erregchen	ἔρρεγχεν	was snoring	**7:**496
ēsan tetagmēnoi	ἦσαν τεταγμένοι	were appointed	**10:**196
eschatē hōra	ἐσχάτη ὥρα	last hour	**12:**404
eschatos tēs gēs	ἔσχατός τῆς γῆς	end of the earth	**10:**15
eschediazomen	ἐσχεδιάζομεν	to be hasty, careless	**6:**952
estēsen	ἔστησεν	cause to stand, carry out	**6:**952
esthiō	ἐσθίω	to eat	**9:**605
estrangalētai	ἐστραγγάληται	strangled, exposed	**3:**1001
ethnarchēs	ἐθνάρχης	leader of the people	**3:**1113; **4:**165
ethnē	ἔθνη	Gentiles, nations	**8:**211, 456, 503, 688; **10:**83, 308, 334, 420, 778; **11:**749
ethnos	ἔθνος	nation	**4:**107, 269; **8:**415; **9:**816; **10:**360; **11:**215
ethos	ἔθος	custom	**10:**293, 329, 360, 951; **11:**189, 559, 560, 613, 661
etropōthē	ἐτροπώθη	reversal	**4:**81
euangelia	εὐαγγέλια	glad tidings	**11:**205
euangelion	εὐαγγέλιον	gospel	**8:**89, 168, 518, 527–28; **10:**405, 415; **11:**205, 208, 677; **12:**666
euangelistēs	εὐαγγελιστής	evangelist	**10:**289; **11:**422, 855
euangelizō	εὐαγγελίζω	to announce good news	**9:**377; **10:**138; **11:**205, 217, 400; **12:**238, 253, 260, 293, 639
euarestos	εὐάρεστος	well-pleasing, acceptable	**11:**870
eucharisteō	εὐχαριστέω	to give thanks	**8:**471; **9:**420, 691; **10:**352, 934; **11:**554
euchrēstos	εὔχρηστος	useful	**11:**898
eudokeō	εὐδοκέω	to be pleased, to agree	**4:**164; **9:**91; **11:**167
eudokia	εὐδοκία	good pleasure, favor	**11:**488, 746
euergesia	εὐεργεσία	good deed	**10:**89
eugenēs	εὐγενής	highborn	**10:**814
eugenesteroi	εὐγενέστεροι	of more noble character	**10:**239
eugenōs	εὐγενῶς	nobly	**4:**291

Transliteration	Greek	English	Volume and Page
eukairia	εὐκαιρία	opportunity	**8:**468–69
eulogeō	εὐλογέω	to bless	**3:**1051, 1062, 1064; **8:**471; **9:**29, 462; **11:**372
eulogētos	εὐλογητός	blessed	**3:**1062–63
eulogia	εὐλογία	praise, blessing	**11:**128; **12:**291
eunoia	εὔνοια	goodwill	**4:**269
eunouchos	εὐνοῦχος	eunuch	**3:**1158
euōdia	εὐωδία	fragrance	**11:**58
euodoō	εὐοδόω	to prosper, make successful	**3:**982, 1038–39
euperistatos	εὐπερίστατος	surrounding, besetting	**12:**148
euphrainō	εὐφραίνω	to be merry	**4:**55; **9:**256, 316
eupoiia	εὐποιια	the doing of good	**12:**168
euporia	εὐπορία	wealth	**10:**271
euschēmon	εὔσχημον	good order, proper, fitting	**10:**887, 889
euschēmonōs	εὐσχημόνως	decently, properly	**10:**972; **11:**721
eusebeia	εὐσεβεία	piety, godliness	**11:**797–98, 808, 851; **12:**336–37
eutheian hodon	εὐθεῖαν ὁδὸν	straight way	**12:**351
eutheōs	εὐθέως	immediately	**10:**152
euthys	εὐθύς	next, immediately	**8:**110; **9:**125
eutrapelia	εὐτραπελία	vulgar talk	**11:**435
ex	ἐξ	from, out of	**8:**424
ex akoēs pisteōs	ἐξ ἀκοῆς πίστεως	by believing what you heard (?)	**11:**251–52
ex ergōn nomou	ἐξ ἔργων νόμου	by works of the Law	**11:**251
ex hymōn	ἐξ ὑμῶν	your own doing, "from you"	**11:**392
ex kathedra	ἐξ καθέδρα	with authority, "from a chair"	**10:**967
ex ouranou	ἐξ οὐρανου	from heaven	**5:**853
exagorazō	ἐξαγοράζω	to buy back, redeem	**11:**260, 284, 442
exaireō	ἐξαιρέω	to rescue	**10:**338
exechean	ἐξεχεαν	was shed	**4:**190
exēcheomai	ἐξηχέομαι	to ring out, sound for the	**11:**694
exēgeomai	ἐξηγέομαι	to explain, interpret, make known	**1:**124; **9:**523
exēgesis	ἐξήγησις	bringing out	**1:**2
exerchomai	ἐξέρχομαι	to go out	**8:**407; **9:**439, 801
exestin	ἔξεστιν	it is lawful, allowable	**8:**386; **10:**860
exilasketai	ἐξιλάσκεται	make atonement for	**10:**474

Transliteration	Greek	English	Volume and Page
existēmi	ἐξίστημι	to amaze, astound	**10:**153, 180; **11:**91
exō	ἔξω	outside	**8:**481
exolethreuo	ἐξολεθρεύω	to ruin, destroy	**4:**94
exomologeō	ἐξομολογέω	to give thanks, acknowledge	**3:**1062, 1064
exousia	ἐξουσία	power, licence	**8:**20, 177, 220, 222, 477, 550; **9:**436, 671, 821; **10:**139, 790, 896, 900, 904–6, 908; **11:**141, 383, 390, 460; **12:**589, 594
exousia tou aeros	ἐξουσὶα τοῦ ἀέρος	power of the air	**11:**390
exoutheneō	ἐξουθενέω	to make light of	**11:**140, 294
exthros	ἐχθρός	enemy	**4:**125
exypnizō	ἐξυπνίζω	to awaken	**9:**687
ezeugisthēsan	ἐζευγίσθησαν	yoke themselves	**4:**32

G

Transliteration	Greek	English	Volume and Page
gangraina	γάγγραινα	gangrene, cancer	**11:**845
gar	γάρ	for, since, then	**5:**674; **6:**987, 995, 998, 1008; **10:**423, 428, 440, 448, 490, 495–96, 518, 546, 562, 565–67, 574, 581, 583, 592, 595, 614, 652, 654, 662, 673, 683, 687, 708, 725, 737, 741–42, 745, 754, 764; **11:**176, 271, 320, 323, 393, 535, 698; **12:**36
gar pantas hēmas	γάρ πάντας ἡμᾶς	"for we, all of us"	**11:**87
gē	γῆ	land	**8:**492; **9:**559
geenna	γέεννα	gehenna, "Valley of Hinnom"	**9:**252
gelaō	γελάω	to laugh	**9:**144
genesis	γένεσις	beginning, generation	**8:**126, 160
genetes	γενέτης	father, begetter	**5:**498
genetis	γενέτις	begetter (feminine)	**5:**498
gennaō	γεννάω	to beget	**9:**550; **12:**429, 430, 435
genos	γένος	race, people, family	**11:**526
gerousia	γερουσία	senate, council of elders	**3:**1114, 1123; **4:**6, 269; **5:**626

Transliteration	Greek	English	Volume and Page
ginesthe oun mimētai tou Theou	γίνεσθε οὖν μιμῆταὶ τοῦ θεου	imitate God	**11:**353
ginomai	γίνομαι	to be, become	**9:**522, 646; **10:**688; **11:**93–94; **12:**643
ginōskō	γινώσκω	to know	**9:**372, 611, 635, 670, 763; **10:**269, 566; **11:**436; **12:**336, 389, 429
glōssai hōsei pyros	γλῶσσαι ὡσει πυρος	tongues of fire	**10:**54
glossalalia	γλωσσαλαλία	speaking in tongues	**8:**201; **10:**55, 599, 944, 959, 961; **11:**91
gnōmē	γνώμη	mind, will, opinion	**10:**806, 860, 884; **11:**123
gnōsis	γνῶσις	knowledge	**11:**783; **12:**334, 336, 337
gnous	γνούς	having known	**8:**466
goētes	γόητες	sorcerers, magicians	**11:**851
gongysmos	γογγυσμός	complaint	**11:**512
gongyzō	γογγύζω	to grumble	**9:**128, 603–4, 609, 617, 621
gramma	γράμμα	a letter, what is written	**11:**72
grammateus	γραμματεύς	officer, scribe	**4:**80, 95, 236; **9:**627; **10:**273
graphē	γραφή	writing, Scripture	**10:**238; **12:**25
graphō	γράφω	to write	**12:**398
grēgoreō	γρηγορέω	to keep awake, keep watch	**8:**451; **10:**283; **12:**583
gymnazō	γυμνάζω	to exercise, train	**12:**152
gynē	γυνή	woman	**9:**536; **10:**928; **11:**801

H

Transliteration	Greek	English	Volume and Page
hagia hagiōn	ἅγια ἁγίων	holy of holies	**12:**103
hagiasmos	ἁγιασμός	upright behavior, holy living	**10:**815; **11:**718
hagiazō	ἁγιάζω	to make holy	**9:**611, 678, 792–93; **11:**700; **12:**115, 154, 291
hagiographa	ἅγιόγραφα	Holy Writings	**1:**45, 70
hagioi	ἅγιοι	priests, saints, "holy ones"	**4:**39; **11:**360, 370, 382, 410, 419, 435, 481, 593, 714

Transliteration	Greek	English	Volume and Page
hagios	ἅγιος	holy	**9**:792; **11**:114, 606; **12**:103
hagios kai amōmos	ἅγιός καὶ ἄμωμος	holy and blameless	**11**:361
hagiotēs	ἁγιότης	holiness, moral purity	**11**:45
hagnizō	ἁγνίζω	to purify	**12**:259
hagnos	ἁγνός	pure, blameless	**12**:410
hai diathēkai	αἱ διαθῆκαι	the covenants	**11**:76
haimarmenē	αἱμαρμένη	necessity, fate	**8**:349
hairesis	αἵρεσις	sect	**10**:319–20, 335, 361; **12**:344
hairetikos	αἱρετικός	heretical	**11**:878
hallēlouia	ἁλληλουιά	Hallelujah	**12**:695
hama	ἅμα	at the same time	**3**:1056
hamartanō	ἁμαρτάνω	to sin	**9**:579; **10**:457
hamartia	ἁμαρτία	iniquity, sin	**5**:673; **9**:235, 528, 634, 764, 772, 821, 847; **10**:457, 647; **11**:150, 355, 596
hamartōlos	ἁμαρτωλός	sinner	**9**:170; **10**:454, 457, 544; **11**:236
hapanta koina	ἅπαντα κοινά	community of goods	**10**:15
hapax	ἅπαξ	once	**6**:1379; **11**:828, 830, 864, 870, 878; **12**:75
hapax legomenon	ἅπαξ λεγόμενον	a word occuring only once in the biblical text, "once being said"	**3**:918; **6**:1092, 1377, 1388, 1393, 1523, 1595; **11**:578, 603, 778
haplotēs	ἁπλότης	sincerity, integrity	**11**:45, 131
haptō	ἅπτω	to take hold of	**9**:842
harpagmos	ἁρπαγμός	something to be exploited, grasped	**11**:507
harpazō	ἁρπάζω	to snatch, seize	**12**:649
hautai hēmerai	αὗται ἡμέραι	these days	**10**:83
hautē	αὕτη	she	**5**:522
hē agapē anypokritos	ἡ ἀγάπη ἀνυπόκριτος	genuine love	**10**:711
hē agapē tou theou	ἡ ἀγάπη τοῦ θεοῦ	the love of God	**12**:419
hē akrobystia ton nomon telousa	ἡ . . . ἀκροβυστία τὸν νόμον τελοῦσα	the uncircumcision which fulfills the law	**10**:657
hē basileia tōn ouranōn homoia estin	ἡ βασιλεία τῶν οὐρανον ὁμοία ἐστίν	the kingdom of heaven is like	**8**:301

Transliteration	Greek	English	Volume and Page
hē basileia tou theou	ἡ βασιλεία τοῦ θεοῦ	the reign, kingdom of God	**8:**537
hē charis	ἡ χάρις	the grace	**10:**996
hē diakonia tou pneumatos	ἡ διακονία τοῦ πνεύματος	the ministry of the Spirit	**11:**72
hē didachē tōn apostolōn	ἡ διδαχὴ τῶν ἀποστόλων	the teaching of the apostles	**10:**71
hē Dikē	ἡ Δίκη	justice	**10:**356
hē dynamis tou Christou	ἡ δύναμις τοῦ Χριστοῦ	the power of Christ	**11:**167
hē ek physeōs akrobystia ton nomon telousa	ἡ ἐκ φύσεως ἀκροβυστία τὸν νόμον τελοῦσα	the by-nature uncircumcision that fulfills the Torah	**10:**442
hē ek pisteōs dikaiosynē	ἡ ἐκ πίστεως δικαιοσύνη	the righteousness from faith	**10:**663
hē ek theou dikaiosynē	ἡ ἐκ θεοῦ δικαιοσύνη	a righteousness from God	**10:**403, 465
hē eklektē kyria	ἡ ἐκλεκτή κυρία	the elect lady	**12:**449
hē entolē	ἡ ἐντολὴ	the commandment	**10:**562
hē epangelia	ἡ ἐπαγγελία	the promise	**10:**68
hē gar agapē tou Christou	ἡ γὰρ ἀγάπη τοῦ Χριστοῦ	the love of Christ	**11:**91
hē gē	ἡ γῆ	the earth, land	**9:**405
hē genea tēs skolias tautēs	ἡ γενεὰ τῆς σκολιᾶς ταύτης	this crooked generation	**10:**68
hē graphē	ἡ γραφή	Scripture	**11:**256
hē hikanotēs hēmōn	ἡ ἱκανότης ἡμῶν	our competence	**11:**73
hē hodos	ἡ ὁδός	the way	**9:**741
hē hodos tou kyriou	ἡ ὁδός τοῦ κυρίου	the way of the Lord	**10:**261
hē hodos tou theou	ἡὁδός τοῦ θεοῦ	the way of God	**10:**261
hē klasei tou artou	ἡ κλάσει τοῦ ἄρτου	the breaking of bread	**10:**71
hē ktisis	ἡ κτίσις	the creation, world	**10:**511
hē orgē tou theou	ἡ ὀργὴ τοῦ θεοῦ	God's wrath	**9:**559
hē pentateuchos biblos	ἡ πεντάτευχος βίβλος	the fivefold book	**1:**305
hē psychē mou	ἡ ψυχή μου	my soul	**3:**1065
hē sarx mou	ἡ σάρξ μου	my flesh	**10:**553
hē skēnē	ἡ σκηνή	the Tabernacle	**10:**128
hē tou kosmou lypē	ἡ τοῦ κόσμου λύπη	worldly grief	**11:**110
heautō	ἑαυτῷ	by himself	**9:**829

Transliteration	Greek	English	Volume and Page
heauton ekenōsen	ἑαυτὸν ἐκένωσεν	he emptied himself	**11:**503
hebdomē kontakis hepta	ἑβδομηκοντάκιϛ ἑπτά	seventy seven times	**8:**380
Hebraios	Ἑβραῖος	Hebrew	**10:**111
hegeomai	ἡγέομαι	to regard, consider	**11:**500, 527, 730; **12:**164
hēgoumenōn	ἡγουμένων	leaders	**12:**164
hēgoumenos	ἡγούμενος	leader	**4:**51; **7:**162; **9:**425
hekastos	ἕκαστος	each, every	**4:**280
hēkō	ἥκω	to be, come, arrive	**9:**641
hekousiōs	ἑκουσίως	willfully	**12:**122
heleopolis	ἑλεόπολις	siege engine	**4:**156
helkō	ἕλκω	to haul, draw	**9:**858
Hellēnes	Ἕλληνες	Greeks	**9:**710
Hellēnistai	Ἑλληνίσται	Greek-speaking Jews	**9:**710
hēmas	ἡμᾶς	us	**11:**690
hēmeis	ἡμεῖς	we	**8:**202
hēmeis de pantes	ἡμεῖς δὲ πάντες	we all	**11:**67
hēmera	ἡμέρα	day	**3:**1028; **9:**331
hēmera tou kyriou	ἡμέρα τοῦ κυρίου	the day of the Lord	**10:**847
hēmin enekainisen	ἡμῖν ἐνεκαίνισεν	he inaugurated for us	**12:**120
hēmōn	ἡμῶν	our	**9:**234; **11:**745
hen	ἕν	one	**9:**677; **11:**420
hen eisin	ἕν εἰσιν	are one	**10:**827
heortē	ἑορτή	celebration, festival	**6:**946
heōs	ἕως	until	**8:**136, 268
heōs telous	ἕως τέλους	until the end, fully, completely	**11:**46
hestēkota	ἑστηκότα	standing	**8:**443
hestos	ἑστός	standing	**8:**443
hēsychasen	ἡσύχασεν	quiet	**4:**118
hēsychia	ἡσυχία	quietness	**4:**118; **11:**800
hetaire	ἑταῖρε	friend	**8:**394, 477
heteron nomon	ἕτερον νόμον	another law	**10:**570, 725
heteros	ἕτερος	other, different	**10:**55; **12:**89
heterozygeō	ἑτεροζυγέω	to be yoked with an animal of a different kind, be mismatched	**11:**103
heurethē pistos	εὑρέθη πίστός	he was found faithful	**10:**498
heuriskō	εὑρίσκω	to find	**4:**87; **9:**294; **10:**489, 569; **11:**527; **12:**357

Transliteration	Greek	English	Volume and Page
heuriskō ara ton nomon	εὑρίσκω ἄρα τὸν νόμον	this is what I find about the law	**10:**570
hēxei ek Siōn ho rhyomenos	ἥξει ἐκ Σιὼν ὁ ῥυόμενος	the deliverer shall come out of Zion	**10:**692
hidrōs	ἱδρώς	sweat	**9:**433
hieron	ἱερόν	temple complex	**8:**405
hierothytos	ἱερόθυτος	something sacrificed in a temple to a deity	**10:**893
hikanos	ἱκανός	sufficient, competent	**11:**58
hilaskomai	ἱλάσκομαι	to atone, expiate	**12:**41, 388
hilasmos	ἱλασμός	atoning sacrifice	**12:**376, 388
hilastērion	ἱλαστήριον	mercy seat, expiation	**1:**998–99, 1111; **8:**34; **10:**474–76; **12:**104
himation	ἱμάτιον	garment, cloak	**8:**194; **9:**831; **12:**613
himatismos	ἱματισμός	clothing	**9:**831
hina	ἵνα	in order that	**8:**146, 305; **9:**702, 765–66, 792; **10:**565–66, 578, 580, 625; **11:**536
hina dikaiōthēsontai pantes hoi pisteuontes	ἵνα δικαιωθήσονται πάντες οἱ πιστεύοντες	so that all who believe may be justified	**10:**656
hina mē ha ean thelēte tauta poiēte	ἵνα μή ἅ ἐὰν θέλητε ταῦτα ποιῆτε	so that you do not do what you want	**11:**326
hina plērōthē	ἵνα πληρωθῇ	to fulfill, result	**8:**152
hina sōthēte	ἵνα σωθῆτε	so that you may be saved	**5:**659
hippeis	ἱππεις	horseman, charger	**7:**609
histēmi	ἵστημι	to stand	**9:**357–58; **10:**131, 914; **11:**50, 461
ho anaplērōn ton topon tou idiōtou	ὁ ἀναπληρῶν τὸν τόπον τοῦ ἰδιώτου	one who is in the situation of a novice/beginner	**10:**965
ho anthrōpos	ὁ ἄνθρωπος	the man	**9:**819
ho anthrōpos tēs anomias	ὁ ἄνθρωπός τῆς ἀνομίας	the man of lawlessness	**11:**758
ho archēgos tēs zōēs	ὁ ἀρχηγός τῆς ζωῆς	the Author of life	**10:**80
ho areios pagos	ὁ Αρειος Πάγος	the Areopagus	**10:**245
ho Christos	ὁ Χριστὸς	the Messiah	**10:**709, 746

Transliteration	Greek	English	Volume and Page
ho Christos to kata sarka ho ōn epi pantōn theos eulogētos eis tous aiōnas amēn	ὁ Χριστὸς τὸ κατὰ σάρκα ὁ ὢν ἐπὶ πάντων θεὸς εὐλογητὸς εἰς τοὺς αἰῶνας ἀμήν	From them, according to the flesh, comes the Messiah, who is over all, God blessed for ever. Amen	**10:**629
ho diabolos	ὁ διάβολος	the devil	**12:**412
ho diakonōn	ὁ διακονῶν	the one who serves	**9:**425
ho diakrinomenos	ὁ διακρινόμενος	the one who disputes, doubts	**10:**742
ho dikaios	ὁ δίκαιος	the Righteous One	**11:**259
ho dikaios	ὁ δίκαιος	the righteous one	**10:**80, 129
ho dikaiōsas me	ὁ δικαιώσας με	the one who vindicates me	**11:**237
ho eleōn	ὁ ἐλεῶν	the merciful	**11:**422
ho erchomenos	ὁ ἐρχόμενος	the one coming	**8:**266, 354, 358; **12:**126
ho esō	ὁ ἔσω	the inner nature	**11:**83
ho estin	ὅ ἐστιν	which is	**11:**578
ho exō anthrōpos	ὁ ἔξω ἄνθρωπος	the outer man	**11:**83
ho hagios kai ho dikaios	ὁ ἅγιος καὶ ὁ δίκαιος	the Holy and Righteous One	**10:**80
ho hēgoumenos	ὁ ἡγούμενος	the leader	**9:**425
ho heōrakamen martyroumen	ὅ ἑωράκαμεν μαρτυροῦμεν	what we know we say	**9:**551
ho hosios	ὁ ὅσιος	the Holy One	**10:**193
ho huios tēs apōleias	ὁ υἱὸς τῆς ἀπωλείας	the son of destruction	**9:**793
ho huios tou anthrōpou	ὁ υἱὸς τοῦ ἀνθρώπου	the Son of Man	**8:**360, 470; **9:**819
ho kairos tōn karpōn	ὁ καιρὸς τῶν καρπῶν	the season of fruits	**8:**413
ho katēchoumenos	ὁ κατηχούμενος	the one who is taught	**11:**335
ho kosmos	ὁ κόσμος	the world	**10:**511
ho kosmos holos	ὁ κοσμός ὅλός	the whole world	**12:**446
ho laos	ὁ λαός	the people	**9:**376, 378, 446, 477; **10:**334
ho laos autou	ὁ λαός αὐτοῦ	his people	**6:**78
ho laos ho Ioudaios	ὁ λαός ὁ Ἰουδαῖος	the Jewish people	**10:**179
ho lithos	ὁ λίθος	the stone	**10:**89
ho logos	ὁ λόγος	the word	**9:**176; **10:**84, 166
ho logos tou kyriou	ὁ λόγος τοῦ κύριου	the word of the Lord	**10:**196
ho logos tou theou	ὁ λόγος τοῦ θεοῦ	the word of God	**10:**196

Transliteration	Greek	English	Volume and Page
ho menōn	ὁ μένων	the one who abides	**12:**453
ho metadidous	ὁ μεταδιδούς	the giver	**11:**422
ho Nazōraios	ὁ Ναζωραῖος	the Nazorean	**9:**354
ho neōteros	ὁ νεώτερος	the younger	**9:**425
ho nomos	ὁ νόμος	the law	**10:**570, 577
ho nous	ὁ νοῦς	the mind	**10:**962
ho ōn epi pantōn	ὁ ὢν ἐπὶ πάντων	who is over all	**10:**630
ho ophis	ὁ ὄφις	the serpent	**12:**651
ho palaios hēmōn anthrōpos	ὁ παλαιὸς ἡμῶν ἄνθρωπος	old self, "our old man"	**10:**539
ho patēr tēs doxēs	ὁ πατήρ τῆς δόξης	Father of glory	**11:**381
ho planos	ὁ πλάνος	the deceiver	**12:**452
ho poiēsas auta	ὁ ποιήσας αὐτὰ	the one who does these things	**11:**259
ho poiōn	ὁ ποιῶν	the one who makes	**12:**29
ho ponēros	ὁ πονηρός	the evildoer	**8:**194
ho presbyteros	ὁ πρεσβύτερος	the elder	**12:**365, 449, 460
ho proagōn	ὁ προάγων	the one who goes ahead	**12:**453
ho theos	ὁ θεός	the God	**10:**246, 571, 600
ho theos exelexato	ὁ θεός ἐξελέξατο	God chose	**10:**814
ho zophos tou skotous	ὁ ζόφος τοῦ σκότους	the deepest darkness	**12:**492
hōde	ὧδε	here	**8:**476
hodēgeō	ὁδηγέω	to guide	**9:**773
hodos	ὁδός	road, way	**1:**178; **5:**719; **6:**961, 966; **9:**742, 773; **12:**672
hoi agapōntes se	οἱ ἀγαπῶντές σε	those who love you	**3:**1065
hoi dōdeka	οἱ δώδεκα	the twelve	**9:**611
hoi dokountes	οἱ δοκοῦντες	those who seem (to be something)	**11:**223
hoi ek peritomēs	οἱ ἐκ περιτομῆς	the circumcision faction, "the ones from circumcision"	**11:**234, 256
hoi ek pisteōs	οἱ ἐκ πίστεως	those whose identity is derived from faith, "the ones from faith"	**11:**256–57
hoi hagioi	οἱ ἅγιοι	the saints	**11:**402, 415, 480
hoi Hebraioi	οἱ Ἑβραῖοί	the Hebrews	**10:**110
hoi Hellēnistai	οἱ Ἑλληνισταί	the Hellenists	**10:**110
hoi idioi	οἱ ἴδιοι	his own	**9:**574, 670

Transliteration	Greek	English	Volume and Page
hoi Ioudaioi	οἱ Ἰουδαῖοι	"the Jews"	**4:**278; **9:**527, 579, 809
hoi men oun	οἱ μὲν οὖν	now those, now after	**10:**138, 140
hoi neaniskoi	οἱ νεανίσκοι	the young men	**9:**425
hoi pateres hēmōn	οἱ πατέρες ἡμῶν	our ancestors	**10:**913
hoi peritemnomenoi	οἱ περιτεμνόμενοι	those who are circumcised	**11:**343
hoi phoboumenoi se	οἱ φοβούμενοί σε	those who fear you	**3:**1065
hoi phoboumenoiton theon	οἱ φοβούμενοιτὸν θεόν	those who fear God God	**10:**191
hoi polloi	οἱ πολλοὶ	ordinary citizens	**5:**688; **11:**59
hoi pseudeis theoi	οἱ ψευδεῖς θεοί	false gods	**6:**1008
hoi rhabdouchoi	οἱ ῥαβδοῦχοι	the police	**10:**234
hoi tarassontes	οἱ ταράσσοντες	those who disturb	**11:**205
hoi zōntes	οἱ ζῶντες	the ones who are living	**11:**92
Holōs akouetai	Ὅλως ἀκούεται	it is actually reported	**10:**846
homoia	ὅμοια	like	**8:**426
homoiōma	ὁμοίωμα	likeness	**10:**539, 578
homoiopathēs	ὁμοιοπαθής	of the same nature, mortal	**10:**199
homologeō	ὁμολογέω	to confess	**9:**657; **10:**320
homothymadon	ὁμοθυμαδόν	with one mind	**10:**746
hon phileis	ὅν φιλεῖς	he whom you love	**9:**686
hōn to telos estai kata ta erga autōn	ὧν το τέλος ἔσται κατὰ τὰ ἔργα αὐτῶν	their end will be according to their works	**11:**87
hopla	ὅπλα	armor, military equipment	**10:**728; **11:**138
hopōs	ὅπως	in order that, for the purpose that	**4:**164; **10:**625
hōra	ὥρα	hour	**9:**537, 539, 686
horaō	ὁράω	to see, perceive	**9:**481, 529, 599, 646, 841; **12:**252
horkōmosia	ὁρκωμοσία	the taking of an oath	**12:**91
hos	ὅς	who	**11:**501, 602; **12:**23, 62
hōs	ὡς	as	**11:**97, 633; **12:**506, 566
hōs despotais douleusei	ὡς δεσπόταίς δουλεύσει	he will follow his parents just like masters	**5:**659
hōs dia pyros	ὡς διὰ πυρός	as through fire	**10:**829
hos en zōē autou	ὃς ἐν ζωη αὐτου	in whose life	**5:**858

Transliteration	Greek	English	Volume and Page
hos ge tou idiou huiou ouk epheisato	ὅς γε τοῦ ἰδίου υἱοῦ οὐκ ἐφείσατο	he did not withhold his own son	**10:**580
hōs mē	ὡς μὴ	as if not	**10:**785, 887; **11:**97, 104
hōs nēpiois	ὡς νηπίοις	as babies	**11:**103
hōs pleonexian	ὡς πλεονεξίαν	as grudgingly granted	**11:**128
hōs talantiaia	ὡς ταλαντιαία	as a talent, about a hundred pounds	**12:**678
hōs teknois	ὡς τέκνοις	as children	**11:**103
hōsanna	ὡσαννά	hosanna	**8:**403
hōsautōs	ὡσαύτως	in the same way	**10:**598
hosios	ὅσιος	holy	**10:**193; **12:**93
hosoi ex ergōn nomou	ὅσοι ἐξ ἔργων νόμου	those who are from works of Law	**11:**257
hosous an proskalesētai kyrios ho theos hēmōn	ὅσούς ἂν προσκαλέσηται κύριος ὁ Θεός ἡμῶν	everyone whom the Lord our God calls to him	**10:**68
hōsper	ὥσπερ	just as	**8:**398
hotan aphelōmai tas hamartias auton	ὅταν ἀφέλωμαι τὰς ἁμαρτίας αὐτῶν	whenever I take away their sins	**10:**693
hotan gar ethnē ta mē nomon echonta physei ta tou nomou poiōsin	ὅταν γὰρ ἔθνη τὰ μὴ νόμον ἔχοντα φύσει τὰ τοῦ νόμου ποιῶσιν	for when nations not having Torah by nature do the things of Torah	**10:**441–42
hote	ὅτε	when	**9:**717
hoti	ὅτι	because, for	**8:**178, 188, 305; **9:**634, 717, 741, 772; **10:**144, 687; **12:**292, 398
hoti airetai	ὅτι αἴρεται	for it is taken	**10:**144
hou	οὗ	this, him	**12:**67
houtoi	οὗτοι	these	**11:**255; **12:**478
houtoi eisin	οὗτοι εἰσιν	these are	**12:**478
houtōs	οὕτως	thus, so	**8:**334, 372; **10:**197, 691
houtōs kai	οὕτως καί	in the same way	**8:**365
huioi hosioi	υἱοὶ ὅσιοι	faithful children	**5:**817
huioi theou	υἱοί θεοῦ	children of God	**5:**485
huios	υἱός	son	**8:**195, 358; **9:**224, 583; **12:**39, 620

Transliteration	**Greek**	**English**	**Volume and Page**
huios tou theou	υἱὸς τοῦ θεοῦ	Son of God	**8:**354
huiothesia	υἱοθεσία	sonship, adoption	**10:**597, 643; **11:**284
hybris	ὕβρις	arrogance	**12:**123
hydōr zōn	ὕδωρ ζῶν	living water	**9:**566
hygiainō	ὑγιαίνω	to be well	**3:**982, 1023, 1038, 1051, 1055
hygiainōn elthois	ὑγιαίνων ἔλθοις	welcome	**3:**983
hygiainōn poreusetai/ hypostrepsei hygiainōn	ὑγιαίνων πορεύσεται/ ὑποστρέψει ὑγιαίνων	will leave in good health/ return in good health	**3:**983
hygiainontōn logōn	ὑγιαινόντων λόγων	sound teaching	**11:**837
hygiēs genesthai	ὑγιὴς γενέσθαι	be made well	**9:**578
hymas . . . parastēsai tō Christō	ὑμᾶς . . . παραστῆσαι τῷ Χριστω	to present you to Christ	**11:**82
hymeis	ὑμεῖς	you (plural)	**8:**181, 344, 480; **9:**330; **10:**336
hymōn	ὑμῶn	your (plural)	**10:**991
hypagō	ὑπάγω	to go, go away	**1:**178; **8:**349; **9:**633
hypakoē	ὑπακοή	obedience	**10:**420; **11:**695
hypakoē pisteōs	ὑπακοή πίστεως	the obedience of faith	**10:**482
hypakouein tais epithymiais autou	ὑπακούειν ταῖς ἐπιθυμίαις αὐτοῦ	obedience to passions	**11:**695
hypakouō	ὑπακούω	to obey	**10:**482, 668; **11:**512; **12:**72
hypantaō	ὑπαντάω	to meet someone	**8:**500
hypar ti	ὕπαρ τι	a certain waking reality	**4:**296
hyparchō	ὑπάρχω	to be	**11:**536
hypeikō	ὑπείκω	to submit	**12:**168
hypēkoos	ὑπήκοος	obedient	**11:**509
hyper	ὑπὲρ	over, for	**8:**472; **11:**502, 510
hyper Christou	ὑπὲρ Χριστοῦ	for/on behalf of Christ	**11:**497
hyper dynamin	ὑπὲρ δύναμιν	beyond ability	**11:**42
hyper egō	ὑπὲρ ἐγώ	I am more	**11:**156
hyper hēmōn	ὑπὲρ ἡμῶν	for us	**11:**92
hyper pantōn	ὑπὲρ πάντων	for all	**11:**92
hyper ti	ὕπὲρ τι	beyond measure	**4:**296
hyperauxanō	ὑπεραυξάνω	to grow abundantly	**11:**745
hyperēphania	ὑπερηφανία	arrogance	**12:**211, 215
hypēretai	ὑπηρέται	followers, "servants"	**9:**817

Transliteration	Greek	English	Volume and Page
hypēretēs	ὑπηρέτης	assistant, helper	**10:**337
hyperlian apostoloi	ὑπερλίαν ἀπόστολοι	superapostles	**11:**133, 149
hypermachos	ὑπέρμαχος	defender	**4:**250
hyperypsōsen	ὑπερύψωσεν	highly exalted	**11:**502, 510
hypo	ὑπὸ	under	**11:**281
hypo pantōn anthrōpōn	ὑπὸ πάντων ἀνθρώπων	by all people	**11:**63
hypodeiknymi	ὑποδείκνυμι	to recount, show	**3:**1064
hypodikos	ὑπόδικος	accountable	**10:**458
hypogrammos	ὑπογραμμός	example, pattern	**12:**282
hypokrinomenos	ὑποκρινόμενός	hypocrite	**5:**786
hypokritēs	ὑποκριτής	hypocrite, “an actor”	**9:**151, 268; **11:**234
hypokrisis	ὑπόκρισις	insincerety	**8:**435; **9:**251; **11:**234
hypomimnēskō	ὑπομιμνῆσκω	to remember	**9:**439, 751
hypomonē	ὑπομονη	patient endurance	**11:**42, 97; **12:**129, 148, 337, 575
hypōpiazō	ὑπωπιάζω	to treat roughly, impose discipline	**10:**909
hypostasis	ὑπόστασις	the very essence of a matter	**12:**50, 131
hypostellō	ὑποστέλλω	to draw back	**11:**233
hypostēnai	ὑποστῆναι	stand before, resist	**4:**80
hypostrephō	ὑποστρέφω	to return	**9:**469
hypotagē	ὑποταγή	submission	**11:**801
hypotassō	ὑποτάσσω	to subject, subordinate	**11:**442, 450, 654, 870, 875; **12:**274, 315
hypsistos pambasileus	ὕψιστός παμβασιλέυς	the Most High, the king of all	**5:**846
hypsoō	ὑψόω	to exalt, lift up	**3:**1062, 1064; **9:**552, 635, 713, 830, 842
hysterēma	ὑστέρημα	deficiency, need	**11:**613
hystereō	ὑστερέω	to fall short	**12:**154

I

Transliteration	Greek	English	Volume and Page
iaomai	ἰάομαι	to heal	**9:**436
ichthys	ἰχθύς	fish	**9:**196
idein peri	ἰδεῖν περὶ	to consider, “look into”	**10:**208
idios	ἴδιος	one’s own	**9:**521, 574, 580; **10:**284
idiōtēs	ἰδιώτης	untrained person	**10:**965; **11:**150
idou	ἰδού	behold	**6:**980; **11:**93

Transliteration	Greek	English	Volume and Page
Iēsou Christou	Ἰησοῦ Χριστοῦ	of Jesus Christ	**11:**239
Iēsous	Ἰησοῦς	Jesus	**8:**134, 252; **12:**659
Iēsous Christos	Ἰησοῦς Χριστός	Jesus Christ	**8:**46; **10:**386
ios	ἰός	rust	**6:**1336; **8:**210
Ioudaia	Ἰουδαία	Judea	**3:**1131
Ioudaios	Ἰουδαῖος	Jews	**9:**464
Ioudaismos	Ἰουδαισμός	Judaism	**11:**213, 228
ioudaizō	ἰουδαΐζω	to live according to Jewish customs	**11:**185, 235
ischyō	ἰσχύω	to be strong, prevail	**10:**269
ischyroi dynamei	ἰσχυροὶ δυνάμει	mighty warriors	**4:**47
ischyros	ἰσχυρός	strong, mighty	**11:**140, 141; **12:**693
ischys	ἰσχύς	might	**9:**227
isopsychos	ἰσόψυχος	soul mate	**11:**38
isotēs	ἰσότης	equality	**11:**115, 124
K			
kagō	κἀγώ	I too	**11:**156
kai	καί	and	**4:**30; **6:**966; **8:**110, 254; **10:**154, 495, 684; **11:**237, 369, 500
kai dontos hēmin tēn diakonian tēs katallagēs	καί δόντος ἡμῖν τὴν διακονίαν τῆς καταλλαγῆς	and has given us the ministry of reconciliation	**11:**95
kai egeneto	καὶ ἐγένετο	and it came to pass	**4:**30; **9:**119, 133, 174
kai euangelizomenoi hous kyrios proskeklētai	καὶ εὐαγγελιζόμενοι οὓς κύριος προσκέκληται	and among the survivors shall be those whom the Lord calls	**10:**666
kai gar egō	καὶ γὰρ ἐγὼ	For I also	**8:**226
kai gar ou dedoxastai to dedoxasmenon	καὶγάρ οὐ δεδόξασται τὸ δεδοξασμένον	what was glorified has no glory	**11:**66
kai hapax kai dis	καὶ ἅπαξ καὶ δὶς	again and again, "once and twice"	**11:**707
kai hēmeis	καὶ ἡμεῖς	even we	**11:**237
kai houtōs	καὶ οὕτως	and so	**10:**69–91
kai houtōs pas Israēl sothēsetai	καὶ οὕτως πᾶς Ἰσραὴλ σωθήσεται	and so all Israel shall be saved	**10:**688
kai idou	καὶ ἰδού	and behold	**9:**284
kai nyn	καὶ νῦν	and now	**10:**284, 335
kai nyn idou	καὶ νῦν ἰδοῦ	and now I	**10:**282

Transliteration	Greek	English	Volume and Page
kai ou pollois estin phanera	καὶ οὐ πολλοίς ἐστιν φανερά	and is not manifest to the populace	**5:**688
kai peri hamartias	καὶ περὶ ἁμαρτίας	and concerning sin	**10:**579
kai theos ēn ho logos	καὶ θεὸς ἦν ὁ λόγος	and the word was God	**9:**519
kai tou euangeliou	καὶ τοῦ εὐαγγελίου	and the gospel	**9:**201
kainē ktisis	καινὴ κτίσις	new creation	**11:**93–94
kainos	καινός	new, fresh	**11:**93–94
kairos	καιρός	appointed time	**1:**179; **5:**651, 672; **6:**946; **8:**341, 468–69; **9:**49, 268, 436, 616; **10:**83, 728; **11:**337, 442, 758; **12:**105–6, 311, 638, 661, 713
kaka	κακα	evils, calamaties	**6:**957
kakia	κακία	badness, depravity	**10:**848; **11:**643
kakoētheia	κακοήθεια	wickedness, malice	**12:**163
kakologeō	κακολογέω	to speak evil of	**10:**267
kakon poiōn	κακὸν ποιῶν	doing wrong	**9:**816
kakoō	κακόω	to poison, "make evil"	**10:**197
kakos	κακός	bad, evil	**11:**177
kakōs omosantes	κακῶς ὀμόσαντες	wicked oaths	**5:**559
kakourgos	κακοῦργος	criminal	**9:**452
kalamon hypo anemou saleuomenon	κάλαμον ὑπὸ ἀνέμου σαλευόμενον	a reed shaken by the wind	**9:**163
kaleō	καλέω	to call	**8:**418; **11:**204, 701
kalon ergon	καλὸν ἔργον	good work	**8:**698
kalon estin	καλόν ἐστίν	it would be better if . . .	**8:**640
kalopoieō	καλοποιέω	to do what is right	**11:**765
kalos	καλός	well, good	**10:**874
kalos	καλός	noble, beautiful	**3:**984; **8:**606, 678; **9:**669, 677; **11:**126
kalou kai agathou, dikaiou kai eleēmopoiou	καλοῦ καὶ ἀγαθοῦ, δικαίου καὶ ἐλεημοποιοῦ	good and noble, righteous and charitable	**3:**1045
kamēlos	κάμηλος	camel	**8:**395; **9:**348
kamilos	κάμιλος	rope	**8:**395; **9:**348
kanōn	κανών	reed, measuring stick, sphere of influence	**1:**7, 44, 305; **11:**16, 143, 144, 345

Transliteration	Greek	English	Volume and Page
kardia	καρδία	heart	**9:**227; **11:**68, 428, 754; **12:**422
kardia kai psychē mia	καρδία καὶ ψυχὴ μία	of one heart and soul	**10:**96
kardiais sarkinais	καρδίαις σαρκίναις	flesh-and-blood hearts	**11:**63
karpophoreō	καρποφορέω	to bear fruit	**11:**591
karpos	καρπος	fruit	**5:**473; **11:**491
kati' idian	κατ᾿ ἰδίαν	by himself	**8:**327
kati' onar	κατ᾿ ὄναρ	by a dream	**8:**486
kata	κατά	according to, down	**11:**861
kata anthrōpon	κατὰ ἄνθρωπον	according to a human being	**11:**211
kata apokalypsin	κατὰ ἀποκάλυψιν	according to revelation	**11:**223
kata Isaak	κατὰ ᾿Ισαάκ	in the line of Isaac	**11:**305
KATA MATHTHAION	ΚΑΤΑ ΜΑΘΘΑΙΟΝ	according to Matthew	**8:**106
kata sarka	κατὰ σάρκα	according to the flesh	**10:**629; **11:**25, 92–93, 137–38, 154
kata tēn oikoumenēn	κατὰ τὴν οἰκουμένην	throughout the world	**10:**318
kata tēn praxin	κατὰ τὴν πράξιν	according to one's practice	**8:**351
kata tēn sarka	κατὰ τὴν σάρκα	according to the flesh	**9:**633
kata theon	κατὰ θεὸν	godly, according to God	**11:**109, 429; **12:**303
katabainō	καταβαίνω	to come down	**9:**575; **10:**259; **12:**630
katabrabeuō	καταβραβεύω	to disqualify	**11:**632
katakrima	κατάκριμα	condemnation	**10:**550, 566, 577, 580
katakrinō	κατακρίνω	to condemn	**8:**392
katakrisis	κατάκρισις	condemnation	**11:**102
katalalia	καταλαλιά	evil speech, slander	**12:**215
katalambanō	καταλαμβάνω	to seize, overpower	**9:**520; **11:**533
kataleipō	καταλείπω	to abandon, leave behind	**8:**341, 407
katallagē	καταλλαγή	reconcilliation	**4:**184
katallassō	καταλλάσσω	to reconcile	**4:**184, 188; **11:**600
katangeleus	καταγγελεύς	a proclaimer	**10:**246
katangellō	καταγγέλλω	to proclaim	**10:**246, 935
katapateō	καταπατέω	to trample	**12:**123
katapausis	κατάπαυσις	rest	**12:**52
katapetasma	καταπέτασμα	curtain	**1:**898; **12:**120
katapheugō	καταφεύγω	to flee	**12:**81
kataphileō	καταφιλέω	to kiss profusely	**5:**775
katapinō	καταπίνω	to gulp down, swallow	**11:**84

Transliteration	Greek	English	Volume and Page
kataraomai	καταράομαι	to curse	**11:**260
katargeō	καταργέω	to make powerless, abolish	**10:**815, 974; **11:**67, 68; **12:**40
katartisis	κατάρτισις	completion	**11:**70, 177
katartizō	καταρτίζω	to put in order, arrange	**11:**177–78, 332; **12:**172
katastrēniaō	καταστρηνιάω	to have strong desire	**11:**820
katastrophē	καταστροφή	ruin, destruction	**11:**844
katathematizō	καταθεματίζω	to curse	**8:**481
katatomē	κατατομή	mutilation, a cutting into	**11:**524
katechō	κατέχω	to restrain	**11:**758
katēgoreō	κατηγορέω	to accuse	**8:**279
kateidōlos	κατείδωλος	full of idols	**10:**244
katenanti	κατέναντι	alongside	**4:**152; **11:**59
katēnenka psēphon	κατήνεγκα ψῆφον	to cast a voting pebble	**10:**336
katergazomai	κατεργάζομαι	to do, accomplish	**11:**84, 512
kath hēmeran	καθ᾽ ἡμέραν	daily	**9:**201
kath hyperbolēn	καθ᾽ ὑπερβολὴν	beyond measure, beyond our ability	**11:**42
kathairesis	καθαίρεσις	destruction	**11:**141, 177
kathairō	καθαίρω	to prune	**9:**757
kathaper apo kyriou pneumatos	καθάπερ ἀπὸ κυρίου πνεύματος	as from the Lord, the Spirit	**11:**71
katharizō	καθαρίζω	to cleanse	**9:**121; **11:**105
katharos	καθαρός	pure, clean	**4:**242; **9:**724; **12:**723
kathēgētēs	καθηγητής	instructor, teacher	**8:**432
katheudō	καθεύδω	to sleep	**11:**727
kathexēs	καθεξῆς	afterwards	**9:**174
kathizō	καθίζω	to sit	**2:**608; **9:**822
kathōs	καθώς	just as	**8:**527; **9:**792, 794; **10:**691; **11:**255
kathōs gegraptai	καθὼς γέγραπται	as it is written	**10:**691
kathōs . . . houtōs	καθὼς . . . οὕτως	just as . . . even so	**10:**691
kathōs proegrapsa	καθὼς προέγραψα	as I wrote before briefly	**11:**409
katoikeō	κατοικέω	to dwell, live in	**12:**650
katoptrizomai	κατοπτρίζομαι	to see by reflection	**11:**69
kauchaomai	καυχάομαι	to boast, rejoice	**10:**816; **11:**525
kauchēma	καύχημα	boasting	**11:**491
kauchēsis	καύχησις	pride, boasting	**11:**45
keimai	κεῖμαι	to stand, be appointed	**11:**488
kenodoxia	κενοδοξία	vain pride, groundless boasting	**11:**499

Transliteration	Greek	English	Volume and Page
kenoō	κενόω	to empty	**11:**508
kenosis	κένοσις	an emptying	**4:**670
kēnsos	κῆνσος	poll tax	**8:**673; **9:**386
kentron	κέντρον	goad, spur	**10:**337
kephalaion	κεφάλαιον	sum, main point	**12:**97
kephalē	κεφαλή	head, source	**10:**928; **11:**450, 599
kēphas	κηφᾶς	Cephas	**12:**245
kēpos	κῆπος	garden	**9:**801
kerdainō	κερδαίνω	to profit, win	**10:**907; **11:**527
kerdos	κέρδος	gain	**11:**490–91, 527
kērygma	κήρυγμα	good news, proclamation	**4:**843; **8:**220; **9:**201; **10:**74, 80, 84, 382; **11:**858; **12:**375, 427, 428, 441
kēryssō	κηρύσσω	to preach, proclaim	**9:**103; **10:**138, 367; **12:**293–94
kētos	κῆτος	large fish, sea monster	**7:**505
kinounta staseis	κινοῦντα στάσεις	stirring up discord	**10:**318
klaiō	κλαίω	to weep	**9:**439, 779, 841
kleptēs	κλέπτης	thief	**9:**702
klēronomeō	κληρονομέω	to inherit	**9:**346; **11:**375
klēronomia	κληρονομία	inheritance	**11:**265
klēronomos	κληρονόμος	inheritor, heir	**10:**511; **11:**281
klēros	κλῆρός	lot, portion	**5:**476, 485; **11:**593
klēsis	κλῆσις	calling, invitation	**10:**814; **12:**337
klinidion	κλινίδιον	bed	**9:**125
klōntes . . . kat' oikon arton	κλωντές . . . κατ᾽οἶκον ἄρτον	breaking bread at home	**10:**72
kodrantēs	κοδράντης	quadrans	**9:**171
koimaomai	κοιμάομαι	to fall asleep	**9:**687; **11:**723
koinōneō	κοινωνέω	to share, participate	**11:**483; **12:**40
koinōnia	κοινωνία	community, fellowship	**10:**5, 23, 71, 231, 918, 935; **11:**105, 114, 179 , 201, 226, 272, 483, 499, 529, 544, 892, 895, 899; **12:**168, 310, 316, 383, 454
koinōnia tēs pisteōs	κοινωνία τῆς πίστεως	fellowship of faith	**10:**700
koinōnoi . . . tōn pathēmatōn . . . tēs paraklēseōs	κοινωνοὶ . . . τῶν παθημὰτων . . . τῆς παρακλὴσεως	partners in suffering . . . and encouragement	**11:**42

Transliteration	Greek	English	Volume and Page
koinos	κοινός	common, vulgar	**8:**13, 17; **12:**123, 178
kolaphizō	κολαφίζω	to treat roughly, torment	**11:**164
kolpoS	κόλπος	lap, bosom	**9:**148
kōlyō	κωλύω	to hinder	**9:**249, 345; **10:**226
komizō	κομίζω	to receive a recompense	**11:**87
kopiaō	κοπιάω	to work hard	**10:**1000; **11:**288
kopos	κόπος	work, labor	**10:**991; **11:**730
koptō	κόπτω	to mourn, lament	**8:**444
korasion	κοράσιον	girl, maiden	**8:**321
korban	κορβᾶν	Corban, dedicated to the temple	**8:**606
korē	κόρη	maiden, pupil	**12:**351
koros	κόρος	kor (unit of dry measurement)	**9:**308
kosmeō	κοσμέω	to order, arrange	**5:**729; **11:**870
kosmikos	κοσμικός	earthly	**11:**871; **12:**103
kosmios	κόσμιος	moderate, orderly	**11:**805, 871
kosmokratores	κοσμοκράτορες	cosmic powers	**11:**460
kosmos	κόσμος	world	**5:**523; **9:**521–52, 559, 617, 632, 653, 678, 708, 763, 783, 792, 794, 809, 825; **10:**246–47; **11:**92, 344, 633; **12:**400
krabattos	κράβαττος	pallet	**9:**125
kraipalē	κραιπάλη	dissipation	**9:**409
krateō	κρατέω	to retain, arrest	**9:**847; **10:**78, 319; **11:**567
kratesai	κρατῆσαι	to take hold of	**8:**563
krazō	κράζω	to cry out	**9:**355; **11:**285
kreittōn	κρείττων	better	**12:**100
krima	κρίμα	judgment	**10:**322
krinantas touto, hoti	κρίναντας τοῦτο ὅτι	"being convinced of this, that . . ."	**11:**91
krinō	κρίνω	to judge	**8:**211, 392, 444; **9:**426, 583, 772; **10:**91, 194
krisei	κρῖσει	judged	**5:**730
krisis	κρίσις	judgment	**8:**444; **9:**583
kryptō	κρύπτω	to hide	**9:**276; **11:**639
ktaomai	κτάομαι	to control, take	**11:**718
ktisis	κτίσις	creation	**5:**730, 808

Transliteration	Greek	English	Volume and Page
ktistēs	κτίστης	creator	**12:**240, 312
ktisthentes en Christō	κτισθέντες ἐν Χριστῷ	created in Christ	**11:**393
kynarion	κυνάριον	little dog	**8:**336, 610
kyōn	κύων	dog	**8:**336; **12:**733
kyriakos	κυριακός	belonging to the Lord	**12:**566
kyrie	κύριε	sir, Lord	**8:**497
kyrie eleēson	κύριε ἐλέησον	Lord have mercy	**8:**368
kyrios	κύριος	Lord, master	**1:**1164; **3:**956, 1101; **5:**818; **8:**354, 358, 414, 432, 477; **9:**307–8; **10:**64, 68, 150, 175, 419, 630, 665, 732, 738, 815; **11:**68, 71–72, 590, 657; **12:**330, 494, 624, 699
Kyrios ek Sina hēkei	Κύριος ἐκ Σινα ἥκει	The Lord comes from Sinai	**10:**692
kyrios Iēsous	κύριος Ἰησοῦς	Jesus is Lord	**10:**663
Kyrios Pantokratōr	Κυριός Παντοκράτωρ	Lord Almighty	**6:**957
kyrōsai eis auton agapēn	κυρῶσαι είς αὐτὸν ἀγάπην	confirm love for him	**11:**54

L

Transliteration	Greek	English	Volume and Page
labete, phagete, touto estin to sōma mou	λάβετε φάγετε· τοῦτό ἐστιν τὸ σῶμά μου	Take, eat; this is my body	**8:**703
labete, touto estin to sōma mou	λάβετε· τοῦτό ἐστιν τὸ σῶμά μου	Take; this is my body	**8:**703
laleō	λαλέω	to speak	**10:**599
lalia	λαλιά	language	**9:**641
lambanō	λαμβάνω	to take, receive	**12:**700
lampra	λαμπρά	radiant	**5:**491
lampros	λαμπρός	splendid	**9:**316
lamprōs	λαμπρῶς	sumptuously	**9:**316
lanthanō	λανθάνω	to be unaware	**12:**163
laos	λαός	people	**4:**130, 163; **9:**142, 412, 414, 447; **10:**19, 78, 83, 179, 193, 218, 255, 360

Transliteration	Greek	English	Volume and Page
latreia	λατρεία	service, worship	**9:**766
latreuō	λατρεύω	to worship, minister	**10:**422; **11:**525; **12:**108, 625
legei ho theos	λέγει ὁ θεός	God declares	**10:**64
legiōn	λεγιών	mob, legion	**9:**188
legō	λέγω	to say	**9:**654; **10:**675; **12:**47
legō gar	λέγω γάρ	for I say	**10:**746
legō oun	λέγω οὖν	I say then	**10:**675
leimma	λεῖμμα	remnant	**10:**676
leitourgeō	λειτουργέω	to serve, minister	**10:**756
leitourgia	λειτουργία	service, offering	**11:**514, 520
leitourgos	λειτουργός	servant, minister	**10:**721; **11:**520; **12:**31
lepra	λέπρα	a scaly condition	**1:**1094–95
leptos	λεπτός	small coin, mite, "leptos"	**9:**171, 269, 395
lēstēs	λῃστής	bandit, one leading a rebellion	**8:**478, 491, 663, 710, 723; **9:**818
leukainō	λευκαίνω	to make white	**12:**624
Libertinos	Λιβερτῖνος	Freedman	**10:**121
limoi kai loimoi	λιμοὶ καὶ λοιμοί	famines and plagues	**9:**400
litras	λίτρας	one hundred	**9:**836
logeia	λογεία	collection	**10:**995; **11:**114
logikos	λογικός	rational, reasonable	**10:**705; **12:**264
logios	λόγιος	eloquent	**10:**261
logizomai	λογίζομαι	to consider, reckon	**10:**481, 502, 595; **11:**150, 541
logomacheō	λογομαχέω	to argue over words	**11:**844
logomachia	λογομαχία	an argument over words	**11:**844
logon apodōsontes	λόγον ἀποδώσοντες	give an account	**12:**169
logos	λόγος	word	**1:**91; **5:**15, 759; **8:**41, 501; **9:**176, 506, 517, 519, 522, 587, 632, 637, 641, 742, 746; **10:**113, 207–8, 284, 668, 705, 810; **11:**189, 323–24, 559–60; **12:**23, 67, 264, 584
logos protreptikos	λόγος προτρεπτικός	persuasive word	**5:**2
logos tēs paraklēseōs	λόγος τῆς παρακλήσεως	word of exhortation	**10:**191; **12:**371
loidoreō	λοιδορέω	to revile	**9:**659

Transliteration	Greek	English	Volume and Page
loimos	λοιμός	scoundrel	**4:**168–69
loipos	λοιπός	remaining, left over	**11:**522, 682, 693, 717, 754
louō	λούω	to bathe	**9:**724
lychnos	λύχνος	lamp	**9:**586
lyo	λύω	to loose, release	**12:**563, 601
lypē	λύπη	sorrow, pain	**9:**771, 779; **10:**628; **11:**50, 109–10, 520
lytron	λύτρον	ransom	**1:**787; **8:**399
lytrosis	λυτρωσίς	redemption	**12:**107
M			
machaira	μάχαιρα	sword	**8:**477; **12:**612
magoi	μάγοι	wise men, astrologers	**8:**140
makarios	μακάριος	happy, blessed	**3:**1065; **8:**176; **9:**145; **10:**334; **12:**291, 310
makariōtera	μακαριωτέρα	more blessed, happier	**10:**891
makarismos	μακαρισμός	a pronouncement of blessing	**11:**294
makrothymeō	μακροθυμέω	to have patience, be forbearing	**9:**338
makrothymia	μακροθυμία	patience, endurance	**10:**642; **11:**97, 420; **12:**221
makrothymōs	μακροθύμως	patiently	**10:**334
malakoi	μαλακοί	male prostitutes	**10:**858
mallon ephobēthē	μᾶλλον ἐφοβήθη	more afraid	**9:**820
mania	μανία	insanity	**10:**340
manthanō	μανθάνω	to learn	**9:**604; **11:**544; **12:**63
Marana tha	μαράνα θά (Aramaic)	our Lord, come	**10:**778, 1002; **12:**531, 734
martyreō	μαρτυρέω	to bear witness	**9:**30, 529, 586, 729, 764, 776; **10:**113; **12:**90, 130, 145, 438
martyria	μαρτυρία	witness, testimony	**9:**30, 527, 570, 586; **12:**438, 465
martyria Iēsou	μαρτυρία Ἰησοῦ	the testimony of Jesus	**12:**696
martyrion	μαρτύριον	confession, martyrdom	**8:**352; **9:**30; **10:**128
martyromai	μαρτύρομαι	to testify, insist	**11:**700, 719
martyros	μάρτυρος	a witness	**10:**166, 199
martys	μάρτυς	a martyr, witness	**9:**30, 488; **10:**337; **12:**315
mastigoō	μαστιγόω	to afflict, punish	**3:**1064; **9:**352; **12:**151

Transliteration	Greek	English	Volume and Page
mataioō	ματαιόω	to become worthless	**11:**427
mataios	μάταιος	empty, worthless	**10:**983
mataiotēs	ματαιότης	emptiness, worthlessness	**11:**427
mathete	μάθετε	learn	**8:**694
mathētēs	μαθητής	disciple	**8:**297; **9:**808, 846; **10:**262, 267
mē	μὴ	not (interrogative particle)	**9:**566, 645, 661, 808, 810, 816–17
mē antilege tē alētheia	μὴ ἀντίλεγε τη ἀληθεία	do not oppose the truth	**5:**674
mē apanainou	μὴ ἀπαναινου	do not refuse	**5:**688
mē entrapēs	μὴ ἐντραπῄς	do not be ashamed	**5:**673
mē genoito	μὴ γένοιτο	May it not happen	**9:**382; **10:**537, 569, 603; **11:**268
mē moi kopous pareche	μή μοι κόπους πάρεχε	do not bother me	**9:**337
mē planēthēte	μὴ πλανηθῆτε	do not be led astray	**9:**398–99
mē pros thanaton	μὴ πρὸς θάνατον	not toward death	**12:**443
mē poreuthēte	μὴ πορευθῆτε	do not go	**9:**398–99
mē ptoēthēte	μὴ πτοηθῆτε	do not be terrified	**9:**398–99
mēchanē	μηχανή	siege engine	**4:**156
mechri	μέχρι	until	**8:**268; **11:**509
mechri thanatou	μέχρι θανάτου	unto death	**11:**503, 520
mēdemian en mēdeni	μηδεμίαν ἐν μηδενὶ	no one in any way	**11:**97
mēden diakrinomenos	μηδὲν διακρινόμενος	without hesitation	**10:**164, 209
megalōs	μεγάλως	greatly	**11:**543
megalynō	μεγαλύνω	to exalt	**11:**490
megas	μέγας	great	**10:**138
meizonos kai teleioteras	μείζονος και τελειοτέρας	greater and more perfect	**12:**106
meletaō	μελετάω	to attend to, practice doing a thing	**11:**814
melos	μέλος	member, limb, part	**10:**710
membrana	μεμβράνα	parchment	**11:**857
men	μέν	surely, indeed	**12:**100
men . . . de	μὲν . . . δε	meanwhile	**9:**831
men oun	μὲν οὖν	so therefore	**10:**179, 197, 335–36
menō	μένω	to stay, dwell	**9:**531, 570, 608, 637, 643, 739, 741, 750,

Transliteration	Greek	English	Volume and Page
			758–59, 776, 862; **11:**491; **12:**390, 394, 404, 407, 423, 430, 431, 450
menoun	μενοῦν	rather, on the contrary	**9:**243
merimnaō	μεριμνάω	to worry, be anxious	**9:**258–59
meris	μερίς	part, share	**11:**105, 593
merizō	μερίζω	to separate, measure out	**11:**143
meros	μέρος	part, share	**9:**264, 723
mesitēs	μεσίτης	mediator	**12:**100
mesiteuō	μεσιτεύω	to guarantee, confirm	**12:**81
mesos	μέσος	middle	**9:**460
mestoō	μεστόω	to be filled with	**10:**62
meta	μετά	with	**8:**476; **12:**721
meta pantōn	μετὰ πάντων	with all	**12:**734
meta pasēs sarkos	μετὰ πάσης σαρκὸς	upon all flesh	**5:**647
meta tauta	μετὰ ταῦτα	after these things	**10:**64, 218
metakaleō	μετακαλέω	to send a message	**10:**282
metamelomai	μεταμέλομαι	to regret, repent	**8:**483
metamorphoō	μεταμορφόω	to undergo a metamorphosis, be transformed	**8:**363; **11:**70
metanoeō	μετανοέω	to repent, change one's mind	**1:**179; **8:**167, 483–95; **10:**67
metanoia	μετάνοια	repentance	**10:**67; **11:**54, 110; **12:**633
metaschēmatizō	μετασχηματίζω	to change the form of	**10:**803; **11:**151
metastrephō	μεταστρέφω	to change, cause to be different	**11:**206
metatithēmi	μετατίθημι	to transfer, transplant	**11:**204
metechō	μετέχω	to participate in	**12:**40
mētēr	μήτηρ	mother	**4:**1024; **9:**182
methistēmi	μεθίστημι	to remove, turn away	**10:**271
methodeia	μεθοδεία	scheming	**11:**423
methyskō	μεθύσκω	to get drunk	**5:**651; **11:**442
mēti	μήτι	sign of interrogative	**8:**470; **9:**569, 816, 857
metochē	μετοχή	partnership	**11:**105
metriopatheō	μετριοπαθέω	to deal gently	**12:**60
metron	μέτρον	a measure, standard	**11:**143, 423

Transliteration	Greek	English	Volume and Page
mia sabbatou	μία σαββάτου	the first day of the week, Sabbath	**10:**778
miainō	μιαίνω	to corrupt, defile	**11:**866; **12:**154
mikros	μικρός	small, little	**9:**321, 778
mimētai mou ginesthe	μιμηταί μου γίνεσθε	be imitators of me	**10:**840
mimētai tou Theou	μιμηταί τοῦ θεου	imitators of God	**11:**434
mimnēskomai	μιμνῄσκομαι	to remember	**9:**751
miseō	μισέω	to hate	**9:**292, 402, 763–64
misthapodosia	μισθαποδοσία	recompense, reward	**12:**34
misthapodotēs	μισθαποδότης	rewarder	**12:**133
misthos	μισθός	reward, compensation	**12:**644, 733
misthōtos	μισθωτός	hired worker, mercenary	**3:**1123
mna	μνᾶ	mina (unit of money)	**9:**353
mnēmoneuō	μνημονεύω	to recall, remember	**5:**479; **9:**765; **11:**114
mnēmosynon	μνημόσυνον	memorial	**6:**974
modios	μόδιος	bushel basket	**8:**182
moi	μοι	to/for me	**8:**469
moicheia	μοιχεία	adultery	**8:**190, 192
moicheuō	μοιχεύω	to commit adultery	**8:**191
molynō	μολύνω	to defile	**4:**286
molysmos	μολυσμός	defilement	**11:**105
mōmētos	μωμητός	blameworthy	**11:**512
monē	μονή	dwelling place, room	**9:**740–41, 748
monogenēs	μονογενής	unique, one and only	**5:**15; **12:**430
monos	μόνος	alone, only	**8:**327; **9:**100, 124, 635; **11:**496, 707
monos menei	μόνος μένει	remains alone	**9:**711
mōros	μωρός	foolish	**8:**218
morphē	μορφή	form, external appearance	**11:**504, 506–7, 509, 529, 536
morphōsis	μόρφωσις	outward manifestation	**10:**447; **11:**849
mou	μου	my	**10:**64
myeō	μυέω	to initiate, instruct	**11:**544
myrias	μυριάς	myriad, ten thousand	**8:**382
myron	μύρον	perfume	**8:**466
mystērion	μυστήριον	secret, mystery	**5:**496; **8:**571, 572; **10:**988; **11:**351, 353, 355, 357, 359–60, 370, 374, 376, 381, 408, 451–52, 615, 760, 807; **12:**681

Transliteration	Greek	English	Volume and Page
mystērion tou euangeliou	μυστήριον τοῦ εὐαγγελίου	mystery of the gospel	**11**:458
mystis	μυστίς	one initiated	**5**:509
mythos	μῦθος	myth	**12**:342

N

naos	ναός	temple sanctuary	**8**:405
Nazarēnos	Ναζαρηνός	Nazarene	**9**:354
neanias	νεανίας	young man	**10**:312
neaniskos	νεανίσκος	young man	**8**:390; **12**:398
nekrōsis	νέκρωσις	death	**11**:81, 346
neophytos	νεόφυτος	newly planted, a new convert	**11**:806
nēphalios	νηφάλιος	temperate	**11**:805
nephelē	νεφέλη	cloud	**10**:43
nēphō	νήφω	to be disciplined, sober	**12**:257, 303
nephos	νέφος	cloud, a crowd of people	**12**:148
nēpioi en Christo	νήπιοι ἐν Χριστῷ	babies in Christ	**10**:825
nēpios	νήπιος	baby, infant	**11**:699
Nēro Kaisar	Νέρων Καῖσαρ	Nero Caesar	**12**:659
neuō	νεύω	to nod	**9**:730
nikaō	νικάω	to conquer	**12**:576, 611–12
niptō	νίπτω	to wash	**9**:724
nomikos	νομικός	lawyer	**8**:424
nomon dikaiosynēs	νόμον δικαιοσύνης	the law of righteousness	**10**:656
nomon kai krisin	νόμον καὶ κρίσιν	statutes and ordinances	**4**:50
nomos	νόμος	law, law code	**1**:38; **8**:30; **9**:677; **10**:374–75, 480, 569, 570–71, 576, 656; **11**:72, 356
nosphizō	νοσφίζω	to steal, misappropriate	**11**:870
nosseuō	νοσσεύω	to build a nest	**5**:651
nōthros	νωθρός	sluggish	**12**:68
nounechōs	νουνεχῶς	wisely	**8**:678
nous	νοῦς	understanding, intellect	**10**:806
nouthesia	νουθεσία	instruction	**11**:453
noutheteō	νουθετέω	to instruct, admonish	**10**:753; **11**:730, 768
nun	νῦν	now	**9**:143, 770, 783; **11**:398; **12**:649
nux	νύξ	night	**3**:1028; **9**:548

O

ochlos	ὄχλος	crowd	**8**:297, 486; **9**:142

Transliteration	Greek	English	Volume and Page
odynē	ὀδύνη	anguish	**10:**628
oida	οἶδα	to know	**5:**563; **11:**84, 237, 436, 687, 730; **12:**442
oikeioi	οἰκεῖοι	members of the household	**11:**402
oiketēs	οἰκέτης	houseslave	**12:**280
oikia	οἰκία	house	**10:**252; **12:**46
oikia tou skēnous	οἰκία τοῦ σκήνους	earthly tent	**11:**167
oikiakos	οἰκιακός	member of a household	**8:**262
oikodomē	οἰκοδομή	building, building up	**10:**950; **11:**70, 84, 141, 422
oikodomeō	οἰκοδομέω	to build	**8:**345; **10:**284; **12:**265
oikonomia	οἰκονομία	management of a household	**4:**770; **11:**374, 408, 791
oikonomos	οικονόμος	manager of a household	**11:**374
oikos	οἶκος	house	**9:**543; **10:**213, 234, 254, 269
oikoumenē	οἰκουμένη	world, empire	**10:**178, 248
oikourgos	οἰκουργός	working at home	**11:**870
oiktirmos	οἰκτιρμός	compassion	**6:**956; **10:**639, 703; **11:**41
oiktirō	οἰκτίρω	to have pity upon	**10:**639
olethros	ὄλεθρος	destruction	**11:**749
oligopistos	ὀλιγόπιστος	little faith	**8:**214, 324, 342, 368
oligopsychos	ὀλιγόψυχος	faint-hearted	**11:**730–31
oikodespotēs	οἰκοδεσπότης	landowner	**8:**413–14
oneidismos	ὀνειδισμός	reproach	**3:**1008
Onēsimos	᾿Ονήσιμος	Onesimus, “useful”	**11:**898
onoma	ὄνομα	name	**9:**791; **10:**90, 336
onoma mou	ὄνομά μου	my name	**10:**152
opheilē	ὀφειλή	debt	**9:**235; **10:**724
ōpheleō	ὠφελέω	to help	**10:**952
ophis	ὄφις	snake	**1:**85
ophlēsis	ὄφλησίς	punished	**6:**957
ophthalmos	ὀφθαλμός	eye	**11:**382
opisō mou	ὀπίσω μου	behind me	**8:**349
opsarion	ὀψάριον	fish	**9:**858
opse de sabbatōn	ὀψὲ δὲ σαββάτων	late on the sabbath	**8:**498
opsias de genomenēs	ὀψίας δὲ γενομένης	when evening came	**8:**494
opsias genomenēs	ὀψίας γενομένης	when it was evening	**8:**470
opsōnion	ὀψώνιον	wages, pay	**11:**137
optasia	ὀπτασία	vision, appearance	**9:**478; **12:**518

Transliteration	Greek	English	Volume and Page
oregomai	ὀρέγομαι	to long for	**12:**137
orgē	ὀργή	anger	**11:**643, 695; **12:**675
orgistheis	ὀργισθείς	becoming angry	**8:**544
orgizomai	ὀργίζομαι	to be angry	**11:**430
orphanos	ὀρφανός	orphan	**9:**748
orthopodeō	ὀρθοποδέω	to walk straight	**11:**235
orthrinai	ὀρθριναί	early in the morning	**9:**478
orthrou batheōs	ὄρθρου βαθέως	early dawn	**9:**478
osmē	ὀσμή	aroma	**11:**58
osmēn euōdias	ὀσμὴν εὐωδίας	a fragrant aroma	**11:**58
othonē	ὀθόνη	linen cloth	**9:**472
ōtion	ὠτίον	ear	**12:**115
ou	οὐ	not	**11:**533
ou . . . alla	οὐ . . . ἀλλά	not . . . but	**12:**342, 356
ou diekrithē tē apistia	οὐ διεκρίθη τῇ ἀπιστίᾳ	he did not waver in unbelief	**10:**742
ou dikaiōseis ton asebē	οὐ δικαιώσεις τὸν ἀσεβῆ	you shall not justify the ungodly	**10:**492
ou gar hikanos	οὐ γὰρ ἱκανός	I am not worthy	**9:**155
ou lambaneis prosōpon	οὐ λαμβάνεις πρόσωπον	makes no distinction between persons, "does not receive faces"	**9:**385
ou mē	οὐ μη	never	**11:**325
ou mē kataischynthē ho laos mou	οὐ μὴ καταισχυνθῇ ὁ λαός μου	my people shall never again be put to shame	**10:**666
ou mē kataischynthōsin ouketi pas ho laos mou eis ton aiōna	οὐ μη καταισχυνθῶσιν οὐκέτι πᾶς ὁ λαός μου εἰς τὸν αἰῶνα	all my people shall never, ever, ever again be put to shame	**10:**666
ou pisteuousin	οὐ πιστεύουσιν	they do not believe	**9:**772
ou syniēmi	οὐ συνίημι	without understanding	**11:**143
ouai	οὐαι	woe to	**5:**655
ouch	οὐχ	no, not	**8:**317
ouchi	οὐχί	no, not	**8:**317, 376
oudeis etolma kollasthai	οὐδεὶς ἐτόλμα κολλᾶσθαι	dared not join	**10:**99
ouk adikēsei	οὐκ ἀδικήσει	will not harm	**4:**92
ouk ara	οὐκ ἄρα	then you are not . . .	**10:**298
ouk eimi	οὐκ εἰμί	I am not	**9:**808
ouk ekzētēsomen kakon	οὐκ ἐκζητήσομεν κακόν	will not seek evil	**4:**92

Transliteration	Greek	English	Volume and Page
ouk ēsan ek tou spermatos	οὐκ ἦσαν ἐκ τοῦ σπέρματος	not belong to the family, "not of the seed of"	**4:**81
ouk estēken	οὐκ ἔστηκεν	does not stand	**9:**643
ouk ēthelon elthein	οὐκ ἤθελον ἐλθεῖν	but they refused to come	**8:**417
ouk oligos	οὐκ ὀλίγος	no little	**10:**270
ouketi eimi	οὐκέτι εἰμί	I am no longer	**9:**792
oun	οὖν	therefore, then	**6:**987; **8:**362; **9:**658, 696; **11:**126, 498, 533; **12:**215
oupō	οὔπω	not yet	**8:**617–18; **11:**533
ouranos	οὐρανός	sky, heaven	**8:**341; **10:**90; **12:**94
outhen diekrinen	οὐθὲν διέκρινεν	made no distinction	**10:**209
oxos	ὄξος	sour wine	**9:**454, 832
P			
p	π	p (Greek letter)	**12:**21, 33
paianōn	παιάνων	paeans	**4:**297
paidagōgos	παιδαγωγός	guardian, trainer, instructor	**11:**267, 269–70, 281
paideia	παιδεία	instruction, discipline	**5:**652, 670; **11:**453; **12:**151, 282
paideuō	παιδεύω	to instruct, discipline	**9:**448; **12:**151
paidion	παιδίον	child	**3:**983; **9:**344, 857; **12:**398
paiō	παίω	to strike	**8:**481
pais	παίς	child, servant	**5:**463; **11:**503
palin	πάλιν	again	**8:**188, 193, 417; **9:**634
palingenesia	παλιγγενεσία	renewal, rebirth	**8:**126, 392
pan	πᾶν	all, every	**11:**130
pan . . . esthiete	πᾶν . . . ἐσθίετε	eat everything	**10:**921
pan hamartēma	πᾶν ἁμάρτημα	all sin	**10:**864
panēgyris	πανήγυρις	festal gathering	**12:**158
panourgeumata	πανουργεύματα	secrets	**5:**648
panourgia	πανουργία	craftiness, trickery	**11:**74, 147
panourgos	πανοῦργος	crafty	**5:**142
panta	πάντα	all	**9:**832; **10:**909, 953; **11:**384, 527
panta ta ethnē	πάντα τὰ ἔθνη	all the nations	**8:**456
pantas	πάντας	all	**10:**682; **11:**410
pantes	πάντες	all	**11:**271
pantokratōr	παντοκράτωρ	Almighty	**11:**105–6; **12:**593
pantōn	πάντων	all	**11:**689

Transliteration	Greek	English	Volume and Page
pantote	πάντοτε	always	**11**:57, 689, 704, 712
pantote peri hymōn	πάντοτε περὶ ὑμῶν	always . . . for you	**11**:744
pari' hēmin	παρ' ἡμῖν	with us	**8**:422
para tēn hodon	παρὰ τὴν ὁδόν	by the highway	**1**:178
parabasis	παράβασις	transgression, disobedience	**11**:266–67
parabolē	παραβολή	parable	**7**:468; **8**:298, 300, 334, 564; **9**:667–68; **12**:105
parachrēma	παραχρῆμα	immediately, "at that moment"	**9**:125, 439
paradeisos	παράδεισος	garden	**7**:177; **9**:458; **11**:163; **12**:576
paradidōmi	παραδίδωμι	to betray, deliver up	**8**:166, 254, 258, 348–49, 467, 470, 536; **9**:210, 400, 414, 469, 816, 821, 833; **10**:201, 475; **11**:81; **12**:352, 485
paradosis	παράδοσις	tradition, teaching	**10**:926
paradoxa	παράδοξα	strange things	**9**:125
parakaleō	παρακαλέω	to encourage, have compassion	**4**:240; **9**:747; **10**:276, 703; **11**:41, 53, 137, 178, 419, 424, 540, 700, 710, 729, 855; **12**:81, 169, 272, 314
paraklēsis	παρὰκλησις	appeal, exhortation, comfort	**11**:33, 41, 101, 499; **12**:6, 173
paraklētos	παράκλητος	paraclete, Spirit	**9**:497, 747, 762, 771; **10**:154; **12**:376, 388
parakoē	παρακοή	an unwillingness to listen	**12**:34
parakypsas blepei ta othonia	παρακύψας βλέπει τὰ ὀθόνια	stooping, he saw the linen cloths	**9**:471
paralambanō	παραλαμβάνω	to take along, bring along	**11**:620, 717; **12**:159, 485
paramenō	παραμένω	to remain	**11**:491
paramytheomai	παραμυθέομαι	to encourage	**11**:700, 730
parangellō	παραγγέλλω	to command	**9**:200
paranomos	παράνομος	renegade	**4**:21
parapiptō	παραπίπτω	to fall beside, go astray	**12**:75
paraptōma	παράπτωμα	transgression, trespass	**10**:681; **11**:596
paratērēsis	παρατήρησις	things that can be observed	**9**:329

Transliteration	Greek	English	Volume and Page
parathēkē	παραθήκη	a deposit, goods entrusted to someone else	**11:**830, 837, 842
paratithēmi	παρατίθημι	to prove, entrust	**10:**238; **11:**842
parautika	παραυτίκα	momentary	**11:**83
pareisagō	παρεισάγω	to bring in	**12:**344
pareisdyō	παρεισδύω	to secretly slip in	**12:**485
pareiserchomai	παρεισέρχομαι	to come in alongside	**10:**530
parekomizeto	παρεκομίζετο	brought back	**4:**257
parenochleō	παρενοχλέω	to cause trouble, annoy	**10:**219
parepidēmos	παρεπίδημος	exiled, sojourning	**12:**246
paristēmi	παρίστημι	to prove, offer	**10:**320; **11:**82, 148, 606
paroikos	πάροικος	stranger, alien, neighbor	**6:**976; **11:**402
paroimia	παροιμία	figure of speech	**8:**61; **9:**667–68, 676, 781–82
parousia	παρουσία	arrival, coming	**11:**491–92, 511, 677, 725, 758; **12:**323, 342, 409, 702, 704
parousia tou kyriou	παρουσία τοῦ κυρίου	the return of the Lord	**12:**221
paroxysmos	παροξυσμός	provocation, sharp disagreement	**10:**225; **12:**121
parrēsia	παρρησία	openly, plainly, boldly	**9:**620, 668, 676, 687, 781; **10:**15, 367, 803; **11:**29, 50, 73, 101–2, 109, 411; **12:**409, 422
parrēsiazomai	παρρησιάζομαι	to speak freely, boldly	**10:**194, 341
parthenos	παρθένος	virgin, young woman	**6:**112; **8:**135; **10:**884
pas	πᾶς	all, everyone	**3:**1062; **9:**167, 313, 410, 602; **10:**368, 665; **11:**479, 483, 602, 729; **12:**305, 494
pas ho	πᾶς ὁ	everyone who	**8:**188
pas ho eis makran	πᾶς ὁ εἱς μακράν	for all who are far away	**10:**68
pas ho laos	πᾶς ὁ λαός	the people as a whole	**8:**486
pasa sarx	πᾶσα σὰρξ	all flesh	**10:**459, 814
pascha	πάσχα	Passover	**8:**697; **9:**419
paschō	πάσχω	to suffer	**9:**201, 419; **11:**40, 252; **12:**63
pasēs sarkos	πάσης σαρκός	all flesh	**9:**789

Transliteration	Greek	English	Volume and Page
pasin tois ethnesin	πᾶσιν τοῖς ἔθνεσιν	to all the nations	**8:**442
pasin tois Ioudaiois	πᾶσιν τοῖς Ἰουδαίοις	among all the Jews	**10:**318
patassō	πατάσσω	to strike	**8:**481
patēr	πατήρ	father, ancestor	**4:**129; **8:**202–3; **9:**224, 433, 583, 640, 691, 789; **10:**803, 826, 857; **11:**370, 414, 656; **12:**398
pater dikaie	πατέρ δίκαιε	righteous father	**9:**796
pathēma	πάθημα	suffering, misfortune	**11:**40–41
pathos	πάθος	experience, passion, emotion	**11:**189, 559–60, 613, 661
patria	πατριά	ancestral family	**3:**994; **10:**83; **11:**414
patris	πατρίς	homeland, hometown	**4:**250; **8:**317, 592; **9:**106–7, 574
pēgnymi	πήγνυμι	to establish, build	**12:**97
peirasmos	πειρασμός	test, trial	**8:**476, 708; **9:**425, 433; **12:**187–88, 585
peirazō	πειράζω	to put to the test	**3:**1138; **8:**162, 341, 385, 424; **9:**241; **11:**176, 711; **12:**188
peithō	πείθω	to persuade	**4:**268; **10:**238, 361; **11:**525
pempō	πέμπω	to send	**9:**552, 764
pentēkostē	πεντηκοστή	fiftieth, Pentecost	**1:**1158; **3:**1001
pephōtismenous tous ophthalmous tēs kardias	πεφωτισμένούς τούς ὀφθαλμοὺς τής καρδίας	the eyes of your heart enlightened	**11:**381
peri	περί	concerning, for	**4:**64; **8:**472
peri de	περί δέ	now concerning	**11:**725
peri de tōn pneumatikōn	περὶ δὲ τῶν πνευματικῶν	now concerning spiritual things/ persons	**10:**941
peri hypomonēs	περὶ ὑπομονης	on patience	**5:**654
peri men gar	περὶ μὲν γάρ	so concerning	**11:**8
periaireō	περιαιρέω	to remove, give up	**10:**348
periergazomai	περιεργάζομαι	to work around, bustle about uselessly	**11:**768
perilypos	περίλυπος	deeply grieved	**8:**321
periodos	περίοδος	a going around	**12:**21

Transliteration	Greek	English	Volume and Page
peripateite en agapē	περιπατεῖτε ἐν ἀγάπῃ	live in love	**11:**435
peripateō	περιπατέω	to walk around, go about	**10:**811, 825; **11:**137, 325, 620, 700–701, 717; **12:**386
peripherō	περιφέρω	to carry here and there	**11:**81
peripoieō	περιποιέω	to obtain	**10:**284
peripoiēsis	περιποίησις	possession	**11:**376
perisseuō	περισσεύω	to be over and above, plentiful	**11:**41, 118, 130, 720
perissoterōs de pros hymas	περισσοτὲρως δὲ πρὸς ὑμᾶς	and all the more toward you	**11:**45
peritomē	περιτομή	circumcision	**11:**524
perysi	πέρυσι	since last year	**11:**12
petra	πέτρα	rock	**8:**562
Petros	Πέτρος	Peter, "rock"	**8:**345, 562
phage kai pie	φάγε καὶ πίε	eat and drink	**3:**983
phagein arton	φαγεῖν ἄρτον	to eat bread	**9:**284
phaneroō	φανερόω	to reveal	**9:**856, 859; **10:**768; **11:**81, 662; **12:**412, 518
phaneros	φανερός	visible, apparent	**12:**412
phaneros ginomai	φανερός γίνομαι	to make manifest, known, clear	**11:**488
phanerōthentos de nun	φανερωθέντος δὲ νῦν	but is now disclosed	**10:**768
phaulos	φαῦλος	worthless, bad	**11:**87
pheidomai	φείδομαι	to spare, refrain	**11:**49, 175
phēmi	φημί	to say	**11:**140
pherō	φέρω	to carry	**12:**70
philadelphia	φιλαδελφία	affection for fellow believer	**10:**711; **11:**719 **12:**162, 259, 337
philanthrōpia	φιλανθρωπία	goodness, kindness	**11:**876
philanthrōpōs	φιλανθρώπως	kindly	**10:**346
philei ton kyrion	φιλεῖ τὸν κύριον	he loves the Lord	**10:**1002
phileō	φιλέω	to love	**8:**425; **9:**686, 758, 782, 860; **11:**878
philia	φιλία	friendship, love	**8:**425; **11:**690
philoneikia	φιλονεικία	dispute, love of strife	**9:**424
philos	φίλος	friend	**9:**236, 758, 781
philos pistos pharmakon zōēs	φίλος πιστὸς φάρμακον ζωῆς	a faithful friend is a medicine of life	**5:**683

Transliteration	Greek	English	Volume and Page
philotimeomai	φιλοτιμέομαι	to be ambitious, aspire to	**11:**720
philoxenia	φιλοξενία	hospitality	**12:**162
philoxenos	φιλόξενος	hospitable	**11:**805
phobeomai	φοβέομαι	to fear	**9:**252; **11:**452
phobos	φόβος	fear	**10:**71
phōnē	φωνή	voice	**10:**150
phronimos	φρόνιμος	wise, intelligent	**8:**218, 448; **10:**764
phoros	φόρος	tax, tribute	**9:**386
phōs	φῶς	light	**5:**504; **9:**506, 586, 632; **10:**150, 195, 334
phōs ek tou ouranou	φῶς ἐκ τοῦ οὐρανοῦ	a light from heaven	**10:**150
phōs lampsei	φῶς λάμψει	let light shine	**11:**68
phōstēres	φωστῆρες	stars, light-giving bodies	**11:**513
phōtizō	φωτίζω	to enlighten	**11:**410
phragelloō	φραγελλόω	to scourge	**9:**352
phronēsis	φρόνησις	prudence	**6:**961, 963, 966–67
phroneō	φρονέω	to think, feel	**11:**483–84, 499, 506–7, 533, 535, 541, 543
phthanō	φθάνω	to precede, attain	**11:**704
phtheirō	φθείρω	to destroy, ruin	**10:**831, 851
phthonos	φθόνος	envy, jealousy	**12:**210–11
phthora	φθορά	destruction, corruption	**11:**336
phylarchos	φύλαρχος	Phylarchos, "commander"	**4:**250
phylassesthai ta dikaiōmata	φυλάσσεσθαι τὰ δικαιώματα	keep the decrees	**10:**448
phylassō	φυλάσσω	to keep	**11:**343; **12:**478, 482
physei	φύσει	by nature, instinctively	**10:**441; **11:**391, 393
physioō	φυσιόω	to puff up, be arrogant	**10:**841, 846
physis	φύσις	nature	**11:**391
piazō	πιάζω	to take hold of, arrest	**12:**700
piete ex autou pantes, touto gar estin to haima mou tēs diathēkēs to peri pollōn ekchynnomenon eis aphesin hamartiōn	πίετε ἐξ αὐτοῦ πάντες· τοῦτο γάρ ἐστιν τὸ αἷμά μου της διαθήκης τὸ περὶ πολλῶν ἐκχυννόμενον εἰς ἄφεσιν ἁμαρτιῶν	Drink from it, all of you; for this is my blood of the covenant, which is poured out for many for the forgiveness of sins	**8:**704

Transliteration	Greek	English	Volume and Page
pimplēmi	πίμπλημι	to be filled with	**10:**62, 78
pinō	πίνω	to drink	**8:**653; **9:**623
piptō	πίπτω	to fall	**9:**690; **10:**914; **12:**630
pisteōs sou	πίστεως σου	your faith	**11:**895
pisteuō	πιστεύω	to trust, believe	**5:**654; **9:**190, 546, 559, 599, 611, 688–89, 739, 740, 743, 782–83, 841, 851; **10:**84, 196; **11:**240, 251, 256; **12:**422, 435
pistin Iēsou	πίστιν ᾿Ιησου	faith of Jesus	**12:**667
pistis	πίστις	faith	**5:**652; **9:**190; **10:**386, 453, 470, 835; **11:**217, 240, 244, 251–52, 256, 265, 270–71, 275–76, 328, 528, 530, 684, 894–95; **12:**45, 131, 259, 422
pistis Christou	πίστις Χριστοῦ	the faith of Christ	**10:**502; **11:**528
pistis di' agapēs energoumenē	πίστις δι' ἀγάπης ἐνεργουμένη	faith working through love	**11:**87
pistis Iēsou Christou	πίστις ᾿Ιησοῦ Χριστοῦ	Jesus's trustworthiness	**10:**470; **11:**240
pistis theou	πίστις θεοῦ	God's trustworthiness	**10:**453
pistos	πιστός	faithful	**5:**652; **9:**850; **10:**835; **11:**256, 370, 588; **12:**386, 422, 462
planaō	πλανάω	to lead astray, deceive	**9:**399, 617; **12:**412
planē	πλάνη	deception	**8:**497; **12:**352
planos	πλάνος	imposter	**8:**497
plastois logois	πλαστοῖς λόγοις	made-up stories	**12:**344
platynō	πλατύνω	to widen, make wide	**11:**106
plēgē	πληγή	plague, blow	**12:**693
plēn	πλήν	nevertheless, but	**5:**775; **9:**422; **10:**929
pleonazō	πλεονάζω	to be more than enough, greatly abound	**11:**745
pleonekteō	πλεονεκτέω	to take advantage of, exploit	**11:**170–71
pleonexia	πλεονεξία	covetousness	**11:**642
plērēs	πλήρης	full	**10:**113

Transliteration	Greek	English	Volume and Page
plērōma	πλήρωμα	fullness, full measure	**10:**680; **11:**358, 384–85, 415–16, 450
plērōma tōn kairōn	πλήρωμα τῶν καιρῶν	the fullness of time	**11:**374
plērōma tou Theou	πλήρωμα τοῦ Θεοῦ	fullness of God	**11:**416
plēroō	πληρόω	to fully come	**9:**617; **11:**322–23, 384–85, 421
plērophorētheis	πληροφορηθείς	being fully convinced	**10:**742
plērousthe en pneumati	πληροῦσθε ἐν πνεύματι	be filled with the Spirit	**11:**442
plēssō	πλήσσω	to strike	**12:**630
plēthos	πλῆθος	multitude, people	**4:**107, 269–70; **8:**561
plousios	πλούσιος	rich	**11:**389
plousios en eleei	πλούσιος ἐν ἐλέει	rich in mercy	**11:**391
ploutos tēs charitos	πλοῦτος τῆς χάριτος	riches of grace	**11:**389
pneuma	πνεῦμα	spirit, wind	**4:**209; **5:**546, 579; **9:**550, 833; **10:**113, 226, 261, 419, 962; **11:**72, 148, 391, 496; **12:**31, 210, 264
pneuma sophias	πνεῦμα σοφίας	spirit of wisdom	**11:**381
pneuma theou	πνεῦμα θεοῦ	Spirit of God	**11:**71
pneuma tou kosmou	πνεῦμα τοῦ κόσμου	Spirit of the world	**10:**822
pneumata akatharta	πνεύματα ἀκάθαρτα	unclean spirits	**12:**677
pneumatikos	πνευματικός	spiritual, pertaining to the spirit	**10:**705; **11:**73, 649
poia	ποῖα	what things?	**9:**477
poiei sēmeia megala	ποιεῖ σημεῖα μεγάλα	it performs great signs	**12:**658
poiēma	ποίημα	what has been made, a work	**11:**393
poieō	ποιέω	to make, do	**7:**188; **9:**151, 599, 639, 642; **10:**341; **11:**765
poiēsei eleēmosynēn	ποιήσει ἐλεημοσύνην	do alms	**3:**1064
poimainō	ποίμαινω	to shepherd, care for	**12:**699
poimēn	ποιμήν	shepherd, pastor, minister	**11:**360, 422

Transliteration	Greek	English	Volume and Page
polemos	πόλεμος	war, battle	**12:**631
polis	πόλις	city	**4:**10, 60, 233
politarchai	πολιτάρχαι	city authorities	**10:**239–40
politeia	πολιτεία	polity, citizenship	**1:**38; **4:**281; **11:**397
politeuma	πολίτευμα	place of citizenship	**5:**439; **11:**535; **12:**711
politeuomai	πολιτεύομαι	to conduct one's life, live	**4:**269; **11:**496, 535
polla grammata	πολλὰ γράμματα	great learning	**10:**340–41
polla terata kai semēia	πολλὰ τέρατα καῖ σημεία	many wonders and signs	**10:**71
pollō agōni	πολλῷ ἀγῶνι	great opposition	**11:**698
polloi	πολλοὶ	many	**9:**696
polloi episteusan	πολλοὶ ἐπίστευσαν	many believed	**9:**635
polloi planoi	πολλοὶ πλάνοι	many deceivers	**12:**452
pōlos	πῶλος	a young donkey	**9:**367
polyn karpon pherei	πολὺν καρπὸν φέρει	bearing much fruit	**9:**711
polys	πολύς	much, many	**10:**818
polytelēs	πολυτελής	precious	**12:**284
ponēria	πονηρία	wickedness, baseness	**10:**848
ponēroi anthrōpoi	πονηροί ἄνθρωποι	evil persons	**11:**765
ponēros	πονηρός	wicked, Satan	**7:**161; **12:**418, 464
poreuomai	πορεύομαι	to go, journey	**9:**108, 112, 232, 424; **10:**180; **12:**294
pornē	πόρνη	prostitute	**10:**862–63, 865; **12:**351, 579, 680
porneia	πορνεία	fornication, illicit sex	**8:**190–93; **9:**313, 640; **10:**220, 844–51, 855, 857, 859, 861–66, 869, 871–73, 877, 883, 913–14; **11:**172–73, 435, 642; **12:**579, 680–81
pornos	πόρνος	fornicator, sexually immoral person	**10:**848–50, 855, 865, 869; **11:**104; **12:**579
pōrōsis	πώρωσις	hardening	**10:**688
pōs	πῶς	how	**8:**427
poson autō dōsō ton misthon/ poson autō eti dō misthon	πόσον αὐτῷ δώσω τόν μισθόν/ πόσον αὐτῷ ἔτι δῶ μισθόν	how much shall I pay him?	**3:**984
potērion	ποτήριον	cup	**8:**653; **9:**433

Transliteration	Greek	English	Volume and Page
pothen toutō	πόθεν τούτῳ	where did this come from?	**8:**317
pou estin	ποῦ ἐστιν	where is	**12:**355
pragma	πρᾶγμα	matter	**11:**718–19
praitōrion	πραιτώριον	imperial guard	**11:**488
praotēs	πραότης	humility	**5:**652
prassō	πράσσω	to do, accomplish	**11:**327
praus	πραΰς	meek, humble	**8:**150, 161, 179, 275, 370, 403
prautēs	πραύτης	gentleness, humility	**11:**136, 420
praxeis	πρᾶξεις	work, activity	**10:**29
prepō	πρέπω	to be suitable, proper	**12:**93
presbeuō	πρεσβεύω	to be an ambassador, envoy	**11:**95
presbyteros	πρεσβύτερος	elders	**10:**200, 282, 325; **11:**480, 481, 818, 822, 864, 869
presbytēs	πρεσβύτης	old man, aged person, ambassador	**11:**869, 898–99
pro emou	πρὸ ἐμοῦ	before me	**9:**669
pro me	πρὸ με	for me	**10:**464
proagō	προάγω	to go before	**8:**705
proaulion	προαύλιον	forecourt	**8:**715
procheirizomai	προχειρίζομαι	to appoint	**10:**337
prodotēs	προδότης	betrayer	**9:**139
prodromos	πρόδρομος	forerunner	**12:**82
proeirēka kai prolegō	προείρηκα καὶ προλέγω	I said beforehand in warning and I tell before it happens	**11:**175
proepangellō	προεπαγγέλλω	to promise in advance	**11:**128
proeuangelizomai	προευαγγελίζομαι	to bring good news in advance	**11:**256
prognōsis	πρόγνωσις	foreknowledge	**12:**247
prographō	προγράφω	to write beforehand, set forth publicly	**11:**250
proistēmi	προΐστημι	to place before, stand before	**11:**422, 806
prokatartizō	προκαταρτίζω	to arrange in advance	**11:**128
prokopē	προκοπή	progress	**11:**70, 491, 814
prokoptō	προκόπτω	to make progress, advance	**11:**213
prolegō	προλέγω	to tell in advance	**11:**711
pronoeō	προνοέω	to think of beforehand	**10:**714; **11:**126

Transliteration	Greek	English	Volume and Page
pronoia	πρόνοια	forethought, foresight	**10:**318
proorizō	προορίζω	to determine in advance	**10:**602; **11:**373
propathontes kai hybristhentes	προπαθόντες καὶ ὑβρισθέντες	we had already suffered and been shamefully mistreated	**11:**698
propempō	προπέμπω	to send on one's way	**12:**462
prophētēs	προφήτης	prophet	**6:**4; **7:**162; **11:**402
prophēteusousin	προφητεύσουσιν	and they shall prophesy	**10:**64
pros	πρός	to, toward, with	**12:**382, 443
pros heautous	πρὸς ἑαυτούς	to one another	**8:**466
pros phthonon	πρὸς φθόνον	toward envy	**12:**210
pros thanaton	πρὸς θάνατον	toward death	**12:**443
pros to sympheron	πρὸς τὸ συμφέρον	for the common good	**10:**944
pros tous exō	πρός τούς ἔξω	outsiders	**11:**720
prosagōgē	προσαγωγή	access, privilege of entrance	**11:**401
prosanaplēroō	προσαναπληρόω	to replenish	**11:**138
prosanatithēmi	προσανατίθημι	to consult	**11:**216
prosballō	προσβάλλω	to strike, attack	**7:**101
prosechō	προσέχω	to keep watch, be on guard	**9:**409; **10:**283; **12:**33
prosēlytos	προσήλυτος	a convert	**10:**194
proserchomai	προσέρχομαι	to approach, come	**8:**368, 500; **12:**158, 265
proseuchē	προσευχή	prayer	**10:**71, 231
proskairos	πρόσκαιρος	temporary, transitory	**11:**83
prosklēraomai	προσκληράομαι	to join, "cast one's lot with"	**10:**238
proskyneō	προσκυνέω	to worship	**8:**224, 500; **9:**99, 661; **10:**128; **12:**585, 604
proslambanō	προσλαμβάνω	to welcome	**10:**730
proslēmpsis	πρόσλημψις	acceptance, receiving	**10:**683
prosōpon	πρόσωπον	face	**11:**707
prosphatos	πρόσφατος	new	**12:**120
prospherō	προσφέρω	to offer	**12:**104, 138
prostatis	προστάτις	captain	**4:**206
prostithēmi	προστίθημι	to add to	**11:**267
prothesis	πρόθεσις	purpose, a setting forth	**11:**850
prothymia	προθυμία	willingness, eagerness	**11:**118, 126
prōtoi	πρῶτοι	leaders	**10:**325
prōtos	πρῶτος	first	**9:**539
prōtotokos	πρωτότοκος	firstborn	**11:**597; **12:**29

Transliteration	Greek	English	Volume and Page
prōtotokos ek tōn nekrōn	πρωτότοκος ἐκ τῶν νεκρῶν	firstborn from the dead	**11:**573
protreptomai	προτρέπτομαι	to encourage	**10:**261
psalmos	ψαλμός	psalm	**4:**657
pseudapostoloi	ψευδαπόστολοι	false apostles	**11:**133
pseustēs	ψεύστης	liar	**9:**646
psychē	ψυχή	life principle, soul	**8:**351; **9:**227, 256, 258, 711; **10:**720; **11:**496; **12:**253, 273, 461, 613
psychikos	ψυχικός	natural, unspiritual	**10:**821, 987
ptōchos	πτωχός	the poor	**11:**114
pylē	πύλη	iron gate	**10:**179
pylōn	πυλών	outer gate	**10:**179
pynthanomai	πυνθάνομαι	to inquire, interrogate	**10:**297
pyr	πῦρ	fire	**5:**692; **10:**54; **12:**310
Pythōn	Πυθῶν	the Python, a spirit of divination	**10:**232

R

rabbi	ῥαββί	rabbi	**8:**374, 470
rabbouni	ῥαββουνί (Aramaic)	rabbi	**9:**842
rakos katamēniōn	ῥάκος καταμηνίων	filthy, menstruous rag	**3:**959
rapizō	ῥαπίζω	to strike	**8:**480
rhadiourgia	ῥαδιουργία	villainy	**10:**190
rhēma	ῥῆμα	word, command	**4:**39; **10:**166, 668–69; **11:**462
rhētōr	ῥήτωρ	attorney	**10:**318
rhiza	ῥίζα	root	**4:**31
romphaia	ῥομφαία	sword	**12:**612
ryomai	ῥύομαι	to deliver, save	**11:**43, 596

S

sagēnē	σαγήνη	drag net	**9:**116
sainomai	σαίνομαι	to be shaken, disturbed	**11:**711
sapra	σαπρά	rotten	**8:**314
sarkikos	σαρκικός	in the manner of the flesh	**10:**566, 756, 849; **11:**138; **12:**272
sarkinos	σάρκινος	fleshy, consisting of flesh	**10:**566, 825; **12:**90
sarx	σάρξ	flesh	**1:**24; **9:**485, 522, 610; **10:**417, 566; **11:**321, 336, 491, 526, 606, 613, 634; **12:**105, 120, 401

Transliteration	Greek	English	Volume and Page
sarx genomenos	σὰρξ γενόμενος	the one who became flesh	**9:**790
Satanas	Σατανᾶς	Satan	**11:**356; **12:**577, 650
schēma	σχῆμα	form, outward structure	**10:**886, 887; **11:**104, 509, 536
schēma tou kosmou	σχῆμα τοῦ κόσμου	the schema of the world	**10:**887
schinos	σχινος	mastic tree	**7:**182
schizō	σχίζω	to cut in two, divide	**7:**182; **8:**724
schoinoi	σχοινοί	a Persian measure	**4:**266
scholē	σχολή	lecture hall	**10:**267
sebomenos	σεβόμενος	devout	**10:**194, 196
seiō	σείω	to shake, tremble	**8:**403
seismos	σεισμός	earthquake	**8:**230
semaino	σημαίνω	to signify, indicate	**12:**560
sēmeia kai terata	σημεία καῖ τέρατα	signs and wonders	**8:**246; **9:**575; **10:**15, 64
sēmeion	σημεῖον	sign	**8:**62, 76; **9:**407, 446, 502, 539, 544, 546, 599, 656, 851; **11:**168
sēmeron	σήμερον	today	**9:**359; **11:**67
sēmeron hēmeras	σήμερον ἡμέρας	this day	**11:**68
semnos	σεμνός	respectable, serious	**11:**807
semnotēs	σεμνότης	dignity, seriousness	**11:**798
Simōn	Σίμων	Simeon	**5:**607
sindōn	σινδών	linen cloth	**9:**472
skandalizō	σκανδαλίζω	to stumble over, fall away	**8:**267, 317, 333, 357, 372, 442, 474, 640; **9:**765; **11:**158
skandalon	σκάνδαλον	stumbling block	**8:**270, 350, 357, 372; **9:**321; **10:**811, 813; **11:**316; **12:**394
skēnē	σκηνη	tent, booth	**3:**1133; **8:**363–64; **10:**213, 252; **12:**106, 721
skēnoō	σκηνόω	to tent, dwell	**4:**290; **5:**15; **9:**522; **12:**591, 650, 721
skēnopoios	σκηνοποιός	tent-maker	**10:**213, 252
skēnos	σκῆνος	tent, tabernacle	**11:**84
skeuē	σκευή	ship gear, rigging	**10:**348
skeuos	σκεῦος	body, vessel	**11:**718–19
sklēros	σκληρός	hard	**10:**337

Transliteration	Greek	English	Volume and Page
sklērotrachēlos	σκληροτράχηλος	stiff-necked	**10:**129
sklērynō	σκληρύνω	to act stubbornly	**10:**267
skōlēx	σκωληξ	worm	**5:**692
skolops	σκόλοψ	thorn, stake	**11:**164–65
skopeō	σκοπέω	to look at	**11:**533
skopos	σκοπός	goal	**11:**533
skybalon	σκύβαλον	rubbish, excrement	**11:**527
skyllō	σκύλλω	to harass, trouble	**9:**155
skythrōpos	σκυθρωπός	downcast, gloomy	**9:**477
soi	σοι	to/for you	**8:**469
sōma	σῶμα	body	**10:**862, 866, 909–10, 936, 989; **11:**383–84, 422, 490, 599, 603, 606, 613, 648; **12:**115, 163, 694
sōma tou Christou	σῶμα τοῦ Χριστου	body of Christ	**11:**358
sōmatikos	σωματικός	bodily	**9:**91; **11:**623
sophia	σοφία	wisdom	**5:**2, 96, 648, 652; **6:**961, 966; **9:**73, 519; **11:**415; **12:**23
sophia kai phronēsis	σοφία καὶ φρόνησις	wisdom and insight	**11:**373–74
sophia logou	σοφία λόγου	wisdom of speech	**10:**808
sophizō	σοφίζω	to instruct, be cleverly thought up	**12:**342
sophos	σοφός	wise	**10:**765, 814, 828
sōphrōn	σώφρων	moderate, respectable	**11:**805, 870–71
sōphroneō	σωφρονέω	to be of sound mind	**11:**91; **12:**303
sōphronizō	σωφρονίζω	to advise, encourage, urge	**11:**869
sōphrosynē	σωφροσύνη	reasonable	**10:**340–41
sōtēr	σωτήρ	savior	**3:**966; **10:**107; **11:**535, 677
sōtēria	σωτηρία	salvation, safety	**5:**674, 823; **8:**176; **10:**352; **11:**490
sōtērios	σωτήριος	salvific, relating to salvation	**9:**71; **11:**871
sōthē	σωθῇ	be saved	**8:**590
sou	σου	your(s)	**8:**202; **11:**895
soudarion	σουδάριον	head cloth	**9:**841
sōzō	σῴζω	to save	**9:**190, 687; **10:**89–90, 169, 198, 348, 811

Transliteration	Greek	English	Volume and Page
speira	σπεῖρα	a division of soldiers	**4:**249; **9:**801
spendō	σπένδω	to offer a libation	**11:**856
sperma	σπέρμα	descendants, seed	**9:**638, 640; **10:**675; **11:**261, 264, 305; **12:**413, 651
spermologos	σπερμόλογος	babbler, "seed-picker"	**10:**244–45
sphazō	σφάζω	to slaughter	**12:**603
sphēx	σφήξ	wasp, hornet	**5:**542
sphragizō	σφραγίζω	to set one's seal to, certify	**9:**559
spilades	σπιλάδες	blemishes, spots	**12:**492
splagchnismos	σπλαγχνισμός	the eating of sacrifices	**4:**242
splagchnistheis	σπλαγχνισθείς	filled with compassion, moved with pity	**8:**544
splagchnizomai	σπλαγχνίζομαι	to have compassion	**9:**158; **10:**50
splagchnon	σπλάγχνον	inward part, bowels	**10:**50; **11:**101, 499; **12:**419
spoudē	σπουδή	zeal, eagerness	**11:**118, 127
stadia	στάδια	stadia	**4:**266
statēr	στατήρ	coin, "stater"	**9:**171
stauroō	σταυρόω	to crucify	**9:**469; **11:**251
stegō	στέγω	to give a hindrance to	**10:**905
stēkō	στήκω	to stand	**11:**306
stenagmos	στεναγμός	complaint, groan	**12:**221
stenazō	στενάζω	to groan, sigh	**12:**169
stephanos	στέφανος	crown	**5:**476; **11:**536
stereōma	στερέωμα	firmness	**11:**617
stērizō	στηρίζω	to strengthen	**11:**754; **12:**339, 583
stigmata	στίγματα	marks	**11:**346
stippyon synēgmenon synagōgē anomōn	στιππύον συνηγμένον συναγωγὴ ἀνομων	a bundle of tow is like a band of lawless ones	**5:**742
stoicheia	στοιχεῖα	rudimentary principles, elements	**11:**282–84, 287, 288–89, 296, 302, 329, 565–66; **12:**357
stoicheia tou kosmou	στοιχεῖα τοῦ κόσμου	basic principles of the world (?)	**11:**344
stoicheō	στοιχέω	to go in a line, row	**11:**328, 345, 534
stratēgos	στρατήγος	general of the army	**3:**1113; **4:**255
strateuō	στρατεύω	to serve as a soldier	**11:**138
stratiōtai	στρατιῶται	soldiers	**8:**501
stratopedon	στρατόπεδον	armies, "camps"	**9:**404

Transliteration	Greek	English	Volume and Page
strephō	στρέφω	to turn	**9:**439
su	σύ	you	**8:**480; **9:**660
su eipas	σὺ εἶπας	you said it	**8:**470
su legeis	σὺ λέγεις	you say so	**8:**470
sygchairō	συγχαίρω	to rejoice with	**11:**483, 514
sygchronizō	συγχρονίζω	to spend some time in a place (often implies simultaneity)	**5:**610, 643
sygkatathesis	συγκατάθεσις	union	**11:**105
sygkathizō	συγκαθίζω	to seat together with	**11:**392
sygklēronomos	συγκληρονόμος	joint heir	**11:**357
sygkoinōneō	συγκοινωνέω	to share together in	**11:**544
sygkoinōnos	συγκοινωνός	partner, fellow participant	**11:**484, 544
sygkrinō	συγκρίνω	to compare, explain	**11:**143
sykophanteō	συκοφαντέω	to accuse falsely	**9:**85
sylaō	συλάω	to strip off	**11:**137
syllambanō	συλλαμβάνω	to capture, seize	**4:**118
symballō	συμβάλλω	to debate	**10:**244
symbibazō	συμβιβάζω	to unite, bring together	**11:**423
symbouleuomai	συμβουλεύομαι	to counsel	**4:**118
symboulion labontes	συμβούλιον λαβόντες	held an official consultation	**8:**501
symmachos	σύμμαχος	ally	**4:**250
symmetochos	συμμέτοχος	partaking in jointly	**11:**357, 437
symmorphoō	συμμορφόω	to become like	**11:**529
sympheron	συμφέρον	common good, what is helpful	**10:**944–45
symphōnēsis	συμφώνησις	agreement	**11:**105
symphōnia	συμφωνία	music	**7:**63
sympolitai	συμπολῖται	citizens with	**11:**402
symporeuomai	συμπορεύομαι	to travel together	**8:**642
sympresbyteros	συμπρεσβύτερος	fellow elder	**12:**315
syn	σὺν	with	**10:**535, 538–40; **11:**725–26, 835
syn autois	σὺν αὐτοῖς	with them	**10:**78
synagō	συνάγω	to gather, assemble	**4:**20; **8:**464, 479, 488, 497, 605
synagōgai hosiōn	συναγωγαί ὁσίων	synagogues of the pious	**8:**35
synagōgē	συναγωγή	company, synagogue	**4:**20; **12:**192, 585
synagōnisasthai moi	συναγωνίσασθαι μοι	wrestle together with me	**10:**757
synanameignymi	συναναμείγνυμι	to mix, mingle	**10:**848–49

Transliteration	Greek	English	Volume and Page
synantilambanomai	συναντιλαμβάνομαι	to grasp hold, help	**10:**598
synathleō	συναθλέω	to strive together with	**11:**540
syncheō	συγχέω	to confound	**10:**153
syndeō	συνδέω	to gather	**5:**787
syndesmos	σύνδεσμος	bond, link	**11:**420
synechō	συνέχω	to hold, enclose	**9:**111; **11:**92
synedrion	συνέδριον	council, assembly	**3:**1114, 1123
synegeirō	συνεγείρω	to raise up together	**11:**392
syneidēsin theou	συνείδησιν θεοῦ	awareness of God	**12:**281
syneidēsis	συνείδησις	a person's moral consciousness	**10:**900; **11:**45, 74, 91; **12:**105, 296
synekeraunōsan	συνεκεραύνωσαν	struck down, "strike with a thunderbolt"	**4:**193
synepitithēmi	συνεπιτίθημι	to join a movement	**10:**319
synergeō	συνεργέω	to work together with	**10:**600, 1000; **11:**96
synergos	συνεργός	fellow worker, helper	**10:**827; **11:**730; **12:**463
synesis	σύνεσις	understanding	**6:**961, 966–67
synestaurōmai	συνεσταύρωμαι	to be crucified with	**11:**243
synesthiō	συνεσθίω	to eat together	**11:**233
synetelesen	συνετέλεσεν	kept doing	**4:**174
syngenēs	συγγενής	of common origin, related	**10:**766
syngnōmē	συγγνώμη	concession	**10:**872
synkoinōnos	συγκοινωνός	partner	**10:**907
syntithemai	συντίθεμαι	to agree	**9:**657
syntribō	συντρίβω	to crush	**4:**58, 80, 110
syntrophos	σύντροφος	brought up with	**4:**255
synypourgeō	συνυπουργέω	to cooperate with	**11:**43
syssōmos	σύσσωμος	belonging to the same body	**11:**357
systoicheō	συστοιχέω	to correspond to	**11:**303
systratiōtēs	συστρατιώτης	fellow soldier	**11:**892
systrephomenōn	συστρεφομένων	gathering	**8:**369
syzaō	συζάω	to co-live	**10:**540
syzōopoieō	συζωοποιέω	to make alive together with	**11:**391–92

T

ta agenē	τὰ ἀγενῆ	the insignificant, common	**10:**812
ta archaia	τὰ ἀρχαῖα	the old	**11:**94
ta archaia	τὰ ἀρχαῖα	everything old has passed	**11:**93

Transliteration	Greek	English	Volume and Page
parēlthen, idou gegonen kaina	παρῆλθεν ἰδοὺ γέγονεν καινα	away; see, everything has become new	
ta aresta	τὰ ἀρεστά	pleasing actions	**9:**635; **12:**422
ta auta poieite	τὰ αὐτὰ ποιεῖτε	do the same	**11:**453
ta de panta	τὰ δὲ πάντα	everything	**11:**172
ta ema	τὰ ἐμα	my own	**9:**670
ta eschata	τὰ ἔσχατα	the destiny, end	**4:**402
ta epigeia	τὰ ἐπίγεια	earthly things	**9:**551
ta epourania	τὰ ἐπουράνια	heavenly things	**9:**551
ta ethnē	τὰ ἔθνη	the Gentiles	**10:**778; **11:**428
ta katōtera mera tēs gēs	τὰ κατώτερα μέρα τῆς γῆς	lower regions of the earth	**11:**421
ta logia	τὰ λόγια	the oracles	**10:**453
ta loipa	τὰ λοιπὰ	the rest	**10:**99
ta miasmata tou kosmou	τὰ μίασματα τοῦ κόσμου	the defilements of the world	**12:**352
ta noēmata	τὰ νοήματα	the minds	**11:**74
ta noēmata autōn	τὰ νοήματα αὐτῶν	their minds	**11:**68
ta panta	τὰ πάντα	all of this, everything	**11:**82, 94, 375
ta pros ton theon	τὰ πρὸς τὸν θεόν	concerning the things of God	**10:**754
ta rhēmata autōn	τὰ ῥήματα αὐτῶν	their words	**10:**668
ta stoicheia tou kosmou	τὰ στοιχεῖα τοῦ κόσμου	the basic principles of the world (?)	**11:**282, 565
ta telē tōn aiōnōn	τὰ τέλη τῶν αἰώνων	ends of the ages	**10:**914
ta thelēmata tēs sarkos kai tōn dianoiōn	τὰ θελήματα τῆς σαρκός καὶ τῶν διανοιῶν	the desires or urgings of flesh and thoughts	**11:**391
tameion	ταμεῖον	inner room, closet	**8:**201
tapeinoō	ταπεινόω	to make low, humiliate	**11:**499, 536, 544
tapeinophrosynē	ταπεινοφροσύνη	humility	**11:**420, 499, 562, 647
tapeinos	ταπεινός	oppressed, humble	**3:**1178; **11:**137
tapeinōsis	ταπείνωσις	humiliation	**10:**144; **11:**536
tarassō	ταράσσω	to be agitated, disturb	**9:**690, 729, 740; **11:**205
tauta	ταῦτα	these things	**8:**693
taxis	τάξις	morale	**11:**617
tē doxē mou	τῇ δόξῃ μου	my glory	**11:**69
tē sarki	τῇ σαρκί	in the flesh	**11:**164
technitēs	τεχνίτης	artisan	**5:**546
tegos	τέγος	terrace, roof	**6:**995

Transliteration	Greek	English	Volume and Page
tekmērion	τεκμήριον	convincing proof	**10:**40
tekna agapēta	τέκνα ἀγαπητά	beloved children	**10:**840
tekna autou	τεκνα αὐτου	his children	**5:**720
teknon	τέκνον	child	**5:**654–55; **8:**358; **9:**640, 732, 857; **11:**103, 452, 656, 898; **12:**388, 398
tektōn	τέκτων	carpenter	**8:**592
teleioō	τελειόω	to complete	**9:**795, 832; **10:**825; **11:**532–33; **12:**39, 68, 430, 431, 611
teleios	τέλειος	complete, perfect	**8:**391; **10:**825; **11:**533–34
teleiōs	τελείως	entirely	**12:**257
teleiōtēs	τελειωτής	perfecter, completion	**12:**149
teleō	τελέω	to finish	**9:**832; **10:**657; **11:**166, 325
teleutēsei	τελευτησει	will die	**5:**719
telōnai	τελῶναι	tax collectors	**9:**167
telos	τέλος	end	**5:**476, 678; **10:**625, 655, 657, 842, 980; **11:**68
telos gar nomou Christos	τέλός γὰρ νόμου Χριστός	for Christ is the fulfillment, goal of the law	**10:**645
telos nomou	τέλος νόμου	fulfillment, goal of the law	**10:**656, 692
tēn archēn	τὴν ἀρχήν	from the beginning	**9:**634
tēn autēn eikona	τὴν αὐτὴν εἰκόνα	into the same image	**11:**70
tēn charin tautēn	τὴν χάριν ταύτην	this grace	**11:**121
tēn dikaian krisin	τὴν δικαίαν κρίσιν	right judgment	**9:**620
tēn dorean tou hagiou pneumatos	τὴν δωρεὰν τοῦ ἁγίου πνεύματος	the gift of the Holy Spirit	**10:**67
tēn idian dikaiosynēn	τὴν ἰδίαν δικαιοσύνην	their own righteousness	**10:**654
tēn pistin	τὴν πίστιν	the faith	**11:**269
tēn prosagōgēn . . . pros ton patera	τὴν προσαγωγὴν πρὸς τὸν πατέρα	access to the Father	**11:**401
tēn tritēn	τὴν τρίτην	third	**3:**994
teras	τέρας	wonder, marvel	**11:**168
tēreō	τηρέω	to keep, watch over	**12:**478, 482

Transliteration	Greek	English	Volume and Page
tē rēsis dēmosia	τήρησις δημοσία	the public prison	**10:**104
tē s apeitheias	τῆς ἀπειθείας	those who are disobedient	**11:**373
tē s doxēs tou Christou	τῆς δόξης τοῦ Χριστοῦ	the glory of Christ	**11:**74
tē s thlipseōs tēs megalēs	τῆς θλίψεως τῆς μεγάλης	the great ordeal	**12:**624
tetelestai	τετέλεσται	it is finished	**1:**977
teteleiōmai	τετελείωμαι	to be complete, finished	**10:**825
tethēriōmenos tē psychē	τεθηριωμένος τῇ ψυχῇ	inwardly raging, "wild beast-like in soul"	**4:**228
Thaiman	θαιμαν	Thaiman, teman	**6:**966
thallos	θαλλός	olive branch	**4:**286
thambos	θάμβος	astonishment, amazement	**9:**110
thanatos	θάνατος	death	**9:**584; **10:**982; **11:**529
tharreō	θαρρέω	to be confident, courageous	**11:**84
tharseō	θάρσέω	to take courage	**3:**983, 1040, 1042; **6:**974; **10:**357
tharsei paidion	θάρσει παιδίον	take courage, child	**3:**983
tharsei thygater	θάρσει θύγατερ	take courage, daughter	**3:**983
tharsos	θάρσος	courage	**10:**357
thaumazō	θαυμάζω	to marvel, be astonished	**8:**420, 592
theaomai	θεάομαι	to see, look at	**9:**127; **12:**382
theis ta gonata	θεὶς τὰ γόνατα	kneeling, "placing the knees"	**9:**433
thelēma	θέλημα	will	**9:**795; **12:**301
thelēma Theou	θέλημα Θεοῦ	will of God	**11:**369–70
thelō	θέλω	to want, wish	**8:**350, 469; **9:**795; **10:**641; **11:**567
theodidaktos	θεοδίδακτος	taught by God	**11:**719–20
theopneustos	θεόπνευστος	God-breathed	**11:**851
theōros	θεωρός	sacred envoy	**4:**218
theos	θεός	God	**6:**960; **10:**630, 738
theosebēs	θεοσεβής	one who worships God	**9:**660
theosebēs	θεοσεβής	pious	**1:**291
theou oikodomē	θεοῦ οἰκοδομή	God's building	**10:**831
theou zōntos	θεοῦ ζῶντος	the living God	**11:**105
therapōn	θεράπων	servant	**12:**46
thēsauros	θησαυρός	treasure	**8:**314; **9:**347; **11:**81

Transliteration	Greek	English	Volume and Page
-thētō	-θήτω	third person imperative ending	**8:**202
thinganō	θιγγάνω	to touch	**11:**633
thlibō	θλίβω	to oppress, afflict	**11:**40, 81, 109
thlipsis	θλῖψις	tribulation, anguish, persecution	**8:**442; **9:**780, 783; **10:**200, 885, 983; **11:**40–41, 55, 83, 97, 109, 118, 120, 613–14, 695, 708, 711, 745, 771; **12:**565, 576
thrēneō	θρηνέω	to mourn	**9:**779
Thrēnoi	θρῆνοι	Lamentations	**6:**1024
thrēskeia	θρησκεία	religion, worship	**10:**335; **11:**564
thriambeuō	θριαμβεύω	to celebrate a victory	**11:**58
throeō	θροέω	to agitate	**11:**756
thromboi	θρόμβοι	drops	**9:**433
thygatēr	θυγάτηρ	daughter	**9:**190
thymos	θυμός	wrath, rage	**11:**643; **12:**675
thyra pisteōs	θύρα πίστεως	door of faith	**10:**205
thyreos	θυρεός	large shield	**11:**461
thyrsos	θύρσος	ivy-wreathed wand	**4:**257
thysia	θυσία	sacrifice	**11:**514
thysian zōsan	θυσίαν ζῶσαν	a living sacrifice	**11:**58
ti hymin dokei	τί ὑμῖν δοκεῖ	How does it seem to you?	**8:**376
ti kainoteron	τι καινότερον	something new	**10:**245
ti oun	τί οὖν	why then	**8:**364; **10:**489
ti oun eroumen	τί οὖν ἐροῦμεν	what then shall we say?	**10:**489
ti poiēsō	τί ποιήσω	What will I do?	**9:**381
timaō	τιμάω	to honor, revere	**9:**252, 645
timē	τιμή	honor	**9:**107; **11:**819; **12:**285, 593
tinas	τινὰς	some	**10:**682
tines	τινές	some	**9:**696
tis	τίς	certain	**9:**233; **10:**986; **11:**622
tis anthrōpos ex hymōn	τίς ἄνθρωπος ἐξ ὑμῶν	which one of you	**9:**294
tis hetera entolē	τις ἑτέρα ἐντολή	any other commandment	**10:**725
tithēmi	τίθημι	to lay down, give up	**9:**690, 722, 759; **10:**907
titlos	τίτλος	inscription, notice	**9:**830
to	τὸ	the	**10:**837; **11:**302

Transliteration	Greek	English	Volume and Page
to agathon	τὸ ἀγαθόν	the good	**12:**465
to auto phroneite	τὸ αὐτὸ φρονεῖτε	be of one mind, "think the same thing"	**11:**178
to chyma tōn arithmōn	τὸ χύμα τῶν ἀριθμῶν	flood of statistics, large number of lines	**4:**202
tō de theō charis	τῷ δε`θεῷ χάρις	thanks be to God	**11:**57
tō didonti	τῷ διδόντι	the giver	**10:**989
to ethnos	τὸ ἔθνος	the nations	**9:**407
to ethnos hēmōn	τὸ ἔθνος ἡμῶν	our nation	**9:**447
to euangelion to euangelisthen hyp'emou	τὸ εὐαγγέλιον τὸ εὐαγγελισθὲν ὑπ'ἐμοῦ	the gospel that was gospeled by me	**11:**211
to hyperballon	τὸ ὑπερβάλλον	the exceeding	**11:**416
to kakon	τὸ κακόν	the evil	**12:**465
to kalon	τὸ καλόν	the good	**11:**177
to krima	τὸ κρίμα	the condemnation	**12:**477, 485
to loipon	τὸ λοιπόν	finally, and so	**11:**522, 541
to menon	τὸ μένον	that which remains	**11:**65
to mesotoichon	τὸ μεσότοιχον	dividing wall, fence	**11:**399
to mesotoichon tou phragmou	τὸ μεσότοιχον τοῦ φραγμοῦ	the dividing wall of the hedge, fence	**11:**399
to nikos	τὸ νῖκος	the victory	**11:**57
to parechein moi kopon	τὸ παρέχειν μοι κόπον	keeps on bothering me	**9:**337
to phronēma tēs sarkos	τὸ φρόνημα τῆς σαρκός	the mind of flesh	**10:**582
to phronēma tou pneumatos	τὸ φρόνημα τοῦ πνεύματος	the mind of spirit	**10:**582
to plērōma touta panta en pasin plēroumenou	τὸ πλήρωμα τοῦτά πάντα ἐν πᾶσιν πληρουμένου	the fullness of him who fills all in all	**11:**381
to pneuma autou en autō	τὸ πνεῦμα αὐτοῦ ἐν αὐτῷ	his spirit within him	**10:**244
tō pneumati	τῷ πνεύματι	the Spirit, spirit	**10:**961
to ponēros	τὸ πονηρός	the evil, devil	**12:**465
to sōma	τὸ σῶμα	the body	**10:**909
to telos	τὸ τὲλος	the end	**11:**27
toigaroun	τοιγαροῦν	therefore	**12:**148
tois ergois tois ponerois	τοῖς ἔργοις τοῖς πονηροῖς	with wicked works	**12:**454
tois eusebesin	τοις εὐσεβέσιν	to the devout ones	**5:**833
tois hagiois autou	τοῖς ἁγίοις αὐτοῦ	his holy ones	**11:**750

Transliteration	Greek	English	Volume and Page
tois huiois tēs apeitheias	τοῖς υἱοις τῆς ἀπειθείας	sons of disobedience	**11**:389
tois ousin	τοῖς οὖσιν	who are	**11**:369
tois pasin gegona panta, hina pantōs tinas sōsō	τοῖς πᾶσιν γέγονα πάντα ἵνα πάντως τινὰς σώσω	I have become all things to all people so that by all means I might save . . . some	**10**:682
ton adelphon	τὸν ἀδελφον	the brother	**12**:393
tōn alisgēmatōn tōn eidōlōn	τῶν ἀλισγημάτων τῶν εἰδώλων	polluted by idols	**10**:221
ton bion	τὸν βίον	means of livelihood	**12**:419
ton ek pisteōs Iēsou	τὸν ἐκ πίστεως Ἰησοῦ	out of the faith(fulness) of Jesus	**10**:473
tōn ergōn	τῶν ἔργων	of works	**10**:480
ton estaurōmenon	τὸν ἐσταυρωμένον	the crucified one	**8**:499
ton heautou huion	τὸν ἑαυτοῦ υἱόν	his own son	**10**:580
ton heteron nomon	τὸν ἕτερον νόμον	the other law	**10**:725
ton kainon anthrōpon	τὸν καινὸν ἄνθρωπον	new humanity	**11**:414
ton logon tou theou	τὸν λόγον τοῦ θεοῦ	the word of God	**9**:232
ton neon	τὸν νέον	the new self	**11**:643
ton nomon telousa	τὸν νόμον τελοῦσα	fulfillment of Torah	**10**:480
ton nomon tōn entolōn en dogmasin	τὸν νόμον τῶν ἐντολῶν ἐν δόγμασιν	the law with its commandments and ordinances	**11**:399
ton oikon tēs pisteōs	τὸν οἶκον τής πίστεως	the house of faith	**11**:337
ton palaion anthrōpon	τὸν παλαιόν ἄνθρωπον	the old self	**11**:643
tōn planōntōn	τῶν πλανώντων	the ones who deceive, lead astray	**12**:406, 412, 452
toparchēs	τοπάρχης	governor	**3**:953
tote	τότε	then	**4**:47; **8**:287, 427–28, 442, 477
tote ērxato	τότε ἤρξατο	then he began	**8**:271
tou adikēsantos	τοῦ ἀδικήσαντος	the one who did the wrong	**11**:52
tou aiōnos toutou	τοῦ αἰῶνος τούτου	of this age	**10**:822
tou kosmou	τοῦ κόσμου	of the world	**11**:622

Transliteration	Greek	English	Volume and Page
tou plērōmatos tou Christou	τοῦ πληρώματος τοῦ Χριστοῦ	the fullness of Christ	**11:**360
tou ponērou	τοῦ πονηροῦ	the evil one	**11:**765
tous dialogismous autōn	τοὺς διαλογισμούς αὐτῶν	what they (are) thinking	**9:**211
tous kynas . . . tous kakous ergatas . . . tēn katatomēn	τοὺς κὺνας . . . τοὺς κακους ἐργάτας . . . τὴν κατατομήν	the dogs . . . the evildoers . . . the mutilators of flesh	**11:**524
tous opthalmous tes kardias	τούς ὀφθαλμοὺς τής καρδίας	eyes of your heart	**11:**381
touto	τοῦτό	this	**10:**89
Touto estin to haima mou tēs diathēkēs to ekchynnomenon hyper pollōn	τοῦτό ἐστιν τὸ αἵμά μου τῆς διαθήκης τὸ ἐκχυννόμενον ὑπὲρ πολλῶν	This is my blood of the covenant, which is poured out for many	**8:**704
Touto estin to sōma mou to hyper hymōn didomenon	τοῦτό ἐστιν τὸ σῶμά μου τὸ ὑπὲρ ὑμῶν διδόμενον	This is my body, which is given for you	**8:**703
Touto mou estin to sōma to hyper hymōn	τοῦτό μού ἐστιν τὸ σῶμα τὸ ὑπὲρ ὑμῶν	This is my body that is for you	**8:**703
Touto to potērion hē kainē diathēkē en tō haimati mou to hyper hymōn ekchynnomenon	τοῦτο τὸ ποτήριον ἡ καινὴ διαθήκη ἐν τῷ αἵματι μου τὸ ὑπὲρ ὑμῶν ἐκχυννόμενον	This cup that is poured out for you is the new covenant in my blood	**8:**704
Touto to potērion hē kainē diathēkē estin en tō emō haimati	τοῦτο τὸ ποτήριον ἡ καινὴ διαθήκη ἐστὶν ἐν τῷ ἐμῷ αἵματι	This cup is the new covenant in my blood	**8:**704
toxon	τόξον	bow	**12:**611
triboi	τρίβοι	paths	**6:**966
tropē	τροπή	reversal	**4:**69
tympanizō	τυμπανίζω	to beat, torture	**12:**144
tympanon	τύμπανον	drum, stick, wagon wheel	**4:**236
tynchanō	τυγχάνω	to help	**10:**339

Transliteration	Greek	English	Volume and Page
tynchanō	τυγχάνω	to receive, attain, experience	**12:**100
typos	τύπος	type, example	**1:**91; **11:**694; **12:**295
tyrannoi	τύραννοι	monarchs	**5:**490
X			
xenia daimonia	ξενία δαιμόνια	foreign deities	**10:**242–44
xenizō	ξενίζω	to receive as a guest, surprise	**4:**232; **12:**162, 310
xenoi	ξένοι	strangers, aliens	**11:**402
xylon	ξυλον	wood, tree	**5:**552; **12:**694
Z			
zaō	ζάω	to live	**9:**575, 583, 688; **10:**335; **11:**633
zēloō	ζηλόω	to be zealous	**10:**126; **11:**295
zēlos	ζῆλος	zeal, jealousy	**10:**126; **12:**211
zēlos kai eris	ζῆλος καὶ ἔρις	jealousy and quarreling	**10:**825
zēlōtēs	ζηλωτής	zealot, enthusiast	**10:**292–93, 306; **11:**213
zēmia	ζημία	loss	**11:**527
zemioō	ζημιόω	to lose	**11:**527
zeōn	ζέων	lively	**10:**261
zeōn tō pneumati	ζέων τῷ πνεύματι	burning enthusiasm	**10:**261
zizania	ζιζάνια	weeds (?)	**8:**308
zōē	ζωή	life	**9:**583–84, 632, 742
zōē aiōnios	ζωὴ αἰώνιός	eternal life	**9:**552, 789; **12:**447
zōnnyō	ζωννύω	to gird	**9:**861
zygos	ζυγός	yoke	**4:**106; **12:**612

MAPS, CHARTS, ILLUSTRATIONS

A

Abijah's Conquests (911 BCE)
3:531
Adam Compared to Christ
11:505
Aegean Region, The
11:4
Agricultural and Civil Calendar
1:275
Ancient Near East in Maccabean Times
4:4
Ancient Near East Second Millennium BCE
1:423
Apostles Identified in Matthew, Mark, Luke/Acts, John, and Paul
8:254
Around the Sea of Galilee
8:583; **9:**537

B

Banquets in Esther, The
3:857

C

Canaan at the Time of Abraham
1:474
Canaan at the Time of the Conquest
2:17
Capture and Return of the Ark, The
2:1000
Central Corinth at the Time of Paul (about 50 CE)
10:894
Christ Hymn 1, The
11:502
Christ Hymn 2, The
11:503
Chronology of 1 and 2 Maccabees
4:14
Chronology of Jesus' Final Days in Jerusalem, The
8:401
Chronology of the Holy Week and Resurrection Appearances in the Gospels, The
9:704
Chronology of the Kings of the Divided Monarchy, The
3:101
Circuit of Love in 1 John, The
12:436
Cities of Benjamin in Neh 11:25-30 Compared to Ezra 2:1 or Joshua 15:1
3:828
Cities of Judah in Neh 11:25-30 Compared to Joshua 15:1
3:827
Coin Depicting the Deified Emperor Augustus
11:401
Coins in the Gospels
9:171
Corinth and Vicinity
10:774
Cultic Calendars in Leviticus 23:1 and Numbers 28:1-29
2:231

D

David as Fugitive from Saul
2:1143
David's Battles Against the Arameans (990 BCE)
3:414
David's Empire
2:1275
Death and the Strange Woman in Proverbs 1–9
5:71
Defeat at Mt. Gilboa, The
2:1197
Diagram of 1 Thess 5:16-22, A
11:730
Dialogue Between Job and the Three Friends
4:320

E

Eastern Early Roman Empire, The
10:4
Eastern Mediterranean in Paul's Time, The
11:782
Eph 3:1-13 and Col 1:23-28
11:407
Eph 4:17-19 and Rom 1:21, 24
11:427
Eph 4:17-24 and Col 3:5-10
11:427
Eph 5:15-20 and Col 3:16-17; 4:5
11:441
Eph 5:22–6:9 as Household Code
11:447
Eph 5:3-8 and Col 3:5-8
11:434

Eph 6:14-17 and the Armor of God
11:459
Eph 6:21-24 and Col 4:7-9, 18
11:466
External Design: A Study in Symmetry
7:475

F

Family Tree of David, The
2:1286
Family Tree of Ruth and Boaz, The
2:944
Fertile Crescent at the Turn of the 7th/6th Centuries BCE, The
6:557
Five Diptychs and the Seven Antitheses in the Book of Wisdom, The
5:446

G

Galatia
11:192
Geographical Setting of Jacob's Journey
1:554
Geographical Setting of the Exodus
1:807

H

Hearing and Seeing in the Book of Revelation
12:622
"Heart" in the Old Testament, The
5:60
Hebrew Alphabet, The
4:718; **7:**601
High Priests During New Testament Times
9:807
Hill Country of Ephraim and Benjamin, The
2:974
Historical Setting of the Prophetic Books
7:844
Homelands of the Pentecost Pilgrims in Acts 2:9-11
10:56

I

"I AM" Sayings in John, The
9:602
Israel, Judah, and the Surrounding Nations, 8th-7th Centuries BCE
7:201
Israel's Wilderness Travel in Exodus–Numbers and in Numbers 33:1
2:251

J

Jerusalem at the Time of David
2:1239
Jerusalem at the Time of Jeremiah (640–586 BCE)
6:1014
Jerusalem at the Time of Jesus
9:368
Jerusalem at the Time of Paul
10:6
Jerusalem at the Time of Solomon
3:27
Jesus' Journey Through Samaria
9:564
Jesus' Journey to Jerusalem
8:644
Jesus' Works in the Gospel of Luke as Fulfillment of the Prophets
9:161
Jewish Religious Festivals in John
9:542
Judea at the Time of Jesus
9:685

K

Kings of Israel and Judah
1:263

L

Late Assyrian Kings, The
7:594
Levites Who Signed the Firm Agreement, The
3:816
Levitical Ancestral Houses, The
2:52
Literary Relationships Between Psalms of Solomon 11 and Baruch 5
6:972

M

Macedonia and Achaia
11:676
Main Roadways of Asia Minor
11:581
Major Individual Sacrifices Prescribed by Leviticus
1:1008
Meaning of ἐξ ἀκοῆς πὶστεως (ex akoēs pisteōs), The
11:252
Miracle Stories in the Gospels
8:242

N

Narrative Structure of Job, The
4:324

Nebuchadnezzar's First Campaign (605–604 BCE)
3:650
Nehemiah's Reconstruction of the Wall of Jerusalem
3:760

O

Old Testament and Other Texts Alluded to in Revelation
12:737
Oppositional Columns in Paul's Allegory
11:303
Oracles of Amos, The
7:356

P

Palestine at the Time of Jesus
8:141; **9:**64
Palestine at the Turn of the 7th/6th Centuries BCE
6:558
Parables in the Synoptic Gospels
9:297
Paraclete Passages in the Gospel of John
9:775
Parallels Between Gal 3:23-29 and 4:1-7
11:281
Parallels Between Gal 4:4-6 and 3:13-14
11:286
Partial Family Tree of Herod the Great
8:320; **9:**89
Partial Geneaology of Levi from Exod 6:14-25
2:48
Paul's Relation with the Corinthians
11:11
Persian Empire, The
3:879
Philistine Conquests (734 BCE), The
3:599
Post-Exilic Priests
3:831

R

Reconstruction of the Iron Age City of Lachish, A
1:222
Rehoboam's Fortresses (928–920 BCE)
3:520
Roman Emperors 4 BCE–138 CE
12:683

S

Saul and Jonathan at Michmash
2:1069
Saul Rescues Jabesh-gilead
2:1054
Selected Literary and Epigraphical Evidence from the Ancient Near East
1:235
Selection of Exilic Prayers of Confession and Deliverance, A
7:127
Seleucid and Jewish Leaders in 1 and 2 Maccabees
4:135
Sequence of Seven Seals, Trumpets, and Bowls, The
12:610
Seven Churches of Revelation, The
12:572
Signers of the Firm Agreement, The
3:816
Site Plan of Beer Sheba
1:223
Solomon's Temple
3:62
Structure and Number of the Clans, The
2:208
Structure of Matthew 1:1–12:21, The
8:116
Structure of Matthew 8:1–9:34, The
8:223
Structure of Matthew 13:1-52, The
8:301
Structure of Matthew's Narrative of Jesus' Passion and Resurrection, The
8:461
Structure of the Gospel of Matthew, The
8:117
Structure of the Judgment Discourse, The
8:429
Structure of the Sermon on the Mount, The
8:173
Structure of the Toledot from Genesis 2 to Numbers 3, The
2:49
Synopsis of the Sermon on the Mount/Sermon on the Plain
9:140
Synoptic Chart of Antiochus's Persecution, A
4:9
Syria and Israel/Judea in Maccabean Times
4:79

T

Temple Mount of Herod the Great, The
8:662

Temple of Ezekiel's Vision, The
6:1535
Texts and Versions of Esther
3:861
Twelve Identified in Matthew, Mark, Luke, and Acts, The
9:138
Twelve Tribes of Israel, The
3:318
Two Ministries and Their Consequences, The
11:65
Tyre, Sidon, and Caesarea Philippi
8:610

V

Variants of the Word for "Bread"
8:703
Variants of the Word for "Cup"
8:704
Via Egnatia
11:470

W

Women at the Crucifixion or the Tomb of Jesus
9:470

EXCURSUSES

A

Afterlife of Jonah, The
7:526
Almsgiving (Tobit)
3:1015
Are the Levites Punished or Restored in Ezek 44:10-14?
6:1575

B

Beliefs About Death (Tobit)
3:1004
Biblical Suspicion of the Temple
12:725

C

Call Narrative Form in 1 Samuel 9:1–10:16, The
2:1040
Cities as Females
6:1121

D

Daniel and Nonviolence
7:144
Day and Night (Tobit)
3:1028
Deuteronomistic Repression of Patriarchal Authority
2:628

E

Existence, Structure, and Background of a Possible Hymn, The
11:601
Extra-textual Traditions and Ezekielian Innovations
6:1118
Ezekiel's Oracles Against Foreign Nations and Rulers
6:1355
Ezekiel's Oracles Against Pharoah/Egypt
6:1401

F

Fall in 1 Enoch, The
12:645
Food and Power
7:40
"Fornication" and Idolatry
12:579

G

God's Throne, the Heavenly Merkabah, and the Human Figure
12:596

H

Hebrew Poetry
6:190
"The Household Code": Its Origin and Adaptation
11:652
Household Tables, The
12:278

I

Imprisonment and Exile
7:89
Interpreting the Miracle Stories in Matthew
8:244
Israel's "High Places"
6:1159

J

Jerusalem Conference and the Collection for the Poor, The
11:113
Jesus' Return to Glory
9:790
John 6:51*c*-58 in Critical Scholarship
9:605
John 9:22 and the Benediction Against Heretics
9:657
John's Portrayal of Pilate
9:815

K

Kingdom of Heaven in Matthew
8:288

L

Language of Righteousness, The
11:238

M

Matthean Christology
8:353
Matthew as Interpreter of Scripture
8:151
Millennium, The
12:708
Monotheism and the Song of Moses
2:529

O

On Fasting, Communal Prayer, and Heavenly Warfare
7:123

P

Paraclete, The
9:774
Parousia in the New Testament, The
12:702
Paul's Discussion of Multiple Covenants
11:76
Perimeters of Paradise, The
6:1597
"Period of Wrath" and Modern Theology, The
7:115
Phoenician City of Sidon, The
6:1398
Prophetic Sign Acts
6:1143

R

Reign of God in Mark
8:537
Role of Satan in the Old Testament, The
4:347

S

Suffering in 1 Peter
12:251

T

Theory of Retribution (Tobit)
3:995
"Third Isaiah"
6:472
Tithes (Tobit)
3:993
Tribulations of the Messianic Age, The
12:635
Tyre "in the Heart of the Seas"
6:1359

U

Uncleanness and Purification (Tobit)
3:1002

REFERENCE LISTS

1. The Old Testament

Genesis (Vol. 1)
Exodus (Vol. 1)
Leviticus (Vol. 1)
Numbers (Vol. 2)
Deuteronomy (Vol. 2)
Joshua (Vol. 2)
Judges (Vol. 2)
Ruth (Vol. 2)
1 Samuel (Vol. 2) = 1 Kingdoms
2 Samuel (Vol. 2) = 2 Kingdoms
1 Kings (Vol. 3) = 3 Kingdoms
2 Kings (Vol. 3) = 4 Kingdoms
1 Chronicles (Vol. 3)
2 Chronicles (Vol. 3)
Ezra (Vol. 3)
Nehemiah (Vol. 3)
Esther (Vol. 3)
Job (Vol. 4)
Psalms (Vol. 4)
Proverbs (Vol. 5)
Ecclesiastes (Vol. 5)
Song of Solomon (Vol. 5)
Isaiah (Vol. 6)
Jeremiah (Vol. 6)
Lamentations (Vol. 6)
Ezekiel (Vol. 6)
Daniel (Vol. 7)
Hosea (Vol. 7)
Joel (Vol. 7)
Amos (Vol. 7)
Obadiah (Vol. 7)
Jonah (Vol. 7)
Micah (Vol. 7)
Nahum (Vol. 7)
Habakkuk (Vol 7)
Zephaniah (Vol. 7)
Haggai (Vol. 7)
Zechariah (Vol. 7)
Malachi (Vol. 7)

2. Apocryphal and Deuterocanonical Books

Tobit (Vol. 3)
Judith (Vol. 3)
Esther Additions (Vol. 3)
Wisdom of Solomon (Vol. 5)
Sirach (Vol. 5) Ecclesiasticus = Wisdom of Jesus Son of Sirach = Ben Sirach
Baruch (Vol. 6)
The Letter of Jeremiah (Vol. 6) = Baruch, Chap. 6
Daniel Additions (Vol. 7)
- The Prayer of Azariah and the Song of the Three Jews
- Susanna
- Bel and the Dragon

1 Maccabees (Vol. 4)
2 Maccabees (Vol. 4)

3. The New Testament

Matthew (Vol. 8)
Mark (Vol. 8)
Luke (Vol. 9)
John (Vol. 9)
Acts (Vol. 10) = The Acts of the Apostles
Romans (Vol. 10)
1 Corinthians (Vol. 10)
2 Corinthians (Vol. 11)
Galatians (Vol. 11)
Ephesians (Vol. 11)
Philippians (Vol. 11)
Colossians (Vol. 11)
1 Thessalonians (Vol. 11)
2 Thessalonians (Vol. 11)
1 Timothy (Vol. 11)
2 Timothy (Vol. 11)
Titus (Vol. 11)
Philemon (Vol. 11)
Hebrews (Vol. 12)
James (Vol. 12)
1 Peter (Vol. 12)
2 Peter (Vol. 12)
1 John (Vol. 12)
2 John (Vol. 12)
3 John (Vol. 12)
Jude (Vol. 12)
Revelation (Vol. 12) = Apocalypse

4. The Pentateuch (Torah)

Genesis
Exodus
Leviticus
Numbers
Deuteronomy

5. The Agricultural and Civil Calendar

See the chart on page 275 in volume 1

6. The Ten Commandments

(Exod 20:1-17)

1. No other gods
2. No handmade images of, God
3. No false use of God's name
4. No work on the Sabbath
5. No dishonor toward parents
6. No murder
7. No adultery
8. No stealing
9. No lying or false witness
10. No coveting

7. The Plagues on Egypt

The Plague of Blood (Exod 7:14-25)
The Plague of Frogs (Exod 8:1-15)
The Plague of Gnats (Exod 8:16-19)
The Plague of Flies (Exod 8:20-32)
The Plague on Livestock (Exod 9:1-7)
The Plague of Boils (Exod 9:8-12)
The Plague of Hail (Exod 9:13-35)
The Plague of Locusts (Exod 10:1-20)
The Plague of Darkness (Exod 10:21-29)
The Death of the Firstborn (Exod 12:29-39)

8. Megillot

Song of Songs
Ruth
Lamentations
Ecclesiastes
Esther

9. Wisdom Literature

Job
Ecclesiastes
Proverbs
Song of Songs
Sirach
Book of Wisdom

10. Historical Books

Joshua
Judges
Ruth
1 Samuel
2 Samuel
1 Kings
2 Kings
1 Chronicles
2 Chronicles
Ezra
Nehemiah
Esther
1 Maccabees
2 Maccabees

11. Old Testament Prophets

(Literary)
Isaiah
Jeremiah
Ezekiel
Daniel
Hosea
Joel
Amos
Obadiah
Jonah
Micah
Nahum
Habakkuk
Zephaniah
Haggai
Zechariah
Malachi

12. Minor Prophets

Hosea
Joel
Amos
Obadiah
Jonah
Micah
Nahum
Habakkuk
Zephaniah
Haggai
Zechariah
Malachi

13. Major Prophets

Isaiah
Jeremiah
Ezekiel
Daniel

14. The Kings of Israel and Judah

See figure 1 on page 263 in volume 1

15. Pre-exilic Prophets

Hosea
Amos

Micah
First Isaiah

16. Exilic Prophets

Jeremiah
Ezekiel
Second Isaiah

17. Post-exilic (and Second Temple) Prophets

Third Isaiah
Daniel
Joel
Jonah
Nahum
Obadiah
Habakkuk
Zephaniah
Haggai
Zechariah
Malachi

18. Some Other Prophets

David
Deborah
Elijah
Elisha
Ezra
Hannah
Huldah
Isaiah's wife
Micaiah
Miriam
Moses
Nathan
Samuel
Shemaiah
Zedekiah

19. Seleucid Rulers in 1 and 2 Maccabees

Antiochus III
Seleucus IV Philopator
Antiochus IV Epiphanes
Antiochus V Eupator
Demetrius I Soter
Alexander (Balas) V Epiphanes
Demetrius II Nicator
Antiochus VI Epiphanes
Antiochus VII Sidetes

20. Maccabean Leaders (1 and 2 Maccabees)

Mattathias
Judas Maccabeus
Jonathan
Simon

21. Jewish High Priests in 1 and 2 Maccabees

Onias III
Jason
Menelaus
Alcimus
Jonathan
Simon
John Hyrcanus

22. Job's Friends

Eliphaz
Bildad
Zophar

23. Types of Psalms

Entrance Liturgy
Hymn or Song of Praise
Lament of an Individual
Lament of the Community
Mixed Types
Prophetic Exhortation
Psalms of Confidence/Trust
Royal Psalm
Thanksgiving Song of an Individual
Wisdom/Torah Psalm

24. Some Psalm Groups or Types

Entrance Liturgies (15, 24)
Enthronement (24, 47, 93, 95, 96, 97, 98, 99)
Penitential Psalms (6, 32, 38, 51, 102, 130, 143)
Prophetic Exhortation (50, 81, 95)
Royal Psalms (2, 18, 20, 21, 45, 72, 89, 110, 132)
Psalms of David (3–17, 23–32, 34–41, 51–65, 68–70, 86, 101, 103, 108–10, 122, 124, 131, 138–45)
Psalms of Solomon (72, 127)
Psalms of the Asaphites (50, 73–83)
Psalms of the Korahites (42, 44–49, 84–85, 87–88)
Psalms of Jeduthin (39, 62, 77)
Songs of Ascents (120–134)
Songs of Zion (46, 48, 76, 84, 87, 122)

25. Apocalyptic Writings

Isaiah 24–27
Ezekiel 40–48

Apocalyptic Writings *(continued)*
- Daniel
- Matthew 24
- Mark 13
- Revelation

26. The Gospels
- Matthew
- Mark
- Luke
- John

27. The Synoptic Gospels
- Matthew
- Mark
- Luke

28. Johannine Literature
- John (Gospel of)
- 1 John
- 2 John
- 3 John
- Revelation

29. Miracle Stories in the Gospels
See figure 6 on page 242 in volume 8

30. "Signs" in the Gospel of John
- Wine miracle at the Cana wedding (2:1-11)
- Healing the royal official's son (4:46-54)
- Healing a lame man (5:1-18)
- Feeding of 5,000 (6:1-14)
- Jesus walks on water (6:16-21)
- Healing a blind man (9:1-41)
- Raising of Lazarus (11:1-44)
- Miraculous catch of fish (21:1-14)

31. Jewish Religious Festivals in the Gospel of John
- Sabbath
- Passover-Unleavened Bread
- Feast of Tabernacles
- Feast of Dedication

See also figure 9 on page 542 in volume 9

32. The "I AM" Sayings in the Gospel of John
- "I AM the one who is speaking to you." (4:26)
- "I AM; do not be afraid." (6:20)
- "I am the bread of life." (6:35)
- "I am the living bread that came down from heaven." (6:51)
- "I am the light of the world." (8:12)
- "I told you that you would die in your sins, for you will die in your sins unless you believe that I AM." (8:24)
- "When you have lifted up the Son of Man, then you will realize that I AM, and I do nothing on my own, but I speak these things as the Father instructed me." (8:28)
- "Very truly, I tell you, before Abraham was, I AM." (8:58)
- "I am the light of the world." (9:5)
- "Very truly, I tell you, I am the gate for the sheep." (10:7, 9)
- "I am the good shepherd." (10:11, 14)
- "I am the resurrection and the life." (11:25-26)
- "I tell you this now, before it occurs, so that when it does occur, you may believe that I AM." (13:19)
- "I am the way, and the truth, and the life." (14:6)
- "I am the true vine, and my Father is the vine grower." (15:1, 5)
- "I AM." (18:5, 7)

33. Pastoral Epistles
- 1 Timothy
- 2 Timothy
- Titus

34. Letters Attributed to Paul
- Romans
- 1 Corinthians
- 2 Corinthians
- Galatians
- Ephesians
- Philippians
- Colossians
- 1 Thessalonians
- 2 Thessalonians
- 1 Timothy
- 2 Timothy
- Titus
- Philemon

35. Undisputed Letters of Paul
- Romans
- 1 Corinthians
- 2 Corinthians
- Galatians
- Philippians
- 1 Thessalonians
- Philemon

36. Disputed Letters Attributed to Paul

Ephesians
Colossians
2 Thessalonians

37. General Epistles

James
1 Peter
2 Peter
1 John
2 John
3 John
Jude

38. Birth Accounts (Birth of Jesus)

Matt 1:18–2:18
Luke 1:5–2:52

39. The Twelve Disciples

See figure 2 on page 138 in volume 9

40. Miracles of Jesus

Blind and mute man healed (Matt 12:22-30)
Blind man at Bethsaida healed (Mark 8:22-26)
Blind man healed (John 9:1-41)
Blind man/men healed (Matt 9:27-31; 20:29-34; Mark 10:46-52; Luke 18:35-43)
Boy possessed by a spirit (Matt 17:14-21; Mark 9:14-29; Luke 9:37-43*a*)
Centurion of Capernaum (Matt 8:5-13)
Cleansing of a leper (Matt 8:1-4; Mark 1:40-45; Luke 5:12-16)
Deaf Man (Mark 7:31-37)
Demoniac in Capernaum healed (Mark 1:21-28; Luke 4:31-37)
Feeding of 5,000 (Matt 13:13-21; Mark 6:32-34; Luke 9:10-17; John 6:1-14)
Feeding of 4,000 (Matt 15:32-39; Mark 8:1-10)
Fig tree withers (Matt 21:18-22; Mark 11:12-13, 20-26)
Gadarene demoniac(s) (Matt 8:28-34; Mark 5:1-20; Luke 8:26-39)
Jairus's daughter and the woman with a hemorrhage healed (Matt 9:18-26; Mark 5:21-43)
Jesus walks on water (John 6:16-21)
Lame man healed (John 5:1-18)
Man with dropsy (Luke 14:1-6)
Miraculous catch of fish (John 21:1-14)
Paralytic healed (Matt 9:1-8; Mark 2:1-12; Luke 5:17-26)
Payment of the Temple tax (Matt 17:24-27)
Peter's mother-in-law healed (Matt 8:14-15; Mark 1:29-31; Luke 4:38-39)
Raising of Lazarus (John 11:1-44)
Raising the widow's son (Luke 7:11-17)
Royal official's son healed (John 4:46-54)
Sick healed (Luke 4:40-41)
Speechless demoniac (Matt 9:32-34)
Stilling of the storm (Matt 8:23-27; Mark 4:35-41; Luke 8:22-25)
Stooped woman healed (Luke 13:10-17)
Syro-Phoenician woman (Matt 15:21-28; Mark 7:24-30)
Ten lepers (Luke 17:11-19)
Walking on water (Matt 14:22-33; Mark 6:45-52)
Wine at the Cana wedding (John 2:1-11)
Withered hand (Matt 12:9-14; Mark 3:1-6; Luke 6:6-11)

41. Parables in the Synoptic Gospels

See figure 6 on page 297 in volume 9

42. Coins in the Gospels

argyria
assarion
chalkon
denarius
drachma
lepton
quadrans
stater
See also figure 5 on page 171 in volume 9

43. Passion Predictions

First Prediction (Matt 16:21-23; Mark 8:31-33)
Second Prediction (Matt 17:22-23; Mark 9:30-32; Luke 9:43*b*-45)
Third Prediction (Matt 20:17-19; Mark 10:32-34; Luke 18:31-34)

44. Chronology of Jesus' Final Days in Jerusalem

See figure 10 on page 401 in volume 8

45. Passion Narratives

Matthew 26:1–28:28
Mark 14–15
Luke 22:1–23:56
John 18:1–19:42

46. Words of Christ from the Cross

"My God, my God, why have you forsaken me?" (Matt 27:46; Mark 15:34)
"Father, forgive them; for they know not what they are doing." (Luke 23:34)
"Truly, I tell you, today you will be with me in Paradise." (Luke 23:43)
"Father, into your hands I commend my spirit." (Luke 23:46)
"Woman, here is your son." "Here is your mother." (John 19:25*b*-27)
"I am thirsty." (John 19:28)
"It is finished." (John 19:30)

47. Resurrection Accounts

Matt 28:1-10 (15)
Mark 16:1-8
Luke 24:1-12
John 20:1-18

48. Resurrection Appearances

Matt 28:16-20
Mark 16:9-18
Luke 24:13-53
John 20:19–21:23

49. Ascension Accounts

Mark 16:19-20
Luke 24:50-52

50. The Apostles

See figure 7 on page 254 in volume 8

51. Some Prayers of the Bible

Abraham's prayer for an heir (Gen 15)
Abraham's prayer for Ishmael (Gen 17)
Abraham's prayer for a wicked city (Gen 18–19)
Blessing upon the tribes (Gen 49)
Eliezer's prayer for a bride (Gen 24)
Jacob's vow (Gen 28:20)
Jacob's prayer about his brother (Gen 32:9-12)
Moses' prayer and calling (Exod 3:11-14; 4:10-13; 5:22)
Moses' first prayer for Israel (Exod 32:9-14)
Moses' second prayer for Israel (Exod 32:30-34)
Moses' third prayer for Israel (Exod 33:12-23)
Moses and the children of Israel (Exod 15:1-19)
Moses prays for a delay of judgment (Exod 32:31)
Prayer of a leper (Matt 8:1-4; Mark 1:40-45; Luke 5:12-14)
Jesus' prayer of gratitude (Matt 11:25-27)
Jesus' Gethsemane prayer (Matt 26:26, 36-46; Mark 14:32-42; Luke 22:39-46)
Jesus' prayer from the cross (Matt 27:46-50; Luke 23:34, 46)
Jesus' farewell prayer (John 17:1-26)
The Lord's Prayer (Matt 6:8-13; Luke 11:1-4)

52. Named Women of the Bible

Adah, wife of Lamech (Gen 4:19-23)
Adah, wife of Esau (Gen 26:34; 36:2)
Aholibamah/Oholibamah (Gen 36:2-25)
Anah (Gen 36:2, 18, 25)
Anna (Luke 2:36-38)
Antiochis (2 Macc 4:30)
Asenath (Gen 41:45-50; 46:20)
Bashemath/Basemeth/Basmath (Gen 26:34; 36:10; 36:3, 4, 13)
Bilhah (Gen 29:29; 30:3-5, 7; 35:22, 25; 37:2; 46:25; 1 Chr 4:29; 7:13)
Cleopatra (1 Macc 10:57-58; 11:8-12)
Deborah (Gen 24:59; 35:8)
Dinah (Gen 34)
Elisheba (Exod 6:23)
Elizabeth (Luke 1:5-80)
Eve (Gen 2; 3; 2 Cor 11:3; 1 Tim 2:13)
Hagar (Gen 16; 21:9-17; 25:12; Gal 4:24-25)
Herodias (Matt 14:3-12; Mark 6:14-24; Luke 3:19-20)
Iscah (Gen 11:29)
Jemima (Job 42:14)
Jochebed (Exod 1; 2:1-11; 6:20; Num 26:59; Heb 11:23)
Joanna (Luke 8:1-3; 23:55; 24:10)
Judith (Gen 26:34)
Keren-Happuch (Job 1:2; 42:14)
Keturah (Gen 25:1-6; 1 Chr 1:32, 33)
Kezia (Job 42:14)
Leah (Gen 29; 30; 49:31; Ruth 4:11)
Macchah (Gen 22:24)
Mahalah/Mahlah (Gen 28:9)
Martha (Luke 10:38-41; John 11; 12:1-3)
Mary (Matt 1:2; 12:46; Luke 1:2; John 2:1-11; 19:25; Acts 1:14)
Mary Magdalene (Matt 27:56, 61; 28:1; Mark 15:40, 47; 16:1-19; Luke 8:2; 24:10; John 11; 12:1-3)
Mary, mother of James and Joseph (Matt 27:55-61; Mark 15:40, 47; 16:1; Luke 24:10)
Mary of Bethany (Luke 10:38-41; John 11; 12:1-3)
Matred (Gen 36:39; 1 Chr 1:50)
Mehetabel (Gen 36:39; 1 Chr 1:50)

Milcah (Gen 11:29; 22:20, 23; 24:15, 24, 47)
Miriam (Exod 15:20, 21; Num 12:1-15; 20:1; 26:59; Deut 24:9; Micah 6:4)
Naamah (Gen 4:22)
Puah (Exod 1:15)
Rachel (Gen 29; 30; 31; 33:1, 2, 7; 35:16-26; 46:19, 22, 25; 48:7; Ruth 4:11; 1 Sam 10:2; Jer 31:15; Matt 2:18)
Rahab (Josh 2:1, 3; 6:17-25; Matt 1:5; Heb 1:31)
Rebekah/Rebecca (Gen 22:23; 24; 25:20-28; 26:6-35; 27; 28:5; 29:12; 35:8; 49:31; Rom 9:6-16)
Reumah (Gen 22:24)
Ruth, (book of Ruth; Matt 1:5)
Salome, daughter of Herodias (Matt 14:6-11; Mark 6:22-28)
Salome the disciple (Mark 15:40, 41)
Sarah/Sarai/Sara (Gen 11:29-32; 12:5-17; 16:1-8; 17:15-21; 18; 20:2-18; 21:1-12; 23:1-19; 24:36-37; 25:10, 12; 49:31; Isa 51:2; Rom 4:19; 9:9; Heb 11:11; 1 Pet 3:6)
Serah (Gen 46:17; 1 Chr 7:30)
Shelomith (Lev 24:10-13)
Shiphrah (Exod 1:15)
Shua (Gen 38:1, 2; 1 Chr 7:32)
Susanna (Luke 8:2, 3)
Tamar (Gen 38:6-30; Ruth 4:12; 1 Chr 2:4; Matt 1:3)
Timna (Gen 36:12, 22; 1 Chr 1:39)
Zillah (Gen 4:19-23)
Zilpah (Gen 29:24; 30:9, 10; 35:26; 37:2; 46:18)
Zipporah (Exod 2:21-22; 4:24-25; 18:1-6)

53. Unnamed Women of the Bible

Cain's wife (Gen 4:17)
Cainan's daughters (Gen 5:12-14)
Daughters of Jerusalem (Luke 23:28)
Daughters of Men (Gen 6:1-8)
Daughters of Putiel (Exod 6:25)
Daughters of Reuel (Exod 2:15-22)
Enoch's daughters (Gen 5:21-24)
Enos' daughters (Gen 5:9-11)
Jairus's daughter (Matt 9:18-25; Mark 5:21-43; Luke 8:41-56)
Jared's daughters (Gen 5:18-20)
Jesus' sisters (Matt 13:55-56; Mark 6:3)
Job's wife (Job 2:9, 10; 19:17; 31:10)
Lamech's daughters (Gen 5:28-31)
Lot's daughters (Gen 19:12-17, 30-38)
Lot's wife (Gen 19:15-26; Luke 17:29-33)
Mahaleel's daughters (Gen 5:15-17)
Methuselah's daughters (Gen 5:25-27)
Noah's wife, sons' wives (Gen 6:18; 7:1, 7, 13; 8:16, 18)
Peter's mother-in-law (Matt 8:14-18; Mark 1:29-34; Luke 4:38-41)
Peter's wife (Matt 8:14-18; Mark 1:29-34; Luke 4:38-41)
Pharaoh's daughter (Exod 2:5-10; Acts 7:21; Heb 11:24)
Pilate's wife (Matt 27:19)
Potiphar's wife (Gen 39)
Priestly daughters (Lev 21:9)
Seth's daughters (Gen 5:6-8)
Shaul's mother (Gen 46:10; Exod 6:15)
Shem's daughters (Gen 11:10-32)
Stooped woman healed by Jesus (Luke 13:11-13)
Syro-Phoenician woman (Matt 15:21-28; Mark 7:24-30)
Tabernacle women (Exod 38:8)
Widow of Nain (Luke 7:11-18)
Widow of Zarephath (1 Kgs 17:8-24; Luke 4:25, 26)
Widow with two mites (Mark 12:41-44; Luke 21:1-4)
Wife sold for debt (Matt 18:25; Luke 17:3-4)
Wise-hearted women (Exod 35:22-29)
Woman of Samaria (John 4)
Woman taken in adultery (Deut 17:5-6; John 8:1-11)
Woman who responded to a healing (Luke 11:27-28)
Woman who sinned yet loved much (Luke 7:36-50)
Woman with the hemorrhage (Matt 9:20-22; Mark 5:25-34; Luke 8:43-48)
Women at Peter's denial (Matt 26:69-71; Mark 14:66-69; Luke 22:56-59; John 18:16-17)
Women at the cross (Matt 27:55)

This set of lists was published on the CD-ROM edition of *The New Interpreter's Bible.* It has been thoroughly revised and included here in the print index for the reader's convenience. The first three lists point to the volume of the commentary in which a biblical book is discussed. For additional tables in the commentary, see the "List of Maps, Charts, and Illustrations," which can also be found in this index volume.

ABBREVIATIONS

General

BCE	Before the Common Era
CE	Common Era
c.	circa
cent.	century
cf.	compare
chap(s).	chapter(s)
d.	died
Dtr	Deuteronomistic historian
esp.	especially
fem.	feminine
f(f).	and following
HB	Hebrew Bible
lit.	literally
l(l).	line(s)
LXX	Septuagint
MS(S)	manuscript(s)
mg.	margin
masc.	masculine
MT	Masoretic Text
n(n).	note(s)
neut.	neuter
NT	New Testament
OG	Old Greek
OL	Old Latin
OT	Old Testament
par(s).	parallel(s)
pl(s).	plate(s)
sing.	singular
SP	Samaritan Pentateuch
v(v).	verse(s)
Vg	Vulgate
\\	between Scripture references indicates parallelism

Bible Translations

ASV	American Standard Version
CEV	Contemporary English Version
CSB	Catholic Study Bible
GNB	Good News Bible
JB	Jerusalem Bible
KJV	King James Version
NAB	New American Bible

NCB	New Century Bible
NEB	New English Bible
NIV	New International Version
NJB	New Jerusalem Bible
NKJV	New King James Version
NRSV	New Revised Standard Version
REB	Revised English Bible
RSV	Revised Standard Version
TLB	The Living Bible
TNK	Tanakh

Biblical Books (with the Apocrypha)

Gen	Nah	1–4 Kgdms	John
Exod	Hab	Add Esth	Acts
Lev	Zeph	Bar	Rom
Num	Hag	Bel	1–2 Cor
Deut	Zech	1–2 Esdr	Gal
Josh	Mal	4 Ezra	Eph
Judg	Ps (Pss)	Jdt	Phil
1–2 Sam	Job	Ep Jer	Col
1–2 Kgs	Prov	1–4 Macc	1–2 Thess
Isa	Ruth	Pr Azar	1–2 Tim
Jer	Cant	Pr Man	Titus
Ezek	Eccl	Sir	Phlm
Hos	Lam	Sus	Heb
Joel	Esth	Tob	Jas
Amos	Dan	Wis	1–2 Pet
Obad	Ezra	Matt	1–3 John
Jonah	Neh	Mark	Jude
Mic	1–2 Chr	Luke	Rev

Pseudepigraphical and Early Patristic Books

Apoc. Ab.	*Apocalypse of Abraham*
Apoc. Adam	*Apocalypse of Adam*
2 Apoc. Bar.	Syriac *Apocalypse of Baruch*
3 Apoc. Bar.	Greek *Apocalypse of Baruch*
Apoc. Mos.	*Apocalypse of Moses*
As. Mos.	*Assumption of Moses*
Ascen. Isa.	*Ascension of Isaiah*
Barn.	*Barnabas*
1–2 Clem.	*1–2 Clement*
Did.	*Didache*
1 Enoch	Ethiopic Book of *Enoch*
2 Enoch	Slavonic Book of *Enoch*
3 Enoch	Hebrew Book of *Enoch*
Ep. Arist.	*Epistle of Aristeas*

Gos. Pet.	*Gospel of Peter*
Herm. *Sim.*	Shepherd of Hermas, *Similitude*
Ign. *Eph.*	Ignatius, *To the Ephesians*
Ign. *Magn.*	Ignatius, *To the Magnesians*
Ign. *Phld.*	Ignatius, *To the Philadelphians*
Ign. *Pol.*	Ignatius, *To Polycarp*
Ign. *Rom.*	Ignatius, *To the Romans*
Ign. *Smyrn.*	Ignatius, *To the Smyrnaeans*
Ign. *Trall.*	Ignatius, *To the Trallians*
Jub.	*Jubilees*
P. Oxy.	*Oxyrynchus Papyri.* Edited by B. P. Grenfell and A. S. Hunt.
Pss. Sol.	*Psalms of Solomon*
Sib. Or.	*Sibylline Oracles*
T. Benj.	*Testament of Benjamin*
T. Dan	*Testament of Dan*
T. Iss.	*Testament of Issachar*
T. Job	*Testament of Job*
T. Jud.	*Testament of Judah*
T. Levi	*Testament of Levi*
T. Naph.	*Testament of Naphtali*
T. Reu.	*Testament of Reuben*
T. Sim.	*Testament of Simeon*

Dead Sea Scrolls and Related Texts

CD	Cairo Genizah text of the *Damascus Document*
DSS	Dead Sea Scrolls
8Ḥev XIIgr	Greek Scroll of the Minor Prophets from Naḥal Ḥever
Q	Qumran
1Q, 2Q, 3Q, etc.	Numbered caves of Qumran yielding written material followed by abbreviation of biblical or apocryphal book (e.g., 1Q pHab) or numbered document (e.g., 1Q7)
1Q28b	Appendix b *(Rule of the Blessings)* to 1QS
1QH^{a}	*Hodayot^{a} (Thanksgiving Hymns^{a})*
1QM	*Milḥamah (War Scroll)*
1QpHab	*Pesher Habakkuk*
1QS	*Serek Hayaḥad (Rule of the Community, Manual of Discipline)*
1QS^{a}	Appendix a *(Rule of the Congregation)* to 1QS
1QS^{b}	Appendix b *(Rule of the Blessings)* to 1QS
4Q175	*Testimonia* (4QTest)
4Q246	*Apocryphon of Daniel* (Aramaic Apocalypse)
4Q298	*Cryptic A: Words of the Sage to the Sons of Dawn*
4Q385^{b}	4QApocryphon of Jeremiah^{c}
4Q389^{a}	4QApocryphon of Jeremiah^{e}
4Q390	4QPseudo-Moses^{e}
4Q394	*Miqsat Maʿaśê ha- Torah^{a}* (4QMMT^{a})
4Q416	*Sapiential Work Ab*
4Q521	*Messianic Apocalypse*

4Q5504Qproto-Esther $^{a-f}$	ProtoEsther, Aramaic, copies to
4QFlor (MidrEschat^{a})	*Florilegium* (or *Midrash on Eschatology*^{a})
4QMMT	*Halakhic Letter*
4QpaleoDeutr	Copy of Deuteronomy in paleo-Hebrew script
4QpaleoExod^{m}	Copy of Exodus in paleo-Hebrew script
4QpNah	*Nahum Pesher*
4QpPss^{a}	*Psalm Pesher A*
4QprNab ar	*Prayer of Nabonidus*
4QPs37	*Psalms Scroll*
4QpsDan	Pseudo-Daniel
4Qsam^{a}	First copy of Samuel
4QTob	Copy of Tobit
11QMelch	*Melchizedek*
11QpHab	A fragment of the Habakkuk scroll
11QPs^{a}	*Psalms Scroll*^{a}
11QTemple	*Temple Scroll*
11QtgJob	*Targum of Job*

Orders and Tractates in Mishnaic and Related Literature

To distinguish between the same-named tractates in the Mishna, Tosepta, Babylonian Talmud, and Jerusalem Talmud, *m., t., b.,* or *y.* precedes the title of the tractate.

ʾAbot	*ʾAbot*
ʾArak.	*ʾArakin*
B. Bat.	*Baba Batra*
B. Men	*Baba Meniʿa*
B. Qam.	*Baba Qamma*
Ber.	*Berakot*
Dem.	*Demai*
Git.	*Giṭṭin*
Ḥag.	*Ḥagigah*
Hor.	*Horayot*
Ḥul.	*Ḥullin*
Ketub.	*Ketubbot*
Maʿaś.	*Maʿaśerot*
Meg.	*Megillah*
Menaḥ.	*Menaḥot*
Mid.	*Middot*
Moʾed Qaṭ.	*Moʾed Qaṭan*
Ned.	*Nedarim*
Pesaḥ.	*Pesaḥim*
Qidd.	*Qiddušin*
Šabb.	*Šabbat*
Sanh.	*Sanhedrin*
Shekal	*Pesahim Shekalim*
Soïa	*Soïa*
Sukk.	*Sukka*
Taʿan.	*Taʿanit*

Tg. Neof.	*Targum Neofiti*
Yad.	*Yadayim*
Yoma	*Yoma (= Kippurim)*

Targumic Material

Tg. Esth. I, II	*First or Second Targum of Esther*
Tg. Neb.	*Targum of the Prophets*

Other Rabbinic Works

ʾAbot R. Nat.	*ʾAbot de Rabbi Nathan*
Pesiq. Rab.	*Pesiqta Rabbati*
Rab.	*Rabbah* (following abbreviation of biblical book—e.g., Gen. Rab. = Genesis Rabbah)
Sipra	*Sipra*
Song Rab.	*Song of Songs Rabbah*

Names of Nag Hammadi Tractates

Ap. John	*Apocryphon of John*
Apoc. Adam	*Apocalypse of Adam*
Ep. Pet. Phil.	*Letter of Peter to Philip*
Exeg. Soul	*Exegesis on the Soul*
Gos. Phil.	*Gospel of Philip*
Gos. Truth	*Gospel of Truth*

Greek Manuscripts and Ancient Versions

Papyrus Manuscripts

𝔓1	Third-century Greek Papyrus manuscript of the Gospels
𝔓29	Third- or fourth-century Greek Papyrus manuscript of Acts
𝔓33	Sixth-century Greek Papyrus manuscript of Acts
𝔓37	Third- or fourth-century Greek Papyrus manuscript of the Gospels
𝔓38	Fourth-century Greek Papyrus manuscript of Acts
𝔓45	Third-century Greek Papyrus manuscript of the Gospels
𝔓46	Third-century Greek Papyrus manuscript of the Gospels
𝔓47	Third-century Greek Papyrus manuscript of the Gospels
𝔓48	Third-century Greek Papyrus manuscript of Acts
𝔓52	Second-century Greek Papyrus manuscript of John 18:31-33, 37-38
𝔓58	Sixth-century Greek Papyrus manuscript of Acts
𝔓64	Third-century Greek Papyrus fragment of Matthew
𝔓66	Third-century Greek Papyrus manuscript of the Gospels
𝔓67	Third-century Greek Papyrus fragment of Matthew
𝔓69	Late second-century Greek Papyrus manuscript of the Gospel of Luke
𝔓75	Third-century Greek Papyrus manuscript of the Gospels

Lettered Uncials

ℵ	Codex Sinaiticus, fourth-century manuscript of LXX, NT, *Epistle of Barnabas,* and *Shepherd of Hermas*
A	Codex Alexandrinus, fifth-century manuscript of LXX, NT, *1 & 2 Clement,* and *Psalms of Solomon*
B	Codex Vaticanus, fourth-century manuscript of LXX and parts of the NT
C	Codex Ephraemi, fifth-century manuscript of parts of LXX and NT
D	Codex Bezae, fifth-century bilingual (Greek and Latin) manuscript of the Gospels and Acts
G	Ninth-century manuscript of the Gospels
K	Ninth-century manuscript of the Gospels
L	Eighth-century manuscript of the Gospels
W	Washington Codex, fifth-century manuscript of the Gospels
X	Codex Monacensis, ninth- or tenth-century miniscule manuscript of the Gospels
Z	Sixth-century manuscript of Matthew
Θ	Koridethi Codex, ninth-century manuscript of the Gospels
Y	Athous Laurae Codex, eighth- or ninth-century manuscript of the Gospels (incomplete), Acts, The Catholic and Pauline Epistles, and Hebrews

Numbered Uncials

058	Fourth-century fragment of Matthew 18
074	Sixth-century fragment of Matthew
078	Sixth-century fragment of Matthew, Luke, and John
0170	Fifth- or sixth-century uncial manuscript of Matthew
0181	Fourth- or fifth-century partial manuscript of Luke 9:59–10:14

Numbered Minuscules

33	Tenth-century manuscript of the Gospels
174	Eleventh-century manuscript of the Gospels
565	Ninth-century miniscule manuscript of the Gospels
700	Eleventh-century miniscule manuscript of the Gospels
892	Ninth-century miniscule manuscript of the Gospels

Ancient Versions

bo	The Bohairic (Memphitic) Coptic Version
bo^{mss}	Some manuscripts in the Bohairic tradition
bo^{pt}	Some manuscripts in the Bohairic tradition
d	The Latin text of Codex Bezae
e	Codex Palatinus, fifth-century Latin manuscript of the Gospels
ff^2	Old Latin manuscript, fifth-century translation of the Gospels
Ir^{lat}	The Latin translation of Iraneaus
latt	The whole Latin tradition (including the Vulgate)
mae	Middle Egyptian
sa	The Sahidic (Thebaic) Coptic Version
sy	The Syriac Version
sy^s	The Sinaitic Syriac Version

Other Abbreviations

pc	A few other manuscripts

f^{1}	Family 1: miniscule manuscripts belonging to the Lake Group (1, 118, 131, 209, 1582)
f^{13}	Family 13: miniscule manuscripts belonging to the Ferrar Group (13, 69, 124, 174, 230, 346, 543, 788, 826, 828, 983, 1689, 1709)
a*	The original reading of Codex Sinaiticus
a^{1}	The first corrector of Codex Sinaiticus
a^{2}	The second corrector of Codex Sinaiticus
D*	The original reading of Codex Bezae
D^{2}	The second corrector (c. fifth century) of Codex Bezae
𝔐	The Majority text (the mass of later manuscripts)
C^{2}	The corrected text of Codex Ephraemi
700*	The original reading of manuscript 700
NA^{27}	*Novum Testamentum Graece*, Nestle-Aland, 27th ed.
UBS^{4}	*The Greek New Testament*, United Bible Societies, 4th ed.

Periodicals, Reference Works, and Serials

AB	Anchor Bible
ABD	*Anchor Bible Dictionary.* Edited by D. N. Freedman. 6 vols. New York, 1992
ABR	*Australian Biblical Review*
ABRL	Anchor Bible Reference Library
ACNT	Augsburg Commentaries on the New Testament
AcOr	*Acta orientalia*
AfO	*Archiv für Orientforschung*
AfOB	Archiv für Orientforschung: Beiheft
AGJU	Arbeiten zur Geschichte des antiken Judentums und des Urchristentums
AJP	*American Journal of Philology*
AJSL	*American Journal of Semitic Languages and Literature*
AJT	*American Journal of Theology*
AnBib	Analecta biblica
ANEP	*The Ancient Near East in Pictures Relating to the Old Testament.* Edited by J. B. Pritchard. Princeton, 1954
ANET	*Ancient Near Eastern Texts Relating to the Old Testament.* Edited by J. B. Pritchard. 3rd ed. Princeton, 1969
ANF	*The Ante-Nicene Fathers*
ANRW	*Aufstieg und Niedergang der römischen Welt: Geschichte und Kultur Roms im Spiegel der neueren Forschung.* Edited by H. Temporini and W. Haase. Berlin, 1972–
ANTC	Abingdon New Testament Commentaries
ANTJ	Arbeiten zum Neuen Testament und Judentum
APOT	*Apocrypha and Pseudepigrapha of the Old Testament.* Edited by R. H. Charles. 2 vols. Oxford, 1913
ASNU	Acta seminarii neotestamentici upsaliensis
ATANT	Abhandlungen zur Theologie des Alten und Neuen Testaments
ATD	Das Alte Testament Deutsch
ATDan	Acta theological danica
Aug	*Augustinianum*
BA	*Biblical Archaeologist*

BAGD	Bauer, W., W. F. Arndt, F. W. Gingrich, and F. W. Danker. *Greek-English Lexicon of the New Testament and Other Early Christian Literature.* 2nd ed. Chicago, 1979
BAR	*Biblical Archaeology Review*
BASOR	*Bulletin of the American Schools of Oriental Research*
BBB	Bonner biblische Beiträge
BBET	Beiträge zur biblischen Exegese und Theologie
BBR	*Bulletin for Biblical Research*
BDAG	Bauer, W., F. W. Danker, W. F. Arndt, and F. W. Gingrich. *Greek-English Lexicon of the New Testament and Other Early Christian Literature.* 3rd ed. Chicago, 2000
BDB	Brown, F., S. R. Driver, and C. A. Briggs. *A Hebrew and English Lexicon of the Old Testament.* Oxford, 1907
BDF	Blass, F., A. Debrunner, and R. W. Funk. *A Greek Grammar of the New Testament and Other Early Christian Literature.* Chicago, 1961
BEATAJ	Beiträge zur Erforschung des Alten Testaments und des antiken Judentum
BETL	Bibliotheca ephemeridum theologicarum lovaniensium
BEvT	Beiträge zur evangelischen Theologie
BHS	*Biblia Hebraica Stuttgartensia.* Edited by K. Elliger and W. Randolph. Stuttgart, 1983
BHT	Beiträge zur historischen Theologie
Bib	*Biblica*
BibInt	*Biblical Interpretation*
BibOr	Biblica et orientalia
BJRL	*Bulletin of the John Rylands University Library of Manchester*
BJS	Brown Judaic Studies
BK	*Bibel und Kirche*
BKAT	Biblischer Kommentar, Altes Testament. Edited by M. Noth and H. W. Wolff
BLS	Bible and Literature Series
BN	*Biblische Notizen*
BNTC	Black's New Testament Commentaries
BR	*Biblical Research*
BSac	*Bibliotheca sacra*
BSOAS	*Bulletin of the School of Oriental and African Studies*
BT	*The Bible Translator*
BTB	*Biblical Theology Bulletin*
BVC	*Bible et vie chrétienne*
BWA(N)T	Beiträge zur Wissenschaft vom Alten (und Neuen) Testament
BZ	*Biblische Zeitschrift*
BZAW	Beihefte zur Zeitschrift für die alttestamentliche Wissenschaft
BZNW	Beihefte zur Zeitschrift für die neutestamentliche Wissenschaft
CAD	*The Assyrian Dictionary of the Oriental Institute of the University of Chicago.* Chicago, 1956–
CB	*Cultura bíblica*
CBC	Cambridge Bible Commentary
CBQ	*Catholic Biblical Quarterly*
CBQMS	Catholic Biblical Quarterly Monograph Series
ConBNT	Coniectanea neotestamentica or Coniectanea biblica: New Testament Series
ConBOT	Coniectanea biblica: Old Testament Series
CP	*Classical Philology*

CRAI	Comptes rendus del l'Académie des inscriptions et belles-lettres
CRINT	Compendia rerum iudaicarum ad Novum Testamentum
CTM	*Concordia Theological Monthly*
DJD	Discoveries in the Judaean Desert
EB	Echter Bibel
EI	*Encyclopaedia of Islam.* 9 of 13 projected vols. 2nd ed. Leiden, 1954–
EKKNT	Evangelisch-katholischer Kommentar zum Neuen Testament
Enc	*Encounter*
EncJud	*Encyclopaedia Judaica.* 16 vols. Jerusalem, 1972
EPRO	Etudes préliminairies aux religions orientales dans l'empire romain
ErIsr	*Eretz-Israel*
EstBib	*Estudios bíblicos*
ETL	*Ephemerides theologicae lovanienses*
ETS	Erfurter theologische Studien
EvQ	*Evangelical Quarterly*
EvT	*Evangelische Theologie*
ExAud	*Ex auditu*
ExpTim	*Expository Times*
FAT	Forschungen zum Alten Testament
FB	Forschung zur Bibel
FBBS	Facet Books, Biblical Series
FFNT	Foundations and Facets: New Testament
FOTL	Forms of the Old Testament Literature
FRLANT	Forschungen zur Religion und Literatur des Alten und Neuen Testaments
FTS	Frankfurter Theologische Studien
GBS.OTS	Guides to Biblical Scholarship. Old Testament Series
GCS	Die griechische christliche Schriftsteller der ersten [drei] Jahrhunderte
GKC	*Gesenius' Hebrew Grammar.* Edited by E. Kautzsch. Translated by A. E. Cowley. 2nd ed. Oxford, 1910
GNS	*Good News Studies*
GTA	Göttinger theologischer Arbeiten
HAL	Koehler, L., W. Baumgartner, and J. J. Stamm. *Hebräisches und aramäisches Lexikon zum Alten Testament.* Fascicles 1–5, 1967–1995 (KBL3). ET: *HALOT*
HAR	*Hebrew Annual Review*
HAT	Handbuch zum Alten Testament
HBC	*Harper's Bible Commentary.* Edited by J. L. Mays et al. San Francisco, 1988
HBT	*Horizons in Biblical Theology*
HDB	*Hastings Dictionary of the Bible*
HDR	Harvard Dissertations in Religion
HeyJ	*Heythrop Journal*
HNT	Handbuch zum Neuen Testament
HNTC	Harper's New Testament Commentaries
HR	*History of Religions*
HSM	Harvard Semitic Monographs
HSS	Harvard Semitic Studies
HTKNT	Herders theologischer Kommentar zum Neuen Testament
HTR	*Harvard Theological Review*
HTS	Harvard Theological Studies
HUCA	*Hebrew Union College Annual*

IB	*Interpreter's Bible.* Edited by G. A. Buttrick et al. 12 vols. New York, 1951–1957
IBC	Interpretation: A Bible Commentary for Teaching and Preaching
IBS	*Irish Biblical Studies*
ICC	International Critical Commentary
IDB	*The Interpreter's Dictionary of the Bible.* Edited by G.A. Buttrick. 4 vols. Nashville, 1962
IDBSup	*Interpreter's Dictionary of the Bible: Supplementary Volume.* Edited by K. Crim. Nashville, 1976
IEJ	*Israel Exploration Journal*
Int	*Interpretation*
IRT	Issues in Religion and Theology
ITC	International Theological Commentary
JAAR	*Journal of the American Academy of Religion*
JAL	Jewish Apocryphal Literature Series
JANESCU	*Journal of the Ancient Near Eastern Society of Columbia University*
JAOS	*Journal of the American Oriental Society*
JBL	*Journal of Biblical Literature*
JETS	*Journal of the Evangelical Theological Society*
JJS	*Journal of Jewish Studies*
JNES	*Journal of Near Eastern Studies*
JNSL	*Journal of Northwest Semitic Languages*
JPS	Jewish Publication Society
JPSV	Jewish Publication Society Version
JQR	*Jewish Quarterly Review*
JR	*Journal of Religion*
JRH	*Journal of Religious History*
JSJ	*Journal for the Study of Judaism in the Persian, Hellenistic, and Roman Periods*
JSNT	*Journal for the Study of the New Testament*
JSNTSup	Journal for the Study of the New Testament: Supplement Series
JSOT	*Journal for the Study of the Old Testament*
JSOTSup	Journal for the Study of the Old Testament: Supplement Series
JSP	*Journal for the Study of the Pseudepigrapha*
JSPTSS	Journal of the Study of Pentecostal Theology Supplement Series
JSS	*Journal of Semitic Studies*
JTC	*Journal for Theology and the Church*
JTS	*Journal of Theological Studies*
KAT	Kommentar zum Alten Testament
KEK	Kritisch-exegetischer Kommentar über das Neue Testament (Meyer-Kommentar)
KPG	Knox Preaching Guides
LCL	Loeb Classical Library
LTQ	*Lexington Theological Quarterly*
MNTC	Moffatt New Testament Commentary
NA^{27}	*Novum Testamentum Graece*, Nestle-Aland, 27th ed.
NCBC	New Century Bible Commentary
NHS	Nag Hammadi Studies
NIB	*The New Interpreter's Bible*
NICNT	New International Commentary on the New Testament
NICOT	New International Commentary on the Old Testament
NIGTC	New International Greek Testament Commentary

NJBC	*The New Jerome Biblical Commentary.* Edited by R. E. Brown et al. Englewood Cliffs, 1990
NovT	*Novum Testamentum*
NovTSup	Supplements to Novum Testamentum
NPNF	*Nicene and Post-Nicene Fathers,* Series 1 and 2
NTC	New Testament in Context
NTD	Das Neue Testament Deutsch
NTG	New Testament Guides
NTS	*New Testament Studies*
NTTS	New Testament Tools and Studies
OBC	Oxford Bible Commentary
OBO	Orbis biblicus et orientalis
OBT	Overtures to Biblical Theology
OIP	Oriental Institute Publications
Or	*Orientalia* (NS)
OTG	Old Testament Guides
OTL	Old Testament Library
OTM	Old Testament Message
OTP	*Old Testament Pseudepigrapha.* Edited by J. H. Charlesworth. 2 vols. New York, 1983
OtSt	*Oudtestamentische Studiën*
PAAJR	*Proceedings of the American Academy of Jewish Research*
PEQ	*Palestine Exploration Quarterly*
PGM	*Papyri graecae magicae: Die griechischen Zauberpapyri.* Edited by K. Preisendanz. Berlin, 1928
PTMS	Pittsburgh Theological Monograph Series
QD	Quaestiones disputatae
RANE	Records of the Ancient Near East
RB	*Revue biblique*
ResQ	*Restoration Quarterly*
RevExp	*Review and Expositor*
RevQ	*Revue de Qumran*
RevScRel	*Revue des sciences religieuses*
RSR	*Recherches de science religieuse*
RTL	*Revue théologique de Louvain*
SAA	State Archives of Assyria
SBB	Stuttgarter biblische Beiträge
SBL	Society of Biblical Literature
SBLDS	Society of Biblical Literature Dissertation Series
SBLMS	Society of Biblical Literature Monograph Series
SBLRBS	Society of Biblical Literature Resources for Biblical Study
SBLSCS	Society of Biblical Literature Septuagint and Cognate Studies
SBLSP	*Society of Biblical Literature Seminar Papers*
SBLSS	Society of Biblical Literature Semeia Studies
SBLSymS	Society of Biblical Literature Symposium Series
SBLWAW	Society of Biblical Literature Writings from the Ancient World
SBM	Stuttgarter biblische Monographien
SBS	Stuttgarter Bibelstudien
SBT	Studies in Biblical Theology
SEÅ	*Svensk exegetisk årsbok*

SJLA	Studies in Judaism in Late Antiquity
SJOT	*Scandinavian Journal of the Old Testament*
SJT	*Scottish Journal of Theology*
SKK	Stuttgarter kleiner Kommentar
SNTSMS	Society for New Testament Studies Monograph Series
SOTSMS	Society for Old Testament Study Monograph Series
SP	Sacra pagina
SR	*Studies in Religion*
SSN	Studia semitica neerlandica
Str-B	Strack, H. L., and P. Billerbeck. *Kommentar zum Neuen Testament aus Talmud und Midrasch.* 6 vols. Munich, 1922–6161
SUNT	Studien zur Umwelt des Neuen Testaments
SVTP	Studia in Veteris Testamenti pseudepigrapha
TB	Theologische Bücherei: Neudrucke und Berichte aus dem 20. Jahrhundert
TD	*Theology Digest*
TDNT	*Theological Dictionary of the New Testament.* Edited by G. Kittel and G. Friedrich. Translated by G. W. Bromiley. 10 vols. Grand Rapids, 1964–1976
TDOT	*Theological Dictionary of the Old Testament.* Edited by G. J. Botterweck and H. Ringgren. Translated by J. T. Willis, G. W. Bromiley, and D. E. Green. 8 vols. Grand Rapids, 1974–
THKNT	Theologischer Handkommentar zum Neuen Testament
ThTo	*Theology Today*
TLZ	*Theologische Literaturzeitung*
TOTC	Tyndale Old Testament Commentaries
TQ	*Theologische Quartalschrift*
TS	Texts and Studies
TS	*Theological Studies*
TSK	*Theologische Studien und Kritiken*
TSSI	*Textbook of Syrian Semitic Inscriptions.* J. C. L. Gibson. Oxford, 1971–1982
TynBul	*Tyndale Bulletin*
TZ	*Theologische Zeitschrift*
UBS	United Bible Societies
UBS^4	*The Greek New Testament*, United Bible Societies, 4th ed.
UF	*Ugarit-Forschungen*
USQR	*Union Seminary Quarterly Review*
UUA	Uppsala Universitetsårskrift
VC	*Vigiliae christianae*
VT	*Vetus Testamentum*
VTSup	Vetus Testamentum Supplements
WA	*Weimar Ausgabe.* (Weimer ed.). M. Luther
WBC	Word Biblical Commentary
WBT	*Word Biblical Themes*
WMANT	Wissenschaftliche Monographien zum Alten und Neuen Testament
WTJ	*Westminster Theological Journal*
WUNT	Wissenschaftliche Untersuchungen zum Neuen Testament
ZAH	*Zeitschrift für Althebräistik*
ZAW	*Zeitschrift für die alttestamentliche Wissenschaft*
ZNW	*Zeitschrift für die neutestamentliche Wissenschaft und die Kunde de älteren Kirche*
ZTK	*Zeitschrift für Theologie und Kirche*